Psychology 3e

A Journey

DENNIS COON

JOHN O. MITTERER
Brock University

THOMSON

WADSWORTH

Australia • Brazil • Canada • Mexico • Singapore • Spain
United Kingdom • United States

THOMSON

WADSWORTH

Psychology: A Journey
Third Edition
Dennis Coon / John O. Mitterer

Publisher: Michele Sordi
Development Editors: Kristin Makarewycz, Jeremy Judson
Assistant Editor: Magnolia Molcan
Editorial Assistant: Rachel Guzman
Technology Project Manager: Lauren Keyes
Marketing Manager: Sara Swangard
Marketing Communications Manager: Linda Yip
Project Manager, Editorial Production: Jerilyn Emori
Creative Director: Rob Hugel

Art Director: Vernon Boes
Print Buyer: Karen Hunt
Permissions Editor: Sue Howard
Production Service: Carol O'Connell, Graphic World Inc.
Text and Cover Designer: Lisa Buckley
Photo Researcher: Kathleen Olson
Cover Image: Jim Reed/Getty Images
Text and Cover Printer: Courier Corporation/Kendallville
Compositor: Graphic World Inc.

ExamView® and ExamView Pro® are registered trademarks of FSCreations, Inc. Windows is a registered trademark of the Microsoft Corporation used herein under license. Macintosh and Power Macintosh are registered trademarks of Apple Computer, Inc. Used herein under license.

Library of Congress Control Number: 2006937382

Student Edition:
ISBN-13: 978-0-495-09553-8
ISBN-10: 0-495-09553-2

Loose-leaf Edition:
ISBN-13: 978-0-495-10480-3
ISBN-10: 0-495-10480-9

Thomson Higher Education
10 Davis Drive
Belmont, CA 94002-3098
USA

For more information about our products, contact us at:
Thomson Learning Academic Resource Center
1-800-423-0563

For permission to use material from this text or product, submit a request online at **http://www.thomsonrights.com.**
Any additional questions about permissions can be submitted by e-mail to **thomsonrights@thomson.com.**

Brief Contents

Contents

CHAPTER 2   Brain and Behavior   52

CHAPTER 3   Human Development   87

CHAPTER 4 Sensation and Perception 130

CHAPTER 5 States of Consciousness 179

CHAPTER 6   Conditioning and Learning   223

CHAPTER 9   Motivation and Emotion   343

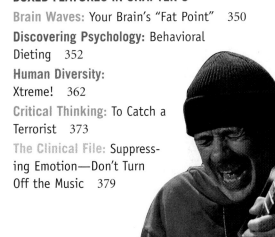

CHAPTER 10   Personality   387

CHAPTER 11   Health, Stress, and Coping   430

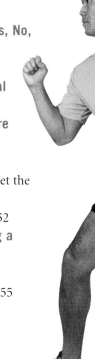

CHAPTER 14   Social Behavior   553

Appendix   Behavioral Statistics   598
Glossary   G-1
Refs   R-1

Preface

TO THE STUDENT—THE JOURNEY BEGINS

Psychology is an exciting field. It is at once familiar, exotic, surprising, and challenging. Most of all, psychology is changing. Indeed, this book is just a "snapshot" of a colorful passing scene. Yet, change makes psychology especially fascinating: What, really, could be more intriguing than our evolving understanding of human behavior?

Psychology is about each of us. It asks us to adopt a reflective attitude as we inquire, "How can we step outside of ourselves to look objectively at how we live, think, feel, and act?" Psychologists believe the answer is through careful thought, observation, and inquiry. As simple as that may seem, thoughtful reflection takes practice to develop. It is the guiding light for all that follows in this text.

Each chapter of this book will take you into a different realm of psychology, such as personality, abnormal behavior, memory, consciousness, or child development. Each realm is complex and fascinating in its own right, with many pathways, landmarks, and interesting detours to discover. The title of this book, *Psychology: A Journey,* reflects the fact that learning is an adventure. Like any journey of discovery, your "tour" of psychology will help you to better understand yourself, others, and the world around you. It's definitely a trip worth taking.

Please view this book as a long letter from your authors to you. It is, in a very real sense, written about you, for you, and to you. We sincerely hope you will find human behavior as fascinating as we do. In the pages that follow, we have done all that we could imagine to make your first journey through psychology enjoyable and worthwhile.

Getting Started

None of us likes to start out a new adventure by reading the manual. We just want to get right into our new computer game, step off the plane and get on with our vacation, or just start using our new digital camera or cell phone. You might be similarly tempted to just start reading this textbook.

Please be patient. We probably don't have to tell you that learning psychology depends on how you study this book, as well as how you read it. *Psychology: A Journey* is your passport to an adventure in learning, and not just reading. To help you get off to a good start, we strongly encourage you to read our short Introduction, which precedes Chapter 1. The Introduction describes study skills, including the SQ4R method, which you can use to get the most out of this text and your psychology course. It also tells how you can explore psychology through the Internet, electronic databases, and interactive CDs.

TO THE INSTRUCTOR—A CONCISE SURVEY OF PSYCHOLOGY

Psychology: A Journey was written to provide a concise, but complete, first course in psychology. It is organized into 14 chapters so that the entire field can be covered in a single term, at a pace of one chapter per week. *Journey's* brevity prompted us to select only the very "best" material from the many topics that could be presented. Nevertheless, *Journey* covers not only the heart of psychology, but also many topics at the cutting edge of current knowledge. New information, anecdotes, perspectives, and narratives appear throughout the Third Edition. The result is a concise text that is readable, manageable, informative, and motivating.

At the same time, Marcel Proust wrote, "The real voyage of discovery consists not in seeing new landscapes but in having new eyes." It is in this spirit that we invite you to make full use of this book to help you promote an interest in human behavior, including an appreciation of the practical applications of psychology, the richness of human diversity, and the field of positive psychology.

In this edition we have also updated the SQ4R method. The steps are now Survey, Question, Read, Recite, Reflect, Review. This update has allowed us to expand the Reflect step to strengthen the relationship between learning and doing the kinds of active, elaborative processing and critical thinking that characterize the reflective student (Gadzella, 1995). The end result is a more effective promotion of active learning, better long-term retention of ideas, and a reflective attitude that lies at the heart of critical thinking. Without such skills, students cannot easily go, as Jerome Bruner put it, "beyond the information given" (Bruner, 1973).

Readability and Narrative Emphasis

Selecting a textbook is half the battle in teaching a successful course. A good text does much of the work of imparting information to your students. This frees class time for your discussion, extra topics, or media presentations. It also leaves students asking for more. When a book overwhelms students or cools their interest, teaching and learning suffer.

Many introductory psychology students are reluctant readers. No matter how interesting a text may be, its value is lost if students fail to read it. That's why we've worked hard to make this a clear, readable, and engaging text. We want students to read this book with genuine interest and enthusiasm, not merely as an obligation.

To encourage students to read, we made a special effort to weave narrative threads through every chapter. Everyone loves a good story, and the story of psychology is among the most compelling to be told. Throughout *Psychology: A Journey*, we have used intriguing anecdotes and examples to propel reading and sustain interest. As students explore concepts, they are encouraged to think about ideas and relate them to their own experiences.

Practical Applications

Psychology: A Journey is designed to give students a clear grasp of major concepts, without burying them in details. At the same time, it offers a broad overview that reflects psychology's rich heritage of ideas. We think students will find this book informative and intellectually stimulating. Moreover, we have emphasized the many ways that psychology relates to practical problems in daily life.

A major feature of this book is the *Psychology in Action* section found at the end of each chapter. These high-interest discussions bridge the gap between theory and practical applications. We believe it is fair for students to ask, "Does this mean anything to me? Can I use it? Why should I learn it if I can't?" The Psychology in Action features show students how to solve practical problems and manage their own behavior. This allows them to see the benefits of adopting new ideas, and it breathes life into psychology's concepts.

An Integrated Study Guide

The chapters of this text are divided into short segments by special sections called *Study Breaks.* Each Study Break challenges students to relate concepts to their own experiences, to quiz themselves, and to think critically about psychology. In addition, each chapter concludes with a self-assessment called *Test Your Knowledge.* The multiple-choice questions in Test Your Knowledge provide a way for students to judge how well they are doing in their studies, by taking a sample test. These tests now include 20 questions that are comparable in difficulty to in-class exams.

If students would like more feedback and practice, a great new printed supplement, *Practice Exams with Visual Guides,* is bundled with this text, a traditional *Study Guide* is available, and students can use a Web-based course management tool called *Web Tutor Toolbox* to practice with electronic flashcards or take online quizzes.

Electronic Resources

To encourage further explorations, students will find a section called *Interactive Learning* at the end of each chapter. The Web sites described there offer a wealth of information on topics related to psychology. Students are also directed to *Psychology: A Journey Companion Website,* which offers online quizzes, flash cards, animations, video clips, experiments, interactive assessments, and other helpful study aids for this text. All chapters also include a link to modules in *ThomsonNOW,* an excellent online study tool from Wadsworth that provides students with a rich assortment of interactive learning experiences, animations, and simulations.

Human Diversity

Today's students reflect the multicultural, multifaceted nature of contemporary society. In *Psychology: A Journey,* students will find numerous discussions of human diversity, including differences in race, ethnicity, culture, gender, abilities, sexual orientation, and age. Too often, such differences needlessly divide people into opposing groups. Our aim throughout this text is to discourage stereotyping, prejudice, discrimination, and intolerance. We've tried to make this book gender neutral and sensitive to diversity issues. All pronouns and examples involving females and males are equally divided by gender. In artwork, photographs, and examples, we have tried to portray the rich diversity of humanity. In addition, a boxed feature, *Human Diversity,* appears throughout the book, providing the student with examples of how to be more reflective about human diversity. Many topics and examples in this book encourage students to appreciate social, physical, and cultural differences and to accept them as a natural part of being human.

Positive Psychology

In January 2000, Martin Seligman and Mihaly Csikszentmihalyi co-edited a special issue of *American Psychologist* devoted to optimal functioning, happiness, and "positive psychology." Over the past 100 years, psychologists have paid ample attention to the negative side of human behavior. This is easy to understand because we urgently need to find remedies for human problems. However, Seligman and Csikszentmihalyi have urged us to also study positive psychology. What do we know, for instance, about love, happiness, creativity, well-being, self-confidence, and achievement? Throughout this book, we have attempted to answer such questions for students. Our hope is that students who read this book will gain an appreciation for the potential we all have for optimal functioning. Also, of course, we hope that they will leave introductory psychology with emotional and intellectual tools they can use to enhance their lives.

■ Table 1 Human Diversity and Culture in *Psychology: A Journey*

Chapter 1: Introducing Psychology and Research Methods

- Cultural psychology
- Human diversity, appreciating social and cultural differences
- The impact of culture
- Cultural relativity
- A broader view of diversity
- Human diversity and representative samples

Chapter 2: Brain and Behavior

- Nerve grafting for people with spinal injuries
- Hypopituitary dwarfism
- Handedness and laterality
- Computer aids for people with total paralysis

Chapter 3: Human Development

- Ethnic differences in child-rearing
- The relationship between culture and babbling
- Parentese in different cultures
- Piagetian stages and cultural influences
- Sociocultural influences on cognitive development (Vygotsky)
- Adolescent status and culture
- Diversity and the adolescent search for identity
- Ethnicity and personal identity
- Culture and moral reasoning
- 20-somethings and emerging adulthood
- Ageism and myths about the elderly

Chapter 4: Sensation and Perception

- The "other race" effect in facial recognition
- Culture and the recognition of pictorial depth cues
- Culture and the Müller-Lyer illusion

- Cross-racial perceptions (eyewitness accuracy)
- Cultural differences in perception

Chapter 5: States of Consciousness

- States of consciousness and culture
- The cultural context of drug use

Chapter 6: Conditioning and Learning

- Comparing U.S. television content with cultures that limit televised violence

Chapter 7: Memory

- Aging and memory
- Cultural influences on memory
- Eyewitnesses and cross-racial recognition
- Labeling and the ability to remember people from other social groups

Chapter 8: Intelligence, Cognition, Language, and Creativity

- Cultural barriers to problem solving
- Age and IQ
- The developmentally disabled
- Race, culture, ethnicity, and intelligence
- Cultural differences in intelligence (as taught to children)
- Culture-fair intelligence testing
- A critique of *The Bell Curve*
- Social stereotypes and cognition
- The effects of unconscious prejudice on word recognition
- Affect of word meanings on thinking (of celebrity names)
- Linguistic misunderstandings between cultures
- The pros and cons of bilingualism
- Cultural differences in the use of phonemes
- The deaf community and gestural languages

- Bias in the use of IQ tests for educational placement

Chapter 9: Motivation and Emotion

- Cultural values and food preferences
- Culture, ethnicity, and dieting
- Pain avoidance and cultural conditioning
- The influence of culture on emotional expressions
- Cultural differences in the occurrence of emotion
- Cultural differences in facial expressions
- Cultural learning and body language

Chapter 10: Personality

- Self-esteem and culture

Chapter 11: Health, Stress, and Coping

- Scapegoating of ethnic group members
- Culture shock and acculturative stress

Chapter 12: Psychological Disorders

- How culture affects judgments of psychopathology
- Culture-specific psychological "disorders"
- Ethnic group differences in psychopathology

Chapter 13: Therapies

- Cultural issues in counseling and psychotherapy
- Culturally aware therapists

Chapter 14: Social Behavior

- Cultural differences in norms governing personal space
- Gendered friendships
- Male-female differences in mate preferences
- Evolutionary perspectives on male and female mate selection

How Chapter Features Support Active Learning

Psychology: A Journey uses an SQ4R, active-learning, format to make studying psychology a rewarding experience. Notice how the steps of the SQ4R method—*survey, question, read, reflect, relate,* and *review*—are incorporated into the chapter design.

Survey At the front of each chapter, several features help students build cognitive maps of upcoming topics, thus serving as advance organizers. A short opening vignette arouses interest, provides an entry point into the main topic of the chapter, and focuses attention. Next, a list of *Survey Questions* provides a focused overview of the chapter. These same Survey Questions appear in the main body of the chapter to help students structure their learning. Later, the Survey Questions are used to organize the chapter Summary, and they also appear in the *Study Guide.* In this way, students are given a consistent framework for studying and learning. These chapter-opening features invite students to read with a purpose, and thus engage in active information processing.

■ Table 2   Gender in *Psychology: A Journey*

Chapter 1: Introducing Psychology and Research Methods
- The psychology of gender
- Women in psychology
- A broader view of diversity
- Gender bias in research

Chapter 2: Brain and Behavior
- Oversecretion of sex hormones (and virilism and pre-puberty)
- Male-female differences in brain lateralization

Chapter 3: Human Development
- Parenting styles and gender role development
- Comparing male and female moral reasoning
- Comparing male and female mid-life transitions
- Menopause versus the climacteric
- Gender and happiness

Chapter 5: States of Consciousness
- Lung cancer deaths caused by smoking
- Metabolism of alcohol

- Affects of alcohol on sexual performance
- Sexual affects of Ecstasy

Chapter 6: Conditioning and Learning
- Affects of television on children's perceptions of sex roles
- Affects of television on children's level of aggression

Chapter 8: Intelligence, Cognition, Language, and Creativity
- Sex and IQ
- Gender and genetic mutations

Chapter 9: Motivation and Emotion
- Pain avoidance and cultural conditioning
- Social obstacles to achievement for women
- How hormones affect sex drive
- Gender differences in emotion

Chapter 10: Personality
- Social learning of male and female traits

Chapter 12: Psychological Disorders
- How gender affects judgments of psychopathology

- Gender differences in rates of anxiety disorders
- Sex differences in rates of clinical depression
- Gender differences in suicide (attempt and completion)

Chapter 14: Social Behavior
- Gender differences in touching (as related to status)
- Double standards for male and female performance
- Influence of physical attractiveness
- Male-female differences in mate preferences
- Gendered friendships
- Male-female differences in loving and liking
- Evolutionary perspectives on male and female mate selection

■ Table 3   **Positive Psychology in** *Psychology: A Journey*

Appreciating human diversity (Ch. 1)
Characteristics of the gifted (Ch. 8)
Constructive child discipline (Ch. 3)
Dreams and creativity (Ch. 5)
Elements of positive mental health (Ch. 12)
Emotional intelligence (Ch. 9)
Enhancing creativity (Ch. 8)
Enriching early development (Ch. 3)
Ethical research (Ch. 1)
Exceptional memory (Ch. 7)
Facilitating cognitive development (Ch. 3)
Friendship and attraction (Ch. 14)
Fully functioning person (Ch. 10)
Hardiness and happiness (Ch. 11)

Health promoting behaviors (Ch. 11)
Health-promoting conditions in therapy (Ch. 13)
High achievers (Ch. 9)
Hope (Ch. 11)
Humanistic psychology (Chs. 1, 9, 10, 13)
Improving memory (Ch. 7)
Intrinsic motivation and creativity (Ch. 9)
Loving and liking (Ch. 14)
Meditation (Ch. 11)
Meta-needs (Ch. 9)
Moral behavior (Ch. 3)
Multiple intelligences (Ch. 8)
Optimal caregiving (Ch. 3)
Peak performance (Ch. 9)

Perceptual awareness (Ch. 4)
Positive states of consciousness (Ch. 5)
Promoting secure attachment (Ch. 3)
Promoting self-esteem in children (Ch. 3)
Quality day care (Ch. 3)
Repair of brain damage (Ch. 2)
Self-actualization (Chs. 1, 9, 10)
Self-efficacy (Ch. 10)
Self-confidence (Ch. 10)
Self-esteem (Ch. 10)
Self-regulated learning (Introduction)
Successful aging (Ch. 3)
Wellness (Ch. 11)
Well-being and happiness (Ch. 3)

Question   Throughout each chapter, italicized Guide Questions also serve as advance organizers. That is, Guide Questions prompt students to look for important ideas as they read and thus promote active learning. They also establish a dialogue in which the questions and reactions of students are anticipated. This clarifies difficult points—in a lively give-and-take between questions and responses.

Read   We've made every effort to make this a clear, readable text. To further aid comprehension, we've used a full array of traditional learning aids. These include: boldface terms (with phonetic pronunciations), bullet summaries, a robust illustration program, summary tables, a name index, a subject index, and a detailed glossary. As an additional aid, figure and table references in the text are marked with small geometric shapes. These "place holders" make it easier for students to return to reading after they have paused to view a table or figure.

An integrated Glossary aids reading comprehension by providing precise definitions directly in context. When important terms first appear, they are immediately defined. In this way, students get clear definitions when and where they need them—in the general text itself. In addition, a parallel Running Glossary defines key terms in the margins of pages. The Running Glossary makes it easier for students to find, study, and review important terms.

Recite   Every few pages, a *Study Break* gives students a chance to test their understanding and recall of preceding topics. The Study Breaks are small, built-in study guides that include a *Learning Check* (a short, noncomprehensive quiz), which help students actively process information and assess their progress. Learning Check questions are not as difficult as in-class tests, and they are just a sample of what students could be asked about various topics. Students who miss any items are asked to backtrack and clarify their understanding before reading more. Completing Learning Checks serves as a form of recitation to enhance learning.

Reflect   Cognitive psychology tells us that elaboration, the reflective processing of new information, is one of the best ways to actively foster understanding and form lasting memories (Gadzella, 1995). The more elaborated that processing, the richer the understanding and the better the resulting memory.

Self-reference, a particularly powerful form of elaboration, makes new information more meaningful by relating it to what is already known (Klein and Kihlstrom, 1986). New in this edition are the *Discovering Psychology* boxes. These "try-it" demonstrations allow students to observe interesting facets of their own behavior or do self-assessment exercises, thus linking new chapter information to the student's concrete experience.

To help students further elaborate their new understanding, each Study Break includes a series of *Reflect* questions. These questions also encourage students to associate new concepts with personal experiences and prior knowledge.

A course in psychology also naturally contributes to deeper forms of reflection, such as the development of critical-thinking abilities. To further facilitate reflection, each Study Break also includes one or more *Critical Thinking* questions. These stimulating questions challenge students to think critically and analytically about psychology. Each is followed by a brief answer with which students can compare their own thoughts. Many of these answers are based on research and are informative in their own right.

In addition, several boxed highlights encourage other forms of reflective thought. The *Critical Thinking* features model a reflective approach to the theoretical and empirical foundations of critical thinking in psychology. In addition, *Human Diversity* features encourage reflection on the variability of the human experience, *The Clinical File* features encourage reflection on the clinical applications of psychology, and *Brain Waves* features encourage reflection on the role of the brain in understanding psychological phenomena.

Review   As noted previously, all important terms appear in a Running Glossary throughout the book, which aids review. As also noted, a Psychology in Action section shows students how psychological concepts relate to practical problems, including problems in their own lives. The information found in Psychology in Action helps reinforce learning by illustrating psychology's practicality.

To help students consolidate their learning, the *Chapter in Review* section restates all of the major ideas presented earlier in the chapter. This section begins with a list of *Major Points* that summarize the "take home" concepts every student should be able to remember 10 years after reading this text. Next, a point-by-point *Summary* provides a detailed synopsis of the chapter. As mentioned before, the Summary is organized around the same Survey Questions found at the beginning of the chapter. This brings the SQ4R process full-circle and reinforces the learning objectives for the chapter. Every chapter concludes with Test Your Knowledge, the brief multiple-choice test described earlier. Students who miss any questions on this test are urged to review further, using various supplements available with this text.

Critical Thinking

The active, questioning nature of the SQ4R method is, in itself, an inducement to think critically. Many of the Guide Questions that introduce topics in the text act as models of critical thinking. So do the Critical Thinking, Human Diversity, Discovering Psychology, The Clinical File, and Brain Waves boxed highlights. Further, Chapter 1 contains a discussion of critical thinking skills and a rational appraisal of pseudo-psychologies. In addition, the discussion of research methods in Chapter 1 is actually a short course on how to think clearly about behavior. It is augmented by suggestions about how to critically evaluate claims in the popular media. Chapter 8, "Intelligence, Cognition, Language, and Creativity," includes many topics that focus on thinking skills. Throughout the text, many boxed highlights promote critical thinking about specific topics that students should approach with healthy skepticism. As mentioned earlier, every Study Break includes Critical Thinking questions. Taken together, these features will help students gain thinking skills of lasting value.

PSYCHOLOGY: A JOURNEY—WHAT'S NEW IN THE THIRD EDITION?

Thanks to psychology's vitality and suggestions from professors, this edition has improved in many ways. The Third Edition of *Psychology: A Journey* features some of the most recent and interesting information in psychology and features fully updated references and statistics. The following annotations highlight some of the new topics and features that appear in this edition.

Introduction: The Psychology of Studying

The SQ4R framework has been updated to place more emphasis on critical thinking. Throughout this book, the term *Relate* has been replaced by the term *Reflect* to make it clear that relating new information to personal experience and thinking critically about new information are both forms of reflective cognition. The Introduction, which we recommend students be asked to read, offers students updated information on how to read effectively, study more efficiently, take good notes, prepare for tests, perform well on various types of tests, create study schedules, and avoid procrastination.

Chapter 1: Introducing Psychology and Research Methods

The major modern viewpoints in psychology have now been grouped into three major perspectives: biological, psychological, and sociocultural. This organization provides a better framework for students to apply to the remainder of the book, as well as giving greater prominence to the sociocultural perspective. A new Discovering Psychology feature asks students to explore if a career in psychology is right for them. An updated Clinical File feature explores false media images of psychologists.

Chapter 2: Brain and Behavior

This chapter has been lengthened to reflect the growing importance of neuroscience to psychology. In addition, some other chapters now include Brain Waves boxes to further highlight neuroscience. A new section on neural networks has been added to the discussion of the neurons and neural functioning. Material on plasticity and brain repair has been reorganized and enhanced in this section. The section on research methods in biopsychology has been more clearly reorganized around the key concept of localization of function. Brain imaging methods that reveal brain structure have been clearly differentiated from those that reveal brain function. A new Discovering Psychology feature invites students to think about reaction times in terms of neural conduction. Finally, a new Clinical File feature introduces a striking case study of a stroke that a neuroscientist self-diagnosed.

Chapter 3: Human Development

The opening section on nature-nurture has been reworked to reflect the necessary interplay of heredity and environment rather than casting them as an either-or debate. The previous edition's stress on parenting has been lightened to make room for more material on adolescence and early adulthood. For example, a new Discovering Psychology feature invites students to reflect on the possibility that their adult attachment style is related to their childhood experiences. Similarly, a new Critical Thinking feature introduces the phenomenon of delayed adulthood.

Chapter 4: Sensation and Perception

The chapter opening section on the general properties of sensory systems has been more clearly reorganized around the functions of selection, analysis, and sensory coding. The bottom-up–top-down processing distinction has been more clearly highlighted. The sections on attention, gating, perception and reality, motives, and emotions now more clearly reflect this distinction. The treatment of depth cues now more clearly distinguishes between binocular and monocular cues. The treatment of hearing loss has been rewritten to reflect the National Institutes of Health typology of conduction and sensorineural hearing loss. Noise-induced hearing loss is now treated as a type of sensorineural hearing loss. Finally, a new Brain Waves feature presents a discussion of phantom limb pain and neuromatrix theory as an example of top-down processing.

Chapter 5: States of Consciousness

Many sections of this chapter, including those on sleep patterns, insomnia, and several subsections on drugs, have been rewritten for greater clarity. The section on hypnosis has been upgraded. Hilgard's hidden observer hypothesis is now included and a new Discovering Psychology feature gives students an exercise to explore suggestibility. A new section on meditation and sensory deprivation offers a more fully integrated treatment of these important topics. Various statistics presented in this chapter (such as drug abuse rates and accidents related to sleepiness or drug use) have been updated. The section on recognizing problem drinking has been simplified and now includes an adaptation of the College Alcohol Problems Scale. The old conclusion that marijuana does not produce physical dependence has been tempered with the inclusion of recent data to the contrary. The closing section on dreams has been updated. In particular, the chapter-closing section on dream analysis now relies on the Hall–Van de Castle system of dream content analysis. A new Critical Thinking feature introduces students to the distinction between objective and subjective perspectives on consciousness. Finally, a reworked Clinical File feature on hypnopompic hallucinations highlights the mystery of sleep and introduces students to a naturalistic explanation of out-of-body experiences, alien abductions, and even some false memories of sexual abuse.

Chapter 6: Conditioning and Learning

The section on observational learning and television has been updated to reflect the new mix of digital media. A new Critical Thinking feature updates the discussion of violence in video games. A new Clinical File feature highlights classical conditioning by discussing the side effects of chemotherapy and the use of classical conditioning to minimize the effects of conditioned nausea. Finally, a new Brain Waves feature explores the self-stimulation phenomenon.

Chapter 7: Memory

In the interest of clarity, recognition is no longer referred to as a type of partial memory; it is more consistently treated as a retrieval strategy. There have also been several significant omissions from this chapter. Bahrick's permastore notion, an idea that is little referred to today, is no longer discussed. Overlearning is also no longer stressed as a memory strategy, in light of recent negative evidence. Finally, Lashley's search for the engram is no longer mentioned since many neuroscientists now treat his pioneering work as of historical interest only. This allows a more consistent treatment of the neuroscience of memory. A new Critical Thinking feature draws together previously presented information on hypnosis and memory as well as the cognitive interview technique to better stress the role of false positives in memory retrieval. Finally, a new Human Diversity feature stresses the role of cultural values in shaping what we see as important and, are hence more likely to encode, store, and recall.

Chapter 8: Intelligence, Cognition, Language, and Creativity

This chapter has been renamed *Intelligence, Cognition, Language, and Creativity*. The chapter opener introduces Kim Peek, a remarkable autistic savant. The material on intelligence is now presented at the start of the chapter. The distinction between intelligence as "g" and multiple intelligences is given more prominence, and the material on multiple intelligences has been lengthened to become a chapter section. Artificial intelligence is now given a different treatment and included in the Intelligence section. The material on expertise is now in the section on problem solving. New features on bilingualism, thin-slicing (rapid intuitive judgments), and culture and intelligence have been added while material on madness and creativity has been deleted. The Psychology in Action section now addresses the socially important topic of race, intelligence, and IQ.

Chapter 9: Motivation and Emotion

This chapter now opens with a case study of alexythymia, introducing a chapter theme of "emotions as music." Material on circadian rhythms now appears in the opening section of the chapter and the section on stimulus drives has been restructured. The section on hunger has been restructured into major sections on internal and external factors in hunger. Material on sexual scripts now appears later in the section on sexuality. The result is that the discussion of the lower drives always begins with internal factors and then moves to external factors. Features on sensation seeking and lie detection have been reworked and updated, as has the feature on suppressing emotions. A new Brain Waves feature discusses fat set points.

Chapter 10: Personality

Information on when personality "hardens" has been updated. The distinction between direct and indirect aggression has been clearly linked to issues of personality and gender. Androgyny has been related to emotional intelligence. The overview of personality theories has been reworked. A previous feature on identical twins features a new pair of twins, Carolyn Spiro and Pamela Spiro Wagner. These identical twins were reared together and yet one developed schizophrenia while the other became a psychiatrist. Two new features have been added, on the concept of a musical personality and on perfectionism.

Chapter 11: Health, Stress, and Coping

The material on the general adaptation syndrome and psychoneuroimmunology has been moved toward the beginning of the chapter. A number of specific examples and most of the statistics reported in this chapter have been updated. A new feature on acculturative stress has been added to the chapter, and a feature on coping with traumatic stress has been updated.

Chapter 12: Psychological Disorders

Many incidence statistics and some of the case study examples of the major disorders have been updated in this chapter. A new Brain Waves feature updates the treatment of the schizophrenic brain. A new Discovering Psychology feature invites students to get a sense of how social norms define "normality" in daily life. Features on the politics of mental disorders and culture-bound disorders have been reworked and updated.

Chapter 13: Therapies

This chapter has received a light update, including many of the references and small changes in the main chapter text. Features on quitting smoking and EMDR have been absorbed into the main chapter text while information on how to relax has been promoted to the status of a feature. Finally an existing feature on cultural issues in counseling and psychotherapy has been reworked and updated.

Chapter 14: Social Behavior

The introduction to this chapter now updates Milgram's small world phenomenon for the Internet era. In general, the treatment of the Internet as a tool for social communication has been updated throughout this chapter. The material on TV violence has been reworked and incorporated into an updated section on media violence. The treatment of topics in social influence has been reordered from conformity to compliance and then obedience (in increasing order of directness). The self-assertiveness section now follows the treatment of all three forms of social influence. The treatment of the chance conditioning of attitudes is now included in the section on direct contact. The *Quack Like a Duck* demonstration is now presented as a Discovering Psychology feature, and a new Critical Thinking feature on political polarization in America has been added.

A COMPLETE COURSE—TEACHING AND LEARNING SUPPLEMENTS

A rich array of supplements accompanies *Psychology: A Journey,* including several that make use of the latest technologies. These supplements are designed to make teaching and learning more effective. Many are available free to professors or students. Others can be packaged with this text at a discount. For more information on any of the listed resources, please call the Thomson Learning™ Academic Resource Center at 800-423-0563.

Student Support Materials

Introductory students must learn a multitude of abstract concepts, which can make a first course in psychology difficult. The materials listed here will greatly improve students' chances for success.

Practice Exams with Visual Guides   This free booklet is included with every copy of *Psychology: A Journey* (ISBN: 0-495-10477-9). The Visual Guides present important topics from each chapter in an easy-to-use flow chart. The Visual Guides were created by Art VanDeventer of Thomas Nelson Community College to help students connect ideas and build cognitive maps of key concepts. The Practice Exams, written by Shawn Talbot of Kellogg Community College, consist of 20 multiple-choice questions that students can use to evaluate their understanding and prepare for classroom tests.

Study Guide   To facilitate learning, the *Study Guide* provides abundant opportunities for practice, self-testing, and rehearsal. The *Study Guide* is structured around the SQ4R method and closely coordinated with this text. Each chapter includes the following sections: Chapter Overview (a concise chapter summary), Learning Objectives (a detailed list of what students need to know), Recite and Review (a survey of major terms and concepts), Connections (matching items), Check Your Memory (true-false items), Final Survey and Review (fill-in-the-blank questions), and a Mastery Test (multiple-choice questions similar to in-class test items). The *Study Guide* also includes a Language Development Guide. For some students, language and culture can be major barriers to comprehension. The Language Development Guide helps clarify idioms and special phrases, cultural and historic allusions, and tricky vocabulary. All terms and phrases in the manual are page-referenced to the text and followed by concise definitions. (*Study Guide,* by Joseph Karafa of Ferris State University, ISBN: 0-495-10374-8.)

Careers in Psychology: Opportunities in a Changing World   This informative new booklet, written by Tara L. Kuther, is a Wadsworth exclusive. The pamphlet describes the field of psychology, as well as how to prepare for a career in psychology. Career options and resources are also discussed. *Careers in Psychology* can be packaged with this text at no additional cost to students (ISBN 0-495-09078-6).

Multimedia CD-ROM

Interactive CD-ROMs make it possible for students to directly experience some of the phenomena they are studying. The following CD from Wadsworth provides a wealth of engaging modules and exercises.

Sniffy™ *the Virtual Rat, Lite Version 2.0*   There's no better way to master the basic principles of learning than working with a real laboratory rat. However, this is usually impractical in introductory psychology courses. *Sniffy the Virtual Rat* offers a fun, interactive alternative to working with lab animals. This innovative and entertaining software teaches students about operant and classical conditioning by allowing them to condition a virtual rat. Users begin by training Sniffy to press a bar to obtain food. Then they progress to studying the effects of reinforcement schedules and simple classical conditioning. In addition, special "Mind Windows" enable students to visualize how Sniffy's experiences in the Skinner Box produce learning. The Sniffy CD-ROM includes a Lab Manual that shows students how to set up various operant and classical conditioning experiments. *Sniffy*™ *the Virtual Rat, Lite Version 2.0* may be packaged with this text for a discount (ISBN: 0-534-63357-9).

Internet Resources

The Internet is providing new ways to exchange information and enhance education. In psychology, Wadsworth is at the forefront in making use of this exciting technology.

Book Companion Website   As users of this text, you and your students will have access to the *Psychology: A Journey* section of the Wadsworth Psychology Resource Center (http://psychology.wadsworth.com). Access is free and no pincode is required. The site includes learning objectives, a glossary, flash cards, crossword puzzles, and extensive Web links. It also offers chapter quizzing—multiple-choice and essay questions.

ThomsonNOW   This valuable study aid is available free to students. The new Self-Study Assessments, written by Christopher Mayhorn of North Carolina State University, work in tandem with this text's SQ4R learning system. For every Study Break in the text, the Self-Study Assessment program offers a *Pre-Test* (20–25 questions) that students can complete to determine what they know. A second *Post-Test* (with 20–25 different questions) lets students see what they've learned after further study. Then, personalized *Integrated Study Plans* (with page numbers) are generated automatically, based on their responses to the *Pre-Tests* and *Post-Tests.*

After they read a text chapter, students can access a Pre-Test using the free Pin Code that came with their text. (Please note: This Pin Code is not automatically packaged with *Journey*, it must be requested as a bundle.)

After submitting the Pre-Test, a Personalized Study Plan is created, which directs students to specific topics (and specific page references) they need to review. For convenience, students can print the Personalized Study Plan to use as a guide. Students are also given access to numerous digital resources, such as ABC videos, simulations, narrated animations, glossary terms, and Web links, all of which are tied to specific topics in the text. Extensive, media-rich Learning Modules with strong pedagogy are also available for key concepts.

Following their review of specific topics in *Psychology: A Journey,* students take a Post-Test to verify their understanding of the chapter. ThomsonNOW also includes a gradebook for instructors to track students' progress through the Pre-Test and Post-Test process (ISBN: 0-495-10496-5).

Thomson Learning *Web Tutor Toolbox*™   This online supplement helps students succeed by taking them into an environment rich with study and mastery tools, communication aids, and additional course content. For students, *Web Tutor* offers real-time access to a full array of study tools, including flashcards (with audio), practice quizzes and tests, online tutorials, exercises, asynchronous discussion, a whiteboard, and an integrated e-mail system. Students will also have integrated access to the online library, as well as to the *Newbury House Online Dictionary,* an interactive dictionary that gives users instant access to definitions (including audio pronunciations).

Professors can use *Web Tutor Toolbox*™ to offer virtual office hours, to post syllabi, to set up threaded discussions, to track student progress on quizzes, and more. You can customize the content of *Web Tutor* in any way you choose, including uploading images and other resources, adding Web links, and creating course-specific practice materials. (*Web Tutor Toolbox* on *WebCT*, ISBN: 0-495-10494-9; Toolbox on *Blackboard*, ISBN: 0-495-10493-0.)

Essential Teaching Resources

As every professor knows, teaching an introductory psychology course is a tremendous amount of work. The supplements listed here should not only make life easier for you, they should also make it possible for you to concentrate on the more creative and rewarding facets of teaching.

Instructor's Resource Manual   The *Instructor's Resource Manual* (ISBN: 0-495-10376-4) was prepared by Susan Weldon of Henry Ford Community College. For every chapter in the text, this manual includes: learning objectives and detailed chapter outlines; discussion topics, classroom activities, and handouts; Web links; and video suggestions. The manual also includes a detailed *Resource Integration Guide* that shows, at a glance, how each of this text's supplements correlates to each chapter of the text.

Test Bank   The *Test Bank* was prepared by Jeannette Murphey of Meridian Community College. It includes over 4,000 multiple-choice questions organized by chapter and by Learning Objectives. All items, which are classified as factual, conceptual, or applied, include correct answers and page references from the text. To encourage students to study, 15 items per chapter in the *Test Bank* are drawn from the printed *Study Guide,* and 20 items are taken from online Web quizzes. Every chapter of the *Test Bank* also includes 35–40 fill-in-the-blank and 20 essay questions that tie into the learning objectives (ISBN: 0-495-10377-2).

Multimedia Manager Instructor's Resource **CD-ROM**   This CD-ROM includes PowerPoint® lecture outline slides with video clips, animations, and art from the book—as well as the complete *Instructor's Resource Manual* and *Test Bank* in Word® format (ISBN: 0-495-10479-5).

JoinIn™ *on TurningPoint*®   JoinIn turns your ordinary PowerPoint application into powerful audience response software, allowing you to take attendance, poll students on key issues to spark discussion, check student comprehension of difficult concepts, collect student demographics to better assess student needs, and even administer quizzes without collecting paper or grading. In addition, we provide interactive slide sets that you can modify and merge with any existing PowerPoint lecture slides for a seamless classroom presentation (ISBN: 0-495-10425-6).

ExamView **Computerized Testing**   This software helps you create, deliver, and customize tests and study guides (both in print and online). In just minutes, this easy-to-use system can generate the assessment and tutorial materials your students need. *ExamView* offers both a Quick Test Wizard and an Online Test Wizard that guide you step-by-step through the process of creating tests. *ExamView* shows the test you are creating on the screen exactly as it will print or display online. Using a database prepared by Sandra Madison, you can build tests of up to 250 questions using up to 12 question types. *ExamView's* complete word processing capabilities also allow you to enter an unlimited number of new questions or edit existing questions (ISBN: 0-495-10378-0).

Videotapes and Films

Wadsworth offers a variety of videotapes and films to enhance classroom presentations. Many video segments in the Wadsworth collection pertain directly to major topics in this text, making them excellent lecture supplements.

Wadsworth Film and Video Library for Introductory Psychology   Adopters can select from a variety of continually updated film and video options. The Wadsworth Film and Video Library includes selections from the *Discovering Psychology* series, the *Annenberg* series, and *Films for Humanities*. It also includes the exclusive CNN offerings described below. Contact your local sales representative or Wadsworth Marketing at 877-999-2350 for details.

ABC® *Videos for Introductory Psychology*   These one- to four-minute video clips, a Wadsworth exclusive, allow you to integrate the newsgathering and programming power of ABC into the classroom to show students the relevance of psychology to daily life. Organized by course topics, these compelling clips are ideal for launching lectures and encouraging discussion. Adopters receive one new, updated video each year. A Wadsworth/Thomson Learning Exclusive!

Psychology Digital Video Library Version 3.0 CD-ROM   This CD-ROM contains a diverse selection of more than 100 classic and contemporary clips, including "Little Albert," the "Action Potential of a Neuron," "Parts of the Brain," and many more! The digital library offers a convenient way to access an appropriate clip for every lecture. An accompanying *Digital Video Handbook* offers a detailed description, approximate running time, and references to related media clips. It also offers objective quizzing and critical-thinking questions for each clip, as well as instructions on how to embed clips into your *PowerPoint* presentations. Available exclusively to instructors who adopt Wadsworth psychology texts (ISBN: 0-495-09063-8).

Supplementary Books

No text can cover all of the topics that might be included in an introductory psychology course. If you would like to enrich your course, or make it more challenging, the Wadsworth titles listed here may be of interest.

Critical Thinking in Psychology: Separating Sense from Nonsense, Second Edition

The second edition of *Critical Thinking in Psychology: Separating Sense from Nonsense* (ISBN: 0-534-63459-1) provides the tools to distinguish between the true science of human thought and behavior from pop psychology. John Ruscio's book provides a tangible and compelling framework for making that distinction. Because we are inundated with "scientific" claims, the author does not merely differentiate science and pseudoscience, but goes further to teach the fundamentals of scientific reasoning on which students can base their evaluation of information.

Challenging Your Preconceptions: Thinking Critically about Psychology, Second Edition

This paperbound book (ISBN: 0-534-26739-4), written by Randolph Smith, helps students strengthen their critical thinking skills. Psychological issues such as hypnosis and repressed memory, statistical seduction, the validity of pop psychology, and other topics arc used to illustrate the principles of critical thinking.

Writing Papers in Psychology: A Student Guide

The seventh edition of *Writing Papers in Psychology* (ISBN: 0-534-53331-0), by Ralph and Mimi Rosnow, is a valuable "how to" manual for writing term papers and research reports. This new edition has been updated to reflect the latest APA guidelines. The book covers each task with examples, hints, and two complete writing samples. Citation ethics, how to locate information, and new research technologies are also covered.

Your Guide to College Success: Strategies for Achieving Your Goals, Concise Edition (with Instant Access Code-ThomsonNOW™)

Authored by John Santrock, a prominent developmental psychologist, and Jane Halonen, an educational leader in critical thinking, this fourth edition (ISBN: 1-413-02073-9) emphasizes student self-awareness in the pursuit of college success goals, as well as active learning strategies.

College Survival Guide: Hints and References to Aid College Students

This fourth edition of Bruce Rowe's *College Survival Guide* (ISBN: 0-534-35569-2) is designed to help students succeed. Rowe provides valuable tips on how to finance an education, how to manage time, how to study for and take exams, and more. Other sections focus on maintaining concentration, credit by examination, use of the credit/no credit option, cooperative education programs, and the importance of a liberal arts education.

Cross-Cultural Perspectives in Psychology

How well do the concepts of psychology apply to various cultures? What can we learn about human behavior from cultures different from our own? These questions lie behind a collection of original articles written by William F. Price and Rich Crapo. The fourth edition of *Cross-Cultural Perspectives in Psychology* (ISBN: 0-534-54653-6) contains articles on North American ethnic groups as well as cultures from around the world.

Wadsworth Quick Guide for Career Planning

This quick guide (ISBN: 1-413-02264-2) provides highly useful tools for students needing step-by-step advice on career planning.

Wadsworth Quick Guide to Our Diverse World

This booklet (ISBN: 1-413-02259-6) tackles the topic of diversity, including how to fight the natural tendency to stereotype, discriminate, and hold prejudicial views of others.

Culture and Psychology: People Around the World, Third Edition

David Matsumoto and Linda Juang's unique book (ISBN: 0-534-53591-7) discusses similarities and differences in research findings in the United States and other cultures. By doing so, it helps students see psychology and their own behavior from a broader, more culturally aware perspective.

College Success Internet at a Glance (Trifold Brochure)

This handy one-page laminated reference (ISBN: 0-534-56411-9) for students has a host of URL addresses related to college success—to give you a guided tour of the Internet!

Summary

We sincerely hope that teachers and students will consider this book and its supporting materials a refreshing change from the ordinary. Creating it has been quite an adventure. In the pages that follow, we think students will find an attractive blend of the theoretical and the practical, plus many of the most exciting ideas in psychology. Most of all, we hope that students using this book will discover that reading a college textbook can be entertaining and enjoyable.

ACKNOWLEDGMENTS

Psychology is a cooperative effort requiring the talents and energies of a large community of scholars, teachers, researchers, and students. Like most endeavors in psychology, this book reflects the efforts of many people. We deeply appreciate the contributions of all those who have supported this text's evolution, including the following psychologists:

Jean Brown, Cambrian College
Anice Bullock, Tomball College
Lisa Clark, Clark Atlanta University
Eric Comstock, Heald College, Concord
David Das, Elgin Community College
Michael Gardner, California State University, Northridge
Dorothy Gomez, Bunker Hill Community College
Frank Hager, Allegany College of Maryland
John Haworth, Florida Community College at Jacksonville
John S. Klein, Castleton State College
Patricia Lanzon, Henry Ford Community college
Denis Laplante, Lambton College
Laura Madson, New Mexico State University
Errol Magidson, Richard J. Daley College
Horace Marchant, Westfield State College
Richard Mascolo, El Camino Community College
Shawn Mikulay, Elgin Community College
Pike Nelson, Chicago State University
Alysia Ritter, Murray State University
Moises Salinas, Central Connecticut State University
Matthew Westra, Longview Community College

We especially wish to thank the following professors, whose sage advice helped improve the second edition of *Psychology: A Journey:*

Dana Albright, Clovis Community College

Saundra Ciccarelli, Gulf Coast Community College

Ellen Cotter, Georgia Southwestern State University

Keith Davis, University of South Carolina

Mary Ellen Dello Stritto, Ball State University

Mylo Egipciaco, Los Angeles Pierce College

Richard Epro, Nassau County Community College

Sabra Jacobs, Prestonsburg Community College

Thuy Karafa, Ferris State University

Jimi Leopold, Tarleton State University

Feleccia Moore-Davis, Houston Community College

Todd Nelson, California State University, Stanislaus

Randall Osborne, Southwest Texas State University

Sandra Phipps, Hazard Community College

Robert Wellman, Fitchburg State College

Matthew Zagumny, Tennessee Tech University

Producing *Psychology: A Journey* and its supplements was a formidable task. We are especially indebted to each of the following individuals for supporting this book:

Susan Badger

Eve Howard

Sean Wakely

We also wish to thank the individuals at Wadsworth who so generously shared their knowledge and talents over the past year. These are the people who made it happen:

Vernon Boes

Sara Swangard

Jerilyn Emori

Jeremy Judson

Kristin Makarewycz

Magnolia Molcan

Margaret Parks

Laura Stowe

Barbara Kushmier and Kayleigh Hagerman also helped with several aspects of the preparation of this book. It has been a pleasure to work with such a gifted group of professionals and many others at Wadsworth. We would especially like to express our gratitude to former editor Marianne Taflinger for plotting a new course for *Journey*. Her editorial guidance will make life easier for professors and students who use this book. Special thanks also to Kristin Makarewycz and Jeremy Judson for helping to bring the itinerary into sharper focus.

Last of all, we would like to thank our wives, Sevren and Heather, for making the journey worthwhile.

The Psychology of Studying

E Even if you're an excellent student, you may be able to improve your study skills. Students who get good grades tend to work *smarter,* not just longer or harder (Santrock & Halonen, 2007). To help you get a good start, let's look at several ways to improve studying.

THE SQ4R METHOD—HOW TO TAME A TEXTBOOK

How much do you typically remember after you've read a textbook chapter? If the answer is "Nada," "Zilch," or simply "Not enough," it may be time to try the **SQ4R method.** SQ4R stands for *survey, question, read, recite, reflect,* and *review.* These six steps can help you learn as you read, remember more, and review effectively:

S = *Survey.* Skim through a chapter before you begin reading it. Start by looking at topic headings, figure captions, and summaries. Try to get an overall picture of what lies ahead. Because this book is organized into short sections, you can survey just one section at a time if you prefer.

Q = *Question.* As you read, turn each topic heading into one or more questions. For example, when you read the heading "Stages of Sleep" you might ask: "Is there more than one stage of sleep?" "What are the stages of sleep?" "How do they differ?" Asking questions helps you read with a purpose.

R1 = *Read.* The first R in SQ4R stands for read. As you read, look for answers to the questions you asked. Read in short "bites," from one topic heading to the next, then stop. For difficult material you may want to read only a paragraph or two at a time.

R2 = *Recite.* After reading a small amount, you should pause and recite or rehearse. That is, try to mentally answer your questions. Better yet, summarize what you just read in brief notes. Making notes will show you what you know and don't know, so you can fill gaps in your knowledge (Peverly et al., 2003).

If you can't summarize the main ideas, skim over each section again. Until you can remember what you just read, there's little point to reading more.

After you've studied a short "bite" of text, turn the next topic heading into questions. Then read to the following heading. Remember to look for answers as you read and to recite or take notes before moving on. Ask yourself repeatedly, "What is the main idea here?" Repeat the question-read-recite cycle until you've finished an entire chapter (or just from one Study Break to the next, if you want to read shorter units).

R3 = *Reflect.* As you read, try to relate new facts, terms, and concepts to information you already know well or to your own experiences. You've probably noticed that it is especially easy to remember ideas that are personally meaningful so try to relate the ideas you encounter to your own life. This may be the most important step in the SQ4R method. The more genuine interest you can bring to your reading, the more you will learn (Hartlep & Forsyth, 2000).

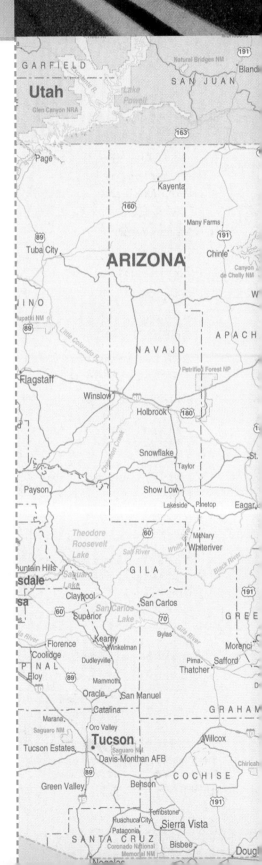

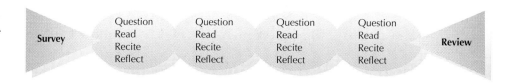

R4 = *Review.* When you're done reading, skim back over the chapter, or read your notes. Then check your memory by reciting and quizzing yourself again. Try to make frequent, active review a standard part of your study habits. (See ►►Fig. I.1.)

Does this really work? Yes. Using a reading strategy improves learning and course grades (Taraban, Rynearson, & Kerr, 2000). Simply reading straight through a chapter can give you "intellectual indigestion." That's why it's better to stop often to think, question, recite, relate, review, and "digest" information as you read.

HOW TO USE *PSYCHOLOGY: A JOURNEY*

You can apply the SQ4R method to any text. However, this book is specifically designed to help you actively learn psychology.

Survey
Each chapter opens with a preview called *Journey into Psychology* and a list of *Survey Questions.* You can use these features to identify important ideas as you begin reading. The previews should help you get interested in the topics you will be reading about and Survey Questions are a good guide to the kinds of information you should look for as you read. After you've studied these features, take a few minutes to do your own survey of the chapter. Doing so will help you build a "mental map" of upcoming topics.

Question
How can I use the SQ4R method to make reading more interesting and effective? One of the key steps is to ask yourself lots of questions while you read. The Survey Questions are repeated throughout each chapter to help you recognize key topics. In addition, questions like the one that began this paragraph appear throughout each chapter. They will help you focus on seeking information as you read. However, be sure to ask your own questions, too. Try to actively interact with your textbooks as you read.

Read
As an aid to reading, important terms are printed in **boldface type** and defined where they first appear. (Some are followed by pronunciations—capital letters show which syllables are accented.) You'll also find a *running glossary* on the page you are reading, so you never have to guess about the meaning of technical terms. If you need to look up a term from lecture or another chapter, check the main *Glossary.* This "mini-dictionary" is located near the end of the book. Perhaps you should take a moment to find it now.

Recite and Reflect
Every few pages, a learning guide called a *Study Break* provides chances to think, rehearse, reflect, and test your memory. (Don't forget to also take notes or recite on your own.) If you want to study chapters in smaller "bites," Study Breaks make good stopping points.

This book also encourages you to reflect more deeply about what you are reading. Near the end of each chapter, you'll find a section called *Psychology in Action.* These discussions are filled with practical ideas you can put to use in your own life. *Discovering Psychology* boxes also invite you to relate psychology to your own life. The *Critical Thinking* boxes will help you reflect on intriguing questions and apply critical thinking skills to psychology. In addition, *Human Diver-*

SQ4R method An active study-reading technique based on these steps: survey, question, read, recite, reflect, and review.

sity boxes encourage you to reflect on the rich variability of human experience, *Brainwaves* boxes invite you to reflect on how the brain relates to psychology, and *The Clinical File* encourages you to reflect on ways that psychology can be applied to treat clinical problems.

Review

Each chapter concludes with a summary, called *Chapter in Review,* to help you identify key ideas to remember. Each Chapter in Review begins with a list of *Major Points* that make up the most important concepts or "big ideas" of the chapter. Then, a point-by-point *Summary* reviews the chapter in greater detail. These summaries are organized around the same Survey Questions you read at the beginning of the chapter. You can also return to the glossary items throughout each chapter for further review.

On the last page of every chapter you will find a brief quiz called *Test Your Knowledge.* You can use this quiz to get a preliminary idea about how well you remember ideas and concepts from your reading. But don't stop studying just because you do well on one of these quizzes. Additional review and practice will add greatly to your understanding—not to mention your test scores.

■ Table I.1 summarizes how this text helps you apply the SQ4R method. Even with all this help, there is still much more you can do on your own.

EFFECTIVE NOTE-TAKING— GOOD STUDENTS, TAKE NOTE!

Reading strategies may be good for studying, but what about taking notes in class? Sometimes it's hard to know what's important. Like effective reading, good notes come from actively seeking information. People who are **active listeners** avoid distractions and skillfully gather ideas. Here's a listening/note-taking plan that works for many students. The letters LISAN, pronounced like the word *listen,* will help you remember the steps.

L = *Lead. Don't follow.* Try to anticipate what your teacher will say by asking yourself questions. Questions can come from study guides, reading assignments, or your own curiosity.

I = *Ideas.* Every lecture is based on a core of ideas. Usually, an idea is followed by examples or explanations. Ask yourself often, "What is the main idea now? What ideas support it?"

S = *Signal words.* Listen for words that tell you what direction the instructor is taking. For instance, here are some signal words:

There are three reasons why . . .	Here come ideas
Most important is . . .	Main idea
On the contrary . . .	Opposite idea
As an example . . .	Support for main idea
Therefore . . .	Conclusion

A = *Actively listen.* Sit where you can get involved and ask questions. Bring questions you want answered from the last lecture or from your text. Raise your hand at the beginning of class or approach your professor before the lecture. Do anything that helps you stay active, alert, and engaged.

N = *Note taking.* Students who take accurate lecture notes tend to do well on tests (Williams & Eggert, 2002). However, don't try to be a tape recorder. Listen to everything, but be selective and write down only key points. If you are too busy writing, you may not grasp what your professor is saying. When you're taking notes, it might help to think of yourself as a reporter who is trying to get a good story (Ryan, 2001).

■ Table I.1 Using the SQ4R Method

Survey
Preview
Survey Questions
Figure Captions
Chapter in Review

Question
Topic Headings
Survey Questions
In-text dialogue questions

Read
Topic Headings
Boldface Terms
Running Glossary (in margins)
Figures and Tables

Recite
Learning Check Questions (in Study Breaks)
Practice Quizzes (online)
Notes (make them while reading)

Reflect
Reflect Questions (in Study Breaks)
Critical Thinking Questions (in Study Breaks)
Boxed Features (throughout the text)

Review
Chapter in Review
Boldface Terms
Running Glossary (in margins)
Tables
Test Your Knowledge
Practice Quizzes (online)
Study Guide

Active listener A person who knows how to maintain attention, avoid distractions, and actively gather information from lectures.

Actually, most students take reasonably good notes—and then don't use them! Many students wait until just before exams to review. By then, their notes have lost much of their meaning. If you don't want your notes to seem like "chicken scratches," it pays to review them every day (Rowe, 2007).

Using and Reviewing Your Notes

When you review, you will learn more if you take the extra steps listed here (Knaus & Ellis, 2002; Rowe, 2007; Santrock & Halonen, 2007).

- As soon as you can, improve your notes by filling in gaps, completing thoughts, and looking for connections among ideas.
- Remember to link new ideas to what you already know.
- Summarize your notes. Boil them down and *organize* them.
- After each class session, write down at least seven major ideas, definitions, or details that are likely to become test questions. Then, make up questions from your notes and be sure you can answer them.

Summary

The letters LISAN are a guide to active listening, but listening and good note taking are not enough. You must also review, organize, reflect, and extend, and think about new ideas. Use active listening to get involved in your classes and you will undoubtedly learn more (Rowe, 2007).

STUDY STRATEGIES— MAKING A HABIT OF SUCCESS

Grades depend nearly as much on effort as they do on "intelligence." However, don't forget that good students work more *efficiently*, not just harder. Many study practices are notoriously poor, such as recopying lecture notes, studying class notes but not the textbook (or the textbook but not class notes), outlining chapters, answering study questions with the book open, and "group study" (which often becomes a party). The best students emphasize *quality:* They study their books and notes in depth and attend classes regularly. It's a mistake to blame poor grades on events "beyond your control." Students who are motivated to succeed usually get better grades (Perry et al., 2001). Let's consider a few more things you can do to improve your study habits.

Study in a Specific Place

Ideally, you should study in a quiet, well-lighted area free of distractions. If possible, you should also have at least one place where you *only study.* Do nothing else at that spot: Keep magazines, iPods, friends, cell phones, pets, posters, video games, puzzles, food, lovers, sports cars, elephants, pianos, televisions, kazoos, and other distractions out of the area. In this way, the habit of studying will become strongly linked with one specific place. Then, rather than trying to force yourself to study, all you have to do is go to your study area. Once there, you'll find it is relatively easy to get started.

Use Spaced Study Sessions

It is reasonable to review intensely before an exam. However, you're taking a big risk if you are only "cramming" (learning new information at the last minute). Spaced practice is much more efficient (Anderson, 2005). **Spaced practice** consists of a large number of relatively short study sessions. Long, uninterrupted study sessions are called **massed practice.** (If you "massed up" your studying, you probably messed it up too.)

Spaced practice Practice spread over many relatively short study sessions.

Massed practice Practice done in a long, uninterrupted study session.

Cramming places a big burden on memory. Usually, you shouldn't try to learn anything new about a subject during the last day before a test. It is far better to learn small amounts every day and review frequently (Anderson, 2005).

Try Mnemonics

Learning has to start somewhere, and memorizing is often the first step. Let's consider just one technique here.

A **mnemonic** (nee-MON-ik) is a memory aid. Most mnemonics link new information to ideas or images that are easy to remember. For example, what if you want to remember that the Spanish word for duck is *pato* (pronounced POT-oh)? To use a mnemonic, you could picture a duck in a pot or a duck wearing a pot for a hat. Likewise, to remember that the cerebellum controls coordination, you might picture someone named "Sarah Bellum" who is very coordinated. For best results, make your mnemonic images exaggerated or bizarre, vivid, and interactive (Macklin & McDaniel, 2005). There are many ways to create mnemonics. If you would like to learn more about memory strategies, see Chapter 7.

Test Yourself

A great way to improve grades is to take practice tests before the real one in class. In other words, studying should include **self-testing,** in which you pose questions to yourself. You can use flash cards, "Learning Check" questions, "Test Your Knowledge" questions, online quizzes, a study guide, or other means. As you study, ask many questions and be sure you can answer them. Studying without self-testing is like practicing for a basketball game without shooting any baskets.

For more convenient self-testing, your professor may make a *Study Guide* or a separate booklet of *Practice Quizzes* available. You can use either to review for tests. Practice quizzes are also available on the Book Companion website, as described later. However, don't use practice quizzes as a substitute for studying your textbook and lecture notes. Trying to learn from quizzes alone will probably *lower* your grades. It is best to use quizzes to find out what topics you need to study more (Brothen & Wambach, 2001).

Overlearn

Many students *underprepare* for exams, and most *overestimate* how well they will do. A solution to both problems is **overlearning,** in which you continue studying beyond your initial mastery of a topic. In other words, plan to do extra study and review *after* you think you are prepared for a test. One way to overlearn is approach all tests as if they will be essays. That way, you will learn more completely, so you really "know your stuff."

SELF-REGULATED LEARNING— ACADEMIC ALL-STARS

Think of a topic you are highly interested in, such as music, sports, fashion, cars, cooking, politics, or movies. Whatever the topic, you have probably learned a lot about it—painlessly. How could you make your college work more like voluntary learning? An approach called self-regulated learning might be a good start. **Self-regulated learning** is active, self-guided study (Hofer & Yu, 2003). Here's how you can change passive studying into goal-oriented learning:

1. *Set specific, objective learning goals.* Try to begin each learning session with specific goals in mind. What knowledge or skills are you trying to master? What do you hope to accomplish? (Knaus & Ellis, 2002).

2. *Plan a learning strategy.* How will you accomplish your goals? Make daily, weekly, and monthly plans for learning. Then put them into action.

Mnemonics make new information more familiar and memorable. Forming an image of a duck wearing a pot for a hat might help you remember that *pato* is the Spanish word for duck.

Mnemonic A memory aid or strategy.

Self-testing Evaluating learning by posing questions to yourself.

Overlearning Continuing to study and learn after you first think you've mastered a topic.

Self-regulated learning Active, self-guided learning.

3. *Be your own teacher.* Effective learners silently give themselves guidance and ask themselves questions. For example, as you are learning, you might ask yourself, "What are the important ideas here? What do I remember? What don't I understand? What do I need to review? What should I do next?"

4. *Monitor your progress.* Self-regulated learning depends on self-monitoring. Exceptional learners keep records of their progress toward learning goals (pages read, hours of studying, assignments completed, and so forth). They quiz themselves, use study guides, and find other ways to check their understanding while learning.

5. *Reward yourself.* When you meet your daily, weekly, or monthly goals, reward your efforts in some way, such as going to a movie or buying a new CD. Be aware that self-praise also rewards learning. Being able to say, "Hey, I did it!" or "Good work!" and know that you deserve it can be very rewarding. In the long run, success, self-improvement, and personal satisfaction are the real payoffs for learning.

6. *Evaluate your progress and goals.* It is a good idea to frequently evaluate your performance records and goals. Are there specific areas of your work that need improvement? If you are not making good progress toward long-range goals, do you need to revise your short-term targets?

7. *Take corrective action.* If you fall short of your goals you may need to adjust how you budget your time. You may also need to change your learning environment, to deal with distractions such as watching TV, daydreaming, talking to friends, or testing the structural integrity of the walls with your stereo system.

If you discover that you lack necessary knowledge or skills, ask for help, take advantage of tutoring programs, or look for information beyond your courses and textbooks. Knowing how to regulate and control learning can be a key to life-long enrichment and personal empowerment.

PROCRASTINATION—AVOIDING THE LAST-MINUTE BLUES

All of these study techniques are fine. But what can I do about procrastination? A tendency to procrastinate is almost universal. (When campus workshops on procrastination are offered, many students never get around to signing up!) Even when procrastination doesn't lead to failure, it can cause much suffering. Procrastinators work only under pressure, skip classes, give false reasons for late work, and feel ashamed of their last-minute efforts. They also tend to feel frustrated, bored, and guilty more often (Blunt & Pychyl, 2005).

Why do so many students procrastinate? Many students equate grades with their *personal worth.* That is, they act as if grades tell whether they are good, smart people who will succeed in life. By procrastinating they can blame poor work on a late start, rather than a lack of ability (Beck, Koons, & Milgrim, 2000). After all, it wasn't their best effort, was it? Perfectionism is a related problem. If you expect the impossible, it's hard to start an assignment. Students with high standards often end up with all-or-nothing work habits (Onwuegbuzie, 2000).

Time Management

Most procrastinators must eventually face the self-worth issue. Nevertheless, most can improve by learning study skills and better time management. We have already discussed general study skills, so let's consider time management in a little more detail.

A **weekly time schedule** is a written plan that allocates time for study, work, and leisure activities. To prepare your schedule, make a chart showing all of the hours in each day of

Weekly time schedule A written plan that allocates time for study, work, and leisure activities during a one-week period.

the week. Then fill in times that are already committed: sleep, meals, classes, work, team practices, lessons, appointments, and so forth. Next, fill in times when you will study for various classes. Finally, label the remaining hours as open or free times.

Each day, you can use your schedule as a checklist. That way you'll know at a glance which tasks are done and which still need attention (Knaus & Ellis, 2002).

You may also find it valuable to make a **term schedule** that lists the dates of all quizzes, tests, reports, papers, and other major assignments for each class.

The beauty of sticking to a schedule is that you know you are making an honest effort. It will also help you avoid feeling bored while you are working or guilty when you play.

Be sure to treat your study times as serious commitments, but respect your free times, too. And remember, students who study hard and practice time management *do* get better grades (Rau & Durand, 2000).

Goal Setting

As mentioned earlier, students who are active learners set **specific goals** for studying. Such goals should be clear-cut and measurable (Knaus & Ellis, 2002). If you find it hard to stay motivated, try setting goals for the semester, the week, the day, and even for single study sessions. Also, be aware that more effort early in a course can greatly reduce the "pain" and stress you will experience later. If your professors don't give frequent assignments, set your own day-by-day goals. That way, you can turn big assignments into a series of smaller tasks that you can actually complete (Ariely & Wertenbroch, 2002). An example would be reading, studying, and reviewing 8 pages a day to complete a 40-page chapter in 5 days. For this book, reading from one Study Break to the next each day might be a good pace. Remember, many small steps can add up to an impressive journey. (See ▸▸Fig. I.2 for a summary of study skills.)

Make Learning an Adventure

A final point to remember is that you are most likely to procrastinate if you think a task will be unpleasant (Pychyl et al., 2000). Learning can be hard work. Nevertheless, many students find ways to make schoolwork interesting and enjoyable. Try to approach your schoolwork as if it were a game, a sport, an adventure, or simply a way to become a better person. The best educational experiences are challenging, yet fun (Ferrari & Scher, 2000).

Virtually every topic is interesting to someone, somewhere. You may not be particularly interested in the sex life of South American tree frogs. However, a biologist might be fascinated. (Another tree frog might be, too.) If you wait for teachers to "make" their courses interesting, you are missing the point. Interest is a matter of *your attitude.*

TAKING TESTS—ARE YOU "TEST WISE"?

If I read and study effectively, is there anything else I can do to improve my grades? You must also be able to show what you know on tests. Here are some suggestions for improving your test-taking skills.

General Test-Taking Skills

You'll do better on all types of tests if you observe the following guidelines (Wood & Willoughby, 1995):

1. Read all directions and questions carefully. They may give you good advice or clues.
2. Quickly survey the test before you begin.

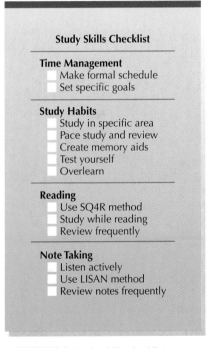

Study Skills Checklist

Time Management
- [ ] Make formal schedule
- [ ] Set specific goals

Study Habits
- [ ] Study in specific area
- [ ] Pace study and review
- [ ] Create memory aids
- [ ] Test yourself
- [ ] Overlearn

Reading
- [ ] Use SQ4R method
- [ ] Study while reading
- [ ] Review frequently

Note Taking
- [ ] Listen actively
- [ ] Use LISAN method
- [ ] Review notes frequently

▸▸**FIGURE I.2** Study skills checklist.

Term schedule A written plan that lists the dates of all major assignments for each of your classes for an entire semester or quarter.

Specific goal A goal with a clearly defined and measurable outcome.

3. Answer easy questions before spending time on more difficult ones.
4. Be sure to answer all questions.
5. Use your time wisely.
6. Ask for clarification when necessary.

Objective Tests

Several additional strategies can help you do better on objective tests. Objective tests (multiple-choice and true-false items) require you to recognize a correct answer among wrong ones or a true statement versus a false one. Here are some strategies for taking objective tests.

1. First, relate the question to what you know about the topic. Then, read the alternatives. Does one match the answer you expected to find? If none match, reexamine the choices and look for a *partial* match.
2. Read *all* the choices for each question before you make a decision. Here's why: If you immediately think that *a* is correct and stop reading, you might miss seeing a better answer like "both *a* and *d*."
3. Read rapidly and skip items you are unsure about. You may find "free information" in later questions that will help you answer difficult items.
4. Eliminate certain alternatives. With a four-choice multiple-choice test, you have one chance in four of guessing right. If you can eliminate two alternatives, your guessing odds improve to 50-50.
5. Unless there is a penalty for guessing, be sure to answer any skipped items. Even if you are not sure of the answer, you may be right. If you leave a question blank, it is automatically wrong. When you are forced to guess, don't choose the longest answer or the letter you've used the least. Both strategies lower scores more than random guessing does.
6. There is a bit of folk wisdom that says "Don't change your answers on a multiple-choice test. Your first choice is usually right." This is *false*. If you change answers you are more likely to gain points than to lose them. This is especially true if you are uncertain of your first choice or it was a hunch, and if your second choice is more reflective (Higham & Gerrard, 2005).
7. Remember, you are searching for the one *best* answer to each question. Some answers may be partly true, yet flawed in some way. If you are uncertain, try rating each multiple-choice alternative on a 1-to-10 scale. The answer with the highest rating is the one you are looking for.
8. Few circumstances are *always* or *never* present. Answers that include superlatives such as *most, least, best, worst, largest,* or *smallest* are often false.

Essay Tests

Essay questions are a weak spot for students who lack organization, don't support their ideas, or don't directly answer the question (Rowe, 2007). When you take an essay exam try the following:

1. Read the question carefully. Be sure to note key words, such as *compare, contrast, discuss, evaluate, analyze,* and *describe.* These words all demand a certain emphasis in your answer.
2. Think about your answer for a few minutes and list the main points you want to make. Just write them as they come to mind. Then rearrange the ideas in a logical order and begin writing. Elaborate plans or outlines are not necessary.
3. Don't beat around the bush or pad your answer. Be direct. Make a point and support it. Get your list of ideas into words.
4. Look over your essay for errors in spelling and grammar. Save this for last. Your *ideas* are of first importance. You can work on spelling and grammar separately if they affect your grades.

Short-Answer Tests

Tests that ask you to fill in a blank, define a term, or list specific items can be difficult. Usually, the questions themselves contain little information. If you don't know the answer, you won't get much help from the questions.

The best way to prepare for short-answer tests is to overlearn the details of the course. As you study, pay special attention to lists of related terms.

Again, it is best to start with the questions you're sure you know. Follow that by completing items you think you probably know. Questions you have no idea about can be left blank.

Again, for your convenience, Figure I.2 provides a checklist summary of the main study skills we have covered.

USING DIGITAL MEDIA— NETTING NEW KNOWLEDGE

The Internet and digital media are providing exciting new ways to explore topics ranging from amnesia to zoophobia. Let's see how you can use these technologies to learn more about psychology.

Digital Journeys

The **Internet** is a network of computers that communicate through the phone system and other digital links. An important subpart of the Internet is the **World Wide Web,** or just plain "web," an interlinked system of information "sites" or "pages." If you know the URL, the "address" of a website, you can view the information it contains. Almost all web pages also have links to other websites. These **links** let you "jump" from one site to the next to find more information.

Google It

To find psychological information on the Internet you'll need a computer and an Internet connection. If you don't own a computer, you can usually use one on campus to access the Internet. Various software browsers make it easier to navigate around the web. A **browser** allows you to see text, images, sounds, and video clips stored on other computers. Browsers also keep lists of your favorite URLs so that you can return to them.

The Book Companion Website

How would I find information about psychology on the Internet? Your first stop on the Internet should be the companion website for this book at *www.thomsonedu.com/psychology/ coon.* Here's what you'll find there:

Online Quizzes. You can use these chapter-by-chapter multiple choice quizzes to practice for tests and check your understanding.

Interactive Activities. The demonstrations and mini-experiments in this feature allow you to directly experience various psychological principles.

Internet Resources. This area is a "launching pad" that will take you to other psychology-related sites on the Internet. If a site sounds interesting, a click of the mouse will link you to it.

Online Flash Cards. These online flash cards allow you to practice terms and concepts interactively.

Psych in the News. This section features a news item or current event that is explored from a psychological perspective. After you've thought about a topic, you can share your opinions with others in an online discussion.

Internet A digital network that enables computers to communicate with one another through the phone system and other digital links.

World Wide Web A system of information "sites" accessible through the Internet.

Links Connections built into Internet sites that let you "jump" from one site to the next.

Browser Software that facilitates access to text, images, sounds, video, and other information stored in formats used on the Internet.

The Book Companion website gives you online access to a variety of valuable learning aids and interesting materials.

Discussion Forum. In the Discussion Forum you'll have a chance to share your ideas with those of psychology students from all over the country.

Research and Teaching Showcase. Here you'll find regularly updated summaries of presentations, articles, or other teaching and research materials.

Archives. Using the Archives, you can quickly search for current and past articles from Psych in the News and the Research and Teaching Showcase.

Be sure to visit the Book Companion website for valuable information about how to improve your grades and enhance your appreciation of psychology.

ThomsonNOW

Students can also make use of *ThomsonNOW for Coon/Mitterer's Psychology: A Journey 3e,* a web-based, personalized study system that provides a pre-test and a post-test for each chapter and separate chapter quizzes. *ThomsonNOW,* located at www.thomsonedu.com, can also create personalized study plans—which include rich media such as videos, animations, and learning modules—that point students to areas in the text that will help them master course content (▸Fig. I.3). An additional set of integrative questions helps students pull all of the material together.

Psych Sites

You'll find a list of interesting websites you may want to explore at the end of each chapter in this book. The best way to reach these sites is through the Book Companion website. We have not included website addresses in the book because they often change or may become inactive. At the Book Companion site you'll find up-to-date links for websites listed in this book. The sites we've listed are generally of high quality. However, be aware that information on the Internet is not always accurate. It is wise to approach all websites with a healthy dose of skepticism.

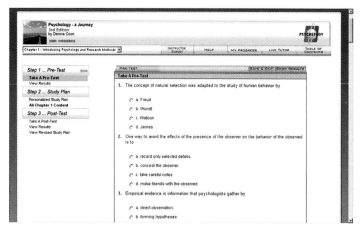

▸▸**FIGURE I.3** A sample screen from *ThomsonNOW.*

PsycINFO

Psychological knowledge can also be found in specialized online databases. One of the best is PsycINFO, offered by the American Psychological Association. **PsycINFO** provides summaries of the scientific and scholarly literature in psychology. Each record in PsycINFO consists of an abstract (short summary), plus notes about the author, title, source, and other details (⇥Fig. I.4). All entries are indexed using key terms. Thus, you can search for various topics by entering words such as *drug abuse, postpartum depression,* or *creativity.*

You can gain access to PsycINFO in several ways. Many colleges and universities subscribe to PsycINFO or to a related CD-ROM version called PsycLIT. If this is the case, you can usually search PsycINFO from a terminal in the college library or computer center—for free. PsycINFO can also be accessed through the Internet, either directly or through APA's PsycDIRECT service. For more information on how to gain access to PsycINFO, check this website: www.apa.org/psycinfo.

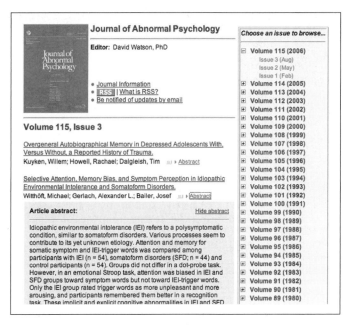

The APA Website

The APA maintains an online library of free general interest articles on aging, anger, children and families, depression, divorce, emotional health, kids and the media, sexuality, stress, women and men, and other topics. They are well worth consulting when you have questions about psychological issues. You'll find them at www.apa.org. For links to recent articles in newspapers and magazines, be sure to check the APA's PsycPORT page at www.psycport.com.

Please do take some of the "digital journeys" described here. You might be surprised by the fascinating information that awaits you. Investigating psychology on your own is one of the best ways to enrich an already valuable course.

▶FIGURE I.4 This is a sample abstract from the PsycINFO database. If you search for the term *idiopathic environmental intolerance* you will find this article and many more in PsychINFO. (This record is reprinted with permission of the American Psychological Association, publisher of the PsycINFO Database, all rights reserved. May not be reproduced without prior permission.)

A Final Word

There is a distinction in Zen between "live words" and "dead words." Live words come from personal experience; dead words are "about" a subject. This book can only be a collection of dead words unless you accept the challenge of making an intellectual journey. You will find many helpful, useful, and exciting ideas in the pages that follow. To make them yours, you must set out to *actively* learn as much as you can. The ideas presented here should get you off to a good start. Good luck!

For more information, consult any of the following books.

Hettich, P. I. (2005). *Connect College to Career: Student Guide to Work and Life Transition.* Belmont, CA: Wadsworth.

Knaus, W. J., & Ellis, A. (2002). *The Procrastination Workbook: Your Personalized Program for Breaking Free from the Patterns That Hold You Back.* Oakland, CA: New Harbinger Press.

Rosnow, R. L. (2006). *Writing Papers in Psychology: A Student Guide to Research Papers, Essays, Proposals, Posters, and Handouts* (7th ed.). Belmont, CA: Wadsworth.

Rowe, B. (2007). *College Awareness Guide: What Students Need to Know to Succeed in College.* Upper Saddle River, NJ: Prentice Hall.

Santrock, J. W., & Halonen, J. S. (2007). *Connections to College Success.* Belmont, CA: Wadsworth.

PsycINFO A searchable, online database that provides brief summaries of the scientific and scholarly literature in psychology.

Study Break Study Skills

Reflect

Which study skills do you think would help you the most? Which techniques do you already use? Which do you think you should try? To what extent do you already engage in self-regulated learning? What additional steps could you take to become a more active, goal-oriented learner?

Learning Check

1. The four R's in SQ4R stand for "read, recite, reflect, and review." T or F?
2. When using the LISAN method, students try to write down as much of a lecture as possible so that their notes are complete. T or F?
3. Spaced study sessions are usually superior to massed practice. T or F?

4. According to recent research, you should almost always stick with your first answer on multiple-choice tests. T or F?
5. To use the technique known as overlearning, you should continue to study after you feel you have begun to master a topic. T or F?
6. Setting learning goals and monitoring your progress are important parts of _____ learning.
7. Procrastination is related to seeking perfection and equating self-worth with grades. T or F?
8. An Internet browser is typically used to search CD-ROM databases for articles on various topics. T or F?

Critical Thinking

9. How are the SQ4R method and the LISAN method related?

Answers

1. T 2. F 3. T 4. F 5. T 6. self-regulated 7. T 8. F 9. Both encourage people to actively seek information as a way of learning more effectively.

---

www Interactive Learning

Internet addresses frequently change. To find the sites listed here, visit www.thomsonedu.com/psychology/coon for an updated list of Internet addresses and direct links to relevant sites.

***Psychology: A Journey* Companion Website**   Find online quizzes, flash cards, animations, video clips, experiments, interactive assessments, and other helpful study aids for this text at www.thomsonedu.com/psychology/coon.

How to Succeed as a Student   Advice on how to be a college student. Topics from studying to housing to preparation for work are included.

Library Research in Psychology   Hints on how to do library research in psychology.

Psychology Glossary   You can use this glossary to get additional definitions for common psychological terms.

Introducing Psychology and Research Methods

JOURNEY INTO PSYCHOLOGY:
THE MYSTERIES OF HUMAN BEHAVIOR

As your authors we are often asked, "Why did you become a psychologist?" Because we are just getting acquainted, let us answer this way:

> You are a universe, a collection of worlds within worlds. Your brain is possibly the most complicated system in existence. Through its action you are capable of art, music, science, philosophy, love, hatred, and charity. You are the most challenging riddle ever written, a mystery even to yourself at times. Your thoughts, emotions, and actions—and those of your family and friends—are the most fascinating subject we can imagine. We both chose to study psychology because everything of interest and importance in the world is ultimately related to human behavior.

Look around you: The Internet, television, newspapers, radio, and magazines are brimming with psychological topics. Psychology is an ever-changing panorama of people and ideas. You really can't call yourself educated without knowing something about it. And, although we might envy those who have walked on the moon or explored the ocean's depths, the ultimate frontier lies much closer to home. What could be more fascinating than a journey of self-discovery?

As you read, think of this book as a travel guide. Ultimately, each person's path through life is unique. Nonetheless, psychology can show you much about human behavior and help you better understand yourself and others. Your guide awaits you. We hope you enjoy the journey.

Royalty-Free/Corbis

▽ **Survey Questions**

- What is psychology? What are its goals?
- How did the field of psychology emerge?
- What are the major trends and specialties in psychology?
- Why is the scientific method important to psychologists? How do psychologists collect information?
- How is an experiment performed?
- What other research methods do psychologists use?
- What is critical thinking?
- How does psychology differ from false explanations of behavior?
- How good is psychological information found in the popular media?

PSYCHOLOGY—SPOTLIGHT ON BEHAVIOR

>SURVEY QUESTION< *What is psychology? What are its goals?*

Psychology touches our lives in many ways. Psychology is about happiness, memory, stress, therapy, love, persuasion, hypnosis, perception, death, conformity, creativity, learning, personality, aging, intelligence, sexuality, emotion, and much more.

Jeff Greenberg/PhotoEdit

Psychologists are highly trained professionals who have specialized skills in counseling and therapy, measurement and testing, research and experimentation, statistics, diagnosis, treatment, and many other areas.

Psychology is both a *science* and a *profession*. As scientists, some psychologists do research to discover new knowledge. Others are teachers who pass this knowledge on to students. Still others apply psychology to solve problems in mental health, education, business, sports, law, and medicine. Later we will return to the profession of psychology. For now, let's focus on how knowledge is created. Whether they work in a lab, a classroom, or a clinic, all psychologists rely on information from scientific research.

Defining Psychology

The word *psychology* comes from the roots *psyche,* which means "mind," and *logos,* meaning "knowledge or study." However, when did you last see or touch a "mind"? Because the mind can't be studied directly, **psychology** is now defined as the scientific study of behavior and mental processes.

What does behavior refer to in the definition of psychology? Anything you do—eating, sleeping, talking, or sneezing—is a behavior. So are snowboarding, gambling, watching television, picking your nose, learning Spanish, and reading this book. Naturally, we are interested in *overt behaviors* (directly observable actions and responses). But psychologists also study *covert behaviors.* These are private, internal activities, such as thinking, dreaming, remembering, and other mental events (Leary, 2004).

Empiricism

When it comes to psychology, it seems we are all expert "people watchers." "Commonsense" theories abound. However, you may be surprised to learn how often self-appointed authorities and long-held commonsense beliefs about human behavior are wrong. For example, have you ever heard that blind people have amazingly accurate organs of touch? Or that the more motivated you are, the better you will do at solving a complex problem? It turns out that these commonsense beliefs, and many others, are wrong (Landau & Bavaria, 2003).

Psychology The scientific study of behavior and mental processes.

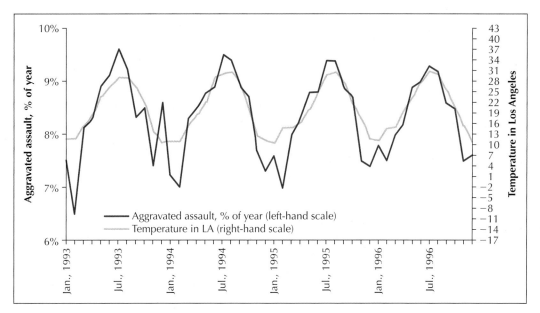

▸▸**FIGURE 1.1** Results of an empiri-cal study. The graph shows that aggravated assaults in Los Angeles become more likely as air temperature increases. This suggests that physical discomfort is associated with interpersonal hostility (Data from Simister & Cooper, 2005.)

Because of the limitations of common sense, psychologists have a special respect for *empirical evidence* (information gained from direct observation), especially when it is collected systematically. We study behavior directly and collect data (observed facts) so that we can draw valid conclusions. Would you say it's true, for instance, that "You can't teach an old dog new tricks"? Why argue about it? As psychologists, we would simply get ten "new" dogs, ten "used" dogs, and ten "old" dogs and then try to teach them all a new trick to find out!

Basically, the empirical approach says, "Let's take a look" (Stanovich, 2004). Have you ever wondered if people become more hostile when it's blazing hot outside? John Simister and Cary Cooper (2005) decided to find out. They obtained data on temperatures and criminal activity in Los Angeles over a 4-year period. When temperature and the frequency of aggravated assaults was graphed, a clear relationship emerged. (See ▸▸Figure 1.1.) Temperatures and crime rates rise and fall more or less in synchrony (so there may be something to the phrase "hot under the collar").

Isn't the outcome of this study fairly predictable? Sometimes the results of studies are consistent with commonsense knowledge and sometimes they come as a surprise. In this instance, you may have guessed the outcome. However, hostile actions that require more extreme physical exertion, such as fistfights, become *less* likely at very high temperatures. Without systematically gathering data, we wouldn't know for sure if overheated Angelenos become more lethargic or more aggressive. Thus, the study tells us something interesting about frustration, discomfort, and aggression.

Psychological Research

Many fields, such as history, law, art, and business are interested in human behavior. How is psychology different? Psychology's great strength is that it uses **scientific observation** to systematically answer questions about behavior (Stanovich, 2004).

Of course, some topics can't be studied because of ethical or practical concerns. More often, questions go unanswered for lack of a suitable **research method** (a systematic process for answering scientific questions). In the past, for example, we had to take the word of people who say they never dream. Then the EEG (electroencephalograph, or brain-wave machine) was invented. Certain EEG patterns, and the presence of eye movements, can reveal that a person is dreaming. People who "never dream," it turns out, dream frequently. If they are awakened during a dream they vividly remember it. Thus, the EEG helped make the study of dreaming more scientific.

Scientific observation A systematic empirical investigation that is structured to answer questions about the world.

Research method A systematic approach to answering scientific questions.

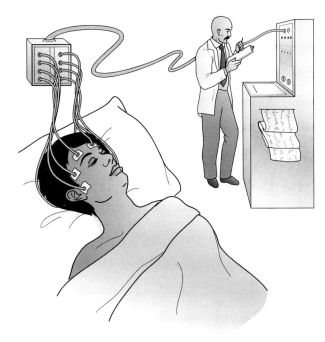

The scientific study of dreaming was made possible by use of the EEG, a device that records the tiny electrical signals generated by the brain as a person sleeps. The EEG converts these electrical signals to a written record of brain activity. Certain shifts in brain activity, coupled with the presence of rapid eye movements, are strongly related to dreaming. (See Chapter 5 for more information.)

The variety and complexity of human behavior make psychological investigation challenging. How would you explain the behaviors shown here?

Research Specialties

What kinds of topics do psychologists study? Here's a sample of what various psychologists might say about their work.

"In general, *developmental psychologists* study the course of human growth and development, from conception until death. I'm especially interested in the transition from the teenage years to early adulthood."

"I'm also interested in how people get to be the way they are. Like other *learning theorists,* I study how and why learning occurs in humans and animals. Right now I'm investigating how patterns of reward affect learning."

"I'm a *personality theorist.* I study personality traits, motivation, and individual differences. I am especially interested in the personality profiles of highly creative college students."

"As a *sensation and perception psychologist,* I investigate how we discern the world through our senses. I am using a perceptual theory to study how we are able to recognize faces."

"*Comparative psychologists* study and compare the behavior of different species, especially animals. Personally, I'm fascinated by the communication abilities of porpoises."

"*Biopsychologists* are interested in how behavior relates to biological processes, especially activities in the nervous system. I've been doing some exciting research on how the brain controls hunger."

"*Cognitive psychologists* are primarily interested in thinking. I want to know how reasoning, problem solving, memory, and other mental processes relate to human behavior."

"*Gender psychologists* study differences between females and males. I want to understand how gender differences are influenced by biology, child rearing, education, and stereotypes."

Warren Morgan/Corbis

"*Social psychologists* explore human social behavior, such as attitudes, persuasion, riots, conformity, leadership, racism, and friendship. My own interest is interpersonal attraction. I place two strangers in a room and analyze how strongly they are attracted to each other."

"*Cultural psychologists* study the ways in which culture affects human behavior. The language you speak, the foods you eat, how your parents disciplined you, what laws you obey, who you regard as 'family,' whether you eat with a spoon or your fingers—these and countless other details of behavior are strongly influenced by culture."

"*Evolutionary psychologists* are interested in how our behavior is guided by patterns that evolved during the long history of humankind. I am studying some interesting trends in male and female mating choices that don't seem to be merely learned or based on culture."

This small sample should give you an idea of the diversity of psychological research. It also hints at some of the kinds of information we will explore in this book.

Animals and Psychology

Research involving animals was mentioned in some of the preceding examples. Why is that? You may be surprised to learn that psychologists are interested in the behavior of *any* living creature—from flatworms to humans. Indeed, some comparative psychologists spend their entire careers studying rats, cats, dogs, turtles, or chimpanzees.

Although only a small percentage of psychological research involves animals, many different types of research are carried out (Ord et al., 2005). Some psychologists use **animal models** to discover principles that apply to humans. For instance, animal studies have helped us understand stress, learning, obesity, aging, sleep, and many other topics. Psychology also benefits animals. For example, caring for domestic animals, as well as endangered species in zoos, relies on behavioral studies.

Stink

Some of the most interesting research with animals has focused on attempts to teach primates to communicate with sign language. Psychologist Penny Patterson has spent 25 years teaching Koko over 1000 signs. Here, Koko signs that something stinks (for more, visit www.koko.org). Such research has led to better methods for teaching language to aphasic children (children with serious language impairment). (See Chapter 8 for more information.)

Psychology's Goals

What do psychology's goals mean in practice? Imagine that we would like to answer questions such as these: What happens when the right side of the brain is injured? Why are some people risk seekers while others avoid risk at all costs? Do autistic children react abnormally to their parents?

Description

Answering psychological questions requires a careful description of behavior. **Description,** or naming and classifying, is typically based on making a detailed record of behavioral observations.

But a description doesn't explain anything, does it? Right. Useful knowledge begins with accurate description, but descriptions fail to answer the important "why" questions. *Why* do more women attempt suicide, and *why* do more men complete it? *Why* are people more aggressive when they are uncomfortable? *Why* are bystanders often unwilling to help in an emergency?

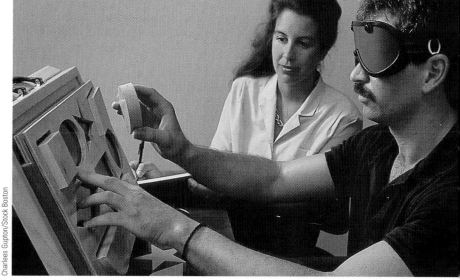

Some psychologists specialize in administering, scoring, and interpreting psychological tests, such as tests of intelligence, creativity, personality, or aptitude. This specialty, which is called psychometrics, is an example of using psychology to predict future behavior. For instance, psychological tests are frequently used to select people for jobs and admission to colleges.

Understanding

We have met psychology's second goal when we can explain an event. That is, **understanding** usually means we can state the causes of a behavior. Take our last "why" question as an example: Research on "bystander apathy" reveals that people often fail to help when *other* possible helpers are nearby. Why? Because a "diffusion of responsibility" occurs. Basically, no one feels personally obligated to pitch in. As a result, the more potential helpers there are, the less likely it is that anyone will help (Darley, 2000; Darley & Latané, 1968). Now we can explain a perplexing problem.

Prediction

Psychology's third goal, **prediction,** is the ability to forecast behavior accurately. Notice that our explanation of bystander apathy makes a prediction about the chances of getting help. If you've ever been stranded on a busy freeway with car trouble, you'll recognize the accuracy of this prediction: Having many potential helpers nearby is no guarantee that anyone will stop to help.

Animal model In research, an animal whose behavior is used to discover principles that may apply to human behavior.
Description In scientific research, the process of naming and classifying.
Understanding In psychology, understanding is achieved when the causes of a behavior can be stated.
Prediction An ability to accurately forecast behavior.

Control

Description, explanation, and prediction seem reasonable, but is control a valid goal? Control may seem like a threat to personal freedom. However, to a psychologist, **control** simply refers to altering conditions that affect behavior. If you suggest changes in a classroom that help children learn better, you have exerted control. If a clinical psychologist helps a person overcome a terrible fear of heights, control is involved. Control is also involved in designing airplanes to keep pilots from making fatal errors. Clearly, psychological control must be used wisely and humanely.

In summary, psychology's goals are a natural outgrowth of our desire to understand behavior. Basically, they boil down to asking the following questions:

What is the nature of this behavior? (description)

Why does it occur? (understanding and explanation)

Can we forecast when it will occur? (prediction)

What conditions affect it? (control)

→ Study Break   The Science of Psychology

Reflect

At first, many students think that psychology is primarily about abnormal behavior and psychotherapy. Did you? How would you describe the field now?

Learning Check

To check your memory, see if you can answer these questions. If you miss any, skim over the preceding material before continuing, to make sure you understand what you just read.

1. Psychology is the _____ study of _____ _____ and _____ processes.
2. Information gained through direct observation and measurement is called _____ evidence.
3. In psychological research, animal _____ may be used to discover principles that apply to human behavior.
4. Which of the following questions relates most directly to the goal of *understanding* behavior?
   a. Do the scores of men and women differ on tests of thinking abilities?
   b. Why does a blow to the head cause memory loss?

c. Will productivity in a business office increase if room temperature is raised or lowered?
d. What percentage of college students suffer from test anxiety?

Match the following research areas with the topics they cover.

_____ 5. Developmental psychology
_____ 6. Learning
_____ 7. Personality
_____ 8. Sensation and perception
_____ 9. Biopsychology
_____ 10. Social psychology
_____ 11. Comparative psychology

A. Attitudes, groups, leadership
B. Conditioning, memory
C. The psychology of law
D. Brain and nervous system
E. Child psychology
F. Individual differences, motivation
G. Animal behavior
H. Processing sensory information

Critical Thinking

12. All sciences are interested in controlling the phenomena they study. True or false?

Answers

1. scientific, behavior, mental   2. empirical   3. models   4. b   5. E   6. B   7. F   8. H   9. D   10. A   11. G   12. False. Astronomy and archaeology are examples of sciences that do not share psychology's fourth goal.

A BRIEF HISTORY OF PSYCHOLOGY— PSYCHOLOGY'S FAMILY ALBUM

>SURVEY QUESTION< *How did the field of psychology emerge?*

People have been informally observing and speculating about human behavior for thousands of years. In contrast, psychology's short history as a science dates back only about 130 years. Of course, to some students any history is "not short enough!" Nevertheless, to understand psychology now, we need to explore its past.

Psychology's history as a science began in 1879 in Leipzig, Germany. There, the "father of psychology," Wilhelm Wundt (VILL-helm Voont), set up the first psychological laboratory to study conscious experience. What happens, he wondered, when we have sensations, images, and feelings? To find out, Wundt systematically observed and measured stimuli of various kinds (lights, sounds, weights). A **stimulus** is any physical energy that affects a per-

Control Altering conditions that influence behavior.

Stimulus Any physical energy that has some effect on an organism and that evokes a response.

son and evokes a response (stimulus: singular; stimuli [STIM-you-lie]: plural). Wundt then used **introspection,** or "looking inward," and careful measurement to probe his reactions to various stimuli. (If you carefully examine your thoughts, feelings, and sensations for a moment, you will have done some introspecting.) Over the years, Wundt studied vision, hearing, taste, touch, memory, time perception, and many other topics. By insisting on systematic observation and measurement, he asked some interesting questions and got psychology off to a good start.

Structuralism

Wundt's ideas were carried to the United States by a man named Edward Titchener (TICH-in-er). Titchener called Wundt's ideas **structuralism** and tried to analyze the structure of mental life into basic "elements" or "building blocks."

How could they do that? You can't analyze experience like a chemical compound, can you? Perhaps not, but the structuralists tried, mostly by using introspection. For instance, an observer might heft an apple and decide that she had experienced the elements "hue" (color), "roundness," and "weight." Another example of a question that might have interested a structuralist is, What basic tastes mix together to create complex flavors as different as liver, lime, bacon, and burnt-almond fudge?

Introspection proved to be a poor way to answer many questions. Why? Because no matter how systematic the observations, the structuralists frequently disagreed. And when they did, there was no way to settle differences. Think about it. If you and a friend both introspect on your experiences of an apple and end up listing different basic elements, who would be right? Despite such limitations, "looking inward" is still used in studies of hypnosis, meditation, problem solving, moods, and many other topics (Mayer & Hanson, 1995).

Functionalism

William James, an American scholar, broadened psychology to include animal behavior, religious experience, abnormal behavior, and other interesting topics. James's brilliant first book, *Principles of Psychology* (1890), helped establish the field as a separate topic (Hergenhahn, 2005).

The term **functionalism** comes from James's interest in how the mind functions to help us adapt to the environment. James regarded consciousness as an ever-changing stream or flow of images and sensations—not a set of lifeless building blocks, as the structuralists claimed.

The functionalists admired Charles Darwin, who deduced that creatures evolve in ways that favor survival. According to Darwin's principle of **natural selection,** physical features that help animals adapt to their environments are retained in evolution. Similarly, the functionalists wanted to find out how the mind, perception, habits, and emotions help us adapt and survive.

Behaviorism

Functionalism and structuralism were soon challenged by **behaviorism,** the study of observable behavior. Behaviorist John B. Watson objected strongly to the study of the "mind" or "conscious experience." "Introspection," he said, "is unscientific" because there is no way to settle disagreements between observers. Watson realized that he could study the overt behavior of animals even though he couldn't ask them questions, or know what they were thinking (Watson, 1913/1994). He simply observed the relationship between stimuli (events in the environment) and an animal's **responses** (any muscular action, glandular

Wilhelm Wundt, 1832–1920. Wundt is credited with making psychology an independent science, separate from philosophy. Wundt's original training was in medicine, but he became deeply interested in psychology. In his laboratory, Wundt investigated how sensations, images, and feelings combine to make up personal experience.

William James, 1842–1910. William James was the son of philosopher Henry James, Sr., and the brother of novelist Henry James. During his long academic career, James taught anatomy, physiology, psychology, and philosophy at Harvard University. James believed strongly that ideas should be judged in terms of their practical consequences for human conduct.

Introspection To look within; to examine one's own thoughts, feelings, or sensations.

Structuralism The school of thought concerned with analyzing sensations and personal experience into basic elements.

Functionalism School of psychology concerned with how behavior and mental abilities help people adapt to their environments.

Natural selection Darwin's theory that evolution favors those plants and animals best suited to their living conditions.

Behaviorism School of psychology that emphasizes the study of overt, observable behavior.

Response Any muscular action, glandular activity, or other identifiable aspect of behavior.

John B. Watson, 1878–1958. Watson's intense interest in observable behavior began with his doctoral studies in biology and neurology. Watson became a psychology professor at Johns Hopkins University in 1908 and advanced his theory of behaviorism. He remained at Johns Hopkins until 1920 when he left for a career in the advertising industry!

B. F. Skinner, 1904–1990. Skinner studied simple behaviors under carefully controlled conditions. The "Skinner Box" you see here has been widely used to study learning in simplified animal experiments. In addition to advancing psychology, Skinner hoped that his radical brand of behaviorism would improve human life.

activity, or other identifiable behavior). These observations were *objective* because they did not involve introspecting on *subjective* experience. Why not, he asked, apply the same objectivity to human behavior?

Watson soon adopted Russian physiologist Ivan Pavlov's (ee-VAHN PAV-lahv) concept of *conditioning* to explain most behavior. (A *conditioned response* is a learned reaction to a particular stimulus.) Watson eagerly claimed, "Give me a dozen healthy infants, well-formed, and my own special world to bring them up in and I'll guarantee to take any one at random and train him to become any type of specialist I might select—doctor, lawyer, artist, merchant-chief, and yes, beggarman and thief" (Watson, 1913/1994).

Would most psychologists agree with Watson's claim? No, today it is regarded as an overstatement. Just the same, behaviorism helped make psychology a natural science, rather than a branch of philosophy (Benjafield, 2004).

One of the best-known behaviorists, B. F. Skinner (1904–1990), believed that our actions are controlled by rewards and punishments. To study learning, Skinner created his

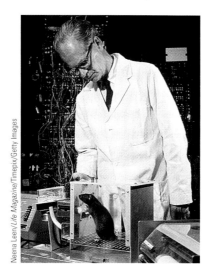

famous conditioning chamber or "Skinner box." With it, he could present stimuli to animals and record their responses (see Chapter 6, "Operant Conditioning"). Many of Skinner's ideas about learning grew out of work with rats and pigeons. Nevertheless, he believed that the same laws of behavior apply to humans. As a "radical behaviorist," Skinner also believed that mental events, such as thinking, are not needed to explain behavior (Hergenhahn, 2005).

Skinner was convinced that a "designed culture" based on positive reinforcement could encourage desirable behavior. (Skinner disliked the use of punishment because it doesn't teach correct responses.) Too often, he believed, misguided rewards lead to destructive actions that create problems such as overpopulation, pollution, and war.

Gestalt Psychology

Imagine that you just played "Happy Birthday" on a tuba. Next, you play it on a high-pitched violin. None of the tuba's sounds are duplicated by the violin. Yet, we notice something interesting: The melody is still recognizable—as long as the *relationship* between notes remains the same.

Now, what would happen if you played the notes of "Happy Birthday" in the correct order, but at a rate of one per hour? What would we have? Nothing! The separate notes would no longer be a melody. Perceptually, the melody is somehow more than the individual notes that define it.

It was observations like these that launched the Gestalt school of thought. **Gestalt psychologists** studied thinking, learning, and perception as whole units, not by analyzing experiences into parts. Their slogan was, "The whole is greater than the sum of its parts." (See ▸▸Figure 1.2.)

In Germany, Max Wertheimer (VERT-hi-mer) was the first psychologist to advance the Gestalt viewpoint. It is a mistake, he said, to analyze psychological events into pieces, or "elements," as the structuralists did. Like a melody, many experiences cannot be broken into smaller units. For this reason, studies of perception and personality have been especially influenced by the Gestalt viewpoint.

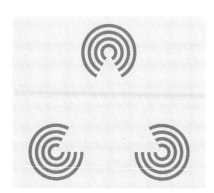

▸▸**FIGURE 1.2** The design you see here is entirely made up of broken circles. However, as the Gestalt psychologists discovered, our perceptions have a powerful tendency to form meaningful patterns. Because of this tendency, you will probably see a triangle in this design, even though it is only an illusion. Your whole perceptual experience exceeds the sum of its parts.

Gestalt psychology A school of psychology emphasizing the study of thinking, learning, and perception in whole units, not by analysis into parts.

Psychoanalytic Psychology

As American psychology grew more scientific, an Austrian doctor named Sigmund Freud was developing his own theories. Freud believed that mental life is like an iceberg: Only a small part is exposed to view. He called the area of the mind that lies outside of personal awareness the **unconscious.** According to Freud, our behavior is deeply influenced by unconscious thoughts, impulses, and desires—especially those concerning sex and aggression. Freud's ideas opened new horizons in art, literature, and history, as well as psychology (Jacobs, 2003).

Freud theorized that many unconscious thoughts are *repressed* (held out of awareness) because they are threatening. But sometimes, he said, they are revealed by dreams, emotions, or slips of the tongue. ("Freudian slips" are often humorous, as when a student who is tardy for class says, "I'm sorry I couldn't get here any later.")

Freud believed that all thoughts, emotions, and actions are *determined*. In other words, nothing is an accident: If we probe deeply enough we will find the causes of every thought or action. Freud was also among the first to appreciate that childhood affects adult personality ("The child is father to the man"). Most of all, perhaps, Freud is known for creating **psychoanalysis,** the first "talking cure." Freud's method of psychotherapy explores unconscious conflicts and emotional problems (see Chapter 13). Today, his ideas have been altered so much that few strictly psychoanalytic psychologists are left. However, Freud's legacy is still evident in various **psychodynamic theories,** which continue to emphasize internal motives, conflicts, and unconscious forces (Gedo, 2002).

Humanistic Psychology

Humanism is a view that focuses on subjective human experience. Humanistic psychologists are interested in human problems, potentials, and ideals.

How is the humanistic approach different from others? Carl Rogers, Abraham Maslow, and other humanists rejected the Freudian idea that we are ruled by unconscious forces. They were also uncomfortable with the behaviorist emphasis on conditioning. Both views have a strong undercurrent of **determinism** (the idea that behavior is determined by forces beyond our control). Instead, the humanists stress **free will,** our ability to make voluntary choices. Of course, past experiences do affect us. Nevertheless, humanists believe that people can freely *choose* to live more creative, meaningful, and satisfying lives.

Humanists are interested in psychological needs for love, self-esteem, belonging, self-expression, creativity, and spirituality. Such needs, they believe, are as important as our biological urges for food and water. For example, newborn infants deprived of human love may die just as surely as they would if deprived of food.

How scientific is the humanistic approach? Initially, humanists were less interested in treating psychology as a science. They stressed more subjective factors, such as one's self-image, self-evaluation, and frame of reference. (*Self-image* is your perception of your own body, personality, and capabilities. *Self-evaluation* refers to appraising yourself as good or bad. A *frame of reference* is a mental perspective used to interpret events.) Today, humanists still seek to understand how we perceive ourselves and experience the world. However, most now do research to test their ideas, just as other psychologists do (Schneider, Bugental, & Pierson, 2001).

Max Wertheimer, 1880–1941. Wertheimer first proposed the Gestalt viewpoint to help explain perceptual illusions. He later promoted Gestalt psychology as a way to understand not only perception, problem solving, thinking, and social behavior, but also art, logic, philosophy, and politics.

Sigmund Freud, 1856–1939. For more than 50 years, Freud probed the unconscious mind. In doing so, he altered modern views of human nature. His early experimentation with a "talking cure" for hysteria is regarded as the beginning of psychoanalysis. Through psychoanalysis, Freud added psychological treatment methods to psychiatry.

Abraham Maslow, 1908–1970. As a founder of humanistic psychology, Maslow was interested in studying people of exceptional mental health. Such self-actualized people, he believed, make full use of their talents and abilities. Maslow offered his positive view of human potential as an alternative to the schools of behaviorism and psychoanalysis.

Unconscious Contents of the mind that are beyond awareness, especially impulses and desires not directly known to a person.

Psychoanalysis A Freudian approach to psychotherapy emphasizing the exploration of unconscious conflicts.

Psychodynamic theory Any theory of behavior that emphasizes internal conflicts, motives, and unconscious forces.

Humanism An approach to psychology that focuses on human experience, problems, potentials, and ideals.

Determinism The idea that all behavior has prior causes that would completely explain one's choices and actions if all such causes were known.

Free will The idea that human beings are capable of freely making choices or decisions.

■ Table 1.1   The Early Development of Psychology

Perspective	Date	Notable Events
Experimental psychology	1875	■ First psychology course offered by William James
	1878	■ First American Ph.D. in psychology awarded
	1879	■ Wilhelm Wundt opens first psychology laboratory in Germany
	1883	■ First American psychology lab founded at Johns Hopkins University
	1886	■ First American psychology textbook written by John Dewey
Structuralism	1898	■ Edward Titchener advances psychology based on introspection
Functionalism	1890	■ William James publishes *Principles of Psychology*
	1892	■ American Psychological Association founded
Psychodynamic psychology	1895	■ Sigmund Freud publishes first studies
	1900	■ Freud publishes *The Interpretation of Dreams*
Behaviorism	1906	■ Ivan Pavlov reports his research on conditioned reflexes
	1913	■ John Watson presents behavioristic view
Gestalt psychology	1912	■ Max Wertheimer and others advance Gestalt viewpoint
Humanistic psychology	1942	■ Carl Rogers publishes *Counseling and Psychotherapy*
	1943	■ Abraham Maslow publishes "A theory of human motivation."

Maslow's concept of self-actualization is a special feature of humanism. **Self-actualization** refers to developing one's potential fully and becoming the best person possible. According to humanists, everyone has this potential. Humanists seek ways to help it emerge. (See ▥ Table 1.1 for a summary of psychology's early development.)

The Role of Women in Psychology's Early Days

Were all the early psychologists men? Even though most of the early psychologists were men, women have contributed to psychology from the beginning (Minton, 2000). By 1906 in America, about 1 psychologist in 10 was a woman. Who were these "foremothers" of psychology? Three who became well known are Mary Calkins, Christine Ladd-Franklin, and Margaret Washburn.

Mary Calkins did valuable research on memory. She was also the first woman president of the American Psychological Association, in 1905. Christine Ladd-Franklin studied color vision. In 1906 she was ranked among the 50 most important psychologists in America. In 1908 Margaret Washburn published an influential textbook on animal behavior, titled *The Animal Mind.*

The first woman to be awarded a Ph.D. in psychology was Margaret Washburn, in 1894. Over the next 15 years many more women followed her pioneering lead. Today, two out of three graduate students in psychology are women. And, in recent years, nearly 75 percent of all college graduates with a major in psychology have been women. Clearly, psychology has become fully open to both men and women (Hyde, 2004; Martin, 1995).

Self-actualization The process of fully developing one's personal potentials.

Mary Calkins, 1863–1930.

Christine Ladd-Franklin, 1847–1930.

Margaret Washburn, 1871–1939.

■ Table 1.2 **Contemporary Ways to Look at Behavior**

Biological Perspective

Biopsychological View

Key Idea: *Human and animal behavior is the result of internal physical, chemical, and biological processes.*
Seeks to explain behavior through activity of the brain and nervous system, physiology, genetics, the endocrine system, and biochemistry; neutral, reductionistic, mechanistic view of human nature.

Evolutionary View

Key Idea: *Human and animal behavior is the result of the process of evolution.*
Seeks to explain behavior through evolutionary principles based on natural selection; neutral, reductionistic, mechanistic view of human nature.

Psychological Perspective

Behavioristic View

Key Idea: *Behavior is shaped and controlled by one's environment.*
Emphasizes the study of observable behavior and the effects of learning; stresses the influence of external rewards and punishments; neutral, scientific, somewhat mechanistic view of human nature.

Cognitive View

Key Idea: *Much human behavior can be understood in terms of the mental processing of information.*
Concerned with thinking, knowing, perception, understanding, memory, decision making, and judgment; explains behavior in terms of information processing; neutral, somewhat computer-like view of human nature.

Psychodynamic View

Key Idea: *Behavior is directed by forces within one's personality that are often hidden or unconscious.*
Emphasizes internal impulses, desires, and conflicts—especially those that are unconscious; views behavior as the result of clashing forces within personality; somewhat negative, pessimistic view of human nature.

Humanistic View

Key Idea: *Behavior is guided by one's self-image, by subjective perceptions of the world, and by needs for personal growth.*
Focuses on subjective, conscious experience, human problems, potentials, and ideals; emphasizes self-image and self-actualization to explain behavior; positive, philosophical view of human nature.

Sociocultural Perspective

Sociocultural View

Key Idea: *Behavior is influenced by one's social and cultural context.*
Emphasizes that behavior is related to the social and cultural environment within which a person is born, grows up, and lives from day to day; neutral, interactionist view of human nature.

PSYCHOLOGY TODAY—THREE COMPLEMENTARY PERSPECTIVES ON BEHAVIOR

>SURVEY QUESTION< *What are the major trends and specialties in psychology?*

At one time, loyalty to each school of thought was fierce, and clashes were common. Over the last 60 years, viewpoints such as functionalism and Gestalt psychology have blended into newer, broader perspectives. Also, some early systems, such as structuralism, have disappeared entirely while new ones have gained prominence. Certainly, loyalties and specialties still exist. But today, many psychologists are *eclectic* (ek-LEK-tik), because they realize that a single perspective is unlikely to fully explain complex forms of human behavior. As a result, psychologists commonly draw insight from a variety of perspectives. The three broad views that shape modern psychology are the *biological, psychological,* and *sociocultural* perspectives (■ Table 1.2).

The Biological Perspective

Biopsychologists seek to explain all behavior in terms of physical mechanisms, such as brain activity. By using new techniques for studying the brain, they are producing exciting new insights about how the brain relates to thinking, feelings, perception, abnormal behavior, and other topics. Biopsychologists and others who study the brain and nervous system, such as biologists and biochemists, form the broader field of *neuroscience*. *Evolutionary psychologists* attempt to explain our current behavior by looking back at human history to learn how evolutionary principles and genetics affect us.

The Psychological Perspective

The *psychological perspective* continues the tradition of objective observation that began with the *behavioristic view*. But the radical behaviorism of B. F. Skinner has been widely criticized. Basically, Skinner ignored the role that thinking plays in our lives. One critic even charged that Skinnerian psychology had "lost consciousness"!

Over the last 50 years, a "cognitive revolution" has taken place as *cognitive psychologists* have successfully applied objective observation to study covert mental behaviors, such as thinking, memory, language, perception, problem solving, consciousness, and creativity. Cognitive psychologists and other researchers interested in cognition, such as computer scientists and linguists, form the broader field of *cognitive science*. With all this renewed interest in thinking, it can be said that psychology has finally "regained consciousness" (Robins, Gosling, & Craik, 1998).

Freudian psychoanalysis continues to evolve into the broader *psychodynamic view*. Although many of Freud's ideas have been challenged, psychodynamic psychologists continue to trace human behavior to unconscious processes. They also seek to develop therapies to help people lead happier, fuller lives. *Humanistic psychologists* do, too, but they stress subjective, conscious experience and the positive side of human nature.

Positive Psychology

Psychologists have always paid attention to the negative side of human behavior. This is easy to understand because of the pressing need to solve human problems. However, psychologists have recently begun to ask, What do we know about love, happiness, creativity, well-being, self-confidence, and achievement? Together, such topics make up **positive psychology,** the study of human strengths, virtues, and optimal behavior (Compton, 2005; Seligman & Csikszentmihalyi, 2000). Many topics from positive psychology can be found in this book. Ideally, they will help make your own life more positive and fulfilling (Simonton & Baumeister, 2005).

The Sociocultural Perspective

As you can see, it is helpful to view human behavior from more than one perspective. This is also true in another sense. We are rapidly becoming a multicultural society, made up of people from many different nations. How has this affected psychology? Let us introduce you to Jerry, who is Japanese American and is married to an Irish Catholic American. Here is what Jerry, his wife, and their children did one New Year's Day:

> We woke up in the morning and went to Mass at St. Brigid's, which has a black gospel choir. . . . Then we went to the Japanese-American Community Center for the Oshogatsu New Year's program and saw Buddhist archers shoot arrows to ward off evil spirits for the year. Next, we ate traditional rice cakes as part of the New Year's service and listened to a young Japanese-American storyteller. On the way home, we stopped in Chinatown and after that we ate Mexican food at a taco stand. (Njeri, 1991)

Jerry and his family reflect a new social reality: Cultural diversity is becoming the norm. About one third of the population in the United States is now African American, Hispanic, Asian American, Native American, or Pacific Islander. In some large cities "minority" groups are already the majority (Schmitt, 2001).

In the past, psychology was based mostly on the cultures of North America and Europe. Now, we must ask, Do the principles of Western psychology apply to people in all cultures?

Positive psychology The study of human strengths, virtues, and effective functioning.

Are some psychological concepts invalid in other cultures? Are any universal? As psychologists have probed such questions, one thing has become clear: Most of what we think, feel, and do is influenced in one way or another by the social and cultural worlds in which we live (Lehman, Chiu, & Schaller, 2004).

Cultural Relativity

Imagine that you are a psychologist. Your client, Linda, who is a Native American, tells you that spirits live in the trees near her home. Is Linda suffering from a delusion? Is she abnormal? Obviously, you will misjudge Linda's mental health if you fail to take her cultural beliefs into account. **Cultural relativity** (the idea that behavior must be judged relative to the values of the culture in which it occurs) can greatly affect the diagnosis and treatment of mental disorders (Alarcon, 1995; Draguns, Gielen, & Fish, 2004). Cases like Linda's teach us to be wary of using narrow standards when judging others or comparing groups.

A Broader View of Diversity

In addition to cultural differences, age, ethnicity, gender, religion, disability, and sexual orientation all affect the **social norms** that guide behavior. Social norms are rules that define acceptable and expected behavior for members of various groups. All too often, the unstated standard for judging what is "average," "normal," or "correct" is the behavior of white, middle-class males (Reid, 2002). To fully understand human behavior, psychologists need to know how people differ, as well as the ways in which we are all alike (APA, 2003). For the same reason, an appreciation of human diversity can enrich your life, as well as your understanding of psychology (Denmark, Rabinowitz, & Sechzer, 2005).

In a moment, we will further explore what psychologists do. First, here's a chance to improve your next test score.

I Patrick Giardino/Corbis

To fully understand human behavior, personal differences based on age, race, culture, ethnicity, gender, and sexual orientation must be taken into account.

Cultural relativity The idea that behavior must be judged relative to the values of the culture in which it occurs.

Social norms Unspoken rules that define acceptable and expected behavior for members of a group.

→ **Study Break** **History and Major Perspectives**

Reflect

Which school of thought most closely matches your own view of behavior? Do you think any of the early schools offers a complete explanation of why we behave as we do? What about the three contemporary perspectives? Can you explain why so many psychologists are eclectic?

Learning Check

Match:

1. _____ Philosophy
2. _____ Wundt
3. _____ Structuralism
4. _____ Functionalism
5. _____ Behaviorism
6. _____ Gestalt
7. _____ Psychodynamic
8. _____ Humanistic
9. _____ Cognitive
10. _____ Washburn
11. _____ Biopsychology

A. Against analysis; studied whole experiences
B. "Mental chemistry" and introspection
C. Emphasizes self-actualization and personal growth
D. Interested in unconscious causes of behavior
E. Interested in how the mind aids survival
F. First woman Ph.D. in psychology

G. Studied stimuli and responses, conditioning
H. Part of psychology's "long past"
I. Concerned with thinking, language, problem solving
J. Used introspection and careful measurement
K. Relates behavior to the brain, physiology, and genetics
L. Also known as engineering psychology

12. Universal norms exist for judging the behavior of people in various cultural and social groups. T or F?

Critical Thinking

13. Modern sciences like psychology are built on observations that can be verified by two or more independent observers. Did structuralism meet this standard? Why or why not?

Answers

1. H 2. J 3. B 4. E 5. G 6. A 7. D 8. C 9. I 10. F 11. K 12. F 13. No, it did not. The downfall of structuralism was that each observer examined the contents of his or her own mind—which is something that no other person can observe.

The Golden Psi

As you read this book you may find yourself wondering whether a particular concept can be used to solve mental and behavioral problems. That's good. Applying concepts is an excellent way to reflect on and better understand new ideas. These "Clinical File" boxes are designed to encourage you to reflect on how psychology can be applied to help people.

Public impressions of psychologists are often inaccurate, perhaps because of stereotyped images appearing in the media. For example, in the 2005 comedy *Prime* a therapist listens to a patient describe intimate details of her relationship with a man, but fails to tell the patient that the man is her son. Other films have featured psychologists who are more disturbed than their patients (such as Jack Nicholson's character in *Anger Management*) or psychologists who are bumbling buffoons (such as Billy Crystal's character in *Analyze This*). Such characters may be dramatic and entertaining, but they seriously distort public perceptions of responsible and hardworking psychologists (Schultz, 2004). Real psychologists follow an ethical code that stresses respect for people's privacy, dignity, confidentiality, and welfare ("Ethical," 2002; Sullivan et al., 1998).

In the film *Prime*, Meryl Streep plays a therapist who listens to her patient, played by Uma Thurman, describe intimate details of her relationship with a man. However, the therapist neglects to tell her patient that the man is her son. No ethical therapist would ever engage in such behavior. Such premises are typical of the way psychologists and psychotherapy are misrepresented in the media.

In response, the American Psychological Association created the Golden Psi Media Award for the responsible portrayal of mental health professionals. (The Greek letter psi, written Ψ, symbolizes psychology.) The 2004 Golden Psi went to two episodes of the television program *Law & Order: Special Victims Unit*. In both episodes, a psychiatrist acts professionally, despite intense pressures to act otherwise. In one episode, the psychiatrist refuses to medicate a schizophrenic man (without his permission) to force him to reveal the location of an abducted child. In a second episode, the psychiatrist testifies at the trial of a man accused of raping and killing Arabs. The defense attorney argues that these acts are "in the man's genes" and out of his control. The psychiatrist testifies about environmental influences on behavior and how the killer is, in fact, responsible for his crimes. Interestingly, the Golden Psi has never been awarded to a movie, going instead to television programs, probably because most movies try to be dramatic and sensational, whereas some television programs try to be more realistic (Schultz, 2004).

PSYCHOLOGISTS—GUARANTEED NOT TO SHRINK

Psychologists are all shrinks, right? Nope. "Shrinks" (a slang term derived from "head shrinkers") are *psychiatrists,* a different type of mental health professional. To read about some other popular misconceptions about psychologists, see "The Golden Psi."

A **psychologist** is highly trained in the methods, knowledge, and theories of psychology. Psychologists usually have a doctorate or a master's degree. These degrees typically require from 3 to 8 years of postgraduate training. Psychologists may teach, do research, give psychological tests, or serve as consultants to business, industry, government, or the military.

Even without media distortions, misconceptions about psychologists are common. For instance, most psychologists are not therapists in private practice. Instead, they are employed by schools, businesses, and social agencies. Likewise, only 14 percent work in clinics or hospitals.

One perception of psychologists is accurate: Most do help people in one way or another. Psychologists interested in emotional problems specialize in clinical or counseling psychology (see ▦ Table 1.3). **Clinical psychologists** treat psychological problems or do research on therapies and mental disorders. In contrast, **counseling psychologists** tend to treat milder problems, such as poor adjustment at work or school. However, such differences are fading, and many counseling psychologists now work full time as therapists.

To enter the profession of psychology, it is best to have a doctorate (Ph.D., Psy.D., or Ed.D.). Most clinical psychologists have a Ph.D. degree and follow a scientist-practitioner model. That is, they are trained to do either research or therapy. Many do both. Other clini-

Psychologist A person highly trained in the methods, factual knowledge, and theories of psychology.

Clinical psychologist A psychologist who specializes in the treatment of psychological and behavioral disturbances or who does research on such disturbances.

Counseling psychologist A psychologist who specializes in the treatment of milder emotional and behavioral disturbances.

■ Table 1.3 Kinds of Psychologists and What They Do

Specialty		Typical Activities
Biopsychology	B*	Does research on the brain, nervous system, and other physical origins of behavior
Clinical	A	Does psychotherapy; investigates clinical problems; develops methods of treatment
Cognitive	B	Studies human thinking and information processing abilities
Community	A	Promotes community-wide mental health through research, prevention, education, and consultation
Comparative	B	Studies and compares the behavior of different species, especially animals
Consumer	A	Researches packaging, advertising, marketing methods, and characteristics of consumers
Counseling	A	Does psychotherapy and personal counseling; researches emotional disturbances and counseling methods
Cultural	B	Studies the ways in which culture, subculture, and ethnic group membership affect behavior
Developmental	A, B	Conducts research on infant, child, adolescent, and adult development; does clinical work with disturbed children; acts as consultant to parents and schools
Educational	A	Investigates classroom dynamics, teaching styles, and learning; develops educational tests, evaluates educational programs
Engineering	A	Does applied research on the design of machinery, computers, airlines, automobiles, and so on, for business, industry, and the military
Environmental	A, B	Studies the effects of urban noise, crowding, attitudes toward the environment, and human use of space; acts as a consultant on environmental issues
Forensic	A	Studies problems of crime and crime prevention, rehabilitation programs, prisons, courtroom dynamics; selects candidates for police work
Gender	B	Does research on differences between males and females, the acquisition of gender identity, and the role of gender throughout life
Health	A, B	Studies the relationship between behavior and health; uses psychological principles to promote health and prevent illness
Industrial-organizational	A	Selects job applicants, does skills analysis, evaluates on-the-job training, improves work environments and human relations in organizations and work settings
Learning	B	Studies how and why learning occurs; develops theories of learning
Medical	A	Applies psychology to manage medical problems, such as the emotional impact of illness, self-screening for cancer, compliance in taking medicine
Personality	B	Studies personality traits and dynamics; develops theories of personality and tests for assessing personality traits
School	A	Does psychological testing, referrals, emotional and vocational counseling of students; detects and treats learning disabilities; improves classroom learning
Sensation and perception	B	Studies the sense organs and the process of perception; investigates the mechanisms of sensation and develops theories about how perception occurs
Social	B	Investigates human social behavior, including attitudes, conformity, persuasion, prejudice, friendship, aggression, helping, and so forth

*Research in this area is typically applied (A), basic (B), or both (A, B).

cians earn the Psy.D. (Doctor of Psychology) degree, which emphasizes therapy skills rather than research.

Have you ever wondered what it takes to become a psychologist? See "Is a Career in Psychology Right for You?"

Other Mental Health Professionals

A **psychiatrist** is a medical doctor who treats mental disorders, usually by doing psychotherapy. However, psychiatrists can also prescribe drugs, which is something a psychologist cannot do. This may change, however. Psychologists in New Mexico and Louisiana can now

Psychiatrist A medical doctor with additional training in the diagnosis and treatment of mental and emotional disorders.

DISCOVERING PSYCHOLOGY

Is a Career in Psychology Right for You?

As you read this book we encourage you to frequently reflect on new ideas by relating them to your own life in order to better understand and remember them. "Discovering Psychology" boxes like this one are designed to help you be more reflective about how psychology relates to your own life. Answer the following questions to explore whether you would enjoy becoming a psychologist:

1. I have a strong interest in human behavior. True or False?
2. I am good at recognizing patterns, evaluating evidence, and drawing conclusions. True or False?
3. I am emotionally stable. True or False?
4. I have good communication skills. True or False?
5. I find theories and ideas challenging and stimulating. True or False?

6. My friends regard me as especially sensitive to the feelings of others. True or False?
7. I enjoy planning and carrying out complex projects and activities. True or False?
8. Programs and popular books about psychology interest me. True or False?
9. I enjoy working with other people. True or False?
10. Clear thinking, objectivity, and keen observation appeal to me. True or False?

If you answered "True" to most of these questions, a career in psychology might be a good choice. And remember that many psychology majors also succeed in occupations such as management, public affairs, social services, business, sales, and education.

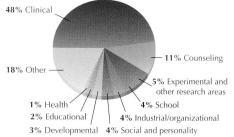

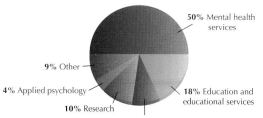

▶▶**FIGURE 1.3** (a) Specialties in psychology (APA, 2005). Percentages are approximate. (b) Where psychologists work (APA, 2000). (c) This chart shows the main activities psychologists do at work (APA, 2000). Any particular psychologist might do several of these activities during a work week. As you can see, most psychologists specialize in applied areas and work in applied settings.

Psychoanalyst A mental health professional (usually a medical doctor) trained to practice psychoanalysis.

Counselor A mental health professional who specializes in helping people with problems not involving serious mental disorder; for example, marriage counselors, career counselors, or school counselors.

Psychiatric social worker A mental health professional trained to apply social science principles to help patients in clinics and hospitals.

legally prescribe drugs. It will be interesting to see whether other states grant similar privileges (Munsey, 2006).

To be a psychoanalyst, you must have a moustache and goatee, spectacles, a German accent, and a well-padded couch—or so the TV and movie stereotype goes. Actually, to become a **psychoanalyst,** you must have an M.D. or Ph.D. degree plus further training in Freudian psychoanalysis. In other words, either a physician or a psychologist may become an analyst by learning a specific type of psychotherapy.

In many states, counselors also do mental health work. A **counselor** is an adviser who helps solve problems with marriage, career, school, work, or the like. To be a licensed counselor (such as a marriage and family counselor, a child counselor, or a school counselor) typically requires a master's degree plus 1 or 2 years of full-time supervised counseling experience. Counselors learn practical helping skills and do not treat serious mental disorders.

Psychiatric social workers play an important role in many mental health programs. **Psychiatric social workers** apply social science principles to help patients in clinics and hospitals. Most hold an M.S.W. (Master of Social Work) degree. Often, they assist psychologists and psychiatrists as part of a team. Their typical duties include evaluating patients and families, conducting group therapy, or visiting a patient's home, school, or job to alleviate problems.

Specialties in Psychology

Do all psychologists do therapy and treat abnormal behavior? No. Only about 58 percent are clinical and counseling psychologists. The rest are found in other specialties. At present, the American Psychological Association (APA) consists of more than 50 divisions, each reflecting special skills or areas of interest. Some of the major specialties are listed in ▪ Table 1.3

(also see ▸▸Fig. 1.3). Nearly 30 percent of all psychologists are employed full-time at colleges or universities, where they teach and do research, consulting, or therapy. Some do *basic research,* in which they seek knowledge for its own sake. For example, a psychologist might study memory simply to understand how it works. Others do *applied research* to solve immediate practical problems, such as finding ways to improve the memory of eyewitnesses to crimes. Some do both types of research.

In a moment we'll take a closer look at how research is done. Before that, here's a chance to do a little research on how much you've learned.

 Study Break **Psychologists and Their Specialties**

Reflect

You're going to meet four psychologists at a social gathering. How many would you expect to be therapists in private practice? Odds are that only two will be clinical (or counseling) psychologists and only one of these will work in private practice. On the other hand, at least one out of the four (and probably two) will work at a college or university.

Learning Check

See if you can answer these questions before continuing.

1. Which of the following can prescribe drugs?

   a. a psychologist   b. a psychiatrist
   c. a psychotherapist   d. a counselor

2. A psychologist who specializes in treating human emotional difficulties is called a _____ psychologist.
3. Roughly 40 percent of psychologists specialize in counseling psychology. T or F?
4. Who among the following would most likely be involved in the detection of learning disabilities?

   a. a consumer psychologist   b. a forensic psychologist
   c. an experimental   d. a school psychologist
      psychologist

Critical Thinking

5. If most psychologists work in applied settings, why is basic research still of great importance?

Answers

1. b 2. clinical or counseling 3. F 4. d 5. Because practitioners benefit from basic psychological research in the same way that physicians benefit from basic research in biology. Discoveries in basic science form the knowledge base that leads to useful applications.

SCIENTIFIC RESEARCH—HOW TO THINK LIKE A PSYCHOLOGIST

>SURVEY QUESTIONS< *Why is the scientific method important to psychologists? How do psychologists collect information?*

Drawing valid conclusions in psychology is more challenging than you might think. In the course of a day, you probably hear dozens of false statements about human behavior. How can you separate fact from fiction and reality from fantasy? Psychologists have found that the tools of science provide an elegant way to investigate human and animal behavior.

Carefully recording facts and events is the heart of all sciences. As we mentioned previously, to be *scientific,* our observations must be *systematic,* so that they reveal something about behavior (Stanovich, 2004). To use an earlier example, if you are interested in heat and aggression, you will learn little by driving around and making haphazard observations of aggressive behavior. To be of value, your observations must be planned and systematic.

The Scientific Method

The **scientific method** is based on careful collection of evidence, accurate description and measurement, precise definition, controlled observation, and repeatable results (Leary, 2004). In its ideal form the scientific method has six elements:

1. Making observations
2. Defining a problem

Scientific method Testing the truth of a proposition by careful measurement and controlled observation.

Applying the scientific method to the study of behavior requires careful observation. Here, a psychologist videotapes a session in which a child's thinking abilities are being tested.

Dan McCoy/Rainbow

3. Proposing a hypothesis
4. Gathering evidence/testing the hypothesis
5. Publishing results
6. Theory building

Let's take a closer look at some elements of the scientific method.

Hypothesis Testing

Yes, what exactly is a hypothesis? A **hypothesis** (hi-POTH-eh-sis) is a tentative explanation of an event or relationship. In common terms, a hypothesis is a *testable* hunch or educated guess about behavior. For example, you might hypothesize that "Frustration encourages aggression." How could you test this hypothesis? First you would have to decide how you are going to frustrate people. (This part might be fun.) Then you will need to find a way to measure whether or not they become more aggressive. (Not so much fun if you plan to be nearby.) Your observations would then provide evidence to confirm or disconfirm the hypothesis.

Conceptual Level

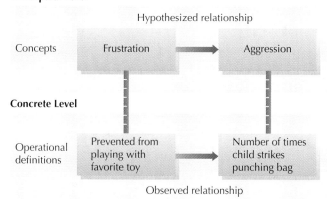

▸▸FIGURE 1.4 Operational definitions are used to link concepts with concrete observations. Do you think the examples given are reasonable operational definitions of frustration and aggression? Operational definitions vary in how well they represent concepts. For this reason, many different experiments may be necessary to draw clear conclusions about hypothesized relationships in psychology.

Hypothesis The predicted outcome of an experiment or an educated guess about the relationship between variables.

Operational definition Defining a scientific concept by stating the specific actions or procedures used to measure it. For example, "hunger" might be defined as "the number of hours of food deprivation."

Operational Definitions

Because we cannot see or touch frustration, it must be defined operationally. An **operational definition** states the exact procedures used to represent a concept. Operational definitions allow abstract ideas to be tested in real-world terms. (See ▸▸Figure 1.4.) For example, you might define frustration as "interrupting an adult before he or she can finish a puzzle and win a $200 prize." And aggression might be defined as "the number of times a frustrated individual insults the person who prevented work on the puzzle." Covert behaviors are operationally defined in terms of overt behavior in order to permit scientific study.

Clever Hans

Several steps of the scientific method can be illustrated with the story of Clever Hans, a horse who became famous in Germany 100 years ago (Rosenthal, 1965). Clever Hans seemed to solve difficult math problems, which he answered by tapping his hoof. If you asked Hans, "What is 12 times 2, minus 18," Hans would tap his hoof six times. This was so astonishing that one skeptical scientist decided to find out if Hans really could do arithmetic. Assume that you are the scientist and that you are just itching to discover how Hans *really* does his trick.

Can a Horse Add?

Your investigation of Hans's math skills would probably begin with careful *observation* of both the horse and his owner. Assume that these observations fail to reveal any obvious cheating. Then the *problem* becomes more clearly *defined*: What signals Hans to start and stop tapping his hoof? Your first *hypothesis* might be that the owner is giving Hans a signal. Your proposed *test* would be to make the owner leave the room. Then someone else could ask Hans questions. Your test would either confirm or deny the owner's role. This *evidence* would support or eliminate the cheating hypothesis. By changing the conditions under which you observe Hans, you have *controlled* the situation to gain more information from your observations.

Incidentally, Hans could still answer when his owner was out of the room. But a brilliant series of controlled observations revealed Hans's secret. If Hans couldn't see the questioner, he couldn't answer. It seems that questioners always *lowered their heads* (to look at Hans's hoof) after asking a question. This was Hans's cue to start tapping. When Hans had tapped the correct number, a questioner would always *look up* to see if Hans was going to stop. This was Hans's cue to stop tapping!

Theories

What about theory formulation? Since Clever Hans's ability to do math was an isolated problem, no theorizing was involved. However, in actual research, a **theory** acts as a map of knowledge. Good theories summarize observations, explain them, and guide further research (▶▶Fig. 1.5). Without theories of forgetting, personality, stress, mental illness, and the like, psychologists would drown in a sea of disconnected facts (Stanovich, 2004).

Publication

Scientific information must always be *publicly available.* The results of psychological studies are usually published in professional journals. (See ▪ Table 1.4.) That way, anyone willing to make appropriate observations can see whether or not a claim is true (Leary, 2004).

Summary

Now let's summarize more realistically. All the basic elements of the scientific method are found in the example that follows.

Observation: Isidora, a psychologist, observes that some computer game designers seem to experience less work-related stress than others do.

Defining a Problem: Isidora's problem is to identify the ways in which high-stress and low-stress game designers are different.

Observation: Isidora carefully questions game designers about how much stress they experience. These additional observations suggest that low-stress game designers feel they have more control over their work.

Proposing a Hypothesis: Isidora hypothesizes that having control over difficult tasks reduces stress.

Gathering Evidence/Testing the Hypothesis: Isidora designs an experiment in which people must solve a series of very difficult problems. In one group, people solve the problems at a forced pace, dictated by Isidora. In another group, they are allowed to set the pace themselves. While working, the second group reports lower stress levels than the first did. This suggests that Isidora's hypothesis is correct.

Publishing Results: In a scholarly article, Isidora carefully describes the question she investigated, the methods she used, and the results of her experiment. The article is published in the *Journal of Clinical Psychology.*

Theory Building: Drawing on the results of similar experiments, Isidora and other psychologists create a theory to explain why having control over a task helps reduce stress.

▶▶**FIGURE 1.5** Psychologists use the logic of science to answer questions about behavior. Specific hypotheses can be tested in a variety of ways, including naturalistic observation, correlational studies, controlled experiments, clinical studies, and the survey method. Psychologists revise their theories to reflect the evidence they gather. New or revised theories then lead to new observations, problems, and hypotheses.

▪ Table 1.4 **Outline of a Research Report**

- *Abstract* Research reports begin with a very brief summary of the study and its findings. The abstract allows you to get an overview without reading the entire article.

- *Introduction* The introduction describes the question to be investigated. It also provides background information by reviewing prior studies on the same or related topics.

- *Method* This section tells how and why observations were made. It also describes the specific procedures used to gather data. That way, other researchers can repeat the study to see if they get the same results.

- *Results* The outcome of the investigation is presented. Data may be graphed, summarized in tables, or statistically analyzed.

- *Discussion* The results of the study are discussed in relation to the original question. Implications of the study are explored and further studies may be proposed.

Theory A system of ideas designed to interrelate concepts and facts in a way that summarizes existing data and predicts future observations.

Research Methods

Psychologists gather evidence and test hypotheses in many ways: They observe behavior as it unfolds in natural settings (**naturalistic observation**); they make measurements to discover relationships between events (**correlational method**); they use the powerful technique of controlled experimentation (**experimental method**); they study psychological problems and therapies in clinical settings (**clinical method**); and they use questionnaires to poll large groups of people (**survey method**). Let's see how each of these is used to advance psychological knowledge.

NATURALISTIC OBSERVATION— PSYCHOLOGY STEPS OUT!

Psychologists sometimes actively observe behavior in a *natural setting* (the typical environment in which a person or animal lives). The work of Jane Goodall provides a good example. She and her staff have been observing chimpanzees in Tanzania since 1960. A quote from her book, *In the Shadow of Man,* captures the excitement of a scientific discovery:

> Quickly focusing my binoculars, I saw that it was a single chimpanzee, and just then he turned my direction. . . . He was squatting beside the red earth mound of a termite nest, and as I watched I saw him carefully push a long grass stem into a hole in the mound. After a moment he withdrew it and picked something from the end with his mouth. I was too far away to make out what he was eating, but it was obvious that he was actually using a grass stem as a tool (»Fig. 1.6). (Van Lawick-Goodall, 1971)

Notice that naturalistic observation only provides *descriptions* of behavior. In order to *explain* observations we may need information from other research methods. Just the same, Goodall's discovery showed that humans are not the only tool-making animals (Nakamichi, 2004).

Chimpanzees in zoos use objects as tools. Doesn't that demonstrate the same thing? Not necessarily. Naturalistic observation allows us to study behavior that hasn't been tampered with or altered by outside influences. Only by observing chimps in their natural environment can we tell if they use tools without human interference.

»**FIGURE 1.6** A special moment in Jane Goodall's naturalistic study of chimpanzees. A chimp uses a grass stem to extract a meal from a termite nest. Goodall's work also documented the importance of long-term emotional bonds between chimpanzee mothers and their offspring, as well as fascinating differences in the behavior and "personalities" of individual chimps (Goodall, 1990).

Baron Hugo van Lawick/National Geographic Society

Limitations

Doesn't the presence of human observers affect the animals' behavior? Yes. The observer effect is a major problem. The **observer effect** refers to changes in a subject's behavior caused by an awareness of being observed. Naturalists must be very careful to keep their distance and avoid "making friends" with the animals they are watching. Likewise, if you are interested in why automobile drivers have traffic accidents, you can't simply get in people's cars and start taking notes. As a stranger, your presence would probably change the driver's behaviors. When possible, this problem can be minimized by concealing the observer. Another solution is to use hidden recorders. For example, a naturalistic study of traffic accidents was done with video cameras installed in 100 cars (Dingus et al., 2006). It turns out that most accidents are caused by failing to look at the traffic in front of the car (eyes forward!).

Observer bias is a related problem in which observers see what they expect to see or record only selected details. For instance, teachers in one classic study were told to watch normal elementary school children who had been labeled (for the study) as "learning disabled," "mentally retarded," "emotionally disturbed," or "normal." Sadly, teachers gave the children very different ratings, depending on the labels used (Foster & Ysseldyke, 1976). In some situations, observer bias can have serious consequences (Leary, 2004). For example,

Naturalistic observation Observing behavior as it unfolds in natural settings.

Correlational method Making measurements to discover relationships between events.

Experimental method Investigating behavior through controlled experimentation.

Clinical method Studying psychological problems and therapies in clinical settings.

Survey method Using questionnaires and surveys to poll large groups of people.

Observer effect Changes in behavior brought about by an awareness of being observed.

Observer bias The tendency of an observer to distort observations or perceptions to match his or her expectations.

psychotherapists tend to get better results with the type of therapy they favor (Lambert, 1999).

The Anthropomorphic Error

A special mistake to avoid while observing animals is the **anthropomorphic** (AN-thro-po-MORE-fik) **error**. This is the error of attributing human thoughts, feelings, or motives to animals—especially as a way of explaining their behavior (Wynne, 2004). The temptation to assume that an animal is "angry," "jealous," "bored," or "guilty" can be strong. If you have pets at home, you probably already know how difficult it is to avoid anthropomorphizing. But it can lead to false conclusions. For example, if your dog growls at your girlfriend every time she visits, you might assume the dog doesn't like her. But maybe she wears a perfume that bothers the dog's nose.

Recording Observations

Psychologists doing naturalistic studies make a special effort to minimize bias by keeping an *observational record,* or detailed summary of data and observations. As suggested by the study of traffic accidents, video recording often provides the most objective record of all.

Despite its problems, naturalistic observation can supply a wealth of information and raise many interesting questions. In most scientific research it is an excellent starting point.

CORRELATIONAL STUDIES—IN SEARCH OF THE PERFECT RELATIONSHIP

Let's say a psychologist notes an association between the IQs of parents and their children, or between beauty and social popularity, or between anxiety and test performance, or even between crime and the weather. In each case, two observations or events are **correlated** (linked together in an orderly way).

A **correlational study** finds the degree of relationship, or correlation, between two existing traits, behaviors, or events. First, two factors are measured. Then a statistical technique is used to find their degree of correlation. (See the Statistics Appendix near the end of this book for more information.) For example, we could find the correlation between the number of hours slept at night and afternoon sleepiness. If the correlation is large, knowing how long a person sleeps at night would allow us to predict his or her degree of sleepiness in the afternoon. Likewise, afternoon sleepiness could be used to predict the duration of nighttime sleep.

Correlation Coefficients

How is the degree of correlation expressed? The strength and direction of a relationship can be expressed as a **coefficient of correlation.** This is simply a number falling somewhere between +1.00 and −1.00 (see the Statistics Appendix). If the number is zero or close to zero, the association between two measures is weak or nonexistent. For example, the correlation between shoe size and intelligence is zero. (Sorry, size 12 readers.) If the correlation is +1.00, a perfect positive relationship exists; if it is −1.00, a perfect negative relationship has been discovered.

Correlations in psychology are rarely perfect. But the closer the coefficient is to +1.00 or −1.00, the stronger the relationship. For example, identical twins tend to have almost identical IQs. In contrast, the IQs of parents and their children are only generally similar. The correlation between the IQs of parents and children is .35; between identical twins it's .86.

What do the terms "positive" and "negative" correlation mean? A positive correlation shows that increases in one measure are matched by increases in the other (or decreases correspond with decreases). For example, there is a positive correlation between high school grades and college grades; students who do well in high school tend to do well in college (and the reverse). In a negative correlation, increases in the first measure are associated with decreases in the sec-

Anthropomorphic error The error of attributing human thoughts, feelings, or motives to animals, especially as a way of explaining their behavior.

Correlation The existence of a consistent, systematic relationship between two events, measures, or variables.

Correlational study A nonexperimental study designed to measure the degree of relationship (if any) between two or more events, measures, or variables.

Coefficient of correlation A statistical index ranging from −1.00 to +1.00 that indicates the direction and degree of correlation.

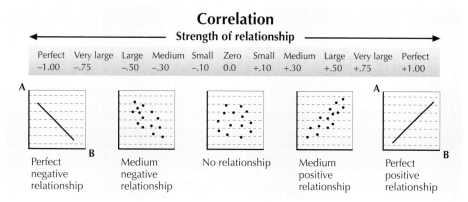

Correlation
Strength of relationship

Perfect	Very large	Large	Medium	Small	Zero	Small	Medium	Large	Very large	Perfect
−1.00	−.75	−.50	−.30	−.10	0.0	+.10	+.30	+.50	+.75	+1.00

Perfect
negative
relationship

Medium
negative
relationship

No relationship

Medium
positive
relationship

Perfect
positive
relationship

▶▶FIGURE 1.7 The correlation coefficient tells how strongly two measures are related. These graphs show a range of relationships between two measures, A and B. If a correlation is negative, increases in one measure are associated with decreases in the other. (As B gets larger, A gets smaller.) In a positive correlation, increases in one measure are associated with increases in the other. (As B gets larger, A gets larger.) The center-left graph ("medium negative relationship") might result from comparing anxiety level (B) with test scores (A): Higher anxiety is associated with lower scores. The center graph ("no relationship") would result from plotting a person's shoe size (B) and his or her IQ (A). The center-right graph ("medium positive relationship") could be a plot of grades in high school (B) and grades in college (A) for a group of students: Higher grades in high school are associated with higher grades in college.

ond (see ▶▶Fig. 1.7). We might observe, for instance, that students who play many hours of computer games get lower grades than those who play few hours. (This is the well-known computer-game-zombie effect.)

Wouldn't that show that playing computer games too much causes lower grades? It might seem so, but we cannot be sure without performing an experiment.

Correlation and Causation

Correlational studies help us discover relationships and make predictions. However, correlation *does not* demonstrate *causation* (a cause-effect relationship) (Halpern, 2003). It could be, for instance, that students who aren't interested in their classes have more time for computer games. If so, then their lack of study and lower grades would *both* result from disinterest, not from excess game playing. Just because one thing *appears* to be related to another does not mean that a cause-and-effect connection exists.

Here is another example of mistaking correlation for causation: What if a psychologist discovers that the blood of patients with schizophrenia contains a certain chemical not found in the general population? Does this show that the chemical *causes* schizophrenia? It may seem so, but schizophrenia could cause the chemical to form. Or, both schizophrenia and the chemical might be caused by some unknown third factor, such as the typical diet in mental hospitals. Just because one thing *appears* to cause another does not *confirm* that it does. The best way to be confident that a cause-and-effect relationship exists is to perform a controlled experiment. You'll learn how in the next section.

 Study Break **Research Methods, Naturalistic Observation, and Correlation**

Reflect

You probably hypothesize daily about why people act the way they do. Do you seek to verify your hypotheses? Usually we closely observe others to determine if our "educated guesses" about them are correct. But casual observation can be misleading. To really test a hypothesis, systematic observation and formal research methods are necessary.

Learning Check

1. Most of psychology can rightfully be called common sense because psychologists prefer naturalistic observation to controlled observation. T or F?
2. A hypothesis is any careful observation made in a controlled experiment. T or F?
3. Two major problems in naturalistic observation are the effects of the observer and observer bias. T or F?

4. The _____ fallacy involves attributing human feelings and motives to animals.
5. Correlation typically does not demonstrate causation. T or F?
6. Which correlation coefficient represents the strongest relationship?

   a −0.86   b. +0.66   c. +0.10   d. +0.09

Critical Thinking

7. Can you think of some "commonsense" statements that contradict each other?
8. Attributing mischievous motives to a car that is not working properly is a thinking error similar to anthropomorphizing. T or F?
9. Adults who often ate Frosted Flakes cereal as children now have half the cancer rate seen in adults who never ate Frosted Flakes. What do you think explains this strange correlation?

Answers

1. F 2. F 3. T 4. anthropomorphic 5. T 6. a 7. There are many examples. Here are more to add to the ones you thought of: "You can't make a silk purse out of a sow's ear," versus "Clothes make the man (or woman)." "He (or she) who hesitates is lost," versus "Haste makes waste." "Birds of a feather flock together," versus "Opposites attract." 8. True. It appears to be difficult for humans to resist thinking of other species and even machines in human terms. 9. The correlation is related to an age bias in the group of people studied. Older adults have higher cancer rates than younger adults, and Frosted Flakes weren't available during the childhoods of older people. Thus, Frosted Flakes appear to be related to cancer, when age is the real connection (Tierny, 1987).

THE PSYCHOLOGY EXPERIMENT—WHERE CAUSE MEETS EFFECT

>SURVEY QUESTION< *How is an experiment performed?*

The most powerful research tool is an **experiment** (a formal trial undertaken to confirm or disconfirm a hypothesis). Psychologists carefully control conditions in experiments to identify cause-and-effect relationships. To perform an experiment you would do the following:

1. Directly vary a condition you think might affect behavior.
2. Create two or more groups of subjects. These groups should be alike in all ways *except* the condition you are varying.
3. Record whether varying the condition has any effect on behavior.

Assume that you want to find out if hunger affects memory. First, you would form two groups of people. Then you could give the members of one group a memory test while they are hungry. The second group would take the same test after eating a meal. By comparing average memory scores for the two groups, you could tell if hunger affects memory.

As you can see, the simplest psychological experiment is based on two groups of *subjects* (animals or people whose behavior is investigated). One group is called the *experimental group;* the other becomes the *control group.* The control group and the experimental group are treated exactly alike except for the condition you intentionally vary. This condition is called the *independent variable.*

Variables and Groups

A *variable* is any condition that can change and that might affect the outcome of the experiment. Identifying causes and effects in an experiment involves three types of variables:

CONTROL GROUP   OUT OF CONTROL GROUP

1. **Independent variables** are conditions altered or varied by the experimenter, who sets their size, amount, or value. Independent variables are suspected causes for differences in behavior.
2. **Dependent variables** measure the results of the experiment. That is, they reveal the *effects* that independent variables have on *behavior*. Such effects are often revealed by measures of performance, such as test scores.
3. **Extraneous variables** are conditions that a researcher wishes to prevent from affecting the outcome of the experiment.

We can apply these terms to our hunger/memory experiment in this way: Hunger is the independent variable—we want to know if hunger affects memory. Memory (defined by scores on the memory test) is the dependent variable—we want to know if the ability to memorize depends on how hungry a person is. All other variables that could affect memory scores are extraneous. Examples are the number of hours slept the night before the test, intelligence, or difficulty of the questions.

As you can see, an **experimental group** consists of subjects exposed to the independent variable (hunger in the preceding example). Members of the **control group** are exposed to all conditions except the independent variable.

Let's examine another simple experiment. Suppose you notice that you seem to study better while listening to your iPod. This suggests the hypothesis that music improves learning. We could test this idea by forming an experimental group that studies with music. A control group would study without music. Then we could compare their scores on a test.

Is a control group really needed? Can't people just study while listening to their iPods to see if they do better? Without a control group it would be impossible to tell if music had any effect on learning. The control group provides a *point of reference* for comparison with the scores in the experimental group. If the average test score of the experimental group is

Experiment A formal trial undertaken to confirm or disconfirm a fact or principle.

Independent variable In an experiment, the condition being investigated as a possible cause of some change in behavior. The values that this variable takes are chosen by the experimenter.

Dependent variable In an experiment, the condition (usually a behavior) that is affected by the independent variable.

Extraneous variables Conditions or factors excluded from influencing the outcome of an experiment.

Experimental group In a controlled experiment, the group of subjects exposed to the independent variable or experimental condition.

Control group In a controlled experiment, the group of subjects exposed to all experimental conditions or variables *except* the independent variable.

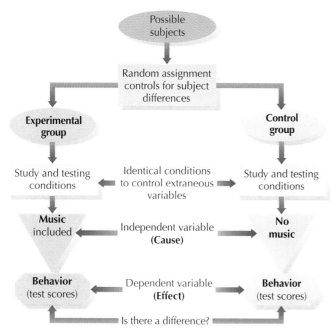

⟩⟩**FIGURE 1.8** Elements of a simple psychological experiment to assess the effects of music during study on test scores.

higher than the average of the control group, we can conclude that music improves learning. If there is no difference, it's obvious that the independent variable had no effect on learning.

In this experiment, the amount learned (indicated by scores on the test) is the *dependent variable.* We are asking, Does the independent variable *affect* the dependent variable? (Does music affect or influence learning?)

Experimental Control

How do we know that the people in one group aren't more intelligent than those in the other group? It's true that personal differences might affect the experiment. However, they can be controlled by randomly assigning people to groups. **Random assignment** means that a subject has an equal chance of being in either the experimental group or the control group. Randomization evenly balances personal differences in the two groups. In our musical experiment, this could be done by simply flipping a coin for each subject: Heads, and the subject is in the experimental group; tails, it's the control group. This would result in few differences in the number of people in each group who are women or men, geniuses or dunces, hungry, hung over, tall, music lovers, or whatever.

Other *extraneous,* or outside, variables—such as the amount of study time, the temperature in the room, the time of day, the amount of light, and so forth—must also be prevented from affecting the outcome of an experiment. But how? Usually this is done by making all conditions (except the independent variable) *exactly* alike for both groups. When all conditions are the same for both groups—*except* the presence or absence of music—then a difference in the amount learned *must* be caused by the music (⟩⟩Fig. 1.8).

⟩⟩**FIGURE 1.9** Experimental control is achieved by balancing extraneous variables for the experimental group and the control group. For example, the average age (A), education (B), and intelligence (C) of group members could be made the same for both groups. Then we could apply the independent variable to the experimental group. If their behavior (the dependent variable) changes (in comparison with the control group), the change must be caused by the independent variable.

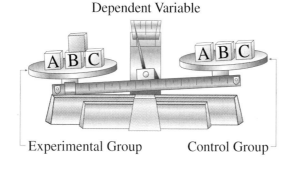

Dependent Variable

Experimental Group   Control Group

▢ Extraneous Variables
▢ Independent Variable

Cause and Effect

Now let's summarize. In an experiment two or more groups of subjects are treated differently with respect to the independent variable. In all other ways they are treated the same. That is, extraneous variables are equalized for all groups. The effect of the independent variable (or variables) on some behavior (the dependent variable) is then measured. In a carefully controlled experiment, the independent variable is the only possible *cause* for any *effect* noted in the dependent variable. This allows clear cause-and-effect connections to be identified (⟩⟩Fig. 1.9).

Placebo Effects, Sugar Pills, and Saltwater

Now let's do an experiment to see if the drug amphetamine (a stimulant) affects learning: Before studying, members of our experimental group take an amphetamine pill. Control group members get nothing. Later, we assess how much each subject learned. Does this experiment seem valid? Actually, it is seriously flawed.

Why? The experimental group took the drug and the control group didn't. Differences in the amount they learned must have been caused by the drug, right? No, because the drug wasn't the only difference between the groups. People in the experimental group swallowed a pill, and control subjects did not. Without using a placebo (plah-SEE-bo), it is impossible to tell if the drug affects learning. It could be that those who swallowed a pill *expected* to do better. This alone might have affected their performance, even if the pill didn't.

Random assignment The use of chance (for example, flipping a coin) to assign subjects to experimental and control groups.

What is a placebo? Why would it make a difference? A *placebo* is a fake drug. Inactive substances such as sugar pills and saline (saltwater) injections are commonly used as placebos. If a placebo has any effect, it must be based on suggestion, rather than chemistry (Thompson, 2005).

The **placebo effect** (changes in behavior caused by belief that one has taken a drug) can be powerful. For instance, a saline injection is 70 percent as effective as morphine in reducing pain. That's why doctors sometimes prescribe placebos—especially for complaints that seem to have no physical basis. Placebos have been shown to affect pain, anxiety, depression, alertness, tension, sexual arousal, cravings for alcohol, and many other processes (Wampold et al., 2005).

How could an inert substance have any effect? Placebos alter our expectations about our own emotional and physical reactions. Because we associate taking medicine with feeling better, we expect placebos to make us feel better, too (Stewart-Williams, 2004). After a person takes a placebo, there is a reduction in brain activity linked with pain, so the effect is not imaginary (Wager et al., 2004).

The placebo effect is a major factor in medical treatments. Would you also expect the placebo effect to occur in psychotherapy? (It does, which complicates studies on the effectiveness of new psychotherapies.)

Controlling Placebo Effects

To control for placebo effects, we could use a **single-blind experiment.** In this case, subjects do not know if they are receiving a real drug or a placebo. All subjects get a pill or injection. People in the experimental group get a real drug and the control group gets a placebo. Because subjects are *blind* as to whether they received the drug, their expectations are the same. Any difference in their behavior must be caused by the drug. Even this is not enough because researchers themselves sometimes affect experiments by influencing the behavior of their subjects. Let's see how this occurs.

The Experimenter Effect

How could a researcher influence subjects? The **experimenter effect** (changes in behavior caused by the unintended influence of an experimenter) is a common problem in psychological research. In essence, experimenters run the risk of finding what they expect to find. This occurs because humans are very sensitive to hints about what is expected of them (Rosenthal, 1994).

The experimenter effect even applies outside the laboratory. Psychologist Robert Rosenthal (1973) reports a classic example of how expectations can influence people: At the U.S. Air Force Academy Preparatory School, 100 airmen were randomly assigned to five different math classes. Their teachers did not know about this random placement. Instead, each teacher was told that his or her students had unusually high or low ability. Students in the classes labeled "high ability" improved much more in math scores than those in "low-ability" classes. Yet, initially, all of the classes had students of equal ability.

Apparently, the teachers subtly communicated their expectations to students. Most likely, they did this through tone of voice, body language, and by giving encouragement or criticism. Their "hints," in turn, created a self-fulfilling prophecy that affected the students. A *self-fulfilling prophecy* is a prediction that prompts people to act in ways that make the prediction come true. In short, people sometimes become what we prophesy for them. It is wise to remember that others tend to live *up* or *down* to our expectations for them (Jussim & Harber, 2005).

Because of the experimenter effect, it is common to keep both subjects and researchers "blind." In a **double-blind experiment** neither subjects nor experimenters know who has received a drug and who has taken a placebo. This also keeps researchers from unconsciously influencing subjects. Typically, someone else prepares the pills or injections so that experimenters don't know until after testing who got what. Double-blind testing has shown that about 50 percent of the effectiveness of antidepressant drugs, such as the "wonder drug" Prozac, is due to the placebo effect (Kirsch & Sapirstein, 1998). It's very likely that much of the current popularity of herbal health remedies is also based on the placebo effect (Seidman, 2001).

Placebo effect Changes in behavior due to expectations that a drug (or other treatment) will have some effect.

Single-blind experiment An arrangement in which subjects remain unaware of whether they are in the experimental group or the control group.

Experimenter effect Changes in subjects' behavior caused by the unintended influence of an experimenter's actions.

Double-blind experiment An arrangement in which both subjects and experimenters are unaware of whether subjects are in the experimental group or the control group.

Study Break The Psychology Experiment

Reflect

In a sense, we all conduct little experiments to detect cause-and-effect connections. If you are interested in cooking, for example, you might try steaming your broccoli in beef broth one time but not another. The question then becomes, Does the use of beef broth to steam broccoli (the independent variable) improve the taste of the broccoli (the dependent variable)? By comparing broccoli steamed in water (the control group) to broccoli steamed in broth (the experimental group) you could find out if broth is worth using to steam broccoli. Can you think of at least one informal experiment you've run in the last month? What were the variables? What was the outcome?

Learning Check

1. To understand cause and effect, a simple psychological experiment is based on creating two groups: the _____ group and the _____ group.
2. There are three types of variables to consider in an experiment: _____ variables (which are manipulated by the experimenter); _____ variables (which measure the outcome of the experiment); and _____ variables (factors to be excluded in a particular experiment).

3. A researcher performs an experiment to learn if room temperature affects the amount of aggression displayed by college students under crowded conditions in a simulated prison environment. In this experiment, the independent variable is which of the following?

   a. room temperature
   c. crowding
   b. the amount of aggression
   d. the simulated prison environment

4. A procedure used to control both the placebo effect and the experimenter effect in drug experiments is the

   a. correlation method
   c. double-blind technique
   b. extraneous prophecy
   d. random assignment of subjects

Critical Thinking

5. There is a loophole in the statement, "I've been taking vitamin C tablets, and I haven't had a cold all year. Vitamin C is great!" What is the loophole?
6. How would you determine if sugary breakfasts affect children's activity levels and their ability to learn in school?
7. People who believe strongly in astrology have personality characteristics that actually match, to a degree, those predicted by their astrological signs. Can you explain why this occurs?

Answers

1. experimental, control 2. independent, dependent, extraneous 3. a 4. c 5. The statement implies that vitamin C prevented colds. However, not getting a cold could just be a coincidence. A controlled experiment with a group given vitamin C and a control group not taking vitamin C would be needed to learn if vitamin C actually has any effect on susceptibility to colds. 6. An actual experiment on this question used a double-blind design in which children were given a breakfast drink containing either 50 grams of sucrose (sugar), a placebo (aspartame), or only a very small amount of sucrose. Observed changes in activity levels and in scores on a learning task did not support the view that sugar causes major changes in children's behavior (Rosen et al., 1988). 7. Belief in astrology can create a self-fulfilling prophecy in which people alter their behaviors and self-concepts to match their astrological signs (van Rooij, 1994).

THE CLINICAL METHOD—DATA BY THE CASE

>SURVEY QUESTION< *What other research methods do psychologists use?*

It can be difficult or impossible to use the experimental method to study mental disorders, such as depression or psychosis. Many experiments are impractical, unethical, or impossible to do. In such instances, a **case study** (an in-depth focus on a single subject) may be the best source of information. Clinical psychologists rely heavily on case studies, especially as a way to investigate rare or unusual problems.

Case studies may sometimes be thought of as **natural clinical tests** (accidents or other natural events that provide psychological data). Gunshot wounds, brain tumors, accidental poisonings, and similar disasters provide much information about the human brain. One remarkable case from the history of psychology is reported by Dr. J. M. Harlow (1868). Phineas Gage, a young foreman on a work crew, had a 13-pound steel rod blown through the front of his brain by a dynamite explosion (»Fig. 1.10). Amazingly, he survived the accident. Within 2 months Gage could walk, talk, and move normally. But the injury forever changed his personality. Instead of the honest and dependable worker he had been before, Gage became a surly, foul-mouthed liar. Dr. Harlow carefully recorded all details of what was perhaps the first in-depth case study of an accidental frontal lobotomy (the destruction of front brain matter).

When a Los Angeles carpenter named Michael Melnick suffered a similar injury, he recovered completely, with no sign of lasting ill effects. Melnick's very different reaction to

Case study An in-depth focus on all aspects of a single person.

Natural clinical test A natural event that provides data on a psychological phenomenon.

a similar injury shows why psychologists prefer controlled experiments and often use lab animals for studies of the brain. Case studies lack formal control groups. This, of course, limits the conclusions that can be drawn from clinical observations. Nonetheless, case studies are especially valuable for studying rare events, such as unusual mental disorders, childhood "geniuses," or "rampage" school shootings (Harding, Fox, & Mehta, 2002). Also, case studies of psychotherapy have provided many useful ideas about how to treat emotional problems (Wedding & Corsini, 2005).

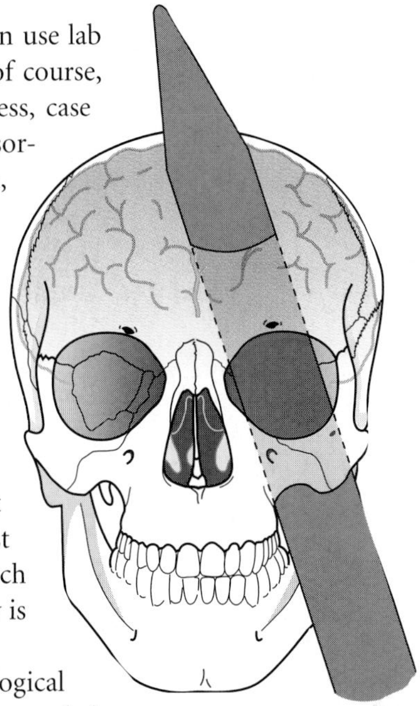

SURVEY METHOD—HERE, HAVE A SAMPLE

Sometimes psychologists would like to ask everyone in the world a few well-chosen questions: "Do you drink alcoholic beverages? How often per week?" "What form of discipline did your parents use when you were a child?" "What is the most creative thing you've done?" Honest answers to such questions can reveal much about behavior. But because it is impossible to question everyone, doing a survey is often more practical.

In the **survey method,** public polling techniques are used to answer psychological questions. Typically, people in a representative sample are asked a series of carefully worded questions. A **representative sample** is a small group that accurately reflects a larger population. A good sample must include the same proportion of men, women, young, old, professionals, blue-collar workers, Republicans, Democrats, whites, African Americans, Native Americans, Latinos, Asians, and so on, as found in the population as a whole.

A *population* is an entire group of animals or people belonging to a particular category (for example, all college students or all single women). Ultimately, we are interested in entire populations. But by selecting a smaller sample, we can draw conclusions about the larger group without polling each and every person. Representative samples are often obtained by *randomly* selecting who will be included (►►Fig. 1.11). (Notice that this is similar to randomly assigning subjects to groups in an experiment.)

How accurate is the survey method? Modern surveys like the Gallup and Harris polls are quite accurate. The Gallup poll has erred in its election predictions by only 1.5 percent since 1954. However, if a survey is based on a biased sample, it may paint a false picture. A *biased sample* does not accurately reflect the population from which it was drawn. Surveys done by magazines, websites, and online information services can be quite biased. Surveys on the use of illicit drugs done by *Fitness* and *Rolling Stone* would probably produce very different results—neither of which would represent the general population. That's why psychologists using the survey method go to great lengths to ensure that their samples are representative. Fortunately, people can often be polled by telephone, which makes it easier to obtain large samples. Even if one person out of three refuses to answer survey questions, the results are still likely to be valid (Hutchinson, 2004).

Internet Surveys

Recently, psychologists have started doing surveys and experiments on the Internet. Web-based research has the advantage of low cost and it can reach very large groups of people. Internet studies have provided interesting information about topics such as anger, decision making, racial prejudice, what disgusts people, religion, sexual attitudes, and much more. Biased samples can limit web-based research, but psychologists are finding ways to gather valid information with it (Birnbaum, 2004; Gosling et al., 2004).

►► **FIGURE 1.10** Some of the earliest information on the effects of damage to frontal areas of the brain came from a case study of the accidental injury of Phineas Gage.

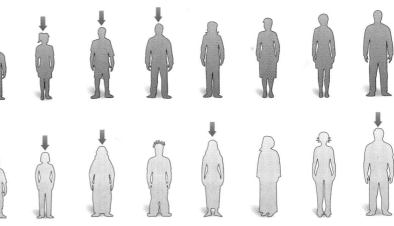

►► **FIGURE 1.11** If you were conducting a survey in which a person's height might be an important variable, the nonrandom sample of shorter people would be very unrepresentative. The random sample, selected using a table of random numbers, better represents the group as a whole.

Survey method The use of public polling techniques to answer psychological questions.

Representative sample A small, randomly selected part of a larger population that accurately reflects characteristics of the whole population.

Social Desirability

Even well-designed surveys may be limited by another problem. If a psychologist were to ask you detailed questions about your sexual history and current sexual behavior, how accurate would your replies be? Would you exaggerate? Would you be embarrassed? Replies to survey questions are not always accurate or truthful. Many people show a distinct *courtesy bias* (a tendency to give "polite" or socially desirable answers). For example, answers to questions concerning sex, drinking or drug use, income, and church attendance tend to be less than truthful. Likewise, the week after an election, more people will say they voted than actually did (Hutchinson, 2004).

Summary

Despite their limitations, surveys frequently produce valuable information. For instance, the survey method was used to find out about the attitudes of Muslims in the Middle East towards U.S. policies in the region and to clarify the debate about Islam and violence that has arisen since the terrorist attacks of 9/11 (Haddad, 2003). To sum up, the survey method can be a powerful research tool. Like other methods, it has limitations, but new techniques and strategies are providing valuable information about our behavior (Tourangeau, 2004).

SCIENCE AND CRITICAL THINKING— HEALTHY SKEPTICISM

>SURVEY QUESTION< *What is critical thinking?*

Is so much emphasis on research really necessary in psychology? In a word, yes. As we have seen, science is a powerful way of asking questions about the world and getting trustworthy answers. Your awareness of this fact should help make you a more critical observer of human behavior. ■ Table 1.5 summarizes many of the important ideas we have covered.

Most of us would be skeptical when buying a used car. But all too often, we may be tempted to "buy" outrageous claims about topics such as those of psychics "channeling" dead people, the occult, UFOs, Tarot cards, healing crystals, some herbal remedies, and so forth. Likewise, most of us easily accept our ignorance of sub-atomic physics. But because we deal with human behavior every day, we tend to think that we already know what is true in psychology.

■ Table 1.5   Comparison of Psychological Research Methods

	Advantages	Disadvantages
Naturalistic Observation	Behavior is observed in a natural setting; much information is obtained, and hypotheses and questions for additional research are formed	Little or no control is possible; observed behavior may be altered by the presence of the observer; observations may be biased; causes cannot be conclusively identified
Correlational Method	Demonstrates the existence of relationships; allows prediction; can be used in lab, clinic, or natural setting	Little or no control is possible; relationships may be coincidental; cause-and-effect relationships cannot be confirmed
Experimental Method	Clear cause-and-effect relationships can be identified; powerful controlled observations can be staged; no need to wait for natural event	May be somewhat artificial; some natural behavior not easily studied in laboratory (field experiments may avoid these objections)
Clinical Method	Takes advantage of "natural clinical trials" and allows investigation of rare or unusual problems or events	Little or no control is possible; does not provide a control group for comparison, subjective interpretation is often necessary, a single case may be misleading or unrepresentative
Survey Method	Allows information about large numbers of people to be gathered; can address questions not answered by other approaches	Obtaining a representative sample is critical and can be difficult to do; answers may be inaccurate; people may not do what they say or say what they do

For these and many more reasons, learning to think critically is one of the lasting benefits of a college education. **Critical thinking** refers to an ability to evaluate, compare, analyze, critique, and synthesize information. Critical thinkers are willing to ask the hard questions, including those that challenge conventional wisdom. For example, many people believe that punishment (a spanking) is a good way to reinforce learning in children. Actually, nothing could be farther from the truth (Gershoff, 2002). That's why a critical thinker would immediately ask: "Does punishment work? If so, when? Under what conditions does it not work? What are its drawbacks? Are there better ways to guide learning?"

Thinking about Behavior

The core of critical thinking is a willingness to actively *evaluate* ideas. Critical thinkers analyze the evidence supporting their beliefs and probe for weaknesses in their reasoning. They question assumptions and look for alternate conclusions. True knowledge, they recognize, comes from constantly revising our understanding of the world. As Susan Blackmore (2001) said when her studies caused her to abandon some long-held beliefs, "Admitting you are wrong is always hard—even though it's a skill that every psychologist has to learn."

Critical thinking is built upon a few basic principles (Browne & Keeley, 2007; Gill, 1991):

1. *Few "truths" transcend the need for empirical testing.* It is true that religious beliefs and personal values may be held as matters of faith, without supporting evidence. But most other ideas can be evaluated by applying the rules of logic and evidence.
2. *Judging the quality of evidence is crucial.* Imagine that you are a juror in a courtroom, judging claims made by two battling lawyers. To decide correctly, you can't just weigh the amount of evidence. You must also critically evaluate the *quality* of the evidence. Then you can give greater weight to the most credible facts.
3. *Authority or claimed expertise does not automatically make an idea true.* Just because a teacher, guru, celebrity, or authority is convinced or sincere doesn't mean you should automatically believe them. Always ask, "What evidence convinced her or him? How good is it? Is there a better explanation?"
4. *Critical thinking requires an open mind.* Be prepared to consider daring departures and go wherever the evidence leads. However, don't become so "open-minded" that you are simply gullible. Critical thinkers strike a balance between open-mindedness and healthy skepticism. They are ready to change their views when new evidence arises (Bartz, 2002).

To put these principles into action, here are some questions to ask over and over again as you evaluate new information (Browne & Keeley, 2007):

1. What claims are being made?
2. What test (if any) of these claims has been made?
3. Who did the test? How good is the evidence?
4. What was the nature and quality of the tests? Are they credible? Can they be repeated?
5. How reliable and trustworthy were the investigators? Do they have conflicts of interest? Do their findings appear to be objective? Has any other independent researcher duplicated the findings?
6. Finally, how much credibility can the claim be given? High, medium, low, provisional?

A course in psychology naturally enriches thinking skills. To add to the process, all upcoming chapters include Critical Thinking questions like the ones you have seen here. Tackling these questions will sharpen your thinking abilities and make learning more lively. For an immediate thinking challenge, let's take a critical look at several nonscientific systems that claim to explain behavior.

Critical thinking An ability to evaluate, compare, analyze, critique, and synthesize information.

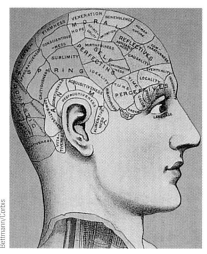

Phrenology was an attempt to assess personality characteristics by examining various areas of the skull. Phrenologists used charts such as the one shown here as guides. Like other pseudopsychologists, phrenologists made no attempt to empirically verify their concepts.

PSEUDOPSYCHOLOGIES—PALMS, PLANETS, AND PERSONALITY

>SURVEY QUESTION< *How does psychology differ from false explanations of behavior?*

A **pseudopsychology** (SUE-doe-psychology) is any unfounded system that resembles psychology. Many pseudopsychologies give the appearance of science but are actually false. (*Pseudo* means "false.") Pseudopsychologies change little over time because their followers avoid evidence that contradicts their beliefs. Scientists, in contrast, actively look for contradictions as a way to advance knowledge. They are skeptical critics of their own theories (Schick & Vaughn, 2001).

Can you give some examples of false psychologies? An early pseudopsychology is *phrenology*, which claimed that personality traits are revealed by the shape of the skull. Phrenology was popularized in the nineteenth century by Franz Gall, a German anatomy teacher. Modern research has long since shown that bumps on the head have nothing to do with talents or abilities. In fact, the phrenologists were so far off that they listed the part of the brain that controls hearing as a center for "combativeness"! *Palmistry* is a similar false system that claims lines on the hand reveal personality traits and predict the future. Despite the overwhelming evidence against this, palmists can still be found separating the gullible from their money in many cities.

At first glance, a pseudopsychology called *graphology* might seem more reasonable. Graphologists claim that personality traits are revealed by handwriting. Based on such claims, some companies use graphologists to select job candidates. This is troubling because graphologists score close to zero on tests of accuracy in rating personality (Furnham, Chamorro-Premuzic, & Callahan, 2003). In fact, graphologists do no better than untrained college students in rating personality and job performance (Neter & Ben-Shakhar, 1989). Even a graphological society recently concluded that handwriting analysis should not be used to select people for jobs (Simner & Goffin, 2003). (By the way, graphology's failure at revealing personality should be separated from its value for detecting forgeries.)

Would you hire this man? Here's a sample of your author's handwriting. What do you think it reveals? Your interpretations are likely to be as accurate (or inaccurate) as those of a graphologist.

Graphology might seem harmless enough. However, this false system has been used to determine who is hired, given bank credit, or selected for juries. In these and similar situations, pseudopsychologies do, in fact, harm people (Beyerstein & Beyerstein, 1992).

If pseudopsychologies have no scientific basis, how do they survive and why are they popular? There are several reasons, all of which can be demonstrated by a critique of astrology.

Problems in the Stars

Astrology is probably the most popular pseudopsychology. Astrology holds that the positions of the stars and planets at the time of one's birth determine personality traits and affect behavior. Like other pseudopsychologies, astrology has repeatedly been shown to have no scientific validity (Hartmann, Reuter, & Nyborg, 2006; Kelly, 1999). The objections to astrology are numerous and devastating:

1. The zodiac has shifted in the sky by one full constellation since astrology was first set up. However, most astrologers simply ignore this shift. (In other words, if astrology calls you a Scorpio you are really a Libra, and so forth.)
2. Astrologers have failed to explain why the moment of birth should be more important than, say, the moment of conception.

Pseudopsychology Any false and unscientific system of beliefs and practices that is offered as an explanation of behavior.

Bettmann/Corbis

3. There is no connection between the "compatibility" of couples' astrological signs and their marriage and divorce rates.

4. Studies have found no connection between astrological signs and leadership, physical characteristics, career choices, or personality traits.

5. A study of more than 3,000 predictions by famous astrologers found that only a small percentage were fulfilled. These "successful" predictions tended to be vague ("There will be a tragedy somewhere in the east in the spring") or easily guessed from current events.

6. If astrologers are asked to match people with their horoscopes, they do no better than would be expected by chance (Kelly, 1999).

7. A few astrologers have tried to test astrology. Their results have been just as negative as those obtained by critics (Hartmann, Reuter, & Nyborg, 2006; Kelly, 1999; Martens & Trachet, 1998).

In short, astrology doesn't work.

Then why does astrology often seem to work? The following discussion tells why.

Uncritical Acceptance

If you have ever had your astrological chart done, you may have been impressed with its apparent accuracy. However, such perceptions are typically based on **uncritical acceptance** (the tendency to believe positive or flattering descriptions of yourself). Many astrological charts are made up of mostly flattering traits. Naturally, when your personality is described in *desirable* terms, it is hard to deny that the description has the "ring of truth." How much acceptance would astrology receive if a birth sign read like this:

> **Virgo:** You are the logical type and hate disorder. Your nitpicking is unbearable to your friends. You are cold, unemotional, and usually fall asleep while making love. Virgos make good doorstops.

Positive Instances

Even when an astrological description contains a mixture of good and bad traits it may seem accurate. To find out why, read the following personality description.

> **Your Personality Profile**
> You have a strong need for other people to like you and for them to admire you. You have a tendency to be critical of yourself. You have a great deal of unused energy which you have not turned to your advantage. While you have some personality weaknesses, you are generally able to compensate for them. Your sexual adjustment has presented some problems for you. Disciplined and controlled on the outside, you tend to be worrisome and insecure inside. At times you have serious doubts as to whether you have made the right decision or done the right thing. You prefer a certain amount of change and variety and become dissatisfied when hemmed in by restrictions and limitations. You pride yourself on being an independent thinker and do not accept other opinions without satisfactory proof. You have found it unwise to be too frank in revealing yourself to others. At times you are extroverted, affable, sociable, while at other times you are introverted, wary, and reserved. Some of your aspirations tend to be pretty unrealistic.*

Does this describe your personality? A psychologist read this summary individually to college students who had taken a personality test. Only 5 students out of 79 felt that the description was inaccurate. Another study found that people rated this "personality profile" as more accurate than their actual horoscopes (French et al., 1991).

---

*Reprinted with permission of author and publisher from: R. E. Ulrich, T. J. Stachnik, and N. R. Stainton, "Student acceptance of generalized personality interpretations," *Psychological Reports, 13,* 1963, 831–834.

Uncritical acceptance The tendency to believe generally positive or flattering descriptions of oneself.

Reread the description and you will see that it contains both sides of several personality dimensions ("At times you are extroverted . . . while at other times you are introverted"). Its apparent accuracy is an illusion based on the **fallacy of positive instances,** in which we remember or notice things that confirm our expectations and forget the rest. The pseudo-psychologies thrive on this effect. For example, you can always find "Leo characteristics" in a Leo. If you looked, however, you could also find "Gemini characteristics," "Scorpio characteristics," or whatever.

The fallacy of positive instances is used by various "psychic mediums" who pretend to communicate with the deceased friends and relatives of audience members. An analysis of their performances shows that the number of "hits" (correct statements) made by these fakes tends to be very low. Nevertheless, many viewers are impressed because of the natural tendency to remember apparent hits and ignore misses. Also, embarrassing misses are edited out before the shows appear on television (Nickell, 2001).

Non Sequitur

Non Sequitur © 1993 Wiley Miller. Distributed by Universal Press Syndicate. Reprinted with permission. All rights reserved.

The Barnum Effect

Pseudopsychologies also take advantage of the **Barnum effect,** which is a tendency to consider personal descriptions accurate if they are stated in general terms. P. T. Barnum, the famed circus showman, had a formula for success: "Always have a little something for everybody." Like the all-purpose personality profile, palm readings, fortunes, horoscopes, and other products of pseudopsychology are stated in such general terms that they can hardly miss. There is always "a little something for everybody." To observe the Barnum effect, read *all 12* of the daily horoscopes found in newspapers for several days. You will find that predictions for other signs fit events as well as those for your own sign do. You can also give a friend the wrong horoscope for his sign. Your friend may well still be quite impressed with the accuracy of his horoscope.

Astrology's popularity shows that many people have difficulty separating valid psychology from systems that seem valid but are not. The goal of this discussion, then, has been to make you a more critical observer of human behavior and to clarify what is, and what is not, psychology. Here is what the "stars" say about your future:

> Emphasis now on education and personal improvement. A learning experience of lasting value awaits you. Take care of scholastic responsibilities before engaging in recreation. The word *psychology* figures prominently in your future.

Pseudopsychologies may seem like no more than a nuisance, but they can do harm. For instance, people seeking treatment for psychological disorders may become the victims of self-appointed "experts" who offer ineffective, pseudoscientific "therapies" (Kalal, 1999; Lilienfeld et al., 2005). Valid psychological principles are based on observation and evidence, not fads, opinions, or wishful thinking.

A Look Ahead

Now that you have an overview of psychology, We'd like to let psychologists Gary VandenBos and Brenda Bryant summarize:

> Psychologists are explorers and discoverers. They explore the reactions of human beings to small frustrations and great successes, to pleasing colors and the aftermath of disaster, always looking for answers to how and why people think, feel, and behave as they do. . . . The psychologist, regardless of where she or he may work, is always applying what is known in an effort to resolve the unknown. The psychologist, no matter how small the question being asked may appear to be, is looking for the larger answer (VandenBos & Bryant, 1987).

To help you get the most out of psychology, each chapter of this text includes a "Psychology in Action" section like the one that follows. There you will find ideas you can actually

Fallacy of positive instances The tendency to remember or notice information that fits one's expectations, while forgetting discrepancies.

Barnum effect The tendency to consider a personal description accurate if it is stated in very general terms.

use, now or in the future. To complete our discussion, let's take a critical look at information reported in the popular press. You should find this an interesting way to conclude our first tour of psychology and its methods.

Study Break   Clinical and Survey Methods, Critical Thinking

Reflect

It is nearly impossible to get through a day without encountering people who believe in pseudopsychologies or who make unscientific or unfounded statements. How stringently do you evaluate your own beliefs and the claims made by others? Critical thinking requires effort and discipline, but high-quality information is the reward.

Learning Check

1. Case studies can often be thought of as natural tests and are frequently used by clinical psychologists. T or F?
2. For the survey method to be valid, a representative sample of people must be polled. T or F?
3. Amnesia would most likely be investigated by use of
   a. a representative sample   b. field experiments
   c. the double-blind   d. case studies
      procedure

4. _____ is the outdated theory that personality is revealed by the skull. It was popularized by Franz _____.
5. The fallacy of positive instances refers to graphology's accepted value for the detection of forgeries. T or F?
6. Personality descriptions provided by pseudopsychologies are stated in general terms that provide "a little something for everybody." This fact is the basis of the
   a. palmist's fallacy   b. uncritical acceptance pattern
   c. fallacy of positive   d. Barnum effect
      instances

Critical Thinking

7. A psychologist conducting a survey at a shopping mall (The Gallery of Wretched Excess) flips a coin before stopping passersby. If the coin shows heads, he interviews the person; if it shows tails he skips that person. Has the psychologist obtained a random sample?

Answers

1. T 2. T 3. d 4. Phrenology, Gall 5. F 6. d 7. The psychologist's coin flips *might* produce a reasonably good sample of people *at the mall*. The real problem is that people who go to the mall may be mostly from one part of town, from upper income groups, or from some other nonrepresentative group. The psychologist's sample is likely to be seriously flawed.

Psychology in Action

Psychology in the Media—Separating Fact from Fiction

>SURVEY QUESTION< *How good is psychological information found in the popular media?*

Psychology is a popular topic in contemporary media. Unfortunately, much of what you will encounter is based on wishful thinking rather than science. Here are some suggestions for separating high-quality information from misleading fiction.

Suggestion 1: Be skeptical.

Reports in the popular media tend to be made uncritically and with a definite bias toward reporting "astonishing" findings. Remember, saying, "That's incredible" means, "That's not believable"—which is often true.

Example 1: The Internet is awash with rumors, hoaxes, half-truths, and urban legends. One classic is a story about the health department in Oregon seeking a Klingon interpreter for mental health patients who only speak in the fictional language used on the Star Trek TV series. This tale started when a newspaper reported that Klingon was on a list of languages that some psychiatric patients claimed they could speak. The article specifically noted that "in reality, no patient has yet tried to communicate in Klingon." Nevertheless, as the story spread around the web, the idea that Oregon was looking for someone fluent in Klingon had become a "fact" (O'Neill, 2003).

Example 2: Some years ago, news articles described an amazing new "sixth sense" called "dermo-optical perception." A few gifted people, the articles claimed, could use their fingertips to identify colors and read print while blindfolded.

In reality, such "abilities" are based on what stage magicians call a "nose peek." It is impossible to prepare a blindfold (without damaging the eyes) that does not leave a tiny space on each side of the nose. Were the people who claimed to have "X-ray eyes" taking nose peeks? Apparently they were, because "dermo-optical abilities" disappeared as soon as the opportunity to peek was controlled.

Suggestion 2: Consider the source of information.

It should come as no surprise that information used to sell a product often reflects a desire for profit rather than the objective truth. Here is a typical advertising claim: "Government tests prove that no pain reliever is stronger or more effective than Brand X aspirin." A statement like this usually means that there was *no difference* between the products tested. No other pain reliever was stronger or more effective. But none was weaker either.

Keep the source in mind when reading the claims of makers of home biofeedback machines, sleep-learning devices, subliminal tapes, and the like. Remember that psychological services may be merchandised as well. Be wary of expensive courses that promise instant mental health and happiness, increased efficiency, memory, ESP or psychic ability, control of the unconscious mind, an end to smoking, and so on. Usually they are promoted with a few testimonials and many unsupported claims (Lilienfeld, 2005).

Psychic claims should be viewed with special caution. Stage mentalists make a living by deceiving the public. Understandably, they are highly interested in promoting belief in their nonexistent powers. Psychic phenomena, when (and if) they do occur, are quite unpredictable. It would be impossible for a mentalist to do three shows a night, six nights a week without consistently using deception. The same is true of the so-called "psychic advisers" promoted in TV commercials. These charlatans make use of the Barnum effect to create an illusion that they know private information about the people who call them (Nickell, 2001). Check out magician James Randi's Million Dollar Challenge. Randi is offering $1,000,000 to anyone demonstrating such abilities under controlled conditions (www.randi.org). Are you surprised to learn that no one has even passed the preliminary tests yet?

Suggestion 3: Ask yourself if there was a control group.

The key importance of a control group in any experiment is frequently overlooked by the unsophisticated—an error to which you are no longer susceptible! The popular press is full of reports of "experiments" performed without control groups: "Talking to Plants Speeds Growth"; "Special Diet Controls Hyperactivity in Children"; "Food Shows Less Spoilage in Pyramid Chamber"; "Graduates of Firewalking Seminar Risk Their Soles."

Consider the last example for a moment. Expensive commercial courses have long been promoted to teach people to walk barefoot on hot coals. (Why anyone would want to do this is itself an interesting question.) Firewalkers supposedly protect their feet with a technique called "neurolinguistic programming." Many people have paid good money to learn the technique, and most do manage a quick walk on the coals. But is the technique necessary? And is anything remarkable happening? We need a comparison group!

Fortunately, physicist Bernard Leikind has provided one. Leikind showed with volunteers that anyone (with reasonably callused feet) can walk over a bed of coals without being burned. The reason is that the coals, which are light, fluffy carbon, transmit little heat when touched. The principle involved is similar to briefly putting your hand in a hot oven. If you touch a pan, you will be burned because metal transfers heat efficiently. But if your hand stays in the heated air you'll be fine because air transmits little heat (Mitchell, 1987). Mystery solved.

Suggestion 4: Look for errors in distinguishing between correlation and causation.

As you now know, it is dangerous to presume that one thing *caused* another just because they are correlated. In spite of this, you will see many claims based on questionable correlations. Here's an example of mistaking correlation for causation: Jeanne Dixon, an astrologer, once answered a group of prominent scientists—who had declared that there

John Nordell/The Image Works

Firewalking is based on simple physics, not on any form of supernatural psychological control. The temperature of the coals may be as high as 1,200° F. However, coals are like the air in a hot oven: They are very inefficient at transferring heat during brief contact.

is no scientific foundation for astrology—by saying, "They would do well to check the records at their local police stations, where they will learn that the rate of violent crime rises and falls with lunar cycles." Dixon, of course, believes that the moon affects human behavior.

If it is true that violent crime is more frequent at certain times of the month, doesn't that prove her point? Far from it. Increased crime could be due to darker nights, the fact that many people expect others to act crazier, or any number of similar factors. More importantly, direct studies of the alleged "lunar effect" have shown that it doesn't occur (Dowling, 2005). Moonstruck criminals, influenced by "a bad moon rising," are a fiction (Iosif & Ballon, 2005).

Suggestion 5: Be sure to distinguish between observation and inference.

If you see a person *crying*, is it correct to assume that she or he is *sad?* Although it seems reasonable to make this assumption, it is actually quite risky. We can observe objectively that the person is crying, but to *infer* sadness may be an error. It could be that the individual has just peeled 5 pounds of onions. Or maybe he or she just won a million-dollar lottery or is trying contact lenses for the first time.

Psychologists, politicians, physicians, scientists, and other experts often go far beyond the available facts in their claims. This does not mean that their inferences, opinions, and interpretations have no value; the opinion of an expert on the causes of mental illness, criminal behavior, learning problems, or whatever can be revealing. But be careful to distinguish between fact and opinion.

Suggestion 6: Beware of oversimplifications, especially those motivated by monetary gain.

Courses or programs that offer a "new personality in three sessions," "six steps to love and fulfillment in marriage," or newly discovered "secrets of unlocking the powers of the mind" should be immediately suspect.

An excellent example of oversimplification is provided by a brochure entitled "Dr. Joyce Brothers Asks: How Do You Rate as a 'Superwoman'?" Dr. Brothers, a "media" psychologist who has no private practice and is not known for research, once wrote the brochure as a consultant for the Aerosol Packaging Council of the Chemical Specialties Manufacturers Association. A typical suggestion in this brochure tells how to enhance a marriage: "Sweep him off to a weekend hideaway. Tip: When he's not looking spray a touch of your favorite *aerosol* cologne mist on the bed sheets and pillows" (italics added). Sure, Joyce.

Suggestion 7: Remember, "for example" is no proof.

After reading this chapter you should be sensitive to the danger of selecting single examples. If you read, "Law student passes state bar exam using sleep-learning device," don't rush out to buy one. Systematic research has long ago shown that these devices are of little or no value (Druckman & Bjork, 1994). A corollary to this suggestion is to ask, Are the reported observations important or widely applicable?

Examples, anecdotes, single cases, and testimonials are all potentially deceptive. Unfortunately, *individual cases* tell nothing about what is true *in general* (Stanovich, 2004). For instance, studies of large groups of people show that smoking increases the likelihood of lung cancer. It doesn't matter if you know a lifelong heavy smoker who is 95 years old. The general finding is the one to remember.

Summary

We are all bombarded daily with such a mass of new information that it is difficult to absorb it. The available knowledge, even in a limited area like psychology, biology, medicine, or contemporary hip-hop music, is so vast that no single person can completely know and comprehend it. With this situation in mind, it becomes increasingly important that you become a critical, selective, and informed consumer of information.

Study Break **Psychology in the Media**

Reflect

Do you tend to assume that a statement must be true if it is in print, on television, or made by an authority? How actively do you evaluate and question claims found in the media? Could you be a more critical consumer of information? *Should* you be a more critical consumer of information?

Learning Check

1. Newspaper accounts of dermo-optical perception have generally reported only the results of carefully designed psychological experiments. T or F?
2. Stage mentalists and psychics often use deception in their acts. T or F?

3. Blaming the lunar cycle for variations in the rate of violent crime is an example of mistaking correlation for causation. T or F?
4. If a law student uses a sleep-learning device to pass the bar exam, it proves that the device works. T or F?

Critical Thinking

5. Many parents believe that children become "hyperactive" when they eat too much sugar, and some early studies seemed to confirm this connection. However, we now know that eating sugar rarely has any effect on children. Why do you think that sugar appears to cause hyperactivity?

Answers

1. F 2. T 3. T 4. F 5. This is another case of mistaking correlation for causation. Children who are hyperactive may eat more sugar (and other foods) to fuel their frenetic activity levels.

CHAPTER IN REVIEW

Major Points

- Psychology is the science of behavior and mental processes. Psychology provides objective answers to questions about human behavior.
- Psychologists gather scientific data in order to describe, understand, predict, and control behavior.
- The scientific method consists of highly refined procedures for observing the natural world, testing hypotheses, and drawing valid conclusions.
- Psychologists use several specialized research methods. Each has strengths and weaknesses, so all are needed to fully investigate human behavior.
- Experimentation is the most powerful way to identify cause-and-effect relationships.
- Critical thinking is central to the scientific method, to psychology, and to effective behavior in general.
- The popular media are rife with inaccurate information. It is essential to critically evaluate information, no matter what its source may be.

Summary

What is psychology? What are its goals?

- Psychology is the scientific study of behavior and mental processes.
- Some major areas of research in psychology are comparative, learning, sensation, perception, personality, biopsychology, motivation and emotion, social, cognitive, developmental, the psychology of gender, cultural psychology, and evolutionary psychology.

- Psychologists may be directly interested in animal behavior, or they may study animals as models of human behavior.
- As a science, psychology's goals are to describe, understand, predict, and control behavior.

How did the field of psychology emerge?

- Historically, psychology is an outgrowth of philosophy.
- The first psychological laboratory was established in Germany by Wilhelm Wundt, who tried to study conscious experience.
- The first school of thought in psychology was structuralism, a kind of "mental chemistry" based on introspection and analysis.
- Structuralism was followed by functionalism, behaviorism, and Gestalt psychology.
- Psychodynamic approaches, such as Freud's psychoanalytic theory, emphasize the unconscious origins of behavior.
- Humanistic psychology accentuates subjective experience, human potentials, and personal growth.

What are the major trends and specialties in psychology?

- Three main streams of thought in modern psychology are the biological perspective, including biopsychology and evolutionary psychology; the psychological perspective, including behaviorism, cognitive psychology, the psychodynamic approach, and humanism; and the sociocultural perspective.

- Although psychologists, psychiatrists, psychoanalysts, and counselors all work in the field of mental health, their training and methods differ considerably.
- Clinical and counseling psychologists, who do psychotherapy, represent only two of dozens of specialties in psychology.
- Psychological research may be basic or applied.

Why is the scientific method important to psychologists?

- Important elements of a scientific investigation include observing, defining a problem, proposing a hypothesis, gathering evidence/testing the hypothesis, publishing results, and forming a theory.
- Before they can be investigated, psychological concepts must be given operational definitions.

How do psychologists collect information?

- Naturalistic observation is a starting place in many investigations.
- Three problems with naturalistic observation are the effects of the observer on the observed, observer bias, and an inability to explain observed behavior.
- In the correlational method, relationships between two traits, responses, or events are measured.
- A correlation coefficient is computed to gauge the strength of the relationship. Correlations allow prediction, but they do not demonstrate cause-and-effect connections.
- Cause-and-effect relationships are best identified by controlled experiments.

How is an experiment performed?

- In an experiment, two or more groups of subjects are formed. These groups differ only with regard to the independent variable (condition of interest as a cause in the experiment).
- Effects on the dependent variable are then measured. All other conditions (extraneous variables) are held constant.
- In experiments that involve drugs, a placebo must be given to control for the effects of expectations. If a double-blind procedure is used, neither subjects nor experimenters know who received a drug.
- A related problem is the experimenter effect (a tendency for experimenters to unconsciously influence the outcome of an experiment). Expectations can create a self-fulfilling prophecy, in which a person changes in the direction of the expectation.

What other research methods do psychologists use?

- The clinical method employs case studies, which are in-depth records of a single subject. Case studies provide important information on topics that cannot be studied any other way.
- In the survey method, people in a representative sample are asked a series of carefully worded questions.

What is critical thinking?

- Critical thinking is the ability to evaluate, compare, analyze, critique, and synthesize information.
- To judge the validity of a claim, it is important to gather evidence for and against the claim and to evaluate the quality of the evidence.

How does psychology differ from false explanations of behavior?

- Numerous pseudopsychologies exist. These false systems are frequently confused with valid psychology. Belief in pseudopsychologies is based in part on uncritical acceptance, the fallacy of positive instances, and the Barnum effect.

How good is psychological information found in the popular media?

- Information in the mass media varies greatly in quality and accuracy.
- It is wise to approach such information with skepticism and caution. This is especially true with regard to the source of information, uncontrolled observation, correlation and causation, inferences, oversimplification, single examples, and unrepeatable results.

Interactive Learning

Internet addresses frequently change. To find the sites listed here, visit www.thomsonedu.com/psychology/coon for an updated list of Internet addresses and direct links to relevant sites.

Psychology: A Journey Companion Website   Find online quizzes, flash cards, animations, video clips, experiments, interactive assessments, and other helpful study aids for this text at www.thomsonedu.com/psychology/coon.

American Psychological Association   Home page of the APA, with links to PsychNET, student information, member information, and more.

American Psychological Society   Home page of the APS, with links to information, services, and Internet resources.

Ethical Principles of Psychologists and Code of Conduct   The full text of the ethical principles that guide professional psychologists.

Psychweb   This award-winning page provides a multitude of services and links.

Psycoloquy   An online journal with short articles on all areas of psychology.

PsycPORT   This site is a large database of psychological information, including daily updates on news related to psychology.

The Jane Goodall Institute   Information about Goodall's work at Gombe, in Tanzania, where she has studied and protected wild chimpanzees for more than 40 years.

Today in the History of Psychology   Events in the history of psychology by the date.

ThomsonNOW   Go to www.thomsonedu.com/login to link to ThomsonNOW, your online study tool. First take the **Pre-Test** for this chapter to get your **Personalized Study Plan,** which will identify topics you need to review and direct you to online resources. Then take the **Post-Test** to determine what concepts you have mastered and what you still need work on.

TEST YOUR KNOWLEDGE

Psychology and Research Methods

For additional review, get more practice with *ThomsonNOW*, *WebTutor*, the *Practice Quizzes*, and/or the printed *Study Guide* available with this book.

1. Psychology is the _____ of _____ and mental processes.
   a. study, the mind
   b. knowledge, philosophy
   c. study, personality
   d. science, behavior

2. The best psychological information is typically based on
   a. proven theories
   b. opinions of experts and authorities
   c. anthropomorphic measurements
   d. empirical evidence

3. Who among the following is most interested in the growth of young children?
   a. learning theorist
   b. personality theorist
   c. comparative psychologist
   d. developmental psychologist

4. Cognitive psychologists are primarily interested in
   a. thinking and information processing
   b. the behavior of various species
   c. attitudes, persuasion, riots, conformity, and leadership
   d. how the brain evolved to produce human intelligence

5. Research that can explain why people remember better if they relate new information to familiar ideas meets which of psychology's goals?
   a. describe
   b. understand
   c. predict
   d. control

6. Introspection was especially important to which school of thought in psychology?
   a. structuralism
   b. functionalism
   c. behaviorism
   d. Gestalt

7. Which two schools of thought have largely disappeared from contemporary psychology?
   a. behaviorism, Gestalt
   b. humanism, cognitive behaviorism
   c. functionalism, structuralism
   d. structuralism, humanism

8. Who among the following was NOT an historic woman psychologist?
   a. Calkins
   b. Ladd-Franklin
   c. Washburn
   d. Watson

9. Who among the following is LEAST likely to treat serious behavioral and emotional disturbances?
   a. psychologist
   b. counselor
   c. psychiatrist
   d. psychoanalyst

10. Modern psychodynamic theories owe much to the work of
    a. Titchener
    b. Freud
    c. Darwin
    d. Wertheimer

11. A psychotherapist is working with a person from an ethnic group other than her own. She should be aware of how cultural relativity and _____ affect behavior.
    a. the anthropomorphic error
    b. operational definitions
    c. biased sampling
    d. social norms

12. After you identify an interesting problem or question about behavior, you will need to establish _____ of important variables before you begin to make controlled observations.
    a. correlations
    b. operational definitions
    c. double-blind controls
    d. a theory

13. A psychologist does a study to see if having control over difficult tasks reduces stress. In the study he will be testing an
    a. experimental hypothesis
    b. operational definition
    c. empirical definition
    d. anthropomorphic theory

14. Because correlation does not demonstrate causation, psychologists often use _____ to answer questions about behavior.
    a. experimentation
    b. naturalistic observation
    c. the survey method
    d. the clinical method

15. Observer bias and the observer effect are problems in using
    a. naturalistic observation
    b. the correlational method
    c. the experimental method
    d. naturalistic experiments

16. The outcome of a psychology experiment is revealed by measuring changes in behavior. Such measures are the _____ variable of the experiment.
    a. independent
    b. correlational
    c. dependent
    d. extraneous

17. Double-blind experiments are designed to control for the
    a. placebo effect
    b. anthropomorphic fallacy
    c. unintended influence of operational definitions
    d. courtesy bias

18. Obtaining a representative sample is especially important in psychological research involving
    a. the placebo effect
    b. hypothesis testing
    c. the experimenter effect
    d. the clinical method

19. Belief in astrology is based on the fallacy of positive instances, which is a failure to
    a. collect relevant correlations
    b. make use of introspection
    c. distinguish between observation and inference
    d. engage in critical thinking

20. An article in a magazine claims that "Special Diet Controls Hyperactivity in Children." This claim is meaningless unless
    a. the author is an authority on hyperactivity
    b. the diet has been tested empirically
    c. an animal model was used
    d. the author knows of a specific child who benefited from the diet

ANSWERS   1. d 2. d 3. d 4. a 5. b 6. a 7. c 8. d 9. b 10. b 11. d 12. b 13. a 14. a 15. a 16. c 17. a 18. d 19. d 20. b

Brain and Behavior

JOURNEY INTO PSYCHOLOGY: FINDING MUSIC IN TOFU

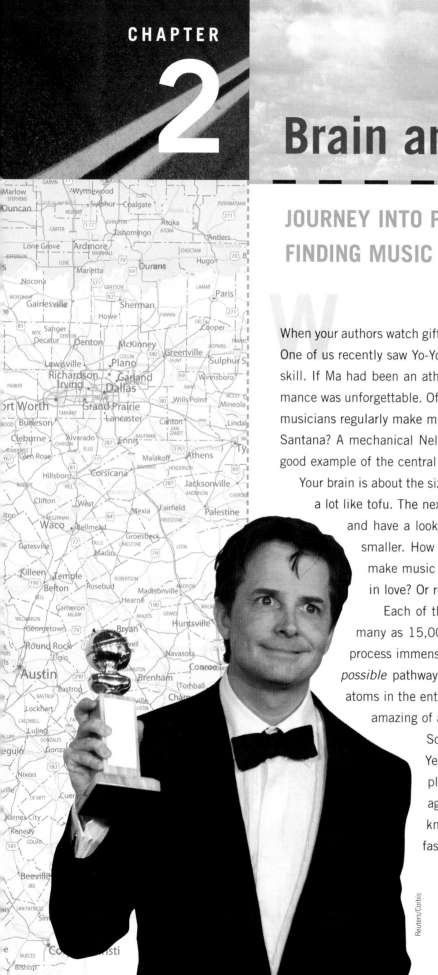

When your authors watch gifted musicians, we often think about the brain (Really!). One of us recently saw Yo-Yo Ma, a master cellist, play a Bach suite with amazing skill. If Ma had been an athlete, you would say he was "in the zone." His performance was unforgettable. Of course, in everything from classical to jazz to hip-hop, musicians regularly make music that no machine could duplicate. A virtual Carlos Santana? A mechanical Nelly Furtado? We don't think so. That's why music is a good example of the central role the brain plays in all that is human.

Your brain is about the size of a grapefruit. It weighs around 3 pounds and looks a lot like tofu. The next time you are in a market that sells beef brains, stop and have a look. What you will see is similar to your own brain, only smaller. How could such a squishy little blob of tissue allow us to make music of exquisite beauty? To seek a cure for cancer? To fall in love? Or read a book like this one?

Each of the billions of nerve cells in your brain is linked to as many as 15,000 others. The resulting network makes it possible to process immense amounts of information. In fact, there may be more *possible* pathways between the neurons in your brain than there are atoms in the entire universe! Undeniably, the human brain is the most amazing of all computers.

Scientists use the power of the brain to study the brain. Yet, even now we must wonder if the brain will ever completely understand itself. Nevertheless, answers to many age-old questions about the mind, consciousness, and knowledge lie buried within the brain. Let's visit this fascinating realm.

Reuters/Corbis

- How do nerve cells operate and communicate?
- What are the functions of the major parts of the nervous system?
- How do we know how the brain works?
- How is the brain organized, and what do its higher structures do?
- What kinds of behaviors are controlled by the subcortex?
- Does the glandular system affect behavior?
- In what ways do right- and left-handed individuals differ?

NEURONS—BUILDING A "BIOCOMPUTER"

>SURVEY QUESTION< *How do nerve cells operate and communicate?*

The brain consists of some 100 billion **neurons** (NOOR-ons: individual nerve cells). Neurons carry and process information. They also activate muscles and glands. Thus, everything you do, think, or feel can be traced back to these tiny cells. A single neuron is not very smart—it would take at least several just to make you blink. Yet, when neurons form vast networks, they produce intelligence and consciousness. Neurons link to one another in tight clumps and long "chains." Each neuron receives messages from many others and sends its own message on. Millions of neurons must send messages at the same time to produce even the most fleeting thought (Kalat, 2007). When a musician such as Eric Clapton plays a guitar riff, literally billions of neurons may be involved.

Parts of a Neuron

What does a neuron look like? What are its main parts? No two neurons are exactly alike, but most have four basic parts (⟫Fig. 2.1). The **dendrites** (DEN-drytes), which look like tree roots, receive messages from other neurons. The **soma** (SOH-mah: cell body) does the same. In addition, the soma sends messages of its own (nerve impulses) down a thin fiber called the **axon** (AK-sahn).

Most axons end in **axon terminals.** These "branches" link up with the dendrites and somas of other neurons. This allows information to pass from neuron to neuron. Some axons are only 0.1 millimeter long. (That's about the width of a pencil line.) Others stretch up to a meter through the nervous system. (From the base of your spine to your big toe, for instance.) Like miniature cables, axons carry messages through the brain and nervous system. Altogether, your brain contains about 3 million miles of axons (Rosenzweig, Breedlove, & Watson, 2004).

Now let's summarize with a metaphor. Imagine that you are standing in a long line of people who are holding hands. A person on the far right end of the line wants to silently send a message to the person on the left end. She does this by pressing the hand of the person to her left, who presses the hand of the person to his left, and so on. The message arrives at your right hand (your dendrites). You decide whether to pass it on (you are the soma). The message goes out through your left arm (the axon). With your left hand (the axon terminals), you squeeze the hand of the person to your left, and the message moves on.

The Nerve Impulse

Electrically charged molecules called *ions* (EYE-ons) are found inside each neuron (⟫Fig. 2.2). Other ions lie outside the cell. Some ions have a positive electrical charge, and some are negative. Different numbers of these "plus" and "minus" charges exist inside and outside of nerve cells. As a result, the inside of each neuron in your brain has an electrical charge of

Neuron An individual nerve cell.

Dendrites Neuron fibers that receive incoming messages.

Soma The main body of a neuron or other cell.

Axon Fiber that carries information away from the cell body of a neuron.

Axon terminals Branching fibers at the ends of axons.

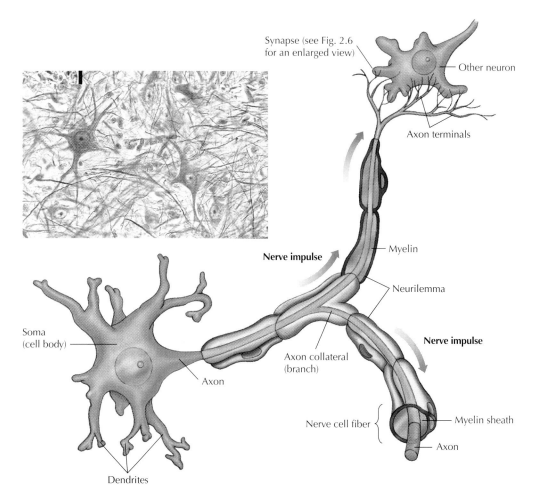

▸▸FIGURE 2.1 A neuron, or nerve cell. In the right foreground you can see a nerve cell fiber in cross section. The upper left photo gives a more realistic picture of the shape of neurons. Nerve impulses usually travel from the dendrites and soma to the branching ends of the axon. The nerve cell shown here is a motor neuron. The axons of motor neuron stretch from the brain and spinal cord to muscles or glands of the body.

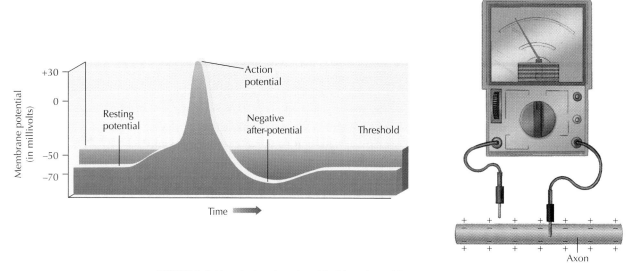

▸▸FIGURE 2.2 Electrical probes placed inside and outside an axon measure its activity. (The scale is exaggerated here. Such measurements require ultra-small electrodes, as described later in this chapter.) The inside of an axon at rest is about –60 to –70 millivolts, compared with the outside. Electrochemical changes in a neuron generate an action potential. When sodium ions (Na^+) that have a positive charge rush into the cell, its interior briefly becomes positive. This is the action potential. After the action potential, positive potassium ions (K^+) flow out of the axon and restore its negative charge. (See Fig. 2.3 for further explanation.)

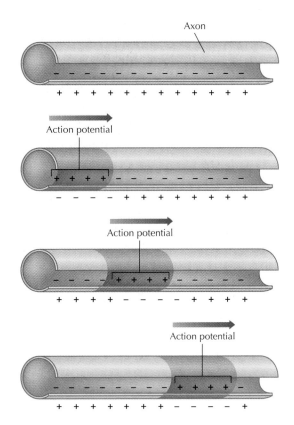

1. In its resting state, the axon has a negatively charged interior.

2. During an action potential, positively charged atoms (ions) rush into the axon. This briefly changes the electrical charge inside the axon from negative to positive. Simultaneously, the charge outside the axon becomes negative.

3. The action potential advances as positive and negative charges reverse in a moving zone of electrical activity that sweeps down the axon.

4. After an action potential passes, positive ions rapidly flow out of the axon to quickly restore its negative charge. An outward flow of additional positive ions returns the axon to its resting state.

▸▸**FIGURE 2.3** The electrical charge inside an axon is normally negative. The fluid surrounding an axon is normally positive. As an action potential passes along the axon, these charges reverse so that the interior of the axon briefly becomes positive. This process is described in more detail in Figure 2.4.

about minus 70 millivolts. (A millivolt is one thousandth of a volt.) This charge allows each neuron in your brain to act like a tiny biological battery.

The electrical charge of an inactive neuron is called its **resting potential.** But neurons seldom get much rest: Messages arriving from other neurons raise and lower the resting potential. If the electrical charge rises to about minus 50 millivolts, the neuron will reach its *threshold,* or trigger point for firing (see ▸▸Fig. 2.2). It's as if the neuron says "Ah ha! It's time to send a message to my neighbors." When a neuron reaches −50 millivolts, an **action potential,** or nerve impulse, sweeps down the axon at up to 200 miles per hour (▸▸Fig. 2.3). That may seem fast, but it still takes at least a split second to react. That's one reason why hitting a 95-mile-per-hour major league fastball is so difficult. (See "Dollars, Drag Racing, and the Nervous System.")

What happens during an action potential? The axon membrane is pierced by tiny tunnels or "holes," called *ion channels.* Normally, these tiny openings are blocked by molecules that act like "gates" or "doors." During an action potential, the gates pop open. This allows sodium ions (Na^+) to rush into the axon (Carlson, 2005). The channels first open near the soma. Then, gate after gate opens down the length of axon as the action potential zips along (▸▸Fig. 2.4).

Each action potential is an *all-or-nothing event* (a nerve impulse occurs completely or not at all). You might find it helpful to picture the axon as a row of dominoes set on end. Tipping over the dominoes is an all-or-nothing act. Once the first domino drops, a wave of falling blocks will zip rapidly to the end of the line. Similarly, when a nerve impulse is triggered near the soma, a wave of activity (the action potential) travels down the length of the axon. This is what happens in long chains of neurons as Yo-Yo Ma's brain tells his hands what to do next, note after note.

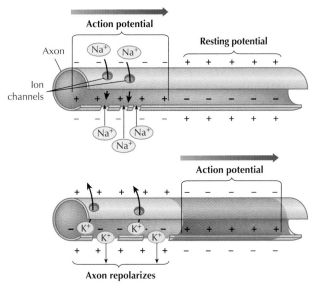

▸▸**FIGURE 2.4** The interior of an axon. The right end of the top axon is at rest. Thus, it has a negative charge inside. An action potential begins when ion channels open and sodium ions (Na^+) rush into the axon. In this drawing, the action potential would travel from left to right along the axon. In the lower axon, the action potential has moved to the right. After it passes, potassium ions (K^+) flow out of the axon. This quickly renews the negative charge inside the axon, so that it can fire again. Sodium ions that enter the axon during an action potential are pumped out more slowly. Removing them restores the original resting potential.

Resting potential The electrical charge of a neuron at rest.

Action potential The nerve impulse.

Dollars, Drag Racing, and the Nervous System

In the sport of drag racing, victory depends on a driver's reaction time. When a light signals the start of a race, the driver must react as quickly as possible, usually in less than a half second. To test your own reaction time, have a friend hold a dollar bill from the top, as shown in ▸▸Figure 2.5. Spread your thumb and fingers about 2 inches apart and place them around the bill, near the middle of Washington's portrait. Watch the bill intently. Without warning, your friend should release the bill. When you see it begin to move, try to catch it by pressing your thumb and fingers together. Most likely, the bill will slip through your fingers. It takes a split second for you to see the bill's movement, process that information in your brain, and send signals to your hand, causing it to move. Because neural processing takes time, our experiences and reactions lag slightly behind events in the world. In fact, your sense of control over your actions is partly an illusion. For instance, if you decide to wiggle your finger, your brain will begin a series of events that leads to finger movement. This activity will start before you begin to feel that you are intentionally moving your finger (Obhi & Haggard, 2004)!

▸▸**FIGURE 2.5**

After each nerve impulse, the cell briefly drops below its resting level, and it becomes less willing to fire. This **negative after-potential** occurs because potassium ions (K^+) flow out of the neuron while the membrane gates are open (▸▸Fig. 2.4). After a nerve impulse, ions flow both into and out of the axon, recharging it for more action. In our model, the row of dominoes is quickly set up again. Soon, the axon is ready for another wave of activity.

Synapses and Neurotransmitters

How does information move from one neuron to another? The nerve impulse is primarily electrical. That's why electrically stimulating the brain affects behavior. To prove the point, researcher José Delgado once entered a bullring with a cape and a radio transmitter. The bull charged. Delgado retreated. At the last instant the speeding bull stopped short. Why? Because Delgado's radio activated electrodes (metal wires) that were placed deep within the bull's brain. These, in turn, stimulated "control centers" that brought the bull to a halt (Horgan, 2005).

In contrast to the nerve impulse, communication between neurons is chemical. The microscopic space between two neurons, over which messages pass, is called a **synapse** (SIN-aps) (▸▸Fig. 2.6). When an action potential reaches the tips of the axon terminals, **neurotransmitters** (NOOR-oh-TRANS-mit-ers) are released into the synaptic gap. Neurotransmitters are chemicals that alter activity in neurons.

Let's return to the people standing in a line. To be more accurate, you and the others shouldn't be holding hands. Instead, each person should have a toy squirt gun in his or her left hand. To pass along a message, you would squirt the right hand of the person to your left. When that person notices this "message," he or she would squirt the right hand of the person to the left, and so on.

When chemical molecules cross over a synapse, they attach to special receiving areas on the next neuron (▸▸Fig. 2.6). These tiny *receptor sites* on the cell membrane are sensitive to neurotransmitters. The sites are found in large numbers on nerve cell bodies and on dendrites. Muscles and glands have receptor sites, too.

Negative after-potential A drop in electrical charge below the resting potential.

Synapse The microscopic space between two neurons, over which messages pass.

Neurotransmitter Any chemical released by a neuron that alters activity in other neurons.

Do neurotransmitters always trigger an action potential in the next neuron? No. Some transmitters *excite* the next neuron (move it closer to firing). Others *inhibit* it (make firing less likely).

More than 100 transmitter chemicals are found in the brain. Some examples are acetylcholine, epinephrine, norepinephrine, serotonin, dopamine, histamine, and various amino acids. Disturbances of any of these substances can have serious consequences. For example, too little dopamine can cause the shaking and muscle tremors of Parkinson's disease. Too much dopamine may cause schizophrenia.

Many drugs imitate, duplicate, or block neurotransmitters. For example, *acetylcholine* (ah-SEET-ul-KOH-leen) normally activates muscles. Without acetylcholine, our musical friend Yo-Yo Ma couldn't even move, much less play Bach. That's exactly why the drug curare (cue-RAH-ree) causes paralysis. By attaching to receptor sites on muscles, curare competes with acetylcholine. This prevents acetylcholine from activating muscle cells. As a result, a person or animal given curare cannot move—a fact known to South American Indians of the Amazon River Basin, who use curare as an arrow poison for hunting.

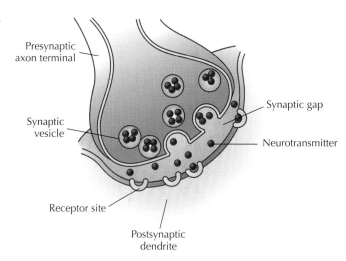

▸▸FIGURE 2.6 A highly magnified view of a synapse. Neurotransmitters are stored in tiny sacs called synaptic vesicles (VES-ih-kels). When a nerve impulse reaches the end of an axon, the vesicles move to the surface and release neurotransmitters. These molecules cross the synaptic gap to affect the next neuron. The size of the gap is exaggerated here; it is actually only about one millionth of an inch. Some transmitter molecules excite the next neuron and some inhibit its activity.

Neural Regulators

More subtle brain activities are affected by chemicals called **neuropeptides** (NOOR-oh-PEP-tides). Neuropeptides do not carry messages directly. Instead, they *regulate* the activity of other neurons. By doing so, they affect memory, pain, emotion, pleasure, moods, hunger, sexual behavior, and other basic processes. For example, when you touch something hot, you jerk your hand away. The messages for this action are carried by neurotransmitters. At the same time, pain may cause the brain to release *enkephalins* (en-KEF-ah-lins). These opiate-like neural regulators relieve pain and stress. Related chemicals called *endorphins* (en-DORF-ins) are released by the pituitary gland. Together, these chemicals reduce the pain so that it is not too disabling (Drolet et al., 2001).

Such discoveries help explain the painkilling effect of placebos (fake pills or injections), which raise endorphin levels (Stewart-Williams, 2004). A release of endorphins also seems to underlie "runner's high," masochism, acupuncture, and the euphoria sometimes associated with childbirth and painful initiation rites, and even sport parachuting (Janssen & Arntz, 2001). In each case, pain and stress cause the release of endorphins. These in turn induce feelings of pleasure or euphoria similar to being "high" on morphine. People who say they are "addicted" to running or eating hot chilies may be closer to the truth than they realize. And more important, we may at last know why some hardy souls take hot saunas followed by cold showers! Ultimately, brain regulators may help explain depression, schizophrenia, drug addiction, and other puzzling topics. For example, women who suffer from severe premenstrual pain and distress have unusually low endorphin levels (Straneva et al., 2002).

Neural Networks

Let's put together what we now know about the nerve impulse and synapses to see how *neural networks* process information in our brains. ▸▸Figure 2.7 shows a small part of a neural network. Five neurons synapse with a single neuron that, in turn, connects with three more neurons. At the point in time depicted in the diagram, the single neuron is receiving three excitatory messages (+) and two inhibitory ones (−). At any instant, an actual neuron may receive hundreds or thousands of messages. Does it fire an impulse? It depends: If several "exciting" messages arrive close in time, the neuron will fire—but only if it doesn't get too many "inhibiting" messages that push it *away* from its trigger point. In this way, messages are *combined* before a neuron "decides" to fire its all-or-nothing action potential.

Neuropeptides Brain chemicals, such as enkephalins and endorphins, that regulate the activity of neurons.

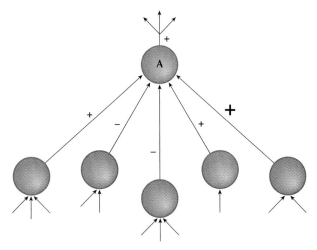

▸▸**FIGURE 2.7** A small neural network. Neuron A receives inputs from three excitatory connections (+) and two inhibitory connections (−) and combines the inputs into a "decision" to launch an action potential which may help trigger further synaptic transmissions in other neurons.

Let's try another metaphor. You are out shopping for new blue jeans with five friends. Three of them think you should buy the jeans (your best friend is especially positive) and two think you shouldn't. Because, on balance, their input is positive, you go ahead and buy the jeans. Maybe you even tell some other friends they should buy those jeans as well. Similarly, any single neuron in a neural network "listens" to the neurons that synapse with it and combines that input into an output. After the neuron recovers from the resulting action potential, it again combines the inputs, which may well have changed in the meantime, into another output, and another, and another.

In this way, each neuron in your brain functions as a tiny computer. Compared with the average laptop computer, a neuron is terribly simple and slow. But multiply these events by 100 billion neurons and 100 trillion synapses, all operating at the same time, and you have an amazing computer—one that could easily fit inside a shoebox.

Plasticity

The term **plasticity** refers to the capacity of our brains to change in response to experience. The neural networks in your brain constantly change. New synapses may form between neurons or they may grow stronger (▸▸Figure 2.7 shows one particularly strong synapse—the large +). Other synaptic connections weaken and might even die. Every new experience you have is reflected in changes in your brain. For example, rats raised in a complex environment have more synapses and longer dendrites in their brains than rats raised in a simpler environment (Kolb, Gibb, & Gorny, 2003).

Brain Repair

Until only a few years ago, it was widely believed that we are born with all the brain cells we will ever have. This led to the depressing idea that we all slowly go downhill, as the brain loses thousands of neurons every day. However, we now know that a healthy 75-year-old brain has just as many neurons as it did when it was careening through life in the body of a 25-year-old. Although it is true that the brain loses cells daily, it simultaneously grows new neurons to replace them. This process is called **neurogenesis** (noor-oh-JEN-uh-sis: the production of new brain cells) (Gould, Reeves, & Gross, 1999). Each day, thousands of new cells originate deep within the brain, move to the surface, and link up with other neurons to become part of the brain's circuitry. This is stunning news to brain scientists, who must now figure out what the new cells do. Most likely they are involved in learning, memory, and our ability to adapt to changing circumstances (Gould & Gross, 2002).

The discovery of neurogenesis in adult brains has raised new hopes that some types of brain damage can be repaired. For example, doctors are testing a new method to treat strokes. Their attempts involve injecting millions of immature nerve cells into damaged areas of the brain. If the technique is successful, the new cells will link up with existing neurons and repair some of the stroke damage (Borlongan, Sanberg, & Freeman, 1999). Researchers are also trying to nudge immature brain cells to develop into particular types of neurons. If they succeed, cures for blindness, Parkinson's disease, and other problems might follow (Kolb & Whishaw, 1998).

THE NERVOUS SYSTEM—WIRED FOR ACTION

>SURVEY QUESTION< *What are the functions of the major parts of the nervous system?*

Jamal and Vicki are playing catch with a Frisbee. This may look fairly simple. However, to merely toss the Frisbee or catch it, a huge amount of information must be sensed, interpreted, and directed to countless muscle fibers. As they play, Jamal and Vicki's neural cir-

Plasticity The capacity of the brain to change in response to experience.
Neurogenesis The production of new brain cells.

cuits are ablaze with activity. Let's explore the "wiring diagram" that makes their Frisbee game possible.

Neurons and Nerves

Are neurons the same as nerves? No. Neurons are tiny cells. You would need a microscope to see one. **Nerves** are large bundles of axons and dendrites. You can easily see nerves without magnification.

Many nerves are white because they contain axons coated with a fatty layer called *myelin* (MY-eh-lin). Small gaps in the myelin help nerve impulses move faster. Instead of passing down the entire length of the axon, the action potential leaps from gap to gap. Without the added speed this allows, it would probably be impossible to brake in time to avoid many automobile accidents. When the myelin layer is damaged, a person may suffer from numbness, weakness, or paralysis. That, in fact, is what happens in multiple sclerosis, a disease that occurs when the immune system attacks and destroys the myelin in a person's body.

A thin layer of cells called the *neurilemma* (NOOR-rih-LEM-ah) is also wrapped around most axons outside the brain and spinal cord. (Return to ▸Figure 2.1.) The neurilemma forms a "tunnel" that damaged fibers can follow as they repair themselves.

Subparts of the Nervous System

As you can see in ▸Figure 2.8, the **central nervous system (CNS)** consists of the brain and spinal cord. The brain is the central "computer" of the nervous system. Jamal must use this "computer" to anticipate when and where the Frisbee will arrive. Jamal's brain communicates with the rest of his body through a large "cable" called the spinal cord. From there, messages flow through the **peripheral nervous system (PNS).** This intricate network of nerves carries information to and from the CNS.

A serious injury to the brain or spinal cord is usually permanent. However, as we have noted, scientists are starting to make progress in repairing damaged neurons in the CNS. For instance, they have been able to partially repair cut spinal cords in rats. First they closed the gap with nerve fibers from outside the spinal cord. Then they biochemically coaxed the severed spinal nerve fibers to grow through the "tunnels" provided by the implanted fibers. Within 2 months, the rats had regained some use of their hind legs (Cheng, Cao, & Olson, 1996). Similarly, medical researchers recently began the first human trials in which nerve grafts will be used to repair damaged spinal cords (Féron et al., 2005). Imagine what that could mean to a person confined to a wheelchair. Although it is unwise to raise false hopes, solutions to such problems are beginning to emerge. Nevertheless, it is wise to take good

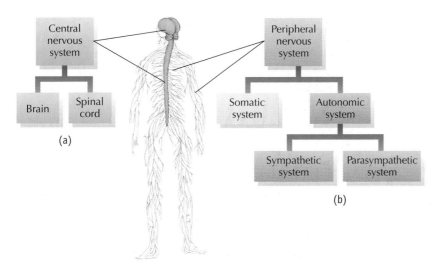

(a)

(b)

▸**FIGURE 2.8** Subparts of the nervous system. *(a)* Central and peripheral nervous systems. *(b)* Spinal nerves, cranial nerves, and the autonomic nervous system.

Nerve A bundle of neuron fibers.

Central nervous system The brain and spinal cord.

Peripheral nervous system All parts of the nervous system outside the brain and spinal cord.

Each year spinal cord injuries rob many thousands of people of the ability to move. Yet, there is growing hope that nerve grafting techniques may someday make it possible for some of these people to walk again.

Phanie/Photo Researchers, Inc.

care of your own CNS. That means using seatbelts when you drive, a helmet if you ride a motorcycle or bicycle, wearing protective gear for sports, and avoiding activities that pose a risk to the head or spinal cord.

The Peripheral Nervous System

The peripheral system can be divided into two major parts (see ▸Fig. 2.8). The **somatic system** carries messages to and from the sense organs and skeletal muscles. In general, it controls voluntary behavior, such as when Vicki tosses the Frisbee or B.B. King plays the blues. In contrast, the **autonomic system** serves the internal organs and glands of the body. The word *autonomic* means "self-governing." Activities governed by the autonomic nervous system (ANS) are mostly "vegetative" or automatic, such as heart rate, digestion, or perspiration. Thus, messages carried by the somatic system can make your hand move, but they cannot cause your eyes to dilate. Likewise, messages carried by the ANS can stimulate digestion, but they cannot help you carry out a voluntary action, such as writing a letter. If Jamal feels a flash of anger when he misses a catch, a brief burst of activity will spread through his autonomic system.

The ANS can be divided into the sympathetic and parasympathetic branches. Both are related to emotional responses, such as crying, sweating, heart rate, and other involuntary behavior (▸Fig. 2.9). The ANS and the somatic system work together to coordinate the body's internal reactions with events in the world outside. For example, if a snarling dog lunges at you, the somatic system will control your leg muscles so that you can run. At the same time, the autonomic system will raise your blood pressure, quicken your heart, and so forth.

How do the branches of the autonomic system differ? The **sympathetic branch** is an "emergency" system. It prepares the body for "fight or flight" during times of danger or high emotion. In essence, it arouses the body for action. (Yo-Yo Ma once left his $2 million cello

▸**FIGURE 2.9** Sympathetic and parasympathetic branches of the autonomic nervous system. Both branches control involuntary actions. The sympathetic system generally activates the body. The parasympathetic system generally quiets it. The sympathetic branch relays its messages through clusters of nerve cells outside the spinal cord.

Parasympathetic   **Sympathetic**

Constricts pupil
Stimulates tears
Stimulates salivation

Inhibits heart rate
Constricts respiration
Constricts blood vessels
Stimulates digestion

Dilates pupil
Inhibits tears
Inhibits salivation
Activates sweat glands
Increases heart rate
Increases respiration
Inhibits digestion
Release of adrenaline
Release of sugar from liver
Relaxes bladder
Inhibits elimination
Inhibits genitals
Ejaculation in males

Contracts bladder
Stimulates elimination
Stimulates genitals

Somatic system The system of nerves linking the spinal cord with the body and sense organs.

Autonomic system The system of nerves carrying information to and from the internal organs and glands.

Sympathetic system A branch of the ANS that arouses the body.

in a taxi. No doubt his sympathetic nervous system was quite active when he first noticed his error.)

The **parasympathetic branch** quiets the body and returns it to a lower level of arousal. It is most active soon after an emotional event. The parasympathetic branch also helps keep vital processes such as heart rate, breathing, and digestion at moderate levels.

Of course, both branches of the ANS are always active. At any given moment, their combined activity determines if your body is relaxed or aroused.

The Spinal Cord

As mentioned earlier, the spinal cord acts like a cable connecting the brain to other parts of the body. If you were to cut through this "cable," you would see columns of *white matter* in areas that have lots of myelin. This tissue is made up of axons that eventually leave the spinal cord. Outside the cord, they are bundled together into nerves. Thirty-one **spinal nerves** carry sensory and motor messages to and from the spinal cord. In addition, 12 pairs of **cranial nerves** leave the brain directly. Together, these nerves keep your entire body in communication with your brain.

How is the spinal cord related to behavior? The simplest behavior pattern is a **reflex arc,** which occurs when a stimulus provokes an automatic response. Such reflexes occur within the spinal cord, without any help from the brain (see ▸▸Fig. 2.10). Imagine that Vicki steps on a thorn. (Yes, they're still playing catch.) Pain is detected in her foot by a *sensory neuron* (a nerve cell that carries messages from the senses toward the CNS). Instantly, the sensory neuron fires off a message to Vicki's spinal cord.

Inside the spinal cord, the sensory neuron synapses with a *connector neuron* (a nerve cell that links two others). The connector neuron activates a *motor neuron* (a cell that carries commands from the CNS to muscles and glands). The muscle fibers are made up of *effector cells* (cells capable of producing a response). The muscle cells contract and cause Vicki's foot to withdraw. Note that no brain activity is required for a reflex arc to occur. Vicki's body will react automatically to protect itself.

In reality, even a simple reflex usually triggers more complex activity. For example, muscles of Vicki's other leg must contract to support her as she shifts her weight. Even this can be done by the spinal cord, but it involves many more cells and several spinal nerves. Also, the spinal cord normally informs the brain of the actions it has taken. As her foot pulls away from the thorn, Vicki will feel the pain and think "Ouch, what was that?"

Perhaps you have realized how adaptive it is to have a spinal cord capable of responding on its own. Such automatic responses leave the brains of our Frisbee aces free to deal with more important information—such as the location of trees, lampposts, and attractive onlookers—as they take turns making grandstand catches.

In a few moments, we will probe more deeply into the brain. Before we do, it might be wise to explore some of the research tools biopsychologists use. Uncovering the brain's mysteries has not been easy. Let's consider some of the basics.

RESEARCH METHODS—CHARTING THE BRAIN'S INNER REALMS

>SURVEY QUESTION< *How do we know how the brain works?*

Biopsychology is the study of how biological processes, the brain, and the nervous system relate to behavior. When it comes to the brain, a basic research strategy is to **localize function.** That is, we try to identify which structures in the brain control specific psychological or behavioral functions, such as recognizing faces or moving your hands.

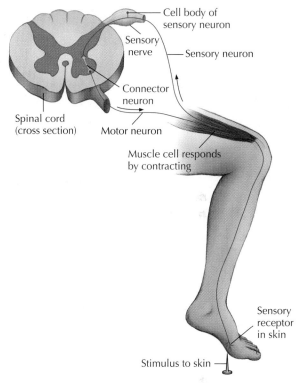

▸▸**FIGURE 2.10** A sensory-motor arc, or reflex, is set in motion by a stimulus to the skin (or other part of the body). The nerve impulse travels to the spinal cord and then back out to a muscle, which contracts. Such reflexes provide an "automatic" protective device for the body.

Parasympathetic system A branch of the ANS that quiets the body.

Spinal nerves Major nerves that carry sensory and motor messages in and out of the spinal cord.

Cranial nerves Major nerves that leave the brain without passing through the spinal cord.

Reflex arc The simplest behavior, in which a stimulus provokes an automatic response.

Localization of function The research strategy of linking specific structures in the brain with specific psychological or behavioral functions.

Mapping Brain Structure

Anatomists have learned much about brain structure by dissecting (cutting apart) autopsied human and animal brains and examining them under a microscope. Dissection reveals that the brain is made up of many anatomically distinct areas or "parts." More modern methods, such as the CT scan and the MRI scan, can be used to map brain structures in living brains.

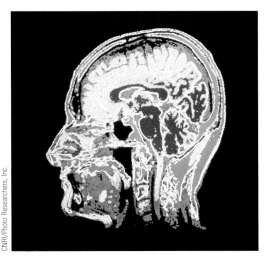

CNRI/Photo Researchers, Inc.

▶▶**FIGURE 2.11** A colored MRI scan of the brain reveals many details. Can you identify any brain regions?

CT Scan

Computerized scanning equipment has revolutionized the study of brain diseases and injuries. At best, conventional X-rays produce only shadowy images of the brain. **Computed tomographic (CT) scanning** is a specialized type of X-ray that does a much better job of making the brain visible. In a CT scan, X-ray information is collected by a computer and formed into an image of the brain. A CT scan can reveal the effects of strokes, injuries, tumors, and other brain disorders.

MRI Scan

Magnetic resonance imaging (MRI) uses a very strong magnetic field, rather than X-rays, to produce an image of the body's interior. During an MRI scan, the body is placed inside a magnetic field. Processing by a computer then creates a three-dimensional model of the brain or body. Any two-dimensional plane, or slice, of the body can be selected and displayed as an image on a computer screen. MRI scans produce more detailed images than are possible with CT scans, allowing us to peer into the living brain almost as if it were transparent (▶▶Fig. 2.11).

Mapping Brain Function

How does the brain allow us to think, feel, perceive, or act? In order to localize such functions, we must link psychological or behavioral capacities with particular brain structures. In many instances, this has been done through **clinical case studies.** Such studies examine changes in personality, behavior, or sensory capacity caused by brain diseases or injuries. If damage to a particular part of the brain consistently leads to a particular loss of function, then we say the function is localized in that structure. Presumably, that part of the brain controls the same function in all of us.

Consider, for example, the story of Kate Adamson (Adamson, 2004). At the age of 33, she had a stroke that caused catastrophic damage to her brainstem. This event left her with *locked-in syndrome:* One moment she was fine, and the next she was totally paralyzed, trapped in her own body and barely able to breathe. As you can see, this clinical case suggests that our brainstems play a role in the control of vital life functions, such as movement and breathing.

But what happened to Kate? Oh, yes. Unable to move a muscle, but still fully awake and aware, Kate thought she was going to die. Her doctors, who thought she was brain dead, did not administer painkillers as they inserted breathing and feeding tubes down her throat. However, in time Kate discovered that she could communicate by blinking her eyes. Ultimately, she appeared before the U.S. Congress, after a recovery that has been miraculous, by any measure.

Instead of relying on clinical studies, much has been learned from **ablation** (ab-LAY-shun: surgical removal) of parts of the brain (▶▶Fig. 2.12). When ablation causes changes in behavior or sensory capacity, we also gain insight into the purpose of the missing "part." An alternate approach is to use electrical stimulation to "turn on" brain structures. For example, the surface of the brain can be activated by touching it with a small electrified wire called an *electrode*. When this is done during brain surgery, the patient can tell what effect the stimulation had. (The brain has no pain receptors so surgery can be done while a patient is awake. Only local painkillers are used for the scalp and skull.) (Any volunteers?)

Even structures below the surface of the brain can be activated or removed. In **deep lesioning** (LEE-zhun-ing), a thin wire electrode, insulated except at the tip, is lowered into

CT scan Computed tomography scan; a computer-enhanced X-ray image of the brain or body.

MRI scan Magnetic resonance imaging; a three-dimensional image of the brain or body, based on its response to a magnetic field.

Clinical case study A detailed investigation of a single person, especially one suffering from some injury or disease.

Ablation Surgical removal of tissue.

Deep lesioning Removal of tissue within the brain by use of an electrode.

a target area inside the brain (▸▸Fig. 2.12). An electric current is then used to destroy a small amount of brain tissue. Again, changes in behavior give clues about the function of the affected area. Using a weaker current, it is also possible to *activate* target areas, rather than remove them. This is called ESB, for **electrical stimulation of the brain.** ESB can call forth behavior with astonishing power. Instantly, it can bring about aggression, alertness, escape, eating, drinking, sleeping, movement, euphoria, memories, speech, tears, and more. By using ablation and ESB, researchers are creating a three-dimensional brain map. This "atlas" shows the sensory, motor, and emotional responses that can be elicited from various parts of the brain. It promises to be a valuable guide for medical treatment, as well as for exploring the brain (Kalat, 2007; Yoshida, 1993).

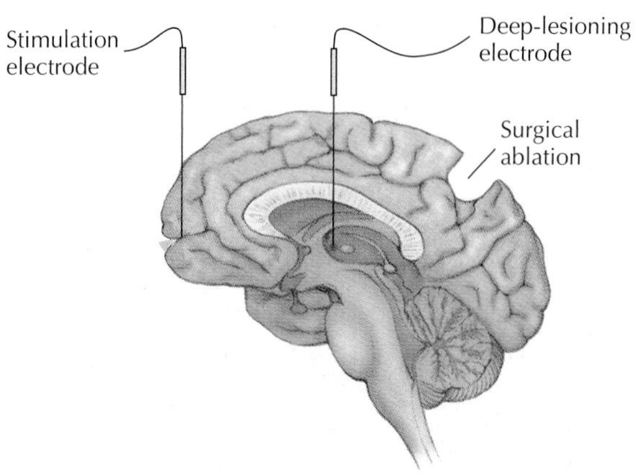

Could ESB be used to control a person against his or her will? It might seem that ESB could be used to control a person like a robot. But the details of emotions and behaviors elicited by ESB are modified by personality and circumstances. Sci-fi movies to the contrary, it would be impossible for a ruthless dictator to enslave people by "radio controlling" their brains.

To find out what individual neurons are doing, we need to do a microelectrode recording. A *microelectrode* is an extremely thin glass tube filled with a salty fluid. The tip of a microelectrode is small enough to detect the electrical activity of a *single* neuron. Watching the action potentials of just one neuron provides a fascinating glimpse into the true origins of behavior. (The action potential shown in ▸▸Figure 2.2 was recorded with a microelectrode.)

Are any less invasive techniques available for studying brain function? Yes, several techniques allow us to observe the activity of parts of the brain without doing any damage at all. These include the EEG, PET scan, and fMRI. Such techniques are allowing scientists to pinpoint areas in the brain responsible for thoughts, feelings, and actions.

EEG

Electroencephalography (ee-LEK-tro-in-SEF-ah-LOG-ruh-fee) measures the waves of electrical activity produced by the surface of the brain. Small disk-shaped metal plates are placed on a person's scalp. Electrical impulses from the brain are detected by these electrodes and sent to an **electroencephalograph (EEG).** The EEG amplifies these very weak signals (brain waves) and records them on a moving sheet of paper or a computer screen (▸▸Fig. 2.13). Various brain-wave patterns can identify the presence of tumors, epilepsy, and

▸▸**FIGURE 2.12** The functions of brain structures are explored by selectively activating or removing them. Brain research is often based on electrical stimulation, but chemical stimulation is also used at times.

Stimulation electrode · Deep-lesioning electrode · Surgical ablation

▸▸**FIGURE 2.13** An EEG recording.

AJPhoto/Photo Researchers, Inc.

Electrical stimulation of the brain (ESB) Direct electrical stimulation and activation of brain tissue.

Electroencephalograph (EEG) A device that detects, amplifies, and records electrical activity in the brain.

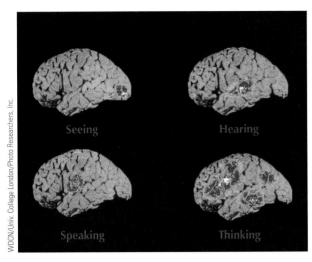

WDCN/Univ. College London/Photo Researchers, Inc.

▸▸**FIGURE 2.14** Colored PET scans reveal different patterns of brain activation when we engage in different tasks.

other diseases. The EEG also reveals changes in brain activity during sleep, daydreaming, hypnosis, and other mental states.

PET Scan

A newer technology, called positron emission tomography (PET), provides much more detailed images of activity both *on* the surface and *below* the surface of the brain. A **PET scan** detects positrons (subatomic particles) emitted by weakly radioactive glucose (sugar) as it is consumed by the brain. Because the brain runs on glucose, a PET scan shows which areas are using more energy. Higher energy use corresponds with higher activity. Thus, by placing positron detectors around the head and sending data to a computer, it is possible to create a moving, color picture of changes in brain activity. As you can see in ▸▸Figure 2.14, PET scans reveal that very specific brain areas are active when you see, hear, speak, or think.

More active brains are good, right? Surprisingly, although we might assume that smart brains are hardworking brains, the reverse appears to be true. Using PET scans, psychologist Richard Haier and his colleagues found that the brains of people who perform well on a difficult reasoning test consume less energy than those of poor performers (Haier et al., 1988) (▸▸Fig. 2.15). Haier believes this shows that intelligence is related to brain efficiency: Less efficient brains work harder and still accomplish less (Haier, White, & Alkire, 2003). We've all had days like that!

Is it true that most people use only 10 percent of their brain capacity? This is one of the lasting myths about the brain. Brain scans show that all parts of the brain are active during waking hours. Obviously, some people make better use of their innate brainpower than others do. Nevertheless, there are no great hidden or untapped reserves of mental capacity in a normally functioning brain.

fMRI

A **functional MRI (fMRI)** uses MRI technology to make brain activity visible. Like PET scans, functional MRIs also provide images of activity on the surface of the brain and *below* the surface, as well. For example, if we scanned Carlos Santana while he played his guitar, the motor areas on the surface of his brain would be highlighted in an fMRI image. Psychiatrist David Langleben and his colleagues have even used fMRI images to tell if a person is lying (Langleben et al., 2005). It is just a matter of time until even brighter beacons are flashed into the shadowy inner world of thought.

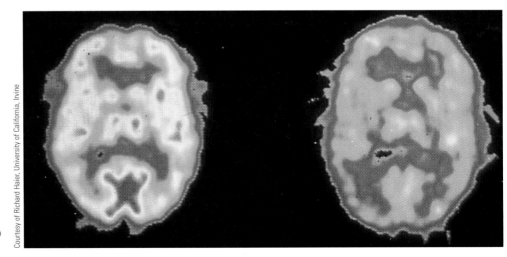

Courtesy of Richard Haier, University of California, Irvine

PET scan Positron emission tomography; a computer-generated image of brain activity, based on glucose consumption in the brain.

fMRI scan Functional magnetic resonance imaging that records brain activity.

▸▸**FIGURE 2.15**   In the images you see here, red, orange, and yellow indicate high consumption of glucose; green, blue, and pink show areas of low glucose use. The PET scan of the brain on the left shows that a man who solved 11 out of 36 reasoning problems burned more glucose than the man on the right, who solved 33.

Reflect

To cope with all of the technical terms in this chapter it might help to think of neurons as strange little creatures. How do they act? What excites them? How do they communicate? To remember the functions of major branches of the nervous system, think about what you *couldn't* do if each part were missing. How does a neural network differ from the central processing unit of a computer?

You suspect that a certain part of the brain is related to risk-taking. How could you use clinical studies, ablation, deep lesioning, and ESB to study the structure? You are interested in finding out how single neurons in the optic nerve respond when the eye is exposed to light. What technique will you use? You want to know which areas of the brain's surface are most active when a person sees a face. What methods will you use?

Learning Check

1. The _____ and _____ are receiving areas where information from other neurons is accepted.
2. Nerve impulses are carried down the _____ to the _____ _____.
3. The _____ potential becomes a(n) _____ potential when a neuron passes the threshold for firing.

4. Neuropeptides are transmitter substances that help regulate the activity of neurons. T or F?
5. The somatic and autonomic systems are part of the _____ nervous system.
6. Sodium and potassium ions flow through ion channels in the synapse to trigger a nerve impulse in the receiving neuron. T or F?
7. The simplest behavior sequence is a(n) _____ _____.
8. The parasympathetic nervous system is most active during times of high emotion. T or F?
9. Which of the following research techniques has the most in common with clinical studies of the effects of brain injuries?

   a. EEG recording   b. deep lesioning
   c. microelectrode recording d. PET scan

Critical Thinking

10. What effect would you expect a drug to have if it blocked passage of neurotransmitters across the synapse?
11. Deep lesioning is used to ablate an area in the hypothalamus of a rat. After the operation, the rat seems to lose interest in food and eating. Why would it be a mistake to conclude that the ablated area is a "hunger center"?

Answers

1. dendrites, soma 2. axon, axon terminals 3. resting, action 4. T 5. peripheral 6. F 7. reflex arc 8. F 9. b 10. Such a drug could have wide-ranging effects. If the drug blocked excitatory synapses it would depress brain activity. If it blocked inhibitory messages it would act as a powerful stimulant. 11. Because other factors might explain the apparent loss of appetite. For example, the taste or smell of food might be affected, or the rat might simply have difficulty swallowing. It is also possible that hunger originates elsewhere in the brain and the ablated area merely relays messages that cause the rat to eat.

THE CEREBRAL CORTEX—MY, WHAT A BIG BRAIN YOU HAVE!

>SURVEY QUESTION< *How is the brain organized, and what do its higher structures do?*

Many parts of your brain are surprisingly similar to corresponding brain areas in lower animals, such as lizards. Superior human intelligence is related to the fact that our brains have a large cerebrum. The wrinkled surface of the cerebrum can be divided into smaller areas known as lobes. Parts of various lobes are responsible for the ability to see, hear, move, think, and speak. Thus, a map of the cerebrum is in some ways like a map of human behavior, as we shall see.

Cerebrum

In many ways we are pretty unimpressive creatures. Animals surpass humans in almost every category of strength, speed, and sensory sensitivity. The one area in which we excel is intelligence.

Do humans have the largest brains? Surprisingly, no. Elephant brains weigh 13 pounds, and whale brains, 19 pounds. At 3 pounds, the human brain seems puny—until we compare brain weight to body weight. We then find that an elephant's brain is 1/1,000 of its weight; the ratio for sperm whales is 1 to 10,000. The ratio for humans is 1 to 60. If someone tells you that you have a "whale of a brain," be sure to find out if they mean size or ratio!

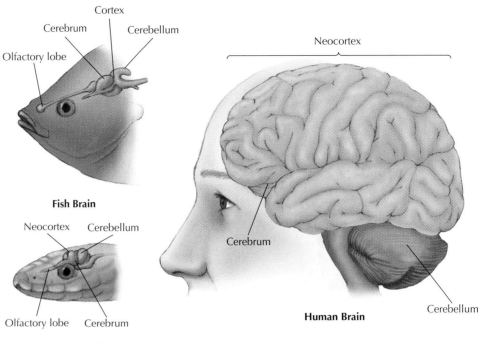

▸▸**FIGURE 2.16**

The *cerebrum* consists of the two large hemispheres that cover the upper part of the brain. Its outer layer is known as the **cerebral** (seh-REE-brel or ser-EH-brel) **cortex,** which looks a little like a giant, wrinkled walnut. It covers most of the brain with a mantle of *gray matter* (spongy tissue made up mostly of cell bodies). The cortex in lower animals is small and smooth. In humans it is twisted, folded, and the largest brain structure (see ▸▸Figure 2.16). The fact that humans are more intelligent than other animals is related to this **corticalization** (KORE-tih-kal-ih-ZAY-shun), or increase in the size and wrinkling of the cortex.

Although the cortex is only 3 millimeters thick (one tenth of an inch), it contains 70 percent of the neurons in the central nervous system. It is largely responsible for our ability to use language, make tools, acquire complex skills, and live in complex social groups (Gibson, 2002). Without the cortex, humans wouldn't be much smarter than toads.

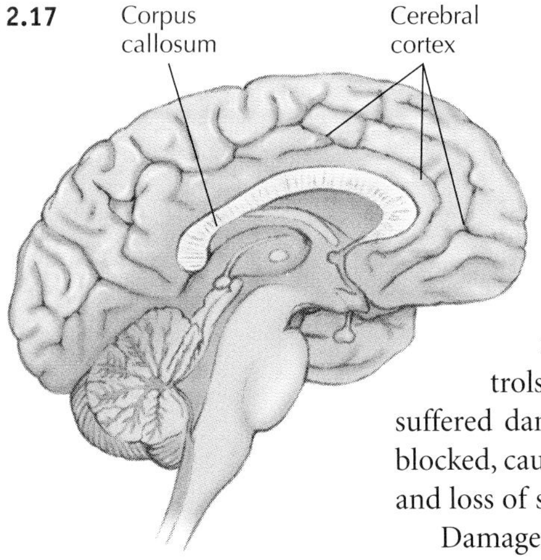

Cerebral Hemispheres

The cortex is composed of two sides, or *cerebral hemispheres* (half-globes). The two hemispheres are connected by a thick band of fibers called the *corpus callosum* (KORE-pus kah-LOH-sum) (▸▸Fig. 2.17). The left side of the brain mainly controls the right side of the body. Likewise, the right brain mainly controls left body areas. When our friend Marge had a stroke, her right hemisphere suffered damage. (A stroke occurs when an artery carrying blood to the brain becomes blocked, causing some brain tissue to die.) In Marge's case, the stroke caused some paralysis and loss of sensation on the left side of her body.

Damage to the right hemisphere may also cause a curious problem called *spatial neglect.* Affected patients pay no attention to the left side of visual space. (See ▸▸Figure 2.18.) Often, the patient will not eat food on the left side of a plate. Some even refuse to acknowledge a paralyzed left arm as their own (Springer & Deutsch, 1998). If you point to the "alien" arm, the patient is likely to say, "Oh, that's not my arm. It must belong to someone else." (To learn more about strokes, see "A Stroke of Bad Luck").

▸▸**FIGURE 2.17**

Corpus callosum

Cerebral cortex

Cerebral cortex The outer layer of the cerebrum.

Corticalization An increase in the relative size of the cerebral cortex.

A Stroke of Bad Luck

One morning Bryan Kolb lost his left hand. Up early to feed his cat, he could not see his hand, or anything else to his upper left side. Kolb, a Canadian biopsychologist, instantly realized that he had suffered a right hemisphere stroke. He drove to the hospital where he argued with the doctors about his own diagnosis. (He was right, of course!) He eventually resumed his career and even wrote a fascinating account of his case (Kolb, 1990).

Strokes and other brain injuries can hit like a thunderbolt. Almost instantly, victims realize that something is wrong. You would, too, if you suddenly found that you couldn't move, or feel parts of your body, or see, or speak. However, some brain injuries are not so obvious. Many involve less dramatic, but equally dis-

abling, changes in personality, thinking, judgment, or emotions (Banich, 2004; Borod et al., 2002). Although major brain injuries are easy enough to spot, psychologists also look for more subtle signs that the brain is not working properly. Neurological soft signs, as they are called, include clumsiness, an awkward gait, poor hand-eye coordination, and other problems with perception or fine muscle control (Stuss & Levine, 2002). These telltale signs are "soft" in the sense that they aren't direct tests of the brain, like an EEG or CT scan. Bryan Kolb initially diagnosed himself entirely with soft signs. Likewise, soft signs help psychologists diagnose problems ranging from childhood learning disorders to full-blown psychosis (Ward, 2006).

Hemispheric Specialization

In 1981, Roger Sperry (1914–1994) won a Nobel Prize for his remarkable discovery that the right and left brain hemispheres perform differently on tests of language, perception, music, and other capabilities.

How is it possible to test only one side of the brain? One way is to work with people who've had a **"split-brain" operation.** In this rare type of surgery, the corpus callosum is cut to control severe epilepsy. The result is essentially a person with two brains in one body (Gazzaniga, 2005). After the surgery, it is a simple matter to send information to one hemisphere or the other (see ▸▸Fig. 2.19).

"Split Brains"

After the right and left brain are separated, each hemisphere will have its own separate perceptions, concepts, and impulses to act.

How does a split-brain person function after the operation? Having "two brains" in one body can create some interesting dilemmas. In one famous case, when a split-brain patient dressed himself, he sometimes pulled his pants down with one hand and up with the other. Once, he grabbed his wife with his left hand and shook her violently. Gallantly, his right hand came to her aid and grabbed the aggressive left hand (Gazzaniga, 1970). However, such conflicts are actually rare. That's because both halves of the brain normally have about the same experience at the same time. Also, if a conflict arises, one hemisphere usually overrides the other.

Split-brain effects are easiest to see in specialized testing. For example, we could flash a dollar sign to the right brain and a question mark to the left brain of a patient named Tom. (Figure 2.19 shows how this is possible.) Next, Tom is asked to draw what he saw, using his left hand, out of sight. Tom's left hand draws a dollar sign. If Tom is then asked to point with his right hand to a picture of what his hidden left hand drew, he will point to a question mark (Sperry, 1968). In short, for the split-brain person, one hemisphere may not know what is happening in the other. This has to be the ultimate case of the "right hand not knowing what the left hand is doing"! ▸▸Figure 2.20 provides another example of split-brain testing.

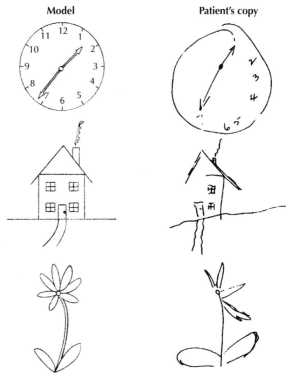

Model Patient's copy

▸▸**FIGURE 2.18** Spatial neglect. A patient with right-hemisphere damage was asked to copy three model drawings. Notice how he neglected the left side in his drawings. Similar neglect occurs in other patients with right-hemisphere damage. (From *Left Brain, Right Brain,* Revised Edition by S. P. Springer and G. Deutsch, copyright 1981, 1985, 1989, 1993, 1998. Reprinted with the permission of W. H. Freeman and Company.)

"Split-brain" operation Cutting the corpus callosum.

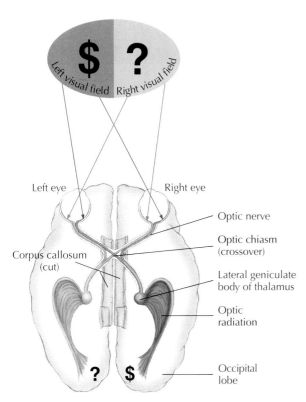

▶▶**FIGURE 2.19** Basic nerve pathways of vision. Notice that the left portion of each eye connects only to the left half of the brain; likewise, the right portion of each eye connects to the right brain. When the corpus callosum is cut, a "split brain" results. Then visual information can be sent to just one hemisphere by flashing it in the right or left visual field as the person stares straight ahead.

Right Brain/Left Brain

Earlier it was stated that the hemispheres differ in abilities; in what ways are they different? The brain divides its work in interesting ways. Roughly 95 percent of us use our left brain for language (speaking, writing, and understanding). In addition, the left hemisphere is superior at math, judging time and rhythm, and coordinating the order of complex movements, such as those needed for speech.

In contrast, the right hemisphere can produce only the simplest language and numbers. Working with the right brain is like talking to a child who can say only a dozen words or so. To answer questions, the right hemisphere must use nonverbal responses, such as pointing at objects (see ▶▶Fig. 2.20).

Although it is poor at producing language, the right brain has it own talents. The right brain is especially good at perceptual skills, such as recognizing patterns, faces, and melodies, putting together a puzzle, or drawing a picture. It also helps you express emotions and detect the emotions that other people are feeling (Borod et al., 2002; Stuss & Alexander, 2000).

One Brain, Two Styles

In general, the left hemisphere is mainly involved with *analysis* (breaking information into parts). It also processes information *sequentially* (in order, one item after the next). The right hemisphere appears to process information *simultaneously* and *holistically* (all at once) (Springer & Deutsch, 1998).

Left Brain

- Language
- Speech
- Writing
- Calculation
- Time sense
- Rhythm
- Ordering of complex movements

Right Brain

- Nonverbal
- Perceptual skills
- Visualization
- Recognition of patterns, faces, melodies
- Recognition and expression of emotion
- Spatial skills
- Simple language comprehension

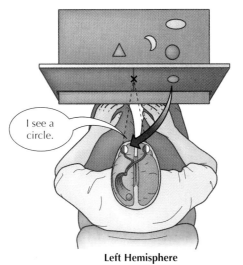
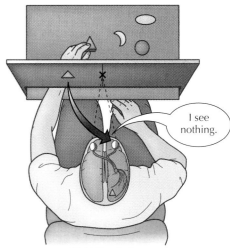

Left Hemisphere   **Right Hemisphere**

▶▶**FIGURE 2.20** A circle is flashed to the left brain of a split-brain patient and he is asked what he saw. He easily replies, "a circle." He can also pick out the circle by merely touching shapes with his right hand, out of sight behind a screen. However, his left hand can't identify the circle. If a triangle is flashed to the patient's right brain, he can't say what he saw (speech is controlled by the left hemisphere). He also can't identify the triangle by touch with the right hand. Now, however, the left hand has no difficulty picking out the triangle. In other tests, the hemispheres reveal distinct skills, as listed above the drawing.

To summarize further, you could say that the right hemisphere is better at assembling pieces of the world into a coherent picture; it sees overall patterns and general connections. The left brain focuses on small details. (See ▸▸Figure 2.21.) The right brain sees the wide-angle view; the left zooms in on specifics. The focus of the left brain is local, the right is global (Heinze et al., 1998; Huebner, 1998).

Do people normally do puzzles or draw pictures with just the right hemisphere? Do they do other things with only the left? Numerous books have been written about how to use the right brain to manage, teach, draw, ride horses, learn, cook, and even make love (Carter, 1998). But such books drastically oversimplify right-brain and left-brain differences. People normally use both sides of the brain at all times. It's true that some tasks may make more use of one hemisphere or the other. But in most "real world" activities, the hemispheres share the work. Each does the parts it does best and shares information with the other side. Popular books and courses that claim to teach "right-brain thinking" ignore the fact that everyone already uses the right brain for thinking (Clark, Boutros, & Mendez, 2005). To do anything well requires the talents and processing abilities of both hemispheres. A smart brain is one that grasps both the details and the overall picture at the same time. Notice, for instance, that during a concert Yo-Yo Ma will use his left brain to judge time and rhythm and coordinate the order of his hand movements. At the same time, he will use his right brain to recognize and organize melodies.

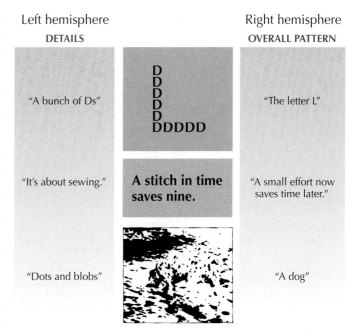

▸▸**FIGURE 2.21** The left and right brain have different information processing styles. The right brain gets the big pattern; the left focuses on small details. (Photograph by R. C. James.)

Lobes of the Cerebral Cortex

In addition to the two big hemispheres, the cerebral cortex can be divided into several smaller *lobes* (areas bordered by major grooves or fissures or defined by their functions). Many of the lobes of the cerebral cortex are defined by larger fissures on the surface of the cerebrum. Others are regarded as separate areas because their functions are quite different. (See ▸▸Fig. 2.22.)

The Occipital Lobes

At the back of the brain, we find the **occipital lobes** (awk-SIP-ih-tal), the primary visual area of the cortex. Patients with tumors (cell growths that interfere with brain activity) in the occipital lobes experience blind spots in their vision.

Do the visual areas of the cortex correspond directly to what is seen? Images are mapped onto the cortex, but the map is greatly stretched and distorted (Carlson, 2005). It is important to avoid thinking of the visual area as being like a little TV screen in the brain. Visual information creates complex patterns of activity in nerve cells; it does *not* make a TV-like image.

The Parietal Lobes

Bodily sensations register in the **parietal lobes** (puh-RYE-ih-tal), located just above the occipital lobes. Touch, temperature, pressure, and other somatic sensations flow into the **somatosensory area** (SO-mat-oh-SEN-so-ree) on the parietal lobes. Again, we find that the map of bodily sensations is distorted. The drawing in ▸▸Figure 2.23 shows that the cortex reflects the *sensitivity* of body areas, not their size. For example, the lips are large in the

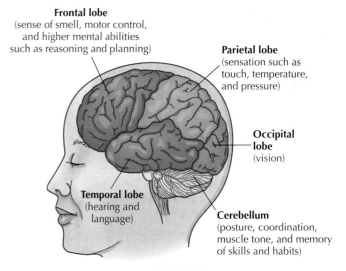

▸▸**FIGURE 2.22**

Occipital lobes Portion of the cerebral cortex where vision registers in the brain.
Parietal lobes Area of the brain where bodily sensations register.
Somatosensory area A receiving area for bodily sensations.

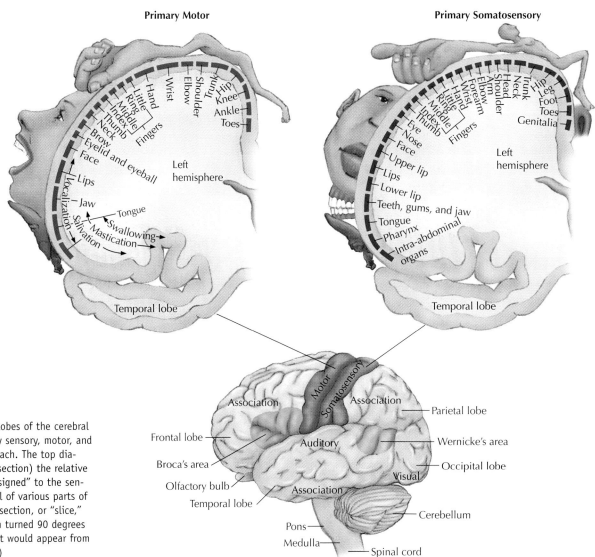

Primary Motor

Primary Somatosensory

⏩**FIGURE 2.23** The lobes of the cerebral cortex and the primary sensory, motor, and association areas on each. The top diagrams show (in cross section) the relative amounts of cortex "assigned" to the sensory and motor control of various parts of the body. (Each cross section, or "slice," of the cortex has been turned 90 degrees so that you see it as it would appear from the back of the brain.)

Temporal lobes Areas that include the sites where hearing registers in the brain.

Frontal lobes A brain area associated with movement, the sense of smell, and higher mental functions.

drawing because of their great sensitivity, while the back and trunk, which are less sensitive, are much smaller. Notice that the hands are also large in the map of body sensitivity—which is obviously an aid to musicians, typists, watchmakers, massage therapists, lovers, and brain surgeons.

The Temporal Lobes

The temporal lobes are located on each side of the brain. Auditory information projects directly to the **temporal lobes,** making them the main site where hearing registers. If we did a PET scan of your brain, and then played your favorite MP3 tune, your temporal lobes would light up. Likewise, if we could stimulate the auditory area of your temporal lobe, you would "hear" a series of sound sensations.

For most people, the left temporal lobe also contains a language "center." (For 5 percent of all people, the area is on the right temporal lobe.) Damage to the temporal lobe can severely limit ability to use language. (More on this later.)

The Frontal Lobes

The **frontal lobes** are associated with higher mental abilities. This area is also responsible for the control of movement. Specifically, an arch of tissue over the top of the brain, called the **motor cortex,** directs the body's muscles. If this area is stimulated with an electrical current, various parts of the body will twitch or move. Like the somatosensory area, the motor cortex corresponds to the importance of bodily areas, not to their size. The hands, for example, get more area than the feet (see ▸▸Fig. 2.23). If you've ever wondered why your hands are more dexterous than your feet, it's partly because more motor cortex is devoted to the hands.

The frontal lobes are also related to more complex behaviors. If the frontal lobes are damaged, a patient's personality and emotional life may change dramatically. (Remember Phineas Gage, the railroad foreman described in Chapter 1?) Reasoning or planning may also be affected (Goel & Dolan, 2004). Patients with frontal lobe damage often get "stuck" on mental tasks and repeat the same wrong answers over and over (Goel & Grafman, 1995). PET scans suggest that much of what we call intelligence is related to increased activity in the frontal areas of the cortex (Duncan et al., 2000). Sadly, drug abuse can damage this important area of the brain (Liu et al., 1998).

Association Areas

Only a small part of the cerebral cortex directly controls the body and receives information from the senses. All the surrounding areas, which are called the **association cortex,** combine and process information from the senses. If you see a rose, the association areas will help you recognize it and name it. The association cortex also contributes to higher mental abilities. For example, a person with damage to association areas on the left hemisphere may suffer an **aphasia** (ah-FAZE-yah: impaired ability to use language).

One type of aphasia is related to **Broca's area** (BRO-cahs), a "speech center" on the left frontal lobe (Ward, 2006). Damage to Broca's area causes great difficulty in speaking or writing. Typically, a patient's grammar and pronunciation are poor and speech is slow and labored. For example, the person may say "bife" for bike, "seep" for sleep, or "zokaid" for zodiac. Generally, the person knows what she or he wants to say but can't seem to utter the words (Geschwind, 1979).

A second language site, called **Wernicke's area** (VER-nick-ees; see ▸▸Fig. 2.23), lies on the left temporal lobe. If it is damaged, the person has problems with the *meaning* of words, not their pronunciation. Someone with Broca's aphasia might say "tssair" when shown a picture of a chair. In contrast, a Wernicke's patient might say "stool" (Ward, 2006).

One of the most fascinating results of brain injury is **agnosia** (ag-KNOW-zyah: an inability to identify seen objects). This condition is sometimes referred to as "mindblindness." For example, if we show Alicia, an agnosia patient, a candle, she will describe it as "a long narrow object that tapers at the top." Alicia can even draw the candle accurately, but she cannot name it. However, if she is allowed to *feel* the candle, she will name it immediately (Farah, 2004). In short, Alicia can still see color, size, and shape. She just can't perceive the meanings of objects.

Are agnosias limited to objects? No. A fascinating form of "mindblindness" is **facial agnosia,** an inability to perceive familiar faces. A patient with facial agnosia won't be able to recognize her family members when they visit him in the hospital or is shown their pictures. However, as soon as family members speak, he will recognize them immediately by their voices.

Areas devoted to recognizing faces lie on the underside of the occipital lobes. These areas appear to have no other function. Why would part of the brain be set aside solely for identifying faces? From an evolutionary standpoint it is not really so surprising. After all, we are social animals, for whom facial recognition is very important. This specialization is just one example of what a marvelous organ of consciousness we possess. But do the brains of different people differ? Could we find specialization from brain to brain? Perhaps. "His and Her Brains?" explains why.

Motor cortex A brain area associated with control of movement.

Association cortex All areas of the cerebral cortex that are not primarily sensory or motor in function.

Aphasia A speech disturbance resulting from brain damage.

Broca's area A language area related to grammar and pronunciation.

Wernicke's area An area related to language comprehension.

Agnosia An inability to identify seen objects.

Facial agnosia An inability to perceive familiar faces.

His and Her Brains?

As you read this book you may be curious about the many ways people can differ from each other. These "Human Diversity" boxes are designed to help you be more reflective about the rich variety of humanity.

Are men's and women's brains specialized? Yes, to some extent. Many physical differences between the brains of men and women have been reported, although the interpretation of these differences remains controversial. In one group of studies, researchers used brain imaging to observe brain activity while people did language tasks. As they worked, both men and women showed increased activity in Broca's area, on the left side of the brain, exactly as expected. Surprisingly, however, both the left *and* the right brain were activated in more than half the women tested (Shaywitz & Gore, 1995; see ▸▸Fig. 2.24). Despite this difference, in one of the studies, the two sexes performed equally well on the task, which involved sounding out words (Shaywitz et al., 1995). The researchers concluded that nature has given the brain different routes to the same ability.

In a study of men and women with similar IQs, brain images revealed major differences in the parts of their brains involved in intelligence (Haier et al., 2004). In general, the men had more gray matter (neuron cell bodies) and the women had more white matter (neuron axons coated in myelin). Further, both the gray and white matter of the women was more concentrated in their frontal lobes than was that of the men. In contrast, the men's gray matter was split between the frontal and parietal lobes and their white matter was concentrated in the temporal lobe. Whatever else these

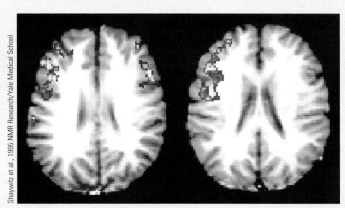

Shaywitz et al., 1995 NMR Research/Yale Medical School

▸▸**FIGURE 2.24** Language tasks activate both sides of the brain in many women but only the left side in men.

differences mean, they show that the human brain can be specialized in different ways to arrive at the same capabilities.

In summary, the bulk of our daily experience and all of our understanding of the world can be traced to the sensory, motor, and association areas of the cortex. The human brain is among the most advanced and sophisticated of the brain-bearing species on earth. This, of course, is no guarantee that this marvelous "biocomputer" will be put to full use. Still, we must stand in awe of the potential it represents.

 Study Break **Cerebral Cortex and Lobes of the Brain**

Reflect

Learning the functions of the brain lobes is like learning areas on a map. Try drawing a map of the cortex. Can you label all of the different "countries" (lobes)? Can you name their functions? Where is the motor cortex? The somatosensory area? Broca's area? Keep redrawing the map until it becomes more detailed and you can do it easily.

Learning Check

See if you can match the following.

1. _____ Corpus callosum
2. _____ Occipital lobes
3. _____ Parietal lobes
4. _____ Temporal lobes
5. _____ Frontal lobes
6. _____ Association cortex
7. _____ Aphasias
8. _____ Corticalization

9. _____ Left hemisphere
10. _____ Right hemisphere
11. _____ "Split brain"

A. Visual area
B. Language, speech, writing
C. Motor cortex and abstract thinking
D. Spatial skills, visualization, pattern recognition
E. Speech disturbances
F. Causes sleep
G. Increased ratio of cortex in brain
H. Bodily sensations
I. Treatment for severe epilepsy
J. Hearing
K. Fibers connecting the cerebral hemispheres
L. Cortex that is not sensory or motor in function

Critical Thinking

12. If you wanted to increase the surface area of the cerebrum so that more cerebral cortex would fit within the skull, how would you do it?
13. What would be some of the possible advantages and disadvantages to having a "split brain"?
14. If your brain were removed, replaced by another, and moved to a new body, which would you consider to be yourself, your old body with the new brain, or your new body with the old brain?

Answers 1. K 2. A 3. H 4. J 5. C 6. L 7. E 8. G 9. B 10. D 11. I 12. One solution would be to gather the surface of the cortex into folds, just as you might if you were trying to fit a large piece of cloth into a small box. This, in fact, is probably why the cortex is more convoluted (folded or wrinkled) in higher animals. 13. If information were properly routed to each brain hemisphere, it would be possible to have both hands working simultaneously on conflicting tasks. However, such possible benefits would apply only under highly controlled conditions. 14. Although there is no "correct" answer to this question, your personality, knowledge, personal memories, and self-concept all derive from brain activity—which makes a strong case for your old brain in a new body being more nearly the "real you."

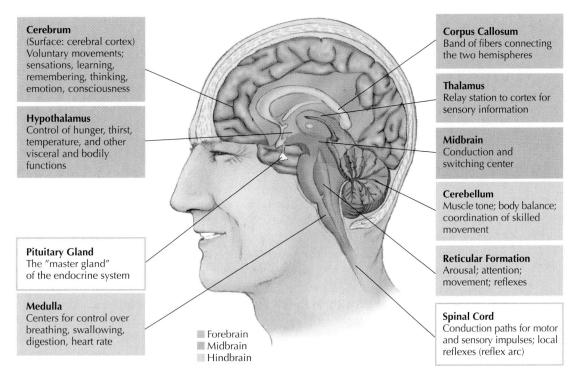

Cerebrum
(Surface: cerebral cortex)
Voluntary movements; sensations, learning, remembering, thinking, emotion, consciousness

Hypothalamus
Control of hunger, thirst, temperature, and other visceral and bodily functions

Pituitary Gland
The "master gland" of the endocrine system

Medulla
Centers for control over breathing, swallowing, digestion, heart rate

Corpus Callosum
Band of fibers connecting the two hemispheres

Thalamus
Relay station to cortex for sensory information

Midbrain
Conduction and switching center

Cerebellum
Muscle tone; body balance; coordination of skilled movement

Reticular Formation
Arousal; attention; movement; reflexes

Spinal Cord
Conduction paths for motor and sensory impulses; local reflexes (reflex arc)

■ Forebrain
■ Midbrain
■ Hindbrain

▸▸**FIGURE 2.25** This simplified drawing shows the main structures of the human brain and describes some of their most important features. (You can use the color code in the foreground to identify which areas are part of the forebrain, midbrain, and hindbrain.)

THE SUBCORTEX—AT THE CORE OF THE (BRAIN) MATTER

>SURVEY QUESTION< *What kinds of behaviors are controlled by the subcortex?*

You could lose large portions of your cerebrum and still survive. Not so with the brain areas below the cortex. Serious damage to the subcortex (lower brain) can be fatal. Hunger, thirst, sleep, attention, sex, breathing, and many other vital functions are localized in parts of the subcortex. (Remember Kate Adamson and locked-in syndrome?) Let's take a quick tour of these brain areas.

The **subcortex** lies immediately below the cerebral hemispheres. This area can be divided into the brainstem (or hindbrain), the midbrain, and the forebrain. (The forebrain also includes the cerebral cortex, which we have already discussed because of its size and importance.) For our purposes the midbrain can be viewed as a link between the forebrain and the brainstem. Therefore, let us focus on the rest of the subcortex (see ▸▸Fig. 2.25).

The Hindbrain

Why are the lower brain areas so important? As the spinal cord joins the brain, it widens into the brainstem. The **brainstem** consists mainly of the medulla (meh-DUL-ah) and the cerebellum (ser-ah-BEL-uhm). The **medulla** contains centers important for the reflex control of vital life functions, including heart rate, breathing, swallowing, and the like. Various drugs, diseases, and injuries can disrupt the medulla and end or endanger life. That's why a karate chop to the back of the neck can be extremely dangerous.

The **pons,** which looks like a small bump on the brainstem, acts as a bridge between the medulla and other brain areas. In addition to connecting with many other locations, including the cerebellum, the pons influences sleep and arousal.

The cerebellum, which looks like a miniature cerebral cortex, lies at the base of the brain. The **cerebellum** primarily regulates posture, muscle tone, and muscular coordination. The

Subcortex All brain structures below the cerebral cortex.

Brainstem The lowest portions of the brain, including the cerebellum, medulla, pons, and reticular formation.

Medulla The structure that connects the brain with the spinal cord and controls vital life functions.

Pons An area on the brainstem that acts as a bridge between the medulla and other structures.

Cerebellum A brain structure that controls posture and coordination.

cerebellum also stores memories related to skills and habits (Christian & Thompson, 2005).

What happens if the cerebellum is injured? Without the cerebellum, tasks like walking, running, or playing catch would be impossible. The first symptoms of a crippling disease called *spinocerebellar degeneration* are tremor, dizziness, and muscular weakness. Eventually, victims have difficulty merely standing, walking, or feeding themselves.

Reticular Formation

A network of fibers and cell bodies called the **reticular** (reh-TICK-you-ler) **formation** (RF) lies inside the medulla and brainstem. As messages flow into the brain, the RF gives priority to some while turning others aside. By doing so, the RF influences *attention.* The RF doesn't fully mature until adolescence, which may be why children have such short attention spans. The RF also modifies outgoing commands to the body. In this way the RF affects muscle tone, posture, and movements of the eyes, face, head, body, and limbs. At the same time, the RF controls reflexes involved in breathing, sneezing, coughing, and vomiting.

Keeping us vigilant, alert, and awake is another important task of the reticular formation. Incoming messages from the sense organs branch into a part of the RF called the **reticular activating system (RAS).** The RAS bombards the cortex with stimulation, keeping it active and alert. For instance, let's say a sleepy driver rounds a bend and sees a deer standing in the road. The driver snaps to attention and applies the brakes. She can thank her RAS for arousing the rest of her brain and averting an accident. If you're getting sleepy while reading this chapter, try pinching your ear—a little pain will cause the RAS to momentarily arouse your cortex.

The Forebrain

Like hidden gemstones, two of the most important parts of your body lie buried deep within your brain. The thalamus (THAL-uh-mus) and an area just below it called the hypothalamus (HI-po-THAL-uh-mus) are key parts of the forebrain (see ▸▸Fig. 2.25).

The **thalamus** acts as a final "switching station" for sensory messages on their way to the cortex. Vision, hearing, taste, and touch all pass through this small, football-shaped structure. Thus, injury to even small areas of the thalamus can cause deafness, blindness, or loss of any other sense, except smell.

The human hypothalamus is about the size of a small grape. Small as it may be, the **hypothalamus** is a kind of master control center for emotion and many basic motives (Carlson, 2005). The hypothalamus affects behaviors as diverse as sex, rage, temperature control, hormone release, eating and drinking, sleep, waking, and emotion. The hypothalamus is basically a "crossroads" that connects many areas of the brain. It is also the final pathway for many kinds of behavior. That is, the hypothalamus is the last place where many behaviors are organized or "decided on" before messages leave the brain, causing the body to react.

The Limbic System

As a group, the hypothalamus, parts of the thalamus, the amygdala, the hippocampus, and other structures make up the limbic system (▸▸Fig. 2.26). The **limbic system** has a major role in producing emotion and motivating behavior. Rage, fear, sexual response, and intense arousal can be obtained from various points in the limbic system. Laughter, a delightful part of human social life, also has its origins in the limbic system (Cardoso, 2000).

During evolution, the limbic system was the earliest layer of the forebrain to develop. In lower animals, the limbic system helps organize basic survival responses: feeding, fleeing, fighting, or reproduction. In humans, a clear link to emotion remains. The **amygdala** (ah-MIG-dah-luh), in particular, is strongly related to fear.

The amygdala provides a primitive, "quick pathway" to the cortex. Like lower animals, we are able to react to dangerous stimuli before we fully know what is going on. In situations

Reticular formation A network within the medulla and brainstem; associated with attention, alertness, and some reflexes.

Reticular activating system (RAS) A part of the reticular formation that activates the cerebral cortex.

Thalamus A brain structure that relays sensory information to the cerebral cortex.

Hypothalamus A small area of the brain that regulates emotional behaviors and motives.

Limbic system A system in the forebrain that is closely linked with emotional response.

Amygdala A part of the limbic system associated with fear responses.

where true danger exists, such as in military combat, the amygdala's rapid response may aid survival. However, disorders of the brain's fear system can be very disruptive. An example is the war veteran who involuntarily dives into the bushes when he hears a car backfire (Fellous & LeDoux, 2005; LaBar & LeDoux, 2002). The role of the amygdala in emotion may also explain why people who suffer from phobias and disabling anxiety often feel afraid without knowing why (LeDoux, 1999).

People who suffer damage to the amygdala become "blind" to emotion. An armed robber could hold a gun to the person's head and the person wouldn't feel fear. Such people are also unable to "read" or understand other people's emotions. Many lose their ability to relate normally to friends, family, and coworkers (Goleman, 1995).

Some parts of the limbic system have taken on additional, higher level functions. A part called the **hippocampus** (HIP-oh-CAMP-us) is important for forming lasting memories (Kumaran & Maguire, 2005). The hippocampus lies inside the temporal lobes, which is why stimulating the temporal lobes can produce memory-like or dream-like experiences. The hippocampus also helps us navigate through space. Your right hippocampus will become more active, for instance, if you mentally plan a drive across town (Maguire et al., 1997).

Psychologists have discovered that animals will learn to press a lever to deliver a rewarding dose of electrical stimulation to the limbic system. The animals act like the stimulation is satisfying or pleasurable. Indeed, several areas of the limbic system act as reward, or "pleasure," pathways. Many are found in the hypothalamus, where they overlap with areas that control thirst, sex, and hunger. Commonly abused drugs such as cocaine, amphetamine, heroin, nicotine, marijuana, and alcohol activate many of the same pleasure pathways. This appears to explain, in part, why these drugs are so powerfully rewarding (Kandel, Schwartz, & Jessell, 2003).

You might also be interested to know that music you would describe as "thrilling," activates pleasure systems in your brain. This may explain some of the appeal of music that can send shivers down your spine (Blood & Zatorre, 2001). (It may also explain why people will pay so much for concert tickets!)

Punishment, or "aversive," areas have also been found in the limbic system. When these locations are activated, animals show discomfort and will work hard to turn off the stimulation. Because much of our behavior is based on seeking pleasure and avoiding pain, these discoveries continue to fascinate psychologists.

The Magnificent Brain

Given the amount of information covered in our journey through the brain, a short review is in order. We have seen that the human brain is an impressive assembly of billions of sensitive cells and nerve fibers. The brain controls vital bodily functions, keeps track of the external world, issues commands to the muscles and glands, responds to current needs, creates the magic of consciousness, and regulates its own behavior—*all* at the same time.

A final note of caution is now in order. For the sake of simplicity we have assigned functions to each "part" of the brain as if it were a computer. This is only a half-truth. In reality, the brain is a vast information-processing system. Incoming information scatters all over the brain and converges again as it goes out through the spinal cord, to muscles and glands. The overall system is much, much more complicated than our discussion of separate "parts" implies. In addition, the brain constantly revises its circuits in response to changing life experiences (Kolb & Whishaw, 2005).

We began our exploration of the brain with a virtuoso musician. Imagine the other extreme of being completely unable to move or speak. Even though you would remain alert

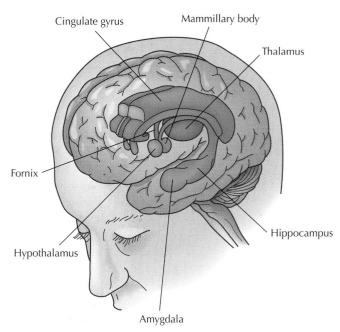

▶▶**FIGURE 2.26** Parts of the limbic system. Although only one side is shown here, the hippocampus and the amygdala extend out into the temporal lobes at each side of the brain. The limbic system is a sort of "primitive core" of the brain strongly associated with emotion.

Rod Planck/Photo Researchers, Inc.

The limbic system is responsible for many of our emotional responses. The amygdala, in particular, produces rapid fear, which can help protect us from danger. If you unexpectedly saw a rattlesnake, it is likely that you would instantly jump back in fear, without having to first think about whether you were in danger.

Hippocampus A part of the limbic system associated with storing memories.

and intelligent, you would be unable to communicate your simplest thoughts and feelings to others. Each year, this is the fate of thousands of people, like Kate Adamson, who are paralyzed by stroke, disease, or injury. In a very real sense, these people become prisoners in their own bodies (Christensen, 1999). What if they could "will" a computer to speak for them?

In pioneering studies, doctors Roy Bakay and Philip Kennedy have inserted special electrodes into the motor cortex of paralyzed patients. When the patient thinks certain thoughts, bursts of activity in the brain are detected by the implanted wires. Instantly, these signals are transmitted to a computer, where they control the movements of a cursor on the screen (Kennedy & Bakay, 1998). More recently, German researchers have developed a brain–computer interface that translates patient's EEG recordings into commands that can be used to control a computer (Hinterberger et al., 2003).

Neuroscientists realize that they have only taken baby steps toward freeing "locked-in" patients. Nevertheless, what was merely science fiction a few years ago is starting to become reality. The human brain is just beginning to understand itself. What an adventure the next decade of brain research will be.

THE ENDOCRINE SYSTEM— HORMONES AND BEHAVIOR

>SURVEY QUESTION< *Does the glandular system affect behavior?*

Our behavior is not solely a product of the nervous system. The endocrine glands (EN-duh-krin) serve as a second great communication system in the body. The **endocrine system** is made up of glands that pour chemicals directly into the bloodstream or lymph system (see ▸Fig. 2.27). These chemicals, called **hormones,** are carried throughout the body, where

Endocrine system Glands whose secretions pass directly into the bloodstream or lymph system.

Hormone A glandular secretion that affects bodily functions or behavior.

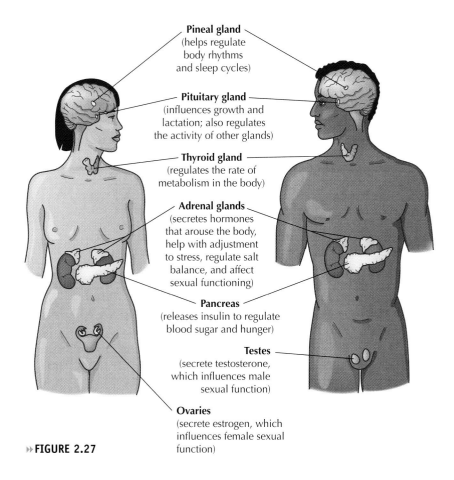

Pineal gland
(helps regulate body rhythms and sleep cycles)

Pituitary gland
(influences growth and lactation; also regulates the activity of other glands)

Thyroid gland
(regulates the rate of metabolism in the body)

Adrenal glands
(secretes hormones that arouse the body, help with adjustment to stress, regulate salt balance, and affect sexual functioning)

Pancreas
(releases insulin to regulate blood sugar and hunger)

Testes
(secrete testosterone, which influences male sexual function)

Ovaries
(secrete estrogen, which influences female sexual function)

▸**FIGURE 2.27**

they affect both internal activities and visible behavior. Hormones are related to neurotransmitters. Like other such chemicals, hormones activate cells in the body. To respond, the cells must have receptor sites for the hormone. Hormones can affect everything from puberty to personality, gigantism to jet lag.

How do hormones affect behavior? Although we are seldom aware of them, hormones affect us in many ways. Here is a brief sample: Hormone output from the adrenal glands rises during stressful situations; androgens ("male" hormones) are related to the sex drive in both males and females; hormones secreted during times of high emotion intensify memory formation; at least some of the emotional turmoil of adolescence is due to elevated hormone levels; different hormones prevail when you are angry, rather than fearful. Something as routine as watching a movie can alter hormone levels. After watching violent scenes from *The Godfather,* men had higher levels of the male hormone testosterone. For both men and women, watching a romantic film boosted a hormone that's linked to relaxation and reproduction (Schultheiss, Wirth, & Stanton, 2004). Because these are just samples, let's consider some additional effects hormones have on the body and behavior.

The pituitary is a pea-sized globe hanging from the base of the brain (return to »Fig. 2.25). One of the pituitary's more important roles is to regulate growth. During childhood, the pituitary secretes a hormone that speeds body development. If too little **growth hormone** is released, a person may remain far smaller than average. If this condition is not treated, a child may be 6 to 12 inches shorter than age-mates. As adults, some will have *hypopituitary dwarfism* (HI-po-pih-TU-ih-ter-ee). Such individuals are perfectly proportioned, but tiny. Regular injections of growth hormone can raise a hypopituitary child's height by several inches, usually to the short side of average.

Too much growth hormone produces *gigantism* (excessive bodily growth). Secretion of too much growth hormone late in the growth period causes *acromegaly* (AK-row-MEG-uh-lee), a condition in which the arms, hands, feet, and facial bones become enlarged. Acromegaly produces prominent facial features, which some people have used as a basis for careers as character actors, wrestlers, and the like.

The pituitary also governs the functioning of other glands (especially the thyroid, adrenal glands, and ovaries or testes). These glands in turn regulate such bodily processes as metabolism, responses to stress, and reproduction. In women, the pituitary controls milk output during pregnancy.

The **pituitary** is often called the "master gland" because it influences other endocrine glands. But the master has a master: The pituitary is directed by the hypothalamus, which lies directly above it. In this way, the hypothalamus can affect glands throughout the body. This, then, is the major link between the brain and hormones (Carlson, 2005).

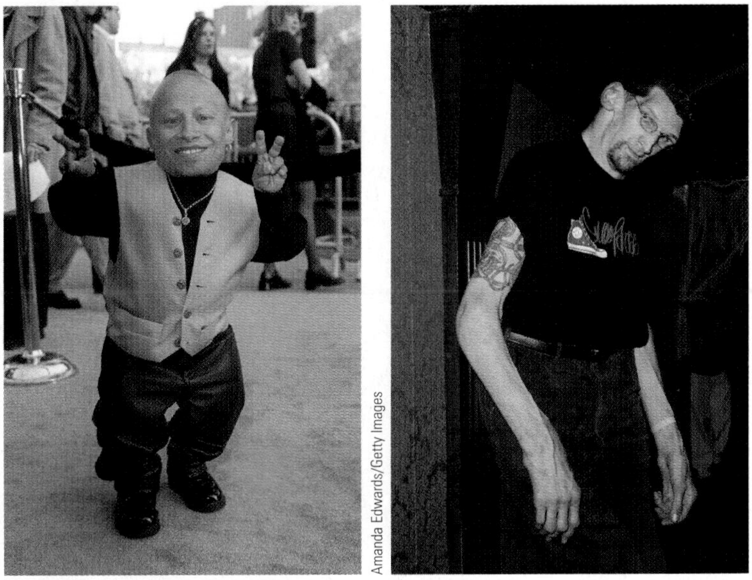

Getty Images

Amanda Edwards/Getty Images

Underactivity of the pituitary gland may produce a dwarf. Verne Troyer, best known for playing Mini-Me in the *Austin Powers* movies, has enjoyed an impressive career as an actor. Overactivity of the pituitary gland may produce a giant. Until his premature death in 2005, actor Matthew McGrory was best know for his role of Karl the Giant in the 2003 movie *Big Fish*.

The pineal gland (pin-EE-ul) was once considered a useless remnant of evolution. However, in humans its function is now coming to light (so to speak). The **pineal gland** releases a hormone called **melatonin** (mel-ah-TONE-in) in response to daily variations in light. Melatonin levels in the bloodstream rise at dusk and peak around midnight. They fall again as morning approaches. This light-driven cycle helps control body rhythms and sleep cycles. As far as the brain is concerned, it's bedtime when melatonin levels rise (Kennaway & Wright, 2002).

The **thyroid gland,** located in the neck, regulates metabolism. As you may remember from a biology course, *metabolism* is the rate at which energy is produced and expended in the body. By altering metabolism, the thyroid can have a sizable effect on personality. A person suffering from *hyperthyroidism* (an overactive thyroid) tends to be thin, tense, excit-

Growth hormone A hormone, secreted by the pituitary gland, that promotes bodily growth.

Pituitary gland The "master gland" whose hormones influence other endocrine glands.

Pineal gland Gland in the brain that helps regulate body rhythms and sleep cycles.

Melatonin Hormone released by the pineal gland in response to daily cycles of light and dark.

Thyroid gland Endocrine gland that helps regulate the rate of metabolism.

able, and nervous. An underactive thyroid (*hypothyroidism*) in an adult can cause inactivity, sleepiness, slowness, and obesity. In infancy, hypothyroidism limits development of the nervous system, leading to severe mental retardation.

When you are frightened or angry, some important reactions prepare your body for action: Your heart rate and blood pressure rise; stored sugar is released into the bloodstream for quick energy; your muscles tense and receive more blood; and your blood is prepared to clot more quickly in case of injury. As we discussed earlier, these changes are controlled by the autonomic nervous system. Specifically, the sympathetic branch of the ANS causes the hormones *epinephrine* and *norepinephrine* to be released by the adrenal glands. (Epinephrine is also known as adrenaline, which may be more familiar to you.) **Epinephrine** (ep-eh-NEF-rin), which is associated with fear, tends to arouse the body. **Norepinephrine** also tends to arouse the body, but it is linked with anger.

The **adrenal glands** are located just under the back of the rib cage, atop the kidneys. The *adrenal medulla*, or inner core of the adrenal glands, is the source of epinephrine and norepinephrine. The *adrenal cortex*, or outer "bark" of the adrenal glands, produces a set of hormones called corticoids (KOR-tih-coids). One of their jobs is to regulate salt balance in the body. A deficiency of certain corticoids can evoke a powerful craving for the taste of salt in humans. The corticoids also help the body adjust to stress, and they are a secondary source of sex hormones.

Brad Mangin/Getty Images

As we write this book, Barry Bonds just passed Babe Ruth on the all-time home run list. Unfortunately, his achievement has been overshadowed by allegations of steroid use. In response, major league baseball has begun to make steroids illegal. Many athletes in other sports have been disqualified, banned from competing, or stripped of medals for steroid use.

An oversecretion of the adrenal sex hormones can cause *virilism* (exaggerated male characteristics). For instance, a woman may grow a beard or a man's voice may become so low it is difficult to understand. Oversecretion early in life can cause *premature puberty* (full sexual development during childhood). One of the most remarkable cases on record is that of a 5-year-old Peruvian girl who gave birth to a son.

While we are on the topic of sex hormones, there is a related issue worth mentioning. One of the principal androgens, or "male" hormones, is testosterone, which is supplied in small amounts by the adrenal glands. (The testes are the main source of testosterone in males.) Perhaps you have heard about the use of anabolic steroids by athletes who want to "bulk up" or promote muscle growth. Most of these drugs are synthetic versions of testosterone.

Although there is some disagreement about whether steroids actually improve athletic performance, it is widely accepted that they may cause serious side effects. Problems include voice deepening or baldness in women and shrinkage of the testicles, sexual impotence, or breast enlargement in men (Millman & Ross, 2003). Dangerous increases in hostility and aggression ("roid rage") have also been linked with steroid use (Hartgens & Kuipers, 2004). Also common when steroids are used by younger adolescents are an increased risk of heart attack and stroke, liver damage, or stunted growth. Understandably, almost all major sports organizations ban the use of anabolic steroids.

In this brief discussion of the endocrine system we have considered only a few of the more important glands. Nevertheless, this should give you an appreciation of how completely behavior and personality are tied to the ebb and flow of hormones in the body.

A Look Ahead

In the upcoming Psychology in Action section, we will return to the brain to see how hand preference relates to brain organization. You'll also find out if being right- or left-handed affects your chances of living to a ripe old age.

Epinephrine An adrenal hormone that tends to arouse the body; epinephrine is associated with fear. (Also known as adrenaline.)

Norepinephrine An adrenal hormone that tends to arouse the body; norepinephrine is associated with anger. (Also known as noradrenaline.)

Adrenal glands Endocrine glands that arouse the body, regulate salt balance, adjust the body to stress, and affect sexual functioning.

Study Break **Subcortex and Endocrine System**

Reflect

If Mr. Medulla met Ms. Cerebellum at a party, what would they say their roles are in the brain? Would a marching band in a "reticular formation" look like a network? Would it get your attention? If you were standing in the final path for behavior leaving the brain, would you be in the thalamus? Or in the hy-**path**-alamus (please forgive the misspelling)? When you are emotional do you wave your limbs around (and does your limbic system become more active)?

Name as many of the endocrine glands as you can. Which did you leave out? Can you summarize the functions of each of the glands?

Learning Check

1. Three major divisions of the brain are the brainstem or
   _____, the _____, and the _____.
2. Reflex centers for heartbeat and respiration are found in the

   a. cerebellum   b. thalamus
   c. medulla   d. RF

3. A portion of the reticular formation, known as the RAS, serves
   as an _____ system in the brain.

   a. activating   b. adrenal
   c. adjustment   d. aversive

4. The _____ is a final relay, or "switching station," for sensory information on its way to the cortex.
5. "Reward" and "punishment" areas are found throughout the _____ system, which is also related to emotion.
6. Undersecretion from the thyroid can cause

   a. dwarfism   b. gigantism
   c. obesity   d. mental retardation

7. The body's ability to resist stress is related to the action of the adrenal _____.

Critical Thinking

8. Subcortical structures in humans are quite similar to corresponding lower brain areas in animals. Why would knowing this allow you to predict, in general terms, what functions are controlled by the subcortex?
9. Where in all the brain's "hardware" do you think the mind is found? What is the relationship between mind and brain?

Answers

1. hindbrain, midbrain, forebrain 2. c 3. a 4. thalamus 5. limbic 6. c, d (in infancy) 7. cortex 8. Because the subcortex must be related to basic functions common to all higher animals: motives, emotions, sleep, attention, and vegetative functions, such as heartbeat, breathing, and temperature regulation. The subcortex also routes and processes incoming information from the senses and outgoing commands to the muscles. 9. This question, known as the mind-body problem, has challenged thinkers for centuries. One recent view is that mental states are "emergent properties" of brain activity. That is, brain activity forms complex patterns that are, in a sense, more than the sum of their parts. Or, to use a rough analogy, if the brain were a musical instrument, then mental life would be like music played on that instrument.

Psychology in Action

Handedness—If Your Brain Is Right, What's Left?

>**SURVEY QUESTION**< *In what ways do right- and left-handed individuals differ?*

Around the world, left-handedness has long been considered to be negative. The Latin word for "left" is actually *sinister!* "Lefties" have often been characterized as clumsy, awkward, unlucky, or insincere. In contrast, right-handedness is the paragon of virtue. The Latin word for "right" is *dexter,* and "righties" are more likely to be referred to as dexterous, coordinated, skillful, and even just. But is there any basis in fact for these attitudes?

What causes **handedness** (a preference for the right or left hand)? Why are there more right-handed than left-handed people? How do left-handed and right-handed people differ? Does being left-handed create any problems—or benefits? The answers to these questions lead us back to the brain, where handedness begins. Let's see what research has revealed about handedness, the brain, and you.

Hand Dominance Take a moment and write your name on a sheet of paper, first using your right hand and then your left. You were probably much more comfortable writing with your dominant hand. This is interesting because there's no real difference in the strength or dexterity of the hands themselves. The agility of your dominant hand is an outward expression of superior motor control on one side of the brain. If you are right-handed, there is literally more area on the left side of your brain devoted to controlling your right hand. If you are left-handed, the reverse applies (Annett, 2002).

Handedness A preference for the right or left hand in most activities.

The preceding exercise implies that you are either entirely right- or left-handed. But handedness is a matter of degree. To better assess your handedness, complete the following questions adapted from the Waterloo Handedness Questionnaire (Brown et al., 2006) by circling an answer for each of the questions. The more "Rights" you circle, the more right-handed you are.

Are You Right- or Left-Handed?

1. Which hand would you use to spin a top?	Right	Left	Either
2. With which hand would you hold a paintbrush to paint a wall?	Right	Left	Either
3. Which hand would you use to pick up a book?	Right	Left	Either
4. With which hand would you use a spoon to eat soup?	Right	Left	Either
5. Which hand would you use to flip pancakes?	Right	Left	Either
6. Which hand would you use to pick up a piece of paper?	Right	Left	Either
7. Which hand would you use to draw a picture?	Right	Left	Either
8. Which hand would you use to insert and turn a key in a lock?	Right	Left	Either
9. Which hand would you use to insert a plug into an electrical outlet?	Right	Left	Either
10. Which hand would you use to throw a ball?	Right	Left	Either
11. In which hand would you hold a needle while sewing?	Right	Left	Either
12. Which hand would you use to turn on a light switch?	Right	Left	Either
13. With which hand would you use the eraser at the end of a pencil?	Right	Left	Either
14. Which hand would you use to saw a piece of wood with a hand saw?	Right	Left	Either
15. Which hand would you use to open a drawer?	Right	Left	Either
16. Which hand would you turn a doorknob with?	Right	Left	Either
17. Which hand would you use to hammer a nail?	Right	Left	Either
18. With which hand would you use a pair of tweezers?	Right	Left	Either
19. Which hand do you use for writing?	Right	Left	Either
20. Which hand would you turn the dial of a combination lock with?	Right	Left	Either

Most people (about 75 percent) are strongly right- or left-handed. The rest show some inconsistency in hand preference. As you can see in the following list, such differences can affect performance in some sports (Coren, 1992).

Sport	Handedness Advantage
Boxing	Left
Fencing	Left
Basketball	Mixed and ambidextrous
Ice hockey	Mixed and ambidextrous
Field hockey	Mixed and ambidextrous
Squash	Strong left or strong right
Badminton	Strong left or strong right

By the way, chalk up one more for the left-handers, who have also done well in professional tennis (Holtzen, 2000). Away from sports, though, left-handedness has an undeserved bad reputation. The supposed clumsiness of lefties is merely a result of living in a right-handed world: If it can be gripped, turned, or pulled, it's probably designed for the right hand. Even toilet handles are on the right side.

If a person is strongly left-handed does that mean the right hemisphere is dominant? Not necessarily. It's true that the right hemisphere controls the left hand, but a left-handed per-

Left-handers have an advantage in sports such as fencing, boxing, and tennis. Most likely, their movements are less familiar to opponents, who usually face right-handers (Coren, 1992).

Bob Daemmrich/The Image Works

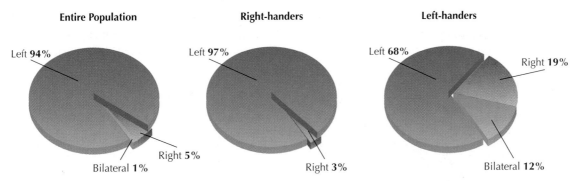

Entire Population

Left **94%**

Bilateral **1%**

Right **5%**

Right-handers

Left **97%**

Right **3%**

Left-handers

Left **68%**

Right **19%**

Bilateral **12%**

▸▸**FIGURE 2.28** Language is controlled by the left side of the brain in the majority of right- and left-handers.

son's language-producing, **dominant hemisphere** may be on the opposite side of the brain.

Brain Dominance   About 97 percent of right-handers process speech in the left hemisphere and are left-brain dominant (▸▸Fig. 2.28). A good 68 percent of left-handers produce speech from the left hemisphere, just as right-handed people do. About 19 percent of all lefties and 3 percent of righties use their right brain for language. Some left-handers (approximately 12 percent) use both sides of the brain for language processing. All totaled, 94 percent of the population uses the left brain for language (Coren, 1992).

Is there any way for a person to tell which of his or her hemispheres is dominant? One interesting clue is based on the way you write. Right-handed individuals who write with a straight hand, and lefties who write with a hooked hand, are usually left-brain dominant for language. Left-handed people who write with their hand below the line, and righties who use a hooked position, are usually right-brain dominant (Levy & Reid, 1976). Another hint is provided by the hand gestures. If you gesture mostly with your right hand as you talk, you probably process language in your left hemisphere. Gesturing with your left hand is associated with right-brain language processing (Hellige, 1993). Are your friends right brained or left brained? (See ▸▸Figure 2.29.)

Before you leap to any conclusions, be aware that writing position is not foolproof. The only sure way to check brain dominance is to do a medical test that involves briefly anesthetizing one cerebral hemisphere at a time (Springer & Deutsch, 1998).

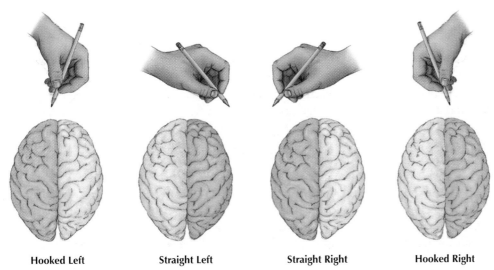

Hooked Left   **Straight Left**   **Straight Right**   **Hooked Right**

▸▸**FIGURE 2.29** Research suggests that the hand position used in writing may indicate which brain hemisphere is used for language. (Redrawn from an illustration by M. E. Challinor.)

Dominant hemisphere A term usually applied to the side of a person's brain that produces language.

Handedness How common is left-handedness, and what causes it? Ninety percent of all humans are right-handed; 10 percent are left-handed. In the past, many left-handed children were forced to use their right hand for writing, eating, and other skills. But clear hand preferences are apparent even before birth, as can be seen in a fetal ultrasound image (»Fig. 2.30). Further, British psychologist Peter Hepper has shown that prenatal handedness preferences persist for at least 10 years after birth (Hepper, McCartney, & Shannon, 1998; Hepper, Wells, & Lynch, 2005). This suggests that handedness cannot be dictated. Parents should never try to force a left-handed child to use the right hand. To do so may create speech or reading problems.

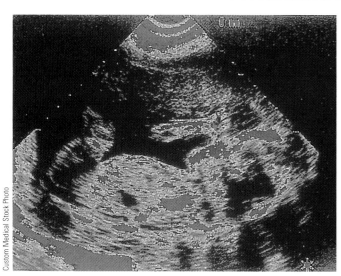

»**FIGURE 2.30** In this ultrasound image, a 4-month-old fetus sucks her right thumb. Research by British psychologist Peter Hepper suggests that she will continue to prefer her right hand long after she is born and that she will be right-handed as an adult.

Is handedness inherited from parents? Studies of twins show that hand preferences are not directly inherited like eye color or skin color (Ooki, 2005; Reiss et al., 1999). Yet, two left-handed parents are more likely to have a left-handed child than two right-handed parents are (McKeever, 2000). This suggests that handedness is influenced by heredity, at least to a degree. The best evidence to date shows that handedness is influenced by a single gene on the X (female) chromosome (Jones & Martin, 2001). However, learning, birth traumas, and social pressure to use the right hand may also affect which hand you end up favoring (Bailey & McKeever, 2004; McKeever et al., 2000).

Are there any drawbacks to being left-handed? A minority of lefties owe their hand preference to birth traumas (such as prematurity, low birth weight, and breech birth). These individuals have a higher incidence of allergies, learning disorders, and other problems (Betancur et al., 1990). But in most instances, left-handedness is unrelated to intelligence or the overall rate of illness and accidental injury (Porac et al., 1998). However, people with inconsistent handedness (as opposed to consistent left-handers) may be at risk for more immune-related diseases (Bryden, Bruyn, & Fletcher, 2005).

Then why do right-handed people seem to live longer than left-handed people? It is true that there is a shortage of very old lefties. However, this does not mean that the left-handed die early. It just reflects the fact that, in the past, more left-handed children were forced to become right-handed. That makes it look like many lefties don't survive to old age. In reality, they do, but many of them are masquerading as righties (Martin & Freitas, 2002)!

Advantage Left Throughout history a notable number of artists have been lefties, from Leonardo da Vinci and Michelangelo to Pablo Picasso and M. C. Escher. Conceivably, because the right hemisphere is superior at imagery and visual abilities, there is some advantage to using the left hand for drawing or painting (Springer & Deutsch, 1998). At the least, lefties are definitely better at visualizing three-dimensional objects. This may be why there are more left-handed architects, artists, and chess players than would be expected (Coren, 1992).

Lateralization refers to specialization in the abilities of the brain hemispheres. One striking feature of lefties is that they are generally less lateralized than the right-handed. In fact, even the physical size and shape of their cerebral hemispheres are more alike. If you are a lefty you can take pride in the fact that your brain is less lopsided than most! In general, left-handers are more symmetrical on almost everything, including eye dominance, fingerprints—even foot size (Polemikos & Papaeliou, 2000).

In some situations less lateralization may be a real advantage. For instance, individuals who are moderately left-handed or ambidextrous seem to have better than average pitch memory, which is a basic musical skill. Correspondingly, more musicians are ambidextrous than would normally be expected (Springer & Deutsch, 1998).

Math abilities may also benefit from fuller use of the right hemisphere. Students who are extremely gifted in math are much more likely to be left-handed or ambidextrous (Benbow,

Lateralization Differences between the two sides of the body; especially, differences in the abilities of the brain hemispheres.

1986). Even where ordinary arithmetic skills are concerned, lefties seem to excel (Annett, 2002; Annett & Manning, 1990).

The clearest advantage of being left-handed shows up when there is a brain injury. Because of their milder lateralization, left-handed individuals typically experience less language loss after damage to either brain hemisphere, and they recover more easily (Geschwind, 1979). Maybe having "two left feet" isn't so bad after all.

 Study Break **Handedness and Brain Lateralization**

Reflect

Think for a moment about what you "knew" about handedness and left-handed people before you read this section. Which of your beliefs were correct? How has your knowledge about handedness changed?

Learning Check

1. About 97 percent of left-handed people process language on the left side of the brain, the same as right-handed people do. T or F?
2. Left-handed individuals who write with their hand below the line are likely to be right-brain dominant. T or F?

3. People basically learn to be right- or left-handed. T or F?
4. In general, left-handed individuals show less lateralization in the brain and throughout the body. T or F?

Critical Thinking

5. News reports that left-handed people tend to die younger have been flawed in an important way: The average age of people in the left-handed group was younger than that of subjects in the right-handed group. Why would this make a difference in the conclusions drawn?

Answers

1. F 2. T 3. F 4. T 5. Because we can't tell if handedness or average age accounts for the difference in death rates. For example, if we start with a group of 20- to 30-year-old people, in which some die, the average age of death has to be between 20 and 30. If we start with a group of 30- to 40-year-old people, in which some die, the average age of death has to be between 30 and 40. Thus, the left-handed group might have an earlier average age at death simply because members of the group were younger to start with.

CHAPTER IN REVIEW

Major Points

- Biopsychologists study how processes in the body, brain, and nervous system relate to behavior.
- Ultimately, all behavior can be traced to the activity of nerve cells.
- To map the brain, researchers activate or disable specific areas and observe changes in behavior.
- Bioelectrical recordings and computer-generated images of brain activity provide further insights into the structure and function of the brain.
- Sensations, thoughts, feelings, motives, actions, memories, and all other human capacities are associated with brain activities and structures.
- Endocrine glands serve as a chemical communication system within the body. Behavior is greatly influenced by the ebb and flow of hormones in the bloodstream.
- Brain dominance and brain activity determine if you are right-handed, left-handed, or ambidextrous.

Summary

How do nerve cells operate and communicate?

- The nervous system is made up of linked neurons that pass information from one to another through synapses.
- The basic conducting fibers of neurons are axons, but dendrites, the soma, and axon terminals are also involved in communication.
- The firing of an action potential (nerve impulse) is basically electrical. Communication between neurons is chemical.
- Neurotransmitters cross the synapse, attach to receptor sites, and excite or inhibit the receiving cell.
- By combining information, neurons act as simple computers, which become very powerful when they operate together as neural networks.
- Chemicals called neuropeptides appear to regulate activity in the brain.

- Nerves are made of axons and associated tissues. Neurons and nerves in the peripheral nervous system can often regenerate. At present, damage in the central nervous system is usually permanent, although scientists are working on ways to repair damaged neural tissue.

What are the functions of the major parts of the nervous system?

- The nervous system can be divided into the central nervous system and the peripheral nervous system, which includes the somatic (bodily) and autonomic (involuntary) nervous systems.
- The autonomic system has a sympathetic branch and a parasympathetic branch.

How do we know how the brain works?

- Brain structure is investigated though dissection and less intrusive CT scans and MRI scans.
- Brain function is investigated through clinical case studies, electrical stimulation, ablation, deep lesioning, electrical recording, and microelectrode recording, as well as less intrusive EEG recording, PET scans, and fMRI scans.

How is the brain organized, and what do its higher structures do?

- The human brain is marked by advanced corticalization, or enlargement of the cerebral cortex.
- The left cerebral hemisphere contains speech or language "centers" in most people. It also specializes in writing, calculating, judging time and rhythm, and ordering complex movements.
- The right hemisphere is largely nonverbal. It excels at spatial and perceptual skills, visualization, and recognition of patterns, faces, and melodies.
- "Split brains" have been created in animals and humans by cutting the corpus callosum. The split-brain individual shows a remarkable degree of independence between the right and left hemispheres.
- The most basic functions of the lobes of the cerebral cortex are as follows: occipital lobes—vision; parietal lobes—bodily sensation; temporal lobes—hearing and language; frontal lobes—motor control, speech, and abstract thought. Damage to any of these areas will impair the named functions.
- Association areas on the cortex are neither sensory nor motor in function. They are related to more complex skills such as language, memory, recognition, and problem solving.
- Damage to either Broca's area or Wernicke's area causes speech and language problems known as aphasias.

What kinds of behaviors are controlled by the subcortex?

- The brain can be subdivided into the forebrain, midbrain, and hindbrain. The subcortex includes several crucial brain structures found at all three levels, below the cortex.
- The medulla contains centers essential for reflex control of heart rate, breathing, and other "vegetative" functions.
- The cerebellum maintains coordination, posture, and muscle tone.
- The reticular formation directs sensory and motor messages, and part of it, known as the RAS, acts as an activating system for the cerebral cortex.
- The thalamus carries sensory information to the cortex. The hypothalamus exerts powerful control over eating, drinking, sleep cycles, body temperature, and other basic motives and behaviors.
- The limbic system is strongly related to emotion. It also contains distinct reward and punishment areas and an area known as the hippocampus that is important for forming memories.

Does the glandular system affect behavior?

- The endocrine system provides chemical communication in the body by releasing hormones into the bloodstream. Endocrine glands influence moods, behavior, and personality.
- Many of the endocrine glands are influenced by the pituitary (the "master gland"), which is in turn influenced by the hypothalamus. Thus, the brain controls the body through the fast nervous system and the slower endocrine system.

In what ways do right- and left-handed individuals differ?

- Hand dominance ranges from strongly left- to strongly right-handed, with mixed handedness and ambidexterity in between. Ninety percent of the population is basically right-handed, 10 percent left-handed.
- The vast majority of people are right-handed and therefore left-brain dominant for motor skills. Ninety-seven percent of right-handed persons and 68 percent of the left-handed also produce speech from the left hemisphere.
- In general, the left-handed are less strongly lateralized in brain function than are right-handed persons.

Interactive Learning

Internet addresses frequently change. To find the sites listed here, visit www.thomsonedu.com/psychology/coon for an updated list of Internet addresses and direct links to relevant sites.

Psychology: A Journey Companion Website   Find online quizzes, flash cards, animations, video clips, experiments, interactive assessments, and other helpful study aids for this text at www.thomsonedu.com/psychology/coon.

Brain Briefings   Articles on a variety of topics in neuroscience.

Brain Connection   Explains brain research to the public, including common myths about the brain, the effects of various chemicals, how brain research applies to education, and more.

Lorin's Left-handedness Site   Answers to common questions about left-handedness.

Probe the Brain   Explore the motor homunculus of the brain interactively.

The Brain Quiz   Answer questions about the brain and get instant feedback.

The Brain: A Work in Progress   A set of related articles about the brain.

The Human Brain: Dissections of the Real Brain   Detailed photographs and drawings of the human brain.

The Endocrine System   Describes the endocrine system and hormones.

ThomsonNOW   Go to www.thomsonedu.com/login to link to ThomsonNOW, your online study tool. First take the **Pre-Test** for this chapter to get your **Personalized Study Plan**, which will identify topics you need to review and direct you to online resources. Then take the **Post-Test** to determine what concepts you have mastered and what you still need work on.

TEST YOUR KNOWLEDGE

Brain and Behavior

For additional review, get more practice with *ThomsonNOW*, *WebTutor*, the *Practice Quizzes*, and/or the printed *Study Guide* available with this book.

1. The point at which information is passed from one neuron to another links the
   a. neurilemma and myelin
   b. soma and ion channels
   c. axon terminals and dendrites
   d. enkephalin and myelin

2. The activity of neurons is regulated by _____, which affect memory, pain, moods, hunger, and other processes.
   a. neuropeptides
   b. neurilemmas
   c. resting potentials
   d. dendrites

3. Muscles are activated by a transmitter substance called
   a. neuropeptide
   b. acetylcholine
   c. enkephalin
   d. endorphin

4. The brain grows new neurons to replace those that are lost. This process is known as
   a. neurogenesis
   b. neuileminal regeneration
   c. autonomic regeneration
   d. neuropeptosis

5. Nerves are made up of bundles of dendrites and
   a. action potentials
   b. neurotransmitters
   c. synapses
   d. axons

6. The somatic nervous system is part of the
   a. PNS
   b. ANS
   c. sympathetic branch
   d. axon terminal

7. Quieting the body and returning it to a lower level of arousal after an emotional event is a specialty of the
   a. parasympathetic system
   b. peripheral nervous system
   c. spinal nerves
   d. effector cells

8. To record the electrical activity of a single neuron, you would need to use
   a. an EEG
   b. ESB
   c. a microelectrode
   d. surface ablation

9. Which research technique provides an image of ongoing brain activity?
   a. ESB
   b. deep lesioning
   c. PET
   d. surface ablation

10. Among animals and humans, greater corticalization is associated with increased
    a. muscular coordination
    b. intelligence
    c. fight-or-fight responses
    d. conduction speed in the axon

11. The left hemisphere of the brain processes information sequentially, and it is superior at
    a. recognizing patterns
    b. holistic thinking
    c. expressing and detecting emotions
    d. analysis

12. In a "split-brain" operation, the _____ is cut, thereby separating the two cerebral _____.
    a. corpus callosum, hemispheres
    b. chiasm, medullas
    c. motor cortex, lobes
    d. occipital region, reticulums

13. Impaired hearing could result from damage to the _____ lobes of the brain.
    a. frontal
    b. temporal
    c. occipital
    d. parietal

14. Damage to Broca's area causes
    a. a loss of coordination
    b. disturbed sleep patterns
    c. aphasia
    d. an inability to remember recent events

15. Structures in the brain that play a major role in producing emotion and motivating behavior are called the
    a. thalamic branch of the RAS
    b. cerebellar activating system
    c. medial brainstem
    d. limbic system

16. Which of the following parts of the brain is most involved in forming lasting memories?
    a. amygdala
    b. hippocampus
    c. thalamus
    d. hypothalamus

17. The endocrine gland that most influences the activities of other glands is the
    a. pituitary
    b. adrenal
    c. pineal
    d. thyroid

18. Dwarfism and gigantism can be caused by problems in the
    a. pituitary gland
    b. adrenal glands
    c. pineal gland
    d. thyroid gland

19. A majority of both right-handed and left-handed people produce speech from the
    a. right brain hemisphere
    b. corpus callosum
    c. left brain hemisphere
    d. hippocampus

20. One consistent finding about left-handed people is that they are
    a. less lateralized
    b. more likely to die at an early age
    c. unable to use the right brain to produce language
    d. usually also ambidextrous

ANSWERS 1. c 2. a 3. b 4. a 5. d 6. a 7. a 8. c 9. c 10. b 11. d 12. a 13. b 14. c 15. d 16. b 17. a 18. a 19. c 20. a

Human Development

JOURNEY INTO PSYCHOLOGY: A STAR IS BORN—HERE'S AMY!

Olivia has just given birth to her first child, Amy. Frankly, at the moment Amy looks something like a pink prune, with pudgy arms, stubby legs, and lots of wrinkles. She also has the face of an angel—at least in her parents' eyes. As Olivia and her husband Tom look at Amy they wonder, "How will her life unfold? What kind of a person will she be?"

What if we could skip ahead through Amy's life and observe her at various ages? What could we learn? Seeing the world through her eyes would be fascinating and instructive. For example, a child's viewpoint can make us more aware of things we take for granted. Younger children, in particular, are very literal in their use of language. When she was 3, Amy thought her bath was too hot and said to Tom, "Make it warmer, daddy." At first, Tom was confused. The bath was already fairly hot. But then he realized that what she really meant was, "Bring the water closer to the temperature we call *warm*." It makes perfect sense if you look at it that way.

Today we can merely guess about Amy's future. However, developmental psychologists have studied many thousands of children, adolescents, and adults. Their findings tell a fascinating story about human growth and development. Let's let Olivia, Tom, and Amy represent parents and children everywhere, as we see what psychology can tell us about the challenges of growing up. Tracing Amy's development might even help you answer two very important questions, How did I become the person I am today? and Who will I become tomorrow?

Blend Images/jupiterimages

- How do heredity and environment affect development?
- What can newborn babies do?
- What influence does maturation have on early development?
- Of what significance is a child's emotional bond with parents?
- How important are parenting styles?
- How do children acquire language?
- How do children learn to think?
- How do we develop morals and values?
- What are the typical tasks and dilemmas through the life span?
- How do effective parents discipline and communicate with their children?

HEREDITY AND ENVIRONMENT— IT TAKES TWO TO TANGO

>SURVEY QUESTION< *How do heredity and environment affect development?*

When we think of development we naturally think of children "growing up" into adults. But even as adults we never really stop growing. **Developmental psychology,** the study of progressive changes in behavior and abilities, involves every stage of life from conception to death (or "the womb to the tomb"). Heredity and environment also affect us throughout life. Some events, such as when Amy achieves sexual maturity, are mostly governed by heredity. Others, such as when Amy learns to swim, read, or drive a car, are primarily a matter of environment.

But which is more important, heredity or environment? Actually, neither. Biopsychologist D. O. Hebb (1904–1985) once offered a useful analogy: To define the area of a rectangle, what is more important, height or width? Of course, both dimensions are absolutely essential. If either is reduced to zero, there is no rectangle. Similarly, if Amy grows up to become an attractive, popular, intelligent girl and is elected the valedictorian of her senior high school class, her success will be due to both heredity and environment.

While heredity gives each of us a variety of potentials and limitations, these are, in turn, affected by environmental influences, such as learning, nutrition, disease, and culture. Thus, the person you are today reflects a constant *interaction,* or interplay, between the forces of nature and nurture (Gopnik, Meltzoff, & Kuhl, 2000). Let's look in more detail at this dance between heredity and environment.

Heredity

Heredity ("nature") refers to the genetic transmission of physical and psychological characteristics from parents to their children. An incredible number of personal features are set at conception, when a sperm and an ovum (egg) unite.

How does heredity operate? The nucleus of every human cell contains **DNA,** deoxyribonucleic acid (dee-OX-see-RYE-bo-new-KLEE-ik). DNA is a long, ladder-like chain of pairs of chemical molecules (▸Fig. 3.1). The order of these molecules, or organic bases, acts as a code for genetic information. The DNA in each cell contains a record of all the instructions needed to make a human—with room left over to spare. A major scientific milestone was reached with the completion in 2003 of the Human Genome Project, a project of the U.S. government to completely determine the sequence of all 3 billion chemical base pairs in human DNA (U.S. Department of Energy Office of Science, 2005).

Developmental psychology The study of progressive changes in behavior and abilities from conception to death.

Heredity ("nature") The transmission of physical and psychological characteristics from parents to offspring through genes.

DNA Deoxyribonucleic acid, a molecular structure that contains coded genetic information.

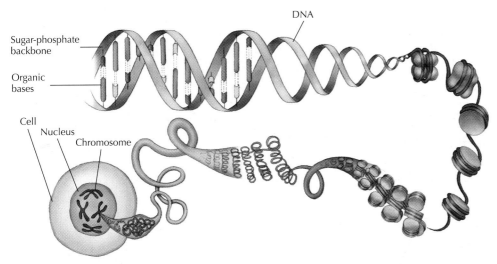

DNA

Sugar-phosphate backbone

Organic bases

Cell
Nucleus
Chromosome

▸▸**FIGURE 3.1** *(Top left)* Linked molecules (organic bases) make up the "rungs" on DNA's twisted "molecular ladder." The order of these molecules serves as a code for genetic information. The code provides a genetic blueprint that is unique for each individual (except identical twins). The drawing shows only a small section of a DNA strand. An entire strand of DNA is composed of billions of smaller molecules. *(Bottom left)* The nucleus of each cell in the body contains chromosomes made up of tightly wound coils of DNA. (Don't be misled by the drawing: Chromosomes are microscopic in size and the chemical molecules that make up DNA are even smaller.)

Human DNA is organized into 46 **chromosomes.** (The word chromosome means "colored body.") These thread-like structures hold the coded instructions of heredity (▸▸Fig. 3.2). A notable exception is sperm cells and ova, which contain only 23 chromosomes. Thus, Amy received 23 chromosomes from Olivia and 23 from Tom. This is her genetic heritage.

Genes are small areas of DNA that affect a particular process or personal characteristic. Sometimes, a single gene is responsible for an inherited feature, such as Amy's eye color. Most characteristics, however, are **polygenic** (pol-ih-JEN-ik), or controlled by many genes working in combination.

Genes may be dominant or recessive. When a gene is **dominant,** the feature it controls will appear every time the gene is present. When a gene is **recessive,** it must be paired with a second recessive gene before its effect will be expressed. For example, if Amy got a blue-eye gene from Tom and a brown-eye gene from Olivia, Amy will be brown-eyed, because brown-eye genes are dominant.

If brown-eye genes are dominant, why do two brown-eyed parents sometimes have a blue-eyed child? If one or both parents have two brown-eye genes, the couple's children can only be brown-eyed. But what if each parent has one brown-eye gene and one blue-eye gene? In that case, both parents would have brown eyes. Yet, there is 1 chance

Twins who share identical genes (identical twins) demonstrate the powerful influence of heredity. Even when they are reared apart, identical twins are strikingly alike in motor skills, physical development, and appearance. At the same time, twins are less alike as adults than they were as children, which shows environmental influences are at work (Larsson, Larsson, & Lichtenstein, 2004).

Myrleen Ferguson Cate/PhotoEdit

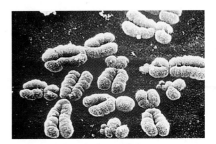

▸▸**FIGURE 3.2** This image, made with a scanning electron microscope, shows several pairs of human chromosomes. (Colors are artificial.) (Biophoto Associates/Science-Source/Photo Researchers, Inc.)

Chromosomes Thread-like "colored bodies" in the nucleus of each cell that are made up of DNA.

Genes Specific areas on a strand of DNA that carry hereditary information.

Polygenic characteristics Personal traits or physical properties that are influenced by many genes working in combination.

Dominant gene A gene whose influence will be expressed each time the gene is present.

Recessive gene A gene whose influence will be expressed only when it is paired with a second recessive gene.

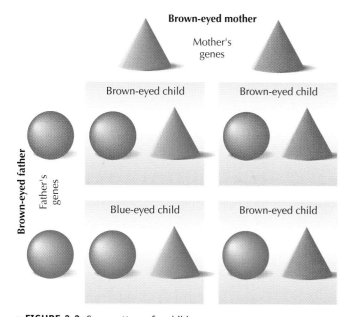

Brown-eyed mother

Mother's genes

Brown-eyed father

Father's genes

Brown-eyed child

Brown-eyed child

Blue-eyed child

Brown-eyed child

▸▸**FIGURE 3.3** Gene patterns for children of brown-eyed parents, where each parent has one brown-eye gene and one blue-eye gene. Because the brown-eye gene is dominant, 1 child in 4 will be blue-eyed. Thus, there is a significant chance that two brown-eyed parents will have a blue-eyed child.

in 4 that their children will get two blue-eye genes and have blue eyes (▸▸Fig. 3.3).

Heredity exerts a powerful influence on the *human growth sequence,* or overall pattern of physical development (see ▪ Table 3.1). Heredity also determines eye color, skin color, and susceptibility to some diseases. To a degree, genetic instructions affect body size and shape, height, intelligence, athletic potential, personality traits, sexual orientation, and a host of other details (Cummings, 2006).

Temperament

How soon do hereditary differences appear? Some appear right away. For instance, newborn babies differ noticeably in **temperament.** This is the physical core of personality. It includes sensitivity, irritability, distractibility, and typical mood (Kagan, 2004). About 40 percent of all newborns are *easy children* who are relaxed and agreeable. Ten percent are *difficult children* who are moody, intense, and easily angered. *Slow-to-warm-up children* (about 15 percent) are restrained, unexpressive, or shy. The remaining children do not fit neatly into a single category (Chess & Thomas, 1986).

▪ **Table 3.1   Human Growth Sequence**

Period	Duration	Descriptive Name
Prenatal Period	From conception to birth	
Germinal period	First 2 weeks after conception	Zygote
Embryonic period	2–8 weeks after conception	Embryo
Fetal period	From 8 weeks after conception to birth	Fetus
Neonatal Period	From birth to a few weeks after birth	Neonate
Infancy	From a few weeks after birth until child is walking securely; some children walk securely at less than a year, while others may not be able to until age 17–18 months	Infant
Early Childhood	From about 15–18 months until about 2–2½ years	Toddler
	From age 2–3 to about age 6	Preschool child
Middle Childhood	From about age 6 to age 12	School-age child
Pubescence	Period of about 2 years before puberty	
Puberty	Point of development at which biological changes of pubescence reach a climax marked by sexual maturity	
Adolescence	From the beginning of pubescence until full social maturity is reached (difficult to fix duration of this period)	Adolescent
Adulthood Young adulthood (19–25) Adulthood (26–40) Maturity (41 plus)	From adolescence to death; sometimes subdivided into other periods as shown at left	Adult
Senescence	No defined limit that would apply to all people; extremely variable; characterized by marked physiological and psychological deterioration	Adult (senile), "old age"

*Note: There is no exact beginning or ending point for various growth periods. The ages are approximate, and each period may be thought of as blending into the next. (Table courtesy of Tom Bond.)

Temperament The physical core of personality, including emotional and perceptual sensitivity, energy levels, typical mood, and so forth.

Imagine that we start with some infants who are very shy and some who are very bold. By the time they are 4 to 5 years old, most of these children will be only moderately shy or bold. This suggests that inherited temperaments are modified by learning (Kagan, 2005). In other words, nurture also immediately enters the picture.

Environment

Environment ("nurture") refers to the sum of all external conditions that affect a person. The environments in which a child grows up can have a powerful impact on development. Humans today are genetically very similar to cave dwellers who lived 30,000 years ago. Nevertheless, a bright baby born today could learn to become almost anything—a ballet dancer, an engineer, a gangsta rapper, or a biochemist who likes to paint in watercolors. But an Upper Paleolithic baby could have only become a hunter or food gatherer.

Early experiences can have very lasting effects. For example, children who are abused may suffer lifelong emotional problems (Goodwin, Fergusson, & Horwood, 2005). At the same time, extra care can sometimes reverse the effects of a poor start in life (Bornstein & Tamis-LeMonda, 2001). In short, environmental forces guide human development, for better or worse, throughout life.

Sensitive Periods

Why do some experiences have more lasting effects than others? Part of the answer lies in **sensitive periods.** These are times when children are more susceptible to particular types of environmental influences. Events that occur during a sensitive period can permanently alter the course of development (Bruer, 2001). For example, forming a loving bond with a caregiver early in life seems to be crucial for optimal development. Likewise, babies who don't hear normal speech during their first year may have impaired language abilities (Thompson & Nelson, 2001).

Prenatal Influences

The interplay of nature and nurture actually starts before birth. Although the intrauterine environment (interior of the womb) is highly protected, environmental conditions can affect the growth sequence of the developing child. For example, when Olivia was pregnant, Amy's fetal heart rate and movements increased when loud sounds or vibrations penetrated the womb (Kisilevsky et al., 2004).

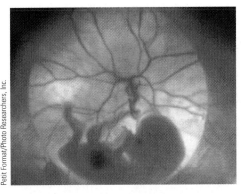

Petit Format/Photo Researchers, Inc.

Because of the rapid growth of basic structures, the developing fetus is sensitive to a variety of diseases, drugs, and sources of radiation. This is especially true during the first trimester (3 months) of gestation (pregnancy).

If Olivia's health or nutrition had been poor, or if she had German measles, syphilis, or HIV, or used drugs, or was exposed to X-rays or atomic radiation, Amy might have been harmed. In such cases babies can suffer from **congenital problems** or "birth defects." These problems affect the developing fetus and become apparent at birth. In contrast, **genetic disorders** are inherited from parents. Examples are sickle-cell anemia, hemophilia, cystic fibrosis, muscular dystrophy, albinism, and some types of mental retardation.

Fetal Vulnerability

How is it possible for the embryo or the fetus to be harmed? No direct intermixing of blood takes place between a mother and her unborn child. Yet some substances—especially drugs—do reach the fetus. Anything capable of directly causing birth defects is called a **teratogen** (teh-RAT-uh-jen). Sometimes women are exposed to powerful teratogens, such as radiation, lead, pesticides, or PCBs, without knowing it (Eliot, 1999). But pregnant women do have direct control over many teratogens. For example, a woman who takes cocaine runs a serious risk of injuring her fetus (Schuetze & Eiden, 2006). In short, when a pregnant woman takes drugs, her unborn child does too.

Environment ("nurture") The sum of all external conditions affecting development, including especially the effects of learning.

Sensitive period During development, a period of increased sensitivity to environmental influences. Also, a time during which certain events must take place for normal development to occur.

Congenital problems Problems or defects that originate during prenatal development in the womb.

Genetic disorders Problems caused by defects in the genes or by inherited characteristics.

Teratogen Radiation, a drug, or other substance capable of altering fetal development in nonheritable ways that cause birth defects.

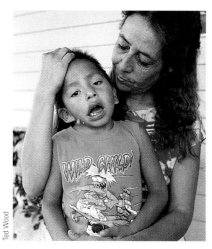

Some of the typical features of children suffering from fetal alcohol syndrome (FAS) include a small nonsymmetrical head, a short nose, a flattened area between the eyes, oddly shaped eyes, and a thin upper lip. Many of these features become less noticeable by adolescence. However, mental retardation and other problems commonly follow the FAS child into adulthood. The child shown here represents a moderate example of FAS.

Unfortunately, in the United States this is one of the greatest risk factors facing unborn children (Coles & Black, 2006). If a mother is addicted to morphine, heroin, or methadone, her baby may be born with an addiction. Repeated heavy drinking during pregnancy causes *fetal alcohol syndrome (FAS)*. Affected infants have low birth weight, a small head, bodily defects, and facial malformations. Many also suffer from emotional, behavioral, and mental handicaps (Golden, 2005).

Tobacco is also harmful. Smoking during pregnancy greatly reduces oxygen to the fetus. Heavy smokers risk miscarrying or having premature, underweight babies who are more likely to die soon after birth (Slotkin, 1998). Children of smoking mothers score lower on tests of language and mental ability (Fried et al., 1992). In other words, an unborn child's future can go "up in smoke." That goes for marijuana as well (Viveros et al., 2005).

Deprivation and Enrichment

Nature and nurture also continue to interact after birth, right? Yes. The brain of a newborn baby has fewer *dendrites* (nerve cell branches) and *synapses* (connections between nerve cells) than an adult brain. However, the newborn brain is highly *plastic*. During the first 3 years of life, millions of new connections form in the brain every day. At the same time, unused connections disappear. As a result, early learning environments literally shape the developing brain, through "blooming and pruning" of synapses (Nelson, 1999). This is especially true of environments that can be described as *enriched* or *deprived*. **Deprivation** refers to a lack of normal stimulation, nutrition, comfort, or love. **Enrichment** exists when an environment is deliberately made more complex and intellectually stimulating.

What happens when children suffer severe deprivation? Tragically, a few mistreated children have spent their first years in closets, attics, and other restricted environments. When first discovered, these children are usually mute, retarded, and emotionally damaged. Fortunately, such extreme deprivation is unusual.

Nevertheless, milder levels of perceptual, intellectual, or emotional deprivation occur in many families, especially those that must cope with poverty. Poverty can effect the development of children in at least two ways (Sobolewski & Amato, 2005). First, poor parents may not be able to give their children needed resources such as nutritious meals and access to health care or home computers and learning materials (Bradley & Corwyn, 2002). As a result, impoverished children tend to have more health problems and they may lag in cognitive development and achievement at school. Second, the stresses of poverty can also be hard on parents, leading to marriage problems, less positive parenting, and poorer parent-child relationships. The resulting emotional turmoil can damage a child's socioemotional development. In the extreme, it may increase the risk of mental illness and delinquent behavior (Bradley & Corwyn, 2002).

Adults who grew up in poverty often remain trapped in a vicious cycle of continued poverty. Because one in seven American families fall below the poverty line, this grim reality plays itself out in millions of American homes every day (Sobolewski & Amato, 2005).

Children who grow up in poverty run a high risk of experiencing many forms of deprivation. There is evidence that lasting damage to social, emotional, and cognitive development occurs when children must cope with severe early deprivation.

Enriched Environments

Can an improved environment enhance development? To answer this question, psychologists have created *enriched environments* that are especially novel, complex, and stimulating. Enriched environments may be the "soil" from which brighter children grow. To illustrate, let's consider the effects of raising rats in a sort of "rat wonderland." The walls of their cages were decorated with colorful patterns, and each cage was filled with platforms, ladders, and cubbyholes. As adults, these rats were superior at learning mazes. In addition, they had

Deprivation In development, the loss or withholding of normal stimulation, nutrition, comfort, love, and so forth; a condition of lacking.

Enrichment Deliberately making an environment more novel, complex, and perceptually or intellectually stimulating.

larger, heavier brains, with a thicker cortex (Benloucif, Bennett, & Rosenzweig, 1995). Of course, it's a long leap from rats to people, but an actual increase in brain size is impressive. If extra stimulation can enhance the "intelligence" of a lowly rat, it's likely that human infants also benefit from enrichment. Many studies have shown that enriched environments improve abilities or enhance development. It would be wise for Tom and Olivia to make a point of nourishing Amy's mind, as well as her body (Dieter & Emory, 1997).

What can parents do to enrich a child's environment? They can encourage exploration and stimulating play by paying attention to what holds the baby's interest. It is better to "child-proof" a house than to strictly limit what a child can touch. There is also value in actively enriching sensory experiences. Babies should be surrounded by colors, music, people, and things to see, taste, smell, and touch. Infants are not vegetables. It makes perfect sense to take them outside, to hang mobiles over their cribs, to place mirrors nearby, to play music for them, or to rearrange their rooms now and then. Children progress most rapidly when they have responsive parents and stimulating play materials at home (Luster & Dubow, 1992). In light of this, it is wise to view all of childhood as a relatively sensitive period (Nelson, 1999).

Reciprocal Influences

Because of differences in temperament, some babies are more likely than others to smile, cry, vocalize, reach out, or pay attention. As a result, babies rapidly become active participants in their own development. Growing infants alter their parents' behavior at the same time they are changed by it. For example, Amy is an easy baby who smiles frequently and is easily fed. This encourages Olivia to touch, feed, and sing to Amy. Olivia's affection rewards Amy, causing her to smile more. Soon, a dynamic relationship blossoms between mother and child. The reverse also occurs: Difficult children make parents unhappy and elicit more negative parenting (Parke, 2004).

A person's **developmental level** is his or her current state of physical, emotional, and intellectual development. To summarize, three factors combine to determine your developmental level at any stage of life. These are *heredity, environment,* and your *own behavior,* each tightly interwoven with the others.

Developmental level An individual's current state of physical, emotional, and intellectual development.

Study Break   Heredity and Environment

Reflect

Can you think of clear examples of some ways in which heredity and environmental forces have combined to affect your development?

What kind of temperament did you have as an infant? How did it affect your relationship with your parents or caregivers?

What advice would you give a friend who has just become pregnant? Be sure to consider the prenatal environment and sensitive periods.

Learning Check

1. Areas of the DNA molecule called genes are made up of dominant and recessive chromosomes. T or F?
2. Most inherited characteristics can be described as polygenic. T or F?
3. If one parent has a one dominant brown-eye gene and one recessive blue-eye gene and the other parent has two dominant brown-eye genes, what is the chance that their child will have blue eyes?
   a. 25 percent   b. 50 percent
   c. 0 percent   d. 75 percent
4. "Slow-to-warm-up" children can be described as restrained, unexpressive, or shy. T or F?
5. A(n) _____ _____ is a time of increased sensitivity to environmental influences.
6. As a child develops there is a continuous _____ between the forces of heredity and environment.

Critical Thinking

7. Environmental influences can interact with hereditary programming in an exceedingly direct way. Can you guess what it is?

Answers

1. F 2. T 3. c 4. T 5. sensitive period 6. interaction 7. Environmental conditions sometimes turn specific genes on or off, thus directly affecting the expression of genetic tendencies (Gottlieb, 1998).

THE NEWBORN BABY—THE BASIC MODEL COMES WITH OPTIONS

Margaret Miller/Photo Researchers, Inc.

Newborn babies display a special interest in the human face. A preference for seeing their mother's face develops rapidly and encourages social interactions between mother and baby.

>SURVEY QUESTION< *What can newborn babies do?*

Infants have mental capacities that continue to surprise researchers and delight parents. The emergence of a baby's mental life, physical abilities, and emotions is closely related to maturation of the brain, nervous system, and body. Let's see how the infant's world unfolds.

At birth the human *neonate* (NEE-oh-NATE: newborn infant) will die if not cared for by adults. Newborn babies cannot lift their heads, turn over, or feed themselves. Does this mean they are inert and unfeeling? Definitely not! Neonates like Amy can see, hear, smell, taste, and respond to pain and touch. Although their senses are less acute, babies are very responsive. Amy will follow a moving object with her eyes and will turn in the direction of sounds.

Amy also has a number of adaptive infant reflexes (Siegler, DeLoache, & Eisenberg, 2006). To elicit the *grasping reflex,* press an object in the neonate's palm and she will grasp it with surprising strength. Many infants, in fact, can hang from a raised bar, like little trapeze artists. The grasping reflex aids survival by helping infants avoid falling. You can observe the *rooting reflex* (reflexive head turning and nursing) by touching Amy's cheek. Immediately, she will turn toward your finger, as if searching for something.

How is such turning adaptive? The rooting reflex helps infants find a bottle or a breast. Then, when a nipple touches the infant's mouth, the *sucking reflex* (rhythmic nursing) helps her obtain needed food. Like other reflexes, this is a genetically programmed action (Koepke & Bigelow, 1997). At the same time, food rewards nursing. Because of this, babies quickly learn to nurse more actively. Again, we see how the interplay of nature and nurture alters a baby's behavior.

The *Moro reflex* is also interesting. If Amy's position is changed abruptly or if she is startled by a loud noise, she will make a hugging motion. This reaction has been compared to the movements baby monkeys use to cling to their mothers. (We leave it to the reader's imagination to decide if there is any connection.)

The World of the Neonate

Thirty years ago, many people thought of newborn babies as mere bundles of reflexes, like the ones just described. But infants are capable of much more. For example, University of Washington psychologist Andrew Meltzoff has found that babies are born mimics (Meltzoff, 2005). ▸Figure 3.4 shows Meltzoff as he sticks out his tongue, opens his mouth, and purses his lips at a 20-day-old girl. Will she imitate him? Videotapes of babies confirm that they imitate adult facial gestures. As early as 9 months of age, infants can imitate actions a day after seeing them (Heimann & Meltzoff, 1996). Such mimicry obviously aids rapid learning in infancy.

How intelligent are neonates? Babies are smarter than many people think. From the earli-

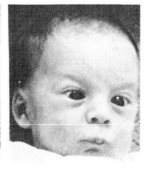

▸**FIGURE 3.4** Infant imitation. In the top row of photos, Andrew Meltzoff makes facial gestures at an infant. The bottom row records the infant's responses. Videotapes of Meltzoff and of tested infants helped ensure objectivity. (Photos courtesy of Andrew N. Meltzoff.)

est days of life, babies are learning how the world works. They immediately begin to look, touch, taste, and otherwise explore their surroundings. From an evolutionary perspective, a baby's mind is designed to soak up information, which it does at an amazing pace (Meltzoff & Prinz, 2002).

In the first months of life, babies are increasingly able to think, to learn from what they see, to make predictions, and to search for explanations. For example, Jerome Bruner (1983) observed that 3- to 8-week-old babies seem to understand that a person's voice and body should be connected. If a baby hears his mother's voice coming from where she is standing, the baby will remain calm. If her voice comes from a loudspeaker several feet away, the baby will become agitated and begin to cry.

Another look into the private world of infants can be drawn from testing their vision. However, such testing is a challenge because infants cannot talk. Robert Fantz invented a device called a *looking chamber* to find out what infants can see and what holds their attention (▶Fig. 3.5*a*). Imagine that Amy is placed on her back inside the chamber, facing a lighted area above. Next, two objects are placed in the chamber. By observing the movements of Amy's eyes and the images they reflect, we can tell what she is looking at. Such tests show that adult vision is about 30 times sharper, but babies can see large patterns, shapes, and edges.

Fantz found that 3-day-old babies prefer complex patterns, such as checkerboards and bull's-eyes, to simpler colored rectangles. Other researchers have learned that infants are excited by circles, curves, and bright lights (▶Fig. 3.5*b*) (Brown, 1990). Immediately after birth, Amy will be aware of changes in the position of objects (Slater et al., 1991). When she is 6 months old, she will be able to recognize categories of objects that differ in shape or color. By 9 months of age she will be able to tell the difference between dogs and birds or other groups of animals (Mandler & McDonough, 1998). So, there really is a person inside that little body!

Neonates can most clearly see objects about a foot away from them. It is as if they are best prepared to see the people who love and care for them (Gopnik, Meltzoff, & Kuhl, 2000). Perhaps that's why babies have a special fascination with human faces. Just *hours* after they are born, babies begin to prefer seeing their mother's face, rather than a stranger's (Walton, Bower, & Bower, 1992). When babies are only 2 to 5 days old, they will pay more

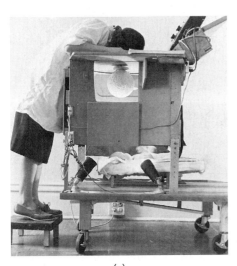

(a)

(b)

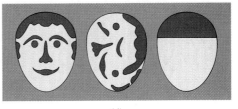

(c)

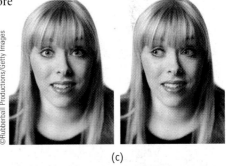

(d)

▶**FIGURE 3.5** *(a)* Eye movements and fixation points of infants are observed in Fantz's "looking chamber." *(b)* Thirteen-week-old infants prefer concentric and curved patterns like those on the left to nonconcentric and straight-line patterns like those on the right. *(c)* When they are just days old, infants pay more attention to the faces of people who are gazing directly at them. *(d)* Infants look at normal faces longer than at scrambled faces and at both faces longer than designs, like the one on the right. (Photo *a* courtesy of David Linton. Drawing from "The Origin of Form Perception" by Robert L. Fantz, Copyright © 1961 by Scientific American, Inc. All rights reserved.)

attention to a person who is gazing directly at them, rather than one who is looking away (⇒Fig. 3.5*c*) (Farroni et al., 2004).

In a looking chamber, most infants will spend more time looking at a human face pattern than a scrambled face or a colored oval (⇒Fig. 3.5*d*). When real human faces are used, infants prefer familiar faces to unfamiliar faces. However, this reverses at about age 2. At that time, unusual objects begin to interest the child. For instance, in a classic study Jerome Kagan (1971) showed face masks to 2-year-olds. Kagan found that the toddlers were fascinated by a face with eyes on the chin and a nose in the middle of the forehead. He believes the babies' interest came from a need to understand why the scrambled face differed from what they had come to expect. Such behavior is further evidence that babies actively try to make sense of their surroundings (Gopnik, Meltzoff, & Kuhl, 2000).

MATURATION

>SURVEY QUESTION< *What influence does maturation have on early development?*

The emergence of many basic abilities is closely tied to **maturation** (physical growth and development of the body, brain, and nervous system). Maturation will be especially evident as Amy learns motor skills, such as crawling and walking. Of course, the *rate* of maturation varies from child to child. Nevertheless, the *order* of maturation is almost universal. For instance, Amy will be able to sit without support from Tom before she has matured enough to crawl. Indeed, infants around the world typically sit before they crawl, crawl before they stand, and stand before they walk (⇒Fig. 3.6).

What about my weird cousin Emo who never crawled? Like cousin Emo, a few children substitute rolling, creeping, or shuffling for crawling. A very few move directly from sitting to standing and walking (Robson, 1984). Even so, their motor development is orderly. In

1. Fetal posture (newborn)

2. Holds chin up (1 month)

3. Holds chest up (2 months)

4. Sits when supported (4 months)

5. Sits alone (7 months)

6. Stands holding furniture (9 months)

7. Crawls (10 months)

8. Walks if led (11 months)

9. Stands alone (11 months)

10. Walks alone (12 months)

⇒**FIGURE 3.6** Motor development. Most infants follow an orderly pattern of motor development. Although the order in which children progress is similar, there are large individual differences in the ages at which each ability appears. The ages listed are averages for American children. It is not unusual for many of the skills to appear 1 or 2 months earlier than average or several months later (Harris & Liebert, 1991). Parents should not be alarmed if a child's behavior differs some from the average.

Maturation The physical growth and development of the body and nervous system.

general, muscular control spreads in a pattern that is *cephalocaudal* (SEF-eh-lo-KOD-ul: from head to toe) and *proximodistal* (PROK-seh-moe-DIS-tul: from the center of the body to the extremities). Even if cousin Emo flunked Elementary Crawling, his motor development followed the standard top-down, center-outward pattern (Piek, 2006).

Motor Development

Although maturation has a big impact, motor skills don't simply "emerge." Amy must learn to control her actions. When babies are beginning to crawl or walk, they actively try new movements and select those that work. Amy's first efforts may be flawed—a wobbly crawl or some shaky first steps. However, with practice, babies "tune" their movements to be smoother and more effective. Such learning is evident from the very first months of life (Piek, 2006; Thelen, 2000). (See ▸▸Fig. 3.7.)

Readiness

At what ages will Amy be ready to feed herself, to walk alone, or to say goodbye to diapers? Such milestones tend to be governed by a child's **readiness** for rapid learning. That is, minimum levels of maturation must occur before some skills can be learned. Parents are asking for failure when they try to force a child to learn skills too early (Schum et al., 2002). It is impossible, for instance, to teach children to walk or use a toilet before they have matured enough to control their bodies.

Consider the eager parents who toilet trained an 18-month-old child in 10 trying weeks of false alarms and "accidents." If they had waited until the child was 24 months old, they might have succeeded in just 3 weeks. Parents may control when toilet training starts, but maturation tends to dictate when it will be completed (Schum et al., 2002). The average age for *completed* toilet training is about 3 years (girls a little earlier, boys a little later) (Schum et al., 2001). So why fight nature? (The wet look is in.)

Emotional Development

Early emotional development also follows a pattern closely tied to maturation (Panksepp & Pasqualini, 2005). Even the basic emotions of *anger, fear,* and *joy*—which appear to be unlearned—take time to develop. General *excitement* is the only emotion newborn infants clearly express. However, as Tom and Olivia can tell you, a baby's emotional life blossoms rapidly. One researcher (Bridges, 1932) observed that all the basic human emotions appear before age 2. Bridges found that emotions appear in a consistent order and that the first basic split is between pleasant and unpleasant emotions (▸▸Fig. 3.8).

Experts do not yet agree on how quickly emotions unfold (Oster, 2005). For example, psychologist Carroll Izard thinks that infants can express several basic emotions as early as 10 weeks of age. When Izard looks carefully at the faces of babies he sees abundant signs of emotion. (See ▸▸Fig. 3.9.) The most common infant expression, he found, is not excitement, but *interest*—followed by *joy, anger,* and *sadness* (Izard et al., 1995).

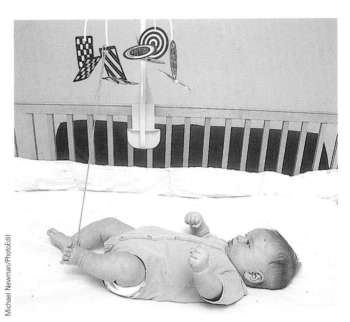

Michael Newman/PhotoEdit

▸▸**FIGURE 3.7** Psychologist Carolyn Rovee-Collier has shown that babies as young as 3 months old can learn to control their movements. In her experiments, babies lie on their backs under a colorful crib mobile. A ribbon is tied around the baby's ankle and connected to the mobile. Whenever babies spontaneously kick their legs, the mobile jiggles and rattles. Within a few minutes, infants learn to kick faster. Their reward for kicking is a chance to see the mobile move (Hayne & Rovee-Collier, 1995).

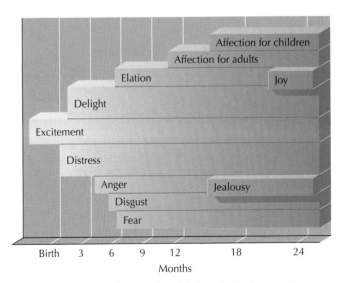

▸▸**FIGURE 3.8** The traditional view of infancy holds that emotions are rapidly differentiated from an initial capacity for excitement. (After K. M. B. Bridges, 1932. Reprinted by permission of the Society for Research in Child Development, Inc.)

Readiness A condition that exists when maturation has advanced enough to allow the rapid acquisition of a particular skill.

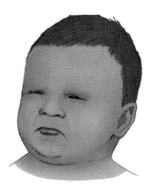

▸▸**FIGURE 3.9** Infants display many of the same emotional expressions as adults do. Carroll Izard believes such expressions show that distinct emotions appear within the first months of life. Other theorists argue that specific emotions come into focus more gradually, as an infant's nervous system matures. Either way, parents can expect to see a full range of basic emotions by the end of a baby's first year.

If Izard is right, then emotions are "hardwired" by heredity and related to evolution. Perhaps that's why smiling is one of a baby's most common reactions. Smiling probably helps babies survive by inviting parents to care for them (Izard et al., 1995).

At first, a baby's smiling is haphazard. By the age of 8–12 months, however, infants smile more frequently when another person is nearby (Jones & Hong, 2001). They can even communicate interest in another object through their smile (Venezia et al., 2004). This **social smile** is especially rewarding to parents. On the other hand, when new parents see and hear a crying baby, they feel annoyed, irritated, disturbed, or unhappy. Babies the world over, it seems, rapidly become capable of letting others know what they like and dislike. (Prove this to yourself sometime by driving a baby buggy.)

With dazzling speed, human infants are transformed from helpless babies to independent persons. Early growth is extremely rapid. By her third year, Amy will have a unique personality and she will be able to stand, walk, talk, and explore. At no other time after birth does development proceed more rapidly. During the same period, Amy's relationships with other people will expand as well. Before we explore that topic, here's a chance to review what you've learned.

Social smile Smiling elicited by social stimuli, such as seeing a parent's face.

 Study Break   The Neonate and Maturation

Reflect

What infant reflexes have you observed? How would maturation affect the chances of teaching an infant to eat with a spoon? Can you give an example of how heredity and environment interact during motor development?

To know what a baby is feeling would it be more helpful to be able to detect delight and distress (Bridges) or joy, anger, and sadness (Izard)?

Learning Check

1. If an infant is startled, it will make movements similar to an embrace. This is known as the

   a. grasping reflex   b. rooting reflex
   c. Moro reflex   d. adaptive reflex

2. During infancy, a capacity for imitating others first becomes evident at about 9 months of age. T or F?

3. After age 2, infants tested in a looking chamber show a marked preference for familiar faces and simpler designs. T or F?
4. The orderly sequence observed in the unfolding of many basic responses can be attributed to _____.
5. General excitement or interest is the clearest emotional response present in newborn infants, but meaningful expressions of delight and distress appear soon after. T or F?
6. Neonates display a social smile as early as 10 days after birth. T or F?

Critical Thinking

7. If you were going to test newborn infants to see if they prefer their own mother's face to that of a stranger, what precautions would you take?

Answers

1. c 2. F 3. F 4. maturation 5. T 6. F 7. In one study of the preferences of newborns, the hair color and complexion of strangers was matched to that of the mothers. Also, only the mother's or stranger's face was visible during testing. And finally, a scent was used to mask olfactory (smell) cues so that an infant's preference could not be based on the mother's familiar odor (Bushnell, Sai, & Mullin, 1989).

SOCIAL DEVELOPMENT— BABY, I'M STUCK ON YOU

>SURVEY QUESTION< *Of what significance is a child's emotional bond with parents?*

Like all humans, babies are social creatures. Their early **social development** lays a foundation for relationships with parents, siblings, friends, and relatives. A first basic step into the social world involves becoming aware of oneself as a person. When you look in a mirror, you recognize the image staring back as your own—except, perhaps, early on Monday mornings. Would Amy recognize herself at age 1? At age 2? Like many such events, initial self-awareness depends on maturation of the nervous system. In a typical test of self-recognition, infants are shown images of themselves on a TV. Most infants have to be 18 months old before they recognize themselves (Nielsen & Dissanayake, 2004).

A sense of self, or self-awareness, develops at about age 18 months. Before children develop self-awareness, they do not recognize their own image in a mirror. Typically, they think they are looking at another child. Some children hug the child in the mirror or go behind it looking for the child they see there (Lewis, 1995).

Attachment

The real core of social development is found in the **emotional attachment,** or close emotional bond, that babies form with their primary caregivers. There is a sensitive period (roughly the first year of life) during which this must occur for optimal development. Returning to Amy's story, we find that attachment keeps her close to Olivia, who provides safety, stimulation, and a secure "home base" from which Amy can go exploring.

Mothers usually begin to cultivate a parent-child bond within hours of giving birth. For example, they touch their own infants more and hold them closer than they do other babies (Kaitz et al., 1995). You may have heard that bonding is especially powerful during the first few hours after birth (Klaus, Kennell, & Klaus, 1995). However, careful studies have generally failed to support a "superglue" version of bonding. Whereas long-term infant attachments are a reality, "instant bonding" appears to be a myth (Eyer, 1994).

Most parents are familiar with the storm of crying that sometimes occurs when babies are left alone at bedtime. Bedtime distress can be a mild form of separation anxiety. As many parents know, it is often eased by the presence of "security objects," such as a stuffed animal or favorite blanket (Morelli et al., 1992).

A direct sign that an emotional bond has formed appears around 8 to 12 months of age. At that time Amy will display **separation anxiety** (crying and signs of fear) when she is left alone or with a stranger. Mild separation anxiety is normal. When it is more intense, it may reveal a problem. At some point in their lives, about 5 percent of all children (1 in 20) suffer from *separation anxiety disorder*. These children are miserable when they are separated from their parents, whom they cling to or constantly follow. Some fear that they will get lost and never see their parents again. Seventy-five percent refuse to go to school, which can be a serious handicap.

What causes separation anxiety disorder? Some children are more vulnerable to the disorder, indicating a genetic component (Cronk et al., 2005). As you might expect, environmental stressors also play a role. The problem may begin after a child faces such stresses as illness, the death of a relative or pet, moving to a new neighborhood, or changing schools. Whatever the triggering event, separation anxiety should not be ignored because it can seriously impair emotional development. Children tend

Social development The development of self-awareness, attachment to parents or caregivers, and relationships with other children and adults.

Emotional attachment An especially close emotional bond that infants form with their parents, caregivers, or others.

Separation anxiety Distress displayed by infants when they are separated from their parents or principal caregivers.

What's Your Attachment Style?

Do our first attachments continue to affect us as adults? Some psychologists believe they do, by influencing how we relate to friends and lovers (Bridges, 2003; Sroufe et al., 2005). Read the following statements and see which best describes your adult relationships.

Secure Attachment Style

In general, I think most other people are well intentioned and trustworthy.
I find it relatively easy to get close to others.
I am comfortable relying on others and having others depend on me.
I don't worry much about being abandoned by others.
I am comfortable when other people want to get close to me emotionally.

Avoidant Attachment Style

I tend to pull back when things don't go well in a relationship.
I am somewhat skeptical about the idea of true love.
I have difficulty trusting my partner in a romantic relationship.
Other people tend to be too eager to seek commitment from me.
I get a little nervous if anyone gets too close emotionally.

Ambivalent Attachment Style

I have often felt misunderstood and unappreciated in my romantic relationships.
My friends and lovers have been somewhat unreliable.
I love my romantic partner, but I worry that she or he doesn't really love me.
I would like to be closer to my romantic partner, but I'm not sure I trust her or him.

Do any of the preceding statements sound familiar? If so, they may describe your adult attachment style. Most adults have a secure attachment style that is marked by caring, supportiveness, and understanding. However, it's not unusual to have an avoidant attachment style that reflects a tendency to resist intimacy and commitment to others (Collins et al., 2002). An ambivalent attachment style is marked by mixed feelings about love and friendship (Tidwell, Reis, & Shaver, 1996). Do you see any similarities between your present relationships and your attachment experiences as a child?

Attachment Category

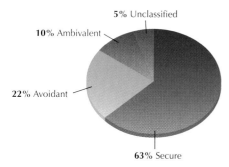

5% Unclassified
10% Ambivalent
22% Avoidant
63% Secure

▸▸**FIGURE 3.10** In the United States, about two thirds of all children from middle-class families are securely attached. About 1 child in 3 is insecurely attached. (Percentages are approximate. From Kaplan, 1998.)

Secure attachment A stable and positive emotional bond.

Insecure-avoidant attachment An anxious emotional bond marked by a tendency to avoid reunion with a parent or caregiver.

Insecure-ambivalent attachment An anxious emotional bond marked by both a desire to be with a parent or caregiver and some resistance to being reunited.

to grow out of the disorder (Kearney et al., 2003), but if separation anxiety is intense or lasts for more than a month, parents should seek professional help for their child (Masi, Mucci, & Millepiedi, 2001).

Attachment Quality

According to psychologist Mary Ainsworth (1913–1999), the quality of attachment is revealed by how babies act when their mothers return after a brief separation. Infants who are **securely attached** have a stable and positive emotional bond. They are upset by the mother's absence and seek to be near her when she returns. **Insecure-avoidant** infants have an anxious emotional bond. They tend to turn away from the mother when she returns. **Insecure-ambivalent** attachment is also an anxious emotional bond. In this case, babies have mixed feelings: They both seek to be near the returning mother and angrily resist contact with her. (See ▸▸Fig. 3.10.)

Attachment can have lasting effects. Infants who are securely attached at the age of 1 year show more resiliency, curiosity, problem-solving ability, and social skill in preschool (Collins & Gunnar, 1990). In contrast, attachment failures can be quite damaging. Consider, for example, the plight of children raised in severely overcrowded Romanian orphanages. These children got almost no attention from adults for the first year or two of their lives. Some have now been adopted by American and Canadian families, but many are poorly attached to their new parents. Some, for instance, will wander off with strangers, they are anxious and remote, and they don't like to be touched or make eye contact with others (O'Conner et al., 2003). In short, for some children, a lack of affectionate care early in life leaves a lasting emotional impact well into adulthood (see "What's Your Attachment Style?").

Promoting Secure Attachment

The key to secure attachment is a mother who is accepting and sensitive to her baby's signals and rhythms. Poor attachment occurs when a mother's actions are inappropriate, inadequate, intrusive, overstimulating, or rejecting. An example is the mother who tries to play with a drowsy infant or who ignores a baby who is looking at her and vocalizing. The link between sensitive caregiving and secure attachment appears to apply to all cultures (Posada et al., 2002).

What about attachment to fathers? Fathers of securely attached infants tend to be outgoing, agreeable, and happy in their marriage. In general, a warm family atmosphere—one that includes sensitive mothering *and* fathering—produces secure children (Belsky, 1996).

Day Care

Does commercial day care interfere with the quality of attachment? It depends on the quality of day care. Overall, *high-quality* day care does not adversely affect attachment to parents (National Institute of Child Health and Human Development, 1999). In fact, children in high-quality day care tend to have better relationships with their mothers and fewer behavior problems. They also have better cognitive skills and language abilities (Burchinal et al., 2000; Vandell, 2004). Thus, high-quality day care can actually improve children's social and mental skills (Mercer, 2006).

However, all of the positive effects just noted are *reversed* for low-quality day care. Poor-quality day care can actually create behavior problems that didn't exist beforehand (Pierre-humbert et al., 2002). Parents are wise to carefully evaluate and monitor the quality of day care their children receive (▸▸ Fig. 3.11).

What should parents look for when they evaluate the quality of child care? Low-quality day care *is* risky and it *may* weaken attachment. Parents seeking quality should insist on *at least* the following: (1) a small number of children per caregiver, (2) small overall group size (12 to 15), (3) trained caregivers, (4) minimal staff turnover, and (5) stable, consistent care (Howes, 1997). (Also, avoid any child-care center with the words *zoo, menagerie,* or *stockade* in its name.)

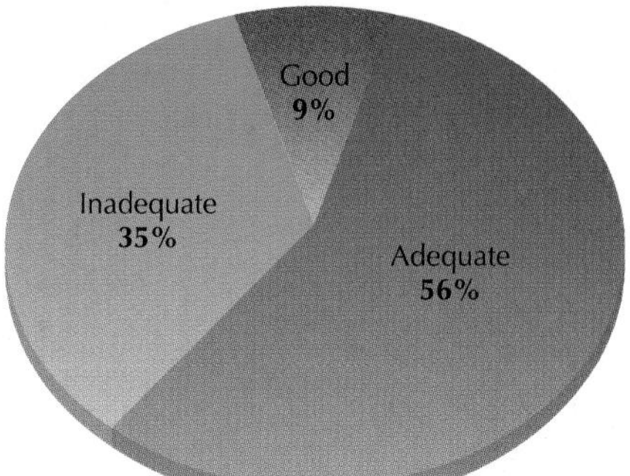

Attachment and Affectional Needs

A baby's **affectional needs** (needs for love and affection) are every bit as important as more obvious needs for food, water, and physical care. All things considered, creating a bond of trust and affection between the infant and at least one other person is a key event during the first year of life. Parents are sometimes afraid of "spoiling" babies with too much attention, but for the first year or two this is nearly impossible. In fact, a later capacity to experience warm and loving relationships may depend on it.

▸▸**FIGURE 3.11** This graph shows the results of a study of child care in homes other than the child's. In most cases, parents paid for this care, although many of the caregivers were unlicensed. As you can see, child care was "good" in only 9 percent of the homes. In 35 percent of the homes it was rated as inadequate (Mehren, 1994).

Affectional needs Emotional needs for love and affection.

Study Break   Social Development

Reflect

Think of a child you know who seems to be securely attached and one who seems to be insecurely attached. How do the children differ? Do their parents treat them differently?

Do you think that your experiences as a child, such as your early attachment pattern, really affect your life as an adult? Can you think of any examples from your own life?

Learning Check

1. Clear signs of self-awareness or self-recognition are evident in most infants by the time they reach 8 months of age. T or F?
2. The development of separation anxiety in an infant corresponds to the formation of an attachment to parents. T or F?

3. In Mary Ainsworth's system for rating the quality of attachment, secure attachment is revealed by a lack of distress when an infant is left alone with a stranger. T or F?
4. High-quality day care can actually improve children's social and mental skills. T or F?

Critical Thinking

5. Can you think of another way to tell if infants have self-awareness?
6. Can emotional bonding begin before birth?
7. Attachment quality is usually attributed to the behavior of parents or caregivers. How might infants contribute to the quality of attachment?

Answers

1. F 2. T 3. F 4. T 5. Another successful method is to secretly rub a spot of rouge on an infant's nose. The child is then placed in front of a mirror. The question is, Will the child touch the red spot, showing recognition of the mirror image as his or her own? The probability that a child will do so jumps dramatically during the second year. 6. It certainly can for parents. When a pregnant woman begins to feel fetal movements she becomes aware that a baby is coming to life inside of her. Likewise, prospective parents who hear a fetal heartbeat at the doctor's office or see an ultrasound image of the fetus begin to become emotionally attached to the unborn child (Santrock, 2007). 7. An infant's behavior patterns, temperament, and emotional style may greatly influence parents' behavior. As a result, infants can affect attachment as much as parents do (Oatley & Jenkins, 1992).

"All right now, give Mommy the super-glue."

PARENTAL INFLUENCES— LIFE WITH MOM AND DAD

>SURVEY QUESTION< *How important are parenting styles?*

From the first few years of life, when caregivers are the center of a child's world, through to adulthood, the style and quality of mothering and fathering very important.

Parenting Styles

Psychologist Diana Baumrind (1991, 2005) has studied the effects of three major **parental styles,** identifiable patterns of parental caretaking and interaction with children. See if you recognize the styles she describes.

Authoritarian parents enforce rigid rules and demand strict obedience to authority. Typically they view children as having few rights but adult-like responsibilities. The child is expected to stay out of trouble and to accept, without question, what parents regard as right or wrong. ("Do it because I say so.") The children of authoritarian parents are usually obedient and self-controlled. But they also tend to be emotionally stiff, withdrawn, apprehensive, and lacking in curiosity.

Overly permissive parents give little guidance, allow too much freedom, or don't hold children accountable for their actions. Typically, the child has rights similar to an adult's but few responsibilities. Rules are not enforced, and the child usually gets his or her way. ("Do whatever you want.") Permissive parents tend to produce dependent, immature children who misbehave frequently. Such children are aimless and likely to "run amok."

Baumrind describes **authoritative parents** as those who supply firm and consistent guidance, combined with love and affection. Such parents balance their own rights with those of their children. They control their children's behavior in a caring, responsive, non-authoritarian way. ("Do it for this reason.") Effective parents are firm and consistent, not harsh or rigid. In general, they encourage the child to act responsibly, to think, and to make good decisions. This style produces children who are *resilient* (good at bouncing back after bad experiences) and develop the strengths they need to thrive even in difficult circumstances (Kim-Cohen et al., 2004; Masten, 2001). The children of authoritative parents are competent, self-controlled, independent, assertive, and inquiring (Baumrind, 1991). They know how to manage their emotions and use positive coping skills (Eisenberg et al., 2003; Lynch et al., 2004). To read more about effective parenting, see this chapter's "Psychology in Action" section.

Maternal and Paternal Influences

Don't mothers and fathers parent differently? Yes. Although **maternal influences** (all the effects a mother has on her child) generally have a greater impact, fathers do make a unique contribution to parenting (Santrock, 2007). Although fathers are spending more time with their children, mothers still do most of the nurturing and caretaking, especially of young children (Craig, 2006).

Studies of **paternal influences** (the sum of all effects a father has on his child) reveal that fathers are more likely to play with their children and tell them stories. In contrast, mothers are typically responsible for the physical and emotional care of their children (▸▸Fig. 3.12).

It might seem that the father's role as a playmate makes him less important. Not so. From birth onward, fathers pay more visual attention to children than mothers do. Fathers are much more tactile (lifting, tickling, and handling the baby), more physically arousing

Parental styles Identifiable patterns of parental caretaking and interaction with children.

Authoritarian parents Parents who enforce rigid rules and demand strict obedience to authority.

Overly permissive parents Parents who give little guidance, allow too much freedom, or do not require the child to take responsibility.

Authoritative parents Parents who supply firm and consistent guidance combined with love and affection.

Maternal influences The aggregate of all psychological effects mothers have on their children.

Paternal influences The aggregate of all psychological effects fathers have on their children.

(engaging in rough-and-tumble play), and more likely to engage in unusual play (imitating the baby, for example) (Crawley & Sherrod, 1984). In comparison, mothers speak to infants more, play more conventional games (such as peekaboo), and, as noted, spend much more time in caregiving. Amy's playtime with Tom is actually very valuable. Young children who spend a lot of time playing with their fathers tend to be more competent in many ways (Pettit et al., 1998).

Overall, fathers can be as affectionate, sensitive, and responsive as mothers are. Nevertheless, infants and children tend to get very different views of males and females. Females, who offer comfort, nurturance, and verbal stimulation, tend to be close at hand. Males come and go, and when they are present, action, exploration, and risk-taking prevail. It's no wonder, then, that the parental styles of mothers and fathers have a major impact on children's gender role development (Lindsay, Mize, & Pettit, 1997; Videon, 2005).

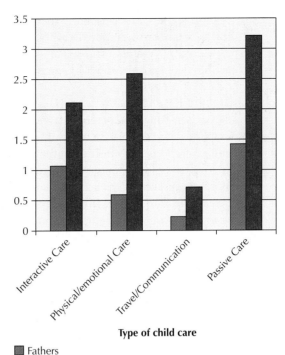

Type of child care

Fathers (light bars)
Mothers (dark bars)

▸▸**FIGURE 3.12** Mother-child and father-child interactions. This graph shows what occurred on routine days in a sample of more than 1,400 Australian homes. Mothers spend about twice as long each day on child care, compared to fathers. Further, mothers spend more time on physical and emotional care (e.g., feeding, bathing, soothing) than on interactive care (e.g., playing, reading, activities); fathers show the reverse pattern. Finally, mothers spend more time on travel (e.g., driving children to sports or music lessons), communication (e.g., talking to teachers about their children), and passive care (e.g., supervising children while they play). (Adapted from Craig, 2006.)

Ethnic Differences: Four Flavors of Parenting

Do ethnic differences in parenting affect children in distinctive ways? Diana Baumrind's work provides a good overall summary of the effects of parenting. However, her conclusions are probably most valid for families whose roots lie in Europe. Child-rearing in other ethnic groups often reflects different customs and beliefs. Cultural differences are especially apparent with respect to the meaning attached to a child's behavior. Is a particular behavior "good" or "bad"? Should it be encouraged or discouraged? The answer will depend greatly on parents' cultural values (Leyendecker et al., 2005).

Making generalizations about groups of people is always risky. Nevertheless, some typical differences in child-rearing patterns have been observed in North American ethnic communities (Kaplan, 1998; Parke, 2004).

African-American Families

Traditional African-American values emphasize loyalty and interdependence among family members, security, developing a positive identity, and not giving up in the face of adversity. African-American parents typically stress obedience and respect for elders.

BananaStock/SuperStock

Fathering typically makes a contribution to early development that differs in emphasis from mothering.

© Baby Blues Partnership. King Features Syndicate.

Child discipline tends to be fairly strict (Parke, 2004), but many African-American parents see this as a necessity, especially if they live in urban areas where safety is a concern. Self-reliance, resourcefulness, and an ability to take care of oneself in difficult situations are also qualities that African-American parents seek to promote in their children.

Hispanic Families

Like African-American parents, Hispanic parents tend to have relatively strict standards of discipline. They also place a high value on family values, family pride, and loyalty. Hispanic families are typically affectionate and indulgent toward younger children. However, as children grow older, they are expected to learn social skills and to be calm, obedient, courteous, and respectful. In fact, such social skills may be valued more than cognitive skills (Delgado & Ford, 1998). In addition, Hispanic parents tend to stress cooperation more than competition. Such values can put Hispanic children at a disadvantage in highly competitive, European-American culture.

Asian-American Families

Asian cultures tend to be group-oriented, and they emphasize interdependence among individuals. In contrast, Western cultures value individual effort and independence. This difference is often reflected in Asian-American child-rearing practices (Chao & Tseng, 2002). Asian-American children are taught that their behavior can bring either pride or shame to the family. Therefore, they are obliged to set aside their own desires when the greater good of the family is at stake (Parke, 2004). Parents tend to act as teachers who encourage hard work, moral behavior, and achievement. For the first few years, parenting is lenient and permissive. However, after about age 5, Asian-American parents begin to expect respect, obedience, self-control, and self-discipline from their children.

Arab-American Families

In Middle Eastern cultures, children are expected to be polite, obedient, disciplined, and conforming. Punishment generally consists of spankings, teasing, or shaming in front of others. Arab-American fathers tend to be strong authority figures who demand obedience so that the family will not be shamed by a child's bad behavior. Success, generosity, and hospitality are highly valued in Arab-American culture. The pursuit of family honor encourages hard work, thrift, conservatism, and educational achievement. The welfare of the family is emphasized over individual identity. Thus, Arab-American children are raised to respect their parents, members of their extended family, and other adults as well (Erickson & Al-Timimi, 2001; Medhus, 2001).

Implications

Child-rearing is done in a remarkable variety of ways around the world. In fact, many of the things we do in North America, such as forcing young children to sleep alone, would be considered odd or wrong in other cultures. In the final analysis, parenting can only be judged if we know what culture or ethnic community a child is being prepared to enter (Leyendecker et al., 2005).

In ethnic communities, norms for effective parenting often differ in subtle ways from parenting styles in Euro-American culture.

Jeff Greenberg/PhotoEdit

Study Break Parental Influences

Reflect

Do you know any parents who have young children and who are authoritarian, permissive, or authoritative? What are their children like?

How do mothers and fathers differ in their influence on children? How did your own parents influence you?

Do you think parenting depends on ethnicity? If so, why? If not, why not?

Learning Check

1. Three important elements of effective mothering are _____ maternal involvement; parental _____ to a child's feelings; needs, rhythms, and signals, and compatibility between parent and child _____.

2. Fathers are more likely to act as playmates for their children, rather than caregivers. T or F?

3. According to Diana Baumrind's research, effective parents are authoritarian in their approach to their children's behavior. T or F?

4. Authoritarian parents view children as having few rights but many responsibilities. T or F?

5. Asian-American parents tend to be more individually oriented than parents whose ethnic roots are European. T or F?

Critical Thinking

6. Why is it risky to make generalizations about child-rearing differences for various ethnic groups?

7. If power assertion is a poor way to discipline children, why do so many parents use it?

Answers

1. proactive, responsiveness, temperaments   2. T   3. F   4. T   5. F   6. Because there may be as much variation within ethnic groups as there is between them. For example, there are sizable differences in the child-rearing styles of Hispanic parents from Puerto Rico, Argentina, and Guatemala.   7. Most parents discipline their children in the same ways that they themselves were disciplined. Parenting is a responsibility of tremendous importance, for which most people receive almost no training.

LANGUAGE DEVELOPMENT—FAST-TALKING BABIES

>SURVEY QUESTION< *How do children acquire language?*

There's something almost miraculous about a baby's first words. As infants, how did we manage to leap into the world of language? Even a quick survey like this one reveals that both maturation and social development provide a foundation for language learning.

How We Acquire Language

Language development is closely tied to maturation (Gleason, 2005). As every parent knows, babies can cry from birth on. By 1 month of age they use crying to gain attention. Typically, parents can tell if an infant is hungry, angry, or in pain from the tone of the crying (Kaplan, 1998). Around 6 to 8 weeks of age, babies begin *cooing* (the repetition of vowel sounds such as "oo" and "ah").

By 7 months of age, Amy's nervous system will mature enough to allow her to grasp objects, to smile, laugh, sit up, and *babble*. In the babbling stage, the consonants *b, d, m,* and *g* are combined with the vowel sounds to produce meaningless language sounds: *dadadadada* or *bababa*. At first, babbling is the same around the world. But soon, the language spoken by

© Baby Blues Partnership. King Features Syndicate.

parents begins to have an influence. That is, Japanese babies start to babble in a way that sounds like Japanese, Mexican babies babble in Spanish-like sounds, and so forth (Gopnik, Meltzoff, & Kuhl, 2000; Kuhl, 2004).

At about 1 year of age, children respond to real words such as *no* or *hi.* Soon afterward, the first connection between words and objects forms, and children may address their parents as "Mama" or "Dada." By age 18 months to 2 years, Amy's vocabulary may include from 24 to 200 words. At first there is a *single-word stage,* during which children use one word at a time, such as "go," "juice," or "up." Soon after, words are arranged in simple two-word sentences called *telegraphic speech:* "Want-Teddy," "Mama-gone."

Language and the Terrible Twos

At about the same time that children begin to put two or three words together they become much more independent. Two-year-olds understand some of the commands parents make, but they are not always willing to carry them out. A child like Amy may assert her independence by saying "No drink," "Me do it," "My cup, my cup," and the like. It can be worse, of course. A 2-year-old may look at you intently, make eye contact, listen as you shout "No, no," and still pour her juice on the cat.

During their second year, children become increasingly capable of mischief and temper tantrums. Thus, calling this time "the terrible twos" is not entirely inappropriate. One-year-olds can do plenty of things parents don't want them to do. However, it's usually 2-year-olds who do things *because* you don't want them to (Gopnik, Meltzoff, & Kuhl, 2000).

Perhaps parents can take some comfort in knowing that a stubborn, negative 2-year-old is simply becoming more independent. When Amy is 2, Olivia and Tom would be wise to remember that "This, too, shall pass." After age 2, the child's comprehension and use of words takes a dramatic leap forward (Reznick & Goldfield, 1992). From this point on, vocabulary and language skills grow at a phenomenal rate (Fernald, Perfors, & Marchman, 2006). By first grade, Amy will be able to understand around 8,000 words and use about 4,000. She will have truly entered the world of language.

The Roots of Language

What accounts for this explosion of language development? One possibility is that language recognition is innate. Linguist Noam Chomsky (1975, 1986) has long claimed that humans have a **biological predisposition** or hereditary readiness to develop language. According to Chomsky, language patterns are inborn, much like a child's ability to coordinate walking. If such inborn language recognition does exist, it may explain why children around the world use a limited number of patterns in their first sentences. Typical patterns include (Mussen et al., 1979):

Identification:	"See kitty."
Nonexistence:	"Allgone milk."
Possession:	"My doll."
Agent-Action:	"Mama give."
Negation:	"Not ball."
Question:	"Where doggie?"

Does Chomsky's theory explain why language develops so rapidly? It is certainly part of the story. But many psychologists feel that Chomsky underestimates the importance of learning (Tomasello, 2003) and the social contexts that shape language development (Hoff, 2006). *Psycholinguists* (specialists in the psychology of language) have shown that imitation of adults and rewards for correctly using words (as when a child asks for a cookie) are an important part of language learning. Also, babies actively participate in language learning by asking questions, such as "What dis?" (Domingo & Goldstein-Alpern, 1999).

When a child makes a language error, parents typically repeat the child's sentence, with needed corrections (Bohannon & Stanowicz, 1988) or ask a clarifying question to draw the

Biological predisposition The presumed hereditary readiness of humans to learn certain skills, such as how to use language, or a readiness to behave in particular ways.

 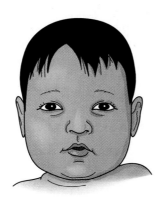 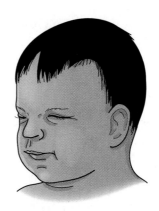

85
Medium high positive

50
Neutral attention

20
Avert

▸▸**FIGURE 3.13** Infant engagement scale. These samples from a 90-point scale show various levels of infant engagement, or attention. Babies participate in prelanguage "conversations" with parents by giving and withholding attention and by smiling, gazing, or vocalizing. (From Beebe et al., 1982.)

child's attention to the error (Saxton, Houston-Price, & Dawson, 2005). More important is the fact that parents and children begin to communicate long before the child can speak. A readiness to interact *socially* with parents may be as important as innate language recognition. The next section explains why.

Early Communication

How do parents communicate with infants before they can talk? Parents go to a great deal of trouble to get babies to smile and vocalize (▸▸Fig. 3.13). In doing so, they quickly learn to change their actions to keep the infant's attention, arousal, and activity at optimal levels. A familiar example is the "I'm-Going-to-Get-You Game." In it, the adult says, "I'm gonna getcha . . . . I'm gonna getcha . . . . I'm gonna getcha . . . . Gotcha!" Through such games, adults and babies come to share similar rhythms and expectations (Stern, 1982). Soon a system of shared **signals** is created, including touching, vocalizing, gazing, and smiling. These help lay a foundation for later language use (Tamis-LeMonda, Bornstein, & Baumwell, 2001). Specifically, signals establish a pattern of "conversational" *turn-taking* (alternate sending and receiving of messages).

Olivia	*Amy*
	(smiles)
"Oh what a nice little smile!"	
"Yes, isn't that nice?"	
"There."	
"There's a nice little smile."	(burps)
"Well, pardon you!"	
"Yes, that's better, isn't it?"	
"Yes."	(vocalizes)
"Yes."	(smiles)
"What's so funny?"	

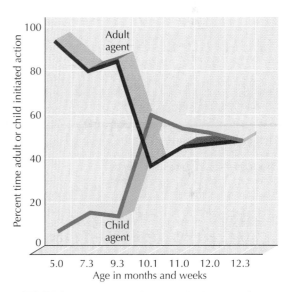

▸▸**FIGURE 3.14** This graph shows the development of turn-taking in games played by an infant and his mother. For several months Richard responded to games such as peeka-boo and "hand-the-toy-back" only when his mother initiated action. At about 9 months, however, he rapidly began to initiate action in the games. Soon, he was the one to take the lead about half of the time. Learning to take turns and to direct actions toward another person underlie basic language skills. (From Bruner, 1983.)

From the outside, such exchanges may look meaningless. In reality, they represent real communication. Amy's vocalizations and attention provide a way of interacting emotionally with Olivia and Tom. Infants as young as 4 months engage in vocal turn-taking with adults (also, see ▸▸Fig. 3.14) (Jaffe et al., 2001). The more children interact with parents, the faster they learn to talk and the faster they learn thinking abilities (Dickinson & Tabors, 2001). One study found that 6-week-old babies gaze at an adult's face in rhythm with the adult's speech (Crown et al., 2002). Unmistakably, social relationships contribute to early language learning (Hoff, 2006).

Signal In early language development, any behavior, such as touching, vocalizing, gazing, or smiling, that allows nonverbal interaction and turn-taking between parent and child.

As with motherese, parents use a distinctive style when singing to an infant. Even people who speak another language can tell if a tape-recorded song was sung to an infant or an adult. Likewise, lullabies remain recognizable when electronic filtering removes words (Trehub et al., 1993a, 1993b).

Gary Conner/Index Stock Imagery

Parentese

When they talk to infants, parents use an exaggerated pattern of speaking called **motherese** or **parentese.** Typically, they raise their tone of voice, use short, simple sentences, repeat themselves more, and use frequent gestures (Gogate, Bahrick, & Watson, 2000). They also slow their rate of speaking and use exaggerated voice inflections: "Did Amy eat it A-L-L UP?"

What is the purpose of such changes? Parents are apparently trying to help their children learn language. When a baby is still babbling, parents tend to use long, adult-style sentences. But as soon as the baby says its first word they switch to parentese. By the time babies are 4 months old they prefer parentese over normal speech (Cooper et al., 1997).

In addition to being simpler, parentese has a distinct "musical" quality (Trainors & Desjardins, 2002). No matter what language mothers speak, the melodies, pauses, and inflections they use to comfort, praise, or give warning are universal. Psychologist Anne Fernald has found that mothers of all nations talk to their babies with similar changes in pitch. For instance, we praise babies with a rising, then falling pitch ("BRA-vo!" "GOOD girl!"). Warnings are delivered in a short, sharp rhythm ("Nein! Nein!" "Basta! Basta!" "Not! Dude!"). To give comfort, parents use low, smooth, drawn-out tones ("Oooh poor baaa-by." "Oooh pobrecito.") A high-pitched, rising melody is used to call attention to objects ("See the pretty BIRDIE?") (Fernald, 1989).

Parentese helps parents get babies' attention, communicate with them, and teach them language (Thiessen, Hill, & Saffran, 2005). Later, as a child's speaking improves, parents tend to adjust their speech to the child's language ability. Especially from 18 months to 4 years of age, parents seek to clarify what a child says and prompt the child to say more.

In summary, some elements of language are innate. Nevertheless, our inherited tendency to learn language does not determine if we will speak English or Vietnamese, Spanish or Russian. Environmental forces also influence whether a person develops simple or sophisticated language skills. The first 7 years of life are a sensitive period in language learning (Eliot, 1999). Clearly, a full flowering of speech requires careful cultivation.

Motherese (or parentese) A pattern of speech used when talking to infants, marked by a higher-pitched voice; short, simple sentences; repetition, slower speech; and exaggerated voice inflections.

➡ Study Break   Language Development

Reflect

In order, see if you can name and imitate the language abilities you had as you progressed from birth to age 2 years. Now see if you can label and imitate some basic elements of parentese.

In your own words, state at least one argument for and against Chomsky's view of language acquisition.

You are going to spend a day with a person who speaks a different language than you do. Do you think you would be able to communicate with the other person? How does this relate to language acquisition?

Learning Check

1. The development of speech and language usually occurs in which order?

   a. crying, cooing, babbling, telegraphic speech
   b. cooing, crying, babbling, telegraphic speech
   c. babbling, crying, cooing, telegraphic speech
   d. crying, babbling, cooing, identification

2. Simple two-word sentences are characteristic of _____ speech.

3. Noam _____ has advanced the idea that language acquisition is built on innate patterns.

4. Prelanguage turn-taking and social interactions would be of special interest to a psycholinguist. T or F?

5. The style of speaking known as _____ is higher in pitch and has a musical quality.

Critical Thinking

6. The children of professional parents hear more words per hour than the children of welfare parents, and they also tend to score higher on tests of mental abilities. How else could their higher scores be explained?

Answers

1. a 2. telegraphic 3. Chomsky 4. T 5. parentese 6. Children in professional homes receive many educational benefits that are less common in welfare homes. Yet, even when such differences are taken into account, brighter children tend to come from richer language environments (Hart & Risley, 1999).

COGNITIVE DEVELOPMENT—HOW DO CHILDREN LEARN TO THINK?

>SURVEY QUESTION< *How DO children learn to think?*

Now that we have Amy talking, let's move on to a broader view of intellectual development. Jean Piaget (Jahn pea-ah-ZHAY) provided some of the first great insights into how children develop thinking abilities.

How different is a child's understanding of the world from that of an adult? Generally speaking, their thinking is less abstract. Children use fewer generalizations, categories, and principles. They also tend to base their understanding on particular examples and objects they can see or touch.

Before the age of 6 or 7, thinking is very concrete. Younger children cannot make **transformations** in which they must mentally change the shape or form of a substance (such as clay or water). Let's visit Amy at age 5: If you show her a short, wide glass full of milk and a taller, narrow glass (also full), she will most likely tell you that the taller glass contains more milk (even if it doesn't). Amy will tell you this even if she watches you pour milk from the short glass into an empty, tall glass. She is not bothered by the fact that the milk appears to be transformed from a smaller to a larger amount. Instead, she responds only to the fact that *taller* seems to mean *more.* (See ▸▸Fig. 3.15.) After about age 7, children are no longer fooled by this situation. Perhaps that's why 7 has been called the "age of reason." From age 7 on, we see a definite trend toward more logical, adult-like thought (Flavell, 1992).

Is there any pattern to the growth of intellect in childhood? According to the Swiss psychologist and philosopher Jean Piaget (1951, 1952), there is.

Piaget's Theory of Cognitive Development

Jean Piaget believed that all children pass through a series of distinct stages in intellectual development. Many of his ideas came from observing his own children as they solved various thought problems. (It is tempting to imagine that Piaget's illustrious career was launched one day when his wife said to him, "Watch the children for a while, will you, Jean?")

Mental Adaptations

Piaget was convinced that intellect grows through processes he called assimilation and accommodation. **Assimilation** refers to using existing mental patterns in new situations. Let's say that a plastic hammer is the favorite toy of a boy named Benjamin, who pounds on blocks with it. For his birthday Benjamin gets an oversized toy wrench. If he uses the wrench for pounding, it has been assimilated to an existing knowledge structure.

In **accommodation,** existing ideas are modified to fit new requirements. For instance, a younger child might think that a dime is worth less than a (larger) nickel. However, as children begin to spend money, they must alter their ideas about what "more" and "less" mean. Thus, new situations are assimilated to existing ideas, and new ideas are created to accommodate new experiences.

Piaget's ideas have deeply affected our view of children (Feldman, 2004). The following is a brief summary of what he found.

The Sensorimotor Stage (0–2 Years)

In the first 2 years of life, Amy's intellectual development will be largely nonverbal. She will be mainly concerned with learning to coordinate her movements with information from her senses. Also, **object permanence** (an understanding that objects continue to exist when

▸▸**FIGURE 3.15** Children under age 7 intuitively assume that a volume of liquid increases when it is poured from a short, wide container into a taller, thinner one. This boy thinks the tall container holds more than the short one. Actually each holds the same amount of liquid. Children make such judgments based on the height of the liquid, not its volume.

Jean Piaget—philosopher, psychologist, and keen observer of children.

Transformation The mental ability to change the shape or form of a substance (such as clay or water) and to perceive that its volume remains the same.

Assimilation In Piaget's theory, the application of existing mental patterns to new situations (that is, the new situation is assimilated to existing mental schemes).

Accommodation In Piaget's theory, the modification of existing mental patterns to fit new demands (that is, mental schemes are changed to accommodate new information or experiences).

Sensorimotor stage Stage of intellectual development during which sensory input and motor responses become coordinated.

Object permanence Concept, gained in infancy, that objects continue to exist even when they are hidden from view.

they are out of sight) emerges at this time. Sometime during their first year, babies begin to actively pursue disappearing objects. By age 2, they can anticipate the movement of an object behind a screen. For example, when watching an electric train, Amy will look ahead to the end of a tunnel, rather than staring at the spot where the train disappeared.

In general, developments in this stage indicate that the child's conceptions are becoming more *stable*. Objects cease to appear and disappear magically, and a more orderly and predictable world replaces the confusing and disconnected sensations of infancy.

The Preoperational Stage (2–7 Years)

During this period, children begin to think *symbolically* and use language. But the child's thinking is still very **intuitive** (it makes little use of reasoning and logic). (Do you remember thinking as a child that the sun and the moon followed you when you took a walk?) In addition, the child's use of language is not as sophisticated as it might seem. Children have a tendency to confuse words with the objects they represent. If Benjamin calls a toy block a "car" and you use it to make a "house," he may be upset. To children, the name of an object is as much a part of the object as its size, shape, and color. This seems to underlie a preoccupation with name calling. To the preoperational child, insulting words may really hurt. Consider one rather protected youngster who was angered by her older brother. Searching for a way to retaliate against her larger and stronger foe, she settled on, "You pantygirdle!" It was the worst thing she could think of saying.

During the preoperational stage, the child is also quite **egocentric** (unable to take the viewpoint of other people). The child's ego seems to stand at the center of his or her world. To illustrate, show Amy a two-sided mirror. Then hold it between you and her, so she can see herself in it. If you ask her what she thinks *you* can see, she imagines that you see *her* face reflected in the mirror, instead of your own. Such egocentrism explains why children can seem exasperatingly selfish or uncooperative at times. If Benjamin blocks your view by standing in front of the TV, he assumes that you can see it if he can. If you ask him to move so you can see better, he may move so that he can see better! Benjamin is not being selfish, in the ordinary sense. He just doesn't realize that your view differs from his.

Crossing a busy street can be dangerous for the preoperational child. Because their thinking is still egocentric, younger children cannot understand why the driver of a car can't see them if they can see the car. Children under the age of 7 also cannot consistently judge speeds and distances of oncoming cars. Adults can easily overestimate the "street smarts" of younger children. It is advisable to teach children to cross with a light, in crosswalks, or with assistance.

The Concrete Operational Stage (7–11 Years)

An important development during this stage is mastery of **conservation** (the concept that mass, weight, and volume remain unchanged when the shape of objects changes). Children have learned conservation when they understand that rolling a ball of clay into a "snake" does not increase the amount of clay. Likewise, pouring liquid from a tall, narrow glass into a shallow dish does not reduce the amount of liquid. In each case the volume remains the same despite changes in shape or appearance. The original amount is *conserved* (see ▶▶ Fig. 3.15).

During the concrete operational stage, children begin to use concepts of time, space, and number. The child can think logically about very concrete objects or situations, categories, and principles. Such abilities explain why children stop believing in Santa Claus when they reach this stage. Because they can conserve volume, they realize that Santa's sack couldn't possibly hold enough toys for millions of girls and boys.

Another important development at this time is the ability to *reverse* thoughts or mental operations. A 4-year-old boy in the preoperational stage might have a conversation like this (showing what happens when a child's thinking *lacks* reversibility):

"Do you have a brother?"
"Yes."
"What's his name?"

Preoperational stage Period of intellectual development during which children begin to use language and think symbolically, yet remain intuitive and egocentric in their thought.

Intuitive thought Thinking that makes little or no use of reasoning and logic.

Egocentric thought Thought that is self-centered and fails to consider the viewpoints of others.

Concrete operational stage Period of intellectual development during which children become able to use the concepts of time, space, volume, and number, but in ways that remain simplified and concrete, rather than abstract.

Conservation In Piaget's theory, mastery of the concept that the weight, mass, and volume of matter remains unchanged (is conserved) even when the shape or appearance of objects changes.

FogStock LLC/Index Stock Imagery

"Sam."

"Does Sam have a brother?"

"No."

Reversibility of thought allows children in the concrete operational stage to recognize that if $4 \times 2 = 8$, then 2×4 does, too. Younger children must memorize each relationship separately. Thus, a preoperational child may know that $4 \times 9 = 36$, without being able to tell you what 9×4 equals.

The Formal Operations Stage (11 Years and Up)

After about the age of 11, children begin to break away from concrete objects and specific examples. Thinking is based more on abstract principles, such as "democracy," "honor," or "correlation." Children who reach this stage can think about their thoughts, and they become less egocentric. Older children and young adolescents also gradually become able to consider hypothetical possibilities (suppositions, guesses, or projections). For example, if you ask a younger child, "What do you think would happen if it suddenly became possible for people to fly?" the child might respond, "People can't fly." Older children are able to consider such possibilities.

Full adult intellectual ability is attained during the stage of formal operations. Older adolescents are capable of inductive and deductive reasoning, and they can comprehend math, physics, philosophy, psychology, and other abstract systems. They can learn to test hypotheses in a scientific manner. Of course, not everyone reaches this level of thinking. Also, many adults can think formally about some topics, but their thinking becomes concrete when the topic is unfamiliar. This implies that formal thinking may be more a result of culture and learning than maturation. In any case, after late adolescence, improvements in intellect are based on gaining knowledge, experience, and wisdom, rather than on any leaps in basic thinking capacity.

How can parents apply Piaget's ideas? Piaget's theory suggests that the ideal way to guide intellectual development is to provide experiences that are only slightly novel, unusual, or challenging. Remember, a child's intellect develops mainly through accommodation. It is usually best to follow a *one-step-ahead strategy*, in which your teaching efforts are aimed just beyond a child's current level of comprehension (Brainerd, 2003).

Parents should avoid *forced teaching*, or "hothousing," which is like trying to force plants to bloom prematurely. Forcing children to learn reading, math, gymnastics, swimming, or music at an accelerated pace can bore or oppress them. True intellectual enrichment respects the child's interests. It does not make the child feel pressured to perform (Alvino et al., 1996).

For your convenience, ▨ Table 3.2 briefly summarizes each Piagetian stage. To help you remember Piaget's theory, the table describes what would happen at each stage if we played a game of *Monopoly* with the child. You'll also find brief suggestions about how to relate to children in each stage.

Piaget Today

Piaget's theory is a valuable "road map" for understanding how children think. However, many psychologists are convinced that Piaget gave too little credit to the effects of learning. For example, children who grow up in villages where pottery is made can correctly answer questions about the conservation of clay at an earlier age than Piaget would have predicted.

According to learning theorists, children continuously gain specific knowledge; they do not undergo stage-like leaps in general mental ability (Siegler, 2004). On the other hand, the growth in connections between brain cells occurs in waves that parallel some of Piaget's stages (see ▸▸ Fig. 3.16). Thus, the truth may lie somewhere between Piaget's stage theory and modern learning theory.

On a broad scale, many of Piaget's *observations* have held up well. However, his *explanations* of childhood thinking abilities continue to be debated (Feldman, 2004). Where early

Formal operations stage Period of intellectual development characterized by thinking that includes abstract, theoretical, and hypothetical ideas.

■ Table 3.2 Piaget—A Guide for Parents

Piaget	*Monopoly* Game	Guidelines for Parents
Sensorimotor Stage (0–2 Years) The stage during which sensory input and motor responses become coordinated.	The child puts houses, hotels, and dice in her mouth and plays with "Chance" cards.	Active play with a child is most effective at this stage. Encourage explorations in touching, smelling, and manipulating objects. Peekaboo is a good way to establish the permanence of objects.
Preoperational Stage (2–7 Years) The period of cognitive development when children begin to use language and think symbolically, yet remain intuitive and egocentric.	The child plays *Monopoly,* but makes up her own rules and cannot understand instructions.	Specific examples and touching or seeing things continues to be more useful than verbal explanations. Learning the concept of conservation may be aided by demonstrations with liquids, beads, clay, and other substances.
Concrete Operational Stage (7–11 Years) The period of cognitive development during which children begin to use concepts of time, space, volume, and number, but in ways that remain simplified and concrete.	The child understands basic instructions and will play by the rules, but is not capable of hypothetical transactions dealing with mortgages, loans, and special pacts with other players.	Children are beginning to use generalizations, but they still require specific examples to grasp many ideas. Expect a degree of inconsistency in the child's ability to apply concepts of time, space, quantity, and volume to new situations.
Formal Operations Stage (11 Years and Up) The period of intellectual development marked by a capacity for abstract, theoretical, and hypothetical thinking.	The child no longer plays the game mechanically; complex and hypothetical transactions unique to each game are now possible.	It is now more effective to explain things verbally or symbolically and to help children master general rules and principles. Encourage the child to create hypotheses and to imagine how things could be.

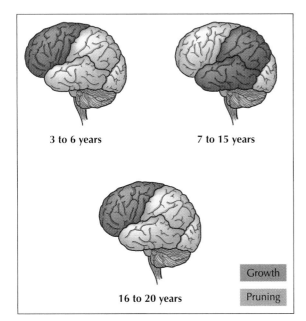

3 to 6 years   7 to 15 years

16 to 20 years

Growth

Pruning

▸▸**FIGURE 3.16** Between the ages of 3 and 6 a tremendous wave of growth occurs in connections among neurons in the frontal areas of the brain. This corresponds to the time when children make rapid progress in their ability to think symbolically. Between ages 7 and 15, peak synaptic growth shifts to the temporal and parietal lobes. During this period children become increasingly adept at using language, a specialty of the temporal lobes. In the late teens, the brain actively destroys unneeded connections, especially in the frontal lobes. This pruning of synapses sharpens the brain's capacity for abstract thinking (Restak, 2001).

infancy is concerned, even Piaget's observations may need updating. It looks like Piaget greatly underestimated the mental abilities of infants.

Infant Cognition

What evidence is there that Piaget underestimated infant abilities? Piaget believed that infants under the age of 1 year cannot think. Babies, he said, have no memory of people and objects that are out of sight. Yet, we now know that infants begin forming representations of the world very early in life. For example, babies as young as 3 months of age appear to know that objects are solid and do not disappear when out of view (Baillargeon, 2004).

Why did Piaget fail to detect the thinking skills of infants? Most likely, he mistook babies' limited physical skills for mental incompetence. Piaget's tests required babies to search for objects or reach out and touch them. Newer, more sensitive methods are uncovering abilities Piaget missed. One such method takes advantage of the fact that

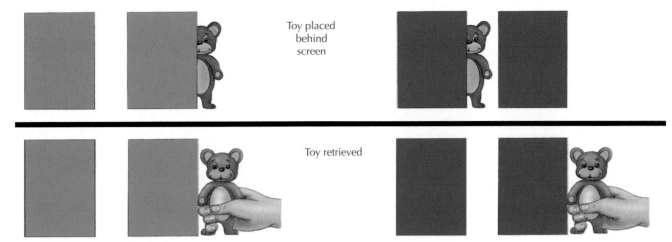

>>**FIGURE 3.17** The panels on the left show a possible event, in which an infant watches as a toy is placed behind the right of two screens. After a delay of 70 seconds, the toy is brought into view from behind the right screen. In the two panels on the right, an impossible event occurs. The toy is placed behind the left screen and retrieved from behind the right. (A duplicate toy was hidden there before testing.) Eight-month-old infants react with surprise when they see the impossible event staged for them. Their reaction implies that they remember where the toy was hidden. Infants appear to have a capacity for memory and thinking that greatly exceeds what Piaget claimed is possible during the sensorimotor period. (Adapted from Baillargeon et al., 1989.)

babies, like adults, act surprised when they see something "impossible" or unexpected occur. To use this effect, psychologist Renee Baillargeon (1991, 2004) puts on little "magic shows" for infants. In her "theater" babies watch as possible and impossible events occur with toys or other objects. Some 3-month-old infants act surprised and gaze longer at impossible events. An example is seeing two solid objects appear to pass through each other. By the time they are 8 months old, babies can remember where objects are (or should be) for at least 1 minute (>>Fig. 3.17).

Piaget believed that abilities like those described in Figure 3.17 emerge only after a long period of sensorimotor development. However, it's clear that babies quickly acquire the capacity to form concepts about the world (Eimas, Quinn, & Cowan, 1994). It looks as if further study is likely to refine and amend the ideas that grew from Piaget's fateful decision to "watch the children for a while."

Another criticism of Piaget is that he underestimated the impact of culture on mental development. The next section tells how Amy will master the intellectual tools valued by her culture.

Vygotsky's Sociocultural Theory

Psychologists are also interested in the *sociocultural theory* of Russian scholar Lev Vygotsky (1896–1934). Vygotsky's key insight is that children's thinking develops through dialogues with more capable persons (Vygotsky, 1962, 1978).

How does that relate to intellectual growth? So far, no one has ever published *A Child's Guide to Life on Earth*. Instead, children must learn about life from various "tutors," such as parents, teachers, and older siblings. Even if *A Child's Guide to Life on Earth* did exist, we would need a separate version for every culture. It is not enough for children to learn how to think. They must also learn specific intellectual skills valued by their culture.

Like Piaget, Vygotsky believed that children actively seek to discover new principles. However, Vygotsky emphasized that many of a child's most important "discoveries" are guided by skillful tutors. Psychologist David Shaffer (2002) offers the following example:

> Annie, a 4-year-old, has just received her first jigsaw puzzle as a birthday present. She attempts to work the puzzle but gets nowhere until her father comes along, sits down beside her, and gives her some tips. He suggests that it would be a good idea to put together the corners first, points to the pink area at the edge of one corner piece and says, "Let's look for another pink piece." When Annie seems frustrated, he places two interlocking pieces near each other so that she will notice them, and when Annie succeeds, he offers words of encouragement. As Annie gradually gets the hang of it, he steps back and lets her work more and more independently. (p. 260)

Interactions like this are most helpful when they take place within a child's **zone of proximal development.**

What did Vygotsky mean by that? The word *proximal* means close or nearby. Vygotsky realized that, at any given time, some tasks are just beyond a child's reach. The child is close to having the mental skills needed to do the task, but it is a little too complex to be mastered alone. However, children working within this zone can make rapid progress if they receive sensitive guidance from a skilled partner (LeBlanc & Bearison, 2004).

Vygotsky also emphasized a process he called **scaffolding.** A scaffold is a framework or temporary support. Vygotsky believed that adults help children learn how to think by "scaffolding," or supporting, their attempts to solve problems or discover principles (Daniels, 2005). To be most effective, scaffolding must be responsive to a child's needs. For example, as Annie's father helped her with the puzzle, he tailored his hints and guidance to match her evolving abilities. The two of them worked together, step by step, so that Annie could better understand how to assemble a puzzle. In a sense, Annie's father set up a series of temporary bridges that helped her move into new mental territory. As predicted by Vygotsky's theory, the cognitive skills of 3- to 6-year-old children are closely related to the amount of scaffolding their parents provide (Smith, Landry, & Swank, 2000).

During their collaborations with others, children learn important cultural beliefs and values. For example, imagine that a boy wants to know how many hockey cards he has. His mother helps him stack and count the cards, moving each card to a new stack as they count it. She then shows him how to write the number on a slip of paper so he can remember it. This teaches the child not only about counting, but also that writing is valued in our culture. In other parts of the world, a child learning to count might be shown how to make notches on a stick or tie knots in a cord.

Implications

Vygotsky saw that grown-ups play a crucial role in what children know. As they try to decipher the world, children rely on adults to help them understand how things work. Vygotsky further noticed that adults unconsciously adjust their behavior to give children the information they need to solve problems that interest the child. In this way, children use adults to learn about their culture and society (Gopnik, Meltzoff, & Kuhl, 2000; LeBlanc & Bearison, 2004).

MORAL DEVELOPMENT— GROWING A CONSCIENCE

>SURVEY QUESTION< *How do we develop morals and values?*

A person with a terminal illness is in great pain. She is pleading for death. Should extraordinary medical efforts be made to keep her alive? A friend of yours desperately needs to pass a test and asks you to help him cheat. Will you do it? These are *moral* questions, or questions of conscience.

Zone of proximal development Refers to the range of tasks a child cannot yet master alone, but that she or he can accomplish with the guidance of a more capable partner.

Scaffolding The process of adjusting instruction so that it is responsive to a beginner's behavior and supports the beginner's efforts to understand a problem or gain a mental skill.

Moral development starts in childhood and continues into adulthood (Turiel, 2006). Through this process, we acquire values, beliefs, and thinking patterns that guide responsible behavior. Moral values are especially likely to come into sharper focus during adolescence, as capacities for self-control and abstract thinking increase (Hart & Carlo, 2005). Let's take a brief look at this interesting aspect of personal development.

Levels of Moral Development

How are moral values acquired? In his influential account, psychologist Lawrence Kohlberg (1981a) held that we learn moral values through thinking and reasoning. To study moral development, Kohlberg posed dilemmas to children of different ages. The following is one of the moral dilemmas he used (Kohlberg, 1969, adapted).

A woman was near death from cancer, and there was only one drug that might save her. It was discovered by a druggist who was charging 10 times what it cost to make the drug. The sick woman's husband could only pay $1,000, but the druggist wanted $2,000. He asked the druggist to sell it cheaper or to let him pay later. The druggist said no. So the husband became desperate and broke into the store to steal the drug for his wife. Should he have done that? Was it wrong or right? Why?

Each child was asked what action the husband should take. Kohlberg classified the reasons given for each choice and identified three levels of moral development. Each is based not so much on the choices made, but on the reasoning used to arrive at a choice.

At the lowest, **preconventional level,** moral thinking is guided by the consequences of actions (punishment, reward, or an exchange of favors). For example, a person at this level might reason that "The man shouldn't steal the drug because he could get caught and sent to jail" (avoiding punishment) or "It won't do him any good to steal the drug because his wife will probably die before he gets out of jail" (self-interest).

At the second, or **conventional level,** reasoning is based on a desire to please others or to follow accepted authority, rules, and values. For example, a person at this intermediate level might say "He shouldn't steal the drug because others will think he is a thief. His wife would not want to be saved by thievery" (avoiding disapproval) or "Although his wife needs the drug, he should not break the law to get it. Everyone has to obey the law. His wife's condition does not justify stealing" (traditional morality of authority).

At the highest, or **postconventional level,** moral behavior is directed by self-chosen ethical principles that tend to be general, comprehensive, or universal. People at this level place high value on justice, dignity, and equality. For example, a highly principled person might say "He should steal the drug and then inform the authorities that he has done so. He will have to face a penalty, but he will have saved a human life" (self-chosen ethical principles).

Does everyone eventually reach the highest level? People advance at different rates, and many fail to reach the postconventional level of moral reasoning. In fact, many do not even reach the conventional level. For instance, one English survey revealed that 11 percent of men and 3 percent of women would commit murder for $1 million if they could be sure of getting away with the crime ("They'd kill," 1991).

The preconventional level is most characteristic of young children and delinquents (Forney, Forney, & Crutsinger, 2005). Conventional, group-oriented morals are typical of older children and most adults. Kohlberg estimated that only about 20 percent of the adult population achieves postconventional morality, representing self-direction and higher principles. (It would appear that few of these people enter politics!)

Developing a "moral compass" is an important part of growing up. Many of the choices we make every day involve fundamental questions of right and wrong. Being able to think clearly about such questions is essential to becoming a responsible adult.

Moral development The development of values, beliefs, and thinking abilities that act as a guide regarding what is acceptable behavior.

Preconventional moral reasoning Moral thinking based on the consequences of one's choices or actions (punishment, reward, or an exchange of favors).

Conventional moral reasoning Moral thinking based on a desire to please others or to follow accepted rules and values.

Postconventional moral reasoning Moral thinking based on carefully examined and self-chosen moral principles.

Study Break   Cognitive Development and Moral Development

Reflect

You are going to make cookies with children of various ages. See if you can name each of Piaget's stages and give an example of what a child in that stage might be expected to do.

You have been asked to help a child learn to use a pocket calculator to do simple addition. How would you go about identifying the child's zone of proximal development for this task? How would you scaffold the child's learning?

At what stage of moral development do you think most terrorists function?

Learning Check

Match each item with one of the following stages.

A. Sensorimotor   B. Preoperational   C. Concrete operational
D. Formal operations

1. _____ egocentric thought
2. _____ abstract or hypothetical
3. _____ purposeful movement
4. _____ intuitive thought

5. _____ conservation
6. _____ reversibility thought
7. _____ object permanence
8. _____ nonverbal development

9. Assimilation refers to applying existing thought patterns or knowledge to new situations. T or F?
10. Newer methods for testing infant thinking abilities frequently make note of whether an infant is _____ by seemingly _____ events.
11. Vygotsky called the process of providing a temporary framework of supports for learning new mental abilities _____.
12. According to Kohlberg, the conventional level of moral development is marked by a reliance on outside authority. T or F?
13. Self-interest and avoiding punishment are elements of post-conventional morality. T or F?

Critical Thinking

14. Using Piaget's theory as a guide, at what age would you expect a child to recognize that a Styrofoam cup has weight?

Answers

1. B 2. D 3. A 4. B 5. C 6. C 7. A 8. A 9. T 10. surprised, impossible 11. scaffolding 12. T 13. F 14. Seventy-five percent of 4- to 6-year-olds say that a Styrofoam cup has no weight after lifting it! Most children judge weight intuitively (by the way an object feels) until they begin to move into the concrete operational stage (Smith, Carey, & Wiser, 1985).

THE STORY OF A LIFETIME—ROCKY ROAD OR GARDEN PATH?

>SURVEY QUESTION< *What are the typical tasks and dilemmas through the life span?*

At the beginning of this chapter we noted that developmental psychologists are interested in every phase of life from the womb to the tomb. Thus far, we have concentrated on Amy's early years because development during childhood can have a large impact on a person's life. It is not possible here to satisfy Olivia and Tom's curiosity about Amy's future. Nevertheless, we can at least sketch the general outlines of her life to come. Every life is marked by a number of *developmental milestones.* These are notable events, markers, or turning points in personal development. Some examples include graduating from school, voting for the first time, getting married, watching a child leave home (or move back!), the death of a parent, becoming a grandparent, retirement, and one's own death.

Erikson's Psychosocial Theory

Perhaps the best way to get a preview of Amy's life is to consider some of the major psychological challenges she is likely to encounter. Broad similarities can be found in the life stages of infancy, childhood, adolescence, young adulthood, middle adulthood, and old age. Each stage confronts a person with new **developmental tasks** that must be mastered for optimal development. Examples are learning to read in childhood, adjusting to sexual maturity in adolescence, and establishing a vocation as an adult.

In an influential book entitled *Childhood and Society* (1963), personality theorist Erik Erikson (1903–1994) suggests that we face a specific *psychosocial dilemma,* or "crisis," at each stage of life. A **psychosocial dilemma** is a conflict between personal impulses and the social world. Resolving each dilemma creates a new balance between a person and society. A string

Developmental task Any skill that must be mastered, or personal change that must take place, for optimal development.

Psychosocial dilemma A conflict between personal impulses and the social world.

of "successes" produces healthy development and a satisfying life. Unfavorable outcomes throw us off balance, making it harder to deal with later crises. Life becomes a "rocky road" and personal growth is stunted. ■ Table 3.3 lists Erikson's dilemmas.

What are the major developmental tasks and life crises? A brief description of each psychosocial dilemma follows.

Stage One, First Year of Life: Trust versus Mistrust

During the first year of life, children are completely dependent on others. Erikson believes that a basic attitude of trust or mistrust is formed at this time. **Trust** is established when babies are given warmth, touching, love, and physical care. **Mistrust** is caused by inadequate or unpredictable care and by parents who are cold, indifferent, or rejecting. Basic mistrust may later cause insecurity, suspiciousness, or an inability to relate to others. Notice that trust comes from the same conditions that help babies become securely attached to their parents.

Stage Two, 1–3 Years: Autonomy versus Shame and Doubt

In stage two, children express their growing self-control by climbing, touching, exploring, and trying to do things for themselves. Tom and Olivia can foster Amy's sense of **autonomy** by encouraging her to try new skills. However, her first efforts may be crude, involving spilling, falling, wetting, and other "accidents." If Tom and Olivia ridicule or overprotect Amy, they may cause her to **doubt** her abilities and feel **shameful** about her actions.

Stage Three, 3–5 Years: Initiative versus Guilt

In stage three, children move beyond simple self-control and begin to take initiative. Through play, children learn to make plans and carry out tasks. Parents reinforce **initiative** by giving children freedom to play, ask questions, use imagination, and choose activities. Feelings of **guilt** about initiating activities are formed if parents criticize severely, prevent play, or discourage a child's questions.

Stage Four, 6–12 Years: Industry versus Inferiority

Many events of middle childhood are symbolized by that fateful day when you first entered school. With dizzying speed your world expanded beyond your family, and you faced a whole series of new challenges.

The elementary school years are a child's "entrance into life." In school, children begin to learn skills valued by society, and success or failure can affect a child's feelings of adequacy. Children learn a sense of **industry** if they win praise for productive activities, such as building, painting, cooking, reading, and studying. If a child's efforts are regarded as messy, childish, or inadequate, feelings of **inferiority** result. For the first time, teachers, classmates, and adults outside the home become as important as parents in shaping attitudes toward oneself.

Stage Five, Adolescence: Identity versus Role Confusion

Adolescence is often a turbulent time. Caught between childhood and adulthood, the adolescent faces some unique problems. Erikson considers a need to answer the question "Who am I?" the primary task during this stage of life. As Amy matures mentally and physically, she will have new feelings, a new body, and new attitudes (▶ Fig. 3.18). Like other adolescents, she will need to build a consistent **identity** out of her talents, values, life history, rela-

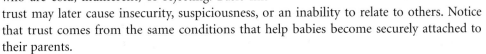

Personality theorist Erik Erikson (1903–1994) is best known for his life-stage theory of human development.

■ Table 3.3	Erikson's Psychosocial Dilemmas
Age	**Characteristic Dilemma**
Birth to 1 year	Trust versus mistrust
1 to 3 years	Autonomy versus shame and doubt
3 to 5 years	Initiative versus guilt
6 to 12 years	Industry versus inferiority
Adolescence	Identity versus role confusion
Young adulthood	Intimacy versus isolation
Middle adulthood	Generativity versus stagnation
Late adulthood	Integrity versus despair

Trust versus mistrust A conflict early in life about learning to trust others and the world.

Autonomy versus shame and doubt A conflict created when growing self-control (autonomy) is pitted against feelings of shame or doubt.

Initiative versus guilt A conflict between learning to take initiative and overcoming feelings of guilt about doing so.

Industry versus inferiority A conflict in middle childhood centered around lack of support for industrious behavior, which can result in feelings of inferiority.

Identity versus role confusion A conflict of adolescence, involving the need to establish a personal identity.

Ethnic Diversity and Identity

For adolescents of ethnic descent, the question is often not just "Who am I?" Rather, it is "Who am I at home? Who am I at school? Who am I with friends from my neighborhood?"

Ethnic heritage can have a powerful influence on personal identity (Weisskirch, 2005). Yet, at a time when teens are trying to find their place in society, they may feel rejected or excluded because of their ethnic heritage. In America, popular culture is loaded with images that dismiss anyone who doesn't look like Scarlett Johansson or Orlando Bloom. Also, ethnic adolescents often face degrading stereotypes concerning their intelligence, sexuality, social status, manners, and so forth. The result can be lowered self-esteem and confusion about roles, values, and personal identity (de las Fuentes & Vasquez, 1999).

In forming an identity, adolescents of ethnic descent face the question of how they should think of themselves. Is Lori an American or a Chinese American or both? Is Jaime a Latino, a Chicano, or a Mexican American? The answer typically depends on how strongly adolescents identify with their family and ethnic community. Teens who take pride in their ethnic heritage have higher self-esteem, a better self-image, and a stronger sense of personal identity (Roberts et al., 1999; Tse, 1999). They are also less likely to engage in drug use (Marsiglia et al., 2004) or violent behavior (French, Kim, & Pillado, 2006).

Group pride, positive models, and a more tolerant society could do much to keep a broad range of options open to *all* adolescents.

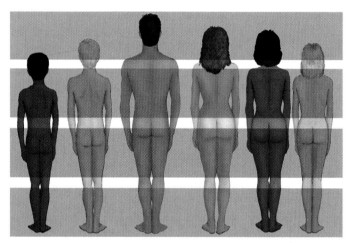

▶▶FIGURE 3.18 Dramatic differences in physical size and maturity are found in adolescents of the same age. The girls pictured are all 13, the boys 16. Maturation that occurs earlier or later than average can affect the "search for identity." (Adapted from "Growing Up" by J. M. Tanner. Copyright © September 1973 by Scientific American, Inc. All rights reserved.)

tionships, and the demands of her culture (Côté & Levine, 2002). Her conflicting experiences as a student, friend, athlete, worker, daughter, lover, and so forth, must be integrated into a unified sense of self. (See "Ethnic Diversity and Identity.") Persons who fail to develop a sense of identity suffer from **role confusion,** an uncertainty about who they are and where they are going.

Stage Six, Young Adulthood: Intimacy versus Isolation

What does Erikson believe is the major conflict in early adulthood? In stage six, the individual feels a need for *intimacy* in his or her life. After establishing a stable identity, a person is prepared to share meaningful love or deep friendship with others. By **intimacy,** Erikson means an ability to care about others and to share experiences with them. In line with Erikson's view, 75 percent of college-age men and women rank a good marriage and family life as important adult goals (Bachman & Johnson, 1979). And yet, marriage or sexual involvement is no guarantee of intimacy: Many adult relationships remain superficial and unfulfilling. Failure to establish intimacy with others leads to a deep sense of **isolation** (feeling alone and uncared for in life). This often sets the stage for later difficulties.

The challenges of young adulthood are quite daunting. More and more young people today are deferring young adulthood, preferring to prolong identity explorations into their 20s before they commit to long-term choices in love and work (Arnett, 2000, 2004; Arnett & Tanner, 2006). (See "The Twixters.")

Stage Seven, Middle Adulthood: Generativity versus Stagnation

According to Erikson, an interest in guiding the next generation provides emotional balance in mature adulthood. Erikson called this quality **generativity.** It is expressed by caring about oneself, one's children, and future generations. Generativity may be achieved by guiding one's own children or by helping other children (as a teacher or coach, for example). Productive or creative work can also express generativity. In any case, a person's concerns and energies must broaden to include the welfare of others and society as a whole. Failure to do this is marked by a **stagnant** concern with one's own needs and comforts. Life loses meaning, and the person feels bitter, dreary, and trapped (Friedman, 2004).

Intimacy versus isolation The challenge of overcoming a sense of isolation by establishing intimacy with others.

Generativity versus stagnation A conflict of middle adulthood in which self-interest is countered by an interest in guiding the next generation.

The Twixters

As you read this book, we encourage you to frequently reflect on new ideas and psychological concepts by thinking critically about them. Consider, for example, the term *adulthood*. Is becoming an adult strictly a biological event? Meet 22-year-old Kirsten:

"When our mothers were our age, they were engaged. . . . They at least had some idea what they were going to do with their lives. . . . I, on the other hand, will have a dual degree in majors that are ambiguous at best and impractical at worst (English and political science), no ring on my finger and no idea who I am, much less what I want to do. . . . Under duress, I will admit that this is a pretty exciting time. Sometimes, when I look out across the wide expanse that is my future, I can see beyond the void. I realize that having nothing ahead to count on means I now have to count on myself; that having no direction means forging one of my own." (Page, 1999).

Kirsten is a "twixter": twentysomething, still living at home, not yet married, with no children, and no settled career. In England,

twixters are called "kippers" (Kids In Parents' Pockets Eroding Retirement Savings). In Australia they are "boomerang kids" (they always come back home). And in Germany they are "Nesthocker" (nest squatters). Are twixters adolescents who are taking longer to find their identity? Or are they young adults avoiding their need to establish themselves in the adult world? Are they self-indulgent individuals trapped in a "maturity gap" (Galambos, Barker, & Tilton-Weaver, 2003)? Or are they part of a culturally defined new status that could be called "emerging adulthood" (Arnett & Tanner, 2006)?

According to American psychologist Jeffrey Arnett, emerging adulthood is increasingly common in affluent Westernized cultures that allow young people to take longer to settle into their adult roles (Arnett, 2000, 2004). However, in less affluent countries, as in poorer parts of America, most adolescents continue to "become adults" at much younger ages (Arnett & Galambos, 2003). Thus, words like *adolescent* or *adulthood* cannot be defined solely in terms of physical maturation. Sociocultural factors also play a role in defining when we stop being children or become adults (Arnett, 2004).

Stage Eight, Late Adulthood: Integrity versus Despair

What does Erikson see as the conflicts of old age? Old age is a time of reflection. According to Erikson, when Amy grows old she must be able to look back over her life with acceptance and satisfaction. People who have lived richly and responsibly develop a sense of **integrity** (self-respect). This allows them to face aging and death with dignity. If previous life events are viewed with regret, the elderly person experiences **despair** (heartache and remorse). In this case, life seems like a series of missed opportunities. The person feels like a failure and knows it's too late to reverse what has been done. Aging and the threat of death then become sources of fear and depression.

To squeeze a lifetime into a few pages, we had to ignore countless details. Although much is lost, the result is a clearer picture of an entire life cycle. Is Erikson's description, then, an exact map of Amy's future—or your own? Probably not. Still, psychosocial dilemmas are major events in many lives. Knowing about them may allow you to anticipate typical trouble spots in your own life. You may also be better prepared to understand the problems and feelings of friends and relatives at various points in the life cycle.

Midlife and Old Age

Erikson's dilemmas are not the only challenges of adulthood. Others are all too familiar: marital strife, divorce, career difficulties, unemployment, health problems, financial pressures, legal conflicts, and personal tragedies—to name but a few. How do people maintain a state of well-being as they run the gauntlet of modern life? Psychologist Carol Ryff (1995; Ryff, Singer, & Palmersheim, 2004) believes that well-being during adulthood has six elements:

1. Self-acceptance
2. Positive relations with others
3. Autonomy (personal freedom)
4. Environmental mastery
5. A purpose in life
6. Continued personal growth

Jeff Greenberg/PhotoEdit

According to Erikson, an interest in future generations characterizes optimal adult development.

Integrity versus despair A conflict in old age between feelings of integrity and the despair of viewing previous life events with regret.

At age 77, John Glenn became the oldest person to fly into space, in October 1998. Glenn was also the first American astronaut to orbit Earth, in 1962. As Glenn's space adventure shows, aging does not inevitably bring an end to engaging in challenging activities.

Ryff found that for many older adults, age-related declines are offset by positive relationships and greater mastery of life's demands (Ryff & Keyes, 1995). Thus, sharing life's joys and sorrows with others, coupled with a better understanding of how the world works, can help carry people through midlife and into their later years (Ryff & Singer, 2000; Ryff, Singer, & Palmersheim, 2004). Despite the emphasis on youth in our culture, middle age and beyond can be a rich period of life in which people feel secure, happy, and self-confident (Rubenstein, 2002).

After the late 50s, personal development is complicated by physical aging. However, it is wrong to believe that most elderly people are sickly, infirm, or senile. (Nowadays, 60 is the new 40, an idea both of your authors whole-heartedly agree with!) Only about 5 percent of those older than 65 are in nursing homes. Mentally, many elderly persons are at least as capable as the average young adult. On intellectual tests, top scorers over the age of 65 match the average for men younger than 35. What sets these silver-haired stars apart? Typically they are people who have continued to work and remain intellectually active (Salthouse, 2004). Gerontologist Warner Schaie (1994, 2005) found that you are most likely to stay mentally sharp in old age if:

1. You remain healthy.
2. You live in a favorable environment (you are educated, have a stimulating occupation, above-average income, and an intact family).
3. You are involved in intellectually stimulating activities (reading, travel, cultural events, continuing education, clubs, professional associations).
4. You have a flexible personality.
5. You are married to a smart spouse.
6. You maintain your perceptual processing speed.
7. You were satisfied with your accomplishments in midlife.

A shorter summary of this list is "Those who live by their wit die with their wits."

Aging and Ageism

You have almost certainly encountered ageism in one way or another. **Ageism,** which refers to discrimination or prejudice based on age, can oppress the young as well as the old. For instance, a person applying for a job may just as well be told "You're too young" as "You're too old." In some societies ageism is expressed as respect for the elderly. In Japan, for instance, aging is seen as positive, and greater age brings more status and respect. In most Western nations, however, ageism tends to have a negative impact on older individuals (Ng, 2002).

Ageism is often expressed through patronizing language. Older people are frequently spoken to in an overly polite, slow, loud, and simple way implying that they are infirm, even when they are not (Nelson, 2005). Popular stereotypes of the "dirty old man," "meddling old woman," "senile old fool," and the like, also help perpetuate myths about aging. But such stereotypes are clearly wrong: A tremendous diversity exists among the elderly—ranging from the infirm to aerobic-dancing grandmothers.

In many occupations, older workers perform well in jobs that require *both* speed and skill. Of course, people do experience a gradual loss of *fluid abilities* (those requiring speed or rapid learning) as they age but, often, this can be offset by many *crystallized abilities* (learned knowledge and skills), such as vocabulary and stored-up facts, which may actually improve—at least into the 60s (Schaie, 2005). Overall, very little loss of job performance occurs as workers grow older. In the professions, wisdom and expertise can usually more than compensate for any loss of mental quickness (Ericsson, 2000). Basing retirement solely on a person's age makes little sense.

Ageism Discrimination or prejudice based on a person's age.

Successful Aging

What are the keys to successful aging? They are not unlike the elements of well-being at midlife. Four psychological characteristics shared by the healthiest, happiest older people are (de Leon, 2005; Vaillant, 2002):

Optimism, hope, and an interest in the future

Gratitude and forgiveness; an ability to focus on what is good in life

Empathy; an ability to share the feelings of others and see the world through their eyes

Connection with others; an ability to reach out, to give and receive social support

Actually, these are excellent guidelines for well-being at any stage of adulthood.

In summary, enlightened views of aging call for an end to the forced obsolescence of the elderly. As a group, older people represent a valuable source of skill, knowledge, and energy that we can't afford to cast aside. As we face the challenges of this planet's uncertain future, we need all the help we can get!

 Study Break Psychosocial Dilemmas, Midlife, and Aging

Reflect

See if you can think of a person you know who is facing one of Erikson's psychosocial dilemmas. Now see if you can think of specific people who seem to be coping with each of the other dilemmas.

See if you can describe three instances of ageism you have witnessed.

Do you know any twixters? (Are you one?) Do you think twixters are adolescents taking longer to find their identity or young adults avoiding their need to establish themselves in the world of adults?

Learning Check

As a way to improve your memory, you might find it helpful to summarize Erikson's eight life stages. Complete this do-it-yourself summary and compare your answers to those given below.

Stage	Crisis	Favorable Outcome
First year of life	1. _____ vs. 2. _____	Faith in the environment and in others
Ages 1–3	Autonomy vs. 3. _____	Feelings of self-control and adequacy
Ages 3–5	4. _____ vs. guilt	Ability to begin one's own activities
Ages 6–12	Industry vs. 5. _____	Confidence in productive skills, learning how to work

Adolescence	6. _____ vs. role confusion	An integrated image of oneself as a unique person
Young adulthood	Intimacy vs. 7. _____	Ability to form bonds of love and friendship with others
Middle adulthood	Generativity vs. 8. _____	Concern for family, society, and future generations
Late adulthood	9. _____ vs. 10. _____	Sense of dignity and fulfillment, willingness to face death

11. After age 65, a large proportion of older people show significant signs of mental disability and most require special care. T or F?

12. Job performance tends to decline rapidly in older workers. T or F?

Critical Thinking

13. Trying to make generalizations about development throughout life is complicated by at least one major factor. What do you think it is?

Answers

1. Trust 2. mistrust 3. shame or doubt 4. Initiative 5. inferiority 6. Identity 7. isolation 8. stagnation 9. Integrity 10. despair 11. F 12. F 13. Different cohorts (groups of people born in different historical times. People born in various decades may have very different life experiences. This makes it difficult to identify universal patterns (Stewart & Ostrove, 1998).

Psychology in Action

Effective Parenting—Raising Healthy Children

>SURVEY QUESTION< *How do effective parents discipline and communicate with their children?*

Authoritative parents help their children grow up with a capacity for love, joy, fulfillment, responsibility, and self-control through *positive parent-child interactions*. Positive interac-

image 100/SuperStock

tions occur when parents spend enjoyable time encouraging their children in a loving and mutually respectful fashion (Dinkmeyer, McKay, & Dinkmeyer, 1997).

As any parent can tell you, it is all well and good to talk about positive interactions until little Johnny misbehaves (and he will, count on it!). As children mature and become more independent, parents must find ways to control their children's behavior. ("No, you may not smear banana pudding on daddy's face.") When parents fail to provide *discipline* (guidance regarding acceptable behavior), children become antisocial, aggressive, and insecure. And yet, it is not easy to have a positive interaction while disciplining your child. This is one reason why overly permissive parents avoid disciplining their children.

Effective discipline is created through communication that is fair but loving, authoritative yet sensitive. It socializes a child without destroying the bond of love and trust between parent and child. Children should feel free to express their deepest feelings. However, this does not mean they can do whatever they please. Rather, the child is allowed to move freely within consistent, well-defined boundaries for acceptable behavior.

Effective Discipline

Parents typically discipline children in one of three ways. **Power assertion** refers to physical punishment or a show of force, such as taking away toys or privileges. As an alternative, some parents use **withdrawal of love** (withholding affection) by refusing to speak to a child, threatening to leave, rejecting the child, or otherwise acting as if the child is temporarily unlovable. **Management techniques** combine praise, recognition, approval, rules, reasoning, and the like to encourage desirable behavior. Each of these approaches can control a child's behavior, but their side effects differ considerably.

What are the side effects? Power-oriented techniques—particularly harsh or severe physical punishment—are associated with fear, hatred of parents, and a lack of spontaneity and warmth. Most children show no signs of long-term damage from spanking—*if* spanking is backed up by supportive parenting (Baumrind, Larzelere, & Cowan, 2002). However, emotional damage does occur if spankings are severe, frequent, or coupled with harsh parenting. In addition, frequent spanking tends to increase aggression, and it leads to *more* problem behaviors, not fewer (McLoyd & Smith, 2002). After reviewing many studies, psychologist Elizabeth Gershoff concludes that parents should minimize spanking or avoid it entirely (Gershoff, 2002).

Withdrawal of love produces children who tend to be self-disciplined. You could say that such children have developed a good conscience. Often, they are described as "model" children or as unusually "good." But as a side effect, they are also frequently anxious, insecure, and dependent on adults for approval.

Management techniques also have limitations. Most important is the need to carefully adjust to a child's level of understanding. Younger children don't always see the connection between rules, explanations, and their own behavior. Nevertheless, management techniques receive a big plus in another area: There is a direct connection between discipline and a child's self-esteem.

How does discipline affect self-esteem? If you regard yourself as a worthwhile person, you have **self-esteem.** High self-esteem is essential for good emotional health. In elementary school, children with high self-esteem tend to be more popular, cooperative, and successful in class. Children with low self-esteem are more withdrawn and tend to perform below average (Amato & Fowler, 2002).

Low self-esteem is related to physical punishment and the withholding of love. And why not? What message do children receive if a parent beats them or tells them they are not worthy of love? Thus, it is best to minimize physical punishment and avoid withdrawal of love. In contrast, high self-esteem is promoted by management techniques. Children who

Power assertion The use of physical punishment or coercion to enforce child discipline.

Withdrawal of love Withholding affection to enforce child discipline.

Management techniques Combining praise, recognition, approval, rules, and reasoning to enforce child discipline.

feel that their parents support them emotionally tend to have high self-esteem (Amato & Fowler, 2002; Nielsen & Metha, 1994).

Consistent Discipline   Individual parents choose limits on behavior that are more "strict" or less "strict." But this choice is less important than **consistency** (maintaining stable rules of conduct). Consistent discipline gives a child a sense of security and stability. Inconsistency makes the child's world seem insecure and unpredictable.

What does consistent discipline mean in practice? To illustrate the errors parents often make, let's consider a few examples of inconsistency (Fontenelle, 1989). The following are mistakes to avoid:

Saying one thing and doing something else. You tell the child, "Bart, if you don't eat your brussels sprouts you can't have any dessert." Then you feel guilty and offer him some dessert.

Making statements you don't mean. "If you don't quiet down, I'm going to stop the car and make you walk home."

Changing *no* to *yes,* especially to quiet a nagging child. A good example is the parent who first refuses to buy the child a toy and later gives in and buys it.

Responding differently to the same misbehavior. One day a child is sent to his room for fighting with his sister. The next day the fighting is overlooked.

Inconsistency makes children feel angry and confused because they cannot control the consequences of their own behavior. Inconsistency also gives children the message: "Don't believe what I say because I usually don't mean it."

Using Discipline Constructively   At one time or another, most parents use power assertion, withdrawal of love, or management techniques to control their children. Each mode of discipline has its place. However, physical punishment and withdrawal of love should always be used with caution. Here are some guidelines.

1. Parents should separate disapproval of the act from disapproval of the child. Instead of saying, "I'm going to punish you because you are bad," say, "I'm upset about what you did."
2. State specifically what misbehavior you are punishing. Explain why you have set limits on this kind of conduct.
3. Punishment should never be harsh or injurious. Don't physically punish a child while you are angry. Also remember that the message "I don't love you right now" can be more painful and damaging than any spanking.
4. Punishment, such as a scolding or taking away privileges, is most effective when done immediately. This statement is especially true for younger children.

Self-esteem Regarding oneself as a worthwhile person; a positive evaluation of oneself.

Consistency With respect to child discipline, the maintenance of stable rules of conduct.

5. Spanking and other forms of physical punishment are not particularly effective for children younger than age 2. The child will only be confused and frightened. Spankings also become less effective after age 5 because they tend to humiliate the child and breed resentment.

6. As discussed earlier, many psychologists believe that children should never be spanked. If you do use physical punishment, reserve it for situations that pose an immediate danger to younger children; for example, when a child runs into the street.

7. Remember, too, that it is usually more effective to reward children when they are being good than it is to punish them for misbehavior.

After age 5, management techniques are the most effective form of discipline, especially techniques that emphasize communication and the relationship between parent and child.

Communicating Effectively with Children

Creative communication is another important ingredient of successful child management (Bath, 1996). Child expert Haim Ginott (1965) believed that making a distinction between feelings and behavior is the key to clear communication. Because children (and parents, too) do not choose how they feel, it is important to allow free expression of feelings.

Accepting Feelings   The child who learns to regard some feelings as "bad," or unacceptable, is being asked to deny a very real part of his or her experience. Ginott encouraged parents to teach their children that all feelings are appropriate; it is only actions that are subject to disapproval. Consider this typical conversation excerpted from Ginott's classic book (1965):

Son: I am stupid, and I know it. Look at my grades in school.
Father: You just have to work harder.
Son: I already work harder and it doesn't help. I have no brains.
Father: You are smart, I know.
Son: I am stupid, I know.
Father: (loudly) You are not stupid!
Son: Yes, I am!
Father: You are not stupid. Stupid!

By debating with the child, the father misses the point that his son *feels* stupid. It would be far more helpful for the father to encourage the boy to talk about his feelings. For instance, he might say, "You really feel that you are not as smart as others, don't you? Do you feel this way often?" In this way, the child is given a chance to express his emotions and to feel understood. The father might conclude by saying, "Look, son, in my eyes you are a fine person. But I understand how you feel. Everyone feels stupid at times." He might also offer some encouragement: "You're improving. Look at the progress you've made."

I-Messages   Child psychologist Thomas Gordon (2000) believes that parents should send *I-messages* to their children, rather than *you-messages.*

What's the difference? **You-messages** take the form of threats, name-calling, accusing, bossing, lecturing, or criticizing. Generally, you-messages tell children what's "wrong" with them. An **I-message** tells children what effect their behavior had on you. For example, after a hard day's work, Maria wants to sit down and rest awhile. She begins to relax with a newspaper when her 5-year-old daughter starts banging loudly on a toy drum. Many parents would respond with a you-message such as "You go play outside this instant" (bossing) or "Don't you ever make such a racket when someone is reading" (lecturing). Gordon suggests sending an I-message such as, "I am very tired, and I would like to read. I feel upset and can't read with so much noise." This forces the child to accept responsibility for the effects of her actions (Dinkmeyer, McKay, & Dinkmeyer, 1997).

You-message Threatening, accusing, bossing, lecturing, or criticizing another person.

I-message A message that states the effect someone else's behavior has on you.

Using Natural and Logical Consequences   Sometimes events automatically discourage misbehavior. For example, a child who refuses to eat dinner will get uncomfortably hungry. A child who throws a temper tantrum may gain nothing but a sore throat and a headache if the tantrum is ignored (Fontenelle, 1989). In such instances, a child's actions have **natural consequences** (intrinsic effects). In situations that don't produce natural consequences, parents can set up **logical consequences** (rational and reasonable effects). For example, a parent might say, "We'll go to the zoo when you've picked up all those toys," or "You can play with your dolls as soon as you've taken your bath," or "You two can stop arguing or leave the table until you're ready to join us."

The concept of logical, parent-defined consequences can be combined with I-messages to handle many day-to-day instances of misbehavior. The key idea is to use an I-message to set up consequences and then give the child a choice to make: "Michelle, we're trying to watch TV. You can settle down and watch with us or go play elsewhere. You decide which you'd rather do" (Dinkmeyer, McKay, & Dinkmeyer, 1997).

How could Maria have dealt with her 5-year-old—the one who was banging on a drum? A response that combines an I-message with logical consequences would be, "I would like for you to stop banging on that drum; otherwise, please take it outside." If the child continues to bang on the drum inside the house, then she has caused the toy to be put away. If she takes it outside, she has made a decision to play with the drum in a way that respects her mother's wishes. In this way, both parent and child have been allowed to maintain a sense of self-respect and a needless clash has been averted.

After you have stated consequences and let the child decide, be sure to respect the child's choice. If the child repeats the misbehavior, you can let the consequences remain in effect longer. But later, give the child another chance to cooperate.

With all child management techniques, remember to be firm, kind, consistent, respectful, and encouraging. And most of all, try every day to live the message you wish to communicate.

Natural consequences The effects that naturally tend to follow a particular behavior.

Logical consequences Reasonable consequences that are defined by parents.

 Study Break   **Parenting and Child Discipline**

Reflect

What do you think are the best ways to discipline children? How would your approach be classified? What are its advantages and disadvantages?

Parents can probably never be completely consistent. Think of a time when your parents were inconsistent in disciplining you. How did it affect you?

Think of a you-message you have recently given a child, family member, roommate, or spouse. Can you change it into an I-message?

Learning Check

1. Effective discipline gives children freedom within a structure of consistent and well-defined limits. T or F?
2. One good way to maintain consistency in child management is to overstate the consequences for misbehavior. T or F?

3. Spankings and other physical punishments are most effective for children under the age of 2. T or F?
4. Giving recognition for progress and attempts to improve is an example of parental _____.
5. I-messages are a gentle way of accusing a child of misbehavior. T or F?
6. In situations where natural consequences are unavailable or do not discourage misbehavior, parents should define logical consequences for a child. T or F?

Critical Thinking

7. Several Scandinavian countries have made it illegal for parents to spank their own children. Does this infringe on the rights of parents?

Answers

1. T 2. F 3. F 4. encouragement 5. F 6. T 7. Such laws are based on the view that it should be illegal to physically assault any person, regardless of their age. Although parents may believe they have a "right" to spank their children, it can be argued that children need special protection because they are small, powerless, and dependent (Durrant & Janson, 2005).

CHAPTER IN REVIEW

Major Points

- You are a product of both your genetic heritage and the environments in which you have lived.
- Infant development is strongly influenced by heredity. However, environmental factors such as nutrition, parenting, and learning are also important.
- Forming an emotional bond with a caregiver is a crucial event during infancy.
- Learning to use language is a cornerstone of early intellectual development.
- Piaget's stage theory provides a valuable map of how thinking abilities unfold.
- Vygotsky's theory reminds us that a child's mind is shaped by culture and human relationships.
- Acquiring moral standards depends, in part, on the development of thinking and reasoning abilities.
- Erik Erikson identified a series of challenges that occur across the lifespan. These range from a need to gain trust in infancy to the need to live with integrity in old age.
- Effective child discipline is consistent, humane, encouraging, and based on respectful communication.

Summary

How do heredity and environment affect development?

- Heredity (nature) and environment (nurture) are both necessary for human development.
- Hereditary instructions are carried by the chromosomes and genes in each cell of the body. Most characteristics are polygenic and reflect the combined effects of dominant and recessive genes.
- Temperament is hereditary. Most infants fall into one of three temperament categories: easy children, difficult children, and slow-to-warm-up children.
- During sensitive periods in development, infants are more sensitive to specific environmental influences.
- Prenatal development influenced by environmental factors, such as diseases, drugs, radiation, various teratogens, and the mother's diet, health, and emotions.
- Early perceptual, intellectual, or emotional deprivation seriously retards development.
- Deliberate enrichment of the environment has a beneficial effect on infants.
- Heredity and environment are interacting forces. A child's developmental level reflects heredity, environment, and the effects of the child's own behavior.

What can newborn babies do?

- The human neonate has a number of adaptive reflexes, including the grasping, rooting, sucking, and Moro reflexes. Neonates begin to learn immediately and they appear to be aware of the effects of their actions.
- Testing with a looking chamber reveals that neonates prefer bright lights and circular or curved designs.
- Infants prefer human face patterns, especially familiar faces. In later infancy, interest in the unfamiliar emerges.

What influence does maturation have on early development?

- Maturation of the body and nervous system underlies the orderly development of motor skills, cognitive abilities, emotions, and language.
- The rate of maturation varies from person to person. Also, learning contributes greatly to the development of basic motor skills.
- Emotions develop in a consistent order, starting with generalized excitement in newborn babies. Three of the basic emotions—fear, anger, and joy—may be unlearned.
- Many early skills are subject to the principle of readiness.

Of what significance is a child's emotional bond with parents?

- Emotional attachment of human infants is a critical early event.
- Infant attachment is reflected by separation anxiety. The quality of attachment can be classified as secure, insecure-avoidant, or insecure-ambivalent.
- High-quality day care does not appear to harm children. Low-quality care can be risky.
- Meeting a baby's affectional needs is as important as meeting needs for physical care.

How important are parenting styles?

- Studies suggest that parental styles have a substantial impact on emotional and intellectual development.
- Three major parental styles are authoritarian, permissive, and authoritative (effective). Authoritative parenting appears to benefit children the most.
- Whereas mothers typically emphasize caregiving, fathers tend to function as playmates for infants.
- Parenting styles vary across cultures.

How do children acquire language?

- Language development proceeds from crying, to cooing, then babbling, the use of single words, and then to telegraphic speech.
- The underlying patterns of telegraphic speech suggest a biological predisposition to acquire language. This innate tendency is augmented by learning.
- Prelanguage communication between parent and child involves shared rhythms, nonverbal signals, and turn-taking.
- Motherese or parentese is a simplified, musical style of speaking that parents use to help their children learn language.

How do children learn to think?

- Jean Piaget theorized that intellectual growth occurs through a combination of assimilation and accommodation.
- Piaget also held that children go through a fixed series of cognitive stages. The stages and their approximate age ranges are sensorimotor (0–2), preoperational (2–7), concrete operational (7–11), and formal operations (11–adult).
- Learning principles provide an alternate explanation that assumes cognitive development is continuous; it does not occur in stages.
- Recent studies of infants under the age of 1 year suggest that they are capable of thought well beyond that observed by Piaget.
- Lev Vygotsky's sociocultural theory emphasizes that a child's mental abilities are advanced by interactions with more competent partners. Mental growth takes place in a child's zone of proximal development, where a more skillful person may scaffold the child's progress.

How do we develop morals and values?

- Lawrence Kohlberg identified preconventional, conventional, and postconventional levels of moral reasoning.
- Most people function at the conventional level of morality, but some never get beyond the selfish, preconventional level. Only a minority of people attain the highest, or postconventional, level of moral reasoning.

What are the typical tasks and dilemmas through the life span?

- According to Erikson, each life stage provokes a specific psychosocial dilemma.
- In addition to the dilemmas identified by Erikson, we recognize that each life stage requires successful mastery of certain developmental tasks.

- Well-being during adulthood consists of six elements: self-acceptance, positive relations with others, autonomy, environmental mastery, having a purpose in life, and continued personal growth.
- Intellectual declines associated with aging are limited, at least through one's 70s. This is especially true of individuals who remain mentally active.
- Ageism refers to prejudice, discrimination, and stereotyping on the basis of age. It affects people of all ages but is especially damaging to older people. Most ageism is based on stereotypes, myths, and misinformation.

How do effective parents discipline their children?

- Positive parent-child interactions occur when parents spend enjoyable time encouraging their children in a loving and mutually respectful fashion.
- Effective parental discipline tends to emphasize child management techniques (especially communication), rather than power assertion or withdrawal of love.
- Consistency is also an important aspect of effective parenting.
- Effective parents allow their children to express their feeling but place limits on their behavior.
- Much misbehavior can be managed by use of I-messages and the application of natural and logical consequences.

Interactive Learning

Internet addresses frequently change. To find the sites listed here, visit www.thomsonedu.com/psychology/coon for an updated list of Internet addresses and direct links to relevant sites.

Psychology: **A Journey Companion Website**   Online quizzes, flash cards, and other helpful study aids for this text. Find online quizzes, flash cards, animations, video clips, experiments, interactive assessments, and other helpful study aids for this text at www.thomsonedu .com/psychology/coon.

Choosing Quality Child Care   Provides information on issues related to quality child care.

Depression after Delivery   A site devoted to providing information about postpartum depression.

Diving into the Gene Pool   From the Exploratorium, teaches about modern genetics.

Human Relations Publications   Covers more than 50 topics spanning the entire range of human development.

I Am Your Child   Information for parents of children up to 3 years of age.

Jean Piaget Archives: Biography   The life of Jean Piaget, plus five photos from birth to old age.

Parenthood Web   A comprehensive site for parents.

Sesame Street Parents   An expert description of physical development from birth to 11.

The Parent's Page   Comprehensive site full of links for expectant couples and new parents.

ThomsonNOW   Go to www.thomsonedu.com/login to link to ThomsonNOW, your online study tool. First take the **Pre-Test** for this chapter to get your **Personalized Study Plan**, which will identify topics you need to review and direct you to online resources. Then take the **Post-Test** to determine what concepts you have mastered and what you still need work on.

TEST YOUR KNOWLEDGE

Human Development

For additional review, get more practice with *ThomsonNOW*, *WebTutor*, the *Practice Quizzes*, and/or the printed *Study Guide* available with this book.

1. In the "nature-nurture" debate, the term *nature* primarily refers to
   a. senescence
   b. the existence of sensitive periods
   c. prenatal teratogens
   d. heredity

2. If a personal trait is controlled by a single dominant gene, the trait cannot be
   a. hereditary
   b. related to DNA sequences
   c. influenced by chromosomes
   d. polygenic

3. The influence of heredity on early child development is most clearly shown by
   a. differences in temperament
   b. the existence of sensitive periods
   c. congenital problems
   d. the effects of teratogens

4. Deprivation has an especially strong impact on development during
   a. the reciprocal stage
   b. sensitive periods
   c. the polygenic stage
   d. the social play phase

5. Cephalocaudal and proximodistal patterns show the effects of _____ on motor development.
   a. enriched environments
   b. maturation
   c. scaffolding
   d. sensitive periods

6. Early in life, the learning of basic skills is most effective when parents respect the
   a. Mozart effect
   b. value of reactive maternal involvement
   c. principle of readiness
   d. fact that babies cannot imitate adult actions until they are 18 months old

7. In infancy, an early step toward social development is revealed by the emergence of
   a. self-awareness
   b. cephalodistal attachment
   c. the Moro reflex
   d. the congenital period

8. A clear sign that infant attachment is beginning to occur is found in the presence of
   a. a social smile
   b. separation anxiety
   c. social scaffolding
   d. affectional needs

9. A baby who turns away from his mother when she returns after a brief separation shows signs of having which type of attachment?
   a. insecure-avoidant
   b. insecure-ambivalent
   c. solitary-ambivalent
   d. maternal-disaffectional

10. Which of the following is NOT an element of optimal caregiving?
    a. you-messages
    b. proactive involvement
    c. goodness of fit
    d. responsiveness

11. Psychologist Diana Baumrind describes parents who enforce rigid rules and demand strict obedience as
    a. authoritative
    b. permissive-repressive
    c. proactive-reactive
    d. authoritarian

12. Which form of child discipline tends to make children insecure, anxious, and hungry for approval?
    a. withdrawal of love
    b. management techniques
    c. power assertion
    d. authoritative techniques

13. Turn-taking with nonverbal signals is a first step toward
    a. secure attachment
    b. motor development
    c. using language
    d. an ability to make transformations

14. Parents talk to young children with a raised tone of voice and an exaggerated pattern of speaking that is called
    a. transformational grammar
    b. telegraphic speech
    c. signal switching
    d. parentese

15. Piaget believed that a child's understanding of the world grows through the mental processes of assimilation and
    a. intuition
    b. accommodation
    c. egocentricism
    d. reversibility

16. According to Piaget, a child's mastery of conservation occurs during the
    a. formal operations stage
    b. preoperational stage
    c. concrete operational stage
    d. sensorimotor stage

17. Vygotsky believed that adults help children learn how to think by using a process he called
    a. reversible thinking
    b. scaffolding
    c. accommodation
    d. moral reasoning

18. According to Erikson, the dilemma faced by most 3- to-5-year-olds is
    a. autonomy versus shame and doubt
    b. initiative versus guilt
    c. trust versus mistrust
    d. industry versus inferiority

19. Erikson's theory states that mature adults are best able to avoid stagnation when they express
    a. integrity
    b. generativity
    c. intimacy
    d. preconventional moral reasoning

20. Which type of child discipline takes the form of threats, name-calling, accusing, bossing, lecturing, or criticizing?
    a. I-messages
    b. you-messages
    c. logical consequences
    d. natural consequences

ANSWERS 1. d 2. d 3. a 4. b 5. b 6. c 7. a 8. b 9. a 10. a 11. d 12. a 13. c 14. d 15. b 16. c 17. b 18. b 19. b 20. b

Sensation and Percepton

JOURNEY INTO PSYCHOLOGY: MURDER ON AISLE NINE

One of your authors was in a supermarket when an 8-year-old girl suddenly came running around a corner. She looked back and screamed, "Stop! Stop! You're killing him! You're killing my father!" Here is your author's account of what followed:

I retraced the girl's path and saw two men on the floor, struggling violently. The guy on top had his victim by the throat. There was blood everywhere. It was a murder in progress! As a witness, I would have told a jury what I just told you, were it not for an important fact: No murder ever took place that day at the supermarket. When the police arrived, they quickly discovered that the "guy on the bottom" had passed out and hit his head. That caused the cut (actually quite minor) that explained the "blood everywhere." The "guy on top" saw the first man fall and was trying to loosen his collar. Obviously, the girl had misunderstood what was happening to her father. As a psychologist, I still find it fascinating that her words so dramatically influenced what I saw.

At this very moment you are bathed in a swirling kaleidoscope of light, heat, pressure, vibrations, molecules, radiation, and mechanical forces. Without the senses, all of this would seem like nothing more than a void of darkness and silence. The next time you drink in the beauty of a sunset, a flower, or a friend, remember this: Sensation makes it all possible.

Yet, sensing the world is not enough. As our murder-in-the-supermarket story shows, sensory information can be interpreted in various ways. In this chapter we will begin with a look at how the senses operate. Then we will discuss how we assemble sensations into a meaningful "picture" or model of the world. Our perceptions create faces, melodies, works of art, illusions, and on occasion, "murders" out of the raw material of sensation. Let's see how this takes place.

John Lund/Annabelle Breakey/Getty Images

- In general, how do sensory systems function?
- How is vision accomplished?
- What are the mechanisms of hearing?
- How do the chemical senses operate?
- What are the somesthetic senses and why are they important?
- Why are we more aware of some sensations than others?
- How do perceptual constancies and Gestalt organizing principles shape our perceptions?
- How is it possible to see depth and judge distance?
- How is perception altered by expectations, motives, emotions, and learning?
- Is extrasensory perception possible?
- How can I learn to perceive events more accurately?

SENSORY SYSTEMS—WHAT YOU GET IS WHAT YOU SEE

>SURVEY QUESTION< *In general, how do sensory systems function?*

Vision gives us amazingly wide access to the world. In one instant you can view a star light-years away, and in the next, you can peer into the microscopic universe of a dewdrop. Yet, vision also narrows what we can possibly observe. Like the other senses, vision acts as a *data reduction system.* It selects and analyzes information in order to code and send to the brain only the most important data (Sekuler & Blake, 2006).

Selection

How does data reduction take place? Some selection occurs because sensory receptors are *biological transducers,* devices that convert one kind of energy into another (Fain, 2003). For example, a guitar transduces string vibrations into sound waves. Pluck a string and the guitar will produce a sound. However, stimuli that don't cause the string to move will have no effect. For instance, if you shine a light on the string, or pour cold water on it, the guitar will remain silent. (The owner of the guitar, however, might get quite loud at this point!) Thus, the eye transduces electromagnetic radiation, the ear transduces sound waves, and so on. Other types of energy are not selected for conversion to nerve impulses and hence we cannot sense them directly.

Further, sense receptors transduce only part of their target energy range (Fain, 2003). For example, your eyes transduce only a tiny fraction of the entire range of electromagnetic energies, which we call the *visible spectrum.* The eyes of honeybees can transduce, and therefore see, parts of the electromagnetic spectrum invisible to us humans. Similarly, the ears of bats can transduce, and hear, sound waves that we humans cannot. If, by chance, a bat ever silently flies by you at night, remember that it is, nonetheless, shouting and listening for echoes. This ability, called *echolocation,* allows bats to fly in pitch darkness. As you can see, our rich sensory experience is only a small part of what *could* be sensed and what some animals *can* sense.

Analysis

What we experience is also influenced by **sensory analysis.** As they process information, the senses divide the world into important **perceptual features** (basic stimulus patterns). The visual system, for example, has a set of *feature detectors* that are attuned to very specific

Sensory analysis Separation of sensory information into important elements.

Perceptual features Basic elements of a stimulus, such as lines, shapes, edges, or colors.

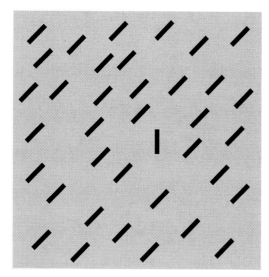

▸▸**FIGURE 4.1** Visual pop-out. Pop-out is so basic that babies as young as 3 months respond to it. (Adapted from Adler & Orprecio, 2006).

stimuli, such as lines, shapes, edges, spots, colors, and other patterns (Hubel & Wiesel, 2005). Look at ▸▸ Figure 4.1 and notice how eye-catching the single vertical line is among a group of slanted lines. This effect, which is called *pop-out,* occurs because your visual system is highly sensitive to perceptual features (Adler & Orprecio, 2006).

Similarly, frog eyes are highly sensitive to small, dark, moving spots. In other words, they are basically "tuned" to detect bugs flying nearby (Lettvin, 1961). But the insect (spot) must be moving, or the frog's "bug detectors" won't work. A frog could starve to death surrounded by dead flies.

Our sensitivity to perceptual features is an innate characteristic of the nervous system. Like other inborn capacities, this sensitivity is influenced by early experience. For instance, Colin Blakemore and Graham Cooper of Cambridge University raised kittens in a room with only vertical stripes on the walls. Another set of kittens saw only horizontal stripes. When returned to normal environments, the "horizontal" cats could easily jump onto a chair, but when walking on the floor, they bumped into chair legs. "Vertical" cats, on the other hand, easily avoided chair legs, but they missed when trying to jump to horizontal surfaces. The cats raised with vertical stripes were "blind" to horizontal lines, and the "horizontal" cats acted as if vertical lines were invisible (Blakemore & Cooper, 1970). Other experiments show that there is an actual decrease in brain cells tuned to the missing features (Grobstein & Chow, 1975).

Sensory Coding

As they select and analyze information, sensory systems *code* it. **Sensory coding** refers to converting important features of the world into neural messages understood by the brain (Hubel & Wiesel, 2005). To see coding at work, try closing your eyes for a moment. Then take your fingertips and press firmly on your eyelids. Apply enough pressure to "squash" your eyes slightly. Do this for about 30 seconds and observe what happens. (Readers with eye problems or contact lenses should not try this.)

Did you "see" stars, checkerboards, and flashes of color? These are called *phosphenes* (FOSS-feens: visual sensations caused by mechanical excitation of the retina). They occur because the eye's receptor cells, which normally respond to light, are also somewhat sensitive to pressure. Notice though, that the eye is only prepared to code stimulation—including pressure—into visual features. As a result, you experience light sensations, not pressure. Also important in producing this effect is *sensory localization* in the brain.

Sensory localization means that the type of sensation you experience depends on which brain area is activated. Some brain areas receive visual information; others receive auditory information, and still others receive taste or touch (see Chapter 2). Knowing which brain areas are active tells us, in general, what kinds of sensations you are feeling.

Sensory localization may someday make it possible to artificially restore sight, hearing, or other senses. In fact, researchers have already used a miniature television camera to send electrical signals to the brain (▸▸Fig. 4.2) (Dobelle, 2000; Warren & Normann, 2005). In July 2006, a woman named Cheri Robinson became the 16th person in the world with an implant of this type. She can now "see" 100 dots of light. Like a sports scoreboard, these lights can be used to form crude letters (Dobelle, 2000). Eventually, a larger number of dots could make reading and "seeing" large objects, such as furniture and doorways, possible.

It is fascinating to realize that "seeing" and "hearing" take place in your brain, not your eyes or ears. Information arriving from the sense organs creates **sensations.** When the brain organizes sensations into meaningful patterns, we speak of **perception,** which we will discuss later. For now, let's begin with vision, the most magnificent sensory system of all.

Sensory coding Codes used by the sense organs to transmit information to the brain.

Sensation A sensory impression; also, the process of detecting physical energies with the sensory organs.

Perception The mental process of organizing sensations into meaningful patterns.

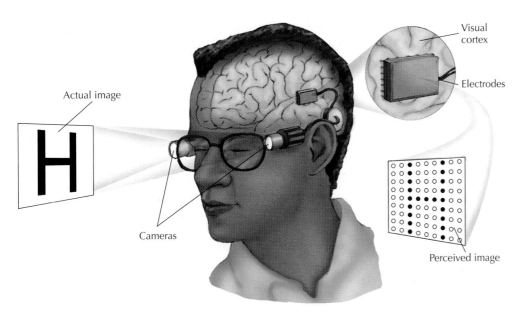

▸▸**FIGURE 4.2** An artificial visual system.

Actual image

Visual cortex

Electrodes

Cameras

Perceived image

VISION—CATCHING SOME RAYS

>SURVEY QUESTION< *How is vision accomplished?*

What are the basic dimensions of light and vision? Various wavelengths of light make up the *visible spectrum* (entire spread of electromagnetic energies to which the eyes respond). Visible light starts at "short" wavelengths of 400 *nanometers* (nan-OM-et-er: one billionth of a meter), which we sense as purple or violet. Longer light waves produce blue, green, yellow, orange, and red, which has a wavelength of 700 nanometers (▸▸Fig. 4.3).

The term *hue* refers to the basic color categories of red, orange, yellow, green, blue, indigo, and violet. As just noted, various hues (or color sensations) correspond to the wavelength of the light that reaches our eyes (Sekuler & Blake, 2006). White light, in contrast, is a mixture of many wavelengths. Hues (colors) from a narrow band of wavelengths are very *saturated*, or "pure." (An intense "fire-engine" red is more saturated than a muddy "brick" red.) A third dimension of vision, *brightness*, corresponds roughly to the

▸▸**FIGURE 4.3** The visible spectrum.

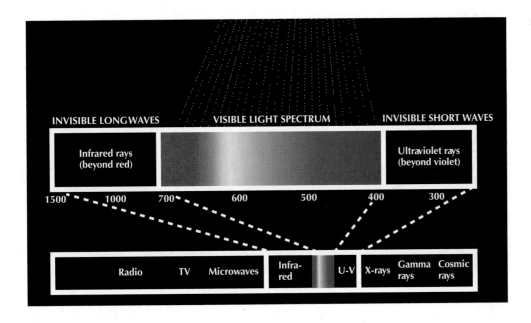

INVISIBLE LONGWAVES   VISIBLE LIGHT SPECTRUM   INVISIBLE SHORT WAVES

Infrared rays (beyond red)

Ultraviolet rays (beyond violet)

1500   1000   700   600   500   400   300

Radio   TV   Microwaves   Infra-red   U-V   X-rays   Gamma rays   Cosmic rays

amplitude, or height, of light waves. Waves of greater amplitude are "taller," carry more energy, and cause the colors we see to appear brighter or more intense. For example, the same "brick" red would look bright under intense, high-energy illumination and drab under dim light.

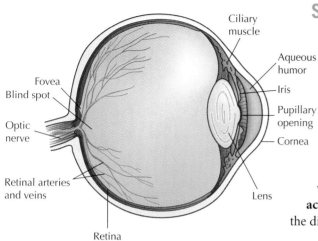

>>**FIGURE 4.4** The human eye, a simplified view.

Structure of the Eye

Is it true that the eye is like a camera? In some ways, it is. Both cameras and eyes have a *lens* to focus images on a light-sensitive layer at the back of a closed space. In a camera, this layer is the film. In the eye, it is a layer of *photoreceptors* (light-sensitive cells) in the **retina,** an area about the size and thickness of a postage stamp (>>Fig. 4.4).

How does the eye focus? Most focusing is done at the front of the eye by the *cornea,* a clear membrane that bends light inward. The lens makes additional, smaller adjustments. Your eye's focal point changes when muscles attached to the lens alter its shape. This process is called **accommodation.** In cameras, focusing is done more simply—by changing the distance between the lens and the film.

Visual Problems

Focusing is also affected by the shape of the eye. If your eye is too short, nearby objects will be blurred, but distant objects will be sharp. This is called **hyperopia** (HI-per-OPE-ee-ah: farsightedness). If your eyeball is too long, images fall short of the retina and you won't be able to focus distant objects. This results in **myopia** (my-OPE-ee-ah: nearsightedness). When the cornea or the lens is misshapen, part of vision will be focused and part will be fuzzy. In this case, the eye has more than one focal point, a problem called **astigmatism** (ah-STIG-mah-tiz-em). All three visual defects can be corrected by placing glasses (or contact lenses) in front of the eye to change the path of light (>>Fig. 4.5).

As people age, the lens becomes less flexible and less able to accommodate. The result is **presbyopia** (prez-bee-OPE-ee-ah: old vision, or farsightedness due to aging). Perhaps you have seen a grandparent or older friend reading a newspaper at arm's length because of presbyopia. If you now wear glasses for nearsightedness, you may need bifocals as you age. (Just like your authors.) Bifocal lenses correct near vision *and* distance vision.

Rods and Cones

The eye has two types of "film," consisting of receptor cells called *rods* and *cones.* The 6.5 million **cones** in each eye work best in bright light. They also produce color sensations and fine details. In contrast, the **rods,** numbering about 100 million, can't detect colors (>>Fig. 4.6). Pure rod vision is black and white. However, the rods are much more sensitive to light than the cones are. The rods therefore allow us to see in very dim light.

Surprisingly, the retina has a "hole" in it: Each eye has a *blind spot* because there are no receptors where the optic nerve leaves the eye (>>Fig. 4.7a). The blind spot shows that vision depends greatly on the brain. If you close one eye, part of what you see will fall on the blind spot of your open eye. Why isn't there a gap in your vision? The answer is that the visual cortex of the brain actively fills in the gap with patterns from surrounding areas (>>Fig. 4.7b). By closing one eye, you can visually "behead" other people by placing their images on your blind spot. (Just a hint for some classroom fun.) The brain can also "erase" distracting information. Roll your eyes all the way to the right and then close your right eye. You should clearly see your nose in your left eye's field of vision. Now, open your right eye again and your nose will nearly disappear as your brain disregards its presence.

Retina The light-sensitive layer of cells at the back of the eye.

Accommodation Changes in the shape of the lens of the eye.

Hyperopia Difficulty focusing nearby objects (farsightedness).

Myopia Difficulty focusing distant objects (nearsightedness).

Astigmatism Defects in the cornea, lens, or eye that cause some areas of vision to be out of focus.

Presbyopia Farsightedness caused by aging.

Cones Visual receptors for colors and daylight visual acuity.

Rods Visual receptors for dim light that produce only black and white sensations.

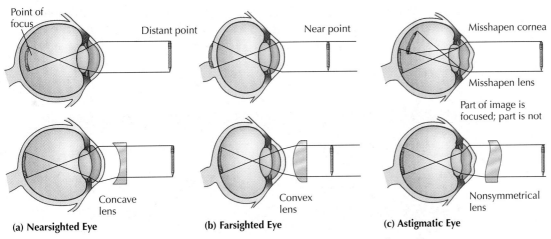

FIGURE 4.5 Visual defects and corrective lenses: *(a)* A myopic (longer than usual) eye. The concave lens spreads light rays just enough to increase the eye's focal length. *(b)* A hyperopic (shorter than usual) eye. The convex lens increases refraction (bending), to focus light on the retina. *(c)* An astigmatic (lens or cornea not symmetrical) eye. In astigmatism, parts of vision are sharp and parts are unfocused. Lenses that correct astigmatism are non-symmetrical.

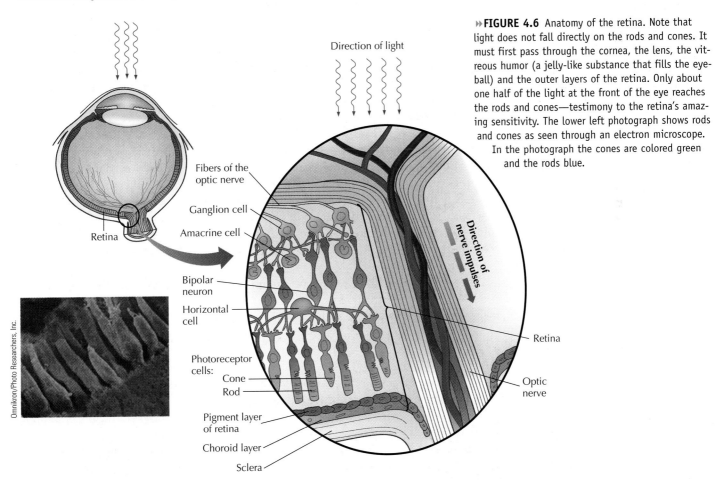

FIGURE 4.6 Anatomy of the retina. Note that light does not fall directly on the rods and cones. It must first pass through the cornea, the lens, the vitreous humor (a jelly-like substance that fills the eyeball) and the outer layers of the retina. Only about one half of the light at the front of the eye reaches the rods and cones—testimony to the retina's amazing sensitivity. The lower left photograph shows rods and cones as seen through an electron microscope. In the photograph the cones are colored green and the rods blue.

Omnikron/Photo Researchers, Inc.

Visual Acuity

The rods and cones also affect **visual acuity,** or sharpness. The cones lie mainly at the center of the eye. In fact, the *fovea* (FOE-vee-ah: a small cup-shaped area in the middle of the retina) contains only cones—about 50,000 of them. Like a newspaper photograph made of many small dots, the tightly packed cones in the fovea produce the sharpest images. Normal acuity

Visual acuity The sharpness of visual perception.

FIGURE 4.7 Experiencing the blind spot. *(a)* With your right eye closed, stare at the upper right cross. Hold the book about 1 foot from your eye and slowly move it back and forth. You should be able to locate a position that makes the black spot to disappear. When it does, it is on your blind spot. With a little practice you can learn to make people or objects you dislike disappear too! *(b)* Repeat the procedure described, but stare at the lower cross. When the white space falls on the blind spot, the black lines will appear to be continuous. This may help you understand why you do not usually notice a blind spot in your visual field.

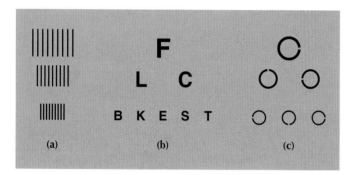

FIGURE 4.8 Tests of visual acuity. Here are some common tests of visual acuity. In *(a)*, sharpness is indicated by the smallest grating still seen as individual lines. The Snellen chart *(b)* requires that you read rows of letters of diminishing size until you can no longer distinguish them. The Landolt rings *(c)* require no familiarity with letters. All that is required is a report of which side has a break in it.

is designated as 20/20 vision: At 20 feet in distance, you can distinguish what the average person can see at 20 feet (Fig. 4.8). If your vision is 20/40, you can only see at 20 feet what the average person can see at 40 feet. If your vision is 20/200, everything is a blur and you need glasses! Vision that is 20/12 would mean that you can see at 20 feet what the average person must be 8 feet nearer to see, indicating better than average acuity. American astronaut Gordon Cooper, who claimed to see railroad lines in northern India from 100 miles above, had 20/12 acuity.

Peripheral Vision

What is the purpose of the rest of the retina? Areas outside the fovea also get light, creating a large region of **peripheral** (side) **vision.** The rods are most numerous about 20 degrees from the center of the retina, so much of our peripheral vision is rod vision. Although rod vision is not very sharp, the rods are quite sensitive to *movement* in peripheral vision. To experience this characteristic of the rods, look straight ahead and hold your hand beside your head, at about 90 degrees. Wiggle your finger and slowly move your hand forward until you can detect motion. You will become aware of the movement before you can actually "see" your finger.

The rods are also highly responsive to dim light. Because most rods are 20 degrees to each side of the fovea, the best night vision comes from looking *next to* an object you wish to see. Test this yourself some night by looking at, and next to, a very dim star.

Color Vision

How do the cones produce color sensations? The **trichromatic theory** (TRY-kro-MAT-ik) of color vision holds that there are three types of cones, each most sensitive to either red, green, or blue. Other colors result from combinations of these three. Black and white sensations are produced by the rods.

A basic problem with the trichromatic theory is that four colors of light—red, green, blue, and yellow—seem to be primary (you can't get them by mixing other colors). Also, why is it impossible to have a reddish green or a yellowish blue? These problems led to the development of a second view, known as the **opponent-process theory,** which states that vision analyzes colors into "either-or" messages. That is, the visual system can produce messages for either red or green, yellow or blue, black or white. Coding one color in a pair (red, for instance) seems to block the opposite message (green) from coming through. As a result, a reddish green is impossible, but a yellowish red (orange) can occur.

Peripheral vision Vision at the edges of the visual field.

Trichromatic theory Theory of color vision based on three cone types: red, green, and blue.

Opponent-process theory Theory of color vision based on three coding systems (red or green, yellow or blue, black or white).

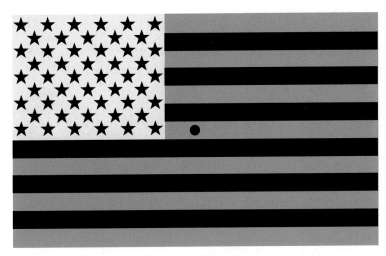

▸▸**FIGURE 4.9** Negative afterimages. Stare at the dot near the middle of the flag for at least 30 seconds. Then look immediately at a plain sheet of white paper or a white wall. You will see the American flag in red, white, and blue. Reduced sensitivity to green, black, and yellow in the visual system, caused by prolonged staring, produces the complementary colors.

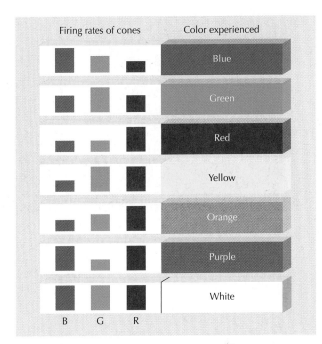

▸▸**FIGURE 4.10** Firing rates of blue, green, and red cones in response to different colors. The taller the colored bar, the higher the firing rates for that type of cone. As you can see, colors are coded by differences in the activity of all three types of cones in the normal eye. (Adapted from Goldstein, 2007.)

According to opponent-process theory, fatigue caused by making one response produces an afterimage of the opposite color as the system recovers. *Afterimages* are visual sensations that persist after a stimulus is removed—like seeing a spot after a flashbulb goes off. To see an afterimage of the type predicted by opponent-process theory, look at ▸▸Figure 4.9 and follow the instructions there.

Which color theory is correct? Both! The three-color theory applies to the retina, where three different types of *visual pigments* (light-sensitive chemicals) have been found in cones. As predicted, each pigment is most sensitive to light in roughly the red, green, or blue region. The three types of cones fire nerve impulses at different rates to produce various color sensations (▸▸Fig. 4.10).

In contrast, the opponent-process theory better explains what happens in optic pathways and the brain *after* information leaves the eye. For example, some nerve cells in the brain are excited by the color red and inhibited by the color green. So both theories are "correct." One explains what happens in the eye itself. The other explains how colors are analyzed after messages leave the eye (Gegenfurtner & Kiper, 2003).

Color Blindness

Do you know anyone who regularly draws hoots of laughter by wearing clothes of wildly clashing colors? Or someone who sheepishly tries to avoid saying what color an object is? If so, you probably know someone who is color-blind.

What is it like to be color-blind? What causes color blindness? A person who is **color-blind** cannot perceive colors. It is as if the world is a black-and-white movie. The color-blind person either lacks cones or has cones that do not function normally (Deeb, 2004). Such total color blindness is rare. In **color weakness,** or partial color blindness, a person can't see certain colors. Approximately 8 percent of Caucasian males (but fewer Asian, African and Native American males and less than 1 percent of women) are red-green color-blind (Delpero et al., 2005). These people see reds and greens as the same color, usually a yellowish brown (see ▸▸Fig. 4.11). Another form of color blindness, involving yellow and blue, is quite rare (Hsia & Graham, 1997). (See "Are You Color-Blind?")

How can color-blind individuals drive? Don't they have trouble with traffic lights? Red-green color-blind individuals have normal vision for yellow and blue, so the main problem is telling red lights from green. In practice, that's not difficult. The red light is always on top,

Color blindness A total inability to perceive colors.
Color weakness An inability to distinguish some colors.

(a)   (b)   (c)

▶▶**FIGURE 4.11** Color blindness and color weakness. *(a)* Photograph illustrates normal color vision. *(b)* Photograph is printed in blue and yellow and gives an impression of what a red-green color-blind person sees. *(c)* Photograph simulates total color blindness. If you are totally color-blind, all three photos will look nearly identical.

DISCOVERING PSYCHOLOGY

Are You Color-Blind?

How can I tell if I am color-blind? Surprisingly, it is not as obvious as you might think; some people reach adulthood without knowing that some colors are missing. The *Ishihara test* is commonly used to measure color blindness and weakness. In the test, numbers and other designs made of dots are placed on a background also made of dots (▶▶Fig. 4.12). The background and the numbers are of different colors (red and green, for example). A person who is color-blind sees only a jumble of dots. If you have normal color vision you can detect the numbers or designs (Birch & McKeever, 1993; Coren, Ward, & Enns, 2004). The chart below Figure 4.12 lists what people with normal color vision, and those with color blindness, see. Because Figure 4.12 is just a replica, it is not a definitive test of color blindness. Nevertheless, if you can't see all of the embedded designs, you may be color-blind or color weak.

ARE YOU COLOR BLIND?

NO.	NORMAL EYE	COLOR BLIND EYE	NO.	NORMAL EYE	COLOR BLIND EYE
1	12	12	9	NOTHING	45
2	8	3	10	26	2 OR 6
3	29	70	11	2 LINES X TO X	LINE X TO X
4	5	2	12	NOTHING	LINE X TO X
5	74	21	13	LINE X TO X	NOTHING
6	45	NOTHING	14	LINE X TO X	NOTHING
7	5	NOTHING	15	LINE X TO X	NOTHING
8	NOTHING	5	16	LINE X TO X	LINE X TO X

▶▶**FIGURE 4.12** A replica of the Ishihara test for color blindness.

and the green light is brighter than the red. Also, "red" traffic signals have yellow light mixed in with the red and a "green" light that is really blue-green.

Dark Adapting to Dim Light

What happens when the eyes adjust to a dark room? **Dark adaptation** is the dramatic increase in retinal sensitivity to light that occurs after a person enters the dark (Goldstein, 2007). Consider walking into a theater. If you enter from a brightly lighted lobby, you practically need to be led to your seat. After a short time, however, you can see the entire room in detail (including the couple kissing over in the corner). It takes about 30 to 35 minutes of complete darkness to reach maximum visual sensitivity (▶▶Fig. 4.13). At that point, your eye will be 100,000 times more sensitive to light.

What causes dark adaptation? Like the cones, the rods contain a light-sensitive visual pigment. When struck by light, visual pigments *bleach,* or break down chemically. The afterimages you have seen after looking at a flashbulb are a result of this bleaching. In fact, a few seconds of exposure to bright white light can completely wipe out dark adaptation. That's why you should be sure to avoid looking at oncoming headlights when you are driving at night—especially the new bluish-white zenon lights. To restore light sensitivity, the visual pigments in the rods must recombine, which takes time.

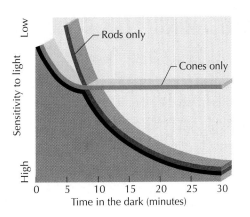

▶▶**FIGURE 4.13** Typical course of dark adaptation. The black line shows how the threshold for vision lowers as a person spends time in the dark. (A lower threshold means that less light is needed for vision.) The green line shows that the cones adapt first, but they soon cease adding to light sensitivity. Rods, shown by the red line, adapt more slowly. However, they continue to improve night vision long after the cones are fully adapted.

Dark adaptation Increased retinal sensitivity to light.

Study Break Sensory Systems and Vision

Reflect

How does sensation affect what you are experiencing right now? What if data reduction didn't occur? What if you could transduce other energies? What if your senses were tuned to detect different perceptual features? How would the sensory world you live in change? What would it be like to be a bat?

   Pretend you are a beam of light. What will happen to you at each step as you pass into the eye and land on the retina? What will happen if the eye is not perfectly shaped? How will the retina know you've arrived? How will it tell what color of light you are? What will it tell the brain about you?

Learning Check

1. Sensory receptors are biological _____, or devices for converting one type of energy to another.
2. Lettvin found that a frog's eyes are especially sensitive to phosphenes. T or F?
3. Important features of the environment are transmitted to the brain through a process known as

   a. phosphenation   b. coding
   c. detection   d. programming

4. Match:
   ____ Myopia   A. Farsightedness
   ____ Hyperopia   B. Elongated eye
   ____ Presbyopia   C. Farsightedness due to aging
   ____ Astigmatism   D. Lack of cones in the fovea
                      E. Misshapen cornea or lens

5. In dim light, vision depends mainly on the _____. In brighter light, color and fine detail are produced by the

   _____.

6. The fovea has the greatest visual acuity due to the large concentration of rods found there. T or F?

7. The eyes become more sensitive to light at night because of a process known as _____ _____.

Critical Thinking

8. William James once said, "If a master surgeon were to cross the auditory and optic nerves, we would hear lightning and see thunder." Can you explain what James meant?

9. Sensory transduction in the eye takes place first in the cornea, then in the lens, then in the retina. True or false?

Answers

1. transducers 2. F 3. b 4. B, A, C, E 5. rods, cones 6. F 7. dark adaptation 8. The explanation is based on sensory localization: Even if a lightning flash caused rerouted messages from the eyes to activate auditory areas of the brain, we would nevertheless experience a sound sensation. Likewise, if the ears transduced a thunderclap, and sent impulses to the visual area, a sensation of light would occur. 9. False. The cornea and lens bend and focus light rays, but they do not change light to another form of energy. No change in the *type* of energy takes place until the retina converts light to nerve impulses.

HEARING—GOOD VIBRATIONS

>SURVEY QUESTION< *What are the mechanisms of hearing?*

Rock, classical, jazz, rap, country, hip-hop—whatever your musical taste, you have probably been moved by the riches of sound. Hearing also collects information from all around the body, such as detecting the approach of an unseen car (Yost, 2007).

What is the stimulus for hearing? If you throw a stone into a quiet pond, a circle of waves will spread in all directions. In much the same way, sound travels as a series of invisible waves of *compression* (peaks) and *rarefaction* (RARE-eh-fak-shun: valleys) in the air. Any vibrating object—a tuning fork, the string of a musical instrument, or the vocal cords—will produce sound waves (rhythmic movement of air molecules). Other materials, such as fluids or solids, can also carry sound. But sound does not travel in a vacuum or the airless realm of outer space. Movies that show characters reacting to the "roar" of alien starships or titanic battles in deep space are in error.

The *frequency* of sound waves (the number of waves per second) corresponds to the perceived *pitch* (higher or lower tone) of a sound. The *amplitude,* or physical "height," of a sound wave tells how much energy it contains. Psychologically, amplitude corresponds to sensed *loudness* (sound intensity) (▶Fig. 4.14).

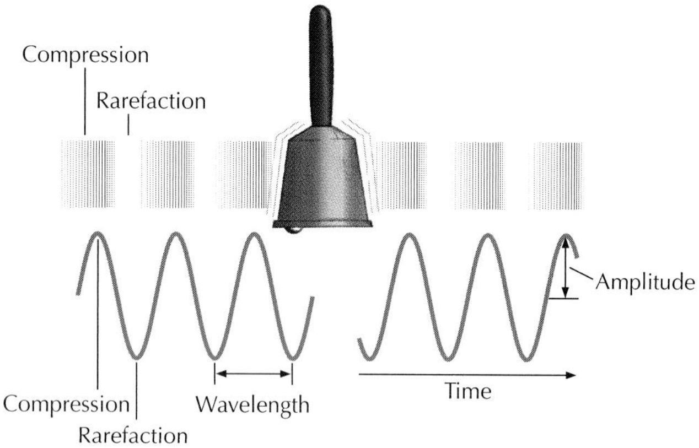

▶**FIGURE 4.14** Waves of compression in the air, or vibrations, are the stimulus for hearing. The frequency of sound waves determines their pitch. The amplitude determines loudness.

Mechanisms of Hearing

How are sounds converted to nerve impulses? Hearing begins with the *pinna* (PIN-ah: the visible, external part of the ear). In addition to being a good place to hang earrings or balance pencils, the pinna acts like a funnel to concentrate sounds. After they are guided into the ear canal, sound waves collide with the *tympanic membrane* (eardrum), setting it in motion. This, in turn, causes three small bones (the *auditory ossicles*) (OSS-ih-kuls) to vibrate (▶Fig. 4.15). The ossicles are the malleus (MAL-ee-us), incus, and stapes (STAY-peas). Their common names are the hammer, anvil, and stirrup. The ossicles link the eardrum with the *cochlea* (KOCK-lee-ah: a snail-shaped organ that makes up the inner ear). The stapes is attached to a membrane on the cochlea called the *oval window.* As the oval window moves back and forth, it makes waves in the fluid inside the cochlea.

Inside the cochlea tiny **hair cells** detect waves in the fluid. The hair cells are part of the **organ of Corti** (KOR-tee), which makes up the center part of the cochlea (▶Fig. 4.16). A set of *stereocilia* (STER-ee-oh-SIL-ih-ah), or "bristles," atop each hair cell brush against the tectorial membrane when waves ripple through the fluid surrounding the organ of Corti. As the stereocilia are bent, nerve impulses are triggered, which then flow to the brain. (Are your ears "bristling" with sound?)

How are higher and lower sounds detected? The **frequency theory** of hearing states that as pitch rises, nerve impulses of a corresponding frequency are fed into the auditory nerve. That is, an 800-hertz tone produces 800 nerve impulses per second. (*Hertz* refers to the number of vibrations per second.) This explains how sounds up to about 4,000 hertz reach the brain. But what about higher tones? **Place theory** states that higher and lower tones excite specific areas of the cochlea. High tones register most strongly at the base of the cochlea (near the oval window). Lower tones, on the other hand, mostly move hair cells near the outer tip of the cochlea (▶Fig. 4.17). Pitch is signaled by the area of the cochlea most strongly activated. Incidentally, place theory also explains why hunters sometimes lose hearing in a narrow pitch range. "Hunter's notch," as it is called, occurs when hair cells are damaged in the area affected by the pitch of gunfire.

Hair cells Receptor cells within the cochlea that transduce vibrations into nerve impulses.

Organ of Corti Center part of the cochlea, containing hair cells, canals, and membranes.

Frequency theory Holds that tones up to 4,000 hertz are converted to nerve impulses that match the frequency of each tone.

Place theory Theory that higher and lower tones excite specific areas of the cochlea.

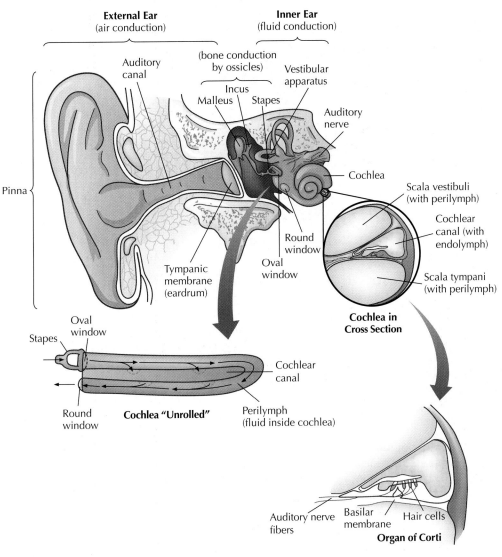

External Ear
(air conduction)

Inner Ear
(fluid conduction)

(bone conduction
by ossicles)

Auditory
canal

Incus

Malleus   Stapes

Vestibular
apparatus

Auditory
nerve

Pinna

Cochlea

Tympanic
membrane
(eardrum)

Round
window

Oval
window

Scala vestibuli
(with perilymph)

Cochlear
canal (with
endolymph)

Scala tympani
(with perilymph)

**Cochlea in
Cross Section**

Oval
window

Stapes

Round
window

Cochlear
canal

Perilymph
(fluid inside cochlea)

Cochlea "Unrolled"

Auditory nerve
fibers

Basilar
membrane

Hair cells

Organ of Corti

> **FIGURE 4.15** Anatomy of the ear. The inset in the foreground (Cochlea "Unrolled") shows that as the stapes moves the oval window, the round window bulges outward, allowing waves to ripple through fluid in the cochlea. The waves move membranes near the hair cells, causing cilia or "bristles" on the tips of the cells to bend. The hair cells then generate nerve impulses carried to the brain. (See an enlarged cross section of cochlea in > Fig. 4.16.)

> **FIGURE 4.16** A closer view of the hair cells shows how movement of fluid in the cochlea causes the bristling "hairs" or cilia to bend, generating a nerve impulse.

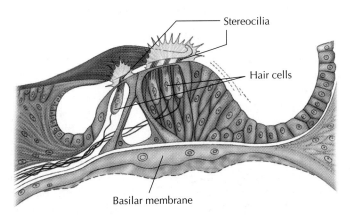

Stereocilia

Hair cells

Basilar membrane

Hearing Loss

What causes other types of hearing loss? There are two main types of hearing loss (also referred to as deafness). **Conductive hearing loss** occurs when the transfer of vibrations from the outer ear to the inner ear is weak. For example, the eardrums or ossicles may be damaged or immobilized by disease or injury. In many cases, conductive hearing loss can be overcome with a hearing aid, which makes sounds louder and clearer.

Conductive hearing loss Poor transfer of sounds from the eardrum to the inner ear.

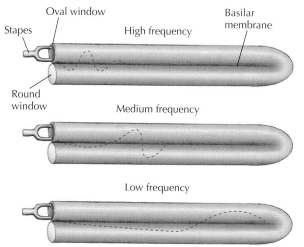

Oval window
Stapes
Round window

High frequency
Basilar membrane

Medium frequency

Low frequency

» **FIGURE 4.17** Here we see a simplified side view of the cochlea "unrolled." Remember that the basilar membrane is the elastic "roof" of the lower chamber of the cochlea. The organ of Corti, with its sensitive hair cells, rests atop the basilar membrane. The colored line shows where waves in the cochlear fluid cause the greatest deflection of the basilar membrane. (The amount of movement is exaggerated in the drawing.) The area of greatest movement helps identify sound frequency.

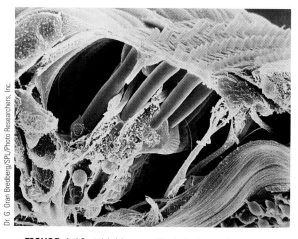

Dr. G. Oran Bredberg/SPL/Photo Researchers, Inc.

»**FIGURE 4.18** A highly magnified electron microscope photo of the cilia (orange bristles) on the top of human hair cells. (Colors are artificial.)

Sensorineural hearing loss results from damage to the inner ear hair cells or auditory nerve. Many jobs, hobbies, and pastimes can cause **noise-induced hearing loss,** a form of sensorineural hearing loss that occurs when very loud sounds damage hair cells (as in hunter's notch). The hair cells, which are about as thin as a cobweb, are very fragile (» Fig. 4.18). By the time you are 65, more than 40 percent of them will be gone. If you work in a noisy environment or enjoy loud music, motorcycling, snowmobiling, hunting, or similar pursuits, you may be risking noise-induced hearing loss. Dead hair cells are never replaced: When you abuse them you lose them.

How loud must a sound be to be hazardous? Daily exposure to 85 decibels or more may cause permanent hearing loss (Sekuler & Blake, 2006). Decibels are a measure of sound intensity. Every 20 decibels increases the sound pressure by a factor of 10. In other words, a rock concert at 120 decibels is 1,000 times stronger than a voice at 60 decibels. Even short periods at 120 decibels can cause temporary hearing loss. Brief exposure to 150 decibels (a jet airplane nearby) may cause permanent hearing loss. You might find it interesting to check the decibel ratings of some of your activities in » Figure 4.19. Be aware that amplified musical concerts, iPod-style headphones, and "boom-box" car stereos can also damage your hearing.

Hearing aids are of no help in cases of sensorineural hearing loss because auditory messages are blocked from reaching the brain. However, artificial hearing systems are making it possible for some persons with this form of hearing loss to break through the wall of silence.

Artificial Hearing

In many cases of sensorineural hearing loss, the auditory nerve is actually intact. This finding has spurred the development of cochlear implants that bypass hair cells and stimulate the auditory nerves directly (» Fig. 4.20). Wires from a microphone carry electrical signals to an external coil. A matching coil under the skin picks up the signals and carries them to one or more areas of the cochlea. The latest implants make use of place theory to separate higher and lower channels. This has allowed some formerly deaf persons to hear human voices, music, and other higher frequency sounds. About 60 percent of all multichannel implant patients can understand some spoken words and appreciate music (Leal et al., 2003; Tye-Murray et al., 1995). Some deaf children learn to speak. Those who receive a cochlear implant before age 2 learn spoken language at a near normal rate (Dorman & Wilson, 2004). At present, artificial hearing remains crude. All but the most successful cochlear implant patients describe the sound as "like a radio that isn't quite tuned in." Nevertheless, it is hard to argue with enthusiasts like Kristen Cloud. Shortly after Kristen received an implant, she

Sensorineural hearing loss Loss of hearing caused by damage to the inner ear hair cells or auditory nerve.

Noise-induced hearing loss Damage caused by exposing the hair cells to excessively loud sounds.

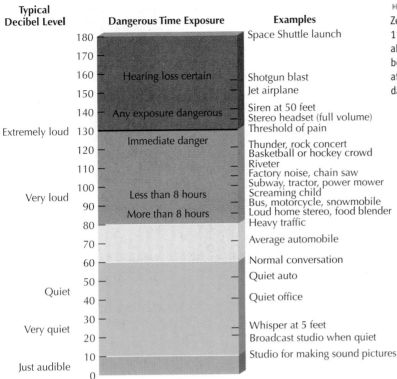

Typical Decibel Level	Dangerous Time Exposure	Examples
180		Space Shuttle launch
170		
160	Hearing loss certain	Shotgun blast
150		Jet airplane
140	Any exposure dangerous	Siren at 50 feet
		Stereo headset (full volume)
Extremely loud 130		Threshold of pain
120	Immediate danger	Thunder, rock concert
		Basketball or hockey crowd
110		Riveter
		Factory noise, chain saw
100	Less than 8 hours	Subway, tractor, power mower
		Screaming child
Very loud 90		Bus, motorcycle, snowmobile
	More than 8 hours	Loud home stereo, food blender
80		Heavy traffic
70		Average automobile
60		Normal conversation
50		Quiet auto
Quiet 40		Quiet office
30		
Very quiet 20		Whisper at 5 feet
		Broadcast studio when quiet
10		Studio for making sound pictures
Just audible 0		

▸▸**FIGURE 4.19** The loudness of sound is measured in decibels. Zero decibels is the faintest sound most people can hear. Sounds of 110 decibels are uncomfortably loud. Prolonged exposure to sounds above 85 decibels may damage the inner ear. Rock music, which may be 120 decibels, has caused hearing loss in musicians and may affect audiences as well. Sounds of 130 decibels pose an immediate danger to hearing.

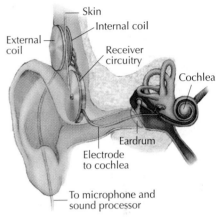

▸▸**FIGURE 4.20** A cochlear implant, or "artificial ear."

was able to hear a siren and avoid being struck by a speeding car. She says simply, "The implant saved my life."

SMELL AND TASTE—THE NOSE KNOWS WHEN THE TONGUE CAN'T TELL

>SURVEY QUESTION< *How do the chemical senses operate?*

Unless you are a wine taster, a perfume blender, a chef, or a gourmet, you may think of **olfaction** (smell) and **gustation** (taste) as minor senses. Certainly you could survive without these *chemical senses* (receptors that respond to chemical molecules). Just the same, smell and taste occasionally prevent poisonings and they certainly add pleasure to our lives (Wolfe et al., 2005). Let's see how they operate.

The Sense of Smell

Smell receptors respond to airborne molecules. As air enters the nose, it flows over roughly 5 million nerve fibers in the upper nasal passages (▸▸Fig. 4.21). Receptor proteins on the surface of the fibers are sensitive to various airborne molecules. When a fiber is stimulated it sends signals to the brain.

How are different odors produced? This is still an unfolding mystery. One hint comes from a problem called *anosmia* (an-OZE-me-ah: defective smell), a sort of "smell blindness" for a single odor. Anosmia suggests there are receptors for specific odors. Indeed, molecules having a particular odor are quite similar in shape. Specific shapes produce the following types of odors: floral (flower-like), camphoric (camphor-like), musky (have you ever smelled a sweaty musk ox?), minty (mint-like), and etherish (like ether or cleaning fluid). This does not mean, however, that there are just five different olfactory receptors. In humans, about 1,000 types of smell receptors are believed to exist (Bensafi et al., 2004).

Olfaction The sense of smell.
Gustation The sense of taste.

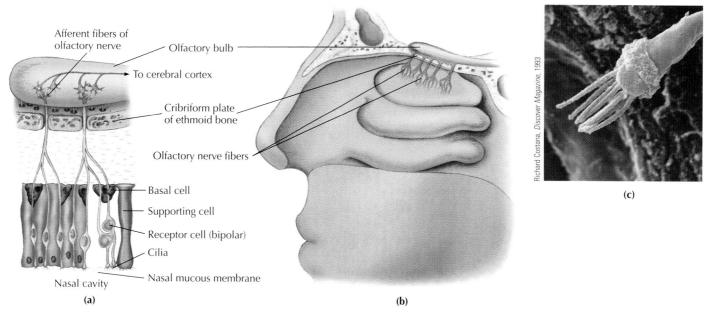

Richard Costana, *Discover Magazine*, 1993

(a)

(b)

(c)

▸▸**FIGURE 4.21** *(a)* Olfactory nerve fibers respond to gaseous molecules. Receptor cells are shown in cross section to the left. *(b)* Olfactory receptors are located in the upper nasal cavity. *(c)* An extreme close-up of an olfactory receptor shows fibers that sense gaseous molecules of various shapes.

Does the existence of 1,000 different types of receptors mean that we can sense only 1,000 different odors? No, molecules trigger activity in different *combinations* of odor receptors. Thus, humans can detect at least 10,000 different odors. Just as you can make many thousands of words from the 26 letters of the alphabet, many combinations of receptors are possible, resulting in many different odors. The brain uses the distinctive patterns of messages it gets from the olfactory receptors to recognize particular scents (Laurent et al., 2001).

It appears that different-shaped "holes," or "pockets," exist on the surface of olfactory receptors. Like a piece fits in a puzzle, chemicals produce odors when part of a molecule matches a hole of the same shape. This is the **lock and key theory.** Scents are also identified, in part, by the *location* of the receptors in the nose that are activated by a particular odor. And finally, the *number of activated receptors* tells the brain how strong an odor is (Bensafi et al., 2004).

What causes anosmia? Risks include infections, allergies, and blows to the head (which may tear the olfactory nerves). Exposure to chemicals such as ammonia, photo-developing chemicals, and hair-dressing potions can also cause anosmia. If you value your sense of smell, be careful what you breathe (Herz, 2001).

Taste and Flavors

There are at least four basic taste sensations: *sweet, salt, sour,* and *bitter.* We are most sensitive to bitter, less sensitive to sour, even less sensitive to salt, and least sensitive to sweet. This order may have helped prevent poisonings when most humans foraged for food, because bitter and sour foods are more likely to be inedible.

Many experts now believe that a fifth taste quality exists. The Japanese word *umami* (oo-MAH-me) describes a pleasant savory or "brothy" taste associated with certain amino acids in chicken soup, some meat extracts, kelp, tuna, human milk, cheese, and soybeans. The receptors for *umami* are sensitive to glutamate, a substance found in MSG (Sugimoto & Ninomiya, 2005). Perhaps MSG's reputation as a "flavor enhancer" is based on the pleasant *umami* taste (Lindemann, 2000). At the very least, we may finally know why chicken soup is such a "comfort food."

If there are only four or five tastes, how can there be so many different flavors? Flavors seem more varied because we tend to include sensations of texture, temperature, smell, and even pain ("hot" chili peppers) along with taste. Smell is particularly important in determining flavor. If you plug your nose and eat small bits of apple, potato, and onion, they will "taste" almost exactly alike. So do gourmet jelly beans! It is probably fair to say that subjective flavor is one half smell. That's why food loses its "taste" when you have a cold.

Lock and key theory Holds that odors are related to the shapes of chemical molecules.

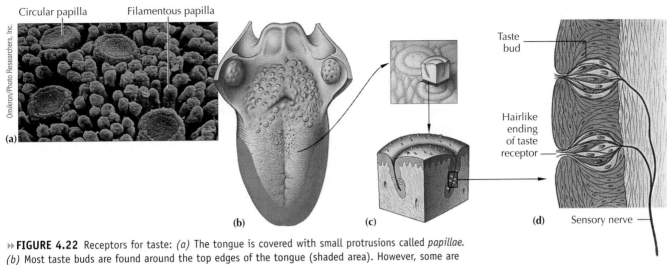

Circular papilla   Filamentous papilla

Omikron/Photo Researchers, Inc.

(a)   (b)   (c)   (d)

Taste bud

Hairlike ending of taste receptor

Sensory nerve

▸▸**FIGURE 4.22** Receptors for taste: *(a)* The tongue is covered with small protrusions called *papillae*. *(b)* Most taste buds are found around the top edges of the tongue (shaded area). However, some are located elsewhere, including under the tongue. Stimulation of the central part of the tongue causes no taste sensations. All four primary taste sensations occur anywhere that taste buds exist. *(c)* An enlarged drawing shows that taste buds are located near the base of papillae. *(d)* Detail of a taste bud. These receptors also occur in other parts of the digestive system, such as the lining of the mouth.

Taste buds (taste-receptor cells) are mainly located on the top side of the tongue, especially around the edges. However, a few are found elsewhere inside the mouth (▸▸Fig. 4.22). As food is chewed, it dissolves and enters the taste buds, where it sets off nerve impulses to the brain (Northcutt, 2004). Much like smell, sweet and bitter tastes appear to be based on a lock-and-key match between molecules and intricately shaped receptors. Saltiness and sourness, however, are triggered by a direct flow of charged atoms into the tips of taste cells (Lindemann, 2001).

Taste bud The receptor organ for taste.

Study Break   Hearing, Smell, and Taste

Reflect

Close your eyes and listen to the sounds around you. As you do, try to mentally trace the events necessary to convert vibrations in the air into the sounds you are hearing. Review the discussion of hearing if you leave out any steps.

What is your favorite food odor? What is your favorite taste? Can you explain how you are able to sense the aroma and taste of foods?

Learning Check

1. The frequency of a sound wave corresponds to how loud it is. T or F?

2. Which of the following is not a part of the cochlea?

   a. ossicles   b. pinna
   c. tympanic membrane   d. all of the above

3. According to the place theory of hearing, higher tones register most strongly near the base of the cochlea. T or F?

4. Sensorineural hearing loss occurs when the auditory ossicles are damaged. T or F?

5. Daily exposure to sounds with a loudness of _____ decibels may cause permanent hearing loss.

6. Cochlear implants have been used primarily to overcome

   a. conduction hearing loss   b. noise-induced hearing loss
   c. sensorineural hearing loss   d. hunter's notch

7. Olfaction appears to be at least partially explained by the _____ _____ _____ theory of molecule shapes and receptor sites.

8. *Umami* is a type of "smell blindness" for a particular odor. T or F?

Critical Thinking

9. Why do you think your voice sounds so different when you hear a tape recording of your speech?

10. Smell and hearing differ from vision in a way that may aid survival. What is it?

Answers

1. F 2. d 3. T 4. F 5. 85 6. c 7. lock and key 8. F 9. The answer lies in another question: How else might vibrations from the voice reach the cochlea? Other people hear your voice only as it is carried through the air. You hear not only that sound, but also vibrations conducted by the bones of your skull. 10. Both smell and hearing can detect stimuli (including signals of approaching danger) around corners, behind objects, and behind the head.

THE SOMESTHETIC SENSES—FLYING BY THE SEAT OF YOUR PANTS

>SURVEY QUESTION< *What are the somesthetic senses and why are they important?*

A gymnast "flying" through a routine on the uneven bars may rely as much on the **somesthetic senses** as on vision (*soma* means "body," *esthetic* means "feel"). Even the most routine activities, such as walking, running, or passing a sobriety test, would be impossible without the **skin senses** (touch), the **kinesthetic senses** (receptors in muscles and joints that detect body position and movement), and the **vestibular senses** (receptors in the inner ear for balance, gravity, and acceleration). Because of their importance, let's begin with the skin senses.

The Skin Senses

It's difficult to imagine what life would be like without the sense of touch, but the plight of Ian Waterman gives a hint. After an illness, Waterman permanently lost all feeling below his neck. Now, in order to know what position his body is in he has to be able to see it. If he moves with his eyes closed, he has no idea where he is moving. If the lights go out in a room, he's in big trouble (Cole, 1995).

Skin receptors produce at least five different sensations: *light touch, pressure, pain, cold,* and *warmth.* Receptors with particular shapes appear to specialize somewhat in various sensations (▸Fig. 4.23). However, free nerve endings alone can produce all five sensations (Carlson, 2005). Altogether, the skin has about 200,000 nerve endings for temperature, 500,000 for touch and pressure, and 3 million for pain.

Does the number of receptors in an area of skin relate to its sensitivity? Yes. Your skin could be "mapped" by applying heat, cold, touch, pressure, or pain to points all over your body. Such testing would show that the number of skin receptors varies, and that sensitivity generally matches the number of receptors in a given area. Generally speaking, important areas such as the lips, tongue, face, hands, and genitals have a higher density of receptors.

▸▸**FIGURE 4.23** The skin senses include touch, pressure, pain, cold, and warmth. This drawing shows different forms the skin receptors can take. The only clearly specialized receptor is the Pacinian corpuscle, which is highly sensitive to pressure. Free nerve endings are receptors for pain and any of the other sensations. For reasons that are not clear, cold is sensed near the surface of the skin, and warmth is sensed deeper (Carlson, 2005).

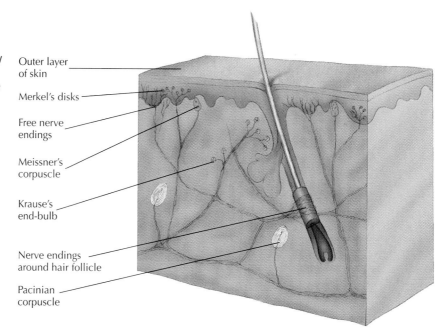

Outer layer of skin

Merkel's disks

Free nerve endings

Meissner's corpuscle

Krause's end-bulb

Nerve endings around hair follicle

Pacinian corpuscle

Somesthetic senses Sensations produced by the skin, muscles, joints, viscera, and organs of balance.

Skin senses The senses of touch, pressure, pain, heat, and cold.

Kinesthetic senses The senses of body movement and positioning.

Vestibular senses The senses of balance, position in space, and acceleration.

Pain

The number of pain receptors also varies, right? Yes, like the other skin senses, pain receptors vary in their distribution. About 230 pain points per square centimeter (about a half inch) are found behind the knee, 180 per centimeter on the buttocks, 60 on the pad of the thumb, and 40 on the tip of the nose. (Is it better, then, to be pinched on the nose or behind the knee? It depends on what you like!)

Pain carried by *large nerve fibers* is sharp, bright, fast, and seems to come from specific body areas (McMahon & Koltzenburg, 2005). This is the body's **warning system.** Give yourself a small jab with a pin and you will feel this type of pain. As you do this, notice that warning pain quickly disappears. Much as we may dislike warning pain, it is usually a signal that the body has been, or is about to be, damaged. Without warning pain, we would be unable to detect or prevent injury. Children who are born with a rare inherited insensitivity to pain repeatedly burn themselves, break bones, bite their tongues, and become ill without knowing it (Larner et al., 1994).

A second type of somatic pain is carried by *small nerve fibers*. This type is slower, nagging, aching, widespread, and very unpleasant (McMahon & Koltzenburg, 2005). It gets worse if the pain stimulus is repeated. This is the body's **reminding system.** It reminds the brain that the body has been injured. For instance, lower back pain often has this quality. Sadly, the reminding system can cause agony long after an injury has healed, or in terminal illnesses, when the reminder is useless.

Pain Control

In some cultures, people endure tattooing, stretching, cutting, and burning with little apparent pain. How do they do it? Very likely the answer lies in a reliance on psychological factors that anyone can use to reduce pain, such as anxiety reduction, control, and attention (Mailis-Gagnon & Israelson, 2005).

In general, unpleasant emotions such as fear and anxiety increase pain; pleasant emotions decrease it (Rainville, 2004). Anytime you can anticipate pain (such as a trip to the doctor, dentist, or tattoo parlor), you can lower anxiety by making sure you are *fully informed.* Be sure everything that will happen is explained. In general, the more control you *feel* you have over a painful stimulus, the less pain you will experience. To apply this principle, you should arrange a signal so your doctor, dentist, or body piercer will know when to start and stop a painful procedure. Finally, distraction also reduces pain. Instead of listening to the whirr of a dentist's drill, for example, you might imagine that you are lying in the sun at a beach, listening to the roar of the surf. Or, take an iPod along and crank up your favorite MP3s (Bushnell, Villemure, & Duncan, 2004).

The Vestibular System

Space flight might look like fun. But if you ever get a ride into space, it is about 70 percent likely that your first experience in orbit will be throwing up. Weightlessness and space flight affect the vestibular system, often causing severe motion sickness. Within the vestibular system, fluid-filled sacs called *otolith organs* (OH-toe-lith) are sensitive to movement, acceleration, and gravity (►Fig. 4.24). The otolith organs contain tiny crystals in a soft, gelatin-like mass. The tug of gravity or rapid head movements can cause the mass to shift. This, in turn, stimulates hair-like receptor cells, allowing us to sense gravity, acceleration, and movement through space (Lackner & DiZio, 2005).

Three fluid-filled tubes called the *semicircular canals* are the sensory organs for balance. If you could climb inside these tubes, you would find that head movements cause the fluid to swirl about. As the fluid moves, it bends a small "flap," or "float," called the *crista*, that detects movement in the semicircular canals. The bending of each crista again stimulates hair cells and signals head rotation.

Weightlessness presents astronauts with a real challenge in sensory adaptation.

Warning system Pain based on large nerve fibers; warns that bodily damage may be occurring.

Reminding system Pain based on small nerve fibers; reminds the brain that the body has been injured.

Many people become nauseated the first time they experience virtual reality. Why? Because virtual reality also creates a sensory conflict: Computer-generated visual images change as if the viewer's body is in motion, but the vestibular system tells viewers that they are standing still. The result? The scenery may not be real but the nausea is.

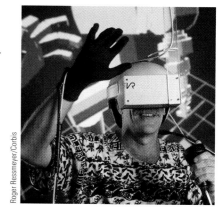

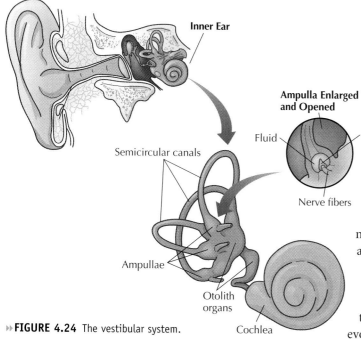

Inner Ear

Ampulla Enlarged and Opened

Fluid

Crista

Nerve fibers

Semicircular canals

Ampullae

Otolith organs

Cochlea

>> **FIGURE 4.24** The vestibular system.

What causes motion sickness? According to **sensory conflict theory,** dizziness and nausea occur when sensations from the vestibular system don't match sensations from the eyes and body (Flanagan, May, & Dobie, 2004). On solid ground, information from the vestibular system, vision, and kinesthesis usually matches. However, in a heaving, pitching boat, car, or airplane, a serious mismatch can occur—causing disorientation and heaving of another kind.

Why would sensory conflict cause nausea? You can probably blame (or thank) evolution. Many poisons disturb the vestibular system, vision, and the body. Therefore, we may have evolved so that we react to sensory conflict by vomiting to expel poison. The value of this reaction, however, may be of little comfort to anyone who has ever been "green" and miserable with motion sickness. To minimize such conflicts, try to keep your head still, fix your vision on a distant immobile object, and lie down if you can.

ADAPTATION, GATING, AND ATTENTION— TUNING IN AND TUNING OUT

>SURVEY QUESTION< *Why are we more aware of some sensations than others?*

You are surrounded by a rich mix of sights, sounds, odors, tastes, and touch sensations. As we saw earlier, the senses actively reduce the amount of information they send to the brain. In addition, many sensory events never reach awareness because of *sensory adaptation, sensory gating,* and *selective attention.* Let's see how these processes further filter sensory information.

Sensory Adaptation

Think about walking into a house where fried fish, sauerkraut, and head cheese were prepared for dinner. (Some dinner!) You would probably pass out at the door, yet people who had been in the house for some time wouldn't be aware of the food odors. Why? Because sensory receptors respond less to unchanging stimuli, a process called **sensory adaptation.**

Fortunately, the olfactory (smell) receptors adapt quickly. When exposed to a constant odor, they send fewer and fewer nerve impulses to the brain until the odor is no longer noticed. Adaptation to pressure from a wristwatch, waistband, ring, or glasses is based on

Sensory conflict theory Explains motion sickness as the result of a mismatch between information from vision, the vestibular system, and kinesthesis.

Sensory adaptation A decrease in sensory response to an unchanging stimulus.

Roger Ressmeyer/Corbis

the same principle. Sensory receptors generally respond best to *changes* in stimulation. No one wants or needs to be reminded 16 hours a day that his or her shoes are on.

Sensory Gating

Are sensory messages ever blocked before they reach the brain? Yes, a process called *sensory gating* blocks some incoming nerve impulses while allowing others to pass through (Melzack & Katz, 2004). A fascinating example of sensory gating is provided by Ronald Melzack and Patrick Wall, who study "pain gates" in the spinal cord (Melzack & Wall, 1996). Melzack and Wall noticed (as you may have) that one type of pain will sometimes cancel another. Their **gate control theory** suggests that pain messages from different nerve fibers pass through the same neural "gate" in the spinal cord. If the gate is "closed" by one pain message, other messages may not be able to pass through (Humphries, Johnson, & Long, 1996).

How is the gate closed? Messages carried by large, fast nerve fibers seem to close the spinal pain gate directly. Doing so can prevent slower, "reminding system" pain from reaching the brain. As a pain control technique, this is called *counterirritation*. Pain clinics use it by applying a mild electrical current to the skin. This causes only a mild tingling that can greatly reduce more agonizing pain (Köke et al., 2004). You can use counterirritation to control your own pain. For instance, if you are having a tooth filled, try pinching yourself or digging a fingernail into a knuckle while the dentist is working. Focus your attention on the pain you are creating, and increase it anytime the dentist's work becomes more painful. This strategy may seem strange, but it works. Generations of children have used it to take the edge off a spanking.

Messages from small, slow fibers seem to take a different route. After going through the pain gate, they pass on to a "central biasing system" in the brain. Under some circumstances, the brain then sends a message back down the spinal cord, closing the pain gates (▶ Fig. 4.25). Melzack and Wall believe that gate control theory explains the painkilling effects of acupuncture (but see "The Matrix: Do Phantoms Live Here?").

Acupuncture is the Chinese medical art of relieving pain and illness by inserting thin needles into the body. As the acupuncturist's needles are twirled, heated, or electrified, they activate small pain fibers. These relay through the biasing system to close the gates to intense or chronic pain (Melzack & Wall, 1996). Studies have shown that acupuncture produces short-term pain relief for many patients (Cardenas & Jensen, 2006; Witt et al., 2006).

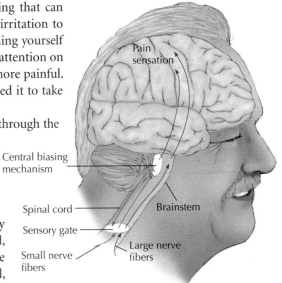

▶▶**FIGURE 4.25** Diagram of a sensory gate for pain. A series of pain impulses going through the gate may prevent other pain messages from passing through. Or pain messages may relay through a "central biasing mechanism" that exerts control over the gate, closing it to other impulses.

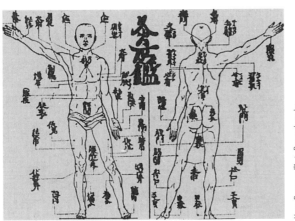

(Left) An acupuncturist's chart. *(Right)* Thin stainless steel needles are inserted into areas defined by the chart. Modern research has begun to explain the painkilling effects of acupuncture (see text). Acupuncture's claimed ability to cure diseases is more debatable.

Gate control theory Proposes that pain messages pass through neural "gates" in the spinal cord.

The Matrix: Do Phantoms Live Here?

As you read this book, you may find yourself wondering why psychologists are so interested in the brain. "Brainwaves" boxes like this one are designed to help you think about how the biopsychological perspective contributes to a better understanding of human behavior.

In the popular *Matrix* films, Neo, as played by Keanu Reeves, discovers that machines have imprisoned humans in a phantom world called the Matrix in order to steal human energy for their own use. Actually, the idea of a "matrix" is not totally farfetched. In fact, your own brain may be creating a *neuromatrix* that is responsible for your perceptions of your own body.

A person who suffers an amputation doesn't need to believe in the Matrix to encounter phantoms. Most amputees have phantom limb sensations, including pain, for months or years after losing a limb (Fraser, 2002; Halbert, Crotty, & Cameron, 2002). Because the phantom limb feels so "real," a patient with a recently amputated leg may inadvertently try to walk on it, risking further injury. Sometimes, phantom limbs feel like they are stuck in awkward positions. For instance, one man can't sleep on his back because his missing arm feels like it is twisted behind him.

What causes phantom limbs? Gate control theory cannot explain phantom limb pain (Hunter, Katz, & Davis, 2003).

Because pain can't be coming from the missing limb, it cannot pass through pain gates to the brain (after all, it's missing!). Instead, according to Ronald Melzack (1999), the brain creates a body image called the *neuromatrix*. This internal model of the body generates our sense of bodily self. Although amputation may remove a limb, as far as the neuromatrix in the brain is concerned, the limb still exists. Functional MRI imaging confirms that sensory and motor areas of the brain are more active when a person feels a phantom limb (Rosen et al., 2001). Even though pain signals no longer come from the amputated limb, the neuromatrix evidently interprets other sensory experiences as pain from the missing limb.

Sometimes the brain gradually reorganizes to adjust for the sensory loss (Wu & Kaas, 2002). For example, a person who loses an arm may at first have a phantom arm and hand. After many years, the phantom may shrink, until only a hand is felt at the shoulder. Perhaps more vividly than others, people with phantom limbs are reminded that the sensory world as we know it is constructed, moment by moment, not by some futuristic machines but by our very own neuromatrix in our brains.

Selective Attention

As you sit reading this page, receptors for touch and pressure in the seat of your pants are sending nerve impulses to your brain. Although these sensations have been present all along, you were probably not aware of them until just now. This "seat-of-the-pants phenomenon" is an example of **selective attention** (voluntarily focusing on a specific sensory input). Selective attention appears to be based on the ability of brain structures to select and divert incoming sensory messages (Freiwald & Kanwisher, 2004). We are able to "tune in on" a single sensory message while excluding others. Another familiar example of this is the "cocktail party effect."

When you are in a group of people, surrounded by voices, you can still select and attend to the voice of the person you are facing. Or if that person gets dull, you can eavesdrop on conversations all over the room. (Be sure to smile and nod your head occasionally!) Actually, no matter how interesting your companion may be, your attention will probably shift away if you hear your own name spoken somewhere in the room (Conway, Cowan, & Bunting, 2001). We do find what others say about us to be very interesting, don't we?

At times, we can even suffer from *inattentional blindness* (Most et al., 2005). That is, we may not see something that is plainly before our eyes when our attention is narrowly focused (Mack, 2002). Inattentional blindness is vividly illustrated by the work of psychologists Daniel Simons and Christopher Chabris. In one study, Simons and Chabris showed people a film of two basketball teams, one wearing black shirts and the other wearing white. Observers were asked to watch the film closely and count how many times a basketball passed between members of one of the teams, while ignoring the other team. As observers watched and counted, a person wearing a gorilla suit walked into the middle of the basketball game, faced the camera, thumped its chest, and walked out of view. Half the observers failed to notice this rather striking event (Simons & Chabris, 1999). This effect probably explains why fans of opposing sports teams often act as if they had seen two completely different games. In a similar way, using a cell phone while driving can cause inattentional

Selective attention Giving priority to a particular incoming sensory message.

blindness. Instead of ignoring a gorilla, you might miss seeing another car, a motorcyclist, or a pedestrian while your attention is focused on the phone (Strayer, Drews, & Johnson, 2003).

You might find it helpful to think of selective attention as a *bottleneck,* or narrowing in the information channel linking the senses to perception. When one message enters the bottleneck, it seems to prevent others from passing through (see ▸Fig. 4.26). Imagine, for instance, that you are a pilot preparing to land a jumbo jet. You need to be sure the flaps are down. Just as you are about to check them, your copilot says something to you. If you then fail to notice the flaps are still up, an air disaster is just seconds away.

The senses supply raw data to the brain, but the information remains mostly meaningless until it is interpreted. It's as if the senses provide only the jumbled pieces of a complex puzzle. Melzack's (1999) concept of a neuromatrix is one theory of how the brain tries to make sense of sensory input. In the remainder of this chapter we will further explore how we put the puzzle together.

▸**FIGURE 4.26** The attentional "bottleneck," or "spotlight," can be widened or narrowed. If you focus on local details in this drawing you will see the letter *A* repeated 13 times. If you broaden your field of attention to encompass the overall pattern, you will see the letter *H*. (After Lamb & Yund, 1996.)

 Study Break ## Somesthetic Senses, Adaptation, Gating, and Attention

Reflect

Stand on one foot with your eyes closed. Now touch the tip of your nose with your index finger. Which of the somesthetic senses did you use to perform this feat?

Imagine you are on a boat ride with a friend who starts to feel queasy. Can you explain to your friend what causes motion sickness and what she or he can do to prevent it?

As you sit reading this book, which sensory inputs have undergone adaptation? What new inputs can you become aware of by shifting your focus of attention?

Think about a strategy you have used for reducing pain at the doctor, dentist, or some other painful situation. Did you alter anxiety, control, or attention? Can you think of any ways in which you have used counterirritation to lessen pain?

Learning Check

1. Which of the following is a somesthetic sense?
   a. gustation   b. olfaction
   c. rarefaction   d. kinesthesis
2. Warning pain is carried by _____ nerve fibers.
3. Head movements are detected primarily in the semicircular canals, gravity by the otolith organs. T or F?
4. Sensory conflicts appear to explain nausea caused by poisoning, but not the nausea associated with motion sickness. T or F?

5. Sensory adaptation refers to an increase in sensory response that accompanies a constant or unchanging stimulus. T or F?
6. The brain-centered ability to influence what sensations we will receive is called
   a. sensory gating   b. central adaptation
   c. selective attention   d. sensory biasing
7. The painkilling effects of acupuncture appear to result from _____ _____ .
8. Like heightened anxiety, increased control tends to increase subjective pain. T or F?
9. Phantom limb pain cannot be explained by gate-control theory. T or F?

Critical Thinking

10. Drivers are less likely to become carsick than passengers are. Why do you think drivers and passengers differ in susceptibility to motion sickness?
11. What special precautions would you have to take to test the ability of acupuncture to reduce pain?
12. What measures would you take to ensure that an experiment involving pain is ethical?

Answers

1. d   2. large   3. T   4. F   5. F   6. c   7. sensory gating   8. F   9. T   10. Drivers experience less sensory conflict because they control the car's motion. This allows them to anticipate the car's movements and to coordinate their head and eye movements with those of the car.   11. At the very least, you would have to control for the placebo effect by giving fake acupuncture to control group members. However, a true double-blind study would be difficult to do. Acupuncturists would always know if they were giving a placebo treatment or the real thing, which means they might unconsciously influence subjects.   12. Experiments that cause pain must be handled with care and sensitivity. Participation must be voluntary; the source of pain must be noninjurious; and subjects must be allowed to quit at any time.

Visual perception involves finding meaningful patterns in complex stimuli. If you look closely at this painting by the artist Yvaral, you will see that it is entirely made up of small, featureless squares. An infant or newly sighted person would see only a jumble of meaningless colors. But because the squares form a familiar pattern, you should easily see Marilyn Monroe's face. (Or is that Madonna?) ("Marilyn Numerisée," 1990, courtesy Circle Gallery.)

PERCEPTION—MAKING SENSE OF YOUR SENSES

>SURVEY QUESTION< *How do perceptual constancies and Gestalt organizing principles shape our perceptions?*

What would it be like to have your vision restored after a lifetime of blindness? Actually, a first look at the world can be disappointing because your newfound ability to *sense* the world does not guarantee that you can *perceive* it. Newly sighted persons must *learn* to identify objects, to read clocks, numbers, and letters, and to judge sizes and distances (Gregory, 2003). For instance, a cataract patient named Mr. S. B. had been blind since birth. After an operation restored his sight at age 52, Mr. S. B. struggled to use his vision. At first, he could only judge distance in familiar situations (Gregory, 1990). One day he was found crawling out of a hospital window to get a closer look at traffic on the street. It's easy to understand his curiosity, but he had to be restrained. His room was on the fourth floor!

Perceptual Constancies

Why would Mr. S. B. try to crawl out of a fourth-story window? Couldn't he at least tell distance from the size of the cars? No, you must be familiar with objects to use their size to judge distance. Try holding your left hand a few inches in front of your nose and your right hand at arm's length. Your right hand should appear to be about half the size of your left hand. Still, you know your right hand did not suddenly shrink, because you have seen it many times at various distances. We call this **size constancy:** The perceived size of an object remains the same, even though the size of its image on the retina changes.

To perceive your hand accurately, you had to draw on past experience. Some perceptions are so basic they seem to be *native* (inborn). An example is the ability to see a line on a piece of paper. Likewise, even newborn babies show some evidence of size constancy (Slater, Mattock, & Brown, 1990). However, many of our perceptions are *empirical*, or based on prior experience. For instance, cars, houses, and people look like toys when seen from a great distance or from an unfamiliar perspective, such as from the top of a skyscraper. This suggests that although some size constancy is innate, it is also affected by learning (Granrud, 2004).

In **shape constancy** the shape of an object remains stable, even though the shape of its retinal image changes. You can demonstrate shape constancy by looking at this page from directly overhead and then from an angle. Obviously, the page is rectangular, but most of the images that reach your eyes are distorted. Yet, though the book's image changes, your perception of its shape remains constant. (For additional examples, see ▸▸Fig. 4.27.) On the highway, alcohol intoxication impairs size and shape constancy, adding to the accident rate among drunk drivers (Farrimond, 1990).

Let's say that you are outside in bright sunlight. Beside you, a friend is wearing a gray skirt and a white blouse. Suddenly a cloud shades the sun. It might seem that the blouse would grow dimmer, but it still appears to be bright white. This happens because the blouse continues to reflect a larger *proportion* of light than nearby objects. **Brightness constancy**

Almost everyone's family album has at least one photo like this. Extreme viewing angles can make maintaining size constancy difficult, even for familiar objects.

Mark Richards/PhotoEdit

Size constancy The perceived size of an object remains constant, despite changes in its retinal image.

Shape constancy The perceived shape of an object is unaffected by changes in its retinal image.

Brightness constancy The apparent (or relative) brightness of objects remains the same as long as they are illuminated by the same amount of light.

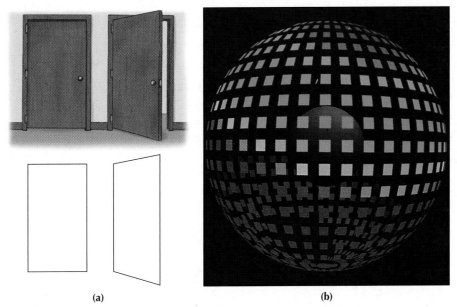

(a)   (b)

▶▶**FIGURE 4.27** Shape constancy. *(a)* When a door is open its image actually forms a trapezoid. Shape constancy is indicated by the fact that it is still perceived as a rectangle. *(b)* With great effort you may be able to see this design as a collection of flat shapes. However, if you maintain shape constancy the distorted squares strongly suggest the surface of a sphere. (From *Spherescapes-1* by Scott Walter and Kevin McMahon, 1983.)

refers to the fact that the brightness of objects appears to stay the same as lighting conditions change. However, this holds true only if the blouse and other objects are all illuminated by the same amount of light. You could make an area on your friend's gray skirt look whiter than the shaded blouse by shining a bright spotlight on the skirt.

To summarize, the energy patterns reaching our senses are constantly changing, even when they come from the same object. Size, shape, and brightness constancy rescue us from a confusing world in which objects would seem to shrink and grow, change shape as if made of rubber, and light up or fade like neon lamps. Gaining these constancies was only one of the hurdles Mr. S. B. faced in learning to see. In the next section, we will consider some others.

Gestalt Organizing Principles

Mr. S. B. soon learned to tell time from a large clock and to read block letters he had known only from touch. At a zoo, he recognized an elephant from descriptions he had heard. However, handwriting meant nothing to him for more than a year after he regained sight, and many objects were meaningless until he touched them. Thus, Mr. S. B. slowly learned to organize his sensations into meaningful perceptions.

How are sensations organized? The Gestalt psychologists (see Chapter 1) proposed that the simplest organization involves grouping some sensations into an object, or figure, that stands out on a plainer background. **Figure-ground organization** is probably inborn, because it is the first perceptual ability to appear after cataract patients regain sight. In normal figure-ground perception, only one figure is seen. In *reversible figures*, however, figure and ground can be switched. In ▶▶Figure 4.28 it is equally possible to see either a wineglass figure on a dark background or two face profiles on a light back-

▶▶**FIGURE 4.28** A reversible figure-ground design. Do you see two faces in profile, or a wineglass?

Figure-ground organization Part of a stimulus appears to stand out as an object (figure) against a less prominent background (ground).

ground. As you shift from one pattern to the other, you should get a clear sense of what figure-ground organization means.

Are there other Gestalt organizing principles? The Gestalt psychologists identified several other principles that bring some order to your perceptions (»Fig. 4.29).

1. **Nearness.** All other things being equal, stimuli that are near each other tend to be grouped together (Kubovy & Gepshtein, 2003). Thus, if three people stand near each other and a fourth person stands 10 feet away, the adjacent three will be seen as a group and the distant person as an outsider (see »Fig. 4.29*a*).

2. **Similarity.** "Birds of a feather flock together," and stimuli that are similar in size, shape, color, or form tend to be grouped together (see »Fig. 4.29*b*). Picture two bands marching side by side. If their uniforms are different colors, the bands will be seen as two separate groups, not as one large group.

3. **Continuation, or continuity.** Perceptions tend toward simplicity and continuity. In »Figure 4.29*c* it is easier to visualize a wavy line on a squared-off line than it is to see a complex row of shapes.

4. **Closure.** Closure refers to the tendency to *complete* a figure, so that it has a consistent overall form. Each of the drawings in »Figure 4.29*d* has one or more gaps, yet

»**FIGURE 4.29** How we organize perceptions.

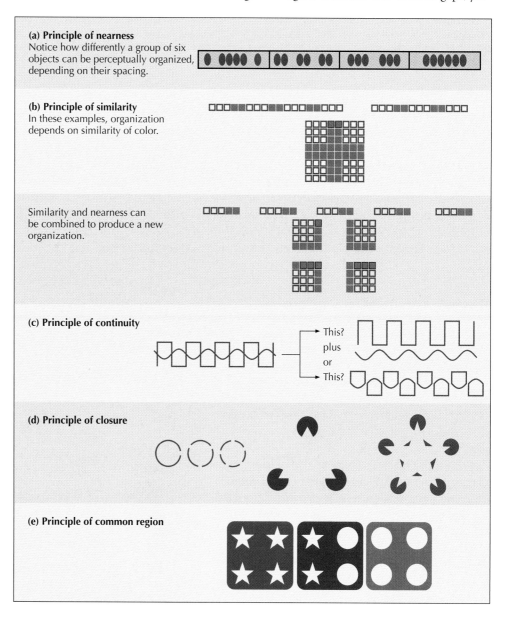

each is perceived as a recognizable figure. Our tendency to form shapes—even with minimal cues—is powerful.

5. **Contiguity.** A principle that can't be shown in ➠ Figure 4.29 is contiguity, or nearness in time *and* space. Contiguity is often responsible for the perception that one thing has *caused* another (Buehner & May, 2003). A psychologist friend of ours demonstrates this principle in class by knocking on his head with one hand while knocking on a wooden table (out of sight) with the other. The knocking sound is perfectly timed with the movements of his visible hand. This leads to the irresistible perception that his head is made of wood.

6. **Common region.** As you can see in ➠ Figure 4.29*e*, stimuli that are found within a common area tend to be seen as a group (Palmer, 1992). On the basis of similarity and nearness, the stars in ➠ Figure 4.29*e* should be one group and the dots another. However, the colored backgrounds define regions that create three groups of objects (four stars, two stars plus two dots, and four dots). Perhaps the principle of common region explains why we tend to mentally group together people from a particular country, state, province, or geographic region.

Clearly, the Gestalt principles shape our day-to-day perceptions, but so does learning and past experience. Take a moment and look for the camouflaged animal pictured in ➠ Figure 4.30. (Camouflage patterns break up figure-ground organization). If you had never seen similar animals before, could you have located this one? Mr. S. B. would have been at a total loss to find meaning in such a picture.

In a way, we are all detectives, seeking patterns in what we see. In this sense, a meaningful pattern represents a **perceptual hypothesis,** or initial guess about how to organize sensations. Have you ever seen a "friend" in the distance, only to have the person turn into a stranger as you drew closer? Pre-existing ideas and expectations *actively* guide our interpretation of sensations (Most et al., 2005).

The active nature of perception is perhaps most apparent for *ambiguous stimuli* (patterns allowing more than one interpretation). If you look at a cloud, you may discover dozens of ways to organize its contours into fanciful shapes and scenes. Even clearly defined stimuli may permit more than one interpretation. Look at Necker's cube in ➠ Figure 4.31 if you doubt that perception is an active process. Visualize the top cube as a wire box. If you stare at the cube, its organization will change. Sometimes it will seem to project upward, like the lower left cube; other times it will project downward. The difference lies in how your brain interprets the same information. In short, we actively *construct* meaningful perceptions; we do not passively record the events and stimuli around us (Coren, Ward, & Enns, 2004).

In some instances, a stimulus may offer such conflicting information that perceptual organization becomes impossible. For example, the tendency to make a three-dimensional object out of a drawing is frustrated by the "three-pronged widget" (➠ Fig. 4.32), an *impossible figure.* Such patterns cannot be organized into stable, consistent, or meaningful perceptions. If you cover either end of the drawing in Figure 4.32, it makes sense perceptually. However, a problem arises when you try to

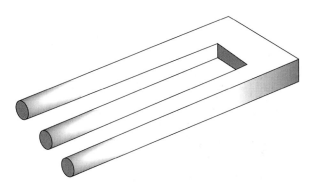

➠ **FIGURE 4.30** A challenging example of perceptual organization. Once the camouflaged insect (known as a giant walkingstick) becomes visible, it is almost impossible to view the picture again without seeing the insect.

E. R. Degginger/Animals Animals

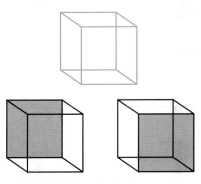

➠ **FIGURE 4.31** Necker's cube.

➠ **FIGURE 4.32** *(Left)* An impossible figure—the "three-pronged widget." *(Right)* It might seem that including more information in a drawing would make perceptual conflicts impossible. However, Japanese artist Shigeo Fukuda has shown otherwise. ("Disappearing Column" © Shigeo Fukuda, 1985.)

Perceptual hypothesis An initial guess regarding how to organize (perceive) a stimulus pattern.

organize the entire drawing. Then, the conflicting information it contains prevents you from forming a stable perception.

One of the most amazing perceptual feats is our capacity to create three-dimensional space from flat retinal images. We'll explore that topic in a moment, but first here's a chance to rehearse what you've learned.

 Study Break **Perceptual Constancies and Gestalt Organizing Principles**

Reflect

If you needed to explain the perceptual constancies to a friend, what would you say? Why are the constancies important for maintaining a stable perceptual world?

As you look around the area in which you are now, how are the Gestalt organizing principles helping to organize your perceptions? Try to find a specific example for each principle.

Learning Check

1. Which among the following are subject to basic perceptual constancy?

   a. figure-ground organization   b. size
   c. ambiguity   d. brightness
   e. continuity   f. closure
   g. shape   h. nearness

2. The first and most basic perceptual organization to emerge when sight is restored to a blind person is

   a. continuity   b. nearness constancy
   c. recognition of numbers   d. figure-ground
     and letters

3. At times, meaningful perceptual organization represents a(n) _____, or "guess," held until the evidence contradicts it.

4. The design known as Necker's cube is a good example of an impossible figure. T or F?

Critical Thinking

5. People who have taken psychedelic drugs, such as LSD or mescaline, often report that the objects and people they see appear to be changing in size, shape, and brightness. This suggests that such drugs disrupt what perceptual process?

Answers

1. b, d, g   2. d   3. hypothesis   4. F   5. Perceptual constancies (size, shape, and brightness).

DEPTH PERCEPTION—WHAT IF THE WORLD WERE FLAT?

>SURVEY QUESTION< *How is it possible to see depth and judge distance?*

Close one of your eyes, hold your head very still, and stare at a single point across the room. If you don't move your head or eyes, your surroundings will appear to be almost flat, like a painting or photograph. But even under these conditions you will still have some sense of depth. Now, open both eyes and move your head and eyes as usual. Suddenly, the "3-D" perceptual world returns. Perceptual processes in the brain take in sensory information from the eyes to construct a three-dimensional experience of the world. How are we able to perceive depth and space?

Depth perception is the ability to see three-dimensional space and to accurately judge distances. Without depth perception, you would be unable to drive a car or ride a bicycle, shoot baskets, thread a needle, or simply navigate around a room (Howard & Rogers, 2001a). The world would look like a flat surface.

Mr. S. B. had trouble with depth perception after his sight was restored. Is depth perception learned? Studies done with a visual cliff suggest that depth perception is partly learned and partly innate (Witherington et al., 2005). Basically, a visual cliff is a glass-topped table (»Fig. 4.33). On one side a checkered surface lies directly beneath the glass. On the other side, the checkered surface is 4 feet below. This makes the glass look like a tabletop on one side and a cliff, or drop-off, on the other.

To test for depth perception, 6- to 14-month-old infants were placed in the middle of the visual cliff. This gave them a choice of crawling to the shallow side or the deep side. (The glass prevented them from doing any "skydiving" if they chose the deep side.) Most infants chose the shallow side. In fact, most refused the deep side even when their mothers tried to call them toward it (Gibson & Walk, 1960).

Depth perception The ability to see three-dimensional space and to accurately judge distances.

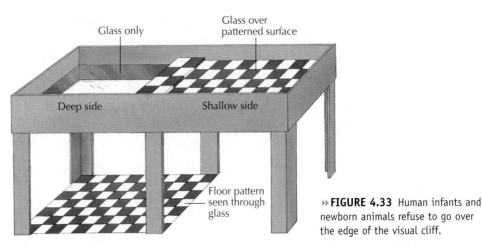

Glass only

Glass over patterned surface

Deep side

Shallow side

Floor pattern seen through glass

Mark Richards/PhotoEdit

▶▶**FIGURE 4.33** Human infants and newborn animals refuse to go over the edge of the visual cliff.

If the infants were at least 6 months old when they were tested, isn't it possible that they learned to perceive depth? Yes. More recent research has shown that depth perception begins to develop as early as 2 weeks of age (Yonas, Elieff, & Arterberry, 2002). It is very likely that at least a basic level of depth perception is innate (Aslin & Smith, 1988). Yet, the development of depth perception is not complete until about 6 months, suggesting that it depends on both brain maturation and individual experience.

We also learn to use a variety of *depth cues* as aids to perceiving three-dimensional space. **Depth cues** are features of the environment and messages from the body that supply information about distance and space. Some cues require two eyes (*binocular cues*) whereas others will work with just one eye (*monocular cues*).

Binocular Depth Cues

The most basic source of depth perception is *retinal disparity* (a discrepancy in the images that reach the right and left eyes). Retinal disparity, which is a binocular cue, is based on the fact that the eyes are about 2.5 inches apart. Because of this, each eye receives a slightly different view of the world. When the two images are fused into one overall image, **stereoscopic vision** (three-dimensional sight) occurs (Howard & Rogers, 2001b). The result is a powerful sensation of depth (▶▶Fig. 4.34 and ▶▶Fig. 4.35).

Convergence is a second binocular depth cue. When you look at a distant object, the lines of vision from your eyes are parallel. However, when you look at something 50 feet or less in distance, your eyes must converge (turn in) to focus the object (▶▶Fig. 4.36).

You can feel convergence by exaggerating it: Focus on your fingertip and bring it toward your eyes until they almost cross. At that point you can feel the sensations from the muscles that control eye movement. You are normally not aware of it, but whenever you estimate a distance under 50 feet (as when you play catch or zap flies with your personal laser), you are using convergence. How? Muscles attached to the eyeball feed information on eye position to the brain to help it judge distance.

Stereoscopic: optic nerve transmissions from each eye are relayed to both sides of brain

Binocular: both eyes have overlapping fields of vision

Allows depth perception with accurate distance estimation

(a)

Bob Western

(b)

▶▶**FIGURE 4.34** *(a)* Stereoscopic vision. *(b)* The photographs show what the right and left eyes would see when viewing a plant. Hold the page about 6 to 8 inches from your eyes. Allow your eyes to cross and focus on the overlapping image between the two photos. Then try to fuse the leaves into one image. If you are successful the third dimension will appear like magic.

Depth cues Perceptual features that impart information about distance and three-dimensional space.

Stereoscopic vision Perception of space and depth caused chiefly by the fact that the eyes receive different images.

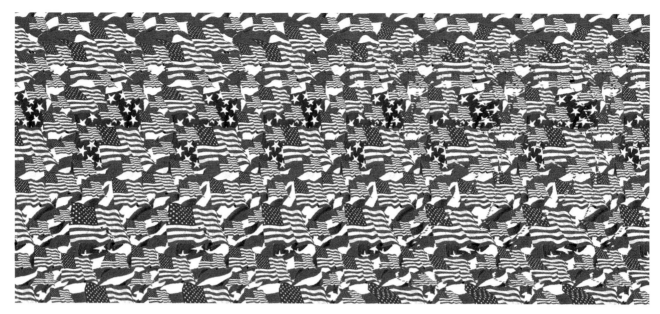

▸▸**FIGURE 4.35** This computer-generated art creates a 3-D illusion by superimposing two patterns. There are mismatches between some areas of the two patterns. This simulates retinal disparity and creates a sensation of depth. To get the 3-D effect, hold the stereogram about 8 inches from the end of your nose. Relax your eyes and look *through* the art, as if you were focusing on something in the distance. If you're patient, you may see a 3-D globe. (Stereogram © 2007 Magic Eye Inc.)

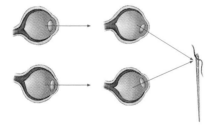

▸▸**FIGURE 4.36** The eyes must converge, or turn in toward the nose, to focus close objects.

Pictorial depth cues Features found in paintings, drawings, and photographs that impart information about space, depth, and distance.

Can a person with one eye perceive depth? Yes, but not as well as a person with two eyes. Overall, stereoscopic vision is 10 times better for judging depth than perception based on just one eye (Rosenberg, 1994). Try driving a car or riding a bicycle with one eye closed. You will find yourself braking too soon or too late, and you will have difficulty estimating your speed. ("But officer, my psychology text said to . . .") Despite this, you will be able to drive, although it will be more difficult than usual. This is possible because your single eye is making use of monocular depth cues.

Monocular Depth Cues

As their name implies, monocular depth cues can be perceived with just one eye. One such cue is *accommodation,* the bending of the lens to focus on nearby objects. Sensations from muscles attached to each lens flow back to the brain. Changes in these sensations help us judge distances within about 4 feet of the eyes. This information is available even if you are just using one eye, so accommodation is a monocular cue. Beyond 4 feet, accommodation has limited value. Obviously, it is more important to a watchmaker or a person trying to thread a needle than it is to a basketball player or someone driving an automobile. Other monocular depth cues are referred to as pictorial depth cues, because a good movie, painting, or photograph can create a convincing sense of depth where none exists.

How is the illusion of depth created on a two-dimensional surface? **Pictorial depth cues** are features found in paintings, drawings, and photographs that impart information about space, depth, and distance. To understand how these cues work, imagine that you are looking outdoors through a window. If you trace everything you see onto the glass, you will have an excellent drawing, with convincing depth. Then, if we analyze what is on the glass, we will find the following features.

1. **Linear perspective.** This cue is based on the apparent convergence of parallel lines in the environment. If you stand between two railroad tracks, they appear to meet near the horizon. Because you know they are parallel, their convergence implies great distance (▸▸Fig. 4.37a).

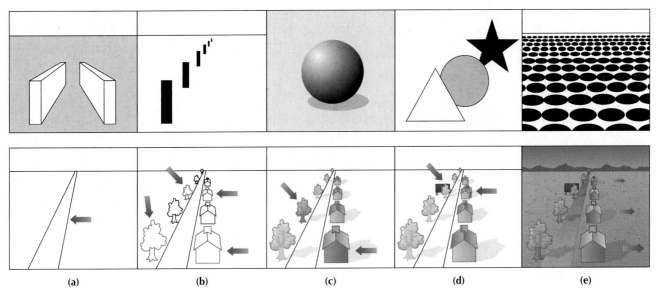

▶▶**FIGURE 4.37** *(a)* Linear perspective. *(b)* Relative size. *(c)* Light and shadow. *(d)* Overlap. *(e)* Texture gradients. Drawings in the top row show fairly "pure" examples of each of the pictorial depth cues. In the bottom row, the pictorial depth cues are used to assemble a more realistic scene.

2. **Relative size.** If an artist wishes to depict two objects of the same size at different distances, the artist makes the more distant object smaller (▶▶ Fig. 4.37*b*). Special effects in films create sensational illusions of depth by rapidly changing the image size of planets, airplanes, monsters, or what have you. (Also see ▶▶ Figure 4.38.)

3. **Height in the picture plane.** Objects that are placed higher (closer to the horizon line) in a drawing tend to be perceived as more distant. In the upper frame of ▶▶ Figure 4.37*b* the black columns look like they are receding into the distance partly because they become smaller, but also because they move higher in the drawing.

4. **Light and shadow.** Most objects are lighted in ways that create clear patterns of light and shadow. Copying such patterns of light and shadow can give a two-dimensional design a three-dimensional appearance (▶▶ Fig. 4.37*c*). (Also, look ahead to ▶▶ Fig. 4.39 for more information on light and shadow.)

5. **Overlap.** Overlap (or *interposition*) is a depth cue that occurs when one object partially blocks another object. Hold your hands up and ask a friend across the room which is nearer. Relative size will give the answer if one hand is much nearer to your friend than the other. But if one hand is only slightly closer than the other, your friend may not be able to see it—until you slide one hand in front of the other. Overlap then removes any doubt (▶▶ Fig. 4.37*d*).

6. **Texture gradients.** Changes in texture also contribute to depth perception. If you stand in the middle of a cobblestone street, the street will look coarse near your feet. However, its texture will get smaller and finer if you look into the distance (▶▶ Fig. 4.37*e*).

7. **Aerial perspective.** Smog, fog, dust, and haze add to the apparent distance of an object. Because of aerial perspective, distant objects tend to be hazy, washed out in color, and lacking in detail. Aerial haze is often most noticeable when it is missing. If you have ever seen a distant mountain range on a crystal-clear day, it might have looked like it was only a few miles away.

Linear perspective is a very powerful cue for depth. Because of the depth cues implied in this drawing, the upper cross on the vertical line appears to be diagonal. It is actually a right angle. The lower cross, which appears to be a right angle, is actually diagonal to the vertical line. (After Enns & Coren, 1995.)

Dennis Coon

▶▶**FIGURE 4.38** On a dry lake bed, relative size is just about the only depth cue available for judging the camera's distance from this vintage aircraft. What do you estimate the distance to be? For the answer, look ahead to ▶▶ Figure 4.42.

FIGURE 4.39 *(Left)* When judging depth we usually assume that light comes mainly from one direction, usually from above. Squint a little to blur the image you see here. You should perceive a collection of globes projecting outward. If you turn this page upside down, the globes should become cavities. (After Ramachandran, 1995.)
(Right) The famed Dutch artist M. C. Escher violated our assumptions about light to create the dramatic illusions of depth found in his 1955 lithograph *Convex and Concave*. In this print, light appears to come from all sides of the scene. (© 2007 The M. C. Escher Company—Holland. All rights reserved. www.mcescher.com.)

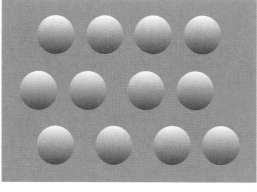

8. **Relative motion.** Relative motion, also known as *motion parallax* (PAIR-ah-lax), can be seen by looking out a window and moving your head from side to side. Notice that nearby objects appear to move a sizable distance as your head moves. In comparison, trees, houses, and telephone poles that are farther away appear to move slightly in relation to the background. Distant objects like hills, mountains, or clouds don't seem to move at all.

When combined, pictorial cues can create a powerful illusion of depth. (See Table 4.1 for a summary of all the depth cues we have discussed.)

Is motion parallax really a pictorial cue? Strictly speaking it is not, except in the two-dimensional world of movies, television, or animated cartoons. However, when parallax is present, we almost always perceive depth. Much of the apparent depth of a good movie comes from relative motion captured by the camera. Figure 4.40 illustrates an interesting feature of motion parallax. Imagine that you are in a bus and watching the passing scenery (with your gaze at a right angle to the road). Under these conditions, nearby objects will appear to rush *backward*. Those farther away, such as distant mountains, will seem to move very little or not at all. Objects that are more remote, such as the sun or moon, will appear to move in the *same* direction you are traveling. (That's why the moon appears to "follow" you when you take a stroll at night.)

The Moon Illusion

How do the depth perception cues relate to daily experience? We constantly use both pictorial cues and bodily cues to sense depth and judge distances. Consider an intriguing effect called the *moon illusion* (perceiving the moon as larger when it is low in the sky). When the moon

■ Table 4.1 **Summary of Visual Depth Cues**

Binocular Cues
- Convergence
- Retinal disparity

Monocular Cues
- Accommodation
- Pictorial depth cues
  Linear perspective
  Relative size
  Height in the picture plane
  Light and shadow
  Overlap
  Texture gradients
  Aerial perspective
  Relative motion (motion parallax)

FIGURE 4.40 The apparent motion of objects viewed during travel depends on their distance from the observer. Apparent motion can also be influenced by an observer's point of fixation. At middle distances, objects closer than the point of fixation appear to move backward; those beyond the point of fixation appear to move forward. Objects at great distances, such as the sun or moon, always appear to move forward.

← Direction of travel

FIGURE 4.41 The Ponzo illusion may help you understand the moon illusion. Picture the two white bars as resting on the railroad tracks. In the drawing, the upper bar is the same length as the lower bar. However, because the upper bar appears to be farther away than the lower bar, we perceive it as longer. The same logic applies to the moon illusion.

FIGURE 4.42 Before you can use familiar size to judge distance, objects must actually be the size you assume they are. Either these men are giants, or the model airplane was closer than you may have thought when you looked at Figure 4.38.

is on the horizon, it tends to look like a silver dollar. When it is directly overhead, it looks more like a dime. Contrary to what some people believe, the moon is not magnified by the atmosphere. But the moon *looks* nearly twice as large when it's low in the sky (Ross & Plug, 2002). This occurs, in part, because the moon's *apparent distance* is greater when it is near the horizon than when it is overhead (Kaufman & Kaufman, 2000).

But if it seems farther away, shouldn't it look smaller? No. When the moon is overhead, few depth cues surround it. In contrast, when you see the moon on the horizon, it is behind houses, trees, telephone poles, and mountains. These objects add numerous depth cues, which cause the horizon to seem more distant than the sky overhead. Picture two balloons, one 10 feet away and the second 20 feet away. Suppose the more distant balloon is inflated until its image matches the image of the nearer balloon. How do we know the more distant balloon is larger? Because its image is the same size as a balloon that is closer. Similarly, the moon makes the same-size image on the horizon as it does overhead. However, the horizon seems more distant because more depth cues are present. As a result, the horizon moon must be perceived as larger (Kaufman & Kaufman, 2000). (See Fig. 4.41.)

This explanation is known as the **apparent-distance hypothesis** (the horizon seems more distant than the night sky). You can test it by removing depth cues while looking at a horizon moon. Try looking at the moon through a rolled-up paper tube, or make your hands into a "telescope" and look at the next large moon you see. It will immediately appear to shrink when viewed without depth cues (Ross & Plug, 2002).

Apparent-distance hypothesis An explanation of the moon illusion stating that the horizon seems more distant than the night sky.

Study Break Depth Perception

Reflect

Part of the rush of excitement produced by action movies and video games is based on the sense of depth they create. Return to the list of pictorial depth cues. What cues have you seen used to portray depth? Try to think of specific examples in a movie or game you have seen recently.

Learning Check

1. The visual cliff is used to test for infant sensitivity to linear perspective. T or F?
2. Write an *M* or a *B* after each of the following to indicate if it is a monocular or binocular depth cue.

accommodation _____ convergence _____ retinal disparity _____ linear perspective _____ motion parallax _____ overlap _____ relative size _____

3. Which of the depth cues listed in Question 2 are based on muscular feedback? _____.
4. Interpretation of pictorial depth cues requires no prior experience. T or F?
5. The moon's image is greatly magnified by the atmosphere near the horizon. T or F?

Critical Thinking

6. What hearing ability would you say is most closely related to stereoscopic vision?

Answers

1. F 2. accommodation (M), convergence (M), retinal disparity (B), linear perspective (B), motion parallax (M), overlap (M), relative size (M) 3. accommodation or convergence 4. F 5. F 6. If you close your eyes, you can usually tell the direction and perhaps the location of a sound source, such as a hand-clap. Locating sounds in space is heavily dependent on having two ears, just as stereoscopic vision depends on having two eyes.

The Boiled Frog Syndrome

Until something surprising happens, like the "murder" one of your authors saw that wasn't a murder at all, we tend to take perception for granted. But make no mistake, the world as we know it is created from sensory impressions. In fact, it takes about 50 milliseconds for a visual signal to move from the retina to the brain. Therefore, our perceptions always lag slightly behind the "real world." An event that happens quickly, like the pop of a flash-bulb, may be over by the time we perceive it.

On the other end of the time scale, perception can blind us to very slow events and gradual changes. Humans evolved to detect sharp changes, such as the sudden appearance of a lion, a potential mate, or sources of food. However, many of the threats facing us today develop very slowly. Examples include the stockpiling of nuclear warheads, degradation of the environment, global deforestation, global warming, erosion of the ozone layer, and runaway human population growth.

Randy Ury/Corbis

Robert Ornstein, a psychologist, and Paul Ehrlich, a biologist, believe that many of the large-scale threats we face are similar to the "boiled frog syndrome." Frogs placed in a pan of water that is slowly heated cannot detect the gradual rise in temperature. They will sit still until they die. Like the doomed frogs, many people seem unable to detect gradual but deadly trends in modern civilization (Ornstein & Ehrlich, 1989).

To avoid disasters, it may take a conscious effort by large numbers of people to construct the "big picture" and reverse lethal but easily overlooked patterns (O'Neill, 2005). The relatively new field of *community psychology* is dedicated to helping overcome our own narrow perspectives to perceive important larger patterns (Nelson & Prilleltensky, 2005). Understanding how perception shapes "reality" may ultimately prove to be a matter of life or death. Are you paying attention?

PERCEPTION AND OBJECTIVITY— BELIEVING IS SEEING

>SURVEY QUESTION< *How is perception altered by expectations, motives, emotions, and learning?*

At the beginning of this chapter one of your authors described an apparent murder that turned out to be something quite different. If he had never returned to "the scene of the crime," he would have sworn that he had seen a homicide. The girl's description completely shaped his own perceptions. This perhaps is understandable. But he'll never forget the added shock he felt when he met the "murderer"—the man he had seen a few moments before as huge, vicious, and horrible-looking. The man was not a stranger. He was a neighbor who your author had seen dozens of times before and knows by name. Stories such as this show that our experiences are **perceptual constructions** or mental models of external events. Perceptions are filtered through our needs, expectations, attitudes, values, and beliefs (⟩⟩ Fig. 4.43). Clearly, we don't just believe what we see. We also see what we believe. Let's explore the process of perceptual construction and some factors that shape or even distort it. (Also see "The Boiled Frog Syndrome.")

On a piece of paper, draw a circle about 3 inches in diameter. Inside the circle, above and to the left of center, make a large black dot, about one-half inch in diameter. Make another dot inside the circle above and to the right of center. Now, still inside the circle, draw an arc, curved upward and about 2 inches long just below the center of the circle. If you followed these instructions, your reaction might now be, "Oh! Why didn't you just say to draw a happy face?"

Like the happy face drawing, perceptual construction seems to proceed in two major ways. In **bottom-up processing,** we analyze information starting at the "bottom" with small sensory units (features) and build upward to a complete perception. The reverse also seems

⟩⟩**FIGURE 4.43** It is difficult to look at this simple drawing without perceiving depth. Yet, the drawing is nothing more than a collection of flat shapes. Turn this page counterclockwise 90 degrees and you will see three Cs, one within another. When the drawing is turned sideways, it seems nearly flat. However, if you turn the page upright again, a sense of depth will reappear. Clearly, you have used your knowledge and expectations to *construct* an illusion of depth. The drawing itself would only be a flat design if you didn't invest it with three-dimensional meaning.

Perceptual construction A mental model of external events.

Bottom-up processing Organizing perceptions by beginning with low-level features.

to occur. In **top-down processing** pre-existing knowledge is used to rapidly organize features into a meaningful whole. Bottom-up processing is like putting together a picture puzzle you've never seen before: You must assemble small pieces until a recognizable pattern appears. Top-down processing is like putting together a puzzle you have solved many times: After only a few pieces are in place you begin to see outlines of the final picture.

Both types of processing are illustrated by ▸▸Figure 4.44. Also, return to ▸▸Figure 4.30, the giant walkingstick. The first time you saw the photo you probably processed it bottom-up, picking out features until the insect was recognizable. This time, because of top-down processing, you should see the insect instantly. Another good example of top-down processing is found in perceptual expectancies.

Perceptual Expectancies

What is a perceptual expectancy? A runner in the starting blocks at a track meet is *set* to respond in a certain way. Likewise, past experience, motives, context, or suggestions may create a **perceptual expectancy** (or **set**) that prepares you to perceive in a certain way. If a car backfires, runners at a track meet may jump the gun. As a matter of fact, we all frequently jump the gun when perceiving. In essence, an expectancy is a perceptual hypothesis we are *very likely* to apply to a stimulus—even if applying it is inappropriate.

Perceptual sets often lead us to see what we *expect* to see. One of your authors thought he saw a murder in the supermarket because he had just heard the girl's description of what was happening. Here's another example: Let's say you are driving across the desert and you're very low on gas. Finally, you see a sign approaching. On it are the words FUEL AHEAD. You relax, knowing you will not be stranded. But as you draw nearer, the words on the sign become FOOD AHEAD. Most people have had similar experiences in which expectations altered their perceptions. To observe perceptual expectancies firsthand, perform the demonstration described in ▸▸Figure 4.45.

Perceptual expectancies are frequently created by *suggestion*. This is especially true of perceiving other people. In one classic experiment, a psychology professor arranged for a guest lecturer to teach his class. Half the students in the class were given a page of notes that described the lecturer as a "rather *cold* person, industrious, critical, practical, and determined." The other students got notes describing him as a "rather *warm* person, industrious, critical, practical, and determined" (Kelley, 1950; italics added). Students who received the "cold" description perceived the lecturer as unhappy and irritable and didn't volunteer in class discussion. Those who got the "warm" description saw the lecturer as happy and good natured, and they actively took part in discussion with him. In the same way, labels such as "punk," "mental patient," "queer," "illegal immigrant," "bitch," and so on, are very likely to distort perceptions.

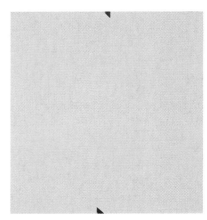

▸▸**FIGURE 4.44** This painting by abstract artist Al Held is 9 feet by 9 feet. If you process the painting "bottom-up," all you will see is two small dark geometric shapes. Would you like to try some top-down processing? Knowing the painting's title will allow you to apply your knowledge and see the painting in an entirely different way. The title? It's *The Big N*. Can you see it now? (Held, Al [1928–] *The Big N*. 1964. Synthetic polymer paint on canvas, $9'3/8'' \times 9'$. Mrs. Armand P. Bartos Fund. [104.1973] The Museum of Modern Art, New York, NY. Digital image © The Museum of Modern Art/Licensed by SCALA.)

View I

View II

View III

▸▸**FIGURE 4.45** "Young woman/old woman" illustrations. As an interesting demonstration of perceptual expectancy, show some of your friends view I and some view II (cover all other views). Next show your friends view III and ask them what they see. Those who saw view I should see the old woman in view III; those who saw view II should see the young woman in view III. Can you see both? (After Leeper, 1935.)

Top-down processing Applying higher level knowledge to rapidly organize sensory information into a meaningful perception.

Perceptual expectancy (or set) A readiness to perceive in a particular manner, induced by strong expectations.

Motives, Emotions, and Perception

Our motives and emotions also play a role in shaping our perceptions. For example, if you are hungry, food-related words are more likely to gain your attention than non-food words (Mogg et al., 1998). Advertisers take advantage of two motives that are widespread in our society: *anxiety* and *sex.* Everything from mouthwash to automobile tires is merchandised by using sex to gain attention. Other ads combine sex with anxiety. Deodorant, soaps, toothpaste, and countless other articles are pushed in ads that play on desires to be attractive, to have "sex appeal," or to avoid embarrassment.

By directing attention, motives may alter what is perceived. As part of a supposed study of "the dating practices of college students," male volunteers were shown a picture of a female student and asked to give a first impression of how attractive she was. Before making these ratings, each person read one of two short written passages: One was sexually arousing and the other was not. The important finding was that men who read the more arousing passage rated the female as more attractive (Stephan et al., 1971). This result may come as no surprise if you have ever been infatuated with someone and then fallen out of love. A person who once seemed highly attractive may look quite different when your feelings change.

Our emotions can also shape our perceptions. According to psychologist Barbara Frederickson, negative emotions generally narrow our perceptual focus, increasing the likelihood of inattentional blindness, whereas positive emotions can actually broaden the scope of attention (Fredrickson & Branigan, 2005). For example, positive emotions can affect how well people recognize people from other races. In recognizing faces, a consistent *other-race effect* occurs. This is a sort of "They all look alike to me" bias in perceiving persons from other racial and ethnic groups. In tests of facial recognition, people are much better at recognizing faces of their own race than others. But when people are in positive moods, their ability to recognize people from other races improves (Johnson & Fredrickson, 2005).

Another reason for the other-race effect is that we typically have more experience with people from our own race. As a result, we become very familiar with the features that help us recognize different persons. For other groups, we lack the perceptual expertise needed to accurately separate one face from another (Sporer, 2001). This indicates the importance of perceptual learning, a topic we turn to next.

Charles Platiau/Reuters/Corbis

In many sports, expert players are much better than beginners at paying attention to key information. Compared with novices, experts scan actions and events more quickly, and they focus on only the most meaningful information. This helps experts to make decisions and react more quickly (Bard, Fleury, & Goulet, 1994).

Perceptual learning Changes in perception that can be attributed to prior experience; a result of changes in how the brain processes sensory information.

Perceptual Learning

England is one of the few countries in the world where people drive on the left side of the road. In view of this reversal, it is not unusual for visitors to step off curbs in front of cars—after carefully looking for traffic in the *wrong* direction. As this example suggests, learning has a powerful impact on perception.

How does learning affect perception? The term **perceptual learning** refers to changes in the brain that alter how we process sensory information (Fahle & Poggio, 2002). For example, to use a computer, you must learn to pay attention to specific stimuli, such as icons, commands, and signals. We also learn to tell the difference between stimuli that seemed identical at first. An example is the novice chef who discovers how to tell the difference between dried basil, oregano, and tarragon. In other situations, we learn to focus on just one part of a group of stimuli. This saves us from having to process all of the stimuli in the group. For instance, a linebacker in football may be able to tell if the next play will be a run or a pass by watching one or two key players, rather than the entire opposing team (Seitz & Watanabe, 2005).

In general, learning creates *perceptual habits* (ingrained patterns of organization and attention) that affect our daily experience. Stop for a moment and look at ⟩⟩ Figure 4.46. The

Bettmann/Corbis

▶▶**FIGURE 4.46** The effects of prior experience on perception. The doctored face looks far worse when viewed right side up because it can be related to past experience.

left face looks somewhat unusual, to be sure. But the distortion seems mild—until you turn the page upside down. Viewed this way, the face looks quite grotesque. Why is there a difference? Apparently, most people have little experience with upside-down faces. Perceptual learning, therefore, has less impact on our perceptions of an upside-down face. With a face in the normal position, you know what to expect and where to look. Also, you tend to see the entire face as a recognizable pattern. When a face is inverted, we are forced to perceive its individual features separately (Bartlett & Searcy, 1993).

Illusions

Perceptual learning is responsible for a number of *illusions.* In an **illusion,** length, position, motion, curvature, or direction is consistently misjudged. For example, you are probably in the perceptual habit of assuming that a room is shaped roughly like a box. This need not be true, however. An *Ames room* (named for the man who designed it) is a lopsided space that appears square when viewed from a certain point (▶▶Fig. 4.47). This illusion is achieved by carefully distorting the proportions of the walls, floor, ceiling, and windows. Because the left corner of the Ames room is farther from a viewer than the right, a person standing in that corner looks very small; one standing in the nearer, shorter right corner looks very large. A person who walks from the left to the right corner, will seem to "magically" grow larger.

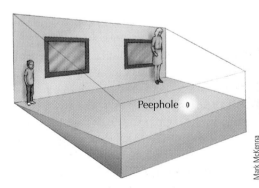

Peephole

Mark McKenna

▶▶**FIGURE 4.47** The Ames room. From the front, the room looks normal; actually, the right-hand corner is very short, and the left-hand corner is very tall. In addition, the left side of the room slants away from viewers. The diagram shows the shape of the room and reveals why people appear to get bigger as they cross the room toward the nearer, shorter right corner.

Illusion A misleading or distorted perception.

Staying in Touch with Reality

Just imagine that often, and without warning, you hear a voice shouting "Buckets of blood!" or see blood spattering across the walls of your bedroom. Chances are people would think you are mentally disturbed. Hallucinations are a major symptom of psychosis, dementia, epilepsy, migraine headaches, alcohol withdrawal, and drug intoxication (Spence & David, 2004). They are also one of the clearest signs that a person has "lost touch with reality."

Yet consider the case of mathematician John Nash (the subject of *A Beautiful Mind,* the winner of the 2002 Oscar for best film). Even though Nash suffered from schizophrenia, he eventually learned to use his ability to engage in reality testing to sort out which of his experiences were perceptions and which were hallucinations. Unlike John Nash, most people who experience full-blown

hallucinations also have a limited ability to reality test (Hohwy & Rosenberg, 2005).

Curiously, "sane hallucinations" also occur. *Charles Bonnet syndrome* is a rare condition which afflicts mainly older people who are partially blind but not mentally disturbed. They may "see" people, animals, buildings, plants, and other objects appear and disappear in front of their eyes. One older man suffering from partial blindness and leukemia complained of seeing animals in his house, including cattle and bears (Jacob et al., 2004). However, people experiencing "sane hallucinations" can more easily tell that their hallucinations aren't real because their capacity to reality test is not impaired.

Such unusual experiences show how powerfully the brain seeks meaningful patterns in sensory input and the role reality testing plays in our normal perceptual experience.

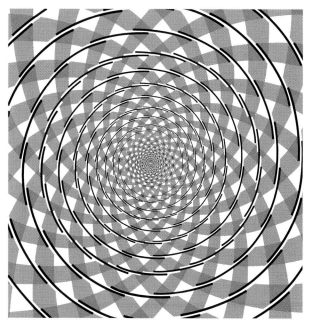

▶▶**FIGURE 4.48** The limits of pure perception. Even simple designs are easily misperceived. Fraser's spiral is actually a series of concentric circles. The illusion is so powerful that people who try to trace one of the circles sometimes follow the illusory spiral and jump from one circle to the next. (After Seckel, 2000.)

Hallucination An imaginary sensation—such as seeing, hearing, or smelling something that does not exist in the external world.

Reality testing Obtaining additional information to check on the accuracy of perceptions.

Müller-Lyer illusion Two equal-length lines tipped with inward or outward pointing V's appear to be of different lengths.

Note that illusions are distorted perceptions of stimuli that actually exist. In a **hallucination,** people perceive objects or events that have no external reality (Lepore, 2002). For example, they hear voices that are not there (see "Staying in Touch with Reality"). If you think you are experiencing an illusion or a hallucination, try engaging in some reality testing.

What do you mean by reality testing? In any situation having an element of doubt or uncertainty, **reality testing** involves obtaining additional information to check your perceptions. If you think you see a 3-foot-tall butterfly, you can confirm you are hallucinating by trying to touch its wings. To detect an illusion, you may have to measure a drawing or apply a straight-edge to it. ▶▶Figure 4.48 shows a powerful illusion called Fraser's spiral. What appears to be a spiral is actually made up of a series of closed circles. Most people cannot spontaneously see this reality. Instead, they must carefully trace one of the circles to confirm what is "real" in the design.

Can illusions be explained? Not in all cases, or to everyone's satisfaction. In general, size and shape constancy, habitual eye movements, continuity, and perceptual habits combine in various ways to produce the illusions in ▶▶Figure 4.49. Rather than attempt to explain all of them, let's focus on one deceptively simple example.

Consider the drawing in ▶▶Figure 4.49*a*. This is the familiar **Müller-Lyer** (MEOO-ler-LIE-er) **illusion** in which the horizontal line with arrowheads appears shorter than the line with V's. A quick measurement will show that they are the same length. How can we explain this illusion? Evidence suggests it is based on a lifetime of experience with the edges and corners of rooms and buildings. Richard Gregory (1990) believes you see the horizontal line with the V's as if it were the corner of a room viewed from inside (▶▶Fig. 4.50). The line with arrowheads, on the other hand, suggests the corner of a room or building seen from outside. In other words, cues that suggest a three-dimensional space alter our perception of a two-dimensional design (Enns & Coren, 1995).

Earlier, to explain the moon illusion, we said that if two objects make images of the same size, the more distant object must be larger. This is known formally as *size-distance invariance* (the size of an object's image is precisely related to its distance from the eyes). Gregory believes the same concept explains the Müller-Lyer illusion. If the V-tipped line looks farther away than the arrowhead-tipped line, you must compensate by seeing the V-tipped line

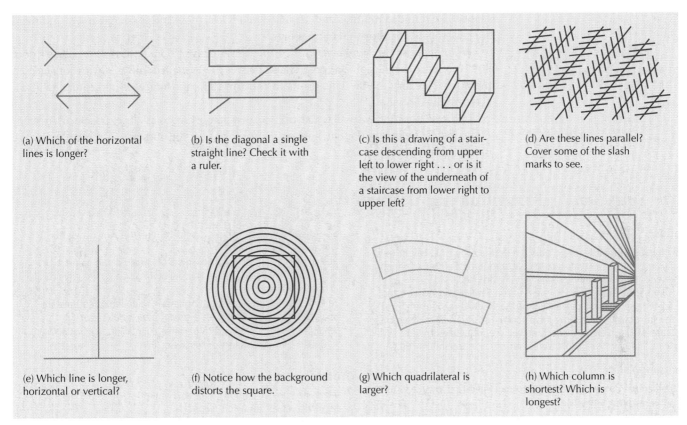

(a) Which of the horizontal lines is longer?

(b) Is the diagonal a single straight line? Check it with a ruler.

(c) Is this a drawing of a staircase descending from upper left to lower right . . . or is it the view of the underneath of a staircase from lower right to upper left?

(d) Are these lines parallel? Cover some of the slash marks to see.

(e) Which line is longer, horizontal or vertical?

(f) Notice how the background distorts the square.

(g) Which quadrilateral is larger?

(h) Which column is shortest? Which is longest?

▸▸**FIGURE 4.49** Some interesting perceptual illusions. Such illusions are a normal part of visual perception.

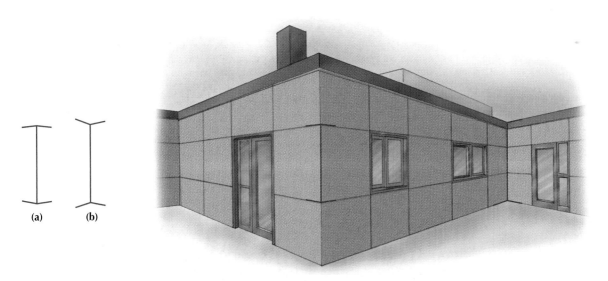

(a) (b)

▸▸**FIGURE 4.50** Why does line *(b)* in the Müller-Lyer illusion look longer than line *(a)*? Probably because it looks more like a distant corner than a nearer one. Because the vertical lines form images of the same length, the more "distant" line must be perceived as larger. As you can see in the drawing on the right, additional depth cues accentuate the Müller-Lyer illusion. (After Enns & Coren, 1995.)

as longer. This explanation presumes that you have had years of experience with straight lines, sharp edges, and corners—a pretty safe assumption in our culture.

Is there any way to show that past experience causes the illusion? If we could test someone who saw only curves and wavy lines as a child, we would know if experience with a "square" culture is important. Fortunately, the Zulus, a group of people in South Africa, live in a "round" culture. In their daily lives, Zulus rarely encounter a straight line: Their houses are shaped like rounded mounds and arranged in a circle, tools and toys are curved, and there are few straight roads or square buildings.

What happens if a Zulu looks at the Müller-Lyer design? The typical Zulu villager does not experience the illusion. At most, she or he sees the V-shaped line as *slightly* longer than the other (Gregory, 1990). This seems to confirm the importance of perceptual habits in determining our view of the world.

In the next section, we will go beyond normal perception to ask, Is extrasensory perception possible? Before we do that, here's a chance to answer the question, Is remembering the preceding discussion possible?

Study Break **Perception and Objectivity**

Reflect

How has perceptual learning affected your ability to safely drive a car? For example, what do you pay attention to at intersections? Where do you habitually look as you are driving?

If you spent a year hiking the Amazon River Basin, what effect might it have on your perception of the Müller-Lyer illusion?

You have almost certainly misperceived a situation at some time because of a perceptual expectancy or the influence of your motives and emotions. How were your perceptions influenced?

Learning Check

1. Perceptual habits may become so ingrained that they lead us to misperceive a stimulus. T or F?
2. Perceptual learning seems to program the brain for sensitivity to important _____ of the environment.
3. The Ames room is used to test infants for depth perception. T or F?

4. Size-distance relationships appear to underlie which two illusions? _____ and _____
5. Research shows that heightened sexual arousal can cause a person to perceive members of the opposite sex as more physically attractive. T or F?
6. In top-down processing of information, individual features are analyzed and assembled into a meaningful whole. T or F?
7. When a person is prepared to perceive events in a particular way, it is said that a perceptual expectancy or _____ exists.

Critical Thinking

8. What size object do you think you would have to hold at arm's length to cover up a full moon?
9. Cigarette advertisements in the United States are required to carry a warning label about the health risks of smoking. How have tobacco companies made these labels less visible?

Answers

1. T 2. features 3. F 4. moon illusion, Müller-Lyer illusion 5. T 6. F 7. set 8. The most popular answers range from a quarter to a softball. Actually, a pea held in the outstretched hand will cover a full moon (Kunkel, 1993). If you listed an object larger than a pea, be aware that perceptions, no matter how accurate they seem, may distort reality. 9. Advertisers place health warnings in the corners of ads, where they attract the least possible attention. Also, the labels are often placed on "busy" backgrounds so that they are partially camouflaged. Finally, the main images in ads are designed to strongly attract attention. This further distracts readers from seeing the warnings.

EXTRASENSORY PERCEPTION— DO YOU BELIEVE IN MAGIC?

>SURVEY QUESTION<   *Is extrasensory perception possible?*

Uri Geller, a self-proclaimed "psychic," once agreed to demonstrate his claimed paranormal abilities. During testing, it seemed that Geller could sense which of 10 film canisters contained a hidden object, he correctly guessed the number that would come up on a die shaken in a closed box, and he reproduced drawings sealed in envelopes.

Was Geller cheating, or was he using some ability beyond normal perception? There is little doubt that Geller was cheating (Randi, 1997). But how? The answer lies in a discussion of **extrasensory perception (ESP)**—the purported ability to perceive events in ways that cannot be explained by known sensory capacities.

Parapsychology is the study of ESP and other **psi phenomena** (events that seem to defy accepted scientific laws). (Psi is pronounced like "sigh.") Parapsychologists seek answers to the questions raised by three basic forms that ESP could take. These are:

1. **Telepathy.** The purported ability to communicate directly with another person's mind. When the other person is dead, the communications are called *mediumship*.

Extrasensory perception The purported ability to perceive events in ways that cannot be explained by known capacities of the sensory organs.

Psi phenomena Events that seem to lie outside the realm of accepted scientific laws.

2. **Clairvoyance.** The purported ability to perceive events or gain information in ways that appear unaffected by distance or normal physical barriers.

3. **Precognition.** The purported ability to perceive or accurately predict future events. Precognition may take the form of prophetic dreams that foretell the future.

While we are at it, we might as well toss in another purported psi ability:

4. **Psychokinesis.** The purported ability to exert influence over inanimate objects by willpower ("mind over matter"). (Psychokinesis cannot be classed as a type of ESP, but it is frequently studied by parapsychologists.)

An Appraisal of ESP

Psychologists as a group are highly skeptical about psi abilities. If you've ever had an apparent clairvoyant or telepathic experience you might be convinced that ESP exists. However, the difficulty of excluding *coincidence* makes such experiences less conclusive than they might seem.

Consider a typical "psychic" experience: During the middle of the night, a woman away for a weekend visit suddenly had a strong impulse to return home. When she arrived she found the house on fire with her husband asleep inside (Rhine, 1953). An experience like this is striking, but it does not confirm the reality of ESP. If, by coincidence, a hunch turns out to be correct, it may be *reinterpreted* as precognition or clairvoyance (Marks, 2000). If it is not confirmed, it will simply be forgotten. Most people don't realize it, but such coincidences occur quite often.

Susan Van Etten/PhotoEdit

Formal investigation of psi events owes much to the late J. B. Rhine, who tried to study ESP objectively. Many of Rhine's experiments made use of the *Zener cards* (a deck of 25 cards, each bearing one of five symbols) (▸▸Fig. 4.51). In a typical clairvoyance test, people tried to guess the symbols on the cards as they were turned up from a shuffled deck. Pure guessing in this test will produce an average score of 5 "hits" out of 25 cards.

Most so-called psychics are simply keen observers. The "psychic" begins a "cold reading" by making general statements about a person. The "psychic" then plays "hot and cold" by attending to the person's facial expressions, body language, or tone of voice. When the "psychic" is "hot" (on the right track) the "psychic" continues to make similar statements about the person. If the person's reactions signal that the "psychic" is "cold" the psychic drops that topic or line of thought and tries another (Schouten, 1994).

Fraud and Skepticism

Unfortunately, some of Rhine's most dramatic early experiments used badly printed Zener cards that allowed the symbols to show faintly on the back. It is also very easy to cheat, by marking cards with a fingernail or by noting marks on the cards caused by normal use. Even if this were not the case, there is evidence that early experimenters sometimes unconsciously gave people cues about cards with their eyes, facial gestures, or lip movements. In short, none of the early studies in parapsychology were done in a way that eliminated the possibility of fraud or "leakage" of helpful information (Alcock, Burns, & Freeman, 2003).

Modern parapsychologists are now well aware of the need for double-blind experiments, security and accuracy in record keeping, meticulous control, and repeatability of experiments (Milton & Wiseman, 1997; O'Keeffe & Wiseman, 2005). In the last 10 years, hundreds of experiments have been reported in parapsychological journals. Many of them seem to support the existence of psi abilities.

Then why do most psychologists remain skeptical about psi abilities? Fraud continues to plague the field. As one critic put it, positive ESP results usually mean "Error Some Place"

▸▸**FIGURE 4.51** ESP cards used by J. B. Rhine, an early experimenter in parapsychology.

(Marks, 2000). The more closely psi experiments are examined, the more likely it is that claimed successes will evaporate (Alcock, 2003; Stokes, 2001).

The need for skepticism is especially great anytime there's money to be made from purported psychic abilities. For example, the owners of the "Miss Cleo" TV-psychic operation were convicted of felony fraud in 2002. "Miss Cleo," supposedly a Jamaican-accented psychic, was really just an actress from Los Angeles. People who paid $4.99 a minute for a "reading" from "Miss Cleo" actually reached one of several hundred operators. These people were hired through ads that read "No experience necessary." Despite being entirely faked, the "Miss Cleo" scam brought in more than $1 billion before it was shut down.

Anyone can learn to do "cold readings" (Wood et al., 2003) well enough to produce satisfied customers. *Cold reading* is a set of techniques that are used to lead people to believe in the truth of what a psychic or medium is saying about them. These include a reliance on many of the same techniques used by practitioners of the horoscope, such as uncritical acceptance, positive instances and the Barnum effect (see Chapter 1).

Statistics and Chance

Inconsistency is another major problem in psi research. For every study with positive results, there are many others that fail and are never published (Alcock, 2003). It is rare—in fact, almost unheard of—for a person to maintain psi ability over any sustained period of time (Alcock, Burns, & Freeman, 2003). ESP researchers believe this "decline effect" shows that parapsychological skills are very fragile. But critics argue that a person who only temporarily scores above chance has just received credit for a **run of luck** (a statistically unusual outcome that could occur by chance alone). When the run is over, it is not fair to assume that ESP is temporarily gone. We must count *all* attempts.

To understand the run-of-luck criticism, imagine that you flip a coin 100 times and record the results. You then flip another coin 100 times, again recording the results. The two lists are compared. For any 10 pairs of flips, we would expect heads or tails to match 5 times. Let's say that you go through the list and find a set of 10 pairs where 9 out of 10 matched. This is far above chance expectation. But does it mean that the first coin "knew" what was going to come up on the second coin? The idea is obviously silly.

Now, what if a person guesses 100 times what will come up on a coin. Again, we might find a set of 10 guesses that matches the results of flipping the coin. Does this mean that the person, for a time, had precognition—then lost it? Parapsychologists tend to believe the answer is yes. Skeptics assume that nothing more than random matching occurred, as in the two-coin example.

Inconclusive Research

Unfortunately, many of the most spectacular findings in parapsychology simply cannot be replicated (reproduced or repeated) (Hyman, 1996a). Even the same researchers using the same experimental subjects typically can't get similar results every time (Schick & Vaughn, 2001). More importantly, improved research methods usually result in fewer positive results (Hyman, 1996b; O'Keeffe & Wiseman, 2005).

Reinterpretation is also a problem in psi experiments. For example, ex-astronaut Edgar Mitchell claimed he did a successful telepathy experiment from space. Yet news accounts never mentioned that on some trials Mitchell's "receivers" scored above chance, and on others they scored *below* chance. Although you might assume that below chance trials were failures to find telepathy, Mitchell reinterpreted them as "successes," claiming that they represented intentional "psi missing." But, as skeptics have noted, if both high scores and low scores count as successes, how can you lose?

Of course, in many ESP tests the outcome is beyond debate. A good example is provided by recent ESP experiments done through newspapers, radio, and television. In these mass media studies, people attempted to identify ESP targets from a distance. The results of one study of over 1.5 million ESP trials done through the mass media are easy to summarize: There was no significant ESP effect (Milton & Wiseman, 1999). Zero. Zip. Nada. Clearly, state lottery organizers have nothing to fear!

Run of luck A statistically unusual outcome (as in getting 5 heads in a row when flipping a coin) that could still occur by chance alone.

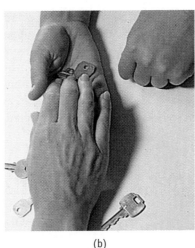

(a)   (b)   (c)

▸▸**FIGURE 4.52** Fake psychokinesis. *(a)* The performer shows an observer several straight keys. While doing so, he bends one of the keys by placing its tip in the slot of another key. Normally, this is done out of sight, behind the "psychic's" hand. It is clearly shown here so you can see how the deception occurs. *(b)* Next, the "psychic" places the two keys in the observer's hand and closes it. By skillful manipulation, the observer has been kept from seeing the bent key. The performer then "concentrates" on the keys to "bend them with psychic energy." *(c)* The bent key is revealed to the observer. "Miracle" accomplished! (Adapted from Randi, 1983.)

Stage ESP

Stage ESP simulates ESP for the purpose of entertainment. If psychic phenomena do occur, they certainly can't be controlled well enough to be used by entertainers. Like stage magic, it is based on sleight of hand, deception, and patented gadgets (▸▸Fig. 4.52). A case in point is Uri Geller, a former nightclub magician who "astounded" audiences—and some scientists—with apparent telepathy, psychokinesis, and precognition.

It's now clear that tests of Geller's performance were incredibly sloppy. For instance, Geller reproduced sealed drawings in a room next to the one where the drawings were made. Original reports failed to mention that there was a hole in the wall between the rooms, through which Geller could have heard descriptions of the pictures as they were being drawn. Likewise, in the "die in the box" tests Geller was allowed to hold the box, shake it, and have the honor of opening it (Randi, 1997).

Why weren't such details reported? Sensational and uncritical reporting of apparent paranormal events is widespread. Hundreds of books, articles, and television programs are produced each year by people who are getting rich by promoting unsupported claims. If a person did have psychic powers, he or she would not have to make a living by entertaining others. A quick trip to a casino would allow the person to retire for life.

Implications

After close to 130 years of investigation, it is still impossible to say conclusively whether psi events occur. As we have seen, a close look at psi experiments often reveals serious problems of evidence, procedure, and scientific rigor (Alcock, Burns, & Freeman, 2003; Hyman, 1996b; Stokes, 2001). It is also interesting to note that a survey of leading parapsychologists and skeptics found that almost all in both camps said their belief in psi had decreased (Blackmore, 1989). Yet, being a skeptic does not mean a person is against something. It means that you are unconvinced. The purpose of this discussion, then, has been to counter the *uncritical* acceptance of psi events that is rampant in the media (But then, you already knew we were going to say that, didn't you!)

What would it take to scientifically demonstrate the existence of ESP? Quite simply, a set of instructions that would allow any competent, unbiased observer to produce a psi event under standardized conditions that rule out any possibility of fraud (Schick & Vaughn, 1995). In fact, professional magician and skeptic James Randi even offers a $1,000,000 prize

Stage ESP The simulation of ESP for the purpose of entertainment.

to anyone who can demonstrate evidence of psi events under standardized conditions. No one has claimed the prize yet (you can read all about it at www.randi.org).

A Look Ahead

In this chapter we have moved from basic sensations to the complexities of perceiving people and events. We have also probed some of the controversies concerning ESP. In the Psychology in Action section, we will return to "everyday" perception, for a look at perceptual awareness.

Study Break   Extrasensory Perception

Reflect

Let's say that a friend of yours is an avid fan of TV shows that feature paranormal themes. See if you can summarize for her or him what is known about ESP. Be sure to include evidence for and against the existence of ESP and some of the thinking errors associated with non-skeptical belief in the paranormal.

Learning Check

1. Four purported psi events investigated by parapsychologists are clairvoyance, telepathy, precognition, and _____.
2. The _____ cards were used by J. B. Rhine in early tests of ESP.
3. Natural, or "real life," occurrences are regarded as the best evidence for the existence of ESP. T or F?

4. Skeptics attribute positive results in psi experiments to statistical runs of luck. T or F?
5. Replication rates are very high for ESP experiments. T or F?

Critical Thinking

6. What would you estimate is the chance that two people will have the same birthday (day and month, but not year) in a group of 30 people?
7. A "psychic" on television offers to fix broken watches for viewers. Moments later, dozens of viewers call the station to say that their watches miraculously started running again. What have they overlooked?

Answers

1. psychokinesis   2. Zener   3. F   4. T   5. F   6. Most people assume that this would be a relatively rare event. Actually there is a 71 percent chance that two people will share a birthday in a group of 30. Most people probably underestimate the natural rate of occurrence of many seemingly mysterious coincidences (Alcock, 2003).   7. When psychologists handled watches awaiting repair at a store, 57 percent began running again, with no help from a "psychic." Believing the "psychic's" claim also overlooks the impact of big numbers: If the show reached a large audience, at least a few "broken" watches would start working merely by chance.

Psychology in Action

Becoming a Better Eyewitness to Life

>SURVEY QUESTION< *How can I learn to perceive events more accurately?*

In the courtroom, the claim "I saw it with my own eyes" carries a lot of weight with a jury. Most jurors (unless they have taken a psychology course) tend to assume that eyewitness testimony is nearly infallible (Durham & Dane, 1999). Even U.S. judges are vulnerable to overoptimism about eyewitness testimony (Wise & Safer, 2004). But to put it bluntly, eyewitness testimony is frequently wrong. Recall, for instance, that one of your authors would have sworn in court that he had seen a murder taking place at the supermarket—*if* he hadn't received more information to correct his misperceptions.

What about witnesses who are certain that their perceptions were accurate? Should juries believe them? Actually, having confidence in your testimony has almost no bearing on its accuracy (Brewer & Wells, 2006)! Psychologists are gradually convincing lawyers, judges, and police that eyewitness errors are common (Yarmey, 2003). Even so, thousands of people have been wrongfully convicted (Scheck, Neufeld, & Dwyer, 2000).

Unfortunately, perception rarely provides an "instant replay" of events. Impressions formed when a person is surprised, threatened, or under stress are especially prone to distortion. One study of eyewitness cases found that the *wrong person* was chosen from police lineups 25 percent of the time (Levi, 1998).

Wouldn't the victim of a crime remember more than a mere witness? Not necessarily. A revealing study found that eyewitness accuracy is virtually the same for witnessing a crime (seeing a pocket calculator stolen) as it is for being a victim (seeing one's own watch stolen) (Hosch & Cooper, 1982). Placing more weight on the testimony of victims may be a serious mistake. In many crimes, victims fall prey to *weapon focus*. Understandably, they fix their entire attention on the knife, gun, or other weapon used by an attacker. In doing so, they fail to notice details of appearance, dress, or other clues to identity (Pickel, French, & Betts, 2003; Steblay, 1992). Additional factors that consistently lower eyewitness accuracy are summarized in ■ Table 4.2 (Kassin et al., 2001).

Implications   Now that DNA testing is available, more than 100 people who were convicted of murder, rape, and other crimes in the United States have been exonerated. Each of these innocent people was convicted mainly on the basis of eyewitness testimony. Each also spent *years* in prison before being cleared (Foxhall, 2000). How often are everyday perceptions as inaccurate or distorted as those of an emotional eyewitness? The answer is, very frequently. Bearing this in mind may help you be more tolerant of the views of others and more cautious about your own objectivity. It may also encourage more frequent *reality testing* on your part.

If you have ever concluded that someone was angry, upset, or unfriendly without checking the accuracy of your perceptions, you have fallen into a subtle trap. Personal objectivity is an elusive quality, requiring frequent reality testing to maintain. At the very least, it pays to ask a person what she or he is feeling when you are in doubt. Clearly, most of us could learn to be better "eyewitnesses" to daily events.

Even in broad daylight, eyewitness testimony is untrustworthy. In 2001 an airliner crashed near Kennedy International Airport in New York. Hundreds of people saw the plane go down. Half of them said the plane was on fire. Flight recorders showed there was no fire. One witness in five saw the plane make a right turn. An equal number saw it make a left turn! As one investigator noted, the best witness may be a "kid under 12 years old who doesn't have his parents around." Adults, it seems, are easily swayed by their expectations.

■ Table 4.2	**Factors Affecting the Accuracy of Eyewitness Perceptions**
Sources of Error	**Summary of Findings**
1. Wording of questions	An eyewitness's testimony about an event can be affected by how the questions put to that witness are worded.
2. Postevent information	Eyewitness testimony about an event often reflects not only what was actually seen but also information obtained later on.
3. Attitudes, expectations	An eyewitness's perception and memory for an event may be affected by his or her attitudes and expectations.
4. Alcohol intoxication	Alcohol intoxication impairs later ability to recall events.
5. Cross-racial perceptions	Eyewitnesses are better at identifying members of their own race than they are at identifying people of other races.
6. Weapon focus	The presence of a weapon impairs an eyewitness's ability to accurately identify the culprit's face.
7. Accuracy-confidence	An eyewitness's confidence is not a good predictor of his or her accuracy.
8. Exposure time	The less time an eyewitness has to observe an event, the less well she or he will perceive and remember it.
9. Unconscious transference	Eyewitnesses sometimes identify as a culprit someone they have seen in another situation or context.
10. Color perception	Judgments of color made under monochromatic light (such as an orange street light) are highly unreliable.
11. Stress	Very high levels of stress impair the accuracy of eyewitness perceptions.

Source: Adapted from Kassin et al., 2001.

Perceptual Awareness

Do some people perceive things more accurately than others? Humanistic psychologist Abraham Maslow (1969) believed that some people perceive themselves and others with unusual accuracy. Maslow characterized these people as especially alive, open, aware, and mentally healthy. He found that their perceptual styles were marked by immersion in the present; a lack of self-consciousness; freedom from selecting, criticizing, or evaluating; and a general "surrender" to experience. The kind of perception Maslow described is like that of a mother with her newborn infant, a child at Christmas, or two people in love.

In daily life, we quickly habituate (respond less) to predictable and unchanging stimuli. **Habituation** is a type of learning—basically, we learn to cease paying attention to familiar stimuli. For instance, when you download a new MP3, the music initially holds your attention all the way through. But when the MP3 becomes "old," the song may play without your really attending to it. When a stimulus is repeated *without change,* our response to it habituates, or decreases. Interestingly, creative people habituate *more slowly* than average. We might expect that they would rapidly become bored with a repeated stimulus. Instead, it seems that creative people actively attend to stimuli, even those that are repeated (Colin, Moore, & West, 1996).

The Value of Paying Attention Whereas the average person has not reached perceptual restriction of the "if you've seen one tree, you've seen them all" variety, the fact remains that most of us tend to look at a tree and classify it into the perceptual category of "trees in general" without really appreciating the miracle standing before us. How, then, can we bring about **dishabituation** (a reversal of habituation) on a day-to-day basis? Does perceptual clarity require years of effort? Fortunately, a more immediate avenue is available. The deceptively simple key to dishabituation is: Pay attention. The following story summarizes the importance of attention:

> One day a man of the people said to Zen Master Ikkyu: "Master, will you please write for me some maxims of the highest wisdom?"
>
> Ikkyu immediately took his brush and wrote the word "Attention."
>
> "Is that all?" asked the man. "Will you not add something more?"
>
> Ikkyu then wrote twice running: "Attention. Attention."
>
> "Well," remarked the man rather irritably, "I really don't see much depth or subtlety in what you have just written."
>
> Then Ikkyu wrote the same word three times running: "Attention. Attention. Attention." Half angered, the man demanded, "What does that word 'Attention' mean anyway?"
>
> And Ikkyu answered gently: "Attention means attention." (Kapleau, 1966)

To this we can add only one thought, provided by the words of poet William Blake: "If the doors of perception were cleansed, man would see everything as it is, infinite."

How to Become a Better "Eyewitness" to Life

Here's a summary of ideas from this chapter to help you maintain and enhance perceptual awareness and accuracy.

1. *Remember that perceptions are constructions of reality.* Learn to regularly question your own perceptions. Are they accurate? Could another interpretation fit the facts? What assumptions are you making? Could they be false? How might your assumptions be distorting your perceptions?

2. *Break perceptual habits and interrupt habituation.* Each day, try to do some activities in new ways. For example, take different routes when you travel to work or school. Do routines, such as brushing your teeth or combing your hair, with your nonpreferred hand. Try to look at friends and family members as if they are persons you just met for the first time.

Habituation A decrease in perceptual response to a repeated stimulus.

Dishabituation A reversal of habituation.

3. *Shift adaptation levels and broaden frames of reference by seeking out-of-the-ordinary experiences.* The possibilities here range from trying foods you don't normally eat to reading opinions very different from your own. Experiences ranging from a quiet walk in the woods to a trip to an amusement park may be perceptually refreshing.

4. *Beware of perceptual sets.* Anytime you pigeonhole people, objects, or events, there is a danger that your perceptions will be distorted by expectations or pre-existing categories. Be especially wary of labels and stereotypes. Try to see people as individuals and events as unique, one-time occurrences.

5. *Be aware of the ways in which motives and emotions influence perceptions.* It is difficult to avoid being swayed by your own interests, needs, desires, and emotions. But be aware of this trap and actively try to see the world through the eyes of others. Taking the other person's perspective is especially valuable in disputes or arguments. Ask yourself, "How does this look to her or him?"

6. *Make a habit of engaging in reality testing.* Actively look for additional evidence to check the accuracy of your perceptions. Ask questions, seek clarifications, and find alternate channels of information. Remember that perception is not automatically accurate. You could be wrong—we all are frequently.

7. *Pay attention.* Make a conscious effort to pay attention to other people and your surroundings. Don't drift through life in a haze. Listen to others with full concentration. Watch their facial expressions. Make eye contact. Try to get in the habit of approaching perception as if you are going to have to testify later about what you saw and heard.

 Study Break **Perceptual Awareness and Accuracy**

Reflect

Because perceptions are constructions or models of external events, we should all engage in more frequent reality testing. Can you think of a recent event when a little reality testing would have saved you from misjudging a situation?

In order to improve your own perceptual awareness and accuracy, which strategies would you emphasize first?

Learning Check

1. Most perceptions can be described as active constructions of external reality. T or F?

2. Inaccuracies in eyewitness perceptions obviously occur in "real life," but they cannot be reproduced in psychology experiments. T or F?

3. Eyewitnesses choose the wrong person from police lineups as much as 25 percent of the time. T or F?

4. Victims of crimes are more accurate eyewitnesses than are impartial observers. T or F?

5. *Reality testing* is another term for dishabituation. T or F?

Critical Thinking

6. Return for a moment to the incident described at the beginning of this chapter. What perceptual factors were involved in the first version of the "murder"? How did the girl affect what one of your authors saw?

Answers

1. T 2. F 3. T 4. F 5. F 6. The girl's misperception, communicated so forcefully to your author, created a powerful expectancy that influenced what your author perceived. Also, the event happened quickly (the exposure time was brief) and the stressful or emotional nature of the incident encouraged your author's misperception.

CHAPTER IN REVIEW

Major Points

- Sensory systems select, analyze, and transduce information from the surrounding world.
- All of the senses rely on a complex series of mechanical, chemical, and neural events to generate messages understood by the brain.
- Sensory adaptation, sensory gating, and selective attention significantly modify our experiences.
- Perception is an active process of assembling sensations into meaningful patterns.
- We unconsciously use Gestalt organizing principles to organize sensations into meaningful patterns.
- Our wondrous ability to perceive three-dimensional space is based on binocular and monocular depth cues.
- Perception is greatly affected by expectations, motives, emotions, and learning.
- Perceptual accuracy can be improved by conscious effort and an awareness of factors that contribute to erroneous perceptions.

Summary

In general, how do sensory systems function?

- Because of transduction, selectivity, limited sensitivity, feature detection, and coding patterns, the senses act as data reduction systems.
- Sensation can be partially understood in terms of sensory localization in the brain.

How is vision accomplished?

- The eye is a visual system, not a photographic one. The entire visual system is structured to analyze visual information.
- Four common visual defects are myopia, hyperopia, astigmatism, and presbyopia.
- The rods and cones are photoreceptors in the retina of the eye.
- The rods specialize in peripheral vision, night vision, seeing black and white, and motion detection. The cones specialize in color vision, acuity, and daylight vision.
- Color vision is explained by the trichromatic theory in the retina and by the opponent-process theory in the visual system beyond the eyes.
- Total color blindness is rare, but 8 percent of males and 1 percent of females are red-green color-blind or color-weak.
- Dark adaptation is caused mainly by an increase in the amount of visual pigments in the rods.

What are the mechanisms of hearing?

- Sound waves are the stimulus for hearing. They are transduced by the eardrum, auditory ossicles, oval window, cochlea, and ultimately, the hair cells.
- The frequency theory and place theory of hearing together explain how pitch is sensed.
- Two basic types of hearing loss are conductive hearing loss and sensorineural hearing loss. Loud noise is a common cause of sensorineural hearing loss and is referred to as noise-induced hearing loss.

How do the chemical senses operate?

- Olfaction (smell) and gustation (taste) are chemical senses responsive to airborne or liquefied molecules.
- The lock-and-key theory partially explains smell. In addition, the location of the olfactory receptors in the nose helps identify various scents.
- Sweet and bitter tastes are based on a lock-and-key coding of molecule shapes. Salty and sour tastes are triggered by a direct flow of ions into taste receptors.

What are the somesthetic senses and why are they important?

- The somesthetic senses include the skin senses, vestibular senses, and kinesthetic senses (receptors that detect muscle and joint positioning).
- The skin senses are touch, pressure, pain, cold, and warmth. Sensitivity to each is related to the number of receptors found in an area of skin.
- Distinctions can be made between warning pain and reminding pain.
- Pain is greatly affected by anxiety, attention, and control over a stimulus. Pain can be reduced by controlling these factors.
- Various forms of motion sickness are related to messages received from the vestibular system, which detects gravity and movement.

Why are we more aware of some sensations than others?

- Incoming sensations are affected by sensory adaptation, sensory gating, and selective attention.
- Selective gating of pain messages takes place in the spinal cord, as explained by gate control theory.
- Gate control theory cannot explain phantom limb pain.

How do perceptual constancies and Gestalt organizing principles shape our perceptions?

- Perception is the process of assembling sensations into a usable mental representation of the world.

- In vision, the image projected on the retina is constantly changing, but the external world appears stable and undistorted because of size, shape, and brightness constancy.
- Separating figure and ground is the most basic perceptual organization.
- The following Gestalt principles also help organize sensations: nearness, similarity, continuity, closure, contiguity, and common region.
- A perceptual organization may be thought of as a hypothesis held until evidence contradicts it.

How is it possible to see depth and judge distance?

- A basic capacity for depth perception is present soon after birth.
- Depth perception depends on binocular cues of retinal disparity and convergence.
- Depth perception also depends on the monocular cue of accommodation. Other things depth perception depends on include the following: the monocular "pictorial" depth cues of linear perspective, relative size, height in the picture plane, light and shadow, overlap, texture gradients, aerial haze, and motion parallax.
- The moon illusion can be explained by the apparent distance hypothesis, which emphasizes that many depth cues are present when the moon is on the horizon.

How is perception altered by expectations, motives, emotions, and learning?

- Perception is an active construction of events.
- Perceptions may be based on top-down or bottom-up processing of information.
- Suggestion, motives, emotions, attention, and prior experience combine in various ways to create perceptual sets, or expectancies.
- Personal motives and values often alter perceptions by changing the evaluation of what is seen or by altering attention to specific details.
- Perceptual learning influences the ways in which we organize and interpret sensations.
- One of the most familiar of all illusions, the Müller-Lyer illusion, seems to be related to perceptual learning, linear perspective, and size-distance invariance relationships.

Is extrasensory perception possible?

- Parapsychology is the study of purported psi phenomena, including telepathy (including mediumship), clairvoyance, precognition, and psychokinesis.
- Research in parapsychology remains controversial because of a variety of problems and shortcomings.

The bulk of the evidence to date is against the existence of ESP.
- Stage ESP is based on deception and tricks.

How can I learn to perceive events more accurately?

- Eyewitness testimony is surprisingly unreliable. Eyewitness accuracy is further damaged by weapon focus, and a number of similar factors.
- When a stimulus is repeated without change, our response to it undergoes habituation.
- Perceptual accuracy is enhanced by reality testing, dishabituation, and conscious efforts to pay attention.
- It is also valuable to break perceptual habits, to broaden frames of reference, to beware of perceptual sets, and to be aware of the ways in which motives and emotions influence perceptions.

Interactive Learning

Internet addresses frequently change. To find the sites listed here, visit www.thomsonedu.com/psychology/coon for an updated list of Internet addresses and direct links to relevant sites.

Psychology: A Journey Companion Website   Find online quizzes, flash cards, animations, video clips, experiments, interactive assessments, and other helpful study aids for this text at www.thomsonedu.com/psychology/coon.

HEARNET   A page that promotes ear protection for rock musicians.

IllusionWorks   A large collection of visual illusions.

Questions and Answers About Pain Control Answers common questions about pain control.

Smell and Taste Disorders FAQ   Questions and answers about smell and taste disorders.

Stereogram Links   Provides links to stereograms and information about stereograms, including how to create your own.

The Joy of Visual Perception   An online book about visual perception.

Vestibular Disorders Association   Provides links to sites concerned with vestibular problems.

Vision Test   An on-screen vision test.

ThomsonNOW   Go to www.thomsonedu.com/login to link to ThomsonNOW, your online study tool. First take the **Pre-Test** for this chapter to get your **Personalized Study Plan**, which will identify topics you need to review and direct you to online resources. Then take the **Post-Test** to determine what concepts you have mastered and what you still need work on.

TEST YOUR KNOWLEDGE

Sensation and Perception

For additional review, get more practice with *ThomsonNOW*, *WebTutor*, the *Practice Quizzes*, and/or the printed *Study Guide* available with this book.

1. The senses divide the world into basic perceptual features and sensory patterns, a process known as
   a. sensory localization
   b. sensory analysis
   c. accommodation
   d. phosphenation

2. If you press on your closed eyelids you will experience phosphenes. This illustrates the concept of
   a. visual saturation
   b. sensory coding
   c. accommodation
   d. hyperopia

3. People who become farsighted as they get older have the condition known as
   a. hyperopia
   b. myopia
   c. astigmatism
   d. presbyopia

4. The greatest visual acuity is associated with the _____ and the _____.
   a. trichromat, rods
   b. vitreous humor, cones
   c. fovea, cones
   d. nanometer, cones

5. Black and white vision and a high degree of sensitivity to movement are characteristic of
   a. rod vision
   b. cone vision
   c. the blind spot
   d. the fovea

6. Colored afterimages are best explained by
   a. trichromatic theory
   b. the effects of astigmatism
   c. sensory localization
   d. opponent-process theory

7. Dark adaptation is directly related to an increase in
   a. visual pigments in the rods
   b. astigmatism
   c. accommodation
   d. saturation

8. The loudness of a sound is determined by the _____ of sound waves.
   a. frequency
   b. amplitude
   c. rarefaction
   d. ossicle

9. Sounds are ultimately transduced by movements of the
   a. pinna
   b. malleus
   c. cochlea
   d. hair cells

10. The term *umami* refers to
    a. smell blindness
    b. temporary damage to the hair cells
    c. secondary olfaction
    d. a taste quality

11. The lock and key theory appears to partly explain
    a. motion sickness
    b. olfaction and gustation
    c. dark adaptation
    d. color blindness

12. Which of the following is NOT a somesthetic sense?
    a. taste
    b. touch
    c. balance
    d. kinesthesis

13. As time passes, nerve endings in the skin under your wristwatch send fewer signals to the brain and you become able to feel the watch. This process is called
    a. sensory gating
    b. the sensory bottleneck
    c. reverse attention
    d. sensory adaptation

14. The fact that a mild surface pain can greatly reduce more agonizing pain is consistent with
    a. gate control theory
    b. the concept of sensory adaptation
    c. sensory conflict theory
    d. perceptual constancy theory

15. Which of the following is LEAST likely to contribute to the formation of a perceptual figure?
    a. continuity
    b. closure
    c. similarity
    d. separation

16. The clearest example of a binocular depth cue is
    a. linear perspective
    b. retinal disparity
    c. aerial perspective
    d. motion parallax

17. The apparent distance hypothesis provides a good explanation of the
    a. moon illusion
    b. horizontal-vertical illusion
    c. Zulu illusion
    d. effects of inattentional blindness

18. Top-down perceptual processing is closely related to
    a. perceptual expectancies
    b. the Müller-Lyer illusion
    c. size-distance invariances
    d. precognition

19. The Zener cards were used in early studies of
    a. psi phenomena
    b. inattentional blindness
    c. the Müller-Lyer illusion
    d. top-down processing

20. A good antidote to perceptual habituation can be found in conscious efforts to
    a. reverse sensory gating
    b. pay attention
    c. achieve visual accommodation
    d. counteract shape constancy

ANSWERS 1. b 2. b 3. d 4. c 5. a 6. d 7. a 8. b 9. d 10. d 11. b 12. a 13. d 14. a 15. d 16. b 17. a 18. a 19. a 20. b

States of Consciousness

JOURNEY INTO PSYCHOLOGY: A VISIT TO SEVERAL STATES (OF CONSCIOUSNESS)

In New Zealand, a Maori tohunga (priest) performs a nightlong ritual to talk to the spirits who created the world in the mythical period the Aborigines call Dreamtime.

In Toronto, Canada, three businessmen head for a popular tavern after a stressful day.

In the American Southwest, a Navajo elder gives his congregation peyote tea, a sacrament in the Native American Church, as a drumbeat resounds in the darkness.

In Big Bend National Park in southern Texas, a college student spends a day walking through the wilderness, in a quiet state of mindfulness meditation.

In Northern Ireland, a nun living in a convent spends an entire week in silent prayer and contemplation.

In Los Angeles, California, an aspiring actor consults a hypnotist for help in reducing her stage fright.

In Berkeley, California, an artist spends 2 hours in a flotation chamber, to clear her head before resuming work on a large painting.

At a park in Amsterdam, a group of street musicians smoke a joint and sing for spare change.

In Tucson, Arizona, one of your authors pours himself another cup of coffee.

Each of these people seeks to alter consciousness—in different ways, to different degrees, and for different reasons. As these examples suggest, consciousness can take many forms. In the discussion that follows, we will begin with the familiar realms of sleep and dreaming and then move to more exotic states of consciousness.

Iconica/Getty Images

▽ **Survey Questions**

- What is an altered state of consciousness?
- What are the effects of sleep loss or changes in sleep patterns?
- Are there different stages of sleep?
- What are the causes of sleep disorders and unusual sleep events?
- Do dreams have meaning?
- How is hypnosis done, and what are its limitations?
- What are meditation and sensory deprivation? Do they have any benefits?
- What are the effects of the more commonly used psychoactive drugs?
- How are dreams used to promote personal understanding?

STATES OF CONSCIOUSNESS—THE MANY FACES OF AWARENESS

>SURVEY QUESTION< *What is an altered state of consciousness?*

To be conscious means to be aware. **Consciousness** consists of all the sensations, perceptions, memories, and feelings you are aware of at any instant (Hobson, 2001; Koch, 2004). (See "What Is It Like to Be a Bat?"). We spend most of our lives in waking consciousness, a state of clear, organized alertness. In waking consciousness we perceive times, places, and events as real, meaningful, and familiar. But states of consciousness related to fatigue, delirium, hypnosis, drugs, and euphoria may differ markedly from "normal" awareness. Everyone experiences at least some altered states, such as sleep, dreaming, and daydreaming (Blackmore, 2004). In everyday life, changes in consciousness may also accompany long-distance running, listening to music, making love, or other circumstances.

Altered States of Consciousness

How are altered states distinguished from normal awareness? During an **altered state of consciousness** (**ASC**) changes occur in the *quality* and *pattern* of mental activity. Typically there are distinct shifts in perceptions, emotions, memories, time sense, thoughts, feelings of self-control, and suggestibility (Siegel, 2005). Definitions aside, most people know when they have experienced an ASC.

Are there other causes of ASCs? In addition to the ones mentioned, we could add: sensory overload (for example, a rave, Mardi Gras crowd, or mosh pit), monotonous stimulation (such as "highway hypnotism" on long drives), unusual physical conditions (high fever, hyperventilation, dehydration, sleep loss, near-death experiences), restricted sensory input, and many other possibilities. In some instances, altered states have important cultural meanings. (See "Consciousness and Culture" for more information.)

An unconscious person will die without constant care. Yet, as crucial as consciousness is, we can't really explain how it occurs. Nevertheless, it is possible to identify various states of consciousness and to explore the role they play in our lives. Let's begin with a look at sleep and dreaming.

Consciousness Mental awareness of sensations, perceptions, memories, and feelings.

Altered state of consciousness (ASC) A condition of awareness distinctly different in quality or pattern from waking consciousness.

SLEEP—A NICE PLACE TO VISIT

>SURVEY QUESTION< *What are the effects of sleep loss or changes in sleep patterns?*

Each of us will spend some 25 years of life asleep. Contrary to common belief, you are not totally unresponsive during sleep. For instance, you are more likely to awaken if you hear

What Is It Like to Be a Bat?

Imagine hurtling through the air on leather wings while shrieking noisily. Suddenly, the echo of your own voice draws your attention to a moth that is frantically trying to evade you. You careen after it, twisting through the pitch-black jungle. Dodging trees and other bats, you catch the moth and savor your first meal of the still-young night.

In his famous essay, *What Is It Like to Be a Bat?*, Thomas Nagel (1974) points out that we can learn a lot about bats from an objective, *third-person* point of view. Scientifically, we know that bats use echolocation (they emit sounds and interpret the echoes to locate objects) to hunt insects at night. But what does that *feel* like from a subjective, *first-person* point of view? Have you ever been curious about what it is like to be a bat, or a dog,

or a cat? What runs through Rover's mind when he sniffs other dogs? Does Rover have dreams? Are they as strange as ours? Do cats ever worry about the future? Do they like music? Do animals feel joy?

According to Nagel, we cannot directly know the first-person experience of animals (or even other people, for that matter). The difficulty of knowing other minds is why the early behaviorists distrusted introspection. (Remember Chapter 1?) A key challenge for psychology is to use objective studies of the brain and behavior to help us understand the mind and consciousness, which are basically private phenomena (Blackmore, 2004; Koch, 2004). This chapter summarizes some of what we have learned about states of consciousness.

---

your own name spoken, instead of another. Likewise, a sleeping mother may ignore a jet thundering overhead but wake at the slightest whimper of her child. It's even possible to do simple tasks while asleep. In one experiment, people learned to avoid an electric shock by touching a switch each time a tone sounded. Eventually, they could do it without waking. (This is much like the basic survival skill of turning off your alarm clock without waking.) Of course, sleep does impose limitations. Don't expect to learn math, a foreign language, or other complex skills while asleep—especially if the snooze takes place in class (Druckman & Bjork, 1994). But do expect that a good sleep will help you to consolidate what you learned the day before (Fenn, Nusbaum, & Margoliash, 2003).

Because sleep is familiar, many people think they know all about it. Before reading more, test your knowledge with the following Sleep Quiz. Were you surprised by any of the answers? Let's see what we know about our "daily retreat from the world."

The Need for Sleep

How strong is the need for sleep? Sleep is an innate **biological rhythm** that can never be entirely ignored (Lavie, 2001; Mistlberger, 2005). Of course, sleep will give way temporarily, especially at times of great danger. As comedian and filmmaker Woody Allen once put it, "The lion and the lamb shall lie down together, but the lamb will not be very sleepy." However, there are limits to how long humans can go without sleep. A rare disease that prevents sleep always ends with stupor, coma, and death (Dauvilliers et al., 2004). (See ▸Fig. 5.1.)

Sleep Quiz

1. People can learn to sleep for just a few hours a night and still function well. T or F?
2. Everyone dreams every night. T or F?
3. The brain rests during sleep. T or F?
4. Resting during the day can replace lost sleep. T or F?
5. As people get older they sleep more. T or F?
6. Alcohol may help a person get to sleep but it disturbs sleep later during the night. T or F?
7. If a person goes without sleep long enough, death will occur. T or F?
8. Dreams mostly occur during deep sleep. T or F?
9. A person prevented from dreaming would soon go crazy. T or F?
10. Sleepwalking occurs when a person acts out a dream. T or F?

Answers

1. F 2. T 3. F 4. F 5. F 6. T 7. T 8. T 9. F 10. F

Timothy Ross/The Image Works

▸▸**FIGURE 5.1** Not all animals sleep, but like humans, those that do have powerful sleep needs. For example, dolphins must voluntarily breathe air, which means they face the choice of staying awake or drowning. The dolphin solves this problem by sleeping on just one side of its brain at a time! The other half of the brain, which remains awake, controls breathing (Jouvet, 1999).

Biological rhythm Any repeating cycle of biological activity, such as sleep and waking cycles or changes in body temperature.

Consciousness and Culture

Throughout history, people have found ways to alter consciousness (Siegel, 2005). A dramatic example is the sweat lodge ceremony of the Sioux Indians. During the ritual, several men sit in total darkness inside a small chamber heated by coals. Cedar smoke, bursts of steam, and sage fill the air. The men chant rhythmically. The heat builds. At last they can stand it no more. The door is thrown open. Cooling night breezes rush in. And then? The cycle begins again—often to be repeated four or five times more.

Like the yoga practices of Hindu mystics or the dances of the Whirling Dervishes of Turkey, the ritual "sweats" of the Sioux are meant to cleanse the mind and body. When they are especially intense, they bring altered awareness and personal revelation.

People seek some altered states for pleasure, as is often true of drug intoxication. Yet as the Sioux illustrate, many cultures regard altered

Joel Gordon, 1991

consciousness as a pathway to personal enlightenment. Indeed, all cultures and most religions recognize and accept some alterations of consciousness. However, the meaning given to these states varies greatly—from signs of "madness" and "possession" by spirits, to life-enhancing breakthroughs. Thus, cultural conditioning greatly affects what altered states we recognize, seek, consider normal, and attain (de Rios & Grob, 2005).

In many cultures, rituals of healing, prayer, purification, or personal transformation are accompanied by altered states of consciousness.

Imagine placing an animal on a moving treadmill, over a pool of water. Even under these conditions, animals soon drift into repeated microsleeps. A **microsleep** is a brief shift in brain activity to the pattern normally recorded during sleep. When you drive, remember that microsleeps can lead to macroaccidents. Even if your eyes are open, you can fall asleep for a few seconds. A hundred thousand crashes every year are caused by sleepiness (Rau, 2005). Although coffee helps (Kamimori et al., 2005), if you are struggling to stay awake while driving, you should stop, quit fighting it, and take a short nap.

Sleep Deprivation

How long could a person go without sleep? With few exceptions, 4 days or more without sleep becomes hell for everyone. For example, a disc jockey named Peter Tripp once stayed awake for 200 hours, to raise money for charity. After 100 hours, Tripp began to hallucinate: He saw cobwebs in his shoes and watched in terror as a tweed coat became a suit of "furry worms." By the end of 200 hours, Tripp was unable to distinguish between his hallucinations and reality (Luce, 1965). Despite Tripp's breakdown, longer sleepless periods are possible. The world record is held by Randy Gardner—who at age 17 went 268 hours (11 days) without sleep. Surprisingly, Randy needed only 14 hours of sleep to recover. As Randy found, most symptoms of **sleep deprivation** (sleep loss) are reversed by a single night's rest.

What are the costs of sleep loss? Age and personality make a big difference. Although Peter Tripp's behavior became quite bizarre, Randy Gardner was less impaired. However,

Microsleep A brief shift in brain-wave patterns to those of sleep.

Sleep deprivation Being prevented from getting desired or needed amounts of sleep.

Calvin and Hobbes © 1996 Watterson. Distributed by Universal Press Syndicate. Reprinted with permission. All rights reserved.

Teenage Sleep Zombies

Did you ever have to fight to stay awake in a high school class? *Hypersomnia* (hi-per-SOM-nee-ah: excessive daytime sleepiness) is a common problem during adolescence (Carskadon, Acebo, & Jenni, 2004). The reason? Rapid physical changes during puberty increase the need for sleep. However, the quality and quantity of sleep time tends to decrease during the teen years (Fukuda & Ishihara, 2001). At a time when they need more sleep, many adolescents get less.

If teenagers are sleep deprived, why don't they just sleep more? As children enter puberty, they begin to stay up later at night. However, they must get up early to attend school, regardless of when they went to bed. As a result, many teens are seriously sleep deprived during the week. Then, on the weekend, they sleep longer and get up late in the morning (LaBerge et al., 2001). After sleeping extra amounts for 2 days, many teens have difficulty falling asleep Sunday night. On Monday, they have to get up early for school, and the sleep loss cycle begins again.

What can be done about teenage sleep deprivation? Psychologists have persuaded some school districts to start classes later so that high school students can sleep longer. Studies suggest that this schedule improves learning and reduces behavior problems. In fact, it looks like some of the "storm and stress" of adolescence may be ordinary grouchiness caused by sleep loss (Mitru, Millrood, & Mateika, 2002).

---

make no mistake: Sleep is a necessity. At various times, Randy's speech was slurred, and he couldn't concentrate, remember clearly, or name common objects (Coren, 1996). Sleep loss also typically causes trembling hands, drooping eyelids, inattention, irritability, staring, increased pain sensitivity, and general discomfort (Doran, Van Dongen, & Dinges, 2001).

Most people who have not slept for 2 or 3 days can still do interesting or complex mental tasks (Binks, Waters, & Hurry, 1999). But they have trouble paying attention, staying alert, and doing simple or boring routines (Belenky et al., 2003). For a driver, pilot, or machine operator, this can spell disaster. If a task is monotonous (such as factory work or air traffic control), no amount of sleep loss is safe (Gillberg & Akerstedt, 1998). In fact, if you lose just 1 hour of sleep a night, it can affect your mood, memory, ability to pay attention, and even your health (Maas, 1999). (See "Teenage Sleep Zombies.")

How can I tell how much sleep I really need? Pick a day when you feel well rested. Then sleep that night until you wake without an alarm clock. If you feel rested when you wake up, that's your natural sleep need. If you're sleeping fewer hours than you need, you're building up a sleep debt (Maas, 1999).

Severe sleep loss can cause a temporary **sleep-deprivation psychosis** (loss of contact with reality) like Peter Tripp suffered. Confusion, disorientation, delusions, and hallucinations are typical of this reaction. Fortunately, such "crazy" behavior is uncommon. Hallucinations and delusions rarely appear before 60 hours of wakefulness (Naitoh, Kelly, & Englund, 1989).

Sleep Patterns

Sleep was described as an innate biological rhythm. What does that mean? Daily sleep and waking periods create a variety of sleep patterns. Rhythms of sleep and waking are so steady that they continue for many days, even when clocks and light–dark cycles are removed. However, under such conditions, humans eventually shift to a sleep–waking cycle that averages slightly more than 24 hours (Czeisler et al., 1999). (See ▸▸Fig. 5.2.) This suggests that external time markers, especially light and dark, help tie our sleep rhythms to days that are exactly 24 hours long. Otherwise, many of us would drift into our own unusual sleep cycles (Duffy & Wright, Jr., 2005).

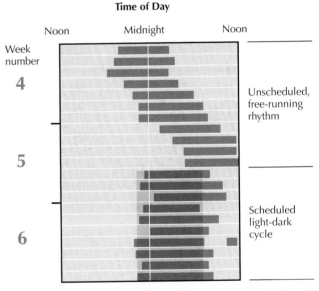

▸▸**FIGURE 5.2** Sleep rhythms. Bars show periods of sleep during the fourth, fifth, and sixth weeks of an experiment with a human subject. During unscheduled periods, the subject was allowed to select times of sleep and lighting. The result was a sleep rhythm of about 25 hours. Notice how this free-running rhythm began to advance around the clock as they fell asleep later each day. When periods of darkness (shaded area) were imposed during the fifth week, the rhythm quickly resynchronized with 24-hour days. (Adapted from Czeisler et al., 1981.)

Sleep-deprivation psychosis A major disruption of mental and emotional functioning brought about by sleep loss.

What is the normal range of sleep? A few rare individuals can get by on an hour or two of sleep a night—and feel perfectly fine. Only a small percentage of the population are *short sleepers,* averaging 5 hours of sleep or less per night. On the other end of the scale we find *long sleepers,* who doze 9 hours or more (Grandner & Kripke, 2004). The majority of us sleep on a familiar 7- to 8-hour-per-night schedule. For a few people, however, it is quite normal to sleep as little as 5 hours per night or as much as 11. Urging everyone to sleep 8 hours would be like advising everyone to wear medium-size shoes.

We need less sleep as we get older, right? Yes, total sleep time declines throughout life. Those older than 50 average only 6 hours of sleep a night. In contrast, infants spend up to 20 hours a day sleeping, usually in 2- to 4-hour cycles. As they mature, most children go through a "nap" stage and eventually settle into a steady cycle of sleeping once a day. Perhaps we should all continue to take an afternoon "siesta." Midafternoon sleepiness is a natural part of the sleep cycle. Brief, well-timed naps can help maintain alertness in people like truck drivers and hospital interns, who often must fight to stay alert (Garbarino et al., 2004).

Busy people may be tempted to sleep less. However, people on *shortened* cycles—for example, 3 hours of sleep to 6 hours awake—often can't get to sleep when the cycle calls for it. That's why astronauts continue to sleep on their normal earth schedule while in space. Adapting to *longer* than normal days is more promising. Such days can be tailored to match natural sleep patterns, which have a ratio of 2 to 1 between time awake and time asleep (16 hours awake and 8 hours asleep). For instance, one study showed that 28-hour "days" work for some people. Overall, however, sleep is a "gentle tyrant." Sleep patterns may be bent and stretched, but they rarely yield entirely to human whims (Akerstedt et al., 1993).

STAGES OF SLEEP—THE NIGHTLY ROLLER-COASTER RIDE

>SURVEY QUESTION< *Are there different stages of sleep?*

What causes sleep? Early sleep experts thought that something in the bloodstream must cause sleep. But conjoined twins, whose bodies are joined at birth, show that this is false. It's not unusual for one twin to be asleep while the second is awake (Fig. 5.3). During waking hours, a **sleep hormone** (sleep-promoting chemical) collects in the brain and spinal cord, *not* in the blood. If this substance is extracted from one animal and injected into another, the second animal will sleep deeply for many hours (Cravatt et al., 1995). Notice, however, that this explanation is incomplete. For example, why would a well-rested person have to fight to stay awake during a boring midday meeting?

Whether you are awake or asleep right now depends on the *balance* between separate sleep and waking systems. Brain circuits and chemicals in one of the systems promote sleep. A network of brain cells in the other system responds to chemicals that inhibit sleep. The two systems seesaw back and forth, switching the brain between sleep and wakefulness (Lavie, 2001). Note that the brain does not "shut down" during sleep. Rather, the *pattern* of activity changes.

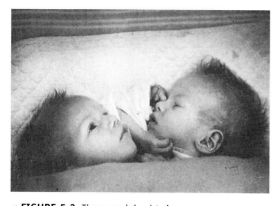

FIGURE 5.3 These conjoined twins share the same blood supply, yet one sleeps while the other is awake. (Photo by Yale Joel, *Life Magazine.* © 1954 Time, Inc.)

Sleep hormone A sleep-promoting substance found in the brain and spinal cord.

Electroencephalograph (EEG) A device designed to detect, amplify, and record electrical activity in the brain.

Beta waves Small fast brain waves associated with being awake and alert.

Alpha waves Large, slow brain waves associated with relaxation and falling asleep.

Sleep stages Levels of sleep identified by brain-wave patterns and behavioral changes.

Stages of Sleep

How does brain activity change when you fall asleep? Sleep activity can be measured with an **electroencephalograph** (eh-LEK-tro-en-SEF-uh-lo-graf), or **EEG.** The brain generates tiny electrical signals (brain waves) that can be amplified and recorded. When you are awake and alert, the EEG reveals a pattern of small fast waves called **beta** (Fig. 5.4). Immediately before sleep, the pattern shifts to larger and slower waves called **alpha.** (Alpha waves also occur when you are relaxed and allow your thoughts to drift.) As the eyes close, breathing becomes slow and regular, the pulse rate slows, and body temperature drops. Soon after, four separate **sleep stages** occur.

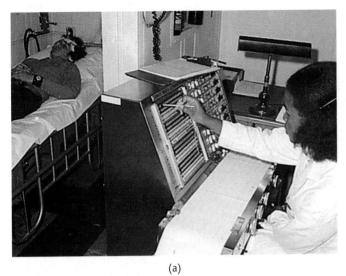

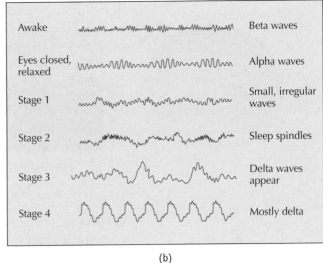

(a)

(b)

» **FIGURE 5.4** *(a)* Photograph of an EEG recording session. The man in the background is asleep. *(b)* Changes in brain-wave patterns associated with various stages of sleep. Actually, most wave types are present at all times, but they occur more or less frequently in various sleep stages.

Stage 1

As you enter **light sleep** (stage 1 sleep), your heart rate slows even more. Breathing becomes more irregular. The muscles of your body relax. This may trigger a reflex muscle twitch called a *hypnic jerk* (HIP-nik: sleep). (This is quite normal, so have no fear about admitting to your friends that you fell asleep with a hypnic jerk.) In stage 1 sleep the EEG is made up mainly of small, irregular waves with some alpha. Persons awakened at this time may or may not say they were asleep.

Stage 2

As sleep deepens, body temperature drops further. Also, the EEG begins to include **sleep spindles,** which are short bursts of distinctive brain-wave activity (Gottselig, Bassetti, & Achermann, 2002). Spindles seem to mark the true boundary of sleep. Within 4 minutes after spindles appear, most people will say they were asleep.

Stage 3

In stage 3, a new brain wave called delta begins to appear. **Delta waves** are very large and slow. They signal a move to deeper sleep and a further loss of consciousness.

Stage 4

Most people reach **deep sleep** (the deepest level of normal sleep) in about an hour. Stage 4 brain waves are almost pure delta and the sleeper is in a state of oblivion. If you make a loud noise during stage 4, the sleeper will wake up in a state of confusion and may not remember the noise. After spending some time in stage 4, the sleeper returns (through stages 3 and 2) to stage 1. Further shifts between deeper and lighter sleep occur throughout the night (» Fig. 5.5).

Two Basic Kinds of Sleep

If you watch a person sleep, you will soon notice that the sleeper's eyes occasionally move under the eyelids. These **rapid eye movements** (or **REMs**) are associated with dreaming (» Fig. 5.5*b*). Roughly 85 percent of the time, people awakened during REMs report vivid dreams. In addition to rapid eye movements, **REM sleep** is marked by a return to fast, irregular EEG patterns similar to stage 1 sleep. In fact, the brain is so active during REM sleep that

Light sleep Stage 1 sleep, marked by small, irregular brain waves and some alpha waves.

Sleep spindles Distinctive bursts of brain-wave activity that indicate a person is asleep.

Delta waves Large, slow brain waves that occur in deeper sleep (stages 3 and 4).

Deep sleep Stage 4 sleep; the deepest form of normal sleep.

Rapid eye movements (REMs) Swift eye movements during sleep.

REM sleep Sleep marked by rapid eye movements and a return to stage 1 EEG patterns.

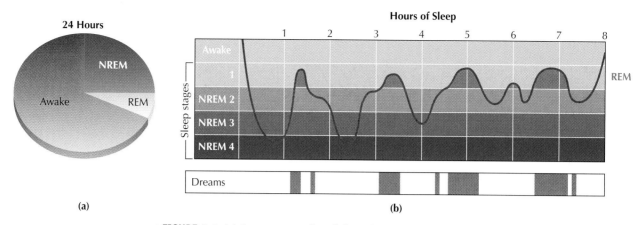

FIGURE 5.5 *(a)* Average proportion of time adults spend daily in REM sleep and NREM sleep. REM periods add up to about 20 percent of total sleep time. *(b)* Typical changes in stages of sleep during the night. Notice that dreams mostly coincide with REM periods.

it looks as if the person is awake (Hobson et al., 1998). REM sleep is easy to observe in pets, such as dogs and cats. Watch for eye and face movements and irregular breathing. (You can forget about your pet iguana, though. Reptiles show no signs of REM sleep.)

REM and NREM Sleep

The two most basic states of sleep are REM sleep with its associated dreaming and **non-REM (NREM) sleep,** which occurs during stages 1, 2, 3, and 4 (Jouvet, 1999). NREM sleep is dream free about 90 percent of the time. Your first period of stage 1 sleep usually lacks REMs and dreams. Each later return to stage 1 is usually accompanied by rapid eye movements. Dreams during REM sleep tend to be longer, clearer, more detailed, more bizarre, and more "dream-like" than thoughts and images that occur in NREM sleep (Hobson, Pace-Schott, & Stickgold, 2000). Also, brain areas associated with imagery and emotion become more active during REM sleep. This may explain why REM dreams tend to be more vivid than NREM dreams (Braun, Balkin, & Herscovitch, 1998).

What is the function of NREM sleep? NREM sleep increases after physical exertion and may help us recover from bodily fatigue. In comparison, daytime stress tends to increase REM sleep. REM sleep totals only about 90 minutes per night (about the same as a feature movie). Yet, its link with dreaming makes it as important as NREM sleep. REM sleep may rise dramatically when there is a death in the family, trouble at work, a marital conflict, or other emotionally charged events.

REM Sleep and Dreaming

What happens to the body when a person dreams? REM sleep is a time of high emotion. The heart beats irregularly. Blood pressure and breathing waver. Both males and females appear to be sexually aroused: Males usually have an erection, and genital blood flow increases in women. This occurs for all REM sleep, so it is not strictly related to erotic dreams (Jouvet, 1999).

During REM sleep your body becomes quite still, as if you were paralyzed. Imagine for a moment the results of acting out some of your recent dreams. Very likely, REM-sleep paralysis prevents some hilarious—and dangerous—nighttime escapades. When it fails, some people thrash violently, leap out of bed, and may attack their bed partners. A lack of muscle paralysis during REM sleep is called *REM behavior disorder* (Ochoa & Pulido, 2005). One patient suffering from the disorder tied himself to his bed every night. That way, he couldn't jump up and crash into furniture or walls (Shafton, 1995). And yet, sometimes sleep paralysis can go a little too far (see "Abducted by Space Aliens?").

In a moment we will survey some additional sleep problems—if you are still awake. First, here are a few questions to check your memory of our discussion so far.

NREM sleep Non-rapid eye movement sleep characteristic of stages 2, 3, and 4.

THE CLINICAL FILE

Abducted by Space Aliens?

Imagine opening your eyes shortly before dawn, attempting to roll over in your bed, and suddenly realizing that you are entirely paralyzed. While lying helplessly on your back and unable to cry out for help, you become aware of sinister figures lurking in your bedroom. As they move closer to your bed, your heart begins to pound violently and you feel as if you are suffocating. You hear buzzing sounds, and feel electrical sensations shooting throughout your body. Within moments, the visions vanish and you can move once again. Terrified, you wonder what has just happened. (McNally & Clancy, 2005, p. 114.)

Sleep paralysis, which normally prevents us from moving during REM sleep, can also occur just as you begin to wake up. During such episodes, people sometimes have *hypnopompic* (hip-neh-POM-pik: "upon awakening") hallucinations. According to psychologist Al Cheyne, these hallucinations may include bizarre experiences, such as sensing that an alien being is in your bedroom; feeling something pressing on your chest, suffocating you; or feeling like you are

Detroit Institute of the Arts/SuperStock

floating out of your body (Cheyne, 2005; Cheyne, Rueffer, & Newby-Clark, 1999).

Although most of us shrug off these weird experiences, some people try to make sense of them. Earlier in history, people interpreted these hallucinated intruders as angels, demons, or witches, and believed that their out-of-the-body experiences were real. However, as our culture changes, so do our interpretations of sleep experiences. Today, for example, some people who have sleep-related hallucinations believe they have been abducted by aliens or sexually abused (McNally & Clancy, 2005).

Folklore and legends often develop as attempts to explain human experiences, including some of the stranger aspects of sleep. By studying hypnopompic hallucinations, psychologists hope to offer natural explanations for many experiences that might otherwise seem supernatural or paranormal (Cheyne, Rueffer, & Newby-Clark, 1999).

Swiss artist Henry Fuseli drew on hypnopompic imagery as an inspiration for his famous painting *The Nightmare*.

→ Study Break   Altered States and Sleep

Reflect

Make a quick list of some altered states of consciousness you have experienced. What do they have in common? How are they different? What conditions caused them?

Imagine that you are a counselor at a sleep clinic. You must explain the basics of sleep and dreaming to a new client who knows little about these topics. Can you do it?

Learning Check

1. Changes in the quality and pattern of mental activity define

    a. an EEG   b. an REM
    c. SIDS   d. an ASC

2. Alyssa experiences a microsleep while driving. Most likely, this indicates that she

    a. was producing mostly beta waves
    b. had high levels of sleep hormones in her bloodstream
    c. switched from delta waves to alpha waves
    d. was sleep deprived

3. Delusions and hallucinations typically continue for several days after a sleep-deprived individual returns to normal sleep. T or F?
4. Older adults, and particularly the elderly, sleep more than children do because the elderly are more easily fatigued. T or F?
5. Which of the following would normally be most incompatible with moving your arms and legs while asleep?

    a. REM sleep   b. sleep spindles
    c. delta waves   d. NREM sleep

6. Rapid eye movements indicate that a person is in deep sleep. T or F?
7. Alpha waves are to presleep drowsiness as _____ _____ are to stage 4 sleep.

Critical Thinking

8. Why might it be better for the unscheduled human sleep–waking cycle to average more than 24 hours, instead of less?
9. Biologically, what advantages might sleeping provide?

Answers

1. d 2. d 3. F 4. F 5. a 6. F 7. delta waves 8. Sleep experts theorize that the 25-hour average leaves a little "slack" in the cycle. External time markers can then retard the bodily cycle slightly to synchronize it with light–dark cycles. If the bodily cycle were shorter than 24 hours, we all might have to "stretch" every day to adjust. 9. Lowering bodily activity and metabolism during sleep may help conserve energy and lengthen life. Also, natural selection may have favored sleep because sleep kept animals that remained active at night probably had a higher chance of being killed. (We'll bet they had more fun, though.)

SLEEP DISTURBANCES—SHOWING NIGHTLY: SLEEP WARS!

>SURVEY QUESTION< *What are the causes of sleep disorders and unusual sleep events?*

Sleep quality has taken a beating in North America. Artificial lighting, frenetic schedules, exciting pastimes, smoking, drinking, overstimulation, and many other factors have contributed to a near epidemic of sleep problems. Sleep disturbances are a serious risk to health and happiness (Shneerson, 2005). Sleep clinics treat thousands of people each year who suffer from sleep disturbances. (See ■ Table 5.1.) Let's explore some of the more interesting problems these people face.

Insomnia

Staring at the ceiling at 2 A.M. is pretty low on most people's list of favorite pastimes. Yet, about 30 percent of all adults have had insomnia. Roughly 9 percent have a serious or chronic problem. **Insomnia** includes difficulty in going to sleep, frequent nighttime awakenings, waking too early, or a combination of these problems. Insomnia can harm people's work, health, and relationships (Sateia & Nowell, 2004).

Types and Causes of Insomnia

Worry, stress, and excitement can cause *temporary insomnia* and a self-defeating cycle. First, excess mental activity ("I can't stop turning things over in my mind") and heightened arousal block sleep. Then, frustration and anger over not being able to sleep cause more worry and arousal. This further delays sleep, which causes more frustration, and so on (Espie, 2002). A good way to beat this cycle is to avoid fighting it. It is usually best to get up

---

■ Table 5.1 **Sleep Disturbances—Things That Go Wrong in the Night**

Hypersomnia Excessive daytime sleepiness. This can result from depression, insomnia, narcolepsy, sleep apnea, sleep drunkenness, periodic limb movements, drug abuse, and other problems.

Insomnia Difficulty in getting to sleep or staying asleep; also, not feeling rested after sleeping.

Narcolepsy Sudden, irresistible, daytime sleep attacks that may last anywhere from a few minutes to a half hour. Victims may fall asleep while standing, talking, or even driving.

Nightmare disorder Vivid, recurrent nightmares that significantly disturb sleep.

Periodic limb movement syndrome Muscle twitches (primarily affecting the legs) that occur every 20 to 40 seconds and severely disturb sleep.

REM behavior disorder A failure of normal muscle paralysis, leading to violent actions during REM sleep.

Restless legs syndrome An irresistible urge to move the legs in order to relieve sensations of creeping, tingling, prickling, aching, or tension.

Sleep apnea During sleep, breathing stops for 20 seconds or more until the person wakes a little, gulps in air, and settles back to sleep; this cycle may be repeated hundreds of times per night.

Sleep drunkenness A slow transition to clear consciousness after awakening; sometimes associated with irritable or aggressive behavior.

Sleep terror disorder The repeated occurrence of night terrors that significantly disturb sleep.

Sleep-wake schedule disorder A mismatch between the sleep-wake schedule demanded by a person's bodily rhythm and that demanded by the environment.

Sleepwalking disorder Repeated incidents of leaving bed and walking about while asleep.

Sources: Carney, Geyer, & Berry, 2005; Shneerson, 2005

Insomnia Difficulty in getting to sleep or staying asleep.

and do something useful or satisfying when you can't sleep. (Reading a textbook might be a good choice of useful activities.) Return to bed only when you begin to feel that you are struggling to stay awake. If sleeping problems last for more than 3 weeks, then a diagnosis of *chronic insomnia* can be made.

Drug-dependency insomnia (sleep loss caused by withdrawal from sleeping pills) can also occur. North Americans spend a billion dollars a year on sleeping pills. There is real irony in this expense. Nonprescription sleeping pills such as *Sominex, Nytol,* and *Sleep-Eze* have little sleep-inducing effect. Barbiturates are even worse. These prescription sedatives decrease both stage 4 sleep and REM sleep, drastically lowering sleep quality. In addition, many users become "sleeping-pill junkies" who need an ever-greater number of pills to get to sleep. Victims must be painstakingly weaned from their sleep medicines. Otherwise, terrible nightmares and "rebound insomnia" may drive them back to drug use. It's worth remembering that although alcohol and other depressant drugs may help a person get to sleep, they greatly reduce sleep quality (Nau & Lichstein, 2005).

Behavioral Remedies for Insomnia

If sleeping pills are a poor way to treat insomnia, what can be done? Sleep specialists prefer to treat insomnia with lifestyle changes and behavioral techniques (Montgomery & Dennis, 2004). Treatment for chronic insomnia usually begins with a careful analysis of a patient's sleep habits, lifestyle, stress levels, and medical problems. All of the approaches discussed in the following list are helpful for treating insomnia (Nau & Lichstein, 2005). Of the methods listed, stimulus control and sleep restriction are the most effective (Chesson et al., 1999):

1. **Stimulus control.** Insisting on a regular schedule helps establish a firm body rhythm, greatly improving sleep. This is best achieved by exercising **stimulus control,** which refers to linking a response with specific stimuli. It is important to get up and go to sleep at the same time each day, including weekends (Bootzin & Epstein, 2000). (As noted earlier regarding adolescent sleep loss, many people upset their sleep rhythms by staying up late on weekends.) In addition, insomniacs are told to avoid doing anything but sleeping when they are in bed. They are not to study, eat, watch TV, read, pay the bills, worry, or even think in bed. (Lovemaking is okay, however.) In this way, only sleeping and relaxation become associated with going to bed at specific times (Bootzin & Epstein, 2000).

2. **Sleep Restriction.** Even if an entire night's sleep is missed, it is important not to sleep late in the morning, nap more than an hour, sleep during the evening, or go to bed early the following night. Instead, restricting sleep to normal bedtime hours avoids fragmenting sleep rhythms (Shneerson, 2005).

3. **Paradoxical Intention.** Another helpful approach is to remove the pressures of *trying* to go to sleep. Instead, the goal becomes trying to keep the eyes open (in the dark) and stay awake as long as possible (Nau & Lichstein, 2005). This allows sleep to come unexpectedly and lowers performance anxiety (Espie, 2002).

4. **Relaxation.** Some insomniacs lower their arousal before sleep by using a physical or mental strategy for relaxing, such as progressive muscle relaxation (see Chapter 13), meditation, or blotting out worries with calming images. It is also helpful to schedule time in the early evening to write down worries or concerns and plan what to do about them the next day, in order to set them aside before going to bed.

5. **Exercise.** Strenuous exercise during the day promotes sleep. It is best if done about 6 hours before bedtime (Maas, 1999). However, exercise in the evening is helpful only if it is very light.

6. **Food intake.** What you eat can affect how easily you get to sleep. Eating starchy foods increases the amount of *tryptophan* (TRIP-tuh-fan: an amino acid) reaching the brain. More tryptophan, in turn, increases the amount of serotonin in the brain, which is associated with relaxation, a positive mood, and sleepiness. Thus, to promote sleep, try eating a starchy snack, such as cookies, bread, pasta, oatmeal,

Stimulus control Linking a particular response with specific stimuli.

pretzels, or dry cereal. If you really want to drop the bomb on insomnia, try eating a baked potato (which may be the world's largest sleeping pill!) (Sahelian, 1998).

7. **Stimulants.** Stimulants such as coffee and cigarettes should be avoided.

Sleepwalking and Sleeptalking

Sleepwalking is eerie and fascinating. **Somnambulists** (som-NAM-bue-lists: those who sleepwalk) avoid obstacles, descend stairways, and on rare occasions may step out of windows or in front of automobiles. The sleepwalker's eyes are usually open, but a blank face and shuffling feet reveal that the person is still asleep. If you find someone sleepwalking, you should gently guide the person back to bed. Awakening a sleepwalker does no harm, but it is not necessary.

Does sleepwalking occur during dreaming? No. Remember that people are normally immobilized during REM sleep. EEG studies have shown that somnambulism occurs during NREM stages 3 and 4 (Stein & Ferber, 2001). **Sleeptalking** also occurs mostly in NREM stages of sleep. The link with deep sleep explains why sleeptalking makes little sense and why sleepwalkers are confused and remember little when awakened (DSM-IV-TR, 2000).

Nightmares and Night Terrors

Stage 4 sleep is also the realm of night terrors. These frightening episodes are quite different from ordinary nightmares. A **nightmare** is simply a bad dream that takes place during REM sleep. Frequently occurring nightmares (one a week or more) are associated with higher levels of psychological distress (Levin & Fireman, 2002). During stage 4 **night terrors,** a person suffers total panic and may hallucinate frightening dream images into the bedroom. An attack may last 15 or 20 minutes. When it is over, the person awakens drenched in sweat but only vaguely remembers the terror. Because night terrors occur during NREM sleep (when the body is not immobilized), victims may sit up, scream, get out of bed, or run around the room. Victims remember little afterward. (Other family members, however, may have a story to tell.) Night terrors are most common in childhood, but they continue to plague about 2 out of every 100 adults (Kataria, 2004; Ohayon, Guilleminault, & Priest, 1999).

How to Eliminate a Nightmare

Is there any way to stop a recurring nightmare? A bad nightmare can be worse than any horror movie. It's easy to leave a theater, but we often remain trapped in terrifying dreams. Nevertheless, most nightmares can be banished by following three simple steps. First, write down your nightmare, describing it in detail. Next, change the dream any way you wish, being sure to spell out the details of the new dream. The third step is *imagery rehearsal,* in which you mentally rehearse the changed dream before you fall asleep again (Krakow & Zadra, 2006). Imagery rehearsal may work because it makes upsetting dreams familiar while a person is awake and feeling safe. Or perhaps it mentally "re-programs" future dream content. In any case, the technique has helped many people (Krakow & Krakow, 2002).

Sleep Apnea

Some sage once said, "Laugh and the whole world laughs with you; snore and you sleep alone." Nightly "wood sawing" is often harmless, but it can signal a serious problem. A person who snores loudly, with short silences and loud gasps or snorts, may suffer from apnea (AP-nee-ah: interrupted breathing). In **sleep apnea,** breathing stops for periods of 20 seconds to 2 minutes. As the need for oxygen becomes intense, the person wakes a little and gulps in air. She or he then settles back to sleep. But soon, breathing stops again. This cycle is repeated hundreds of times a night. As you might guess, apnea victims are extremely sleepy during the day (Collop, 2005).

Somnambulism Sleepwalking; occurs during NREM sleep.

Sleeptalking Speaking that occurs during NREM sleep.

Nightmare A bad dream that occurs during REM sleep.

Night terror A state of panic during NREM sleep.

Sleep apnea Repeated interruption of breathing during sleep.

What causes sleep apnea? Some cases occur because the brain stops sending signals to the diaphragm to maintain breathing. Another cause is blockage of the upper air passages. The most effective treatments are the use of a CPAP (continuous positive airway pressure) mask to aid breathing during sleep, weight loss, and surgery for breathing obstructions (Collop, 2005).

SIDS

Sleep apnea is suspected as one cause of **sudden infant death syndrome (SIDS),** or "crib death." Each year 1 out of every 500 babies is a victim of SIDS. In the "typical" crib death, a slightly premature or small baby with some signs of a cold or cough is bundled up and put to bed. A short time later, parents find the child has died. A baby deprived of air will normally struggle to begin breathing again. However, SIDS babies seem to have a weak arousal reflex. This prevents them from changing positions and resuming breathing after an episode of apnea (Horne et al., 2001).

Babies at risk for SIDS must be carefully watched for the first 6 months of life. To aid parents in this task, a special monitor may be used that sounds an alarm when breathing or pulse becomes weak (▶▶Fig. 5.6). The list that follows gives some danger signals for SIDS.

- The mother is a teenager.
- The baby is premature.
- The baby has a shrill, high-pitched cry.
- The baby engages in "snoring," breath-holding, or frequent awakening at night.
- The baby breathes mainly through an open mouth.
- The baby remains passive when its face rolls into a pillow or blanket.
- The baby's bed contains soft objects such as pillows, quilts, comforters, or sheepskins.
- Parents or other adults in the home are smokers.

"Back to Sleep"

Pop quiz: Should babies be placed face down or face up in bed? Sleeping position is another major risk factor for SIDS. Healthy infants are better off sleeping on their backs or sides. (Premature babies, those with respiratory problems, and those who often vomit may need to sleep face down. Ask a pediatrician for guidance.) At least one third of all SIDS cases involve babies who were placed face down. Remember, "*back* to sleep" is the safest position for most infants (Hauck et al., 2002).

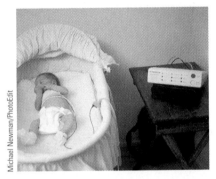

Michael Newman/PhotoEdit

▶▶**FIGURE 5.6** Infants at risk for SIDS are often attached to devices that monitor breathing and heart rate during sleep. An alarm sounds to alert parents if either pulse or respiration falters. SIDS rarely occurs after an infant is 1 year old. Babies at risk for SIDS should be placed on their sides or on their backs.

DREAMS—A SEPARATE REALITY?

>SURVEY QUESTION< *Do dreams have meaning?*

When REM sleep was discovered in 1952, it ushered in a "Golden Era" of dream inquiry. To conclude our discussion of sleep, let's consider some age-old questions about dreaming.

Does everyone dream? Do dreams occur in an instant? Most people dream four or five times a night, but not all people remember their dreams. "Non-dreamers" are often surprised by their dreams when first awakened during REM sleep. Dreams are usually spaced about 90 minutes apart. The first dream lasts only about 10 minutes; the last averages 30 minutes and may run as long as 50. Dreams, therefore, occur in real time, not as a "flash" (Shafton, 1995).

REM Sleep Revisited

How important is REM sleep? Is it essential for normal functioning? To answer these questions, sleep expert William Dement awakened volunteers each time they entered REM sleep. Soon, their need for "dream time" grew more urgent. By the fifth night, many had to be

Sudden infant death syndrome (SIDS)
The sudden, unexplained death of an apparently healthy infant.

awakened 20 or 30 times to prevent REM sleep. When the volunteers were finally allowed to sleep undisturbed, they dreamed extra amounts. This effect, called a **REM rebound,** explains why alcoholics have horrible nightmares after they quit drinking. Alcohol suppresses REM sleep and sets up a powerful rebound when it is withdrawn. It's worth remembering that alcohol, like other depressant drugs, greatly reduces sleep quality (Stein & Friedmann, 2005).

Dement's volunteers complained of memory lapses, poor concentration, and anxiety. For a while, it was thought that people deprived of REM sleep might go crazy. But later experiments showed that missing *any* sleep stage can cause a rebound for that stage. In general, daytime disturbances are related to the *total amount* of sleep lost, not to the *type* of sleep lost (Devoto et al., 1999).

The Value of REM Sleep

What then, is the purpose of REM sleep? Early in life, REM sleep may stimulate the developing brain. Newborn babies spend a hearty 8 or 9 hours a day in REM sleep. That's about 50 percent of their total sleep time. In adulthood, REM sleep may prevent sensory deprivation during sleep, and it may help us process emotional events. REM sleep also seems to help us sort and integrate memories, especially memories about strategies that help us solve problems (Walker & Stickgold, 2006). Speaking very loosely, it's as if the dreaming brain were reviewing messages left on a telephone answering machine, to decide which are worth keeping. During the day, when information is streaming in, the brain may be too busy to efficiently select useful memories. When the conscious brain is "off-line" we are better able to build new memories. Although we have much to learn, it's clear that REM sleep and dreaming are valuable for keeping the brain in good working order.

Dream Worlds

Most dreams reflect everyday events (Hall, 1966; Pesant & Zadra, 2006). For example, athletes dream about athletic activities of the previous day (Erlacher & Schredl, 2004). The favorite dream setting is a familiar room in a house. Action usually takes place between the dreamer and two or three other emotionally important people—friends, enemies, loved ones, or employers. Dream actions are also mostly familiar: running, jumping, riding, sitting, talking, and watching. About half of all dreams have sexual elements. Dreams of flying, floating, and falling occur less frequently.

Are most dreams happy or sad? If you ask people in the morning what they dreamed about, they mention more unpleasant emotions than pleasant emotions (Merritt et al., 1994). However, it may be that dreams of fear, anger, or sadness are easier to remember. When people are awakened during REM sleep, they report equal numbers of positive and negative emotions (Fosse, Stickgold, & Hobson, 2001).

Dream Theories

How meaningful are dreams? Most theorists agree that dreams reflect our waking thoughts, fantasies, and emotions (Beck, 2004). Thus, the real question might be, How deep should we dig in interpreting dreams? Some theorists believe that dreams have deeply hidden meanings. Others regard dreams as nearly meaningless. Let's examine both views.

Psychodynamic Dream Theory

Sigmund Freud's landmark book, *The Interpretation of Dreams* (1900), first advanced the idea that many dreams are based on *wish fulfillment* (an expression of unconscious desires). Thus, a student who is angry with a teacher might dream of embarrassing the teacher in class; a lonely person may dream of romance; or a hungry child may dream of food.

REM rebound The occurrence of extra rapid eye movement sleep following REM sleep deprivation.

Freud's **psychodynamic theory** of dreaming emphasizes internal conflicts and unconscious forces. Although many of his ideas are attractive, there is evidence against them. For example, volunteers in a study of starvation showed no particular increase in dreams about food and eating. In general, dreams show few signs of directly expressing hidden wishes (Domhoff, 2003; Fisher & Greenberg, 1996).

Freud's response to critics, no doubt, would have been that dreams rarely express needs so directly. One of Freud's key insights is that ideas in dreams are expressed as *images* or pictures, rather than in words. Freud believed that dreams express unconscious desires and conflicts as disguised **dream symbols** (images that have deeper symbolic meaning). For instance, death might be symbolized by a journey, children by small animals, or sexual intercourse by horseback riding or dancing. Similarly, a woman sexually attracted to her best friend's husband might dream of stealing her friend's wedding ring and placing it on her own hand, an indirect symbol of her true desires.

Do all dreams have hidden meanings? Probably not. Even Freud realized that some dreams are trivial "day residues" or carryovers from ordinary waking events. On the other hand, dreams do tend to reflect a person's current concerns, so Freud wasn't entirely wrong.

The Activation-Synthesis Hypothesis

Psychiatrists Allan Hobson and Robert McCarley have a radically different view of dreaming. They believe that during REM sleep, brain cells are activated that normally control eye movements, balance, and actions. However, messages from the cells are blocked from reaching the body, so no movement occurs. Nevertheless, the cells continue to tell higher brain areas of their activities. Struggling to interpret this information, the brain searches through stored memories and manufactures a dream (Hobson, 2000, 2005).

How does that help explain dream content? Let's use the classic chase dream as an example. In such dreams we feel we are running but not going anywhere. This occurs because the brain is told the body is running, but it gets no feedback from the motionless legs. To make sense of this information, the brain creates a chase drama. A similar process probably explains dreams of floating or flying.

Hobson and McCarley call their view the **activation-synthesis hypothesis.** Hobson explains that several parts of the brain are "turned on" (activated) during REM sleep. This triggers sensations, motor commands, and memories. The cortex of the brain, which also becomes more active during REM sleep, synthesizes this activity into stories and visual images. However, frontal areas of the cortex, which control higher mental abilities, are mostly shut down during REM sleep. This explains why dreams are more primitive and more bizarre than daytime thoughts (Hobson, 2000). Viewed this way, dreams are merely a different type of thinking that occurs during sleep (McCarley, 1998).

Note that the activation-synthesis hypothesis doesn't rule out the idea that dreams have meaning. Because dreams are created from memories and past experiences, they can tell us quite a lot about each person's mental life, emotions, and concerns (Hobson, 2000). However, many psychologists continue to believe that dreams have deeper meaning (White & Taytroe, 2003; Wilkinson, 2006).

There seems to be little doubt that dreams can make a difference in our lives: Veteran sleep researcher William Dement once dreamed that he had lung cancer. In the dream a doctor told Dement he would die soon. At the time, Dement was smoking two packs of cigarettes a day. He says, "I will never forget the surprise, joy, and exquisite relief of waking up. I felt reborn." Dement quit smoking the following day. (For more information about dreaming, see the "Psychology in Action" section later in this chapter.)

Kactus Foto/SuperStock

According to Freudian theory, dream imagery often has symbolic meaning. How would you interpret Chilean artist Matias Morales's *Dream in Blue?* The fact that dreams don't have a single unambiguous meaning is one of the shortcomings of Freudian dream theory.

Psychodynamic theory Any theory of behavior that emphasizes internal conflicts, motives, and unconscious forces.

Dream symbols Images in dreams that serve as visible signs of hidden ideas, desires, impulses, emotions, relationships, and so forth.

Activation-synthesis hypothesis An attempt to explain how dream content is affected by motor commands in the brain that occur during sleep, but are not carried out.

Reflect

Almost everyone suffers from insomnia at least occasionally. Are any of the techniques for combating insomnia similar to strategies you have discovered on your own?

How many sleep disturbances can you name (including those listed in ▪ Table 5.1)? Are there any that you have experienced? Which do you think would be most disruptive?

Do you think the activation-synthesis theory provides an adequate explanation of your own dreams? Have you had dreams that seem to reflect Freudian wish fulfillment? Do you think your dreams have symbolic meaning?

Learning Check

1. Eating a snack that is nearly all starch can promote sleep because it increases _____ in the brain.

   a. beta waves
   b. tryptophan
   c. EEG activity
   d. hypnic cycling

2. Night terrors, sleepwalking, and sleeptalking all occur during stage 1, NREM sleep. T or F?

3. Sleep _____ is suspected as one cause of SIDS.

4. Which of the following is *not* a behavioral remedy for insomnia?

   a. daily hypersomnia
   b. stimulus control
   c. progressive relaxation
   d. paradoxical intention

5. The favored setting for dreams is

   a. work
   b. school
   c. outdoors or unfamiliar places
   d. familiar rooms

6. Sorting and integrating memories is one function of

   a. activation-synthesis cycles
   b. REM sleep
   c. deep sleep
   d. NREM sleep

7. According to the activation-synthesis model of dreaming, dreams are constructed from _____ to explain messages received from nerve cells controlling eye movement, balance, and bodily activity.

Critical Thinking

8. Even without being told that somnambulism is an NREM event, you could have predicted that sleepwalking doesn't occur during dreaming. Why?

Answers

1. b 2. F 3. apnea 4. a 5. c 6. d 7. memories 8. Because people are immobilized during REM sleep and REM sleep is strongly associated with dreaming. This makes it unlikely that sleepwalkers are acting out dreams.

HYPNOSIS—LOOK INTO MY EYES

>SURVEY QUESTION< *How is hypnosis done, and what are its limitations?*

"Your body is becoming heavy. You can barely keep your eyes open. You are so tired you can't move. Relax. Let go. Relax. Close your eyes and relax." These are the last words a textbook should ever say to you, and the first a hypnotist might say.

Interest in hypnosis began in the 1700s with Austrian doctor Franz Mesmer, whose name gave us the term *mesmerize* (to hypnotize). Mesmer believed he could cure disease with magnets. Mesmer's strange "treatments" are related to hypnosis because they actually relied on the power of suggestion, not magnetism (Waterfield, 2002). For a time, Mesmer enjoyed quite a following. In the end, however, his theories of "animal magnetism" were rejected and he was branded a fraud.

The term *hypnosis* was later coined by English surgeon James Braid. The Greek word *hypnos* means "sleep," and Braid used it to describe the hypnotic state. Today we know that hypnosis is *not* sleep. Confusion about this point remains because some hypnotists give the suggestion, "Sleep, sleep." However, EEG patterns recorded during hypnosis are different from those observed when a person is asleep or pretending to be hypnotized (Barabasz, 2000).

Theories of Hypnosis

If hypnosis isn't sleep, then what is it? That's a good question. **Hypnosis** is often defined as an altered state of consciousness, characterized by narrowed attention and an increased openness to suggestion (Kallio & Revonsuo, 2003; Kosslyn et al., 2000). Notice that this definition assumes hypnosis is a distinct state of consciousness.

The best-known *state theory* of hypnosis was proposed by Ernest Hilgard (1904–2001), who argued that hypnosis causes a *dissociative state*, or "split" in awareness. To illustrate, he asked

Hypnosis An altered state of consciousness characterized by narrowed attention and increased suggestibility.

Swinging Suggestions

Here's a demonstration you can use to gain insight into hypnosis. Tie a short length of string (about 6 inches) to a small, heavy object, such as a ring or a small metal nut. Hold the ring at eye level, about a foot from your face. Concentrate on the ring and notice that it will begin to move, ever so slightly. As it does, focus all your attention on the ring. Narrow your attention to a beam of energy and mentally push the ring away from you. Each time the ring swings away, push on it, using only mental force. Then release it and let it swing back toward you. Continue to mentally push and release the ring until it is swinging freely. For the best results, try this now, before reading more.

Did the ring move? If it did, you used *autosuggestion* to influence your own behavior in a subtle way. Sug-

gestions that the ring would swing caused your hand to make tiny micromuscular movements. These, in turn, caused the ring to move—no special mental powers or supernatural forces are involved.

As is true of hypnotic suggestion, the ring's movement probably seemed to be automatic. Obviously, you could just intentionally swing the ring. However, if you responded to suggestion, the movement seemed to happen without any effort on your part. In the same way, when people are hypnotized, their actions seem to occur without any voluntary intent. Incidentally, autosuggestion likely underlies other phenomena such as how Ouija boards spell out answers to questions despite no apparent conscious interference. Autosuggestion also plays a role in many forms of self-therapy.

Dennis Coon

hypnotized subjects to plunge one hand into a painful bath of ice water. Subjects told to feel no pain said they felt none. The same subjects were then asked if there was any part of their mind that did feel pain. With their free hand, many wrote, "It hurts," or "Stop it, you're hurting me," while they continued to act pain-free (Hilgard, 1977, 1994). Thus, one part of the hypnotized person says there is no pain and acts as if there is none. Another part, which Hilgard calls the *hidden observer,* is aware of the pain but remains in the background. The **hidden observer** is a detached part of the hypnotized person's awareness that silently observes events.

In contrast, *nonstate theorists* argue that hypnosis is not a distinct state at all. Instead it is merely a blend of conformity, relaxation, imagination, obedience, and role-playing (Kirsch, 2005). For example, many theorists believe that all hypnosis is really self-hypnosis (autosuggestion). From this perspective, a hypnotist merely helps another person to follow a series of suggestions. These suggestions, in turn, alter sensations, perceptions, thoughts, feelings, and behaviors (Lynn & Kirsch, 2006). (See "Swinging Suggestions.")

Regardless of which theoretical approach finally prevails, hypnosis can be explained by normal principles. It is not mysterious or "magical," despite what stage hypnotists might have you think.

Stage Hypnosis

On stage the hypnotist intones, "When I count to three, you will imagine that you are on a train to Disneyland and growing younger and younger as the train approaches." Responding to these suggestions, grown men and women begin to giggle and squirm like children on their way to a circus.

How do stage entertainers use hypnosis to get people to do strange things? They don't. Little or no hypnosis is needed to do a good hypnosis act. **Stage hypnosis** is often merely a simulation of hypnotic effects. Stage hypnotists make use of several features of the stage setting to perform their act (Barber, 2000).

1. **Waking suggestibility.** We are all more or less open to suggestion, but on stage people are unusually cooperative because they don't want to "spoil the act." As a result, they will readily follow almost any instruction given by the entertainer.

2. **Selection of responsive subjects.** Participants in stage hypnotism (all *volunteers*) are first "hypnotized" as a group. Then, anyone who doesn't yield to instructions is eliminated.

Hidden observer A detached part of the hypnotized person's awareness that silently observes events.

Stage hypnosis Use of hypnosis to entertain; often, merely a simulation of hypnosis for that purpose.

Dennis Coon

▸▸**FIGURE 5.7** Arrange three chairs as shown. Have someone recline as shown. Ask him to lift slightly while you remove the middle chair. Accept the applause gracefully! (Concerning hypnosis and similar phenomena, the moral, of course, is "Suspend judgment until you have something solid to stand on.")

3. **The hypnosis label disinhibits.** Once a person has been labeled "hypnotized," she or he can sing, dance, act silly, or whatever, without fear or embarrassment. On stage, being "hypnotized" takes away personal responsibility for one's actions.

4. **The hypnotist as a "director."** After volunteers loosen up and respond to a few suggestions, they find that they are suddenly the stars of the show. Audience response to the antics on stage brings out the "ham" in many people. All the "hypnotist" needs to do is direct the action.

5. **The stage hypnotist uses tricks.** Stage hypnosis is about 50 percent taking advantage of the situation and 50 percent deception. One of the more impressive stage tricks is to rigidly suspend a person between two chairs. This is astounding only because the audience does not question it. Anyone can do it, as is shown in the photographs and instructions in ▸▸Figure 5.7. Try it!

To summarize, hypnosis is real, and it can significantly alter private experience. Hypnosis is a useful tool in a variety of settings. Nightclubs, however, are not one of these settings. Stage "hypnotists" entertain; they rarely hypnotize. Let's conclude our exploration of hypnosis by looking into how it is done and what effects it has.

The Reality of Hypnosis

How is hypnosis done? Could I be hypnotized against my will? Hypnotists use many different methods. Still, all techniques encourage a person (1) to focus attention on what is being said, (2) to relax and feel tired, (3) to "let go" and accept suggestions easily, and (4) to use vivid imagination (Druckman & Bjork, 1994). Basically, you must cooperate to become hypnotized.

What does it feel like to be hypnotized? You might be surprised at some of your actions during hypnosis. You also might have mild feelings of floating, sinking, anesthesia, or separation from your body. Personal experiences vary widely. A key element in hypnosis is the **basic suggestion effect** (a tendency of hypnotized persons to carry out suggested actions as if they were involuntary). Hypnotized persons feel like their actions and experiences are *automatic*—they seem to happen without effort. Here is how one person described his hypnotic session:

> I felt lethargic, my eyes going out of focus and wanting to close. My hands felt real light. . . . I felt I was sinking deeper into the chair. . . . I felt like I wanted to relax more and more. . . . My responses were more automatic. I didn't have to *wish* to do things so much or *want* to do them . . . I just did them. . . . I felt floating . . . very close to sleep. (Hilgard, 1968)

Contrary to the way hypnosis is portrayed in movies, hypnotized people generally remain in control of their behavior and aware of what is going on. For instance, most people will

Basic suggestion effect The tendency of hypnotized persons to carry out suggested actions as if they were involuntary.

■ Table 5.2 **Standard Hypnotic Susceptibility Scale**	
Suggested Behavior	**Criterion of Passing**
1. Postural sway	Falls without forcing
2. Eye closure	Closes eyes without forcing
3. Hand lowering (left)	Lowers at least 6 inches by end of 10 seconds
4. Immobilization (right arm)	Arm rises less than 1 inch in 10 seconds
5. Finger lock	Incomplete separation of fingers at end of 10 seconds
6. Arm rigidity (left arm)	Less than 2 inches of arm bending in 10 seconds
7. Hands moving together	Hands at least as close as 6 inches after 10 seconds
8. Verbal inhibition (name)	Name unspoken in 10 seconds
9. Hallucination (fly)	Any movement, grimacing, acknowledgment of effect
10. Eye catalepsy	Eyes remain closed at end of 10 seconds
11. Posthypnotic (changes chairs)	Any partial movement response
12. Amnesia test	Three or fewer items recalled

Source: Adapted from Weitzenhoffer & Hilgard, 1959.

not act out hypnotic suggestions that they consider immoral or repulsive (such as disrobing in public or harming someone) (Kirsch & Lynn, 1995).

Hypnotic Susceptibility

Can everyone be hypnotized? About 8 people out of 10 can be hypnotized, but only 4 out of 10 will be good hypnotic subjects. People who are imaginative and prone to fantasy are often highly responsive to hypnosis (Kallio & Revonsuo, 2003). But people who lack these traits may also be hypnotized. If you are willing to be hypnotized, chances are good that you could be. Hypnosis depends more on the efforts and abilities of the hypnotized person than the skills of the hypnotist. But make no mistake, people who are hypnotized are not merely faking their responses (Perugini et al., 1998).

Hypnotic susceptibility refers to how easily a person can become hypnotized. It is measured by giving a series of suggestions and counting the number of times a person responds. A typical hypnotic test is the *Stanford Hypnotic Susceptibility Scale,* shown in ■ Table 5.2. In the test, various suggestions are made, and the person's response is noted. For instance, you might be told that your left arm is becoming more and more rigid and that it will not bend. If you can't bend your arm during the next 10 seconds, you have shown susceptibility to hypnotic suggestions. (Also see ▸▸Fig. 5.8.)

Effects of Hypnosis

What can (and cannot) be achieved with hypnosis? Many abilities have been tested during hypnosis, leading to the following conclusions (Burgess & Kirsch, 1999; Chaves, 2000):

1. **Superhuman acts of strength.** Hypnosis has no more effect on physical strength than instructions that encourage a person to make his or her best effort.
2. **Memory.** There is some evidence that hypnosis can enhance memory (Wagstaff et al., 2004). However, it frequently increases the number of false memories as well. For this reason, many states now bar persons from testifying in court if they were hypnotized to improve their memory of a crime they witnessed.
3. **Amnesia.** A person told not to remember something heard during hypnosis may claim not to remember. In some instances this may be nothing more than a deliberate attempt to avoid thinking about specific ideas. However, brief memory loss of this type actually does seem to occur (Barnier, McConkey, & Wright, 2004).
4. **Pain relief.** Hypnosis can relieve pain (Keefe, Abernethy, & Campbell, 2005). It can be especially useful when chemical painkillers are ineffective. For instance, hypnosis can reduce phantom limb pain (Oakley, Whitman, & Halligan, 2002). (As discussed

Dennis Coon

▸▸**FIGURE 5.8** In one test of hypnotizability, subjects attempt to pull their hands apart after hearing suggestions that their fingers are "locked" together.

Hypnotic susceptibility One's capacity for becoming hypnotized.

in Chapter 4, amputees sometimes feel phantom pain that seems to come from a missing limb.)

5. **Age regression.** Given the proper suggestions, some hypnotized people appear to "regress" to childhood. However, most theorists now believe that "age-regressed" subjects are only acting out a suggested role.

6. **Sensory changes.** Hypnotic suggestions concerning sensations are among the most effective. Given the proper instructions, a person can be made to smell a small bottle of ammonia and respond as if it were a wonderful perfume. It is also possible to alter color vision, hearing sensitivity, time sense, perception of illusions, and many other sensory responses.

Hypnosis is a valuable tool. It can help people relax, feel less pain, and make better progress in therapy (Chapman, 2006). Generally, hypnosis is more successful at changing subjective experience than it is at modifying behaviors such as smoking or overeating.

MEDITATION AND SENSORY DEPRIVATION—CHILLING, THE HEALTHY WAY

>SURVEY QUESTION< *What are meditation and sensory deprivation? Do they have any benefits?*

Throughout history, meditation and sensory deprivation have been widely used means of altering consciousness by relaxing. Let's see what they have in common and how they differ.

Meditation

Meditation is a mental exercise used to alter consciousness. In general, meditation focuses attention and interrupts the typical flow of thoughts, worries, and analysis. People who use meditation to reduce stress often report less daily physical tension and anxiety (Andresen, 2000). PET and fMRI scans reveal changes in the activity of the frontal lobes of the brain during meditation, which suggests that it may represent a distinct state of consciousness (Cahn & Polich, 2006).

Meditation takes two major forms. In **concentrative meditation,** you attend to a single focal point, such as an object, a thought, or your own breathing. In contrast, **mindfulness meditation** is "open," or expansive. In this case, you widen your attention to embrace a total, nonjudgmental awareness of the world (Lazar, 2005). An example is losing all self-consciousness while walking in the wilderness with a quiet and receptive mind. Although it may not seem so, mindfulness meditation is more difficult to attain than concentrative meditation. For this reason, we will discuss concentrative meditation as a practical self-control method.

Performing Concentrative Meditation

How is concentrative meditation done? The basic idea is to sit still and quietly focus on some external object or on a repetitive internal stimulus, such as your own breathing or humming (Blackmore, 2004). As an alternative, you can silently repeat a *mantra* (a word used as the focus of attention in concentrative meditation). Typical mantras are smooth, flowing sounds that are easily repeated. A widely used mantra is the word "om." A mantra could also be any pleasant word or a phrase from a familiar song, poem, or prayer. If other thoughts arise as you repeat a mantra, just return attention to it as often as necessary to maintain meditation.

The Relaxation Response

Medical researcher Herbert Benson believes that the core of meditation is the **relaxation response**—an innate physiological pattern that opposes your body's fight-or-flight mechanisms. Benson feels, quite simply, that most of us have forgotten how to relax deeply. People

Meditation A mental exercise for producing relaxation or heightened awareness.

Concentrative meditation Mental exercise based on attending to a single object or thought.

Mindfulness meditation Mental exercise based on widening attention to become aware of everything experienced at any given moment.

Relaxation response The pattern of internal bodily changes that occurs at times of relaxation.

in his experiments have learned to produce the relaxation response by following these instructions:

> Sit quietly in a comfortable position. Close your eyes. Deeply relax all your muscles, beginning at your feet and progressing up to your face. Keep them deeply relaxed. Breathe through your nose. Become aware of your breathing. As you breathe out, say the word "one" silently to yourself. Do not worry about whether you are successful in achieving a deep level of relaxation. Maintain a passive attitude and permit relaxation to occur at its own pace. Expect distracting thoughts. When these distracting thoughts occur, ignore them and continue repeating "one." (Adapted from Benson, 1977; Lazar et al., 2000.)

As a stress-control technique, meditation may be a good choice for people who find it difficult to "turn off" upsetting thoughts when they need to relax. In one study, a group of college students that received just 90 minutes of training in the relaxation response experienced greatly reduced stress levels (Deckro et al., 2002). The physical benefits of meditation include lowered heart rate, blood pressure, muscle tension, and other signs of stress (Lazar et al., 2000) as well as improved immune system activity (Davidson et al., 2003).

According to Roger Walsh and Shauna Shapiro (2006), meditation is about more than just relaxing. Practiced regularly, meditation may foster mental well-being and the development of desired psychological skills such as clarity, concentration, and calm. In this sense, meditation may share much in common with psychotherapy. Indeed, research has shown that mindfulness meditation lessens the symptoms of a variety of psychological disorders, from insomnia to anxiety disorders, as well as reducing aggression and the illegal use of psychoactive drugs (Walsh & Shapiro, 2006). Regular meditation may even help develop self-awareness and maturity (Travis, Arenander, & DuBois, 2004).

Sensory Deprivation

The relaxation response can also be produced by brief sensory deprivation. **Sensory deprivation** (SD) refers to any major reduction in the amount or variety of sensory stimulation.

What happens when stimulation is greatly reduced? A hint comes from reports by prisoners in solitary confinement, arctic explorers, high-altitude pilots, long-distance truck drivers, and radar operators. When faced with limited or monotonous stimulation, people sometimes have bizarre sensations, dangerous lapses in attention, and wildly distorted perceptions. Oddly enough, brief periods of sensory restriction can be very relaxing.

Psychologists have explored the possible benefits of sensory restriction using small isolation tanks like the one pictured in ▸▸Figure 5.9. An hour or two spent in a flotation tank, for instance, causes a large drop in blood pressure, muscle tension, and other signs of stress (van Dierendonck & Te Nijenhuis, 2005). Of course, it could be argued that a warm bath has the same effect. Nevertheless, brief sensory deprivation appears to be one of the surest ways to induce deep relaxation (Suedfeld & Borrie, 1999).

Like meditation, sensory restriction may also help with more than relaxation. Mild sensory deprivation can help people quit smoking, lose weight, and reduce their use of alcohol and drugs (van Dierendonck & Te Nijenhuis, 2005). Psychologist Peter Suedfeld calls such benefits Restricted Environmental Stimulation Therapy, or **REST.** Deep relaxation makes people more open to suggestion, and sensory restriction interrupts habitual behavior patterns. As a result, REST can "loosen" belief systems and make it easier to change bad habits (Suedfeld & Borrie, 1999).

REST also shows promise as a way to stimulate creative thinking (Norlander, Anonymous, & Archer, 1998). Other researchers have reported that REST sessions can enhance performance in skilled sports, such as gymnastics, tennis, basketball, darts, and marksman-

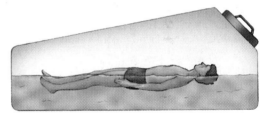

▸▸**FIGURE 5.9** A sensory isolation chamber. Small flotation tanks like the one pictured have been used by psychologists to study the effects of mild sensory deprivation. Subjects float in darkness and silence. The shallow body-temperature water contains hundreds of pounds of Epsom salts, so that subjects float near the surface. Mild sensory deprivation produces deep relaxation.

Sensory deprivation Any major reduction in the amount or variety of sensory stimulation.

REST Restricted Environmental Stimulation Therapy.

ship (Druckman & Bjork, 1994; Norlander, Bergman, & Archer, 1999). There is also evidence that REST can relieve chronic pain and reduce stress (Kjellgren et al., 2001). Clearly, there is much yet to be learned from studying "nothingness."

Summary

To summarize, research suggests that meditation and sensory deprivation are ways to elicit the relaxation response. For many people, sitting quietly and "resting" can be as effective. Similar stress reduction occurs when people set aside time daily to engage in other restful activities, such as muscle relaxation, positive daydreaming, and even leisure reading. However, if you are the type of person who finds it difficult to ignore upsetting thoughts, then concentrative meditation might be a good way to promote relaxation. Practiced regularly, meditation and REST may even help improve overall mental health—something almost everyone could use in our fast-paced society.

Study Break Hypnosis, Meditation, and Sensory Deprivation

Reflect

How have your beliefs about hypnosis changed after reading the preceding section? Can you think of specific examples in which hypnosis was misrepresented? For example, in high school assemblies, stage acts, movies, or TV dramas?

Various activities can produce the relaxation response. When do you experience states of deep relaxation, coupled with a sense of serene awareness? What similarities do these occurrences have to meditation or sensory deprivation?

Learning Check

1. The term *hypnotism* was coined by a British surgeon named
   a. Franz Mesmer   b. James Stanford
   c. T. A. Kreskin   d. James Braid

2. Only 4 out of 10 people can be hypnotized. T or F?

3. Which of the following can most definitely be achieved with hypnosis?
   a. unusual strength   b. pain relief
   c. improved memory   d. sleep-like brain waves

4. The focus of attention in concentrative meditation is "open," or expansive. T or F?

5. Mantras are words said silently to oneself to end a session of meditation. T or F?

6. The most immediate benefit of meditation appears to be its capacity for producing the relaxation response. T or F?

7. Prolonged periods of extreme sensory deprivation lower anxiety and induce deep relaxation. T or F?

Critical Thinking

8. What kind of control group would you need in order to identify the true effects of hypnosis?

9. Regular meditators report lower levels of stress and a greater sense of well-being. What other explanations must we eliminate before this effect can be regarded as genuine?

Answers

1. d 2. F 3. b 4. F 5. F 6. T 7. F 8. Most experiments on hypnosis include a control group in which people are asked to simulate being hypnotized. Without such controls, the tendency of subjects to cooperate with experimenters makes it difficult to identify true hypnotic effects. 9. Studies on the effects of meditation must control for the placebo effect and the fact that those who choose to learn meditation may not be a representative sample of the general population. Studies controlling for such factors still show that meditation is beneficial (Pagano & Warrenburg, 1983).

DRUG-ALTERED CONSCIOUSNESS—THE HIGH AND LOW OF IT

>SURVEY QUESTION< *What are the effects of the more commonly used psychoactive drugs?*

The surest way to alter human consciousness is to administer a **psychoactive drug** (a substance capable of altering attention, judgment, memory, time sense, self-control, emotion, or perception) (Julien, 2005). The fact that most Americans regularly use psy-

Psychoactive drug A substance capable of altering attention, memory, judgment, time sense, self-control, mood, or perception.

choactive drugs attests to the popularity of altering consciousness (don't forget that caffeine, alcohol, and nicotine are mildly psychoactive). Because of their profound effects, the more powerful psychoactive drugs are controlled substances. Nevertheless, more than 20 million Americans are currently illicit drug users (SAMHAS, 2005). Most psychoactive drugs can be placed on a scale ranging from stimulation to depression. A **stimulant** is a substance that increases activity in the body and nervous system. A **depressant** does the reverse. ⟩⟩Figure 5.10 shows various drugs and their approximate effects. A more complete summary of frequently abused psychoactive drugs is given in ▒ Table 5.3.

How Drugs Affect the Brain

How do drugs alter consciousness? Psychoactive drugs influence the activity of brain cells. Typically, drugs imitate or alter neurotransmitters, the chemicals that carry messages between brain cells. Some drugs, such as Ecstasy, amphetamine, and some antidepressants, cause more neurotransmitters to be released, increasing the activity of brain cells. Other drugs, such as cocaine, slow the removal of neurotransmitters after they are released. This prolongs the action of transmitter chemicals and typically has a stimulating effect. Other drugs, such as nicotine and opiates, directly stimulate brain cells by mimicking neurotransmitters. Another possibility is illustrated by alcohol and tranquilizers. These drugs affect certain types of brain cells that cause relaxation and relieve anxiety. Some drugs fill receptor sites on brain cells and block incoming messages. Other possibilities also exist, which is why drugs can have such a wide variety of effects on the brain (Julien, 2005).

All addictive drugs stimulate the brain's reward circuitry, producing feelings of pleasure. As one expert put it, addictive drugs fool brain-reward pathways: "As a result, the reward pathway signals, 'That felt good. Let's do it again. Let's remember exactly how we did it.'" This creates a compulsion to repeat the drug experience. It's the hook that eventually snares the addict (Restak, 2001). Adolescents are especially susceptible to addiction because brain systems that restrain risk-taking are not as mature as those that reward pleasure-seeking (Chambers, Taylor, & Potenza, 2003).

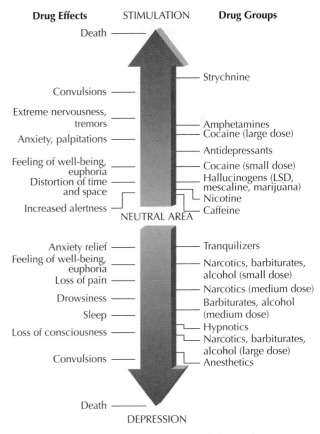

⟩⟩**FIGURE 5.10** Spectrum and continuum of drug action. Many drugs can be rated on a stimulation-depression scale according to their effects on the central nervous system. Although LSD, mescaline, and marijuana are listed here, the stimulation-depression scale is less relevant to these drugs. The principal characteristic of such hallucinogens is their mind-altering quality.

Dependence

Drug dependence falls into two broad categories. When a person compulsively uses a drug to maintain bodily comfort, a **physical dependence** (addiction) exists. Addiction occurs most often with drugs that cause **withdrawal symptoms** (physical illness that follows removal of a drug) (Julien, 2005). Withdrawal from drugs such as alcohol, barbiturates, and opiates can cause violent flu-like symptoms of nausea, vomiting, diarrhea, chills, sweating, and cramps. Addiction is often accompanied by a **drug tolerance** (reduced response to a drug). This leads users to take larger and larger doses to get the desired effect.

Persons who develop a **psychological dependence** feel that a drug is necessary to maintain feelings of comfort or well-being. Usually, they intensely crave the drug and its rewarding qualities (Winger et al., 2005). Psychological dependence can be just as powerful as physical addiction. That's why some psychologists define addiction as any compulsive habit pattern. By this definition, a person who has lost control over drug use, for

Stimulant A substance that increases activity in the body and nervous system.

Depressant A substance that decreases activity in the body and nervous system.

Physical dependence Physical addiction, as indicated by the presence of drug tolerance and withdrawal symptoms.

Withdrawal symptoms Physical illness and discomfort following the withdrawal of a drug.

Drug tolerance A reduction in the body's response to a drug.

Psychological dependence Drug dependence that is based primarily on emotional or psychological needs.

■ Table 5.3   Comparison of Psychoactive Drugs

Name	Classification	Medical Use	Usual Dose	Duration of Effect
Alcohol	Sedative-hypnotic	Solvent, antiseptic	Varies	1–4 hours
Amphetamines	Stimulant	Relief of mild depression, control of narcolepsy and hyperactivity	2.5–5 milligrams	4 hours
Barbiturates	Sedative-hypnotic	Sedation, relief of high blood pressure, anticonvulsant	50–100 milligrams	4 hours
Benzodiazepines	Anxiolytic (antianxiety drug)	Tranquilizer	2–100 milligrams	10 minutes–8 hours
Caffeine	Stimulant	Counteract depressant drugs, treatment of migraine headaches	Varies	Varies
Cocaine	Stimulant, local anesthetic	Local anesthesia	Varies	Varied, brief periods
Codeine	Narcotic	Ease pain and coughing	30 milligrams	4 hours
GHB	Sedative-hypnotic	Experimental treatment of narcolepsy, alcoholism	1–3 grams (powder)	1–3 hours
Heroin	Narcotic	Pain relief	Varies	4 hours
LSD	Hallucinogen	Experimental study of mental function, alcoholism	100–500 milligrams	10 hours
Marijuana (THC)	Relaxant, euphoriant; in high doses, hallucinogen	Treatment of glaucoma and side effects of chemotherapy	1–2 cigarettes	4 hours
MDMA	Stimulant/hallucinogen	None	125 milligrams	4–6 hours
Mescaline	Hallucinogen	None	350 micrograms	12 hours
Methadone	Narcotic	Pain relief	10 milligrams	4–6 hours
Morphine	Narcotic	Pain relief	15 milligrams	6 hours
PCP	Anesthetic	None	2–10 milligrams	4–6 hours, plus 12-hour recovery
Psilocybin	Hallucinogen	None	25 milligrams	6–8 hours
Tobacco (nicotine)	Stimulant	Emetic (nicotine)	Varies	Varies

Question marks indicate conflict of opinion. It should be noted that illicit drugs are frequently adulterated and thus pose unknown hazards to the user.

whatever reason, is addicted. In fact, most people who answer yes to both of the following questions have an alcohol or drug problem and should seek professional help (Brown et al., 1997):

- In the last year, did you ever drink or use drugs more than you meant to?
- Have you felt you wanted or needed to cut down on your drinking or drug use in the last year?

Effects Sought	Long-Term Symptoms	Physical Dependence Potential	Psychological Dependence Potential	Organic Damage Potential
Sense alteration, anxiety reduction, sociability	Cirrhosis, toxic psychosis, neurologic damage, addiction	Yes	Yes	Yes
Alertness, activeness	Loss of appetite, delusions, hallucinations, toxic psychosis	Yes	Yes	Yes
Anxiety reduction, euphoria	Addiction with severe withdrawal symptoms, possible convulsions, toxic psychosis	Yes	Yes	Yes
Anxiety relief	Irritability, confusion, depression, sleep disorders	Yes	Yes	No, but can affect fetus
Wakefulness, alertness	Insomnia, heart arrhythmias, high blood pressure	No?	Yes	Yes
Excitation, talkativeness	Depression, convulsions	Yes	Yes	Yes
Euphoria, prevent withdrawal discomfort	Addiction, constipation, loss of appetite	Yes	Yes	No
Intoxication, euphoria, relaxation	Anxiety, confusion, insomnia, hallucinations, seizures	Yes	Yes	No?
Euphoria, prevent withdrawal discomfort	Addiction, constipation, loss of appetite	Yes	Yes	No*
Insightful experiences, exhilaration, distortion of senses	May intensify existing psychosis, panic reactions	No	No?	No?
Relaxation; increased euphoria, perceptions, sociability	Possible lung cancer, other health risks	No	Yes	Yes?
Excitation, euphoria	Personality change, hyperthermia, liver damage	No	Yes	Yes
Insightful experiences, exhilaration, distortion of senses	May intensify existing psychosis, panic reactions	No	No?	No?
Prevent withdrawal discomfort	Addiction, constipation, loss of appetite	Yes	Yes	No
Euphoria, prevent withdrawal discomfort	Addiction, constipation, loss of appetite	Yes	Yes	No*
Euphoria	Unpredictable behavior, suspicion, hostility, psychosis	Debated	Yes	Yes
Insightful experiences, exhilaration, distortion of senses	May intensify existing psychosis, panic reactions	No	No?	No?
Alertness, calmness, sociability	Emphysema, lung cancer, mouth and throat cancer, cardiovascular damage, loss of appetite	Yes	Yes	Yes

*Persons who inject drugs under nonsterile conditions run a high risk of contracting AIDS, hepatitis, abscesses, or circulatory disorders.

Drugs of Abuse

Note in ■ Table 5.3 that the drugs most likely to lead to physical dependence are alcohol, amphetamines, barbiturates, cocaine, codeine, heroin, methadone, morphine, and tobacco (nicotine). Using *any* of the drugs listed in ■ Table 5.3 can result in psychological dependence. Note too that people who take drugs intravenously are at high risk for developing hepatitis and AIDS (see Chapter 11). The discussion that follows focuses on the drugs most often abused by students.

UPPERS—AMPHETAMINES, COCAINE, MDMA, CAFFEINE, NICOTINE

Amphetamines are synthetic stimulants. Common street names for amphetamine are "speed," "bennies," "dex," "go," and "uppers." These drugs were once widely prescribed for weight loss or depression. Today, the only fully legitimate medical use of amphetamines is to treat narcolepsy, childhood hyperactivity, and overdoses of depressant drugs. Illicit use of amphetamines is widespread, however, especially by people seeking to stay awake and by those who think drugs can improve mental or physical performance.

Methamphetamine is a more potent variation of amphetamine. It can be snorted, injected, or eaten. Of the various types of amphetamine, methamphetamine has created the largest drug problem. "Crank," "speed," "meth," or "crystal," as it is known on the street, can be made cheaply in backyard labs and sold for massive profits. In addition to ruining lives through addiction, it has fueled a violent criminal subculture.

Amphetamines rapidly produce a drug tolerance. Most abusers end up taking ever larger doses to get the desired effect. Eventually, some users switch to injecting methamphetamine ("speed") directly into the bloodstream. True speed freaks typically go on binges lasting several days, after which they "crash" from lack of sleep and food.

Abuse

How dangerous are amphetamines? Amphetamines pose many dangers. Large doses can cause nausea, vomiting, extremely high blood pressure, fatal heart attacks, and disabling strokes. It is important to realize that amphetamines speed up the use of bodily resources; they do not magically supply energy. After an amphetamine binge, people suffer from crippling fatigue, depression, confusion, uncontrolled irritability, and aggression. Repeated amphetamine use damages the brain. Amphetamines can also cause *amphetamine psychosis,* a loss of contact with reality. Affected users have paranoid delusions that someone is out to get them. Acting on these delusions, they may become violent, resulting in suicide, self-injury, or injury to others (Kratofil, Baberg, & Dimsdale, 1996).

A potent smokable form of crystal methamphetamine has added to the risks of stimulant abuse. This drug, known as "ice" on the street, is highly addictive. Like "crack," the smokable form of cocaine, it produces an intense high. But also like crack (discussed in a moment), crystal methamphetamine leads very rapidly to compulsive abuse and severe drug dependence.

Cocaine

Cocaine ("coke," "snow," "blow") is a powerful central nervous system stimulant extracted from the leaves of the coca plant. Cocaine produces feelings of alertness, euphoria, well-being, power, boundless energy, and pleasure (Julien, 2005). At the turn of the twentieth century, dozens of nonprescription potions and cure-alls contained cocaine. It was during this time that Coca-Cola was indeed the "real thing." From 1886 until 1906, when the U.S. Pure Food and Drug Act was passed, Coca-Cola contained cocaine (which has since been replaced with caffeine).

How does cocaine differ from amphetamines? The two are very much alike in their effects on the central nervous system. The main difference is that amphetamine lasts several hours; cocaine is snorted and quickly metabolized, so its effects last only about 15 to 30 minutes.

Abuse

How dangerous is cocaine? Cocaine is one of the most dangerous drugs of abuse. When rats and monkeys are given free access to cocaine, they find it irresistible. Many, in fact, end up dying of convulsions from self-administered overdoses of the drug. Cocaine increases the chemical messengers dopamine (DOPE-ah-meen) and noradrenaline (nor-ah-DREN-ah-lin). Noradrenaline arouses the brain, and dopamine produces a "rush" of pleasure. This combination is so powerfully rewarding that cocaine users run a high risk of becoming compulsive abusers (Ridenour et al., 2005). Even casual or first-time users risk having convulsions, a heart attack, or a stroke (Lacayo, 1995).

A person who stops using cocaine does not experience heroin-like withdrawal symptoms. But cocaine can be highly addictive. The brain adapts to cocaine abuse in ways that upset its chemical balance, causing depression when cocaine is withdrawn. First, there is a jarring "crash" of mood and energy. Within a few days, the person enters a long period of fatigue, anxiety, paranoia, boredom, and **anhedonia** (an-he-DAWN-ee-ah: an inability to feel pleasure). Before long, the urge to use cocaine becomes intense. So, although cocaine does not fit the classic pattern of addiction, it is ripe for compulsive abuse. Even a person who gets through withdrawal may crave cocaine months or years later (Withers et al., 1995). If cocaine were cheaper, 9 out of 10 users would progress to com-

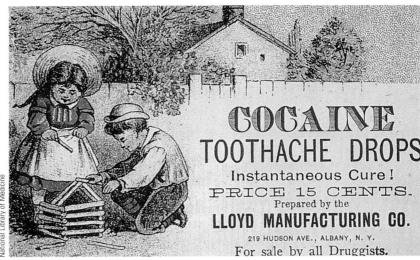

Cocaine was the main ingredient in many nonprescription elixirs before the turn of the twentieth century. Today cocaine is recognized as a powerful and dangerous drug. Its high potential for abuse has damaged the lives of countless users.

pulsive abuse. In fact, rock cocaine ("crack," "rock," or "*roca*"), which is cheaper, produces very high abuse rates. Here are some signs of cocaine abuse:

- *Compulsive use.* If cocaine is available—say, at a party—you can't say no to it.
- *Loss of control.* Once you have had some cocaine, you will keep using it until you are exhausted or the cocaine is gone.
- *Disregarding consequences.* You don't care if the rent gets paid, your job is endangered, your lover disapproves, or your health is affected, you'll use cocaine anyway.

Cocaine's capacity for abuse and social damage rivals that of heroin. Anyone who thinks she or he has a cocaine problem should seek advice at a drug clinic or a Cocaine Anonymous meeting. Quitting cocaine is extremely difficult (Sinha et al., 2006). Nevertheless, three out of four cocaine abusers who remain in treatment do succeed in breaking their coke dependence (Simpson et al., 1999).

MDMA ("Ecstasy")

The drug MDMA (methylenedioxymethamphetamine, or "Ecstasy") is also chemically similar to amphetamine. In addition to producing a rush of energy, users say it makes them feel closer to others and heightens sensory experiences. Ecstasy causes brain cells to release extra amounts of serotonin. The physical effects of MDMA include dilated pupils, elevated blood pressure, jaw clenching, loss of appetite, and elevated body temperature (Braun, 2001). Although some users believe that Ecstasy increases sexual pleasure, it *diminishes* sexual performance, impairing erection in 40 percent of men, and retarding orgasm in both men and women (Zemishlany, Aizenberg, & Weizman, 2001).

Abuse

Ecstasy use in North America has declined slightly from a peak around 2002, perhaps because of widespread negative publicity. Regardless, every year more than half a million Americans try Ecstasy for the first time (SAMHSA, 2005). Every year, emergency room doctors see many MDMA cases, including MDMA-related deaths. Some of these incidents are caused by elevated body temperature (hyperthermia) or heart arrhythmias, which can lead to collapse. Ecstasy users at "rave" parties try to prevent overheating by drinking water to cool themselves. This may help to a small degree, but the risk of fatal heat exhaustion is real. MDMA can also cause severe liver damage, which can be fatal (Braun, 2001). In addition, Ecstasy users are more likely to abuse alcohol and other drugs, to neglect studying, to party excessively, and to engage in risky sex (Strote, Lee, & Wechsler, 2002).

Anhedonia An inability to feel pleasure.

It may take another decade before Ecstasy's full impact on health emerges. For now, we know that repeated use of MDMA damages serotonergic brain cells. This damage lasts for years. It leads to feelings of anxiety or depression that can persist for months after a person stops taking Ecstasy. In addition, heavy users typically do not perform well in tests of learning and memory and show signs of underlying brain damage (Quednow et al., 2006). Despite its street name, Ecstasy may be a ticket to agony for many users (Kuhn & Wilson, 2001).

Caffeine

Caffeine is the most frequently used psychoactive drug in North America. (And that's not counting Seattle!) Caffeine stimulates the brain by blocking chemicals that normally inhibit or slow nerve activity (Julien, 2005). Its effects become apparent with doses as small as 50 milligrams, the amount found in about one-half cup of brewed coffee. Physically, caffeine causes sweating, talkativeness, tinnitus (ringing in the ears), and hand tremors (Nehlig, 2004). Psychologically, caffeine suppresses fatigue or drowsiness and increases feelings of alertness (Wesensten et al., 2002). Some people have a hard time starting a day (or writing another paragraph) without it.

How much caffeine did you consume today? It is common to think of coffee as the major source of caffeine, but there are many others. Caffeine is found in tea, many soft drinks (especially colas), chocolate, and cocoa (▇ Table 5.4). More than 2,000 nonprescription drugs also contain caffeine, including stay-awake pills, cold remedies, and many name-brand aspirin products.

Abuse

Are there any serious drawbacks to using caffeine? Overuse of caffeine may result in an unhealthy dependence known as **caffeinism.** Insomnia, irritability, loss of appetite, chills, racing heart, and elevated body temperature are all signs of caffeinism. Many people with these symptoms drink 15 or 20 cups of coffee a day. However, even at lower dosages, caffeine can intensify anxiety and other psychological problems (Hogan, Hornick, & Bouchoux, 2002).

Caffeine poses a variety of health risks. Caffeine encourages the growth of breast cysts in women, and it may contribute to bladder cancer, heart problems, and high blood pressure. Pregnant women should consider giving up caffeine entirely because of a suspected link between caffeine and birth defects. Pregnant women who consume as little as 2 cups of coffee a day increase the risk of having a miscarriage (Cnattingius et al., 2000).

It is customary to think of caffeine as a nondrug. But as few as 2.5 cups of coffee a day (or the equivalent) can be a problem. People who consume even such modest amounts may experience anxiety, depression, fatigue, headaches, and flu-like symptoms during withdrawal (Juliano & Griffiths, 2004). About half of all caffeine users show some signs of dependence (Hughes et al., 1998). It is wise to remember that caffeine *is* a drug and to use it in moderation.

Nicotine

Nicotine is a natural stimulant found mainly in tobacco. Next to caffeine and alcohol, it is the most widely used psychoactive drug (Julien, 2005).

How does nicotine compare with other stimulants? Nicotine is a potent drug. It is so toxic that it is sometimes used to kill insects! In large doses it causes stomach pain, vomiting and diarrhea, cold sweats, dizziness, confusion, and muscle tremors. In very large doses, nicotine may cause convulsions, respiratory failure, and death. For a nonsmoker, 50 to 75 milligrams of nicotine taken in a single dose could be lethal. (Chain-smoking about 17 to 25 cigarettes will produce this dosage.) Most first-time smokers get sick on one or two cigarettes. In contrast, a heavy smoker may inhale 40 cigarettes a day without feeling ill. This indicates that regular smokers build a tolerance for nicotine.

■ Table 5.4 **Average Caffeine Content of Various Foods**

Instant coffee (5 ounces), 64 milligrams
Percolated coffee (5 ounces), 108 milligrams
Drip coffee (5 ounces), 145 milligrams
Decaf. coffee (5 ounces), 3 milligrams
Black tea (5 ounces), 42 milligrams
Canned ice tea (17 ounces), 30 milligrams
Cocoa drink (6 ounces), 8 milligrams
Chocolate drink (8 ounces), 14 milligrams
Sweet chocolate (1 ounce), 20 milligrams
Colas (12 ounces), 50 milligrams
Soft drinks (12 ounces), 0–52 milligrams

Caffeinism Excessive consumption of caffeine, leading to dependence and a variety of physical and psychological complaints.

Abuse

How addictive is nicotine? A vast array of evidence confirms that nicotine is very addictive (Spinella, 2005). Among regular smokers who are 15 to 24 years old, 60 percent are addicted (Breslau et al., 2001). For many smokers, withdrawal from nicotine causes headaches, sweating, cramps, insomnia, digestive upset, irritability, and a sharp craving for cigarettes (Killen & Fortmann, 1997; NIDA, 2006). These symptoms may last from 2 to 6 weeks and may be worse than heroin withdrawal. Indeed, relapse patterns are nearly identical for alcoholics, heroin addicts, cocaine abusers, and smokers who try to quit (Stolerman & Jarvis, 1995). Up to 90 percent of people who quit smoking relapse within a year and 20 percent relapse even after 2 years of abstinence (Krall, Garvey, & Garcia, 2002).

Impact on Health

How serious are the health risks of smoking? If you think smoking is harmless, or that there's no connection between smoking and cancer, you're kidding yourself. A burning cigarette releases a large variety of potent *carcinogens* (car-SIN-oh-jins: cancer-causing substances). According to the U.S. Surgeon General (USDHHS, 2004), "smoking harms nearly every organ of the body," leading to an increased risk of many cancers (such as lung cancer), cardiovascular diseases (such as stroke), respiratory diseases (such as chronic bronchitis), and reproductive disorders (such as decreased fertility). Together, these health risks combine to reduce the life expectancy of the average smoker by 10 to 15 years. (Skeptics please note: Wayne McLaren, who portrayed the rugged "Marlboro Man" in cigarette ads, died of lung cancer at age 51.) More people die every year from tobacco use than from motor vehicle injuries, murders, suicides, alcohol use, illegal drug use, and AIDS *combined* (NCCDPHP, 2004).

Smokers don't just risk their own health, they also endanger those who live and work nearby. Secondary smoke causes about 3,000 lung cancer deaths and as many as 62,000 heart disease deaths each year in the United States alone. It is particularly irresponsible of smokers to expose young children, who are especially vulnerable, to secondhand smoke (American Lung Association, 2006).

Quitting Smoking

What is the best way to quit smoking? Most people try to quit by themselves. Some try to quit cold turkey while others try to taper down gradually. Although going cold turkey has its advocates, gradually quitting works better for more people.

Going cold turkey makes quitting an all-or-nothing proposition. Smokers who smoke even one cigarette after "quitting forever" tend to feel they've failed. Many figure they might just as well resume smoking. Those who quit gradually accept that success may take many attempts, spread over several months. If you are going to quit by going cold turkey, you will have a better chance of success if you decide to quit *now* rather than at some time in the future (West & Sohal, 2006).

The best way to taper off is *scheduled gradual reduction* (Riley et al., 2002). There are many ways in which smoking can be

THE FAR SIDE® BY GARY LARSON

The real reason dinosaurs became extinct

The Everett Collection

Actress and comedienne Lily Tomlin, here shown portraying one of her comedic characters, Ernestine, once took up smoking for a role in a movie *(Shadows and Fog)* and developed a 4-pack-a-day habit. As Tomlin's experience shows, the best way to avoid developing a nicotine addiction is to not begin smoking in the first place.

gradually reduced. For example, the smoker can (1) delay having a first cigarette in the morning and then try to delay a little longer each day, (2) gradually reduce the total number of cigarettes smoked each day, or (3) quit completely, but for just 1 week, then quit again, a week at a time, for as many times as necessary to make it stick. Deliberately scheduling the gradually stretching of time periods between cigarettes is a key part of this program. Scheduled smoking apparently helps people learn to cope with the urge to smoke. As a result, people using this method are more likely to succeed. Also, they more often remain permanent nonsmokers than people using other approaches (Cinciripini, Wetter, & McClure, 1997).

Whatever approach is taken, quitting smoking is not easy (Abrams et al., 2003). Many people find that using nicotine patches or gum helps them get through the withdrawal period (Shiffman et al., 2006). Also, as we have noted, anyone trying to quit should be prepared to make several attempts before succeeding. But the good news is tens of millions of people have quit.

DOWNERS—SEDATIVES, TRANQUILIZERS, AND ALCOHOL

How do downers differ from the stimulant drugs? The most widely used downers, or depressant drugs, are alcohol, barbiturates, GHB, and benzodiazepine (ben-zoe-die-AZ-eh-peen) tranquilizers. These drugs are much alike in their effects. In fact, barbiturates and tranquilizers are sometimes referred to as "solid alcohol." Let's examine the properties of each.

Barbiturates

Barbiturates are sedative drugs that depress brain activity. Common barbiturates include amobarbital, pentobarbital, secobarbital, and tuinal. On the street they are known as "downers," "blue heavens," "yellow jackets," "purple hearts," "goof balls," "reds," "pink ladies," "rainbows," or "tooies." Medically, barbiturates are used to calm patients or to induce sleep. At mild dosages, barbiturates have an effect similar to alcohol intoxication. Higher dosages can cause severe mental confusion or even hallucinations. Barbiturates are often taken in excess amounts because a first dose may be followed by others, as the user becomes uninhibited or forgetful. Overdoses first cause a loss of consciousness. Then they severely depress brain centers that control heartbeat and breathing. The result is death (McKim, 2003).

GHB

Would you swallow a mixture of degreasing solvent and drain cleaner to get high? Apparently, a lot of people would. A mini-epidemic of GHB (gamma-hydroxybutyrate) use has taken place in recent years, especially at nightclubs and raves. GHB ("goop," "scoop," "max," "Georgia Home Boy") is a central nervous system depressant that relaxes and sedates the body. Users describe its effects as being similar to alcohol. Mild GHB intoxication tends to produce euphoria, a desire to socialize, and a mild loss of inhibitions. GHB's intoxicating effects typically last 3 to 4 hours, depending on the dosage.

Abuse

At lower dosages, GHB can relieve anxiety and produce relaxation. However, as the dose increases, its sedative effects may result in nausea, a loss of muscle control, and either sleep or a loss of consciousness. Potentially fatal doses of GHB are only three times the amount typically taken by users. This narrow margin of safety has led to numerous overdoses, especially when GHB was combined with alcohol. An overdose causes coma, breathing failure, and death. Also, GHB inhibits the gag reflex, so some users choke to death on their own vomit.

In March 2000, the U.S. government classified GHB as a controlled substance, making its possession a felony crime. Clinical evidence increasingly suggests that GHB is addictive and a serious danger to users. Two out of three frequent users have lost consciousness after taking GHB. Heavy users who stop taking GHB have withdrawal symptoms that include anxiety, agitation, tremor, delirium, and hallucinations (Miotto et al., 2001).

As if the preceding weren't enough reason to be leery of GHB, here's one more to consider: GHB is often manufactured in homes with recipes and ingredients purchased on the Internet. As mentioned earlier, it can be produced by combining degreasing solvent with drain cleaner (Falkowski, 2000). If you want to degrease your brain, GHB will do the trick.

Tranquilizers

A **tranquilizer** is a drug that lowers anxiety and reduces tension. Doctors prescribe benzodiazepine tranquilizers to alleviate nervousness and stress. Valium is the best-known drug in this family; others are Xanax, Halcion, and Librium. Even at normal dosages these drugs can cause drowsiness, shakiness, and confusion. When used at too high a dosage or for too long a time, benzodiazepines have strong addictive potential (McKim, 2003).

A drug sold under the trade name Rohypnol (ro-HIP-nol) has added to the problem of tranquilizer abuse. This drug, which is related to Valium, is cheap and 10 times more potent. It lowers inhibitions and produces relaxation or intoxication. Large doses induce short-term amnesia and sleep. "Roofies," as they are known on the street, are odorless and tasteless. They have been used to spike drinks, which are given to the unwary. Victims of this "date rape" drug are then sexually assaulted or raped while they are unconscious. (Be aware, however, that drinking too much alcohol is by far the most common prelude to rape.)

Abuse

Repeated use of barbiturates can cause physical dependence. Some abusers suffer severe emotional depression that may end in suicide. Similarly, when tranquilizers are used at too high a dosage or for too long a time, addiction can occur. Many people have learned the hard way that their legally prescribed tranquilizers are as dangerous as many illicit drugs (McKim, 2003).

Combining barbiturates or tranquilizers with alcohol is especially risky. When mixed, the effects of both drugs are multiplied by a **drug interaction** (one drug enhances the effect of another). Drug interactions are responsible for many hundreds of fatal drug overdoses every year. All too often, depressants are gulped down with alcohol or added to a spiked punch bowl. This is the lethal brew that left a young woman named Karen Ann Quinlan in a coma that lasted 10 years, ending with her death. It is no exaggeration to restate that mixing depressants with alcohol can be deadly.

Alcohol

Alcohol is the common name for ethyl alcohol, the intoxicating element in fermented and distilled liquors. Contrary to popular belief, alcohol is not a stimulant. The noisy animation at drinking parties is due to alcohol's effect as a *depressant*. As ▸▸Figure 5.11 shows, small amounts of alcohol reduce inhibitions and produce feelings of relaxation and euphoria. Larger amounts cause ever-greater impairment of the brain until the drinker loses consciousness. Alcohol is also not an aphrodisiac. Rather than enhancing sexual arousal, it usually impairs performance, especially in males. As William Shakespeare observed long ago, drink "provokes the desire, but it takes away the performance."

Tranquilizer A drug that lowers anxiety and reduces tension.

Drug interaction A combined effect of two drugs that exceeds the addition of one drug's effects to the other.

▶▶**FIGURE 5.11** The behavioral effects of alcohol are related to blood alcohol content and the resulting suppression of higher mental function. Arrows indicate the typical threshold for legal intoxication in the United States. (From Jozef Cohen, *Eyewitness Series in Psychology*, p. 44. Copyright © by Rand McNally and Company. Reprinted by permission.)

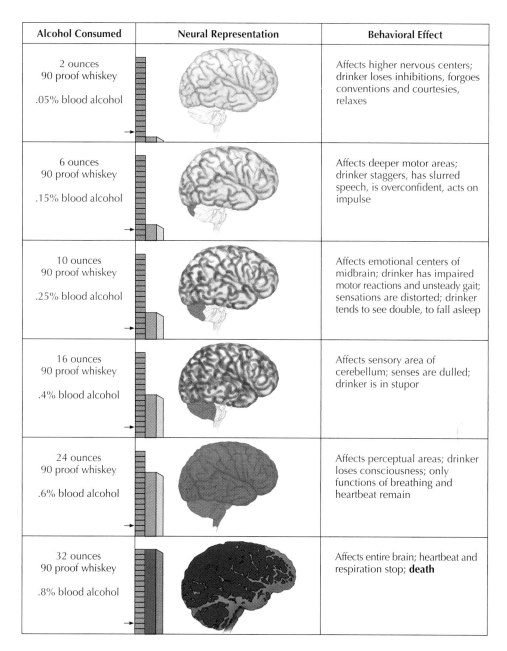

Alcohol Consumed	Neural Representation	Behavioral Effect
2 ounces 90 proof whiskey .05% blood alcohol		Affects higher nervous centers; drinker loses inhibitions, forgoes conventions and courtesies, relaxes
6 ounces 90 proof whiskey .15% blood alcohol		Affects deeper motor areas; drinker staggers, has slurred speech, is overconfident, acts on impulse
10 ounces 90 proof whiskey .25% blood alcohol		Affects emotional centers of midbrain; drinker has impaired motor reactions and unsteady gait; sensations are distorted; drinker tends to see double, to fall asleep
16 ounces 90 proof whiskey .4% blood alcohol		Affects sensory area of cerebellum; senses are dulled; drinker is in stupor
24 ounces 90 proof whiskey .6% blood alcohol		Affects perceptual areas; drinker loses consciousness; only functions of breathing and heartbeat remain
32 ounces 90 proof whiskey .8% blood alcohol		Affects entire brain; heartbeat and respiration stop; **death**

Abuse

Alcohol, the world's favorite depressant, breeds our biggest drug problem. More than 20 million people in the United States and Canada have serious drinking problems. One American dies every 20 minutes in an alcohol-related car crash. The level of alcohol abuse among adolescents and young adults is alarming. Of 18-year-olds, 15 percent are heavy drinkers, and 40 percent have engaged in binge drinking (SAMHAS, 2005). For fraternity and sorority members, the figure is much higher. **Binge drinking** is defined as downing five or more drinks in a short time (four drinks for women). Apparently, many students think it's entertaining to get completely wasted and throw up on their friends. However, binge drinking is a serious sign of alcohol abuse. It is responsible for 1,400 college student deaths each year and thousands of trips to the ER (Wechsler et al., 2002).

Binge drinking is of special concern because the brain continues to develop into the early 20s. Research has shown that teenagers and young adults who drink too much may lose as much as 10 percent of their brain power—especially their memory capacity (Brown et al., 2000). Such losses can have a long-term impact on a person's chances for success in

Binge drinking Consuming five or more drinks in a short time.

life. In short, getting drunk is a slow but sure way to get stupid (Wechsler & Wuethrich, 2002).

Positive reinforcement—drinking for pleasure—motivates most people who consume alcohol. What sets alcohol abusers apart from other drinkers is that they also drink to cope with negative emotions, such as anxiety and depression. That's why alcohol abuse increases with the level of stress in people's lives. People who drink to cope with bad feelings are at risk of becoming alcoholics (Kenneth, Carpenter, & Hasin, 1998).

Recognizing Problem Drinking

What are the signs of alcohol abuse? Because alcohol abuse is such a common problem, it is important to recognize the danger signals. If you can answer yes to even one of the following questions, you may have a problem with drinking (adapted from the College Alcohol Problems Scale, revised; Maddock et al., 2001):

As a result of drinking alcoholic beverages I . . .

1. engaged in unplanned sexual activity.
2. drove under the influence.
3. did not use protection when engaging in sex.
4. engaged in illegal activities associated with drug use.
5. felt sad, blue, or depressed.
6. was nervous or irritable.
7. felt bad about myself.
8. had problems with appetite or sleeping.

Creasource/Series/PictureQuest

Binge drinking and alcohol abuse have become serious problems among college students. Many alcohol abusers regard themselves as "moderate" drinkers, which suggests that they are in denial about how much they actually drink (Grant & Dawson, 1997).

Moderated Drinking

Many social-recreational drinkers could do a far better job of managing their use of alcohol. Almost everyone has been to a party spoiled by someone who drank too much too fast. Those who avoid overdrinking have a better time, and so do their friends. But how do you avoid drinking too much? After all, as one wit once observed, "The conscience dissolves in alcohol." It takes skill to regulate drinking in social situations, where the temptation to drink can be strong. If you choose to drink, here are some guidelines that may be helpful (adapted from Miller & Munoz, 2005; Vogler & Bartz, 1992):

Paced Drinking

1. Think about your drinking beforehand and plan how you will manage it.
2. Drink slowly, eat while drinking or drink on a full stomach, and make every other drink (or more) a nonalcoholic beverage.
3. Limit drinking primarily to the first hour of a social event or party.
4. Practice how you will politely but firmly refuse drinks.
5. Learn how to relax, meet people, and socialize without relying on alcohol.

And remember, research has shown that you are likely to overestimate how much your fellow students are drinking (Maddock & Glanz, 2005). So don't let yourself be lured into overdrinking just because you have the (probably false) impression that other students are drinking more than you. Limiting your own drinking may help others as well. When people are tempted to drink too much, their main reason for stopping is that "other people were quitting and deciding they'd had enough" (Johnson, 2002).

Treatment

Treatment for alcohol dependence begins with sobering up the person and cutting off the supply. This phase is referred to as **detoxification** (literally, "to remove poison"). It frequently produces all the symptoms of drug withdrawal and can be extremely unpleasant.

Detoxification In the treatment of alcoholism, the withdrawal of the patient from alcohol.

The next step is to try to restore the person's health. Heavy abuse of alcohol usually causes severe damage to body organs and the nervous system. After alcoholics have "dried out" and some degree of health has been restored, they may be treated with tranquilizers, antidepressants, or psychotherapy. Unfortunately, the success of these procedures has been limited.

One mutual-help approach that has been fairly successful is Alcoholics Anonymous (AA). AA takes a spiritual approach while acting on the premise that it takes a former alcoholic to understand and help a current alcoholic. Participants at AA meetings admit that they have a problem, share feelings, and resolve to stay "dry" one day at a time. Other group members provide support for those struggling to end dependency. (Other "12-step" programs, such as Cocaine Anonymous and Narcotics Anonymous, use the same approach.)

Eighty percent of those who remain in AA for more than 1 year get through the following year without a drink. However, AA's success rate may simply reflect the fact that members join voluntarily, meaning they have admitted they have a serious problem (Morgenstern et al., 1997). Sadly, it seems that alcohol abusers will often not face their problems until they have "hit rock bottom." If they are willing, though, AA presents a practical approach to the problem (Vaillant, 2005).

Other groups offer a rational, nonspiritual approach to alcohol abuse that better fits the needs of some people. Examples include Rational Recovery and Secular Organizations for Sobriety (SOS). Other alternatives to AA include medical treatment, group therapy, and individual psychotherapy (Buddie, 2004). There is a strong tendency for abusive drinkers to deny they have a problem. The sooner they seek help, the better.

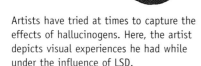

Artists have tried at times to capture the effects of hallucinogens. Here, the artist depicts visual experiences he had while under the influence of LSD.

HALLUCINOGENS—TRIPPING THE LIGHT FANTASTIC

Marijuana is the most popular illicit drug in America (SAMHAS, 2005). The main active chemical in marijuana is tetrahydrocannabinol (tet-rah-hydro-cah-NAB-ih-nol), or THC, for short. THC is a mild **hallucinogen** (hal-LU-sin-oh-jin: a substance that alters sensory impressions). Other hallucinogenic drugs include LSD and PCP.

LSD and PCP

The drug LSD (lysergic acid diethylamide, or "acid") is perhaps the best-known hallucinogen. Even when taken in tiny amounts, LSD can produce hallucinations and psychotic-like disturbances in thinking and perception. Two other common hallucinogens are mescaline (peyote) and psilocybin ("magic mushrooms," or "shrooms"). Incidentally, the drug PCP (phencyclidine, or "angel dust") can have hallucinogenic effects. However, PCP, which is an anesthetic, also has stimulant and depressant effects. This potent combination can cause extreme agitation, disorientation, violence—and too often, tragedy. All of the hallucinogens, including marijuana, typically affect neurotransmitter systems that carry messages between brain cells (Julien, 2005).

Marijuana

Marijuana and hashish are derived from the hemp plant *Cannabis sativa*. Marijuana ("pot," "herb," "weed") consists of the leaves and flowers of the hemp plant. Hashish is a resinous material scraped from Cannabis leaves.

Marijuana's psychological effects include a sense of euphoria or well-being, relaxation, altered time sense, and perceptual distortions. At high dosages, however, paranoia, hallucinations, and delusions can occur (Ksir, Hart, & Ray, 2006). All considered, marijuana intoxi-

Hallucinogen A substance that alters or distorts sensory impressions.

cation is relatively subtle by comparison to drugs such as LSD or alcohol. Despite this, driving a car while high on marijuana can be extremely hazardous. As a matter of fact, driving under the influence of any intoxicating drug is dangerous.

No overdose deaths from marijuana have been reported. However, marijuana cannot be considered harmless. Particularly worrisome is the fact that THC accumulates in the body's fatty tissues, especially in the brain and reproductive organs. Even if a person smokes marijuana just once a week, the body is never entirely free of THC. Scientists have located a specific receptor site on the surface of brain cells where THC binds to produce its effects (▶Fig. 5.12). These receptor sites are found in large numbers in the cerebral cortex, which is the seat of human consciousness (Julien, 2005). In addition, THC receptors are found in areas involved in the control of skilled movement. Naturally occurring chemicals similar to THC may help the brain cope with pain and stress. However, when THC is used as a drug, high dosages can cause paranoia, hallucinations, and dizziness.

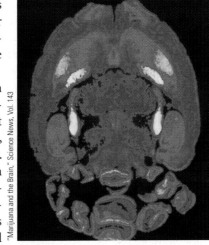

"Marijuana and the Brain," Science News, Vol. 143

▶**FIGURE 5.12** This thin slice of a rat's brain has been washed with a radioactive THC-like drug. Yellowish areas show where the brain is rich in THC receptors. In addition to the cortex, or outer layer of the brain, THC receptors are found in abundance in areas involved in the control of coordinated movement. Naturally occurring chemicals similar to THC may help the brain cope with pain and stress. However, when THC is used as a drug, high doses can cause paranoia, hallucinations, and dizziness (Julien, 2005).

Does marijuana produce physical dependence? Yes, according to recent studies (Lichtman & Martin, 2006). Frequent users of marijuana find it very difficult to quit, so dependence is a risk (Budney & Hughes, 2006). But marijuana's potential for abuse lies primarily in the realm of psychological dependence, not physical addiction.

Dangers of Marijuana Use

There have been very alarming reports in the press about the dangers of marijuana. Are they accurate? In the past it was widely reported that marijuana causes brain damage, genetic damage, and a loss of motivation. Each of these charges can be criticized for being based on poorly done or inconclusive research. But that doesn't mean that marijuana gets a clean bill of health. For about a day after a person smokes marijuana, his or her attention, coordination, and short-term memory are impaired (Pope, Gruber, & Yurgelun-Todd, 1995). Frequent marijuana users show small declines in learning, memory, attention, and thinking abilities (Solowij et al., 2002). When surveyed at age 29, nonusers are healthier, earn more, and are more satisfied with their lives than people who smoke marijuana regularly (Ellickson, Martino, & Collins, 2004).

People who smoke five or more joints a week score 4 points lower on IQ tests. This is enough to dull their learning capacity. In fact, many people who have stopped using marijuana say they quit because they were bothered by short-term memory loss and concentration problems. Fortunately, IQ scores and other cognitive measures rebound in about a month after a person quits using marijuana (Grant et al., 2001). In other words, people who smoke dope may act like dopes, but if they quit, there's a good chance they will regain their mental abilities.

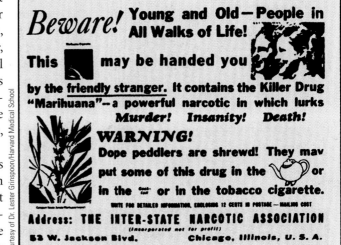

Courtesy of Dr. Lester Grinspoon/Harvard Medical School

An outdated anti-marijuana poster demonstrates the kind of misinformation that has long been attached to this drug. Research has finally begun to sort out what risks are associated with use of marijuana.

Health Risks

After many years of conflicting information, some of marijuana's health hazards are also being clarified. Marijuana's long-term effects include the following health risks.

1. Marijuana smoke contains 50 percent more cancer-causing hydrocarbons and 16 times more tar than tobacco smoke does. Thus, smoking several "joints" a week

may be the equivalent of smoking a dozen cigarettes a day. In regular users, marijuana increases the risk of a variety of cancers, including prostate and cervical cancer (Hashibe, 2005).

2. Marijuana temporarily lowers sperm production in males, and users produce more abnormal sperm. This could be a problem for a man who is marginally fertile and wants to have a family (Schuel et al., 1999).

3. In experiments with female monkeys, THC causes abnormal menstrual cycles and disrupts ovulation. Other animal studies show that THC causes a higher rate of miscarriages and that it can reach the developing fetus. As is true for so many other drugs, it appears that marijuana should be avoided during pregnancy.

4. THC can suppress the body's immune system, increasing the risk of disease.

5. In animals, marijuana causes genetic damage within cells of the body. It is not known to what extent this happens in humans, but it does suggest that marijuana can be detrimental to health.

6. Activity levels in the cerebellum are lower than normal in marijuana abusers. This may explain why chronic marijuana users tend to show some loss of coordination (Volkow et al., 1996).

7. There is some evidence that THC damages parts of the brain important for memory (Chan et al., 1998).

8. Children whose mothers smoked marijuana during pregnancy show lowered ability to succeed in challenging, goal-oriented activities (Fried & Smith, 2001; Noland et al., 2005).

Although much is still unknown, marijuana appears to pose a wide range of health risks, as do two other potent drugs in widespread use—tobacco and alcohol. Only future research will tell for sure "what's in the pot."

A few of the known poisons found in second-hand tobacco smoke.

arsenic Mercury
formaldehyde
Nicotine Vinyl chloride
Lead
Benzene DDT
Hydrogen cyanide Nickel
ammonia

Scientists around the world agree the only safe level of exposure to second-hand tobacco smoke is no exposure at all.

It's time to clear the air... about Brantford's Clean Air Bylaw

CTFB COUNCIL FOR A TOBACCO FREE BRANT

For more information about Brantford's Clean Air Bylaw, call the Tobacco Information Line (519) 732-6222 www.bchu.org

Courtesy of the Brant County Health Unit

Well-crafted information and education can discourage drug use. This poster emphasizes the dangers of secondhand smoke. Research has shown that this is one of several issues that motivates children and adolescents to resist pressures to begin smoking.

Summary

Why is drug abuse such a common problem? People seek drug experiences for many reasons, ranging from curiosity and a desire to belong to a group, to a search for meaning or an escape from feelings of inadequacy. The best predictors of adolescent drug use and abuse are drug use by peers, parental drug use, delinquency, parental maladjustment, poor self-esteem, social nonconformity, and stressful life changes. One study found that adolescents who abuse drugs tend to be maladjusted, alienated, impulsive, and emotionally distressed (Masse & Tremblay, 1997). Antisocial behavior, school failure, and risky sexual behavior are also commonly associated with drug abuse (Ary et al., 1999). Such patterns make it clear that taking drugs is a symptom, rather than a cause, of personal and social maladjustment (Ksir, Hart, & Ray, 2006).

Many abusers turn to drugs in a self-defeating attempt to cope with life. All of the frequently abused drugs produce immediate feelings of pleasure. The negative consequences follow much later. This combination of immediate pleasure and delayed punishment allows abusers to feel good on demand. In time, of course, most of the pleasure goes out of drug abuse, and the abuser's problems get worse. But if an abuser merely feels better (however briefly) after taking a drug, drug taking can become compulsive. In contrast, people who stop using drugs often say that they quit because the drawbacks had come to exceed the benefits (Toneatto et al., 1999).

Although billions of dollars have been spent on drug enforcement in recent years, there has been an increase in the overall level of drug use in the United States. Most drug use begins in early adolescence (Chen & Kandel, 1995). Given this fact, some experts believe that prevention through education and early intervention is the answer to drug problems (Julien, 2005). What do you think?

A Look Ahead

Of the many states of consciousness we have discussed, dreaming remains one of the most familiar—and the most surprising. Are there lessons to be learned from dreams? What personal insights lie hidden in the ebb and flow of your dream images? Let's find out.

→ **Study Break** **Psychoactive Drugs**

Reflect

What legal drugs did you use in the last year? Did any have psychoactive properties? How do psychoactive drugs differ from other substances in their potential for abuse?

Learning Check

1. Which of the drugs listed below are known to cause a physical dependence?

   a. heroin　　　　　　b. morphine
   c. codeine　　　　　　d. methadone
   e. barbiturates　　　　f. alcohol
   g. marijuana　　　　　h. amphetamines
   i. nicotine　　　　　　j. cocaine
   k. GHB

2. Amphetamine psychosis is similar to extreme _____, in which the individual feels threatened and suffers from delusions.

3. Cocaine is very similar to which of the following in its effects on the central nervous system?

   a. Seconal　　b. codeine　　c. *Cannabis*　　d. amphetamine

4. The combination of _____ or _____ and alcohol can be fatal.

5. College students may overdrink as they try to keep up with how much they falsely imagine that their peers drink. T or F?

6. This country's biggest drug problem centers on abuse of

   a. marijuana　　b. alcohol　　c. tobacco　　d. cocaine

7. MDMA and GHB are classified as depressants. T or F?

Critical Thinking

8. The U.S. government, which helps fund antismoking campaigns and smoking-related health research, also continues to subsidize tobacco growers. Can you explain this contradiction?

9. Why do you think there is such a contrast between the laws regulating marijuana and those regulating alcohol and tobacco?

Answers

1. All of them do　2. paranoia　3. d　4. barbiturates, tranquilizers　5. T　6. b　7. F　8. Neither can we.　9. Drug laws in Western societies reflect cultural values and historical patterns of use. Inconsistencies in the law often cannot be justified on the basis of pharmacology, health risks, or abuse potential.

Psychology in Action

Exploring and Using Dreams

>SURVEY QUESTION< *How are dreams used to promote personal understanding?*

In many ways, dreams can be thought of as a message *from* yourself *to* yourself. Thus, the way to understand dreams is to remember them, write them down, look for the messages they contain, and become deeply acquainted with *your own* symbol system. Here's how.

How to Catch a Dream

1. Before going to sleep, plan to remember your dreams. Keep a pen and paper or a tape recorder beside your bed.

2. If possible, arrange to awaken gradually without an alarm. Natural awakening almost always follows soon after a REM period.

3. If you rarely remember your dreams, you may want to set an alarm clock to go off an hour before you usually awaken. Although less desirable than awakening naturally, this may let you catch a dream.

4. Upon awakening, lie still and review the dream images with your eyes closed. Try to recall as many details as possible.

■ Table 5.5 **Effects of Selected Drugs on Dreaming**

Drug	Effect on REM Sleep
Alcohol	Decrease
Amphetamines	Decrease
Barbiturates	Decrease
Caffeine	None
Cocaine	Decrease
LSD	Slight increase
Marijuana	Slight decrease or no effect
Opiates	Decrease
Valium	Decrease

How would you try to find the meaning of a dream? A traditional approach is to look for symbolic messages, as well as literal meanings. If you find yourself wearing a mask in a dream, for instance, it could relate to important roles that you play at school, work, or home. It could also mean that you want to hide or that you are looking forward to a costume party. However, to accurately interpret a dream, it is important to learn your own "vocabulary" of dream images and meanings. Keeping a dream diary is the first step toward gaining valuable insights.

Dream processes Mental filters that hide the true meanings of dreams.

Condensation Combining several people, objects, or events into a single dream image.

Displacement Directing emotions or actions toward safe or unimportant dream images.

Symbolization The nonliteral expression of dream content.

Secondary elaboration Making a dream more logical and complete while remembering it.

5. If you can, make your first dream record (whether by writing or by tape) with your eyes closed. Opening your eyes will disrupt dream recall.

6. Review the dream again and record as many additional details as you can remember. Dream memories disappear quickly. Be sure to describe feelings as well as the plot, characters, and actions of the dream.

7. Put your dreams into a permanent dream diary. Keep dreams in chronological order and review them periodically. This procedure will reveal recurrent themes, conflicts, and emotions. It almost always produces valuable insights.

8. Remember, a number of drugs suppress dreaming by interfering with REM sleep (see ■ Table 5.5).

Dream Work

At one time or another almost everyone has had a dream that seemed to have deep meaning (Rock, 2004). Exploring everyday dream life can be a source of personal enrichment and personal growth (Cartwright & Lamberg, 1992). What strategies do psychologists use to interpret dreams? Let's start with Sigmund Freud's pioneering approach.

To unlock dreams, Freud identified four **dream processes,** or mental filters, that disguise the meanings of dreams. The first is **condensation,** in which several people, objects, or events are combined into a single dream image. A dream character that looks like a teacher, acts like your father, talks like your mother, and is dressed like your employer might be a condensation of authority figures in your life.

Courtesy of Maryanne Mott

Displacement is a second way of disguising dream content. Displacement may cause important emotions or actions of a dream to be redirected toward safe or seemingly unimportant images. Thus, a student angry at his parents might dream of accidentally wrecking their car instead of directly attacking them.

A third dream process is **symbolization.** As mentioned earlier, Freud believed that dreams are often expressed in images that are symbolic rather than literal. That's why it helps to ask what feelings or ideas a dream image might symbolize. Let's say, for example, that a student dreams of coming to class naked. A literal interpretation would be that the student is an exhibitionist! A more likely symbolic meaning is that the student feels vulnerable or unprepared in the class.

Secondary elaboration is the fourth method by which dream meanings are disguised. **Secondary elaboration** is the tendency to make a dream more logical and to add details when remembering it. The fresher a dream memory is, the more useful it is likely to be.

Looking for condensation, displacement, symbolization, and secondary elaboration may help you unlock your dreams. But there are other techniques that may be more effective. Dream theorist Calvin Hall (1974) preferred to think of dreams as plays and the dreamer as a playwright. Although dream images and ideas tend to be more primitive than waking thoughts, much can be learned by simply considering the *setting, cast of characters, plot,* and *emotions* portrayed in a dream.

Another dream theorist, Rosalind Cartwright, suggests that dreams are primarily "feeling statements." According to her, the overall *emotional tone* (underlying mood) of a dream is a major clue to its meaning (Cartwright & Lamberg, 1992). Is the dream comical, threatening, joyous, or depressing? Were you lonely, jealous, frightened, in love, or angry?

Because each dream has several possible meanings or levels of meaning, there is no fixed way to work with it. Telling the dream to others and discussing its meaning can be a good start. Describing it may help you relive some of the feelings in the dream. Also, family members or friends may be able to offer interpretations to which you would be blind. Watch for verbal or visual puns and other playful elements in dreams. For example, if you dream that you are in a wrestling match and your arm is pinned behind your back, it may mean that you feel someone is "twisting your arm" in real life.

The meaning of most dreams will yield to a little detective work. Try asking a series of questions about dreams you would like to understand:

Probing Dreams

1. Who was in the dream? Were there humans, animals, or mythical characters? Do you recognize any of the characters?
2. What social interactions were taking place? Were those interactions friendly? Aggressive? Sexual?
3. What activities were taking place? Were they physical activities or not?
4. Was there striving? Was the striving successful or not?
5. Was the dream about good fortune or misfortune?
6. What emotions were present in the dream? Was there anger, apprehension, confusion, happiness, or sadness?
7. What were the physical surroundings like? What was the setting? Were there any physical objects present? (Adapted from the Hall-Van de Castle system of dream content analysis; Domhoff, 2003.)

If you still have trouble seeing the meaning of a dream, you may find it helpful to use a technique developed by Fritz Perls. Perls, the originator of Gestalt therapy, considered most dreams a special message about what's missing in our lives, what we avoid doing, or feelings that need to be "re-owned." Perls believed that dreams are a way of filling in gaps in personal experience (Perls, 1969).

An approach that Perls found helpful is to "take the part of" or "speak for" each of the characters and objects in the dream. In other words, if you dream about a strange man standing behind a doorway, you would speak aloud to the man, then answer for him. To use Perls's method, you would even speak for the door, perhaps saying something like, "I am a barrier. I keep you safe, but I also keep you locked inside. The stranger has something to tell you. You must risk opening me to learn it."

A particularly interesting dream exercise is to continue a dream as waking fantasy so that it may be concluded or carried on to a more meaningful ending. As the world of dreams and your personal dream language become more familiar, you will doubtless find many answers, paradoxes, intuitions, and insights into your own behavior.

Using Your Dreams

It is possible to learn to use our dreams for our own purposes. For example, as mentioned previously, nightmare sufferers can use imagery rehearsal to modify their own nightmares (Germain et al., 2004; Krakow & Zadra, 2006). Similarly, it is possible to use your dreams to enhance creativity (Stickgold & Walker, 2004).

Dreams and Creativity   History is full of cases where dreams have been a pathway to creativity and discovery. A striking example is provided by Dr. Otto Loewi, a pharmacologist and winner of a Nobel Prize. Loewi had spent years studying the chemical transmission of nerve impulses. A tremendous breakthrough in his research came when he dreamed of an experiment three nights in a row. The first two nights he woke up and scribbled the experiment on a pad. But the next morning, he couldn't tell what the notes meant. On the third night, he got up after having the dream. This time, instead of making notes he went straight to his laboratory and performed the crucial experiment. Loewi later said that if the experiment had occurred to him while awake he would have rejected it.

Loewi's experience gives some insight into using dreams to produce creative solutions. Inhibitions are reduced during dreaming, which may be especially useful in solving problems that require a fresh point of view. Even unimaginative people may create amazing worlds each night in their dreams. For many of us, this rich ability to create is lost in the daily rush of sensory input.

Being able to take advantage of dreams for problem solving is improved if you "set" yourself before retiring. Before you go to bed, try to visualize or think intently about a problem you wish to solve. Steep yourself in the problem by stating it clearly and reviewing all relevant information. Then use the suggestions listed previously to catch your dreams. Although this method is not guaranteed to produce a novel solution or a new insight, it is certain to be an adventure. About half of a group of college students using the method for 1 week recalled a dream that helped them solve a personal problem (Barrett, 1993).

Lucid Dreaming   If you would like to press further into the territory of dreams, you may want to learn lucid dreaming, a relatively rare, but fascinating, experience. During a **lucid dream** a person feels as if she or he is fully awake within the dream world and capable of normal thought and action. If you ask yourself, "Could this be a dream?" and answer "Yes," you are having a lucid dream (LaBerge, 2000).

Stephen LaBerge and his colleagues at the Stanford University Sleep Research Center have used a unique approach to show that lucid dreams are real and that they occur during REM sleep. In the sleep lab, lucid dreamers agree to make prearranged signals when they become aware they are dreaming. One such signal is to look up abruptly in a dream, causing a distinct upward eye movement. Another signal is to clench the right and left fists (in the dream) in a prearranged pattern. In other words, lucid dreamers can partially overcome REM sleep paralysis. Such signals show very clearly that lucid dreaming and voluntary action in dreams is possible (LaBerge, 1985, 2000).

How can a person learn to have lucid dreams? Try following this simple routine: When you awaken spontaneously from a dream, take a few minutes to try to memorize it. Next, engage in 10 to 15 minutes of reading or any other activity requiring full wakefulness. Then while lying in bed and returning to sleep, say to yourself, "Next time I'm dreaming, I want to remember I'm dreaming." Finally, visualize yourself lying in bed asleep while in the dream you just rehearsed. At the same time, picture yourself realizing that you are dreaming. Follow this routine each time you awaken (substitute a dream memory from another occasion if you don't awaken from a dream).

Why would anyone want to have more lucid dreams? Researchers are interested in lucid dreams because they provide a tool for understanding dreaming (Paulsson & Parker, 2006). Using subjects who can signal while they are dreaming makes it possible to explore dreams with firsthand data from the dreamer's world itself.

On a more personal level, lucid dreaming can convert dreams into a nightly "workshop" for emotional growth. Consider, for example, a recently divorced woman who kept dreaming that she was being swallowed by a giant wave. Rosalind Cartwright asked the woman to try swimming the next time the wave engulfed her. She did, with great determination, and the nightmare lost its terror. More important, her revised dream made her feel that she could cope with life again. For reasons such as this, people who have lucid dreams tend to feel a sense of emotional well-being (Wolpin et al., 1992). Dream expert Allan Hobson believes that learning to voluntarily enter altered states of consciousness (through lucid dreaming or self-hypnosis, for example) has allowed him to have enlightening experiences without the risks of taking mind-altering drugs (Hobson, 2001). So, day or night, don't be afraid to dream a little.

Lucid dream A dream in which the dreamer feels awake and capable of normal thought and action.

Study Break Exploring and Using Dreams

Reflect

Some people are very interested in remembering and interpreting their dreams. Others pay little attention to dreaming. What importance do you place on dreams? Do you think dreams and dream interpretation can increase self-awareness?

Learning Check

1. Which is NOT one of the four dream processes identified by Freud?

   a. condensation b. lucidity
   c. displacement d. symbolization

2. In secondary elaboration, one dream character stands for several others. T or F?

3. Calvin Hall's approach to dream interpretation emphasizes the setting, cast, plot, and emotions portrayed in a dream. T or F?

4. Rosalind Cartwright stresses that dreaming is a relatively mechanical process having little personal meaning. T or F?

5. Both alcohol and LSD cause a slight increase in dreaming. T or F?

6. "Taking the part of" or "speaking for" dream elements is a dream interpretation technique originated by Fritz Perls. T or F?

7. Recent research shows that lucid dreaming occurs primarily during NREM sleep or microawakenings. T or F?

Critical Thinking

8. The possibility of having a lucid dream raises an interesting question: If you were dreaming right now, how could you prove it?

Answers

1. b 2. F 3. T 4. F 5. F 6. T 7. F 8. In waking consciousness, our actions have consequences that produce immediate sensory feedback. Dreams lack such external feedback. Thus, trying to walk through a wall or doing similar tests would reveal if you were dreaming.

CHAPTER IN REVIEW

Major Points

- Consciousness and altered states of awareness are core features of mental life.

- Sleep is necessary for survival; dreaming appears to contribute to memory consolidation and perhaps to general mental and emotional health.

- Sleep loss and sleep disorders are serious health problems that should be corrected when they persist.

- Dreams are at least as meaningful as waking thoughts. Whether they have deeper, symbolic meaning is still debated.

- Hypnosis is useful but not "magical." Hypnosis can change private experiences more readily than behaviors or habits.

- Meditation can be used to alter consciousness, as well as to reliably produce deep relaxation.

- Psychoactive drugs, which alter consciousness, are highly prone to abuse.

- Collecting and interpreting your dreams can promote self-awareness.

Summary

What is an altered state of consciousness?

- States of awareness that differ from normal, alert, waking consciousness are called altered states of consciousness (ASCs). Altered states are especially associated with sleep and dreaming, hypnosis, sensory deprivation, and psychoactive drugs.

- Cultural conditioning greatly affects what altered states a person recognizes, seeks, considers normal, and attains.

What are the effects of sleep loss or changes in sleep patterns?

- Sleep is an innate biological rhythm essential for survival. Higher animals and people deprived of sleep experience involuntary microsleeps.

- Moderate sleep loss mainly affects vigilance and performance on routine or boring tasks. Extended sleep loss can (somewhat rarely) produce a temporary sleep-deprivation psychosis.

- Sleep patterns show some flexibility, but 7 to 8 hours remains average. The amount of daily sleep decreases steadily from birth to old age. Once-a-day sleep patterns, with a 2-to-1 ratio of waking and sleep, are most efficient for most people.

Are there different stages of sleep?

- Sleep occurs in four stages. Stage 1 is light sleep, and stage 4 is deep sleep. The sleeper alternates between stages 1 and 4 (passing through stages 2 and 3) several times each night.

How does dream sleep differ from dreamless sleep?

- There are two basic sleep states, rapid eye movement (REM) sleep and non-REM (NREM) sleep. REM sleep is much more strongly associated with dreaming than non-REM sleep is.

- Dreaming and REMs occur mainly during light sleep, similar to stage 1. Dreaming is accompanied by emotional arousal but relaxation of the skeletal muscles.

- People deprived of dream sleep show a REM rebound when allowed to sleep without interruption. However, total sleep loss seems to be more important than loss of a single stage.

- In addition to several other possible functions, REM sleep appears to aid the processing of memories.

What are the causes of sleep disorders and unusual sleep events?

- Sleepwalking and sleeptalking occur during NREM sleep. Night terrors occur in NREM sleep, whereas nightmares occur in REM sleep. Narcolepsy (sleep attacks) and cataplexy are caused by a sudden shift to stage 1 REM patterns during normal waking hours.

- Sleep apnea (interrupted breathing) is one source of insomnia and daytime hypersomnia (sleepiness).

- Apnea is suspected as one cause of sudden infant death syndrome (SIDS). Exposure to secondhand smoke is a major risk factor for SIDS. With only a few exceptions, healthy infants should sleep face up or on their sides.

- Insomnia may be temporary or chronic. When it is treated through the use of drugs, sleep quality is often lowered and drug-dependency insomnia may develop.

- Behavioral approaches to managing insomnia, such as sleep restriction and stimulus control, are quite effective.

Do dreams have meaning?

- Most dream content is about familiar settings, people, and actions. Dreams more often involve negative emotions than positive emotions.

- The Freudian, or psychodynamic, view is that dreams express unconscious wishes, frequently hidden by dream symbols.

- Many theorists have questioned Freud's view of dreams. For example, the activation-synthesis model portrays dreaming as a physiological process.

How is hypnosis done, and what are its limitations?

- Hypnosis is an altered state characterized by narrowed attention and increased suggestibility. (Not all psychologists agree that hypnotic effects require an alteration of consciousness.)

- Stage hypnotism takes advantage of typical stage behavior and uses deception to simulate hypnosis.

- Hypnosis appears capable of producing relaxation, controlling pain, and altering perceptions.

What are meditation and sensory deprivation? Do they have any benefits?

- Concentrative meditation can be used to focus attention, alter consciousness, and reduce stress. Major benefits of meditation are its ability to interrupt anxious thoughts and to elicit the relaxation response.

- Brief exposure to sensory deprivation can also elicit the relaxation response. Under proper conditions, sensory deprivation may help break long-standing habits.

What are the effects of the more commonly used psychoactive drugs?

- A psychoactive drug is a substance that affects the brain in ways that alter consciousness. Most psychoactive drugs can be placed on a scale ranging from stimulation to depression.

- Drugs may cause a physical dependence (addiction) or a psychological dependence, or both. The physically addicting drugs are alcohol, amphetamines, barbiturates, cocaine, codeine, GHB, heroin, methadone, morphine, nicotine, and tranquilizers. All psychoactive drugs can lead to psychological dependence.

- Drug use can be classified as experimental, recreational, situational, intensive, and compulsive. Drug abuse is most often associated with the last three.

- Stimulant drugs are readily abused because of the period of depression that often follows stimulation. The greatest risks are associated with amphetamines (especially methamphetamine), cocaine, MDMA, and nicotine, but even caffeine can be a problem. Nicotine includes the added risk of lung cancer, heart disease, and other health problems.

- Barbiturates and tranquilizers are depressant drugs whose action is similar to that of alcohol. The overdose level for barbiturates and GHB is close to the intoxication dosage, making them dangerous drugs. Mixing barbiturates, tranquilizers, or GHB and alcohol may result in a fatal drug interaction.

- Alcohol is the most heavily abused drug in common use today. Binge drinking is a problem among college students. It is possible to pace the consumption of alcohol.

- Marijuana is subject to an abuse pattern similar to alcohol. Studies have linked chronic marijuana use with lung cancer, various mental impairments, and other health problems.

How are dreams used to promote personal understanding?

- Dreams may be used to promote self-understanding. Freud held that the meaning of dreams is hidden by condensation, displacement, symbolization, and secondary elaboration.
- Hall emphasizes the setting, cast, plot, and emotions of a dream. Cartwright's view of dreams as feeling statements and Perls's technique of speaking for dream elements are also helpful.
- Dreams may be used for creative problem solving, especially when dream awareness is achieved through lucid dreaming.

Interactive Learning

Internet addresses frequently change. To find the sites listed here, visit www.thomsonedu.com/psychology/coon for an updated list of Internet addresses and direct links to relevant sites.

Psychology: A Journey **Companion Website**   Find online quizzes, flash cards, animations, video clips, experiments, interactive assessments, and other helpful study aids for this text at www.thomsonedu.com/psychology/coon.

Alcoholics Anonymous (AA)   Home page of Alcoholics Anonymous.

Circadian Rhythms   Basic information about circadian rhythms and jet lag.

Cocaine Anonymous   Offers advice and information on how to quit cocaine addiction.

Drugs and Behavior Links   Comprehensive links to topics in drugs and behavior.

Marijuana Anonymous   Offers advice and information on how to quit smoking marijuana.

Self-scoring Alcohol Check Up   A short quiz for identifying drinking problems.

SleepNet   Information about sleep and sleep disorders, with many links to other sites.

Sudden Infant Death and Other Infant Death   Information about SIDS, with links to related topics.

The Antidrug.com   Advice to parents and other adults about how to help children resist drug use.

The Reality of Hypnosis   An extended discussion of hypnosis.

ThomsonNOW   Go to www.thomsonedu.com/login to link to ThomsonNOW, your online study tool. First take the **Pre-Test** for this chapter to get your **Personalized Study Plan**, which will identify topics you need to review and direct you to online resources. Then take the **Post-Test** to determine what concepts you have mastered and what you still need work on.

TEST YOUR KNOWLEDGE

States of Consciousness

For additional review, get more practice with *ThomsonNOW*, *WebTutor*, the *Practice Quizzes*, and/or the printed *Study Guide* available with this book.

1. Changes in the quality and pattern of mental activity define
   a. an EEG
   b. an REM
   c. SIDS
   d. an ASC

2. Alyssa experiences a microsleep while driving. Most likely, this indicates that she
   a. was producing mostly beta waves
   b. had high levels of sleep hormones in her bloodstream
   c. switched from delta waves to alpha waves
   d. was sleep deprived

3. A person in deep sleep produces mostly
   a. beta waves
   b. alpha waves
   c. delta waves
   d. REMs

4. Which of the following would normally be most incompatible with moving your arms and legs while asleep?
   a. REM sleep
   b. sleep spindles
   c. delta waves
   d. NREM sleep

5. People who suffer from sudden daytime sleep attacks have which sleep disorder?
   a. narcolepsy
   b. REM behavior disorder
   c. somnambulism
   d. sleep spindling

6. Eating a snack that is nearly all starch can promote sleep because it increases _____ in the brain.
   a. beta waves
   b. tryptophan
   c. EEG activity
   d. hypnic cycling

7. Sleep restriction and stimulus control are techniques used to treat
   a. sleep apnea
   b. sleep talking
   c. night terrors
   d. insomnia

8. Sorting and integrating memories is one function of
   a. activation-synthesis cycles
   b. REM sleep
   c. deep sleep
   d. NREM sleep

9. Wish fulfillment and dream symbols are important concepts in which explanation of dream content?
   a. activation-synthesis
   b. the REST hypothesis
   c. imagery rehearsal
   d. psychodynamic

10. Tests of hypnotic susceptibility measure a person's tendency to respond to
    a. suggestion
    b. imagery rehearsal
    c. stimulus control techniques
    d. the activation-synthesis effect

11. Research has shown that hypnosis cannot produce
    a. unusual strength
    b. improved memory
    c. pain relief
    d. sensory changes

12. Which terms do NOT belong together?
    a. concentrative meditation— relaxation response
    b. sensory deprivation— relaxation response
    c. mindfulness meditation—mantra
    d. sensory deprivation—REST

13. Addictive drugs stimulate the brain's reward circuitry by affecting
    a. neurotransmitters
    b. alpha waves
    c. tryptophan levels
    d. delta spindles

14. Drug tolerance is most closely associated with
    a. psychological dependence
    b. marijuana
    c. withdrawal symptoms
    d. anhedonia

15. Marijuana is most similar to _____ in its effects on the nervous system.
    a. cocaine
    b. benzodiazepine
    c. serotonin
    d. LSD

16. Hyperthermia, heart arrhythmias, and severe liver damage are major risks in the use of
    a. marijuana
    b. benzodiazepine
    c. MDMA
    d. GHB

17. Drug interaction is a special danger when a person combines
    a. marijuana and amphetamine
    b. barbiturates and alcohol
    c. alcohol and cocaine
    d. marijuana and THC

18. Treatment for alcohol dependence begins with sobering up the person and cutting off the supply. This is referred to as
    a. "hitting bottom"
    b. the crucial phase
    c. detoxification
    d. clinical anhedonia

19. Drug abuse is partly explained by the fact that psychoactive drugs produce immediate pleasure and
    a. somnambulism
    b. enhanced self-esteem
    c. delayed punishment
    d. brain carcinogens

20. The Freudian dream process that results when several people, objects, or events are combined into a single dream image is called
    a. symbolization
    b. lucidity
    c. displacement
    d. condensation

Conditioning and Learning

JOURNEY INTO PSYCHOLOGY: WHAT DID YOU LEARN IN SCHOOL TODAY?

When one of your authors was in college, he and other students discovered an intriguing flaw in the dorm plumbing. Flush a toilet while someone was taking a shower and the cold-water pressure would suddenly drop. This caused the shower to become scalding hot. Naturally, the shower victim screamed in terror as his reflexes caused him to leap backward in pain. Soon it was discovered that if *all* the toilets were flushed at once, the effects were multiplied many times over!

A toilet has to be one of the world's most uninspiring stimuli. But for a time, a whole flock of college students twitched involuntarily whenever they heard a toilet flush. Their reactions were the result of classical conditioning, a basic type of learning. Classical conditioning is one of the topics of this chapter.

Now, let's say that you are at school and you feel like you are "starving to death." You locate a vending machine and deposit your last two quarters to buy a candy bar. Then you press the button, and . . . nothing happens. Being civilized and in complete control, you press the other buttons, try the coin return, and look for an attendant. Still nothing. Your stomach growls. Impulsively, you give the machine a little kick (just to let it know how you feel). Then, as you turn away, out pops a candy bar plus 75 cents change. Once this happens, chances are good that you will repeat the "kicking response" in the future. If it pays off several times more, kicking vending machines may become a regular feature of your behavior. In this case, learning is based on operant conditioning (also called instrumental learning).

Classical and operant conditioning reach into every corner of our lives. Are you ready to learn more about learning? If so, read on!

Chris Collins/Corbis

▼ **Survey Questions**

- What is learning?
- How does classical conditioning occur?
- Does conditioning affect emotions?
- How does operant conditioning occur?
- Are there different kinds of operant reinforcement?
- How are we influenced by patterns of reward?
- What does punishment do to behavior?
- What is cognitive learning?
- Does learning occur by imitation?
- How does conditioning apply to practical problems?

WHAT IS LEARNING—DOES PRACTICE MAKE PERFECT?

>SURVEY QUESTION< *What is learning?*

Most behavior is learned. Imagine if you suddenly lost all you had ever learned. What could you do? You would be unable to read, write, or speak. You couldn't feed yourself, find your way home, drive a car, play the bassoon, or "party." Needless to say, you would be totally incapacitated. (Dull, too!)

Learning is a relatively permanent change in behavior due to experience (Domjan, 2006). Notice that this definition excludes temporary changes caused by motivation, fatigue, maturation, disease, injury, or drugs. Each of these can alter behavior, but none qualifies as learning.

Isn't learning the result of practice? It depends on what you mean by practice. Merely repeating a response will not necessarily produce learning. You could close your eyes and swing a tennis racket hundreds of times without learning anything about tennis. Reinforcement is the key to learning. **Reinforcement** refers to any event that increases the probability that a response will occur again. A response is any identifiable behavior. Responses may be observable actions, such as blinking, eating a piece of candy, or turning a doorknob. They can also be internal, such as having a faster heartbeat.

To teach a dog a trick, we could reinforce correct responses by giving the dog some food each time it sits up. Similarly, you could teach a child to be neat by praising her for picking up her toys. Learning can also occur in other ways. For instance, if a girl gets stung by a bee, she may learn to associate pain with bees and to fear them. In this case, the girl's fear is reinforced by the discomfort she feels immediately after seeing the bee. Later, you'll discover how such varied experiences lead to learning.

Antecedents and Consequences

Unlocking the secrets of learning begins with noting what happens before and after a response. Events that precede a response are called **antecedents.** For example, Ashleigh, who is 3, has learned that when she hears a truck pull into the driveway, it means that daddy is home. Ashleigh runs to the front door, where she gets a hug from her father. Effects that follow a response are **consequences.** The hug is what reinforces Ashleigh's tendency to run to the door. As this suggests, paying careful attention to the "before and after" of learning is a key to understanding it.

Learning Any relatively permanent change in behavior that can be attributed to experience.

Reinforcement Any event that increases the probability that a particular response will occur.

Antecedents Events that precede a response.

Consequences Effects that follow a response.

Classical Conditioning

Classical conditioning is based on what happens before we respond. It begins with a stimulus that reliably triggers a response. Imagine, for example, that a puff of air (the stimulus) is aimed at your eye. The air puff will make you blink (a response) every time. The eyeblink is a **reflex** (automatic, nonlearned response).

Now, assume that we sound a horn (another stimulus) just before each puff of air hits your eye. If the horn and the air puff occur together many times, what happens? Soon, the horn alone will make you blink. Clearly, you've learned something. Before, the horn didn't make you blink. Now it does. Similarly, if your mouth waters each time you eat a cookie, you may learn to salivate when you merely *see* a cookie, a picture of cookies, a cookie jar, or other stimuli that preceded salivation.

In **classical conditioning,** an antecedent stimulus that doesn't produce a response is linked with one that does (a horn is associated with a puff of air to the eye, for example). We can say that learning has occurred when the new stimulus will also elicit (bring forth) responses (»Fig. 6.1).

Operant Conditioning

In **operant conditioning,** learning is based on the consequences of responding. A response may be followed by a reinforcer (such as food). Or by punishment. Or by nothing. These results determine whether a response is likely to be made again (»Fig. 6.1). For example, if you wear a particular hat and get lots of compliments (reinforcement), you are likely to wear it more often. If people snicker, insult you, call the police, or scream (punishment), you will probably wear it less often.

Now that you have an idea of what happens in the two basic kinds of learning, let's look at classical conditioning in more detail.

»FIGURE 6.1 In classical conditioning, a stimulus that does not produce a response is paired with a stimulus that does elicit a response. After many such pairings, the stimulus that previously had no effect begins to produce a response. In the example shown, a horn precedes a puff of air to the eye. Eventually the horn alone will produce an eyeblink. In operant conditioning, a response that is followed by a reinforcing consequence becomes more likely to occur on future occasions. In the example shown, a dog learns to sit up when it hears a whistle.

CLASSICAL CONDITIONING—DOES THE NAME PAVLOV RING A BELL?

>SURVEY QUESTION< *How does classical conditioning occur?*

At the beginning of the twentieth century, something happened in the lab of Russian physiologist Ivan Pavlov that brought him the Nobel Prize: Pavlov's subjects drooled at him. Actually, Pavlov was studying digestion. To observe salivation, he placed meat powder or some tidbit on a dog's tongue. After doing this many times, Pavlov noticed that his dogs were salivating *before* the food reached their mouths. Later, the dogs even began to salivate when they saw Pavlov enter the room.

Was this misplaced affection? Pavlov knew better. Salivation is normally a reflex. For the animals to salivate at the mere sight of food, some type of learning must have occurred. Pavlov called it conditioning (»Fig. 6.2). Because of its importance in psychology's history, it is now called classical conditioning (also known as *Pavlovian conditioning* or *respondent conditioning*) (Mackintosh, 2003).

Pavlov's Experiment

How did Pavlov study conditioning? After Pavlov observed that food made his dogs salivate, he began his classic experiments (»Fig. 6.2). To begin, he rang a bell. At first, the bell was a neutral stimulus (the dogs did not respond to it by salivating). Immediately after Pavlov

Reflex An innate, automatic response to a stimulus; for example, an eyeblink.

Classical conditioning A form of learning in which reflex responses are associated with new stimuli.

Operant conditioning Learning based on the consequences of responding.

FIGURE 6.2 An apparatus for Pavlovian conditioning. A tube carries saliva from the dog's mouth to a lever that activates a recording device (far left). During conditioning, various stimuli can be paired with a dish of food placed in front of the dog. The device pictured here is more elaborate than the one Pavlov used in his early experiments.

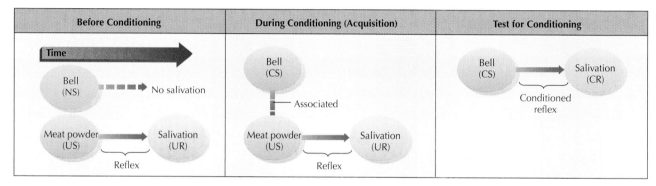

FIGURE 6.3 The classical conditioning procedure.

rang the bell, he placed meat powder on the dog's tongue, which caused reflex salivation. This sequence was repeated a number of times: bell, meat powder, salivation; bell, meat powder, salivation. Eventually (as conditioning took place), the dogs began to salivate when they heard the bell (▸▸Fig. 6.3). By association, the bell, which before had no effect, began to evoke the same response that food did. This was shown by sometimes ringing the bell alone. Then the dog salivated, even though no food had been placed in its mouth.

Psychologists use several terms to describe these events. The meat powder is an **unconditioned stimulus (US)** (a stimulus innately capable of producing a response). Notice that the dog did not have to learn to respond to the US. Such stimuli naturally trigger reflexes or emotional reactions. Because a reflex is innate, or "built in," it is called an **unconditioned** (nonlearned) **response (UR)**. Reflex salivation was the UR in Pavlov's experiment.

The bell starts out as a **neutral stimulus (NS)**. In time, the bell becomes a **conditioned stimulus (CS)** (a stimulus that, because of learning, will elicit a response). When Pavlov's bell also produced salivation, the dog was making a new response. Thus, salivation had also become a **conditioned** (learned) **response (CR)** (▸▸Fig. 6.3). ▪ Table 6.1 summarizes the important elements of classical conditioning.

Are all these terms really necessary? Yes, because they help us recognize similarities in various instances of learning. Let's summarize the terms using an earlier example:

Before Conditioning	Example
US → UR	Puff of air → eyeblink
NS → no effect	Horn → no effect

After Conditioning	Example
CS → CR	Horn → eyeblink

Unconditioned stimulus A stimulus innately capable of eliciting a response.

Unconditioned response An innate reflex response elicited by an unconditioned stimulus.

Neutral stimulus A stimulus that does not evoke a response.

Conditioned stimulus A stimulus that evokes a response because it has been repeatedly paired with an unconditioned stimulus.

Conditioned response A learned response elicited by a conditioned stimulus.

Coping with Chemo

Our hearts go out to children with cancer. Even the treatment, chemotherapy, makes them miserable because it causes nausea and vomiting. In a cruel twist, after a few treatments, nausea can occur even when no chemotherapy is scheduled. Typically, it is triggered by certain sights or tastes, like the sight of the treatment center or the taste of a food the child ate before an earlier chemotherapy session.

In classical conditioning terms, chemotherapy is a US that leads to nausea, which is a UR. The sight of the treatment center or the taste of food eaten before treatment is initially a neutral stimulus that becomes associated with nausea and vomiting, making it a CS. These sights or tastes can now elicit anticipatory nausea (a CR) even at times when the child doesn't receive chemotherapy (Chance, 2006).

In nature, many species are *biologically prepared* to associate specific locations and tastes with nausea. If animals eat contaminated food, get sick, and vomit, later the same locations or tastes may trigger anticipatory nausea and vomiting. These reactions discourage animals from eating potentially dangerous food. Unfortunately, conditioned nausea only complicates treatment for young cancer patients. If Gita eats pizza, her favorite meal, before she has a chemotherapy session, the taste of pizza may come to make her feel sick.

Is there any way to prevent conditioned nausea? No, but classical conditioning can provide some relief (Taylor, 2002). Meals eaten before chemotherapy can be strongly flavored with an unusual taste, such as peppermint. The unique flavor overshadows other tastes, which don't become linked with nausea (Bovbjerg et al., 1992). In this way, Gita can continue to enjoy her favorite meal.

■ Table 6.1 Elements of Classical Conditioning

Element	Symbol	Description	Example
Unconditioned stimulus	US	A stimulus innately capable of eliciting a response	Meat powder
Unconditioned response	UR	An innate reflex response elicited by an unconditioned stimulus	Reflex salivation
Neutral stimulus	NS	A stimulus that does not evoke a response	Bell
Conditioned stimulus	CS	A stimulus that evokes a response because it has been repeatedly paired with an unconditioned stimulus	Bell
Conditioned response	CR	A learned response elicited by a conditioned stimulus	Salivation

---

Now let's see if we can explain the shower and flushing toilet example described earlier. The unconditioned, or nonlearned, response was a reflex jump from the hot water. The unconditioned stimulus was the hot water. The conditioned stimulus was the sound of a flushing toilet. That is, the flushing sound was at first neutral. But as a result of conditioning, it became capable of triggering a reflex. See "Coping with Chemo" for an example of how classical conditioning is being used to solve a clinical problem.

Imagine a boy named Johnny. To observe conditioning, you could ring a bell and squirt lemon juice into Johnny's mouth. By repeating this procedure several times, you could condition Johnny to salivate to the bell. Johnny might then be used to explore other aspects of classical conditioning. Let's see how conditioning occurs.

Acquisition

During **acquisition,** or training, a conditioned response must be reinforced (strengthened) (▶Fig. 6.4). Classical conditioning is reinforced when the CS is followed by, or paired with, an unconditioned stimulus. This type of reinforcement is known as **respondent reinforcement.** For Johnny, the bell is the CS, salivating is the UR, and the sour lemon juice is a US. To reinforce salivating to the bell, we must link the bell with the lemon juice. Conditioning will be most rapid if the US (lemon juice) follows *immediately* after the CS (the bell). With

Acquisition The period in conditioning during which a response is reinforced.

Respondent reinforcement Reinforcement that occurs when an unconditioned stimulus closely follows a conditioned stimulus.

▸▸**FIGURE 6.4** Acquisition and extinction of a conditioned response. (After Pavlov, 1927.)

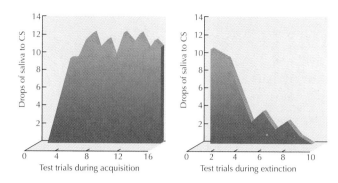

Test trials during acquisition · Test trials during extinction

most reflexes, the optimal delay between CS and US is from one-half second to about 5 seconds (Chance, 2006).

Higher Order Conditioning

Once a response is learned, it can bring about **higher order conditioning.** In this case, a well-learned CS is used to reinforce further learning. That is, the CS has become strong enough to be used like an unconditioned stimulus. Let's illustrate again with our salivating child.

As a result of earlier learning, the bell now makes Johnny salivate. (No lemon juice is now needed.) To go a step further, you could clap your hands and then ring the bell. (Again, no lemon juice would be used.) Through higher order conditioning, Johnny would soon learn to salivate when you clapped your hands (▸▸Fig. 6.5). (This little trick could be a real hit with friends and neighbors.)

Higher order conditioning extends learning one or more steps beyond the original conditioned stimulus. Many advertisers use this effect by pairing images that evoke good feelings (such as people smiling and having fun) with pictures of their products. They hope that you will learn, by association, to feel good when you see their products (Priluck & Till, 2004).

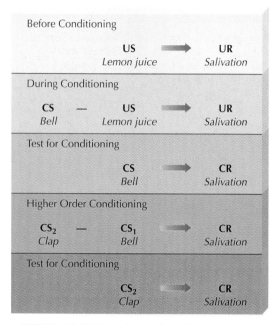

▸▸**FIGURE 6.5** Higher order conditioning takes place when a well-learned conditioned stimulus is used as if it were an unconditioned stimulus. In this example, a child is first conditioned to salivate to the sound of a bell. In time, the bell will elicit salivation. At that point, you could clap your hands and then ring the bell. Soon, after repeating the procedure, the child would learn to salivate when you clapped your hands.

Expectancies

Many psychologists believe that classical conditioning is related to information that might aid survival. According to this **informational view,** we look for associations among events. Doing so creates new mental **expectancies,** or expectations about how events are interconnected.

How does classical conditioning alter expectancies? Notice that the conditioned stimulus reliably precedes the unconditioned stimulus. Because it does, the CS *predicts* the US (Rescorla, 1987). During conditioning, the brain learns to *expect* that the US will follow the CS. As a result, the brain prepares the body to respond to the US. Here's an example: When you are about to get a shot with a hypodermic needle, your muscles tighten and there is a catch in your breathing. Why? Because your body is preparing for pain. You have learned to expect that getting poked with a needle will hurt. This expectancy, which was acquired during classical conditioning, changes your behavior.

Extinction and Spontaneous Recovery

After conditioning has occurred, what would happen if the US no longer followed the CS? If the US never again follows the CS, conditioning will extinguish, or fade away. Let's return to the boy and the bell. If you ring the bell many times and do not follow it with lemon juice, Johnny's expectancy that "bell precedes lemon juice" will weaken. As it does, he will lose his tendency to salivate when he hears the bell. Thus, we see that classical conditioning can be weakened by removing the contingency between the conditioned and unconditioned stimulus (see ▸▸Fig. 6.4). This process is called **extinction.**

Higher order conditioning Classical conditioning in which a conditioned stimulus is used to reinforce further learning; that is, a CS is used as if it were a US.

Informational view Perspective that explains learning in terms of information imparted by events in the environment.

Expectancy An anticipation concerning future events or relationships.

Extinction The weakening of a conditioned response through removal of reinforcement.

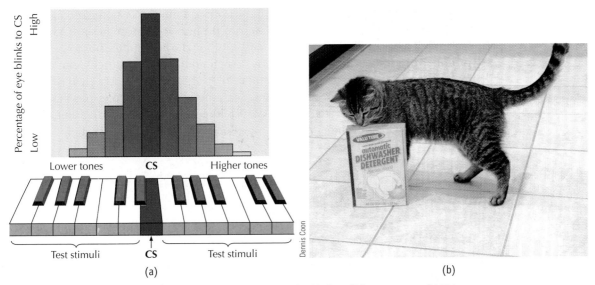

▸▸**FIGURE 6.6** *(a)* Stimulus generalization. Stimuli similar to the CS also elicit a response. *(b)* This cat has learned to salivate when it sees a cat food box. Because of stimulus generalization, it also salivates when shown a similar-looking detergent box.

If conditioning takes a while to build up, shouldn't it take time to reverse? Yes. In fact, it may take several extinction sessions to completely reverse conditioning. Let's say that we ring the bell until Johnny quits responding. It might seem that extinction is complete. However, Johnny will probably respond to the bell again on the following day, at least at first (Rescorla, 2004). The return of a learned response after apparent extinction is called **spontaneous recovery.** It explains why people who have had car accidents may need many slow, calm rides before their fear of driving extinguishes.

Generalization

After conditioning, other stimuli similar to the CS may also trigger a response. This is called **stimulus generalization.** For example, we might find that Johnny salivates to the sound of a ringing telephone or doorbell, even though they were never used as conditioning stimuli.

It is easy to see the value of stimulus generalization. Consider the child who burns her finger while playing with matches. Most likely, lighted matches will become conditioned fear stimuli for her. But will she fear only matches? Because of stimulus generalization, she may also have a healthy fear of flames from lighters, fireplaces, stoves, and so forth. It's fortunate that generalization extends learning to related situations. Otherwise, we would all be far less adaptable.

As you may have guessed, stimulus generalization has limits. As stimuli become less like the original CS, responding decreases. If you condition a person to blink each time you play a particular note on a piano, blinking will decline as you play higher or lower notes. If the notes are *much* higher or lower, the person will not respond at all (▸▸Fig. 6.6). Stimulus generalization explains why many stores carry imitations of nationally known products. For many customers, positive attitudes conditioned to the real products tend to generalize to the cheaper knockoffs (Till & Priluck, 2000).

Discrimination

Let's consider one more idea with Johnny (who by now must be ready to hide in the closet). Suppose we again condition him, with a bell as the CS. As an experiment, we also occasionally sound a buzzer instead of ringing the bell. However, the buzzer is never followed by the US (lemon juice). At first, Johnny salivates when he hears the buzzer (because of generaliza-

Spontaneous recovery The reappearance of a learned response after its apparent extinction.

Stimulus generalization The tendency to respond to stimuli similar to, but not identical to, a conditioned stimulus.

tion). But after we sound the buzzer several times more, Johnny will stop responding to it. Why? In essence, Johnny's generalized response to the buzzer has extinguished. As a result, he has learned to *discriminate,* or respond differently, to the bell and the buzzer.

Stimulus discrimination is the ability to respond differently to various stimuli. As an example, you might remember the feelings of anxiety or fear you had as a child when your mother's or father's voice changed to its you're-in-a-heap-of-trouble tone. (Or the dreaded give-me-that-PlayStation Portable tone.) Most children quickly learn to discriminate voice tones associated with punishment from those associated with praise or affection.

CLASSICAL CONDITIONING IN HUMANS— AN EMOTIONAL TOPIC

>SURVEY QUESTION< *Does conditioning affect emotions?*

How much human learning is based on classical conditioning? At its simplest, classical conditioning depends on reflex responses. As mentioned earlier, a reflex is a dependable, inborn stimulus-and-response connection. For example, your hand reflexively draws back from pain. Bright light causes the pupil of the eye to narrow. A puff of air directed at your eye will make you blink. Various foods elicit salivation. Any of these reflexes, and others as well, can be associated with a new stimulus. At the very least, you have probably noticed how your mouth waters when you see or smell a bakery. Even pictures of food may make you salivate (a photo of a sliced lemon is great for this).

Conditioned Emotional Responses

In addition to simple reflexes, more complex *emotional,* or "gut," responses may be linked to new stimuli. For instance, if your face reddened when you were punished as a child, you may blush now when you are embarrassed or ashamed. Or think about the effects of associating pain with a dentist's office during your first visit. On later visits, did your heart pound and your palms sweat *before* the dentist began?

Many *involuntary,* autonomic nervous system responses ("fight-or-flight" reflexes) are linked with new stimuli and situations by classical conditioning. For example, learned reactions worsen many cases of hypertension (high blood pressure). Traffic jams, arguments with a spouse, and similar situations can become conditioned stimuli that trigger a dangerous rise in blood pressure (Reiff, Katkin, & Friedman, 1999).

Of course, emotional conditioning also applies to animals. One of the most common mistakes people make with pets (especially dogs) is hitting them if they do not come when called. Calling the animal then becomes a conditioned stimulus for fear and withdrawal. No wonder the pet disobeys when called on future occasions. Parents who belittle, scream at, or physically abuse their children make the same mistake.

Learned Fears

Some phobias (FOE-bee-ahs) are also based on emotional conditioning. A *phobia* is a fear that persists even when no realistic danger exists. Fears of animals, water, heights, thunder, fire, bugs, elevators, and the like are common. Psychologists believe that many phobias begin as **conditioned emotional responses (CERs),** learned emotional reactions to a previously neutral stimulus. People who have phobias can often trace their fears to a time when they were frightened, injured, or upset by a particular stimulus, especially in childhood (King, Muris, & Ollendick, 2005). Just one bad experience in which you were frightened or disgusted by a spider may condition fears that last for years (de Jong & Muris, 2002).

Stimulus generalization and higher order conditioning can spread CERs to other stimuli (Gewirtz & Davis, 1998). As a result, what began as a limited fear may become a disabling phobia (▸▸Fig. 6.7). However, a therapy called *desensitization* is now widely used to extin-

Stimulus discrimination The learned ability to respond differently to similar stimuli.

Conditioned emotional response An emotional response that has been linked to a previously nonemotional stimulus by classical conditioning.

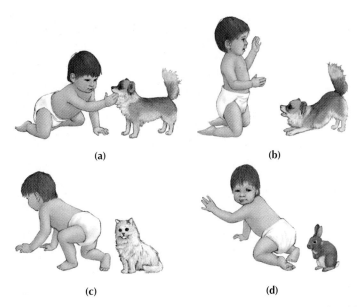

▶▶**FIGURE 6.7** Hypothetical example of a CER becoming a phobia. Child approaches dog *(a)* and is frightened by it *(b)*. Fear generalizes to other household pets *(c)* and later to virtually all furry animals *(d)*.

guish fears, anxieties, and phobias. This is done by gradually exposing the phobic person to feared stimuli while she or he remains calm and relaxed. For example, people have been desensitized for acrophobia (fear of heights) through *virtual reality exposure,* the use of computers to safely simulate the experience of heights (Wiederhold & Wiederhold, 2005). (See Chapter 13 for more information about therapies based on learning principles.)

Undoubtedly, we acquire many of our likes, dislikes, and fears as conditioned emotional responses. As noted before, advertisers try to achieve the same effect by pairing products with pleasant images and music. So do many students on a first date.

Vicarious, or Secondhand, Conditioning

Conditioning also occurs indirectly, which adds to its impact on us. Let's say, for example, that you watch another person get an electric shock. Each time, a signal light comes on before the shock is delivered. Even if you don't receive a shock yourself, you will soon develop a CER to the light. Children who learn to fear thunder by watching their parents react to it have undergone similar conditioning. Many Americans were traumatized as a consequence of watching media coverage of the September 11 terrorist attacks in New York and Washington (Blanchard et al., 2004). Similarly, people who counsel traumatized victims of sexual abuse can develop vicarious trauma (Way et al., 2004).

Vicarious classical conditioning occurs when we learn to respond emotionally to a stimulus by observing another person's emotional reactions. Such "secondhand" learning affects feelings in many situations. For example, "horror" movies filled with screaming actors probably add to fears of snakes, caves, spiders, heights, and other terrors. If movies can affect us, we might expect the emotions of parents, friends, and relatives to have even more impact. How, for instance, does a city child learn to fear snakes and respond emotionally to mere pictures of them? Being told that "snakes are dangerous" may not explain the child's *emotional* response. More likely, the child has observed others reacting fearfully to the word *snake* or to snake images on television (King, Muris, & Ollendick, 2005).

The emotional attitudes we develop toward foods, political parties, ethnic groups, escalators—whatever—are probably conditioned not only by direct experiences, but vicariously as well. No one is born prejudiced—all attitudes are learned. Parents may do well to look in a mirror if they wonder how or where a child "picked up" a particular fear or emotional attitude (Mineka & Hamida, 1998).

Vicarious classical conditioning
Classical conditioning brought about by observing another person react to a particular stimulus.

Reflect

US, CS, UR, CR—How will you remember these terms? First, you should note that we are interested in either a stimulus (S) or a response (R). What else do we need to know? Each S or R can be either conditioned (C) or unconditioned (U).

Can a stimulus provoke a response before any learning has occurred? If it can, then it's a US. Do you have to learn to respond to the stimulus? Then it's a CS.

Does a response occur without being learned? Then it's a UR. If it has to be learned, then it's a CR.

Learning Check

1. The concept of reinforcement applies to both

   a. antecedents and consequences
   b. neutral stimuli and rewards
   c. classical and operant conditioning
   d. acquisition and spontaneous recovery

2. Classical conditioning, studied by the Russian physiologist _____, is also referred to as _____ conditioning.

3. You smell the odor of cookies being baked and your mouth waters. Apparently, the odor of cookies is a _____ and your salivation is a _____.

   a. CR, CS
   b. CS, CR
   c. consequence, neutral stimulus
   d. reflex, CS

4. The informational view says that classical conditioning is based on changes in mental _____ about the CS and US.

5. After you have acquired a conditioned response, it may be weakened by

   a. spontaneous recovery
   b. stimulus generalization
   c. removing reinforcement
   d. following the CS with a US

6. When a conditioned stimulus is used to reinforce the learning of a second conditioned stimulus, higher order conditioning has occurred. T or F?

7. Psychologists theorize that many phobias begin when a CER generalizes to other, similar situations. T or F?

8. Three-year-old Josh sees his five-year-old sister get chased by a neighbor's dog. Now Josh is as afraid of the dog as his sister is. Josh's fear is a result of

   a. stimulus discrimination
   b. vicarious conditioning
   c. spontaneous recovery
   d. higher order conditioning

Critical Thinking

9. Lately you have been getting a shock of static electricity every time you touch a door handle. Now there is a hesitation in your door-opening movements. Can you analyze this situation in terms of classical conditioning?

Answers

1. c 2. Pavlov, respondent 3. b 4. expectancies 5. c 6. T 7. T 8. b 9. Door handles have become conditioned stimuli that elicit the reflex withdrawal and muscle tensing that normally follows getting a shock. This conditioned response has also generalized to other handles.

OPERANT CONDITIONING—CAN PIGEONS PLAY PING-PONG?

>SURVEY QUESTION< *How does operant conditioning occur?*

Operant conditioning applies to all living creatures and explains much day-to-day behavior. The principles of operant learning are among the most powerful tools in psychology. You won't regret learning how to apply them. Operant conditioning can be used to alter the behavior of pets, children, other adults, and your own behavior, too.

As stated earlier, in **operant conditioning** (or instrumental learning) we associate responses with their consequences. The basic principle is simple: Acts that are reinforced tend to be repeated (Mazur, 2006). Pioneer learning theorist Edward L. Thorndike called this the **law of effect** (the probability of a response is altered by the effect it has). Learning is strengthened each time a response is followed by a satisfying state of affairs. Think of the earlier example of the vending machine. Because kicking the machine had the effect of producing food and money, the odds of repeating the "kicking response" increased.

Classical conditioning is passive. It simply "happens to" the learner when a US follows a CS. In operant conditioning, the learner actively "operates on" the environment. Thus, operant conditioning refers mainly to learning *voluntary* responses. For example, pushing buttons on a TV remote control is a learned operant response. Pushing a particular button is reinforced by gaining the consequence you desire, such as changing channels or muting an obnoxious commercial. (See ▪ Table 6.2 for a further comparison of classical and operant conditioning.)

Operant conditioning Learning based on the consequences of responding.

Law of effect Responses that lead to desirable effects are repeated; those that produce undesirable results are not.

■ Table 6.2 Comparison of Classical and Operant Conditioning

	Classical Conditioning	Operant Conditioning
Nature of response	Involuntary, reflex	Spontaneous, voluntary
Reinforcement	Occurs *before* response (CS paired with US)	Occurs *after* response (response is followed by reinforcing stimulus or event)
Role of learner	Passive (response is *elicited* by US)	Active (response is emitted)
Nature of learning	Neutral stimulus becomes a CS through association with a US	Probability of making a response is altered by consequences that follow it
Learned expectancy	US will follow CS	Response will have a specific effect

Positive Reinforcement

The idea that reward affects learning is certainly nothing new to parents (and other trainers of small animals). However, parents, as well as teachers, politicians, supervisors, and even you, may use reward in ways that are inexact or misguided. A case in point is the term *reward*. To be correct, it is better to say *reinforcer*. Why? Because rewards do not always increase responding. If you try to give licorice candy to a child as a "reward" for good behavior, it will work only if the child likes licorice. What is reinforcing for one person may not be for another. As a practical rule of thumb, psychologists define an **operant reinforcer** as any event that follows a response and increases its probability of occurring again (»Fig. 6.8).

Acquiring an Operant Response

Many studies of instrumental learning have been done in a conditioning chamber, an apparatus designed to study operant conditioning in animals. This device is also called a Skinner box, after B. F. Skinner, who invented it. A look into a typical Skinner box will clarify the process of operant conditioning.

The Adventures of Mickey Rat

A hungry rat is placed in a small cage-like chamber. The walls are bare except for a metal lever and a tray into which food pellets can be dispensed (see »Fig. 6.9).

Frankly, there's not much to do in a Skinner box. This increases the chances that our subject will make the response we want to reinforce, which is pressing the bar. Also, hunger

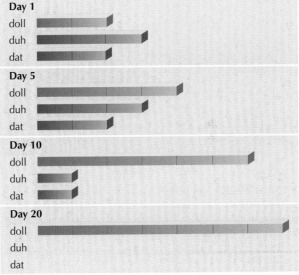

»FIGURE 6.8 Assume that a child who is learning to talk points to her favorite doll and says either "doll," "duh," or "dat" when she wants it. Day 1 shows the number of times the child uses each word to ask for the doll (each block represents one request). At first, she uses all three words interchangeably. To hasten learning, her parents decide to give her the doll only when she names it correctly. Notice how the child's behavior shifts as operant reinforcement is applied. By day 20, saying "doll" has become the most probable response.

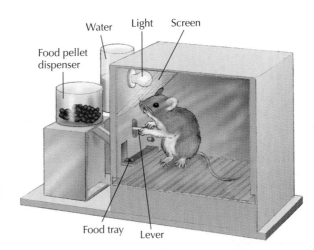

»FIGURE 6.9 The Skinner box. This simple device, invented by B. F. Skinner, allows careful study of operant conditioning. When the rat presses the bar, a pellet of food or a drop of water is automatically released. (A photograph of a Skinner box appears in Chapter 1.)

Operant reinforcer Any event that reliably increases the probability or frequency of responses it follows.

keeps the animal motivated to seek food and actively *emit,* or freely give off, a variety of responses. Now let's take another look at our subject.

Further Adventures of Mickey Rat

For a while our subject walks around, grooms, sniffs at the corners, or stands on his hind legs—all typical rat behaviors. Then it happens. He places his paw on the lever to get a better view of the top of the cage. *Click!* The lever depresses, and a food pellet drops into the tray. The rat walks to the tray, eats the pellet, and then grooms himself. Up and exploring the cage again, he leans on the lever. *Click!* After a trip to the food tray, he returns to the bar and sniffs it, then puts his foot on it. *Click!* Soon the rat settles into a smooth pattern of frequent bar pressing.

Notice that the rat did not acquire a new skill in this situation. He was already able to depress the bar. Reinforcement only alters how *frequently* he presses the bar. In operant conditioning, new behavior patterns are molded by changing the probability that various responses will be made.

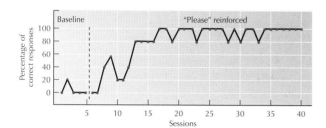

» **FIGURE 6.10** Reinforcement and human behavior. The percentage of times that a severely disturbed child said "Please" when he wanted an object was increased dramatically by reinforcing him for making a polite request. Reinforcement produced similar improvements in saying "Thank you" and "You're welcome," and the boy applied these terms in new situations as well. (Adapted from Matson et al., 1990.)

Information and Contingency

Like classical conditioning, operant learning is based on information and expectancies. In operant conditioning, *we learn to expect that a certain response will have a certain effect at certain times* (Pierce & Cheney, 2004). That is, we learn that a particular stimulus is associated with a particular response that is associated with reinforcement (Hergenhahn & Olson, 2005). Further, operant reinforcement works best when it is *response contingent* (kon-TIN-jent). That is, it must be given only after a desired response has occurred. From this point of view, a reinforcer tells a person or an animal that a response was "right" and worth repeating.

» Figure 6.10 shows how operant reinforcement can change behavior. The results are from an effort to teach a severely disturbed 9-year-old child to say "Please," "Thank you," and "You're welcome." As you can see, during the initial, baseline period, the child rarely used the word *please.* Typically, he just grabbed objects and became angry if he couldn't have them. However, when he was reinforced for saying "Please," he soon learned to use the word nearly every time he wanted something. When the child said "Please" he was reinforced in three ways: He received the object he asked for (a crayon, for example); he was given a small food treat, such as a piece of candy, popcorn, or a grape; and he was praised for his good behavior (Matson et al., 1990).

The Timing of Reinforcement

Operant reinforcement is most effective when it rapidly follows a correct response (Mazur, 2006). For rats in a Skinner box, little learning, if any, occurs when the delay between bar pressing and receiving food exceeds 50 seconds (»Fig. 6.11). In general, you will be most

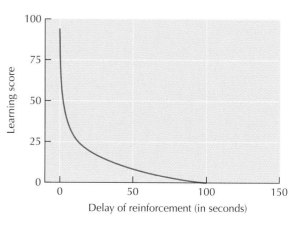

» **FIGURE 6.11** The effect of delay of reinforcement. Notice how rapidly the learning score drops when reward is delayed. Animals learning to press a bar in a Skinner box showed no signs of learning if food reward followed a bar press by more than 100 seconds (Perin, 1943).

successful if you present a reinforcer *immediately* after a response you wish to change. Thus, a child who is helpful or courteous should be immediately praised for her good behavior.

Let's say I work hard all semester in a class to get an A grade. Wouldn't the delay in reinforcement keep me from learning anything? No, for several reasons. First, as a mature human you can anticipate future reward. Second, you get reinforced by quiz and test grades all through the semester. Third, a single reinforcer can often maintain a long **response chain** (a linked series of actions that lead to reinforcement). A classic example of response chaining is provided by Barnabus, a rat trained by psychologists at Brown University.

The Great Barnabus

By carefully working from the last response to the first, Barnabus was trained to make an ever-longer chain of responses to obtain a single food pellet. When in top form, Barnabus was able to climb a spiral staircase, cross a narrow bridge, climb a ladder, pull a toy car with a chain, get into the car, pedal it to a second staircase, climb the staircase, wriggle through a tube, climb onto an elevator and descend to a platform, press a lever to receive a food pellet, and . . . start over! (Pierrel & Sherman, 1963)

Many of the things we do every day involve similar response chains. The long series of events necessary to prepare a meal is rewarded by the final eating. A violinmaker may carry out thousands of steps for the final reward of hearing a first musical note. And as a student, you have built up a long response chain for the final reward of a good grade (right?).

Are You Superstitious?

Reinforcers affect not only the specific response they follow but also other responses that occur shortly before. This helps explain many human superstitions. If a golfer taps her club on the ground three times and then hits a great shot, what happens? The successful shot reinforces not only the correct swing but also the three taps. During operant training, animals often develop similar unnecessary responses. If this happens a few times more, the golfer may superstitiously tap her club three times before every shot. Some examples of actual superstitious behaviors of professional baseball players include drawing four lines in the dirt before getting in the batter's box, eating chicken before each game, and always playing in the same athletic supporter—for four years (phew!) (Burger & Lynn, 2005).

Superstitious behaviors are repeated because they appear to produce reinforcement, even though they are actually unnecessary (Burger & Lynn, 2005). If you walk under a ladder and then break a leg, you may avoid ladders in the future. Each time you avoid a ladder and nothing bad happens, your superstitious action is reinforced. Belief in magic can also be explained along such lines. Rituals to bring rain, ward off illness, or produce abundant crops very likely earn the faith of participants because they occasionally appear to succeed. Besides, better safe than sorry.

Shaping

How is it possible to reinforce responses that rarely occur? Even in a barren Skinner box, it could take a long time for a rat to accidentally press the bar and get a food pellet. We might wait forever for more complicated responses to occur. For example, you would have to wait a long time for a duck to accidentally walk out of its cage, turn on a light, play a toy piano, turn off the light, and walk back to its cage. If this is what you wanted to reward, you would never get the chance.

Then how are the animals on TV and at amusement parks taught to perform complicated tricks? The answer lies in **shaping,** which is the gradual molding of responses to a desired pattern. Let's look again at our subject, Mickey Rat.

Mickey Rat Shapes Up

Assume that the rat has not yet learned to press the bar. He also shows no signs of interest in the bar. Instead of waiting for the first accidental bar press, we can shape his behavior. At first, we settle for just getting him to face the bar. Any time he turns toward the bar, he is reinforced with a bit of food. Soon Mickey spends much

---

Response chaining The assembly of separate responses into a series of actions that lead to reinforcement.

Superstitious behavior A behavior repeated because it seems to produce reinforcement, even though it is actually unnecessary.

Shaping Gradually molding responses to a final desired pattern.

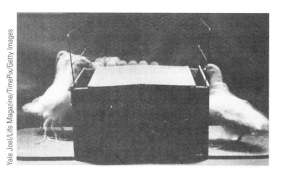

FIGURE 6.12 Operant conditioning principles were used to train these pigeons to play Ping-Pong.

of his time facing the bar. Next, we reinforce him every time he takes a step toward the bar. If he turns toward the bar and walks away, nothing happens. But when he faces the bar and takes a step forward, *click!* His responses are being shaped.

By changing the rules about what makes a successful response, we can gradually train the rat to approach the bar and press it. In other words, *successive approximations* (ever-closer matches) to a desired response are reinforced during shaping. B. F. Skinner once taught two pigeons to play Ping-Pong in this way (Fig. 6.12). Shaping applies to humans, too. Let's say you want to study more, clean the house more often, or exercise more. In each case, it would be best to set a series of gradual, daily goals. Then you can reward yourself for small steps in the right direction (Watson & Tharp, 2007).

Operant Extinction

Would a rat stop bar pressing if no more food arrived? Yes, but not immediately. Through **operant extinction,** learned responses that are not reinforced gradually fade away. Just as acquiring an operant response takes time, so does extinction. For example, if a TV program repeatedly bores you, watching the program will probably extinguish over time.

Even after extinction seems complete, the previously reinforced response may return. If a rat is removed from a Skinner box after extinction and given a short rest, the rat will press the bar again when returned to the box. Similarly, a few weeks after they give up on buying state lottery tickets, many people are tempted to try again.

Does extinction take as long the second time? If reinforcement is still withheld, a rat's bar pressing will extinguish again, usually more quickly. The brief return of an operant response after extinction is another example of spontaneous recovery (mentioned earlier regarding classical conditioning). Spontaneous recovery is very adaptive. After a rest period, the rat responds again in a situation that produced food in the past: "Just checking to see if the rules have changed!"

Marked changes in behavior occur when reinforcement and extinction are combined. For example, parents often unknowingly reinforce children for *negative attention seeking* (using misbehavior to gain attention). Children are generally ignored when they are playing quietly. They get attention when they become louder and louder, yell "Hey, Mom!" at the top of their lungs, throw tantrums, show off, or break something. Granted, the attention they get is often a scolding, but attention is a powerful reinforcer, nevertheless. Parents report dramatic improvements when they *ignore* their children's disruptive behavior and praise or attend to a child who is quiet or playing constructively.

Negative Reinforcement

Until now, we have stressed **positive reinforcement,** which occurs when a pleasant or desirable event follows a response. How else could operant learning be reinforced? The time has come to consider **negative reinforcement,** which occurs when making a response removes an unpleasant event. Don't be fooled by the word *negative.* Negative reinforcement also increases responding. However, it does so by ending (negating) discomfort.

Let's say that you have a headache and take an aspirin. Your aspirin taking will be negatively reinforced if the headache stops. Likewise, a rat could be taught to press a bar to get food (positive reinforcement), or the rat could be given a continuous mild shock (through the floor of its cage) that is turned off by a bar press (negative reinforcement). Either way, the rat will learn to press the bar more often. Why? Because it leads to a desired state of affairs (food or an end to pain). Here's another example of negative reinforcement: A politician who irritates you is being interviewed on the evening news. You change channels so you won't have to listen to him. (Channel changing is negatively reinforced.)

Operant extinction The weakening or disappearance of a nonreinforced operant response.

Positive reinforcement Occurs when a response is followed by a reward or other positive event.

Negative reinforcement Occurs when a response is followed by an end to discomfort or by the removal of an unpleasant event.

■ Table 6.3 Behavioral Effects of Various Consequences

	Consequence of Making a Response	Example	Effect on Response Probability
Positive reinforcement	Positive event begins	Food given	Increase
Negative reinforcement	Negative event ends	Pain stops	Increase
Punishment	Negative event begins	Pain begins	Decrease
Punishment (response cost)	Positive event ends	Food removed	Decrease
Nonreinforcement	Nothing	—	Decrease

Punishment

Many people mistake negative reinforcement for punishment. However, **punishment** refers to following a response with an *aversive* (unpleasant) consequence. Punishment *decreases* the likelihood that the response will occur again. As noted, negative reinforcement *increases* responding. The difference can be seen in a hypothetical example. Let's say you live in an apartment and your neighbor's stereo is blasting so loudly that your ears hurt. If you pound on the wall and the volume suddenly drops (negative reinforcement), future wall pounding will be more likely. But if you pound on the wall and the volume increases (punishment) or if the neighbor comes over and pounds on you (more punishment), wall pounding becomes less likely. Here's another example of punishment, in which an unpleasant result follows a response: Every time you give advice to a friend she suddenly turns cold and distant. Lately, you've stopped offering her advice. (Giving advice was punished by rejection.)

Isn't it also punishing to have privileges, money, or other positive things taken away for making a particular response? Yes. Punishment also occurs when a reinforcer or positive state of affairs is removed, such as losing privileges. This second type of punishment is called **response cost.** Parents who "ground" their teenage children for misbehavior are applying response cost. Parking tickets and other fines are also based on response cost. For your convenience, ■ Table 6.3 summarizes four basic consequences of making a response.

OPERANT REINFORCERS— WHAT'S YOUR PLEASURE?

>SURVEY QUESTION< *Are there different kinds of operant reinforcement?*

For humans, learning may be reinforced by anything from an M&M candy to a pat on the back. In categorizing reinforcers, useful distinctions can be made between *primary reinforcers, secondary reinforcers,* and *feedback.* Operant reinforcers of all types have a large impact on our lives. Let's examine them in more detail.

Primary Reinforcers

Primary reinforcers are natural, nonlearned, and rooted in biology: They produce comfort, end discomfort, or fill an immediate physical need. Food, water, and sex are obvious examples. Every time you open the refrigerator, walk to a drinking fountain, turn up the heat, or order a double latte, your actions reflect primary reinforcement. In addition to obvious examples, there are other, less obvious, primary reinforcers, such as psychoactive drugs. One of the most powerful is *intracranial self-stimulation,* which involves the direct activation of "pleasure centers" in the brain (see "Tickling Your Own Fancy").

Punishment Any event that follows a response and *decreases* its likelihood of occurring again.

Response cost Removal of a positive reinforcer after a response is made.

Primary reinforcers Nonlearned reinforcers; usually those that satisfy physiological needs.

Tickling Your Own Fancy

Suppose you could have an electrode permanently implanted in your brain and connected to an iPod-style controller. Twirl the controller and electrical impulses stimulate one of your brain's "pleasure centers." The very few humans who have ever had a chance to try direct brain stimulation report feeling intense pleasure that is better than food, water, sex, drugs, or any other primary reinforcer (Heath, 1963). (See ▸▸Fig 6.13.)

Most of what we know about intracranial self-stimulation (ICSS) comes from studying rats with similar implants (Olds & Fobes, 1981). A rat "wired for pleasure" can be trained to press the bar in a Skinner box to deliver electrical stimulation to its own limbic system (refer back to Fig 2.26). Some rats will press the bar thousands of times per hour to obtain brain stimulation. After 15 or 20 hours of constant pressing, animals sometimes collapse from exhaustion. When they revive, they begin pressing again. If the reward circuit is not turned off, an animal will ignore food, water, and sex in favor of bar pressing.

Many natural primary reinforcers activate the same pleasure pathways in the brain that make ICSS so powerful (McBride, Murphy, & Ikemoto, 1999). So do psychoactive drugs, such as alcohol and cocaine (Eisler, Justice, Jr., & Neill, 2004; Rodd et al., 2005). One shudders to think what might happen if brain implants were easy and practical to do. (They are not.) Every company from Playboy to Microsoft would have a device on the market, and we would have to keep a closer watch on politicians than usual!

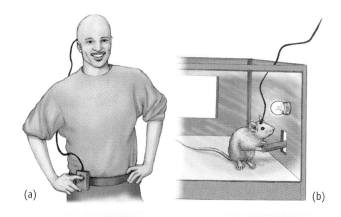

(a)   (b)

▸▸**FIGURE 6.13** Humans have been "wired" for brain stimulation, as shown in *(a)*. However, in humans, this has been done only as an experimental way to restrain uncontrollable outbursts of violence. Implants have not been done merely to produce pleasure. Most research has been carried out with rats. Using the apparatus shown in *(b)*, the rat can press a bar to deliver mild electric stimulation to a "pleasure center" in the brain.

Secondary Reinforcers

Much human learning is still strongly tied to food, water, and other primary reinforcers. Regardless, humans also respond to a broader range of rewards and reinforcers. Money, praise, attention, approval, success, affection, grades, and the like, all serve as learned or **secondary reinforcers.**

How does a secondary reinforcer gain its ability to promote learning? Some secondary reinforcers are simply associated with a primary reinforcer. For example, if you would like to train a dog to follow you ("heel") when you take a walk, you could reward the dog with small food treats for staying near you. If you praise the dog each time you give it a treat, praise will become a secondary reinforcer. In time, you will be able to skip giving treats and simply praise your pup for doing the right thing. The same principle applies to children. One reason that parents' praise becomes a secondary reinforcer is because it is frequently associated with food, candy, hugs, and other primary reinforcers.

Tokens

Secondary reinforcers that can be *exchanged* for primary reinforcers gain their value more directly (Mazur, 2006). Printed money obviously has little or no value of its own. You can't eat it, drink it, or sleep with it. However, it can be exchanged for food, water, lodging, and other necessities.

A **token reinforcer** is a tangible secondary reinforcer, such as money, gold stars, poker chips, and the like. In a series of classic experiments, chimpanzees were taught to work for tokens. The chimps were first trained to put poker chips into a "Chimp-O-Mat" vending machine. Each chip dispensed a few grapes or raisins. Once the animals had learned to exchange tokens for food, they would learn new tasks to earn the chips. To maintain the

Secondary reinforcer A learned reinforcer; often one that gains reinforcing properties by association with a primary reinforcer.

Token reinforcer A tangible secondary reinforcer such as money, gold stars, poker chips, and the like.

value of the tokens, the chimps were occasionally allowed to use the "Chimp-O-Mat" (Cowles, 1937) (▶Fig. 6.14).

A major advantage of tokens is that they don't lose reinforcing value as quickly as primary reinforcers do. For instance, if you use candy to reinforce a retarded child for correctly naming things, the child might lose interest once he is satiated (fully satisfied) or no longer hungry. It would be better to use tokens as immediate rewards for learning. Later, the child can exchange his tokens for candy, toys, or other treats.

Tokens have been used with troubled children and adults in special programs, and even in ordinary elementary school classrooms (Spiegler & Guevremont, 2003) (▶Fig. 6.15). In each case the goal is to provide an immediate reward for learning. Typically, tokens may be exchanged for food, special privileges, or trips to movies, amusement parks, and so forth. Many parents find that tokens greatly reduce discipline problems with younger children. For example, children can earn points or gold stars during the week for good behavior. If they earn enough tokens, they are allowed on Sunday to choose one item out of a "grab bag" of small prizes.

Social Reinforcers

As we have noted, learned desires for attention and approval, which are called **social reinforcers,** often influence human behavior. This fact can be used in a classic, if somewhat mischievous, demonstration.

Shaping a Teacher

For this activity, about one half (or more) of the students in a classroom must participate. First, select a target behavior. This should be something like "lecturing from the right side of the room." (Keep it simple, in case your teacher is a slow learner.) Begin training in this way: Each time the instructor turns toward the right or takes a step in that direction, participating students should look *really* interested. Also, smile, ask questions, lean forward, and make eye contact. If the teacher turns to the left or takes a step in that direction, participating students should lean back, yawn, check out their split ends, close their eyes, or generally look bored. Soon, without being aware of why, the instructor should be spending most of his or her time each class period lecturing from the right side of the classroom.

This trick has been a favorite of psychology graduate students for decades. For a time, one of your author's professors delivered all of her lectures from the right side of the room while toying with the cords on the window shades. (We added the cords the second week!) The point to remember from this example is that attention and approval can change the behavior of children, family members, friends, roommates, and coworkers. Be aware of what you are reinforcing.

Feedback

His eyes, driven and blazing, dart from side to side. His left hand twitches, dances, rises, and strikes, hitting its target again and again. At the same time, his right hand furiously spins in circular motions. Does this describe some strange neurological disorder? Actually, it depicts

Chimp-O-Mat, Yukes Regional Primate Research Center, Emory University

▶**FIGURE 6.14** Poker chips normally have little or no value for chimpanzees, but this chimp will work hard to earn them once he learns that the "Chimp-O-Mat" will dispense food in exchange for them.

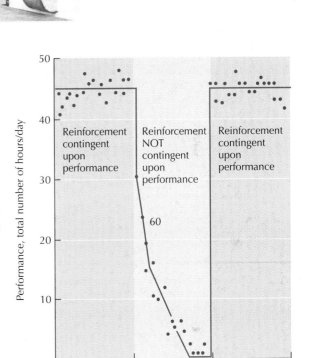

▶**FIGURE 6.15** Reinforcement in a token economy. This graph shows the effects of using tokens to reward socially desirable behavior in a mental hospital ward. Desirable behavior was defined as cleaning, making the bed, attending therapy sessions, and so forth. Tokens earned could be exchanged for basic amenities such as meals, snacks, coffee, game-room privileges, or weekend passes. The graph shows more than 24 hours per day because it represents the total number of hours of desirable behavior performed by all patients in the ward. (Adapted from Ayllon & Azrin, 1965.)

Social reinforcer Reinforcement based on receiving attention, approval, or affection from another person.

10-year-old Vikram as he plays his favorite video game, an animated skateboarding adventure!

How did Vikram learn the complex movements needed to excel at virtual skateboarding? After all, he was not rewarded with food or money. The answer lies in the fact that Vikram's favorite video game provides *feedback,* a key element that underlies learning. **Feedback** (information about the effect a response had) is particularly important in human learning.

Every time a player moves, a video game responds instantly with sounds, animated actions, and a higher or lower score. The machine's responsiveness and the information flow it provides can be very motivating if you want to win. The same principle applies to many other learning situations: If you are trying to learn to use a computer, to play a musical instrument, to cook, or to solve math problems, reinforcement comes from feedback that you achieved a desired result.

The adaptive value of feedback helps explain why much human learning occurs in the absence of obvious reinforcers, such as food or water. Humans readily learn responses that merely have a desired effect or that bring a goal closer. Let's explore this idea further.

Knowledge of Results

Imagine that you are asked to throw darts at a target. Each dart must pass over a screen that prevents you from telling if you hit the target. If you threw 1,000 darts, we would expect little improvement in your performance because no feedback is provided. Vikram's video game did not explicitly reward him for correct responses. Yet, because it provided feedback, rapid learning took place.

How can feedback be applied? Increased feedback (also called **knowledge of results,** or **KR**) almost always improves learning and performance (Horn et al., 2005). If you want to learn to play a musical instrument, to sing, to speak a second language, tape-recorded feedback can be very helpful. In sports, video-taped replays are used to provide feedback on everything from tennis serves to pick-off moves in baseball. Whenever you are trying to learn a complex skill, it pays to get more feedback (Wulf et al., 2002). (Also, see "Conditioning and Conservation.")

Learning Aids

How do these techniques make use of feedback? Feedback is most effective when it is *frequent, immediate,* and *detailed. Programmed instruction* teaches students in a format that presents information in small amounts, gives immediate practice, and provides continuous feedback to learners. Frequent feedback keeps learners from practicing errors. It also lets students work at their own pace. (A small sample of programmed instruction is shown in ▸Figure 6.16 so that you can see what the format looks like.) Programmed learning can be done in book form or presented by a computer or through the web (Emurian, 2005; McDonald, Yanchar, & Osguthorpe, 2005).

In *computer-assisted instruction (CAI),* learning is aided by computer-presented information and exercises. In addition to giving learners immediate feedback, the computer can give hints about why an answer was wrong and what is needed to correct it (Timmerman & Kruepke, 2006). Although the final level of skill or knowledge gained is not necessarily higher, CAI can save much time and effort. In addition, people often do better with feedback from a computer because they can freely make mistakes and learn from them (Norton, 2003). For example, CAI can give medical students unlimited practice at diagnosing diseases from symptoms, such as "acute chest pain" (Papa, Aldrich, & Schumacker, 1999).

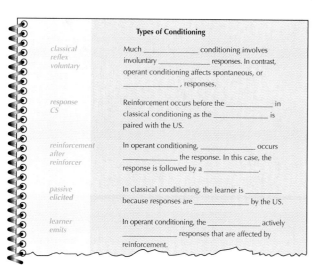

▸**FIGURE 6.16** To sample a programmed instruction format, try covering the terms on the left with a piece of paper. As you fill in the blanks, uncover one new term for each response. In this way, your correct (or incorrect) responses will be followed by immediate feedback.

Feedback Information returned to a person about the effects a response has had; also known as knowledge of results.

Knowledge of results (KR) Informational feedback.

Conditioning and Conservation

Psychologists enjoy seeing behavioral principles used to solve practical problems. One area of behavior very much in need of attention is our "throw-away" society. We burn fossil fuels, destroy forests, use chemical products, and strip, clear, and farm the land. In doing so, we alter the very face of the Earth. What can be done? One approach involves changing the *consequences* of wasteful energy use, polluting, and the like. For example, energy taxes can be used to increase the cost of using fossil fuels (response cost). On the reinforcement side of the equation, rebates can be offered for installing insulation, or buying energy-efficient appliances or cars, and tax breaks can be given to companies that take steps to preserve the environment.

On a daily level, people can help recycle materials such as paper, steel, glass, aluminum, and plastic. Again, behavioral principles come into play. For instance, people who set their own goals for recycling tend to meet them. Likewise, when families, work groups, factories, and dorms receive feedback, on a weekly basis, about how much they recycled, they typically recycle more. Recycling is also more effective when entire families participate, with some family members (usually mom, of course) reinforcing the recycling behavior of other family members (Meneses & Beerlipalacio, 2005). We also know that people are more likely to continue recycling if they feel a sense of satisfaction from helping protect the environment (Ewing, 2001). Is such satisfaction sufficiently reinforcing to encourage more people to reduce, reuse, and recycle? We certainly hope so.

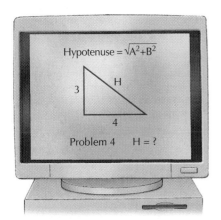

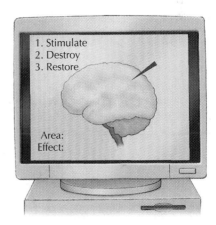

▸▸**FIGURE 6.17** Computer-assisted instruction. The screen on the left shows a typical drill-and-practice math problem, in which students must find the hypotenuse of a triangle. The center screen presents the same problem as an instructional game to increase interest and motivation. In the game, a child is asked to set the proper distance on a ray gun in the hovering spaceship to "vaporize" an attacker. The screen on the right depicts an educational simulation. Here, students place a "probe" at various spots in a human brain. They then "stimulate," "destroy," or "restore" areas. As each area is altered, it is named on the screen and the effects on behavior are described. This allows students to explore basic brain functions on their own.

Some CAI programs, called *serious games,* make use of instructional games in which stories, competition with a partner, sound effects, and game-like graphics increase interest and motivation (Michael & Chen, 2006) (▸▸Fig. 6.17). Educational simulations allow students to explore an imaginary situation or "microworld" that simulates real-world problems. By seeing the effects of their choices, students discover basic principles of physics, biology, psychology, or other subjects (Grabe, 2006).

Psychologists are only now beginning to fully explore the value and limits of computer-assisted instruction. Nevertheless, it seems likely that their efforts will improve not only education but our understanding of human learning as well.

Let's pause now for some learning exercises so that you can get some feedback about your mastery of the preceding ideas.

Study Break   Operant Conditioning

Reflect

How have your thoughts about the effects of "rewards" changed now that you've read about operant conditioning? Can you explain the difference between positive reinforcement, negative reinforcement, and punishment? Can you give an example of each concept from your own experience?

A friend of yours punishes his dog all the time. What advice would you give him about how to use reinforcement, extinction, and shaping, instead of punishment?

Learning Check

1. Responses in operant conditioning are _____, whereas those in classical conditioning are passive, _____ responses.

2. Changing the rules in small steps so that an animal (or person) is gradually trained to respond as desired is called _____.

3. Extinction in operant conditioning is also subject to _____ of a response.

   a. successive approximations   b. shaping
   c. automation   d. spontaneous recovery

4. Positive reinforcers increase the rate of responding and negative reinforcers decrease it. T or F?

5. Primary reinforcers are those learned through classical conditioning. T or F?

6. Which is a correct match?

   a. social reinforcer–primary   b. token reinforcer–secondary
      reinforcement   reinforcement
   c. ICS–secondary   d. negative reinforcer–
      reinforcement   punishment

7. Superstitious responses are those that are

   a. shaped by secondary   b. extinguished
      reinforcement
   c. prepotent   d. unnecessary to obtain
                                         reinforcement

8. Knowledge of results, or KR, is also known as _____.

9. CAI is based on the same principles as

   a. negative reinforcement   b. programmed instruction
   c. higher order conditioning   d. stimulus generalization

Critical Thinking

10. How might operant conditioning principles be used to encourage people to pick up litter? (What rewards could be offered, and how might the cost of rewards be kept low?)

Answers

1. voluntary, involuntary, emitted, elicited   2. shaping   3. d   4. F   5. F   6. b   7. d   8. feedback   9. b   10. A strategy that has been used with some success is to hold drawings for various prizes, such as movie or concert passes. Each time a person turns in a specific amount of litter, he or she receives one chance (a token) to enter in the drawing. Giving refunds for cans and bottles is another way to reinforce recycling of litter.

PARTIAL REINFORCEMENT—LAS VEGAS, A HUMAN SKINNER BOX?

>SURVEY QUESTION< *How are we influenced by patterns of reward?*

Anyone wishing to influence operant learning would be ill-equipped to do so without knowing how various patterns of reinforcement affect behavior. Imagine, for example, that a mother wants to reward her child for turning off the lights when he leaves a room. Contrary to what you might think, she would be well advised to reinforce only some of her son's correct responses. Why should this be so? You'll find the answer in the following discussion.

Until now, we have treated operant reinforcement as if it were continuous. *Continuous reinforcement* means that a reinforcer follows every correct response. This is fine for the lab, but it has little to do with the real world. Most of our responses are more inconsistently rewarded. In daily life, learning is usually based on **partial reinforcement,** in which reinforcers do not follow every response. Partial reinforcement can be given in several patterns, called **schedules of reinforcement** (plans for determining which responses will be reinforced). Each has a distinct effect on behavior. In addition to these (which will be explored in a moment), there is a general effect: Responses acquired by partial reinforcement are highly resistant to extinction. For some obscure reason, lost in the lore of psychology, this is called the **partial reinforcement effect.**

How does getting reinforced part of the time make a habit stronger? If you have ever visited Las Vegas or a similar gambling mecca, you have probably seen row after row of people playing slot machines. To gain insight into partial reinforcement, imagine that you are mak-

Partial reinforcement A pattern in which only a portion of all responses are reinforced.

Schedule of reinforcement A rule or plan for determining which responses will be reinforced.

Partial reinforcement effect Responses acquired with partial reinforcement are more resistant to extinction.

ing your first visit to Las Vegas. You put a dollar in a slot machine and pull the handle. Ten dollars spills into the tray. Using one of your newly won dollars, you pull the handle again. Another payoff! Let's say this continues for 15 minutes. Every pull is followed by a payoff. Suddenly each pull is followed by nothing. Obviously, you would respond several times more before giving up. However, when continuous reinforcement is followed by extinction, the message soon becomes clear: No more payoffs.

Contrast this with partial reinforcement. Again, imagine that this is your first encounter with a slot machine. You put a dollar in the machine five times without a payoff. You are just about to quit, but decide to play once more. Bingo! The machine returns $20. After this, payoffs continue on a partial schedule; some are large, and some are small. All are unpredictable. Sometimes you hit 2 in a row, and sometimes 20 or 30 pulls go unrewarded.

Now let's say the payoff mechanism is turned off again. How many times do you think you would respond this time before your handle-pulling behavior extinguished? Because you have developed the expectation that any play may be "the one," it will be hard to resist just one more play . . . and one more . . . and one more. Also, because partial reinforcement includes long periods of nonreward, it will be harder to discriminate between periods of reinforcement and extinction. It is no exaggeration to say that the partial reinforcement effect has left many people penniless. Even psychologists visiting Las Vegas may get "cleaned out" (not your authors, of course!).

Christoph Wilhelm/Getty Images

The one-armed bandit (slot machine) is a dispenser of partial reinforcement.

Schedules of Partial Reinforcement

Partial reinforcement can be given in many different patterns (Domjan, 2006). Let's consider the four most basic, which have some interesting effects on us. Typical responses to each pattern are shown in ▸▸Figure 6.18. Results such as these are obtained when a cumulative recorder is connected to a Skinner box. The device consists of a moving strip of paper and a mechanical pen that jumps upward each time a response is made. Rapid responding causes the pen to draw a steep line; a horizontal line indicates no response. Small tick marks on the lines show when a reinforcer was given.

Fixed Ratio (FR)

What would happen if a reinforcer followed only every other response? Or what if we followed every third, fourth, fifth, or other number of responses with reinforcement? Each of these patterns is a **fixed ratio (FR) schedule** (a set number of correct responses must be made to obtain a reinforcer). Notice that in an FR schedule the ratio of reinforcers to responses is fixed: FR-2 means that every other response is rewarded; FR-3 means that every third response is reinforced; in an FR-10 schedule, exactly 10 responses must be made to obtain a reinforcer.

Fixed ratio schedules produce *very high response rates* (▸▸Fig. 6.18). A hungry rat on an FR-10 schedule will quickly run off 10 responses, pause to eat, and will then run off 10 more. A similar situation occurs when factory or farm workers are paid on a piecework basis. When a fixed number of items must be produced for a set amount of pay, work output is high.

Variable Ratio (VR)

In a **variable ratio (VR) schedule** a varied number of correct responses must be made to get a reinforcer. Instead of reinforcing every fourth response (FR-4), for example, a person or animal on a VR-4 schedule gets rewarded *on the average* every fourth response. Sometimes 2 responses must be made to obtain a reinforcer; sometimes it's 5, sometimes 4, and so on. The actual number varies, but it averages out to 4 (in this example). Variable ratio schedules also produce high response rates.

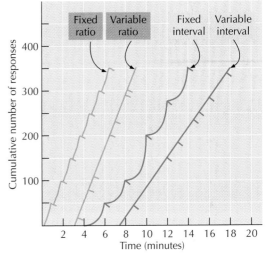

▸▸**FIGURE 6.18** Typical response patterns for reinforcement schedules.

Fixed ratio schedule A set number of correct responses must be made to get a reinforcer. For example, a reinforcer is given for every four correct responses.

Variable ratio schedule A varied number of correct responses must be made to get a reinforcer. For example, a reinforcer is given after three to seven correct responses; the actual number changes randomly.

VR schedules seem less predictable than FR. Does that have any effect on extinction? Yes. Because reinforcement is less predictable, VR schedules tend to produce greater resistance to extinction than fixed ratio schedules. Playing a slot machine is an example of behavior maintained by a variable ratio schedule. Another would be a child asking for a "treat" at the supermarket. The number of times the child must ask before getting reinforced varies, so the child becomes quite persistent. Golf, tennis, and many other sports are also reinforced on a variable ratio basis: An average of perhaps one good shot in 5 or 10 may be all that's needed to create a sports fanatic.

Fixed Interval (FI)

In another pattern, reinforcement is given only when a correct response is made after a fixed amount of time has passed. This time interval is measured from the last reinforced response. Responses made during the time interval are not reinforced. In a **fixed interval (FI) schedule** the first correct response made after the time period has passed is reinforced. Thus, a rat on an FI-30-second schedule has to wait 30 seconds after the last reinforced response before a bar press will pay off again. The rat can press the bar as often as it wants during the interval, but it will not be rewarded.

Fixed interval schedules produce *moderate response rates.* These are marked by spurts of activity mixed with periods of inactivity. Animals working on an FI schedule seem to develop a keen sense of the passage of time (Eckerman, 1999). For example:

> **Mickey Rat Takes a Break**
> Mickey Rat, trained on an FI-60-second schedule, has just been reinforced for a bar press. What does he do? He saunters around the cage, grooms himself, hums, whistles, reads magazines, and polishes his nails. After 50 seconds, he walks to the bar and gives it a press—just testing. After 55 seconds, he gives it two or three presses, but there's still no payoff. Fifty-eight seconds, and he settles down to rapid pressing, 59 seconds, 60 seconds, and he hits the reinforced press. After one or two more presses (unrewarded), he wanders off again for the next interval.

Is getting paid weekly an FI schedule? Pure examples of fixed interval schedules are rare, but getting paid each week at work does come close. Notice, however, that most people do not work faster just before payday, as an FI schedule predicts. A closer parallel would be having a report due every 2 weeks for a class. Right after turning in a paper, your work would probably drop to zero for a week or more. Then, as the next due date draws near, a work frenzy occurs (Chance, 2006).

Variable Interval (VI)

Variable interval (VI) schedules are a variation on fixed intervals. Here, reinforcement is given for the first correct response made after a varied amount of time. On a VI-30-second schedule, reinforcement is available after an interval that *averages* 30 seconds.

VI schedules produce *slow, steady response rates* and tremendous resistance to extinction (Lattal, Reilly, & Kohn, 1998). When you dial a phone number and get a busy signal, reward (getting through) is on a VI schedule. You may have to wait 30 seconds or 30 minutes. If you are like most people, you will doggedly dial over and over again until you get a connection. Success in fishing is also on a VI schedule—which may explain the bulldog tenacity of many anglers (Chance, 2006).

STIMULUS CONTROL—RED LIGHT, GREEN LIGHT

When you are driving, your behavior at intersections is controlled by the red or green light. In similar fashion, many of the stimuli we encounter each day act like stop or go signals that guide our behavior. To state the idea more formally, stimuli that consistently precede a rewarded response tend to influence when and where the response will occur. This effect is called **stimulus control.** Notice how it works with our friend Mickey Rat.

Fixed interval schedule A reinforcer is given only when a correct response is made after a set amount of time has passed since the last reinforced response. Responses made during the time interval are not reinforced.

Variable interval schedule A reinforcer is given for the first correct response made after a varied amount of time has passed since the last reinforced response. Responses made during the time interval are not reinforced.

Stimulus control Stimuli present when an operant response is acquired tend to control when and where the response is made.

Lights Out for Mickey Rat

While learning the bar-pressing response, Mickey has been in a Skinner box illuminated by a bright light. During several training sessions, the light is alternately turned on and off. When the light is on, a bar press will produce food. When the light is off, bar pressing goes unrewarded. We soon observe that the rat presses vigorously when the light is on and ignores the bar when the light is off.

In this example, the light signals what consequences will follow if a response is made. Evidence for stimulus control could be shown by turning the food delivery *on* when the light is *off*. A well-trained animal might never discover that the rules had changed. A similar example of stimulus control would be a child learning to ask for candy when her mother is in a good mood, but not asking at other times. Likewise, we pick up phones that are ringing, but rarely answer phones that are silent. Thus, a simplified summary of stimulus control is: Notice something, do something, get something (Powell, Symbaluk, & Macdonald, 2005).

Stimulus control. Operant shaping was used to teach this whale to "bow" to an audience. Fish were used as reinforcers. Notice the trainer's hand signal, which serves as a discriminative stimulus to control the performance.

Generalization

Two important aspects of stimulus control are generalization and discrimination. Let's return to the example of the vending machine (from the chapter preview) to illustrate these concepts. First, generalization.

Is generalization the same in operant conditioning as it is in classical conditioning? Basically, yes. **Operant stimulus generalization** is the tendency to respond to stimuli similar to those that preceded operant reinforcement. That is, a reinforced response tends to be made again when similar antecedents are present. Assume, for instance, that you have been reliably rewarded for kicking one particular vending machine. Your kicking response tends to occur in the presence of that machine. It has come under stimulus control. Now let's say that there are three other machines on campus identical to the one that pays off. Because they are similar, your kicking response may well transfer to them. If each of these machines also pays off when kicked, your kicking response may *generalize* to other machines only mildly similar to the original. Similar generalization explains why children may temporarily call all men *daddy*—much to the embarrassment of their parents.

Discrimination

Meanwhile, back at the vending machine. . . . As stated earlier, to discriminate means to respond differently to varied stimuli. Because one vending machine reinforced your kicking response, you began kicking other identical machines (generalization). Because these also paid off, you began kicking similar machines (more generalization). If kicking these new machines has no effect, the kicking response that generalized to them will extinguish because of nonreinforcement. Thus, your response to machines of a particular size and color is consistently rewarded, whereas the same response to different machines is extinguished. Through **operant stimulus discrimination** you have learned to differentiate between antecedent stimuli that signal reward and nonreward. As a result, your response pattern will shift to match these **discriminative stimuli** (stimuli that precede reinforced and nonreinforced responses).

A discriminative stimulus that most drivers are familiar with is a police car on the freeway. This stimulus is a clear signal that a specific set of reinforcement contingencies applies. As you have probably observed, the presence of a police car brings about rapid reductions in driving speed, lane changes, and tailgating.

The role of discriminative stimuli may be clarified by an interesting feat achieved by Jack, a psychologist friend of one of your authors. Here is his account of what Jack did:

Jack decided to teach his cat to say its name. To begin, he gave the cat a pat on the back. If the cat meowed in a way that sounded anything like its name, Jack immediately gave the cat a small amount of food. If the cat made this unusual meow at other times, it received nothing. This process was repeated many times each day.

Operant stimulus generalization The tendency to respond to stimuli similar to those that preceded operant reinforcement.

Operant stimulus discrimination The tendency to make an operant response when stimuli previously associated with reward are present and to withhold the response when stimuli associated with nonreward are present.

Discriminative stimuli Stimuli that precede rewarded and nonrewarded responses in operant conditioning.

By gradual shaping, the cat's meow was made to sound very much like its name. Also, this peculiar meow came under stimulus control: When it received a pat on the back, the cat said its name; without the pat, it remained silent or meowed normally.

I should add at this point that I was unaware that Jack had a new cat or that he had trained it. I went to visit him one night and met the cat on the front steps. I gave the cat a pat on the back and said, "Hi kitty, what's your name?" Imagine my surprise when the cat immediately replied, "Ralph"!

Psychologists symbolize a stimulus that precedes reinforced responses as an S+. Discriminative stimuli that precede unrewarded responses are symbolized as S− (Chance, 2006). Thus, ▸▸Figure 6.19 summarizes Ralph's training.

Stimulus discrimination is also aptly illustrated by the "sniffer" dogs that locate drugs and explosives at airports and border crossings. Operant discrimination is used to teach these dogs to recognize contraband. During training, they are reinforced only for approaching containers baited with drugs or explosives.

Stimulus discrimination clearly has a tremendous impact on human behavior. Learning to recognize different automobile brands, birds, animals, wines, types of music, and even the answers on psychology tests all depend, in part, on operant discrimination learning.

▸▸**FIGURE 6.19** A diagram of Ralph the cat's discrimination training.

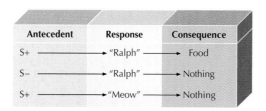

 Study Break   Partial Reinforcement and Stimulus Control

Reflect

Think of something you do that is reinforced only part of the time. Do you pursue this activity persistently? How have you been affected by partial reinforcement?

See if you can think of at least one everyday example of the four basic schedules of reinforcement.

Doors that are meant to be pushed outward have metal plates on them. Those that are meant to be pulled inward have handles. Do these discriminative stimuli affect your behavior? (If they don't, how's your nose doing?)

Learning Check

1. Two aspects of stimulus control are _____ and _____.

2. Responding tends to occur in the presence of discriminative stimuli associated with reinforcement and tends not to occur in the presence of discriminative stimuli associated with nonreinforcement. T or F?

3. Stimulus generalization refers to making an operant response in the presence of stimuli similar to those that preceded reinforcement. T or F?

4. Moderate response rates that are marked by spurts of activity and periods of inactivity are characteristic of

   a. FR schedules   b. VR schedules
   c. FI schedules   d. VI schedules

5. Partial reinforcement tends to produce slower responding and reduced resistance to extinction. T or F?

6. The schedule of reinforcement associated with playing slot machines and other types of gambling is

   a. fixed ratio   b. variable ratio
   c. fixed interval   d. variable interval

Critical Thinking

7. A business owner who pays employees an hourly wage wants to increase productivity. How could the owner make more effective use of reinforcement?

8. How could you use conditioning principles to teach a dog or a cat to come when called?

Answers

1. generalization, discrimination   2. T   3. T   4. c   5. F   6. b   7. Continuing to use fixed interval rewards (hourly wage or salary) would guarantee a basic level of income for employees. To reward extra effort, the owner could add some fixed ratio reinforcement (such as incentives, bonuses, commissions, or profit sharing) to employees' pay.   8. An excellent way to train a pet to come when you call is to give a distinctive call or whistle each time you feed the animal. This makes the signal a secondary reinforcer and a discriminative stimulus for reward (food). Of course, it also helps to directly reinforce an animal with praise, petting, or food for coming when called.

PUNISHMENT—PUTTING THE BRAKES ON BEHAVIOR

>SURVEY QUESTION< *What does punishment do to behavior?*

Spankings, reprimands, fines, jail sentences, firings, failing grades, and the like are commonly used to control behavior. Clearly, the story of learning is unfinished without a return to the topic of punishment. Recall that **punishment** lowers the probability that a response will occur again. To be most effective, punishment must be given contingently (only after an undesired response occurs).

Punishers, like reinforcers, are defined by observing their effects on behavior. A **punisher** is any consequence that reduces the frequency of a target behavior. It is not always possible to know ahead of time what will act as a punisher for a particular person. For example, when Jason's mother reprimanded him for throwing toys, he stopped doing it. In this instance, the reprimand was a punisher. However, Chris is starved for attention of any kind from his parents, who both work full-time. For Chris, a reprimand, or even a spanking, might actually reinforce toy throwing. Remember, too, that a punisher can be either the onset of an unpleasant event or the removal of a positive state of affairs (response cost).

Punishers are consequences that lower the probability that a response will be made again. Receiving a traffic citation is directly punishing because the driver is delayed and reprimanded. Paying a fine and higher insurance rates add to the punishment in the form of response cost.

Variables Affecting Punishment

How effective is punishment? Although many people assume that punishment stops unacceptable behavior, the effectiveness of punishers depends greatly on their *timing, consistency,* and *intensity.* Punishment works best when it occurs as the response is being made, or *immediately* afterward (timing), and when it is given *each time* a response occurs (consistency). Thus, you could effectively (and humanely) punish a dog that barks incessantly by spraying water on its nose each time it barks. About 10 to 15 such treatments are usually enough to greatly reduce barking. This would not be the case if you applied punishment haphazardly or long after the barking stopped. If you discover that your dog dug up a tree and ate it while you were gone, punishing the dog hours later will do little good. Likewise, the commonly heard childhood threat, "Wait 'til your father comes home, then you'll be sorry," just makes the father a feared brute; it doesn't effectively punish an undesirable response.

Severe punishment (following a response with an intensely aversive or unpleasant stimulus) can be extremely effective in stopping behavior. If 3-year-old Beavis sticks his finger in a light socket and gets a shock, that may be the last time he *ever* tries it. However, mild punishment only temporarily *suppresses* a response. If the response is still reinforced, punishment may be particularly ineffective.

This fact was demonstrated by slapping rats on the paw as they were bar pressing in a Skinner box. Two groups of well-trained rats were placed on extinction. One group was punished with a slap for each bar press, and the other group was not. It might seem that the slap would cause bar pressing to extinguish more quickly. Yet, this was not the case, as you can see in ⊳Figure 6.20. Punishment temporarily slowed responding, but it did not cause more rapid extinction. Slapping the paws of rats or children has little permanent effect on a reinforced response.

Similarly, if 7-year-old Alyssa sneaks a snack from the refrigerator before dinner and is punished for it, she may pass up snacks for a short time. But because snack sneaking was also rewarded by the sneaked snack, she will probably try sneaky snacking again, sometime later (the sneaky little devil). It is worth stating again, however, that intense punishment

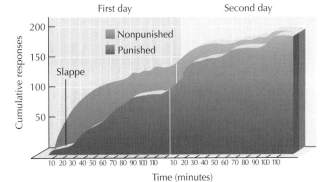

⊳**FIGURE 6.20** The effect of punishment on extinction. Immediately after punishment, the rate of bar pressing is suppressed, but by the end of the second day, the effects of punishment have disappeared. (After B. F. Skinner, *The Behavior of Organisms*. © 1938. D. Appleton-Century Co., Inc. Reprinted by permission of Prentice-Hall, Inc.)

Punishment The process of suppressing a response.

Punisher Any event that decreases the probability or frequency of responses it follows.

may permanently suppress responding, even for actions as basic as eating. Animals severely punished while eating may never eat again (Bertsch, 1976).

Side Effects of Punishment

Are there drawbacks of using punishment? There are several, all of which become more of a problem as punishment increases in severity. Basically, punishment is aversive (painful or uncomfortable). As a result, people and situations associated with punishment tend, through classical conditioning, to become feared, resented, or disliked. The aversive nature of punishment makes it especially poor to use when teaching children to eat politely or in toilet training.

Escape and Avoidance

A second major problem is that aversive stimuli encourage escape and avoidance learning. In **escape learning** we learn to make a response in order to end an aversive stimulus. For example, if you work with a loud and obnoxious person, you may at first escape from conversations with him to obtain relief. (Notice that escape learning is based on negative reinforcement.) Later you may dodge him altogether. This is an example of **avoidance learning** (making a response in order to postpone or prevent discomfort). Each time you sidestep him, your avoidance is again reinforced by a sense of relief. In many situations involving frequent punishment, similar desires to escape and avoid are activated. For example, children who run away from punishing parents (escape) may soon learn to lie about their behavior (avoidance) or to spend as much time away from home as possible (also an avoidance response).

Aggression

A third problem with punishment is that it can greatly increase *aggression.* Animals react to pain by attacking whomever or whatever else is around. A common example is the faithful dog that nips its owner during a painful procedure at the veterinarian's office. Likewise, humans who are in pain have a tendency to lash out at others.

We also know that one of the most common responses to frustration is aggression. Generally speaking, punishment is painful, frustrating, or both. Punishment, therefore, sets up a powerful environment for learning aggression. When spanked, a child may feel angry, frustrated, and hostile. What if that child then goes outside and hits a brother, a sister, or a neighbor? The danger is that aggressive acts may feel good because they release anger and frustration. If so, aggression has been rewarded and will tend to occur again in other frustrating situations.

One study found that children who are physically punished are more likely to engage in aggressive, impulsive, antisocial behavior (Thomas, 2004). Similarly, a classic study of angry adolescent boys found that they were severely punished at home. This suppressed their misbehavior at home but made them more aggressive elsewhere. Parents were often surprised to learn that their "good boys" were in trouble for fighting at school (Bandura & Walters, 1959). Fortunately, at least for younger children, if parents change to less punitive parenting their children's levels of aggression will decline (Thomas, 2004).

In the classroom, physical punishment, yelling, and humiliation are also generally ineffective. Positive reinforcement, in the form of praise, approval, and reward, is much more likely to quell classroom disruptions, defiance, and inattention (Alberto & Troutman, 2006).

Using Punishment Wisely

In light of its limitations and drawbacks, should punishment be used to control behavior? Parents, teachers, animal trainers, and the like have three basic tools to control simple learning: (1) Reinforcement strengthens responses; (2) nonreinforcement causes responses to extinguish; (3) punishment suppresses responses. (Consult ▸Figure 6.21 to refresh your memory

Escape learning Learning to make a response in order to end an aversive stimulus.

Avoidance learning Learning to make a response in order to postpone or prevent discomfort.

about the different types of reinforcement and punishment.) These tools work best in combination. It is usually best to begin by making liberal use of positive reinforcement, especially praise, to encourage good behavior. Also, try extinction first: See what happens if you ignore a problem behavior, or shift attention to a desirable activity and then reinforce it with praise. Remember, it is much more effective to strengthen and encourage desirable behaviors than it is to punish unwanted behaviors (Gershoff, 2002). When all else fails, it may be necessary to use punishment to help manage the behavior of an animal, child, or even another adult. For those times, here are some tips to keep in mind:

1. *Apply punishment during, or immediately after, misbehavior.* Of course, immediate punishment is not always possible. With older children and adults, you can bridge the delay by clearly stating what act you are punishing. If you cannot punish an animal or young child immediately, wait for the next instance of misbehavior.

2. *Be consistent.* Be very clear about what you regard as misbehavior. Punish every time the misbehavior occurs. Don't punish for something one day and ignore it the next. If you are usually willing to give a child three chances, don't change the rule and explode without warning after a first offense. Both parents should try to punish their children for the same things and in the same way.

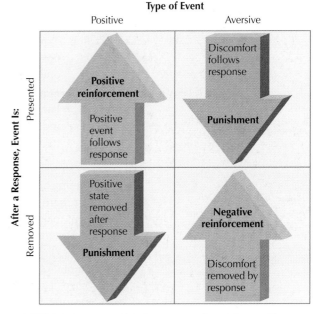

Type of Event

▶▶ **FIGURE 6.21** Types of reinforcement and punishment. The impact of an event depends on whether it is presented or removed after a response is made. Each square defines one possibility: Arrows pointing upward indicate that responding is increased; downward-pointing arrows indicate that responding is decreased.

3. *Use the minimum punishment necessary to suppress misbehavior.* If punishment is used at all, it should always be mild. In a situation that poses immediate danger, such as when a child reaches for something hot or a dog runs into the street, mild punishment may prevent disaster. Punishment in such cases works best when it produces actions *incompatible* with the response you want to suppress. Let's say a child reaches toward a stove burner. Would a swat on the bottom serve as an effective punisher? Probably so. It would be better, however, to slap the child's outstretched hand so that it will be *withdrawn* from the source of danger. Taking away privileges or other positive reinforcers (response cost) is usually best for older children and adults. Often, a verbal rebuke or a scolding is enough.

4. *Avoid harsh punishment.* Harsh or excessive punishment has serious negative drawbacks (never slap a child's face, for instance). "Sparing the rod" will not spoil a child. In fact, the reverse is true. As we just discussed, harsh punishment can lead to negative emotional reactions, avoidance and escape behaviors, and increased aggression.

What about spanking? Parents should minimize spanking or avoid it entirely (Gershoff, 2002). Although most children show no signs of long-term damage from spanking if it is backed up by supportive parenting, emotional damage does occur if spankings are severe, frequent, or coupled with harsh parenting (Baumrind, Larzelere, & Cowan, 2002). Like all harsh punishment, frequent spanking tends to increase aggression and leads to more problem behaviors, not fewer (McLoyd & Smith, 2002; Saadeh, Rizzo, & Roberts, 2002). In fact, anti-spanking laws have been passed in a number of countries around the world.

5. *Don't rely exclusively on punishment.* Mild punishment tends to be ineffective if reinforcers are still available in the situation. That's why it is best to also reward an alternate, desired response. For example, a child who has a habit of taking toys from her sister should not just be reprimanded for it. She should also be praised for cooperative play and sharing her toys with others. Besides, punishment only tells a person or an animal that a response was "wrong." Punishment does not say what

the "right" response is, so it *does not teach new behaviors.* If reinforcement is missing, punishment becomes less effective (Gershoff, 2002).

6. *Expect anger from a punished person.* Briefly acknowledge this anger but be careful not to reinforce it. Be willing to admit your mistake if you wrongfully punish someone or if you punished too severely.

7. *Punish with kindness and respect.* Allow the punished person to retain self-respect. For instance, do not punish a person in front of others, if possible. A strong, trusting relationship tends to minimize behavior problems. Ideally, others should want to behave well to get your praise, not because they fear punishment.

To summarize, the most common error in using punishment is to over-rely on it for training or discipline. The overall emotional adjustment of a child or pet disciplined mainly by reward is usually superior to one disciplined mainly by punishment. Frequent punishment makes a person or an animal unhappy, confused, anxious, aggressive, and fearful.

Parents and teachers should also be aware that using punishment can be "habit forming." When children are being noisy, messy, disrespectful, or otherwise misbehaving, the temptation to punish them can be strong. The danger is that punishment often works. When it does, a sudden end to the adult's irritation acts as a negative reinforcer. This encourages the adult to use punishment more often in the future (Alberto & Troutman, 2006). Immediate silence may be "golden," but its cost can be very high in terms of a child's emotional health.

Study Break   Punishment

Reflect

Think of how you were punished as a child. Was the punishment immediate? Was it consistent? What effect did these factors have on your behavior? Was the punishment effective? Which of the side effects of punishment have you witnessed or experienced?

Learning Check

1. Negative reinforcement increases responding; punishment suppresses responding. T or F?
2. Three factors that greatly influence the effects of punishment are timing, consistency, and _____.
3. Mild punishment tends to only temporarily _____ a response that is also reinforced.

   a. enhance   b. aggravate
   c. replace   d. suppress

4. Three undesired side effects of punishment are (1) conditioning of fear and resentment, (2) encouragement of aggression, and (3) the learning of escape or _____ responses.
5. Using punishment can be "habit forming" because putting a stop to someone else's irritating behavior can _____ _____ the person who applies the punishment.

Critical Thinking

6. Using the concept of partial reinforcement, can you explain why inconsistent punishment is especially ineffective?
7. Escape and avoidance learning have been applied to encourage automobile seat belt use. Can you explain how?

Answers

1. T 2. intensity 3. d 4. avoidance 5. negatively reinforce 6. An inconsistently punished response will continue to be reinforced on a partial schedule, which makes it even more resistant to extinction. 7. Many automobiles have an unpleasant buzzer that sounds if the ignition key is turned before the driver's seat belt is fastened. Most drivers quickly learn to fasten the belt to stop the annoying sound. This is an example of escape conditioning. Avoidance conditioning is evident when a driver learns to buckle up before the buzzer sounds.

COGNITIVE LEARNING—BEYOND CONDITIONING

>SURVEY QUESTION< *What is cognitive learning?*

Is all learning just a connection between stimuli and responses? Much learning can be explained by classical and operant conditioning. But, as we have seen, even basic conditioning has "mental" elements. As a human, you can anticipate future reward or punishment and react accordingly. (You may wonder why this doesn't seem to work when a doctor or dentist says, "This won't hurt a bit." Here's why: They lie!) There is no doubt that human learning includes a large cognitive, or mental, dimension. As humans, we are greatly affected by information, expectations, perceptions, mental images, and the like.

Loosely speaking, **cognitive learning** refers to understanding, knowing, anticipating, or otherwise making use of information-rich higher mental processes. Cognitive learning extends beyond basic conditioning into the realms of memory, thinking, problem solving, and language. Because these topics are covered in later chapters, our discussion here is limited to a first look at learning beyond conditioning.

Cognitive Maps

How do you navigate around the town you live in? Have you constructed an overall mental picture of how the town is laid out? This *cognitive map* acts as a guide even when you must detour or take a new route (Foo et al., 2005). A **cognitive map** is an internal representation of an area, such as a maze, city, or campus. Even the lowly rat—not exactly a mental giant—learns *where* food is found in a maze, not just which turns to make to reach the food (Tolman, Ritchie, & Kalish, 1946). If you have ever learned your way through some of the levels found in many video games, you will have a good idea of what a cognitive map is. In a sense, cognitive maps also apply to other kinds of knowledge. For instance, it could be said that you have been developing a "map" of psychology while reading this book. That's why students sometimes find it helpful to draw pictures or diagrams of how they envision concepts fitting together.

Latent Learning

Cognitive learning is also revealed by latent (hidden) learning. **Latent learning** occurs without obvious reinforcement and remains hidden until reinforcement is provided (Davidson, 2000). Here's an example from a classic animal study: Two groups of rats were allowed to explore a maze. The animals in one group found food at the far end of the maze. Soon, they learned to rapidly make their way through the maze when released. Rats in the second group were unrewarded and showed no signs of learning. But later, when the "uneducated" rats were given food, they ran the maze as quickly as the rewarded group (Tolman & Honzik, 1930). Although there was no outward sign of it, the unrewarded animals had learned their way around the maze. Their learning, therefore, remained latent at first (▶Fig. 6.22).

It's easy to get lost when visiting a new city if you don't have a cognitive map of the area. Printed maps help, but they may still leave you puzzled until you begin to form a mental representation of major landmarks and directions.

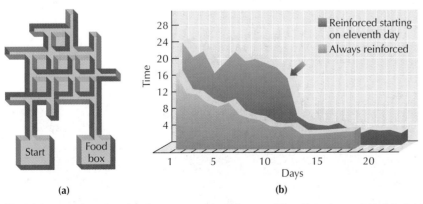

▶**FIGURE 6.22** Latent learning. *(a)* The maze used by Tolman and Honzik to demonstrate latent learning by rats. *(b)* Results of the experiment. Notice the rapid improvement in performance that occurred when food was made available to the previously unreinforced animals. This indicates that learning had occurred but that it remained hidden or unexpressed. (Adapted from Tolman & Honzik, 1930.)

Cognitive learning Higher level learning involving thinking, knowing, understanding, and anticipation.

Cognitive map Internal images or other mental representations of an area (maze, city, campus, and so forth) that underlie an ability to choose alternative paths to the same goal.

Latent learning Learning that occurs without obvious reinforcement and that remains unexpressed until reinforcement is provided.

How did they learn if there was no reinforcement? Just satisfying curiosity can be enough to reward learning (Harlow & Harlow, 1962). In humans, latent learning is related to higher-level abilities, such as anticipating future reward. For example, if you give an attractive classmate a ride home, you may make mental notes about how to get to his or her house, even if a date is only a remote future possibility.

Discovery Learning

Much of what is meant by cognitive learning is summarized by the word *understanding.* Each of us has, at times, learned ideas by **rote** (repetition and memorization). Although rote learning is efficient, many psychologists believe that learning is more lasting and flexible when people *discover* facts and principles on their own. In **discovery learning,** skills are gained by insight and understanding instead of by rote (Swaak, de Jong, & van Joolingen, 2004).

As long as learning occurs, what difference does it make if it is by discovery or by rote? ▶▶Figure 6.23 illustrates the difference. Two groups of students were taught to calculate the area of a parallelogram by multiplying the height by the length of the base. Some were encouraged to see that a "piece" of a parallelogram could be "moved" to create a rectangle. Later, they were better able to solve unusual problems in which the height times base formula didn't seem to work. Students who simply memorized a rule were confused by the same problems (Wertheimer, 1959). As this implies, discovery can lead to a better understanding of new or unusual problems. When possible, people should try new strategies and discover new solutions during learning. However, this doesn't mean that students are supposed to stumble around and rediscover the principles of math, physics, or chemistry. The best teaching strategies are based on *guided discovery,* in which students are given enough freedom to actively think about problems and enough guidance so that they gain useful knowledge (Mayer, 2004).

Rote learning Learning that takes place mechanically, through repetition and memorization, or by learning rules.

Discovery learning Learning based on insight and understanding.

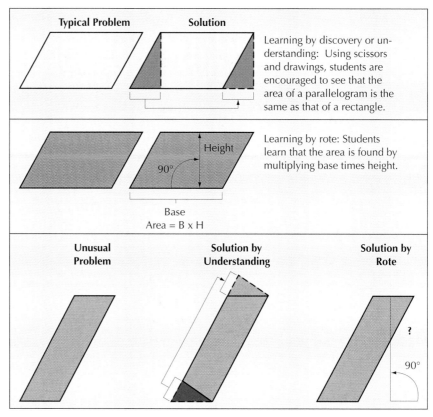

▶▶**FIGURE 6.23** Learning by understanding and by rote. For some types of learning, understanding may be superior, although both types of learning are useful. (After Wertheimer, 1959.)

MODELING—DO AS I DO, NOT AS I SAY

>SURVEY QUESTION< *Does learning occur by imitation?*

Many skills are learned by what Albert Bandura (1971) calls *observational learning,* or *modeling.* **Observational learning** is achieved by watching and imitating the actions of another person or by noting the consequences of the person's actions. In other words, modeling is any process in which information is imparted by example, before direct practice is allowed.

The value of learning by observation is obvious: Imagine trying to *tell* someone how to tie a shoe, do a dance step, or play a guitar. Bandura believes that anything that can be learned from direct experience can be learned by observation. Often, this allows a person to skip the tedious trial-and-error stage of learning.

Observational learning often imparts large amounts of information that would be difficult to obtain by reading instructions or memorizing rules.

Observational Learning

It seems obvious that we learn by observation, but how does it occur? By observing a **model** (someone who serves as an example), a person may (1) learn new responses, (2) learn to carry out or avoid previously learned responses (depending on what happens to the model for doing the same thing), or (3) learn a general rule that can be applied to various situations.

For observational learning to occur, several things must take place. First, the learner must pay *attention* to the model and *remember* what was done. (A beginning auto mechanic might be interested enough to watch an entire tune-up, but unable to remember all the steps.) Next, the learner must be able to *reproduce* the modeled behavior. (Sometimes this is a matter of practice, but it may be that the learner will never be able to perform the behavior. We may admire the feats of world-class gymnasts, but most of us could never reproduce them, no matter how much we practiced.) If a model is *successful* at a task or *rewarded* for a response, the learner is more likely to imitate the behavior. In general, models who are attractive, trustworthy, capable, admired, powerful, or high in status also tend to be imitated (Brewer & Wann, 1998). Finally, once a new response is tried, *normal reinforcement determines whether it will be repeated thereafter.* (Notice the similarity to latent learning, described earlier.)

Imitating Models

Modeling has a powerful effect on behavior. In a classic experiment, children watched an adult attack a large blowup "Bo-Bo the Clown" doll. Some children saw an adult sit on the doll, punch it, hit it with a hammer, and kick it around the room. Others saw a movie of these actions. A third group saw a cartoon version of the aggression. Later, the children were frustrated by having some attractive toys taken away from them. Then, they were allowed to play with the Bo-Bo doll. Most imitated the adult's attack (▸▸Fig. 6.24). Some even added new aggressive acts of their own! Interestingly, the cartoon was only slightly less effective in encouraging aggression than the live adult model and the filmed model (Bandura, Ross, & Ross, 1963).

Then do children blindly imitate adults? No. Remember that observational learning only prepares a person to duplicate a response. Whether it is actually imitated depends on whether the model was rewarded or punished for what was done. Nevertheless, when parents tell a child to do one thing but model a completely different response, children tend to imitate what the parents *do,* and *not* what they *say* (Bryan & Walbek, 1970). Thus, through modeling, children learn not only attitudes, gestures, emotions, and personality traits, but fears, anxieties, and bad habits as well. A good example is the adolescent smoker, who is

Observational learning Learning achieved by watching and imitating the actions of another or noting the consequences of those actions.

Model A person who serves as an example in observational learning.

▸▸**FIGURE 6.24** A nursery school child imitates the aggressive behavior of an adult model he has just seen in a movie. (Photos courtesy of Albert Bandura.)

much more likely to begin smoking if her parents, siblings, and friends smoke (Wilkinson & Abraham, 2004).

Now, consider a typical situation: Little Raymond has just been interrupted at play by his older brother, Robert. Angry and frustrated, he screams at Robert. This behavior interrupts his father Frank's TV watching. Father promptly spanks little Raymond, saying, "This will teach you to hit your big brother." And it will. Because of modeling effects, it is unrealistic to expect a child to "Do as I say, not as I do." The message Frank has given the child is clear: "You have frustrated me; therefore, I will hit you." The next time little Raymond is frustrated, it won't be surprising if he imitates his father and hits his brother (so why does everybody love Raymond, anyway?).

Modeling and the Media

Speaking of television, do the media promote observational learning? According to Roberts, Foehr, and Rideout (2005), today's 8- to 18-year-olds spend an average of 44.5 hours a week engaged with various media, including television, video games, movies, the Internet, music, and print media. Although overall use is falling, television still consumes the lion's share of media attention, averaging 21 hours every week.

By the time the average person has graduated from high school, she or he will have viewed some 15,000 hours of TV, compared with only 11,000 hours spent in the classroom. In that time, viewers will have seen some 18,000 murders and countless acts of robbery, arson, bombing, torture, and beatings. Children watching Saturday morning cartoons see a chilling 26 or more violent acts each hour (Pogatchnik, 1990). Even G-rated cartoons average 10 minutes of violence per hour (Yokota & Thompson, 2000). In short, typical TV viewers are exposed to a massive dose of media violence, which tends to promote observational learning of aggression (Bushman & Anderson, 2001).

Televised Aggression

The last finding comes as no surprise. Studies show conclusively that if large groups of children watch a great deal of televised violence, they will be more prone to behave aggressively (Anderson et al., 2003; Bushman & Anderson, 2001). In other words, not all children will become more aggressive, but many will. More ominously, the effect can last into early adulthood. A group of primary school students with known television viewing habits were later contacted in early adulthood (Huesmann et al., 2003). Those who watched more violence on television as elementary schoolers were more aggressive as adults 15 years later (see ▸▸Fig 6.25).

Does the same conclusion apply to other media? Oh, yes. Children tend to imitate what they observe in all media. From professional wrestling (Bernthal, 2003) to rap music (Wingood et al., 2003) to video games (Carnagey & Anderson, 2004), children have plenty of opportunity to observe and imitate both the good and the bad. (See "You Mean Video Games Might Be Bad for Me?" for some recent evidence.)

You Mean Video Games Might Be Bad for Me?

Today's kids can experience more gore in a day than most people used to experience in a lifetime, even during military combat. For example, in one video game you can kill an entire marching band with a flame-thrower. Some of your victims won't die right away. They will just writhe in pain, begging you to finish them off.

What effects do such experiences have on people who play violent video games? Reviews have concluded that violent video games increase aggressive behavior in children and young adults (Anderson & Bushman, 2001; Anderson, 2004). As with TV, young children are especially susceptible to fantasy violence in video games (Anderson et al., 2003; Bensley & Van Eenwyk, 2001).

One study illustrates the impact of video game violence. First, college students played a violent (Mortal Kombat) or nonviolent (PGA Tournament Golf) video game. Next, they competed with

another student (actually an actor) in a task that allowed aggression and retaliation to take place. Students who played Mortal Kombat were much more likely to aggress, by punishing their competitor (Bartholow & Anderson, 2002). (Don't mess with someone who just played Mortal Kombat!)

How does video game violence increase aggressive behavior? One possibility is that repeated exposure to violence desensitizes players, making them less likely to react negatively to violence and, hence, more prone to engage in it (Bartholow, Sestir, & Davis, 2005; Funk, 2005). Another possibility is that by practicing violence against other people, players may learn to be aggressive in real life (Unsworth & Ward, 2001). (Before you write off video games altogether, read "You Mean Video Games Might Be Good for Me?" in Chapter 8.)

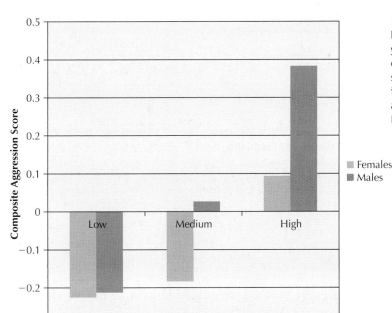

▶▶**FIGURE 6.25** This graph shows that preschoolers who watched low levels of television violence were less aggressive than average as young adults when contacted 15 years later. In contrast, preschoolers who watched high levels of television violence were more aggressive than average as young adults. The composite aggression score includes measures of indirect aggression (e.g., verbal abusiveness) and direct aggression (physical aggression). (Data adapted from Huesmann et al., 2003.)

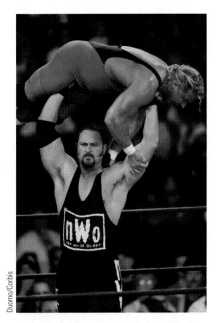

TV heroes can act as powerful models for observational learning of aggression.

Is it fair to say, then, that media violence causes aggression in consumers, especially children? Fortunately, that would be an exaggeration (Kirsh, 2005). Media violence can make aggression more *likely*, but it does not invariably "cause" it to occur for any given child. Many other factors affect the chances that hostile thoughts will be turned into actions. Youngsters who believe that aggression is an acceptable way to solve problems, who believe that TV violence is realistic, and who identify with TV characters are most likely to copy televised aggression (Huesmann et al., 2003). It is particularly sad to find media *heroes* behaving aggressively, as well as villains. Younger children, in particular, are more likely to be influenced because they don't fully recognize that media characters and stories are fantasies (McKenna & Ossoff, 1998).

In view of such findings, it is understandable that countries like Canada, Norway, and Switzerland have restricted the amount of permissible violence on television. Should all countries do the same?

A Look Ahead

Conditioning principles are often derived from animal experiments. However, it should be apparent that the same principles apply to human behavior. Perhaps the best way to appreciate this fact is to observe how reinforcement affects your own behavior. With this in mind, the upcoming Psychology in Action section proposes a personal experiment in operant conditioning. Don't miss this coming attraction!

 Study Break   Cognitive Learning and Imitation

Reflect

Try to think of at least one personal example of each of these concepts: cognitive map, latent learning, discovery learning.

Describe a skill you have learned primarily through observational learning. How did modeling help you learn?

What entertainment or sports personalities did you identify with when you were a child? How did it affect your behavior?

Learning Check

1. An internal representation of relationships is referred to as a _____ _____.

2. Learning that suddenly appears when a reward or incentive for performance is given is called

    a. discovery learning   b. latent learning
    c. rote learning   d. reminiscence

3. Psychologists use the term _____ to describe observational learning.

4. If a model is successful, rewarded, attractive, or high in status, his or her behavior is

    a. difficult to reproduce   b. less likely to be attended to
    c. more likely to be imitated d. subject to positive transfer

5. Children who observed a live adult behave aggressively became more aggressive; those who observed movie and cartoon aggression did not. T or F?

6. Children are most likely to imitate TV characters with whom they identify. T or F?

7. Children who watch a great deal of televised violence are more prone to be aggressive, an effect that is best explained by

    a. negative reinforcement   b. shaping and successive approximations
    c. observational learning   d. vicarious classical conditioning

Critical Thinking

8. Draw a map of your school's campus as you picture it now. Draw a map of the campus as you pictured it after your first visit. Why do the maps differ?

9. Children who watch many aggressive programs on television tend to be more aggressive than average. Why doesn't this observation prove that televised aggression causes aggressive behavior?

Answers

1. cognitive map 2. b 3. modeling 4. c 5. F 6. T 7. c 8. Your cognitive map of the campus has undoubtedly become more accurate and intricate over time as you have added details to it. Your drawings should reflect this change. 9. Because the observation is based on a correlation. Children who are already aggressive may choose to watch more aggressive programs, rather than being made aggressive by them. It took experimental studies to verify that televised aggression promotes aggression by viewers.

Psychology in Action

Behavioral Self-Management—Wouldn't You Like To Reward Yourself?

>SURVEY QUESTION< *How does conditioning apply to practical problems?*

This discussion could be the start of one of the most personal applications of psychology in this book. This is an invitation to carry out a self-management project of your own (Watson & Tharp, 2007). Would you like to increase the number of hours you spend studying each week? Would you like to exercise more, attend more classes, concentrate longer, or read more books? All these activities and many others can be improved by following the rules described here.

Self-Managed Behavior

The principles of operant conditioning can be adapted to manage your own behavior (Martin & Pear, 2003). Here's how:

1. **Choose a target behavior.** Identify the activity you want to change.
2. **Record a baseline.** Record how much time you currently spend performing the target activity or count the number of desired or undesired responses you make each day.
3. **Establish goals.** Remember the principle of shaping, and set realistic goals for gradual improvement on each successive week. Also, set daily goals that add up to the weekly goal.
4. **Choose reinforcers.** If you meet your daily goal, what reward will you allow yourself? Daily rewards might be watching television, eating a candy bar, socializing with friends, listening to your iPod, or whatever you enjoy. Also establish a weekly reward. If you reach your weekly goal, what reward will you allow yourself? A movie? A dinner out? A weekend hike?
5. **Record your progress.** Keep accurate records of the amount of time spent each day on the desired activity or the number of times you make the desired response.
6. **Reward successes.** If you meet your daily goal, collect your reward. If you fall short, be honest with yourself and skip the reward. Do the same for your weekly goal.
7. **Adjust your plan as you learn more about your behavior.** Overall progress will reinforce your attempts at self-management.

Rubberball/SuperStock

If you have trouble finding rewards, remember that anything done often can serve as reinforcement. This is known as the *Premack principle.* It is named after David Premack, a psychologist who popularized its use. For example, if you like to watch television every night and want to study more, make it a rule not to turn on the set until you have studied for an hour (or whatever length of time you choose). Then lengthen the requirement each week. Here is a sample of one student's plan:

1. *Target behavior:* number of hours spent studying for school.
2. *Recorded baseline:* an average of 25 minutes per day for a weekly total of 3 hours.
3. *Goal for the first week:* an increase in study time to 40 minutes per day; weekly goal of 5 hours total study time. *Goal for second week:* 50 minutes per day and 6 hours per week. *Goal for third week:* 1 hour per day and 7 hours per week. *Ultimate goal:* to reach and maintain 14 hours per week study time.
4. *Daily reward for reaching goal:* 1 hour of guitar playing in the evening; no playing if the goal is not met. *Weekly reward for reaching goal:* going to a movie or buying a DVD.

Self-Recording   Even if you find it difficult to give and withhold rewards, you are likely to succeed. Simply knowing that you are reaching a desired goal can be reward enough. The key to any self-management program, therefore, is **self-recording** (keeping records of response frequencies), a form of feedback. The concept was once demonstrated by students in a psychology course. Some of the students recorded their study time and graphed their daily and weekly study behavior. Even though no extra rewards were offered, these students earned better grades than others who were not required to keep records (Johnson & White, 1971).

Feedback can help you decrease bad habits as well as increase desirable responses. Keep track of the number of times daily that you arrive late to class, smoke a cigarette, watch an hour of TV, drink a cup of cappuccino, bite your fingernails, swear, or whatever you are interested in changing. A simple tally on a piece of paper will do, or you can get a small mechanical counter like those used to keep golf scores or count calories. Record keeping helps break patterns, and the feedback can be motivating as you begin to make progress.

Self-recording Self-management based on keeping records of response frequencies.

Good Ways to Break Bad Habits

How can I use learning principles to break a bad habit? By using the methods we have discussed, you can reinforce yourself for *decreasing* unwanted behaviors. However, breaking bad habits may require some additional techniques. Here are four strategies to help you change bad habits.

Alternate Responses A good strategy for change is to try to get the same reinforcement with a new response.

Example: Marta often tells jokes at the expense of others. Her friends sometimes feel hurt by her sharp-edged humor. Marta senses this and wants to change. What can she do? Usually, Marta's joke telling is reinforced by attention and approval. She could just as easily get the same reinforcement by giving other people praise or compliments. Making a change in her behavior should be easy because she will continue to receive the reinforcement she seeks.

Extinction Try to discover what is reinforcing an unwanted response and remove, avoid, or delay the reinforcement.

Example: Fatima has developed a habit of taking longer and longer "breaks" to watch TV when she should be studying. Obviously, TV watching is reinforcing her break taking. To improve her study habits, Fatima could delay reinforcement by studying at the library or some other location a good distance from her TV.

Response Chains Break up response chains that precede an undesired behavior; this will help break the bad habit. The key idea is to scramble the chain of events that leads to an undesired response (Watson & Tharp, 2007).

Example: Most nights Ignacio comes home from work, turns on the TV, and eats a whole bag of cookies or chips. He then takes a shower and changes clothes. By dinnertime he has lost his appetite. Ignacio realizes he is substituting junk food for dinner. Ignacio could solve the problem by breaking the response chain that precedes dinner. For instance, he could shower immediately when he gets home or avoid turning on the television until after dinner.

Cues and Antecedents Try to avoid, narrow down, or remove stimuli that elicit the bad habit.

Example: Raul wants to cut down on smoking. He can take many smoking cues out of his surroundings by removing ashtrays, matches, and extra cigarettes from his house, car, and office. Drug cravings are strongly related to cues conditioned to the drug, such as the odor of cigarettes (Lazev, Herzog, & Brandon, 1999). Raul can try narrowing antecedent stimuli even more. He could begin by smoking only in the lounge at work, never in his office or in his car. He could then limit his smoking to home. Then to only one room at home. Then to one chair at home. If he succeeds in getting this far, he may want to limit his smoking to only one unpleasant place, such as a bathroom, basement, or garage (Riley et al., 2002).

Contracting If you try the techniques described here and have difficulty sticking with them, you may want to try behavioral contracting. In a **behavioral contract,** you state a specific problem behavior you want to control, or a goal you want to achieve. Also state the rewards you will receive, privileges you will forfeit, or punishments you must accept. The contract should be signed by you and a person you trust.

A behavioral contract can be quite motivating, especially when mild punishment is part of the agreement. Here's a classic example, reported by Nurnberger and Zimmerman (1970): A student working on his Ph.D. had completed all requirements but his dissertation, yet for 2 years had not written a single page. A contract was drawn up for him in which he agreed to meet weekly deadlines on the number of pages he would complete. To make sure he would meet the deadlines, he wrote postdated checks. These were to be forfeited if he

Behavioral contract A formal agreement stating behaviors to be changed and consequences that apply.

failed to reach his goal for the week. The checks were made out to organizations he despised (the Ku Klux Klan and American Nazi Party). From the time he signed the contract until he finished his degree, the student's work output was greatly improved.

Getting Help

Attempting to manage or alter your own behavior may be more difficult than it sounds. If you feel you need more information, consult the book listed below. You will also find helpful advice in the Psychology in Action section of Chapter 13. If you do try a self-modification project, but find it impossible to reach your goals, be aware that professional advice is available. For more information, refer to the following article: Watson, D. L., & Tharp, R. G. (2007). *Self-directed behavior* (9th ed.). Belmont, CA: Wadsworth.

Study Break Behavioral Self-Management

Reflect

Even if you don't expect to carry out a self-management project right now, outline a plan for changing your own behavior. Be sure to describe the behavior you want to change, set goals, and identify reinforcers.

Learning Check

1. After a target behavior has been selected for reinforcement, it's a good idea to record a baseline so that you can set realistic goals for change. T or F?
2. Self-recording, even without the use of extra rewards, can bring about desired changes in target behaviors. T or F?
3. The Premack principle states that behavioral contracting can be used to reinforce changes in behavior. T or F?
4. A self-management plan should make use of the principle of shaping by setting a graduated series of goals. T or F?

5. Eleni ends up playing dozens of Solitaire games on her computer each time she tries to work on a term paper for her history class. Eventually she does get to work on the paper, but only after a long delay. To break this bad habit Eleni removes the Solitaire icon from her computer screen so that she won't see it when she begins work. Eleni has used which strategy for breaking bad habits?

a. alternate responses   b. extinction
c. avoid cues   d. contracting

Critical Thinking

6. How does setting daily goals in a behavioral self-management program help maximize the effects of reinforcement?

Answers

1. T 2. T 3. F 4. T 5. c 6. Daily performance goals and rewards reduce the delay of reinforcement, which maximizes its impact.

CHAPTER IN REVIEW

Major Points

- Conditioning is a fundamental type of learning that affects many aspects of daily life.
- In classical conditioning, a neutral stimulus is repeatedly paired with a stimulus that reliably provokes a response. By association, the neutral stimulus also begins to elicit a response.
- In operant conditioning, responses that are followed by reinforcement occur more frequently.
- To understand why people behave as they do, it is important to identify how their responses are being reinforced.
- Cognitive learning involves acquiring higher level information, rather than just linking stimuli and responses.

- We also learn by observing and imitating the actions of others.
- Behavioral principles can be used to manage one's own behavior.

Summary

What is learning?

- Learning is a relatively permanent change in behavior due to experience. Learning resulting from conditioning depends on reinforcement. Reinforcement increases the probability that a particular response will occur.
- Classical, or respondent, conditioning and instrumental, or operant, conditioning are two basic types of learning.

evada

- In classical conditioning, a previously neutral stimulus begins to elicit a response through association with another stimulus.
- In operant conditioning, the frequency and pattern of voluntary responses are altered by their consequences.

How does classical conditioning occur?

- Classical conditioning, studied by Pavlov, occurs when a neutral stimulus (NS) is associated with an unconditioned stimulus (US).
- The US causes a reflex called the unconditioned response (UR). If the NS is consistently paired with the US, it becomes a conditioned stimulus (CS) capable of producing a response by itself. This response is a conditioned (learned) response (CR).
- When the conditioned stimulus is followed by the unconditioned stimulus, conditioning is reinforced (strengthened).
- From an informational view, conditioning creates expectancies, which alter response patterns. In classical conditioning, the CS creates an expectancy that the US will follow.
- Higher order conditioning occurs when a well-learned conditioned stimulus is used as if it were an unconditioned stimulus, bringing about further learning.
- When the CS is repeatedly presented alone, conditioning is extinguished (weakened or inhibited). After extinction seems to be complete, a rest period may lead to the temporary reappearance of a conditioned response. This is called spontaneous recovery.
- Through stimulus generalization, stimuli similar to the conditioned stimulus will also produce a response. Generalization gives way to stimulus discrimination when an organism learns to respond to one stimulus, but not to similar stimuli.

Does conditioning affect emotions?

- Conditioning applies to visceral or emotional responses as well as simple reflexes. As a result, conditioned emotional responses (CERs) also occur.
- Irrational fears called phobias may be CERs. Conditioning of emotional responses can occur vicariously (secondhand) as well as directly.

How does operant conditioning occur?

- Operant conditioning occurs when a voluntary action is followed by a reinforcer. Reinforcement in operant conditioning increases the frequency or probability of a response. This result is based on the law of effect.

- Complex operant responses can be taught by reinforcing successive approximations to a final desired response. This is called shaping. It is particularly useful in training animals.
- If an operant response is not reinforced, it may extinguish (disappear). But after extinction seems complete, it may temporarily reappear (spontaneous recovery).

Are there different kinds of operant reinforcement?

- In positive reinforcement, reward or a pleasant event follows a response. In negative reinforcement, responses that end discomfort tend to be repeated.
- Primary reinforcers are "natural," physiologically based rewards. Intracranial stimulation of "pleasure centers" in the brain can also serve as a primary reinforcer.
- Secondary reinforcers are learned. They typically gain their reinforcing value by direct association with primary reinforcers or because they can be exchanged for primary reinforcers. Tokens and money gain their reinforcing value in this way.
- Feedback, or knowledge of results, aids learning and improves performance. It is most effective when it is immediate, detailed, and frequent.
- Programmed instruction breaks learning into a series of small steps and provides immediate feedback. Computer-assisted instruction (CAI) does the same, but has the added advantage of providing alternative exercises and information when needed. Four variations of CAI are drill and practice, instructional games, educational simulations, and interactive multimedia instruction.

How are we influenced by patterns of reward?

- Delay of reinforcement greatly reduces its effectiveness, but long chains of responses may be built up so that a single reinforcer maintains many responses.
- Superstitious behaviors often become part of response chains because they *appear* to be associated with reinforcement.
- Reward or reinforcement may be given continuously (after every response) or on a schedule of partial reinforcement. Partial reinforcement produces greater resistance to extinction.
- The four most basic schedules of reinforcement are fixed ratio, variable ratio, fixed interval, and variable interval. Each produces a distinct pattern of responding.
- Stimuli that precede a reinforced response tend to control the response on future occasions (stimulus control). Two aspects of stimulus control are generalization and discrimination.

- In generalization, an operant response tends to occur when stimuli similar to those preceding reinforcement are present.
- In discrimination, responses are given in the presence of discriminative stimuli associated with reinforcement (S+) and withheld in the presence of stimuli associated with nonreinforcement (S−).

What does punishment do to behavior?

- Punishment decreases responding. Punishment occurs when a response is followed by the onset of an aversive event or by the removal of a positive event (response cost).
- Punishment is most effective when it is immediate, consistent, and intense. Mild punishment tends to only temporarily suppress responses that are also reinforced or were acquired by reinforcement.
- The undesirable side effects of punishment include the conditioning of fear to punishing agents and situations associated with punishment, the learning of escape and avoidance responses, and the encouragement of aggression.

What is cognitive learning?

- Cognitive learning involves higher mental processes, such as understanding, knowing, or anticipating. Even in relatively simple learning situations, animals and people seem to form cognitive maps (internal representations of relationships).
- In latent learning, learning remains hidden or unseen until a reward or incentive for performance is offered.
- Discovery learning emphasizes insight and understanding, in contrast to rote learning.

Does learning occur by imitation?

- Much human learning is achieved through observation, or modeling. Observational learning is influenced by the personal characteristics of the model and the success or failure of the model's behavior. Studies have shown that aggression is readily learned and released by modeling.
- Media characters can act as powerful models for observational learning. Televised violence increases the likelihood of aggression by viewers.

How does conditioning apply to practical problems?

- Operant principles can be readily applied to manage behavior in everyday settings. When managing one's own behavior, self-reinforcement, self-recording, feedback, and behavioral contracting are all helpful.
- Four strategies that can help change bad habits are reinforcing alternative responses, promoting extinction, breaking response chains, and avoiding antecedent cues.

Interactive Learning

Internet addresses frequently change. To find the sites listed here, visit www.thomsonedu.com/psychology/coon for an updated list of Internet addresses and direct links to relevant sites.

Psychology: A Journey Companion Website Find online quizzes, flash cards, animations, video clips, experiments, interactive assessments, and other helpful study aids for this text at www.thomsonedu.com/psychology/coon.

Animal Training at Sea World Explains how marine mammals are trained at Sea World.

Memory A short tutorial on classical conditioning, operant conditioning, and cognitive learning.

Methods for Changing Behavior Teaches you how to modify your own behavior.

Observational Learning Presents Bandura's original work on modeling, with graphs.

Oppatoons Cartoons of rats undergoing conditioning.

Studying Television Violence An article on television violence.

ThomsonNOW Go to www.thomsonedu.com/login to link to ThomsonNOW, your online study tool. First take the **Pre-Test** for this chapter to get your **Personalized Study Plan,** which will identify topics you need to review and direct you to online resources. Then take the **Post-Test** to determine what concepts you have mastered and what you still need work on.

TEST YOUR KNOWLEDGE

Conditioning and Learning

For additional review, get more practice with *ThompsonNOW*, *WebTutor*, the *Practice Quizzes*, and/or the printed *Study Guide* available with this book.

1. Both classical and operant conditioning involve the concept of
   a. antecedents
   b. consequents
   c. reinforcement
   d. conditioned emotional responses

2. You get out a knife to cut some onions and your eyes begin to water. Apparently, the knife is a(n) _____ and your eyes watering is a(n) _____.
   a. CR, CS
   b. CS, CR
   c. consequence, neutral stimulus
   d. reflex, CS

3. According to the informational view, classical conditioning creates new
   a. expectancies
   b. unconditioned responses
   c. unconditioned stimuli
   d. generalizations

4. Removing reinforcement after a conditioned response has been acquired results in a(n) _____ of that response.
   a. spontaneous recovery
   b. strengthening
   c. weakening
   d. transformation

5. At least some phobias can be thought of as
   a. NS-CR connections
   b. desensitization gradients
   c. extinction responses
   d. CERs

6. Children who receive chemotherapy treatment for cancer sometimes become nauseated by the taste of a particular food or by the sight of their treatment center because of
   a. innate taste aversion
   b. classical conditioning
   c. operant conditioning
   d. punishment

7. Mary watches her best friend get insulted in public by a high school bully. Now Mary is also afraid of the bully. Mary's fear is a result of
   a. stimulus generalization
   b. vicarious conditioning
   c. extinction
   d. higher order conditioning

8. The law of effect defines the role of _____ in learning.
   a. antecedent stimuli
   b. stimulus generalization
   c. operant reinforcers
   d. stimulus approximations

9. Operant reinforcement works best when it is
   a. delayed
   b. an antecedent
   c. response contingent
   d. aversive

10. Negative reinforcement _____ responding.
    a. increases
    b. decreases
    c. reverses
    d. extinguishes

11. Response cost is one form of
    a. discrimination conditioning
    b. generalization
    c. higher order conditioning
    d. punishment

12. Which is a type of primary reinforcer?
    a. social reinforcer
    b. token reinforcer
    c. intracranial stimulation
    d. negative reinforcer

13. Computer-assisted instruction (CAI) is based on the same principles as
    a. negative reinforcement
    b. programmed instruction
    c. higher order conditioning
    d. stimulus generalization

14. Very high response rates are characteristic of
    a. FI schedules
    b. VR schedules
    c. FR schedules
    d. VI schedules

15. The "sniffer" dogs that locate drugs and explosives at airports learn to identify contraband through _____ _____ training.
    a. classical extinction
    b. classical desensitization
    c. vicarious feedback
    d. operant discrimination

16. Punishment tends to encourage escape learning, avoidance learning, and
    a. rapid extinction
    b. aggression
    c. correct responses
    d. the partial reinforcement effect

17. Discovery learning is often superior to its opposite:
    a. rote learning
    b. negative reinforcement
    c. observational learning
    d. cognitive learning

18. Children who watch a great deal of televised violence are more prone to be aggressive, an effect that is best explained by
    a. negative reinforcement
    b. shaping and successive approximations
    c. observational learning
    d. vicarious classical conditioning

19. As a behavioral management strategy, self-recording applies _____ to change personal habits.
    a. vicarious conditioning
    b. feedback
    c. behavioral contracting
    d. the Premack principle

20. Bad habits can be altered by finding ways to remove, avoid, or delay the reinforcement that follows unwanted responses. This strategy is best described as
    a. seek alternate responses
    b. use operant extinction
    c. break up response chains
    d. narrow cues and antecedents

ANSWERS 1. c 2. b 3. a 4. c 5. d 6. b 7. b 8. c 9. c 10. a 11. d 12. b 13. b 14. c 15. d 16. b 17. a 18. c 19. b 20. b

Memory

JOURNEY INTO PSYCHOLOGY: "WHAT THE HELL'S GOING ON HERE?"

It's February and Steven is cross-country skiing on the ice of Lake Michigan. He realizes he is very cold and decides to turn back. In a few minutes comes a new realization: He is lost. Wandering on the ice, he grows numb and very, very tired.

Put yourself in Steven's shoes, and you will appreciate the shock of what happened next. Steven clearly recalls wandering lost and alone on the ice. Immediately after that, he remembers waking up in a field. But as he looked around, Steven knew something was wrong. It was a warm spring day! In his backpack he found running shoes, swimming goggles, and a pair of glasses—all unfamiliar. As he looked at his clothing—also unfamiliar—Steven thought to himself, "What the hell's going on here?" Fourteen months had passed since he left to go skiing (Loftus & Loftus, 1980). How did he get to the field? Steven couldn't say. He had lost more than a year of his life to total amnesia.

As Steven's amnesia vividly shows, life without memory would be meaningless. Imagine the terror of having all your memories wiped out. You would have no identity, no knowledge, and no life history (Behrend, Beike, & Lampinen, 2004). You wouldn't recognize friends or family members. When you looked in a mirror, a stranger would stare back at you. In a very real sense, we are our memories.

This chapter discusses memory and forgetting. By reading it you'll almost certainly discover ways to improve your memory.

▼ Survey Questions

- Is there more than one type of memory?
- What are the features of each type of memory?
- Is there more than one type of long-term memory?
- How is memory measured?
- What are "photographic" memories?
- What causes forgetting?
- How accurate are everyday memories?
- What happens in the brain when memories are formed?
- How can I improve my memory?

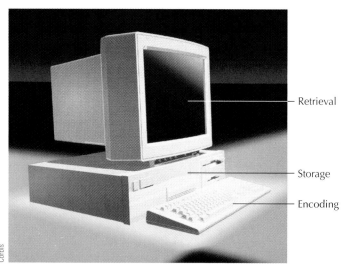

Retrieval

Storage

Encoding

Corbis

»**FIGURE 7.1** In some ways, a computer acts like a mechanical memory system. Both systems process information, and both allow encoding, storage, and retrieval of data.

Memory The mental system for receiving, encoding, storing, organizing, altering, and retrieving information.

Encoding Converting information into a form in which it will be retained in memory.

Storage Holding information in memory for later use.

Retrieval Recovering information from storage in memory.

Sensory memory The first stage of memory, which holds an exact record of incoming information for a few seconds or less.

Icon A mental image or visual representation.

Echo A brief continuation of sensory activity in the auditory system after a sound is heard.

STAGES OF MEMORY—DO YOU HAVE A MIND LIKE A STEEL TRAP? OR A SIEVE?

>SURVEY QUESTION< *Is there more than one type of memory?*

Do you remember what you had for breakfast this morning? Or what happened on September 11, 2001? Of course you do. But how is it possible for us to so easily travel back in time? Let's begin with a look at basic memory systems. An interesting series of events must occur before you can say "I remember."

Many people think of memory as "a dusty storehouse of facts." In reality, **memory** is an active system that receives, stores, organizes, alters, and recovers information (Lieberman, 2004). In some general ways memory acts like a computer (»Fig. 7.1). Incoming information is first **encoded,** or changed into a usable form. This step is like typing data into a computer. Next, information is **stored,** or held, in the system. (As we will see in a moment, human memory can be pictured as three separate storage systems.) Finally, memories must be **retrieved,** or taken out of storage, to be useful. If you're going to remember all of the 9,856 new terms on your next psychology exam, you must successfully encode, store, and retrieve them.

What are the three separate memory systems just mentioned? Psychologists have identified three stages of memory. To be stored for a long time, information must pass through all three stages (»Fig. 7.2).

Sensory Memory

Let's say a friend asks you to pick up several things at a market. How will you remember them? Information first enters **sensory memory,** which can hold an exact copy of what you see or hear, for a few seconds or less. For instance, look at a flower and then close your eyes. An **icon** (EYE-kon), or fleeting mental image, of the flower will persist for about one-half second (Keysers et al., 2005). Similarly, when you hear information, sensory memory stores it as an *echo* for up to 2 seconds (Haenschel et al., 2005). An **echo** is a brief flurry of activity in the auditory system. In general, sensory memory holds information just long enough to move it to the second memory system, short-term memory.

Short-Term Memory

Not everything we see or hear stays in memory. Imagine that a radio is playing in the background as your friend reads her shopping list. Will you remember what the announcer says, too? Probably not, because *selective attention* (focusing on a selected portion of sensory input) controls what information moves on to short-term memory. **Short-term memory (STM)** holds small amounts of information for brief periods. By paying attention to your friend, you will place her shopping list in short-term memory (while you ignore the voice on the radio saying, "Buy Burpo Butter").

How are short-term memories encoded? Short-term memories can be stored as images. But more often they are stored *phonetically* (by sound), especially in recalling words and letters (Neath & Surprenant, 2003). If you are introduced to Tim at a party and you forget his name, you are more likely to call him by a name that sounds like Tim (Jim, Kim, or Slim, for instance), rather than a name that sounds different, such as Bob or Mike. Your friend with the shopping list may be lucky if you don't bring home jam instead of ham and soap instead of soup!

Short-term memory briefly stores small amounts of information. When you dial a phone number or briefly remember a shopping list, you are using STM. Notice that information is quickly "dumped" from STM and forever lost. Short-term memory prevents our minds from storing useless names, dates, telephone numbers, and other trivia.

As you may have noticed when dialing a telephone, STM is very sensitive to interruption, or *interference.* You've probably had something like this happen: Someone leaves a phone number on your answering machine. You repeat the number to yourself as you start to dial. Then the doorbell rings and you rush to see who is there. When you return to the phone, you have completely forgotten the number. You listen to the message again and memorize the number. This time as you begin to dial, someone asks you a question. You answer, turn to the phone, and find that you have forgotten the number. Notice again that STM can handle only small amounts of information. It is very difficult to do more than one task at a time in STM (Miyake, 2001).

▶**FIGURE 7.2** Remembering is thought to involve at least three steps. Incoming information is first held for a second or two by sensory memory. Information selected by attention is then transferred to temporary storage in short-term memory. If new information is not rapidly encoded, or rehearsed, it is forgotten. If it is transferred to long-term memory, it becomes relatively permanent, although retrieving it may be a problem. The preceding is a useful, but highly simplified, *model* of memory; it may not be literally true of what happens in the brain (Goldstein, 2005).

Working Memory

Short-term memory is often used for more than just storing information. When STM is combined with other mental processes, it provides an area of **working memory** where we do much of our thinking. Working memory acts as a sort of "mental scratchpad." It briefly holds the information we need when we are thinking and solving problems (Holmes & Adams, 2006). Whenever you do mental arithmetic, put together a puzzle, plan a meal, follow directions, or read a book, you are using working memory (Baddeley, 2003).

Long-Term Memory

If STM is so limited, how do we remember for longer periods of time? Information that is important or meaningful is transferred to **long-term memory (LTM),** which acts as a lasting storehouse for knowledge. LTM contains everything you know about the world—from aardvark to zucchini, math to *Desperate Housewives,* facts to fantasy. And yet, there appears to be no danger of running out of room. LTM can hold nearly limitless amounts of infor-

Short-term memory (STM) The memory system used to hold small amounts of information for relatively brief time periods.

Working memory Another name for short-term memory, especially as it is used for thinking and problem solving.

Long-term memory (LTM) The memory system used for relatively permanent storage of meaningful information.

Cattle, Memories, and Culture

As noted, we are most likely to remember information that is personally important or meaningful. If you were on a farm and saw 20 cows walk by, do you think you could remember the age, color, sex, and condition of all of them? Unless you are a dairy farmer, doing so would be quite a feat of memory. However, for a Maasai person from East Africa, it would be easy. Livestock are very important in Maasai culture; a Maasai's wealth is measured by the number of cattle owned. Thus, the Maasai are prepared to code and store information about cattle that would be difficult for many people in the United States to remember.

Culture affects our memories in other interesting ways. For example, American culture emphasizes individuals, whereas Chinese culture emphasizes membership in groups. In one study, European-American and Chinese adults were asked to recall 20 memories from any time in their lives. As expected, American memories tended to be self-centered: Most people remembered surprising events and what they did during the events. Chinese adults, in contrast, remembered important social or historical events and their own interactions with family members, friends, and others (Wang & Conway, 2004). Thus, in the United States, personal memories tend to be about "me"; in China they tend to be about "us."

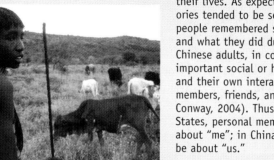

Malcolm Linton/Liaison/Getty Images

mation. In fact, the more you know, the easier it becomes to add new information to memory. This is the reverse of what we would expect if LTM could be "filled up" (Goldstein, 2005). It is also one of many reasons for getting an education.

Are long-term memories also encoded as sounds? They can be. But typically, long-term memories are stored on the basis of *meaning,* not sound. If you make an error in LTM, it will probably be related to meaning. For example, if you are trying to recall the word *barn* from a memorized list, you are more likely to mistakenly say *shed* or *farm* than *yarn* or *darn.* If you can link information in STM to knowledge already stored in LTM, it gains meaning. This makes it easier to remember. As an example, try to memorize this story:

> With hocked gems financing him, our hero bravely defied all scornful laughter. "Your eyes deceive," he had said. "An egg, not a table, correctly typifies this unexplored planet." Now three sturdy sisters sought proof. Forging along, days became weeks as many doubters spread fearful rumors about the edge. At last from nowhere welcome winged creatures appeared, signifying momentous success. (Adapted from Dooling & Lachman, 1971.)

This odd story emphasizes the impact that meaning has on memory. People given the title of the story were able to remember it far better than those not given a title. See if the title helps you as much as it did them. "Columbus Discovers America."

Dual Memory

Most of our daily memory chores are handled by STM and LTM. To summarize their connection, picture short-term memory as a small desk at the front of a huge warehouse full of filing cabinets (LTM). As information enters the warehouse, it is first placed on the desk. Because the desk is small, it must be quickly cleared off to make room for new information. Unimportant items are simply tossed away. Meaningful or personally important information is placed in the files (LTM). (See "Cows, Memories, and Culture.")

When we want to use knowledge from LTM to answer a question, the information is returned to STM. Or, in our analogy, a folder is taken out of the files (LTM) and moved to the desk (STM), where it can be used. Now that you have a general picture of memory it is time to explore STM and LTM in more detail. But first, here's a chance to rehearse what you've learned.

Study Break Memory Systems

Reflect

Wave a pencil back and forth in front of your eyes while focusing on something in the distance. The pencil's image looks transparent. Why? (Because sensory memory briefly holds an image of the pencil. This image persists after the pencil passes by.)

Think of a time today when you used short-term memory (such as briefly remembering a phone number, an Internet address, or someone's name). How long did you retain the information? How did you encode it? How much do you remember now?

How is long-term memory helping you read this sentence? If the words weren't already stored in LTM, could you read at all? How else have you used LTM today?

Learning Check

Match: **A.** Sensory memory **B.** STM **C.** LTM

1. _____ Working memory
2. _____ Holds information for a few seconds or less
3. _____ Stores an icon or echo
4. _____ Permanent, unlimited capacity
5. _____ Temporarily holds small amounts of information
6. _____ Selective attention determines its contents
7. STM is improved by interruption, or interference, because attention is more focused at such times. T or F?

Critical Thinking

8. Why is sensory memory important to filmmakers?

Answers

1. B 2. A 3. A 4. C 5. B 6. B 7. F 8. Without sensory memory, a movie would look like a flickering series of still pictures. The brief persistence of icons in sensory memory is what blends one movie frame into the next.

SHORT-TERM MEMORY—DO YOU KNOW THE MAGIC NUMBER?

>SURVEY QUESTION< *What are the features of each type of memory?*

To make good use of your memory, it is valuable to know more about the characteristics of STM and LTM.

How much information can be held in short-term memory? For an answer, read the following numbers once. Then close the book and write as many as you can in the correct order.

8   5   1   7   4   9   3

This is called a digit-span test. It is a measure of attention and short-term memory. If you were able to correctly repeat 7 digits, you have an average short-term memory. Now try to memorize the following list, reading it only once.

7   1   8   3   5   4   2   9   1   6   3

This series was probably beyond your short-term memory capacity. Psychologist George Miller found that short-term memory is limited to the "magic number" 7 (plus or minus 2) **information bits** (Miller, 1956). A bit is a single meaningful "piece" of information, such as a digit. It is as if short-term memory has 7 "slots" or "bins" into which separate items can be placed. Actually, a few people can remember up to 9 bits, and for some types of information 5 bits is the limit. Thus, an *average* of 7 information bits can be held in short-term memory (Neath & Surprenant, 2003).

When all of the "slots" in STM are filled, there is no room for new information. Picture how this works at a party: Let's say your hostess begins introducing everyone who is there, "Chun, Dasia, Marco, Roseanna, Cholik, Shawn, Kyrene . . . ." "Stop," you think to yourself. But she continues, "Nelia, Jay, Efren, Frank, Marietta, Jorge, Patty, Amit, Ricky." The hostess leaves, satisfied that you have met everyone. And you spend the evening talking with Chun, Dasia, and Ricky, the only people whose names you remember!

Information bits Meaningful units of information, such as numbers, letters, words, or phrases.

Recoding

Before we continue, try your short-term memory again, this time on letters. Read the following letters once, then look away and try to write them in the proper order.

T V I   B M U S   N Y   M C A

Notice that there are 12 letters, or "bits" of information. This should be beyond the 7-item limit of STM. However, because the letters are in four groups, or *chunks* of information, many students are able to memorize them. **Information chunks** are made up of bits of information grouped into larger units.

How does chunking help? Chunking *recodes* (reorganizes) information into units that are already in LTM. For example, you may have noticed that NY is the abbreviation for New York. If so, the two bits N and Y became one chunk. In a classic experiment that used lists like this one, people remembered best when the letters were read as familiar meaningful chunks: TV, IBM, USN, YMCA (Bower & Springston, 1970). If you recoded the letters this way, you probably remembered the entire list.

Chunking suggests that STM holds about 5 to 7 of whatever units we are using. A single chunk could be made up of numbers, letters, words, phrases, or familiar sentences. Picture STM as a small desk again. Through chunking, we combine several items into one "stack" of information. This allows us to place 7 stacks on the desk, where before there was only room for 7 separate items. While you are studying, try to find ways to link 2, 3, or more separate facts or ideas into larger chunks, and your memory will improve. Psychologist Nelson Cowan (2001, 2005) believes that STM may actually hold only 4 items, unless some chunking has occurred. The clear message is that creating information chunks is the key to making good use of your short-term memory.

Rehearsing Information

How long do short-term memories last? They disappear very rapidly. However, you can prolong a memory by silently repeating it, a process called **maintenance rehearsal.** You have probably briefly remembered an address or telephone number this way. In a sense, rehearsing information allows you to "see" it many times, not just once (Nairne, 2002). The more times a short-term memory is rehearsed, the greater its chances of being stored in LTM (Goldstein, 2005).

What if rehearsal is prevented, so a memory cannot be recycled or moved to LTM? Without maintenance rehearsal, STM is quite brief. In one experiment, subjects heard meaningless syllables like XAR followed by a number like 67. As soon as subjects heard the number, they began counting backward by threes (to prevent them from repeating the syllable). After a delay of only 18 seconds, their memory for the syllables fell to zero (Peterson & Peterson, 1959).

After *18 seconds* without rehearsal, the short-term memories were gone forever! Part of this rapid loss can be explained by the testing procedures used (Goldstein, 2005). In daily life, short-term memories usually last longer. Just the same, if you are introduced to someone, and the name slips out of STM, it is gone forever. To escape this awkward situation you might try saying something like, "I'm curious, how do you spell your name?" Unfortunately, the response is often an icy reply like, "B-O-B S-M-I-T-H, it's really not too difficult." To avoid embarrassment, pay careful attention to the name, repeat it to yourself several times, and try to use it in the next sentence or two—before you lose it (Neath & Surprenant, 2003).

Elaborative rehearsal, which makes information more meaningful, is a far better way to form lasting memories. Elaborative rehearsal links new information to memories that are already in LTM. When you are studying, you will remember more if you elaborate, extend, and reflect about the meaning of the information. As you read, try to frequently ask yourself "why" questions, such as "Why would that be true?" (Toyota & Kikuchi, 2005; Willoughby

Information chunks Information bits grouped into larger units.

Maintenance rehearsal Silently repeating or mentally reviewing information to hold it in short-term memory.

Elaborative rehearsal Rehearsal that links new information with existing memories and knowledge.

et al., 1997). Also, try to relate new ideas to your own experiences and knowledge (Hartlep & Forsyth, 2000).

LONG-TERM MEMORY— WHERE THE PAST LIVES

>SURVEY QUESTION< *Is there more than one type of long-term memory?*

An electrode touched the patient's brain. Immediately she said, "Yes, sir, I think I heard a mother calling her little boy somewhere. It seemed to be something happening years ago. It was somebody in the neighborhood where I live." A short time later the electrode was applied to the same spot. Again the patient said, "Yes, I hear the same familiar sounds, it seems to be a woman calling, the same lady" (Penfield, 1958). A woman undergoing brain surgery made these statements. There are no pain receptors in the brain, so the patient was awake as her brain was electrically stimulated (▸▸Fig. 7.3). When activated, some brain areas seemed to produce vivid memories of long-forgotten events.

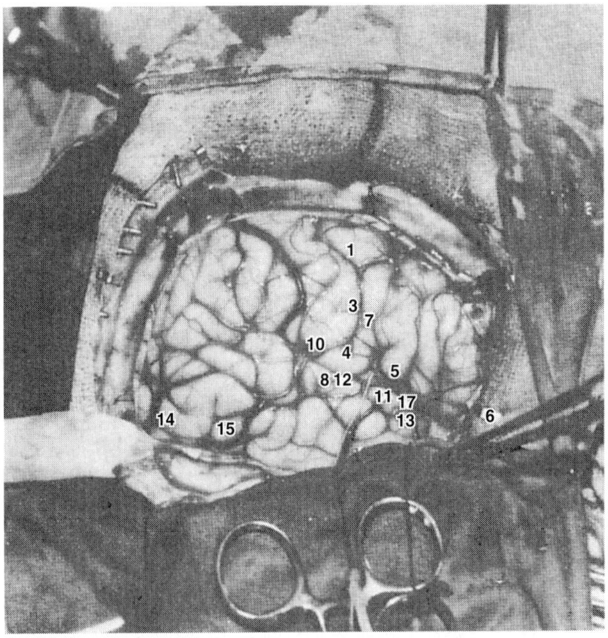

Permanence

Are all of our experiences permanently recorded in memory? Results like those described led neurosurgeon Wilder Penfield to claim that the brain records the past like a "strip of movie film, complete with sound track" (Penfield, 1957). But as you know, this is an exaggeration. Many events never get past short-term memory. Also, brain stimulation produces memory-like experiences in only about 3 percent of cases. Most reports resemble dreams more than memories, and many are clearly imaginary. Memory experts now believe that long-term memories are only *relatively* permanent (Goldstein, 2005). Perfect, eternal memories are a myth.

Try It Yourself: How's Your Memory?
To better appreciate the next topic, pause for a moment and read the words you see here. Read through the list once. Then continue reading the next section of this chapter.

    bed   dream   blanket   doze   pillow   nap   snore   mattress   alarm
     clock   rest   slumber   nod   sheet   bunk   cot   cradle   groggy

Constructing Memories

There's another reason for doubting that all of our experiences are permanently recorded. As new long-term memories are stored, older memories are often updated, changed, lost, or *revised* (Lieberman, 2004). To illustrate this point, Elizabeth Loftus and John Palmer (1974) showed people a filmed automobile accident. Afterward, some participants were asked to estimate how fast the cars were going when they "smashed" into each other. For others the words "bumped," "contacted," or "hit" replaced "smashed." One week later, each person was asked, "Did you see any broken glass?" Those asked earlier about the cars that "smashed" into each other were more likely to say yes. (No broken glass was shown in the film.) The new information ("smashed") was included in memories and altered them.

Try It Yourself: Old or New?
Now, without looking back to the list of words you read a few minutes ago, see if you can tell which of the following are "old" words (items from the list you read)

▸▸**FIGURE 7.3** Exposed cerebral cortex of a patient undergoing brain surgery. Numbers represent points that reportedly produced "memories" when electrically stimulated. A critical evaluation of such reports suggests that they are more like dreams than memories. This fact raises questions about claims that long-term memories are permanent. (Wilder Penfield, *The Excitable Cortex in Conscious Man,* 1958. Courtesy of the author and Charles C Thomas, Publisher, Springfield, IL.)

and which are "new" words (items that weren't on the list). Mark each of the following words as old or new:

sofa   sleep   lamp   kitchen

Updating memories is called **constructive processing.** Gaps in memory, which are common, may be filled in by logic, guessing, or new information (Schacter, Norman, & Koutstaal, 1998). Indeed, it is possible to have "memories" for things that never happened (such as remembering broken glass at an accident when there was none) (Loftus, 2003a, b). In one fascinating study, people who had visited a Disney resort were shown several fake ads for Disney that featured Bugs Bunny. Later, about 16 percent of the people who saw these fake ads claimed that they had met Bugs at Disneyland. This is impossible, of course, because Bugs Bunny is a Warner Brothers character who would never be found at Disneyland (Braun, Ellis, & Loftus, 2002).

Try It Yourself: And Now, the Results

Return now and look at the labels you wrote on the "old or new" word list. Contrary to what you may think you "remembered," all of the listed words are "new." None was on the original list! If you thought you remembered that sleep was on the original list, you had a false memory. The word *sleep* is associated with most of the words on the original list, which creates a strong impression that you saw it before (Roediger & McDermott, 1995).

Eyewitness memories are notoriously inaccurate. By the time witnesses are asked to testify in court, information they learned after an incident may blend into their original memories.

As the preceding examples show, thoughts, inferences, and mental associations may be mistaken for true memories (Loftus, 2003a, b). People in Elizabeth Loftus's experiments who had these *pseudomemories* (false memories) were often quite upset to learn they had given false "testimony" (Loftus & Ketcham, 1994).

False long-term memories are a common problem in police work. For example, a witness may select a photo of a suspect from police files or see a photo in the news. Later, the witness identifies the suspect in a lineup or in court. Did the witness really remember the suspect from the scene of the crime? Or was it from the more recently seen photograph?

Does new information "overwrite" existing memories? No, the real problem is that we often can't remember the *source* of a memory (Simons et al, 2004). This can lead witnesses to "remember" a face that they actually saw somewhere other than the crime scene.

Many tragic cases of mistaken identity occur this way. One famous example involved memory expert Donald Thomson. After appearing live on Australian television, he was accused of rape. It turns out that the victim was watching him on TV when the actual rapist broke into her apartment (Schacter, 1996, 2001).

Is there any way to avoid such problems? Forensic psychologists have tried a variety of techniques to help improve the memory of witnesses. "Telling Wrong from Right in Forensic Memory" examines research on this intriguing question.

To summarize, forming and using memories is an active, creative, highly personal process. Our memories are colored by emotions, judgments, and quirks of personality. If you and a friend were joined at the hip, and you went through life side-by-side, you would still have different memories. What we remember depends on what we pay attention to, what we regard as meaningful or important, and what we feel strongly about (Schacter, 2000).

Organizing Memories

Long-term memory stores huge amounts of information during a lifetime. How are we able to quickly find specific memories? The answer is that each person's "memory index" is highly organized.

Constructive processing Reorganizing or updating memories on the basis of logic, reasoning, or the addition of new information.

Telling Wrong from Right in Forensic Memory

Imagine that you are a forensic psychologist, investigating a crime. Unfortunately, your witness can't remember much of what happened. As a "memory detective," what can you do to help?

Could hypnosis improve the witness's memory? It might seem so. In one case in California, 26 children were abducted from a school bus and held captive for ransom. Under hypnosis, the bus driver recalled the license plate number of the kidnappers' van. This memory helped break the case. Such successes seem to imply that hypnosis can improve memory. But does it?

Research has shown that hypnosis increases false memories more than it does true ones. Eighty percent of the new memories produced by hypnotized subjects in one classic experiment were *incorrect* (Dywan & Bowers, 1983). This is in part because a hypnotized person is more likely than normal to use imagination to fill in gaps in memory. Also, if a questioner asks misleading or suggestive questions, hypnotized persons tend to weave the information into their memories (Scoboria et al., 2002). To make matters worse, even when a memory is completely false, the hypnotized person's confidence in it can be unshakable (Burgess & Kirsch, 1999).

Thus, hypnosis sometimes uncovers more information, as it did with the bus driver (Schreiber & Schreiber, 1999). However, when it does, there is often no sure way to tell which memories are false and which are true (Newman & Thompson, 2001).

Is there a better way to improve eyewitness memory? To help police detectives, R. Edward Geiselman and Ron Fisher created the **cognitive interview,** a technique for jogging the memory of eyewitnesses (Fisher & Geiselman, 1987). The key to this approach is recreating the crime scene. Witnesses revisit the scene in their imaginations or in person. That way, aspects of the crime scene, such as sounds, smells, and objects, provide helpful retrieval cues. Back in the context of the crime, the witness is encouraged to recall events in different orders and from different viewpoints. Every new memory, no matter how trivial it may seem, can serve as a cue to trigger the retrieval of yet more memories. (Later in this chapter, we will see why such cues are so effective for jogging memories.)

When used properly, the cognitive interview produces more correct information than standard questioning (Davis, McMahon, & Greenwood, 2005; Geiselman et al., 1986). This improvement comes without adding to the number of false memories elicited, as occurs with hypnosis, and it is more effective in actual police work (Ginet & Py, 2001; Kebbell & Wagstaff, 1998).

Some police detectives, following the advice of psychologists, recreate crime scenes to help witnesses remember what they saw. Typically, people return to the scene at the time of day the crime occurred. They are also asked to wear the same clothing they wore and go through the same motions as they did before the crime. With so many memory cues available, witnesses sometimes remember key items of information they hadn't recalled before.

Do you mean that information is arranged alphabetically, as in a dictionary? Not a chance! If you are asked to name a black and white animal that lives on ice, is related to a chicken, and cannot fly, you don't have to go from aardvark to zebra to find the answer. You will probably only think of black and white birds living in the Antarctic. *Voila,* the answer is penguin.

Information in LTM may be arranged according to rules, images, categories, symbols, similarity, formal meaning, or personal meaning (Lieberman, 2004). In recent years, psychologists have begun to develop a picture of the *structure*, or organization, of memories. *Memory structure* refers to the pattern of associations among items of information. For example, assume that you are given two statements, to which you must answer yes or no: (1) *A canary is an animal.* (2) *A canary is a bird.* Which do you answer more quickly? Most people can say that *A canary is a bird* faster than they can recognize that *A canary is an animal* (Collins & Quillian, 1969). Why should this be so? Psychologists believe that a **network model** of memory explains why. According to this view, LTM is organized as a network of linked ideas (»Fig. 7.4). When ideas are "farther" apart, it takes a longer chain of associations to connect them. The more two items are separated, the longer it takes to answer. In

Cognitive interview Use of various cues and strategies to improve the memory of eyewitnesses.

Network model A model of memory that views it as an organized system of linked information.

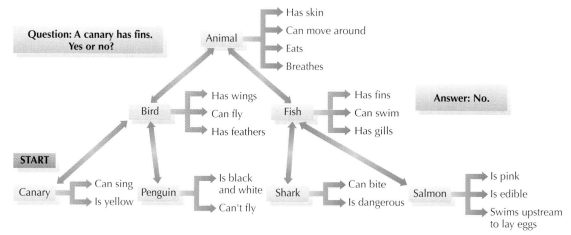

FIGURE 7.4 A hypothetical network of facts about animals shows what is meant by the structure of memory. Small networks of ideas such as this are probably organized into larger and larger units and higher levels of meaning. (Adapted from Collins & Quillian, 1969.)

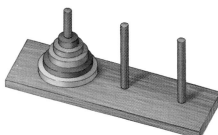

FIGURE 7.5 The tower puzzle. In this puzzle, all the colored disks must be moved to another post, without ever placing a larger disk on a smaller one. Only one disk may be moved at a time, and a disk must always be moved from one post to another (it cannot be held aside). An amnesic patient learned to solve the puzzle in 31 moves, the minimum possible. Even so, each time he began, he protested that he did not remember ever solving the puzzle before and that he did not know how to begin. Evidence like this suggests that memories for skills are distinct from memories for facts. (Adapted from Squire & Zola-Morgan, 1988.)

Redintegrative memories Memories that are reconstructed or expanded by starting with one memory and then following chains of association to other, related memories.

Procedural memory Long-term memories of conditioned responses and learned skills.

terms of information links, *canary* is probably "close" to *bird* in your "memory files." *Animal* and *canary* are farther apart. Remember though, this has nothing to do with alphabetical order. We are talking about a system of linked meanings.

Redintegrative Memories

Networks of associated memories may help explain a common experience: Imagine finding a picture taken on your sixth birthday or tenth Christmas. As you look at the photo, one memory leads to another, which leads to another, and another. Soon you have unleashed a flood of seemingly forgotten details. This process is called redintegration (ruh-DIN-tuh-GRAY-shun).

Redintegrative memories seem to spread through the "branches" of memory networks. Many people find that such memories are also touched off by distinctive odors out of the past—from a farm visited in childhood, Grandma's kitchen, the seashore, a doctor's office, the perfume or aftershave of a former lover, and so on. The key idea in redintegration is that one memory serves as a cue to trigger another. As a result, an entire past experience may be reconstructed from one small recollection.

How many types of long-term memory are there? It is becoming clear that more than one type of long-term memory exists. Let's probe a little farther into the mysteries of memory.

Skill Memory and Fact Memory

A curious thing happens to many people who develop amnesia. Amnesic patients may be unable to learn a telephone number, an address, or a person's name. And yet, the same patients can learn to solve complex puzzles in a normal amount of time (Cavaco et al., 2004) (»Fig. 7.5). These and other observations have led many psychologists to conclude that long-term memories fall into at least two categories. One is called *procedural memory* (or skill memory). The other is *declarative memory* (also sometimes called fact memory).

Skills

Procedural memory includes basic conditioned responses and learned actions, such as those involved in typing, driving, or swinging a golf club. Memories such as these can be fully expressed only as actions (or "know-how"). It is likely that skill memories register in "lower" brain areas, especially the cerebellum. They represent the more basic "automatic" elements of conditioning, learning, and memory (Hermann et al., 2004).

Facts

Declarative memory stores specific factual information, such as names, faces, words, dates, and ideas. Declarative memories are expressed as words or symbols. For example, knowing that Peter Jackson directed both the *Lord of the Rings* trilogy and the latest remake of *King Kong* is a declarative memory. This is the type of memory that a person with amnesia lacks and that most of us take for granted. Declarative memory can be further divided into *semantic memory* and *episodic memory* (Tulving, 2002).

Semantic Memory

Most of our basic factual knowledge about the world is almost totally immune to forgetting. The names of objects, the days of the week or months of the year, simple math skills, the seasons, words and language, and other general facts are all quite lasting. Such impersonal facts make up a part of LTM called **semantic memory.** Semantic memory serves as a mental dictionary or encyclopedia of basic knowledge.

Episodic Memory

Semantic memory has no connection to times or places. It would be rare, for instance, to remember when and where you first learned the names of the seasons. In contrast, **episodic** (ep-ih-SOD-ik) **memory** is an "autobiographical" record of personal experiences. It stores life events (or "episodes") day after day, year after year. Can you remember your seventh birthday? Your first date? An accident you witnessed? What you did yesterday? All are episodic memories. Note that episodic memories are about the "what," "where," and "when" of our lives. More than a simple ability to store information, they make it possible for us to mentally travel back in time and *re-experience* events (Tulving, 2002).

Are episodic memories as lasting as semantic memories? In general, episodic memories are more easily forgotten than semantic memories. This is because new information constantly pours into episodic memory. Stop for a moment and remember where and when you first met your best friend. That was an episodic memory. Notice that you now remember that you just remembered something. You have a new episodic memory in which you remember that you remembered while reading this text! It's easy to see how much we ask of our memory.

How Many Types of Memory?

In answer to the question posed at the beginning of this section, it is very likely that three kinds of long-term memories exist: procedural memory and two types of declarative memory, semantic, and episodic (Squire, 2004) (▸▸Fig. 7.6). Although other types of memory may be discovered, it appears that some pieces of the puzzle are falling into place.

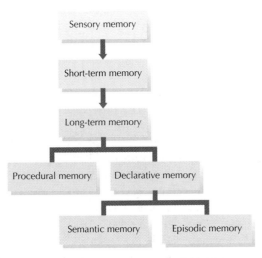

▸▸**FIGURE 7.6** In the model shown here, long-term memory is divided into procedural memory (learned actions and skills) and declarative memory (stored facts). Declarative memories can be either semantic (impersonal knowledge) or episodic (personal experiences associated with specific times and places).

Declarative memory That part of long-term memory containing specific factual information.

Semantic memory A subpart of declarative memory that records impersonal knowledge about the world.

Episodic memory A subpart of declarative memory that records personal experiences that are linked with specific times and places.

Reflect

Telephone numbers are divided into an area code (3 digits) and a 7-digit number that is divided into 3 digits, plus 4 more. Can you relate this practice to STM? How about to chunking and recoding?

Think about how you've used your memory in the last hour. See if you can identify an example of each of the following: a procedural memory, a declarative memory, a semantic memory, and an episodic memory.

Learning Check

1. Information is best transferred from STM to LTM when a person engages in

   a. maintenance chunking   b. maintenance recoding
   c. elaborative networking   d. elaborative rehearsal

2. Constructive processing is often responsible for creating pseudomemories. T or F?

3. Electrical stimulation of the brain has shown conclusively that all memories are stored permanently, but not all memories can be retrieved. T or F?

4. Memories elicited under hypnosis are more vivid, complete, and reliable than normal. T or F?

5. The existence of redintegrative memories is best explained by _____ models of memory.

   a. network   b. TOT
   c. implicit   d. eidetic

6. Which of the following is a type of skill memory?

   a. semantic memory   b. declarative memory
   c. episodic memory   d. procedural memory

Critical Thinking

7. Parents sometimes warn children not to read comic books, fearing that they will learn less in school if they "fill their heads up with junk." Why is this warning unnecessary?

Answers

1. d 2. T 3. F 4. F 5. a 6. d 7. Because the more information you have in long-term memory, the greater the possibilities for linking new information to it. Generally, the more you know, the more you can learn—even if some of what you know is "junk."

MEASURING MEMORY—THE ANSWER IS ON THE TIP OF MY TONGUE

>SURVEY QUESTION< *How is memory measured?*

You either remember something or you don't, right? Wrong. Partial memories are common. For instance, have you ever tried to remember something only to find yourself stuck in a **tip-of-the-tongue (TOT) state**? This is the feeling that a memory is available, but not quite retrievable (Schwartz, 2002). It is as if an answer or a memory is just out of reach—on the "tip of your tongue."

In a classic TOT study, university students read the definitions of words such as *sextant, sampan,* and *ambergris.* Students who "drew a blank" and couldn't name a defined word were asked to give any other information they could. Often, they could guess the first and last letter and the number of syllables of the word they were seeking. They also gave words that sounded like or meant the same thing as the defined word (Brown & McNeill, 1966). In another study, people listened to theme music from popular TV shows. Then they tried to name the program the tune came from. This produced TOT experiences for about 1 out of 5 tunes (Riefer, Keveri, & Kramer, 1995).

Closely related to the TOT state is the fact that people can often tell beforehand if they are likely to remember something. This is called the *feeling of knowing* (Widner, Jr., Otani, & Winkelman, 2005). Feeling-of-knowing reactions are easy to observe on TV game shows, where they often occur when contestant's faces often light up just before they are allowed to answer. *Déjà vu,* the experience that you have previously experienced a new situation, is yet another example of partial retrieval (Brown, 2004).

Because memory is not an all-or-nothing event, there are several ways of measuring it. Three commonly used memory tasks (tests of memory) are *recall, recognition,* and *relearning.* Let's see how they differ.

Tip-of-the-tongue state The feeling that a memory is available but not quite retrievable.

Recalling Information

What is the name of the first song on your favorite CD? Who won the World Series last year? Who wrote *Hamlet?* If you can answer these questions you are using **recall,** a direct retrieval of facts or information. Tests of recall often require *verbatim* (word-for-word) memory. If you study a poem until you can recite it without looking at it, you are recalling it. If you complete a fill-in-the-blank question, you are using recall. When you answer an essay question by providing facts and ideas, you are also using recall, even though you didn't learn your essay verbatim.

The order in which information is memorized has an interesting effect on recall. To experience it, try to memorize the following list, reading it only once:

bread, apples, soda, ham, cookies, rice, lettuce, beets,
mustard, cheese, oranges, ice cream, crackers, flour, eggs

If you are like most people, it will be hardest for you to recall items from the middle of the list. ▸▸Figure 7.7 shows the results of a similar test. Notice that most errors occur with middle items of an ordered list. This is the **serial position effect.** You can remember the last items on a list because they are still in STM. The first items are also remembered well because they entered an "empty" short-term memory. This allows you to rehearse the items so they move into long-term memory (Addis & Kahana, 2004). The middle items are neither held in short-term memory nor moved to long-term memory, so they are often lost.

Recognizing Information

Try to write down everything you can remember learning from a class you took last year. If you actually did this, you might conclude that you had learned very little. However, a more sensitive test based on recognition could be used. In **recognition memory,** previously learned material is correctly identified. For instance, you could take a multiple-choice test on facts and ideas from the course. Because you would only have to recognize correct answers, you would probably find that you had learned a lot.

Recognition memory can be amazingly accurate for pictures and photographs. One investigator showed people 2,560 photographs at a rate of one every 10 seconds. Each person was then shown 280 pairs of photographs. Each pair included an "old" picture (from the first set of photos) and a similar "new" image. Subjects could tell 85 to 95 percent of the time which photograph they had seen before (Haber, 1970).

Recognition is usually superior to recall. That's why people so often say, "I may forget a name, but I never forget a face." (You recall the name but recognize the face.) That's also why police departments use photographs or a lineup to identify criminal suspects. Witnesses who disagree when they try to recall a suspect's height, weight, age, or eye color often agree completely when they merely need to recognize the person.

Is recognition always superior? It depends greatly on the kind of *distractors* used. These are false items included with an item to be recognized. If distractors are very similar to the correct item, memory may be poor. A reverse problem occurs when only one choice looks like it could be correct. This can produce a *false positive,* or false sense of recognition, like the false memory you had earlier when you thought you remembered seeing the word *sleep.*

There have been instances in which witnesses described a criminal as black, tall, or young. Then a lineup was held in which a suspect was the only African American among whites, the only tall suspect, or the only young person. In such cases a false identification is very likely. A better method is to have *all* the distractors look like the person witnesses described. Also, to reduce false positives, witnesses should be warned that the culprit *may not be present.* Many hundreds of people have been put in jail on the basis of mistaken eye-

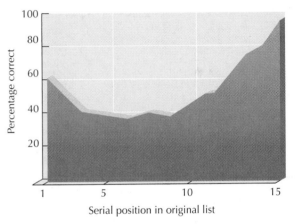

▸▸**FIGURE 7.7** The serial position effect. The graph shows the percentage of subjects correctly recalling each item in a 15-item list. Recall is best for the first and last items. (Data from Craik, 1970.)

Recall To supply or reproduce memorized information with a minimum of external cues.

Serial position effect The tendency to make the most errors in remembering the middle items of an ordered list.

Recognition memory An ability to correctly identify previously learned information.

Police lineups make use of the sensitivity of recognition memory. However, unless great care is taken, false identifications are still possible (Wells, 2001).

SW Productions/Index Stock Imagery

witness memories. To avoid tragic mistakes, it's far better to show witnesses one photo at a time (a sequential lineup). For each photo, the witness must decide whether the person is the culprit before another photo is shown (Wells, 2001; Wells & Olsen, 2003).

Relearning Information

In another classic experiment, a psychologist read a short passage in Greek to his son every day when the boy was between 15 months and 3 years of age. At age 8, the boy was asked if he remembered the Greek passage. He showed no evidence of recall. He was then shown selections from the passage he heard and selections from other Greek passages. Could he recognize the one he heard as an infant? "It's all Greek to me!" he said, indicating a lack of recognition (and drawing a frown from everyone in the room).

Had the psychologist stopped, he might have concluded that no memory of the Greek remained. However, the child was then asked to memorize the original quotation and others of equal difficulty. This time his earlier learning became evident. The boy memorized the passage he had heard in childhood 25 percent faster than the others (Burtt, 1941). As this experiment suggests, **relearning** is typically the most sensitive measure of memory.

When a person is tested by relearning, how do we know a memory still exists? As with the boy described, relearning is measured by a *savings score* (the amount of time saved when relearning information). Let's say it takes you 1 hour to memorize all the names in a telephone book. (It's a small town.) Two years later you relearn them in 45 minutes. Because you "saved" 15 minutes, your savings score would be 25 percent (15 divided by 60 times 100). Savings of this type are a good reason for studying a wide range of subjects. It may seem that learning algebra, history, or a foreign language is wasted if you don't use the knowledge immediately. But when you do need such information, you will be able to relearn it quickly.

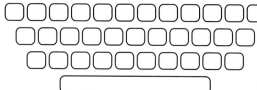

Can you label the letter keys on this blank keyboard? If you can, you probably used implicit memory to do it.

Implicit and Explicit Memories

Many memories remain outside of conscious awareness. For example, if you know how to type, it is apparent that you know where the letters are on the keyboard. But how many typists could correctly label blank keys in a drawing of a keyboard? Many people find that they cannot directly remember such information, even though they "know" it.

Who were the last three presidents of the United States? What did you have for breakfast today? What is the title of The Black Eyed Peas' latest album? Explicit memory is used in answering each of these questions. **Explicit memories** are past experiences that are consciously brought to mind. Recall, recognition, and the tests you take in school rely on explicit memories. In contrast, **implicit memories** lie outside of awareness (Roediger & Amir, 2005). That is, we are not aware that a memory exists. Nevertheless, implicit memories—such as unconsciously knowing where the letters are on a keyboard—greatly influence our behavior (Neath & Surprenant, 2003).

Priming

How is it possible to show that a memory exists if it lies outside of awareness? Psychologists first noticed implicit memory while studying memory loss caused by brain injuries. Let's say, for example, that a patient is shown a list of common words, such as *chair, tree, lamp, table,* and so on. A few minutes later, the patient is asked to recall words from the list. Sadly, he has no memory of the words.

Relearning Learning again something that was previously learned. Used to measure memory of prior learning.

Explicit memory A memory that a person is aware of having; a memory that is consciously retrieved.

Implicit memory A memory that a person does not know exists; a memory that is retrieved unconsciously.

Now, instead of asking the patient to explicitly recall the list, we could "prime" his memory by giving him the first two letters of each word. "We'd like you to say a word that begins with these letters," we tell him. "Just say whatever comes to mind." Of course, many words could be made from each pair of letters. For example, the first item (from chair) would be the letters CH. The patient could say "child," "chalk," "chain," "check," or many other words. Instead, he says "chair," a word from the original list. The patient is not aware that he is remembering the list, but as he gives a word for each letter pair, almost all are from the list. Apparently, the letters **primed** (activated) hidden memories, which then influenced his answers.

Similar effects have been found for people with normal memories. As the preceding example implies, implicit memories are often revealed by giving a person limited cues, such as the first letter of words or partial drawings of objects. Typically, the person believes that he or she is just saying whatever comes to mind. Nevertheless, information previously seen or heard affects his or her answers (Rueckl & Galantucci, 2005). Some nutritionists like to say, "You are what you eat." In the realm of memory it appears that we are what we experience—to a far greater degree than once realized.

EXCEPTIONAL MEMORY—WIZARDS OF RECALL

>SURVEY QUESTION< *What are "photographic" memories?*

Can you remember how many doors there are in your house or apartment? To answer a question like this, many people form **mental images** (mental pictures) of each room and count the doorways they visualize. As this example implies, many memories are stored as mental images (Roeckelein, 2004).

Stephen Kosslyn, Thomas Ball, and Brian Reiser (1978) found an interesting way to show that memories do exist as images. Participants first memorized a sort of treasure map similar to the one shown in ►Figure 7.8*a*. They were then asked to picture a black dot moving from one object, such as one of the trees, to another, such as the hut at the top of the island. Did people really form an image to do this task? It seems they did. As shown in ►Figure 7.8*b*, the time it took to "move" the dot was directly related to actual distances on the map.

Is the "treasure map" task an example of photographic memory? In some ways, internal memory images do have "photographic" qualities. However, the term photographic memory is more often used to describe a type of memory called eidetic imagery.

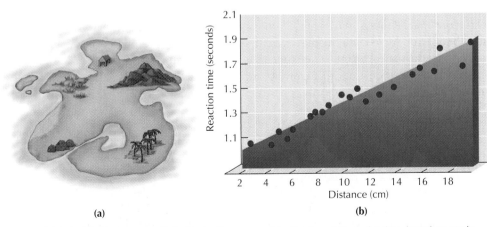

(a) **(b)**

►**FIGURE 7.8** *(a)* "Treasure map" similar to the one used by Kosslyn, Ball, and Reiser (1978) to study images in memory. *(b)* This graph shows how long it took subjects to move a visualized spot various distances on their mental images of the map. (See text for explanation.)

Priming Facilitating the retrieval of an implicit memory by using cues to activate hidden memories.

Mental images Mental pictures or visual depictions used in memory and thinking.

Eidetic Imagery

Eidetic (eye-DET-ik) **imagery** occurs when a person has visual images clear enough to be "scanned" or retained for at least 30 seconds. Internal memory images can be "viewed" mentally with the eyes closed. In contrast, eidetic images are "projected" out in front of a person. That is, they are best "seen" on a plain surface, such as a blank piece of paper. In this respect, eidetic images are somewhat like the after-images you might have after looking at a flashbulb or a brightly lit neon sign (Haber & Haber, 2000).

Eidetic memory is most common in childhood, with about 8 children in 100 having eidetic images. In one series of tests, children were shown a picture from *Alice's Adventures in Wonderland* (▸▸Fig. 7.9). To test your eidetic imagery, look at the picture and read the instructions there.

Now, let's see how much you remember. Can you say (without looking again) which of Alice's apron strings is longer? Are the cat's front paws crossed? How many stripes are on the cat's tail? After the picture was removed from view, one 10-year-old boy was asked what he saw. He replied, "I see the tree, gray tree with three limbs. I see the cat with stripes around its tail." Asked to count the stripes, the boy replied, "There are about 16" (a correct count!). The boy then went on to describe the remainder of the picture in striking detail (Haber, 1969).

Don't be disappointed if you didn't do too well when you tried your eidetic skills. Most eidetic imagery disappears during adolescence and becomes rare by adulthood (Haber & Haber, 2000).

Exceptional Memory

Let's return now to the concept of mental images. In rare instances, such images may be so vivid that it is reasonable to say that a person has "photographic memory." A notable example was reported by Aleksandr Luria (1968) in his book, *The Mind of a Mnemonist.* Luria studied a man he called Mr. S, who had practically unlimited memory for visual images. Mr. S could remember almost everything that ever happened to him with incredible accuracy. Luria tried to test Mr. S's memory by using longer and longer lists of words or numbers. However, he soon discovered that no matter how long the list, Mr. S was able to recall it without error. Mr. S could memorize, with equal ease, strings of digits, meaningless consonants, mathematical formulas, and poems in foreign languages. His memory was so powerful that he had to devise ways to *forget*—such as writing information on a piece of paper and then burning it.

Eidetic imagery The ability to retain a "projected" mental image long enough to use it as a source of information.

Mr. S's abilities might seem fantastic to any college student. However, Mr. S remembered so much that he couldn't separate important facts from trivia or facts from fantasy (Neath & Surprenant, 2003). For instance, if you asked him to read this chapter he might remember every word. Yet, he might also recall all the images each word made him think of and all the sights, sounds, and feelings that occurred as he was reading. Therefore, finding the answer for a specific question, writing a logical essay, or even understanding a single sentence was very difficult for him. If you didn't have selective memory you would recall all the ingredients on your cereal box, every street number you've seen, and countless other scraps of information.

Few people in history have possessed memory abilities like Mr. S's. Nonetheless, you probably know at least one person who has an especially good memory. Is superior memory a biological gift? Or do excellent memorizers merely make better-than-average use of normal memory capacities? Let's investigate further.

Strategies for Remembering

At first, a student volunteer named Steve could remember 7 digits—a typical score for a college student. Could he improve with practice? For 20 months Steve practiced memorizing ever-longer lists of digits. Ultimately, he was able to memorize around 80 digits, like this sample:

9284204805084226895399019025291280799970
6606574717310601080585269726026357332135

How did Steve do it? Basically, he worked by chunking digits into meaningful groups containing 3 or 4 digits each. Steve's avid interest in long-distance running helped greatly. For instance, to him the first three digits above represented 9 minutes and 28 seconds, a good time for a 2-mile run. When running times wouldn't work, Steve used other associations, such as ages or dates, to chunk digits (Ericsson & Chase, 1982). It seems apparent that Steve's success was based on learned strategies. By using similar memory systems, other people have trained themselves to equal Steve's feat (Bellezza, Six, & Phillips, 1992).

Psychologist Anders Ericsson believes that exceptional memory is merely a learned extension of normal memory. As evidence, he notes that Steve's short-term memory did not improve during months of practice. For example, Steve could still memorize only 7 consonants. Steve's phenomenal memory for numbers grew as he figured out new ways to chunk digits at encoding and store them in LTM. Steve began with a normal memory for digits. He extended his memory by diligent practice. Clearly, exceptional memory can be learned (Ericsson et al., 2004). However, we still have to wonder, do some people have naturally superior memories?

Memory Champions

Each year the World Memory Championship is held in England. Contestants must rapidly memorize daunting amounts of information, such as long lists of unrelated words and numbers. Psychologists John Wilding and Elizabeth Valentine saw this event as an opportunity to study exceptional memory and persuaded the contestants to take some additional memory tests. These ranged from ordinary (recall a story), to challenging (recall the telephone numbers of 6 different people), to diabolical (recall 48 numerals arranged in rows and columns; recognize 14 previously seen pictures of snowflakes among 70 new photos) (Maguire et al., 2003; Wilding & Valentine, 1994a).

Exceptional memorizers were found to:

- Use memory strategies and techniques
- Have specialized interests and knowledge that make certain types of information easier to encode and recall
- Have naturally superior memory abilities, often including vivid mental images
- Do not have superior intellectual abilities or different brains

87379268
20117495
01758783
19476069
36168154
45240297

This number matrix is similar to the ones contestants in the World Memory Championship had to memorize. To be scored as correct, digits had to be recalled in their proper positions (Wilding & Valentine, 1994a).

The first two points confirm what we learned from Steve's acquired memory ability. Many of the contestants, for example, actively used memory strategies called *mnemonics* (nee-MON-iks). Specialized interests and knowledge also helped for some tasks. For example, one contestant, who is a mathematician, was exceedingly good at memorizing numbers (Wilding & Valentine, 1994a).

Several of the memory contestants were able to excel on tasks that prevented the use of learned strategies and techniques. This observation implies that superior memory ability can be a "gift" as well as a learned skill. Wilding and Valentine conclude that exceptional memory may be based on either natural ability or learned strategies. Usually it requires both. In fact, most super memorizers use strategies to augment whatever natural talents they have. Some of their strategies are described in this chapter's "Psychology in Action" section. Please do remember to read it.

 Study Break   **Measuring Memory and Exceptional Memory**

Reflect

Have you experienced the TOT state recently? Were you able to retrieve the word you were seeking? If not, what could you remember about it?

Do you prefer tests based primarily on recall or recognition? Have you observed a savings effect while relearning information you studied in the past (such as in high school)?

Can you think of things you do that are based on implicit memories? For instance, how do you know which way to turn various handles in your house, apartment, or dorm? Do you have to explicitly think, "Turn it to the right," before you act?

What kinds of information are you good at remembering? Why do you think your memory is better for those topics?

Learning Check

Unless you have a memory like Mr. S's, it might be a good idea to see if you can answer these questions before reading on.

1. Four techniques for measuring or demonstrating memory are

   _____   _____

   _____   _____

2. Essay tests require _____ of facts or ideas.
3. As a measure of memory, a savings score is associated with

   a. recognition   b. eidetic images
   c. relearning   d. reconstruction

4. The two most sensitive tests of memory are

   a. recall and redintegration   b. recall and relearning
   c. recognition and relearning   d. recognition and digit-span

5. Priming is used to reveal which type of memories?

   a. explicit   b. sensory
   c. skill   d. implicit

6. Children with eidetic imagery typically have no better than average long-term memory. T or F?
7. For most people, having an especially good memory is based on

   a. maintenance rehearsal   b. constructive processing
   c. phonetic imagery   d. learned strategies

Critical Thinking

8. Mr. S had great difficulty remembering faces. Can you guess why?

Answers

1. recall, recognition, relearning, priming   2. recall   3. c   4. c   5. d   6. T   7. d   8. Mr. S's memory was so specific that faces seemed different and unfamiliar if he saw them from a new angle or if a face had a different expression on it than when Mr. S last saw it.

FORGETTING—WHY WE, UH, LET'S SEE; WHY WE, UH . . . FORGET!

>SURVEY QUESTION< *What causes forgetting?*

Forgetting is one of the more vexing aspects of memory. For example, why is it hard to remember facts you learned for a test just a week or two later? Again, the more you know about how we "lose" memories, the better you will be able to hang on to them.

Most forgetting tends to occur immediately after memorization. Herman Ebbinghaus (1885) famously tested his own memory at various intervals after learning. Ebbinghaus wanted to be sure he would not be swayed by prior learning, so he memorized *nonsense syllables.* These are meaningless three-letter words such as CEF, WOL, and GEX. The importance of using meaningless words is shown by the fact that VEL, FAB, and DUZ are no longer used on memory tests. People who recognize these words as detergent names find them very easy to remember. This is another reminder that relating new information to what you already know can improve memory.

By waiting various lengths of time before testing himself, Ebbinghaus plotted a **curve of forgetting.** This graph shows the amount of information remembered after varying lengths of time (▸▸ Fig. 7.10). Notice that forgetting is rapid at first and is then followed by a slow decline. The same applies to meaningful information, but the forgetting curve is stretched over a longer time. As you might expect, recent events are recalled more accurately than those from the remote past (O'Connor et al., 2000). Thus, you are more likely to remember that *Crash* won the "Best Picture" Academy Award for 2005 than you are to remember that *A Beautiful Mind* won it for 2000.

As a student, you should note that a short delay between studying and taking a test minimizes forgetting. However, this is no reason for cramming. Most students make the error of *only* cramming. If you cram, you don't have to remember for very long, but you may not learn enough in the first place. If you use short, daily study sessions and review intensely before a test, you will get the benefit of good preparation and a minimum time lapse.

The Ebbinghaus curve shows less than 30 percent remembered after only 2 days have passed. Is forgetting really that rapid? No, not always. Meaningful information is not lost nearly as quickly as nonsense syllables. After 3 years, students who took a university psychology had forgotten about 30 percent of the facts they learned. After that, little more forgetting occurred (Conway, Cohen, & Stanhope, 1992). Actually, as learning grows stronger, some knowledge may become nearly permanent (Berntsen & Thomsen, 2005).

"I'll never forget old, old . . . oh, what's his name?" Forgetting is both frustrating and embarrassing. Why *do* we forget? The Ebbinghaus curve gives a general picture of forgetting, but it doesn't explain it. For explanations we must search further. Before we do, look at "Card Magic!," where you will find an interesting demonstration.

When Encoding Fails

Whose head is on a U.S. penny? Which way is it facing? What is written at the top of a penny? Can you accurately draw and label a penny? In an interesting experiment, Ray Nickerson and Marilyn Adams (1979) asked a large group of students to draw a penny. Few could. Well then, could the students at least recognize a drawing of a real penny among fakes? (See ▸▸ Fig. 7.11.) Again, few could.

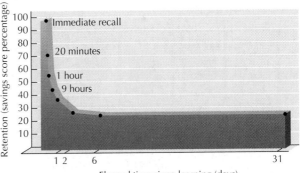

▸▸**FIGURE 7.10** The curve of forgetting. This graph shows the amount remembered (measured by relearning) after varying lengths of time. Notice how rapidly forgetting occurs. The material learned was nonsense syllables. Forgetting curves for meaningful information also show early losses followed by a long gradual decline, but overall, forgetting occurs much more slowly. (After Ebbinghaus, 1885.)

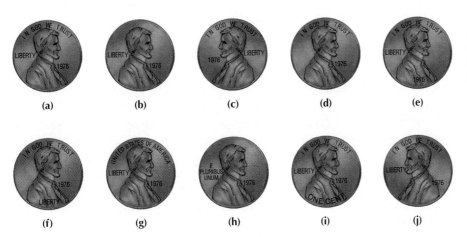

▸▸**FIGURE 7.11** Some of the distractor items used in a study of recognition memory and encoding failure. Penny A is correct but was seldom recognized. Pennies G and J were popular wrong answers. (Adapted from Nickerson & Adams, 1979.)

Curve of forgetting A graph that shows the amount of memorized information remembered after varying lengths of time.

Card Magic!

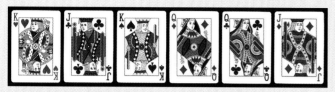

▶▶FIGURE 7.12

Pick a card from the six shown above. Look at it closely and be sure you can remember which card is yours. Now, snap your fingers and look at the cards in ▶▶Figure 7.13, below. Poof! Only five cards remain, and the card you chose has disappeared. Obviously, you could have selected any one of the six cards in ▶▶Figure 7.12. How did we know which one to remove?

This trick is based entirely on an illusion of memory. Recall that you were asked to concentrate on one card among the six cards in

▶▶Figure 7.12. That prevented you from paying attention to the other cards, so they weren't stored in your memory (Mangels, Picton, & Craik, 2001). The five cards you see below are all new (none is shown above, in ▶▶Figure 7.12). Because you couldn't find your card in the "remaining five," it looked like your card disappeared. What looked like "card magic" is actually memory magic. Now return to "When Encoding Fails" and continue reading to learn more about forgetting.

▶▶FIGURE 7.13

The most obvious reason for forgetting is also the most commonly overlooked. Obviously, few of us ever encode the details of a penny. In many cases we "forget" because of **encoding failure.** That is, a memory was never formed in the first place (the card trick you just saw is another example). If you are bothered by frequent forgetting or absentmindedness, it is wise to ask yourself, "Have I been storing the information in the first place?" (Schacter, 2001).

When 140 college professors were asked what they do to improve their memory, the favorite technique was to *write things down* (Park, Smith, & Cavanaugh, 1990). Making notes prevents information from slipping out of short-term memory before you can review it and store it more permanently.

College Students: They're All Alike!

Encoding failures also affect our memories of people. Imagine yourself in this situation: As you are walking on campus, a young man, who looks like a college student, approaches you and asks for directions. While you are talking, two workers carrying a door pass between you and the young man. While your view is blocked by the door, another man takes the place of the first. Now you are facing a different person than the one who was there just seconds earlier. If this happened to you, do you think you would notice the change? Remarkably, only half of the people tested in this way noticed the switch (Simons & Levin, 1998)!

How could anyone fail to notice that one stranger had been replaced by another? The people who didn't remember the first man were all older adults. College students weren't fooled by the switch. Apparently, older adults encoded the first man in very general terms as a "college student." As a result, that's all they remembered about him. Because his replacement also looked like a college student, they thought he was the same person (Simons & Levin, 1998).

Actually, we all tend to categorize strangers in general terms: Is the person young or old, male or female, a member of my ethnic group or another? This tendency is one reason why eyewitnesses are better at identifying members of their own ethnic group than persons from other groups (Burgess & Weaver, 2003; Kassin et al., 2001). It may seem harsh to say so, but during brief social contacts, people really do act as if members of other ethnic groups "all look alike." Of course, this bias disappears when people get acquainted and learn more about one another as individuals.

Encoding failure Failure to store sufficient information to form a useful memory.

Memory Decay

One view of forgetting holds that **memory traces** (changes in nerve cells or brain activity) **decay** (fade or weaken) over time. Decay appears to be a factor in the loss of sensory memories. Such fading also applies to short-term memory. Information stored in STM seems to initiate a brief flurry of activity in the brain that quickly dies out. Short-term memory therefore operates like a "leaky bucket": New information constantly pours in, but it rapidly fades away and is replaced by still newer information. Let's say that you are trying to remember a short list of letters, numbers, or words after seeing or hearing them once. If it takes you more than 4 to 6 seconds to repeat the list, you will forget some of the items (Dosher & Ma, 1998).

Disuse

Is it possible that the decay of memory traces also explains long-term forgetting? That is, could long-term memory traces fade from **disuse** (infrequent retrieval) and eventually become too weak to retrieve? There is evidence that memories not retrieved and "used" or rehearsed become weaker over time (Schacter, 2001). However, disuse alone cannot fully explain forgetting.

Disuse doesn't seem to account for our ability to recover seemingly forgotten memories through redintegration, relearning, and priming. It also fails to explain why some unused memories fade, whereas others are carried for life. A third contradiction will be recognized by anyone who has spent time with the elderly. People growing senile may become so forgetful that they can't remember what happened a week ago. Yet at the same time your Uncle Oscar's recent memories are fading, he may have vivid memories of trivial and long-forgotten events from the past. "Why, I remember it as clearly as if it were yesterday," he will say, forgetting that the story he is about to tell is one he told earlier the same day. In short, disuse offers no more than a partial explanation of long-term forgetting.

If decay and disuse don't fully explain forgetting, what does? Let's briefly consider some additional possibilities.

Cue-Dependent Forgetting

Paul Conklin/PhotoEdit

Often, memories appear to be *available*, but not *accessible*. An example is having an answer on the "tip of your tongue." You know the answer is there (it is available), but it remains just "out of reach" (it is inaccessible). This suggests that many memories are "forgotten" because **memory cues** (stimuli associated with a memory) are missing when the time comes to retrieve information. For example, if you were asked, "What were you doing on Monday afternoon of the third week in May 2 years ago?" your reply might be, "Come on. How should I know?" However, if you were reminded, "That was the day the courthouse burned," or "That was the day Stacy had her automobile accident," you might remember immediately.

The presence of appropriate cues almost always enhances memory (Nairne, 2002). In theory, for instance, memory will be best if you study in the same room where you will be tested. Because this is often impossible, when you study, try to visualize the room where you will be tested. Doing so can enhance memory later (Jerabek & Standing, 1992). Similarly, people remember better if the same odor (such as lemon or lavender) is present when they

External cues like those found in a photograph, in a scrapbook, or during a walk through an old neighborhood often aid recall of seemingly lost memories. For many veterans, finding a familiar name engraved in the Vietnam Veterans Memorial unleashes a flood of memories.

Memory traces Physical changes in nerve cells or brain activity that take place when memories are stored.

Memory decay The fading or weakening of memories assumed to occur when memory traces become weaker.

Disuse Theory that memory traces weaken when memories are not periodically used or retrieved.

Memory cue Any stimulus associated with a particular memory. Memory cues usually enhance retrieval.

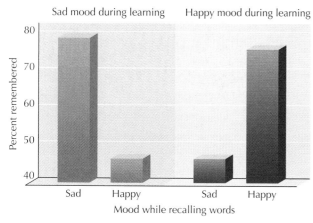

Sad mood during learning   Happy mood during learning

Mood while recalling words

▸▸**FIGURE 7.14** The effect of mood on memory. Subjects best remembered a list of words when their mood during testing was the same as their mood was when they learned the list. (Adapted from Bower, 1981.)

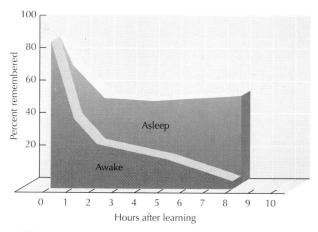

▸▸**FIGURE 7.15** The amount of forgetting after a period of sleep or of being awake. Notice that sleep causes less memory loss than activity that occurs while one is awake. (After Jenkins & Dallenbach, 1924.)

study and are tested (Parker, Ngu, & Cassaday, 2001). If you wear a particular perfume or cologne while you prepare for a test, it might be wise to wear it when you take the test.

State-Dependent Learning

Have you heard the story about the drunk who misplaced his wallet and had to get drunk again to find it? Although this tale is often told as a joke, it is not too farfetched. The bodily state that exists during learning can be a strong cue for later memory, an effect known as **state-dependent learning** (Neath & Surprenant, 2003). Being very thirsty, for instance, might prompt you to remember events that took place on another occasion when you were thirsty. Because of such effects, information learned under the influence of a drug is best remembered when the drugged state occurs again (Slot & Colpaert, 1999).

A similar effect applies to emotional states (Wessel & Wright, 2004). For instance, Gordon Bower (1981) found that people who learned a list of words while in a happy mood recalled them better when they were again happy. People who learned while they felt sad remembered best when they were sad (▸▸Fig. 7.14). Similarly, if you are in a happy mood you are more likely to remember recent happy events. If you are in a bad mood you will tend to have unpleasant memories. Such links between emotional cues and memory could explain why couples who quarrel often end up remembering—and rehashing—old arguments.

Interference

Further insight into forgetting comes from a classic experiment in which college students learned lists of nonsense syllables. After studying, students in one group slept for 8 hours and were then tested for memory of the lists. A second group stayed awake for 8 hours and went about business as usual. When members of the second group were tested, they remembered *less* than the group that slept (▸▸Fig. 7.15.) This difference is based on the fact that new learning can interfere with previous learning. **Interference** refers to the tendency for new memories to impair retrieval of older memories (and the reverse). It seems to apply to both short-term and long-term memory (Lustig, May, & Hasher, 2001; Nairne, 2002).

There is no doubt that interference is a major cause of forgetting (Neath & Surprenant, 2003). College students who memorized 20 lists of words (one list each day) were able to recall only 15 percent of the last list. Students who learned only one list remembered 80 percent (Underwood, 1957) (▸▸Fig. 7.16).

State-dependent learning Memory influenced by one's bodily state at the time of learning and at the time of retrieval. Improved memory occurs when the bodily states match.

Interference The tendency for new memories to impair retrieval of older memories, and the reverse.

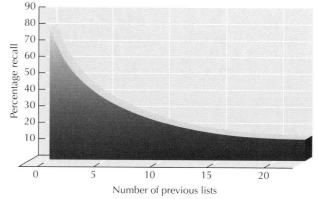

▸▸**FIGURE 7.16** Effects of interference on memory. A graph of the approximate relationship between percentage recalled and number of different word lists memorized. (Adapted from Underwood, 1957.)

Order Effects

The sleeping college students remembered more because retroactive (RET-ro-AK-tiv) interference was held to a minimum. **Retroactive interference** refers to the tendency for new learning to inhibit retrieval of old learning. Avoiding new learning prevents retroactive interference. This doesn't exactly mean you should hide in a closet after you study for an exam. However, you should avoid studying other subjects until the exam. Sleeping after studying can help you retain memories, and reading, writing, or even watching TV may cause interference.

Retroactive interference is easily demonstrated in the laboratory by this arrangement:

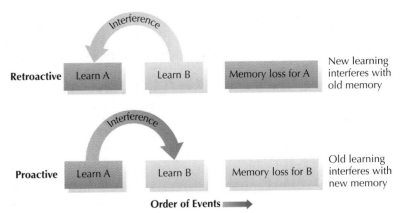

FIGURE 7.17 Retroactive and proactive interference. The order of learning and testing shows whether interference is retroactive (backward) or proactive (forward).

Experimental group:	Learn A	Learn B	Test A
Control group:	Learn A	Rest	Test A

Imagine yourself as a member of the experimental group. In task A, you learn a list of telephone numbers. In task B, you learn a list of Social Security numbers. How do you score on a test of task A (the telephone numbers)? If you do not remember as much as the control group that learns *only* task A, then retroactive interference has occurred. The second thing learned has interfered with memory of the first thing learned; the interference went "backward," or was "retroactive" (▶▶Fig. 7.17).

Proactive (pro-AK-tiv) interference is a second basic source of forgetting. **Proactive interference** occurs when prior learning inhibits recall of later learning. A test for proactive interference would take this form:

Experimental group:	Learn A	Learn B	Test B
Control group:	Rest	Learn B	Test B

Let's assume that the experimental group remembers less than the control group on a test of task B. In that case, learning task A interfered with memory for task B.

Then proactive interference goes "forward"? Yes. For instance, if you cram for a psychology exam and then later the same night cram for a history exam, your memory for the second subject studied (history) will be less accurate than if you had studied only history. (Because of retroactive interference, your memory for psychology would probably also suffer.) The greater the similarity in the two subjects studied, the more interference takes place. The moral, of course, is don't procrastinate in preparing for exams. The more you can avoid competing information, the more likely you are to recall what you want to remember (Anderson & Bell, 2001).

REPRESSION AND SUPPRESSION OF MEMORIES

>SURVEY QUESTION< *How accurate are everyday memories?*

Take a moment and scan over the events of the last few years of your life. What kinds of things most easily come to mind? Many people remember happy, positive events better than disappointments and irritations (Linton, 1979; Ruder & Bless, 2003). A clinical psychologist would call this tendency **repression,** or motivated forgetting. Through repression, painful, threatening, or embarrassing memories are held out of consciousness (Anderson et al., 2004). An example is provided by soldiers who have repressed some of the horrors they saw during combat (Karon & Widener, 1997).

Retroactive interference The tendency for new memories to interfere with the retrieval of old memories.

Proactive interference The tendency for old memories to interfere with the retrieval of newer memories.

Repression Unconsciously pushing unwanted memories out of awareness.

The Recovered Memory/False Memory Debate

Many sexually abused children develop problems that persist into adulthood. In some instances, they repress all memory of the abuse. According to some psychologists, uncovering these hidden memories can be an important step toward regaining emotional health (Palm & Gibson, 1998).

Although the preceding may be true, the search for repressed memories of sexual abuse has itself been a problem. Cases have surfaced in which families were torn apart by accusations of sexual abuse that later turned out to be completely false (Porter et al., 2003). For example, Gary Ramona lost his marriage and his $400,000-a-year job when his daughter Holly alleged that he molested her throughout her childhood. To prove to Holly that her memories were true, the therapists gave her the drug Amytal, and told her that it was a "truth drug." (Amytal is a hypnotic drug that induces a twilight state of consciousness. People do not automatically tell the truth while under its influence.) Ramona sued Holly's therapists, claiming that they had been irresponsible. After reviewing the evidence, a jury awarded Gary Ramona $500,000 in damages. In a way, Gary Ramona was lucky. Most people who are falsely accused have no way to prove their innocence (Loftus & Ketcham, 1994).

Why would anyone have false memories about such disturbing events? Several popular books and a few misguided therapists have actively encouraged people to find repressed memories of abuse. Hypnosis, guided visualization, suggestion, age regression, and similar techniques can elicit fantasies that are mistaken for real memories. As we saw earlier in this chapter, it is easy to create false memories, especially by using hypnosis (Loftus, 2003a, b; Loftus & Bernstein, 2005).

In an effort to illustrate how easy it is to implant false memories and to publicize *false memory syndrome,* memory expert Elizabeth Loftus once deliberately implanted a false memory in actor Alan Alda. As the host of the television series *Scientific American Frontiers,* he was scheduled to interview Loftus. Before the interview, Alda was asked to fill out a questionnaire about his tastes in food. When he arrived, Loftus told Alda that his answers revealed that he must once have gotten sick after eating hard-boiled eggs (which was false). Later that day, at a picnic, Alda would not eat hard-boiled eggs (Loftus, 2003a).

AP/Wide World Photo

Gary Ramona's life was shattered by "recovered" memories that turned out to be false.

Certainly, some memories of abuse that return to awareness are genuine and must be dealt with. However, there is little doubt that some "recovered" memories are pure fantasy. No matter how real a recovered memory may seem, it could be false, unless it can be verified by others, or by court or medical records (Olio, 2004).

A few years ago, an "epidemic" of recovered memories took place. Today, psychologists have developed new guidelines for therapists to minimize the risk of influencing clients' memories. Nevertheless, false claims about childhood abuse still occasionally make the news. The saddest thing about such claims is that they deaden public sensitivity to actual abuse. Childhood sexual abuse is widespread. Awareness of its existence must not be repressed.

The forgetting of past failures, upsetting childhood events, the names of people you dislike, or appointments you don't want to keep may reveal repression. People prone to repression tend to be extremely sensitive to emotional events. As a result, they use repression to protect themselves from threatening thoughts (McNally, Clancy, & Barrett, 2004). See "The Recovered Memory/False Memory Debate" for further cautions.

If I try to forget a test I failed, am I repressing it? No. Repression can be distinguished from **suppression,** an active, conscious attempt to put something out of mind. By not thinking about the test, you have merely suppressed a memory. If you choose to, you can remember the test. Clinicians consider true repression an *unconscious* event. When a memory is repressed we may be unaware that forgetting has even occurred.

Although some psychologists have questioned whether repression exists (Court & Court, 2001), evidence suggests that we can choose to actively suppress remembering upsetting information (Anderson, 2001). If you have experienced a painful emotional event, you will proba-

Suppression A conscious effort to put something out of mind or to keep it from awareness.

bly avoid all thoughts associated with it. This tends to keep cues out of mind that could trigger a painful memory. In time, your active suppression of the memory may become true repression (Anderson & Green, 2001).

Flashbulb Memories

Why are some traumatic events vividly remembered while others are repressed? Psychologists use the term **flashbulb memories** to describe images that seem to be frozen in memory at times of personal tragedy, accident, or other emotionally significant events (Niedzwienska, 2004).

Depending on your age, you may have a "flashbulb" memory for the assassinations of John F. Kennedy and Martin Luther King, the *Challenger* or *Columbia* space shuttle disaster, or the terrorist attack on the World Trade Center in New York. Flashbulb memories are most often formed when an event

AP/Wide World Photo

is surprising, important, or emotional (Paradis et al., 2004). They are frequently associated with public tragedies, but memories of positive events may also have "flashbulb" clarity.

Flashbulb memories seem to be very detailed. Often, they focus primarily on how you reacted to the event. ■ Table 7.1 lists some memories that had "flashbulb" clarity for at least 50 percent of a group of college students. How vivid are the memories they trigger for you? (Note again that both positive and negative events are listed.)

The term *flashbulb memories* was first used to describe recollections that seemed to be unusually vivid and permanent. It has become clear, however, that flashbulb memories are not always accurate (Greenberg, 2004). More than anything else, what sets flashbulb memories apart is that we tend to place great *confidence* in them—even when they are wrong (Niedzwienska, 2004). Perhaps that's because we review emotionally charged events over and over and tell others about them. Also, public events such as wars, earthquakes, and assassinations reappear many times in the news, which highlights them in memory. Over time, flashbulb memories tend to crystallize into consistent, if not entirely accurate, landmarks in our lives (Schmolck, Buffalo, & Squire, 2000).

It is highly likely that you have a flashbulb memory about where you were when you first learned about the terrorist attack on the World Trade Center in New York. If someone alerted you about the news, you will remember that person's call and you will have clear memories about how you reacted to seeing the collapse of the towers.

■ Table 7.1 **Bright Flashes of Memory**	
Memory Cue	Percentage of Students with Flashbulb Memories
A car accident you were in or witnessed	85
When you first met your college roommate	82
The night of your high school graduation	81
The night of your senior prom (if you went or not)	78
An early romantic experience	77
A time you had to speak in front of an audience	72
When you first got your college admissions letter	65
Your first date—the moment you met him/her	57

Source: From Rubin, 1985.

Flashbulb memories Memories created at times of high emotion that seem especially vivid.

MEMORY FORMATION—SOME "SHOCKING" FINDINGS

>SURVEY QUESTION< *What happens in the brain when memories are formed?*

One possibility overlooked in our discussion of forgetting is that memories may be lost as they are being formed. For example, a head injury may cause a "gap" in memories preceding the accident. *Retrograde amnesia,* as this is called, involves forgetting events that occurred before an injury or trauma. In contrast, *anterograde amnesia* involves forgetting events that follow an injury or trauma. (An example of this type of amnesia is discussed in a moment.)

Consolidating Memories

Retrograde amnesia can be understood if we assume that it takes a certain amount of time to move information from short-term memory to long-term memory. The forming of a long-term memory is called **consolidation** (Squire, 2004). You can think of consolidation as being somewhat like writing your name in wet concrete. Once the concrete is set, the information (your name) is fairly lasting, but while it is setting, it can be wiped out (amnesia) or scribbled over (interference).

Consider a classic experiment on consolidation, in which a rat is placed on a small platform. The rat steps down to the floor and receives a painful electric shock. After one shock, the rat can be returned to the platform repeatedly, but it will not step down. Obviously, the rat remembers the shock. Would it remember if consolidation were disturbed?

Interestingly, one way to prevent consolidation is to give a different kind of shock called electroconvulsive shock (ECS). ECS is a mild electric shock to the brain. It does not harm the animal, but it does destroy any memory that is being formed. If each painful shock (the one the animal remembers) is followed by ECS (which wipes out memories during consolidation), the rat will step down over and over. Each time, ECS will erase the memory of the painful shock. (ECS is employed as a psychiatric treatment for severe depression in humans.)

What would happen if ECS were given several hours after the learning? Recent memories are more easily disrupted than older memories. If enough time is allowed to pass between learning and ECS, the memory will be unaffected because consolidation is already complete. That's why people with mild head injuries lose only memories from just before the accident, and older memories remain intact (Lieberman, 2004). Likewise, you would forget more if you studied, stayed awake 8 hours, and then slept 8 hours than you would if you studied, slept 8 hours, and were awake for 8 hours. Either way, 16 hours would pass. However, less forgetting would occur in the second instance, because more consolidation would occur before interference begins (Wixted, 2005).

Where does consolidation take place in the brain? Actually, many parts of the brain are responsible for memory, but the **hippocampus** is particularly important. The hippocampus acts as a sort of "switching station" between short-term and long-term memory (Squire, 2004). The hippocampus does this, in part, by growing new neurons and by making new connections within the brain (Eichenbaum & Fortin, 2005).

Humans who have hippocampal damage usually show a striking inability to store new memories (Zola & Squire, 2001). A patient described by Brenda Milner provides a vivid example. Two years after an operation damaged his hippocampus, the 29-year-old patient continued to give his age as 27. He also reported that it seemed as if the operation had just taken place (Milner, 1965). His memory of events before the operation remained clear, but he found forming new long-term memories almost impossible. When his parents moved to a new house a few blocks away on the same street, he could not remember the new address. Month after month, he read the same magazines over and over without finding them famil-

Consolidation Process by which relatively permanent memories are formed in the brain.

Hippocampus A brain structure associated with emotion and the transfer of information from short-term memory to long-term memory.

iar. If you were to meet this man, he would seem fairly normal because he still has short-term memory. But if you were to leave the room and return 15 minutes later, he would act as if he had never seen you before. Years ago his favorite uncle died, but he suffers the same grief anew each time he is told of the death. Lacking the ability to form new lasting memories, he lives eternally in the present (Corkin, 2002).

The Brain and Long-Term Memory

Somewhere within the 3-pound mass of the human brain lies all we know: ZIP codes, faces of loved ones, history, favorite melodies, the taste of an apple, and much, much more. Where is this information? According to neuroscientist Richard Thompson (2005), many parts of the brain can become active when we learn and form long-term memories but usually one area is more critical for each particular form of memory.

For example, some areas of the cerebral cortex *are* more important to long-term memory than others. Patterns of blood flow in the cerebral cortex (the wrinkled outer layer of the brain) can be used to map brain activity. ▸▸Figure 7.18 shows the results of measuring blood flow while people were thinking about a semantic memory *(a)* or an episodic memory *(b)*. In the map, green indicates areas that are more active during semantic thinking. Reds show areas of greater activity during episodic thinking. The brain in view *c* shows the difference in activity between views *a* and *b*. The resulting pattern indicates that the front of the cortex is related to episodic memory. Back areas are more associated with semantic memory (Tulving, 2002).

To summarize (and simplify greatly), the hippocampus handles memory consolidation (Zola & Squire, 2001). Once declarative long-term memories are formed, they appear to be stored in the cortex of the brain (Squire, 2004). In contrast, as stated previously, long-term procedural (skill) memories are likely stored in the cerebellum (Hermann et al., 2004).

But how are memories recorded in the brain? Scientists are beginning to identify the exact ways in which nerve cells record information. For example, Eric Kandel and his colleagues have studied learning in the marine snail *aplysia* (ah-PLEEZ-yah). Kandel found that learning in *aplysia* occurs when certain nerve cells in a circuit alter the amount of transmitter chemicals they release (Bailey & Kandel, 2004). Learning also alters the activity, structure, and chemistry of brain cells. Such changes determine which connections get stronger and which become weaker. This "reprograms" the brain and records information (Abel & Lattal, 2001; Squire, 2004).

Scientists continue to study various chemicals, especially neurotransmitters that affect memory. If their research succeeds, it may be possible to help the millions of persons who suffer from memory impairment (Elli & Nathan, 2001). Will researchers ever produce a "memory pill" to enhance normal memory? Neuroscientists are confident that memory can be and will be artificially enhanced. However, the possibility of something like a "physics pill" or a "math pill" seems remote.

Jeffrey L. Rotman/Corbis

An *aplysia*. The relatively simple nervous system of this sea animal allows scientists to study memory as it occurs in single nerve cells.

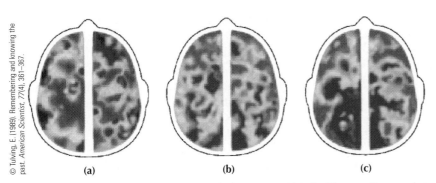

© Tulving, E. (1989). Remembering and knowing the past. *American Scientist, 77*(4), 361–367.

(a)   (b)   (c)

▸▸**FIGURE 7.18** Patterns of blood flow in the cerebral cortex associated with semantic memories and episodic memories.

Study Break Forgetting

Reflect

Which of the following concepts best explains why you have missed some answers on psychology tests: encoding failure, decay, disuse, memory cues, interference?

Do you know someone whose name you have a hard time remembering? Do you like or dislike that person? Do you think your difficulty is an instance of repression? Suppression? Interference? Encoding failure?

Have you had a flashbulb memory? How vivid is the memory today? How accurate do you think it is?

Here's a mnemonic tip: Elephants are supposed to have good memories, but a *hippo campus* is the place to go if you want to learn to consolidate memories.

Learning Check

1. According to the Ebbinghaus curve of forgetting, we forget slowly at first and then a rapid decline occurs. T or F?
2. Which explanation seems to account for the loss of short-term memories?

   a. decay   b. disuse
   c. repression   d. interference

3. When memories are available but not accessible, forgetting may be cue dependent. T or F?
4. When learning one thing makes it more difficult to recall another, forgetting may be caused by _____.

5. You are asked to memorize long lists of telephone numbers. You learn a new list each day for 10 days. When tested on list 3, you remember less than a person who only learned the first three lists. Your larger memory loss is probably caused by

   a. disuse   b. retroactive interference
   c. regression   d. proactive interference

6. If you consciously succeed at putting a painful memory out of mind, you have used

   a. redintegration   b. suppression
   c. negative rehearsal   d. repression

7. Flashbulb memories could be thought of as the reverse of

   a. repressed memories   b. proactive memories
   c. retroactive memories d. eposodic memories

Critical Thinking

8. Based on state-dependent learning, why do you think that music often strongly evokes memories?
9. You must study French, Spanish, psychology, and biology in one evening. What do you think would be the best order in which to study these subjects so as to minimize interference?
10. There may be another way to explain why flashbulb memories are so long lasting. Can you think of one?

Answers

1. F 2. a and d 3. T 4. interference 5. b 6. b 7. a 8. Music tends to affect the mood that a person is in, and moods tend to affect memory (Batch & Lewis, 1996). 9. Any order that separates French from Spanish and psychology from biology would work (for instance: French, psychology, Spanish, biology). 10. Memories of emotionally significant events may be unusually strong because such memories are rehearsed more frequently. People usually mentally review emotionally charged events many times.

IMPROVING MEMORY—KEYS TO THE MEMORY BANK

>SURVEY QUESTION< *How can I improve my memory?*

No matter how good your memory may be, there are probably times when you wish it were better. While we're waiting around for the arrival of a memory pill, this section describes some ways to immediately improve your memory skills.

Tatiana Cooley won a national memory contest held in New York. To win, she had to memorize long lists of words and numbers, the order of the cards in a shuffled deck, a 54-line poem, and 100 names and faces. Tatiana thinks that memorization is fun. You might expect that she would also be good at everyday memory chores. On the contrary, Tatiana describes herself as "incredibly absent-minded." When asked how many brothers and sisters she has, she replies, "Six, er seven, er six." The elementary school grade she was in when she won a regional spelling bee? She can't remember. Ever fearful of forgetting, Tatiana keeps a daily to-do list and surrounds herself with a thicket of Post-it notes (Levinson, 1999).

Memory Strategies

What can we learn about memory from Tatiana? First, we should all be more tolerant of occasional memory lapses. Even memory champions have less than perfect memories! As we have seen in this chapter, memory is not like a tape recorder or a video camera. Information is frequently lost, and memories change as they are stored and retrieved. This can be frustrating at times, but it's also a good thing. The flexibility of human memory allows us to focus on what's important and meaningful, even though it also contributes to some inaccuracies. Tatiana's success as a "memory athlete" also suggests that making full use of memory requires effort and practice. Let's see how you can improve your memory.

Knowledge of Results

Learning proceeds best when feedback, or knowledge of results, allows you to check your progress. Feedback can help you identify ideas that need extra practice. In addition, knowing that you have remembered or answered correctly is rewarding. A prime way to provide feedback for yourself while studying is *recitation*.

Recitation

If you are going to remember something, eventually you will have to retrieve it. *Recitation* refers to summarizing aloud while you are learning. Recitation forces you to practice retrieving information. When you are reading a text, you should stop frequently and try to remember what you have just read by restating it in your own words. In one classic experiment, the best memory score was earned by a group of students who spent 80 percent of their time reciting and only 20 percent reading (Gates, 1958). Maybe students who talk to themselves aren't crazy after all.

Rehearsal

The more you *rehearse* (mentally review) information as you read, the better you will remember it. But remember that maintenance rehearsal alone is not very effective. Elaborative rehearsal, in which you look for connections to existing knowledge, is far better. Thinking about facts helps link them together in memory. To learn college-level information, you must make active use of more reflective rehearsal strategies (Santrock & Halonen, 2007).

Selection

The Dutch scholar Erasmus said that a good memory should be like a fish net: It should keep all the big fish and let the little ones escape. If you boil down the paragraphs in most textbooks to one or two important terms or ideas, your memory chores will be more manageable. Practice very selective marking in your texts and use marginal notes to further summarize ideas. Most students mark their texts too much instead of too little. If everything is underlined, you haven't been selective. And, very likely, you didn't pay much attention in the first place (Peterson, 1992).

Organization

Assume that you must memorize the following list of words: north, man, red, spring, woman, east, autumn, yellow, summer, boy, blue, west, winter, girl, green, south. This rather difficult list could be reorganized into *chunks* as follows: north-east-south-west, spring-summer-autumn-winter, red-yellow-green-blue, man-woman-boy-girl. Organizing class notes and summarizing chapters can be quite helpful (Hettich, 2005). You may even want to summarize your summaries, so that the overall network of ideas becomes clearer and simpler. Summaries improve memory by encouraging better encoding of information (Hadwin, Kirby, & Woodhouse, 1999).

Whole versus Part Learning

If you have to memorize a speech, is it better to try to learn it from beginning to end? Or in smaller parts like paragraphs? Generally it is better to practice whole packages of information rather than smaller parts *(whole learning)*. This is especially true for fairly short, organized information. An exception is that learning parts may be better for extremely long, complicated information. In *part learning,* subparts of a larger body of information are studied (such as sections of a textbook chapter). To decide which approach to use, remember to study the *largest meaningful amount of information* you can at one time.

For very long or complex material, try the *progressive part method,* by breaking a learning task into a series of short sections. At first, you study part A until it is mastered. Next, you study parts A and B; then A, B, and C; and so forth. This is a good way to learn the lines of a play, a long piece of music, or a poem (Ash & Holding, 1990). After the material is learned, you should also practice by starting at points other than A (at C, D, or B, for example). This helps prevent getting "lost" or going blank in the middle of a performance.

Serial Position

Whenever you must learn something in *order,* be aware of the serial position effect. As you will recall, this is the tendency to make the most errors in remembering the middle of a list. If you are introduced to a long line of people, the names you are likely to forget will be those in the middle, so you should make an extra effort to attend to them. You should also give extra practice to the middle of a list, poem, or speech. Try to break long lists of information into short sublists, and make the middle sublists the shortest of all.

Cues

The best memory cues (stimuli that aid retrieval) are those that were present during encoding (Anderson, 2005). For example, students in one study had the daunting task of trying to recall a list of 600 words. As they read the list (which they did not know they would be tested on), the students gave three other words closely related in meaning to each listed word. In a test given later, the words each student supplied were used as cues to jog memory. The students recalled an astounding 90 percent of the original word list (Mantyla, 1986).

The preceding example shows, once again, that it often helps to *elaborate* information as you learn. When you study, try to use new names, ideas, or terms in several sentences. Also, form images that include the new information, and relate it to knowledge you already have. Your goal should be to knit meaningful cues into your memory code to help you retrieve information when you need it (⟫ Fig. 7.19).

Spaced Practice

To keep boredom and fatigue to a minimum, try alternating short study sessions with brief rest periods. This pattern, called **spaced practice,** is generally superior to **massed practice,** in which little or no rest is given between learning sessions. By improving attention and consolidation, three 20-minute study sessions can produce more learning than 1 hour of continuous study. There's an old joke that goes, "How do you get to Carnegie Hall?" The answer is, "Practice, practice, practice." A better answer would be "Practice, wait a while, practice, wait a while, practice" (Neath & Surprenant, 2003).

Perhaps the best way to make use of spaced practice is to *schedule* your time. To make an effective schedule, designate times during the week before, after, and between classes when you will study particular subjects. Then treat these times just as if they were classes you had to attend.

Sleep and Memory

Remember that sleeping after study reduces interference. However, unless you are a "night person," late evening may not be a very efficient time for you to study. Also, you obviously can't sleep after every study session or study everything just before you sleep. That's why your study schedule (see "Spaced Practice") should include ample breaks between subjects, as described above. Using your breaks and free time in a schedule is as important as living up to your study periods.

⟫**FIGURE 7.19** Actors can remember large amounts of complex information for many months, even when learning new roles in between. During testing, they remember their lines best when they are allowed to move and gesture as they would when performing. Apparently their movements supply cues that aid recall (Noice & Noice, 1999).

Spaced practice A practice schedule that alternates study periods with brief rests.

Massed practice A practice schedule in which studying continues for long periods, without interruption.

Hunger and Memory

People who are hungry almost always score lower on memory tests. So mother was right, it's a good idea to make sure you've had a good breakfast or lunch before you take tests at school (Smith, Clark, & Gallagher, 1999). And a coffee won't hurt your test performance, either (Smith, 2005).

Extend How Long You Remember

When you are learning new information, test yourself repeatedly. As you do, gradually lengthen the amount of time that passes before you test yourself again. For example, if you are studying German words on flashcards, look at the first card and then move it a few cards back in the stack. Do the same with the next few cards. When you get to the first "old" card, test yourself on it and check the answer. Then, move it farther back in the stack. Do the same with other "old" cards as they come up. When "old" cards come up for the third time, put them clear to the back of the stack (Cull, Shaughnessy, & Zechmeister, 1996).

Review

If you have spaced your practice and overlearned, review will be like icing on your study cake. Reviewing shortly before an exam cuts down the time during which you must remember details that may be important for the test. When reviewing, hold the amount of new information you try to memorize to a minimum. It may be realistic to take what you have actually learned and add a little more to it at the last minute by cramming. But remember that more than a little new learning may interfere with what you already know.

Using a Strategy to Aid Recall

Successful recall is usually the result of a planned *search* of memory (Herrmann et al., 2006). For example, one study found that students were most likely to recall names that eluded them if they made use of partial information (Reed & Bruce, 1982). The students were trying to answer questions such as, "He is best remembered as the scarecrow in the Judy Garland movie *The Wizard of Oz.*" (The answer is Ray Bolger.) Partial information that helped students remember included impressions about the length of the name, letter sounds within the name, similar names, and related information (such as the names of other characters in the movie). A similar helpful strategy is to go through the alphabet, trying each letter as the first sound of a name or word you are seeking.

The *cognitive interview* described earlier in this chapter (see "Telling Wrong from Right in Forensic Memory") offers some further hints for recapturing context and jogging memories:

1. Say or write down *everything* you can remember that relates to the information you are seeking. Don't worry about how trivial any of it seems; each bit of information you remember can serve as a cue to bring back others.
2. Try to recall events or information in different orders. Let your memories flow out backward or out of order, or start with whatever impressed you the most.
3. Recall from different viewpoints. Review events by mentally standing in a different place. Or try to view information as another person would remember it. When taking a test, for instance, ask yourself what other students or your professor would remember about the topic.
4. Mentally put yourself back in the situation where you learned the information. Try to mentally recreate the learning environment or relive the event. As you do, include sounds, smells, details of weather, nearby objects, other people present, what you said or thought, and how you felt as you learned the information (Fisher & Geiselman, 1987; Milne & Bull, 2002).

A Look Ahead

Psychologists still have much to learn about the nature of memory and how to improve it. For now, one thing stands out clearly: People who have good memories excel at organizing information and making it meaningful. With this in mind, the "Psychology in Action" discussion for this chapter tells how you can combine organization and meaning into a powerful method for improving memory.

Study Break   Improving Memory

Reflect

Return to the topic headings in the preceding pages that list techniques for improving memory. Place a check mark next to those that you have used recently. Review any you didn't mark and think of a specific example of how you could use each technique at school, at home, or at work.

Learning Check

1. To improve memory, it is reasonable to spend as much or more time reciting as reading. T or F?
2. Organizing information while studying has little effect on memory because long-term memory is already highly organized. T or F?

3. The progressive part method of study is best suited to long and complex learning tasks. T or F?
4. Sleeping immediately after studying is highly disruptive to the consolidation of memories. T or F?
5. The cognitive interview helps people remember more by providing

   a. memory cues   b. a serial position effect
   c. phonetic priming   d. massed practice

Critical Thinking

6. What advantages would there be to taking notes as you read a textbook, as opposed to underlining words in the text?

Answers

1. T 2. F 3. T 4. F 5. a 6. Note-taking is a form of recitation, it encourages elaborative rehearsal, facilitates the organization and selection of important ideas, and your notes can be used for review.

Psychology in Action

Mnemonics—Memory Magic

>SURVEY QUESTION< *How can I improve my memory?*

Some stage performers use memory as part of their acts. Do they have eidetic imagery? Various "memory experts" entertain by memorizing the names of everyone at a banquet, the order of all the cards in a deck, long lists of words, or other seemingly impossible amounts of information. Such feats may seem like magic, but if they are, you can have a magic memory too. These tricks are performed through the use of *mnemonics* (nee-MON-iks) (Lieberman, 2004; Neath & Surprenant, 2003). A **mnemonic** is any kind of memory system or aid.

Some mnemonic systems are so common that almost everyone knows them. If you are trying to remember how many days there are in a month, you may find the answer by reciting, "Thirty days hath September . . . ." Physics teachers often help students remember the colors of the spectrum by giving them the mnemonic "Roy G. Biv": **R**ed, **O**range, **Y**ellow, **G**reen, **B**lue, **I**ndigo, **V**iolet. The budding sailor who has trouble telling port from starboard may remember that port and left both have four letters or may remind herself, "I *left* port." And what beginning musician hasn't remembered the notes represented by the lines and spaces of the musical staff by learning "F-A-C-E" and "**E**very **G**ood **B**oy **D**oes **F**ine."

Mnemonic techniques are ways to avoid *rote* learning (learning by simple repetition). The superiority of mnemonic learning as opposed to rote learning has been demonstrated many times (Carney & Levin, 2003; Manalo, 2002).

Stage performers rarely have naturally superior memories. Instead, they make extensive use of memory systems to perform their feats (Wilding & Valentine, 1994b). Few of these systems are of practical value to you as a student, but the principles underlying mnemonics

Mnemonic Any kind of memory system or aid.

are. By practicing mnemonics you should be able to greatly improve your memory with little effort.

Here, then, are the basic principles of mnemonics.

1. **Use mental pictures.** Visual pictures, or images, are generally easier to remember than words. Turning information into mental pictures is therefore very helpful. Make these images as vivid as possible (Neath & Surprenant, 2003).

2. **Make things meaningful.** Transferring information from short-term memory to long-term memory is aided by making it meaningful. If you encounter technical terms that have little or no immediate meaning for you, give them meaning, even if you have to stretch the term to do so. (This point is clarified by the examples following this list.)

3. **Make information familiar.** Connect it to what you already know. Another way to get information into long-term memory is to connect it to information already stored there. If some facts or ideas in a chapter seem to stay in your memory easily, associate other more difficult facts with them.

4. **Form bizarre, unusual, or exaggerated mental associations.** Forming images that make sense is better in most situations. However, when associating two ideas, terms, or especially mental images, you may find that the more outrageous and exaggerated the association, the more likely you are to remember. Bizarre images make stored information more *distinctive* and therefore easier to retrieve (Worthen & Marshall, 1996). Imagine, for example, that you have just been introduced to Mr. Rehkop. To remember his name, you could picture him wearing a police uniform. Then replace his nose with a ray gun. This bizarre image will provide two hints when you want to remember Mr. Rehkop's name: *ray* and *cop.* This technique works for other kinds of information, too. College students who used exaggerated mental associations to remember the names of unfamiliar animals outperformed students who just used rote memory (Carney & Levin, 2001).

   Bizarre images mainly help improve immediate memory, and they work best for fairly simple information (Robinson-Riegler & McDaniel, 1994). Nevertheless, they can be a first step toward learning.

A sampling of typical applications of mnemonics should make these four points clear to you.

Example 1 Let's say you have 30 new vocabulary words to memorize in Spanish. You can proceed by rote memorization (repeat them over and over until you begin to get them), or you can learn them with little effort by using the keyword method (Campos, Amor, & González, 2004). In the **keyword method** a familiar word or image is used to link two other words or items. To remember that the word *pajaro* (pronounced PAH-hah-ro) means bird, you can link it to a "key" word in English: *Pajaro* (to your authors) sounds like "parked car-o." Therefore, to remember that *pajaro* means bird, you might visualize a parked car jam-packed full of birds. You should try to make this image as vivid and exaggerated as possible, with birds flapping and chirping and feathers flying everywhere. Similarly, for the word *carta* (which means "letter") you might imagine a shopping *cart* filled with postal letters.

If you link similar keywords and images for the rest of the list, you may not remember them all, but you will get most without any more practice. As a matter of fact, if you have formed the *pajaro* and *carta* images just now, it is going to be almost impossible for you to see these words again without remembering what they mean. The keyword method is also superior when you want to work "backward" from an English word to a foreign vocabulary word (Hogben & Lawson, 1992).

What about a year from now? How long do keyword memories last? Mnemonic memories work best in the short run. Later, they may be more fragile than conventional memories. That's why it's usually best to use mnemonics during the initial stages of learning (Carney

Ulrike Welsch

Mnemonics can be an aid in preparing for tests. However, because mnemonics help most in the initial stages of storing information, it is important to follow through with other elaborative learning strategies.

Exaggerated mental images can link two words or ideas in ways that aid memory. Here, the keyword method is used to link the English word *letter* with the Spanish word *carta.*

Keyword method As an aid to memory, using a familiar word or image to link two items.

& Levin, 2003). To create more lasting memories, you'll need to use the techniques discussed earlier in this chapter.

Example 2 Let's say you have to learn the names of all the bones and muscles in the human body for biology. You are trying to remember that the jawbone is the *mandible*. This one is easy because you can associate it to a *man nibbling*, or maybe you can picture a *man dribbling* a basketball with his jaw (make this image as ridiculous as possible). If the muscle name *latissimus dorsi* gives you trouble, familiarize it by turning it into *"the ladder misses the door, sigh."* Then picture a ladder glued to your back where the muscle is found. Picture the ladder leading up to a small door at your shoulder. Picture the ladder missing the door. Picture the ladder sighing like an animated character in a cartoon.

This seems like more to remember, not less; and it seems like it would cause you to misspell things. Mnemonics are not a complete substitute for normal memory; they are an aid to normal memory. Mnemonics are not likely to be helpful unless you make extensive use of *images* (Willoughby et al., 1997). Your mental pictures will come back to you easily. As for misspellings, mnemonics can be thought of as a built-in hint in your memory. Often, when taking a test, you will find that the slightest hint is all you need to remember correctly. A mnemonic image is like having someone leaning over your shoulder who says, "Psst, the name of that muscle sounds like 'ladder misses the door, sigh.'" If misspelling continues to be a problem, try to create memory aids for spelling, too.

Here are two more examples to help you appreciate the flexibility of a mnemonic approach to studying.

Example 3 Your art history teacher expects you to be able to name the artist when you are shown slides as part of exams. You have seen many of the slides only once before in class. How will you remember them? As the slides are shown in class, make each artist's name into an object or image. Then picture the object *in* the paintings done by the artist. For example, you can picture Van Gogh as a *van* (automobile) *going* through the middle of each Van Gogh painting. Picture the van running over things and knocking things over. Or, if you remember that Van Gogh cut off his ear, picture a giant bloody ear in each of his paintings.

Example 4 If you have trouble remembering history, try to avoid thinking of it as something from the dim past. Picture each historical personality as a person you know right now (a friend, teacher, parent, and so on). Then picture these people doing whatever the historical figures did. Also, try visualizing battles or other events as if they were happening in your town, or make parks and schools into countries. Use your imagination.

How can mnemonics be used to remember things in order? Here are three techniques that are helpful.

1. **Form a story or a chain.** To remember lists of ideas, objects, or words in order, try forming an exaggerated association (mental image) connecting the first item to the second, then the second to the third, and so on. To remember the following short list in order—elephant, doorknob, string, watch, rifle, oranges—picture a full-sized *elephant* balanced on a *doorknob* playing with a *string* tied to him. Picture a *watch* tied to the string, and a *rifle* shooting *oranges* at the watch. This technique can be used quite successfully for lists of 20 or more items. In one test, people who used a linking mnemonic did much better at remembering lists of 15 and 22 errands (Higbee et al., 1990). Try it next time you go shopping and leave your list at home. Another helpful strategy is to make up a short story that links all of the items on a list you want to remember (McNamara & Scott, 2001).

2. **Take a mental walk.** Ancient Greek orators had an interesting way to remember ideas in order when giving a speech. Their method was to take a mental walk along

a familiar path. As they did, they associated topics with the images of statues found along the walk. You can do the same thing by "placing" objects or ideas along the way as you mentally take a familiar walk (Neath & Surprenant, 2003).

3. **Use a system.** Many times, the first letters or syllables of words or ideas can be formed into another word that will serve as a reminder of order. "Roy G. Biv" is an example. As an alternative, learn the following: 1 is a bun, 2 is a shoe, 3 is a tree, 4 is a door, 5 is a hive, 6 is sticks, 7 is heaven, 8 is a gate, 9 is a line, 10 is a hen. To remember a list in order, form an image associating bun with the first item on your list. For example, if the first item is *frog,* picture a "frog-burger" on a bun to remember it. Then, associate shoe with the second item, and so on.

If you have never used mnemonics, you may still be skeptical, but give this approach a fair trial. Most people find they can greatly extend their memory through the use of mnemonics. But remember, like most things worthwhile, remembering takes effort.

 Study Break   Mnemonics

Reflect

As an exercise, see if you can create mnemonics for the words *icon, implicit memory,* and *mnemonic.* The best mnemonics are your own, but here are some examples to help you get started. An icon is a visual image: Picture an *eye* in a *can* to remember that icons store visual information. Implicit memories are "hidden": Picture an *imp* hiding in memory. A mnemonic is a memory aid: Imagine writing a phone number on your knee to remember it. Imagine your *knee* moaning, *"Ick,* you shouldn't write on me."

Now, go through the glossary items in this chapter and make up mnemonics for any terms you have difficulty remembering.

Learning Check

1. Memory systems and aids are referred to as _____.

Critical Thinking

5. How are elaborative rehearsal and mnemonics alike?

2. Which of the following is least likely to improve memory?
   a. using exaggerated mental images
   b. forming a chain of associations
   c. turning visual information into verbal information
   d. associating new information to information that is already known or familiar

3. Bizarre images make stored information more distinctive and therefore easier to retrieve. T or F?
4. Bower's 1973 study showed that, in general, mnemonics only improve memory for related words or ideas. T or F?

Answers

1. mnemonics 2. c 3. T 4. F 5. Both attempt to relate new information to information stored in long-term memory that is familiar or already easy to retrieve.

CHAPTER IN REVIEW

Major Points

- Remembering is an active process. Our memories are frequently lost, altered, revised, or distorted.
- The best way to remember depends, to an extent, on which memory system you are using.
- Remembering is not an all-or-nothing process. Even when you think you can't recall anything, some information may continue to exist in memory.
- Understanding how and why forgetting occurs will allow you to make better use of your memory.
- Some people have naturally superior memories, but everyone can learn to improve his or her memory.

- Memory systems (mnemonics) greatly improve immediate memory. However, conventional learning tends to create the most lasting memories.

Summary

Is there more than one type of memory?

- Memory is an active, computer-like system that encodes, stores, and retrieves information.
- Humans appear to have three interrelated memory systems. These are sensory memory, short-term memory (STM, also called working memory), and long-term memory (LTM).

What are the features of each type of memory?

- Sensory memory is exact but very brief. Through selective attention, some information is transferred to STM.

- STM has a capacity of about 5 to 7 bits of information, but this can be extended by chunking, or recoding. Short-term memories are brief and very sensitive to interruption, or interference; however, they can be prolonged by maintenance rehearsal.

- LTM functions as a general storehouse of information, especially meaningful information. Elaborative rehearsal helps transfer information from STM to LTM. Long-term memories are relatively permanent, or lasting. LTM seems to have an almost unlimited storage capacity.

- LTM is subject to constructive processing, or ongoing revision and updating. LTM is highly organized to allow retrieval of needed information. The pattern, or structure, of memory networks is the subject of current memory research.

- Redintegrative memories are reconstructed as each memory provides a cue for the next memory.

Is there more than one type of long-term memory?

- Within long-term memory, declarative memories for facts seem to differ from procedural memories for skills.

- Declarative memories may be further categorized as semantic memories or episodic memories.

How is memory measured?

- The tip-of-the-tongue state shows that memory is not an all-or-nothing event. Memories may therefore be revealed by recall, recognition, relearning, or priming.

- In recall, memory proceeds without explicit cues, as in an essay exam. Recall of listed information often reveals a serial position effect (middle items on the list are most subject to errors).

- A common test of recognition is the multiple-choice question.

- In relearning, "forgotten" material is learned again, and memory is indicated by a savings score.

- Recall, recognition, and relearning mainly measure explicit memories. Other techniques, such as priming, are necessary to reveal implicit memories.

What are "photographic" memories?

- Eidetic imagery (photographic memory) occurs when a person is able to project an image onto a blank surface.

- Eidetic imagery is rarely found in adults. However, many adults have internal memory images, which can be very vivid.

- Exceptional memory can be learned by finding ways to directly store information in LTM.

- Learning has no effect on the limits of STM. Some people may have exceptional memories that exceed what can be achieved through learning.

What causes forgetting?

- Forgetting and memory were extensively studied by Herman Ebbinghaus. His work shows that forgetting is most rapid immediately after learning (the curve of forgetting).

- Failure to encode information is a common cause of "forgetting."

- Forgetting in sensory memory and STM probably reflects decay of memory traces in the nervous system. Decay or disuse of memories may also account for some LTM loss.

- Often, forgetting is cue dependent. The power of cues to trigger memories is revealed by state-dependent learning and the link between moods and memory.

- Much forgetting in both STM and LTM can be attributed to interference.

- When recent learning interferes with retrieval of prior learning, retroactive interference has occurred.

- If old learning interferes with new learning, proactive interference has occurred.

How accurate are everyday memories?

- Repression is the forgetting of painful, embarrassing, or traumatic memories.

- Repression is thought to be unconscious, in contrast to suppression, which is a conscious attempt to avoid thinking about something.

- Independent evidence has verified that some recovered memories of childhood sexual abuse are true. However, others have been shown to be false.

- In the absence of confirming or disconfirming evidence, there is currently no way to separate true memories from fantasies. Caution is advised for all concerned with attempts to retrieve supposedly hidden memories.

What happens in the brain when memories are formed?

- Retrograde amnesia and the effects of electroconvulsive shock (ECS) may be explained by the concept of consolidation.

- Consolidation theory holds that permanent memory traces are formed during a critical period after learning. Until they are consolidated, long-term memories are easily destroyed.

- The hippocampus is a brain area that has been linked with consolidation of memories. Once memories are consolidated, declarative memories appear to be stored in the cortex of the brain while procedural memories appear to be stored in the cerebellum.
- Memories are recorded in the brain through nerve cells and how they interconnect.

How can memory be improved?

- Memory can be improved by using feedback, recitation, and rehearsal, by selecting and organizing information, and by using the progressive part method, spaced practice, and active search strategies. Effects of serial position, sleep, review, cues, and elaboration should also be kept in mind when studying or memorizing.
- Mnemonic systems use mental images and unusual associations to link new information with familiar memories already stored in LTM. Such strategies give information personal meaning and make it easier to recall.

Interactive Learning

Internet addresses frequently change. To find the sites listed here, visit www.thomsonedu.com/psychology/coon for an updated list of Internet addresses and direct links to relevant sites.

Psychology: A Journey **Companion Website**   Find online quizzes, flash cards, animations, video clips, experiments, interactive assessments, and other helpful study aids for this text at www.thomsonedu.com/psychology/coon.

Active Brain Areas in Working Memory   A three-dimensional MRI reconstruction of a person's brain while holding letters in working memory.

Exploratorium: Memory   Demonstrations and articles related to memory from an exceptional science museum.

False-Memory Test   Use the materials in this site to induce false memories in others (for demonstration purposes).

Memories Are Made of . . .   Article from *Scientific American* discusses memory-enhancing drugs for Alzheimer's patients.

Memory Techniques and Mnemonics   Links to information on mnemonics.

Questions and Answers about Memories of Childhood Abuse   From the American Psychological Association, a summary of the repressed memory issue.

Repressed and Recovered Memories   Site devoted to the recovered memory controversy; has links to both sides of the controversy.

The Machinery of Thought   *Scientific American* article describes research on the physiology of memory.

The Magical Number Seven, Plus or Minus Two   Full text of George Miller's original article.

ThomsonNOW   Go to www.thomsonedu.com/login to link to ThomsonNOW, your online study tool. First take the **Pre-Test** for this chapter to get your **Personalized Study Plan,** which will identify topics you need to review and direct you to online resources. Then take the **Post-Test** to determine what concepts you have mastered and what you still need work on.

TEST YOUR KNOWLEDGE

Memory

For additional review, get more practice with *ThomsonNOW*, *WebTutor*, the *Practice Quizzes*, and/or the printed *Study Guide* available with this book.

1. The first step in forming a memory is
   a. retrieval
   b. storage
   c. rehearsal
   d. encoding

2. Storing information as an icon or an echo is most characteristic of
   a. sensory memory
   b. short-term memory
   c. long-term memory
   d. procedural memory

3. Selective attention controls which information moves from sensory memory to
   a. phonetic memory
   b. iconic memory
   c. STM
   d. LTM

4. Information in LTM is stored mainly on the basis of
   a. meaning
   b. sounds and phonetics
   c. icons and echos
   d. how it will be retrieved

5. The digit-span test is primarily a measure of
   a. LTM
   b. elaborative rehearsal
   c. recoding
   d. STM

6. Elaborative rehearsal is especially useful for forming
   a. memory icons
   b. long-term memories
   c. skill memories
   d. retroactive memories

7. Network models of memory can explain how remembering one memory can lead to remembering another, a process called
   a. redintegration
   b. TOT
   c. sequential memory
   d. eidetic imagery

8. Which of the following is a type of fact memory?
   a. semantic memory
   b. declarative memory
   c. episodic memory
   d. all of the above

9. The cognitive interview helps people remember more by providing
   a. memory cues
   b. a serial position effect
   c. phonetic priming
   d. massed practice

10. The most sensitive test of memory is
    a. redintegration
    b. recall
    c. relearning
    d. recognition

11. Which type of memory test would be most likely to reveal a serial position effect?
    a. recall
    b. recognition
    c. relearning
    d. implicit

12. Priming is used to reveal which type of memories?
    a. explicit
    b. sensory
    c. skill
    d. implicit

13. Even people who have especially good memories depend on
    a. recalling information
    b. redintegration
    c. maintenance rehearsal
    d. learned strategies

14. Decay of memory traces appears to apply most to the forgetting of
    a. sensory and short-term memories
    b. procedural memories
    c. semantic memories
    d. state-dependent memories

15. A saxophone player learns three new pieces of music, one after the other, in a single afternoon. The next day he is least able to remember the third piece because of
    a. state-dependent learning
    b. the time decay of memory traces
    c. proactive interference
    d. disuse of memory cues

16. If you unconsciously put a painful memory out of mind, you have used
    a. TOT
    b. repression
    c. negative rehearsal
    d. suppression

17. Flashbulb memories could be thought of as the reverse of
    a. repressed memories
    b. proactive memories
    c. retroactive memories
    d. episodic memories

18. Memory consolidation would most likely be disrupted by
    a. rehearsal
    b. ECS
    c. massed practice
    d. sleep

19. Which of the following is BAD advice for improving memory?
    a. Select and organize information.
    b. Use spaced practice.
    c. Study when you are hungry.
    d. Sleep after you study.

20. The keyword method is a commonly used
    a. cognitive interviewing technique
    b. massed practice strategy
    c. mnemonic technique
    d. first step in the progressive-part method

Intelligence, Cognition, Language, and Creativity

JOURNEY INTO PSYCHOLOGY: MEET THE RAIN MAN

Meet Kim Peek, the model for Dustin Hoffman's character in the Academy Award–winning movie *Rain Man.* Kim began memorizing books at 18 months of age. Today, he can recite from memory more than 9,000 books. He knows all of the ZIP codes and area codes in America and can give accurate travel directions between any two major U.S. cities. He can also discuss hundreds of pieces of classical music in detail and is even learning to play all of that music. Amazingly, though, for someone with such skills, Kim has difficulty with abstract thinking and tests of general intelligence. He is poorly coordinated and cannot button his own clothes (Treffert & Christensen, 2005).

Kim Peek is an autistic savant. His *autism* involves impairments in intelligence, communication, and social interaction, as well as repetitive behavior patterns (Dawson & Toth, 2006). Paradoxically, Kim is also a *savant* (highly knowledgeable person). Despite their impaired intelligence, autistic savants may have exceptional abilities in music, mechanics, math, memory, or other mental tasks.

The striking contrast between Kim's limited intelligence and his unusual talents raises many questions. What is intelligence? Is it all in our genes? How do we think? How are we able to solve problems? How do people create works of art, science, and literature? For some preliminary answers, we will investigate intelligence, thinking, problem solving, and creativity in the following pages.

Richard Green

▽ **Survey Questions**

- How is human intelligence defined and measured?
- What are some controversies in the study of intelligence?
- What is the nature of thought?
- In what ways are images related to thinking?
- How do we learn concepts?
- What is the role of language in thinking?
- What do we know about problem solving?
- What is creative thinking?
- How accurate is intuition?
- Are IQ tests fair to all cultural and racial groups?

HUMAN INTELLIGENCE—GEE, ARE YOU SMART!

>SURVEY QUESTION< *How is human intelligence defined and measured?*

Like many important concepts in psychology, intelligence cannot be observed directly. Nevertheless, we feel certain it exists. Let's compare two children:

> When she was 14 months old, Anne H. wrote her own name. She taught herself to read at age 2. At age 5, she astounded her kindergarten teacher by bringing a notebook computer to class—on which she was reading an encyclopedia. At 10 she breezed through an entire high school algebra course in 12 hours.

> Billy A., who is 10 years old, can write his name and can count, but he has trouble with simple addition and subtraction problems and finds multiplication impossible. He has been held back in school twice and is still incapable of doing the work his 8-year-old classmates find easy.

Anne is considered a genius; Billy, a slow learner. There seems little doubt that they differ in intelligence.

Wait! Anne's ability is obvious, but how do we know that Billy isn't just lazy? This is the same question that Alfred Binet faced in 1904 (Jarvin & Sternberg, 2003). The minister of education in Paris had asked Binet to find a way to distinguish slower students from the more capable (or the capable but lazy). In a flash of brilliance, Binet and an associate created a test made up of "intellectual" questions and problems. Next, they learned which questions an average child could answer at each age. By giving children the test, they could tell if a child was performing up to his or her potential (Kaufman, 2000).

Binet's approach gave rise to modern intelligence tests. At the same time, it launched nearly 100 years of heated debate. Part of the debate is related to the basic difficulty of defining intelligence (Sternberg, Grigorenko, & Kidd, 2005).

Defining Intelligence

Isn't there an accepted definition of intelligence? Yes, **intelligence** is the global capacity to act purposefully, to think rationally, and to deal effectively with the environment. The core of intelligence consists of *general mental abilities* (called the **g-factor**) in the areas of reasoning, problem solving, knowledge, memory, and successful adaptation to one's surroundings (Sternberg, 2004). Beyond this there is much disagreement. In fact, many psychologists simply accept an *operational definition* of intelligence by spelling out the procedures they use to measure it. Thus, by selecting items for an intelligence test, a psychologist is saying in

Modern intelligence tests are widely used to measure intellectual abilities. When properly administered, such tests provide an operational definition of intelligence.

David Young-Wolff/PhotoEdit, Inc.

Intelligence An overall capacity to think rationally, act purposefully, and deal effectively with the environment.

g-factor A general ability factor or core of general intellectual ability that involves reasoning, problem-solving ability, knowledge, memory, and successful adaptation to one's surroundings.

Intelligence—How Would a Fool Do It?

You have been asked to sort some objects into categories. Wouldn't it be smart to put the clothes, containers, implements, and foods in separate piles? Not necessarily. When members of the Kpelle culture in Liberia were asked to sort objects, they grouped them together by function. For example, a potato (food) would be placed together with a knife (implement). When the Kpelle were asked why they grouped the objects this way, they often said that's how a wise man would do it. The researchers finally asked the Kpelle, "How would a fool do it?" Only then did the Kpelle sort the objects into the nice, neat categories we Westerners prefer.

This anecdote, related by cultural psychologist Patricia Greenfield (1997), raises serious questions about general definitions of intelligence. For example, among the Cree of Northern Canada, "smart" people are the ones who have visual skills needed to find food on the frozen tundra (Darou, 1992). For the Puluwat people in the South Pacific, being smart means having ocean-going navigation skills necessary to get from island to island (Sternberg, 2004). And so it goes, as each culture teaches its children the kinds of "intelligence" valued in that culture—how the wise man would do it, not a fool (Correa-Chávez, Rogoff, & Arauz, 2005). In view of such differences, psychologists have tried to create "culture-fair" intelligence tests. Some have even questioned the value of intelligence testing itself. We'll discuss both of these ideas in this chapter's "Psychology in Action" section.

a very direct way, "This is what I mean by intelligence." A test that measures memory, reasoning, and verbal fluency offers a very different definition of intelligence than one that measures strength of grip, shoe size, length of the nose, or the person's best *Too Human* video game score. (For a glimpse at how other cultures define "intelligent" behavior, see "Intelligence—How Would a Fool Do It?")

Intelligence Tests

American psychologists quickly saw the value of Alfred Binet's test. In 1916, Lewis Terman and others at Stanford University revised it for use in North America. After more revisions, the *Stanford-Binet Intelligence Scales, Fifth Edition* continues to be widely used. The original Stanford-Binet assumed that a child's intellectual abilities improve with each passing year. Today, the Stanford-Binet (or SB5) is still primarily made up of age-ranked questions. Naturally, these questions get a little harder at each age level. The SB5 is appropriate for people from age 2 to 85+ years (Roid, 2003).

The SB5 measures five cognitive factors (types of mental abilities) that make up general intelligence. These are *fluid reasoning, knowledge, quantitative reasoning, visual-spatial processing,* and *working memory.* Each factor is measured with verbal questions (those involving words and numbers) and nonverbal questions (items that use pictures and objects). Let's see what each factor looks like.

Fluid Reasoning

This factor tests reasoning ability with questions like the following:

How are an apple, a plum, and a banana different from a beet?
An apprentice is to a master as a novice is to an _____.
"I knew my bag was going to be in the last place I looked, so I looked there first."
    What is silly or impossible about that?

Other items ask people to fill in the missing shape in a group of shapes, and to tell a story that explains what's going on in a series of pictures.

Knowledge

This factor assesses the person's knowledge about a wide range of topics.

Why is yeast added to bread dough?
What does cryptic mean?
What is silly or impossible about this picture? (For example, a bicycle has square wheels.)

Quantitative Reasoning

Test items for this factor measure a person's ability to solve problems involving numbers. Here are some samples:

> If I have six marbles and you give me another one, how many marbles will I have?
> Given the numbers 3, 6, 9, 12, what number would come next?
> If a shirt is being sold for 50 percent of the normal price, and the price tag is $60, what is the cost of the shirt?

Visual-Spatial Processing

People who have visual-spatial skills are good at putting picture puzzles together and copying geometric shapes (such as triangles, rectangles, and circles). Other questions ask test takers to reproduce patterns of blocks and choose pictures that show how a piece of paper would look if it were folded or cut. Verbal questions can also require visual-spatial abilities:

> Suppose that you are going east, then turn right, then turn right again, then turn left. In what direction are you facing now?

Working Memory

This part of the SB5 measures the ability to use short-term memory. Some typical memory tasks include:

> Correctly remember the order of colored beads on a stick.
> After hearing several sentences, name the last word from each sentence.
> Repeat a series of digits (forward or backward) after hearing them once.

If you were to take the SB5, it would yield a score for your general intelligence, verbal intelligence, nonverbal intelligence, and each of the five cognitive factors (Bain & Allin, 2005).

Intelligence Quotients

Imagine that a child named Yuan can answer questions that an average 7-year-old can answer. How smart is she? Actually, we can't say yet, because we don't know how old Yuan is. If she is 10, she's not very smart. If she's 5, she is very bright. Thus, to estimate a child's intelligence we need to know both her **mental age** (average intellectual performance) and her **chronological age** (age in years).

Mental age is based on the level of age-ranked questions a person can answer. For example, at ages 8 or 9, very few children can define the word *connection*. At age 10, 10 percent can. At age 13, 60 percent can. Thus, a 13-year-old of average ability can define *connection*. If we had only this item to test children with, those who answered correctly would be given a mental age of 13. When scores from many such items are combined, a child's overall mental age can be found. ■ Table 8.1 is a sample of items that persons of average intelligence can answer at various ages.

Mental age is a good measure of actual ability. But mental age says nothing about whether overall intelligence is high or low, compared with other people of the same age. To find out what a particular mental age means, we must also consider a person's chronological age. Then we can relate mental age to actual age. This yields an **IQ, or intelligence quotient.** A quotient results from dividing one number into another. When the Stanford-Binet was first used, IQ was defined as mental age (MA) divided by chronological age (CA) and multiplied by 100. (Multiplying by 100 changes the IQ into a whole number, rather than a decimal.)

$$\frac{MA}{CA} \times 100 = IQ$$

Mental age The average mental ability people display at a given age.

Chronological age A person's age in years.

Intelligence quotient (IQ) An index of intelligence defined as a person's mental age divided by his or her chronological age and multiplied by 100.

An advantage of the original IQ calculation was that intelligence could be compared among children with different chronological and mental ages. For instance, 10-year-old Justin has a mental age of 12. Thus, his IQ is 120:

■ Table 8.1	Sample Items from the Stanford-Binet Intelligence Scale
2 years old	On a large paper doll, points out the hair, mouth, feet, ears, nose, hands, and eyes. When shown a tower built of four blocks, builds one like it.
3 years old	When shown a bridge built of three blocks, builds one like it. When shown a drawing of a circle, copies it with a pencil.
4 years old	Fills in the missing word when asked, "Brother is a boy; sister is a _____." "In daytime it is light; at night it is _____." Answers correctly when asked, "Why do we have houses?" "Why do we have books?"
5 years old	Defines ball, hat, and stove. When shown a drawing of a square, copies it with a pencil.
9 years old	Answers correctly when examiner says, "In an old graveyard in Spain they have discovered a small skull which they believe to be that of Christopher Columbus when he was about 10 years old. What is foolish about that?" Answers correctly when asked, "Tell me the name of a color that rhymes with head." "Tell me a number that rhymes with tree."
Adult	Can describe the difference between laziness and idleness, poverty and misery, character and reputation. Answers correctly when asked, "Which direction would you have to face so your right hand would be toward the north?"

Source: L. Terman & M. Merrill, Stanford-Binet Intelligence Scale, 1937. Revised edition, 1960b. Houghton Mifflin Co.

$$\frac{(MA)\ 12}{(CA)\ 10} \times 100 = 120\ (IQ)$$

Justin's friend Suke also has a mental age of 12. However, Suke's chronological age is 12, so his IQ is 100:

$$\frac{(MA)\ 12}{(CA)\ 12} \times 100 = 100\ (IQ)$$

The IQ shows that 10-year-old Justin is brighter than his 12-year-old friend Suke, even though their intellectual skills are about the same. Notice that a person's IQ will be 100 when mental age equals chronological age. An IQ score of 100 is therefore defined as average intelligence.

Then does a person with an IQ score below 100 have below average intelligence? Not unless the IQ is well below 100. An IQ of 100 is the *mathematical* average (or mean) for such scores. However, average intelligence is usually defined as any score from 90 to 109. The important point is that IQ scores will be over 100 when mental age is higher than age in years (▶Fig. 8.1). IQ scores below 100 occur when a person's age in years exceeds his or her mental age. An example of the second situation would be a 15-year-old with an MA of 12:

$$\frac{12}{15} \times 100 = 80\ (IQ)$$

Deviation IQs

The preceding examples may give you insight into IQ scores. However, it's no longer necessary to directly calculate IQs. Instead, modern tests use **deviation IQs.** These scores are based on a person's relative standing in his or her age group. That is, they tell how far above or below average the person's score falls. (For more information, see the Statistics appendix near the end of this book.) Tables supplied with the test are then used to convert a person's relative standing in the group to an IQ score. For example, if you score at the 50th percentile, half the people your age who take the test score higher than you and half score lower. In this case, your

AP/Wide World Photo

▶▶**FIGURE 8.1** With a score of 230, Marilyn vos Savant has the highest IQ ever officially recorded. When she was only 7 years and 9 months old, vos Savant could answer questions that the average 13-year-old can answer. At ages 8, 9, and 10, she got perfect scores on the Stanford-Binet scale. Now in her 60s, she is a well-published author and recently became the host of an *Ask Marilyn* segment for CBS TV News.

Deviation IQ An IQ obtained statistically from a person's relative standing in his or her age group; that is, how far above or below average the person's score was relative to other scores.

■ Table 8.2   Sample Items Similar to Those Used on the WAIS-III

Verbal Subtests	Sample Items
Information	How many wings does a bird have? Who wrote *Paradise Lost*?
Digit span	Repeat from memory a series of digits, such as 3 1 0 6 7 4 2 5, after hearing it once.
General Comprehension	What is the advantage of keeping money in the bank? Why is copper often used in electrical wires?
Arithmetic	Three men divided 18 golf balls equally among themselves. How many golf balls did each man receive? If 2 apples cost 15¢, what will be the cost of a dozen apples?
Similarities	In what way are a lion and a tiger alike and/or unalike? In what way are a saw and a hammer alike and/or unalike?
Vocabulary	What is a guitar? What does "robin" mean?
Letter-Number Sequencing	Repeat a list of mixed numbers and letters, numbers first, in numerical order, and letters second, in alphabetical order.

Picture Arrangement

Matrix Reasoning

Performance Subtests	Description of Item
Picture arrangement	Arrange a series of cartoon panels to make a meaningful story.
Picture completion	What is missing from these pictures?
Block design	Copy designs with blocks.
Object assembly	Put together a jigsaw puzzle.
Digit symbol	Fill in the symbols.
Matrix Reasoning	Select the item that completes the matrix:
Symbol Search	Match symbols appearing in separate groups:

Symbol Search

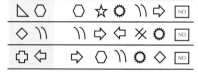

IQ score is 100. If you score at the 84th percentile, your IQ score is 115. If you score at the 97th percentile, your IQ score is 130.

The Wechsler Tests

Is the Stanford-Binet the only intelligence test? A widely used alternative is the *Wechsler Adult Intelligence Scale—Third Edition,* or WAIS-III. A version for children is called the *Wechsler Intelligence Scale for Children—Fourth Edition* (WISC-IV) (Baron, 2005).

The Wechsler tests are similar to the Stanford-Binet but differ in important ways. For one thing, the WAIS-III was specifically designed to test adult intelligence. The original Stanford-Binet was better suited for children and adolescents. The latest Stanford-Binet (the SB5) can now be used for all ages, but the WAIS was the first "adult" IQ test. Like the Stanford-Binet, the Wechsler tests yield a single overall IQ. In addition, the WAIS and WISC give separate scores for **performance** (nonverbal) **intelligence** and **verbal** (language- or symbol-oriented) **intelligence.** (Note that this feature was also recently added to the SB5.) The abilities measured by the Wechsler tests and some sample test items are listed in ▓ Table 8.2.

Group Tests

The SB5 and the Wechsler tests are **individual intelligence tests,** which must be given to a single person by a trained specialist. In contrast, **group intelligence tests** can be given to a large group of people with minimal supervision. Group tests usually require people to read, to follow instructions, and to solve problems of logic, reasoning, mathematics, or spatial

Performance intelligence Intelligence measured by solving puzzles, assembling objects, completing pictures, and other nonverbal tasks.

Verbal intelligence Intelligence measured by answering questions involving vocabulary, general information, arithmetic, and other language- or symbol-oriented tasks.

Individual intelligence test A test of intelligence designed to be given to a single individual by a trained specialist.

Group intelligence test Any intelligence test that can be administered to a group of people with minimal supervision.

skills. If you're wondering if you have ever taken an intelligence test, the answer is probably yes. The well-known *Scholastic Assessment Test* (SAT) measures aptitudes for language, math, and reasoning. The SAT is designed to predict your chances for success in college. Because it measures a number of different mental aptitudes, it can also be used to estimate general intelligence.

Variations in Intelligence

IQ scores are classified as shown in ■ Table 8.3. A look at the percentages reveals a definite pattern. The distribution (or scattering) of IQ scores approximates a **normal** (bell-shaped) **curve**. That is, most scores fall close to the average and very few are found at the extremes. ▶▶Figure 8.2 shows this characteristic of measured intelligence.

The Mentally Gifted

How high is the IQ of a genius? Only 2 people out of 100 score above 130 on IQ tests. These bright individuals are usually described as "gifted." Less than one-half of one percent of the population scores above 140. These people are certainly gifted or perhaps even "geniuses." However, some psychologists reserve the term *genius* for people with even higher IQs or those who are exceptionally creative (Hallahan & Kauffman, 2006).

Gifted Children

Do high IQ scores in childhood predict later ability? To directly answer this question, Lewis Terman selected 1,500 children with IQs of 140 or more. Terman followed this gifted group (the "Termites" as he called them) into adulthood and found that most were quite successful. A majority finished college, earned advanced degrees, or held professional positions, and many had written books or scientific articles (Terman & Oden, 1959).

■ Table 8.3	**Distribution of Adult IQ Scores on WAIS-III**	
IQ	**Description**	**Percent**
Above 130	Very superior	2.2
120–129	Superior	6.7
110–119	Bright normal	16.1
90–109	Average	50.0
80–89	Dull normal	16.1
70–79	Borderline	6.7
Below 70	Mentally retarded	2.2

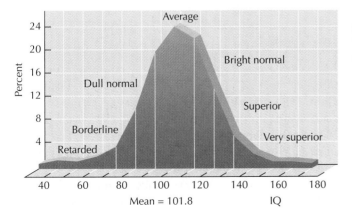

▶▶**FIGURE 8.2** Distribution of Stanford-Binet Intelligence Test scores for 3,184 children. (After Terman & Merrill, 1960.)

Normal curve A bell-shaped curve characterized by a large number of scores in a middle area, tapering to very few extremely high and low scores.

In general, the correlation between IQ scores and school grades is .50, a sizable association. The link would be even stronger, but motivation, special talents, off-campus learning, and many other factors also affect grades. The same is true of "real world" success beyond school. IQ is not at all good at predicting success in art, music, writing, dramatics, science, and leadership. Creativity is much more strongly related to doing well in these areas (Preckel, Holling, & Wiese, 2006; Runco, 2004). Regardless, when people score in the gifted range, their chances for high achievement do seem to rise (Shurkin, 1992).

Were all of the gifted children superior as adults? No. Some had committed crimes, were unemployable, or were emotionally troubled. Remember that a high IQ reveals potential. It does not guarantee success. Marilyn vos Savant, with an IQ of 230, has contributed little to science, literature, or art. Nobel prize–winning physicist Richard Feynman, whom many regarded as a genius, had an IQ of 122 (Michalko, 1998).

How did Terman's more successful Termites differ from the less successful? Most of them had educated parents who taught them to value learning. They also had *intellectual determination,* which is a desire to know, to excel, and to persevere (Winner, 2003). Thus, successful gifted persons tend to be persistent and motivated to learn. No one is paid to sit around being capable of achievement. What you do is always more important than what you should be able to do. That's why a child's talents are most likely to blossom when they are nurtured with support, encouragement, education, and effort (Callahan, 2006).

It is wise to remember that there are many ways in which a child may be gifted. Many schools now offer Gifted and Talented Education programs for students with a variety of special abilities—not just for those who score well on IQ tests.

Identifying Gifted Children

How might a parent spot an unusually bright child? Early signs of giftedness are not always purely "intellectual." **Giftedness** can be either the possession of a high IQ or special talents or aptitudes, such as creativity. Remember, Kim Peek is remarkably gifted *in some ways.*

The following signs may reveal that a child is gifted: A tendency to seek out older children and adults; an early fascination with explanations and problem solving; talking in complete sentences as early as 2 or 3 years of age; an unusually good memory; precocious talent in art, music, or number skills; an early interest in books, along with early reading (often by age 3); showing of kindness, understanding, and cooperation toward others (Alvino et al., 1996).

Notice that this list goes beyond straight g-factor, or "academic," intelligence. Children may be gifted in ways other than having a high IQ. In fact, if artistic talent, mechanical aptitude, musical aptitude, athletic potential, and so on, are considered, many children have a special "gift" of one kind or another. Limiting giftedness to high IQ can shortchange children with special talents. This is especially true of ethnic minority children, who may be the victims of subtle biases in standardized intelligence tests. These children, as well as children with physical disabilities, are less likely to be recognized as gifted (Ford & Moore, 2006; Robinson & Clinkenbeard, 1998).

Mental Retardation

A person with mental abilities far below average is termed **mentally retarded** or **developmentally disabled.** Retardation begins at an IQ of approximately 70 or below. However, a person's ability to perform *adaptive behaviors* (basic skills such as dressing, eating, communicating, shopping, and working) also figures into evaluating retardation (DSM-IV-TR, 2000; Hallahan & Kauffman, 2006). (See ▦ Table 8.4.)

It's important to realize that developmentally disabled persons have no handicap where feelings are concerned. They are easily hurt by rejection, teasing, or ridicule. Likewise, they respond warmly to love and acceptance. Mentally retarded persons have a right to self-respect

Giftedness Either the possession of a high IQ or special talents or aptitudes.

Mental retardation (developmentally disabled) The presence of a developmental disability, a formal IQ score below 70, or a significant impairment of adaptive behavior.

■ Table 8.4	Levels of Mental Retardation		
IQ range	Degree of Retardation	Educational Classification	Required Level of Support
50–55 to 70	Mild	Educable	Intermittent
35–40 to 50–55	Moderate	Trainable	Limited
20–25 to 35–40	Severe	Dependent	Extensive
Below 20–25	Profound	Life support	Pervasive

Sources: DSM-IV-TR, 2000; Luckasson et al., 2002.

and a place in the community (AAMR, 2004). This is especially important during childhood, when support from others adds greatly to the person's chances of becoming a well-adjusted member of society.

Causes of Retardation

What causes mental retardation? About half of all cases of mental retardation are *organic,* or related to physical disorders (Das, 2000). These include *fetal damage* (prenatal damage from teratogens such as disease, infection, or drugs) and *birth injuries* (such as lack of oxygen during delivery). *Metabolic disorders,* which affect energy production and use in the body, also cause retardation. Some forms of retardation are linked to *genetic abnormalities,* such as missing genes, extra genes, or defective genes. Malnutrition and exposure to lead, PCBs, and other toxins early in childhood can also cause organic retardation (Beirne-Smith, Patton, & Shannon, 2006).

Stan Godlew*ski*

These youngsters are participants in the Special Olympics—an athletic event for the mentally retarded. It is often said of the Special Olympics that "everyone is a winner—participants, coaches, and spectators."

In 30 to 40 percent of cases, no known biological problem can be identified. In many such instances, the degree of retardation is mild, in the 50 to 70 IQ range. Often, other family members are also mildly retarded. *Familial retardation,* as this is called, occurs mostly in very poor households where nutrition, intellectual stimulation, medical care, and emotional support may be inadequate. This suggests that familial retardation is based largely on an impoverished environment. Thus, better nutrition, education, and early childhood enrichment programs could prevent many cases of retardation (Beirne-Smith, Patton, & Shannon, 2006).

QUESTIONING INTELLIGENCE—HOW INTELLIGENT ARE INTELLIGENCE TESTS?

>SURVEY QUESTION< *What are some controversies in the study of intelligence?*

Defining intelligence as a g-factor (general ability) has been controversial. As we noted earlier in our discussion of "intelligent" behavior in other cultures, there are many ways to be smart. For example, consider William, a grade-school student two years behind in reading, who shows his teacher how to solve a difficult computer-programming problem. Or what about his classmate, Malika, who is poor in math but plays intricate pieces of piano music? Both of these children show clear signs of intelligence. And yet, each might score below average on a traditional IQ test. And, as we have seen, autistic savants like Kim Peek have even more extreme intellectual strengths and weaknesses. Such observations have convinced many psychologists that it is time to forge new, broader definitions of intelligence. Their basic goal is to better predict "real-world" success—not just the likelihood of success in school (Sternberg & Grigorenko, 2006).

According to Howard Gardner's theory, bodily-kinesthetic skills reflect one of eight distinct types of intelligence.

Multiple Intelligences

One such psychologist is Howard Gardner of Harvard University. Gardner (2003, 2004) theorizes that there are actually eight distinctly different kinds of intelligence. These are different mental "languages" that people use for thinking. Each is listed below, with examples of pursuits that make use of them.

1. *language* (linguistic abilities)—writer, lawyer, comedian
2. *logic and math* (numeric abilities)—scientist, accountant, programmer
3. *visual and spatial thinking* (pictorial abilities)—engineer, inventor, artist
4. *music* (musical abilities)—composer, musician, music critic
5. *bodily-kinesthetic skills* (physical abilities)—dancer, athlete, surgeon
6. *intrapersonal skills* (self-knowledge)—poet, actor, minister
7. *interpersonal skills* (social abilities)—psychologist, teacher, politician
8. *naturalist skills* (an ability to understand the natural environment)—biologist, medicine man, organic farmer

To simplify a great deal, people can be "word smart," "number smart," "picture smart," "musically smart," "body smart," "self smart," "people smart," and/or "nature smart."

Most of us are probably strong in only a few types of intelligence. In contrast, geniuses like Albert Einstein seem to be able to use nearly all of the intelligences, as needed, to solve problems.

If Gardner's theory of **multiple intelligences** is correct, traditional IQ tests measure only a part of real-world intelligence—namely, linguistic, logical-mathematical, and spatial abilities. A further implication is that our schools may be wasting a lot of human potential (Campbell, Campbell, & Dickinson, 2003). For example, some children might find it easier to learn math or reading if these topics were tied into art, music, dance, drama, and so on. Already, many schools are using Gardner's theory to cultivate a wider range of skills and talents (Gardner, 2002; Campbell, Campbell, & Dickinson, 2003). Before we return to human intelligence, let's see what we can learn from some smart machines.

Artificial Intelligence: I Compute, Therefore I Am

How smart are computers and robots? Just as people like Kim Peek challenge our understanding of general intelligence, so too does the difficulty of creating intelligent machines. Let's say you are exchanging instant messages over the Internet with someone you don't know. You are allowed to make any comments and ask any questions you like, for as long as you like. In reality, the "person" you are communicating with is a computer. Do you think a computer could fool you into believing it was human? If it did, wouldn't that qualify it as "intelligent"? You may be surprised to learn that, to date, no machine has come close to passing this test (Moor, 2001).

The problem computers face is that we humans can mentally "shift gears" from one topic to another with incredible flexibility. In contrast, machine "intelligence" is currently "blind" outside its underlying set of rules. As a tiny example, u cann understnd wrds thet ar mizpeld. Computers are very literal and easily stymied by such errors.

Regardless, artificial intelligence has been successful at very specific tasks. **Artificial intelligence (AI)** usually refers to computer programs capable of doing things that require intelligence when done by people (Russell & Norvig, 2003). For example, listeners sometimes mistake music created by Kemal Ebcioglu for that written by Johann Sebastian Bach, the eighteenth-century German composer. Ebcioglu wrote a computer program that creates harmonies remarkably similar to Bach's. By analyzing Bach's music, Ebcioglu came up with 350 rules that govern harmonization. The result is a program that displays artificial intelligence in a specific area.

Much of current artificial intelligence is based on the fact that many tasks—from harmonizing music to diagnosing disease—can be reduced to a set of rules applied to a col-

Multiple intelligences Howard Gardner's theory that there are several specialized types of intellectual ability.

Artificial intelligence Any artificial system (often a computer program) that is capable of human-like problem solving or intelligent responding.

lection of information. AI is valuable in situations where speed, vast memory, and persistence are required. In fact, AI programs are better at some tasks than humans are. An example is world chess champion Garry Kasparov's loss, in 1997, to a computer called Deep Blue.

AI and Cognition

Although AI is a long way from duplicating general human intelligence, artificial intelligence offers a way to probe some of our specific cognitive skills, or intelligences. For instance, computer simulations and expert systems provide good examples of how AI is being used as a research tool.

Computer simulations are programs that attempt to duplicate specific human behaviors, especially thinking, decision making, or problem solving. Here, the computer acts as a "laboratory" for testing models of cognition. If a computer program behaves as humans do (including making the same errors), then the program may be a good model of how we think.

Expert systems are computer programs that respond as a human expert would. They have demystified some human abilities by converting complex skills into clearly stated rules a computer can follow. Expert systems can predict the weather, analyze geological formations, diagnose disease, play chess, read, tell when to buy or sell stocks, and perform many other tasks.

Eventually, AI will almost certainly lead to robots that recognize voices and that speak and act "intelligently" in specific areas of ability. To achieve this, should intelligence be directly programmed into computers? Or should computers be designed to learn from experience, like the human brain does (McClelland & Rogers, 2003)? Only time will tell. For now, it's interesting to note that these questions mirror another area of controversy—whether or not human intelligence is inherited.

Two composers. The one on the left was a genius who wrote sublime, multi-voiced harmonies. The one on the right has created reasonably good, if uninspired, music. Computer models of thought can approximate intelligent human behavior. However, rule-based computer "thinking" still lacks the flexibility, creativity, and common sense of human intelligence.

Heredity, Environment, and Intelligence

Most people are aware that there is a moderate similarity in the intelligence of parents and their children, or between brothers and sisters. As ►Figure 8.3 shows, the similarity in IQ scores among relatives grows in proportion to how close they are on the family tree.

Does that indicate that intelligence is hereditary? Not necessarily. Brothers, sisters, and parents share similar environments as well as similar heredity. To separate nature and nurture, **twin studies** may be done. Such studies compare the IQs of twins who were raised together or separated at birth. This allows us to estimate how much heredity and environment affect intelligence.

Twin Studies

Notice in ►Figure 8.3 that the IQs of fraternal twins are more alike than the IQs of ordinary siblings. *Fraternal twins* come from two separate eggs fertilized at the same time. Genetically, they are no more alike than ordinary siblings. Why, then, should the twins' IQs be more similar? The reason is environmental: Parents treat twins more alike than ordinary siblings, resulting in a closer match in IQs.

More striking similarities are observed with *identical twins*, who develop from a single egg and have identical genes. At the top of ►Figure 8.3 you can see that identical twins who grow up in the same family have highly correlated IQs. This is what we would expect with identical heredity and very similar environments. Now, let's consider what happens when identical twins are reared apart. As you can see, the correlation drops, but only from .86 to

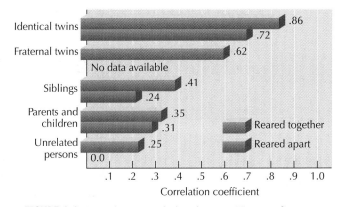

►►**FIGURE 8.3** Approximate correlations between IQ scores for persons with varying degrees of genetic and environmental similarity. Notice that the correlations grow smaller as the degree of genetic similarity declines. Also note that a shared environment increases the correlation in all cases. (Estimates from Bouchard, 1983; Henderson, 1982.)

Twin study A comparison of the characteristics of twins who were raised together or separated at birth; used to identify the relative impact of heredity and environment.

You Mean Video Games Might Be Good for Me?

While rapidly rising Western IQ scores suggest that environmental factors influence intelligence (Schooler, 1998), we are left with the question, Which factors? Writer Steven Johnson (2005) believes that contemporary culture is responsible. Although he agrees that much popular media content is too violent or sexual in nature (see Chapter 6, "You Mean Video Games Might Be Bad for Me?"), he points out that video games, the Internet, and even television are becoming more complex. As a result, they demand ever-greater cognitive effort from us. In other words, it is as important to understand *how* we experience the environment as it is to understand *what* we experience.

For example, early video games, such as *Pong* or *Pac Man*, offered simple, repetitive visual experiences. In contrast, today's popular games, such as *The World of Warcraft* or *The Sims*, offer rich, complicated experiences that can take many hours of intense problem solving to complete. Furthermore, players must usually figure out the rules by themselves. Instructions that fans have written for popular games are typically much longer than chapters in this book. Only a complex and engaging game would prompt players to use such instructions, much less write them for others to use (Johnson, 2005).

According to Johnson, other forms of popular culture have also become more complex, including the Internet, computer software, and even popular television. For example, compared with television dramas of the past, modern dramas weave plot lines and characters through an entire season of programs. In the end, popular culture may well be inviting us to read, reflect, and problem-solve more than ever before.

.72. Psychologists who emphasize genetics believe these figures show that adult intelligence is roughly 50 percent hereditary (Grigorenko & Sternberg, 2003).

How do environmentalists interpret the figures? They point out that the IQs of some separated twins differ by as much as 20 points. Such IQ gaps occur when the twins grow up with big educational and environmental differences. It is more common for separated twins to be placed in homes socially and educationally similar to their biological parents. This fact would tend to inflate apparent genetic effects by making the separated twins' IQs more alike. Another frequently overlooked fact is that twins grow up in the same environment *before birth* (in the womb). If we take such environmental similarities into account, intelligence would seem to be less than 50 percent hereditary (Devlin, Daniels, & Roeder, 1997; Turkheimer et al., 2003).

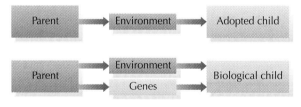

▸▸**FIGURE 8.4** Comparison of an adopted child and a biological child reared in the same family. (After Kamin, 1981.)

IQ and Environment

How much can environment alter intelligence? Strong evidence for an environmental view of intelligence comes from adoption studies. Consider families having one adopted child and one biological child. As ▸▸Figure 8.4 shows, parents contribute genes *and* environment to their biological child. With an adopted child they contribute only environment. If intelligence is highly genetic, the IQs of biological children should be more like their parents' IQs than are the IQs of adopted children. However, one study found that children reared by the same mother tend to resemble her IQ to the same degree. It does not matter whether or not they share her genes (Kamin, 1981; Weinberg, 1989).

In another study, striking increases in IQ occurred in 25 children who were moved from an orphanage and were eventually adopted by parents who gave them love, a family, and a stimulating home environment. Once considered mentally retarded and unadoptable, the children gained an average of 29 IQ points. A second group of initially less "retarded" children, who stayed in the orphanage, *lost* an average of 26 IQ points (Skeels, 1966)!

A particularly dramatic environmental effect is the fact that Westernized nations have shown average IQ gains of 15 points during the last 30 years (Dickens & Flynn, 2001). These IQ boosts occurred in far too short a time for genetics to explain them. It is more likely that the gains reflect environmental forces, such as improved education, nutrition, and living in a technologically complex society (Johnson, 2005). If you've ever tried to play a computer game or set up a wireless network in your home, you'll understand why people may be getting better at answering IQ test questions. (See "You Mean Video Games Might Be Good for Me?")

Summary

In the final analysis, intelligence reflects development as well as potential, nurture as well as nature (Grigorenko, 2005). Moreover, the fact that intelligence is partly determined by heredity tells us little of any real value. Genes are fixed at birth. Improving the environments in which children learn and grow is the main way in which we can assure that they reach their full potential (Grigorenko & Sternberg, 2003).

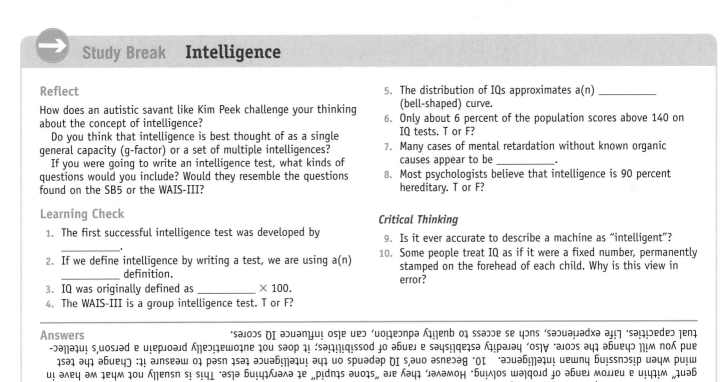

→ Study Break Intelligence

Reflect

How does an autistic savant like Kim Peek challenge your thinking about the concept of intelligence?

Do you think that intelligence is best thought of as a single general capacity (g-factor) or a set of multiple intelligences?

If you were going to write an intelligence test, what kinds of questions would you include? Would they resemble the questions found on the SB5 or the WAIS-III?

Learning Check

1. The first successful intelligence test was developed by _____.
2. If we define intelligence by writing a test, we are using a(n) _____ definition.
3. IQ was originally defined as _____ × 100.
4. The WAIS-III is a group intelligence test. T or F?

5. The distribution of IQs approximates a(n) _____ (bell-shaped) curve.
6. Only about 6 percent of the population scores above 140 on IQ tests. T or F?
7. Many cases of mental retardation without known organic causes appear to be _____.
8. Most psychologists believe that intelligence is 90 percent hereditary. T or F?

Critical Thinking

9. Is it ever accurate to describe a machine as "intelligent"?
10. Some people treat IQ as if it were a fixed number, permanently stamped on the forehead of each child. Why is this view in error?

Answers

1. Alfred Binet 2. operational 3. MA/CA 4. F 5. normal 6. F 7. familial 8. F 9. Rule-driven expert systems may appear "intelligent" within a narrow range of problem solving. However, they are "stone stupid" at everything else. This is usually not what we have in mind when discussing human intelligence. 10. Because one's IQ depends on the intelligence test used to measure it: Change the test and you will change the score. Also, heredity establishes a range of possibilities; it does not automatically preordain a person's intellectual capacities. Life experiences, such as access to quality education, can also influence IQ scores.

WHAT IS COGNITION?—THINK!

>SURVEY QUESTION< *What is the nature of thought?*

Human intelligence allows us to be highly adaptable creatures. We live in deserts, jungles, mountains, frenzied cities, placid retreats, and even space stations. Unlike other species, our success owes more to thinking abilities than it does to physical strength or speed (Solso, MacLin, & MacLin, 2005). Let's see how concepts, language, and mental images make intelligence and thinking possible.

Cognition refers to mentally processing information. Our thoughts take many forms, including daydreaming, problem solving, and reasoning (to name but a few). Although thinking is not limited to humans, imagine trying to teach an animal to match the feats of Shakuntala Devi, who once set a "world's record" for mental calculation by multiplying two 13-digit numbers (7,686,369,774,870 times 2,465,099,745,779) in her head, giving the answer in 28 seconds. (That's 18,947,668,104,042,434,089,403,730 if you haven't already figured it out.)

Cognition The process of thinking or mentally processing information (images, concepts, words, rules, and symbols).

The power of thought is beautifully expressed by Stephen W. Hawking, a theoretical physicist and one of the best-known scientific minds of modern times. Hawking has suffered since age 13 from Lou Gehrig's disease. Today, he can only control his left hand, and he cannot speak. Nevertheless, his brain remains fiercely active. With courage and determination, he has used his intellect to advance our understanding of the universe.

AP/Wide World Photo

Some Basic Units of Thought

At its most basic, thinking is an *internal representation* (mental expression) of a problem or situation. (Picture a chess player who mentally tries out several moves before actually touching a chess piece.) The power of being able to mentally represent problems is dramatically illustrated by chess grand master Miguel Najdorf, who once simultaneously played 45 chess games, while blindfolded. How did Najdorf do it? Like most people, he used the basic units of thought: images, concepts, and language (or symbols). **Images** are picture-like mental representations. **Concepts** are ideas that represent categories of objects or events. **Language** consists of words or symbols, and rules for combining them. Thinking often involves all three units. For example, blindfolded chess players rely on visual images, concepts ("Game 2 begins with a strategy called an English opening"), and the notational system, or "language," of chess.

In a moment we will delve further into imagery, concepts, and language. Be aware, however, that thinking involves attention, pattern recognition, memory, decision-making, intuition, knowledge, and more. The rest of this chapter is just a sample of what cognitive psychology is about.

MENTAL IMAGERY—DOES A FROG HAVE LIPS?

>SURVEY QUESTION< *In what ways are images related to thinking?*

Almost everyone has visual and auditory images. More than half have imagery for movement, touch, taste, smell, and pain. Thus, mental images are sometimes more than just "pictures." For example, your image of a bakery may also include its delicious odor. Most of us use images to think, remember, and solve problems. For instance, we may use mental images to (Kosslyn et al., 1990):

- Make a decision or solve a problem (choosing what clothes to wear; figuring out how to arrange furniture in a room).
- Change feelings (thinking of pleasant images to get out of a bad mood; imagining yourself as thin to stay on a diet).
- Improve a skill or to prepare for some action (using images to improve a swimming stroke; mentally rehearsing how you will ask for a raise).
- Aid memory (picturing Mr. Cook wearing a chef's hat, so you can remember his name).

The Nature of Mental Images

Image Most often, a mental representation that has picture-like qualities; an icon.

Concept An idea representing a category of related objects or events.

Language Words or symbols, and rules for combining them, that are used for thinking and communication.

Mental images are not flat, like photographs. Researcher Stephen Kosslyn showed this by asking people, Does a frog have lips and a stubby tail? Unless you often kiss frogs, you will probably tackle this question by using mental images. Most people picture a frog, "look" at its mouth, and then mentally "rotate" the frog in mental space to check its tail (Kosslyn, 1983). Mental rotation is partly based on imagined movements (▶▶ Fig. 8.5). That is, we mentally "pick up" an object and turn it around (Wraga et al., 2005).

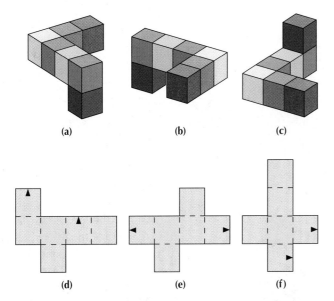

▸▸**FIGURE 8.5** Imagery in thinking. *(Top)* Subjects were shown a drawing similar to *(a)* and drawings of how *(a)* would look in other positions, such as *(b)* and *(c)*. Subjects could recognize *(a)* after it had been "rotated" from its original position. However, the more *(a)* was rotated in space, the longer it took to recognize it. This result suggests that people actually formed a three-dimensional image of *(a)* and rotated the image to see if it matched. (Shepard, 1975.) *(Bottom)* Try your ability to manipulate mental images: Picture each of these shapes as a piece of paper that can be folded to make a cube. After they have been folded, on which cubes do the arrow tips meet? (After Kosslyn, 1985.)

"Reverse Vision"

What happens in the brain when a person has visual images? Seeing something in your "mind's eye" is similar to seeing real objects. Information from the eyes normally activates the brain's primary visual area, creating an image (▸▸ Fig. 8.6). Other brain areas then help us recognize the image by relating it to stored knowledge. When you form a mental image, the system works in reverse. Brain areas where memories are stored send signals back to the visual cortex, where once again, an image is created (Ganis, Thompson, & Kosslyn, 2004; Kosslyn, 2005). For example, if you visualize a friend's face right now, the area of your brain that specializes in perceiving faces will become more active (O'Craven & Kanwisher, 2000).

Using Mental Images

How are images used to solve problems? We use *stored images* (information from memory) to apply past experiences to problem solving. Let's say you are asked, "How many ways can you use an empty egg carton?" You might begin by picturing uses you have already seen, such as sorting buttons into a carton. To give more original answers, you will probably need to use *created* images, which are assembled or invented, rather than simply remembered. Thus, an artist may completely picture a proposed sculpture before beginning work. People with good imaging abilities tend to score higher on tests of creativity (Morrison & Wallace, 2001). In fact, Albert Einstein, Thomas Edison, Lewis Carroll, and many other of history's most original intellects relied heavily on imagery (West, 1991).

Does the "size" of a mental image affect thinking? To find out, first picture a cat sitting beside a housefly. Now try to "zoom in" on the cat's ears so you see them clearly. Next, picture a rabbit sitting beside an elephant. How quickly can you "see" the rabbit's front feet? Did it take longer than picturing the cat's ears?

When a rabbit is pictured with an elephant, the rabbit's image must be small because the elephant is large. Using such tasks, Stephen Kosslyn found that the smaller an image is, the harder it is to "see" its details. To put this finding to use, try forming oversized images of things you want to think about. For example, to understand electricity, picture the wires as

The Church of the Sacred Family in Barcelona, Spain, was designed by Antonio Gaudi. Could a person lacking mental imagery design such a masterpiece? Three people out of 100 find it impossible to produce mental images, and 3 out of 100 have very strong imagery. Most artists, architects, designers, sculptors, and filmmakers have excellent visual imagery.

▸▸**FIGURE 8.6** When you see a flower, its image is represented by activity in the primary visual area of the cortex, at the back of the brain. Information about the flower is also relayed to other brain areas. If you form a mental image of a flower, information follows a reverse path. The result, once again, is activation of the primary visual area.

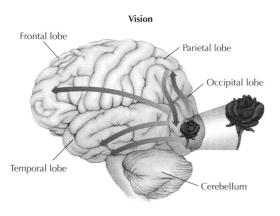

Vision

Frontal lobe

Parietal lobe

Occipital lobe

Temporal lobe

Cerebellum

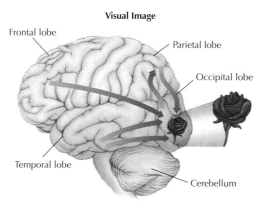

Visual Image

Frontal lobe

Parietal lobe

Occipital lobe

Temporal lobe

Cerebellum

Brian Bailey/Getty Images

A study found that rock climbers use kinesthetic imagery to learn climbing routes and to plan their next few moves (Smyth & Waller, 1998).

Concept formation The process of classifying information into meaningful categories.

large pipes with electrons the size of golf balls moving through them; to understand the human ear, explore it (in your mind's eye) like a large cave; and so forth.

Kinesthetic Imagery

Do muscular responses relate to thinking? In a sense, we think with our bodies as well as our heads. *Kinesthetic images* are created from muscular sensations (Holmes & Collins, 2001). Such images help us think about movements and actions.

As you think and talk, kinesthetic sensations can guide the flow of ideas. For example, if you try to tell a friend how to make bread, you may move your hands as if kneading the dough. Or, try answering this question: Which direction do you turn the hot-water handle in your kitchen to shut off the water? Most people haven't simply memorized the words "Turn it clockwise," or "Turn it counterclockwise." Instead you will probably "turn" the faucet in your imagination before answering. You may even make a turning motion with your hand before answering.

Kinesthetic images are especially important in music, sports, dance, skateboarding, martial arts, and other movement-oriented skills. People with good kinesthetic imagery learn such skills faster than those with poor imagery (Glisky, Williams, & Kihlstrom, 1996).

CONCEPTS—I'M POSITIVE, IT'S A WHATCHAMACALLIT

>SURVEY QUESTION< *How do we learn concepts?*

A concept is an idea that represents a category of objects or events. Concepts help us identify important features of the world. That's why experts in various areas of knowledge are good at classifying objects. Bird watchers, tropical fish fanciers, 5-year-old dinosaur enthusiasts, and other experts all learn to look for identifying details that beginners tend to miss. If you are knowledgeable about a topic, such as horses, flowers, or football, you literally see things differently than less well-informed people do (Johnson & Mervis, 1997).

Forming Concepts

How are concepts learned? **Concept formation** is the process of classifying information into meaningful categories (Ashby & Maddox, 2005). At its most basic, concept formation is based on experience with *positive* and *negative instances* (examples that belong, or do not belong, to the concept class). Concept formation is not as simple as it might seem. Imagine a child learning the concept of *dog.*

Dog Daze

A child and her father go for a walk. At a neighbor's house, they see a medium-sized dog. The father says, "See the dog." As they pass the next yard, the child sees a cat and says, "Dog!" Her father corrects her, "No, that's a *cat*." The child now

▸▸**FIGURE 8.7** When does a cup become a bowl or a vase? Deciding if an object belongs to a conceptual class is aided by relating it to a prototype, or ideal example. Subjects in one experiment chose number 5 as the "best" cup. (After Labov, 1973.)

thinks, "Aha, dogs are large and cats are small." In the next yard, she sees a Pekingese and says, "Cat!" "No, that's a dog," replies her father.

The child's confusion is understandable. At first she might even mistake a Pekingese for a dust mop. However, with more positive and negative instances, the child will eventually recognize everything from Great Danes to Chihuahuas as members of the same category—dogs.

As adults, we often acquire concepts by learning or forming rules. A **conceptual rule** is a guideline for deciding whether objects or events belong to a concept class. For example, a triangle must be a closed shape with three sides made of straight lines. Rules are an efficient way to learn concepts, but examples remain important. It's unlikely that memorizing rules would allow a new listener to accurately categorize *punk, hip-hop, fusion, salsa, metal, country,* and *rap* music.

Types of Concepts

Are there different kinds of concepts? Yes, **conjunctive concepts,** or "and concepts," are defined by the presence of two or more features. In other words, an item must have "this feature *and* this feature *and* this feature." For example, a *motorcycle* must have two wheels *and* an engine *and* handlebars.

Relational concepts are based on how an object relates to something else, or how its features relate to one another. All of the following are relational concepts: *larger, above, left, north,* and *upside down.* Another example is *sister,* which is defined as "a female considered in her relation to another person having the same parents."

Disjunctive concepts have *at least one* of several possible features. These are "either/or" concepts. To belong to the category, an item must have "this feature *or* that feature *or* another feature." For example, in baseball, a *strike* is *either* a swing and a miss *or* a pitch over the plate *or* a foul ball. The either/or quality of disjunctive concepts makes them hard to learn.

Prototypes

When you think of the concept *bird,* do you mentally list the features that birds have? Probably not. In addition to rules and features, we use **prototypes,** or ideal models, to identify concepts (Burnett et al., 2005; Rosch, 1977). A robin, for example, is a prototypical bird; an ostrich is not. In other words, some items are better examples of a concept than others are. Which of the drawings in ▸▸Figure 8.7 best represents a cup? At some point, as a cup grows taller or wider it becomes a vase or a bowl. How do we know when the line is crossed? Probably, we mentally compare objects to an "ideal" cup, like number 5. That's why it's hard to identify concepts when we can't come up with relevant prototypes. What, for example, are the objects shown in ▸▸Figure 8.8? As you can see, prototypes are especially helpful when we try to categorize complex stimuli (Minda & Smith, 2001).

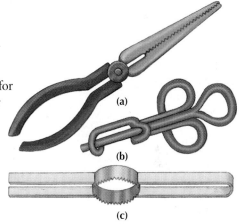

▸▸**FIGURE 8.8** Use of prototypes in concept identification. Even though its shape is unusual, item *(a)* can be related to a model (an ordinary set of pliers) and thus recognized. But what are items *(b)* and *(c)*? If you don't recognize them, look ahead to Figure 8.10. (After Bransford & McCarrell, 1977.)

Conceptual rule A formal rule for deciding if an object or event is an example of a particular concept.

Conjunctive concept A class of objects that have two or more features in common. (For example, to qualify as an example of the concept an object must be both red and triangular.)

Relational concept A concept defined by the relationship between features of an object or between an object and its surroundings (for example, "greater than," "lopsided").

Disjunctive concept A concept defined by the presence of at least one of several possible features. (For example, to qualify an object must be either blue or circular.)

Prototype An ideal model used as a prime example of a particular concept.

▸▸**FIGURE 8.9** This is an example of Osgood's semantic differential. The connotative meaning of the word *jazz* can be established by rating it on the scales. Mark your own rating by placing dots or X's in the spaces. Connect the marks with a line; then have a friend rate the word and compare your responses. It might be interesting to do the same for *rock and roll, classical,* and *rap.* You also might want to try the word *psychology.* (From *Psychological Bulletin,* Vol. 49, No. 3, May 1952.)

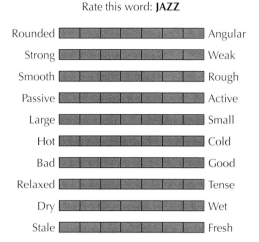

Rate this word: **JAZZ**

Rounded	Angular
Strong	Weak
Smooth	Rough
Passive	Active
Large	Small
Hot	Cold
Bad	Good
Relaxed	Tense
Dry	Wet
Stale	Fresh

▸▸**FIGURE 8.10** Context can substitute for a lack of appropriate prototypes in concept identification.

▸▸**FIGURE 8.11** Wine tasting illustrates the encoding function of language. To communicate their experiences to others, wine connoisseurs must put taste sensations into words. The wine you see here is "Marked by deeply concentrated nuances of plum, blackberry, and currant, with a nice balance of tannins and acid, building to a spicy oak finish." (Don't try this with a Pop-tart!)

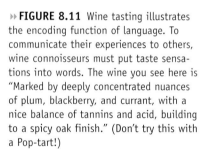

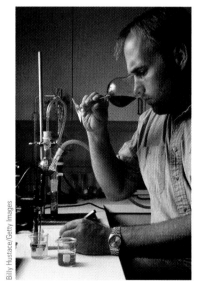

Billy Hustace/Getty Images

Denotative meaning The exact, dictionary definition of a word or concept; its objective meaning.

Connotative meaning The subjective, personal, or emotional meaning of a word or concept.

Semantics The study of meanings in words and language.

Connotative Meaning

Generally speaking, concepts have two types of meaning. The **denotative meaning** of a word or concept is its exact definition. The **connotative meaning** is its emotional or personal meaning. The denotative meaning of the word *naked* (having no clothes) is the same for a nudist as it is for a movie censor, but we could expect their connotations to differ. Connotative differences can influence how we think about important issues. For example, the term *enhanced radiation device* has a more positive connotation than *neutron bomb* does (Gruner & Tighe, 1995).

Can you clarify what a connotative meaning is? Yes, connotative meaning can be measured with a technique called the *semantic differential,* as shown in ▸▸Figure 8.9. When we rate words or concepts, most of their connotative meaning boils down to the dimensions *good/bad, strong/weak,* and *active/passive.* These dimensions give words very different connotations, even when their denotative meanings are similar. For example, I am *conscientious;* you are *careful;* he is *nitpicky!*

Faulty Concepts

Using inaccurate concepts often leads to thinking errors. For example, *social stereotypes* are oversimplified concepts of groups of people. Stereotypes about men, African Americans, women, conservatives, liberals, police officers, or other groups often muddle thinking about members of the group. A related problem is *all-or-nothing thinking* (one-dimensional thought). In this case, we classify things as absolutely right or wrong, good or bad, fair or unfair, black or white, honest or dishonest. Thinking this way prevents us from appreciating the subtleties of most life problems.

LANGUAGE—DON'T LEAVE HOME WITHOUT IT

>SURVEY QUESTION< *What is the role of language in thinking?*

As we have seen, thinking may occur without language. Everyone has searched for a word to express an idea that exists as a vague image or feeling. Nevertheless, most thinking relies heavily on language, because words *encode* (translate) the world into symbols that are easy to manipulate (▸▸Fig. 8.11).

The study of meaning in words and language is known as **semantics.** It is here that the link between language and thought becomes most evident. Suppose, on an intelligence test, you were asked to circle the word that does not belong in this series:

SKYSCRAPER CATHEDRAL TEMPLE PRAYER

If you circled *prayer,* you answered as most people do. Now try another problem, again circling the odd item:

CATHEDRAL PRAYER TEMPLE SKYSCRAPER

Bilingualism—*Si o No, Oui ou Non,* Yes or No?

Are there advantages to being able to speak more than one language? Definitely. **Bilingualism** is the ability to speak two languages. Studies have found that students who learn to speak two languages well have better mental flexibility, general language skills, control of attention, and problem-solving abilities (Craik & Bialystok, 2005).

Unfortunately, millions of minority American children who do not speak English at home experience *subtractive bilingualism.* Immersed in English-only classrooms, where they are expected to "sink or swim," they usually end up losing some of their native language skills. Such children risk becoming less than fully competent in *both* their first and second languages. In addition, they tend to fall behind educationally. As they struggle with English, their grasp of arithmetic, social studies, science, and other subjects may also suffer. In short, English-only instruction can leave them poorly prepared to succeed in the majority culture (Genesee, Paradis, & Crago, 2004; Matthews & Matthews, 2004).

For majority group children, the picture can be quite different, because learning a second language is almost always beneficial. It poses no threat to the child's home language and improves a variety of cognitive skills. This has been called *additive bilingualism* because learning a second language adds to a child's overall competence (Hinkel, 2005).

An approach called **two-way bilingual education** offers a way to retain the benefits of bilingualism and avoid its drawbacks (Lessow-Hurley, 2005). In such programs native speakers and children with limited English skills are taught part of the day in English and part in a second language. Both native and minority language speakers become fluent in two languages and they perform as well or better than single-language students in English and general academic abilities.

Then why isn't two-way bilingual education more widely used? Bilingual education tends to be politically unpopular among majority language speakers. Language is a major sign of group membership. Even where the majority culture is highly dominant, some of its members may feel that recent immigrants and "foreign languages" are eroding their culture. Regardless, an ability to think and communicate in a second language is a wonderful gift.

Did you circle *skyscraper* this time? The new order subtly alters the meaning of the last word (Carroll, 2004). This occurs because words get much of their meaning from *context.* For example, the word *shot* means different things when we are thinking of marksmanship, bartending, medicine, photography, or golf (Miller, 1999).

Semantics affect thinking when the words we use alter meaning: Has one country's army "invaded" another? Or "effected a protective incursion"? Would you rather eat "medium rare prime beef" or "bloody slab of dead cow"?! More subtle effects also occur. For example, most people have difficulty quickly naming the color of the ink used to print the words in the bottom two rows of ▶▶Figure 8.12. The word meanings are just too strong to ignore.

Language also plays a major role in defining ethnic communities and other social groups. Thus, language can be a bridge or a barrier between cultures. Translating languages can cause a rash of semantic problems. Perhaps the San Jose, California, public library can be excused for displaying a large banner that was supposed to say "You are welcome" in a native Philippine language. The banner actually said "You are circumcised." However, in more important situations, such as in international business and diplomacy, avoiding semantic confusion may be vital (see "Bilingualism").

The Structure of Language

What does it take to make a language? First, a language must provide *symbols* that stand for objects and ideas (Jay, 2003). The symbols we call words are built out of **phonemes** (FOE-neems: basic speech sounds) and **morphemes** (MOR-feems: speech sounds collected into meaningful units, such as syllables or words). For instance, in English the sounds *m, b, w,* and *a* cannot form a syllable *mbwa.* In Swahili, they can. (Also, see ▶▶Fig. 8.13.)

Next, a language must have a **grammar,** or set of rules for making sounds into words and words into sentences. One part of grammar, known as **syntax,** concerns rules for word order. Syntax is important because rearranging words almost always changes the meaning of a sentence: "Dog bites man" versus "Man bites dog."

PURPLE	**BLUE**	**GREEN**	**GREEN**
RED	**PURPLE**	**GREEN**	**GREEN**

▶▶**FIGURE 8.12** The Stroop interference task. Test yourself by naming the colors in the top two rows as quickly as you can. Then name the colors of the *ink* used to print the words in the bottom two rows (do not read the words themselves). Was it harder to name the ink colors in the bottom rows? (After MacLeod, 2005.)

Bilingualism An ability to speak two languages.

Two-way bilingual education A program in which English-speaking children and children with limited English proficiency are taught half the day in English and half in a second language.

Phonemes The basic speech sounds of a language.

Morphemes The smallest meaningful units in a language, such as syllables or words.

Grammar A set of rules for combining language units into meaningful speech or writing.

Syntax Rules for ordering words when forming sentences.

Albanian	mak, mak
Chinese	gua, gua
Dutch	rap, rap
English	quack, quack
French	coin, coin
Italian	qua, qua
Spanish	cuá, cuá
Swedish	kvack, kvack
Turkish	vak, vak

➤➤ **FIGURE 8.13** Animals around the world make pretty much the same sounds. Notice, however, how various languages use slightly different phonemes to express the sound a duck makes.

Guy Edwardes/Getty Images

Traditional grammar is concerned with "surface" language—the sentences we actually speak. Linguist Noam Chomsky has focused instead on the unspoken rules we use to change core ideas into various sentences. Chomsky (1986) believes that we do not learn all the sentences we might ever say. Rather, we actively *create* them by applying **transformation rules** to universal, core patterns. We use these rules to change a simple declarative sentence to other voices or forms (past tense, passive voice, and so forth). For example, the core sentence "Dog bites man" can be transformed to these patterns (and others as well):

Past: The dog bit the man.
Passive: The man was bitten by the dog.
Negative: The dog did not bite the man.
Question: Did the dog bite the man?

Children seem to be using transformation rules when they say things such as "I runned home." That is, the child applied the normal past tense rule to the irregular verb *to run*.

A true language is also *productive*—it can generate new thoughts or ideas. In fact, words can be rearranged to produce a nearly infinite number of sentences. Some are silly: "Please don't feed me to the goldfish." Some are profound: "We hold these truths to be self-evident, that all men are created equal." In either case, the productive quality of language makes it a powerful tool for thinking.

Gestural Languages

Contrary to common belief, language is not limited to speech. Consider the case of Ildefonso, a young man who was born deaf. At age 24, Ildefonso had never communicated with another human, except by mime. Then at last, Ildefonso had a breakthrough: After much hard work with a sign language teacher, he understood the link between a cat and the gesture for it. At that magic moment, he grasped the idea that "cat" could be communicated to another person, just by signing the word.

American Sign Language (ASL), a gestural language, made Ildefonso's long-awaited breakthrough possible. ASL is not pantomime or a code. It is a true language, like German, Spanish, or Japanese (Liddell, 2003). In fact, those who use other gestural languages, such as French Sign, Chinese Sign, or Old Kentish Sign, do not understand ASL.

Although ASL has a *spatial* grammar, syntax, and semantics all its own (➤➤ Fig. 8.14), both speech and signing follow similar universal language patterns. Signing children pass through

Look at   **Stare**

 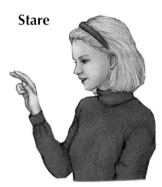

➤➤ **FIGURE 8.14** ASL has only 3,000 root signs, compared with roughly 600,000 words in English. However, variations in signs make ASL a highly expressive language. For example, the sign LOOK-AT can be varied in ways to make it mean look at me, look at her, look at each, stare at, gaze, watch, look for a long time, look at again and again, reminisce, sightsee, look forward to, predict, anticipate, browse, and many more variations.

Transformation rules Rules by which a simple declarative sentence may be changed to other voices or forms (past tense, passive voice, and so forth).

the stages of language development at about the same age as speaking children do. Some psychologists now believe that speech evolved from gestures, far back in human history (Corballis, 2002). Do you ever make hand gestures when you are speaking on the phone? If so, you may be displaying a remnant of the gestural origins of language. Perhaps that's also why the same brain areas become more active when a person speaks or signs (Emmorey et al., 2003).

Sign languages naturally arise out of a need to communicate visually. But they also embody a personal identity and define a distinct community. Those who "speak" sign share not just a language but a rich culture as well (Singleton & Newport, 2004).

Infants can express the idea "pick me up" in gestures before they can make the same request in words. Their progression from gestures to speech may mirror the evolution of human language abilities (Stokoe, 2001).

The Animal Language Debate

Do animals use language? Animals do communicate. The cries, gestures, and mating calls of animals have broad meanings immediately understood by other animals of the same species (Searcy & Nowicki, 2005). For the most part, however, natural animal communication is quite limited. Even apes and monkeys make only a few dozen distinct cries, which carry messages such as "attack," "flee," or "food here." More important, animal communication lacks the productive quality of human language. For example, when a monkey gives an "eagle distress call," it means something like, "I see an eagle." The monkey has no way of saying, "I don't see an eagle," or "Thank heavens that wasn't an eagle," or "That sucker I saw yesterday was some huge eagle" (Pinker & Jackendoff, 2005). Let's consider some of psychology's successes and failures in trying to teach animals to use language.

Talking Chimps

Early attempts to teach chimps to talk were a dismal failure. The world record was held by Viki, a chimp who could say only four words (*mama, papa, cup,* and *up*) after 6 years of intensive training (Fleming, 1974; Hayes, 1951). (Actually, all four words sounded something like a belch.) Then there was a breakthrough. Beatrix and Allen Gardner used operant conditioning and imitation to teach a female chimp named Washoe to use American Sign Language. Washoe was soon able to put together primitive sentence strings like "Come-gimme sweet," "Out please," "Gimme tickle," and "Open food drink." At her peak, Washoe could construct six-word sentences and use about 240 signs (Gardner & Gardner, 1989).

A chimp named Sarah was another well-known pupil of human language. David Premack taught Sarah to use 130 "words" consisting of plastic chips arranged on a magnetized board (▶Fig. 8.15). From the beginning of her training, Sarah was required to use proper word order. She learned to answer questions; to label things "same" or "different"; to classify objects by color, shape, and size; and to form compound sentences (Premack & Premack, 1983). One of Sarah's top achievements was her use of conditional sentences. A *conditional statement* contains a qualification, often in the if/then form: "If Sarah take apple, then Mary give Sarah chocolate." "If Sarah take banana, then Mary no give Sarah chocolate" (▶Fig. 8.16).

Can it be said with certainty that the chimps understand such interchanges? Most researchers working with chimps believe that they have indeed communicated with them. Especially striking are the chimps' spontaneous responses. Washoe once "wet" on psychologist Roger Fouts's back while riding on his shoulders. When Fouts asked, with some annoyance, why she had done it, Washoe signed, "It's funny!"

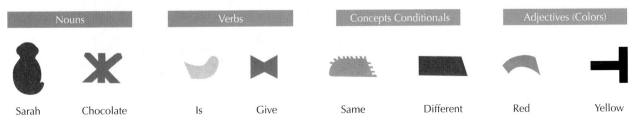

Nouns		Verbs		Concepts Conditionals		Adjectives (Colors)	
Sarah	Chocolate	Is	Give	Same	Different	Red	Yellow

▶▶**FIGURE 8.15** Here is a sample of some of the word-symbols that Sarah the chimpanzee used to communicate with humans. (After Premack & Premack, 1972.)

▸▸ **FIGURE 8.16** After reading the message "Sarah insert apple pail banana dish" on the magnetic board, Sarah performed the actions as directed. (From "Teaching Language to an Ape" by Ann J. Premack and David Premack. Copyright © 1972 by Scientific American, Inc. Reprinted by permission of Eric Mose, Jr.)

Criticisms

Such interchanges are impressive. But communication and real language usage are different things. Even untrained chimps use simple gestures to communicate with humans. For example, a chimp will point at a banana that is out of reach, while glancing back and forth between the banana and a person standing nearby (Leavens & Hopkins, 1998). (The meaning of the gesture is clear. The meaning of the exasperated look on the chimp's face is less certain, but it probably means, "Yes, give me the banana, you idiot.")

Also problems with syntax (word order) have plagued almost all animal language studies. For example, when a chimp named Nim Chimpsky (no relation to Noam Chomsky) wanted an orange, he would typically signal a grammarless string of words: "Give orange me give eat orange me eat orange give me eat orange give me you." This might be communication, but it is not language.

Lexigrams

More recently, Kanzi, a pygmy chimpanzee studied by Duane Rumbaugh and Sue Savage-Rumbaugh, has learned to communicate by pushing buttons on a computer keyboard. Each of the 250 buttons is marked with a *lexigram*, or geometric word-symbol (▸▸ Fig. 8.17). Using the lexigrams, Kanzi can create primitive sentences several words long. He can also understand about 650 spoken sentences. During testing, Kanzi hears spoken words over headphones, so his caretakers cannot visually prompt him (Savage-Rumbaugh & Lewin, 1996; Savage-Rumbaugh, Shanker, & Taylor, 1998).

Kanzi's sentences consistently follow correct word order. Like a child learning language, Kanzi picked up some rules from his caregivers (Segerdahl, Fields, & Savage-Rumbaugh, 2005). However, he has developed other patterns on his own. For example, Kanzi usually places action symbols in the order he wants to carry them out, such as "chase tickle" or "chase hide." In this respect, Kanzi's grammar is on a par with that of a 2-year-old child (Savage-Rumbaugh et al., 1993).

Kanzi's ability to invent a simple grammar may help us better understand the roots of human language. It is certainly the strongest answer yet to critics (Benson et al., 2002). On the other hand, Chomsky insists that if chimps were biologically capable of language they would use it on their own. Although the issue is far from resolved, such research may unravel the mysteries of language learning.

▸▸ **FIGURE 8.17** Kanzi's language learning has been impressive. He can comprehend spoken English words. He can identify lexigram symbols when he hears corresponding words. He can use lexigrams when the objects they refer to are absent, and he can, if asked, lead someone to the object. All these skills were acquired through observation, not conditioning (Savage-Rumbaugh et al., 1990).

Study Break   **Imagery, Concepts, and Language**

Reflect

Name some ways in which you have used imagery in the thinking you have done today.

Write a conceptual rule for the following idea: *unicycle*. Were you able to define the concept with a rule? Would positive and negative instances help make the concept clearer for others?

A true sports car has two seats, a powerful engine, good brakes, and excellent handling. What kind of concept is the term *sports car*? What do you think of as a prototypical sports car?

You must learn to communicate with an alien life form whose language cannot be reproduced by the human voice. Do you think it would be better to use a gestural language or lexigrams? Why?

Learning Check

1. List three primary units of thought:

   _____ _____

   _____

2. Our reliance on imagery in thinking means that problem solving is impaired by the use of language or symbols. T or F?

3. Humans appear capable of forming three-dimensional images that can be moved or rotated in mental space. T or F?

4. A *mup* is defined as anything that is small, blue, and hairy. *Mup* is a(n) _____ concept.

5. The connotative meaning of the word *naked* is "having no clothes." T or F?

6. True languages are _____ because they can be used to generate new possibilities.

7. The basic speech sounds are called _____; the smallest meaningful units of speech are called _____.

Critical Thinking

8. A Democrat and a Republican are asked to rate the word *democratic* on the semantic differential. Under what conditions would their ratings be most alike?

9. Chimpanzees and other apes are intelligent and entertaining animals. If you were doing language research with a chimp, what major problem would you have to guard against?

Answers

1. images, concepts, language or symbols (others could be listed)   2. F   3. T   4. conjunctive   5. F   6. productive   7. phonemes, morphemes   8. If they both assume the word refers to a form of government, not a political party or a candidate.   9. The problem of anthropomorphizing (ascribing human characteristics to animals) is especially difficult to avoid when researchers spend many hours "conversing" with chimps.

PROBLEM SOLVING—GETTING AN ANSWER IN SIGHT

>SURVEY QUESTION< *What do we know about problem solving?*

We all solve many problems every day. Problem solving can be as commonplace as figuring out how to make a nonpoisonous meal out of leftovers or as significant as developing a cure for cancer. How do we solve such problems? A good way to start a discussion of problem solving is to solve a problem. Give this one a try.

A famous ocean liner (the *Queen Latifah*) is steaming toward port at 20 miles per hour. The ocean liner is 50 miles from shore when a seagull takes off from its deck and flies toward port. At the same instant, a speedboat leaves port at 30 miles per hour. The bird flies back and forth between the speedboat and the *Queen Latifah* at a speed of 40 miles per hour. How far will the bird have flown when the two boats pass?

If you don't immediately see the answer to this problem, read it again. (The answer is revealed in the "Insightful Solutions" section.)

Mechanical Solutions

For routine problems, a **mechanical solution** may be adequate. Mechanical solutions are achieved by trial and error or by rote. If you forget the combination to your bike lock, you may be able to discover it by trial and error. In an era of high-speed computers, many trial-and-error solutions are best left to machines. A computer could generate all possible combinations of the five numbers on the lock in a split second. (Of course, it would take a long time to try them all.) When a problem is solved by *rote*, thinking is guided by an **algorithm,** or learned set of rules that always leads to a correct solution. A simple example of an algo-

Mechanical solution A problem solution achieved by trial and error or by a fixed procedure based on learned rules.

Algorithm A learned set of rules that always leads to the correct solution of a problem.

rithm is the steps needed to divide one number into another (by doing arithmetic, not by using a calculator).

If you have a good background in math, you may have solved the problem of the bird and the boats by rote. (Your authors hope you didn't. There is an easier solution.)

Solutions by Understanding

Many problems cannot be solved mechanically. In that case, **understanding** (deeper comprehension of a problem) is necessary. Try this problem:

> A person has an inoperable stomach tumor. A device is available that produces rays that at high intensity will destroy tissue (both healthy and diseased). How can the tumor be destroyed without damaging surrounding tissue? (Also see the sketch in ▸▸Fig. 8.18.)

What does this problem show about problem solving? German psychologist Karl Duncker gave college students this problem in a classic series of studies. Duncker asked them to think aloud as they worked. He found that successful students first had to discover the *general properties* of a correct solution. A **general solution** defines the requirements for success, but not in enough detail to guide further action. This phase was complete when students realized that the intensity of the rays had to be lowered on their way to the tumor. Then, in the second phase, they proposed a number of **functional** (workable) **solutions** and selected the best one (Dunker, 1945). (One solution is to focus weak rays on the tumor from several angles. Another is to rotate the person's body, to minimize exposure of healthy tissue.)

It might help to summarize with a more familiar example. Almost everyone who has tried the Rubik's cube puzzle begins at the mechanical, *trial-and-error level.* If you want to take the easy route, printed instructions are available that give the steps for a *rote* solution. In time, those who persist begin to *understand* the *general properties* of the puzzle. After that, they can solve it consistently.

Heuristics

"You can't get there from here," or so it often seems when facing a problem. Solving problems often requires a strategy. If the number of alternatives is small, a **random search strategy** may work. This is another example of trial-and-error thinking in which all possibilities are tried, more or less randomly. Imagine that you are traveling and you decide to look up an old friend, J. Smith, in a city you are visiting. You open the phone book and find 47 J. Smiths listed. Of course, you could dial each number until you find the right one. "Forget it," you say to yourself. "Is there any way I can narrow the search?" "Oh, yeah! I remember hearing that Janet lives by the beach." Then you take out a map and call only the numbers with addresses near the waterfront (Hunt & Ellis, 2004).

The approach used in this example is a **heuristic** (hew-RIS-tik: a strategy for identifying and evaluating problem solutions). Typically, a heuristic is a "rule of thumb" that *reduces the number of alternatives* thinkers must consider (Solso, MacLin, & MacLin, 2005). Although this raises the odds of success, it does not guarantee a solution. Here are some heuristic strategies that often work:

- Try to identify how the current state of affairs differs from the desired goal. Then find steps that will reduce the difference.
- Try working backward from the desired goal to the starting point or current state.
- If you can't reach the goal directly, try to identify an intermediate goal or subproblem that at least gets you closer.
- Represent the problem in other ways, with graphs, diagrams, or analogies, for instance.

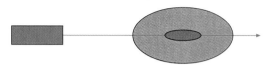

▸▸**FIGURE 8.18** A schematic representation of Duncker's tumor problem. The dark spot represents a tumor surrounded by healthy tissue. How can the tumor be destroyed without injuring surrounding tissue? (After Duncker, 1945.)

Understanding In problem solving, a deeper compression of the nature of the problem.

General solution A solution that correctly states the requirements for success but not in enough detail for further action.

Functional solution A detailed, practical, and workable solution.

Random search strategy Trying possible solutions to a problem in a more or less random order.

Heuristic Any strategy or technique that aids problem solving, especially by limiting the number of possible solutions to be tried.

Real Game

Black

White

Random Placement

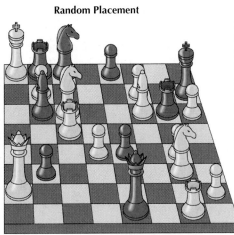

▶▶**FIGURE 8.19** The left chessboard shows a realistic game. The right chessboard is a random arrangement of pieces. Expert chess players can memorize the left board at a glance, yet they are no better than beginners at memorizing the random board. Expert performance at most thinking tasks is based on acquired strategies and knowledge. If you would like to excel at a profession or a mental skill, plan on adding to your knowledge every day (Solso, MacLin, & MacLin, 2005).

- Generate a possible solution and test it. Doing so may eliminate many alternatives, or it may clarify what is needed for a solution.

Experts and Novices

Experts are much more likely than novices to have heuristics available for solving problems. Research on chess masters, for example, shows that they are able to recognize *patterns* that suggest the best lines of play (Anderson, 2005). This helps eliminate a large number of possibilities. The chess master, therefore, doesn't waste time exploring bad moves. Experts are better able to see the true nature of problems and relate them to general principles (Anderson, 2005).

Expertise is based on specific *organized knowledge* (systematic information) and *acquired strategies* (learned tactics). In other words, becoming a star performer does not come from some general strengthening of the mind. Master chess players don't necessarily have better memories than beginners (except for realistic chess positions) (Gobet & Simon, 1996; Solso, MacLin, & MacLin, 2005). (See ▶▶Fig. 8.19.) And, typically, they don't explore more moves ahead than lesser players.

Insightful Solutions

A thinker who suddenly solves a problem has experienced **insight.** Insight is so rapid and clear that we may wonder why we didn't see the solution sooner (Schilling, 2005). Insights are usually based on reorganizing a problem. This allows us to see problems in new ways and makes their solutions seem obvious (Robertson, 2001).

Let's return now to the problem of the boats and the bird. The best way to solve it is by insight. Because the boats will cover the 50-mile distance in exactly 1 hour, and the bird flies 40 miles per hour, the bird will have flown 40 miles when the boats meet. No math is necessary if you have insight into this problem. ▶▶Figure 8.20 lists some additional insight problems you may want to try.

The Nature of Insight

Psychologists Robert Sternberg and Janet Davidson (1982) believe that insight involves three abilities. The first is *selective encoding,* which refers to selecting information that is relevant to a problem, while ignoring distractions. For example, consider the following problem:

If you have white socks and black socks in your drawer, mixed in the ratio of 4 to 5, how many socks will you have to take out to make sure of having a pair of the same color?

Insight A sudden mental reorganization of a problem that makes the solution obvious.

Water lilies

Problem: Water lilies growing in a pond double in area every 24 hours. On the first day of spring, only one lily pad is on the surface of the pond. Sixty days later, the pond is entirely covered. On what day is the pond half-covered?

Twenty dollars

Problem: Jessica and Blair both have the same amount of money. How much must Jessica give Blair so that Blair has $20 more than Jessica?

How many pets?

Problem: How many pets do you have if all of them are birds except two, all of them are cats except two, and all of them are dogs except two?

Between 2 and 3

Problem: What one mathematical symbol can you place between 2 and 3 that results in a number greater than 2 and less than 3?

One word

Problem: Rearrange the letters NEWDOOR to make one word.

▸▸**FIGURE 8.20**

A person who fails to recognize that "mixed in a ratio of 4 to 5" is irrelevant will be less likely to come up with the correct answer of 3 socks.

Insight also relies on *selective combination,* or bringing together seemingly unrelated bits of useful information. Try this sample problem:

> With a 7-minute hourglass and an 11-minute hourglass, what is the simplest way to time the boiling of an egg for 15 minutes?

▸▸**FIGURE 8.21** Solution to the hat rack problem.

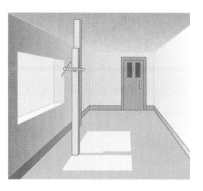

The answer requires using both hourglasses in combination. First, the 7-minute and the 11-minute hourglasses are started running. When the 7-minute hourglass runs out, it's time to begin boiling the egg. At this point, 4 minutes remain on the 11-minute hourglass. Thus, when it runs out it is simply turned over. When it runs out again, 15 minutes will have passed.

A third source of insights is *selective comparison.* This is the ability to compare new problems with old information or with problems already solved. A good example is the hat rack problem, in which subjects must build a structure that can support an overcoat in the middle of a room. Each person is given only two long sticks and a C-clamp to work with. The solution, shown in ▸▸Figure 8.21, is to clamp the two sticks together so that they are wedged between the floor and ceiling. If you were given this problem, you would be more likely to solve it if you first thought of how pole lamps are wedged between floor and ceiling.

Fixations

One of the most important barriers to problem solving is **fixation,** the tendency to get "hung up" on wrong solutions or to become blind to alternatives. Usually this occurs when we place unnecessary restrictions on our thinking (Isaak & Just, 1995). How, for example,

Fixation The tendency to repeat wrong solutions or faulty responses, especially as a result of becoming blind to alternatives.

could you plant four small trees so that each is an equal distance from all the others? (The answer is shown in ▸▸Fig. 8.22.)

A prime example of restricted thinking is **functional fixedness.** This is an inability to see new uses (functions) for familiar objects or for things that were used in a particular way (German & Barrett, 2005). If you have ever used a dime as a screwdriver, you've overcome functional fixedness.

How does functional fixedness affect problem solving? Karl Duncker illustrated the effects of functional fixedness by asking students to mount a candle on a vertical board so the candle could burn normally. Duncker gave each student three candles, some matches, some cardboard boxes, some thumbtacks, and other items. Half of Duncker's subjects received these items *inside* the cardboard boxes. The others were given all the items, including the boxes, spread out on a tabletop.

Duncker found that when the items were in the boxes, solving the problem was very difficult. Why? If students saw the boxes as *containers,* they didn't realize the boxes might be part of the solution. (If you haven't guessed the solution, check ▸▸Fig. 8.23.) Undoubtedly, we could avoid many fixations by being more flexible in categorizing the world (Langer, 2000). For instance, creative thinking could be facilitated in the container problem by saying "This *could be* a box," instead of "This *is* a box." When tested with the candle problem, 5-year-old children show no signs of functional fixedness. Apparently, this is because they have had less experience with the use of various objects. It is sometimes said that to be more creative, you should try to see the world without preconceptions, as if through the eyes of a child. In the case of functional fixedness that may actually be true (German & Defeyter, 2000).

▸▸**FIGURE 8.22** Four trees can be placed equidistant from one another by piling dirt into a mound. Three of the trees are planted equal distances apart around the base of the mound. The fourth tree is planted on the top of the mound. If you were fixated on arrangements that involve level ground, you may have been blind to this three-dimensional solution.

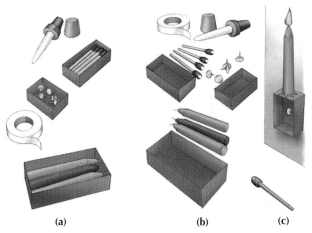

(a)   (b)   (c)

▸▸**FIGURE 8.23** Materials for solving the candle problem were given to subjects in boxes *(a)* or separately *(b)*. Functional fixedness caused by condition *(a)* interfered with solving the problem. The solution to the problem is shown in *(c)*.

Common Barriers to Problem Solving

Functional fixedness is just one of the mental blocks that prevent insight. Here's an example of another: A $5 bill is placed on a table and a stack of objects is balanced precariously on top of the bill. How can the bill be removed without touching or moving the objects? A good answer is to split the bill on one of its edges. Gently pulling from opposite ends will tear the bill in half and remove it without toppling the objects. Many people fail to see this solution because they have learned not to destroy money (Adams, 1988). Notice again the impact of placing something in a category, in this case, "things of value" (which should not be destroyed). Other common mental blocks can hinder problem solving, too, as listed here.

1. **Emotional barriers:** inhibition and fear of making a fool of oneself, fear of making a mistake, inability to tolerate ambiguity, excessive self-criticism
   Example: An architect is afraid to try an unconventional design because she fears that other architects will think it is frivolous.
2. **Cultural barriers:** values that hold that fantasy is a waste of time; that playfulness is for children only; that reason, logic, and numbers are good; that feelings, intuitions, pleasure, and humor are bad or have no value in the serious business of problem solving
   Example: A corporate manager wants to solve a business problem, but becomes stern and angry when members of his marketing team joke playfully about possible solutions.

■ Table 8.5   **Solutions to Insight Problems**

Water lilies: Day 59

Twenty dollars: $10

How many pets?: Three (one bird, one cat, and one dog)

Between 2 and 3: A decimal point

One word: ONE WORD (You may object that the answer is two words, but the problem called for the answer to be "one word," and it is.)

See Figure 8.20 for the problems.

Functional fixedness A rigidity in problem solving caused by an inability to see new uses for familiar objects.

3. **Learned barriers:** conventions about uses (functional fixedness), meanings, possibilities, taboos
   Example: A cook doesn't have any clean mixing bowls and fails to see that he could use a frying pan as a bowl.
4. **Perceptual barriers:** habits leading to a failure to identify important elements of a problem
   Example: A beginning artist concentrates on drawing a vase of flowers without seeing that the "empty" spaces around the vase are part of the composition, too.

 Study Break **Problem Solving**

Reflect

Identify at least one problem you have solved mechanically. Now identify a problem you solved by understanding. Did the second problem involve finding a general solution or a functional solution? Or both? What heuristics did you use to solve the problem? Would you consider yourself an expert or a novice in the solution of problems like the ones you just identified?

What is the best insightful solution you've ever come up with? Did it involve selective encoding, combination, or comparison?

Can you think of a time when you overcame functional fixedness to solve a problem?

Learning Check

1. Insight refers to rote, or trial-and-error, problem solving. T or F?
2. The first phase in problem solving by understanding is to discover the general properties of a correct solution. T or F?
3. Problem-solving strategies that guide the search for solutions are called _____.

4. A common element underlying insight is that information is encoded, combined, and compared

   a. mechanically
   b. by rote
   c. functionally
   d. selectively

5. The term *fixation* refers to the point at which a helpful insight becomes fixed in one's thinking. T or F?
6. Organized knowledge, acquired strategies, and the ability to recognize patterns are all characteristics of human expertise. T or F?

Critical Thinking

7. Do you think that it is true that "a problem clearly defined is a problem half solved"?
8. Sea otters select suitably sized rocks and use them to hammer shellfish loose for eating. They then use the rock to open the shell. Does this qualify as thinking?

Answers

1. F 2. T 3. heuristics 4. d 5. F 6. T 7. Although this might be an overstatement, it is true that clearly defining a starting point and the desired goal can serve as a heuristic in problem solving. 8. Psychologist Donald Griffin (1992) believes it does because thinking is implied by actions that appear to be planned with an awareness of likely results.

CREATIVE THINKING—DOWN ROADS LESS TRAVELED

>SURVEY QUESTION< *What is creative thinking?*

Original ideas have changed the course of human history. Much of what we now take for granted in art, medicine, music, technology, and science was once regarded as radical or impossible. How do creative thinkers achieve the breakthroughs that advance us into new realms? Creativity is elusive. Nevertheless, psychologists have learned a great deal about how creativity occurs and how to promote it.

We have seen that problem solving may be mechanical, insightful, or based on understanding. To this we can add that thinking may be **inductive** (going from specific facts or observations to general principles) or **deductive** (going from general principles to specific situations). Thinking may also be **logical** (proceeding from given information to new conclusions on the basis of explicit rules) or **illogical** (intuitive, associative, or personal).

What distinguishes creative thinking from more routine problem solving? Creative thinking involves all of these thinking styles, plus *fluency, flexibility,* and *originality.* Let's say that you would like to find creative uses for the millions of automobile tires discarded each year. The creativity of your suggestions could be rated in this way: **Fluency** is defined as the total num-

Inductive thought Thinking in which a general rule or principle is gathered from a series of specific examples; for instance, inferring the laws of gravity by observing many falling objects.

Deductive thought Thought that applies a general set of rules to specific situations; for example, using the laws of gravity to predict the behavior of a single falling object.

Logical thought Drawing conclusions on the basis of formal principles of reasoning.

Illogical thought Thought that is intuitive, haphazard, or irrational.

Fluency In tests of creativity, fluency refers to the total number of solutions produced.

■ Table 8.6   Convergent and Divergent Problems

Convergent Problems
- What is the area of a triangle that is 3 feet wide at the base and 2 feet tall?
- Erica is shorter than Zoey but taller than Carlo, and Carlo is taller than Jared. Who is the second tallest?
- If you simultaneously drop a baseball and a bowling ball from a tall building, which will hit the ground first?

Divergent Problems
- What objects can you think of that begin with the letters BR?
- How could discarded aluminum cans be put to use?
- Write a poem about fire and ice.

ber of suggestions you are able to make. **Flexibility** is the number of times you shift from one class of possible uses to another. **Originality** refers to how novel or unusual your ideas are. By counting the number of times you showed fluency, flexibility, and originality, we could rate your creativity, or capacity for *divergent thinking* (Baer, 1993; Runco, 2004).

In routine problem solving or thinking, there is one correct answer, and the problem is to find it. This leads to **convergent thinking** (lines of thought converge on the answer). **Divergent thinking** is the reverse, in which many possibilities are developed from one starting point (Baer, 1993). (See ■ Table 8.6 for some examples.) Rather than repeating learned solutions, creative thinking produces new answers, ideas, or patterns (Michalko, 1998).

Tests of Creativity

There are several ways to measure divergent thinking. In the *Unusual Uses Test,* you would be asked to think of as many uses as possible for some object, such as the tires mentioned earlier. In the *Consequences Test,* you would list the consequences that would follow a basic change in the world. For example, you might be asked "What would happen if everyone suddenly lost the sense of balance and could no longer stay upright?" People try to list as many reactions as possible. If you were to take the *Anagrams Test,* you would be given a word such as *creativity* and asked to make as many new words as possible by rearranging the letters. Each of these tests can be scored for fluency, flexibility, and originality. (For an example of other tests of divergent thinking, see ▶Fig. 8.24.) Tests of divergent thinking seem to tap something quite different from intelligence. Generally, there is little correlation between creativity tests and IQ test scores (Preckel, Holling, & Wiese, 2006).

Creativity tests have been useful, but they are not the whole story. If you want to predict whether a person will be creative in the future, it helps to look at two more kinds of information (Feldhusen & Goh, 1995):

- The *products* of creative thinking (such as essays, poems, drawings, or constructed objects) are often more informative than test results. When creative people are asked to actually produce something, others tend to judge their work as creative.
- A simple listing of a person's *past creative activities and achievements* is an excellent guide to the likelihood that she or he will be creative in the future.

Isn't creativity more than divergent thought? What if a person comes up with a large number of useless answers to a problem? A good question. Divergent thinking is an important

Fluency is an important part of creative thinking. Mozart produced more than 600 pieces of music. Picasso (shown here) created more than 20,000 artworks. Shakespeare wrote 154 sonnets. Not all of these works were masterpieces. However, a fluent outpouring of ideas fed the creative efforts of each of these geniuses.

The first paper clip was patented in 1899. Competition for sales, combined with divergent thinking, has resulted in a remarkable array of alternative designs. These are drawings of just a few of the variations that have appeared over the years. (After Kim, 2000.)

Flexibility In tests of creativity, flexibility is indicated by the number of different types of solutions produced.

Originality In tests of creativity, originality refers to how novel or unusual solutions are.

Convergent thinking Thinking directed toward discovery of a single established correct answer; conventional thinking.

Divergent thinking Thinking that produces many ideas or alternatives; a major element in original or creative thought.

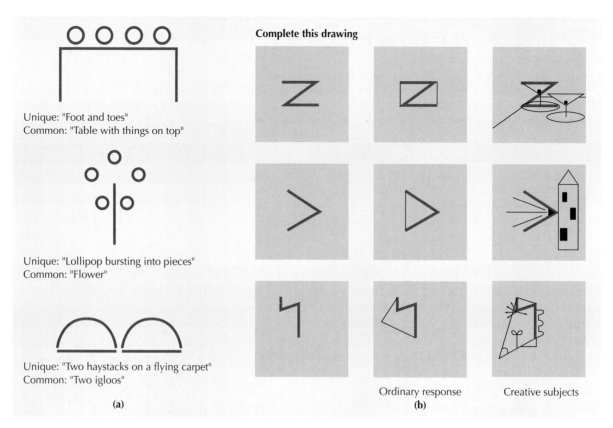

Unique: "Foot and toes"
Common: "Table with things on top"

Unique: "Lollipop bursting into pieces"
Common: "Flower"

Unique: "Two haystacks on a flying carpet"
Common: "Two igloos"

(a)

Complete this drawing

Ordinary response   Creative subjects
(b)

▶▶**FIGURE 8.24** Some tests of divergent thinking. Creative responses are more original and more complex. [*(a)* Adapted from Wallach & Kogan, 1965; *(b)* adapted from Barron, 1958.]

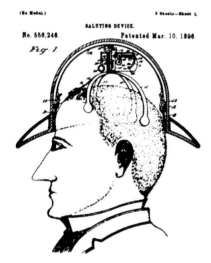

Hat-tipping device. According to the patent, it is for "automatically effecting polite salutations by the elevation and rotation of the hat on the head of the saluting party when said person bows to the person or persons saluted." In addition to being original or novel, a creative solution must fit the demands of the problem. Is this a creative solution to the "problem" of hat tipping?

part of creativity, but there is more to it. To be creative, the solution to a problem must be more than novel, unusual, or original. It must also be *practical* if it is an invention and *sensible* if it is an idea. This is the dividing line between a "harebrained scheme" and a "stroke of genius." In other words, the creative person brings reasoning and critical thinking to bear on new ideas once they are produced (Runco, 2003).

Stages of Creative Thought

Is there any pattern to creative thinking? Typically, five stages occur during creative problem solving:

1. **Orientation.** As a first step, the person defines the problem and identifies its most important dimensions.
2. **Preparation.** In the second stage, creative thinkers saturate themselves with as much information about the problem as possible.
3. **Incubation.** Most major problems produce a period during which all attempted solutions will be futile. At this point, problem solving may proceed on a subconscious level: While the problem seems to have been set aside, it is still "cooking" in the background.
4. **Illumination.** The stage of incubation is often ended by a rapid insight or series of insights. These produce the "Aha!" experience, often depicted in cartoons as a light-bulb appearing over the thinker's head.
5. **Verification.** The final step is to test and critically evaluate the solution obtained during the stage of illumination. If the solution proves faulty, the thinker reverts to the stage of incubation.

Of course, creative thought is not always so neat. Nevertheless, the stages listed are a good summary of the most typical sequence of events.

You may find it helpful to relate the stages to the following more or less true story. Legend has it that the king of Syracuse (a city in ancient Greece) once suspected that his goldsmith had substituted cheaper metals for some of the gold in a crown and kept the extra gold. Archimedes, a famous mathematician and thinker, was given the problem of discovering whether the king had been cheated.

Archimedes began by defining the problem *(orientation):* "How can I tell what metals have been used in the crown without damaging it?" He then checked all known methods of analyzing metals *(preparation).* All involved cutting or melting the crown, so he was forced to temporarily set the problem aside *(incubation).* Then one day as he stepped into his bath, Archimedes suddenly knew he had the solution *(illumination).* He was so excited he is said to have run naked through the streets shouting, "Eureka, eureka!" (I have found it, I have found it!).

On observing his own body floating in the bath, Archimedes realized that different metals of equal weight would displace different amounts of water. A pound of brass, for example, occupies more space than a pound of gold, which is denser. All that remained was to test the solution *(verification).* Archimedes placed an amount of gold (equal in weight to that given the goldsmith) in a tub of water. He marked the water level and removed the gold. He then placed the crown in the water. Was the crown pure gold? If it was, it would raise the water to exactly the same level. Unfortunately, the purity of the crown and the fate of the goldsmith are to this day unknown!

The preceding account is a good general description of creative thinking. However, rather than springing from sudden insights, much creative problem solving is *incremental.* That is, it is the end result of many small steps. This is certainly true of many inventions, which build on earlier ideas.

Some authors believe that truly exceptional creativity requires a rare combination of thinking skills, personality, and a supportive social environment. This mix, they believe, accounts for creative giants such as Edison, Freud, Mozart, Picasso, and others (Runco, 2004; Tardif & Sternberg, 1988).

The development of modern aircraft has been highly creative and quite rapid. Even so, it has been marked more by incremental progress than by dramatic breakthroughs.

Positive Psychology: The Creative Personality

What makes a person creative? According to the popular stereotype, highly creative people are eccentric, introverted, neurotic, socially inept, unbalanced in their interests, and on the edge of madness. Although some artists and musicians cultivate this public image, there is little truth in it. Direct studies of creative individuals paint a very different picture (Winner, 2003):

1. There is a small positive correlation between creativity and IQ. In other words, smarter people have a slight tendency to be more creative. But, for the most part, at

any given level of IQ, some people are creative and some are not (Preckel, Holling, & Wiese, 2006).

2. Creative people usually have a greater-than-average range of knowledge and interests, and they are more fluent in combining ideas from various sources. They are also good at using mental images and metaphors in thinking (Riquelme, 2002).

3. Creative people are open to a wide variety of experiences. They accept irrational thoughts and are uninhibited about their feelings and fantasies. They tend to use broad categories, to question assumptions, to break mental sets, and they find order in chaos. They also experience more unusual states of consciousness, such as vivid dreams and mystical experiences (Ayers, Beaton, & Hunt, 1999).

4. Creative people enjoy symbolic thought, ideas, concepts, and possibilities. They tend to be interested in truth, form, and beauty, rather than in fame or success. Their creative work is an end in itself (Sternberg & Lubart, 1995).

5. Creative people value their independence and prefer complexity. However, they are unconventional and nonconforming primarily in their work; otherwise they do not have unusual, outlandish, or bizarre personalities.

Living More Creatively

Can creativity be learned? It is beginning to look as if some creative thinking skills can be learned. In particular, you can become more creative by practicing divergent thinking, and by taking risks, analyzing ideas, and seeking unusual connections between ideas (Baer, 1993; Sternberg, 2001). Psychologist Mihalyi Csikszentmihalyi (sik-sent-me-HALE-yee) (1997) makes these recommendations about how to become more creative:

- Find something that surprises you every day.
- Try to surprise at least one person every day.
- If something sparks your interest, follow it.
- Make a commitment to doing things well.
- Seek challenges.
- Take time for thinking and relaxing.
- Start doing more of what you really enjoy, less of what you dislike.
- Try to look at problems from as many viewpoints as you can.

Even if you don't become more creative by following these suggestions, they are still good advice. Life is not a standardized test with a single set of correct answers. It is more like a blank canvas on which you can create designs that uniquely express your talents and interests. To live more creatively, you must be ready to seek new ways of doing things. Try to surprise at least one person today—yourself, if no one else.

INTUITIVE THOUGHT—MENTAL SHORTCUT? OR DANGEROUS DETOUR?

>SURVEY QUESTION< *How accurate is intuition?*

At the same time that irrational, intuitive thought may contribute to creative problem solving, it can also lead to thinking errors. To see how this can happen, try the following problems.

Problem 1 An epidemic breaks out, and 600 people are about to die. Doctors have two choices. If they give drug A, 200 lives will be saved. If they give drug B, there is

Have You Ever Thin Sliced Your Teacher?

Think back to your least favorite teacher (not your current one, of course!). How long did it take you to figure out that he or she wasn't going to make your list of star teachers?

In an intriguing study, psychologist Nalini Ambady asked people to watch video clips of teachers they did not know. After watching three ten-second segments, participants were asked to rate the teachers. Amazingly, their ratings correlated highly with year-end course evaluations made by actual students (Ambady & Rosenthal, 1993). Ambady obtained the same result when she presented an even thinner "slice" of teaching behavior, just three two-second clips. A mere six seconds is all that participants needed to form intuitive judgments of the instructors' teaching!

In his book *Blink*, Malcolm Gladwell (2005) argues that this was not a case of hurried irrationality. Instead, it was "thin-slicing," or quickly making sense of thin slivers of experience. According to Gladwell, these immediate, intuitive reactions can sometimes form the basis of more carefully reasoned judgments. They are a testament to the power of the cognitive unconscious, which is a part of the brain that does automatic, unconscious processing (Wilson, 2002). Far from being irrational, intuition may be an important part of how we think.

The trick, of course, is figuring out when thin slicing can be trusted and when it can't. After all, first impressions aren't always right. For example, have you ever had a teacher you came to appreciate only after classes were well under way or only after the course was over? In many circumstances, quick impressions are most valuable when you take the time to verify them through further observation.

---

a one-third chance that 600 people will be saved, and a two-thirds chance that none will be saved. Which drug should they choose?

Problem 2 Again, 600 people are about to die, and doctors must make a choice. If they give drug A, 400 people will die. If they give drug B, there is a one-third chance that no one will die, and a two-thirds chance that 600 will die. Which drug should they choose?

Most people choose drug A for the first problem and drug B for the second. This is fascinating because the two problems are identical. The only difference is that the first is stated in terms of lives saved, the second in terms of lives lost. Yet, even people who realize that their answers are contradictory find it difficult to change them (Kahneman & Tversky, 1972, 1973).

Intuition

As the example shows, we often make decisions intuitively, rather than logically or rationally. **Intuition** is quick, impulsive thought. It may provide fast answers, but it can also be misleading and sometimes disastrous. (See "Have You Ever Thin Sliced Your Teacher?")

Two noted psychologists, Daniel Kahneman (KON-eh-man) and Amos Tversky (tuh-VER-ski) (1937–1996), studied how we make decisions in the face of uncertainty. They found that human judgment is often seriously flawed (Kahneman, 2003; Kahneman, Slovic, & Tversky, 1982). Let's explore some common intuitive thinking errors, so you will be better prepared to avoid them.

Representativeness

One very common pitfall in judgment is illustrated by the question, Which is more probable?

A. Tiger Woods will not be in the lead after the first round of golf of a tournament but win the tournament.

B. Tiger Woods will not be in the lead after the first round of golf of a tournament.

Intuition Quick, impulsive thought that does not make use of formal logic or clear reasoning.

Tversky and Kahneman (1982) found that most people regard statements like A as more probable than B. However, this intuitive answer overlooks an important fact: The likelihood of two events occurring together is lower than the probability of either one alone. (For example, the probability of getting one head when flipping a coin is one half, or .5. The probability of getting two heads when flipping two coins is one fourth, or .25.) Therefore, A is less likely to be true than B.

According to Tversky and Kahneman, such faulty conclusions are based on the **representativeness heuristic.** That is, we tend to give a choice greater weight if it seems to be representative of what we already know. Thus, you probably compared the information about Tiger Woods with your mental model of what a golf pro's behavior should be like. Answer A seems to better represent the model. Therefore, it seems more likely than answer B, even though it isn't. In courtrooms, jurors are more likely to think a defendant is guilty if the person appears to fit the profile of a person likely to commit a crime (Davis & Follette, 2002). For example, a young single male from a poor neighborhood would be more likely to be judged guilty of theft than a middle-aged married father from an affluent suburb.

Underlying Odds

A second common error in judgment involves ignoring the **base rate,** or underlying probability, of an event. People in one experiment were told that they would be given descriptions of 100 people—70 lawyers and 30 engineers. Subjects were then asked to guess, without knowing anything about a person, whether she or he was an engineer or a lawyer. All correctly stated the probabilities as 70 percent for lawyer and 30 percent for engineer. Participants were then given this description:

> Dick is a 30-year-old man. He is married with no children. A man of high ability
> and high motivation, he promises to be quite successful in his field. He is well liked
> by his colleagues.

Notice that the description gives no new information about Dick's occupation. He could still be either an engineer or a lawyer. Therefore, the odds should again be estimated as 70-30. However, most people changed the odds to 50-50. Intuitively it seems that Dick has an equal chance of being either an engineer or a lawyer. But this guess completely ignores the underlying odds.

Perhaps it is fortunate that we do at times ignore underlying odds. Were this not the case, how many people would get married in the face of a 50 percent divorce rate? Or how many would start high-risk businesses? On the other hand, people who smoke, drink and then drive, or skip wearing auto seat belts ignore rather high odds of injury or illness. In many high-risk situations, ignoring base rates is the same as thinking you are an exception to the rule.

Framing

The most general conclusion about intuition is that the way a problem is stated, or **framed,** affects decisions (Tversky & Kahneman, 1981). As the first example in this discussion revealed, people often give different answers to the same problem if it is stated in slightly different ways. To gain some added insight into framing, try another thinking problem:

> A couple are divorcing. Both parents seek custody of their only child, but custody
> can be granted to just one parent. If you had to make a decision based on the fol-
> lowing information, to which parent would you award custody of the child?
>
> **Parent A:** average income, average health, average working hours, reasonable rap-
> port with the child, relatively stable social life.
>
> **Parent B:** above-average income, minor health problems, lots of work-related
> travel, very close relationship with the child, extremely active social life.

Representativeness heuristic A tendency to select wrong answers because they seem to match pre-existing mental categories.

Base rate The basic rate at which an event occurs over time; the basic probability of an event.

Framing In thought, the terms in which a problem is stated or the way that it is structured.

Most people choose to award custody to Parent B, the parent who has some drawbacks but also several advantages (such as above-average income). That's because people tend to look for *positive qualities* that can be *awarded* to the child. However, how would you choose if you were asked this question: Which parent should be denied custody? In this case, most people choose to deny custody to Parent B. Why is Parent B a good choice one moment and a poor choice the next? It's because the second question asked who should be *denied* custody. To answer this question, people tend to look for *negative qualities* that would *disqualify* a parent. As you can see, the way a question is framed can channel us down a narrow path so we attend to only part of the information provided, rather than weighing all the pros and cons (Shafir, 1993).

Usually, the *broadest* way of framing or stating a problem produces the best decisions. However, people often state problems in increasingly narrow terms until a single, seemingly "obvious" answer emerges. For example, to select a career, it would be wise to consider pay, working conditions, job satisfaction, needed skills, future employment outlook, and many other factors. Instead, such decisions are often narrowed to thoughts such as, "I like to write, so I'll be a journalist," "I want to make good money and law pays well," or "I can be creative in photography." Framing decisions so narrowly greatly increases the risk of making a poor choice. If you would like to think more critically and analytically, it is important to pay attention to how you are defining problems before you try to solve them. Remember, short-cuts to answers often short-circuit clear thinking.

Wisdom

People can be intelligent without being wise. For example, a person who does well in school and on IQ tests may make a total mess of her life. Likewise, people can be intelligent without being creative, and clear, rational thinking can lead to correct, but uninspired, answers (Solomon, Marshall, & Gardner, 2005). In many areas of human life, wisdom represents a mixture of convergent thinking, intelligence, and reason, spiced with creativity and originality. People who are wise approach life with openness and tolerance (Helson & Srivastava, 2002).

Study Break **Creative Thinking and Intuition**

Reflect

Make up a question that would require convergent thinking to answer. Now do the same for divergent thinking.

Which of the tests of creativity described in the text do you think you would do best on? (Look back if you can't remember them all.)

To better remember the stages of creative thinking, make up a short story that includes these words: *orient, prepare, in Cuba, illuminate, verify.*

Explain in your own words how representativeness and base rates contribute to thinking errors.

Learning Check

1. Fluency, flexibility, and originality are characteristics of
   a. convergent thought
   b. deductive thinking
   c. creative thought
   d. trial-and-error solutions
2. List the typical stages of creative thinking in the correct order.
   _____ _____ _____ _____ _____

3. Reasoning and critical thinking tend to block creativity; these are noncreative qualities. T or F?
4. To be creative, an original idea must also be practical or feasible. T or F?
5. Intelligence and creativity are highly correlated; the higher a person's IQ, the more likely he or she is to be creative. T or F?
6. Kate is single, outspoken, and very bright. As a college student, she was deeply concerned with discrimination and other social issues and participated in several protests. Which statement is more likely to be true?
   a. Kate is a bank teller.
   b. Kate is a bank teller and a feminist.

Critical Thinking

7. A coin is flipped four times with one of the following results: *(a)* H T T H, *(b)* T T T T, *(c)* H H H H, *(d)* H H T H. Which sequence would most likely precede getting a head on the fifth coin flip?

Answers

1. c 2. orientation, preparation, incubation, illumination, verification 3. F 4. T 5. F 6. a 7. The chance of getting a head on the fifth flip is the same in each case. Each time you flip a coin, the chance of getting a head is 50 percent, no matter what happened before. However, many people intuitively think that *b* is the answer because a head is "overdue," or that *c* is correct because the coin is "on a roll" for heads.

Psychology in Action

Culture, Race, IQ, and You

>SURVEY QUESTION< *Are IQ tests fair to all cultural and racial groups?*

Do you consider yourself intelligent? Okay, then give the Dove Test a try.

If you scored 14 on this exam, your IQ is approximately 100, indicating average intelligence. If you scored 10 or less, you are mentally retarded. With luck and the help of a special educational program, you may be able to learn a few simple skills!

Isn't the Dove Test a little unfair? No, it is *very* unfair. It was written in 1971 by African-American sociologist Adrian Dove as "a half serious attempt to show that we're just not talking the same language." Dove tried to slant his test as much in favor of urban African-American culture as he believes typical IQ tests are biased toward a white middle-class background (Jones, 2003). (Because of its age, the test is probably now also unfair for African Americans under 40.)

Dove's test is a thought-provoking reply to the fact that African-American children score an average of about 15 points lower on standardized IQ tests than European-American children. By reversing the bias, Dove has shown that intelligence tests are not equally valid for all groups. As psychologist Jerome Kagan once said, "If the Wechsler and Binet scales were translated into Spanish, Swahili, and Chinese and given to every 10-year-old in Latin America, East Africa, and China, the majority would obtain IQ scores in the mentally retarded range."

Culture-Fair Testing

Certainly we cannot believe that children of other cultures are all retarded. The fault must lie in the test. As noted earlier, cultural values, knowledge, language patterns, and traditions can greatly affect performance on tests designed for Western cultures (Neisser et al., 1996;

Dove Counterbalance Intelligence Test

Time limit: 5 minutes.
Circle the correct answer.

1. T-bone Walker got famous for playing what?
   a. trombone   b. piano
   c. T-flute   d. guitar
   e. "hambone"

2. A "gas head" is a person who has a
   a. fast-moving car.
   b. stable of "lace."
   c. "process."
   d. habit of stealing cars.
   e. long jail record for arson.

3. If you throw the dice and 7 is showing on the top, what is facing down?
   a. 7   b. snake eyes
   c. boxcars   d. little joes
   e. 11

4. Cheap chitlings (not the kind you purchase at a frozen-food counter) will taste rubbery unless they are cooked long enough. How soon can you quit cooking them to eat and enjoy them?
   a. 45 minutes   b. two hours
   c. 24 hours   d. one week (on a low
                        flame)
   e. one hour

5. Bird or Yardbird was the jacket jazz lovers from coast to coast hung on
   a. Lester Young   b. Peggy Lee
   c. Benny Goodman d. Charlie Parker
   e. Birdman of
      Alcatraz

6. A "handkerchief head" is
   a. a cool cat.   b. a porter.
   c. an Uncle Tom. d. a hoddi.
   e. a preacher.

7. Jet is
   a. an East Oakland motorcycle club.
   b. one of the gangs in West Side Story.
   c. a news and gossip magazine.
   d. a way of life for the very rich.

8. "Bo Diddly" is a
   a. game for children.   b. down-home
                              cheap wine.
   c. down-home singer.   d. new dance.
   e. Moejoe call.

9. Which word is most out of place here?
   a. splib   b. blood
   c. gray   d. spook
   e. black

10. If a pimp is uptight with a woman who gets state aid, what does he mean when he talks about "Mother's Day"?
    a. second Sunday in May
    b. third Sunday in June
    c. first of every month
    d. none of these
    e. first and fifteenth of every month

11. Many people say that "Juneteenth" (June 10th) should be made a legal holiday because this was the day when
    a. the slaves were freed in the United States.
    b. the slaves were freed in Texas.
    c. the slaves were freed in Jamaica.
    d. the slaves were freed in California.
    e. Martin Luther King was born.
    f. Booker T. Washington died.

12. If a man is called a "blood," then he is a
    a. fighter   b. Mexican-American
    c. Black   d. hungry hemophile
    e. red man or
       Indian

13. What are the Dixie Hummingbirds?
    a. a part of the KKK
    b. a swamp disease
    c. a modern gospel group
    d. a Mississippi Negro paramilitary strike force
    e. deacons

14. The opposite of square is
    a. round.   b. up
    c. down.   d. hip
    e. lame

Answers
9. c 10. c 11. b 12. c 13. c 14. d
1. d 2. c 3. a 4. c 5. d 6. c 7. c 8. c

Sternberg & Grigorenko, 2005). To avoid this problem, some psychologists have tried to develop culture-fair tests that do not disadvantage certain groups. A **culture-fair test** is designed to minimize the importance of skills and knowledge that may be more common in some cultures than in others.

Culture-fair tests attempt to measure intelligence without, as much as possible, being influenced by a person's verbal skills, cultural background, and educational level. Their value lies not just in testing people from other cultures. They are also useful for testing children in the United States who come from poor communities, rural areas, or ethnic minority families (Stephens et al., 1999). However, no intelligence test can be entirely free of cultural influences. For instance, our culture is very "visual," because children are constantly exposed to television, movies, video games, and the like. Thus, compared with children in developing countries, a child who grows up in the United States may be better prepared to take *both* nonverbal tests and traditional IQ tests.

Because the concept of intelligence exhibits such diversity across cultures, many psychologists have begun to stress the need to rethink the concept of intelligence itself (Greenfield, 1997; Sternberg & Grigorenko, 2005). If we are to find a truly culture-fair way to measure intelligence, we first need to identify those core cognitive skills, or multiple intelligences, that lie at the heart of human intelligence the world around (Sternberg & Grigorenko, 2006).

The Politics of Race, Culture, and IQ

Biased tests are not the only IQ issue African Americans have confronted. One persistent claim is that African Americans score below average in IQ because of their "genetic heritage" and that they are genetically incapable of climbing out of poverty (Hernstein & Murray, 1994; Rushton & Jensen, 2005). Psychologists have responded to such claims with a number of counterarguments.

First, it is no secret that as a group African Americans are more likely than European Americans to live in environments that are physically, educationally, and intellectually impoverished. As we saw earlier in this chapter, when unequal education is part of the equation, IQs tell us little about how heredity affects intelligence (Sternberg, Grigorenko, & Kidd, 2005; Suzuki & Aronson, 2005). Indeed, one study found that placing African-American children into European-American adoptive families increased the children's IQs by an average of 13 points, bringing them into line with those of European-American children (Nisbett, 2005). That is, providing African-American children with the same environmental experiences available to European-American children erased IQ differences.

Second, the point made by the Dove Test is often overlooked. The assumptions, biases, and content of standard IQ tests do not always allow meaningful comparisons between ethnic, cultural, or racial groups (Helms, 1992; Suzuki & Aronson, 2005). As Leon Kamin (1981) says, "The important fact is that we cannot say which sex (or race) might be more intelligent, because we have no way of measuring 'intelligence.' We have only IQ tests." Kamin's point is that the makers of IQ tests decided in advance to use test items that would give men and women equal IQ scores. It would be just as easy to put together an IQ test that would give African Americans and European Americans equal scores. Differences in IQ scores are not a fact of nature, but a decision by the test makers. That's why European Americans do better on IQ tests written by European Americans, and African Americans do better on IQ tests devised by African Americans.

Third, although IQ predicts school performance, it does not predict later career success (McClelland, 1994). In this regard, "street smarts," or what psychologist Robert Sternberg calls *practical intelligence* (Stemler & Sternberg, 2006), may be seen by minority cultures as more important than "book learning," or what Sternberg calls *analytic intelligence* (Sankofa et al., 2005).

Most psychologists have concluded there is no scientific evidence that group differences in average IQ are based on genetics. In fact, studies that used actual blood group

Culture-fair test A test (such as an intelligence test) designed to minimize the importance of skills and knowledge that may be more common in some cultures than in others.

testing found no significant correlations between ethnic ancestry and IQ scores. According to Bonham, Warshauer-Baker, and Collins (2005), this is because it does not even make genetic sense to talk about "races" at all because obvious external markers, like skin color, have little to do with underlying genetic differences. Group differences in IQ scores are based on cultural and environmental differences, as much as on heredity (Neisser et al., 1996; Nisbett, 2005). To conclude otherwise reflects political beliefs and biases, not scientific facts.

Thinking Beyond the Numbers Game

African Americans are not the only segment of the population with reason to question the validity of intelligence testing and the role of heredity in determining intelligence. The clarifications they have won extend to others as well.

Consider the 9-year-old child confronted with this question on an intelligence test: "Which of the following does not belong with the others? Roller skates, airplane, train, bicycle." If the child fails to answer "airplane," does it reveal a lack of intelligence? It can be argued that an intelligent choice could be based on any of these alternatives: Roller skates are not typically used for transportation; an airplane is the only nonland item; a train can't be steered; a bicycle is the only item with just two wheels. The parents of a child who misses this question may have reason to be angry because educational systems tend to classify children and then make the label stick.

In response to such concerns, court decisions have led some states to outlaw the use of intelligence tests in public schools.

High-Stakes Testing

Widespread reliance on standardized intelligence tests and aptitude tests has raised questions about the relative good and harm they do. On the positive side, tests can open opportunities as well as close them. A high test score may allow a disadvantaged youth to enter college, or it may identify a child who is bright but emotionally disturbed. Test scores may also be fairer and more objective than arbitrary judgments made by admissions officers or employment interviewers. Also, tests *do* accurately predict academic performance. The fact that academic performance *does not* predict later success may call for an overhaul of college course work, not an end to testing.

On the negative side, mass testing can sometimes exclude people of obvious ability. Other complaints relate to the frequent appearance of bad or ambiguous questions on standardized tests, overuse of class time to prepare students for the tests (instead of teaching general skills), and in the case of intelligence tests, the charge that tests are often biased. Also, most standardized tests demand passive recognition of facts, assessed with a multiple-choice format. They do not, for the most part, test a person's ability to think critically or creatively or to apply knowledge to solve problems.

Conclusion

An application of the preceding discussion to your personal understanding of intelligence can be summarized in this way: Intelligence tests are a double-edged sword; we have learned much from their use, yet they have the potential to do great harm. In the final analysis, it is important to remember—as Howard Gardner has pointed out—that creativity, motivation, physical health, mechanical aptitude, artistic ability, and numerous other qualities not measured by intelligence tests contribute to the achievement of life goals. Also remember that IQ is not intelligence. IQ is an *index* of intelligence (as narrowly defined by a particular test). Change the test and you change the score. An IQ is not some permanent number stamped on your forehead (or the foreheads of your friends and classmates) that forever determines your potential. The real issue is what skills people have and how they apply them, not what their test scores are (Hunt, 1995).

Study Break **Intelligence Testing and Culture**

Reflect

Do you think it would be possible to create an intelligence test that is universally culture-fair? What would its questions look like? Can you think of any type of question that wouldn't favor the mental skills emphasized by some culture, somewhere in the world?

Funding for schools in some states varies greatly in rich and poor neighborhoods. Imagine that a politician opposes spending more money on disadvantaged students because she believes it would "just be a waste." What arguments can you offer against her assertion?

In your own opinion, what are the advantages of using standardized tests to select applicants for college, graduate school, and professional schools? What are the disadvantages?

Learning Check

1. The WAIS-III, SB5, and Dove Test are all culture-fair intelligence scales. T or F?
2. The claim that heredity accounts for racial differences in average IQ ignores environmental differences and the cultural bias inherent in standard IQ tests. T or F?
3. IQ scores predict school performance. T or F?
4. IQ is not intelligence; it is one index of intelligence. T or F?

Critical Thinking

5. Assume that a test of memory for words is translated from English to Spanish. Would the Spanish version of the test be equal in difficulty to the English version?

Answers

1. F 2. T 3. T 4. T 5. Probably not, because the Spanish words might be longer or shorter than the same words in English. The Spanish words might also sound more or less alike than the original test. Translating an intelligence test into another language can subtly change the meaning and difficulty of test items.

CHAPTER IN REVIEW

Major Points

- Intelligence is often defined as a single general human quality and operationally defined as performance on an IQ test.
- Simplistic definitions of intelligence have been questioned. IQ is influenced by nurture as well as nature.
- Thinking, problem solving, language, and creativity are the origins of intelligent behavior.
- Thinking is influenced by the form in which information is represented—as images, concepts, or symbols.
- Language is an especially powerful way to encode information and manipulate ideas.
- Understanding problem solving can make you more effective at finding solutions.
- Expert problem solving is based on acquired knowledge and strategies.
- Creative thinking is novel, divergent, and tempered with a dash of practicality.
- Some thinking errors can be avoided if you know the pitfalls of intuitive thought.
- Racial and ethnic minority groups are unfairly stereotyped by culturally biased IQ tests and a tendency to assume that low IQ scores cannot be improved. A high IQ does not automatically lead to high achievement.

Summary

How is human intelligence defined and measured?

- Intelligence refers to the general capacity (or g-factor) to act purposefully, think rationally, and deal effectively with the environment. In practice, intelligence is operationally defined by intelligence tests.
- The first intelligence test was assembled by Alfred Binet. A modern version of Binet's test is the *Stanford-Binet Intelligence Scale.*
- Another major intelligence test is the *Wechsler Adult Intelligence Scale* (WAIS). The WAIS measures both verbal and performance intelligence. Group intelligence tests are also available.
- Intelligence is expressed as an intelligence quotient (IQ), defined as mental age divided by chronological age and then multiplied by 100. The distribution of IQ scores approximates a normal curve.
- People with IQs in the gifted or "genius" range of above 140 tend to be superior in many respects. However, by criteria other than IQ, many children can be considered gifted or talented in one way or another.
- The terms *mentally retarded* and *developmentally disabled* are applied to those whose IQ falls below 70 or who lack various adaptive behaviors. About 50 percent of the cases of mental retardation are organic. Many of the remaining cases are thought to reflect familial retardation.

What are some controversies in the study of intelligence?

- Many psychologists have begun to forge new, broader definitions of intelligence. Howard Gardner's theory of multiple intelligences is a good example.
- Artificial intelligence refers to any artificial system that can perform tasks that require intelligence when done by people. Two principal areas of artificial intelligence research on particular human skills are computer simulations and expert systems.
- Intelligence is partially determined by heredity. However, environment is also important, as revealed by IQ increases induced by education and stimulating environments.

What is the nature of thought?

- Thinking is an internal representation of external stimuli or situations.
- Three basic units of thought are images, concepts, and language (or symbols).

In what ways are images related to thinking?

- Images may be stored in memory or created to solve problems.
- Images can be three-dimensional, they can be rotated in space, and their size may change.
- Kinesthetic images are used to represent movements and actions. Kinesthetic sensations help structure the flow of thoughts for many people.

How do we learn concepts?

- A concept is a generalized idea of a class of objects or events.
- Concept formation may be based on positive and negative instances or rule learning.
- In practice, concept identification frequently makes use of prototypes, or ideal models.
- Concepts may be conjunctive ("and" concepts), disjunctive ("either/or" concepts), or relational.
- The denotative meaning of a word or concept is its dictionary definition. Connotative meaning is personal or emotional. Connotative meaning can be measured with the semantic differential.

What is the role of language in thinking?

- Language allows events to be encoded into symbols for easy mental manipulation. The study of meaning in language is called *semantics*.
- Bilingualism is a valuable ability. Two-way bilingual education allows children to develop additive bilingualism while in school.

- Language carries meaning by combining a set of symbols according to a set of rules (grammar), which includes rules about word order (syntax).
- True languages are productive and can be used to generate new ideas or possibilities.
- Complex gestural systems, such as American Sign Language, are true languages.
- Chimpanzees and other primates have been taught American Sign Language and similar systems. This suggests to some that primates are capable of very basic language use. Others question this conclusion.

What do we know about problem solving?

- The solution to a problem may be arrived at mechanically (by trial and error or by rote application of rules), but mechanical solutions are often inefficient.
- Solutions by understanding usually begin with discovery of the general properties of an answer. Next comes the proposal of a functional solution.
- Problem solving is frequently aided by heuristics, which narrow the search for solutions.
- When understanding leads to a rapid solution, insight has occurred. Three elements of insight are selective encoding, selective combination, and selective comparison.
- Insight and other problem solving can be blocked by fixations. Functional fixedness is a common fixation, but emotional blocks, cultural values, learned conventions, and perceptual habits are also problems.

What is creative thinking?

- To be creative, a solution must be practical and sensible as well as original. Creative thinking requires divergent thought, characterized by fluency, flexibility, and originality. Tests of creativity measure these qualities.
- Five stages often seen in creative problem solving are orientation, preparation, incubation, illumination, and verification. Not all creative thinking fits this pattern.
- Studies suggest that the creative personality has a number of characteristics, most of which contradict popular stereotypes. There is only a very small correlation between IQ and creativity.
- Some creative thinking skills can be learned.

How accurate is intuition?

- Intuitive thinking can be fast and accurate but also often leads to errors. Wrong conclusions may be drawn when an answer seems highly representative of what we already believe is true.

- A second problem is ignoring the base rate (or underlying probability) of an event.
- Clear thinking is usually aided by stating or framing a problem in broad terms.

Are IQ tests fair to all cultural and racial groups?

- Traditional IQ tests often suffer from a degree of cultural bias. For this and other reasons, it is wise to remember that IQ is merely an index of intelligence and that intelligence is narrowly defined by most tests.
- IQ is related to achievement in school, but many other factors are also important. Outside school, the connection between IQ and achievement is even weaker.
- The use of standard IQ tests for educational placement of students (especially into special education classes) has been prohibited by law in some states.

Interactive Learning

Internet addresses frequently change. To find the sites listed here, visit www.thomsonedu.com/psychology/coon for an updated list of Internet addresses and direct links to relevant sites.

Psychology: A Journey **Companion Website**   Find online quizzes, flash cards, animations, video clips, experiments, interactive assessments, and other helpful study aids for this text at www.thomsonedu.com/psychology/coon.

Creativity Web   Multiple links to resources on creativity.

The Psychology of Invention   An exploration of how invention and discovery happen.

The Question of Primate Language   This article from the National Zoo discusses primate communication and intelligence.

Be Careful of How You Define Intelligence   An article about cross-cultural differences in intelligence.

Helping Your Highly Gifted Child   Advice for parents of gifted children.

Introduction to Mental Retardation   Answers to basic question about mental retardation.

IQ Tests   Provides links to a number of IQ tests.

The Knowns and Unknowns of Intelligence   From the American Psychological Association, what is known about intelligence and intelligence tests.

ThomsonNOW   Go to www.thomsonedu.com to link to ThomsonNOW, your online study tool. First take the **Pre-Test** for this chapter to get your **Personalized Study Plan,** which will identify topics you need to review and direct you to online resources. Then take the **Post-Test** to determine what concepts you have mastered and what you still need work on.

TEST YOUR KNOWLEDGE

Cognition, Intelligence, and Creativity

For additional review, get more practice with *ThomsonNOW*, *WebTutor*, the *Practice Quizzes*, and/or the printed *Study Guide* available with this book.

1. Which modern intelligence test originated with attempts to measure the mental abilities of children in Paris?
   a. SB5
   b. WAIS
   c. SAT
   d. WISC

2. By definition, a person has average intelligence when
   a. MA = CA
   b. CA = 100
   c. MA = 100
   d. MA × CA = 100

3. One thing that the mentally gifted and the developmentally disabled have in common is that both have
   a. a tendency to suffer from metabolic disorders
   b. to be tested with the WAIS, rather than the SB5
   c. MAs that are higher than their CAs
   d. extreme IQ scores

4. Which is NOT one of the eight types of intelligence identified by Howard Gardner?
   a. cyber skills
   b. music skills
   c. visual and spatial skills
   d. naturalist skills

5. Computer simulations and expert systems are primary research tools in
   a. psycholinguistics
   b. the field of AI
   c. studies of divergent thinking
   d. studies of the semantic differential

6. From a practical point of view, adult intelligence can most readily be increased by
   a. genetics
   b. teaching adaptive behaviors
   c. stimulating environments
   d. applying deviation IQs

7. Concepts are
   a. picture-like mental representations
   b. generalized ideas about a class of objects or events
   c. symbols and rules for combining symbols
   d. symbolic notational systems

8. A person doing mental rotation would need to use which basic unit of thought?
   a. concepts
   b. language
   c. images
   d. symbols

9. Our ability to think about movements and actions is aided by
   a. kinesthetic imagery
   b. rotational concepts
   c. mental calculation
   d. relational concepts

10. A triangle must be a closed shape and have three sides and the sides must be straight lines. *Triangle* is a
    a. conjuctive concept
    b. relational concept
    c. disjunctive concept
    d. connotative concept

11. When you are trying to categorize complex stimuli _____ are especially helpful.
    a. kinesthetic images
    b. connotative concepts
    c. denotative concepts
    d. prototypes

12. Which of the following is NOT an element of spoken language?
    a. grammar
    b. syntax
    c. phonemes
    d. lexigrams

13. Noam Chomsky believes that we use _____ to change core declarative sentences into other voices and forms.
    a. phonemes
    b. transformation rules
    c. conditional statements
    d. conjunctive encoding

14. Which statement is the best summary of animal language research with chimpanzees?
    a. Chimps can learn to use signs, but they can't make word sounds.
    b. Chimps can learn to communicate with signs.
    c. Chimps who learn signs use language on a par with 5-year-old children.
    d. Because of serious problems with syntax, chimps have been unable to communicate with humans.

15. After you find a general solution to a problem you must usually also find a
    a. heuristic
    b. search strategy
    c. fixation
    d. functional solution

16. Functional fixedness is a major barrier to
    a. insightful problem solving
    b. using random search strategies
    c. mechanical problem solving
    d. achieving fixations through problem solving

17. A test scored for fluency and flexibility is obviously designed to measure
    a. intuitive thinking
    b. convergent thinking
    c. divergent thinking
    d. algorithms

18. The stage of creative thinking that corresponds to insightful problem solving is
    a. verification
    b. incubation
    c. induction
    d. illumination

19. Our decisions are greatly affected by the way a problem is stated, a process called
    a. framing
    b. base rating
    c. induction
    d. selective encoding

20. Traditional IQ tests fail to treat members of ethnic minorities fairly because they are
    a. not culture-fair
    b. scored by applying deviation IQs
    c. out of date
    d. define intelligence too broadly

Motivation and Emotion

JOURNEY INTO PSYCHOLOGY: MOVED BY THE MUSIC OF LIFE

Robert was in his doctor's waiting room when he suffered a "strange attack." Robert recalls that the "atmosphere changed, the walls seemed to close in, and the voices of other patients became a buzz." However, months of therapy were no help because Robert simply couldn't talk about his feelings. When asked how he felt, Robert might reply "Fine" or "I don't know." Or he might describe a bodily sensation, replying "My stomach hurts" (Lumley, 2004). The scientific name for Robert's problem is *alexithymia* (a-LEX-ih-THIGH-me-ah), from the Latin for "can't name emotions."

It could be said that emotion is the "music" that defines the rhythms of our lives. Sadly, Robert is not moved by the music of life as intensely as most of us are. Not only is Robert unable to name his emotions, he is only vaguely aware of them in the first place. It's even hard for him to imagine emotions. As you might suspect, Robert cannot easily empathize with the emotions of others. People like Robert find it hard to form close relationships with others. Their lack of inner awareness can also lead to health problems, such as depression or addictive behaviors (Lumley, 2004).

This chapter is about the motives that provide the drumbeat of human behavior and the emotions that are its rhythm. Derived from the Latin word *movere* (to move), motivation and emotion play complex roles in our everyday lives. Even "simple" motivated activities, such as eating, are not solely under the control of the body. In many instances, external cues, expectations, learning, cultural values, and other factors influence our motives and our emotions (R. C. Beck, 2004).

Let's begin with basic motives, such as hunger and thirst, and then explore how emotions affect us. Although emotions can be the music of life, they are sometimes the music of death as well. Read on to find out why.

AFP/Getty Images

▽ **Survey Questions**

- What is motivation? Are there different types of motives?
- What causes hunger? Overeating? Eating disorders?
- Is there more than one type of thirst? In what ways are pain avoidance and the sex drive unusual?
- What are the typical patterns of human sexual response?
- How does arousal relate to motivation?
- What are social motives? Why are they important?
- Are some motives more basic than others?
- What happens during emotion? Can "lie detectors" really detect lies?
- How accurately are emotions expressed by "body language" and the face?
- How do psychologists explain emotions?
- What does it mean to have "emotional intelligence"?

MOTIVATION—FORCES THAT PUSH AND PULL

>SURVEY QUESTIONS< *What is motivation? Are there different types of motives?*

What are your goals? Why do you pursue them? When are you satisfied? When do you give up? **Motivation** refers to the dynamics of behavior—the ways in which our actions are *initiated, sustained, directed,* and *terminated* (Petri & Govern, 2004).

Can you clarify that? Yes. Imagine that Kendra is studying psychology in the library. Her stomach begins to growl and she can't concentrate. She grows restless and decides to buy an apple from a vending machine. The machine is empty, so she goes to the cafeteria. Closed. Kendra drives home, where she cooks a meal and eats it. At last her hunger is satisfied, and she resumes studying. Notice how Kendra's food seeking was *initiated* by a bodily need. Her search was *sustained* because her need was not immediately met, and her actions were *directed* by possible sources of food. Finally, her food seeking was *terminated* by achieving her goal.

A Model of Motivation

Many motivated activities begin with a **need,** or internal lack or deficiency. The need that initiated Kendra's food search was a shortage of key substances in her body. Needs cause a **drive** (an energized motivational state) to develop. The drive was hunger, in Kendra's case. Drives activate a **response** (an action or series of actions) designed to attain a **goal** (the "target" of motivated behavior). Reaching a goal that satisfies the need will end the chain of events. Thus, a simple model of motivation can be shown in this way:

$$\text{NEED} \longrightarrow \text{DRIVE} \longrightarrow \text{RESPONSE} \longrightarrow \text{GOAL} \atop \text{(NEED REDUCTION)}$$

Aren't needs and drives the same thing? No, because the strength of needs and drives can differ (Franken, 2007). If you begin fasting today, your bodily need for food will increase every day. However, you would probably feel less "hungry" on the seventh day of fasting than you did on the first. Whereas your need for food steadily increases, the hunger drive comes and goes.

Now let's observe Kendra again. It's Saturday night: For dinner, Kendra has soup, salad, a large steak, a baked potato, bread, two pieces of cheesecake, and coffee. After dinner, she

Motivation Internal processes that initiate, sustain, and direct activities.

Need An internal deficiency that may energize behavior.

Drive The psychological expression of internal needs or valued goals. For example, hunger, thirst, or a drive for success.

Response Any action, glandular activity, or other identifiable behavior.

Goal The target or objective of motivated behavior.

complains that she is "too full to move." Soon after, Kendra's roommate arrives with a strawberry pie. Kendra exclaims that strawberry pie is her favorite and she eats three large pieces! Is this hunger? Certainly, Kendra's dinner satisfied her biological needs for food.

How does that change the model of motivation? Kendra's "pie lust" illustrates that motivated behavior can be energized by the "pull" of external stimuli, as well as by the "push" of internal needs.

Incentives

The "pull" of a goal is called its **incentive value** (the goal's appeal beyond its ability to fill a need). Some goals are so desirable (strawberry pie, for example) that they can motivate behavior in the absence of an internal need. Other goals are so low in incentive value that they may be rejected even if they meet the internal need. Fresh, live grubworms, for instance, are highly nutritious. However, it is doubtful that you would eat one no matter how hungry you might be.

Usually, our actions are energized by a mixture of internal needs *and* external incentives. That's why a strong need may change an unpleasant incentive into a desired goal. Perhaps you've never eaten a grubworm, but you may have eaten some pretty horrible leftovers when the refrigerator was bare. The incentive value of goals also helps explain motives that don't seem to come from internal needs, such as drives for success, status, or approval (▸▸ Fig. 9.1).

Types of Motives

For our purposes, motives can be divided into three major categories:

1. **Primary motives** are based on biological needs that must be met for survival. The most important primary motives are hunger, thirst, pain avoidance, and needs for air, sleep, elimination of wastes, and regulation of body temperature. Primary motives are innate.

2. **Stimulus motives** express our needs for stimulation and information. Examples include activity, curiosity, exploration, manipulation, and physical contact. Although such motives also appear to be innate, they are not strictly necessary for survival.

3. **Secondary motives** are based on learned needs, drives, and goals. Learned motives help explain many human activities, such as making music, blogging, or trying to win the skateboarding finals in the X Games. Many secondary motives are related to learned needs for power, affiliation (the need to be with others), approval, status, security, and achievement. Fear and aggression also appear to be greatly affected by learning.

Primary Motives and Homeostasis

How important is air in your life? Water? Sleep? Food? Temperature regulation? Finding a public rest room? For most of us, satisfying biological needs is so routine that we tend to overlook how much of our behavior they direct. But exaggerate any of these needs through famine, shipwreck, poverty, near drowning, bitter cold, or drinking 10 cups of coffee, and their powerful grip on behavior becomes evident. We are, after all, still animals in many ways.

Biological drives are essential because they maintain *homeostasis* (HOE-me-oh-STAY-sis), or bodily equilibrium (Cannon, 1932).

What is homeostasis? The term **homeostasis** means "standing steady," or "steady state." Optimal levels exist for body temperature, for chemicals in the blood, for blood pressure, and so forth. When the body deviates from these "ideal" levels, automatic reactions begin to restore equilibrium (Deckers, 2005). Thus, it might help to think of homeostasis as being similar to a thermostat set at a particular temperature.

(a) High-incentive value goal

(b) Low-incentive value goal

David Austen/Woodfin Cap & Associates

▸▸ **FIGURE 9.1** Needs and incentives interact to determine drive strength *(above)*. *(a)* Moderate need combined with a high-incentive goal produces a strong drive. *(b)* Even when a strong need exists, drive strength may be moderate if a goal's incentive value is low. It is important to remember, however, that incentive value lies "in the eye of the beholder" *(photo)*. No matter how hungry, few people would be able to eat the pictured grubworms.

Incentive value The value of a goal above and beyond its ability to fill a need.

Primary motives Innate motives based on biological needs.

Stimulus motives Innate needs for stimulation and information.

Secondary motives Motives based on learned needs, drives, and goals.

Homeostasis A steady state of bodily equilibrium.

A (Very) Short Course on Thermostats

The thermostat in your house constantly compares the actual room temperature to a *set point,* or ideal temperature, which you can control. When room temperature falls below the set point, the heat is automatically turned on to warm the room. When the heat equals or slightly exceeds the set point, it is automatically turned off or the air conditioning is turned on. In this way room temperature is kept in a state of equilibrium hovering around the set point.

The first reactions to disequilibrium in the human body are also automatic. For example, if you become too hot, more blood will flow through your skin and you will begin to perspire, thus lowering body temperature. Usually, we are not aware of such changes, unless continued disequilibrium drives us to seek shade, warmth, food, or water.

Circadian Rhythms

Our needs and drives can change from moment to moment. After eating, our motivation to eat more food tends to diminish and a few minutes in the hot sun can leave us feeling thirsty. But our motivation can also vary over longer cycles. Scientists have long known that bodily activity is guided by internal "biological clocks." Every 24 hours, your body undergoes a cycle of changes called **circadian** (sur-KAY-dee-an) **rhythms** (*circa:* about; *diem:* a day) (Baehr et al., 2000). Throughout the day, activities in the liver, kidneys, and endocrine glands undergo large changes. Body temperature, blood pressure, and amino acid levels also shift from hour to hour. These activities, and many others, peak once a day (▸▸Fig. 9.2). People are usually more motivated and alert at the high point of their circadian rhythms (Antle & Mistlberger, 2005).

Shift Work and Jet Lag

Circadian rhythms are most noticeable after a major change in time schedules. Businesspersons, athletes, and other time zone travelers tend to perform poorly when their body rhythms are disturbed. If you travel great distances east or west, the peaks and valleys of your circadian rhythms will be out of phase with the sun and clocks. For example, you might be wide-awake at midnight and feel like you're sleepwalking during the day (return to ▸▸Fig. 9.2). Shift work has the same effect, causing fatigue, irritability, upset stomach, and depression (Garbarino, 2002).

How fast do people adapt to rhythm changes? For major time zone shifts (5 hours or more) it can take up to 2 weeks to resynchronize. The *direction* of travel also affects adaptation (Herxheimer & Waterhouse, 2003). If you fly west, adapting is relatively easy; if you fly east, adapting takes much longer (▸▸Fig. 9.3). When you fly east, the sun comes up *earlier* relative to your "home" time. Let's say that you live in San Francisco and fly to Boston. If you get up at 7 A.M. in Boston, it's 4 A.M. back in San Francisco—and your body knows it. If you fly west, the sun comes up later. In this case, it is easier for people to "advance" (stay up later and sleep in) than it is to shift backward.

Adjusting to jet lag is slowest when you stay indoors, where you can sleep and eat on "home time." Getting outdoors speeds adaptation. A few intermittent 5-minute periods of exposure to bright light early in the morning are also helpful for resetting your circadian rhythm (Duffy & Wright, Jr., 2005).

How does this affect those of us who are not world travelers? There are few college students who have not at one time or another "burned the midnight oil," especially for final

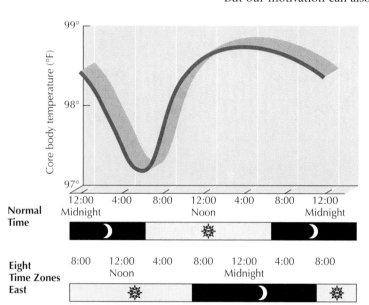

▸▸**FIGURE 9.2** Core body temperature is a good indicator of a person's circadian rhythm. Most people reach a low point 2 to 3 hours before their normal waking time. It's no wonder that both the Chernobyl and Three-Mile Island nuclear power plant accidents occurred around 4 A.M. Rapid travel to a different time zone, shift work, depression, and illness can throw sleep and waking patterns out of synchronization with the body's core rhythm. Mismatches of this kind are very disruptive (Hauri & Linde, 1990).

Circadian rhythms Cyclical changes in bodily functions and arousal levels that vary on a schedule approximating a 24-hour day.

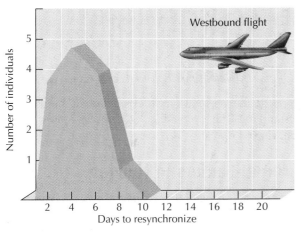

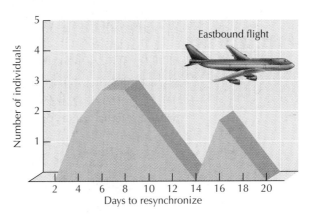

▸▸**FIGURE 9.3** Time required to adjust to air travel across six time zones. The average time to resynchronize was shorter for westbound travel than for eastbound flights. (Data from Beljan et al., 1972; cited by Moore-Ede, Sulzman, & Fuller, 1982.)

exams. At such times it is wise to remember that departing from your regular schedule usually costs more than it's worth. You may be motivated to do as much during 1 hour in the morning as you could have done in 3 hours of work after midnight. You might just as well go to sleep 2 hours earlier.

In general, if you can anticipate an upcoming body rhythm change, it is best to preadapt to your new schedule. *Preadaptation* refers to gradually matching your sleep–waking cycle to a new time schedule. Before traveling, for instance, you should go to sleep 1 hour later (or earlier) each day until your sleep cycle matches the time at your destination.

 Study Break **Overview of Motivation**

Reflect

Motives help explain why we do what we do. See if you can think of something you do that illustrates the concepts of need, drive, response, and goal. Does the goal in your example vary in incentive value? What effects do high- and low-incentive-value goals have on your behavior?

Do your motives vary with your circadian rhythms? At what time of day are you most motivated?

Learning Check

1. Motives _____, sustain, _____, and terminate activities.
2. Needs provide the _____ of motivation, whereas incentives provide the _____.

Classify the following needs or motives by placing the correct letter in the blank.

A. Primary motive **B.** Stimulus motive **C.** Secondary motive

3. _____ curiosity   6. _____ thirst
4. _____ status   7. _____ achievement
5. _____ sleep   8. _____ physical contact

9. Maintaining bodily equilibrium is called thermostasis. T or F?
10. A goal high in incentive value may create a drive in the absence of any internal need. T or F?

Critical Thinking

11. There's an old saying that "You can lead a horse to water, but you can't make him drink." Can you restate this in motivational terms?
12. Many people mistakenly believe that they suffer from "hypoglycemia" (low blood sugar), which is often blamed for fatigue, difficulty concentrating, irritability, and other symptoms. Why is it unlikely that many people actually have hypoglycemia?

Answers

1. initiate, direct 2. push, pull 3. B 4. C 5. A 6. A 7. C 8. B 9. F 10. T 11. Providing an incentive (water) will not automatically lead to drinking in the absence of an internal need for water. 12. Because of homeostasis: Blood sugar is normally maintained within narrow bounds. Whereas blood sugar levels fluctuate enough to affect hunger, true hypoglycemia is an infrequent medical problem.

HUNGER—PARDON ME, MY HYPOTHALAMUS IS GROWLING

>SURVEY QUESTIONS< *What causes hunger? Overeating? Eating disorders?*

You get hungry, you find food, and you eat: Hunger might seem like a "simple" motive, but only recently have we begun to understand it. Hunger provides a good model of how internal and external factors direct our behavior.

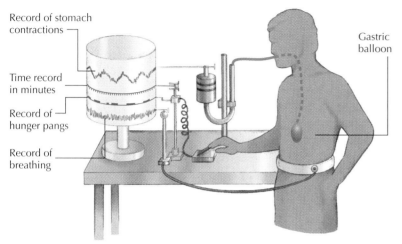

>>**FIGURE 9.4** In Walter Cannon's early study of hunger, a simple apparatus was used to simultaneously record hunger pangs and stomach contractions. (After Cannon, 1934.)

Internal Factors in Hunger

Don't our feelings of hunger originate in our stomach? To find out, Walter Cannon and A. L. Washburn (1912) decided to see if stomach contractions cause hunger. In an early study, Washburn trained himself to swallow a balloon, which could be inflated through an attached tube. This allowed Cannon to record the movements of Washburn's stomach (»Fig. 9.4). When Washburn's stomach contracted, he reported that he felt "hunger pangs." In view of this, the two scientists concluded that hunger is nothing more than the contractions of an empty stomach. (Unfortunately, this proved to be an inflated conclusion.)

For many people, hunger produces an overall feeling of weakness or shakiness, rather than a "growling" stomach. Of course, eating *does* slow when the stomach is stretched or distended (full). (Remember last Thanksgiving?) However, we now know that the stomach is not essential for feeling hunger. Even people who have had their stomachs removed for medical reasons continue to feel hungry and eat regularly (Woods et al., 2000).

Then what does cause hunger? Many different factors combine to promote and suppress hunger. The brain receives many signals from parts of the digestive system, ranging from the tongue and stomach to the intestines and the liver.

The liver? Yes, as the levels of blood sugar (glucose) drop, the liver responds by sending nerve impulses to the brain. These "messages" contribute to a desire to eat (Woods et al., 2000).

Brain Mechanisms

What part of the brain controls hunger? When you are hungry, many parts of the brain are affected, so no single "hunger thermostat" exists. However, a small area called the **hypothalamus** (HI-po-THAL-ah-mus) regulates many motives, including hunger, thirst, and the sex drive (»Fig. 9.5).

The hypothalamus is sensitive to levels of sugar in the blood (and other substances described in a moment). It also receives neural messages from the liver and the stomach. When combined, these signals determine if you are hungry or not (Woods et al., 2000).

One part of the hypothalamus acts as a feeding system that initiates eating. If the *lateral hypothalamus* is "turned on" with an electrified probe, even a well-fed animal will immediately begin eating. (The term *lateral* simply means the sides of the hypothalamus. See »Fig. 9.6.) If the same area is destroyed, the animal will never eat again. The lateral hypothalamus is normally activated in a variety of ways. For example, when you are hungry your stomach lining produces *ghrelin* (GREL-in), a hormone that activates your lateral hypothalamus (Olszewski et al., 2003). (If your stomach is growlin' it's probably releasing ghrelin.) Ghrelin also activates parts of your brain involved in learning. This means you should consider studying before you eat, not immediately afterward (Diano et al., 2006).

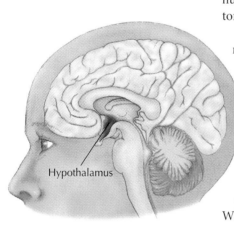

>>**FIGURE 9.5** Location of the hypothalamus in the human brain.

Hypothalamus A small area at the base of the brain that regulates many aspects of motivation and emotion, especially hunger, thirst, and sexual behavior.

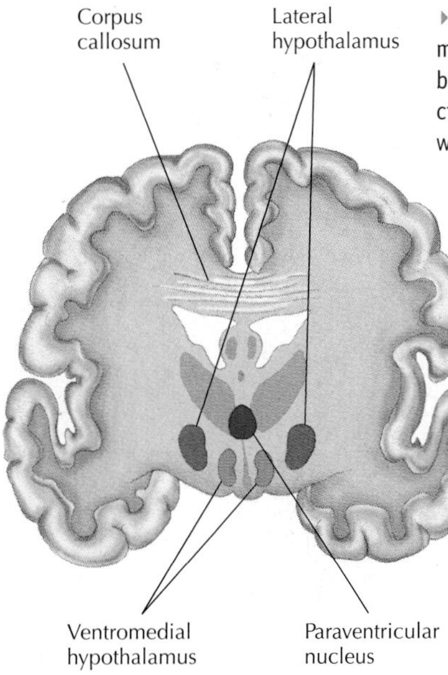

A second area in the hypothalamus is part of a satiety system, or "stop mechanism" for eating. If the *ventromedial hypothalamus* (VENT-ro-MEE-dee-al) is destroyed, dramatic overeating results. (*Ventromedial* refers to the bottom middle of the hypothalamus.) Rats with such damage will eat until they balloon up to weights of 1,000 grams or more (▸▸Fig. 9.7). A normal rat weighs about 180 grams. To put this weight gain in human terms, picture someone you know who weighs 180 pounds growing to a weight of 1,000 pounds.

The *paraventricular nucleus* (PAIR-uh-ven-TRICK-you-ler) of the hypothalamus also affects hunger (▸▸Fig. 9.4). This area helps keep blood sugar levels steady by both starting and stopping eating. The paraventricular nucleus is sensitive to a substance called neu-ropeptide Y (NPY). If NPY is present in large amounts, an animal will eat until it cannot hold another bite (Williams et al., 2004). Incidentally, the hypothalamus also responds to a chemical in marijuana, which can produce intense hunger (the "munchies") (Di Marzo et al., 2001).

How do we know when to stop eating? A chemical called glucagon-like peptide 1 (GLP-1) causes eating to cease. After you eat a meal, GLP-1 is released by the intestines. From there, it travels in the bloodstream to the brain. When enough GLP-1 arrives, your desire to eat ends (Nori, 1998). It takes at least 10 minutes for the hypothalamus to respond after you begin eating. That's why you are less likely to overeat if you eat slowly, which gives your brain time to get the message that you've had enough (Liu et al., 2000).

In addition to knowing when to start eating, and when meals are over, your brain also controls your weight over longer periods of time. (See "Your Brain's 'Fat Point.'")

The substances we have reviewed are only some of the chemical signals that start and stop eating (Geary, 2004). Others continue to be discovered. In time, they may make it possible to artificially control hunger. If so, better treatments for extreme obesity and self-starvation could follow (Batterham et al., 2003).

External Factors in Hunger and Obesity

Our "hunger" is affected by more than just our bodily needs for food. In fact, if internal needs alone controlled eating, fewer people would overeat. Let's consider some external influences on hunger and their role in obesity, a major health risk and, for many, a source of social stigma and low self-esteem.

External Eating Cues

Most of us are sensitive to *external eating cues.* These are signs and signals linked with food. For example, do you tend to eat more when food is highly visible and easy to get? If so, then external cues affect your food intake. In cultures like ours, where food is plentiful, eating cues add greatly to the risk of overeating (Woods et al., 2000). Many college freshmen gain weight rapidly during their first 3 months on campus. All-you-can-eat dining halls in the dorms and nighttime snacking appear to be the culprits (Levitsky et al., 2003). The presence of others can also affect whether people overeat (or undereat) depending on how much everyone else is eating and how important it is to impress them (Pliner & Mann, 2004).

Corpus callosum · Lateral hypothalamus · Ventromedial hypothalamus · Paraventricular nucleus

▸▸**FIGURE 9.6** This is a cross section through the middle of the brain (viewed from the front of the brain). Indicated areas of the hypothalamus are associated with hunger and the regulation of body weight.

John Sholtis, Rockefeller University

▸▸**FIGURE 9.7** Damage to the hunger satiety system in the hypothalamus can produce a very fat rat, a condition called hypothalamic *hyperphagia* (Hi-per-FAGE-yah: overeating). This rat weighs 1,080 grams. (The pointer has gone completely around the dial and beyond.) (Photo courtesy of Neal Miller.)

Your Brain's "Fat Point"

A thermostat set to, say, 72 degrees will constantly turn the heat and/or air conditioning on and off to maintain the temperature at that set point. Like a thermostat, your brain maintains a **set point** in order to control your weight over the long term. It does this by monitoring the amount of fat stored in your body (Ahima & Osei, 2004).

Your set point is the weight you maintain when you are making no effort to gain or lose weight. When your body weight goes below its set point, you will feel hungry most of the time. On the other hand, fat cells release a substance called *leptin* when your "spare tire" is well inflated. Leptin is carried in the bloodstream to the hypothalamus, where it tells us to eat less (Williams et al., 2004).

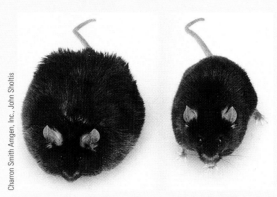

Charron Smith Amgen, Inc., John Sholtis

The mouse on the left has a genetic defect that prevents its fat cells from producing normal amounts of leptin. Without this chemical signal, the mouse's body acts as if its set point for fat storage is, shall we say, rather high.

Can you change your fat set point? Good question. Your leptin levels are partly under genetic control. In rare cases mice (and we humans) inherit a genetic defect that reduces leptin levels in the body, leading to obesity. In such cases, the administration of leptin can help (Williamson et al., 2005).

For the rest of us, the news is not so encouraging because there is currently no known way to lower your set point for fat. To make matters worse, radical diets do not help (but you knew that already, didn't you?). They may even raise the set point for fat, resulting in *diet-induced obesity* (Ahima & Osei, 2004). You may not be able to lose weight by resetting your hypothalamus, but psychologists have studied other approaches to weight loss; we will examine some later in this chapter.

Taste

The availability of a variety of tasty foods can also lead to overeating and obesity in societies where such foods are plentiful. Normally, tastes for foods vary considerably. For example, if you are well fed, leptin dulls the tongue's sensitivity to sweet tastes (Kawai et al., 2000). If you have noticed that you lose your "sweet tooth" when you are full, you may have observed this effect. Actually, if you eat too much of any particular food, it will become less appealing. This probably helps us maintain variety in our diets. However, it also encourages obesity. If you overdose on fried chicken or French fries, moving on to some cookies or chocolate cheesecake certainly won't do your body much good (Pinel, Assanand, & Lehman, 2000).

Emotional Eating

Is it true that people also overeat when they are emotionally upset? Yes. People with weight problems are prone to overeat when they are anxious, angry, or sad (Geliebter & Aversa, 2003). Furthermore, obese individuals are often unhappy in our fat-conscious culture. The result is overeating that leads to emotional distress and still more overeating. This makes weight control extremely difficult (Rutledge & Linden, 1998).

Cultural Factors

Learning to think of some foods as desirable and others as revolting has a large impact on what we eat. In North America we would never consider eating the eyes out of the steamed head of a monkey, but in some parts of the world they are considered a delicacy. By the same token, vegans and vegetarians think it is barbaric to eat any kind of meat. In short, cultural values greatly affect the *incentive value* of foods.

Diet

A diet is not just a way to lose weight. Your current diet is defined by the types and amounts of food you regularly eat. Some diets actually encourage overeating. For instance, placing animals on a "supermarket" diet leads to gross obesity. In one classic experiment, rats were

Set point (for fat) The proportion of body fat that tends to be maintained by changes in hunger and eating.

given meals of chocolate chip cookies, salami, cheese, bananas, marshmallows, milk chocolate, peanut butter, and fat. These pampered rodents overate, gaining almost three times as much weight as rats that ate only laboratory chow (Sclafani & Springer, 1976). (Rat chow is a dry mixture of several bland grains. If you were a rat, you'd probably eat more cookies than rat chow, too.)

People are also sensitive to dietary content. In general, *sweetness*, high *fat content*, and *variety* tend to encourage overeating (Lucas & Sclafani, 1990). Sadly, our culture provides the worst kinds of foods for people who suffer from obesity. Restaurant and fast food tends to be higher in fat and calories than meals made at home (Brownell, 2003). An added problem faced by people who want to control their weight concerns "yo-yo" dieting.

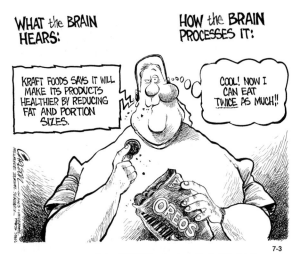

The Paradox of Yo-Yo Dieting

If dieting works, why are hundreds of "new" diets published each year? The answer is that although dieters do lose weight, most regain it soon after they stop dieting. In fact, many people end up weighing even more than before. Why should this be so? Dieting (starving) slows the body's rate of metabolism (the rate at which energy is used up). In effect, a dieter's body becomes highly efficient at *conserving* calories and storing them as fat (Pinel, Assanand, & Lehman, 2000).

Apparently, evolution prepared us to save energy when food is scarce and to stock up on fat when food is plentiful. Briefly starving yourself, therefore, may have little lasting effect on weight. "Yo-yo dieting," or repeatedly losing and gaining weight, is especially dangerous. Frequent changes in weight can dramatically slow the body's metabolic rate. As noted earlier, this may raise the body's set point for fat and makes it harder to lose weight each time a person diets and easier to regain weight when the diet ends. Frequent weight changes also increase the risk of heart disease and premature death (Wang & Brownell, 2005). To avoid bouncing between feast and famine requires a permanent change in eating habits and exercise.

To summarize, eating and overeating are related to internal and external influences, diet, emotions, genetics, exercise, and many other factors. People become obese in different ways and for different reasons. We live in a culture that provides inexpensive, good-tasting food everywhere, and a brain that evolved to say "Eat whenever food is available." Clearly, scientists are still a long way from winning the "battle of the bulge." Nevertheless, many people have learned to take control of eating by applying psychological principles (see "Behavioral Dieting").

Kirstie Alley, the star of the television series *Fat Actress*, has been a lifelong yo-yo dieter who tried many different diets. Ironically, her show pokes fun at the anxieties women like her suffer as they struggle with their weight. As a spokeswoman for a national weight-loss program, Kirstie is again losing weight. Will she maintain her weight loss after she reaches her target weight?

Eating Disorders

Under the sheets of her hospital bed Krystal looks like a skeleton. If her **anorexia nervosa** (AN-uh-REK-see-yah ner-VOH-sah: self-starvation) cannot be stopped, Krystal may die of malnutrition. Victims of anorexia, who are mostly adolescent females (5 to 10 percent are male), suffer devastating weight losses from severe, self-inflicted dieting (Cooper, 2005).

Do anorexics lose their appetite? Although the compulsive attempt to lose weight causes them to not seek or desire food, they often still feel physical hunger. Often, anorexia starts with "normal" dieting that slowly begins to dominate the person's life. In time, anorexics suffer debilitating health problems. Five to eight percent (more than 1 in 20) die

Anorexia nervosa Active self-starvation or a sustained loss of appetite that has psychological origins.

DISCOVERING PSYCHOLOGY

Behavioral Dieting

As we have noted, dieting is usually followed by rapid weight gains. If you really want to lose weight you must overhaul your eating habits, an approach called **behavioral dieting.** Here are some helpful behavioral techniques.

1. **Get yourself committed to weight loss.** Involve other people in your efforts. Programs such as Overeaters Anonymous or Take Off Pounds Sensibly can be a good source of social support.

2. **Exercise.** No diet can succeed for long without an increase in exercise, because exercise burns calories. To lose weight, you must use more calories than you take in. Add activity to your routine in every way you can think of. Stop saving steps and riding elevators. Burning just 200 extra calories a day can help prevent rebound weight gains. The more frequently and vigorously you exercise, the more weight you will lose (Jeffery & Wing, 2001).

3. **Learn your eating habits by observing yourself and keeping a "diet diary."** Begin by making a complete, 2-week record of when and where you eat, what you eat, and the feelings and events that occur just before and after eating. Is a roommate, relative, or spouse encouraging you to overeat? What are your most "dangerous" times and places for overeating?

4. **Learn to weaken your personal eating cues.** When you have learned when and where you do most of your eating, avoid these situations. Try to restrict your eating to one room, and do not read, watch TV, study, or talk on the phone while eating. Require yourself to interrupt what you are doing in order to eat.

5. **Count calories, but don't starve yourself.** To lose weight, you must eat less, and calories allow you to keep a record of your food intake. If you have trouble eating less every day, try dieting 4 days a week. People who diet intensely every other day lose as much as those who diet moderately every day (Viegener et al., 1990).

6. **Develop techniques to control the act of eating.** Begin by taking smaller portions. Carry to the table only what you plan to eat. Put all other food away before leaving the kitchen. Eat slowly, sip water between bites of food, leave food on your plate, and stop eating before you are completely full. Be especially wary of the extra large servings at fast-food restaurants. Saying "super-size me" too often can, indeed, leave you super sized (Murray, 2001).

7. **Avoid snacks.** It is generally better to eat several small meals a day than three large ones because more calories are burned (Assanand, Pinel, & Lehman, 1998). However, high-calorie snacks tend to be eaten *in addition to* meals. If you have an impulse to snack, set a timer for 20 minutes and see if you are still hungry then. Delay the impulse to snack several times if possible. Dull your appetite by filling up on raw carrots, bouillon, water, coffee, or tea.

8. **Chart your progress daily.** Record your weight, the number of calories eaten, and whether you met your daily goal. Set realistic goals by cutting down calories gradually. Losing about a pound per week is realistic, but remember, you are changing habits, not just dieting. Diets don't work!

9. **Set a "threshold" for weight control.** Maintaining weight loss can be even more challenging than losing weight. It is easier to maintain weight losses if you set a regain limit of 3 pounds or less. In other words, if you gain more than 2 or 3 pounds, you immediately begin to make corrections in your eating habits and amount of exercise (Brownell, 2003).

Be patient with this program. It takes years to develop eating habits. You can expect it to take at least several months to change them. If you are unsuccessful at losing weight with these techniques, you might find it helpful to seek the aid of a psychologist familiar with behavioral weight-loss techniques.

of malnutrition (Polivy & Herman, 2002). ■ Table 9.1 lists the symptoms of anorexia nervosa.

Bulimia nervosa (bue-LEE-mee-yah) is a second major eating disorder. Bulimic persons gorge on food, then vomit or take laxatives to avoid gaining weight (see ■ Table 9.1). Like anorexia, most victims of bulimia are girls or women. Approximately 5 percent of college women are bulimic, and as many as 60 percent have milder eating problems. Bingeing and purging can seriously damage health. Typical risks include sore throat, hair loss, muscle

Behavioral dieting Weight reduction based on changing exercise and eating habits, rather than temporary self-starvation.

Bulimia nervosa Excessive eating (gorging) usually followed by self-induced vomiting and/or taking laxatives.

| ■ Table 9.1 | **Recognizing Eating Disorders** |

Anorexia Nervosa

- Body weight below 85 percent of normal for one's height and age.
- Refusal to maintain body weight in normal range.
- Intense fear of becoming fat or gaining weight, even though underweight.
- Disturbance in one's body image or perceived weight.
- Self-evaluation is unduly influenced by body weight.
- Denial of seriousness of abnormally low body weight.
- Absence of menstrual periods.
- Purging behavior (vomiting or misuse of laxatives or diuretics).

Bulimia Nervosa

- Normal or above-normal weight.
- Recurring binge eating.
- Eating within an hour or two an amount of food that is much larger than most people would consume.
- Feeling a lack of control over eating.
- Purging behavior (vomiting or misuse of laxatives or diuretics).
- Excessive exercise to prevent weight gain.
- Fasting to prevent weight gain.
- Self-evaluation is unduly influenced by body weight.

Source: DSM-IV-TR, 2000.

Anorexia nervosa is far more dangerous than many people realize. This haunting photo shows popular singer Karen Carpenter shortly before she died of starvation-induced heart failure. Many other celebrities have struggled with eating disorders, including Paula Abdul, Kirstie Alley, Fiona Apple, Victoria Beckham (Posh Spice), Princess Diana, Tracey Gold, Janet Jackson, and Mary-Kate Olsen.

spasms, kidney damage, dehydration, tooth erosion, swollen salivary glands, menstrual irregularities, loss of sex drive, and even heart attack.

Causes

What causes anorexia and bulimia? Women and men who suffer from eating disorders are extremely dissatisfied with their bodies (Crisp et al., 2006). Usually, they have distorted views of themselves and exaggerated fears of becoming fat. Many overestimate their body size by 25 percent or more. As a result, they think they are disgustingly "fat" when they are actually wasting away (⇢Fig. 9.8) (Polivy & Herman, 2002). Many of these problems are related to harmful messages in the media. Girls who spend a lot of time reading teen magazines are more likely to have distorted body images and unrealistic ideas about how they compare with others (Martinez-Gonzalez et al., 2003).

Anorexic teens are usually described as "perfect" daughters—helpful, considerate, conforming, and obedient. Many seem to be seeking perfect control in their lives by being perfectly slim (Castro et al., 2004). People suffering from bulimia are also concerned with con-

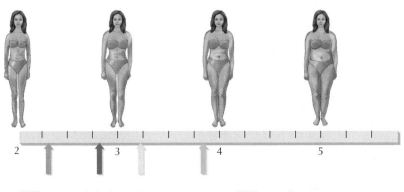

Perceived ideal weight

Perceived as most attractive to men

Actually most attractive to men

Perceived current weight

⇢**FIGURE 9.8** Women with abnormal eating habits were asked to rate their body shape on a scale similar to the one you see here. As a group, they chose ideal figures much thinner than what they thought their current weights were. (Most women say they want to be thinner than they currently are, but to a lesser degree than women with eating problems.) Notice that women with eating problems chose an ideal weight that was even thinner than what they thought men prefer. This is not typical of most women. Only women with eating problems wanted to be thinner than what they thought men find attractive (Zellner, Harner, & Adler, 1989).

trol. Typically they are obsessed with thoughts of weight, food, eating, and ridding themselves of food. As a result, they feel guilt, shame, self-contempt, and anxiety. Vomiting reduces their anxiety, which makes purging highly reinforcing (Powell & Thelen, 1996).

Treatment

Most people suffering from eating disorders will not seek help on their own. Typically, it takes strong urging by family or friends to get victims into treatment.

Treatment for anorexia usually begins with giving drugs to relieve obsessive fears of gaining weight. Then a medical diet is used to restore weight and health. Next, a counselor may help patients work on the emotional conflicts that led to weight loss. For bulimia, behavioral counseling may include self-monitoring of food intake. A related cognitive-behavioral approach focuses on changing the thinking patterns and beliefs about weight and body shape that perpetuate eating disorders (Byrne & McLean, 2002; Cooper, 2005).

PRIMARY MOTIVES REVISITED— THIRST, PAIN, AND SEX

>SURVEY QUESTIONS< *Is there more than one type of thirst? In what ways are pain avoidance and the sex drive unusual?*

Most biological motives work in ways that are similar to hunger. For example, thirst is only partially controlled by dryness of the mouth. If you were to take a drug that made your mouth constantly wet, or dry, your water intake would remain normal. Like hunger, thirst is regulated by separate *thirst* and *thirst satiety* systems in the hypothalamus. Also like hunger, thirst is strongly affected by learning and cultural values.

Thirst

You may not have noticed, but there are actually two kinds of thirst. **Extracellular thirst** occurs when water is lost from the fluids surrounding the cells of your body. Bleeding, vomiting, diarrhea, sweating, and drinking alcohol cause this type of thirst (Petri & Govern, 2004). When a person loses both water and minerals in any of these ways—especially by perspiration—a slightly salty liquid may be more satisfying than plain water.

Why would a thirsty person want to drink salty water? The reason is that before the body can retain water, minerals lost through perspiration (mainly salt) must be replaced. In lab tests, animals greatly prefer saltwater after salt levels in their bodies are lowered (Strickler & Verbalis, 1988). Similarly, some nomadic peoples of the Sahara Desert prize blood as a beverage, probably because of its saltiness. (Maybe they should try Gatorade?)

A second type of thirst occurs when you eat a salty meal. In this instance your body does not lose fluid. Instead, excess salt causes fluid to be drawn out of cells. As the cells "shrink," **intracellular thirst** is triggered. Thirst of this type is best quenched by plain water.

The drives for food, water, air, sleep, and elimination are all similar in that they are generated by a combination of activities in the body and the brain, and they are influenced by various external factors. However, the drive to avoid pain and the sex drive are more unusual.

Pain

How is the drive to avoid pain different? Hunger, thirst, and sleepiness come and go in fairly regular cycles each day. Pain avoidance, by contrast, is an **episodic drive** (ep-ih-SOD-ik). That is, it occurs in distinct episodes when bodily damage takes place or is about to occur. Most drives prompt us to actively seek a desired goal (food, drink, warmth, and so forth). Pain prompts us to *avoid* or *eliminate* sources of discomfort.

Extracellular thirst Thirst caused by a reduction in the volume of fluids found between body cells.

Intracellular thirst Thirst triggered when fluid is drawn out of cells due to an increased concentration of salts and minerals outside the cell.

Episodic drive A drive that occurs in distinct episodes.

Some people feel they must be "tough" and not show any distress. Others complain loudly at the smallest ache or pain. The first attitude raises pain tolerance, and the second lowers it. As this suggests, the drive to avoid pain is partly learned. That's why members of some societies endure cutting, burning, whipping, tattooing, and piercing of the skin that would agonize most people (but apparently not devotees of piercing and "body art"). In general, we learn how to react to pain by observing family members, friends, and other role models (McMahon & Koltzenburg, 2005).

Tolerance for pain and the strength of a person's motivation to avoid discomfort are greatly affected by cultural practices and beliefs.

The Sex Drive

Many psychologists do not think of sex as a primary motive, because sex (contrary to anything your personal experience might suggest) is not necessary for *individual* survival. It is necessary, of course, for *group* survival.

The term **sex drive** refers to the strength of one's motivation to engage in sexual behavior. In lower animals the sex drive is directly related to hormones. Female mammals (other than humans) are interested in mating only when their fertility cycles are in the stage of **estrus,** or "heat." Estrus is caused by a release of **estrogen** (a female sex hormone) into the bloodstream. Hormones are important in males as well. In most animals, castration will abolish the sex drive. But in contrast to females, the normal male animal is almost always ready to mate. His sex drive is primarily aroused by the behavior and scent of a receptive female. Therefore, in many species mating is closely tied to female fertility cycles.

How much do hormones affect human sex drives? Hormones affect the human sex drive, but not as directly as in animals (Crooks & Baur, 2005). The sex drive in men is related to the amount of **androgens** (male hormones) provided by the testes. When the supply of androgens dramatically increases at puberty, so does the male sex drive. Likewise, the sex drive in women is related to their estrogen levels (Hyde & DeLamater, 2006). However, "male" hormones also affect the female sex drive. In addition to estrogen, a woman's body produces small amounts of androgens. When their androgen levels increase, many women experience a corresponding increase in sex drive (Van Goozen et al., 1995). Testosterone levels decline with age, and various medical problems can lower sexual desire. In some instances, taking testosterone supplements can restore the sex drive in both men and women (Crooks & Baur, 2005).

Does alcohol increase the sex drive? In general, no. Alcohol is a *depressant.* As such, it may, in small doses, stimulate erotic desire by lowering inhibitions. This effect no doubt accounts for alcohol's reputation as an aid to seduction. (Humorist Ogden Nash once summarized this bit of folklore by saying "Candy is dandy, but liquor is quicker.") However, in larger doses alcohol suppresses orgasm in women and erection in men. Getting drunk *decreases* sexual desire, arousal, pleasure, and performance (McKay, 2005).

Numerous other drugs are reputed to be aphrodisiacs (af-ruh-DEEZ-ee-aks: substances that increase sexual desire or pleasure). However, like alcohol, many other drugs actually impair sexual response, rather than enhance it (McKay, 2005). Some examples are amphetamines, amyl nitrite, barbiturates, cocaine, Ecstasy, LSD, and marijuana. In the end, love is the best aphrodisiac (Crooks & Baur, 2005).

Perhaps the most interesting fact about the sex drive is that it is largely *nonhomeostatic* (relatively independent of bodily need states). In humans, the sex drive can be aroused at virtually any time by almost anything. It therefore shows no clear relationship to deprivation (the amount of time since the drive was last satisfied). Certainly, an increase in desire may occur as time passes. But recent sexual activity does not prevent sexual desire from occurring again. Notice, too, that people may seek to arouse the sex drive as well as to reduce

Sex drive The strength of one's motivation to engage in sexual behavior.

Estrus Changes in the sexual drives of animals that create a desire for mating; particularly used to refer to females in heat.

Estrogen Any of a number of female sex hormones.

Androgen Any of a number of male sex hormones, especially testosterone.

it. This unusual quality makes the sex drive capable of motivating a wide range of behaviors. It also explains why sex is used to sell almost everything imaginable.

Because sex drive affects the lives of most people, let's explore human sexuality in a little more detail.

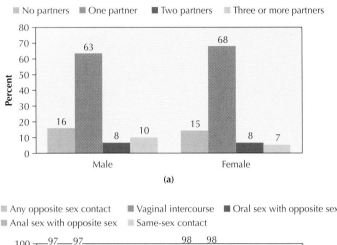

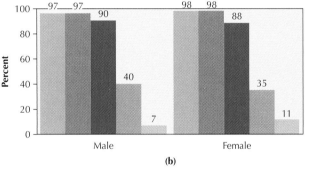

▸▸**FIGURE 9.9** These graphs show the pattern of sexual behavior for American adults. *(a)* Men and women do not differ in their average number of sexual partners or *(b)* in their overall pattern of sexual activity. (Adapted from Mosher, Chandra, & Jones, 2005.)

SEXUAL BEHAVIOR—MAPPING THE EROGENOUS ZONE

>SURVEY QUESTION< *What are the typical patterns of human sexual response?*

Human sexual arousal is complex. It may, of course, be produced by direct stimulation of the body's **erogenous zones** (eh-ROJ-eh-nus: productive of pleasure or erotic desire). Human erogenous zones include the genitals, mouth, breasts, ears, anus, and to a lesser degree, the entire surface of the body. It is clear, however, that more than physical contact is involved: A urological or gynecological exam rarely results in any sexual arousal. Likewise, an unwanted sexual advance may produce only revulsion. Human sexual arousal obviously includes a large mental element.

Sexual Arousal

Are men more easily sexually aroused than women? Overall, women and men have equal potential for sexual arousal and women are no less *physically* responsive than men. However, women tend to place more emphasis on emotional closeness with a lover than men do (Basson et al., 2005; Peplau, 2003).

Based on the frequency of orgasm (from masturbation or intercourse), the peak of male sexual activity is at age 18. The peak rate of female sexual activity appears to occur a little later (Janus & Janus, 1993). However, male and female sexual patterns are rapidly becoming more alike. ▸▸Figure 9.9 presents some of the data on sexual behavior from a major national health survey of American men and women aged 25 to 44. As you can see, in any given year, men and women do not differ in their average number of opposite-sex partners or in their overall pattern of sexual activity (Mosher et al., 2005). Exaggerating the differences between male and female sexuality is not only inaccurate, it can also create artificial barriers to sexual satisfaction (Wiederman, 2001). For example, assuming that men should always initiate sex denies the fact that women have comparable sexual interests and needs.

Human Sexual Response

In a pioneering series of studies, William Masters and Virginia Johnson directly studied sexual intercourse in nearly 700 males and females. The objective information they gained has given us a much clearer picture of human sexuality (Masters & Johnson, 1966, 1970). According to Masters and Johnson, sexual response can be divided into four phases: (1) *excitement*, (2) *plateau*, (3) *orgasm*, and (4) *resolution* (▸▸Fig. 9.10 and ▸▸Fig. 9.11):

Excitement phase The first level of sexual response, indicated by initial signs of sexual arousal.

Plateau phase The second level of sexual response, during which physical arousal intensifies.

Erogenous zones Areas of the body that produce pleasure and/or provoke erotic desire.

Excitement phase The first phase of sexual response, indicated by initial signs of sexual arousal.

Plateau phase The second phase of sexual response during which physical arousal is further heightened.

Orgasm A climax and release of sexual excitement.

Resolution The final phase of sexual response, involving a return to lower levels of sexual tension and arousal.

The four phases are the same for people of all sexual orientations (Garnets & Kimmel, 1991).

Female Response

In women, the excitement phase is marked by a complex pattern of changes in the body. The vagina is prepared for intercourse, the nipples become erect, pulse rate rises, and the skin may become flushed or reddened. If sexual stimulation ends, the excitement phase will gradually subside. If a woman moves into the plateau phase, physical changes and subjective feelings of arousal become more intense. Sexual arousal that ends during this phase tends to ebb more slowly, which may produce considerable frustration. Occasionally, women skip the plateau phase (see ▸▸Fig. 9.10). For some women, this is almost always the case. Orgasm is usually followed by resolution, a return to lower levels of sexual tension and arousal. After orgasm, about 15 percent of all women return to the plateau phase and may have one or more additional orgasms (Mah & Binik, 2001).

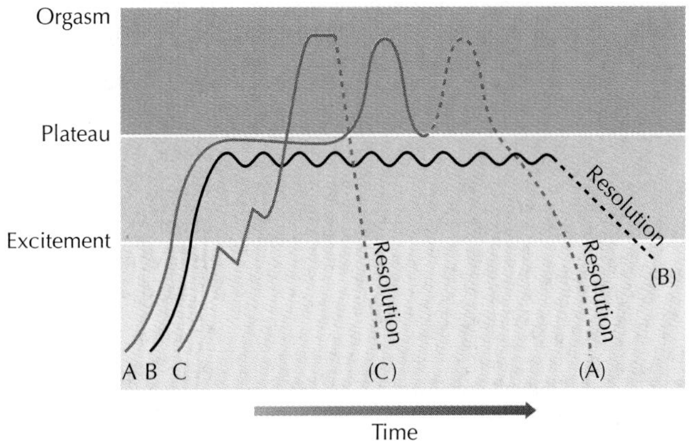

▸▸**FIGURE 9.10** Female sexual response cycle. The green line shows that sexual arousal rises through the excitement phase and levels off for a time during the plateau phase. Arousal peaks during orgasm and then returns to pre-excitement levels. In pattern A, arousal rises from excitement, through the plateau phase, and peaks in orgasm. Resolution may be immediate, or it may first include a return to the plateau phase and a second orgasm (dotted line). In pattern B, arousal is sustained at the plateau phase and slowly resolved without sexual climax. Pattern C shows a fairly rapid rise in arousal to orgasm. Little time is spent in the plateau phase and resolution is fairly rapid. (Reproduced by permission from Frank A. Beach [ed.], *Sex and Behavior,* NY: John Wiley & Sons, Inc., 1965.)

Male Response

Sexual arousal in the male is signaled by erection of the penis during the excitement phase. There is also a rise in heart rate, increased blood flow to the genitals, enlargement of the testicles, erection of the nipples, and numerous other bodily changes. As is true of female sexual response, continued stimulation moves the male into the plateau phase. Again, physical changes and subjective feelings of arousal become more intense. Further stimulation during the plateau phase brings about a reflex release of sexual tension, resulting in orgasm.

In the mature male, orgasm is usually accompanied by *ejaculation* (release of sperm and seminal fluid). Afterward, it is followed by a short *refractory period* during which a second orgasm is impossible. Only rarely is the male refractory period immediately followed by a second orgasm. Both orgasm and resolution in the male usually do not last as long as they do for females.

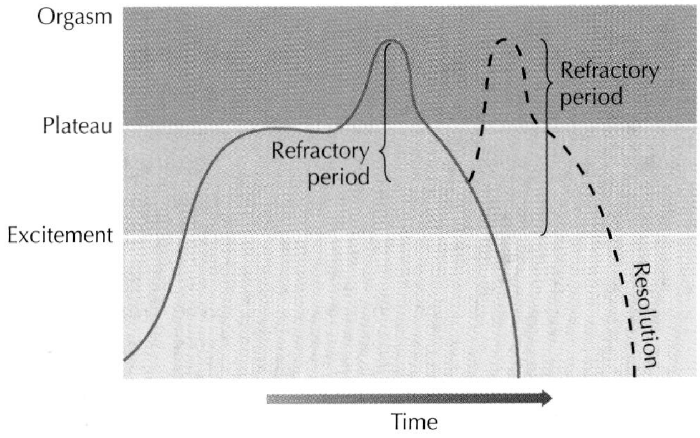

▸▸**FIGURE 9.11** Male sexual response cycle. The green line shows that sexual arousal rises through the excitement phase and levels off for a time during the plateau phase. Arousal peaks during orgasm and then returns to pre-excitement levels. During the refractory period, immediately after orgasm, a second sexual climax is typically impossible. However, after the refractory period has passed, there may be a return to the plateau phase, followed by a second orgasm (dotted line). (Reproduced by permission from Frank A. Beach [ed.], *Sex and Behavior,* NY: John Wiley & Sons, Inc., 1965.)

Comparing Male and Female Responses

Male and female sexual responses are generally quite similar. However, the differences that do exist can affect sexual compatibility. For example, women typically go through the sexual phases more slowly than men do. However, during masturbation, 70 percent of females reach orgasm in 4 minutes or less. This is quite comparable to male response times. It suggests again that women are no less physically responsive than men.

In one regard, women are clearly more responsive. Only about 5 percent of males are capable of multiple orgasm (and then only after an unavoidable refractory period). Most men are limited to a second orgasm at best. In contrast, Masters and Johnson's findings suggest that most women who regularly experience orgasm are capable of multiple orgasm. According to one survey, 48 percent of all women have had multiple orgasms (Darling et al., 1992). Remember, though, that only about 15 percent regularly have multiple orgasms. A woman should not automatically assume that something is wrong if she isn't orgasmic or multiorgasmic. Many women have satisfying sexual experiences even when orgasm is not involved. (For information about common sexual complaints, see "Sexual Problems.")

Orgasm A climax and release of sexual excitement.

Resolution The fourth phase of sexual response, involving a return to lower levels of sexual tension and arousal.

Sexual Scripts

In a restaurant we commonly expect certain things to occur. It could even be said that each of us has a restaurant "script" that defines a plot, dialogue, and actions that should take place. We also learn a variety of **sexual scripts,** or unspoken mental plans that guide our sexual behavior. Such scripts determine when and where we are likely to express sexual feelings, and with whom (Lenton & Bryan, 2005). They provide a "plot" for the order of events in lovemaking and they outline "approved" actions, motives, and outcomes.

When two people follow markedly different scripts, misunderstandings are almost sure to occur. Consider, for instance, what happens when a woman acting out a "friendly-first-date" script is paired with a man following a "seduction" script: The result is often anger, hurt feelings, or worse (Schleicher & Gilbert, 2005). Even newlyweds may find that their sexual "agendas" differ. In such cases, considerable "rewriting" of scripts is often needed for sexual compatibility. For humans the mind (or brain) is the ultimate erogenous zone.

Sexual Orientation—Who Do You Love?

Sexual behavior and romantic relationships are strongly influenced by a person's sexual orientation. **Sexual orientation** refers to your degree of emotional and erotic attraction to members of the same sex, opposite sex, or both sexes. *Heterosexual* people are romantically and erotically attracted to members of the opposite sex. Those who are *homosexual* are attracted to people whose sex matches their own. A person who is *bisexual* is attracted to both men and women. In short, sexual orientation answers these questions: Who are you attracted to? Who do you have erotic fantasies about? Do you love men, or women, or both (Garnets, 2002)?

Sexual orientation is a deep part of personal identity. Starting with their earliest erotic feelings, most people remember being attracted to either the opposite sex or the same sex. The chances are practically nil of an exclusively heterosexual or homosexual person being "converted" from one orientation to the other. If you are heterosexual, you are probably certain that nothing could ever make you have homoerotic feelings. If so, then you know how homosexual persons feel about the prospects for changing *their* sexual orientation (Seligman, 1994).

What determines a person's sexual orientation? Evidence suggests that sexual orientation is at least partly hereditary, although biological, social, cultural, and psychological influences are also involved (Garnets, 2002). Some researchers now estimate that sexual orientation is from 30 to 70 percent genetic (Mustanski, Chivers, & Bailey, 2002).

How could genes affect sexual orientation? Possibly, heredity shapes areas of the brain that orchestrate sexual behavior. Support for this idea comes from the work of neuroscientists who have shown that various brain structures and brain chemicals differ in heterosexuals and homosexuals (Kinnunen et al., 2004; LeVay, 1993).

Homosexuality is not caused by hormone imbalances (Banks & Gartrell, 1995). It is also a mistake to think that parenting makes children homosexual. There is little difference in the development of children with gay or lesbian parents and those who have heterosexual parents (Patterson, 2002; Wainwright et al., 2004). It appears that nature strongly prepares people to be either homosexual or heterosexual. In view of this, discriminating against homosexuals is much like rejecting a person for being blue-eyed or left-handed (Rathus et al., 2005).

Homosexual people are found in all walks of life, at all social and economic levels, and in all cultural groups (Garnets, 2002). Perhaps as more people come to see gay and lesbian people in terms of their humanity, rather than their sexuality, the prejudices they have faced will wane.

Sexual script An unspoken mental plan that defines a "plot," dialogue, and actions expected to take place in a sexual encounter.

Sexual orientation One's degree of emotional and erotic attraction to members of the same sex, opposite sex, or both sexes.

Healthy Sexual Relationships

Regardless of sexual responsiveness or sexual orientation, as a shared pleasure, a form of intimacy, a means of communication, and a haven from everyday tensions, a positive sexual relationship can do much to enhance a couple's mutual understanding and caring. People are most likely to value their sexuality when they develop a respectful, trusting, and intimate relationship with their partner. A sense of closeness helps maintain sexual interest and mutually satisfying lovemaking, especially in long-term relationships (McCarthy, 1995).

Sexual Problems—When Pleasure Fades

Sexual dysfunctions are far more common than many people realize. Most people who seek sexual counseling have one or more of the following types of problems (DSM-IV-TR, 2000; Heiman, 2002):

Desire Disorders: The person has little or no sexual motivation or desire.

Arousal Disorders: The person desires sexual activity but does not become sexually aroused.

Orgasm Disorders: The person does not have orgasms or experiences orgasm too soon or too late.

Sexual Pain Disorders: The person experiences pain that makes lovemaking uncomfortable or impossible.

There was a time when people suffered such problems in silence. However, in recent years effective treatments have been found for many complaints. Medical treatments or drugs (such as Viagra for men) may be helpful for sexual problems that clearly have physical causes. In other cases, counseling or psychotherapy may be the best approach.

For example, many patients benefit from a technique called *sensate focus.* In sensate focus, distressed couples begin by taking turns caressing each other in nonsexual ways. They are told to concentrate on giving pleasure and on signaling what feels good to them. This relieves the pressure to perform and it builds communication skills. Slowly, the couple moves on to mutually satisfying lovemaking, as natural arousal begins to replace fear and anger. Similar solutions exist for many sexual problems. In most communities, professional help can be obtained from appropriately trained psychologists, physicians, or counselors.

 Study Break   Hunger, Thirst, Pain, and Sex

Reflect

Think of the last meal you ate. What caused you to feel hungry? What internal signals told your body to stop eating? How sensitive are you to external eating cues?

A friend of yours seems to be engaging in yo-yo dieting. Can you explain to her or him why such dieting is ineffective?

Even if you're not overweight, reread each of the weight-control techniques listed in the "Using Psychology" box and visualize how you would carry out the suggested behaviors.

If you wanted to provoke extracellular thirst in yourself, what would you do? How could you make intracellular thirst occur?

In what ways are sexual responses of members of the opposite sex similar to your own? In what ways are they different?

Learning Check

1. The hunger satiety system in the hypothalamus signals the body to start eating when it receives signals from the liver or detects changes in blood sugar. T or F?
2. People who diet frequently tend to benefit from practice: They lose weight more quickly each time they diet. T or F?

3. Anorexia nervosa is also known as the binge-purge syndrome. T or F?
4. In addition to burning calories, physical exercise can lower the body's set point. T or F?
5. Thirst may be either intracellular or _____.
6. Pain avoidance is a(n) _____ drive.
7. Sexual behavior in animals is largely controlled by estrogen levels in the female and the occurrence of estrus in the male. T or F?
8. List the four phases of sexual response identified by Masters and Johnson:

   _____

Critical Thinking

9. Kim, who is overweight, is highly sensitive to external eating cues. How might her wristwatch contribute to her overeating?
10. Charting weight loss makes use of a behavioral principle discussed in Chapter 6, "Conditioning and Learning." Can you name it?

Answers

1. F 2. F 3. F 4. T 5. extracellular 6. episodic 7. F 8. excitement, plateau, orgasm, resolution 9. The time of day can influence eating, especially for externally cued eaters, who tend to get hungry at mealtimes, irrespective of their internal needs for food. 10. feedback

▸▸**FIGURE 9.12** Monkeys happily open locks that are placed in their cage. Because no reward is given for this activity, it provides evidence for the existence of stimulus needs. (Photo courtesy of Harry F. Harlow.)

STIMULUS DRIVES—SKYDIVING, HORROR MOVIES, AND THE FUN ZONE

>SURVEY QUESTION< *How does arousal relate to motivation?*

Most people enjoy a steady "diet" of new movies, novels, tunes, fashions, games, news, websites, and adventures. Yet *stimulus drives,* which reflect needs for information, exploration, manipulation, and sensory input, go beyond mere entertainment. Stimulus drives also help us survive. As we scan our surroundings, we constantly identify sources of food, danger, shelter, and other key details. Stimulus drives are readily apparent in animals as well as humans. For example, monkeys will quickly learn to solve a mechanical puzzle made up of interlocking metal pins, hooks, and latches (Butler, 1954) (▸▸Fig. 9.12). No food treats or other external rewards are needed to get them to explore and manipulate their surroundings. The monkeys seem to work for the sheer fun of it. The drive for stimulation can even be observed in infants. By the time a child can walk, there are few things in the home that have not been tasted, touched, viewed, handled, or, in the case of toys, destroyed!

Are you full of energy right now? Are you feeling tired? Clearly, the level of arousal you are experiencing is closely linked with your motivation. Are there ideal levels of arousal for different people and different activities? Let's find out.

Arousal Theory

Are stimulus drives homeostatic? Yes. According to **arousal theory** we try to keep arousal at an optimal level (Franken, 2007; Hancock & Ganey, 2003). In other words, when your level of arousal is too low or too high, you will seek ways to raise or lower it.

What do you mean by arousal? *Arousal* refers to the activation of the body and the nervous system. Arousal is zero at death; it is low during sleep; it is moderate during normal daily activities; and it is high at times of excitement, emotion, or panic. Arousal theory assumes that we become uncomfortable when arousal is too low ("I'm bored") or when it is too high, as in fear, anxiety, or panic ("The dentist will see you now"). Most adults vary their activities to maintain a comfortable level of activation. Music, parties, sports, conversation, sleep, surfing the Internet, and the like, are combined to keep arousal at moderate levels. The right mix of activities prevents boredom *and* overstimulation (Nakamura & Csikszentmihalyi, 2002).

Levels of Arousal

Is there an ideal level of arousal for peak performance? If we set aside individual differences, most people perform best when their arousal level is *moderate.* Let's say that you have to take an essay exam. If you are feeling sleepy or lazy (arousal level too low), your performance will suffer. If you are in a state of anxiety or panic about the test (arousal level too high), you will also perform below par. Thus, the relationship between arousal and performance forms an *inverted U function* (a curve in the shape of an upside-down U) (▸▸Fig. 9.13) (Hancock & Ganey, 2003).

The inverted U tells us that at very low levels of arousal you're not sufficiently energized to perform well. Performance will improve as your arousal level increases, up to the middle of the curve. Then it begins to drop off, as you become emotional, frenzied, or disorganized. For example, imagine trying to start a car stalled on a railroad track, with a speeding train bearing down on you. That's what the high-arousal end of the curve feels like.

Is performance always best at moderate levels of arousal? No, the ideal level of arousal depends on the complexity of a task. If a task is relatively simple, it is best for arousal to be high. When a task is more complex, your best performance will occur at lower levels of

Arousal theory Assumes that people prefer to maintain ideal, or comfortable, levels of arousal.

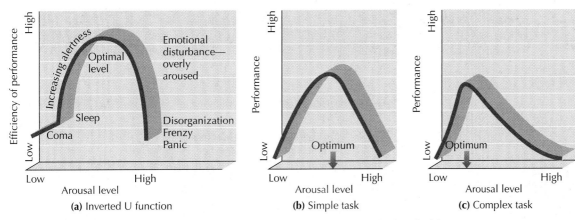

FIGURE 9.13 *(a)* The general relationship between arousal and efficiency can be described by an inverted U curve. The optimal level of arousal or motivation is higher for a simple task *(b)* than for a complex task *(c)*.

arousal. This relationship is called the **Yerkes-Dodson law** (see ▸▸Fig. 9.13). It applies to a wide variety of tasks and to measures of motivation other than arousal.

For example, at a track meet, it is almost impossible for sprinters to get too aroused for a race. The task is direct and simple: Run as fast as you can for a short distance. On the other hand, a golfer making a tournament-deciding putt faces a more sensitive and complex task. Excessive arousal is almost certain to hurt his or her performance. In school, most students have had experience with "test anxiety," a familiar example of how too much arousal can lower performance.

Coping with Test Anxiety

Then is it true that by learning to calm down, a person would do better on tests? Usually, but not always. **Test anxiety** is a mixture of *heightened physiological arousal* (nervousness, sweating, pounding heart) and *excessive worry*. This combination—arousal plus worry—tends to distract students with a rush of upsetting thoughts and feelings (Stipek, 2001). Studies show that students are typically most anxious when they don't know the material. If this is the case, calming down simply means you will remain calm while failing. Here are some suggestions for coping with test anxiety:

Preparation

Hard work is the most direct antidote for test anxiety. Many test-anxious students simply study too little, too late. That's why improving your study skills is a good way to reduce test anxiety (Cassady, 2004). The best solution is to *overprepare* by studying long before the "big day." Well-prepared students score higher, worry less, and are less likely to panic (Zohar, 1998).

Relaxation

Learning to relax is another way to lower test anxiety (Powell, 2004). You can learn self-relaxation skills by looking at Chapter 13, where a relaxation technique is described. Emotional support also helps (Stöber, 2004). If you are test anxious, discuss the problem with your professors or study for tests with a supportive classmate.

Rehearsal

To reduce nervousness, rehearse how you will cope with upsetting events. Before taking a test, imagine yourself going blank, running out of time, or feeling panicked. Then calmly plan how you will handle each situation—by keeping your attention on the task, by focusing on one question at a time, and so forth (Watson & Tharp, 2001).

Yerkes-Dodson law A summary of the relationships among arousal, task complexity, and performance.

Test anxiety High levels of arousal and worry that seriously impair test performance.

Xtreme!

Where would you prefer to go on your next summer vacation? How about a week with your best friends at a cottage on a nearby lake? Or a shopping and museum trip to New York City? Better yet, how about cage diving with great white sharks in South Africa? If the shark adventure attracts you, you are probably high in sensation seeking and would be interested in a vacation which includes activities like bungee-jumping, scuba diving, skiing, skydiving, or white-water rafting (Pizam et al., 2004).

Marvin Zuckerman (1996, 2000) has devised a test to measure differences in sensation seeking. His *Sensation-Seeking Scale* (SSS)

includes statements like the samples shown here (from Zuckerman, 1996):

Thrill and adventure seeking
- I would like to try parachute jumping.
- I think I would enjoy the sensations of skiing very fast down a high mountain slope.

Experience seeking
- I like to explore a strange city or section of town myself, even if it means getting lost.
- I like to try new foods that I have never tasted before.

Disinhibition
- I like wild, "uninhibited" parties.
- I often like to get high (drinking liquor or smoking marijuana).

Boredom susceptibility
- I can't stand watching a movie that I've seen before.
- I like people who are sharp and witty, even if they do sometimes insult others.

So who are the potential cage divers? Perhaps it's not surprising that SSS scores tend to be higher among men and younger people (Butkovic & Bratko, 2003; Roberti, 2004). SSS scores also vary across cultures. In one study of 11 different cultures, people from America, Israel, and Ireland scored higher on the SSS than did people from South Africa, Slovakia, or Gabon (Pizam et al., 2004).

Jeffrey L. Rotman

Thrill seeking is an element of the sensation-seeking personality.

Restructuring Thoughts

Another helpful strategy involves listing the upsetting thoughts you have during exams. Then you can learn to combat these worries with calming, rational replies (Jones & Petruzzi, 1995). (These are called *coping statements;* see Chapter 11 for more information.) Let's say you think, "I'm going to fail this test and everybody will think I'm stupid." A good reply to this upsetting thought would be to say, "If I prepare well and control my worries, I will probably pass the test. Even if I don't, it won't be the end of the world. My friends will still like me, and I can try to improve on the next test."

Students who cope well with exams usually try to do the best they can, even under trying circumstances. Becoming a more confident test taker can actually increase your scores, because it helps you remain calm. With practice, most people can learn to be less testy at test-taking time (Smith, 2002).

Sensation Seekers

Do people vary in their needs for stimulation? Picture a city dweller who is visiting the country. Before long, she begins to complain that it is "too quiet" and seeks some "action." Now imagine a country dweller who is visiting the city. Very soon, she finds the city "overwhelming" and seeks peace and quiet. These examples are extremes, but arousal theory also suggests that people learn to seek particular levels of arousal. Sensation seeking is a trait of people who prefer high levels of stimulation. Which are you? To find out, see "Xtreme!"

Whether you are high or low in sensation seeking is probably based on how your body responds to new, unusual, or intense stimulation (Zuckerman, 1990, 2002). People high in sensation seeking tend to be bold, independent, and value change. They also are more likely to smoke, and they prefer spicy, sour, and crunchy foods over bland foods. Low sensation seekers are orderly, nurturant, giving, and they enjoy the company of others.

There is also a darker side to sensation seeking. High sensation seekers are also more likely to engage in high-risk behaviors such as substance abuse (Horvath et al., 2004) and casual unprotected sex (Gullette & Lyons, 2005).

SOCIAL MOTIVES—IN PURSUIT OF EXCELLENCE

>SURVEY QUESTIONS< *What are social motives? Why are they important?*

Some of your friends are more interested than others in success, achievement, competition, money, possessions, status, love, approval, grades, dominance, power, or belonging to groups—all of which are *social motives* or goals. We acquire **social motives** in complex ways, through socialization and cultural conditioning (Petri & Govern, 2004). The behavior of outstanding artists, scientists, athletes, educators, and leaders is best understood in terms of such learned needs, particularly the need for achievement.

The Need for Achievement

To many people, being "motivated" means being interested in achievement (Wigfield & Eccles, 2002). In a later chapter we will investigate aggression, helping, affiliation, seeking approval, and other social motives. For now, let us focus on the **need for achievement (nAch),** which is a desire to meet an internal standard of excellence (McClelland, 1961). People with a high need for achievement strive to do well any time they are evaluated.

Is that like the aggressive businessperson who strives for success? Not necessarily. Needs for achievement may lead to wealth and prestige, but people who are high achievers in art, music, science, or amateur sports may excel without seeking riches. Such people typically enjoy challenges and they relish a chance to test their abilities (Puca & Schmalt, 1999).

Power

The need for achievement differs from the **need for power,** which is a desire to have impact or control over others (McClelland, 1975). People with strong needs for power want their importance to be visible: They buy expensive possessions, wear prestigious clothes, and exploit relationships. In some ways, the pursuit of power and financial success is the dark side of the American dream. People whose main goal in life is to make lots of money tend to be poorly adjusted and unhappy (Kasser & Ryan, 1993).

Characteristics of Achievers

Using a simple measure, David McClelland (1917–1998) found that he could predict the behavior of high and low achievers. For instance, McClelland compared people's occupations with scores on an achievement test they took as college sophomores. Fourteen years later, those who scored high in nAch tended to have jobs that involved risk and responsibility (McClelland, 1965).

Here's a test: In front of you are five targets. Each is placed at an increasing distance from where you are standing. You are given a beanbag to toss at the target of your choice. Target A, anyone can hit; target B, most people can hit; target C, some people can hit; target D, very few people can hit; target E is rarely if ever hit. If you hit A, you will receive $2; B, $4; C, $8; D, $16; and E, $32. You get only one toss. Which one would you choose? McClelland's research suggests that if you have a high need for achievement, you will select C or perhaps D. Those high in nAch are *moderate* risk takers. When faced with a problem or a challenge, persons high in nAch avoid goals that are too easy.

Why do they pass up sure success? They do it because easy goals offer no sense of satisfaction. They also avoid long shots because there is either no hope of success, or "winning" will

Social motives Learned motives acquired as part of growing up in a particular society or culture.

Need for achievement (nAch) The desire to excel or meet some internalized standard of excellence.

Need for power The desire to have social impact and control over others.

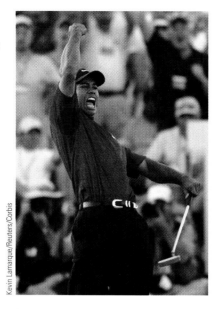

The person with high needs for achievement strives to do well in any situation in which evaluation takes place.

Kevin Lamarque/Reuters/Corbis

be due to luck rather than skill. Persons low in nAch select sure things or impossible goals. Either way, they don't have to take any responsibility for failure.

Desires for achievement and calculated risk taking lead to success in many situations. People high in nAch complete difficult tasks, they earn better grades, and they tend to excel in their occupations. College students high in nAch attribute success to their own ability, and failure to insufficient effort. Thus, high nAch students are more likely to renew their efforts when they perform poorly. When the going gets tough, high achievers get going.

The Key to Success

What does it take to achieve extraordinary success? Psychologist Benjamin Bloom studied America's top concert pianists, Olympic swimmers, sculptors, tennis players, mathematicians, and research neurologists. Bloom (1985) found that drive and determination, not great natural talent, led to exceptional success.

The first steps toward high achievement began when parents exposed their children to music, swimming, scientific ideas, and so forth, "just for fun." At first, many of the children had very ordinary skills. One Olympic swimmer, for instance, remembers repeatedly losing races as a 10-year-old. At some point, however, the children began to actively cultivate their abilities. Before long, parents noticed the child's rapid progress and found an expert instructor or coach. After more successes, the youngsters began "living" for their talent and practiced many hours daily. This continued for many years before they reached truly outstanding heights of achievement.

The upshot of Bloom's work is that talent is nurtured by dedication and hard work (R. C. Beck, 2004). It is most likely to blossom when parents actively support a child's special interest and emphasize doing one's best at all times. Studies of child prodigies and eminent adults also show that intensive practice and expert coaching are common ingredients of high achievement. Elite performance in music, sports, chess, the arts, and many other pursuits requires at least 10 years of dedicated practice (Ericsson & Charness, 1994). The old belief that "talent will surface" on its own is largely a myth.

Self-Confidence

Achieving elite performance may be reserved for the dedicated few. Nevertheless, you may be able to improve everyday motivation by increasing your self-confidence. People with self-confidence believe they can successfully carry out an activity or reach a goal. To enhance self-confidence, it is wise to do the following (Druckman & Bjork, 1994):

- Set goals that are specific and challenging, but attainable.
- Visualize the steps you need to take to reach your goal.
- Advance in small steps.
- When you first acquire a skill, your goal should be to make progress in learning. Later, you can concentrate on improving your performance, compared with other people.
- Get expert instruction that helps you master the skill.
- Find a skilled model (someone good at the skill) to emulate.
- Get support and encouragement from an observer.
- If you fail, regard it as a sign that you need to try harder, not that you lack ability.

Self-confidence affects motivation by influencing the challenges you will undertake, the effort you will make, and how long you will persist when things don't go well. You can be confident that self-confidence is worth cultivating.

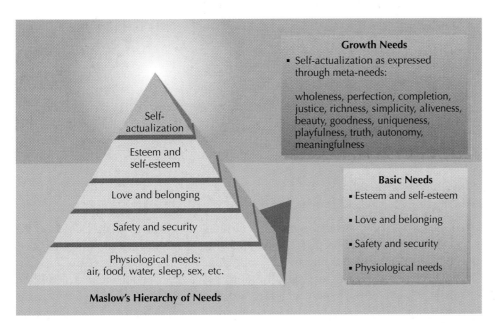

Self-actualization

Esteem and self-esteem

Love and belonging

Safety and security

Physiological needs: air, food, water, sleep, sex, etc.

Maslow's Hierarchy of Needs

Growth Needs
- Self-actualization as expressed through meta-needs:

wholeness, perfection, completion, justice, richness, simplicity, aliveness, beauty, goodness, uniqueness, playfulness, truth, autonomy, meaningfulness

Basic Needs
- Esteem and self-esteem
- Love and belonging
- Safety and security
- Physiological needs

▸▸**FIGURE 9.14** Maslow believed that lower needs in the hierarchy are dominant. Basic needs must be satisfied before growth motives are fully expressed. Desires for self-actualization are reflected in various meta-needs (see text).

MOTIVES IN PERSPECTIVE— A VIEW FROM THE PYRAMID

>SURVEY QUESTION< *Are some motives more basic than others?*

What motivates people who live fully and richly? As you may recall from Chapter 1, Abraham Maslow called the full use of personal potential *self-actualization.* Maslow also described a **hierarchy of human needs,** in which some needs are more basic or powerful than others. Think about the needs that influence your own behavior. Which seem strongest? Which do you spend the most time and energy satisfying? Now look at Maslow's hierarchy (▸▸Fig. 9.14). Note that physiological needs are at the base of the pyramid. Because these needs must be met if we are to survive, they tend to be *prepotent,* or dominant over the higher needs. It could be said, for example, that "to a starving person, food is god."

Maslow believed that higher, more fragile needs are expressed only after we satisfy our physiological needs. This is also true of needs for safety and security. Until they are met, we may have little interest in higher pursuits. For instance, a person who is extremely thirsty might have little interest in writing poetry or even talking with friends. For this reason, Maslow described the first four levels of the hierarchy as **basic needs.** Other basic needs include love and belonging (family, friendship, caring), and needs for esteem and self-esteem (recognition and self-respect).

All of the basic needs are *deficiency* motives. That is, they are activated by a *lack* of food, water, security, love, esteem, or other basic needs. At the top of the hierarchy we find **growth needs,** which are expressed as a need for self-actualization. The need for self-actualization is not based on deficiencies. Rather, it is a positive, life-enhancing force for personal growth (Reiss & Havercamp, 2005). Like other humanistic psychologists, Maslow believed that people are basically good. If our basic needs are met, he said, we will tend to move on to actualizing our potentials.

How are needs for self-actualization expressed? Maslow called the less powerful but humanly important actualization motives **meta-needs** (Maslow, 1970). Meta-needs are an expression of tendencies to fully develop your personal potentials. The meta-needs are:

1. Wholeness (unity)
2. Perfection (balance and harmony)
3. Completion (ending)

Wheelchair athletes engage in vigorous competition. Maslow considered such behavior an expression of the need for self-actualization.

Hierarchy of human needs Abraham Maslow's ordering of needs, based on their presumed strength or potency.

Basic needs The first four levels of needs in Maslow's hierarchy; lower needs tend to be more potent than higher needs.

Growth needs In Maslow's hierarchy, the higher level needs associated with self-actualization.

Meta-needs In Maslow's hierarchy, needs associated with impulses for self-actualization.

4. Justice (fairness)
5. Richness (complexity)
6. Simplicity (essence)
7. Aliveness (spontaneity)
8. Beauty (rightness of form)
9. Goodness (benevolence)
10. Uniqueness (individuality)
11. Playfulness (ease)
12. Truth (reality)
13. Autonomy (self-sufficiency)
14. Meaningfulness (values)

According to Maslow, we tend to move up through the hierarchy of needs, toward the meta-needs. When the meta-needs are unfulfilled, people fall into a "syndrome of decay" marked by despair, apathy, and alienation.

Maslow's point is that mere survival or comfort is usually not enough to make a full and satisfying life. It's interesting to note, in this regard, that college students who are primarily concerned with money, personal appearance, and social recognition score lower than average in vitality, self-actualization, and general well-being (Kasser & Ryan, 1996).

Are many people motivated by meta-needs? Maslow estimated that few people are primarily motivated by needs for self-actualization. Most of us are more concerned with esteem, love, or security. Perhaps this is because rewards in our society tend to encourage conformity, uniformity, and security in schools, jobs, and relationships. When was the last time you met a meta-need?

Intrinsic and Extrinsic Motivation

Some people cook for a living and consider it hard work. Others cook for pleasure and dream of opening a restaurant. For some people, mountain biking, gardening, writing, photography, or jewelry making is fun. For others the same activities are drudgery they must be paid to do. How can the same activity be "work" for one person and "play" for another?

When you do something for enjoyment or to improve your abilities, your motivation is usually *intrinsic*. **Intrinsic motivation** occurs when we act without any obvious external rewards. We simply enjoy an activity or see it as an opportunity to explore, learn, and actualize our potentials. In contrast, **extrinsic motivation** stems from external factors, such as pay, grades, rewards, obligations, and approval. Most of the activities we think of as "work" are extrinsically rewarded (Baard, Deci, & Ryan, 2004; Ryan & Deci, 2000).

Turning Play into Work

Don't extrinsic incentives strengthen motivation? Yes they can, but not always. In fact, *excessive* rewards can decrease intrinsic motivation and spontaneous interest. For instance, in one classic study children who were lavishly rewarded for drawing with felt-tip pens later showed little interest in playing with the pens again (Greene & Lepper, 1974). Apparently, "play" can be turned into "work" by *requiring* people to do something they would otherwise enjoy. When we are coerced or "bribed" to act, we tend to feel as if we are "faking it." Employees who lack initiative and teenagers who reject school and learning are good examples of such reactions (Ryan & Deci, 2000).

Creativity

People are more likely to be creative when they are intrinsically motivated. On the job, for instance, salaries and bonuses may increase the amount of work done. However, work *quality* is affected more by intrinsic factors, such as personal interest and freedom of choice (Nakamura & Csikszentmihalyi, 2003). When a person is intrinsically motivated, a certain amount of challenge, surprise, and complexity makes a task rewarding. When extrinsic

Intrinsic motivation Motivation that comes from within, rather than from external rewards; motivation based on personal enjoyment of a task or activity.

Extrinsic motivation Motivation based on obvious external rewards, obligations, or similar factors.

People who are intrinsically motivated feel free to explore creative solutions to problems. *(left)* Dean Kaman, inventor of the Segway personal transportation device. *(right)* "Caffiends at the Beach," an entrant in the Great Arcata to Ferndale World Championship Cross Country Kinetic Sculpture Race.

motivation is stressed, people are less likely to solve tricky problems and come up with innovative ideas (Amabile, Hadley, & Kramer, 2002).

How can the concept of intrinsic motivation be applied? Both types of motivation are necessary. But extrinsic motivation shouldn't be overused, especially with children. To summarize: (1) If there's no intrinsic interest in an activity to begin with, you have nothing to lose by using extrinsic rewards; (2) if basic skills are lacking, extrinsic rewards may be necessary at first; (3) if extrinsic rewards are used, they should be small and phased out as soon as possible (Cameron & Pierce, 2002; Greene & Lepper, 1974). It also helps to tell children they seem to be *really interested* in drawing, playing the piano, learning a language, or whatever activity you are rewarding (Cialdini et al., 1998).

At work, it is valuable for managers to find out what each employee's interests and career goals are. People are not solely motivated by money. A chance to do challenging, interesting, and intrinsically rewarding work is often just as important. In many situations it is important to encourage intrinsic motivation, especially when children are learning new skills.

Study Break   Stimulus Motives, Learned Motives, Maslow, and Intrinsic Motivation

Reflect

Does arousal theory seem to explain any of your own behavior? Think of at least one time when your performance was impaired by arousal that was too low or too high. Now think of some personal examples that illustrate the Yerkes-Dodson law.

Are you high or low in your need for stimulation?

In situations involving risk and skill, do you like to "go for broke"? Or do you prefer sure things? Do you think you are high, medium, or low in nAch?

Which levels of Maslow's hierarchy of needs occupy most of your time and energy?

Name an activity you do that is intrinsically motivated and one that is extrinsically motivated. How do they differ?

Learning Check

1. Exploration, manipulation, and curiosity provide evidence for the existence of _____ drives.

2. People who score high on the SSS tend to be extroverted, independent, and individuals who value change. T or F?

3. Two key elements of test anxiety that must be controlled are _____ and excessive _____.

4. People high in nAch are attracted to "long shots" and "sure things." T or F?

5. According to Maslow, meta-needs are the most basic and prepotent sources of human motivation. T or F?

6. Intrinsic motivation is often undermined in situations in which obvious external rewards are applied to a naturally enjoyable activity. T or F?

Critical Thinking

7. Many U.S. college freshmen say that "being well-off financially" is an essential life goal and that "making more money" was a very important factor in their decision to attend college. Which meta-needs are fulfilled by "making more money"?

Answers

1. stimulus 2. T 3. arousal, worry 4. F 5. F 6. T 7. None of them.

INSIDE AN EMOTION—HOW DO YOU FEEL?

>SURVEY QUESTIONS<   *What happens during emotion? Can "lie detectors" really detect lies?*

Picture the faces of terrified people fleeing from a tornado or a tsunami and it's easy to see that motivation and emotion are closely related. Emotions create the "music" that shapes our relationships and colors our daily activities. What are the basic parts of an emotion? How does the body respond during emotion?

If a mad scientist replaced your best friend's brain with a computer, how would you know that something was wrong? An absence of emotion might be one of the first telltale signs. **Emotion** is characterized by physiological arousal, and changes in facial expressions, gestures, posture, and subjective feelings. As mentioned earlier, the word *emotion* derives from the Latin word meaning "to move." First, your body is physically aroused during emotion. Such bodily stirrings are what cause us to say we were "moved" by a play, a funeral, or an act of kindness. Second, we are often motivated, or moved to take action, by emotions such as fear, anger, or joy. Many of the goals we seek make us feel good. Many of the activities we avoid make us feel bad. We feel happy when we succeed and sad when we fail (Kalat & Shiota, 2007).

Emotions are linked to many basic **adaptive behaviors,** such as attacking, fleeing, seeking comfort, helping others, and reproducing. Such behaviors help us survive and adjust to changing conditions (Plutchik, 2003). However, it is also apparent that emotions can have negative effects. Stage fright or "choking up" in sports can spoil performances. Hate, anger, contempt, disgust, and fear disrupt behavior and relationships. But more often, emotions aid survival. As social animals, it would be impossible for humans to live in groups, cooperate in raising children, and defend one another without positive emotional bonds of love, caring, and friendship (Buss, 2000).

A pounding heart, sweating palms, "butterflies" in the stomach, and other bodily reactions are a major element of fear, anger, joy, and other emotions. Typical **physiological changes** include changes in heart rate, blood pressure, perspiration, and other bodily stirrings. Most are caused by activity in the sympathetic nervous system and by the hormone *adrenaline,* which the adrenal glands release into the bloodstream.

Emotional expressions, or outward signs of what a person is feeling, are another ingredient of emotion. For example, when you are intensely afraid, your hands tremble, your face contorts, your posture becomes tense and defensive, and your voice changes. In general, these expressions serve to tell others what emotions we are experiencing (Hortman, 2003). **Emotional feelings** (a person's private emotional experience) are a final major element of emotion. This is the part of emotion with which we are usually most familiar.

Primary Emotions

Are some emotions more basic than others? Yes, Robert Plutchik (2003) has identified eight **primary emotions.** These are fear, surprise, sadness, disgust, anger, anticipation, joy, and trust (acceptance). If the list seems too short, it's because each emotion can vary in *intensity.* When you're angry, for instance, you may feel anything from rage to simple annoyance (see ▸▸Fig. 9.15).

As shown in ▸▸ Figure 9.15, each pair of adjacent emotions can be mixed to yield a third, more complex emotion. Other mixtures are also possible. For example, 5-year-old Tupac feels both joy and fear as he eats a stolen cookie. The result? Guilt—as you may recall from your own childhood. Likewise, jealousy could be a mixture of love, anger, and fear.

A *mood* is the mildest form of emotion (▸▸ Fig. 9.16). Moods are low intensity emotional states that can last for many hours, or even days. Moods often affect day-to-day behavior by preparing us to act in certain ways. For example, when your neighbor Roseanne is in an irritable mood she may react angrily to almost anything you say. When she is in a happy mood,

Emotion A state characterized by physiological arousal, changes in facial expression, gestures, posture, and subjective feelings.

Adaptive behaviors Actions that aid attempts to survive and adapt to changing conditions.

Physiological changes (in emotion) Alterations in heart rate, blood pressure, perspiration, and other involuntary responses.

Emotional expression Outward signs that an emotion is occurring.

Emotional feelings The private, subjective experience of having an emotion.

Primary emotions According to Robert Plutchik's theory, the most basic emotions are fear, surprise, sadness, disgust, anger, anticipation, joy, and acceptance.

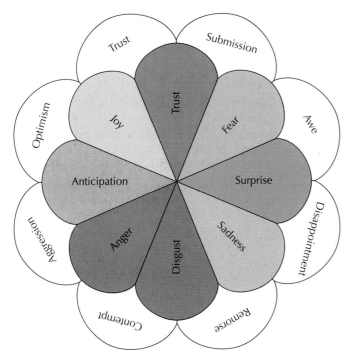

Less intense	Primary emotion	More intense
Interest	Anticipation	Vigilance
Serenity	Joy	Ecstasy
Acceptance	Trust	Admiration
Apprehension	Fear	Terror
Distraction	Surprise	Amazement
Pensiveness	Sadness	Grief
Boredom	Disgust	Loathing
Annoyance	Anger	Rage

▸▸**FIGURE 9.15** Primary and mixed emotions. In Robert Plutchik's model there are eight primary emotions, as listed in the inner areas. Adjacent emotions may combine to give the emotions listed around the perimeter. Mixtures involving more widely separated emotions are also possible. For example, fear plus anticipation produces anxiety. (Adapted from Plutchik, 2001, 2003.)

she can easily laugh off an insult. Happy, positive moods tend to make us more adaptable in several ways. For example, when you are in a good mood, you are likely to make better decisions and you will be more helpful, efficient, creative, and peaceful (Compton, 2005).

Like our motives, our moods are closely tied to circadian rhythms. When your body temperature is at its daily low point, you are more likely to feel "down" emotionally. When body temperature is at its peak, your mood is likely to be positive—even if you missed a night of sleep (Boivin, Czeisler, & Waterhouse, 1997).

The Brain and Emotion

Emotions can be either positive or negative. Ordinarily, we might think that positive and negative emotions are mutually exclusive. But this is not the case. As Tupac's "cookie guilt" implies, it is possible to have positive and negative emotions at the same time. How is that possible? In the brain, positive emotions are processed mainly in the left hemisphere. In contrast, negative emotions are processed in the right hemisphere. The fact that positive and negative emotions are based on different brain areas helps explain why we can feel happy and sad at the same time (Canli et al., 1998). It also explains why your right foot is more ticklish than your left foot! The left hemisphere controls the right side of the body and processes positive emotions (Smith & Cahusac, 2001). Thus, most people are more ticklish on their right side. If you really want to tickle someone, be sure to "do it right."

Later we will attempt to put all the elements of emotion together into a single picture. But first, we need to look more closely at bodily arousal and emotional expressions.

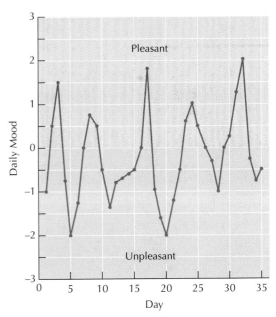

▸▸**FIGURE 9.16** Folklore holds that people who work or attend school on a weekly schedule experience their lowest moods on "Blue Monday." Actually, moods tend to be generally lower for *most* weekdays than they are on weekends. The graph shown here plots the average daily moods of a group of college students over a 5-week period. As you can see, many people find that their moods rise and fall on a 7-day cycle. For most students, a low point tends to occur around Monday or Tuesday and a peak on Friday or Saturday. (Adapted from Larsen & Kasimatis, 1990.) In other words, moods are shaped by weekly schedules.

PHYSIOLOGY AND EMOTION—AROUSAL, SUDDEN DEATH, AND LYING

An African Bushman frightened by a lion and a city dweller frightened by a prowler will react in much the same way. Such encounters usually produce muscle tension, a pounding heart, irritability, dryness of the throat and mouth, sweating, butterflies in the stomach, frequent urination, trembling, restlessness, sensitivity to loud noises, and numerous other bodily changes. These reactions are nearly universal because they are innate. Specifically, they are caused by the **autonomic nervous system (ANS)** (the neural system that connects the brain with internal organs and glands). As you may recall from Chapter 2, activity of the ANS is *automatic,* rather than voluntary (Kalat & Shiota, 2007).

Fight or Flight

The ANS has two divisions, the sympathetic branch and the parasympathetic branch. The two branches are active at all times. Whether you are relaxed or aroused at any moment depends on the combined activity of both branches.

What does the ANS do during emotion? In general, the **sympathetic branch** activates the body for emergency action—for "fighting or fleeing." It does this by arousing some bodily systems and inhibiting others (▸▸ Fig. 9.17). These changes have a purpose. Sugar is released into the bloodstream for quick energy, the heart beats faster to supply blood to the muscles, digestion is temporarily slowed, blood flow in the skin is restricted to reduce bleeding, and so forth. Such reactions improve the chances of surviving an emergency.

The **parasympathetic branch** reverses emotional arousal. This calms and relaxes the body. After a period of high emotion, the heart is slowed, the pupils return to normal size, blood pressure drops, and so forth. In addition to restoring balance, the parasympathetic system helps build up and conserve bodily energy.

The parasympathetic system responds much more slowly than the sympathetic system does. That's why a pounding heart, muscle tension, and other signs of arousal don't fade for 20 or 30 minutes after you feel an intense emotion, such as fear. Moreover, after a strong emotional shock, the parasympathetic system may overreact and lower blood pressure too much. This can cause you to become dizzy or to faint after seeing something shocking, such as a horrifying accident.

Sudden Death

An overreaction to intense emotion is called a **parasympathetic rebound.** If the rebound is severe, it can sometimes cause death. In times of war, for instance, combat can be so savage that some soldiers literally die of fear (Moritz & Zamchech, 1946). Apparently, such deaths occur because the parasympathetic nervous system slows the heart to a stop. Even in civilian life this is possible. In one case, a terrified young woman was admitted to a hospital because she felt she was going to die. A backwoods midwife had predicted that the woman's two sisters would die before their 16th and 21st birthdays. Both died as predicted. The midwife also predicted that this woman would die before her 23rd birthday. She was found dead in her hospital bed the day after she was admitted. It was 2 days before her 23rd birthday (Seligman, 1989). The woman was an apparent victim of her own terror.

Is the parasympathetic nervous system always responsible for such deaths? Probably not. For older persons or those with heart problems, sympathetic effects may be enough to bring about heart attack and collapse. For example, five times more people than usual died of heart attacks on the day of a major 1994 earthquake in Los Angeles (Leor, Poole, & Kloner, 1996). In Asia, the number 4 is considered unlucky, and more heart patients die on the

Autonomic nervous system (ANS) The system of nerves that connects the brain with the internal organs and glands.

Sympathetic branch A part of the ANS that activates the body at times of stress.

Parasympathetic branch A part of the autonomic system that quiets the body and conserves energy.

Parasympathetic rebound Excess activity in the parasympathetic nervous system following a period of intense emotion.

Eyes
Narrow pupil, stimulate tears
Dilate pupil, inhibit tears

Sweat glands
Inhibited, palms
are dry
Perspiration, palms
are wet

Lungs
Bronchi narrow, breathing
relaxed
Bronchi dilate to take in
more oxygen

Skin
Vessels dilate, increase
blood flow
Vessels constrict, skin cold
and clammy

Mouth
Increase saliva
Decrease saliva

Heart
Heartbeat slows
Speed up heartbeat

Hair
Relaxed
Stands on end

Liver
Releases bile for digestion
Releases blood sugar for
quick energy

Stomach and Intestines
Increases digestion and movement
Decreases digestion, diverts blood
to muscles

● **Parasympathetic**
● **Sympathetic**

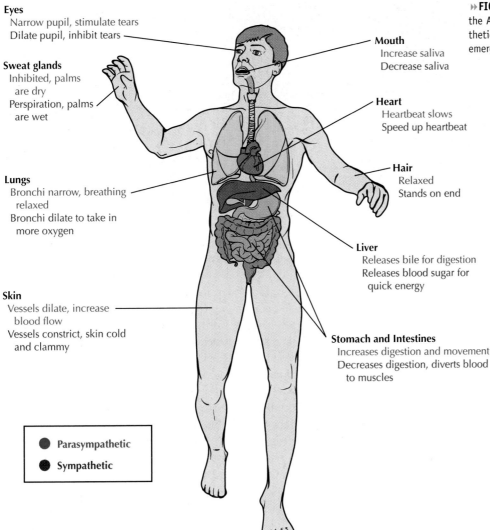

▶▶**FIGURE 9.17** The parasympathetic branch of the ANS calms and quiets the body. The sympathetic branch arouses the body and prepares it for emergency action.

fourth day of the month than any other day. Because they fear they will die on an "unlucky day," their chance of dying actually increases (Phillips et al., 2001).

Lie Detectors

We know that people are not always truthful. As many as 25 percent of all wrongful convictions include false confessions as evidence (Kassin, 2005). If you can't count on someone's word, what can you trust? The most popular method for detecting falsehoods measures the bodily changes that accompany emotion. However, the accuracy of "lie detector" tests is doubtful, and they can be a serious invasion of privacy (Lykken, 2001; National Academy of Sciences, 2002).

What is a lie detector? Do lie detectors really detect lies? The lie detector is more accurately called a **polygraph,** a word that means "many writings" (▶▶Fig. 9.18). A typical polygraph records changes in heart rate, blood pressure, breathing, and the galvanic skin response. The galvanic skin response (GSR) is recorded from the hand by electrodes that measure skin conductance or, more simply, sweating. The polygraph is popularly known as a lie detector because the police use it for that purpose. The polygraph was invented in 1915 by psychologist William Marston, who also created the comic book character *Wonder Woman,* a superhero whose "magic lasso" could force people to tell the truth (Grubin &

Polygraph A device for recording heart rate, blood pressure, respiration, and galvanic skin response; commonly called a "lie detector."

▸▸**FIGURE 9.18** *(left)* A typical polygraph measures heart rate, blood pressure, respiration, and galvanic skin response. Pens mounted on the top of the machine record bodily responses on a moving strip of paper. *(right)* Changes in the area marked by the arrow indicate emotional arousal. If such responses appear when a person answers a question, he or she may be lying, but arousal may have other causes.

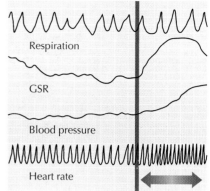

Madsen, 2005). In reality, the polygraph is not a lie detector at all. The device only records *general emotional arousal*—it can't tell the difference between lying and fear, anxiety, or excitement (Lykken, 2001).

When trying to detect a lie, the polygraph operator begins by asking irrelevant (neutral, non-emotional) questions, such as, "Is your name (person's name)?" "Did you eat lunch today?" and so forth. This establishes a "baseline" for normal emotional responses. Then the examiner asks relevant questions: "Did you murder Hensley?" Presumably, only a guilty person will become anxious or emotional if they lie when answering relevant questions.

Wouldn't a person be nervous just from being questioned? Yes, but to minimize this problem, skilled polygraph examiners ask a series of questions with critical items mixed among them. An innocent person may respond emotionally to the whole procedure, but only a guilty person is supposed to respond more to key questions. For example, a suspected bank robber might be shown several pictures and asked, "Was the teller who was robbed this person? Was it this person?"

As an alternative, subjects may be asked **control questions,** which are designed to make almost anyone anxious: "Have ever stolen anything from your place of work?" Typically, such questions are very difficult to answer truthfully with an unqualified no. In theory they show how a person reacts to doubt or misgivings. The person's reaction to critical questions can then be compared with responses to control questions.

Even when questioning is done properly, lie detection may be inaccurate (Grubin & Madsen, 2005). For example, a man named Floyd Fay was convicted of murdering his friend Fred Ery. To prove his innocence, Fay volunteered to take a lie detector test, which he failed. Fay spent 2 years in prison before the real killer confessed to the crime. Psychologist David Lykken (1998, 2001) has documented many cases in which innocent people were jailed after being convicted on the basis of polygraph evidence.

If Floyd Fay was innocent, why did he fail the test? Put yourself in his place, and it's easy to see why. Imagine the examiner asking, "Did you kill Fred?" Because you knew Fred, and you are a suspect, it's no secret that this is a critical question. What would happen to *your* heart rate, blood pressure, breathing, and perspiration under such circumstances?

Proponents of lie detection claim it is 95 percent accurate. But in one study, accuracy was dramatically lowered when people thought about past emotional experiences as they answered irrelevant questions (Ben-Shakhar & Dolev, 1996). Similarly, the polygraph may be thrown off by self-inflicted pain, by tranquilizing drugs, or by people who can lie without anxiety (Waid & Orne, 1982). Worst of all, the test is much more likely to label an innocent person guilty, rather than a guilty person innocent. In studies involving real crimes, an average of one innocent person in five was rated as guilty by the lie detector (Lykken, 2001).

Despite the lie detector's flaws, you may be tested for employment or for other reasons. Should this occur, the best advice is to remain calm; then actively challenge the results if the machine wrongly questions your honesty. And beware; newer, possibly more accurate, methods of detecting lies are under development (see "To Catch a Terrorist").

Control questions In a polygraph exam, questions that almost always provoke anxiety.

CRITICAL THINKING

To Catch a Terrorist

An airport check-in agent asks a passenger if he packed his own luggage. He says he did, but he is sitting in a booth that records infrared images of the heat patterns on his face. The images reveal stress, suggesting that he is lying. His luggage is searched and an otherwise undetectable explosive device is confiscated, averting a potential disaster.

Although the above scenario is not yet a reality, it is not as far-fetched as you might think. The growing realization that polygraph tests are not very accurate could not have come at a worse time for national security (Knight, 2005). The infrared scanner is just one alternative currently under development. Preliminary research indicates that infrared face scans are at least as accurate as polygraphs at detecting lying (Pavlidis, Eberhardt, & Levine, 2002).

Other new techniques look directly at brain activity, thus bypassing the traditional approach of measuring indirect signs of emotional arousal. For example, psychologist Daniel Langleben theorizes that a liar must inhibit telling the truth in order to lie (Langleben et al., 2002). Thus, extra brain areas must be activated to tell a lie, which can be seen in fMRI brain images (see Chapter 2) when people are lying.

Even if new methods are used, the key problem remains: How can we avoid falsely classifying liars as truth tellers and truth tellers as liars? Until that can be done with acceptable accuracy, the new techniques may have no more value than the polygraph does.

 Study Break   Emotion and Physiological Arousal

Reflect

How did your most emotional moment of the past week affect your behavior, expressions, feelings, and bodily state? Could you detect both sympathetic and parasympathetic effects?

Make a list of the emotions you consider to be most basic. To what extent do they agree with Plutchik's list?

What did you think about the lie detector test before reading this chapter? What do you think now?

Learning Check

1. Many of the physiological changes associated with emotion are caused by secretion of the hormone

   a. atropine   b. adrenaline
   c. attributine   d. amoduline

2. Emotional _____ often serve to communicate a person's emotional state to others.

3. Awe, remorse, and disappointment are among the primary emotions listed by Robert Plutchik. T or F?

4. Emotional arousal is closely related to activity of the _____ nervous system.

5. The sympathetic system prepares the body for "fight or flight" by activating the parasympathetic system. T or F?

6. The parasympathetic system inhibits digestion and raises blood pressure and heart rate. T or F?

7. What bodily changes are measured by a polygraph?

   _____

Critical Thinking

8. Can you explain why people "cursed" by shamans or "witch doctors" sometimes actually die?

Answers

1. b   2. expressions   3. F   4. autonomic   5. F   6. F   7. heart rate, blood pressure, breathing rate, galvanic skin response   8. In cultures where there is deep belief in magic or voodoo, a person who thinks that she or he has been cursed may become uncontrollably emotional. After several days of intense terror, a parasympathetic rebound is likely. If the rebound is severe enough, it can lead to physical collapse and death.

EXPRESSING EMOTIONS—MAKING FACES AND TALKING BODIES

>SURVEY QUESTIONS<   *How accurately are emotions expressed by "body language" and the face?*

Next to our own feelings, the expressions of others are the most familiar part of emotion. Are emotional expressions a carryover from human evolution? Charles Darwin thought so. Darwin (1872) observed that angry tigers, monkeys, dogs, and humans all bare their teeth in the same way. Psychologists believe that emotional expressions evolved to communicate

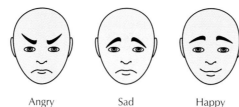

| Angry | Sad | Happy | Scheming | Neutral |

▶▶**FIGURE 9.19** When shown groups of simplified faces (without labels), the angry and scheming faces "jumped out" at people faster than sad, happy, or neutral faces. An ability to rapidly detect threatening expressions probably helped our ancestors survive (Adapted from Tipples, Atkinson, & Young, 2002.)

our feelings to others, which aids survival. Such messages give valuable hints about what other people are likely to do next (Ekman & Rosenberg, 1997). For instance, in one study, people were able to detect angry and scheming faces faster than happy, sad, or neutral faces (▶▶Fig. 9.19). Presumably, we are especially sensitive to threatening faces because they warn us of possible harm (Tipples, Atkinson, & Young, 2002.)

Facial Expressions

Are emotional expressions the same for all people? Basic expressions appear to be fairly universal (▶▶Fig. 9.20). Facial expressions of *fear, anger, disgust, sadness,* and *happiness* (enjoyment) are recognized around the world. *Contempt, surprise,* and *interest* may also be universal, but researchers are less certain of these expressions (Ekman, 1993). Notice that this list covers most of the primary emotions described earlier. Children who are born blind have little opportunity to learn emotional expressions from others. Even so, they also display basic expressions in the same way as sighted people do (Galati, Scherer, & Ricci-Bitti, 1997). It's also nice to note that a smile is the most universal and easily recognized facial expression of emotion.

Some facial expressions are shaped by learning and may be found only in specific cultures. Among the Chinese, for example, sticking out the tongue is a gesture of surprise, not of disrespect or teasing. If a person comes from another culture, it is wise to remember that you may easily misunderstand his or her expressions. At such times, knowing the social *context* in which an expression occurs helps clarify its meaning (Carroll & Russell, 1996; Reeve, 2004).

▶▶**FIGURE 9.20** Is anger expressed the same way in different cultures? Masks that are meant to be frightening or threatening are strikingly similar around the world. Most have an open, downward-curved mouth and diagonal, or triangular eyes, eyebrows, nose, cheeks, and chin. (Keep this list in mind next Halloween.) Obviously, the pictured mask is not meant to be warm and cuddly. Your ability to "read" its emotional message suggests that basic emotional expressions have universal biological roots (Aronoff, Barclay, & Stevenson, 1988).

Cultural Differences in Emotion

How many times have you been angry this week? If it was more than once, you're not unusual. Anger is a very common emotion in Western cultures. Very likely this is because our culture emphasizes personal independence and a free expression of individual rights and needs. In North America, anger is widely viewed as a "natural" reaction to feeling that you have been treated unfairly.

In contrast, many Asian cultures place a high value on group harmony. In Asia, expressing anger in public is less common and anger is regarded as less "natural." The reason for this is that anger tends to separate people. Thus, being angry is at odds with a culture that values cooperation. Culture also influences positive emotions. In America, we tend to have positive feelings such as pride, happiness, and superiority, which emphasize our role as *individuals*. In Japan, positive feelings are more often linked with membership in groups (friendly feelings, closeness to others, and respect) (Kitayama et al., 2000; Markus et al., 2006).

It is common to think of emotion as an individual event. However, as you can see, emotion is shaped by cultural ideas, values, and practices (Mesquita & Markus, 2004).

Gender and Emotion

Women have a reputation for being "more emotional" than men. Are they? Compared with women, men in Western cultures are more likely to have difficulty expressing their emotions, although not to the extent of Robert, the alexithymic man we met at the beginning of the chapter. However, there is little reason to think that most men and women differ in their private experiences of emotion. Further, whereas women are more likely to express sadness, fear, shame, and guilt, men more often express anger and hostility (Fischer et al., 2004).

Why should this be so? The answer again lies in learning. As they are growing up, boys learn to express emotions related to power; girls learn to express emotions related to nurturing others (Wood & Eagly, 2002). For many men, an inability to express feelings is a major barrier to having close, satisfying relationships with others (Levant, 2003). It may even contribute to tragedies like the mass murders at Columbine High School in Littleton, Colorado. For many young males, anger is the only emotion they can freely express.

The expression of emotion is strongly influenced by learning. As you have no doubt observed, women cry more often, longer, and more intensely than men do. Men begin learning early in childhood to suppress crying—possibly to the detriment of their emotional health (Williams & Morris, 1996). Many men are especially unwilling to engage in public displays of emotion, in contrast to these women, who are grieving for the victims of a 2005 school siege in Breslan, Russia, which left hundreds of children dead.

Body Language

If a friend walked up to you and said, "Hey, ugly, what are you doing?" would you be offended? Probably not, because such remarks are usually delivered with a big grin. The facial and bodily gestures of emotion speak a language all their own and add to what a person says.

Kinesics (kih-NEEZ-iks) is the study of communication through body movement, posture, gestures, and facial expressions (Harrigan, 2006). Informally, we call it body language. To see a masterful use of body language, turn off the sound on a television and watch a popular entertainer or politician at work.

What kinds of messages are sent with body language? Again, it is important to realize that cultural learning affects the meaning of gestures. What, for instance, does it mean if you touch your thumb and first finger together to form a circle? In North America it means "Everything is fine" or "A-okay." In France and Belgium it means "You're worth zero." In southern Italy it means "You're an ass!" When the layer of culturally defined meanings is removed, it is more realistic to say that body language reveals an overall emotional tone (underlying emotional state).

Your face can produce some 20,000 different expressions, which makes it the most expressive part of your body. Most of these are *facial blends* (a mixture of two or more basic expressions). Imagine, for example, that you just received an F on an unfair test. Quite likely, your eyes, eyebrows, and forehead would reveal anger, and your mouth would be turned downward in a sad frown.

Most of us believe we can fairly accurately tell what others are feeling by observing their facial expressions. If thousands of facial blends occur, how do we make such judgments? The answer is that facial expressions can be boiled down to three basic dimensions: *pleasantness-unpleasantness, attention-rejection,* and *activation* (or arousal) (Schlosberg, 1954). By smiling when you give a friend a hard time, you add an emotional message of acceptance to the verbal insult, which changes its meaning. As they say in movie Westerns, it makes a big difference to "Smile when you say that, partner."

Emotions are often unconsciously revealed by gestures and body positioning.

The body telegraphs other feelings. The most general "messages" involve *relaxation* or *tension,* and *liking* or *disliking.* Relaxation is expressed by casually positioning the arms and legs, leaning back (if sitting), and spreading the arms and legs. Liking is expressed mainly by leaning toward a person or object. Thus, body positioning can reveal feelings that would normally be concealed. Who do you "lean toward"?

Kinesics Study of the meaning of body movements, posture, hand gestures, and facial expressions; commonly called body language.

THEORIES OF EMOTION—SEVERAL WAYS TO FEAR A BEAR

>SURVEY QUESTION< *How do psychologists explain emotions?*

Is it possible to explain what takes place during emotion? How are arousal, behavior, cognition, expressions, and feelings interrelated? Theories of emotion offer different answers to these questions. Let's explore five views. Each appears to have a part of the truth, so we will try to put them all together in the end.

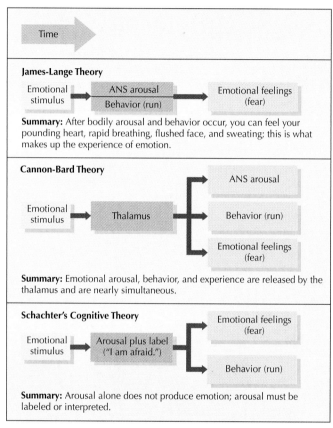

▶▶ FIGURE 9.21 Theories of emotion.

The James-Lange Theory

You're hiking in the woods when a bear suddenly steps out onto the trail. What will happen next? Common sense tells us that we will then feel fear, become aroused, and run (and sweat and yell). But is this the true order of events? In the 1880s, William James and Carl Lange (LON-geh) proposed that common sense had it backward. According to James and Lange, bodily arousal (such as increased heart rate) does not *follow* a feeling such as fear. Instead, they argued, *emotional feelings follow bodily arousal.* Thus, we see a bear, run, are aroused, and *then* feel fear as we become aware of our bodily reactions (▶▶ Fig. 9.21).

To support his ideas, James pointed out that we often do not experience an emotion until after reacting. For example, imagine that you are driving. Suddenly a car pulls out in front of you. You swerve and skid to an abrupt halt at the side of the road. Only after you have come to a stop do you notice your pounding heart, rapid breathing, and tense muscles—and recognize your fear.

The Cannon-Bard Theory

Walter Cannon (1932) and Phillip Bard disagreed with the James-Lange theory. According to them, emotional feelings and bodily arousal *occur at the same time.* Cannon and Bard believed that seeing a bear activates the thalamus in the brain. The thalamus, in turn, alerts the cortex and the hypothalamus for action. The cortex produces our emotional feelings and emotional behavior. The hypothalamus triggers a chain of events that arouses the body. Thus, if you see a dangerous-looking bear, brain activity will simultaneously produce bodily arousal, running, and feeling fear (▶▶ Fig. 9.21).

Schachter's Cognitive Theory of Emotion

The previous theories are mostly concerned with our physical responses. Stanley Schachter realized that cognitive (mental) factors also enter into emotion. According to Schachter, emotion occurs when we apply a particular *label* to general physical *arousal.* Schachter believed that when we are aroused, we have a need to interpret our feelings. Assume, for instance, that someone sneaks up behind you on a dark street and says, "Boo!" No matter who the person is, your body will be aroused (pounding heart, sweating palms, and so on). If the person is a total stranger, you might interpret this arousal as fear; if the person is a close friend, the arousal may be labeled as surprise or delight. The label (such as anger, fear, or happiness) you apply to bodily arousal is influenced by your past experiences, the situation, and the reactions of others (▶▶ Fig. 9.21).

James-Lange theory States that emotional feelings follow bodily arousal and come from awareness of such arousal.

Cannon-Bard theory States that activity in the thalamus causes emotional feelings and bodily arousal to occur simultaneously.

Schachter's cognitive theory States that emotions occur when physical arousal is labeled or interpreted on the basis of experience and situational cues.

Support for the cognitive theory of emotion comes from an experiment in which people watched a slapstick movie (Schachter & Wheeler, 1962). Before viewing the movie, one third of the people received an arousing injection of adrenaline, one third got a placebo (salt water) injection, and one third was given a tranquilizer. People who received the adrenaline rated the movie funniest and laughed the most while watching it. In contrast, those given the tranquilizer were least amused. The placebo group fell in between.

According to the cognitive theory of emotion, individuals who received adrenaline had a stirred-up body, but no explanation for what they were feeling. Consequently, they became happy when the movie implied that their arousal was due to amusement. This and similar experiments make it clear that emotion is much more than just an agitated body. Perception, experience, attitudes, judgment, and many other mental factors also affect the emotions we feel. Schachter's theory would predict, then, that if you met a bear, you would be aroused. If the bear seemed unfriendly, you would interpret your arousal as fear, and if the bear offered to shake your "paw," you would be happy, amazed, and relieved!

Attribution

We now move from slapstick movies and fear of bear bodies to an appreciation of bare bodies. Researcher Stuart Valins (1967) added an interesting wrinkle to Schachter's theory of emotion. According to Valins, arousal can be attributed to various sources—a process that alters our perceptions of emotion. To demonstrate **attribution,** Valins (1966) showed male college students a series of slides of nude females. While watching the slides, each subject heard an amplified heartbeat that he believed was his own. In reality, subjects were listening to a recorded heartbeat carefully designed to beat *louder* and *stronger* when some (but not all) of the slides were shown.

Which theory of emotion best describes the reactions of these people? Given the complexity of emotion, each theory appears to possess an element of truth.

After watching the slides, each student was asked to say which was most attractive. Students who heard the false heartbeat consistently rated slides paired with a "pounding heart" as the most attractive. In other words, when a student saw a slide and heard his heartbeat louder, he attributed his "emotion" to the slide. His interpretation seems to have been, "Now that one I like!" His next reaction, perhaps, was "But why?" Later research suggests that subjects persuaded themselves that the slide really was more attractive in order to explain their apparent arousal (Truax, 1983).

That seems somewhat artificial. Does it really make any difference what arousal is attributed to? Yes. To illustrate attribution in the "real world," consider what happens when parents interfere with the budding romance of a son or daughter. Often, trying to separate a young couple *intensifies* their feelings. Meddling parents add frustration, anger, and fear or excitement (as in seeing each other "on the sly") to the couple's feelings. Because they already care for each other, they are likely to attribute all this added emotion to "true love" (Walster, 1971).

Attribution theory predicts that you are most likely to "love" someone who gets you stirred up emotionally (Foster et al., 1998). This is true even when fear, anger, frustration, or rejection is part of the formula. Thus, if you want to successfully propose marriage, take your intended to the middle of a narrow, windswept suspension bridge over a deep chasm and look deeply into his or her eyes. As your beloved's heart pounds wildly (from being on the bridge, not from your irresistible charms), say, "I love you." Attribution theory predicts that your companion will conclude, "Oh wow, I must love you too."

The preceding is not as far-fetched as it may seem. In an ingenious study, a female psychologist interviewed men in a park. Some were on a swaying suspension bridge 230 feet above a river. The rest were on a solid wooden bridge just 10 feet above the ground. After the interview, the psychologist gave each man her telephone number, so he could "find out about the results" of the study. Men interviewed on the suspension bridge were much more

Attribution The mental process of assigning causes to events. In emotion, the process of attributing arousal to a particular source.

likely to give the "lady from the park" a call (Dutton & Aron, 1974). Apparently, these men experienced heightened arousal, which they interpreted as attraction to the experimenter—a clear case of love at first fright!

The Facial Feedback Hypothesis

Schachter added thinking and interpretation (cognition) to our view of emotion, but the picture still seems incomplete. What about expressions? How do they influence emotion? As Charles Darwin observed, the face is very central to emotion—perhaps it is more than just an "emotional billboard."

Psychologist Carrol Izard (1977, 1990) was among the first to suggest that the face does, indeed, affect emotion. According to Izard, emotions cause innately programmed changes in facial expression. Sensations from the face then provide cues to the brain that help us determine what emotion we are feeling. This idea is known as the **facial feedback hypothesis** (Soussignan, 2002). Stated another way, it says that having facial expressions and becoming aware of them influences emotional experience. Exercise, for instance, arouses the body, but we don't experience this arousal as emotion because it does not trigger emotional expressions.

Dennis Coon

▸▸**FIGURE 9.22** Facial feedback and emotion. Participants in Ekman's study formed facial expressions like those normally observed during emotion. When they did this, emotion-like changes took place in their bodily activity. (After Ekman, Levenson, & Friesen, 1983.)

Psychologist Paul Ekman takes the idea one step further. He believes that "making faces" can actually cause emotion (Ekman, 1993). In one study, participants were guided as they arranged their faces, muscle by muscle, into expressions of surprise, disgust, sadness, anger, fear, and happiness (▸▸ Fig. 9.22). At the same time, each person's bodily reactions were monitored.

Contrary to what you might expect, "making faces" can affect the autonomic nervous system, as shown by changes in heart rate and skin temperature. In addition, each facial expression produces a different pattern of activity. An angry face, for instance, raises heart rate and skin temperature, whereas disgust lowers both (Ekman, Levenson, & Friesen, 1983). Other studies have confirmed that posed expressions alter emotions and bodily activity (Duclos & Laird, 2001; Soussignan, 2002).

In a fascinating experiment on facial feedback, people rated how funny they thought cartoons were while holding a pen crosswise in their mouths. Those who held the pen in their teeth thought the cartoons were funnier than did people who held the pen in their lips. Can you guess why? The answer is that if you hold a pen with your teeth, you are forced to form a smile. Holding it with the lips makes a frown. As predicted by the facial feedback hypothesis, emotional experiences were influenced by the facial expressions that people made (Strack, Martin, & Stepper, 1988). Next time you're feeling sad, bite a pen!

It appears, then, that not only do emotions influence expressions, but expressions influence emotions as shown here (Duclos & Laird, 2001).

Contracted Facial Muscles	Felt Emotion
Forehead	Surprise
Brow	Anger
Mouth (down)	Sadness
Mouth (smile)	Joy

This could explain an interesting effect you have probably observed. When you are feeling "down," forcing yourself to smile will sometimes be followed by an actual improvement in your mood (Kleinke, Peterson, & Rutledge, 1998).

If smiling can improve a person's mood, is it a good idea to inhibit negative emotions? For an answer, see "Suppressing Emotion—Don't Turn Off the Music."

Facial feedback hypothesis States that sensations from facial expressions help define what emotion a person feels.

Suppressing Emotion—Don't Turn Off the Music

Emotional life has its ups and downs. While sharing a beautiful day with friends, you can freely express your happiness. But often we try to appear less emotional than we really are, especially when we are feeling negative emotions. Have you ever been angry with a friend in public? Embarrassed by someone's behavior at a party? Disgusted by someone's table manners? In such circumstances, people are quite good at suppressing outward signs of emotion. However, restraining emotion can actually increase activity in the sympathetic nervous system. In other words, hiding emotion requires a lot of effort.

Suppressing emotions can also impair thinking and memory, as you devote energy to self-control. Thus, while suppressing emotion allows us to appear calm and collected on the outside, this cool appearance comes at a high cost (Richards & Gross, 2000). People who suppress emotions cope poorly with life and are prone to depression and other problems (Lynch et al., 2001). Conversely, people who express their emotions generally experience better emotional and physical health (Lumley, 2004; Pennebaker, 2004). Usually, it's better to manage emotions than it is to suppress them. You will find some suggestions for managing emotions in the upcoming "Psychology in Action" feature.

Emotional Appraisal

According to Richard Lazarus (1991a), the emotions you experience are greatly influenced by how you think about an event in the first place. **Emotional appraisal** refers to evaluating the personal meaning of a stimulus: Is it good/bad, threatening/supportive, relevant/irrelevant, and so on. For example, if another driver "cuts you off" on the highway, you could become very angry. But if you do, you will add 15 minutes of emotional upset to your day. By changing your appraisal, you could just as easily choose to laugh at the other driver's childish behavior—and minimize the emotional wear-and-tear (Gross, 2001). Some examples of emotional appraisals and the emotions they give rise to can be found in ■ Table 9.2.

A Contemporary Model of Emotion

To summarize, James and Lange were right that feedback from arousal and behavior adds to our emotional experiences. Cannon and Bard were right about the timing of events. Schachter showed us that cognition is important. In fact, psychologists are increasingly aware that how you *appraise* a situation greatly affects your emotions (Strongman, 2003). Richard Lazarus stressed the importance of emotional appraisal. To summarize, let's put these ideas together in a single model of emotion (▸▸Fig. 9.23).

■ Table 9.2 **Appraisals and Corresponding Emotions**

Appraisal	Emotion
You have been slighted or demeaned	Anger
You feel threatened	Anxiety
You have experienced a loss	Sadness
You have broken a moral rule	Guilt
You have not lived up to your ideals	Shame
You desire something another has	Envy
You are near something repulsive	Disgust
You fear the worst but yearn for better	Hope
You are moving toward a desired goal	Happiness
You are linked with a valued object or accomplishment	Pride
You have been treated well by another	Gratitude
You desire affection from another person	Love
You are moved by someone's suffering	Compassion

Source: Paraphrased from Lazarus, 1991a.

Emotional appraisal Evaluating the personal meaning of a stimulus or situation.

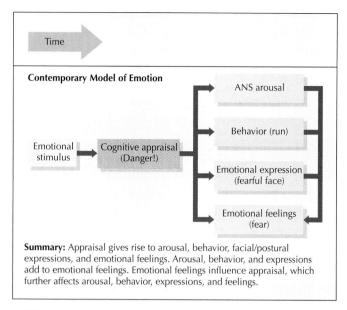

Summary: Appraisal gives rise to arousal, behavior, facial/postural expressions, and emotional feelings. Arousal, behavior, and expressions add to emotional feelings. Emotional feelings influence appraisal, which further affects arousal, behavior, expressions, and feelings.

▶▶**FIGURE 9.23** A contemporary model of emotion.

Imagine that a large snarling dog lunges at you with its teeth bared. A modern view of your emotional reactions goes something like this: An *emotional stimulus* (the dog) is *appraised* (judged) as a threat or other cause for emotion (You think to yourself, "Uh oh, big trouble!"). Your appraisal gives rise to *ANS arousal* (your heart pounds and your body becomes stirred up) and *cognitive labeling*. The appraisal also releases *innate emotional expressions* (your face twists into a mask of fear and your posture becomes tense). At the same time, your appraisal leads to *adaptive behavior* (you run from the dog). It also causes a change in consciousness that you recognize as the subjective experience of fear. (The intensity of this *emotional feeling* is directly related to the amount of ANS arousal taking place in your body.)

Each element of emotion—ANS arousal, labeling, adaptive behavior, subjective experience, and your emotional expressions—may further alter your emotional appraisal of the situation, as well as your thoughts, judgments, and perceptions. Thus, according to the facial feedback hypothesis, your facial expression will further influence your emotion. Such changes affect each of the other reactions, which again alters your appraisal and interpretation of events. Thus, emotion may blossom, change course, or diminish as it proceeds. Note too that the original emotional stimulus can be external, like the attacking dog, or internal, such as a memory of being chased by a dog, rejected by a lover, or praised by a friend. That's why mere thoughts and memories can make us fearful, sad, or happy (Strongman, 2003).

 Study Break **Emotional Expression and Theories of Emotion**

Reflect

Write a list of emotions that you think you can accurately detect from facial expressions. Does your list match Paul Ekman's? Would you be more confident in rating pleasantness-unpleasantness, attention-rejection, and activation? Why?

Which theory seems to best explain your own emotional experiences? Try frowning or smiling for 5 minutes. Did facial feedback have any effect on your mood? Cover the left column of ▣ Table 9.2. Read each emotional label in the right column. What appraisal do you think would lead to the listed emotion? Do the appraisals in the table match your predictions?

Learning Check

1. Charles Darwin held that emotional expressions aid survival for animals. T or F?
2. A formal term for "body language" is _____.
3. Which three dimensions of emotion are communicated by facial expressions?

   a. pleasantness-unpleasantness
   b. complexity
   c. attention-rejection
   d. anger
   e. curiosity-disinterest
   f. activation

4. According to the James-Lange theory, emotional experience precedes physical arousal and emotional behavior. (We see a bear, are frightened, and run.) T or F?
5. The Cannon-Bard theory of emotion says that bodily arousal and emotional experience occur _____.
6. According to Schachter's cognitive theory, bodily arousal must be labeled or interpreted for an emotional experience to occur. T or F?
7. Subjects in Valins's false heart rate study attributed increases in their heart rate to the action of a placebo. T or F?
8. As you try to wiggle your ears, you keep pulling the corners of your mouth back into a smile. Each time you do, you find yourself giggling. Which of the following provides the best explanation for this reaction?

   a. attribution
   b. the Cannon-Bard theory
   c. appraisal
   d. facial feedback

Critical Thinking

9. People with high spinal injuries may feel almost no signs of physiological arousal from their bodies. Nevertheless they still feel emotion, which can be intense at times. What theory of emotion does this observation contradict?

Answers

1. T 2. kinesics 3. a, c, f 4. F 5. simultaneously 6. T 7. F 8. d 9. The James-Lange theory and Schachter's cognitive theory. The facial feedback hypothesis also helps explain the observation.

Psychology in Action

Emotional Intelligence—The Fine Art of Self-Control

>SURVEY QUESTION< *What does it mean to have "emotional intelligence"?*

The Greek philosopher Aristotle had a recipe for handling relationships smoothly: "Be angry with the right person, to the right degree, at the right time, for the right purpose, and in the right way." Psychologists Peter Salovey and John Mayer call such self-control **emotional intelligence,** a combination of skills, such as empathy, self-control, and self-awareness (Salovey & Mayer, 1997). Such skills can make us more flexible, adaptable, and emotionally mature (Bonanno et al., 2004).

Peter Beavis/Getty Images

People who excel in life tend to be emotionally intelligent (Mehrabian, 2000). If our emotions are the music of life then emotionally intelligent people are good musicians. They do not stifle their emotions or overindulge in them. Instead they compose them into sustaining life rhythms that mesh well with other people. Indeed, the costs of poor emotional skills can be high. They range from problems in marriage and parenting to poor physical health. A lack of emotional intelligence can ruin careers and sabotage achievement. Perhaps the greatest toll falls on children and teenagers. For them, having poor emotional skills can contribute to depression, eating disorders, unwanted pregnancy, aggression, violent crime, and poor academic performance (Parker, 2005). Thus, in many life circumstances emotional intelligence is as important as IQ (Dulewicz & Higgs, 2000).

Are there specific skills that make up emotional intelligence? Many elements contribute to emotional intelligence (Larsen & Prizmic, 2004; Mayer et al., 2001). A description of some of the most important skills follows.

Self-Awareness Emotionally intelligent people are tuned in to their own feelings. For example, they are able to recognize quickly if they are angry, or envious, or feeling guilty. This is valuable because many people have disruptive emotions without being able to pinpoint why they are uncomfortable.

Empathy Empathetic people accurately perceive emotions in others and sense what others are feeling. They are good at "reading" facial expressions, tone of voice, and other signs of emotion.

Managing Emotions Emotional intelligence involves an ability to manage your own emotions and those of others. For example, you know how to calm down when you are angry and you also know how to calm others. As Aristotle noted so long ago, people who are emotionally intelligent have an ability to amplify or restrain emotions, depending on the situation (Bonanno et al., 2004).

Understanding Emotions Emotions contain useful information. For instance, anger is a cue that something is wrong; anxiety indicates uncertainty; embarrassment communicates shame; depression means we feel helpless; enthusiasm tells us we're excited. People who are

Emotional intelligence Emotional competence, including empathy, self-control, self-awareness, and other skills.

emotionally intelligent know what causes various emotions, what they mean, and how they affect behavior.

Using Emotion   People who are emotionally intelligent use their feelings to enhance thinking and decision making. For example, if you can remember how you reacted emotionally in the past, it can help you react better to new situations. You can also use emotions to promote personal growth and improve relationships with others. For instance, you may have noticed that helping someone else makes you feel better, too. Likewise, when good fortune comes their way, people who are emotionally smart share the news with others. Almost always, doing so strengthens relationships and increases emotional well-being (Gable et al., 2004).

Emotional Flexibility

In general, being emotionally intelligent means accepting that emotions are an essential part of who we are and how we survive. There is a natural tendency to enjoy positive emotions like joy or love, while treating negative emotions as unwelcome misery. However, negative emotions can also be valuable and constructive. For example, persistent distress may impel a person to seek help, mend a relationship, or find a new direction in life (Plutchik, 2003).

Often, the "right" choices in life can only be defined by taking personal values, needs, and emotions into account. Extremely rational approaches to making choices can produce sensible but emotionally empty decisions. Good decisions often combine emotion with reason. In short, emotional intelligence is the ability to consciously make your emotions work for you.

Positive Psychology and Positive Emotions

It's obvious that joy, interest, contentment, love, and similar emotions are pleasant and rewarding. However, as psychologist Barbara Fredrickson has pointed out, positive emotions have other benefits. Negative emotions are associated with actions that probably helped our ancestors save their skins: escaping, attacking, expelling poison, and the like. As useful as these reactions may be, they tend to narrow our focus of attention and limit our ideas about possible actions. In contrast, positive emotions tend to broaden our focus (Fredrickson & Branigan, 2005). This opens up new possibilities and builds up our personal resources. For instance, emotions such as joy, interest, and contentment create an urge to play, to be creative, to explore, to savor life, to seek new experiences, to integrate, and to grow.

In short, positive emotions are not just a pleasant side effect of happy circumstances. They also encourage personal growth and social connection. Happiness can be cultivated by using the strengths we already possess—including kindness, originality, humor, optimism, and generosity. Such strengths are natural buffers against misfortune, and they can help people live more positive, genuinely happy lives (Seligman, 2002). A capacity for having positive emotions is a basic human strength, and cultivating good feelings is a part of emotional intelligence (Fredrickson, 2003).

Becoming Emotionally Smart

How would a person learn the skills that make up emotional intelligence? Psychologists are still unsure how to teach emotional intelligence. Nevertheless, it's clear that emotional skills can be learned. Accepting that emotions are valuable is an important first step. There are many valuable lessons to learn from paying close attention to your emotions and the emotions of others. It's a good bet that many of the people you admire the most are not just smart, but also emotionally smart. They are people who know how to offer a toast at a wedding, tell a joke at a roast, comfort the bereaved at a funeral, add to the fun at a party, or calm a frightened child. These are skills worth cultivating.

Study Break Emotional Intelligence

Reflect

How do you think you would rate in emotional intelligence? Think of a person you know who is smart, but low in emotional intelligence. Think of another person who is smart cognitively *and* emotionally. How does the second person differ from the first? Which person do you think would make a better parent, friend, supervisor, roommate, or teacher?

Learning Check

1. People who rate high in emotional intelligence tend to be highly aware of their own feelings and unaware of emotions experienced by others. T or F?
2. Using the information imparted by emotional reactions can enhance thinking and decision-making. T or F?

3. Positive emotions may be pleasant, but they tend to narrow our focus of attention and limit the range of possible actions we are likely to consider. T or F?
4. Which of the following is not an element of emotional intelligence?

   a. empathy
   c. misattribution
   b. self-control
   d. self-awareness

Critical Thinking

5. You are angry because a friend borrowed money from you and hasn't repaid it. What would be an emotionally intelligent response to this situation?

Answers

1. F 2. T 3. F 4. c 5. There's no single right answer to this question. However, rather than being angry it might be better to reflect on whether friendship or money is more important in life. If you appreciate your friend's virtues, accept that no one is perfect, and reappraise the loan as a gift; you could save a valued relationship and reduce your anger at the same time.

CHAPTER IN REVIEW

Major Points

- Motives and goals greatly influence what we do and how we expend our energies.
- The brain monitors various internal signals to control basic motives, such as hunger and thirst.
- Motivated behavior is also influenced by learned habits, external cues, and cultural values.
- Many activities are related to needs for stimulation and our efforts to maintain desired levels of arousal.
- Many needs, goals, and drives are learned.
- Emotions can be disruptive, but overall they help us to adapt and survive.
- Personal well-being is a combination of happiness and meaning in life.

Summary

What is motivation? Are there different types of motives?

- Motives initiate, sustain, and direct activities. Motivation typically involves the sequence: need, drive, goal, and goal attainment (need reduction).
- Behavior can be activated either by needs (push) or by goals (pull).
- The attractiveness of a goal and its ability to initiate action are related to its incentive value.

- Three principal types of motives are primary motives, stimulus motives, and secondary motives.
- Most primary motives operate to maintain homeostasis.
- Circadian rhythms are closely tied to sleep, activity, and energy cycles. Time zone travel and shift work can seriously disrupt motivation, sleep, and bodily rhythms.

What causes hunger? Overeating? Eating disorders?

- Hunger is influenced by a complex interplay between fullness of the stomach, blood sugar levels, metabolism in the liver, and fat stores in the body.
- The most direct control of eating comes from the hypothalamus, which is sensitive to both neural and chemical messages that affect eating.
- Other factors influencing hunger are the body's set point, external eating cues, the attractiveness and variety of diet, emotions, learned taste preferences and aversions, and cultural values.
- Obesity is the result of internal and external influences, diet, emotions, genetics, and exercise.
- Behavioral dieting is based on techniques that change eating patterns and exercise habits.
- Anorexia nervosa and bulimia nervosa are two prominent eating disorders. Both tend to involve conflicts about self-image, self-control, and anxiety.

Is there more than one type of thirst? In what ways are pain avoidance and the sex drive unusual?

- Like hunger, thirst and other basic motives are primarily under the central control of the hypothalamus. Thirst may be either intracellular or extracellular.
- Pain avoidance is episodic as opposed to cyclic. Pain avoidance and pain tolerance are partially learned.
- The sex drive is unusual because it is nonhomeostatic.

What are the typical patterns of human sexual response?

- Sexual arousal is related to the body's erogenous zones, but mental and emotional reactions are the ultimate source of sexual responsiveness.
- Sexual orientation refers to one's degree of emotional and erotic attraction to members of the same sex, opposite sex, or both sexes.
- A combination of hereditary, biological, social, and psychological influences combine to produce one's sexual orientation.
- Human sexual response can be divided into four phases: excitement, plateau, orgasm and resolution.
- Overall, male and female sexual responses are similar. However, males experience a refractory period after orgasm, and only 5 percent of men are multiorgasmic. Fifteen percent of women are multiorgasmic.

How does arousal relate to motivation?

- The stimulus drives reflect needs for information, exploration, manipulation, and sensory input.
- Arousal theory states that an ideal level of bodily arousal will be maintained if possible.
- Optimal performance usually occurs at *moderate* levels of arousal, as described by an inverted U function. The Yerkes-Dodson law further states that for simple tasks the ideal arousal level is higher, and for complex tasks it is lower.
- Sensation seeking is a trait of people who prefer high levels of stimulation.

What are social motives? Why are they important?

- Social motives are learned through socialization and cultural conditioning.
- Such motives account for much of the diversity of human motivation.
- A high need for achievement (nAch) is correlated with success in many situations, with career choice, and with *moderate* risk taking.
- Self-confidence greatly affects motivation in everyday life.

Are some motives more basic than others?

- Maslow's hierarchy of motives categorizes needs as either basic or growth oriented. Lower needs are assumed to be prepotent (dominant) over higher needs. Self-actualization, the highest and most fragile need, is reflected in meta-needs.
- Meta-needs are closely related to intrinsic motivation. In some situations, external rewards can undermine intrinsic motivation, enjoyment, and creativity.

What happens during emotion? Can "lie detectors" really detect lies?

- Emotions are linked to many basic adaptive behaviors. Three major elements of emotion are physiological changes in the body, emotional expressions, and emotional feelings.
- The primary emotions are fear, surprise, sadness, disgust, anger, anticipation, joy, and acceptance. Other emotions are mixtures of these primaries.
- Physical changes associated with emotion are caused by the hormone adrenaline and by activity in the autonomic nervous system (ANS).
- The sympathetic branch of the ANS is primarily responsible for arousing the body, the parasympathetic branch for quieting it.
- The polygraph, or "lie detector," measures emotional arousal by monitoring heart rate, blood pressure, breathing rate, and the galvanic skin response (GSR).
- The accuracy of the lie detector can be disturbingly low.

How accurately are emotions expressed by "body language" and the face?

- Basic emotional expressions, such as smiling or baring one's teeth when angry, appear to be unlearned and have universal biological roots. Facial expressions appear to be central to emotion.
- Body gestures and movements (body language) also express feelings, mainly by communicating emotional tone rather than specific universal messages.
- Three dimensions of facial expressions are pleasantness-unpleasantness, attention-rejection, and activation. The formal study of body language is known as kinesics.
- Lying can sometimes be detected from changes in illustrators and from signs of general arousal.

How do psychologists explain emotions?

- The James-Lange theory says that emotional experience follows bodily reactions. In contrast, the Cannon-Bard theory says that bodily reactions and emotional experiences occur simultaneously.

- Schachter's cognitive theory emphasizes the labels we apply to feelings of bodily arousal. In addition, emotions are affected by attribution (ascribing bodily arousal to a particular source).
- The facial feedback hypothesis holds that facial expressions help define the emotions we feel.
- The emotions you experience are greatly influenced by how you emotionally appraise an event in the first place.
- Contemporary views of emotion emphasize that all of the elements of emotion are interrelated and interact with each other.

What does it mean to have "emotional intelligence"?

- Emotional intelligence is the ability to consciously make your emotions work for you in a wide variety of life circumstances.
- Important elements of emotional intelligence include: self-awareness, empathy, an ability to manage emotions, understanding emotion, and knowing how to use emotions to enhance thinking, decision making, and relationships.
- Positive emotions are valuable because they tend to broaden our focus and they encourage personal growth and social connection.

Interactive Learning

Internet addresses frequently change. To find the sites listed here, visit www.thomsonedu.com/psychology/coon for an updated list of Internet addresses and direct links to relevant sites.

Psychology: A Journey **Companion Website** Find online quizzes, flash cards, animations, video clips, experiments, interactive assessments, and other helpful study aids for this text at www.thomsonedu.com/psychology/coon.

Controlling Anger Discusses anger and some strategies for its control.

Eating Disorders Website Home page of a self-help group for those afflicted with eating disorders.

Emotions and Emotional Intelligence Discusses emotional intelligence.

Gestures around the World A description of body language practices in a variety of cultures.

Research on Human Emotions Links to a variety of sources on emotion.

The Validity of Polygraph Examinations Information about the doubtful validity of polygraph examinations.

What's Your Emotional Intelligence Quotient? Visitors may take an online quiz about their E-IQ.

ThomsonNOW Go to www.thomsonedu.com to link to ThomsonNOW, your online study tool. First take the **Pre-Test** for this chapter to get your **Personalized Study Plan,** which will identify topics you need to review and direct you to online resources. Then take the **Post-Test** to determine what concepts you have mastered and what you still need work on.

TEST YOUR KNOWLEDGE

Motivation and Emotion

For additional review, get more practice with *ThomsonNOW*, *WebTutor*, the *Practice Quizzes*, and/or the printed *Study Guide* available with this book.

1. Human needs for activity and exploration are an expression of
   a. secondary motives
   b. primary motives
   c. incentive values
   d. stimulus motives

2. Desirable goals are motivating because they are high in
   a. secondary value
   b. stimulus value
   c. homeostatic value
   d. incentive value

3. The term *jet lag* is commonly used to refer to disruptions of
   a. the inverted U function
   b. circadian rhythms
   c. any of the episodic drives
   d. the body's set point

4. A feeding system exists in the _____ _____ of the brain.
   a. medial leptothalamus
   b. ventral paraventriculum
   c. lateral hypothalamus
   d. leptothalamic nucleus

5. Maintaining your body's set point for fat is closely linked with the amount of _____ in the bloodstream.
   a. hypothalamic factor-1
   b. ventromedial peptide-1
   c. NPY
   d. leptin

6. Bingeing and purging are most characteristic of people who have
   a. taste aversions
   b. anorexia
   c. bulimia
   d. strong sensitivity to external eating cues

7. In addition to changing eating habits, a key element of behavioral dieting is
   a. exercise
   b. well-timed snacking
   c. better eating cues
   d. commitment to "starving" every day

8. One thing that men and women have in common is that their sex drive is
   a. affected by androgens
   b. extracellular
   c. controlled by estrogen
   d. homeostatic and episodic

9. The typical phases of human sexual arousal are
   a. estrus, refractory period, orgasm, resolution
   b. excitement, orgasm, resolution, refractory period
   c. estrus, orgasm, plateau, resolution
   d. excitement, plateau, orgasm, resolution

10. Sensate focus is a technique used to treat
    a. estrus disorders in men
    b. bulimia nervosa
    c. excessive weight cycling
    d. sexual disorders

11. Which of the following is NOT a characteristic of people who score high on the *Sensation-Seeking Scale?*
    a. boredom susceptibility
    b. experience seeking
    c. inhibition
    d. thrill seeking

12. Complex tasks, such as taking a classroom test, tend to be disrupted by high levels of arousal, an effect predicted by
    a. the Sensation-Seeking Scale
    b. the Yerkes-Dodson law
    c. studies of circadian arousal patterns
    d. studies of the need for achievement

13. People high in nAch
    a. prefer long shots
    b. prefer sure things
    c. are moderate risk takers
    d. prefer change and high levels of stimulation

14. The highest level of Maslow's hierarchy of motives involves
    a. meta needs
    b. needs for safety and security
    c. needs for love and belonging
    d. extrinsic needs

15. Polygraph operators try to use which component of emotion to detect deception?
    a. adaptive behaviors
    b. physiological changes
    c. emotional expressions
    d. the parasympathetic rebound

16. Preparing the body for "fighting or fleeing" is largely the job of the
    a. paraventricular nucleus
    b. sympathetic branch
    c. GSR
    d. androgens

17. The idea that labeling arousal helps define what emotions we experience is associated with
    a. the James-Lange theory
    b. Schachter's cognitive theory
    c. the Cannon-Bard theory
    d. Darwin's theory of innate emotional expressions

18. Holding a pen crosswise in your mouth is likely to improve your mood, a result predicted by
    a. The Cannon-Bard theory
    b. attribution theory
    c. the facial-feedback hypothesis
    d. Schachter's cognitive theory

19. Emotionally intelligent people have which of the following skills?
    a. empathy
    b. self-awareness
    c. understanding of emotions
    d. all three of the previously mentioned skills

20. One benefit of positive emotions is the capacity to
    a. broaden our focus
    b. limit our ideas about possible actions
    c. narrow our focus
    d. help our ancestors escape attack

Personality

JOURNEY INTO PSYCHOLOGY:
THE HIDDEN ESSENCE

Rural Colorado. The car banged over one last, brain-jarring rut and lurched toward the dilapidated farmhouse. Annette, a friend of one of your authors, was on the porch, hooting and whooping and obviously happy to see old friends arrive.

If anyone was suited for a move to the "wilds" of Colorado, it was Annette, a strong and resourceful woman. Still, it was hard to imagine a more radical change. After separating from her husband, she had traded a comfortable life in the city for rough times in the high country. Annette was working as a ranch hand and a lumberjack (lumberjill?), trying to make it through some hard winters.

So radical were the changes in Annette's life, we worried that she might be entirely different. She was, on the contrary, more her "old self" than ever.

Perhaps you have had a similar experience. After several years of separation, it is always intriguing to see an old friend. At first you may be struck by how the person has changed. ("Where did you get that haircut?!") Soon, however, you will probably be delighted to discover that the semi-stranger before you is still the person you once knew. It is exactly this core of consistency that psychologists have in mind when they use the term *personality*.

Without doubt, personality touches our daily lives. Falling in love, choosing friends, getting along with coworkers, voting for a president, or coping with your zaniest relatives all raise questions about personality.

What is personality? How does it differ from temperament, character, or attitudes? Is it possible to measure personality? We'll address these questions and more in this chapter.

▽ **Survey Questions**

- How do psychologists use the term *personality?* What core concepts make up the psychology of personality?
- Are some personality traits more basic or important than others?
- How do psychodynamic theories explain personality?
- What do behaviorists and social learning theorists emphasize in personality?
- How do humanistic theories differ from other perspectives?
- How do psychologists measure personality?
- What causes shyness? What can be done about it?

THE PSYCHOLOGY OF PERSONALITY— DO YOU HAVE PERSONALITY?

>SURVEY QUESTIONS< *How do psychologists use the term* personality? *What core concepts make up the psychology of personality?*

Part of the pleasure of getting to know someone is the fascination of learning who the person is and how he or she thinks. Each of us has a unique pattern of thinking, behaving, and expressing our feelings. In short, everyone has a unique personality. As psychologists, we would like to better understand Annette's personality. What models and concepts can we use?

"Annette has a very optimistic personality." "Ramiro's not handsome, but he has a great personality." "My father's business friends think he's a nice guy. They should see him at home where his real personality comes out." "It's hard to believe Tanya and Nikki are sisters. They have such opposite personalities."

It's obvious that we all frequently use the term *personality.* But if you think that personality means "charm," "charisma," or "style," you have misused the term. Psychologists regard **personality** as a person's unique pattern of thinking, emotions, and behavior (Feist & Feist, 2006). In other words, personality refers to the consistency in who you are, have been, and will become. It also refers to the special blend of talents, values, hopes, loves, hates, and habits that makes each of us a unique person.

How is that different from the way most people use the term? Many people confuse personality with character. The term **character** implies that a person has been evaluated, not just described (Skipton, 1997). If, by saying someone has "personality," you mean the person is friendly, outgoing, and attractive, you are describing what we regard as good character in our culture. But in some cultures it is deemed good for people to be fierce, warlike, and cruel. So, whereas everyone in a particular culture has personality, not everyone has character—or at least not good character. (Do you know any good characters?)

Personality is also distinct from *temperament,* the "raw material" from which personalities are formed. **Temperament** refers to the hereditary aspects of your personality, such as your sensitivity, irritability, distractibility, and typical mood (Kagan, 2004). Judging from Annette's adult personality, you might guess that she was an active, happy baby.

Does this man have personality? Do you?

Matthew Mendelsohn/Corbis

Personality A person's unique and relatively stable behavior patterns.

Character Personal characteristics that have been judged or evaluated; a person's desirable or undesirable qualities.

Temperament The hereditary aspects of personality, including sensitivity, activity levels, prevailing mood, irritability, and adaptability.

Psychologists use a large number of terms to explain personality. It might be wise, therefore, to start with a few key concepts. These ideas should help you keep your bearings as you read this chapter.

Traits

We use the idea of traits every day to talk about personality. For instance, Dan is *sociable, orderly,* and *intelligent.* His sister Kayla is *shy, sensitive,* and *creative.* In general, **personality traits** like these are stable qualities that a person shows in most situations (Matthews, Deary, & Whiteman, 2003). Typically, traits are inferred from behavior. If you see Dan talking to strangers—first at a supermarket and later at a party—you might deduce that he is "sociable." Once personality traits are identified, they can be used to predict future behavior. For example, noting that Dan is outgoing might lead you to predict that he will be sociable at school or at work. In fact, such consistencies can span many years. A study of women who appeared to be happy in their college yearbook photos (they had genuine smiles) found that most were still happy people 30 years later (Harker & Keltner, 2001).

When Is the Plaster Set?

As we observed in our reunion with Annette, personality traits are usually quite stable (Gustavsson et al., 1997; Hergenhahn & Olson, 2007). Think about how little the traits of your best friends have changed in the last 5 years. It would be strange indeed to feel like you were talking with a different person every time you met a friend or an acquaintance.

At what age are personality traits firmly established? Personality starts to stabilize at around age 3 and continues to "harden" though age 50 (Caspi, Roberts, & Shiner, 2005). Personality slowly matures during old age as most people continue to become more conscientious and agreeable. It appears that stereotypes of the "grumpy old man" and "cranky old woman" are largely unfounded (Srivastava et al., 2003).

Types

Have you ever asked the question, "What type of person is she (or he)?" A **personality type** refers to people who have *several traits in common* (Larsen & Buss, 2005). Informally, your own thinking might include categories such as the executive type, the athletic type, the motherly type, the hip-hop type, the techno geek, and so forth. If you tried to define these informal types, you would probably list a different collection of traits for each one.

How valid is it to speak of personality "types"? Over the years, psychologists have proposed many ways to categorize personalities into types. For example, Swiss psychiatrist Carl Jung (yoong) proposed that people are either *introverts* or *extroverts.* An **introvert** is a shy, reserved person whose attention is focused inward. An **extrovert** is a bold, outgoing person whose attention is directed outward. These terms are so widely used that you may think of yourself and your friends as being one type or the other. However, the wildest, wittiest, most party-loving "extrovert" you know is introverted at times. Likewise, extremely introverted persons are assertive and sociable in some situations. In short, two categories (or even several) are often inadequate to fully capture

Psychologists and employers are especially interested in the personality traits of individuals who hold high-risk, high-stress positions involving public safety, such as police, air-traffic controllers, and nuclear power plant employees.

THE FAR SIDE®   BY GARY LARSON

The four basic personality types

Personality trait A stable, enduring quality that a person shows in most situations.

Personality type A style of personality defined by a group of related traits.

Introvert A person whose attention is focused inward; a shy, reserved, self-centered person.

Extrovert A person whose attention is directed outward; a bold, outgoing person.

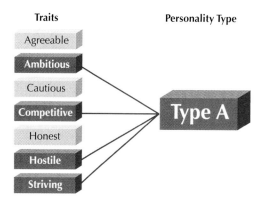

Traits   Personality Type

Agreeable
Ambitious
Cautious
Competitive
Honest
Hostile
Striving

Type A

▶**FIGURE 10.1** Personality types are defined by the presence of several specific traits. For example, several possible personality traits are shown in the left column. A person who has a Type A personality typically possesses all or most of the highlighted traits. Type A persons are especially prone to heart disease (see Chapter 11).

differences in personality. That's why rating people on a list of traits tends to be more informative than classifying them into two or three types.

Even though types tend to oversimplify personality, they do have value. Most often, types are a shorthand way of labeling people who have several key traits in common. For example, in the next chapter we will discuss Type A and Type B personalities. Type A's are people who have personality traits that increase their chance of suffering a heart attack (see ▶Fig. 10.1); Type B's take a more laid-back approach to life. Similarly, you will read in Chapter 12 about unhealthy personality types such as the paranoid personality, the dependent personality, and the antisocial personality. Each problem type is defined by a specific group of maladaptive traits.

Self-Concept

Self-concepts provide another way of understanding personality. The rough outlines of your self-concept could be revealed by this request: "Please tell us about yourself." In other words, your **self-concept** consists of all your ideas, perceptions, and feelings about who you are. It is the mental "picture" you have of your own personality.

We creatively build our self-concepts out of daily experiences. Then we slowly revise them as we have new experiences. Once a stable self-concept exists, it tends to guide what we pay attention to, remember, and think about. Because of this, self-concepts can greatly affect our behavior and personal adjustment—especially when they are inaccurate (Larsen & Buss, 2005). For instance, Alesha is a student who thinks she is stupid, worthless, and a failure, despite getting good grades. With such an inaccurate self-concept, she tends to be depressed regardless of how well she does.

Self-concepts can be remarkably consistent. In an interesting study, very old people were asked how they had changed over the years. Almost all thought they were essentially the same person they were when they were young (Troll & Skaff, 1997).

O'Brien Productions/Corbis

Self-concept A person's perception of his or her own personality traits.

Self-esteem Regarding oneself as a worthwhile person; a positive evaluation of oneself.

Self-Esteem

Note that in addition to having a faulty self-concept, Alesha has low **self-esteem** (a negative self-evaluation). A person with high self-esteem is confident, proud, and self-respecting. One who has low self-esteem is insecure, lacking in confidence, and self-critical. Like Alesha, people with low self-esteem are usually anxious and unhappy.

Self-esteem tends to rise when we experience success or praise. A person who is competent and effective and who is loved, admired, and respected by others will almost always have high self-esteem (Baumeister et al., 2003). (The reasons for having high self-esteem can vary in different cultures. See "Self-Esteem and Culture" for more information.)

What if you "think you're hot," but you're not? Genuine self-esteem is based on an accurate appraisal of your strengths and weak-

Self-Esteem and Culture—Hotshot or Team Player?

You and some friends are playing soccer. Your team wins, in part because you make some good plays. After the game, you bask in the glow of having performed well. You don't want to brag about being a hotshot, but your self-esteem gets a boost from your personal success.

In Japan, Shinobu and some of his friends are playing soccer. His team wins, in part because he makes some good plays. After the game Shinobu is happy because his team did well. However, Shinobu also dwells on the ways in which he let his team down. He thinks about how he could improve, and he resolves to be a better team player.

These sketches illustrate a basic difference in Eastern and Western psychology. In individualistic cultures such as the United States, self-esteem is based on personal success and outstanding performance (Lay & Verkuyten, 1999). For us, the path to higher self-esteem lies in self-enhancement. We are pumped up by our successes and tend to downplay our faults and failures (Ross et al., 2005).

Japanese and other Asian cultures place a greater emphasis on collectivism or interdependence among people. For them, self-esteem is based on a secure sense of belonging to social groups. As a result, people in Asian cultures are more apt to engage in self-criticism (Ross et al., 2005). By correcting personal faults, they add to the well-being of the group (Kitayama, Markus, & Kurokawa, 2000). And, when the *group* succeeds, individual members feel better about themselves, which raises their self-esteem.

Perhaps self-esteem is still based on success in both Eastern and Western cultures. However, it is fascinating that cultures define success in such different ways (Schmitt & Allik, 2005). The North American emphasis on winning is not the only way to feel good about yourself.

nesses. A positive self-evaluation that is bestowed too easily may not be healthy (Twenge & Campbell, 2001). People who think very highly of themselves (and let others know it) may at first seem confident, but their arrogance quickly turns off other people (Paulhus, 1998).

Personality Theories

It would be easy to get lost without a framework for understanding personality. How do our thoughts, actions, and feelings relate to one another? How does personality develop? Why do some people suffer from psychological problems? How can they be helped? To answer such questions, psychologists have created a dazzling array of theories. A **personality theory** is a system of concepts, assumptions, ideas, and principles proposed to explain personality (▸ Fig. 10.2). In this chapter, we can only explore a few of the many personality theories. The four major perspectives we will consider are:

1. **Trait theories** attempt to learn what traits make up personality and how they relate to actual behavior.

2. **Psychodynamic theories** focus on the inner workings of personality, especially internal conflicts and struggles.

3. **Behavioristic and Social Learning theories** place importance on the external environment and on the effects of conditioning and learning. Social learning theories attribute differences in personality to socialization, expectations, and mental processes.

4. **Humanistic theories** stress private, subjective experience and personal growth.

With these broad perspectives in mind, let's take a deeper look at personality.

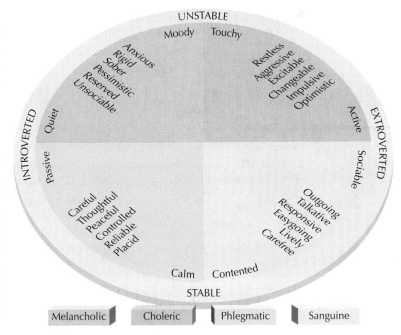

▸ **FIGURE 10.2** English psychologist Hans Eysenck (1916–1997) believed that many personality traits are related to whether you are mainly introverted or extroverted and whether you tend to be emotionally stable or unstable (highly emotional). These characteristics, in turn, are related to four basic types of temperament first recognized by the early Greeks. The types are: *melancholic* (sad, gloomy), *choleric* (hot-tempered, irritable), *phlegmatic* (sluggish, calm), and *sanguine* (cheerful, hopeful). (Adapted from Eysenck, 1981.)

Personality theory A system of concepts, assumptions, ideas, and principles used to understand and explain personality.

THE TRAIT APPROACH—DESCRIBE YOURSELF IN 18,000 WORDS OR LESS

>SURVEY QUESTION< *Are some personality traits more basic or important than others?*

How many words can you think of to describe the personality of a close friend? Your list might be long: More than 18,000 English words refer to personal characteristics. As we have noted, traits are stable qualities that a person shows in most situations (Matthews, Deary, & Whiteman, 2003). For example, if you are usually friendly, optimistic, and cautious, these qualities are traits of your personality.

What if I am also sometimes shy, pessimistic, or uninhibited?   The original three qualities are still traits as long as they are most *typical* of your behavior. Let's say our friend Annette approaches most situations with optimism, but tends to expect the worst each time she applies for a job. If her pessimism is limited to this situation or a few others, it is still accurate and useful to describe her as an optimistic person.

Predicting Behavior

As we have noted, separating people into broad types, such as "introvert" or "extrovert," may oversimplify personality. However, introversion/extroversion can also be thought of as a trait. Knowing how you rate on this single dimension would allow us to predict how you will behave in a variety of settings. Where, for example, do you prefer to meet people, face-to-face or through the Internet? Researchers have found that students high in the trait of introversion are more likely to prefer the Internet because they find it easier to talk with people online (Koch & Pratarelli, 2004). (Other interesting links exist between traits and behavior. See "What's Your Musical Personality?")

Describing People

In general, psychologists try to identify traits that best describe a person. Take a moment to check the traits in ■ Table 10.1 that describe your personality. Are the traits you checked of equal importance? Are some stronger or more basic than others? Do any overlap? For example, if you checked "dominant," did you also check "confident" and "bold"? Answers to these questions would interest a trait theorist. To better understand personality, **trait theorists** attempt to analyze, classify, and interrelate traits.

Classifying Traits

Are there different types of traits? Yes. Psychologist Gordon Allport (1961) identified several kinds. **Common traits** are characteristics shared by most members of a culture. Common traits tell us how people from a particular nation or culture are similar, or which traits a culture emphasizes. In America, for example, competitiveness is a fairly common trait. Among the Hopi of Northern Arizona, however, it is relatively rare.

Of course, common traits don't tell us much about individuals. Although many people are competitive in American culture, various people you know may rate high, medium, or low in this trait. Usually we are also interested in **individual traits,** which describe a person's unique qualities.

Here's an analogy to help you separate common traits from individual traits: If you decide to buy a pet dog, you will want to know the general characteristics of the dog's breed (its common traits). In addition, you will want to know about the "personality" of a specific dog (its individual traits) before you decide to take it home.

Allport also made distinctions between *cardinal traits, central traits,* and *secondary traits.* **Cardinal traits** are so basic that all of a person's activities can be traced to the trait. For instance, compassion was an overriding trait of Mother Teresa's personality. Likewise, Abra-

---

■ Table 10.1   **Adjective Checklist**

Check the traits you feel are characteristic of your personality. Are some more basic than others?

aggressive	ambitious
confident	generous
warm	cautious
sensitive	talented
sociable	funny
dominant	accurate
humble	visionary
thoughtful	helpful
orderly	conforming
liberal	optimistic
meek	passionate
organized	clever
loyal	calm
bold	reliable
mature	jealous
honest	religious
dull	nervous
uninhibited	cheerful
serious	emotional
anxious	good-natured
curious	kind
neighborly	compulsive

Trait theorist A psychologist interested in classifying, analyzing, and interrelating traits to understand personality.

Common traits Personality traits that are shared by most members of a particular culture.

Individual traits Personality traits that define a person's unique individual qualities.

Cardinal trait A personality trait so basic that all of a person's activities relate to it.

What's Your Musical Personality?

Even if you like all kinds of music, you probably prefer some styles to others. Of the styles listed here, which three do you enjoy the most? (Circle your choices.)

blues jazz classical folk rock alternative heavy metal country sound track religious pop rap/hip-hop soul/funk electronic/dance

In one study, Peter Rentfrow and Samuel Gosling found that the types of music people prefer tend to be associated with their personality characteristics. See if your musical tastes match their findings (Rentfrow & Gosling, 2003).

- People who value aesthetic experiences, have good verbal abilities, are liberal, and tolerant of others tend to like music that is reflective and complex (blues, jazz, classical, and folk music).

- People who are curious about new experiences, enjoy taking risks, and are physically active prefer intense, rebellious music (rock, alternative, and heavy metal music).
- People who are cheerful, conventional, extroverted, reliable, helpful, and conservative tend to enjoy upbeat conventional music (country, sound track, religious, and pop music).
- People who are talkative, full of energy, forgiving, physically attractive, and who reject conservative ideals tend to prefer energetic, rhythmic music (rap/hip-hop, soul/funk, and electronic/dance music).

Unmistakably, personality traits affect our everyday behavior.

---

ham Lincoln's personality was dominated by the cardinal trait of honesty. According to Allport, few people have cardinal traits.

Central Traits

How do central and secondary traits differ from cardinal traits? **Central traits** are the basic building blocks of personality. A surprisingly small number of central traits can capture the essence of a person. For instance, just six traits would provide a good description of Annette's personality: dominant, sociable, honest, cheerful, intelligent, and optimistic. When college students were asked to describe someone they knew well, they mentioned an average of seven central traits (Allport, 1961).

Secondary traits are more superficial personal qualities, such as food preferences, attitudes, political opinions, musical tastes, and so forth. In Allport's terms, a personality description might therefore include the following items.

Name: Jane Doe
Age: 22
Cardinal traits: None
Central traits: Possessive, autonomous, artistic, dramatic, self-centered, trusting
Secondary traits: Prefers colorful clothes, likes to work alone, politically liberal, always late.

Source Traits

How can you tell if a personality trait is central or secondary? Raymond B. Cattell (1906–1998) tried to answer this question by directly studying the traits of a large number of people. Cattell began by measuring visible features of personality, which he called **surface traits.** Soon, Cattell noticed that these surface traits often appeared together in groups. In fact, some traits appeared together so often that they seemed to represent a single more basic trait. Cattell called these deeper characteristics, or dimensions, **source traits** (Cattell, 1965). They are the core of each individual's personality.

How do source traits differ from Allport's central traits? Allport classified traits subjectively, and it's possible that he was wrong at times. Cattell used a statistical technique called *factor analysis* to look for connections among traits. For example, he found that imaginative people are almost always *inventive, original, curious, creative, innovative,* and *ingenious.* Thus, *imaginative* is a source trait. If you are an imaginative person, we automatically know that you have several other traits, too.

Central traits The core traits that characterize an individual personality.

Secondary traits Traits that are inconsistent or relatively superficial.

Surface traits The visible or observable traits of one's personality.

Source traits Basic underlying traits, or dimensions, of personality; each source trait is reflected in a number of surface traits.

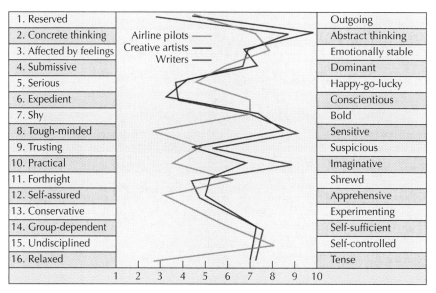

1. Reserved				Outgoing
2. Concrete thinking				Abstract thinking
3. Affected by feelings				Emotionally stable
4. Submissive				Dominant
5. Serious				Happy-go-lucky
6. Expedient				Conscientious
7. Shy				Bold
8. Tough-minded				Sensitive
9. Trusting				Suspicious
10. Practical				Imaginative
11. Forthright				Shrewd
12. Self-assured				Apprehensive
13. Conservative				Experimenting
14. Group-dependent				Self-sufficient
15. Undisciplined				Self-controlled
16. Relaxed				Tense

Airline pilots ——
Creative artists ——
Writers ——

▸▸FIGURE 10.3 The 16 source traits measured by Cattell's 16 PF are listed beside the graph. Scores can be plotted as a profile for an individual or a group. The profiles shown here are group averages for airline pilots, creative artists, and writers. Notice the similarity between artists and writers and the difference between these two groups and pilots. (After Cattell, 1973.)

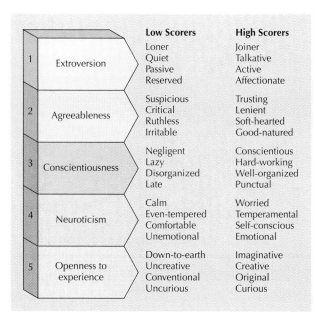

		Low Scorers	High Scorers
1	Extroversion	Loner Quiet Passive Reserved	Joiner Talkative Active Affectionate
2	Agreeableness	Suspicious Critical Ruthless Irritable	Trusting Lenient Soft-hearted Good-natured
3	Conscientiousness	Negligent Lazy Disorganized Late	Conscientious Hard-working Well-organized Punctual
4	Neuroticism	Calm Even-tempered Comfortable Unemotional	Worried Temperamental Self-conscious Emotional
5	Openness to experience	Down-to-earth Uncreative Conventional Uncurious	Imaginative Creative Original Curious

▸▸FIGURE 10.4 The Big Five. According to the five-factor model, basic differences in personality can be "boiled down" to the dimensions shown here. The five-factor model answers these essential questions about a person: Is she or he extroverted or introverted? Agreeable or difficult? Conscientious or irresponsible? Emotionally stable or unstable? Smart or unintelligent? These questions cover a large measure of what we might want to know about someone's personality. (Trait descriptions adapted from McCrae & Costa, 1990.)

Trait profile A graph of the scores obtained on several personality traits.

Five-factor model Proposes that there are five universal dimensions of personality.

Cattell identified 16 source traits. According to him, all 16 are needed to fully describe a personality. Source traits are measured by a test called the *Sixteen Personality Factor Questionnaire* (often referred to as the 16 PF). Like many personality tests, the 16 PF can be used to produce a **trait profile,** or graph of a person's score on each trait. Trait profiles draw a "picture" of individual personalities, which makes it easier to compare them (▸▸Fig. 10.3).

The Big Five

Noel is outgoing and friendly, conscientious, emotionally stable, and smart. His brother Joel is introverted, hostile, irresponsible, emotionally unpredictable, and disinterested in ideas (stupid). You will be spending a week in a space capsule with either Noel or Joel. Who would you choose? If the answer seems obvious, it's because Noel and Joel were described with the **five-factor model,** a system that identifies the five most basic dimensions of personality.

The "Big Five" factors listed in ▸▸Figure 10.4 attempt to further reduce Cattell's 16 factors to just five universal source traits or dimensions (Costa & McCrae, 2006). The Big Five may be the best answer of all to the question, What is the essence of human personality? (McCrae & Terracciano, 2005).

Five Key Dimensions

If you would like to compare the personalities of two people, try rating them informally on the five dimensions shown in ▸▸Figure 10.4. For factor 1, *extroversion,* rate how introverted or extroverted each person is. Factor 2, *agreeableness,* refers to how friendly, nurturant, and caring a person is, as opposed to cold, indifferent, self-centered, or spiteful. A person who is *conscientious* (factor 3) is self-disciplined, responsible, and achieving. People low on this factor are irresponsible, careless, and undependable. Factor 4, *neuroticism,* refers to negative, upsetting emotions.

Perfectly Miserable

Up to a point, wanting to be "perfect" is associated with high achievement. However, having impossibly high standards, a trait called perfectionism, can be a problem. As you might expect, college students who are perfectionists tend to get good grades. Yet, some students cross the line into maladaptive perfectionism, which often lowers performance at school and elsewhere (Accordino et al., 2000).

People who suffer from unhealthy perfectionism set unattainably high standards for themselves. This causes them to feel as if they are always failing. Perfectionistic students are self-critical, terrified of making mistakes, and often seriously depressed (Grzegorek et al., 2004; Sumi & Kanda, 2002).

For many students, maladaptive perfectionism begins with harsh, perfectionistic parenting. There's nothing wrong with having par-

ents who expect a lot of you—if they are also emotionally supportive. However, parents who are demanding and highly critical may leave a student feeling that nothing she or he does is ever quite good enough. As already noted, this is a recipe for self-doubt and depression.

Authentic Navajo rugs always have a flaw in their intricate designs. Navajo weavers intentionally make a "mistake" in each rug as a reminder that humans are not perfect. There is a lesson in this: It is not always necessary, or even desirable, to be "perfect." To learn from your experiences you must feel free to make mistakes (Castro & Rice, 2003). Success, in the long run, is more often based on seeking "excellence" rather than "perfection" (Enns, Cox, & Clara, 2005).

People who are high in neuroticism tend to be anxious, emotionally "sour," irritable, and unhappy. Finally, people who rate high on factor 5, *openness to experience,* are intelligent and open to new ideas (McCrae & Costa, 2001). The beauty of the Big-Five model is that almost any trait you can name will be related to one of the five factors. If you were selecting a college roommate, hiring an employee, or answering a singles ad, you would probably like to know all of the personal dimensions covered by the Big Five. Such traits predict how people will act in various circumstances. For example, people who score high in conscientiousness tend to perform well at work, do well in school, and they rarely have automobile accidents (Arthur & Doverspike, 2001; Barrick et al., 2001; Chamorro-Premuzic & Furnham, 2003). (Is it possible to be too conscientious? See "Perfectly Miserable" for an answer.)

Before you read the next section, take a moment to answer the questions that follow. Doing so will add to your understanding of a long-running controversy in the psychology of personality.

Rate Yourself: How Do You View Personality?

1. My friends' actions are fairly consistent from day to day and in different situations. T or F?
2. Whether a person is honest or dishonest, kind or cruel, a hero or a coward depends mainly on circumstances. T or F?
3. Most people that I have known for several years have pretty much the same personalities now as they did when I first met them. T or F?
4. The reason that people in some professions (such as teachers, lawyers, or doctors) seem so much alike is because their work requires that they act in particular ways. T or F?
5. One of the first things I would want to know about a potential roommate is what the person's personality is like. T or F?
6. I believe that immediate circumstances usually determine how people act at any given time. T or F?
7. To be comfortable in a particular job, a person's personality must match the nature of the work. T or F?
8. Almost anyone would be polite at a wedding reception; it doesn't matter what kind of personality the person has. T or F?

Eleanor Bentall/Corbis

Knowing where a person stands on the "Big Five" personality factors helps predict his or her behavior. For example, people who score high on conscientiousness tend to be safe drivers who are unlikely to have automobile accidents (Arthur & Doverspike, 2001).

Now count the number of times you marked true for the odd-numbered items. Do the same for the even-numbered items.

If you agreed with most of the odd-numbered items, you tend to view behavior as strongly influenced by personality traits or lasting personal dispositions.

If you agreed with most of the even-numbered items, you view behavior as strongly influenced by external situations and circumstances.

What if I answered true about equally for odd and even items? Then you place equal weight on traits and situations as ways to explain behavior. This is the view now held by many personality psychologists (Funder, 2004; Mischel & Shoda, 1998).

Traits, Consistency, and Situations

To predict how a person will act, is it better to focus on personality traits or external circumstances? Actually, it's best to take both into account. Personality traits are quite consistent. As we have seen, they can predict such things as job performance, dangerous driving, or successful marriage (Funder, 2004). Yet, *situations* also greatly influence our behavior. For instance, it would be unusual for you to dance at a movie or read a book at a football game. Likewise, few people sleep in roller coasters or tell off-color jokes at funerals. However, your personality traits may predict whether you choose to read a book, go to a movie, or attend a football game in the first place. Typically, traits *interact* with situations to determine how we will act (Mischel, 2004).

Trait-situation interactions occur when external circumstances influence the expression of personality traits. For instance, imagine what would happen if you moved from a church to a classroom to a party to a football game. As the setting changed, you would probably become louder and more boisterous. This change would demonstrate situational effects on behavior. At the same time, your personality traits would also be apparent: If you were quieter than average in class, you would probably be quieter than average in the other settings, too. Where do such differences come from? The next section explores one source of personality traits.

Do We Inherit Personality?

How much does heredity affect personality traits? Some breeds of dogs have reputations for being friendly, aggressive, intelligent, calm, or emotional. Such differences fall in the realm of **behavioral genetics,** the study of inherited behavioral traits. We know that facial features, eye color, body type, and many other physical characteristics are inherited. So are many of our behavioral tendencies (Bouchard, 2004). Genetic studies have shown that intelligence, some mental disorders, temperament, and other complex qualities are influenced by heredity. In view of such findings, we also might wonder, Do genes affect personality?

Wouldn't comparing the personalities of identical twins help answer the question? It would indeed—especially if the twins were separated at birth or soon after.

Twins and Traits

For several decades, psychologists at the University of Minnesota have been studying identical twins who grew up in different homes. Medical and psychological tests reveal that reunited twins are very much alike, even when they are reared apart (Bouchard et al., 1990; Bouchard, 2004). They may even be similar in appearance, voice quality, facial gestures, hand movements, and nervous tics, such as nail biting. Separated twins also tend to have similar talents. If one twin excels at art, music, dance, drama, or athletics, the other is likely to as well—despite wide differences in childhood environment. However, as the "Critical Thinking" box titled "Amazing Twins" explains, it's wise to be cautious about some reports of extraordinary similarities in reunited twins.

Trait-situation interaction The influence that external settings or circumstances have on the expression of personality traits.

Behavioral genetics The study of inherited behavioral traits and tendencies.

Amazing Twins

Many reunited twins in the Minnesota study have displayed similarities far beyond what would be expected on the basis of heredity. The "Jim twins," James Lewis and James Springer, are one famous example. Both Jims had married and divorced women named Linda. Both had undergone police training. One named his firstborn son James Allan, the other named *his* firstborn son James Alan. Both drove Chevrolets and vacationed at the same beach each summer. Both listed carpentry and mechanical drawing among their hobbies. Both had built benches around trees in their yards. And so forth (Holden, 1980).

Are all identical twins so, well, identical? No, they aren't. Consider identical twins Carolyn Spiro and Pamela Spiro Wagner who, unlike the "Jim Twins," lived together throughout their childhood. While in sixth grade, they found out that President Kennedy had been assassinated. Carolyn wasn't sure why everyone was so upset. Pamela heard voices announcing that she was responsible for his death. After years of hiding her voices from everyone, Pamela tried to commit suicide while the twins were attending Brown University. She was diagnosed with schizophrenia. Never to be cured, she has gone on to write award-winning poetry. Carolyn eventually became a Harvard psychiatrist (Spiro Wagner & Spiro, 2005). Some twins reared apart appear very similar; some reared together appear rather different.

So why are some identical twins, like the Jim Twins, so much alike even if they were reared apart? Although genetics is important, it is preposterous to suggest that there are child-naming genes and bench-building genes. How, then, do we explain the eerie similarities in some separated twins' lives? Imagine that you were separated at birth from a twin brother or sister. If you were reunited with your twin today, what would you do? Quite likely, you would spend the next several days comparing every imaginable detail of your lives. Under such circumstances it is virtually certain that you and your twin would notice and compile a long list of similarities. ("Wow! I use the same brand of toothpaste you do!") Yet, two unrelated persons of the same age, sex, and race could probably rival your list—*if* they were as motivated to find similarities.

In fact, one study compared twins to unrelated pairs of students. The unrelated pairs, who were the same age and sex, were almost as alike as the twins. They had highly similar political beliefs, musical interests, religious preferences, job histories, hobbies, favorite foods, and so on (Wyatt et al., 1984). Why were the unrelated students so similar? Basically, it's because people of the same age and sex live in the same historical times and select from similar societal options.

It appears then that many of the seemingly "astounding" coincidences shared by reunited twins may be a special case of the fallacy of positive instances, described in Chapter 1. Reunited twins tend to notice the similarities and ignore the differences.

Identical twins Pam *(left)* and Carolyn *(right)* were raised together. Regardless, Carolyn became a psychiatrist, and Pamela developed schizophrenia and went on to become an award-winning poet (Spiro, Wagner, & Spiro, 2005). Their story illustrates the complex interplay of forces that shape our adult personalities.

Summary

Studies of twins make it clear that heredity has a sizable effect on each of us. All told, it seems reasonable to conclude that heredity is responsible for about 25 to 50 percent of the variation in many personality traits (Caspi, Roberts, & Shiner, 2005; Loehlin et al., 1998). Notice, however, that the same figures imply personality is shaped as much, or more, by environment as it is by heredity.

Each personality is a unique blend of heredity and environment, biology and culture. We are not—thank goodness—genetically programmed robots whose behavior and personality traits are "wired in" for life. Where you go in life is the result of the choices you make. Although these choices are influenced by inherited tendencies, they are not merely a product of your genes (Funder, 2004).

Study Break Personality and Trait Theories

Reflect

See if you can define or describe the following terms in your own words: personality, character, temperament, trait, type, self-concept, self-esteem.

List six or seven traits that best describe your personality. Which system of traits seems to best match your list, Allport's, Cattell's, or the Big Five?

Choose a prominent trait from your list. Does its expression seem to be influenced by specific situations? Do you think that heredity contributed to the trait?

Learning Check

1. _____ refers to the hereditary aspects of a person's emotional nature.
2. The term _____ refers to the presence or absence of desirable personal qualities.

    a. personality   b. source trait
    c. character   d. temperament

3. A system that classifies all people as either introverts or extroverts is an example of a(n) _____ approach to personality.

4. An individual's perception of his or her own personality constitutes that person's _____.
5. Central traits are those shared by most members of a culture. T or F?
6. Cattell believes that clusters of _____ traits reveal the presence of underlying _____ traits.
7. Which of the following is *not* one of the Big Five personality factors?

    a. submissiveness   b. agreeableness
    c. extroversion   d. neuroticism

8. To understand personality, it is wise to remember that traits and situations _____ to determine our behavior.

Critical Thinking

9. In what way would memory contribute to the formation of an accurate or inaccurate self-image?
10. Are situations equally powerful in their impact on behavior?

Answers

1. Temperament 2. c 3. type 4. self-concept 5. F 6. surface, source 7. a 8. interact 9. As discussed in Chapter 7, memory is highly selective, and long-term memories are often distorted by recent information. Such properties add to the modability of self-concept. 10. No. Circumstances can have a strong or weak influence. In some situations, almost everyone will act the same, no matter what their personality traits may be. In other situations, traits may be of greater importance.

PSYCHODYNAMIC THEORY— ID CAME TO ME IN A DREAM

>SURVEY QUESTION< *How do psychodynamic theories explain personality?*

Psychodynamic theorists are not content with studying traits. Instead, they try to probe under the surface of personality—to learn what drives, conflicts, and energies animate us. Psychodynamic theorists believe that many of our actions are based on hidden, or unconscious, thoughts, needs, and emotions.

Psychoanalytic theory, the best-known psychodynamic approach, grew out of the work of Sigmund Freud, a Viennese physician. As a doctor, Freud was fascinated by patients whose problems seemed to be more emotional than physical. From about 1890 until he died in 1939, Freud evolved a theory of personality that deeply influenced modern thought (Jacobs, 2003). Let's consider some of its main features (Schultz & Schultz, 2005).

The Structure of Personality

How did Freud view personality? Freud's model portrays personality as a dynamic system directed by three mental structures, the **id,** the **ego,** and the **superego.** According to Freud, most behavior involves activity of all three systems. (Freud's theory includes a large number of concepts. For your convenience, they are defined in ■ Table 10.2 rather than in page margins.)

Psychoanalytic theory Freudian theory of personality that emphasizes unconscious forces and conflicts.

■ Table 10.2 Key Freudian Concepts

Anal stage The psychosexual stage corresponding roughly to the period of toilet training (ages 1 to 3).

Anal-expulsive personality A disorderly, destructive, cruel, or messy person.

Anal-retentive personality A person who is obstinate, stingy, or compulsive, and who generally has difficulty "letting go."

Conscience The part of the superego that causes guilt when its standards are not met.

Conscious Region of the mind that includes all mental contents a person is aware of at any given moment.

Ego The executive part of personality that directs rational behavior.

Ego ideal The part of the superego representing ideal behavior; a source of pride when its standards are met.

Electra conflict A girl's sexual attraction to her father and feelings of rivalry with her mother.

Erogenous zone Any body area that produces pleasurable sensations.

Eros Freud's name for the "life instincts."

Fixation A lasting conflict developed as a result of frustration or over-indulgence.

Genital stage Period of full psychosexual development, marked by the attainment of mature adult sexuality.

Id The primitive part of personality that remains unconscious, supplies energy, and demands pleasure.

Latency According to Freud, a period in childhood when psychosexual development is more or less interrupted.

Libido In Freudian theory, the force, primarily pleasure oriented, that energizes the personality.

Moral anxiety Apprehension felt when thoughts, impulses, or actions conflict with the superego's standards.

Neurotic anxiety Apprehension felt when the ego struggles to control id impulses.

Oedipus conflict A boy's sexual attraction to his mother, and feelings of rivalry with his father.

Oral stage The period when infants are preoccupied with the mouth as a source of pleasure and means of expression.

Oral-aggressive personality A person who uses the mouth to express hostility by shouting, cursing, biting, and so forth. Also, one who actively exploits others.

Oral-dependent personality A person who wants to passively receive attention, gifts, love, and so forth.

Phallic personality A person who is vain, exhibitionistic, sensitive, and narcissistic.

Phallic stage The psychosexual stage (roughly ages 3 to 6) when a child is preoccupied with the genitals.

Pleasure principle A desire for immediate satisfaction of wishes, desires, or needs.

Preconscious An area of the mind containing information that can be voluntarily brought to awareness.

Psyche The mind, mental life, and personality as a whole.

Psychosexual stages The oral, anal, phallic, and genital stages, during which various personality traits are formed.

Reality principle Delaying action (or pleasure) until it is appropriate.

Superego A judge or censor for thoughts and actions.

Thanatos The death instinct postulated by Freud.

Unconscious The region of the mind that is beyond awareness, especially impulses and desires not directly known to a person.

The Id

The id is made up of innate biological instincts and urges. It is self-serving, irrational, impulsive, and totally unconscious. The id operates on the **pleasure principle.** That is, it seeks to freely express pleasure-seeking urges of all kinds. If we were solely under control of the id, the world would be chaotic beyond belief.

The id acts as a well of energy for the entire **psyche** (SIGH-key), or personality. This energy, called **libido** (lih-BEE-doe), flows from the **life instincts** (or **Eros**). According to Freud, libido underlies our efforts to survive, as well as our sexual desires and pleasure seeking. Freud also described a **death instinct. Thanatos,** as he called it, produces aggressive and destructive urges. Freud offered humanity's long history of wars and violence as evidence of such urges. Most id energies, then, are aimed at discharging tensions related to sex and aggression.

"All Is Vanity" by Allen Gilbert

Freud considered personality an expression of two conflicting forces, life instincts and the death instinct. Both are symbolized in this drawing by Allan Gilbert. (If you don't immediately see the death symbolism, stand farther from the drawing.)

The Ego

The ego is sometimes described as the "executive," because it directs energies supplied by the id. The id is like a blind king or queen whose power is awesome but who must rely on others to carry out orders. The id can only form mental images of things it desires. The ego wins power to direct behavior by relating the desires of the id to external reality.

Are there other differences between the ego and the id? Yes. Recall that the id operates on the pleasure principle. The ego, in contrast, is guided by the **reality principle.** The ego is the system of thinking, planning, problem solving, and deciding. It is in conscious control of the personality and often delays action until it is practical or appropriate.

The Superego

What is the role of the superego? The superego acts as a judge or censor for the thoughts and actions of the ego. One part of the superego, called the **conscience,** reflects actions for which a person has been punished. When standards of the conscience are not met, you are punished internally by *guilt* feelings.

A second part of the superego is the **ego ideal.** The ego ideal reflects all behavior one's parents approved of or rewarded. The ego ideal is a source of goals and aspirations. When its standards are met, we feel *pride.*

The superego acts as an "internalized parent" to bring behavior under control. In Freudian terms, a person with a weak superego will be a delinquent, criminal, or antisocial personality. In contrast, an overly strict or harsh superego may cause inhibition, rigidity, or unbearable guilt.

The Dynamics of Personality

How do the id, ego, and superego interact? Freud didn't picture the id, ego, and superego as parts of the brain or as "little people" running the human psyche. Instead, they are conflicting mental processes. Freud theorized a delicate balance of power among the three. For example, the id's demands for immediate pleasure often clash with the superego's moral restrictions. Perhaps an example will help clarify the role of each part of the personality.

Freud in a Nutshell

Let's say you are sexually attracted to an acquaintance. The id clamors for immediate satisfaction of its sexual desires, but is opposed by the superego (which finds the very thought of sex shocking). The id says, "Go for it!" The superego icily replies, "Never even think that again!" And what does the ego say? The ego says, "I have a plan!"

Of course, this is a drastic simplification, but it does capture the core of Freudian thinking. To reduce tension, the ego could begin actions leading to friendship, romance, courtship, and marriage. If the id is unusually powerful, the ego may give in and attempt a seduction. If the superego prevails, the ego may be forced to *displace* or *sublimate* sexual energies to other activities (sports, music, dancing, push-ups, cold showers). According to Freud, internal struggles and rechanneled energies typify most personality functioning.

Is the ego always caught in the middle? Basically yes, and the pressures on it can be intense. In addition to meeting the conflicting demands of the id and superego, the overworked ego must deal with external reality.

According to Freud, you feel anxiety when your ego is threatened or overwhelmed. Impulses from the id cause **neurotic anxiety** when the ego can barely keep them under control. Threats of punishment from the superego cause **moral anxiety.** Each person develops habitual ways of calming these anxieties, and many resort to using *ego-defense mechanisms* to lessen internal conflicts. Defense mechanisms are mental processes that deny, distort, or otherwise block out sources of threat and anxiety. (The ego defense mechanisms that Freud identified are used as a form of protection against stress, anxiety, and threatening events. See Chapter 11.)

Levels of Awareness

Like other psychodynamic theorists, Freud believed that our behavior often expresses unconscious (or hidden) forces. The **unconscious** holds repressed memories and emotions, plus the instinctual drives of the id. Interestingly, modern scientists have found that the brain's limbic system does, in fact, seem to trigger unconscious emotions and memories (LeDoux, 1996).

Even though they are beyond awareness, unconscious thoughts, feelings, or urges may slip into behavior in disguised or symbolic form. For example, if you meet someone you would like to know better, you may unconsciously leave a book or a jacket at that person's house to ensure another meeting.

Are the actions of the ego and superego also unconscious, like the id? At times, yes, but they also operate on two other levels of awareness (➡ Fig. 10.5). The **conscious** level includes everything you are aware of at a given moment, including thoughts, perceptions, feelings, and memories. The **preconscious** contains material that can be easily brought to awareness. If you stop to think about a time when you felt angry or rejected, you will be moving this memory from the preconscious to the conscious level of awareness.

The superego's activities also reveal differing levels of awareness. At times we consciously try to live up to moral codes or standards. Yet, at other times a person may feel guilty without knowing why. Psychoanalytic theory credits such guilt to unconscious workings of the superego. Indeed, Freud believed that the unconscious origins of many feelings cannot be easily brought to awareness.

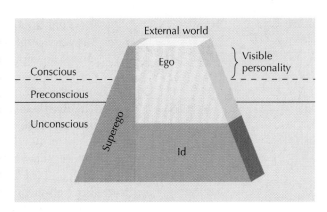

➡**FIGURE 10.5** The approximate relationship between the id, ego, and superego, and the levels of awareness.

Personality Development

How does psychoanalytic theory explain personality development? Freud theorized that the core of personality is formed before age 6 in a series of **psychosexual stages.** Freud believed that erotic urges in childhood have lasting effects on development. As you might expect, this is a controversial idea. However, Freud used the terms *sex* and *erotic* very broadly to refer to many physical sources of pleasure.

A Freudian Fable?

Freud identified four psychosexual stages, the **oral, anal, phallic,** and **genital.** (He also described a period of "latency" between the phallic and genital stages. Latency is explained in a moment.) At each stage, a different part of the body becomes a child's primary **erogenous zone** (an area capable of producing pleasure). Each area then serves as the main source of pleasure, frustration, and self-expression. Freud believed that many adult personality traits can be traced to **fixations** in one or more of the stages.

What is a fixation? A fixation is an unresolved conflict or emotional hang-up caused by overindulgence or by frustration. As we describe the psychosexual stages you'll see why Freud considered fixations important.

The Oral Stage

During the first year of life, most of an infant's pleasure comes from stimulation of the mouth. If a child is overfed or frustrated, oral traits may be created. Adult expressions of oral needs include gum chewing, nail biting, smoking, kissing, overeating, and alcoholism.

What if there is an oral fixation? Fixation early in the oral stage produces an **oral-dependent** personality. Oral-dependent persons are gullible (they swallow things easily!) and passive and need lots of attention (they want to be mothered and showered with gifts). Frustrations later in the oral stage may cause aggression, often in the form of biting. Fixations here create cynical, **oral-aggressive** adults who exploit others. They also like to argue ("biting sarcasm" is their forte!).

The Anal Stage

Between the ages of 1 and 3, the child's attention shifts to the process of elimination. When parents attempt toilet training, the child can gain approval or express rebellion or aggression by "holding on" or by "letting go." Therefore, harsh or lenient toilet training can cause an anal fixation that may lock such responses into personality. Freud described the **anal-retentive** (holding-on) personality as obstinate, stingy, orderly, and compulsively clean. The **anal-expulsive** (letting-go) personality is disorderly, destructive, cruel, or messy.

The Phallic Stage

Adult traits of the **phallic personality** are vanity, exhibitionism, sensitive pride, and narcissism (self-love). Freud theorized that phallic fixations develop between the ages of 3 and 6. At this time, increased sexual interest causes the child to be physically attracted to the parent of the opposite sex. In males this attraction leads to an **Oedipus conflict.** In it, the boy feels a rivalry with his father for the affection of his mother. Freud believed that the male child feels threatened by the father (specifically, the boy fears castration). To ease his anxieties, the boy must identify with the father. Their rivalry ends when the boy seeks to become more like his father. As he does, he begins to accept the father's values and forms a conscience.

What about the female child? Girls experience an **Electra conflict.** In this case, the girl loves her father and competes with her mother. However, according to Freud, the girl identifies with the mother more gradually.

Freud believed that females already feel castrated. Because of this, they are less driven to identify with their mothers than boys are with their fathers. This, he said, is less effective in creating a conscience. This particular part of Freudian thought has been thoroughly (and rightfully) rejected by modern feminists. It is probably best understood as a reflection of the male-dominated times in which Freud lived.

Latency

According to Freud there is a period of **latency** from age 6 to puberty. Latency is not actually a stage. Rather, it is a quiet time during which psychosexual development is dormant. Freud's belief that psychosexual development is "on hold" at this time is hard to accept. Nevertheless, Freud saw latency as a relatively quiet time compared to the stormy first 6 years of life.

The Genital Stage

At puberty an upswing in sexual energies activates all the unresolved conflicts of earlier years. This upsurge, according to Freud, is the reason why adolescence can be filled with emotion and turmoil. The genital stage begins at puberty. It is marked, during adolescence, by a growing capacity for responsible social-sexual relationships. The genital stage ends with a mature capacity for love and the realization of full adult sexuality.

Critical Comments

As bizarre as Freud's theory might seem, it has been influential for several reasons. First, it pioneered the idea that the first years of life help shape adult personality. Second, it identified feeding, toilet training, and early sexual experiences as critical events in personality formation. Third, Freud was among the first to propose that development proceeds through a series of stages. (Erik Erikson's psycho*social* stages, which cover development from birth to old age, are a modern offshoot of Freudian thinking. See Chapter 3.)

Is the Freudian view of development widely accepted? Few psychologists wholeheartedly embrace Freud's theory today. In some cases Freud was clearly wrong. His portrayal of the elementary school years (latency) as free from sexuality and unimportant for personality development is hard to believe. His idea of the role of a stern or threatening father in the development of a strong conscience in males has also been challenged. Studies show that a son is more likely to develop a strong conscience if his father is affectionate and accepting,

Was Freud's ever-present cigar a sign of an oral fixation? Was it a phallic symbol? Was it both? Or was it neither? Once, when he was asked, Freud himself apparently replied, "Sometimes a cigar is just a cigar." An inability to say for sure is one of the shortcomings of psychoanalytic theory.

Bettmann/Corbis

rather than stern and punishing. Freud also overemphasized sexuality in personality development. Other motives and cognitive factors are of equal importance.

Freud has been criticized for his views of patients who believed they were sexually molested as children. Freud assumed that such events were merely childhood fantasies. This view led to a long-standing tendency to disbelieve children who have been molested and women who have been raped (Brannon, 1996).

Another important criticism is that Freud's concepts are almost impossible to verify scientifically. The theory provides numerous ways to explain almost any thought, action, or feeling *after* it has occurred. However, it leads to few predictions, which makes its claims difficult to test. Although more criticisms of Freud could be listed, the fact remains that there is an element of truth to much of what he said (Jacobs, 2003). Because of this, some clinical psychologists continue to regard Freudian theory as a useful way to think about human problems.

 Study Break **Psychodynamic Theory**

Reflect

Try to think of at least one time when your thoughts, feelings, or actions seemed to reflect the workings of each of the following: the id, the ego, and the superego.

Do you know anyone who seems to have oral, anal, or phallic personality traits? Do you think Freud's concept of fixation explains their characteristics?

Do any of your personal experiences support the existence of an Oedipus conflict or an Electra conflict? If not, is it possible that you have repressed feelings related to these conflicts?

Learning Check

1. List the three divisions of personality postulated by Freud.

_____

2. Which division is totally unconscious? _____

3. Which division is responsible for moral anxiety? _____
4. Freud proposed the existence of a life instinct known as Thanatos. T or F?
5. Freud's view of personality development is based on the concept of _____ stages.
6. Arrange these stages in the proper order: phallic, anal, genital, oral. _____
7. Freud considered the anal-retentive personality to be obstinate and stingy. T or F?

Critical Thinking

8. Many adults would find it embarrassing or humiliating to drink from a baby bottle. Can you explain why?

Answers

1. id, ego, superego 2. id 3. superego 4. F 5. psychosexual 6. oral, anal, phallic, genital 7. T 8. A psychoanalytic theorist would say that it is because the bottle rekindles oral conflicts and feelings of vulnerability and dependence.

LEARNING THEORIES OF PERSONALITY— HABIT I SEEN YOU BEFORE?

>SURVEY QUESTION< *What do behaviorists and social learning theorists emphasize in their approach to personality?*

After exploring Freud's psychodynamic theory, you might be relieved to know that behavioral theorists explain personality through straightforward concepts, such as learning, reinforcement, and imitation. Behavioral and social learning theories are based on scientific research, which makes them powerful ways of looking at personality.

How do behaviorists approach personality? According to some critics, behaviorists approach personality as if people are robots like Data of *Star Trek* fame. Actually, the behaviorist position is not nearly that mechanistic, and its value is well established. Behaviorists have shown repeatedly that children can *learn* things like kindness, hostility, generosity, or destructiveness. What does this have to do with personality? Everything, according to the behavioral viewpoint.

Behavioral personality theories emphasize that personality is no more (or less) than a collection of learned behavior patterns. Personality, like other learned behavior, is acquired

Behavioral personality theory Any model of personality that emphasizes learning and observable behavior.

Freud believed that aggressive urges are "instinctual." In contrast, behavioral theories assume that personal characteristics such as aggressiveness are learned. Is this boy's aggression the result of observational learning, harsh punishment, or prior reinforcement?

through classical and operant conditioning, observational learning, reinforcement, extinction, generalization, and discrimination. When Mother says, "It's not nice to make mud pies with Mommy's blender. If we want to grow up to be a big girl, we won't do it again, will we?" she serves as a model and in other ways shapes her daughter's personality.

Strict learning theorists reject the idea that personality is made up of traits. They would assert, for instance, that there is no such thing as a trait of "honesty" (Mischel, 2004).

Certainly some people are honest and others are not. How can honesty not be a trait? Learning theorists recognize that some people are honest *more often* than others. But knowing this does not allow us to predict whether a person will be honest in a specific situation. It would not be unusual, for example, to find that a person honored for returning a lost wallet had cheated on a test, bought a term paper, or broken the speed limit. If you were to ask a learning theorist, "Are you an honest person?" the reply might be, "In what situation?"

As you can see, learning theorists are interested in the **situational determinants** (external causes) of our actions. A good example of how situations can influence behavior is a study in which people were intentionally overpaid for doing an assigned task. Under normal circumstances, 80 percent kept the extra money without mentioning it. But as few as 17 percent were dishonest if the situation was altered. For instance, if people thought the money was coming out of the pocket of the person doing the study, far fewer were dishonest (Bersoff, 1999). Thus, situations always interact with our prior learning history to activate behavior.

Situations vary greatly in their impact. Some are powerful. Others are trivial and have little effect on behavior. The more powerful the situation, the easier it is to see what is meant by situational determinants. For example, each of the following situations would undoubtedly have a strong influence on behavior: an armed terrorist walks into a supermarket; you accidentally sit on a lighted cigarette; you find your lover in bed with your best friend. Yet even these situations could provoke very different reactions from different personalities. That's why behavior is always a product of both prior learning and the situations in which we find ourselves (Mischel, Shoda, & Smith, 2004).

Ultimately, what is predictable about personality is that we respond in consistent ways to certain types of situations. Consider, for example, two people who are easily angered: One person might get angry when she is delayed (for example, in traffic or a checkout line), but not when she misplaces something at home; the other person might get angry whenever she misplaces things, but not when she is delayed. Overall, the two women are equally prone to anger, but their anger tends to occur in different patterns and different types of situations.

Personality = Behavior

How do learning theorists view the structure of personality? The behavioral view of personality can be illustrated with an early theory proposed by John Dollard and Neal Miller (1950). In their view, *habits* (learned behavior patterns) make up the structure of personality. As for the dynamics of personality, habits are governed by four elements of learning: *drive, cue, response,* and *reward.* A *drive* is any stimulus strong enough to goad a person to action (such as hunger, pain, lust, frustration, or fear). *Cues* are signals from the environment. These signals guide *responses* (actions) so that they are most likely to bring about *reward* (positive reinforcement).

How does that relate to personality? Let's say a child named Katrina is frustrated by her older brother Kelvin, who takes a toy from her. Katrina could respond in several ways: She could throw a temper tantrum, hit Kelvin, tell Mother, and so forth. The response she chooses is guided by available cues and the previous effects of each response. If telling Mother has paid off in the past, and the mother is present, telling again may be her immedi-

Situational determinants External conditions that strongly influence behavior.

ate response. If a different set of cues exists (if Mother is absent or if Kelvin looks particularly menacing), Katrina may select some other response. To an outside observer, Katrina's actions seem to reflect her personality. To a learning theorist, they simply express the combined effects of drive, cue, response, and reward.

Doesn't this analysis leave out a lot? Yes. Learning theorists at first set out to provide a simple, clear model of personality. But in recent years they have had to face a fact that they originally tended to overlook: People think. The new breed of behavioral psychologists—who include perception, thinking, expectations, and other mental events in their views—are called social learning theorists. Learning principles, modeling, thought patterns, perceptions, expectations, beliefs, goals, emotions, and social relationships are combined in **social learning theory** to explain personality (Mischel, Shoda, & Smith, 2004).

Social Learning Theory

Someone trips you. How do you respond? Your reaction probably depends on whether you think it was planned or an accident. It is not enough to know the setting in which a person responds. We also need to know the person's **psychological situation** (how the person interprets or defines the situation). As another example, let's say you score low on an exam. Do you consider it a challenge to work harder, a sign that you should drop the class, or an excuse to get drunk? Again, your interpretation is important.

Our actions are affected by an **expectancy,** or anticipation, that making a response will lead to reinforcement. To continue the example, if working harder has paid off in the past, it is a likely reaction to a low test score. But to predict your response, we would also have to know if you *expect* your efforts to pay off in the present situation. In fact, expected reinforcement may be more important than actual past reinforcement. And what about the *value* you attach to grades, school success, or personal ability? The concept of **reinforcement value** states that we attach different subjective values to various activities or rewards. This, too, must be taken into account to understand personality.

Through self-reinforcement we reward ourselves for personal achievements and other "good" behavior.

Self-Efficacy

An ability to control your own life is the essence of what it means to be human. Because of this, Albert Bandura believes that one of the most important expectancies we develop concerns **self-efficacy** (EF-uh-keh-see: a capacity for producing a desired result). You're attracted to someone in your anthropology class. Will you ask him or her out? You're thinking about learning to snowboard. Will you try it this winter? You're beginning to consider a career in psychology. Will you take the courses you need to get into graduate school? In these, and countless other situations, efficacy beliefs play a key role in shaping our lives by influencing the activities and environments we choose to get into (Bandura, 2001).

Self-Reinforcement

One more idea deserves mention. At times, we all evaluate our actions and may reward ourselves with special privileges or treats for "good behavior." With this in mind, social learning theory adds the concept of self-reinforcement to the behavioristic view. **Self-reinforcement** refers to praising or rewarding yourself for having made a particular response (such as completing a school assignment). Thus, habits of self-praise and self-blame become an important part of personality. In fact, self-reinforcement can be thought of as the social learning theorist's counterpart to the superego.

Self-reinforcement is closely related to high self-esteem. The reverse is also true: Mildly depressed college students tend to have low rates of self-reinforcement. It is not known if low self-reinforcement leads to depression, or the reverse. In either case, self-reinforcement

Social learning theory An explanation of personality that combines learning principles, cognition, and the effects of social relationships.

Psychological situation A situation as it is perceived and interpreted by an individual, not as it exists objectively.

Expectancy Anticipation about the effect a response will have, especially regarding reinforcement.

Reinforcement value The subjective value a person attaches to a particular activity or reinforcer.

Self-efficacy Belief in your capacity to produce a desired result.

Self-reinforcement Praising or rewarding oneself for having made a particular response (such as completing a school assignment).

I WISH YOU WOULD QUIT BEING SO HARD ON YOURSELF. IT LEAVES *ME* WITH NOTHING TO DO.

© Vic Lee. Reprinted with special permission of King Features Syndicate.

is associated with less depression and greater life satisfaction (Seybolt & Wagner, 1997). From a behavioral viewpoint, there is value in learning to be "good to yourself."

Behavioristic View of Development

How do learning theorists account for personality development? Many of Freud's ideas can be restated in terms of learning theory. Dollard and Miller (1950) agree with Freud that the first 6 years are crucial for personality development, but for different reasons. Rather than thinking in terms of psychosexual urges and fixations, they ask, "What makes early learning experiences so lasting in their effects?" Their answer is that childhood is a time of urgent drives, powerful rewards and punishments, and crushing frustrations. Also important is *social reinforcement,* which is based on praise, attention, or approval from others. These forces combine to shape the core of personality.

Critical Situations

Dollard and Miller believe that during childhood four **critical situations** are capable of leaving a lasting imprint on personality. These are (1) feeding, (2) toilet or cleanliness training, (3) sex training, and (4) learning to express anger or aggression.

Why are these of special importance? Feeding serves as an illustration. If children are fed when they cry, it encourages them to actively manipulate their parents. The child allowed to cry without being fed learns to be passive. Thus, a basic active or passive orientation toward the world may be created by early feeding experiences. Feeding can also affect later social relationships because the child learns to associate people with pleasure or with frustration and discomfort.

Toilet and cleanliness training can be a particularly strong source of emotion for both parents and children. Rashad's parents were aghast the day they found him smearing feces about with joyful abandon. They reacted with sharp punishment, which frustrated and confused Rashad. Many attitudes toward cleanliness, conformity, and bodily functions are formed at such times. Studies have also long shown that severe, punishing, or frustrating toilet training can have undesirable effects on personality development (Christophersen & Mortweet, 2003). Because of this, toilet and cleanliness training demand patience and a sense of humor.

What about sex and anger? When, where, and how a child learns to express anger and sexual feelings can leave an imprint on personality. Specifically, permissiveness for sexual and aggressive behavior in childhood is linked to adult needs for power (McClelland & Pilon, 1983). This link probably occurs because permitting such behaviors allows children to get pleasure from asserting themselves. Sex training also involves learning socially defined "male" and "female" gender roles—which also affects personality (Pervin, Cervone, & John, 2005).

Personality and Gender

From birth onward, children are labeled as boys or girls and encouraged to learn sex-appropriate behavior (Denmark, Rabinowitz, & Sechzer, 2005).

Critical situations Situations during childhood that are capable of leaving a lasting imprint on personality.

What does it mean to have a "masculine" or "feminine" personality? According to social learning theory, identification and imitation contribute greatly to personality development and to sex training. **Identification** refers to the child's emotional attachment to admired adults, especially those who provide love and care. Identification typically encourages **imitation,** a desire to act like the admired person. Many "male" or "female" traits come from children's attempts to imitate a same-sex parent with whom they identify.

If children are around parents of both sexes, why don't they imitate behavior typical of the opposite sex as well as of the same sex? You may recall from Chapter 6 that learning takes place vicariously as well as directly. This means that we can learn without direct reward by observing and remembering the actions of others. But the actions we choose to imitate depend on their outcomes. For example, boys and girls have equal chances to observe adults and other children acting aggressively. However, girls are less likely than boys to imitate directly aggressive behavior (shouting at or hitting). Instead, girls are more likely to rely on indirectly aggressive behavior (excluding others from friendship, spreading rumors). This may well be because the expression of direct aggression is thought to be inappropriate for girls. As a consequence, girls rarely see direct female aggression rewarded or approved (Richardson & Green, 1999). In others words, "girlfighting" is likely a culturally reinforced pattern (Brown, 2005). Intriguingly, over the last few years, girls have become more willing to engage in direct aggression as popular culture presents more and more images of directly aggressive women (Artz, 2005).

Historically, parents and other adults in Western countries like the United States tended to encourage boys to engage in **instrumental** (goal-directed) **behaviors,** to be directly aggressive, to hide their emotions, and to prepare for the world of work. Girls, on the other hand, were encouraged in **expressive** (emotion-oriented) **behaviors** and, to a lesser degree, were socialized to be indirectly aggressive and for motherhood. Thus, from an early age males and females tended to grow up in different, gender-defined cultures (Martin & Fabes, 2001). But these differences are becoming less and less noticeable as traditional male and female gender roles have been called into question.

Laura Dwight/PhotoEdit

Adult personality is influenced by identification with parents and imitation of their behavior.

ANDROGYNY—ARE YOU MASCULINE, FEMININE, OR ANDROGYNOUS?

Are you aggressive, ambitious, analytical, assertive, athletic, competitive, decisive, dominant, forceful, independent, individualistic, self-reliant, and willing to take risks? If so, you are quite "masculine." Are you affectionate, cheerful, childlike, compassionate, flatterable, gentle, gullible, loyal, sensitive, shy, soft-spoken, sympathetic, tender, understanding, warm, and yielding? If so, then you are quite "feminine." What if you have characteristics from both lists? In that case, you may be androgynous (an-DROJ-ih-nus).

The two lists you just read are from the work of psychologist Sandra Bem. By combining 20 "masculine" traits (self-reliant, assertive, and so forth), 20 "feminine" traits (affectionate, gentle), and 20 neutral traits (truthful, friendly) Bem (1974) created the *Bem Sex Role Inventory* (BSRI). People who take the BSRI are asked to say whether each trait applies to them. Of those surveyed, 50 percent fall into traditional feminine or masculine categories; 15 per-

Identification Feeling emotionally connected to a person and seeing oneself as like him or her.

Imitation An attempt to match one's own behavior to another person's behavior.

Instrumental behaviors Behaviors directed toward the achievement of some goal; behaviors that are instrumental in producing some effect.

Expressive behaviors Behaviors that express or communicate emotion or personal feelings.

Androgynous individuals adapt easily to both traditionally "feminine" and "masculine" situations.

cent score higher on traits of the opposite sex; and 35 percent are androgynous, getting high scores on both feminine and masculine items.

The word **androgyny** (an-DROJ-ih-nee) literally means "man-woman." Psychologically, it refers to having both feminine and masculine traits. Bem is convinced that our complex society requires flexibility about gender-related traits. It is necessary, she believes, for men to be gentle, compassionate, sensitive, and yielding and for women to be forceful, self-reliant, independent, and ambitious—*as the situation requires.* In short, Bem feels that more people should be androgynous.

Adaptability

Bem has shown that androgynous individuals are more adaptable because they are less hindered by narrow images of "feminine" or "masculine" behavior. For example, in one study people were given the choice of doing either a "masculine" activity (oil a hinge, nail boards together, and so forth) or a "feminine" activity (prepare a baby bottle, wind yarn into a ball, and so on). Masculine men and feminine women consistently chose to do gender-appropriate activities, even when the opposite choice paid more!

It appears that having rigid gender traits can seriously restrict behavior, especially for men (Bem, 1974, 1981). Masculine males tend to have great difficulty expressing warmth, playfulness, and concern—even when they are appropriate. Masculine men (let's call them "manly men") also find it hard to accept emotional support from others, particularly from women (Levant, 2001). Highly feminine women face opposite problems. For them, being independent and assertive is difficult, even when these qualities are desirable. In contrast, more androgynous individuals are higher in emotional intelligence (remember Chapter 9?) (Guastello & Guastello, 2003).

Gender in Perspective

Androgyny has been hotly debated over the years. Now, as the dust begins to settle, the picture looks like this:

- Having "masculine" traits primarily means that a person is independent and assertive. Scoring high in "masculinity" is related to high self-esteem and to success in many situations.
- Having "feminine" traits primarily means that a person is nurturant and interpersonally oriented. People who score high in "femininity" tend to experience greater social closeness with others and more happiness in marriage.

In sum, there are advantages to possessing positive "feminine" *and* "masculine" traits (Woodhill & Samuels, 2004). In general, androgynous persons are more flexible when it comes to coping with difficult situations (Hittner & Daniels, 2002; Jurma & Powell, 1994). (See ▸Fig. 10.6.) Androgynous persons also tend to be more satisfied with their lives because they can use both instrumental and emotionally expressive capacities to enhance their lives and relationships (Ramanaiah, Detwiler, & Byravan, 1995).

Androgyny The presence of both "masculine" and "feminine" traits in a single person (as masculinity and femininity are defined within one's culture).

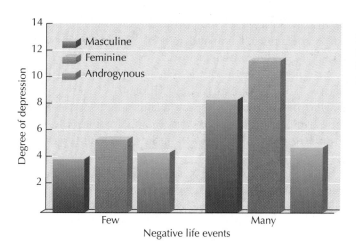

▸▸**FIGURE 10.6** Another indication of the possible benefits of androgyny is found in a study of reactions to stress. When confronted with an onslaught of negative events, strongly masculine or feminine persons become more depressed than androgynous individuals do. (Adapted from Roos & Cohen, 1987.)

It is worth saying again that many people remain comfortable with traditional views of gender. Nevertheless, "feminine" traits and "masculine" traits can readily exist in the same person, and androgyny can be a highly adaptive balance.

 Study Break **Behavioral and Social Learning Theories**

Reflect

What are your favorite foods? Can you relate Dollard and Miller's concepts of habit, drive, cue, response, and reward to explain your preference?

Some people love to shop. Others hate it. How have the psychological situation, expectancy, and reinforcement value affected your willingness to "shop 'til you drop"?

Who did you identify with as a child? What aspects of that person's behavior did you imitate?

Think of three people you know, one who is androgynous, one who is traditionally feminine, and one who is traditionally masculine. What advantages and disadvantages do you see in each collection of traits? How do you think you would be classified if you took the BSRI?

Learning Check

1. Learning theorists believe that personality "traits" really are _____ acquired through prior learning. They also emphasize _____ determinants of behavior.
2. Dollard and Miller consider cues the basic structure of personality. T or F?

3. To explain behavior, social learning theorists include mental elements, such as _____ (the anticipation that a response will lead to reinforcement).
4. Self-reinforcement is to behavioristic theory as superego is to psychoanalytic theory. T or F?
5. Which of the following is *not* a "critical situation" in the behaviorist theory of personality development?

   a. feeding   b. sex training
   c. language training   d. anger training

6. In addition to basic rewards and punishments, a child's personality is also shaped by _____ reinforcement.
7. Social learning theories of development emphasize the impact of identification and _____.
8. A person who is aggressive, ambitious, analytical, assertive would be rated as androgynous on the BSRI. T or F?

Critical Thinking

9. The concept of *reinforcement value* is closely related to a motivational principle discussed in Chapter 9. Can you name it?

Answers 1. habits, situational 2. F 3. expectancies 4. T 5. c 6. social 7. imitation 8. F 9. incentive value

---

HUMANISTIC THEORY—PEAK EXPERIENCES AND PERSONAL GROWTH

>SURVEY QUESTION< *How do humanistic theories differ from other perspectives?*

At the beginning of this chapter you met Annette, an interesting personality. After she remarried, Annette and her second husband spent a year riding mules across the country as a unique way to see America and get to know themselves better. Where do such desires for personal growth come from? Humanistic theories pay special attention to the fuller use of human potentials and they help bring balance to our overall views of personality.

Humanism focuses on human experience, problems, potentials, and ideals. At its core is a positive image of what it means to be human. Humanists reject the Freudian view of personality as a battleground for instincts and unconscious forces. Instead, they view human nature as inherently good. (Human nature consists of the traits, qualities, potentials, and behavior patterns most characteristic of the human species.) Humanists also oppose the machine-like overtones of behaviorism. We are not, they say, merely a bundle of moldable responses. Rather, we are creative beings capable of *free choice* (an ability to choose that is not controlled by genetics, learning, or unconscious forces). In short, humanists seek ways to encourage our potentials to blossom.

To a humanist the person you are today is largely the product of all the choices you have made. Humanists also emphasize immediate *subjective experience* (private perceptions of reality), rather than prior learning. They believe that there are as many "real worlds" as there are people. To understand behavior, we must learn how a person subjectively views the world—what is "real" for her or him.

Who are the major humanistic theorists? Many psychologists have added to the humanistic tradition. Of these, the best known are Carl Rogers (1902–1987) and Abraham Maslow (1908–1970). Because Maslow's idea of self-actualization was introduced in Chapter 1, let's begin with a more detailed look at this facet of his thinking.

Maslow and Self-Actualization

Abraham Maslow became interested in people who were living unusually effective lives. How were they different? To find an answer, Maslow began by studying the lives of great men and women, such as Albert Einstein, William James, Jane Addams, Eleanor Roosevelt, Abraham Lincoln, John Muir, and Walt Whitman. From there he moved on to directly study living artists, writers, poets, and other creative individuals.

Along the way, Maslow's thinking changed radically. At first he studied only people of obvious creativity or high achievement. However, it eventually became clear that a housewife, clerk, student, or someone like our friend Annette could live a rich, creative, and satisfying life. Maslow referred to the process of fully developing personal potentials as **self-actualization** (Maslow, 1954). The heart of self-actualization is a continuous search for personal fulfillment (Ewen, 2003; Reiss & Havercamp, 2005).

Characteristics of Self-Actualizers

A *self-actualizer* is a person who is living creatively and fully using his or her potentials. In his studies, Maslow found that self-actualizers share many similarities. Whether famous or unknown, well-schooled or uneducated, rich or poor, self-actualizers tend to fit the following profile.

1. **Efficient perceptions of reality.** Self-actualizers are able to judge situations correctly and honestly. They are very sensitive to the fake and dishonest.
2. **Comfortable acceptance of self, others, nature.** Self-actualizers accept their own human nature with all its flaws. The shortcomings of others and the contradictions of the human condition are accepted with humor and tolerance.
3. **Spontaneity.** Maslow's subjects extended their creativity into everyday activities. Actualizers tend to be unusually alive, engaged, and spontaneous.
4. **Task centering.** Most of Maslow's subjects had a mission to fulfill in life or some task or problem outside of themselves to pursue. Humanitarians such as Albert Schweitzer and Mother Teresa represent this quality.
5. **Autonomy.** Self-actualizers are free from reliance on external authorities or other people. They tend to be resourceful and independent.
6. **Continued freshness of appreciation.** The self-actualizer seems to constantly renew appreciation of life's basic goods. A sunset or a flower will be experienced as intensely time after time as it was at first. There is an "innocence of vision," like that of an artist or child.

Humanism An approach that focuses on human experience, problems, potentials, and ideals.

Self-actualization The process of fully developing personal potentials.

7. **Fellowship with humanity.** Maslow's subjects felt a deep identification with others and the human situation in general.

8. **Profound interpersonal relationships.** The interpersonal relationships of self-actualizers are marked by deep, loving bonds (Hanley & Abell, 2002).

9. **Comfort with solitude.** Despite their satisfying relationships with others, self-actualizing persons value solitude and are comfortable being alone (Sumerlin & Bundrick, 1996).

10. **Nonhostile sense of humor.** This refers to the wonderful capacity to laugh at oneself. It also describes the kind of humor a man like Abraham Lincoln had. Lincoln probably never made a joke that hurt anybody. His wry comments were a gentle prodding of human shortcomings.

11. **Peak experiences.** All of Maslow's subjects reported the frequent occurrence of *peak experiences* (temporary moments of self-actualization). These occasions were marked by feelings of ecstasy, harmony, and deep meaning. Self-actualizers reported feeling at one with the universe, stronger and calmer than ever before, filled with light, beautiful and good, and so forth.

In summary, self-actualizers feel safe, nonanxious, accepted, loved, loving, and alive.

Maslow's choice of self-actualizing people for study seems pretty subjective. Is it really a fair representation of self-actualization? Although Maslow tried to investigate self-actualization empirically, his choice of people for study was subjective. Undoubtedly there are many ways to make full use of personal potential. Maslow's primary contribution was to draw our attention to the possibility of lifelong personal growth.

What steps can be taken to promote self-actualization? Maslow made few specific recommendations about how to proceed. There is no magic formula for leading a more creative life. Self-actualization is primarily a process, not a goal or an end point. As such, it requires hard work, patience, and commitment. Nevertheless, some helpful suggestions can be gleaned from his writings (Maslow, 1954, 1967, 1971). Here are some ways to begin.

1. **Be willing to change.** Begin by asking yourself, "Am I living in a way that is deeply satisfying to me and that truly expresses me?" If not, be prepared to make changes in your life. Indeed, ask yourself this question often and accept the need for continual change.

2. **Take responsibility.** You can become an architect of self by acting as if you are personally responsible for every aspect of your life. Shouldering responsibility in this way helps end the habit of blaming others for your own shortcomings.

3. **Examine your motives.** Self-discovery involves an element of risk. If your behavior is restricted by a desire for safety or security, it may be time to test some limits. Try to make each life decision a choice for growth, not a response to fear or anxiety.

4. **Experience honestly and directly.** Wishful thinking is another barrier to personal growth. Self-actualizers trust themselves enough to accept all kinds of information without distorting it to fit their fears and desires. Try to see yourself as others do. Be willing to admit, "I was wrong," or, "I failed because I was irresponsible."

5. **Make use of positive experiences.** Maslow considered peak experiences temporary moments of self-actualization. Therefore, you might actively repeat activities that have caused feelings of awe, amazement, exaltation, renewal, reverence, humility, fulfillment, or joy.

6. **Be prepared to be different.** Maslow felt that everyone has a potential for "greatness," but most fear becoming what they might. As part of personal growth, be prepared to trust your own impulses and feelings; don't automatically judge yourself by the standards of others. Accept your uniqueness.

7. **Get involved.** With few exceptions, self-actualizers tend to have a mission or "calling" in life. For these people, "work" is not done just to fill deficiency needs, but to

satisfy higher yearnings for truth, beauty, community, and meaning. Get personally involved and committed. Turn your attention to problems outside yourself.

8. **Assess your progress.** There is no final point at which one becomes self-actualized. It's important to gauge your progress frequently and to renew your efforts. If you feel bored at school, at a job, or in a relationship, consider it a challenge. Have you been taking responsibility for your own personal growth? Almost any activity can be used as a chance for self-enhancement if it is approached creatively.

Carl Rogers' Self Theory

Carl Rogers, another well-known humanist, emphasized the human capacity for inner peace and happiness. The *fully functioning person,* he said, lives in harmony with his or her deepest feelings and impulses. Such people are open to their experiences and they trust their inner urges and intuitions (Rogers, 1961). Rogers believed that this attitude is most likely to occur when a person receives ample amounts of love and acceptance from others.

Personality Structure and Dynamics

Rogers's theory emphasizes the **self,** a flexible and changing perception of personal identity. Much behavior can be understood as an attempt to maintain consistency between our *self-image* and our actions. (Your **self-image** is a total subjective perception of your body and personality.) For example, people who think of themselves as kind tend to be considerate in most situations.

Let's say I know a person who thinks she is kind, but she really isn't. How does that fit Rogers's theory? According to Rogers, we allow experiences that match our self-image into awareness, where they gradually change the self. Information or feelings inconsistent with the self-image are said to be incongruent. Thus, a person who thinks she is kind, but really isn't, is in a state of **incongruence.** In other words, there is a discrepancy between her experiences and her self-image. As another example, it would be incongruent to believe that you are a person who "never gets angry" if you spend much of each day seething inside.

Experiences seriously incongruent with the self-image can be threatening, and are often distorted or denied conscious recognition. Blocking, denying, or distorting experiences prevents the self from changing. This creates a gulf between the self-image and reality. As the self-image grows more unrealistic, the **incongruent person** becomes confused, vulnerable, dissatisfied, or seriously maladjusted (▸▸ Fig. 10.7). In line with Rogers's observations, a

photolibrary/PictureQuest

Humanists consider self-image a central determinant of behavior and personal adjustment.

Self A continuously evolving conception of one's personal identity.

Self-image Total subjective perception of one's body and personality (another term for self-concept).

Incongruence State that exists when there is a discrepancy between one's experiences and self-image or between one's self-image and ideal self.

Incongruent person A person who has an inaccurate self-image or whose self-image differs greatly from the ideal self.

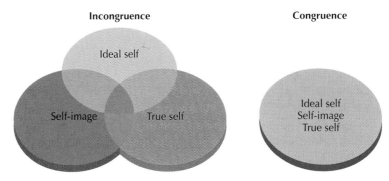

▸▸**FIGURE 10.7** Incongruence occurs when there is a mismatch between any of these three entities: the ideal self (the person you would like to be), your self-image (the person you think you are), and the true self (the person you actually are). Self-esteem suffers when there is a large difference between one's ideal self and self-image. Anxiety and defensiveness are common when the self-image does not match the true self.

study of college students confirmed that being *authentic* is vital for healthy functioning. That is, we need to feel that our behavior accurately expresses who we are (Sheldon et al., 1997). Please note, however, that being authentic doesn't mean you can do whatever you want. Being true to yourself is no excuse for acting irresponsibly or ignoring the feelings of others (Kernis & Goldman, 2005).

When your self-image is consistent with what you really think, feel, do, and experience, you are best able to actualize your potentials. Rogers also considered it essential to have congruence between the self-image and the **ideal self.** The ideal self is similar to Freud's ego ideal. It is an image of the person you would most like to be.

Is it really incongruent not to live up to your ideal self? Rogers was aware that we never fully attain our ideals. Nevertheless, the greater the gap between the way you see yourself and the way you would like to be, the more tension and anxiety you will experience.

Rogers emphasized that to maximize our potentials, we must accept information about ourselves as honestly as possible. In accord with his thinking, researchers have found that people with a close match between their self-image and ideal self tend to be socially poised, confident, and resourceful. Those with a poor match tend to be depressed, anxious, and insecure (Boldero et al., 2005).

According to psychologists Hazel Markus and Paula Nurius (1986), our ideal self is only one of a number of *possible selves* (persons we could become or are afraid of becoming). Annette, who was described earlier, is an interesting personality, to say the least. Annette is one of those people who seems to have lived many lives in the time that most of us manage only one. Like Annette, you may have pondered many possible personal identities.

Possible selves translate our hopes, fears, fantasies, and goals into specific images of who we *could* be. Thus, a beginning law student might picture herself as a successful attorney; an enterprising college student might imagine himself as an Internet entrepreneur; and a person on a diet might imagine both slim and grossly obese possible selves. Such images tend to direct our future behavior (Oyserman et al., 2004).

Of course, almost everyone over age 30 has probably felt the anguish of realizing that some cherished possible selves will never be realized. Nevertheless, there is value in asking yourself not just "Who am I?" but also "Who would I like to become?" As you do, remember Maslow's advice that everyone has a potential for "greatness," but most fear becoming what they might.

Humanistic View of Development

Why do mirrors, photographs, video cameras, and the reactions of others hold such fascination and threat for many people? Carl Rogers's theory suggests it is because they provide information about one's self. The development of a self-image depends greatly on information from the environment. It begins with a sorting of perceptions and feelings: my body, my toes, my nose, I want, I like, I am, and so on. Soon, it expands to include self-evaluation: I am a good person, I did something bad just now, and so forth.

How does development of the self contribute to later personality functioning? Rogers believed that positive and negative evaluations by others cause children to develop internal standards of evaluation called **conditions of worth.** In other words, we learn that some actions win our parents' love and approval whereas others are rejected. More important, parents may label some *feelings* as bad or wrong. For example, a child might be told that it is wrong to feel angry toward a brother or sister—even when anger is justified. Likewise, a little boy might be told that he must not cry or show fear, two very normal emotions.

Learning to evaluate some experiences or feelings as "good" and others as "bad" is directly related to a later capacity for self-esteem, positive self-evaluation, or **positive self-regard,** to use Rogers's term. To think of yourself as a good, lovable, worthwhile person, your behavior and experiences must match your internal conditions of worth. The problem

Ideal self An idealized image of oneself (the person one would like to be).

Conditions of worth Internal standards used to judge the value of one's thoughts, actions, feelings, or experiences.

Positive self-regard Thinking of oneself as a good, lovable, worthwhile person.

is that this can cause incongruence by leading to the denial of many true feelings and experiences.

To put it simply, Rogers blamed many adult emotional problems on attempts to live by the standards of others. He believed that congruence and self-actualization are encouraged by replacing conditions of worth with **organismic valuing** (a natural, undistorted, full-body reaction to an experience). Organismic valuing is a direct, gut-level response to life that avoids the filtering and distortion of incongruence. It involves trusting one's own feelings and perceptions. Organismic valuing is most likely to develop, Rogers felt, when children (or adults) receive **unconditional positive regard** (unshakable love and approval) from others. That is, when they are "prized" as worthwhile human beings, just for being themselves, without any conditions or strings attached. Although this may be a luxury few people enjoy, we are more likely to move toward our ideal selves if we receive affirmation and support from a close partner (Drigotas et al., 1999).

PERSONALITY THEORIES—OVERVIEW AND COMPARISON

Which personality theory is right? To date, each theory has added to our understanding by providing a sort of lens through which human behavior can be viewed. Nevertheless, theories can't be fully proved or disproved. We can only ask, Does the evidence tend to support this theory or disconfirm it? Yet, although theories are neither true nor false, their implications or predictions may be. The best way to judge a theory, then, is in terms of its *usefulness.* Does the theory adequately explain behavior? Does it stimulate new research? Does it suggest how to treat psychological disorders? Each theory has fared differently in these areas (Pervin, Cervone, & John, 2005). ■ Table 10.3 provides an overview of the four principal approaches to personality. In the final analysis, the challenge now facing personality theorists is how to integrate the four major perspectives into a unified, systematic explanation of personality (Mayer, 2005).

Organismic valuing A natural, undistorted, full-body reaction to an experience.
Unconditional positive regard Unshakable love and approval given without qualification.

■ Table 10.3 Comparison of Personality Theories

	Trait Theories	Psychoanalytic Theory	Behavioristic and Social Learning Theories	Humanistic Theory
View of human nature	Neutral	Negative	Neutral	Positive
Is behavior free or determined?	Determined	Determined	Determined	Free choice
Principal motives	Depends on one's traits	Sex and aggression	Drives of all kinds	Self-actualization
Personality structure	Traits	Id, ego, superego	Habits, expectancies	Self
Role of unconscious	Minimized	Maximized	Practically nonexistent	Minimized
Conception of conscience	Traits of honesty, etc.	Superego	Self-reinforcement, punishment history	Ideal self, valuing process
Developmental emphasis	Combined effects of heredity and environment	Psychosexual stages	Critical learning situations, identification, and imitation	Development of self-image
Barriers to personal growth	Unhealthy traits	Unconscious conflicts, fixations	Maladaptive habits, unhealthy environment	Conditions of worth, incongruence

Study Break   Humanistic Theory and Overview of Theories of Personality

Reflect

Do you know anyone who seems to be making especially good use of their personal potentials? Does that person fit Maslow's profile of a self-actualizer?

How much difference do you think there is between your self-image, your ideal self, and your true self? Do you think Rogers is right about the effects of applying conditions of worth to your perceptions and feelings?

Which of the four views of personality has most helped you reflect on your own personality? Have the others helped at all?

Learning Check

1. Humanists view human nature as basically good and they emphasize the effects of subjective learning and unconscious choice. T or F?

2. Maslow used the term _____ to describe the tendency of certain individuals to fully use their talents and potentials.

3. According to Rogers, a close match between the self-image and the ideal self creates a condition called incongruence. T or F?

4. Rogers's theory considers acceptance of conditions of _____ a troublesome aspect of development of the self.

5. According to Maslow, a preoccupation with one's own thoughts, feelings, and needs is characteristic of self-actualizing individuals. T or F?

6. Maslow regarded _____ experiences as times of temporary self-actualization.

Critical Thinking

7. What role has your self-image played in your choice of a college major?

Answers 1. F 2. self-actualization 3. F 4. worth 5. F 6. peak 7. Career decisions almost always involve, in part, picturing oneself occupying various occupational roles. Such "future selves" play a role in many of the major decisions we make (Masters & Holley, 2006).

PERSONALITY ASSESSMENT—PSYCHOLOGICAL YARDSTICKS

>SURVEY QUESTION< *How do psychologists measure personality?*

Measuring personality can help predict how people will behave at work, at school, and in therapy. However, painting a detailed picture can be a challenge. In many instances, it requires several of the techniques described in what follows. To capture a personality as unique as Annette's, it might take all of them!

How is personality "measured"? Psychologists use interviews, observation, questionnaires, and projective tests to assess personality (Derlega, Winstead, & Jones, 2005). Each method has strengths and limitations. For this reason, they are often used in combination.

Formal personality measures are refinements of more casual ways of judging a person. At one time or another, you have probably "sized up" a potential date, friend, or roommate by engaging in conversation (interview). Perhaps you have asked a friend, "When I am delayed I get angry. Do you?" (questionnaire). Maybe you watch your professors when they are angry or embarrassed to learn what they are "really" like when they're caught off-guard (observation). Or possibly you have noticed that when you say, "I think people feel . . . ," you may be expressing your own feelings (projection). Let's see how psychologists apply each of these methods to probe personality.

The Interview

In an **interview,** direct questioning is used to learn about a person's life history, personality traits, or current mental state (Sommers-Flanagan & Sommers-Flanagan, 2002). In an *unstructured interview,* conversation is informal and topics are taken up freely as they arise. In a *structured interview,* information is gathered by asking a planned series of questions.

How are interviews used? Interviews are used to identify personality disturbances; to select people for jobs, college, or special programs; and to study the dynamics of personality.

Interview (personality) A face-to-face meeting held for the purpose of gaining information about an individual's personal history, personality traits, current psychological state, and so forth.

Interviews also provide information for counseling or therapy. For instance, a counselor might ask a depressed person, "Have you ever contemplated suicide? What were the circumstances?" The counselor might then follow by asking, "How did you feel about it?" or, "How is what you are now feeling different from what you felt then?"

In addition to providing information, interviews make it possible to observe a person's tone of voice, hand gestures, posture, and facial expressions. Such "body language" cues are important because they may radically alter the message sent, as when a person claims to be "completely calm" but trembles uncontrollably.

Limitations

Interviews give rapid insight into personality, but they have limitations. For one thing, interviewers can be swayed by preconceptions. A person identified as a "housewife," "college student," "high school athlete," "punk," "geek," or "ski bum" may be misjudged because of an interviewer's personal biases. Second, an interviewer's own personality, or even gender, may influence a client's behavior. When this occurs, it can accentuate or distort the person's apparent traits (Pollner, 1998). A third problem is that people sometimes try to deceive interviewers. For example, a person accused of a crime might try to avoid punishment by pretending to be mentally disabled.

A fourth problem is the **halo effect,** which is the tendency to generalize a favorable (or unfavorable) impression to an entire personality (Lance, LaPointe, & Stewart, 1994). Because of the halo effect, a person who is likable or physically attractive may be rated more mature, intelligent, or mentally healthy than she or he actually is.

What is your impression of the person wearing the black suit? If you think that she looks friendly, attractive, or neat, your other perceptions of her might be altered by that impression. Interviewers are often influenced by the halo effect (see text).

Zia Soleil/Getty Images

Even with their limitations, interviews are a respected method of assessment. In many cases, interviews are the first step in evaluating personality and an essential prelude to therapy. Nevertheless, interviews are usually not enough and must be supplemented by other measures and tests (Meyer et al., 2001).

Direct Observation and Rating Scales

Are you fascinated by airports, bus depots, parks, taverns, subway stations, or other public places? Many people relish a chance to observe the actions of others. When used for assessment, **direct observation** (looking at behavior) is a simple extension of this natural interest in "people watching." For instance, a psychologist might arrange to observe a disturbed child as she plays with other children. Is the child withdrawn? Does she become hostile or aggressive without warning? By careful observation, the psychologist can identify the girl's personality traits and clarify the nature of her problems.

Wouldn't observation be subject to the same problems of misperception as an interview? Yes. Misperceptions can be a difficulty, which is why rating scales are sometimes used (▶▶ Fig. 10.8). A **rating scale** is a list of personality traits or aspects of behavior that can be used to evaluate a person. Rating scales limit the chance that some traits will be overlooked while others are exaggerated (Synhorst et al., 2005). Perhaps they should be a standard procedure for choosing a roommate, spouse, or lover!

An alternative approach is to do a **behavioral assessment** by counting the frequency of specific behaviors. In this case, observers record *actions,* not what traits they think a person has (Ramsay, Reynolds, & Kamphaus, 2002). For example, a psychologist working with hospitalized mental patients might note the frequency of a patient's aggression, self-care, speech, and unusual behaviors. Behavioral assessments can also be used to probe thought

Halo effect The tendency to generalize a favorable or unfavorable impression to unrelated details of personality.

Direct observation Assessing behavior through direct surveillance.

Rating scale A list of personality traits or aspects of behavior on which a person is rated.

Behavioral assessment Recording the frequency of various behaviors.

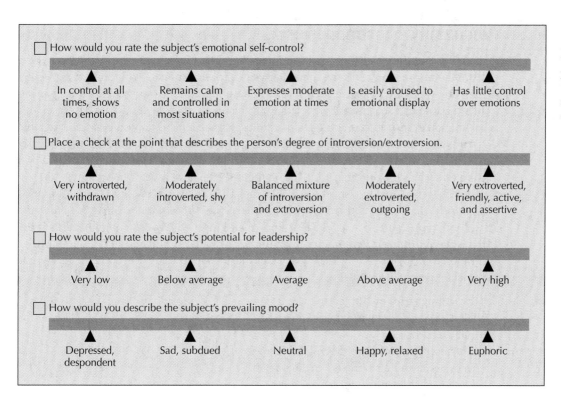

☐ How would you rate the subject's emotional self-control?

▲	▲	▲	▲	▲
In control at all times, shows no emotion	Remains calm and controlled in most situations	Expresses moderate emotion at times	Is easily aroused to emotional display	Has little control over emotions

☐ Place a check at the point that describes the person's degree of introversion/extroversion.

▲	▲	▲	▲	▲
Very introverted, withdrawn	Moderately introverted, shy	Balanced mixture of introversion and extroversion	Moderately extroverted, outgoing	Very extroverted, friendly, active, and assertive

☐ How would you rate the subject's potential for leadership?

▲	▲	▲	▲	▲
Very low	Below average	Average	Above average	Very high

☐ How would you describe the subject's prevailing mood?

▲	▲	▲	▲	▲
Depressed, despondent	Sad, subdued	Neutral	Happy, relaxed	Euphoric

▸▸**FIGURE 10.8** Sample rating scale items. To understand how the scale works, imagine someone you know well. Where would you place check marks on each of the scales to rate that person's characteristics?

processes. In one study, for example, couples were assessed while communicating with each other about their sexuality. Couples with sexual difficulties were less likely to be receptive to talking about their sexuality and more likely to blame each other than were couples with no sexual difficulties (Kelly, Strassberg, & Turner, 2006).

Situational Testing

In **situational testing,** real-life conditions are simulated so that a person's spontaneous reactions can be observed. Such tests assume that the best way to learn how people react is to put them in realistic situations and watch what happens. Situational tests expose people to frustration, temptation, pressure, boredom, or other conditions capable of revealing personality characteristics (Weekley & Jones, 1997). Some popular "reality TV" programs, such as *Survivor* and *The Amazing Race,* bear some similarity to situational tests—which may account for their ability to attract millions of viewers.

How are situational tests done? An interesting example of situational testing is the judgmental firearms training provided by many police departments. At times, police officers must make split-second decisions about using their weapons. A mistake could be fatal. In a typical shoot–don't shoot test, actors play the part of armed criminals. As various high-risk scenes are acted out live or on videotape or by computer, officers must decide to shoot or hold fire. A newspaper reporter who once took the test (and failed it) gives this account (Gersh, 1982):

> I judged wrong. I was killed by a man in a closet, a man with a hostage, a woman interrupted when kissing her lover, and a man I thought was cleaning a shotgun. . . . I shot a drunk who reached for a comb, and a teenager who pulled out a black water pistol. Looked real to me.

In addition to the training it provides, situational testing uncovers police cadets who lack the good judgment needed to carry a gun out on the street.

David McNew Newsmakers/Getty Images

A police officer undergoes judgmental firearms training. Variations on this situational test are used by a growing number of police departments. All officers must score a passing grade.

Situational test Simulating real-life conditions so that a person's reactions may be directly observed.

Personality Questionnaires

Personality questionnaires are paper-and-pencil tests that reveal personality characteristics. Questionnaires are more objective than interviews or observation. (An objective test gives the same score when different people correct it.) Questions, administration, and scoring are all standardized so that scores are unaffected by any biases an examiner may have. However, this is not enough to ensure accuracy. A good test must also be reliable and valid. A test is **reliable** if it yields close to the same score each time it is given to the same person. A test has **validity** if it measures what it claims to measure. Unfortunately, many personality tests you will encounter, such as those in magazines or on the Internet, have little or no validity.

Dozens of personality tests are available, including the *Guilford-Zimmerman Temperament Survey,* the *California Psychological Inventory,* the *Allport-Vernon Study of Values,* the *16 PF,* and many more. One of the best-known and most widely used objective tests is the **Minnesota Multiphasic Personality Inventory-2** (**MMPI-2**) (Butcher, 2005). The MMPI-2 is composed of 567 items to which a test taker must respond "true" or "false." Items include statements such as the following.

> Everything tastes the same.
> There is something wrong with my mind.
> I enjoy animals.
> Whenever possible I avoid being in a crowd.
> I have never indulged in any unusual sex practices.
> Someone has been trying to poison me.
> I daydream often.*

How can these items show anything about personality? For instance, what if a person has a cold so that "everything tastes the same"? For an answer (and a little bit of fun), read the following items. Answer "Yes," "No," or "Don't bother me, I can't cope!"

> I would enjoy the work of a chicken flicker.
> My eyes are always cold.
> Frantic screaming makes me nervous.
> I believe I smell as good as most people.
> I use shoe polish to excess.
> The sight of blood no longer excites me.
> As an infant I had very few hobbies.
> Dirty stories make me think about sex.
> I stay in the bathtub until I look like a raisin.
> I salivate at the sight of mittens.
> I never finish what I

These items were written by humorist Art Buchwald (1965) to satirize personality questionnaires. Such questions may seem ridiculous, but they are not very different from the real thing. How, then, do the items on tests such as the MMPI-2 reveal anything about personality? The answer is that a single item tells little about personality. For example, a person who agrees that "Everything tastes the same" might simply have a cold. It is only through *patterns* of response that personality dimensions are revealed.

Items on the MMPI-2 were selected for their ability to correctly identify persons with particular psychological problems (Butcher, 2005). For instance, if depressed persons consistently answer a series of items in a particular way, it is assumed that others who answer the same way are also prone to depression. As silly as the gag items in the preceding lists may seem, it is possible that some could actually work in a legitimate test. But before an item could be part of a test, it would have to be shown to correlate highly with some trait or dimension of personality.

Personality questionnaire A paper-and-pencil test consisting of questions that reveal aspects of personality.

Reliability The ability of a test to yield nearly the same score each time it is given to the same person.

Validity The ability of a test to measure what it purports to measure.

Minnesota Multiphasic Personality Inventory-2 (MMPI-2) One of the best-known and most widely used objective personality questionnaires.

_____

*Reproduced by permission. Copyright 1989, by the University of Minnesota Press.

■ Table 10.4 MMPI-2 Basic Clinical Subscales

1. **Hypochondriasis** (HI-po-kon-DRY-uh-sis). Exaggerated concern about one's physical health.
2. **Depression.** Feelings of worthlessness, hopelessness, and pessimism.
3. **Hysteria.** The presence of physical complaints for which no physical basis can be established.
4. **Psychopathic deviate.** Emotional shallowness in relationships and a disregard for social and moral standards.
5. **Masculinity/femininity.** One's degree of traditional "masculine" aggressiveness or "feminine" sensitivity.
6. **Paranoia.** Extreme suspiciousness and feelings of persecution.
7. **Psychasthenia** (sike-as-THEE-nee-ah). The presence of obsessive worries, irrational fears (phobias), and compulsive (ritualistic) actions.
8. **Schizophrenia.** Emotional withdrawal and unusual or bizarre thinking and actions.
9. **Mania.** Emotional excitability, manic moods or behavior, and excessive activity.
10. **Social introversion.** One's tendency to be socially withdrawn.

The MMPI-2 measures 10 major aspects of personality (listed in ■ Table 10.4). After the MMPI-2 is scored, results are charted graphically as an **MMPI-2 profile** (▸Fig. 10.9). By comparing a person's profile to scores produced by typical, normal adults, a psychologist can identify various personality disorders (Butcher, 2005). Additional scales identify substance abuse, eating disorders, Type A (heart-attack prone) behavior, repression, anger, cynicism, low self-esteem, family problems, inability to function in a job, and other problems (Butcher, 2006).

How accurate is the MMPI-2? Personality questionnaires are only accurate if people tell the truth about themselves. Because of this, the MMPI-2 has additional **validity scales** that reveal whether a person's scores should be discarded. The validity scales detect attempts by test takers to "fake good" (make themselves look good) or "fake bad" (make it look like they have problems). Other scales uncover defensiveness or tendencies to exaggerate shortcomings and troubles. When taking the MMPI-2, it is best to answer honestly, without trying to second-guess the test.

A clinical psychologist trying to decide if a person has emotional problems would be wise to take more than the MMPI-2 into account. Test scores are informative, but they can incorrectly label some people (Urbina, 2004). (The "Critical Thinking" box titled "Honesty Tests" discusses a related problem.) Fortunately, clinical judgments usually rely on information from interviews, tests, and other sources. Also, despite their limitations, it is reassuring

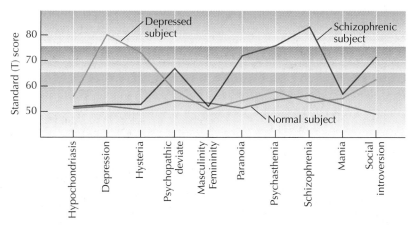

▸▸**FIGURE 10.9** An MMPI-2 profile showing hypothetical scores indicating normality, depression, and psychosis. High scores begin at 66 and very high scores at 76. An unusually low score (40 and below) may also reveal personality characteristics or problems.

MMPI-2 profile A graphic representation of an individual's scores on each of the primary scales of the MMPI-2.

Validity scales Scales that tell whether test scores should be invalidated for lying, inconsistency, or "faking good."

Honesty Tests—Do They Tell the Truth?

Each year, millions of anxious job seekers take paper-and-pencil honesty tests given by companies that hope to avoid hiring dishonest workers (Spector, 2005). **Honesty tests** (also known as integrity tests) assume that poor attitudes toward dishonest acts predispose a person to dishonest behavior. Examples include attitudes toward taking office supplies home or leaving work early. Most of the tests also ask people how honest they think the average person is and how honest they are in comparison. Surprisingly, many job applicants willingly rate their own honesty as below average (Neuman & Baydoun, 1998). (You have to admire them for being honest about it!) Honesty tests also ask about prior brushes with the law, past acts of theft or deceit, and attitudes toward alcohol and drug use.

Is honesty testing valid? This question is still very much in dispute. Some psychologists believe that the best honesty tests are sufficiently valid to be used for making hiring decisions (Ones &

Viswesvaran, 2001). Others, however, remain unconvinced. Most studies have failed to demonstrate that honesty tests can accurately *predict* if a person will be a poor risk on the job (Horn, Nelson, & Brannick, 2004; Ones, Viswesvaran, & Schmidt, 2003). Psychologists are also concerned because honesty tests are often administered by untrained people. Yet another cause for concern is the fact that 96 percent of test takers who fail are *falsely labeled* as dishonest (Camara & Schneider, 1994). In North America alone, that means well over a million workers a year are wrongly accused of being dishonest (Rieke & Guastello, 1995).

Some states have banned the use of honesty tests as the sole basis for deciding whether to hire a person. Yet, it's easy to understand why employers want to do whatever they can to reduce theft and dishonesty in the workplace. The pressures to use honesty tests are intense. No doubt, the debate about honesty testing will continue. Honest.

to note that psychological assessments are at least as accurate as commonly used medical tests (Meyer et al., 2001).

PROJECTIVE TESTS OF PERSONALITY— INKBLOTS AND HIDDEN PLOTS

Projective tests take a different approach to personality. Interviews, observation, rating scales, and inventories try to directly identify overt, observable traits (Leichtman, 2004). By contrast, projective tests seek to uncover deeply hidden or *unconscious* wishes, thoughts, and needs.

As a child you may have delighted in finding faces and objects in cloud formations. Or perhaps you have learned something about your friends' personalities from their reactions to movies or paintings. If so, you will have some insight into the rationale for projective tests. In a **projective test,** a person is asked to describe ambiguous stimuli or make up stories about them. Describing an unambiguous stimulus (a picture of an automobile, for example) tells little about your personality. But when you are faced with an unstructured stimulus, you must organize what you see in terms of your own life experiences. Everyone sees something different in a projective test, and what is perceived can reveal the inner workings of personality.

Projective tests have no right or wrong answers, which makes them difficult to fake (Leichtman, 2004). Moreover, projective tests can be a rich source of information, because responses are not restricted to simple true/false or yes/no answers.

The Rorschach Inkblot Test

Is the inkblot test a projective technique? The inkblot test, or **Rorschach Technique** (ROAR-shock), is one of the oldest and most widely used projective tests. Developed by Swiss psychologist Hermann Rorschach in the 1920s, it consists of 10 standardized inkblots. These vary in color, shading, form, and complexity.

How does the test work? First, a person is shown each blot and asked to describe what she or he sees in it (▸▸Fig. 10.10). Later the psychologist may return to a blot, asking the

Honesty test A paper-and-pencil test designed to detect attitudes, beliefs, and behavior patterns that predispose a person to dishonest behavior.

Projective tests Psychological tests making use of ambiguous or unstructured stimuli.

Rorschach Technique A projective test comprised of ten standardized inkblots.

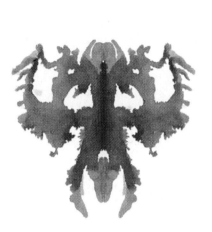

▸▸**FIGURE 10.10** Inkblots similar to those used on the Rorschach. What do you see?

person to identify specific sections of it, to expand previous descriptions, or to give new impressions about what it contains. Obvious differences in content—such as "blood dripping from a dagger" versus "flowers blooming in a field"—are important for identifying personal conflicts and fantasies. But surprisingly, content is less important than what parts of the inkblot are used to organize images. These factors allow psychologists to detect emotional disturbances by observing how a person perceives the world (Hilsenroth, 2000).

The Thematic Apperception Test

Another popular projective test is the **Thematic Apperception Test (TAT)** developed by personality theorist Henry Murray (1893–1988).

How does the TAT differ from the Rorschach? The TAT consists of 20 sketches depicting various scenes and life situations (▸▸Fig. 10.11). During testing, a person is shown each sketch and asked to make up a story about the people in it. Later, the person looks at each sketch a second or a third time and elaborates on previous stories or creates new stories.

To score the TAT, a psychologist analyzes the content of the stories. Interpretations focus on how people feel, how they interact, what events led up to the incidents depicted in the sketch, and how the story will end. For example, TAT stories told by bereaved college students typically include themes of death, grief, and coping with loss (Balk et al., 1998).

A psychologist might also count the number of times the central figure in a TAT story is angry, overlooked, apathetic, jealous, or threatened. Here is a story written by a student to describe ▸▸Figure 10.11:

> The girl has been seeing this guy her mother doesn't like. The mother is telling her that she better not see him again. The mother says, "He's just like your father." The mother and father are divorced. The mother is smiling because she thinks she is right. But she doesn't really know what the girl wants. The girl is going to see the guy again, anyway.

As this example implies, the TAT is especially good at revealing feelings about a person's social relationships (Alvarado, 1994; Aronow, Altman Weiss, & Reznikoff, 2001).

Limitations of Projective Testing

Although projective tests have been popular, their validity is considered lowest among tests of personality (Lilienfeld, 1999; Wood et al., 2003). Objectivity and reliability (consistency) are also low for different users of the TAT and Rorschach. Note that after a person interprets an ambiguous stimulus, the scorer must interpret the person's (sometimes) ambiguous responses. In a sense, the interpretation of a projective test may be a projective test for the scorer!

▸▸**FIGURE 10.11** This is a picture like those used for the Thematic Apperception Test. If you wish to simulate the test, tell a story that explains what led up to the pictured situation, what is happening now, and how the action will end.

Thematic Apperception Test (TAT)
A projective test consisting of 20 different scenes and life situations about which respondents make up stories.

Despite their drawbacks, projective tests still have value (Hilsenroth, 2000). This is especially true when they are used as part of a *test battery* (collection of assessment devices and interviews). In the hands of a skilled clinician, projective tests can be a good way to detect major conflicts, to get clients to talk about upsetting topics, and to set goals for therapy (O'Roark, 2001).

SUDDEN MURDERERS—A RESEARCH EXAMPLE

Personality assessments provide us with clues to some of the most perplexing human events. Consider Fred Cowan, a model student in school and described by those who knew him as quiet, gentle, and a man who loved children. Despite his size (6 feet tall, 250 pounds), Fred was described by a coworker as "someone you could easily push around."

Fred Cowan represents a puzzling phenomenon: We occasionally read in the news about sudden murderers—gentle, quiet, shy, good-natured people who explode without warning into violence (Cartwright, 2002a; Lee, Zimbardo, & Bertholf, 1977). Two weeks after he was suspended from his job, Fred returned to work determined to get even with his supervisor. Unable to find the man, he killed four coworkers and a policeman before taking his own life.

Isn't such behavior contrary to the idea of personality traits? It might seem that sudden murderers are newsworthy simply because they are unlikely candidates for violence. On the contrary, research conducted by Melvin Lee, Philip Zimbardo, and Minerva Bertholf suggests that sudden murderers explode into violence *because* they are shy, restrained, and inexpressive, not in spite of it. These researchers studied prisoners at a California prison. Ten were inmates whose homicide was an unexpected first offense. Nine were criminals with a record of habitual violence prior to murder. Sixteen were inmates convicted of nonviolent crimes.

Did the inmates differ in personality makeup? Each of the inmates took a battery of tests, including the MMPI, a measure of shyness, and an adjective checklist (in which inmates described themselves by selecting relevant adjectives from a list of adjectives used to describe people). Personal interviews were also done with each inmate. As expected, the sudden murderers were passive, shy, and overcontrolled (restrained) individuals. The habitually violent inmates were "masculine" (aggressive), undercontrolled (impulsive), and less likely to view themselves as shy than the inmates convicted of nonviolent crimes (Lee, Zimbardo, & Bertholf, 1977).

Psychologists have learned that quiet, overcontrolled individuals are likely to be especially violent if they ever lose control. Their attacks are usually triggered by a minor irritation or frustration, but the attack reflects years of unexpressed feelings of anger and belittlement. When sudden murderers finally release the strict controls they have maintained on their overcontrolled behavior, a furious and frenzied attack ensues (Cartwright, 2002b). Usually it is totally out of proportion to the offense against them and many have amnesia for their violent actions.

In comparison, the previously violent murderers showed very different reactions. Although they killed, their violence was moderate—usually only enough to do the necessary damage. Typically, they felt they had been cheated or betrayed and that they were doing what was necessary to remedy the situation or maintain their manhood (Lee, Zimbardo, & Bertholf, 1977).

A Look Ahead

The preceding example illustrates how some of the concepts and techniques discussed in this chapter can be applied to further our understanding. The "Psychology in Action" module that follows should add balance to your view of personality. Don't be shy. Read on!

Study Break   Personality Assessment

Reflect

How do *you* assess personality? Do you informally make use of any of the methods described in this chapter?

You are a candidate for a desirable job. Your personality is going to be assessed by a psychologist. What method (or methods) would you prefer that she or he use? Why?

Learning Check

1. The halo effect is the tendency of an interviewer to influence what is said by the interviewee. T or F?
2. Which of the following is considered the most objective measure of personality?

   a. rating scales   b. personality questionnaires
   c. projective tests   d. TAT

3. Situational testing allows direct _____ of personality characteristics.
4. A psychotic person would probably score highest on which MMPI-2 scale?

   a. depression   b. hysteria
   c. schizophrenia   d. mania

5. The use of ambiguous stimuli is most characteristic of

   a. interviews   b. projective tests
   c. personality inventories   d. direct observation

6. The content of one's responses to the MMPI-2 is considered an indication of unconscious wishes, thoughts, and needs. T or F?
7. Doing a behavioral assessment requires direct observation of the person's actions or a direct report of the person's thoughts. T or F?
8. A surprising finding is that sudden murderers are usually undercontrolled, very masculine, and more impulsive than average. T or F?
9. A test is considered valid if it consistently yields the same score when the same person takes it on different occasions. T or F?

Critical Thinking

10. Can you think of one more reason why personality traits may not be accurately revealed by interviews?
11. Projective testing would be of greatest interest to which type of personality theorist?

Answers

1. F 2. b 3. observation 4. c 5. b 6. F 7. T 8. F 9. F 10. Because of trait-situation interactions, a person may not behave in a normal fashion while being evaluated in an interview. 11. Psychodynamic: Because projective testing is designed to uncover unconscious thoughts, feelings, and conflicts.

Psychology in Action

Barriers and Bridges—Understanding Shyness

>SURVEY QUESTIONS< *What causes shyness? What can be done about it?*

As a personality trait, **shyness** refers to a tendency to avoid others, as well as feelings of anxiety, preoccupation, and social inhibition (uneasiness and strain when socializing) (Bruch, 2001). Shy persons fail to make eye contact, retreat when spoken to, speak too quietly, and display little interest or animation in conversations. Do you:

- Find it hard to talk to strangers?
- Lack confidence with people?
- Feel uncomfortable in social situations?
- Feel nervous with people who are not close friends?

Mild shyness may be no more than a nuisance. However, extreme shyness is often associated with depression, loneliness, fearfulness, social anxiety, inhibition, and low self-esteem (Derlega, Winstead, & Jones, 2005; Jackson et al., 2002).

Elements of Shyness

What causes shyness? To begin with, shy persons often lack *social skills* (proficiency at interacting with others). Many simply have not learned how to meet people or how to start a conversation and keep it going. **Social anxiety** (a feeling of apprehension in the presence of others) is also a factor in shyness. Almost everyone feels nervous in some social situations (such as meeting an attractive stranger). Typically, this is a reaction to evaluation fears (fears of being inadequate, embarrassed, ridiculed, or rejected). Although fears of rejection are

Shyness A tendency to avoid others plus uneasiness and strain when socializing.
Social anxiety A feeling of apprehension in the presence of others.

common, they are much more frequent or intense for shy persons (Bradshaw, 2006; Jackson, Towson, & Narduzzi, 1997). A third problem for shy persons is a self-defeating bias (distortion) in their thinking. Specifically, shy persons almost always blame themselves when a social encounter doesn't go well. They are unnecessarily self-critical in social situations (Lundh et al., 2002).

Situational Causes of Shyness Shyness is most often triggered by *novel* or *unfamiliar* social situations. A person who does fine with family or close friends may become shy and awkward when meeting a stranger. Shyness is also magnified by formality, by meeting someone of higher status, by being noticeably different from others, or by being the focus of attention (as in giving a speech) (Larsen & Buss, 2005).

Don't most people become cautious and inhibited in such circumstances? Yes. That's why we need to see how the personalities of shy and non-shy persons differ.

Digital Vision/Getty Images

Dynamics of the Shy Personality

There is a tendency to think that shy persons are wrapped up in their own feelings and thoughts. But surprisingly, researchers Jonathan Cheek and Arnold Buss (1979) found no connection between shyness and **private self-consciousness** (attention to inner feelings, thoughts, and fantasies). Instead, they discovered that shyness is linked to **public self-consciousness** (acute awareness of oneself as a social object).

Persons who rate high in public self-consciousness worry about what others think of them (Cowden, 2005). They worry about saying the wrong thing or appearing foolish. In public, they may feel "naked" or as if others can "see through them." Such feelings trigger anxiety or outright fear during social encounters, leading to awkwardness and inhibition (Cowden, 2005). The shy person's anxiety, in turn, often causes her or him to misperceive others in social situations (Schroeder, 1995).

As mentioned, almost everyone feels anxious in at least some social situations. But there is a key difference in the way shy and not-shy persons *label* this anxiety. Shy persons tend to consider their social anxiety a *lasting personality trait.* Shyness, in other words, becomes part of their self-concept. In contrast, not-shy persons believe that *external situations* cause their occasional feelings of shyness. When not-shy persons feel anxiety or "stage fright," they assume that almost anyone would feel as they do under the same circumstances (Zimbardo, Pilkonis, & Norwood, 1978).

Labeling is important because it affects *self-esteem.* In general, not-shy persons tend to have higher self-esteem than shy persons. This is because not-shy persons give themselves credit for their social successes and they recognize that failures are often due to circumstances. In contrast, shy people blame themselves for social failures, never give themselves credit for successes, and expect to be rejected (Jackson et al., 2002).

Shy Beliefs

What can be done to reduce shyness? Shyness is often maintained by unrealistic or self-defeating beliefs (Antony, 2004; Butler, 2001). Here's a sample of such beliefs.

1. *If you wait around long enough at a social gathering, something will happen.*
   Comment: This is really a cover-up for fear of starting a conversation. For two people to meet, at least one has to make an effort, and it might as well be you.
2. *Other people who are popular are just lucky when it comes to being invited to social events or asked out.*
   Comment: Except for times when a person is formally introduced to someone new, this is false. People who are more active socially typically make an effort to meet and spend time with others. They join clubs, invite others to do things, strike up conversations, and generally leave little to luck.

Private self-consciousness Preoccupation with inner feelings, thoughts, and fantasies.
Public self-consciousness Intense awareness of oneself as a social object.

3. *The odds of meeting someone interested in socializing are always the same, no matter where I am.*
   Comment: This is another excuse for inaction. It pays to seek out situations that have a higher probability of leading to social contact, such as clubs, teams, and school events.

4. *If someone doesn't seem to like you right away, they really don't like you and never will.*
   Comment: This belief leads to much needless shyness. Even when a person doesn't show immediate interest, it doesn't mean the person dislikes you. Liking takes time and opportunity to develop.

Unproductive beliefs like the preceding can be replaced with statements such as the following.

1. I've got to be active in social situations.
2. I can't wait until I'm completely relaxed or comfortable before taking a social risk.
3. I don't need to pretend to be someone I'm not; it just makes me more anxious.
4. I may think other people are harshly evaluating me, but actually I'm being too hard on myself.
5. I can set reasonable goals for expanding my social experience and skills.
6. Even people who are very socially skillful are never successful 100 percent of the time. I shouldn't get so upset when an encounter goes badly. (Adapted from Antony, 2004; Butler, 2001.)

Social Skills

Learning social skills takes practice. There is nothing "innate" about knowing how to meet people or start a conversation. Social skills can be directly practiced in a variety of ways. It can be helpful, for instance, to get a tape recorder and listen to several of your conversations. You may be surprised by the way you pause, interrupt, miss cues, or seem disinterested. Similarly, it can be useful to look at yourself in a mirror and exaggerate facial expressions of surprise, interest, dislike, pleasure, and so forth. By such methods, most people can learn to put more animation and skill into their self-presentation. (For a discussion of related skills, see the section on self-assertion in Chapter 14.)

Conversation One of the simplest ways to make better conversation is by learning to ask questions. A good series of questions shifts attention to the other person and shows you are interested. Nothing fancy is needed. You can do fine with questions such as, "Where do you (work, study, live)? Do you like (dancing, travel, music)? How long have you (been at this school, worked here, lived here)?" After you've broken the ice, the best questions are often those that are *open ended* (they can't be answered yes or no):

"What parts of the country have you seen?" (as opposed to: "Have you ever been to Florida?")

"What's it like living on the west side?" (as opposed to: "Do you like living on the west side?")

"What kinds of food do you like?" (as opposed to: "Do you like Chinese cooking?")

It's easy to see why open-ended questions are helpful. In replying to open-ended questions, people often give "free information" about themselves. This extra information can be used to ask other questions or to lead into other topics of conversation.

This brief sampling of ideas is no substitute for actual practice. Overcoming shyness requires a real effort to learn new skills and test old beliefs and attitudes. It may even require the help of a counselor or therapist. At the very least, a shy person must be willing to take social risks. Breaking down the barriers of shyness will always include some awkward or unsuccessful encounters. Nevertheless, the rewards are powerful: human companionship and personal freedom.

Study Break Understanding Shyness

Reflect

If you are shy, see if you can summarize how social skills, social anxiety, evaluation fears, self-defeating thoughts, and public self-consciousness contribute to your social inhibition. If you're not shy, imagine how you would explain these concepts to a shy friend.

Learning Check

1. Surveys show that 14 percent of American college students consider themselves shy. T or F?
2. Social anxiety and evaluation fears are seen almost exclusively in shy individuals; the non-shy rarely have such experiences. T or F?

3. Unfamiliar people and situations most often trigger shyness. T or F?
4. Public self-consciousness plus a tendency to label oneself as shy are major characteristics of the shy personality. T or F?
5. Changing personal beliefs and practicing social skills can be helpful in overcoming shyness. T or F?

Critical Thinking

6. Shyness is a trait of Vonda's personality. Like most shy people, Vonda is most likely to feel shy in unfamiliar social settings. Vonda's shy behavior demonstrates that the expression of traits is governed by what concept?

Answers

1. F 2. F 3. T 4. T 5. T 6. trait-situation interactions (again)

CHAPTER IN REVIEW

Major Points

- Each of us displays consistent behavior patterns that define our own personalities and allow us to predict how other people will act.
- Personality can be understood by identifying traits, by probing mental conflicts and dynamics, by noting the effects of prior learning and situations, and by knowing how people perceive themselves.
- Psychologists use interviews, direct observation, questionnaires, and projective tests to measure and assess personality.
- Shyness is related to public self-consciousness and other psychological factors that can be altered, which makes it possible for some people to overcome shyness.

Summary

How do psychologists use the term personality?

- Personality is made up of one's unique and enduring behavior patterns.
- Character is personality evaluated, or the possession of desirable qualities.
- Temperament refers to the hereditary and physiological aspects of one's emotional nature.

What core concepts make up the psychology of personality?

- Personality traits are lasting personal qualities that are inferred from behavior.

- Personality types group people into categories on the basis of shared traits.
- Behavior is influenced by self-concept, which is a perception of one's own personality traits.
- A positive self-evaluation leads to high self-esteem. Low self-esteem is associated with stress, unhappiness, and depression.
- Personality theories combine interrelated assumptions, ideas, and principles to explain personality.

Are some personality traits more basic or important than others?

- Trait theories identify qualities that are most lasting or characteristic of a person.
- Allport made useful distinctions between common traits and individual traits and among cardinal, central, and secondary traits.
- Cattell's theory attributes visible surface traits to the existence of 16 underlying source traits.
- Source traits are measured by the *Sixteen Personality Factor Questionnaire* (16 PF).
- The five-factor model identifies five universal dimensions of personality: extroversion, agreeableness, conscientiousness, neuroticism, and openness to experience.
- Traits interact with situations to explain our behavior.
- Behavioral genetics and studies of identical twins suggest that heredity contributes significantly to adult personality traits.

How do psychodynamic theories explain personality?

- Like other psychodynamic approaches, Sigmund Freud's psychoanalytic theory emphasizes unconscious forces and conflicts within the personality.
- In Freud's theory, personality is made up of the id, ego, and superego.
- Libido, derived from the life instincts, is the primary energy running the personality. Conflicts within the personality may cause neurotic anxiety or moral anxiety and motivate us to use ego-defense mechanisms.
- The personality operates on three levels, the conscious, preconscious, and unconscious.
- The Freudian view of personality development is based on a series of psychosexual stages: the oral, anal, phallic, and genital stages. Fixation at any stage can leave a lasting imprint on personality.

What do behaviorists and social learning theorists emphasize in their approach to personality?

- Behavioral theories of personality emphasize learning, conditioning, and immediate effects of the environment (situational determinants).
- Learning theorists Dollard and Miller consider habits the basic core of personality. Habits express the combined effects of drive, cue, response, and reward.
- Social learning theory adds cognitive elements, such as perception, thinking, and understanding to the behavioral view of personality.
- Social learning theory is exemplified by the concepts of psychological situation, expectancies, and reinforcement value.
- The behavioristic view of personality development holds that social reinforcement in four situations is critical. The situations are feeding, toilet or cleanliness training, sex training, and anger or aggression training.
- Identification and imitation are of particular importance in learning to be "male" or "female."
- Psychological androgyny is related to greater behavioral adaptability and flexibility.

How do humanistic theories differ from other perspectives?

- Humanistic theory emphasizes subjective experience and needs for self-actualization.
- Abraham Maslow found that self-actualizers share characteristics that range from efficient perceptions of reality to frequent peak experiences.
- Carl Rogers viewed the self as an entity that emerges from personal experience. We tend to become aware of experiences that match our self-image, and exclude those that are incongruent with it.
- The incongruent person has a highly unrealistic self-image and/or a mismatch between the self-image and the ideal self. The congruent or fully functioning person is flexible and open to experiences and feelings.
- As parents apply conditions of worth to children's behavior, thoughts, and feelings, children begin to do the same. Internalized conditions of worth then contribute to incongruence that disrupts the organismic valuing process.

How do psychologists measure personality?

- Techniques typically used for personality assessment are interviews, observation, questionnaires, and projective tests.
- Structured and unstructured interviews provide much information, but they are subject to interviewer bias and misperceptions. The halo effect may also lower the accuracy of an interview.
- Direct observation, sometimes involving situational tests, behavioral assessment, or the use of rating scales, allows evaluation of a person's actual behavior.
- Personality questionnaires, such as the *Minnesota Multiphasic Personality Inventory-2* (MMPI-2), are objective and reliable, but their validity is open to question.
- Projective tests ask a person to project thoughts or feelings to an ambiguous stimulus or unstructured situation.
- The *Rorschach Technique,* or inkblot test, is a well-known projective technique. A second is the *Thematic Apperception Test* (TAT).
- Projective tests are low in validity and objectivity. Nevertheless, they are considered useful by many clinicians, particularly as part of a test battery.

What causes shyness? What can be done about it?

- Shyness is a mixture of social inhibition and social anxiety. It is marked by heightened public self-consciousness and a tendency to regard one's shyness as a lasting trait.
- Shyness can be lessened by changing self-defeating beliefs and by improving social skills.

Interactive Learning

Internet addresses frequently change. To find the sites listed here, visit www.thomsonedu.com/psychology/coon for an updated list of Internet addresses and direct links to relevant sites.

***Psychology: A Journey* Companion Website**   Find online quizzes, flash cards, animations, video clips,

experiments, interactive assessments, and other helpful study aids for this text at www.thomsonedu.com/psychology/coon.

About Humanistic Psychology   Discusses the history and future of humanistic psychology.

FAQ about Psychological Tests   Answers to commonly asked questions about tests and testing.

Freud Net   Offers links to information on Freud and psychoanalysis.

Personality and IQ Tests   Multiple links to personality tests and IQ tests that are scored online.

ThomsonNOW   Go to www.thomsonedu.com to link to ThomsonNOW, your online study tool. First take the **Pre-Test** for this chapter to get your **Personalized Study Plan**, which will identify topics you need to review and direct you to online resources. Then take the **Post-Test** to determine what concepts you have mastered and what you still need work on.

TEST YOUR KNOWLEDGE

Personality

For additional review, get more practice with *ThomsonNOW*, *WebTutor*, the *Practice Quizzes*, and/or the printed *Study Guide* available with this book.

1. When someone's personality has been evaluated, we are making a judgment about his or her
   a. temperament
   b. character
   c. extroversion
   d. self-esteem

2. A personality type is usually defined by the presence of
   a. all five personality dimensions
   b. a stable self concept
   c. several specific traits
   d. a source trait

3. Personality theorist Raymond Cattell used factor analysis to identify sixteen
   a. common traits
   b. source traits
   c. cardinal traits
   d. trait-situation interactions

4. Which of the following is NOT one of the Big Five personality dimensions?
   a. extroversion
   b. agreeableness
   c. neuroticism
   d. androgyny

5. The research methods of _____ have been used to study the extent to which we inherit personality characteristics.
   a. behavioral genetics
   b. social learning theory
   c. factor analysis
   d. trait profiling

6. According to Freud, which division of personality is governed by the reality principle?
   a. ego
   b. id
   c. ego ideal
   d. superego

7. Freud stated that the mind functions on three levels, the conscious, unconscious, and the
   a. psyche
   b. preconscious
   c. superego
   d. subconscious

8. Freudian theory states that a person who is passive, dependent, and needs lots of attention has a fixation in the
   a. oral stage
   b. superego
   c. Oedipal stage
   d. genital stage

9. The situational determinants of our actions are of special interest and importance to
   a. psychodynamic theorists
   b. humanistic theorists
   c. learning theorists
   d. behavioral geneticists

10. Which of the following is NOT a concept of social learning theory?
    a. incongruence
    b. expectancy
    c. self-efficacy
    d. reinforcement value

11. Maslow thought of peak experiences as temporary moments of
    a. congruence
    b. positive self-regard
    c. self-actualization
    d. self-reinforcement

12. Carl Rogers believed that personal growth is encouraged when conditions of worth are replaced by
    a. self-efficacy
    b. instrumental worth
    c. latency
    d. organismic valuing

13. The halo effect can be a serious problem in accurate personality assessment that is based on
    a. projective testing
    b. behavioral recording
    c. interviewing
    d. the TAT

14. Situational testing is primarily an example of using _____ to assess personality.
    a. direct observation
    b. structured interviewing
    c. cardinal traits
    d. projective techniques

15. Which of the following items does NOT belong with the others?
    a. Rorschach technique
    b. TAT
    c. MMPI-2
    d. projective testing

16. By definition, a test that measures what it claims to measure is
    a. valid
    b. situational
    c. objective
    d. reliable

17. Which of the following is an objective personality questionnaire?
    a. the TAT
    b. the In-basket Test
    c. the NDE-16
    d. the MMPI-2

18. Which MMPI-2 scale is designed to detect phobias and compulsive actions?
    a. Hysteria
    b. Paranoia
    c. Psychasthenia
    d. Mania

19. Contrary to what many people think, shyness is NOT related to
    a. private self-consciousness
    b. social anxiety
    c. self-esteem
    d. blaming oneself for social failures

20. Shy persons tend to consider their social anxiety to be a
    a. situational reaction
    b. personality trait
    c. public efficacy
    d. habit

CHAPTER 11

Health, Stress, and Coping

JOURNEY INTO PSYCHOLOGY: VIOLET'S SERIES OF UNFORTUNATE EVENTS

Somehow, Violet had managed to survive the rush of make-or-break term papers, projects, and classroom speeches. Then it was on to finals, where her tests seemed perfectly timed to inflict as much suffering as possible. Her two hardest exams fell on the same day! Great.

On the last day of finals, Violet got caught in a traffic jam on her way to school. Two drivers cut her off, and another gave her a one-finger salute. When Violet finally got to campus the parking lot was swarming with frantic students. Most of them, like her, were within minutes of missing a final exam. At last, Violet spied an empty space. As she started toward it, an Austin Mini darted around the corner and into "her" place. The driver of the car behind her began to honk impatiently. For a moment, Violet was seized by a colossal desire to run over anything in sight.

Finally, after a week and a half of stress, pressure, and frustration, Violet's finals were over. Sleep deprivation, gallons of coffee, junk food, and equal portions of cramming and complaining had carried her through. She was off for the summer. At last, she could kick back, relax, and have some fun. Or could she? Just 4 days after the end of school, Violet got a bad cold, followed by bronchitis that lasted for nearly a month.

Violet's experience illustrates what happens when stress, emotion, personal habits, and health collide. Though the timing of her cold might have been a coincidence, odds are it wasn't. Periods of stress are frequently followed by illness (Lyons & Chamberlain, 2006).

In the first part of this chapter we will explore a variety of behavioral health risks. Then we will look more closely at what stress is and how it affects us. After that, we will stress ways of coping with stress, so you can do a better job of staying healthy than Violet did.

▼ **Survey Questions**

- What is health psychology? How does behavior affect health?
- What is stress? What factors determine its severity?
- What causes frustration and what are typical reactions to it?
- Are there different types of conflict? How do people react to conflict?
- What are defense mechanisms?
- What do we know about coping with feelings of helplessness and depression?
- How is stress related to health and disease?
- What are the best strategies for managing stress?
- How can sexually transmitted diseases be prevented?

HEALTH PSYCHOLOGY—HERE'S TO YOUR GOOD HEALTH

>SURVEY QUESTIONS< *What is health psychology? How does behavior affect health?*

Despite the high cost of healthcare, one of the most important sources of health is free for the taking. Health psychologists have shown that many of the diseases that bedevil us are caused by unhealthy behavior. Let's see which personal habits contribute the most to leading a long, healthy, and happy life.

Most people agree that health is important—especially their own. Yet, half of all deaths in North America are primarily due to unhealthy behavior (Mokdad et al., 2004). **Health psychology** aims to do something about such deaths by using behavioral principles to prevent illness and promote health. Psychologists working in the allied field of **behavioral medicine** apply psychology to manage medical problems, such as diabetes or asthma. Their interests include pain control, helping people cope with chronic illness, stress-related diseases, self-screening for diseases (such as breast cancer), and similar topics (Brannon & Feist, 2007).

Behavioral Risk Factors

A century ago, people primarily died from infectious diseases and accidents. Today, people generally die from **lifestyle diseases,** which are related to health-damaging personal habits (Mokdad et al., 2004). Examples include heart disease, stroke, and lung cancer (▸Fig. 11.1.). Clearly, some lifestyles promote health, whereas others lead to illness and death. As one observer put it, "We have met the enemy and he is us."

What are some unhealthy behaviors? Some causes of illness are beyond our control, but many behavioral risks can be reduced. **Behavioral risk factors** are actions that increase the chances of disease, injury, or early death. For example, approximately 438,000 people die every year from smoking-related diseases (CDC, 2005). Similarly, being overweight *doubles* the chance of dying from cancer or heart disease. Roughly 60 percent of all American adults are overweight. As a result, obesity may soon overtake smoking as the main cause of preventable deaths. Being fat is not just a matter of fashion—in the long run it could kill you. A person who is overweight at age 20 can expect to lose 5 to 20 years of life expectancy (Fontaine et al., 2003).

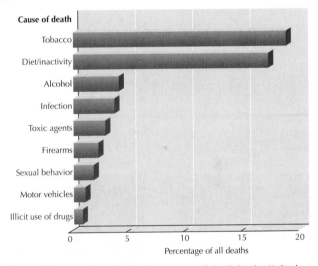

▸▸**FIGURE 11.1** The nine leading causes of death in the United States are shown in this graph. As you can see, eight of the top nine causes are directly related to behavioral risk factors (infection is the exception). At least 45 percent of all deaths can be traced to unhealthful behavior. The percentage of day-to-day health problems related to unhealthful behavior is even higher. (Data from Mokdad et al., 2004.)

Health psychology Study of the ways in which behavioral principles can be used to prevent illness and promote health.

Behavioral medicine The study of behavioral factors in medicine, physical illness, and medical treatment.

Lifestyle disease A disease related to health-damaging personal habits.

Behavioral risk factors Behaviors that increase the chances of disease, injury, or premature death.

Table 11.1 Percentage of U.S. High School Students Who Engaged in Health-Endangering Behaviors	
Risky Behavior in the Previous 30 Days	**Percentage**
Rode with drinking driver	30
Were in a physical fight	33
Carried a weapon	17
Drank alcohol	45
Used marijuana	22
Engaged in sexual intercourse	47
Did not use condom during last sexual intercourse	37
Smoked cigarettes	22
Did not eat enough fruits and vegetables	78
Not enough physical exercise	33

Source: Grunbaum et al., 2004

Each of the following factors is a major behavioral risk (Baum & Posluszny, 1999): High levels of stress, untreated high blood pressure, cigarette smoking, abuse of alcohol or other drugs, overeating, inadequate exercise, unsafe sexual behavior, exposure to toxic substances, violence, excess sun exposure, reckless driving, and disregarding personal safety (accidents). Seventy percent of all medical costs are related to just six of the listed factors—smoking, alcohol and drug abuse, poor diet, insufficient exercise, and risky sexual practices (Orleans, Gruman, & Hollendonner, 1999). (Unsafe sex is discussed later, in this chapter's "Psychology in Action" section.)

■ Table 11.1 shows how many high school students in the United States engage in various kinds of risky behaviors. The health habits you have by the time you are 18 or 19 greatly affect your health, happiness, and life expectancy years later (Vaillant & Mukamal, 2001).

Specific risk factors are not the only concern. Some people have a general **disease-prone personality** that leaves them depressed, anxious, hostile, and . . . frequently ill. In contrast, people who are intellectually resourceful, compassionate, optimistic, and nonhostile tend to enjoy good health (Taylor et al., 2000). Depression, in particular, is likely to damage health. People who are depressed eat poorly, sleep poorly, rarely exercise, fail to use seat belts in cars, smoke more, and so on (Allgower, Wardle, Steptoe, 2001).

Lifestyle

In your mind's eye, fast-forward an imaginary film of your life all the way to old age. Do it twice—once with a lifestyle including a large number of behavioral risk factors, and again without them. It should be obvious that many small risks can add up, dramatically raising the chance of illness. If stress is a frequent part of your life, visualize your body seething with emotion, day after day. If you smoke, picture a lifetime's worth of cigarette smoke blown through your lungs in a week. If you drink, take a lifetime of alcohol's assaults on the brain, stomach, and liver and squeeze them into a month: Your body would be poisoned, ravaged, and soon dead. If you eat a high-fat, high-cholesterol diet, fast-forward a lifetime of heart-killing plaque clogging your arteries.

We don't mean to sermonize. We just want to remind you that risk factors make a difference. To make matters worse, unhealthy lifestyles almost always create multiple risks. That is, people who smoke are also likely to drink excessively. Those who overeat usually do not get enough exercise, and so on (Straub, 2002). Even infectious diseases are often linked to behavioral risks. For example, pneumonia and other infections occur at higher rates in people who have cancer, heart disease, lung disease, or liver disease. Thus, many deaths attributed to infections can actually be traced to smoking, poor diet, or alcohol abuse (Mokdad et al., 2004).

In the long run, behavioral risk factors and lifestyles do make a difference in health and life expectancy.

Disease-prone personality A personality type associated with poor health; marked by persistent negative emotions, including anxiety, depression, and hostility.

Health-Promoting Behaviors

To prevent disease, health psychologists first try to remove behavioral risk factors. All the medicine in the world may not be enough to restore health without changes in behavior. We all know someone who has had a heart attack or lung disease who couldn't change the habits that led to his or her illness.

In some cases, lifestyle diseases can be treated or prevented by making specific, minor changes in behavior. For example, hypertension (high blood pressure) can be deadly. Yet, consuming less sodium (salt) can help fend off this "silent killer." (Losing weight, using alcohol sparingly, and getting more exercise will also help) (Georgiades et al., 2000).

In addition to removing specific risk factors, psychologists are interested in getting people to increase behaviors that promote health. Health-promoting behaviors include such obvious practices as getting regular exercise, controlling smoking and alcohol use, maintaining a balanced diet, getting good medical care, and managing stress (Zarcadoolas, Pleasant, & Greer, 2006). In one study, the risk of dying was cut by 65 percent during a 10-year period for adults who were careful about diet, alcohol, exercise, and smoking (Knoops et al., 2004).

Health-promoting behaviors don't have to be restrictive or burdensome. For instance, maintaining a healthy diet doesn't mean surviving on tofu and wheat grass. The healthiest people in the study just described ate a tasty "Mediterranean diet" high in fruit, vegetables, and fish, and low in red meat and dairy products. Likewise, you don't need to exercise like an Olympic athlete to benefit from physical activity. All you need is 30 minutes of exercise (the equivalent of a brisk walk) 3 or 4 times a week. Almost everyone can fit such "lifestyle physical activity" into his or her schedule (Pescatello, 2001).

What about alcohol? Moderation in drinking doesn't mean that you must be a teetotaler. Consuming one or two alcoholic drinks per day is generally safe for most people, especially if you remain alcohol free two or three days a week. However, having three or more drinks a day greatly increases the risk of stroke, cirrhosis of the liver, cancer, high blood pressure, heart disorders, and other diseases (Knoops et al., 2004).

To summarize, a small number of behavioral patterns accounts for many common health problems (Grunbaum et al., 2004). ■ Table 11.2 lists several major ways to promote good health.

■ Table 11.2　Major Health-Promoting Behaviors

Source	Desirable Behaviors
Nutrition	Eating a balanced, low-fat diet; appropriate caloric intake; maintenance of healthy body weight
Exercise	At least 30 minutes of aerobic exercise, 5 days per week
Blood pressure	Lower blood pressure with diet and exercise, or medicine if necessary
Alcohol and drugs	No more than two drinks per day; abstain from using drugs
Tobacco	Do not smoke; do not use smokeless tobacco
Sleep and relaxation	Avoid sleep deprivation; provide for periods of relaxation every day
Sex	Practice safer sex; avoid unplanned pregnancy
Injury	Curb dangerous driving habits, use seat belts; minimize sun exposure; forgo dangerous activities
Stress	Learn stress management; lower hostility

Early Prevention

Of the behavioral risks we have discussed, smoking is the largest preventable cause of death and the single most lethal factor (Mokdad et al., 2004). As such, it illustrates the prospect for preventing illness.

What have health psychologists done to lessen the risks? Attempts to "immunize" youths against pressures to start smoking are a good example. The smoker who says "Quitting is easy, I've done it dozens of times" states a basic truth—only 1 smoker in 10 has long-term success at quitting. Thus, the best way to deal with smoking is to prevent it before it becomes a lifelong habit. For example, school-based prevention programs have used quizzes about smoking, antismoking art contests, poster and T-shirt giveaways, antismoking pamphlets for parents, and questions for students to ask their parents (Zarcadoolas, Pleasant, & Greer, 2006). Such efforts are designed to persuade kids that smoking is dangerous and "uncool." Apparently, many teens are getting the message, as attitudes toward smoking are now more negative than they were 20 years ago (Chassin et al., 2003).

Celebrities can also help persuade young people to not start smoking in the first place.

Reuters/Corbis

Some antismoking programs include **refusal skills training.** In this case, youths learn to resist pressures to begin smoking (or using other drugs). For example, junior high students can role-play ways to resist smoking pressures from peers, adults, and cigarette ads. Similar methods can be applied to other health risks, such as sexually transmitted diseases and teen pregnancy (Wandersman & Florin, 2003).

Many health programs also teach students general life skills. The idea is to give kids skills that will help them cope with day-to-day stresses. That way, they will be less tempted to escape problems through drug use or other destructive behaviors. **Life skills training** includes practice in stress reduction, self-protection, decision making, goal setting, self-control, and social skills (Tobler et al., 2000).

HEALTH AND WELLNESS—JOB NUMBER ONE

In addition to early prevention, health psychologists have had some success with **community health campaigns.** These are community-wide education projects designed to lessen major risk factors. Health campaigns inform people of risks such as stress, alcohol abuse, high blood pressure, high cholesterol, smoking, STDs, or excessive sun exposure. This is followed by efforts to motivate people to change their behavior. Campaigns sometimes provide *role models* (positive examples) who show people how to improve their own health. They also direct people to services for health screening, advice, and treatment. Health campaigns may reach people through the mass media, public schools, health fairs, their work, or self-help programs. Such programs are increasingly successful in helping people make healthful changes in their behavior (Orleans, 2000).

Positive Psychology: Wellness

Health is not just an absence of disease. People who are truly healthy enjoy a positive state of **wellness** or well-being. Maintaining wellness is a lifelong pursuit and, hopefully, a labor of love. People who attain optimal wellness are both physically and psychologically healthy. They are happy, optimistic, self-confident individuals who can bounce back emotionally from adversity (Tugade, Fredrickson, & Barrett, 2004).

Refusal skills training Program that teaches youths how to resist pressures to begin smoking. (Can also be applied to other drugs and health risks.)

Life skills training A program that teaches stress reduction, self-protection, decision making, self-control, and social skills.

Community health campaign A community-wide education program that provides information about how to lessen risk factors and promote health.

Wellness A positive state of good health; more than the absence of disease.

People who enjoy a sense of well-being also have supportive relationships with others, they do meaningful work, and they live in a clean environment. Many of these aspects of wellness are addressed elsewhere in this book. In this chapter we will give special attention to the effect that stress has on health and sickness. Understanding stress and learning to control it can improve not only your health, but the quality of your life as well (Suinn, 2001). For these reasons, a discussion of stress and stress management follows.

→ Study Break   Health Psychology

Reflect

If you were to work as a health psychologist would you be more interested in preventing disease or managing it?

Make a list of the major behavioral risk factors that apply to you. Are you laying the foundation for a lifestyle disease?

Which of the health-promoting behaviors listed in ▪ Table 11.2 would you like to increase?

If you were designing a community health campaign, who would you use as role models of healthful behavior?

Learning Check

1. Adjustment to chronic illness and the control of pain are topics that would more likely be of interest to a specialist in _____ _____ rather than a health psychologist.

2. With respect to health, which of the following is *not* a major behavioral risk factor?

   a. overexercise
   b. cigarette smoking
   c. stress
   d. high blood pressure

3. According to a major health study, eating breakfast almost every day and rarely eating between meals are the two most important health-promoting behaviors. T or F?

4. Health psychologists tend to prefer _____ rather than modifying habits (like smoking) that become difficult to break once they are established.

5. The disease-prone personality is marked by _____, anxiety, and hostility.

Critical Thinking

6. The general public is increasingly well informed about health risks and healthful behavior. Can you apply the concept of reinforcement to explain why so many people fail to act on this information?

Answers

1. behavioral medicine 2. a 3. F 4. prevention 5. depression 6. Many of the health payoffs are delayed by months or years, greatly lessening the immediate rewards for healthful behavior.

STRESS—THREAT OR THRILL?

>SURVEY QUESTIONS< *What is stress? What factors determine its severity?*

Although stress is a natural part of life, it can be a major behavioral risk factor if it is prolonged or severe. It might seem that stressful events "happen to" people. Although this is sometimes the case, more often stress is a matter of how we perceive events and react to them. Because of this, stress can often be managed or controlled. Let's look into how stress occurs and typical reactions to it.

Stress can be dangerous if it is prolonged or severe but it isn't always bad. As Canadian stress research pioneer Hans Selye (SEL-yay) (1976) observed, "To be totally without stress is to be dead." That's because **stress** is the mental and physical condition that occurs when we adjust or adapt to the environment. Unpleasant events such as work pressures, marital problems, or financial woes naturally produce stress. But so do travel, sports, a new job, mountain climbing, dating, and other positive activities. Even if you aren't a thrill seeker, a healthy lifestyle may include a fair amount of *eustress* (good stress). Activities that provoke "good stress" are usually challenging, rewarding, and energizing.

A **stress reaction** begins with the same autonomic nervous system arousal that occurs during emotion. Imagine you are standing at the top of a wind-whipped ski jump for the first time. Internally, there would be a rapid surge in your heart rate, blood pressure, respiration, muscle tension, and other ANS responses. *Short-term* stresses of this kind can be uncomfortable, but they rarely do any damage. (Your landing might, however.) *Long-term* stresses are another matter entirely (Sternberg, 2000).

Stress The mental and physical condition that occurs when a person must adjust or adapt to the environment.

Stress reaction The physical response to stress, consisting mainly of bodily changes related to autonomic nervous system arousal.

The General Adaptation Syndrome

The impact of long-term stresses can be understood by examining the body's defenses against stress, a pattern known as the general adaptation syndrome.

The **general adaptation syndrome (G.A.S.)** is a series of bodily reactions to prolonged stress. Selye (1976) noticed that the first symptoms of almost any disease or trauma (poisoning, infection, injury, or stress) are almost identical. The body responds in the same way to any stress, be it infection, failure, embarrassment, a new job, trouble at school, or a stormy romance.

How does the body respond to stress? The G.A.S. consists of three stages: an alarm reaction, a stage of resistance, and a stage of exhaustion (»Fig. 11.2) (Selye, 1976).

In the **alarm reaction,** your body mobilizes its resources to cope with added stress. The pituitary gland signals the adrenal glands to produce more adrenaline, noradrenaline, and cortisol. As these stress hormones are dumped into the bloodstream, some bodily processes are speeded up and others are slowed. This allows bodily resources to be applied where they are needed (Lyons & Chamberlain, 2006).

We should all be thankful that our bodies automatically respond to emergencies. But brilliant as this emergency system is, it can also cause problems. In the first phase of the alarm reaction, people have such symptoms as headache, fever, fatigue, sore muscles, shortness of breath, diarrhea, upset stomach, loss of appetite, and a lack of energy. Notice that these are also the symptoms of being sick, of stressful travel, of high-altitude sickness, of final exams week, and (possibly) of falling in love!

During the **stage of resistance,** bodily adjustments to stress stabilize. As the body's defenses come into balance, symptoms of the alarm reaction disappear. Outwardly, everything seems normal. However, this appearance of normality comes at a high cost. The body is better able to cope with the original stressor, but its resistance to other stresses is lowered. For example, animals placed in extreme cold become more resistant to the cold, but more susceptible to infection. It is during the stage of resistance that the first signs of psychosomatic disorders (physical disorders triggered by psychological factors) begin to appear.

Continued stress leads to the **stage of exhaustion,** in which the body's resources are drained and stress hormones are depleted. Some of the typical signs or symptoms of impending exhaustion include (Friedman, 2002):

Emotional signs: Anxiety, apathy, irritability, mental fatigue

Behavioral signs: Avoidance of responsibilities and relationships, extreme or self-destructive behavior, self-neglect, poor judgment

Physical signs: Excessive worry about illness, frequent illness, exhaustion, overuse of medicines, physical ailments and complaints

The G.A.S. may sound melodramatic if you are young and healthy or if you've never endured prolonged stress. However, stress should not be taken lightly. Unless a way of relieving stress is found, the result will be a psychosomatic disease, a serious loss of health, or complete collapse. When Selye examined animals in the later stages of the G.A.S., he found that their adrenal glands were enlarged and discolored. There was intense shrinkage of internal organs, such as the thymus, spleen, and lymph nodes, and many animals had stomach ulcers. In addition to such direct effects, stress can disrupt the body's immune system, as described next.

Stress, Illness, and Your Immune System

How can prolonged stress result in a physical illness? An answer can be found in your body's immune system, which mobilizes defenses (such as white blood cells) against invading microbes and other disease agents. The immune system is regulated, in part, by the brain.

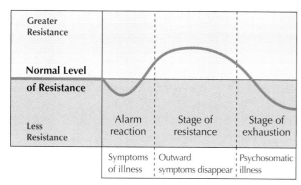

»**FIGURE 11.2** The General Adaptation Syndrome. During the initial alarm reaction to stress, resistance falls below normal. It rises again as bodily resources are mobilized, and it remains high during the stage of resistance. Eventually, resistance falls again as the stage of exhaustion is reached. (From *The Stress of Life* by Hans Selye. Copyright © 1976 by Hans Selye. Used by permission of McGraw-Hill Book Company.)

General adaptation syndrome (G.A.S.) A series of bodily reactions to prolonged stress; occurs in three stages: alarm, resistance, and exhaustion.

Alarm reaction First stage of the G.A.S., during which bodily resources are mobilized to cope with a stressor.

Stage of resistance Second stage of the G.A.S., during which bodily adjustments to stress stabilize, but at a high physical cost.

Stage of exhaustion Third stage of the G.A.S., at which time the body's resources are exhausted and serious health consequences occur.

Because of this link, stress and upsetting emotions can affect the immune system in ways that increase susceptibility to disease (Miller, Cohen, & Ritchey, 2002). By the way, the study of links among behavior, stress, disease, and the immune system is called **psychoneuroimmunology** (Daruna, 2004). (Try dropping that into a conversation sometime if you want to see a stress reaction!)

Studies show that the immune system is weakened in students during major exam times. Immunity is also lowered by divorce, bereavement, a troubled marriage, job loss, depression, and similar stresses (Deinzer et al., 2000; Segerstrom & Miller, 2004). Lowered immunity explains why the "double whammy" of getting sick when you are trying to cope with prolonged or severe stress is so common (Lyons & Chamberlain, 2006). Stress causes the body to release substances that increase inflammation. This is part of the body's self-protective response to threats, but it can prolong infections and delay healing (Kiecolt-Glaser et al., 2002). It's also worth noting again the value of positive emotions. Happiness, laughter, and delight tend to strengthen immune system response. Doing things that make you happy can protect your health (Rosenkranz et al., 2003).

Could reducing stress help prevent illness? Yes. Various psychological approaches, such as support groups, relaxation exercises, guided imagery, and stress management training can actually boost immune system functioning (Dougall & Baum, 2003). By doing so, they help promote and restore health. For example, stress management reduced the severity of cold and flu symptoms in a group of university students (Reid, Mackinnon, & Drummond, 2001).

There is even evidence that stress management can improve the chances of survival following life-threatening diseases, such as cancer, heart disease, and HIV/AIDS (Schneiderman et al., 2001). With some successes to encourage them, psychologists are now searching for the best combination of treatments to help people resist disease (Miller & Cohen, 2001).

When Is Stress a Strain?

It goes almost without saying that some events are more likely to cause stress than others. A **stressor** is a condition or event that challenges or threatens a person. Police officers, for instance, suffer from a high rate of stress-related diseases. The threat of injury or death, plus occasional confrontations with angry, drunk, or hostile citizens, takes a toll. A major factor is the *unpredictable* nature of police work. An officer who stops a car to issue a traffic ticket never knows if a cooperative citizen or an armed gang member is waiting inside.

A revealing study shows how unpredictability adds to stress. In a series of 1-minute trials, college students breathed air through a mask. On some trials, the air contained 20 percent more carbon dioxide (CO_2) than normal. If you were to inhale this air, you would feel anxious, stressed, and a little like you were suffocating. Students tested this way hated the "surprise" doses of CO_2. They found it much less stressful to be told in advance which trials would include a choking whiff of CO_2 (Lejuez et al., 2000).

Pressure is another element of stress, especially job stress. **Pressure** occurs when a person must meet *urgent* external demands or expectations (Weiten, 1998). For example, we feel pressured when activities must be speeded up, when deadlines must be met, when extra work is added, or when we must work near maximum capacity for long periods. Most students who have survived final exams are familiar with the effects of pressure.

What if I set deadlines for myself? Does it make a difference where the pressure comes from? Yes. People generally feel more stress in situations over which they have little or no

Stress and negative emotions lower immune system activity and increase inflammation. This, in turn, raises our vulnerability to infection, worsens illness, and delays recovery.

Air traffic control is stressful work. Employees must pay intense attention for long periods of time, they have little control over the pace of work, and the consequences of making a mistake can be dire.

Psychoneuroimmunology Study of the links among behavior, stress, disease, and the immune system.

Stressor A specific condition or event in the environment that challenges or threatens a person.

Pressure A stressful condition that occurs when a person must meet urgent external demands or expectations.

Burnout—The High Cost of Caring

Margo, a young nurse, realizes with dismay that she has "lost all patience with her patients" and wishes they would "go somewhere else to be sick." Margo's feelings are a clear sign of job **burnout**, a condition in which workers are physically, mentally, and emotionally drained (Greenglass, Burke, & Moore, 2003). Burnout has three aspects (Maslach, Schaufeli, & Leiter, 2001):

- Emotional exhaustion: Affected persons are fatigued, tense, apathetic, and suffer from physical ailments. They feel "used up" and "empty."
- Cynicism or detachment: Burned-out workers have an "I don't give a damn anymore" attitude and they treat clients coldly, as if they were objects.
- Feelings of reduced personal accomplishment: Burned-out workers do poor work and feel helpless, hopeless, or angry.

Burnout may occur in any job, but it is a special problem in emotionally demanding helping professions, such as nursing, teaching, social work, child care, counseling, or police work. Often, the most idealistic and caring workers are the ones who burn out. As some say, "You have to be on fire to burn out" (Maslach, Schaufeli, & Leiter, 2001).

If we wish to keep caring people in the helping professions, it may be necessary to adjust workloads, rewards, and the amount of control people have in their jobs (Leiter & Maslach, 2005).

Can college students experience burnout? Yes they can. If you have a negative attitude toward your studies and feel that your college workload is too heavy, you may be vulnerable to burnout (Jacobs & Dodd, 2003). On the other hand, if you have a positive attitude toward your studies, participate in extracurricular activities, and enjoy good social support from your friends, rock on!

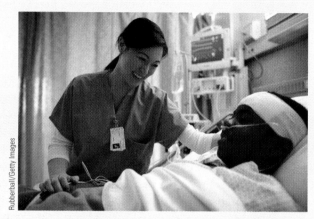

The helping professions require empathy, caring, and emotional involvement. As a result, caregivers risk depleting their emotional resources and ability to cope. Over time, this can lead to burnout.

control (Taris et al., 2005). In one study, nurses with a high sense of control were less likely to get sick, both physically and mentally, than were nurses with a low sense of control (Ganster, Fox, & Dwyer, 2001).

To summarize, when emotional "shocks" are *intense* or *repeated, unpredictable, uncontrollable,* and linked to *pressure,* stress will be magnified and damage is likely to result. At work, people face many of these sources of stress every day. In fact, chronic job stress sometimes results in *burnout,* a pattern of emotional exhaustion (see "Burnout—The High Cost of Caring").

Appraising Stressors

It might seem that stressful events "happen to" us. Sometimes this is true, but as noted in Chapter 10, our emotions are greatly affected by how we appraise situations. That's why some people are distressed by events that others view as a thrill or a challenge (eustress). Ultimately, stress depends on how you perceive a situation. Our friend Akihito would find it stressful to listen to five of his son's hip-hop CDs in a row. His son Takashi would find it stressful to listen to *one* of his father's opera CDs. To know if you are stressed, we must know what meaning you place on events. As we will see in a moment, whenever a stressor is appraised as a *threat* (potentially harmful), a powerful stress reaction follows (Folkman & Moskowitz, 2004; Lazarus, 1991a).

"Am I Okay or in Trouble?"

You have been selected to give a speech to 300 people. Or, a doctor tells you that you must undergo a dangerous and painful operation. Or, the one true love of your life walks out the door. What would your emotional response to these events be? How do you cope with an emotional threat?

Burnout A job-related condition of mental, physical, and emotional exhaustion.

According to Richard Lazarus (1991a), there are two important steps in managing a threat. The first is a **primary appraisal,** in which you decide if a situation is relevant or irrelevant, positive or threatening. In essence, this step answers the question, "Am I okay or in trouble?" Then you make a **secondary appraisal,** in which you assess your resources and choose a way to meet the threat or challenge ("What can I do about this situation?"). Thus, the way a situation is "sized up" greatly affects our ability to cope with it (▶▶Fig. 11.3). Public speaking, for instance, can be appraised as an intense threat or as a chance to perform. Emphasizing the threat—by imagining failure, rejection, or embarrassment—obviously invites disaster (Strongman, 2003).

The Nature of Threat

What does it mean to feel threatened by a stressor? Certainly in most day-to-day situations it doesn't mean you think your life is in danger. (Unless, of course, you owe money to "Eddie The Enforcer.") Threat has more to do with the idea of control. We are particularly prone to feel stressed when we can't—or think we can't—control our immediate environment. In short, a *perceived* lack of control is just as threatening as an actual lack of control. For example, college students who *feel* overloaded experience stress even though their workload may not actually be heavier than that of their classmates (Jacobs & Dodd, 2003).

A sense of control also comes from believing you can reach desired goals. It is threatening to feel that we lack *competence* to cope with life's demands (Bandura, 2001). Because of this, the intensity of your body's stress reaction often depends on what you think and tell yourself about a stressor. That's why it's valuable to learn to think in ways that ward off the body's stress response. (Some strategies for controlling upsetting thoughts are described later in the section on "Stress Management.")

Coping with Threat

You have appraised a situation as threatening. What will you do next? There are two major choices. Both involve thinking and acting in ways that help us handle stressors. In **emotion-focused coping,** we try to control our emotional reactions to the situation. For example, a distressed person may distract herself by listening to music, taking a walk to relax, or seeking emotional support from others. In contrast, **problem-focused coping** is aimed at managing or correcting the distressing situation itself. Some examples are making a plan of action or concentrating on your next step (Folkman & Moskowitz, 2004).

Couldn't both types of coping occur together? Yes. Sometimes the two types of coping aid one another. For instance, quieting your emotions may make it easier for you to find a way to solve a problem. Say, for example, that a woman feels anxious as she steps to the podium to give a speech. If she does some deep breathing to reduce her anxiety (emotion-focused coping) she will be better able to glance over her notes to improve her delivery (problem-focused coping).

It is also possible for coping efforts to clash. For instance, if you have to make a difficult decision, you may suffer intense emotional distress. In such circumstances there is a temptation to make a quick, ill-advised choice, just to end the suffering. Doing so may allow you to cope with your emotions, but it shortchanges problem-focused coping.

In general, problem-focused coping tends to be especially useful when you are facing a controllable stressor—that is, a situation you can actually do something about. Emotion-focused efforts are best suited to managing stressors you cannot control (Folkman & Moskowitz, 2004). To improve your chances of coping effectively, the stress-fighting strategies described in this chapter include a mixture of both techniques.

So far, our discussion has focused on everyday stresses. How do people react to the extreme stresses imposed by war, violence, or disaster? "Coping with Traumatic Stress" discusses this important topic.

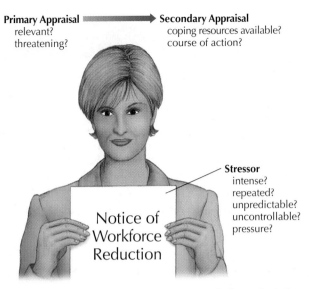

Primary Appraisal
relevant?
threatening?

Secondary Appraisal
coping resources available?
course of action?

Stressor
intense?
repeated?
unpredictable?
uncontrollable?
pressure?

Notice of Workforce Reduction

▶▶**FIGURE 11.3** Stress is the product of an interchange between a person and the environment.

Primary appraisal Deciding if a situation is relevant to oneself and if it is a threat.

Secondary appraisal Deciding how to cope with a threat or challenge.

Emotion-focused coping Managing or controlling one's emotional reaction to a stressful or threatening situation.

Problem-focused coping Directly managing or remedying a stressful or threatening situation.

Coping with Traumatic Stress

Traumatic experiences produce psychological injury or intense emotional pain. Victims of **traumatic stresses,** such as war, torture, rape, assassination, plane crashes, natural disasters, or street violence, may suffer from nightmares, flashbacks, insomnia, irritability, nervousness, grief, emotional numbing, and depression. There is little doubt that the 2005 hurricane season caused these effects in the Gulf Coast states. Like most traumatic stresses, the impact, especially of Hurricanes Katrina and Rita, was overwhelming.

People who personally witness or survive a disaster are most affected by traumatic stress. Twenty percent of the people who lived close to Ground Zero in New York suffered serious stress disorders (Galea et al., 2002). Yet, even those who experience horror at a distance may be traumatized (Galea & Resnick, 2005). Forty-four percent of U.S. adults who only saw the September 11 terrorist attacks on television had at least some stress symptoms (Schuster et al., 2001).

Traumatic stress produces feelings of helplessness and vulnerability (Fields & Margolin, 2001). Victims realize that disaster could strike again without warning. In addition to feeling threatened, many victims sense that they are losing control of their lives (Scurfield, 2002).

What can people do about such reactions? Psychologists recommend the following:

• Identify what you are feeling and talk to others about your fears and concerns.

• Think about the skills that have helped you overcome adversity in the past and apply them to the present situation.
• Continue to do the things that you enjoy and that make life meaningful (LeDoux & Gorman, 2001).
• Get support from others. This is a major element in recovery from all traumatic events.
• Give yourself time to heal. Fortunately, most people are more resilient than they think.

When traumatic stresses are severe or repeated, some people have even more serious symptoms. They suffer from crippling anxiety or become emotionally numb. Typically, they can't stop thinking about the disturbing event; they anxiously avoid anything associated with the event; and they are constantly fearful or nervous. (These are the symptoms of *stress disorders,* which are discussed in Chapter 12.) Such reactions can leave victims emotionally handicapped for months or years after a disaster. If you feel that you are having trouble coping with a severe emotional shock, consider seeking help from a psychologist or other professional.

Ken Cedeno/Corbis

There can be little doubt that Hurricane Katrina's assault on New Orleans was a traumatically stressful event. Even people who merely witnessed the disaster on television suffered from stress symptoms.

FRUSTRATION—BLIND ALLEYS AND LEAD BALLOONS

>SURVEY QUESTION< *What causes frustration and what are typical reactions to it?*

Do you remember how frustrated Violet was when she couldn't find a parking space? **Frustration** is a negative emotional state that occurs when people are prevented from reaching desired goals. In Violet's case, the goal of finding a parking space was blocked by another car.

Obstacles of many kinds cause frustration. A useful distinction can be made between external and personal sources of frustration. *External frustration* is based on conditions outside a person that impede progress toward a goal. All of the following are external frustrations: getting stuck with a flat tire; having a marriage proposal rejected; finding the cupboard bare when you go to get your poor dog a bone; finding the refrigerator bare when you go to get your poor tummy a T-bone; being chased out of the house by your starving dog. In other words, external frustrations are based on *delays, failure, rejection, loss,* and other direct blocking of motivated behavior.

Notice that external obstacles can be either *social* (slow drivers, tall people in theaters, people who cut into lines) or *nonsocial* (stuck doors, a dead battery, rain on the day of the game). If you ask your friends what has frustrated them recently, most will probably mention someone's behavior ("My sister wore one of my dresses when I wanted to wear it," "My supervisor is unfair," "My history teacher grades too hard"). As social animals, we humans

Traumatic stresses Extreme events that cause psychological injury or intense emotional pain.

Frustration A negative emotional state that occurs when one is prevented from reaching a goal.

are highly sensitive to social sources of frustration (Taylor, 2006). That's probably why unfair treatment associated with racial or ethnic prejudice is a major source of frustration and stress in the lives of many African Americans and other minority group members (Clark et al., 1999).

Frustration usually increases as the *strength, urgency,* or *importance* of a blocked motive increases. Violet was especially frustrated in the parking lot because she was late for an exam. Likewise, an escape artist submerged in a tank of water and bound with 200 pounds of chain would become *quite* frustrated if a trick lock jammed. Remember, too, that motivation becomes stronger as we near a goal. As a result, frustration is more intense when a person runs into an obstacle very close to a goal. If you've ever missed an A grade by 5 points, you were probably very frustrated. If you've missed an A by 1 point—well, frustration builds character, right?

A final factor affecting frustration is summarized by the old phrase "the straw that broke the camel's back." The effects of *repeated* frustrations can accumulate until a small irritation sets off an unexpectedly violent response. A case in point is the fact that people with long daily commutes are more likely to display "road rage" (angry, aggressive driving) (Harding et al., 1998).

Personal frustrations are based on personal characteristics. If you are 4 feet tall and aspire to be a professional basketball player, you very likely will be frustrated. If you want to go to medical school, but can earn only D grades, you will likewise be frustrated. In both examples, frustration is actually based on personal limitations. Yet, failure may be *perceived* as externally caused. We will return to this point in a discussion of stress management. In the meantime, let's look at some typical reactions to frustration.

Reactions to Frustration

Aggression is any response made with the intent of harming a person or an object. It is one of the most persistent and frequent responses to frustration (Anderson & Bushman, 2002).

Does frustration always cause aggression? Aren't there other reactions? Although the connection is strong, frustration does not always incite aggression. More often, frustration is met first with *persistence,* often in the form of more vigorous efforts and varied responses (▸▸Fig. 11.4). For example, if you put your last quarter in a vending machine and pressing the button has no effect, you will probably press harder and faster (vigorous effort). Then you will press all the other buttons (varied response). Persistence may help you reach your goal by getting *around* a barrier. However, if the machine *still* refuses to deliver, or return your quarter, you may become aggressive and kick the machine (or at least tell it what you think of it).

Persistence can be very adaptive. Overcoming a barrier ends the frustration and allows the need or motive to be satisfied. The same is true of aggression that removes or destroys a barrier. Picture a small band of nomadic humans, parched by thirst but separated from a water hole by a menacing animal. It is easy to see that attacking the animal may ensure their survival. In modern society such direct aggression is seldom acceptable. If you find a long line at the drinking fountain, aggression is hardly appropriate. Because direct aggression is discouraged, it is frequently *displaced.*

How is aggression displaced? Directing aggression toward a source of frustration may be impossible, or it may be too dangerous. If you are frustrated by your boss at work or by a teacher at school, the cost of direct aggression may be too high (losing your job or failing a class). Instead, the aggression may be displaced, or redirected, toward whomever or whatever is available. Targets of **displaced aggression** tend to be safer, or less likely to retaliate, than the original source of frustration. At one time or another, you have probably lashed out

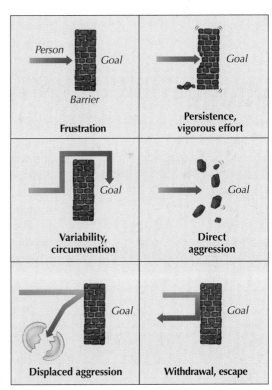

▸▸**FIGURE 11.4** Frustration and common reactions to it.

Aggression Any response made with the intent of causing harm.

Displaced aggression Redirecting aggression to a target other than the actual source of one's frustration.

Bumper cars seem to bring out aggressive impulses in many drivers. Wild smash-ups are part of the fun, but are some drivers displacing aggressive urges related to frustration in other areas of their lives?

at a friend or relative who was not the real cause of your annoyance. As this suggests, excessive anger over a minor irritation is a common form of displaced aggression (Miller et al., 2003).

Psychologists attribute much hostility to displaced aggression. A disturbing example is the finding that unemployment and divorce are associated with increased child abuse (Weissman, Jogerst, & Dawson, 2003). In a pattern known as **scapegoating,** a person or a group is blamed for conditions not of their making. A *scapegoat* is a person who has become a habitual target of displaced aggression. Despite recent progress, many minority groups continue to face hostility based on scapegoating. Think, for example, about the hostility expressed toward illegal immigrants during times of economic hardship. In many communities, layoffs and job losses are closely linked to increased violence (Catalano, Novaco, & McConnell, 1997). Or think about the hostility expressed toward anyone in the United States who looked even vaguely "foreign" right after the September 11 terrorist attacks.

I have a friend who dropped out of school to hitchhike around the country. He seemed very frustrated before he quit. What type of response to frustration is that? Another major reaction to frustration is escape, or withdrawal. It is stressful and unpleasant to be frustrated. If other reactions do not reduce frustration, a person may try to escape. **Escape** may mean actually leaving a source of frustration (dropping out of school, quitting a job, leaving an unhappy marriage), or it may mean psychologically escaping. Two common forms of psychological escape are feigned apathy (pretending not to care) and the use of drugs such as cocaine, alcohol, marijuana, or narcotics. (Notice that these are examples of ineffective emotion-focused coping.) (See ▸▸Fig. 11.4 for a summary of common reactions to frustration.)

Coping with Frustration

In a classic experiment, a psychologist studying frustration placed rats on a small platform at the top of a tall pole. Then he forced them to jump off the platform toward two elevated doors, one locked and the other unlocked. If the rat chose the correct door, it swung open and the rat landed safely on another platform. Rats who chose the locked door bounced off it and fell into a net far below.

The problem of choosing the open door was made unsolvable and very frustrating by randomly alternating which door was locked. After a time, most rats adopted a stereotyped response. That is, they chose the same door every time. This door was then permanently locked. All the rat had to do was to jump to the other door to avoid a fall, but time after time the rat bounced off the locked door (Maier, 1949).

Isn't that an example of persistence? No. Persistence that is *inflexible* can turn into "stupid," stereotyped behavior like that of a rat on a jumping stand. When dealing with frustration, you must know when to quit and establish a new direction. Here are some suggestions to help you avoid needless frustration.

1. Try to identify the source of your frustration. Is it external or personal?
2. Is the source of frustration something that can be changed? How hard would you have to work to change it? Is it under your control at all?
3. If the source of your frustration can be changed or removed, are the necessary efforts worth it?

The answers to these questions help determine if persistence will be futile. There is value in learning to accept gracefully those things that cannot be changed.

It is also important to distinguish between *real* barriers and *imagined* barriers. All too often we create our own imaginary barriers. For example, Corazon wants a part-time job to earn extra money. At the first place she applied, she was told that she didn't have enough

Scapegoating Blaming a person or a group of people for conditions not of their making.

Escape Reducing discomfort by leaving frustrating situations or by psychologically withdrawing from them.

"experience." Now she complains of being frustrated because she wants to work but cannot. She needs "experience" to work, but can't get experience without working. She has quit looking for a job.

Is Corazon's need for experience a real barrier? Unless she applies for *many* jobs it is impossible to tell if she has overestimated its importance. For her the barrier is real enough to prevent further efforts, but with persistence she might locate an "unlocked door." If a reasonable amount of effort does show that experience is essential, it might be obtained in other ways—through temporary volunteer work, for instance.

CONFLICT—YES, NO, YES, NO, YES, NO, WELL, MAYBE

>SURVEY QUESTIONS< *Are there different types of conflict? How do people react to conflict?*

Conflict occurs whenever a person must choose between contradictory needs, desires, motives, or demands. Choosing between college and work, marriage and single life, or study and failure are common conflicts. There are four basic forms of conflict. As we will see, each has its own properties (▸▸Fig. 11.5 and ▸▸Fig. 11.6).

Approach-Approach Conflicts

A simple **approach-approach conflict** comes from having to choose between two positive, or desirable, alternatives. Choosing between tutti-frutti-coconut-mocha-champagne ice and orange-marmalade-peanut butter-coffee swirl at the ice cream parlor may throw you into a temporary conflict. However, if you really like both choices, your decision will be quickly made. Even when more important decisions are at stake, approach-approach conflicts tend to be the easiest to resolve. The old fable about the mule that died of thirst and starvation while standing between a bucket of water and a bucket of oats is obviously unrealistic. When both options are positive, the scales of decision are easily tipped one direction or the other.

Avoidance-Avoidance Conflicts

Being forced to choose between two negative, or undesirable, alternatives creates an **avoidance-avoidance conflict.** A person in an avoidance conflict is caught between "the devil and the deep blue sea," between "the frying pan and the fire," or "a rock and a hard place." In real life, double-avoidance conflicts involve dilemmas such as choosing between unwanted pregnancy and abortion, the dentist and tooth decay, a monotonous job and poverty, or dorm food and starvation.

Suppose I don't object to abortion. Or suppose that I consider any pregnancy sacred and not to be tampered with? Like many other stressful situations, these examples can be defined as conflicts only on the basis of personal needs and values. If a woman wants to end a pregnancy and does not object to abortion, she experiences no conflict. If she would not consider abortion under any circumstances, there is also no conflict.

Avoidance conflicts often have a "damned if you do, damned if you don't" quality. In other words, both choices are negative, but *not choosing* may be impossible or equally undesirable. To illustrate, imagine the plight of a person trapped in a hotel fire 20 stories from the ground. Should she jump from the window and almost surely die on the pavement? Or should she try to dash through the flames and almost surely die of smoke inhalation and burns? When faced with a choice such as this, it is easy to see why people often *freeze*, find-

▸▸**FIGURE 11.5** The three most basic forms of conflict. For this woman, choosing between pie and ice cream is a minor approach-approach conflict; deciding whether to take a job that will require weekend work is an approach-avoidance conflict; and choosing between paying higher rent and moving is an avoidance-avoidance conflict. (Photo: Royalty-Free/Corbis)

Conflict A stressful condition that occurs when a person must choose between incompatible or contradictory alternatives.

Approach-approach conflict Choosing between two positive, or desirable, alternatives.

Avoidance-avoidance conflict Choosing between two negative, undesirable alternatives.

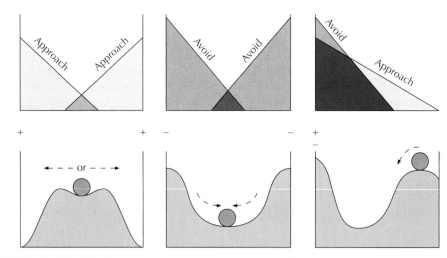

▶▶FIGURE 11.6 Conflict diagrams. As shown by the colored areas in the graphs, desires to approach and to avoid increase near a goal. The effects of these tendencies are depicted below each graph. The "behavior" of the ball in each example illustrates the nature of the conflict above it. An approach conflict *(left)* is easily decided. Moving toward one goal will increase its attraction *(graph)* and will lead to a rapid resolution. (If the ball moves in either direction, it will go all the way to one of the goals.) In an avoidance conflict *(center)*, tendencies to avoid are deadlocked, resulting in inaction. In an approach-avoidance conflict *(right)*, approach proceeds to the point where desires to approach and avoid cancel each other. Again, these tendencies are depicted *(below)* by the action of the ball. (Graphs after Miller, 1944.)

ing it impossible to decide or take action. In actual disasters of this sort, people are often found dead in their rooms, victims of an inability to take action.

Indecision, inaction, and freezing are not the only reactions to double-avoidance conflicts. Because avoidance conflicts are stressful and difficult to solve, people sometimes pull out of them entirely. This reaction, called *leaving the field,* is another form of escape. It may explain the behavior of a student who could not attend school unless he worked. However, if he worked he could not earn passing grades. His solution after much conflict and indecision? He joined the navy.

Approach-Avoidance Conflicts

Approach-avoidance conflicts are also difficult to resolve. A person in an **approach-avoidance conflict** is "caught" by being attracted to, and repelled by, the same goal or activity. Attraction keeps the person in the situation, but its negative aspects cause turmoil and distress. For example, a high school student arrives to pick up his date for the first time. He is met at the door by her father, who is a professional wrestler—7 feet tall, 300 pounds, and entirely covered with hair. The father gives the boy a crushing handshake and growls that he will break him in half if the girl is not home on time. The student considers the girl attractive and has a good time. But does he ask her out again? It depends on the relative strength of his attraction and his fear. Almost certainly he will feel *ambivalent* about asking her out again, knowing that another encounter with her father awaits him.

Ambivalence (mixed positive and negative feelings) is a central characteristic of approach-avoidance conflicts. Ambivalence is usually translated into *partial approach* (Miller, 1944). Because our student is still attracted to the girl, he may spend time with her at school and elsewhere. But he may not actually date her again. Some more realistic examples of approach-avoidance conflicts are planning to marry someone your parents strongly disapprove of, wanting to be in a play but suffering stage fright, wanting to buy a car but not wanting to make monthly payments, and wanting to eat when you're

Approach-avoidance conflict Being attracted to and repelled by the same goal or activity.

already overweight. Many of life's important decisions have approach-avoidance dimensions.

Multiple Conflicts

Aren't real-life conflicts more complex than the ones described here? Yes. Conflicts are rarely as clear-cut as those described. People in conflict are usually faced with several dilemmas at once, so several types of conflict may be intermingled. The fourth type of conflict moves us closer to reality. In a **double approach-avoidance conflict** each alternative has both positive and negative qualities. For example, you are offered two jobs: One has good pay but poor hours and dull work; the second has interesting work and excellent hours, but low pay. Which do you select? This situation is more typical of the choices we must usually make. It offers neither completely positive nor completely negative options.

As with single approach-avoidance conflicts, people faced with double approach-avoidance conflicts feel ambivalent about each choice. This causes them to *vacillate,* or waver between the alternatives. Just as you are about to choose one such alternative, its undesirable aspects tend to loom large. So, what do you do? You swing back toward the other choice. If you have ever been romantically attracted to two people at once—each having qualities you like and dislike—then you have probably experienced vacillation. Another example that may be familiar is trying to decide between two college majors, each with advantages and disadvantages.

In real life it is common to face **multiple approach-avoidance conflicts** in which several alternatives each have positive and negative features. An example would be trying to choose which automobile to buy among several brands. When multiple approach-avoidance conflicts involve major life decisions, such as choosing a career, a school, a mate, or a job, they can add greatly to the amount of stress we experience.

Managing Conflicts

How can I handle conflicts more effectively? Most of the suggestions made earlier concerning frustration also apply to conflicts. However, here are some additional things to remember when you are in conflict or must make a difficult decision.

1. Don't be hasty when making important decisions. Hasty decisions are often regretted. Take time to collect information and to weigh pros and cons. Even if you do make a faulty decision, it will trouble you less if you know that you did everything possible to avoid a mistake.
2. Try out important decisions *partially* when possible. If you are thinking about moving to a new town, try to spend a few days there first. If you are choosing between colleges, do the same. If classes are in progress, sit in on some. If you want to learn to scuba dive, rent equipment for a reasonable length of time before buying.
3. Look for workable compromises. Again it is important to get all available information. If you think that you have only one or two alternatives and they are undesirable or unbearable, seek the aid of a teacher, counselor, minister, or social service agency. You may be overlooking possible alternatives these people will know about.
4. When all else fails, make a decision and live with it. Indecision and conflict exact a high cost. Sometimes it is best to select a course of action and stick with it unless it is very obviously wrong after you have taken it.

Conflicts are a normal part of life. With practice you can learn to manage many of the conflicts you will face.

Double approach-avoidance conflict
Being simultaneously attracted to and repelled by each of two alternatives.

Multiple approach-avoidance conflict
Being simultaneously attracted to and repelled by each of several alternatives.

Study Break Stress, Frustration, and Conflict

Reflect

What impact did pressure, control, predictability, repetition, and intensity have on your last stress reaction?

What type of coping do you tend to use when you face a stressor such as public speaking or taking an important exam?

Think of a time when you were frustrated. What was your goal? What prevented you from reaching it? Was your frustration external or personal?

Have you ever displaced aggression? Why did you choose another target for your hostility?

Review the major types of conflict and think of a conflict you have faced that illustrates each type. Did your reactions match those described in the text?

Learning Check

1. The first stage of the G.A.S. is called the _____ reaction.
2. Whereas stressful incidents suppress the immune system, stress management techniques have almost no effect on immune system functioning. T or F?
3. Emotional exhaustion, cynicism, and reduced accomplishment are characteristics of job _____.
4. Stress tends to be greatest when a situation is appraised as a _____ and a person does not feel _____ to cope with the situation.

5. According to Lazarus, coping with threatening situations can be both problem focused and _____ focused.
6. Which of the following is *not* a common reaction to frustration?

   a. ambivalence   b. aggression
   c. displaced aggression   d. persistence

7. Sampson Goliath is 7 feet tall and weighs 300 pounds. He has failed miserably in his aspirations to become a jockey. The source of his frustration is mainly _____.
8. Inaction and freezing are most characteristic of avoidance-avoidance conflicts. T or F?
9. Approach-avoidance conflicts produce mixed feelings called _____.

Critical Thinking

10. Which do you think would produce more stress: (a) Appraising a situation as mildly threatening but feeling like you are totally incompetent to cope with it? Or, (b) appraising a situation as very threatening but feeling that you have the resources and skills to cope with it?
11. Being frustrated is unpleasant. If some action, including aggression, ends frustration, why might we expect the action to be repeated on other occasions?

Answers

1. alarm 2. F 3. burnout 4. threat, competent 5. emotion 6. a 7. personal 8. T 9. ambivalence 10. There is no correct answer here because individual stress reactions vary greatly. However, the secondary appraisal of a situation often determines just how stressful it is. Feeling incapable of coping is very threatening. 11. If a response ends discomfort, the response has been negatively reinforced. This makes it more likely to occur in the future (see Chapter 6).

PSYCHOLOGICAL DEFENSE—MENTAL KARATE?

>SURVEY QUESTION< *What are defense mechanisms?*

Threatening situations are often accompanied by an unpleasant emotion called **anxiety.** When you are anxious you feel tense, uneasy, apprehensive, worried, and vulnerable. This unpleasant state can lead to emotion-focused coping that is *defensive* in nature (Lazarus, 1991b). Psychodynamic psychologists have identified various defenses that shield us from anxiety. Defense mechanisms allow us to reduce anxiety caused by stressful situations or our own shortcomings.

What are psychological defense mechanisms and how do they reduce anxiety? A **defense mechanism** is any mental process used to avoid, deny, or distort sources of threat or anxiety, including threats to one's self-image. Many of the defenses were first identified by Sigmund Freud, who assumed they operate *unconsciously.* Often, defense mechanisms create large

Anxiety Apprehension, dread, or uneasiness similar to fear but based on an unclear threat.

Defense mechanism A habitual and often unconscious psychological process used to reduce anxiety.

JUMP START © United Feature Syndicate, Inc.

■ Table 11.3 *Psychological Defense Mechanisms*

Compensation Counteracting a real or imagined weakness by emphasizing desirable traits or seeking to excel in the area of weakness or in other areas.

Denial Protecting oneself from an unpleasant reality by refusing to perceive it.

Fantasy Fulfilling unmet desires in imagined achievements or activities.

Identification Taking on some of the characteristics of an admired person, usually as a way of compensating for perceived personal weaknesses or faults.

Intellectualization Separating emotion from a threatening or anxiety-provoking situation by talking or thinking about it in impersonal "intellectual" terms.

Isolation Separating contradictory thoughts or feelings into "logic-tight" mental compartments so that they do not come into conflict.

Projection Attributing one's own feelings, shortcomings, or unacceptable impulses to others.

Rationalization Justifying your behavior by giving reasonable and "rational," but false, reasons for it.

Reaction formation Preventing dangerous impulses from being expressed in behavior by exaggerating opposite behavior.

Regression Retreating to an earlier level of development or to earlier, less demanding habits or situations.

Repression Unconsciously preventing painful or dangerous thoughts from entering awareness.

Sublimation Working off unmet desires, or unacceptable impulses, in activities that are constructive.

blind spots in awareness. For instance, you might know an extremely stingy person who is completely unaware that he is a tightwad.

Everyone has at one time or another used defense mechanisms. Let's consider some of the most common. (A more complete listing is given in ■ Table 11.3.)

Denial

One of the most basic defenses is **denial** (protecting oneself from an unpleasant reality by refusing to accept it or believe it). We are prone to deny death, illness, and similar painful and threatening events. For instance, if you were told that you had only 3 months to live, how would you react? Your first thoughts might be "Aw, come on, someone must have mixed up the X-rays" or "The doctor must be mistaken" or simply "It can't be true!" Similar denial and disbelief are common reactions to the unexpected death of a friend or relative: "It's just not real. I don't believe it!"

Repression

Freud noticed that his patients had tremendous difficulty recalling shocking or traumatic events from childhood. It seemed that powerful forces were holding these painful memories from awareness. Freud called this **repression,** our tendency to protect ourselves by repressing threatening thoughts and impulses. Feelings of hostility toward a family member, the names of people we dislike, and past failures are common targets of repression. Research suggests that you are most likely to repress information that threatens your self-image (Mendolia, 2002).

Reaction Formation

In a **reaction formation,** impulses are not just repressed; they are also held in check by exaggerating opposite behavior. For example, a mother who unconsciously resents her children may, through reaction formation, become absurdly overprotective and overindulgent. Her real thoughts of "I hate them" and "I wish they were gone" are replaced by "I love them" and "I don't know what I would do without them." The mother's hostile impulses are traded for "smother" love, so that she won't have to admit she hates her children. Thus, the basic idea in a reaction formation is that the individual acts out an opposite behavior to block threatening impulses or feelings.

Regression

In its broadest meaning, **regression** refers to any return to earlier, less demanding situations or habits. Most parents who have a second child have to put up with at least some regression by the older child. Threatened by a new rival for affection, an older child may regress to childish speech, bed-wetting, or infantile play after the new baby arrives. If you've ever seen a child get homesick at summer camp or on a vacation, you've observed regression. The child wants to go home, where it's "safe." An adult who throws a temper tantrum or a married adult who "goes home to mother" is also regressing.

Projection

Projection is an unconscious process that protects us from the anxiety we would feel if we were to discern our faults. A person who is projecting tends to see his or her own feelings, shortcomings, or unacceptable impulses in others. **Projection** lowers anxiety by exaggerating negative traits in others. This justifies one's own actions and directs attention away from personal failings.

One of your authors once worked for a greedy shop owner who cheated many of his customers. This same man considered himself a pillar of the community and very religious. How did he justify to himself his greed and dishonesty? He believed that everyone who entered his store was bent on cheating *him* any way they could. In reality, few, if any, of his customers shared his motives, but he projected his own greed and dishonesty onto them.

Rationalization

Every teacher is familiar with this strange phenomenon: On the day of an exam, an incredible wave of disasters sweeps through the city. Mothers, fathers, sisters, brothers, aunts, uncles, grandparents, friends, relatives, and pets become ill or die. Motors suddenly fall out of cars. Books are lost or stolen. Alarm clocks go belly-up and ring no more.

The making of excuses comes from a natural tendency to explain our behavior. **Rationalization** refers to justifying personal actions by giving "rational" but false reasons for them. When the explanation you give for your behavior is reasonable and convincing—but not the real reason—you are *rationalizing.* For example, Violet failed to turn in an assignment made at the beginning of the semester in one of her classes. Here's the explanation she gave her professor:

> My car broke down 2 days ago, and I couldn't get to the library until yesterday. Then I couldn't get all the books I needed because some were checked out, but I wrote what I could. Then last night, as the last straw, the cartridge in my printer ran out, and since all the stores were closed, I couldn't finish the paper on time.

When asked why she left the assignment until the last minute (the real reason it was late), Violet offered another set of rationalizations. Like many people, Violet had difficulty seeing herself without the protection of her rationalizations.

All of the defense mechanisms described seem pretty undesirable. Do they have a positive side? People who overuse defense mechanisms become less adaptable, because they consume great amounts of emotional energy to control anxiety and maintain an unrealistic self-image. Defense mechanisms do have value, though. Often, they help keep us from being overwhelmed by immediate threats. This can provide time for a person to learn to cope in a more effective, problem-focused manner. If you recognize some of your own behavior in the descriptions here, it is hardly a sign that you are hopelessly defensive. As noted earlier, most people occasionally use defense mechanisms.

Two defense mechanisms that have a decidedly more positive quality are compensation and sublimation.

Compensation

Compensatory reactions are defenses against feelings of inferiority. A person who has a defect or weakness (real or imagined) may go to unusual lengths to overcome the weakness or to *compensate* for it by excelling in other areas. One of the pioneers of "pumping iron" in America is Jack LaLanne, who opened the first modern health spa in America. LaLanne made a successful career out of bodybuilding in spite of the fact that he was thin and sickly as a young man. Or perhaps it would be more accurate to say *because* he was thin and sickly.

There are dozens of examples of **compensation** at work. A childhood stutterer may excel in debate at college. As a child, Helen Keller was unable to see or hear, but she became an outstanding thinker and writer. Perhaps Ray Charles, Stevie Wonder, Andrea Bocelli, and other blind entertainers were drawn to music because of their handicap.

Sublimation

The defense called **sublimation** (sub-lih-MAY-shun) is defined as working off frustrated desires (especially sexual desires) through socially acceptable activities. Freud believed that art, music, dance, poetry, scientific investigation, and other creative activities could serve to rechannel sexual energies into productive behavior. Freud also felt that almost any strong desire could be sublimated. For example, a very aggressive person may find social acceptance as a professional soldier, boxer, or football player. Greed may be refined into a successful business career. Lying may be sublimated into storytelling, creative writing, or politics.

Scott Cunningham/Getty Images

For some players—and fans—football probably allows sublimation of aggressive urges. *Grand Theft Auto* and similar computer games may serve the same purpose.

Sexual motives appear to be the most easily and widely sublimated (Jacobs, 2003). Freud would have had a field day with such modern pastimes as surfing, motorcycle riding, drag racing, and dancing to or playing rock music, to name but a few. People enjoy each of these activities for a multitude of reasons, but it is hard to overlook the rich sexual symbolism apparent in each.

LEARNED HELPLESSNESS—IS THERE HOPE?

>SURVEY QUESTION< *What do we know about coping with feelings of helplessness and depression?*

What would happen if a person's defenses failed or if the person appraised a threatening situation as hopeless? Martin Seligman studied the case of a young marine who seemed to have adapted to the stresses of being held prisoner during the Vietnam War. The marine's health was related to a promise made by his captors: If he cooperated, they said, he would be released on a certain date. As the date approached, his spirits soared. Then came a devastating blow. He had been deceived. His captors had no intention of ever releasing him. He immediately lapsed into a deep depression, refused to eat or drink, and died shortly thereafter.

That seems like an extreme example. Does anything similar occur outside of concentration camps? Apparently so. For example, researchers in San Antonio, Texas, asked older people if they were hopeful about the future. Those who answered "No" died at elevated rates (Stern, Dhanda, & Hazuda, 2001).

To explain such patterns psychologists have focused on the concept of **learned helplessness,** an acquired inability to overcome obstacles and avoid aversive stimuli (Seligman, 1989). To observe learned helplessness, let's see what happens when animals are tested in a shuttle box (»Fig. 11.7). If placed in one side of a divided box, dogs will quickly learn to leap to the other side to escape an electric shock. If they are given a warning before the shock occurs (for example, a light that dims), most dogs learn to avoid the shock by leaping the barrier before the shock arrives. This is true of most dogs, but not those who have learned to feel helpless (Overmier & LoLordo, 1998).

Learned helplessness A learned inability to overcome obstacles or to avoid punishment; learned passivity and inaction to aversive stimuli.

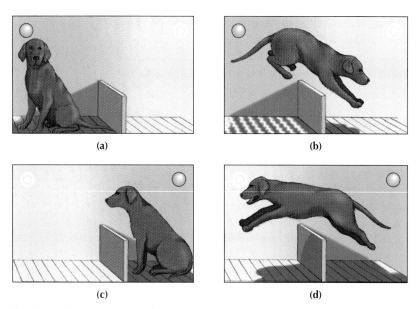

(a)   (b)

(c)   (d)

▸▸**FIGURE 11.7** In the normal course of escape and avoidance learning, a light dims shortly before the floor is electrified *(a)*. Because the light does not yet have meaning for the dog, the dog receives a shock (noninjurious, by the way) and leaps the barrier *(b)*. Dogs soon learn to watch for the dimming of the light *(c)* and to jump before receiving a shock *(d)*. Dogs made to feel "helpless" rarely even learn to escape shock, much less to avoid it.

How is a dog made to feel helpless? Before being tested in the shuttle box, a dog can be placed in a harness (from which the dog cannot escape) and then given several painful shocks. The animal is helpless to prevent these shocks. When placed in the shuttle box, dogs prepared this way react to the first shock by crouching, howling, and whining. None of them try to escape. They helplessly resign themselves to their fate. After all, they have already learned that there is nothing they can do about shock.

As the shuttle box experiments suggest, helplessness is a psychological state that occurs when events *appear to be uncontrollable* (Seligman, 1989). Helplessness also afflicts humans. It is a common reaction to repeated failure and to unpredictable or unavoidable punishment. A prime example is college students who feel helpless about their schoolwork. Such students tend to procrastinate, give up easily, and drop out of school (Perry, 2003).

Where humans are concerned, attributions (discussed in Chapter 9) have a large effect on helplessness. Persons who are made to feel helpless in one situation are more likely to act helpless in other situations if they attribute their failure to *lasting, general* factors. An example would be concluding "I must be stupid" after doing poorly on a test in a biology class. In contrast, attributing a low score to specific factors in the situation ("I'm not too good at the type of test my biology professor uses" or "I'm not very interested in biology") tends to prevent learned helplessness from spreading (Peterson & Vaidya, 2001).

Depression

Seligman and others have pointed out the similarities between learned helplessness and **depression.** Both are marked by feelings of despondency, powerlessness, and hopelessness. "Helpless" animals display decreased activity, lowered aggression, blunted appetite, and a loss of sex drive. Humans suffer from similar effects and also tend to see themselves as failing, even when they're not (LoLordo, 2001; Seligman, 1989).

Depression is one of the most widespread emotional problems, and it undoubtedly has many causes. However, learned helplessness seems to explain many cases of depression and hopelessness. For example, Seligman (1972) describes the fate of Archie, a 15-year-old boy. For Archie, school is an unending series of shocks and failures. Other students treat him as if he's stupid; in class he rarely answers questions because he doesn't know some of the

Depression A state of despondency marked by feelings of powerlessness and hopelessness.

words. He feels knocked down everywhere he turns. These may not be electric shocks, but they are certainly emotional "shocks," and Archie has learned to feel helpless to prevent them. When he leaves school his chances of success will be poor. He has learned to passively endure whatever shocks life has in store for him. Archie is not alone in this regard. Hopelessness is almost always a major element of depression (Ciarrochi, Dean, & Anderson, 2002).

Hope

Does Seligman's research give any clues about how to "unlearn" helplessness? With dogs, an effective technique is to forcibly drag them away from shock into the "safe" compartment. After this is done several times, the animals regain "hope" and feelings of control over the environment. Just how this can be done with humans is a question psychologists are exploring. It seems obvious, for instance, that someone like Archie would benefit from an educational program that would allow him to "succeed" repeatedly.

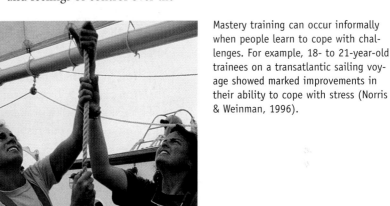

Mastery training can occur informally when people learn to cope with challenges. For example, 18- to 21-year-old trainees on a transatlantic sailing voyage showed marked improvements in their ability to cope with stress (Norris & Weinman, 1996).

In **mastery training,** responses are reinforced that lead to mastery of a threat or control over one's environment. Animals who undergo such training become more resistant to learned helplessness (Volpicelli et al., 1983). For example, animals that first learn to escape shock become more persistent in trying to flee inescapable shock. In effect, they won't give up, even when the situation really is "hopeless."

Such findings suggest that we might be able to "immunize" people against helplessness and depression by allowing them to master difficult challenges. The Outward Bound schools, in which people pit themselves against the rigors of mountaineering, white-water canoeing, and wilderness survival, might serve as a model for such a program.

The value of hope should not be overlooked. As fragile as this emotion seems to be, it is a powerful antidote to depression and helplessness. As an individual, you may find hope in religion, nature, human companionship, or even technology. Wherever you find it, remember its value: Hope is among the most important of all human emotions. Having positive beliefs, such as optimism, hope, and a sense of meaning and control is closely related to overall well-being (Taylor et al., 2003).

Depression: Why Students Get the Blues

During the school year, many college students suffer some symptoms of depression, which can exert a toll on academic performance. In one study, students diagnosed with depression scored half a grade point below nondepressed students (Hysenbegasi, Hass, & Rowland, 2005). Why do students get "blue"? Various problems contribute to depressive feelings. Here are some of the most common:

1. Stresses from college work and pressures to choose a career can leave students feeling that they are missing out on fun or that all their hard work is meaningless.
2. Isolation and loneliness are common when students leave their support groups behind. In the past, family, a circle of high school friends, and often a boyfriend or girlfriend could be counted on for support and encouragement.
3. Problems with studying and grades frequently trigger depression. Many students start college with high aspirations and little prior experience with failure. At the

Mastery training Reinforcement of responses that lead to mastery of a threat or control over one's environment.

same time, many lack basic skills necessary for academic success and are afraid of failure (Martin & Marsh, 2003).

4. Depression can be triggered by the breakup of an intimate relationship, either with a former boyfriend or girlfriend or with a newly formed college romance.
5. Students who find it difficult to live up to their idealized images of themselves are especially prone to depression (Scott & O'Hara, 1993).
6. An added danger is that depressed students are more likely to abuse alcohol, which is a depressant (Weitzman, 2004).

Recognizing Depression

Most people know, obviously enough, when they are "down." Aaron Beck, an authority on depression, suggests you should assume that more than a minor fluctuation in mood is involved when five conditions exist (Beck & Greenberg, 1974):

1. You have a consistently negative opinion of yourself.
2. You engage in frequent self-criticism and self-blame.
3. You place negative interpretations on events that usually wouldn't bother you.
4. The future looks bleak and negative.
5. You feel that your responsibilities are overwhelming.

What can be done to combat depression? Bouts of the college blues are closely related to stressful events. Learning to manage college work and to challenge self-critical thinking can help alleviate mild school-related depression. See "Coping with Depression" for some helpful suggestions.

Attacks of the college blues are common and should be distinguished from more serious cases of depression. Severe depression is a serious problem that can lead to suicide or a major impairment of emotional functioning. In such cases it would be wise to seek professional help.

Coping with Depression

If you don't do well on a test or a class assignment, how do you react? If you see it as a small, isolated setback, you probably won't feel too bad. However, if you feel like you have "blown it" in a big way, depression may follow. Students who strongly link everyday events to long-term goals (such as a successful career or high income) tend to overreact to day-to-day disappointments (McIntosh, Harlow, & Martin, 1995).

What does the preceding tell us about the college blues? The implication is that it's important to take daily tasks one step at a time and chip away at them. That way, you are less likely to feel overwhelmed, helpless, or hopeless. One classic suggestion comes from Aaron Beck and Ruth Greenberg (1974): when you feel "blue," you should make a *daily schedule* for yourself. Try to schedule activities to fill up every hour during the day. It is best to start with easy activities and progress to more difficult tasks. Check off each item as it is completed. That way, you will begin to break the self-defeating cycle of feeling helpless and falling further behind. (Depressed students spend much of their time sleeping.) A series of small accomplishments, successes, or pleasures may be all that you need to get going again. However, if you are lacking skills needed for success in college, ask for help in getting them. Don't remain "helpless."

Feelings of worthlessness and hopelessness are usually supported by self-critical or negative thoughts. Beck and Greenberg recommend writing down such thoughts as they occur, especially those that immediately precede feelings of sadness. After you have collected these thoughts, write a rational answer to each. For example, the thought "No one loves me" should be answered with a list of those who do care. (See Chapter 13 for more information.) One more point to keep in mind is this: When events begin to improve, try to accept it as a sign that better times lie ahead. Positive events are most likely to end depression if you view them as stable and continuing, rather than temporary and fragile (Needles & Abramson, 1990).

Study Break Defense Mechanisms, Helplessness, and Depression

Reflect

We tend to be blind to our own reliance on defense mechanisms. Return to the definitions in ■ Table 11.3 and see if you can think of one example of each defense that you have observed someone else using.

Have you ever felt helpless in a particular situation? What caused you to feel that way? Does any part of Seligman's description of learned helplessness match your own experience?

Imagine that a friend of yours is suffering from the college blues. What advice would you give your friend?

Learning Check

1. Fulfilling frustrated desires in imaginary achievements or activities defines the defense mechanism of

   a. compensation
   b. isolation
   c. fantasy
   d. sublimation

2. Of the defense mechanisms, two that are considered relatively constructive are

   a. compensation
   b. denial
   c. isolation
   d. projection
   e. regression
   f. rationalization
   g. sublimation

3. Depression in humans is similar to _____ _____ observed in animal experiments.

4. At any given time, more than one half of the college student population suffers symptoms of depression. T or F?

5. Frequent self-criticism and self-blame are a natural consequence of doing college work. T or F?

Critical Thinking

6. Learned helplessness is MOST closely related to which of the factors that determine the severity of stress?

Answers

1. c   2. a, g   3. learned helplessness   4. F   5. F   6. Feelings of incompetence and lack of control.

STRESS AND HEALTH—UNMASKING A HIDDEN KILLER

>SURVEY QUESTION< *How is stress related to health and disease?*

At the beginning of this chapter you read about Violet, a student who became ill after a stressful final exam period. As we saw earlier in this chapter, Violet's illness was probably not a coincidence.

What are some factors that influence the health risks we face? Disaster, depression, and sorrow often precede illness (Brannon & Feist, 2007). As Violet (our intrepid student) learned after finals week, stressful events reduce the body's natural defenses against disease. More surprising is the finding that *life changes*—both good and bad—can increase susceptibility to accidents or illness. Major changes in our surroundings or routines require us to be vigilant, on guard, and ready to react. Over long time periods, this can be quite stressful (Sternberg, 2000).

Life Events and Stress

How can I tell if I am subjecting myself to too much stress? Psychiatrist Thomas Holmes and graduate student Richard Rahe developed the first rating scale to estimate the health hazards we face when stresses add up (Holmes & Rahe, 1967). A version of the *Social Readjustment Rating Scale* (SRRS) is reprinted in ■ Table 11.4. Notice that the impact of life events is expressed in *life change units (LCUs)* (numerical values assigned to each life event).

Purestock/SuperStock

Marriage is usually a positive life event. Nevertheless, the many changes it brings can be stressful.

Social Readjustment Rating Scale (SRRS) A scale that rates the impact of various life events on the likelihood of illness.

■ **Table 11.4 Social Readjustment Rating Scale**

Rank	Life Event	Life Change Units	Rank	Life Event	Life Change Units
1	Death of spouse or child	119	22	Child leaving home	44
2	Divorce	98	23	Mortgage or loan greater than $10,000	44
3	Death of close family member	92	24	Change in responsibilities at work	43
4	Marital separation	79	25	Change in living conditions	42
5	Fired from work	79	26	Change in residence	41
6	Major personal injury or illness	77	27	Begin or end school	38
7	Jail term	75	28	Trouble with in-laws	38
8	Death of close friend	70	29	Outstanding personal achievement	37
9	Pregnancy	66	30	Change in work hours or conditions	36
10	Major business readjustment	62	31	Change in schools	35
11	Foreclosure on a mortgage or loan	61	32	Christmas	30
12	Gain of new family member	57	33	Trouble with boss	29
13	Marital reconciliation	57	34	Change in recreation	29
14	Change in health or behavior of family member	56	35	Mortgage or loan less than $10,000	28
			36	Change in personal habits	27
15	Change in financial state	56	37	Change in eating habits	27
16	Retirement	54	38	Change in social activities	27
17	Change to different line of work	51	39	Change in number of family get-togethers	26
18	Change in number of arguments with spouse	51	40	Change in sleeping habits	26
19	Marriage	50	41	Vacation	25
20	Spouse begins or ends work	46	42	Change in church activities	22
21	Sexual difficulties	45	43	Minor violations of the law	22

Source: Miller & Rahe, 1997; reproduced by permission.

As you read the scale, note again that positive life events may be as costly as disasters. Marriage rates 50 life change units, even though it is usually a happy event. You'll also see many items that read "Change in . . ." This means that an improvement in life conditions can be as costly as a decline. A stressful adjustment may be required in either case.

To use the scale shown in ■ Table 11.4, add up the LCUs for all life events you have experienced during the last year and compare the total to the following standards.

> 0–150: No significant problems
> 150–199: Mild life crisis (33 percent chance of illness)
> 200–299: Moderate life crisis (50 percent chance of illness)
> 300 or more: Major life crisis (80 percent chance of illness)

According to Holmes, there is a high chance of illness or accident when your LCU total exceeds 300 points. A more conservative rating of stress can be obtained by totaling LCU points for only the previous 6 months.

Many of the listed life changes don't seem relevant to young adults or college students. Does the SRRS apply to them? The SRRS tends to be more appropriate for older, more established adults. The health of college students is also affected by stressful events, such as entering college, changing majors, or the breakup of a steady relationship. (For a student-oriented rating of stress, see ■ Table 11.7 in the "Stress Management" section.)

Evaluation

People differ greatly in their reactions to the same event. For such reasons, the SRRS is at best a rough index of stress. Nevertheless, it's hard to ignore a classic study in which people were deliberately exposed to the virus that causes common colds. The results were nothing to sneeze at: If a person had a high stress score, she or he was much more likely to actually get a cold (Cohen et al., 1993). In view of such findings, a high LCU score should be taken seriously. If your score goes much over 300, an adjustment in your activities or lifestyle may be needed. Remember, "To be forewarned is to be forearmed."

The Hazards of Hassles

There must be more to stress than major life changes. Isn't there a link between ongoing stresses and health? In addition to having a direct impact, major life events spawn countless daily frustrations and irritations (Pillow, Zautra, & Sandler, 1996). Also, many of us face ongoing stresses at work or at home that do not involve major life changes (Pett & Johnson, 2005). Such minor but frequent stresses are called **hassles,** or **microstressors** (see ■ Table 11.5 for some examples of hassles faced by college students).

In a yearlong study, 100 men and women recorded the hassles they endured. Participants also reported on their physical and mental health. Frequent and severe hassles turned out to be better predictors of day-to-day health than major life events were. However, major life events did predict changes in health 1 or 2 years after the events took place. It appears that daily hassles are closely linked to immediate health and psychological well-being (Crowther et al., 2001). Major life changes have more of a long-term impact.

One way to guarantee that you will experience a large number of life changes and hassles is to live in a foreign culture. The discussion "Acculturative Stress" offers a brief glimpse into some of the consequences of culture shock.

What can be done about a high LCU score or feeling excessively hassled? A good response is to use stress management skills. For serious problems, stress management should be learned directly from a therapist or a stress clinic. When ordinary stresses are involved, there is much you can do on your own. An upcoming discussion of stress management will give you a start. In the meantime, take it easy!

Psychosomatic Disorders

As we have seen, chronic or repeated stress can damage physical health, as well as upset emotional well-being. Prolonged stress reactions are closely related to a large number of psychosomatic (SIKE-oh-so-MAT-ik) illnesses. In **psychosomatic disorders** (*psyche:* mind; *soma:* body), psychological factors contribute to actual bodily damage or to damaging changes in bodily functioning (Asmundson & Taylor, 2005). Psychosomatic problems, therefore, are *not* the same as hypochondria. **Hypochondriacs** (HI-po-KON-dree-aks) imagine that they have diseases. There is nothing imaginary about asthma, a migraine headache, or high blood pressure. Severe psychosomatic disorders can be fatal. The person who says, "Oh it's *just* psychosomatic" doesn't understand how serious stress-related diseases really are.

The most common psychosomatic problems are gastrointestinal and respiratory (stomach pain and asthma, for example), but many others exist. Typical problems include eczema (skin rash), hives, migraine headaches, rheumatoid arthritis, hypertension (high blood pressure), colitis (ulceration of the colon), and heart disease. Actually, these are only the major problems. Many lesser health complaints are also stress related. Typical examples include sore muscles, headaches, neckaches, backaches, indigestion, constipation, chronic diarrhea, fatigue, insomnia, premenstrual problems, and sexual dysfunctions (Taylor, 2006). For some of these problems biofeedback may be helpful. The next section explains how.

■ Table 11.5 **Examples of Common Hassles Faced by College Students**

Too many things to do
Not enough money for housing
Feeling discriminated against
People making gender jokes
Communication problems with friends
Driving to school
People making fun of my religion
Fear of losing valuables
Work schedule
Getting into shape
Parents' expectations

Source: Pett & Johnson, 2005

It is estimated that at least half of all patients who see a doctor have a psychosomatic disorder or an illness that is complicated by psychosomatic symptoms.

Dan McCoy/Rainbow

Hassle (Microstressor) Any distressing, day-to-day annoyance.

Psychosomatic disorders Illnesses in which psychological factors contribute to bodily damage or to damaging changes in bodily functioning.

Hypochondriac A person who complains about illnesses that appear to be imaginary.

HUMAN DIVERSITY

Acculturative Stress—Stranger in a Strange Land

Around the world, an increasing number of emigrants and refugees must adapt to dramatic changes in language, dress, values, and social customs. For many, the result is a period of culture shock or **acculturative stress** (stress caused by adapting to a foreign culture). Typical reactions to acculturative stress are anxiety, hostility, depression, alienation, physical illness, or identity confusion (Rummens, Beiser, & Noh, 2003). For many young immigrants, acculturative stress is a major source of mental health problems (Yeh, 2003).

The severity of acculturative stress is related, in part, to how a person adapts to a new culture. Four main patterns are (Berry, 1990; Berry et al., 2005):

Morton Beebe/Corbis

One of the best antidotes for acculturative stress is a society that tolerates or even celebrates ethnic diversity. Although some people find it hard to accept new immigrants, the fact is, nearly everyone's family tree includes people who were once strangers in a strange land.

Integration—maintain your old cultural identity but participate in the new culture

Separation—maintain your old cultural identity and avoid contact with the new culture

Assimilation—adopt the new culture as your own and have contact with its members

Marginalization—reject your old culture but suffer rejection by members of the new culture

To illustrate each pattern, let's consider a family that has immigrated to the United States from the imaginary country of Farlandia.

The father favors integration. He is learning English and wants to get involved in American life. At the same time, he is a leader in the Farlandian-American community and spends much of his leisure time with other Farlandian-Americans. His level of acculturative stress is low.

The mother only speaks Farlandish and only interacts with other Farlandian-Americans. She remains almost completely separate from American society. Her stress level is high.

The teenage daughter is annoyed by hearing Farlandish spoken at home, by her mother's serving only Farlandian food, and by having to spend her leisure time with her extended Farlandian family. She would prefer to speak English and to be with her American friends. Her desire to assimilate creates moderate stress.

The son doesn't particularly value his Farlandian heritage, yet his schoolmates reject him because he speaks with a Farlandian accent. He feels trapped between two cultures. His position is marginal and his stress level is high.

To summarize, those who feel marginalized tend to be highly stressed; those who seek to remain separate are also highly stressed; those who pursue integration into their new culture are minimally stressed; and those who assimilate are moderately stressed.

As you can see, integration and assimilation are the best options. However, a big benefit of assimilating is that people who embrace their new culture experience fewer social difficulties. For many, this justifies the stress of adopting new customs and cultural values (Ward & Rana-Deuba, 1999).

Biofeedback

Psychologists have discovered that people can learn to control bodily activities once thought to be involuntary. This is done by applying informational feedback to bodily control, a process called **biofeedback.** If I were to say to you, "Raise the temperature of your right hand," you probably couldn't, because you wouldn't know if you were succeeding. To make your task easier, we could attach a sensitive thermometer to your hand. The thermometer could be wired so that an increase in temperature would activate a signal light. Then, all you would have to do is try to keep the light on as much as possible. With practice and the help of biofeedback, you could learn to raise your hand temperature at will.

Biofeedback holds promise as a way to treat some psychosomatic problems (▸▸Fig. 11.8). For instance, people have been trained to prevent migraine headaches with biofeedback. Sensors are taped to patients' hands and foreheads. Patients then learn to redirect blood

Acculturative stress Stress caused by the many changes and adaptations required when a person moves to a foreign culture.

Biofeedback Information given to a person about his or her ongoing bodily activities; aids voluntary regulation of bodily states.

flow away from the head to their extremities. Because migraine headaches involve excessive blood flow to the head, biofeedback helps patients reduce the frequency of their headaches (Andrasik, 2003; Larsson et al., 2005).

Early successes led many to predict that biofeedback would offer a cure for psychosomatic illnesses, anxiety, phobias, drug abuse, and a long list of other problems. In reality, biofeedback has proved helpful, but not an instant cure (Schwartz & Andrasik, 2003). Biofeedback can help relieve muscle-tension headaches, migraine headaches, and chronic pain (Middaugh & Pawlick, 2002). It shows promise for lowering blood pressure and controlling heart rhythms (Rau, Bührer, & Weitkunat, 2003). The technique has been used with some success to control epileptic seizures and hyperactivity in children (Demos, 2005). Insomnia also responds to biofeedback therapy (Gathchel & Oordt, 2003).

How does biofeedback help? Some researchers believe that many of its benefits arise from *general relaxation.* Others stress that there is no magic in biofeedback itself. The method simply acts as a "mirror" to help a person perform tasks involving *self-regulation.* Just as a mirror does not comb your hair, biofeedback does not do anything by itself. It can, however, help people make desired changes in their behavior (Weems, 1998).

The Cardiac Personality

It would be a mistake to assume that stress is the sole cause of psychosomatic diseases. Genetic differences, organ weaknesses, and learned reactions to stress combine to do damage. Personality also enters the picture. As mentioned earlier, a general disease-prone personality type exists. To a degree, there are also "headache personalities," "asthma personalities," and so on. The best documented of such patterns is the "cardiac personality"—a person at high risk for heart disease.

Two cardiologists, Meyer Friedman and Ray Rosenman, offer a glimpse at how some people create stress for themselves. In a landmark study of heart problems, Friedman and Rosenman (1983) classified people as either **Type A personalities** (those who run a high risk of heart attack) or **Type B personalities** (those who are unlikely to have a heart attack). Then they did an 8-year follow-up, finding more than twice the rate of heart disease in Type A's than in Type B's.

Type A

What is the Type A personality like? Type A people are hard driving, ambitious, highly competitive, achievement oriented, and striving. Type A people believe that with enough effort they can overcome any obstacle, and they "push" themselves accordingly.

Perhaps the most telltale signs of a Type A personality are *time urgency* and chronic *anger* or *hostility.* Type A's seem to chafe at the normal pace of events. They hurry from one activity to another, racing the clock in self-imposed urgency. As they do, they feel a constant sense of frustration and anger. Feelings of anger and hostility, in particular, are strongly related to increased risk of heart attack (Boyle et al., 2004; Bunde & Suls, 2006). One study found that 15 percent of a group of 25-year-old doctors and lawyers who scored high on a hostility test were dead by

FIGURE 11.8 In biofeedback training bodily processes are monitored and processed electronically. A signal is then routed back to the patient through headphones, signal lights, or other means. This information helps the patient alter bodily activities not normally under voluntary control.

Individuals with Type A personalities feel a continuous sense of anger, irritation, and hostility.

Type A personality A personality type with an elevated risk of heart disease; characterized by time urgency, anger, and hostility.

Type B personality All personality types other than Type A; a low cardiac-risk personality.

■ Table 11.6 **Characteristics of the Type A Person**

Check the items that apply to you. Do you:

_____ Have a habit of explosively accentuating various key words in ordinary speech even when there is no need for such accentuation (I HATE it when you do THAT!)?

_____ Finish other persons' sentences for them?

_____ *Always* move, walk, and eat rapidly?

_____ Quickly skim reading material and prefer summaries or condensations of books?

_____ Become easily angered by slow-moving lines or traffic?

_____ Feel an impatience with the rate at which most events take place?

_____ Tend to be unaware of the details or beauty of your surroundings?

_____ Frequently strive to think of or do two or more things simultaneously?

_____ Almost always feel vaguely guilty when you relax, vacation, or do absolutely nothing for several days?

_____ Tend to evaluate your worth in quantitative terms (number of A's earned, amount of income, number of games won, and so forth)?

_____ Have nervous gestures or muscle twitches, such as grinding your teeth, clenching your fists, or drumming your fingers?

_____ Attempt to schedule more and more activities into less time and in so doing make fewer allowances for unforeseen problems?

_____ Frequently think about other things while talking to someone?

_____ Repeatedly take on more responsibilities than you can comfortably handle?

Source: Shortened and adapted from Friedman & Rosenman, 1983.

age 50. The most damaging pattern may occur in hostile persons who keep their anger "bottled up." Such people seethe with anger, but don't express it outwardly. This increases their pulse rate and blood pressure and puts a tremendous strain on the heart (Bongard, al'Absi, & Lovallo, 1998).

To summarize, there is growing evidence that anger or hostility may be the core lethal factor of Type A behavior (Krantz & McCeney, 2002; Niaura et al., 2002). To date, hundreds of studies have supported the validity of the Type A concept. In view of this, Type A's would be wise to take their increased health risks seriously.

How are Type A people identified? Characteristics of Type A people are summarized in the short self-identification test presented in ■ Table 11.6. If most of the list applies to you, you might be a Type A. However, confirmation of your type would require more powerful testing methods. Also, remember that the original definition of Type A behavior was probably too broad. The key psychological factors that increase heart disease risk appear to be anger, hostility, and mistrust (Krantz & McCeney, 2002; Smith et al., 2004). Also, although Type A behavior appears to promote heart disease, depression or distress may be what finally triggers a heart attack (Denollet & Van Heck, 2001; Dinan, 2001).

Because our society places a premium on achievement, competition, and mastery, it is not surprising that many people develop Type A personalities. The best way to avoid the self-made stress this causes is to adopt behavior that is the opposite of that listed in ■ Table 11.6 (Williams, Barefoot, & Schneiderman, 2003).

People who frequently feel angry and hostile toward others may benefit from the advice of Redford Williams (1989), a leading expert on Type A behavior. According to

Williams, reducing hostility involves three goals. First, you must stop mistrusting the motives of others. Second, you must find ways to reduce how often you feel anger, indignation, irritation, and rage. Third, you must learn to be kinder and more considerate. It is entirely possible to succeed in life without sacrificing your health or happiness in the process.

Hardy Personality

How do Type A people who do not develop heart disease differ from those who do? Psychologist Salvatore Maddi has studied people who have a **hardy personality.** Such people seem to be unusually resistant to stress. The first study of hardiness began with two groups of managers at a large utility company. All of the managers held high-stress positions. Yet, some tended to get sick after stressful events, whereas others were rarely ill. How did the people who were thriving differ from their "stressed-out" colleagues? Both groups seemed to have traits typical of the Type A personality, so that wasn't the explanation. They were also quite similar in most other respects. The main difference was that the hardy group seemed to hold a worldview that consisted of three traits (Maddi, 2006):

1. They had a sense of personal *commitment* to self, work, family, and other stabilizing values.
2. They felt that they had *control* over their lives and their work.
3. They had a tendency to see life as a series of *challenges,* rather than as a series of threats or problems.

How do such traits protect people from the effects of stress? Persons strong in *commitment* find ways of turning whatever they are doing into something that seems interesting and important. They tend to get involved rather than feeling alienated.

Persons strong in *control* believe that they can more often than not influence the course of events around them. This prevents them from passively seeing themselves as victims of circumstance.

Finally, people strong in *challenge* find fulfillment in continual growth. They seek to learn from their experiences, rather than accepting easy comfort, security, and routine (Maddi, 2006). Indeed, many "negative" experiences can actually enhance personal growth—if you have support from others and the skills needed to cope with challenge (Armeli, Gunthert, & Cohen, 2001).

Positive Psychology: Hardiness and Happiness

Good and bad events occur in all lives. What separates happy people from those who are unhappy is largely a matter of attitude. Happy people tend to see their lives in more positive terms, even when trouble comes their way. For example, happier people tend to find humor in disappointments. They look at setbacks as challenges. They are strengthened by losses (Lyubomirsky & Tucker, 1998). In short, happiness tends to be related to hardiness (Maddi, 2006). Why is there a connection? As psychologist Barbara Fredrickson has pointed out, positive emotions tend to broaden our mental focus. Emotions such as joy, interest, and contentment create an urge to play, to be creative, to explore, to savor life, to seek new experiences, to integrate, and to grow. When you are stressed, experiencing positive emotions can make it more likely that you will find creative solutions to your problems. Positive emotions also tend to reduce the bodily arousal that occurs when we are stressed, possibly limiting stress-related damage (Fredrickson, 2003).

The work we have reviewed here has drawn new attention to the fact that each of us has a personal responsibility for maintaining and promoting health. In the discussion that follows, we will look at what you can do to better cope with stress. But first, the following questions may help you maintain a healthy grade on your next psychology test.

Hardy personality A personality style associated with superior stress resistance.

Study Break Stress and Health

Reflect

Use the SRRS to find your LCU score for the past year. Do you think there is a connection between your LCU score and your health? Or have you observed more of a connection between microstressors and your health?

Suppose you moved to a foreign country. How much acculturative stress do you think you would face? Which pattern of adaptation do you think you would adopt?

Mindy complains about her health all the time, but she actually seems to be just fine. An acquaintance of Mindy's dismisses her problems by saying, "Oh, she's not really sick. It's just psychosomatic." What's wrong with this use of the term *psychosomatic?*

Do you think you are basically a Type A or a Type B personality? To what extent do you possess traits of the hardy personality?

Learning Check

1. Holmes's SRRS appears to predict long-range changes in health, whereas the frequency and severity of daily microstressors is closely related to immediate ratings of health. T or F?

2. Ulcers, migraine headaches, and hypochondria are all frequently psychosomatic disorders. T or F?

3. Which of the following is *not* classified as a psychosomatic disorder?

   a. hypertension   b. colitis
   c. eczema   d. thymus

4. Two major elements of biofeedback training appear to be relaxation and self-regulation. T or F?

5. Evidence suggests that the most important feature of the Type A personality is a sense of time urgency rather than feelings of anger and hostility. T or F?

6. A sense of commitment, challenge, and control characterizes the hardy personality. T or F?

Critical Thinking

7. People with a hardy personality type appear to be especially resistant to which of the problems discussed earlier in this chapter?

Answers

1. T 2. F 3. d 4. T 5. F 6. T 7. Learned helplessness.

STRESS MANAGEMENT—WINNING THE STRESS GAME

>SURVEY QUESTION< *What are the best strategies for managing stress?*

Stress management is the use of behavioral strategies to reduce stress and improve coping skills. As promised, this section describes strategies for managing stress. Before you continue reading, you may want to assess your level of stress again, this time using a scale developed for undergraduate students. (See ▪ Table 11.7.) Like the SRRS, high scores on the *College Life Stress Inventory* suggest that you have been exposed to health-threatening levels of stress (Renner & Mackin, 1998).

The *College Life Stress Inventory* is scored by adding the ratings for all of the items that have happened to you in the last year. The following scale is an approximate guide to the meaning of your score. But remember, stress is an internal state. If you are good at coping with stressors, a high score may not be a problem for you.

> 0–150: Very low
> 151–590: Low
> 591–1030: Below average
> 1031–1470: Average
> 1471–1910: High
> 1911–2350: Very high
> 2351 or more: Extremely high

Stress management The application of behavioral strategies to reduce stress and improve coping skills.

Now that you have a picture of your current level of stress, what can you do about it? The simplest way of coping with stress is to modify or remove its source—by leaving a stressful job, for example. Obviously this is often impossible, which is why learning to manage stress is so important.

■ Table 11.7 College Life Stress Inventory

Circle the "stress rating" number for any item that has happened to you in the last year, then add them.

Event	Stress Rating	Event	Stress Rating
Being raped	100	Talking in front of a class	72
Finding out that you are HIV-positive	100	Lack of sleep	69
Being accused of rape	98	Change in housing situation (hassles, moves)	69
Death of a close friend	97	Competing or performing in public	69
Death of a close family member	96	Getting in a physical fight	66
Contracting a sexually transmitted disease (other than AIDS)	94	Difficulties with a roommate	66
		Job changes (applying, new job, work hassles)	65
Concerns about being pregnant	91	Declaring a major or concerns about future plans	65
Finals week	90	A class you hate	62
Concerns about your partner being pregnant	90	Drinking or use of drugs	61
Oversleeping for an exam	89	Confrontations with professors	60
Flunking a class	89	Starting a new semester	58
Having a boyfriend or girlfriend cheat on you	85	Going on a first date	57
Ending a steady dating relationship	85	Registration	55
Serious illness in a close friend or family member	85	Maintaining a steady dating relationship	55
Financial difficulties	84	Commuting to campus or work, or both	54
Writing a major term paper	83	Peer pressures	53
Being caught cheating on a test	83	Being away from home for the first time	53
Drunk driving	82	Getting sick	52
Sense of overload in school or work	82	Concerns about your appearance	52
Two exams in one day	80	Getting straight A's	51
Cheating on your boyfriend or girlfriend	77	A difficult class that you love	48
Getting married	76	Making new friends; getting along with friends	47
Negative consequences of drinking or drug use	75	Fraternity or sorority rush	47
Depression or crisis in your best friend	73	Falling asleep in class	40
Difficulties with parents	73	Attending an athletic event (e.g., football game)	20

Source: Renner & Mackin, 1998.

As shown in ▸ Figure 11.9, stress triggers *bodily effects, upsetting thoughts,* and *ineffective behavior.* Also shown is the fact that each element worsens the others in a vicious cycle. Indeed, the basic idea of the "Stress Game" is that once it begins, *you lose*—unless you take action to break the cycle. The information that follows tells how.

Managing Bodily Reactions

Much of the immediate discomfort of stress is caused by fight-or-flight emotional responses. The body is ready to act, with tight muscles and a pounding heart. If action is prevented, we merely remain "uptight." A sensible remedy is to learn a reliable, drug-free way of relaxing.

Exercise

Stress-based arousal can be dissipated by using the body. Any full-body exercise can be effective. Swimming, dancing, jumping rope, yoga, most sports, and especially walking are valuable outlets. Regular exercise alters hormones, circulation, muscle tone, and a number of other aspects of physical functioning. Together, such changes can reduce anxiety and lower the risks for disease (Linden, 2005; Salmon, 2001).

Be sure to choose activities that are vigorous enough to relieve tension, yet enjoyable enough to be done repeatedly. Exercising for stress management is most effective when it is done daily. As little as 30 minutes of total exercise per day, even if it occurs in short 10 to 20 minute sessions, can improve mood and energy (Hansen, Stevens, & Coast, 2001).

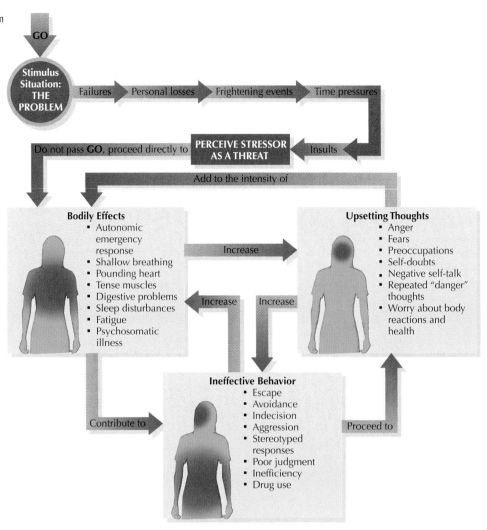

►►**FIGURE 11.9** The Stress Game. (Adapted from Rosenthal and Rosenthal, 1980.)

Meditation

Many stress counselors recommend *meditation* for quieting the body and promoting relaxation. Meditation and its effects were discussed in Chapter 5. For now, it is enough to state that meditation is easy to learn—taking an expensive commercial course is unnecessary.

Meditation is one of the most effective ways to relax (Deckro et al., 2002). But be aware that listening to or playing music, taking nature walks, enjoying hobbies, and the like can be meditations of sorts. Anything that reliably interrupts upsetting thoughts and promotes relaxation can be helpful.

Progressive Relaxation

It is possible to relax systematically, completely, and by choice. To learn the details of how this is done, consult Chapter 13 of this book. The basic idea of **progressive relaxation** is to tighten all the muscles in a given area of your body (the arms, for instance) and then voluntarily relax them. By first tensing and relaxing each area of the body, you can learn what muscle tension feels like. Then when each area is relaxed, the change is more noticeable and more controllable. In this way it is possible, with practice, to greatly reduce tension.

Guided Imagery

In a technique called **guided imagery,** people visualize images that are calming, relaxing, or beneficial in other ways. Relaxation, for instance, can be promoted by visualizing peaceful scenes. Pick several places where you feel safe, calm, and at ease. Typical locations

Progressive relaxation A method for producing deep relaxation of all parts of the body.

Guided imagery Intentional visualization of images that are calming, relaxing, or beneficial in other ways.

might be a beach or lake, the woods, floating on an air mattress in a warm pool, or lying in the sun at a quiet park. To relax, vividly imagine yourself in one of these locations. In the visualized scene, you should be alone and in a comfortable position. It is important to visualize the scene as realistically as possible. Try to feel, taste, smell, hear, and see what you would actually experience in the calming scene. Practice forming such images several times a day for about 5 minutes each time. When your scenes become familiar and detailed they can be used to reduce anxiety and encourage relaxation (Rosenthal, 1993). Remember, too, that imagining that a supportive friend or a loving pet is nearby can reduce tension and anxiety (Allen, Blascovich, & Mendes, 2002; Smith, Ruiz, & Uchino, 2004).

Modifying Ineffective Behavior

Stress is often made worse by our misguided responses to it. The following suggestions may help you deal with stress more effectively.

Slow Down

Remember that stress can be self-generated. Try to deliberately do things at a slower pace—especially if your pace has speeded up over the years. Tell yourself, "What counts most is not if I get there first, but if I get there at all" or "My goal is distance, not speed."

Organize

Disorganization creates stress. Try to take a fresh look at your situation and get organized. Setting priorities can be a real stress fighter. Ask yourself what's really important and concentrate on the things that count. Learn to let go of trivial but upsetting irritations. And above all, when you are feeling stressed, remember to K.I.S.: **K**eep **I**t **S**imple. (Some people prefer K.I.S.S.: Keep It Simple, Stupid.)

Strike a Balance

Work, school, family, friends, interests, hobbies, recreation, community, church—there are many important elements in a satisfying life. Damaging stress often comes from letting one element—especially work or school—get blown out of proportion. Your goal should be quality in life, not quantity. Try to strike a balance between challenging "good stress" and relaxation. Remember, when you are "doing nothing" you are actually doing something very important: Set aside time for "me acts" such as loafing, browsing, puttering, playing, and napping.

Recognize and Accept Your Limits

Many of us set unrealistic and perfectionist goals. Given that no one can ever be perfect, this attitude leaves many people feeling inadequate, no matter how well they have performed. Set gradual, achievable goals for yourself. Also, set realistic limits on what you try to do on any given day. Learn to say no to added demands or responsibilities.

Seek Social Support

Social support (close, positive relationships with others) facilitates good health and morale (Manne, 2003). People with close, supportive relationships have better immune responses and better health (Kiecolt-Glaser et al., 2002). Apparently, support from family and friends serves as a buffer to cushion the impact of stressful events.

Women tend to make better use of social support than men do. Women who are stressed seek support and they nurture others. Men are more likely to become aggressive or to withdraw emotionally (Taylor et al., 2000). This may be why "manly men" won't ask for help, whereas women in trouble call their friends! Where stress is concerned, many men could benefit from adopting women's tendency to tend and befriend others.

Social support Close, positive relationships with other people.

How else might social support help? Most people share positive events, such as marriages, births, graduations, and birthdays, with others. When things go well, we like to tell others. Sharing such events tends to amplify positive emotions and to further increase social support. In many ways, the sharing of good news is an important means by which positive events contribute to individual well-being (Gable et al., 2004).

Write about Your Feelings

If you don't have someone you can talk to about stressful events, you might try expressing your thoughts and feelings in writing. Several studies have found that students who write about their upsetting experiences, thoughts, and feelings are better able to cope with stress. They also experience fewer illnesses, and they get better grades (Pennebaker, 2004; Sterling et al., 1999). Writing about your feelings tends to leave your mind clearer. This makes it easier to pay attention to life's challenges and come up with effective coping strategies (Klein & Boals, 2001a, b). Thus, after you write about your feelings, it helps to make specific plans for coping with upsetting experiences (Cameron & Nicholls, 1998).

As an alternative, you might want to try writing about positive experiences. In one study, college students who wrote about intensely positive experiences had fewer illnesses over the next 3 months. Writing for just 20 minutes a day for 3 days improved the students' moods and had a surprisingly long-lasting effect on their health (Burton & King, 2004).

Avoiding Upsetting Thoughts

Assume you are taking a test. Suddenly you realize that you are running short of time. If you say to yourself, "Oh no, this is terrible, I've blown it now," your body's response will probably be sweating, tenseness, and a knot in your stomach. On the other hand, if you say, "I should have watched the time, but getting upset won't help, I'll just take one question at a time," your stress level will be much lower.

As stated earlier, stress is greatly affected by the views we take of events. Physical symptoms and a tendency to make poor decisions are increased by negative thoughts or "self-talk." In many cases what you say to yourself can be the difference between coping and collapsing (Matheny et al., 1996).

Coping Statements

Psychologist Donald Meichenbaum has popularized a technique called **stress inoculation.** In it, clients learn to fight fear and anxiety with an internal monologue of positive coping statements. First, clients learn to identify and monitor **negative self-statements** (self-critical thoughts that increase anxiety). Negative thoughts are a problem because they tend to directly elevate physical arousal. To counter this effect, clients learn to replace negative statements with coping statements from a supplied list. Eventually they are encouraged to make their own lists (Saunders et al., 1996).

How are coping statements applied? **Coping statements** are reassuring and self-enhancing. They are used to block out, or counteract, negative self-talk in stressful situations. Before giving a short speech, for instance, you would replace "I'm scared," "I can't do this," "My mind will go blank and I'll panic," or "I'll sound stupid and boring" with "I'll give my speech on something I like," or "I'll breathe deeply before I start my speech," or "My pounding heart just means I'm psyched up to do my best." Additional examples of coping statements follow.

Preparing for Stressful Situation
I'll just take things one step at a time.
If I get nervous I'll just pause a moment.
Tomorrow I'll be through it.
I've managed to do this before.
What exactly do I have to do?

Stress inoculation Use of positive coping statements to control fear and anxiety.

Negative self-statements Self-critical thoughts that increase anxiety and lower performance.

Coping statements Reassuring, self-enhancing statements that are used to stop self-critical thinking.

Confronting the Stressful Situation
Relax now, this can't really hurt me.
Stay organized, focus on the task.
There's no hurry, take it step by step.
Nobody's perfect, I'll just do my best.
It will be over soon, just be calm.

Meichenbaum cautions that saying the "right" things to yourself may not be enough to improve stress tolerance. You must practice this approach in actual stress situations. Also, it is important to develop your own personal list of coping statements by finding what works for you. Ultimately, the value of learning this, and other stress management skills, ties back into the idea that much stress is self-generated. Knowing that you can manage a demanding situation is in itself a major antidote for stress. In a recent study, college students who learned stress inoculation not only had less anxiety and depression, but better self-esteem, as well (Schiraldi & Brown, 2001).

Lighten Up

Humor is worth cultivating as a way to reduce stress. A good sense of humor can lower your distress/stress reaction to difficult events (Lefcourt, 2003). In addition, an ability to laugh at life's ups and downs is associated with better immunity to disease (McClelland & Cheriff, 1997). Don't be afraid to laugh at yourself and at the many ways in which we humans make things difficult for ourselves. You've probably heard the following advice about everyday stresses: "Don't sweat the small stuff," and "It's all small stuff." Humor is one of the best antidotes for anxiety and emotional distress because it helps put things into perspective (Henman, 2001; Szabo, 2003). The vast majority of events are only as stressful as you allow them to be. Have some fun. It's perfectly healthy.

A Look Ahead

The ideas we have reviewed here make it clear that each of us has a personal responsibility for maintaining and promoting health. In the Psychology in Action section that follows, we will return to the topic of unsafe sex. This is one risk factor that can be almost completely eliminated by relatively small changes in behavior.

 Study Break   Coping with Stress

Reflect

If you were going to put together a "tool kit" for stress management, what items would you include?

Learning Check

1. Exercise, meditation, and progressive relaxation are considered effective ways of countering negative self-statements. T or F?
2. Research shows that social support from family and friends has little effect on the health consequences of stress. T or F?
3. One element of stress inoculation is training in the use of positive coping statements. T or F?

4. People who write about their feelings tend to dwell on stressful events, which reduces their ability to meet life challenges. T or F?

Critical Thinking

5. Steve always feels extremely pressured when the due date arrives for his major term papers. How could he reduce stress in such instances?

Answers

1. F 2. F 3. T 4. F 5. The stress associated with doing term papers can be almost completely eliminated by breaking up a long-term assignment into many small daily or weekly assignments. Students who habitually procrastinate are often amazed at how pleasant college work can be once they renounce "brinkmanship" (pushing things off to the limits of tolerance).

Psychology in Action

STDs and Safer Sex—Choice, Risk, and Responsibility

>SURVEY QUESTION< *How can sexually transmitted diseases be prevented?*

In general, most adults favor greater freedom of choice for themselves, including choice about sexual behavior. Yet, there is some ambivalence toward greater sexual freedom. As the upcoming discussion of AIDS suggests, there are new and compelling reasons for caution in sexual behavior.

Sexually Transmitted Diseases

A **sexually transmitted disease (STD)** is an infection passed from one person to another by intimate physical contact. Sexually active people run a higher risk of getting chlamydia (klah-MID-ee-ah), gonorrhea, hepatitis B, herpes, syphilis, and other STDs. Many people who carry STDs remain *asymptomatic* (a-SIMP-teh-mat-ik: lacking obvious symptoms). It is easy to have an infection without knowing it. Likewise, it is often impossible to tell if a sexual partner is infectious. Thus, risky sex is a serious hazard. A recent study of sexually active teenage girls engaging in risky sex is a case in point. Nearly 90 percent of the girls thought that they had virtually no chance of getting an STD. In reality, over the next 18 months 1 in 4 got chlamydia or gonorrhea (Ethier et al., 2003).

The AIDS Memorial Quilt was begun in 1985 to commemorate those who have died from AIDS. Today, the quilt has grown to immense size, symbolizing the extent of the AIDS epidemic. Originally the quilt memorialized only homosexual victims. It now includes heterosexual men, women, and children, signifying that AIDS respects no boundaries.

Leonard Lessin/Photo Researchers, Inc.

A major problem is the fact that people who are sexually active may have indirect contact with many other people. One study of sexual relationships at a high school in a Midwestern city found long chains of sexual contact between students. Thus, a student at the end of the chain might have had sex with only one person, but in reality she or he had indirect contact with dozens or even hundreds of others (Bearman, Moody, & Stovel, 2004).

For many sexually active people, the human immunodeficiency virus (HIV) has added a new threat. HIV is a sexually transmitted disease that disables the immune system. Whereas most other STDs are treatable, HIV infections can be lethal. Check your knowledge about HIV against the following summary.

HIV/AIDS

Acquired immune deficiency syndrome (AIDS) is caused by an HIV infection. As the immune system weakens, other "opportunistic" diseases invade the body. Most AIDS victims eventually die of multiple infections (although newer multidrug therapies have greatly improved the odds of survival). The first symptoms of AIDS may show up as little as 2 months after infection, but they typically don't appear for 10 years. Because of this long incubation period, infected persons often pass the AIDS virus on to others without knowing it. Medical testing can detect an HIV infection. However, for at least the first 6 months after becoming infected, a person can test negative while carrying the virus. A negative test result, therefore, is no guarantee that a person is a "safe" sex partner.

Sexually transmitted disease (STD) A disease that is typically passed from one person to the next by intimate physical contact; a venereal disease.

HIV infections are spread by direct contact with body fluids—especially blood, semen, and vaginal secretions. The AIDS virus cannot be transmitted by casual contact. People do not get AIDS from shaking hands, touching or using objects touched by an AIDS patient, eating food prepared by an infected person, or from social kissing, sweat or tears, sharing drinking glasses, sharing towels, and so forth.

HIV can be spread by all forms of sexual intercourse, and it has affected persons of all sexual orientations. Recently, the AIDS epidemic has spread more quickly among heterosexuals, women, African Americans, Hispanics, and children (Taylor-Seehafer & Rew, 2000). Among 13- to 19-year-olds, two thirds of new HIV cases are female ("HIV/AIDS," 2004). HIV infection is the leading cause of death among women and men between the ages of 25 and 44 (Gayle, 2000). Worldwide, 3 million people die each year from HIV/AIDS and 5 million new infections occur.

Behavioral Risk Factors

Sexually active people can do much to protect their own health. The behaviors listed here are risky when performed with an infected person.

Risky Behaviors
- Sharing drug needles and syringes
- Anal sex, with or without a condom
- Vaginal or oral sex with someone who injects drugs or engages in anal sex
- Sex with someone you don't know well, or with someone you know has had several partners
- Unprotected sex (without a condom) with an infected partner
- Having two or more sex partners (additional partners further increase the risk)

In the United States, between 2 and 4 of every 100 adults put themselves at high risk by engaging in the behaviors just listed (Gayle, 2000).

It's important to remember that you can't tell from appearance if a person is infected. Many people would be surprised to learn that their partners have engaged in behavior that places them both at risk (Seal & Palmer-Seal, 1996).

The preceding high-risk behaviors can be contrasted with the following list of safer sexual practices. Note, however, that unless a person completely abstains, sex can be made safer, but not risk-free.

Safer Sex Practices
- Not having sex
- Sex with one mutually faithful, uninfected partner
- Not injecting drugs
- Discussing contraception with partner
- Being selective regarding sexual partners
- Reducing the number of sexual partners
- Discussing partner's sexual health prior to engaging in sex
- Not engaging in sex while intoxicated
- Using a condom

Sexually active persons should practice safer sex until their partner's sexual history and/ or health has been clearly established. It is unwise to count on a sexual partner for protection against HIV infection or any STD, for that matter. Over the next 15 years 65 million more people will die of AIDS unless prevention efforts are greatly expanded (Altman, 2002). Regardless, a study of heterosexually active adults found that 62 percent did not practice safer sex with their last partner. Most of these "gamblers" knew too little about their partners to be assured that they were not taking a big risk. The most common excuses they gave for engaging in risky sex were (Kusseling et al., 1996):

Reasons for Not Having Safer Sex	Percentage Giving Excuse
Condom not available	20
Didn't want to use a condom	19
"Couldn't stop ourselves"	15
Partner didn't want to use a condom	14
Alcohol or drug use	11

One chilling study of HIV patients—who knew they were infectious—found that 41 percent of those who were sexually active did not always use condoms (Sobel et al., 1996)! Thus, responsibility for "safer sex" rests with each sexually active person. And remember, a condom offers little or no protection if it is misused. Sadly, 1 of 3 sexually active teens don't know how to use a condom correctly (and virgins of both sexes are even more clueless) (Crosby & Yarber, 2001).

Isn't it possible that practicing safer sex would be interpreted as a sign that you mistrust your lover? Actually, taking precautions could, instead, be defined as a way of showing that you really care about the welfare of your partner. As is the case with other behavioral risk factors, it's certainly a way of showing that you care about your own health.

→ Study Break   STDs and Safer Sex

Reflect

As a counselor, you are working with a young person who seems to be sexually active. What can you tell this person about STDs and safer sex practices?

Learning Check

1. For at least the first 6 months after becoming infected with HIV, a person can test negative while carrying the virus. T or F?
2. Because HIV is spread by direct contact with body fluids, it can be transmitted by social kissing or contact with food or dishes handled by an AIDS patient. T or F?

3. In the United States, at least 2 of every 100 adults engage in high risk sexual behavior. T or F?
4. If people know they have STDs, it is extremely rare for them to engage in unprotected sex. T or F?

Critical Thinking

5. Of the following reasons that teenage boys and girls give for engaging in sex: love, curiosity, sexual gratification, peer pressure, and "everyone's doing it," which do you think they rank first, and which last?

Answers

1. T 2. F 3. T 4. F 5. Peer pressure ranks first (cited by 30 percent of those surveyed) and love ranked last (cited by 8 percent) ("Teen sex," 1989).

CHAPTER IN REVIEW

Major Points

- A variety of personal habits and behavior patterns affect health.
- Maintaining good health is a personal responsibility, not a matter of luck. Wellness is based on minimizing risk factors and engaging in health-promoting behaviors.
- Stress is a normal part of life; however, it is also a major risk factor for illness and disease.
- Although some events are more stressful than others, stress always represents an interaction between people and the environments in which they live.

- Personality characteristics affect the amount of stress a person experiences and the subsequent risk of illness.
- The body's reactions to stress can directly damage internal organs and stress impairs the body's immune system, increasing susceptibility to disease.
- The damaging effects of stress can be reduced with stress management techniques.

Summary

What is health psychology? How does behavior affect health?

- Health psychologists are interested in behavior that helps maintain and promote health.
- Studies of health and illness have identified a number of behavioral risk factors and health-promoting behaviors.
- Health psychologists have pioneered efforts to prevent the development of unhealthy habits and to improve well-being through community health campaigns.

What is stress? What factors determine its severity?

- Stress occurs when demands are placed on an organism to adjust or adapt.
- The body reacts to stress in a series of stages called the general adaptation syndrome (G.A.S.).
- The stages of the G.A.S. are alarm, resistance, and exhaustion. The G.A.S. appears to explain how psychosomatic disorders develop.
- Studies of psychoneuroimmunology show that stress also lowers the body's immunity to disease.
- Stress is more damaging in situations involving pressure, a lack of control, unpredictability of the stressor, and intense or repeated emotional shocks.
- Stress is intensified when a situation is perceived as a threat and when a person does not feel competent to cope with it.
- In work settings, prolonged stress can lead to burnout.
- The primary appraisal of a situation greatly affects our emotional response to it.
- During a secondary appraisal, a problem-focused or emotion-focused way of coping is selected.

What causes frustration and what are typical reactions to it?

- Frustration is the negative emotional state that occurs when progress toward a goal is blocked.
- External frustrations are based on delay, failure, rejection, loss, and other direct blocking of motives. Personal frustration is related to personal characteristics over which one has little control.
- Frustrations of all types become more intense as the strength, urgency, or importance of the blocked motive increases.
- Major behavioral reactions to frustration include persistence, more vigorous responding, circumvention, direct aggression, displaced aggression (including scapegoating), and escape or withdrawal.

Are there different types of conflict? How do people react to conflict?

- Conflict occurs when one must choose between contradictory alternatives.
- Five major types of conflict are approach-approach, avoidance-avoidance, approach-avoidance, double approach-avoidance, and multiple approach-avoidance.
- Approach-approach conflicts are usually the easiest to resolve.
- Avoidance conflicts are difficult to resolve and are characterized by inaction, indecision, freezing, and a desire to escape.
- People usually remain in approach-avoidance conflicts, but fail to fully resolve them, which leads to ambivalence and partial approach.
- Vacillation is a common reaction to double approach-avoidance conflicts.

What are defense mechanisms?

- Anxiety, threat, or feelings of inadequacy frequently lead to the use of defense mechanisms that reduce anxiety.
- Many defense mechanisms have been identified, including compensation, denial, fantasy, intellectualization, isolation, projection, rationalization, reaction formation, regression, repression, and sublimation.

What do we know about coping with feelings of helplessness and depression?

- Learned helplessness has been used as a model for understanding depression. Mastery training acts as an antidote to helplessness.
- Depression is a major, and surprisingly common, emotional problem. Actions and thoughts that reverse feelings of helplessness tend to reduce depression.
- The college blues are a relatively mild form of depression. Learning to manage college work and to challenge self-critical thinking can help cure the college blues.

How is stress related to health and disease?

- Work with the *Social Readjustment Rating Scale* indicates that multiple life changes tend to increase long-range susceptibility to accident or illness.
- Immediate psychological and mental health is more closely related to the intensity and severity of daily hassles (microstressors).
- Intense or prolonged stress may cause damage in the form of psychosomatic problems.
- During biofeedback training, bodily processes are monitored and converted to a signal that tells what

the body is doing. This allows people to control some bodily activities and alleviate some psychosomatic illnesses.

- People with Type A personalities are competitive, striving, hostile, and impatient. These characteristics—especially hostility—double the risk of heart attack.
- People who have traits of the hardy personality seem to be unusually resistant to stress.

What are the best strategies for managing stress?

- A sizable number of coping skills can be applied to manage stress. Most of these focus on one of three areas: bodily effects, ineffective behavior, and upsetting thoughts.

How can sexually transmitted diseases be prevented?

- Many sexually active people continue to take unnecessary risks with their health by failing to follow safer sex practices.
- Safe-sex practices help protect your own health and they show that you care about the welfare of your partner.

Interactive Learning

Internet addresses frequently change. To find the sites listed here, visit www.thomsonedu/psychology/coon for an updated list of Internet addresses and direct links to relevant sites.

Psychology: A Journey **Companion Website** Find online quizzes, flash cards, animations, video clips, experiments, interactive assessments, and other helpful study aids for this text at www.thomsonedu.com/psychology/coon.

Burnout Test A short questionnaire on job burnout.

Coping with Terrorism Information about emotional reactions to terrorism; provided by the American Psychological Association.

Focus on Stress A series of articles about stress.

HealthyWay A set of pages on health, nutrition, addictions, disabilities, sexuality, fitness, and much more.

Preventive Health Center A general source of information on how to maintain health and prevent disease.

Stress Management: Review of Principles Links to articles on stress management.

Stress, Anxiety, Fears, and Psychosomatic Disorders A comprehensive source on stress, anxiety, and related disorders.

Type A Behavior Describes Type A behavior, with links to an online test and related sites.

ThomsonNOW Go to www.thomsonedu.com to link to ThomsonNOW, your online study tool. First take the **Pre-Test** for this chapter to get your **Personalized Study Plan,** which will identify topics you need to review and direct you to online resources. Then take the **Post-Test** to determine what concepts you have mastered and what you still need work on.

TEST YOUR KNOWLEDGE

Health, Stress, and Coping

For additional review, get more practice with *ThomsonNOW*, *WebTutor*, the *Practice Quizzes*, and/or the printed *Study Guide* available with this book.

1. Lifestyle diseases related to just six behaviors account for 70 percent of all medical costs. The behaviors are smoking, alcohol and drug abuse, poor diet, insufficient exercise, and
   a. driving too fast
   b. excessive sun exposure
   c. unsafe sex
   d. exposure to toxins

2. People who have a disease-prone personality style are anxious and hostile. These traits can also be observed in the _____ personality.
   a. emotion-focused
   b. problem-focused
   c. SSRS-prone
   d. Type A

3. Health promoting behaviors that combat hypertension include the following: lose weight, consume less sodium, use alcohol sparingly, and get more
   a. sleep
   b. exercise
   c. LCUs
   d. cholesterol

4. Which of the following is NOT an STD?
   a. herpes
   b. eczema
   c. chlamydia
   d. hepatitis B

5. For the first _____ after infection, a negative test result for the HIV virus is no guarantee that a person is a "safe" sex partner.
   a. 3 weeks
   b. 6 weeks
   c. 6 months
   d. 3 years

6. A good indication that stress is a normal part of life is provided by the existence of
   a. learned helplessness
   b. hypochondria
   c. sublimation
   d. eustress

7. According to Richard Lazarus, choosing a way to meet a threat or challenge takes place during the
   a. primary stress reaction
   b. secondary stress reaction
   c. primary appraisal
   d. secondary appraisal

8. Aggression is an especially common reaction to
   a. frustration
   b. scapegoating
   c. approach conflicts
   d. ambivalence

9. Displaced aggression is closely related to the pattern of behavior known as
   a. scapegoating
   b. leaving the field
   c. stereotyped responding
   d. burnout

10. You would be most likely to experience vacillation if you found yourself in
    a. an approach-approach conflict
    b. an avoidance-avoidance conflict
    c. a double approach-avoidance conflict
    d. the condition called emotion-focused coping

11. Justifying your actions by making excuses that appear to explain your behavior is called
    a. sublimation
    b. reaction formation
    c. compensation
    d. rationalization

12. Learned helplessness tends to occur when events appear to be
    a. frustrating
    b. in conflict
    c. uncontrollable
    d. problem-focused

13. Ratings on the SRRS are based on the total number of _____ a person has for the preceding year.
    a. hassles
    b. LCUs
    c. STDs
    d. psychosomatic illnesses

14. Anger, hostility, and mistrust appear to be the core lethal factors in
    a. hypochondria
    b. learned helplessness
    c. the G.A.S.
    d. Type A behavior

15. In many ways, a person who has a hardy personality is the opposite of a person who has
    a. a high STD score
    b. a low LCU score
    c. Type A traits
    d. Type B traits

16. The first signs of psychosomatic disorders begin to appear during the stage of
    a. alarm
    b. exhaustion
    c. resistance
    d. appraisal

17. Students taking stressful final exams are more susceptible to the cold virus, a pattern best explained by the concept of
    a. the disease-prone personality
    b. psychoneuroimmunology
    c. emotion-focused coping
    d. reaction formation

18. A person using progressive relaxation for stress management is most likely trying to control which component of stress?
    a. bodily reactions
    b. upsetting thoughts
    c. ineffective behavior
    d. the primary appraisal

19. Exercise, meditation, progressive relaxation, and guided imagery would be least likely to help a person who is in the G.A.S. stage of
    a. alarm
    b. resistance
    c. exhaustion
    d. adaptation

20. While taking a stressful classroom test you say to yourself "Stay organized, focus on the task." It's obvious that you are using
    a. guided imagery
    b. coping statements
    c. LCUs
    d. guided relaxation

Psychological Disorders

Brooke Fasani/Corbis

JOURNEY INTO PSYCHOLOGY:
BEWARE THE HELICOPTERS

"The helicopters. Oh no, not the helicopters. Have come to tear the feathers out of my frontal lobes. Help me, nurse, help me, can't you hear them? Gotta get back into my body to save it. . . . The doctor is thinking I would make good glue."

These are the words of Carol North, a psychiatrist who survived schizophrenia. In addition to being plagued by hallucinated helicopters, Carol heard voices that said: "Be good," "Do bad," "Stand up," "Sit down," "Collide with the other world," "Do you want a cigar?" (North, 1987).

Carol North's painful journey into the shadows of madness left her incapacitated for nearly 20 years. Her case is but one hint of the magnitude of mental health problems. Here are some facts on psychological disorders (NIMH, 2006):

- 1 in 4 American adults suffers from a diagnosable mental disorder in any given year.
- Mental disorders are the leading cause of disability for Americans and Canadians aged 15–44.
- Anxiety disorders are often accompanied by depression and/or substance abuse.
- In 2002, almost 32,000 Americans committed suicide.
- Over 20,000,000 Americans suffer from mood disorders in any given year.

What does it mean to be "crazy"? A hundred years ago, doctors and nonprofessionals alike used terms such as "crazy," "insane," "cracked," and "lunatic" quite freely. The "insane" were thought of as bizarre and definitely different from the rest of us. Today, our understanding of psychological disorders is more sophisticated. To draw the line between normal and abnormal, we must weigh some complex issues. We'll explore some of them in this chapter, as well as an array of psychological problems.

▼ **Survey Questions**

- How is normality defined, and what are the major psychological disorders?
- What is a personality disorder?
- What problems result when a person suffers high levels of anxiety?
- How do psychologists explain anxiety-based disorders?
- What are the general characteristics of psychotic disorders?
- What is the nature of a delusional disorder?
- What forms does schizophrenia take? What causes it?
- What are mood disorders? What causes depression?
- Why do people commit suicide? Can suicide be prevented?

NORMALITY—WHAT IS NORMAL?

>SURVEY QUESTION< *How is normality defined, and what are the major psychological disorders?*

"That guy is really wacko. His porch lights are dimming." "Yeah, the butter's sliding off his waffle. He's ready to go postal." Informally, it's tempting to make such snap judgments about mental health. But to seriously classify people as psychologically unhealthy raises complex and age-old issues. The conservative, churchgoing housewife down the street might be flagrantly psychotic and a lethal danger to her children. The reclusive eccentric who hangs out at the park could be the sanest person in town.

The scientific study of mental, emotional, and behavioral disorders is known as **psychopathology.** The term also refers to mental disorders themselves, such as schizophrenia or depression, and to behavior patterns that make people unhappy and impair their personal growth (Butcher, Mineka, & Hooley, 2004). Defining abnormality can be tricky. We might begin by saying that psychopathology is characterized by *subjective discomfort* (private feelings of pain, unhappiness, or emotional distress) like Carol North endured.

But couldn't a person be seriously disturbed without feeling discomfort? Yes. Psychopathology doesn't always cause personal anguish. A person suffering from mania might feel elated and "on top of the world." Also, a *lack* of discomfort may reveal a problem. For example, if you showed no signs of grief after the death of a close friend, we might suspect psychopathology. In practice, subjective discomfort explains most instances in which people voluntarily seek professional help.

Some psychologists use statistics to define normality more objectively. **Statistical abnormality** refers to scoring very high or low on some dimension, such as intelligence, anxiety, or depression. Anxiety, for example, is a feature of several psychological disorders. To measure it, we could create a test to learn how many people show low, medium, or high levels of anxiety. Usually, the results of such tests will form a *normal* (bell-shaped) *curve.* (*Normal* in this case refers only to the *shape* of the curve.) Notice that most people score near the middle of a normal curve; very few have extremely high and low scores (▸▸Fig. 12.1). A person who deviates from the average by being anxious all the time (high anxiety) might be abnormal. So, too, might a person who never feels anxiety.

Then statistical abnormality tells us nothing about the meaning of deviations from the norm? Right. It is as statistically "abnormal" (unusual) for a person to score above 145 on an IQ test as it is to score below 55. However, only the lower score is regarded as "abnormal"

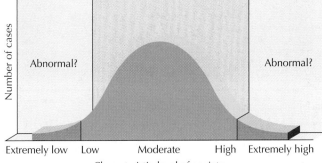

▸▸**FIGURE 12.1** The number of people displaying a personal characteristic may help define what is statistically abnormal.

Psychopathology The scientific study of mental, emotional, and behavioral disorders; also, abnormal or maladaptive behavior.

Statistical abnormality Abnormality defined on the basis of an extreme score on some dimension, such as IQ or anxiety.

Crazy for a Day

Performing a mildly abnormal behavior is a good way to get a sense of how social norms define "normality" in daily life. Here's your assignment: Do something strange in public and observe how people react to you. (Please don't do anything dangerous, harmful, or offensive—and don't get arrested!) Here are some deviant behaviors that other students have staged:

- Sit in the dining area of a fast-food restaurant and loudly carry on a conversation with an imaginary companion.
- Stand in a busy hallway on campus and adopt a Kung Fu stance. Remain in that position for 10 minutes.
- Walk around campus on a sunny day while wearing a raincoat and carrying an open umbrella. Keep the umbrella over your head when you are inside buildings.

- Stick one finger in your nose and another in your ear. Walk through a busy shopping mall.
- Cover your head with aluminum foil for a day.

Does the idea of performing any of these actions make you uncomfortable? If so, you may not need to do anything more to appreciate how powerfully social norms constrain our actions. As we have noted, social nonconformity is just one facet of abnormal behavior. Nevertheless, actions that are regarded as "strange" within a particular culture are often the first sign to others that a person has a problem.

or undesirable. In the same sense, it is unusual for a person to speak four languages or to win an event at the Olympics, but these are desirable, if rare, accomplishments.

Statistical definitions also can't tell us *where to draw the line* between normality and abnormality. To take a new example, we could obtain the average frequency of sexual intercourse for persons of a particular age, sex, sexual orientation, and marital status. Clearly, a person who feels driven to have sex dozens of times a day has a problem. But as we move back toward the norm we face the problem of drawing lines. How often does a normal behavior have to occur before it becomes abnormal? As you can see, statistical boundary lines tend to be somewhat arbitrary (Comer, 2005).

Atypical behavior or nonconformity may underlie some disorders. **Social nonconformity** refers to disobeying public standards for acceptable conduct. Extreme nonconformity can lead to destructive or self-destructive behavior. (Think, for instance, of a drug abuser or a prostitute.) However, we must be careful to separate unhealthy nonconformity from creative lifestyles. Many eccentric "characters" are charming and emotionally stable. Note, too, that strictly following social norms is no guarantee of mental health. In some cases, psychopathology involves rigid conformity. (See "Crazy for a Day.")

Rick Friedman/Corbis

Social nonconformity does not automatically indicate psychopathology.

A young woman ties a thick rubber cord around her ankles, screams hysterically, and jumps head-first off a bridge. Thirty years ago, the woman's behavior might have seemed completely crazy. Today, it is a routine form of entertainment (called "bungee jumping"). Before any behavior can be defined as abnormal, we must consider the *situational context* (social situation, behavioral setting, or general circumstances) in which it occurs. Is it normal to stand outside and water a lawn with a hose? It depends on whether it is raining. Is it abnormal for a grown man to remove his pants and expose himself to another man or woman in a place of business? It depends on whether the other person is a bank clerk or a doctor.

Almost any imaginable behavior can be considered normal in some contexts. In mid-October 1972, an airplane carrying a rugby team crashed in the snowcapped Andes of South America. Incredibly, 16 of the 45 people onboard survived 73 days in deep snow and sub-freezing temperatures. They were forced to use extremely grim measures to do so—they ate the bodies of those who died in the crash.

As implied by our earlier discussion of social norms, culture is one of the most influential contexts in which any behavior is judged. In some cultures it is considered normal to

Social nonconformity Failure to conform to societal norms or the usual minimum standards for social conduct.

A Disease Called Freedom

The year is 1840. You are a slave who has tried repeatedly to escape from a cruel and abusive master. You want to be free. An expert is consulted about your "abnormal" behavior. His conclusion? You are suffering from "drapetomania," a mental "disorder" that causes slaves to run away (Wakefield, 1992). Your "cure"? The expert will cut off your toes.

As this example suggests, psychiatric terms are easily abused. Historically, some have been applied to culturally disapproved behaviors that are not really disorders. Another of our personal favorites is the long-outdated diagnosis of "anarchia," a form of insanity that leads one to seek a more democratic society (Brown, 1990).

All of the following were also once considered disorders: childhood masturbation, lack of vaginal orgasm, self-defeating personality (applied mainly to women), homosexuality, and nymphomania (a woman with a healthy sexual appetite) (Wakefield, 1992). Even today, race, gender, and social class continue to affect the diagnosis of various disorders (Durand & Barlow, 2006; Poland & Caplan, 2004).

Gender is probably the most common source of bias in judging normality because standards tend to be based on males (Nolen-Hoeksema, 2004; Widiger, 2005). According to psychologist Paula Caplan (1995) and others, women are penalized both for conforming to female stereotypes and for ignoring them. If a woman is independent, aggressive, and unemotional, she may be considered "unhealthy." Yet at the same time, a woman who is vain, emotional, irrational, and dependent on others (all "feminine" traits in our culture) may be classified as having a personality disorder (Bornstein, 1996). Indeed, a majority of persons classified as having dependent personality disorder are women. In view of this, Paula Caplan asks, why isn't there a category called "delusional dominating personality disorder" for obnoxious men (Caplan, 1995)?

In view of the subtle influence that culture can have on perceptions of disorder and normality, it is worth being cautious before you leap to conclusions about the mental health of others (DSM-IV-TR, 2000). (They might be doing an assignment for their psychology class!)

defecate or urinate in public or to appear naked in public. In our culture such behaviors would be considered unusual or abnormal. In Muslim cultures, women who remain completely housebound are considered normal or even virtuous. In Western cultures they might be diagnosed as suffering from a disorder called agoraphobia (Fabrega, 2004). (Agoraphobia is described later in this chapter.)

Thus, *cultural relativity*, the idea that judgments are made relative to the values of one's culture, can affect the diagnosis of psychological disorders. (See "A Disease Called Freedom.") Still, *all* cultures classify people as abnormal if they fail to communicate with others or are consistently unpredictable in their actions.

Core Features of Disordered Behavior

If abnormality is so hard to define, how are judgments of psychopathology made? Although the standards we have discussed are *relative*, abnormal behavior does have two core features. First, it is **maladaptive.** Rather than helping people cope successfully, abnormal behavior makes it more difficult for them to meet the demands of day-to-day life. Second, people suffering from psychological disorders *lose the ability to control* their thoughts, behaviors, or feelings adequately. For example, gambling is not a problem if people bet for entertainment and can maintain self-control. However, compulsive gambling is a sign of psychopathology. The voices that Carol North kept hearing are a prime example of what it means to lose control of one's thoughts. In the most extreme cases, people become a danger to themselves or others, which is clearly maladaptive (Hansell & Damour, 2004).

In practice, deciding that a person needs help usually occurs when the person *does something* (hits a person, hallucinates, stares into space, collects rolls of toilet paper, and so forth) that *annoys* or *gains the attention* of a person in a *position of power* in the person's life (an employer, teacher, parent, spouse, or the person himself or herself). That person then *does something* about it. (A police officer may be called, the person may be urged to see a psychologist, a relative may start commitment proceedings, or the person may voluntarily seek help.)

Maladaptive behavior Behavior that makes it difficult to adapt to the environment and meet the demands of day-to-day life.

CLASSIFYING MENTAL DISORDERS— PROBLEMS BY THE BOOK

Psychological problems are classified by using the *Diagnostic and Statistical Manual of Mental Disorders* (DSM-IV-TR, 2000). The DSM helps psychologists correctly identify mental disorders and select the best therapies to treat them (First & Pincus, 2002).

A **mental disorder** is a significant impairment in psychological functioning. If you were to glance through the DSM-IV-TR, you would see many disorders described, including those in ▪ Table 12.2 (on page 479). It's impossible here to discuss all of these problems. Major disorders are listed in the table so you can see the types of problems found in the DSM. (You don't need to memorize all of them.) The descriptions that follow will give you an overview of some selected problems.

An Overview of Psychological Disorders

People suffering from **psychotic disorders** have "retreated from reality." That is, they suffer from hallucinations and delusions and they are socially withdrawn. Psychotic disorders are severely disabling and often lead to hospitalization. Typically, psychotic patients cannot control their thoughts and actions. For example, David often heard the voice of his Uncle Bill: "He told me to turn off the TV. He said, 'It's too damn loud, turn it down, turn it down.' Other times he talks about fishing. 'Good day for fishing. Got to go fishing'" (Durand & Barlow, 2006). Psychotic symptoms occur in schizophrenia, delusional disorders, and some mood disorders. Also, psychosis may be related to medical problems, drug abuse, and other conditions. (▪ Table 12.1 provides a simplified list of major disorders.)

Organic mental disorders are problems caused by brain pathology; that is, by drug damage, diseases of the brain, injuries, poisons, and so on (▶▶ Fig. 12.2). A person with organic disorders may have severe emotional disturbances, impaired thinking, memory loss, personality changes, delirium, or psychotic symptoms (Nolen-Hoeksema, 2004).

Mental disorder A significant impairment in psychological functioning.

Psychotic disorder A severe mental disorder characterized by a retreat from reality, by hallucinations and delusions, and by social withdrawal.

Organic mental disorder A mental or emotional problem caused by brain diseases or injuries.

▪ Table 12.1   Some Selected Categories of Psychopathology

Problem	Primary Symptom	Typical Signs of Trouble
Psychotic disorders	Loss of contact with reality	You hear or see things that others don't; your mind has been playing tricks on you
Mood disorders	Mania or depression	You feel sad and hopeless; or you talk too loud and too fast and have a rush of ideas and feelings that others think are unreasonable
Anxiety disorders	High anxiety or anxiety-based	You have anxiety attacks and distortions of behavior feel like you are going to die; or you are afraid to do things that most people can do; or you spend unusual amounts of time doing things like washing your hands or counting your heartbeats
Somatoform disorders	Bodily complaints without an organic (physical) basis	You feel physically sick, but your doctor says nothing is wrong with you; or you suffer from pain that has no physical basis; or you are preoccupied with thoughts about being sick
Dissociative disorders	Amnesia, feelings of unreality, multiple identities	There are major gaps in your memory of events; you feel like you are a robot or a stranger to yourself; others tell you that you have done things that you don't remember doing
Personality disorders	Unhealthy personality patterns	Your behavior patterns repeatedly cause problems at work, school, and in your relationships with others
Sexual and gender identity disorders	Disturbed gender identity, deviant sexual behavior, problems in sexual adjustment	You feel that you are a man trapped in a woman's body (or the reverse); or you can only gain sexual satisfaction by engaging in highly atypical sexual behavior; or you have problems with sexual desire, arousal, or performance
Substance-related disorders	Disturbances related to drug abuse or dependence	You have been drinking too much, using illegal drugs, or taking prescription drugs more often than you should

In reality, almost all mental disorders are partly biological (Hansell & Damour, 2004). That's why DSM-IV-TR does not list "organic mental disorders" as a separate category. Nevertheless, all of the following problems are closely associated with organic damage: delirium, dementia, amnesia, and other cognitive disorders; mental disorders due to a general medical condition; and substance-related disorders (drug abuse).

Mood disorders are primarily defined by the presence of extreme, intense, and long-lasting emotions. Afflicted persons may be *manic,* meaning agitated, elated, and hyperactive, or they may be *depressed.* Some people with mood disorders alternate between mania and depression and they may have psychotic symptoms as well.

Anxiety disorders are marked by fear or anxiety, and by distorted behavior. Some anxiety disorders involve feelings of panic. Others take the form of phobias (irrational fears) or just overwhelming anxiety and nervousness. Two additional anxiety disorders are posttraumatic stress disorder and acute stress disorder. Obsessive-compulsive behavior patterns are also associated with high anxiety. (These problems are described later in this chapter.)

Somatoform disorders (so-MAT-oh-form) occur when a person has physical symptoms that mimic disease or injury (paralysis, blindness, illness, or chronic pain, for example), for which there is no identifiable physical cause. In such cases, psychological factors appear to explain the symptoms.

A person with a **dissociative disorder** may have temporary amnesia or multiple personalities. Also included in this category are frightening episodes of depersonalization, in which people feel like they are outside of their bodies, are behaving like robots, or are lost in a dream world.

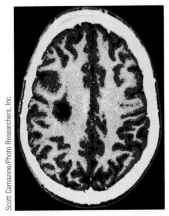

FIGURE 12.2 This MRI scan of a human brain (viewed from the top) reveals a tumor (dark spot). Mental disorders sometimes have organic causes of this sort. However, in many instances no obvious organic damage can be found.

The self-portraits shown here were painted by Andy Wilf during a 4-year period. At that time, Wilf is said to have increasingly abused drugs and alcohol. This dramatic series of images is a record of his self-destructive descent into a private hell. The third painting shows a shrouded skull—and foretells the artist's fate. Wilf died of a drug overdose. Drug abuse is but one of the many psychopathologies, or "problems in living," psychologists seek to alleviate. (Courtesy of Ulrike Kantor, Ulrike Kantor Gallery.)

Personality disorders are deeply ingrained, unhealthy personality patterns. Such patterns usually appear in adolescence and continue through much of adult life. They include paranoid (overly suspicious), narcissistic (self-loving), dependent, borderline, and antisocial personality types, as well as others.

Sexual and gender identity disorders include any of a wide range of difficulties with sexual identity, deviant sexual behavior, or sexual adjustment. In gender identity disorders, sexual identity does not match a person's physical sex and the person may seek a sex-change operation. Deviations in sexual behavior known as *paraphilias* include exhibitionism, fetishism, voyeurism, and so on. Also found in this category are a variety of *sexual dysfunctions* (problems in sexual desire, arousal, or response).

Substance-related disorders involve abuse of, or dependence on, psychoactive drugs. Typical culprits include alcohol, barbiturates, opiates, cocaine, amphetamines, hallucinogens, marijuana, and nicotine. A person with a substance disorder cannot stop using the drug and may also suffer from withdrawal symptoms, delirium, dementia, amnesia, psychosis, emotional outbursts, sexual problems, and sleep disturbances. (Problems related to drug abuse are discussed in Chapter 5.)

Shouldn't neurosis be listed here? Neurosis was once a recognized mental disorder. However, it is no longer included in the DSM because the term *neurosis* is too imprecise. Behavior that psychologists used to refer to as "neurotic" is now part of anxiety, somatoform, or dissociative disorders. Even though **neurosis** is an outdated term, you may still hear it used to loosely refer to problems involving excessive anxiety.

Mood disorder A major disturbance in mood or emotion, such as depression or mania.
Anxiety disorder Disruptive feelings of fear, apprehension, or anxiety, or distortions in behavior that are anxiety related.
Somatoform disorder Physical symptoms that mimic disease or injury for which there is no identifiable physical cause.
Dissociative disorder Temporary amnesia, multiple personality, or depersonalization.
Personality disorder A maladaptive personality pattern.
Sexual and gender identity disorders Any of a wide range of difficulties with sexual identity, deviant sexual behavior, or sexual adjustment.
Substance-related disorder Abuse of or dependence on a mood- or behavior-altering drug.
Neurosis An outdated term once used to refer, as a group, to anxiety disorders, somatoform disorders, dissociative disorders, and some forms of depression.

Running Amok with Cultural Maladies

Every culture recognizes the existence of psychopathology, and most have at least a few folk names for afflictions you won't find in DSM-IV-TR. Called *culture-bound syndromes,* here are some examples from around the world (Durand & Barlow, 2006; López & Guarnaccia, 2000; Sumathipala, Siribaddana, & Bhugra, 2004):

- **Amok** Men in Malaysia, Laos, the Philippines, and Polynesia who believe they have been insulted are sometimes known to go *amok.* After a period of brooding they erupt into an outburst of violent, aggressive, or homicidal behavior randomly directed at people and objects.
- **Susto** Among Latin Americans, the symptoms of *susto* include insomnia, irritability, phobias, and an increase in sweating and heart rate. Susto can result if someone is badly frightened by a black magic curse. In extreme cases, *voodoo death* can result, as the person is literally scared to death.
- **Ghost sickness** Among many American Indian tribes, people who become preoccupied with death and the deceased are said to suffer from *ghost sickness.* The symptoms of ghost sickness include bad dreams, weakness, loss of appetite, fainting, dizziness, fear, anxiety, hallucinations, loss of consciousness, confusion, feelings of futility, and a sense of suffocation.
- **Koro** In southern and eastern Asia, a man may experience sudden and intense anxiety that his penis (or, in females, the vulva and nipples) will recede into the body. In addition to the terror this incites, victims also believe that advanced

cases of *koro* can cause death. A similar fear of shrinking genitals has also been reported from West Africa (Dzokoto & Adams, 2005).
- **Zar** In North African and Middle Eastern societies, *zar* is said to occur when spirits possess an individual. Zar is marked by shouting, laughing, hitting the head against a wall, singing, or weeping. Victims may become apathetic or withdrawn and they may refuse to eat or carry out daily tasks.
- **Dhat** In Indian society, *dhat* is the fear of the loss of semen during nocturnal emissions. A man suffering from dhat will feel anxious and perhaps also guilty. He may also experience fatigue, loss of appetite, weakness, anxiety, and sexual dysfunction.

It's clear that people have a need to label and categorize disturbed behavior. As you can see, however, folk terminology tends to be vague. The terms listed here provide little guidance about the true nature of a person's problems or the best ways to treat them. That's why the DSM is based on empirical data and clinical observations. Otherwise, psychologists and psychiatrists would be no better than folk healers when making diagnoses (Ancis, Chen, & Schultz, 2004).

By the way, culture-bound disorders occur in all societies. For example, American psychologists Pamela Keel and Kelly Klump believe that bulimia is primarily a syndrome of Western cultures, including the United States (Keel & Klump, 2003).

In addition to the formal mental disorders we have reviewed, many cultures have names for "unofficial" psychological "disorders." See "Running Amok with Cultural Maladies" for some examples.

General Risk Factors

What causes mental and psychological disorders like those listed in ■ *Table 12.1?* We will soon explore the causes of some specific problems. For now, here are some general risk factors that contribute to psychopathology:

- **Social conditions:** poverty, stressful living conditions, homelessness, social disorganization, overcrowding
- **Family factors:** parents who are immature, mentally disturbed, criminal, or abusive; severe marital strife; extremely poor child discipline; disordered family communication patterns
- **Psychological factors:** stress, low intelligence, learning disorders, lack of control or mastery
- **Biological/physical factors:** genetic defects or inherited vulnerabilities, poor prenatal care, very low birth weight, chronic physical illness or disability, exposure to toxic chemicals or drugs, head injuries

Insanity

Which of the mental disorders causes insanity? None. **Insanity** is a legal term. It refers to an inability to manage one's affairs or foresee the consequences of one's actions. People who are declared insane are not legally responsible for their actions. If necessary, they can be involuntarily committed to a mental hospital.

Insanity A legal term that refers to a mental inability to manage one's affairs or to be aware of the consequences of one's actions.

■ Table 12.2 Major DSM-IV-TR Categories

- **DISORDERS USUALLY FIRST DIAGNOSED IN INFANCY, CHILDHOOD, OR ADOLESCENCE**
  Mental retardation
      Example: Mild mental retardation
  Learning disorders
      Example: Reading disorder
  Motor skills disorder
      Example: Developmental coordination disorder
  Communication disorders
      Example: Stuttering
  Pervasive developmental disorders
      Example: Autistic disorder
  Attention-deficit and disruptive behavior disorders
      Example: Attention-deficit/hyperactivity disorder
  Feeding and eating disorders of infancy or early childhood
      Example: Pica (eating inedible substances)
  Tic disorders
      Example: Tourette's disorder
  Elimination disorders
      Example: Enuresis (bedwetting)
  Other disorders of infancy, childhood, or adolescence
      Example: Separation anxiety disorder

- **DELIRIUM, DEMENTIA, AMNESTIC, AND OTHER COGNITIVE DISORDERS**
  Delirium
      Example: Delirium due to a general medical condition
  Dementia
      Example: Dementia of the Alzheimer's type
  Amnestic disorders (memory loss)
      Example: Amnestic disorder due to a general medical condition
  Cognitive disorder not otherwise specified

- **MENTAL DISORDERS DUE TO A GENERAL MEDICAL CONDITION NOT ELSEWHERE CLASSIFIED**
  Catatonic disorder due to a general medical condition
  Personality change due to a general medical condition
  Mental disorder not otherwise specified due to a general medical condition

- **SUBSTANCE-RELATED DISORDERS**
  Example: Cocaine use disorders

- **SCHIZOPHRENIA AND OTHER PSYCHOTIC DISORDERS**
  Schizophrenia
      Example: Schizophrenia, paranoid type
  Schizophreniform disorder
  Schizoaffective disorder
  Delusional disorder
      Example: Delusional disorder, grandiose type
  Brief psychotic disorder
  Shared psychotic disorder (folie a deux)
  Psychotic disorder due to a general medical condition
  Substance-induced psychotic disorder
  Psychotic disorder not otherwise specified

- **MOOD DISORDERS**
  Depressive disorders
      Example: Major depressive disorder
  Bipolar disorders
      Example: Bipolar I disorder
  Mood disorder due to a general medical condition
  Substance-induced mood disorder
  Mood disorder not otherwise specified

- **ANXIETY DISORDERS**
  Example: Panic disorder

- **SOMATOFORM DISORDERS**
  Example: Conversion disorder

- **FACTITIOUS DISORDERS** (faked disability or illness)
  Example: Factitious disorder

- **DISSOCIATIVE DISORDERS**
  Example: Dissociative identity disorder

- **SEXUAL AND GENDER IDENTITY DISORDERS**
  Sexual dysfunctions
      Example: Sexual arousal disorders
  Paraphilias
      Example: Voyeurism
  Sexual disorder not otherwise specified
  Gender identity disorders
      Example: Gender identity disorder

- **EATING DISORDERS**
  Example: Anorexia nervosa

- **SLEEP DISORDERS**
  Primary sleep disorders
  Dyssomnias
      Example: Primary insomnia
  Parasomnias
      Example: Sleep terror disorder
  Sleep disorders related to another mental disorder
      Example: Insomnia related to posttraumatic stress disorder
  Other sleep disorders
      Example: Substance-induced sleep disorder

- **IMPULSE CONTROL DISORDERS NOT ELSEWHERE CLASSIFIED**
  Example: Kleptomania

- **ADJUSTMENT DISORDERS**
  Example: Adjustment disorder

- **PERSONALITY DISORDERS**
  Example: Antisocial personality disorder

Legally, insanity is established by testimony from *expert witnesses* (psychologists and psychiatrists) recognized by a court of law as being qualified to give opinions on a specific topic. Involuntary commitments happen most often when people are brought to emergency rooms. People who are involuntarily committed are usually judged to be a danger to themselves or to others, or they are severely mentally disabled (Luchins et al., 2004).

In upcoming sections we will explore some selected problems in more detail, beginning with personality disorders. Before we do, here's a Study Break to help you diagnose your grasp of psychopathology.

Study Break   Normality and Psychopathology

Reflect

Think of an instance of abnormal behavior you have witnessed. By what formal standards would the behavior be regarded as abnormal? In every society? Was the behavior maladaptive in any way?

Learning Check

1. Statistical definitions of abnormality successfully avoid the limitations of other approaches. T or F?

2. One of the most powerful contexts in which judgments of normality and abnormality are made is

   a. the family
   b. occupational settings
   c. religious systems
   d. culture

3. Amnesia, multiple identities, and depersonalization are possible problems in

   a. mood disorders
   b. somatoform disorders
   c. psychosis
   d. dissociative disorders

4. Which among the following is *not* a major psychological problem listed in DSM-IV-TR?

   a. mood disorders
   b. personality disorders
   c. insanity
   d. anxiety disorders

5. A major difference between psychotic disorders and anxiety disorders (or other milder problems) is that in psychosis the individual has lost contact with reality as shown by the presence of _____ or _____.

6. Which of the following is NOT a term used by folk healers to label or categorize disturbed behavior?

   a. amok
   b. delirium
   c. susto
   d. koro

7. Someone who engages in one of the paraphilias has what type of disorder?

   a. dissociative
   b. somatoform
   c. substance
   d. sexual

Critical Thinking

8. Brian, a fan of grunge rock, occasionally wears a skirt in public. Does Brian's cross-dressing indicate that he has a mental disorder?

Answers

1. F   2. d   3. d   4. c   5. delusions, hallucinations   6. b   7. d   8. Probably not. Undoubtedly, Brian's cross-dressing is socially disapproved by many people. Nevertheless, to be classified as a mental disorder it must cause him to feel disabling shame, guilt, depression, or anxiety. The cultural relativity of behavior like Brian's is revealed by the fact that it is fashionable and acceptable for women to wear men's clothing.

PERSONALITY DISORDERS—BLUEPRINTS FOR MALADJUSTMENT

>SURVEY QUESTION< *What is a personality disorder?*

"Get out of here and leave me alone so I can die in peace," Judy screamed at her nurses in the seclusion room of the psychiatric hospital. On one of her arms, long dark red marks mingled with the scars of previous suicide attempts. Judy once bragged that her record was 67 stitches. Today, the nurses had to strap her into restraints to keep her from gouging her own eyes. She was given a sedative and slept for 12 hours. She woke calmly and asked for her therapist—even though her latest outburst began when he canceled a morning appointment and changed it to afternoon.

Judy has a condition called *borderline personality disorder*. Although she is capable of working, Judy has repeatedly lost jobs because of her turbulent relationships with other people. At times she can be friendly and a real charmer. At other times she is extremely unpredictable, moody, and even suicidal. Being a friend to Judy can be a fearsome challenge. Canceling an appointment, forgetting a special date, a wrong turn of phrase—these and similar small incidents may trigger Judy's rage or a suicide attempt. Like other people with borderline personality disorder, Judy is extremely sensitive to ordinary criticism, which leaves her feeling rejected and abandoned. Typically, she reacts with anger, self-hatred, and impulsive behavior. These "emotional storms" damage her personal relationships and leave her confused about who she is (Siever & Koenigsberg, 2000).

Maladaptive Personality Patterns

As stated earlier, a person with a personality disorder has maladaptive personality traits. For example, people with a paranoid personality disorder are suspicious, hypersensitive, and wary of others. Narcissistic persons need constant admiration, and they are lost in fantasies of power, wealth, brilliance, beauty, or love. The dependent personality suffers from extremely low self-confidence. Dependent persons allow others to run their lives and they place everyone else's needs ahead of their own. People with a histrionic personality disorder constantly seek attention by dramatizing their emotions and actions.

Typically, patterns such as the ones just described begin during adolescence or even childhood. Thus, personality disorders are deeply rooted and usually span many years. The list of personality disorders is long (▪ Table 12.3), so let us focus on a single frequently misunderstood problem, the antisocial personality.

Antisocial Personality

What are the characteristics of an antisocial personality? A person with an **antisocial personality** lacks a conscience. Such people are impulsive, selfish, dishonest, emotionally shallow, and manipulative. Antisocial persons, who are sometimes called *sociopaths* or *psychopaths*, are poorly socialized and seem to be incapable of feeling guilt, shame, fear, loyalty, or love (DSM-IV-TR, 2000).

Are sociopaths dangerous? Sociopaths tend to have a long history of conflict with society. Many are delinquents or criminals who may be a threat to the general public (Ogloff, 2006). However, sociopaths are rarely the crazed murderers you may have seen portrayed on TV and in movies. In fact, many sociopaths are "charming" at first. Their "friends" only gradually become aware of the sociopath's lying and self-serving manipulation. One study found that psychopaths are "blind" to signs of disgust in others. This may add to their capacity for

▪ Table 12.3 Personality Disorders and Typical Degree of Impairment

Moderate Impairment

Dependent You lack confidence and you are extremely submissive and dependent on others (clinging)

Histrionic You are dramatic and flamboyant; you exaggerate your emotions to get attention from others

Narcissistic You think you are wonderful, brilliant, important, and worthy of constant admiration

Antisocial You are irresponsible, lack guilt or remorse, and engage in antisocial behavior, such as aggression, deceit, or recklessness

High Impairment

Obsessive-compulsive You demand order, perfection, control, and rigid routine at all times

Schizoid You feel very little emotion and can't form close personal relationships with others

Avoidant You are timid, uncomfortable in social situations, and fear evaluation

Severe Impairment

Borderline Your self-image, moods, and impulses are erratic, and you are extremely sensitive to any hint of criticism, rejection, or abandonment by others

Paranoid You deeply distrust others and are suspicious of their motives, which you perceive as insulting or threatening

Schizotypal You are a loner, you engage in extremely odd behavior, and your thought patterns are bizarre, but you are not actively psychotic

Source: From DSM-IV-TR, 2000.

Antisocial personality A person who lacks a conscience, is emotionally shallow, impulsive, selfish, and tends to manipulate others.

More than 65 percent of all persons with antisocial personalities have been arrested, usually for crimes such as robbery, vandalism, or rape.

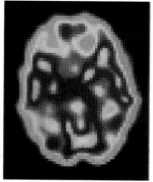
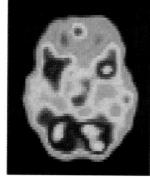

▸▸**FIGURE 12.3** Using PET scans, Canadian psychologist Robert Hare found that the normally functioning brain *(left)* lights up with activity when a person sees emotion-laden words such as "maggot" or "cancer." But the brain of a psychopath *(right)* remains inactive, especially in areas associated with feelings and self-control. When Dr. Hare showed the image at right to several neurologists, one asked, "Is this person from Mars?" (Images courtesy of Robert Hare.)

cruelty and their ability to use others (Kosson et al., 2002). Many successful businesspersons, entertainers, politicians, and other seemingly normal people have psychopathic leanings. Basically, antisocial persons coldly use others and cheat their way through life (Ogloff, 2006).

Causes

What causes sociopathy? Typically, people with antisocial personalities were emotionally deprived and physically abused as children (Pollock et al., 1990). Adult sociopaths also display subtle neurological problems (▸▸ Fig. 12.3). For example, they have unusual brain-wave patterns that suggest underarousal of the brain. This may explain why sociopaths tend to be thrill seekers. Quite likely, they are searching for stimulation strong enough to overcome their chronic underarousal and feelings of "boredom" (Hare, 2006).

In a revealing study, psychopaths were shown extremely grisly and unpleasant photographs of mutilations. The photos were so upsetting that they visibly startled normal people. The psychopaths, however, showed no startle response to the photos (Levenston et al., 2000). (They didn't "bat an eyelash.") Those with antisocial personalities might therefore be described as *emotionally cold.* They simply do not feel normal pangs of conscience, guilt, or anxiety (Blair et al., 2006). Again, this coldness seems to account for an unusual ability to calmly lie, cheat, steal, or take advantage of others.

Can sociopathy be treated? Antisocial personality disorders are rarely treated with success (Hare, 2006). All too often, sociopaths manipulate therapy, just like any other situation. If it is to their advantage to act "cured," they will do so. However, they return to their former behavior patterns as soon as possible. On a more positive note, antisocial behavior does tend to decline somewhat after age 40, even without treatment, because people tend to become more "mellow" as they age (Laub & Sampson, 2003).

An individual with an antisocial personality feels very little anxiety. At the other end of the scale, people who have lots of anxiety also suffer from debilitating problems, as described next.

ANXIETY-BASED DISORDERS— WHEN ANXIETY RULES

>SURVEY QUESTION< *What problems result when a person suffers high levels of anxiety?*

Imagine that you are waiting to take a very important test for which you are unprepared or waiting to give a speech to a large audience of strangers. If you have felt anxiety in one of these situations, then you will understand why anxiety-based disorders are so debilitating. People who suffer from extreme anxiety are miserable and their behavior becomes distorted and self-defeating.

Anxiety refers to feelings of apprehension, dread, or uneasiness. We all feel anxiety, but anxiety that is out of proportion to a situation may reveal a problem. An example is a college student named Jian, who became unbearably anxious when he took exams. By the time Jian went to see a counselor, he had skipped several tests and was in danger of dropping out of school. In general, anxiety-related problems like Jian's involve:

- High levels of anxiety and/or restrictive, self-defeating behavior patterns
- A tendency to use elaborate defense mechanisms or avoidance responses to get through the day
- Pervasive feelings of stress, insecurity, inferiority, and dissatisfaction with life

People with anxiety-related problems feel threatened and often can't do anything constructive about it. They struggle to control themselves, but they remain ineffective and unhappy (Rachman, 2004). In any given year, roughly 18 percent of the adult population suffers from an anxiety disorder (NIMH, 2006).

If anxiety is a normal emotion, when does it signify a problem? A problem exists when intense anxiety prevents people from doing what they want or need to do. Also, their anxieties are out of control—they simply cannot stop worrying.

Adjustment Disorders

Do such problems cause a "nervous breakdown"? People suffering from anxiety-based problems may be miserable, but they rarely experience a "breakdown." Actually, the term *nervous breakdown* has no formal meaning. Nevertheless, a problem known as an *adjustment disorder* does come close to being something of a "breakdown."

Adjustment disorders occur when ordinary stresses push people beyond their ability to cope with life. Examples of such stresses are losing a job, intense marital strife, and chronic physical illness. People suffering from an adjustment disorder may be extremely irritable, anxious, apathetic, or depressed. They also have trouble sleeping, lose their appetite, and suffer from various physical complaints. Often, their problems can be relieved by rest, sedation, supportive counseling, and a chance to "talk through" their fears and anxieties (DSM-IV-TR, 2000).

How is an adjustment disorder different from an anxiety disorder? The outward symptoms are similar. However, adjustment disorders disappear when a person's life circumstances improve. People suffering from anxiety disorders seem to generate their own misery, regardless of what's happening around them. They feel that they must be on guard against *future* threats that *could happen* at any time (Barlow, 2000).

Anxiety Disorders

In most anxiety disorders, distress seems greatly out of proportion to a person's circumstances. For example, consider the following description of Adrian H:

> She becomes very anxious that her children "might have been hurt or killed if they were out of the neighborhood playing and she hadn't heard from them in a couple of hours." But then again, she worries all the time; about her job performance, her children's well-being, and her relationships with men. Noticing that men rarely called back after a date or two, she comments "They can sense I'm not a fun person." She never really relaxes, has difficulty focusing at work, has frequent headaches, and suffers from insomnia. But at least she does not experience extreme anxiety attacks. (Adapted from Brown & Barlow, 2007.)

Distress like Adrian H's is a key ingredient in anxiety disorders. It also may underlie dissociative and somatoform disorders, where maladaptive behavior serves to reduce anxiety and discomfort. To deepen your understanding, let's first examine the anxiety disorders themselves (■ Table 12.4). Then we will see how anxiety contributes to other problems.

Generalized Anxiety Disorder

A person with a **generalized anxiety disorder** has been extremely anxious and worried for at least 6 months. Sufferers typically complain of sweating, a racing heart, clammy hands, dizziness, upset stomach, rapid breathing, irritability, and poor concentration. Overall, more women than men have these symptoms (Brown & Barlow, 2007).

Was Adrian H's problem a generalized anxiety disorder? Yes. If she also experienced *anxiety attacks,* then she would likely be diagnosed with panic disorder.

■ Table 12.4   Anxiety Disorders

Generalized anxiety disorder

Panic disorder
   Without agoraphobia
   With agoraphobia

Agoraphobia (without a history of panic disorder)

Specific phobia

Social phobia

Obsessive-compulsive disorder

Posttraumatic stress disorder

Acute stress disorder

Source: DSM-IV-TR, 2000.

Adjustment disorder An emotional disturbance caused by on-going stressors within the range of common experience.

Generalized anxiety disorder The person is in a chronic state of tension and worries about work, relationships, ability, or impending disaster.

Panic Disorder (without Agoraphobia)

In a **panic disorder (without agoraphobia)** people are highly anxious and also feel sudden, intense, unexpected panic. During a panic attack, victims experience chest pain, a racing heart, dizziness, choking, feelings of unreality, trembling, or fears of losing control. Many believe that they are having a heart attack, are going insane, or are about to die. Needless to say, this pattern leaves victims unhappy and uncomfortable much of the time. Again, the majority of people who suffer from panic disorder are women (Sansone, Sansone, & Righter, 1998).

To get an idea of how a panic attack feels, imagine that you are trapped in your stateroom on a sinking ocean liner (the Titanic?). The room fills with water. When only a small air space remains near the ceiling and you are gasping for air, you'll know what a panic attack feels like.

Panic Disorder (with Agoraphobia)

In a **panic disorder (with agoraphobia)** people suffer from chronic anxiety and sudden panic. In addition, they have agoraphobia (ah-go-rah-FOBE-ee-ah), which is an intense *fear that a panic attack will occur* in a public place or unfamiliar situation. That is, agoraphobics intensely fear leaving their home and familiar surroundings. Typically, they find ways of avoiding places that frighten them—such as crowds, open roads, supermarkets, automobiles, and so on. As a result, some agoraphobics are prisoners in their own homes (DSM-IV-TR, 2000).

Agoraphobia

The problem known as **agoraphobia** can also occur without panic. In this case, people *fear that something extremely embarrassing will happen* if they leave home or enter an unfamiliar situation. For example, an agoraphobic person may refuse to go outside because he or she fears having a sudden attack of dizziness, or diarrhea, or shortness of breath. Going outside the home alone, being in a crowd, standing in line, crossing a bridge, or riding in a car can be impossible for an agoraphobic person (DSM-IV-TR, 2000). About 1.3 percent of all adults suffer from agoraphobia (with or without panic) during their lifetime (Grant et al., 2006).

Specific Phobia

As we noted earlier, phobias are intense, irrational fears that a person cannot shake off, even when there is no real danger. In a **specific phobia,** the person's fear, anxiety, and avoidance are focused on particular objects, activities, or situations. People affected by phobias recognize that their fears are unreasonable, but they cannot control them. For example, a person with a spider phobia would find it impossible to ignore a picture of a spider, even though a photograph can't bite anyone (Miltner et al., 2004). Specific phobias can be linked to nearly any object or situation. Many have been given names, such as these:

Acrophobia—fear of heights	Microphobia—fear of germs
Astraphobia—fear of storms, thunder, lightning	Nyctophobia—fear of darkness
Arachnophobia—fear of spiders	Pathophobia—fear of disease
Aviophobia—fear of airplanes	Pyrophobia—fear of fire
Claustrophobia—fear of closed spaces	Xenophobia—fear of strangers
Hematophobia—fear of blood	Zoophobia—fear of animals

By combining the appropriate root word with the word *phobia,* any number of unlikely fears can be named. Some are *acarophobia,* a fear of itching; *zemmiphobia,* fear of the great mole rat; *phobosophobia,* fear of fear; *arachibutyrophobia,* fear of peanut butter sticking to the roof of the mouth, and *hippopotomonstrosesquipedaliophobia,* fear of long words!

Almost everyone has a few mild phobias, such as fearing heights, closed spaces, or bugs and crawly things. A phobic disorder differs from such garden-variety fears in that it pro-

Panic disorder (without agoraphobia) The person is in a chronic state of anxiety and also has brief moments of sudden, intense, unexpected panic.

Panic disorder (with agoraphobia) A chronic state of anxiety and brief moments of sudden panic. The person fears that these panic attacks will occur in public places or unfamiliar situations.

Agoraphobia (without panic) The person fears that something extremely embarrassing will happen to them if they leave the house or enter unfamiliar situations.

Specific phobia An intense, irrational fear of specific objects, activities, or situations.

duces overwhelming fear. True phobias may lead to vomiting, wild climbing and running, or fainting. For a phobic disorder to exist, the person's fear must disrupt his or her daily life. Phobic persons are so threatened that they will go to almost any length to avoid the feared object or situation, such as driving 50 miles out of the way to avoid crossing a bridge. About 8 percent of all adults have phobic disorders during their lifetime (NIMH, 2001).

For a person with a strong fear of snakes (ophidiophobia), merely looking at this picture may be unsettling.

Social Phobia

In a **social phobia,** people fear situations in which they can be observed, evaluated, embarrassed, or humiliated by others. This leads them to avoid certain social situations, such as eating, writing, using the rest room, or speaking in public. When such situations cannot be avoided, people endure them with intense anxiety or distress. It is common for them to have uncomfortable physical symptoms, such as a pounding heart, shaking hands, sweating, diarrhea, mental confusion, and blushing. Social phobias greatly impair a person's ability to work, attend school, and form personal relationships (DSM-IV-TR, 2000). About 7 percent of all adults are affected by social phobias in a given year (NIMH, 2006).

Obsessive-Compulsive Disorder

People who suffer from **obsessive-compulsive disorder** are preoccupied with certain distressing thoughts and feel compelled to perform certain behaviors. You have probably experienced a mild obsessional thought, such as a song or stupid commercial jingle that repeats over and over in your mind. This may be irritating, but it's usually not terribly disturbing. True obsessions are images or thoughts that force their way into awareness against a person's will. They are so disturbing that they cause intense anxiety. The most common obsessions are about violence or harm (such as poisoning one's spouse or being hit by a car), about being "dirty" or "unclean," about whether one has performed some action (such as turning off the stove), and about committing immoral acts (Barlow, 2002).

The severe obsessions and compulsions of billionaire Howard Hughes led him to live as a recluse for more than 20 years. Hughes had an intense fear of contamination. To avoid infection, he constructed sterile, isolated environments in which his contact with people and objects was strictly limited by complicated rituals. Before handling a spoon, for instance, Hughes had his attendants wrap the handle in tissue paper and seal it with tape. A second piece of tissue was then wrapped around the first before he would touch it (Hodgson & Miller, 1982). A spoon prepared as Hughes required is shown at right.

Obsessions usually give rise to compulsions. These are irrational acts that a person feels driven to repeat. Often, compulsive acts help control or block out anxiety caused by an obsession. For example, a minister who finds profanities popping into her mind might start compulsively counting her heartbeat. Doing this would prevent her from thinking "dirty" words.

Many compulsive people are *checkers* or *cleaners.* For instance, a young mother who repeatedly pictures a knife plunging into her baby might check once an hour to make sure all the knives in her house are locked away. Doing so may reduce her anxieties, but it will probably also take over her life. Likewise, a person who feels "contaminated" from touching ordinary objects because "germs are everywhere" may be driven to wash his hands hundreds of times a day.

Of course, not all obsessive-compulsive disorders are so dramatic. Many simply involve extreme orderliness and rigid routine. Compulsive attention to detail and rigidly following rules helps keep activities totally under control and makes the highly anxious person feel more secure. (Notice that if such patterns are long-standing, but less intense, they are classified as a personality disorder.)

Social phobia An intense, irrational fear of being observed, evaluated, embarrassed, or humiliated by others in social situations.

Obsessive-compulsive disorder An extreme preoccupation with certain thoughts and compulsive performance of certain behaviors.

Stress Disorders

Stress disorders occur when people experience stresses outside the range of normal human experience, such as floods, tornadoes, earthquakes, or horrible accidents. They affect many political hostages, combat veterans, prisoners of war, and victims of terrorism, torture, violent crime, child molestation, rape, domestic violence, or people who have witnessed a death or serious injury (Brown & Barlow, 2007).

Symptoms of stress disorders include repeatedly reliving the traumatic event, avoiding reminders of the event, and blunted emotions. Also common are insomnia, nightmares, wariness, poor concentration, irritability, and explosive anger or aggression. If such reactions last *less* than a month after a traumatic event, the problem is called an **acute stress disorder.** If they last *more* than a month, the person is suffering from **posttraumatic stress disorder (PTSD)** (Shalev, 2001).

If a situation causes distress, anxiety, or fear, we tend to avoid it in the future. This is a normal survival instinct. However, victims of PTSD fail to recover from these reactions (Yehuda, 2002). Military combat is especially likely to cause PTSD. The constant threat of death and the gruesome sights and sounds of war take a terrible toll. Psychologists are already seeing high rates of PTSD among soldiers involved in combat in Iraq (Hoge et al., 2004). Sadly, 8 percent of military veterans still suffer from PTSD decades after they were in combat (Dirkzwager Bramsen, & Van Der Ploeg, 2001). About 3.5 percent of adults suffer from posttraumatic stress in any given year (NIMH, 2006).

In December 2004, a tsunami killed more than 250,000 people in southern Asia. In the aftermath of such disasters, many survivors suffer from acute stress reactions. For some, the flare-up of anxiety and distress occurs months or years after the stressful event, an example of a posttraumatic stress reaction.

Dissociative Disorders

In dissociative reactions we see striking episodes of *amnesia, fugue,* or *multiple identity*. **Dissociative amnesia** is an inability to recall one's name, address, or past. **Dissociative fugue** (FEWG) involves sudden, unplanned travel away from home and confusion about personal identity. Dissociations are often triggered by highly traumatic events (McLewin & Muller, 2006). In such cases, forgetting personal identity and fleeing unpleasant situations appear to be defenses against intolerable anxiety.

A person suffering from a **dissociative identity disorder** has two or more separate identities or personality states. (Note that identity disorders are not the same as schizophrenia. Schizophrenia, which is a psychotic disorder, is discussed later in this chapter.) One famous and dramatic example of multiple identities is described in the book *Sybil* (Schreiber, 1973). Sybil reportedly had 16 different personality states. Each identity had a distinct voice, vocabulary, and posture. One personality could play the piano (not Sybil), but the others could not.

When an identity other than Sybil was in control, Sybil experienced a "time lapse," or memory blackout. Sybil's amnesia and alternate identities first appeared during childhood. As a girl she was beaten, locked in closets, perversely tortured, sexually abused, and almost killed. Sybil's first dissociations allowed her to escape by creating another person who would suffer torture in her place. Identity disorders often begin with unbearable childhood experiences, like Sybil endured. A history of childhood trauma, especially sexual abuse, is found in a high percentage of persons whose personalities split into multiple identities (McLewin & Muller, 2006; Simeon et al., 2002).

Flamboyant cases like Sybil's have led some experts to question the existence of multiple personalities (Casey, 2001). However, a majority of psychologists continue to believe that multiple identity is a real, if rare, problem (Cormier & Thelen, 1998).

Therapy for dissociative identity disorders may make use of hypnosis, which allows contact with the various personality states. The goal of therapy is *integration* and *fusion* of the identities

Stress disorder A significant emotional disturbance caused by stresses outside the range of normal human experience.

Acute stress disorder A psychological disturbance lasting up to 1 month following stresses that would produce anxiety in anyone who experienced them.

Posttraumatic stress disorder A psychological disturbance lasting more than 1 month following stresses that would produce anxiety in anyone who experienced them.

Dissociative amnesia Loss of memory (partial or complete) for important information related to personal identity.

Dissociative fugue Sudden travel away from home, plus confusion abut one's personal identity.

Dissociative identity disorder The presence of two or more distinct personalities (multiple personality).

into a single, balanced personality. Fortunately, multiple identity disorders are far rarer in real life than they are in TV dramas!

Somatoform Disorders

Have you ever known someone who appeared to be healthy but seemed to constantly worry about disease? These people are preoccupied with bodily functions, such as their heartbeat or breathing or digestion. Minor physical problems—even a small sore or an occasional cough—may convince them that they have cancer or some other dreaded disease. Typically, they can't give up their fears of illness, even if doctors can find no medical basis for their complaints (Korol, Craig, & Firestone, 2003).

Are you describing hypochondria? Yes. In **hypochondriasis** (HI-po-kon-DRY-uh-sis), people interpret normal bodily sensations as proof that they have a terrible disease. In a related problem called **somatization disorder** (som-ah-tuh-ZAY-shun), people express their anxieties through various bodily complaints. That is, they suffer from problems such as vomiting or nausea, shortness of breath, difficulty swallowing, or painful menstrual periods. Typically, the person feels ill much of the time and visits doctors repeatedly. Most sufferers take medicines or other treatments, but no physical cause can be found for their distress. Similarly, a person with **pain disorder** is disabled by pain that has no identifiable physical basis.

A rarer somatoform disorder ("body-form" disorder) is called a *conversion reaction*. In a **conversion disorder,** severe emotional conflicts are "converted" into symptoms that actually disturb physical functioning or closely resemble a physical disability. For instance, a soldier might become deaf or lame or develop "glove anesthesia" just before a battle.

What is "glove anesthesia"? "Glove anesthesia" is a loss of sensitivity in the areas of the skin that would normally be covered by a glove. Glove anesthesia shows that conversion symptoms often contradict known medical facts. The system of nerves in the hands does not form a glove-like pattern and could not cause such symptoms (▶▶Fig. 12.4).

Bruce Ayres/Getty Images

Uncontrollable sneezing, which is often a conversion disorder, may continue for days or weeks. In such cases, sneezing is abnormal in rate and rhythm. In addition, the person's eyes do not close during a sneeze and sneezing does not occur during sleep. (A normal sneeze is shown here.) All of these signs suggest that the cause of the sneezing is psychological, not physical (Fochtmann, 1995).

Hypochondriasis A preoccupation with fears of having a serious disease. Ordinary physical signs are interpreted as proof that the person has a disease, but no physical disorder can be found.

Somatization disorder Afflicted persons have numerous physical complaints. Typically, they have consulted many doctors, but no organic cause for their distress can be identified.

Pain disorder Pain that has no identifiable physical cause and appears to be of psychological origin.

Conversion disorder A bodily symptom that mimics a physical disability but is actually caused by anxiety or emotional distress.

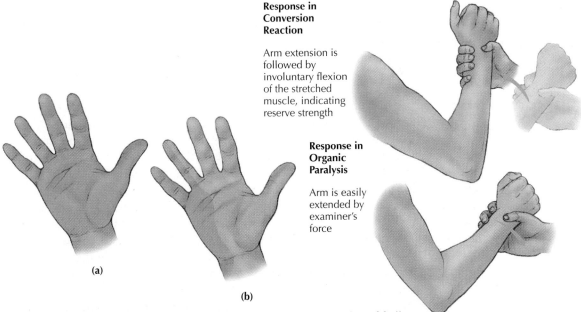

Response in Conversion Reaction

Arm extension is followed by involuntary flexion of the stretched muscle, indicating reserve strength

Response in Organic Paralysis

Arm is easily extended by examiner's force

(a)

(b)

▶▶**FIGURE 12.4** *(left)* "Glove" anesthesia is a conversion reaction involving loss of feeling in areas of the hand that would be covered by a glove *(a)*. If the anesthesia were physically caused, it would follow the pattern shown in *(b)*. *(right)* To test for organic paralysis of the arm, an examiner can suddenly extend the arm, stretching the muscles. A conversion reaction is indicated if the arm pulls back involuntarily. (Adapted from Weintraub, 1983.)

If symptoms disappear when a victim is asleep, hypnotized, or anesthetized, a conversion reaction must be suspected (Russo et al., 1998). Another sign to watch for is that victims of conversion reactions are strangely unconcerned about suddenly being disabled.

ANXIETY AND DISORDER—FOUR PATHWAYS TO TROUBLE

>SURVEY QUESTION< *How do psychologists explain anxiety-based disorders?*

What causes anxiety disorders? Susceptibility to anxiety-based disorders appears to be partly inherited (Rachman, 2004). Studies show that being high strung, nervous, or emotional runs in families. For example, 60 percent of children born to parents suffering from panic disorder have a fearful, inhibited temperament. Such children are irritable and wary as infants, shy and fearful as toddlers, and quiet and cautious introverts in elementary school. By the time they reach adulthood, they are at high risk for anxiety problems, such as panic attacks (Barlow, 2000; Durand & Barlow, 2006).

At least four major psychological perspectives on the causes of dissociative, anxiety-based, and somatoform disorders exist. These are (1) the *psychodynamic* approach, (2) the *humanistic-existential* approach, (3) the *behavioral* approach, and (4) the *cognitive* approach.

Psychodynamic Approach

The term *psychodynamic* refers to internal motives, conflicts, unconscious forces, and other dynamics of mental life. Freud was the first to propose a psychodynamic explanation for what he called "neurosis." According to Freud, disturbances like those we have described represent a raging conflict among subparts of the personality—the id, ego, and superego.

Freud emphasized that intense anxiety can be caused by forbidden id impulses for sex or aggression that threaten to break through into behavior. The person constantly fears doing something "crazy" or forbidden. She or he may also be tortured by guilt, which the superego uses to suppress forbidden impulses. Caught in the middle, the ego is eventually overwhelmed. This forces the person to use rigid defense mechanisms and misguided, inflexible behavior to prevent a disastrous loss of control (see Chapter 10).

Humanistic-Existential Approaches

Humanistic theories emphasize subjective experience, human problems, and personal potentials. Humanistic psychologist Carl Rogers regarded emotional disorders as the end product of a faulty self-image or self-concept (Rogers, 1959). Rogers believed that anxious individuals have built up unrealistic mental images of themselves. This leaves them vulnerable to contradictory information. Let's say, for example, that an essential part of Cheyenne's self-image is the idea that she is highly intelligent. If Cheyenne does poorly in school, she may deny or distort her perceptions of herself and the situation. Should Cheyenne's anxiety become severe, she may resort to using defense mechanisms. A conversion reaction, anxiety attacks, or similar symptoms could also result from threats to her self-image. These symptoms, in turn, would become new threats that provoke further distortions. Soon, she would fall into a vicious cycle of maladjustment and anxiety that feeds on itself once started.

Existentialism focuses on the elemental problems of existence, such as death, meaning, choice, and responsibility. Psychologists who take a more existential view stress that unhealthy anxiety reflects a loss of *meaning* in one's life. According to them, we must show *courage* and *responsibility* in our choices if life is to have meaning. Too often, they say, we give in to "existential anxiety" and back away from life-enhancing choices. Existential anxiety is the unavoidable anguish that comes from knowing we are personally responsible for our lives. Hence, we have a crushing need to choose wisely and courageously as we face life's empty and impersonal void.

From the existential view, people who are anxious are living in "bad faith." That is, they have collapsed in the face of the awesome responsibility to choose a meaningful existence. In short, they have lost their way in life. From this point of view, making choices that don't truly reflect what you value, feel, and believe can make you sick.

Behavioral Approach

Behaviorist approaches emphasize overt, observable behavior and the effects of learning and conditioning. Behaviorists assume that the "symptoms" we have discussed are learned, just as other behaviors are. You might recall from Chapter 6, for instance, that phobias can be acquired through classical conditioning. Similarly, anxiety attacks may reflect conditioned emotional responses that generalize to new situations and the hypochondriac's "sickness behavior" may be reinforced by the sympathy and attention he or she gets. One point that all theorists agree on is that disordered behavior is ultimately self-defeating because it makes the person more miserable in the long run, even though it temporarily lowers anxiety.

But if the person becomes more miserable in the long run, how does the pattern get started? The behavioral explanation is that self-defeating behavior begins with avoidance learning (described in Chapter 6). Avoidance learning occurs when making a response delays or prevents the onset of a painful or unpleasant stimulus. Here's a quick review to refresh your memory:

> An animal is placed in a special cage. After a few minutes a light comes on, followed a moment later by a painful shock. Quickly, the animal escapes into a second chamber. After a few minutes, a light comes on in this chamber, and the shock is repeated. Soon the animal learns to avoid pain by moving before the shock occurs. Once an animal learns to avoid the shock, it can be turned off altogether. A well-trained animal may avoid the nonexistent shock indefinitely.

The same analysis can be applied to human behavior. A behaviorist would say that the powerful reward of immediate relief from anxiety keeps self-defeating avoidance behaviors alive. This view, known as the **anxiety reduction hypothesis,** seems to explain why the behavior patterns we have discussed often look very "stupid" to outside observers.

Cognitive Approach

The cognitive view is that distorted thinking causes people to magnify ordinary threats and failures, which leads to distress (Provencher, Dugas, & Ladouceur, 2004). For example, Bonnie, who is socially phobic, constantly has upsetting thoughts about being evaluated at school. One reason for this is that people with social phobias tend to be perfectionists. Like other social phobics, Bonnie is excessively concerned about mistakes. She also perceives criticism where none exists. Bonnie tends to avoid any social situation she perceives might focus too much attention on herself (Brown & Barlow, 2007). Even when socially phobic persons are successful, distorted thinking leads them to think they have failed (Barlow, 2002). In short, changing the thinking patterns of anxious individuals like Bonnie can greatly lessen their fears (Poulton & Andrews, 1996).

Implications

There is probably a core of truth to all four psychological explanations. For this reason, understanding anxiety-based disorders may be aided by combining parts of each perspective. Each viewpoint also suggests a different approach to treatment. Because there are many possibilities, therapy is discussed later, in Chapter 13.

Anxiety reduction hypothesis Explains the self-defeating nature of avoidance responses as a result of the reinforcing effects of relief from anxiety.

Study Break Personality Disorders and Anxiety-Based Disorders

Reflect

Many of the qualities that define personality disorders exist to a minor degree in normal personalities. Try to think of a person you know who has some of the characteristics described for each type of personality disorder.

Which of the anxiety disorders would you *least* want to suffer from? Why?

What minor obsessions or compulsions have you experienced?

What is the key difference between a stress disorder and an adjustment disorder? (Review both discussions if you don't immediately know the answer.)

Learning Check

1. Which of the following personality disorders is associated with an inflated sense of self-importance and a constant need for attention and admiration?

   a. narcissistic   b. antisocial
   c. paranoid   d. manipulative

2. Antisocial personality disorders are difficult to treat, but there is typically a decline in antisocial behavior a year or two after adolescence. T or F?

3. Excessive anxiety over ordinary life stresses is characteristic of which of the following disorders?

   a. PTSD   b. agoraphobia
   c. hypochondriasis   d. adjustment disorder

4. Panic disorder can occur with or without agoraphobia, but agoraphobia cannot occur alone, without the presence of a panic disorder. T or F?

5. Alice has a phobic fear of blood. What is the formal term for her fear?

   a. nyctophobia   b. hematophobia
   c. pathophobia   d. pyrophobia

6. A person who intensely fears eating, writing, or speaking in public suffers from _____ _____.

7. "Checkers" and "cleaners" suffer from which disorder?

   a. acarophobia   b. panic disorder with agoraphobia
   c. generalized anxiety disorder   d. obsessive-compulsive disorder

8. The symptoms of acute stress disorders last less than 1 month; posttraumatic stress disorders last more than 1 month. T or F?

9. Which of the following is *not* a dissociative disorder?

   a. fugue   b. amnesia
   c. conversion reaction   d. multiple identity

Critical Thinking

10. Many of the physical complaints associated with anxiety disorders are closely related to activity of what part of the nervous system?

Answers

1. a 2. F 3. d 4. F 5. b 6. social phobia 7. d 8. T 9. c 10. The autonomic nervous system (ANS), especially the sympathetic branch of the ANS.

PSYCHOTIC DISORDERS—LIFE IN THE SHADOW OF MADNESS

>SURVEY QUESTION< *What are the general characteristics of psychotic disorders?*

Imagine that a member of your family has been hearing voices, is talking strangely, has covered her head with aluminum foil, and believes that houseflies are speaking to her in code. If you observed such symptoms, would you be concerned? Of course you would, and rightly so. Psychotic disorders are among the most serious of all mental problems.

A person who is psychotic undergoes a number of striking changes in thinking, behavior, and emotion. Basic to all of these changes is the fact that **psychosis** reflects a loss of contact with shared views of reality (psycho*sis*, singular; psycho*ses*, plural). The following comments, made by a psychotic patient, illustrate what is meant by a "split" from reality (Durand & Barlow, 2006):

> When you do the 25 of the clock, it means that you leave the house 25 after 1 to mail letters so they can check on you … and they know where you're at. That's the Eagle.

The Nature of Psychosis

What are the major features of psychotic disorders? Delusions and hallucinations are core features, but there are others as well.

People who suffer from **delusions** hold false beliefs that they insist are true, regardless of how much the facts contradict them. An example is a 43-year-old schizophrenic man who was convinced he was pregnant (Mansouri & Adityanjee, 1995).

Psychosis A withdrawal from reality marked by hallucinations and delusions, disturbed thought and emotions, and by personality disorganization.

Delusion A false belief held against all contrary evidence.

Are there different types of delusions? Yes, some common types of delusions are: (1) *depressive* delusions, in which people feel that they have committed horrible crimes or sinful deeds; (2) *somatic* delusions, such as believing your body is "rotting away" or that it is emitting foul odors; (3) delusions of *grandeur,* in which people think they are extremely important; (4) delusions of *influence,* in which people feel they are being controlled or influenced by others or by unseen forces; (5) delusions of *persecution,* in which people believe that others are "out to get them"; and (6) delusions of *reference,* in which people give great personal meaning to unrelated events. For instance, delusional people sometimes think that television programs are giving them a special personal message (DSM-IV-TR, 2000).

Hallucinations are imaginary sensations, such as seeing, hearing, or smelling things that don't exist in the real world. The most common psychotic hallucination is hearing voices, like the voice that told Carol North to "Collide with the world." Sometimes these voices command patients to hurt themselves. Unfortunately, sometimes people obey (Barrowcliff & Haddock, 2006). More rarely, psychotic people may feel "insects crawling under their skin," taste "poisons" in their food, or smell "gas" their "enemies" are using to "get" them. Sensory changes, such as anesthesia (numbness, or a loss of sensation) or extreme sensitivity to heat, cold, pain, or touch, can also occur.

During a psychotic episode, emotions are often severely disturbed. For instance, the psychotic person may be wildly elated, depressed, hyperemotional, or apathetic. Sometimes psychotic patients display *flat affect,* a condition in which the face is frozen in a blank expression. Brain imaging studies of psychotic patients with "frozen masks" reveals abnormal functioning of the brain areas responsible for processing emotions (Fahim et al., 2005).

Some psychotic symptoms can be thought of as a primitive type of communication. That is, many patients can only use their actions to say "I need help," or "I can't handle it any more." Disturbed verbal communication is a nearly universal symptom of psychosis. In fact, psychotic speech tends to be so garbled and chaotic that it sometimes sounds like a *word salad.*

Major disturbances such as those just described—as well as added problems with thinking, memory, and attention—bring about personality disintegration and a break with reality. *Personality disintegration* occurs when a person's thoughts, actions, and emotions are no longer coordinated. When psychotic disturbances and a fragmented personality are evident for weeks or months, the person has suffered a psychosis (DSM-IV-TR, 2000). (See ■ Table 12.5.)

Organic Psychosis

In a sense, all psychoses are partly organic, involving physical changes in the brain. However, the general term *organic psychosis* is usually reserved for problems involving clear-cut brain injuries or diseases. For example, poisoning by lead or mercury can damage the brain and

A scene in a state mental hospital.

■ Table 12.5 **Warning Signs of Psychotic Disorders and Major Mood Disorders**
• You express bizarre thoughts or beliefs that defy reality.
• You have withdrawn from family members and other relationships.
• You hear unreal voices or sees things others don't.
• You are extremely sad, persistently despondent, or suicidal.
• You are excessively energetic and have little need for sleep.
• You lose your appetite, sleep excessively, and have no energy.
• You exhibit extreme mood swings.
• You believe someone is trying to get you.
• You have engaged in antisocial, destructive, or self-destructive behavior.

Sources: Harvey et al., 1996; Durand & Barlow, 2006.

Hallucination An imaginary sensation, such as seeing, hearing, or smelling things that don't exist in the real world.

▸▸**FIGURE 12.5** The Mad Hatter, from Lewis Carroll's *Alice's Adventures in Wonderland*. History provides numerous examples of psychosis caused by toxic chemicals. Carroll's Mad Hatter character is modeled after an occupational disease of the eighteenth and nineteenth centuries. In that era, hat makers were heavily exposed to mercury used in the preparation of felt. Consequently, many suffered brain damage and became psychotic, or "mad" (Kety, 1979).

cause hallucinations, delusions, and a loss of emotional control (▸▸Fig. 12.5). A particularly dangerous situation is found in old buildings that contain leaded paints. Lead tastes sweet. Thus, young children may be tempted to eat leaded paint flakes as if they were candy. Children who eat leaded paint can become psychotic or retarded (Mielke, 1999).

Leaded paints also release powdered lead into the air. Children may breathe the powder or eat it after handling contaminated toys. Other sources of lead are soldered water pipes, old lead-lined drinking fountains, lead-glazed pottery, and lead deposited years ago from automobile exhaust. On a much larger scale, "poisoning" of another type, in the form of drug abuse, can also produce psychotic symptoms (DSM-IV-TR, 2000).

Are there specific kinds of psychotic disorders? Two major types of psychosis are *delusional disorders* and *schizophrenia*. As you will recall, mood disorders mainly involve emotional extremes. Nevertheless, psychotic symptoms can also occur in some mood disorders. You'll find information on each of these problems in upcoming discussions.

The soil and dust in cities and near busy streets is often heavily contaminated with lead. This lead came from automobile exhaust before leaded gasoline was banned. Young children frequently put objects and their hands in their mouths. This is a major source of lead poisoning for many children. Paving play areas or covering them with clean soil can greatly reduce lead exposure (Mielke, 1999).

DELUSIONAL DISORDERS— AN ENEMY BEHIND EVERY TREE

>SURVEY QUESTION< *What is the nature of a delusional disorder?*

People with delusional disorders usually do not suffer from hallucinations, emotional excesses, or personality disintegration. Even so, their break with reality is unmistakable. The main feature of **delusional disorders** is the presence of deeply held false beliefs, which may take the following forms (DSM-IV-TR, 2000):

- **Erotomanic type** In this disorder, people have erotic delusions that they are loved by another person, especially by someone famous or of higher status.
- **Grandiose type** In this case, people suffer from the delusion that they have some great, unrecognized talent, knowledge, or insight. They may also believe that they have a special relationship with an important person or with God or that they are a famous person. (If the famous person is alive, the deluded person regards her or him as an imposter.)
- **Jealous type** An example of this type of delusion would be having an all-consuming, but unfounded, belief that your spouse or lover is unfaithful.
- **Persecutory type** Delusions of persecution involve belief that you are being conspired against, cheated, spied on, followed, poisoned, maligned, or harassed.
- **Somatic type** People suffering from somatic delusions typically believe that their bodies are diseased or rotting, or infested with insects or parasites, or that parts of their bodies are defective.

Although they are false, and sometimes far-fetched, all of these delusions are about experiences that could occur in real life (Manschreck, 1996). In other types of psychosis, delusions tend to be more bizarre. For example, a person with schizophrenia might believe that space aliens have replaced all of his internal organs with electronic monitoring devices. In contrast, people with ordinary delusions merely believe that someone is trying to steal

Delusional disorder A psychosis marked by severe delusions of grandeur, jealousy, persecution, or similar preoccupations.

their money, that they are being deceived by a lover, that the FBI is watching them, and the like (DSM-IV-TR, 2000).

Paranoid Psychosis

The most common delusional disorder, often called **paranoid psychosis,** centers on delusions of persecution. Many self-styled reformers, crank letter writers, conspiracy theorists, "UFO abductees," and the like, suffer paranoid delusions. Paranoid individuals often believe that they are being cheated, spied on, followed, poisoned, harassed, or plotted against. Usually they are intensely suspicious, believing they must be on guard at all times.

The evidence such people find to support their beliefs usually fails to persuade others. Every detail of the paranoid person's existence is woven into a private version of "what's really going on." Buzzing during a telephone conversation may be interpreted as "someone listening"; a stranger who comes to the door asking for directions may be seen as "really trying to get information"; and so forth.

It is difficult to treat people suffering from paranoid delusions because it is almost impossible for them to accept that they need help. Anyone who suggests that they have a problem simply becomes part of the "conspiracy" to "persecute" them. Consequently, paranoid people frequently lead lonely, isolated, and humorless lives dominated by constant suspicion and hostility.

Although they are not necessarily dangerous to others, they can be. People who believe that terrorists, the Mafia, "government agents," or a street gang is slowly closing in on them may be moved to violence by their irrational fears. Imagine that a stranger comes to the door to ask a paranoid person for directions. If the stranger has his hand in his coat pocket, he could become the target of a paranoid attempt at "self-defense."

Delusional disorders are rare. By far, the most common form of psychosis is schizophrenia. Let's explore schizophrenia in more detail and see how it differs from a delusional disorder.

SCHIZOPHRENIA—SHATTERED REALITY

>SURVEY QUESTIONS< *What forms does schizophrenia take? What causes it?*

Schizophrenia (SKIT-soh-FREN-nee-uh) is marked by delusions, hallucinations, apathy, thinking abnormalities, and a "split" between thought and emotion. In schizophrenia, emotions may become blunted or very inappropriate. For example, if a person with schizophrenia is told his mother just died, he might smile, or giggle, or show no emotion at all. Schizophrenic delusions may include the idea that the person's thoughts and actions are being controlled, that thoughts are being broadcast (so others can hear them), that thoughts have been "inserted" into the person's mind, or that thoughts have been removed. In addition, schizophrenia involves withdrawal from contact with others, a loss of interest in external activities, a breakdown of personal habits, and an inability to deal with daily events (Neufeld et al., 2003). One person in 100 has schizophrenia in any given year (NIMH, 2006).

Many schizophrenic symptoms appear to be related to problems with *selective attention*. In other words, it is hard for people with schizophrenia to focus on one item of information at a time. Having an impaired "sensory filter" in their brains may be why they are overwhelmed by a jumble of thoughts, sensations, images, and feelings (Heinrichs, 2001).

Is there more than one type of schizophrenia? Schizophrenia appears to be a group of related disturbances. It has four major subtypes:

- **Disorganized type** Schizophrenia marked by incoherence, grossly disorganized behavior, bizarre thinking, and flat or grossly inappropriate emotions.
- **Catatonic type** Schizophrenia marked by stupor, rigidity, unresponsiveness, posturing, mutism, and, sometimes, agitated, purposeless behavior.

Paranoid psychosis A delusional disorder centered especially on delusions of persecution.

Schizophrenia A psychosis characterized by delusions, hallucinations, apathy, and a "split" between thought and emotion.

- **Paranoid type** Schizophrenia marked by a preoccupation with delusions or by frequent auditory hallucinations related to a single theme, especially grandeur or persecution.
- **Undifferentiated type** Schizophrenia in which there are prominent psychotic symptoms, but none of the specific features of catatonic, disorganized, or paranoid types.

Disorganized Schizophrenia

The disorder known as disorganized schizophrenia (sometimes called hebephrenic schizophrenia) comes close to matching the stereotyped images of "madness" seen in movies. In **disorganized schizophrenia,** personality disintegration is almost complete: Emotions, speech, and behavior are all highly disorganized. The result is silliness, laughter, and bizarre or obscene behavior, as shown by this intake interview of a patient named Edna:

Peter Granser/Laif/Aurora Photos

In disorganized schizophrenia, behavior is marked by silliness, laughter, and bizarre or obscene behavior.

Dr. I am Dr. _____. I would like to know something more about you.

Patient You have a nasty mind. Lord! Lord! Cats in a cradle.

Dr. Tell me, how do you feel?

Patient London's bell is a long, long dock. Hee! Hee! (Giggles uncontrollably.)

Dr. Do you know where you are now?

Patient D_____n! S_____t on you all who rip into my internals! The grudgerometer will take care of you all! (Shouting) I am the Queen, see my magic, I shall turn you all into smidgelings forever!

Dr. Your husband is concerned about you. Do you know his name?

Patient (Stands, walks to and faces the wall) Who am I, who are we, who are you, who are they, (turns)

I . . . I . . . I . . . I! (Makes grotesque faces.)

Edna was placed in the women's ward where she proceeded to masturbate. Occasionally, she would scream or shout obscenities. At other times she giggled to herself. She was known to attack other patients. She began to complain that her uterus was attached to a "pipeline to the Kremlin" and that she was being "infernally invaded" by Communism. (Suinn, 1975*)

Disorganized schizophrenia typically develops in adolescence or young adulthood. Chances of improvement are limited, and social impairment is usually extreme (DSM-IV-TR, 2000).

Catatonic Schizophrenia

The catatonic person seems to be in a state of total panic (Fink & Taylor, 2003). **Catatonic schizophrenia** brings about a stuporous condition in which odd positions may be held for hours or even days. These periods of rigidity may be similar to the tendency to "freeze" at times of great emergency or panic. Catatonic individuals appear to be struggling desperately to control their inner turmoil. One sign of this is the fact that stupor may occasionally give way to agitated outbursts or violent behavior. The following excerpt describes a catatonic episode.

Manuel appeared to be physically healthy upon examination. Yet he did not regain his awareness of his surroundings. He remained motionless, speechless, and seemingly unconscious. One evening an aide turned him on his side to straighten out the sheet, was called away to tend to another patient, and forgot to return. Manuel

Disorganized schizophrenia
Schizophrenia marked by incoherence, grossly disorganized behavior, bizarre thinking, and flat or grossly inappropriate emotions.

Catatonic schizophrenia Schizophrenia marked by stupor, rigidity, unresponsiveness, posturing, mutism, and, sometimes, agitated, purposeless behavior.

*All Suinn quotes in this chapter are from *Fundamentals of Behavior Pathology* by R. M. Suinn. Copyright © 1975. Reprinted by permission of John Wiley & Sons, Inc.

was found the next morning, still on his side, his arm tucked under his body, as he had been left the night before. His arm was turning blue from lack of circulation, but he seemed to be experiencing no discomfort. (Suinn, 1975)

Notice that Manuel did not speak. *Mutism,* along with a marked decrease in responsiveness to the environment, makes patients with catatonic schizophrenia difficult to "reach." Fortunately, this bizarre disorder has become rare in Europe and North America (DSM-IV-TR, 2000).

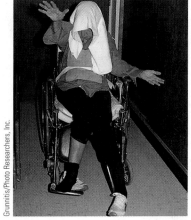

Can the rigid postures and stupor of a person with catatonic schizophrenia be understood in terms of abnormal body chemistry? Environment? Heredity?

Paranoid Schizophrenia

Paranoid schizophrenia is the most common schizophrenic disorder. As in paranoid delusional disorders, **paranoid schizophrenia** centers on delusions of grandeur and persecution. However, paranoid schizophrenics also hallucinate, and their delusions are more bizarre and unconvincing than those in a delusional disorder (Freeman & Garety, 2004).

Thinking that their minds are being controlled by God, the government, or "cosmic rays from space," or that someone is trying to poison them, people suffering from paranoid schizophrenia may feel forced into violence to "protect" themselves (▸▸Fig. 12.6). An example is James Huberty, who brutally murdered 21 people at a McDonald's restaurant in San Ysidro, California. Huberty, who had paranoid schizophrenia, felt persecuted and cheated by life. Shortly before he announced to his wife that he was "going hunting humans," Huberty had been hearing hallucinated voices.

How dangerous are the mentally ill? Horrific crimes, like the San Ysidro murders, lead many people to believe that the mentally ill are dangerous. Are they right? You might be surprised by the answer, found in "Are the Mentally Ill Prone to Violence?"

▸▸**FIGURE 12.6** Over a period of years, Theodore Kaczynski mailed bombs to unsuspecting victims, many of whom were maimed or killed. As a young adult, Kaczynski was a brilliant mathematician. At the time of his arrest, he had become the Unabomber—a reclusive "loner" who deeply mistrusted other people and modern technology. After his arrest, Kaczynski was judged to be suffering from paranoid schizophrenia.

The Causes of Schizophrenia

Former British Prime Minister Winston Churchill once described a question that perplexed him as "a riddle wrapped in a mystery inside an enigma." The same words might describe the causes of schizophrenia.

Environment

What causes schizophrenia? An increased risk of developing schizophrenia may begin at birth or even before. Women who are exposed to the influenza (flu) virus or to rubella (German measles) during the middle of pregnancy have children who are more likely to become schizophrenic (Brown et al., 2001). Malnutrition during pregnancy and complications at the time of birth can have a similar impact. Possibly, such events disturb brain development, leaving people more vulnerable to a psychotic break with reality (Walker et al., 2004).

Early **psychological trauma** (a psychological injury or shock) may also add to the risk. Often, the victims of schizophrenia were exposed to violence, sexual abuse, death, divorce, separation, or other stresses in childhood (Walker et al., 2004). Living in a troubled family is a related risk factor. In a disturbed family environment, stressful relationships, communication patterns, and negative emotions prevail. Deviant communication patterns cause anxiety, confusion, anger, conflict, and turmoil. Typically, disturbed families interact in ways that are laden with guilt, prying, criticism, negativity, and emotional attacks (Bressi, Albonetti, & Razzoli, 1998; Davison & Neale, 2006).

Paranoid schizophrenia Schizophrenia marked by a preoccupation with delusions or by frequent auditory hallucinations related to a single theme, especially grandeur or persecution.

Psychological trauma A psychological injury or shock, such as that caused by violence, abuse, neglect, separation, and so forth.

Are the Mentally Ill Prone to Violence?

News reports and television programs tend to exaggerate the connection between mental illness and violence (Corrigan et al., 2005). Such media reports both create and reflect deeply held beliefs about mental disorders in our society. Such beliefs are important because they affect laws and personal attitudes toward the mentally ill. For example, people who strongly believe that the mentally ill are prone to violence are typically afraid to have for-

Although Jeffrey Dahmer's case is extreme, he is typical of the mentally disordered persons who make the evening news. Most have committed murder or some other heinous crime. This gives the impression that the mentally ill are violent and dangerous. In reality, only a tiny percentage of all mentally disordered persons are more violent than average. (Dahmer was killed in prison by another inmate in 1994.)

mer mental patients as neighbors, coworkers, or friends (Corrigan & Watson, 2005).

The reality is just the opposite. According to the largest study ever conducted on this question, mentally ill individuals who are not also substance abusers are no more prone to violence than are normal individuals (Monahan et al., 2001). There are only a few exceptions to this conclusion and in those cases, the risk is not very large (Noble, 1997; Rice, 1997).

- Only persons who are *actively psychotic* are more violence prone than non-patients. That is, if a person is experiencing delusions and hallucinations, the risk of violence is elevated. Other mental problems are unrelated to violence.
- Only persons *currently* experiencing psychotic symptoms are at increased risk for violence. Violent behavior is not related to having been a mental patient in the past or having had psychotic symptoms in the past.

Thus, most news stories give a false impression. Only a small minority of the actively mentally ill poses an increased risk. Even when we consider people who are actively psychotic, we find that the vast majority are not violent. Former mental patients, in particular, are no more likely to be violent than people in general. No matter how disturbed a person may have been, she or he merits respect and compassion.

The risk of violence from mental patients is actually many times lower than that from persons who have the following attributes: young, male, poor, and intoxicated (Corrigan & Watson, 2005). Remember, people who are not mentally ill commit the overwhelming majority of violent crimes.

Although they are attractive, environmental explanations alone are not enough to account for schizophrenia. For example, when the children of schizophrenic parents are raised away from their chaotic home environment, they are still more likely to become psychotic (Walker et al., 2004).

Does that mean that heredity affects the risk of developing schizophrenia?

Heredity

There is now little doubt that heredity is a factor in schizophrenia. It appears that some individuals inherit a *potential* for developing schizophrenia. They are, in other words, more *vulnerable* to the disorder than others are (Harrison & Weinberger, 2005; Walker et al., 2004).

How has that been shown? If one identical twin becomes schizophrenic (remember, identical twins have identical genes), then the other twin has a *48 percent* chance of also becoming schizophrenic (Lenzenweger & Gottesman, 1994). The figure for twins can be compared to the risk of schizophrenia for the population in general, which is about 1 percent. (See ▸Fig. 12.7 for other relationships.) In general, schizophrenia is clearly more common among close relatives and it tends to run in families. There's even a case on record of *four* identical quadruplets *all* developing schizophrenia (Mirsky et al., 2000). In light of such evidence, researchers are now beginning to search for specific genes related to schizophrenia.

A problem exists with current genetic explanations of schizophrenia: Very few people with schizophrenia have children. How could a genetic defect be passed from one genera-

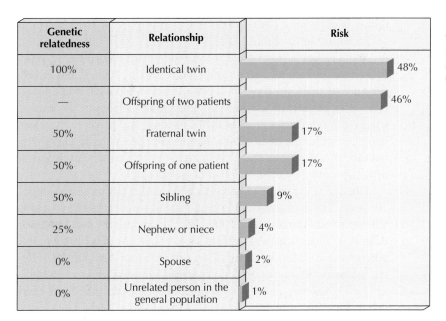

Genetic relatedness	Relationship	Risk
100%	Identical twin	48%
—	Offspring of two patients	46%
50%	Fraternal twin	17%
50%	Offspring of one patient	17%
50%	Sibling	9%
25%	Nephew or niece	4%
0%	Spouse	2%
0%	Unrelated person in the general population	1%

▸▸**FIGURE 12.7** Lifetime risk of developing schizophrenia is associated with how closely a person is genetically related to a schizophrenic person. A shared environment also increases the risk. (Estimates from Lenzenweger & Gottesman, 1994.)

tion to the next if afflicted people don't reproduce? One possible answer is suggested by the fact that the older a man is (even if he doesn't suffer from schizophrenia) when he fathers a child, the more likely it is that the child will develop schizophrenia. Apparently, genetic mutations occur in aging male reproductive cells and increase the risk of schizophrenia (as well as other medical problems) (Malaspina et al., 2005; Sipos et al., 2004).

Brain Chemistry

Amphetamine, LSD, PCP ("angel dust"), and similar drugs produce effects that partially mimic the symptoms of schizophrenia. Also, the same drugs (phenothiazines) used to treat LSD overdoses tend to alleviate psychotic symptoms. Facts such as these suggest that biochemical abnormalities (disturbances in brain chemicals or neurotransmitters) may occur in schizophrenic people. It is possible that the schizophrenic brain produces some substance similar to a *psychedelic* (mind-altering) drug. At present, one likely can-

This series of paintings by Louis Wain reflects a troubled personality. Wain was a British illustrator who became schizophrenic in middle age. As Wain's psychosis progressed, his cat paintings became highly abstract and fragmented. In many ways, Wain's paintings resemble the perceptual changes caused by psychedelic drugs such as mescaline and LSD. Recent research suggests that psychosis may, in fact, be the result of mind-altering changes in brain chemistry. (Derik Bayes/Courtesy Guttman-Maclay *Life* Picture Service.)

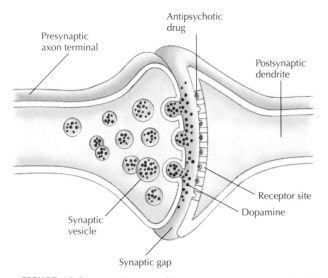

▸▸**FIGURE 12.8** Dopamine normally crosses the synapse between two neurons, activating the second cell. Antipsychotic drugs bind to the same receptor sites as dopamine does, blocking its action. In people suffering from schizophrenia, a reduction in dopamine activity can quiet a person's agitation and psychotic symptoms.

didate is dopamine (DOPE-ah-meen), an important chemical messenger found in the brain.

Many researchers believe that schizophrenia is related to overactivity in brain dopamine systems (Durand & Barlow, 2006; Kapur & Lecrubier, 2003). One possibility is that dopamine receptors become super-responsive to normal amounts of dopamine. Dopamine appears to trigger a flood of unrelated thoughts, feelings, and perceptions, which may account for the voices, hallucinations, and delusions of schizophrenia. The implication is that schizophrenic people may be on a sort of drug trip caused by their own bodies (▸▸ Fig. 12.8).

Dopamine is not the only brain chemical that has caught scientists' attention. The neurotransmitter glutamate also appears to be related to schizophrenia (van Elst et al., 2005). People who take the hallucinogenic drug PCP, which affects glutamate, have symptoms that closely mimic schizophrenia (Murray, 2002). This occurs because glutamate influences brain activity in areas that control emotions and sensory information (Tsai & Coyle, 2002). Another tantalizing connection is the fact that stress alters glutamate levels, which in turn alter dopamine systems (Moghaddam, 2002). The story is far from complete, but it appears that dopamine, glutamate, and other brain chemicals partly explain the devastating symptoms of schizophrenia (Walker et al., 2004). (See "The Schizophrenic Brain.")

Implications

In summary, the emerging picture of psychotic disorders such as schizophrenia takes this form: Anyone subjected to enough stress may be pushed to a psychotic break. (Battlefield psychosis is an example.) However, some people inherit a difference in brain chemistry or brain structure that makes them more susceptible—even to normal life stresses.

Thus, the right mix of inherited potential and environmental stress brings about mind-altering changes in brain chemicals and brain structure. This explanation is called a **stress-vulnerability model.** It attributes psychotic disorders to a blend of environmental stress and inherited susceptibility (Walker et al., 2004). The model seems to apply to other forms of psychopathology as well, such as depression (▸▸ Fig. 12.9).

Despite advances in our understanding, psychosis remains "a riddle wrapped in a mystery inside an enigma." Let us hope that recent progress toward a cure for schizophrenia will continue.

Stress-vulnerability model Attributes psychosis to a combination of environmental stress and inherited susceptibility.

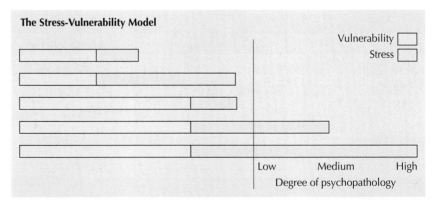

▸▸**FIGURE 12.9** Various combinations of vulnerability and stress may produce psychological problems. The top bar shows low vulnerability and low stress. The result? No problem. The same is true of the next bar down, where low vulnerability is combined with moderate stress. Even high vulnerability (third bar) may not lead to problems if stress levels remain low. However, when high vulnerability combines with moderate or high stress (bottom two bars) the person "crosses the line" and suffers from psychopathology.

The Schizophrenic Brain

Several imaging methods (remember Chapter 2?) have made it possible to directly observe the living schizophrenic brain. CT scans and MRI scans, which can reveal brain structure, suggest that the brains of schizophrenics have shrunk (atrophied). For example, »Figure 12.10 shows a *CT scan* (CT stands for computed tomography, or computer-enhanced X-ray images) of the brain of John Hinkley, Jr., who shot former U.S. President Ronald Reagan and three other men in 1981. In the ensuing trial, Hinkley was declared insane. As you can see, his brain had wider than normal surface fissuring.

Similarly, *MRI scans* (magnetic resonance imaging) indicate that schizophrenic people tend to have enlarged ventricles (fluid-filled spaces within the brain), again suggesting that surrounding brain tissue has withered (Barkataki et al., 2006). Other brain regions also appear to be abnormal. It is telling that the affected areas are crucial for regulating motivation, emotion, perception, actions, and attention (Gur et al., 1998; Walker et al., 2004).

Other methods provide images of brain activity, including PET scans. To make a *PET scan* (positron emission tomography), a radioactive sugar solution is injected into a vein. When the sugar reaches the brain, an electronic device measures how much is used in each area. These data are then translated into a color map, or scan, of brain activity (»Fig. 12.11). Researchers are finding patterns in such scans that are consistently linked with schizophrenia, affective disorders, and other problems. For instance, activity tends to be abnormally low in the frontal lobes of the schizophrenic brain (Durand & Barlow, 2006; Velakoulis & Pantelis, 1996). In the future, PET scans may be used to accurately diagnose schizophrenia. For now, such scans show that there is a clear difference in schizophrenic brain activity.

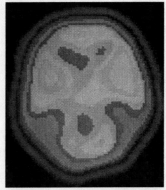

NORMAL

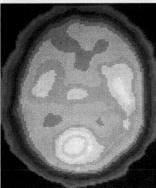

SCHIZOPHRENIC

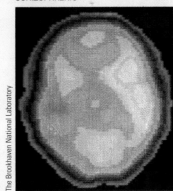

MANIC DEPRESSIVE

The Brookhaven National Laboratory

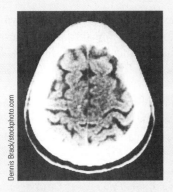

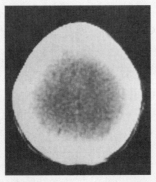

Dennis Brack/stockphoto.com

»**FIGURE 12.10** *(left)* CT scan of would-be presidential assassin John Hinkley, Jr., taken when he was 25. The X-ray image shows widened fissures in the wrinkled surface of Hinkley's brain. *(right)* CT scan of a normal 25-year-old's brain. In most young adults the surface folds of the brain are pressed together too tightly to be seen. As a person ages, surface folds of the brain normally become more visible. Pronounced brain fissuring in young adults may be a sign of schizophrenia, chronic alcoholism, or other problems.

»**FIGURE 12.11** Positron emission tomography produces PET scans of the human brain. In the scans shown here, red, pink, and orange indicate lower levels of brain activity; white and blue indicate higher activity levels. Notice that activity in the schizophrenic brain is quite low in the frontal lobes (top area of each scan) (Velakoulis & Pantelis, 1996). Activity in the manic-depressive brain is low in the left brain hemisphere and high in the right brain hemisphere. The reverse is more often true of the schizophrenic brain. Researchers are trying to identify consistent patterns like these to aid diagnosis of mental disorders.

Study Break Psychosis, Delusional Disorders, and Schizophrenia

Reflect

What did you think psychosis was like before you read about it? How has your understanding changed? If you were writing a "recipe" for psychosis, what would the main "ingredients" be?

If you were asked to play the role of a paranoid person for a theater production, what symptoms would you emphasize?

You have been asked to explain the causes of schizophrenia to the parents of a schizophrenic teenager. What would you tell them?

Learning Check

1. Carol wrongly believes that her body is "rotting away." She is suffering from

   a. depressive hallucinations   b. a delusion
   c. flat affect   d. Alzheimer's disease

2. Colin, who has suffered a psychotic break, is hearing voices. This symptom is referred to as

   a. flat affect   b. hallucination
   c. a word salad   d. organic delusions

3. A psychosis caused by lead poisoning would be regarded as an organic disorder. T or F?

4. Hallucinations and personality disintegration are the principal features of paranoid psychosis. T or F?

5. Environmental explanations of schizophrenia emphasize emotional trauma and

   a. manic parents   b. schizoaffective interactions
   c. psychedelic interactions   d. disturbed family relationships

6. The _____ _____ of a schizophrenic person runs a 48 percent chance of also becoming psychotic.

7. Enlarged surface fissures and ventricles, as revealed by CT scans, are found only in the brains of chronic schizophrenics. T or F?

Critical Thinking

8. Researchers have found nearly double the normal number of dopamine receptor sites in the brains of schizophrenics. Why might that be important?

9. Enlarged surface fissures and ventricles are frequently found in the brains of chronic schizophrenics. Why is it a mistake to conclude that such features cause schizophrenia?

Answers 1. b 2. b 3. T 4. F 5. d 6. identical twin 7. F 8. Because of the extra receptors, schizophrenics may get psychedelic effects from normal levels of dopamine in the brain. 9. Because correlation does not confirm causation. Structural brain abnormalities are merely *correlated* with schizophrenia. They could be additional symptoms, rather than causes, of the disorder.

MOOD DISORDERS—PEAKS AND VALLEYS

>SURVEY QUESTIONS< *What are mood disorders? What causes depression?*

For some people, minor bouts of depression are as common as colds. But extreme swings of mood can be as disabling as a serious physical illness. In fact, depression can be deadly, because depressed persons may be suicidal. It is difficult to imagine how bleak and hopeless the world looks to a person who is deeply depressed, or how "crazy" it can be to ride a wave of mania. Let's explore mood disorders and their causes.

Nobody loves you when you're down and out—or so it seems. Psychologists have come to realize that **mood disorders** (major disturbances in emotion) are among the most serious of all. In any given year, roughly 9.5 percent of the U.S. population suffers from a mood disorder (NIMH, 2006).

Two general types of mood disorder are depressive disorders and bipolar disorders (Nevid & Greene, 2005). (See ■ Table 12.6.) In **depressive disorders,** sadness and despondency are exaggerated, prolonged, or unreasonable. Signs of a depressive disorder are dejection, hopelessness, and an inability to feel pleasure or to take interest in anything. Other common symptoms are fatigue, disturbed sleep and eating patterns, feelings of worthlessness, a very negative self-image, and thoughts of suicide. In **bipolar disorders,** people go both "up" and "down" emotionally (DSM-IV-TR, 2000).

Some mood disorders are long-lasting but relatively moderate problems. If a person is mildly depressed for at least 2 years, the problem is called a **dysthymic disorder** (dis-THY-mik). If depression alternates with periods when the person's mood is cheerful, expansive, or irritable, the problem is a **cyclothymic disorder** (SIKE-lo-THY-mik). Even at this level, mood disorders can be debilitating. However, major mood disorders are much more damaging.

Mood disorder Major disturbances in mood or emotion, such as depression or mania.

Depressive disorders Emotional disorders primarily involving sadness, despondency, and depression.

Bipolar disorders Emotional disorders involving both depression and mania or hypomania.

Dysthymic disorder Moderate depression that persists for 2 years or more.

Cyclothymic disorder Moderate manic and depressive behavior that persists for 2 years or more.

■ Table 12.6 **DSM-IV-TR Classification of Mood Disorders**

Problem	Primary Symptom	Typical Signs of Trouble
Depressive Disorders		
Major depressive disorder	Extreme emotional depression for at least 2 weeks	You feel extremely sad, worthless, fatigued, and empty; you are unable to feel pleasure; you are having thoughts of suicide.
Dysthymic disorder	Moderately depressed mood on most days during the last 2 years	You feel down and depressed more days than not; your self-esteem and energy levels have been low for many months.
Bipolar Disorders		
Bipolar I disorder	Extreme mania and depression	At times you have little need for sleep, can't stop talking, your mind races, and everything you do is of immense importance; at other times you feel extremely sad, worthless, and empty.
Bipolar II disorder	Emotional depression and at least one episode of mild mania	Most of the time you feel extremely sad, worthless, fatigued, and empty; however, at times you feel unusually good, cheerful, energetic, or "high."
Cyclothymic disorder	Periods of moderate depression and moderate mania for at least 2 years	You have been experiencing upsetting emotional ups and downs for many months.

Major Mood Disorders

Major mood disorders are characterized by emotional extremes. The person who only goes "down" emotionally suffers from a **major depressive disorder.** During major depressive episodes everything looks bleak and hopeless. The person has feelings of failure, worthlessness, and total despair. Suffering is intense and the person may become extremely subdued, withdrawn, or intensely suicidal. Suicide attempted during a major depression is rarely a "plea for help." Usually, the person intends to succeed and may give no prior warning.

In a **bipolar I disorder,** people experience both extreme mania and deep depression. During manic episodes, the person is loud, elated, hyperactive, grandiose, and energetic. Manic patients may go bankrupt in a matter of days, get arrested, or go on a binge of promiscuous sex. During periods of depression, the person is deeply despondent and possibly suicidal.

Darren Robb/Getty Images

In a **bipolar II disorder** the person is mostly sad and guilt ridden, but has had one or more mildly manic episodes (called *hypomania*). That is, in a bipolar II disorder both elation and depression occur, but the person's mania is not as extreme as in a bipolar I disorder. Bipolar II patients who are hypomanic usually just manage to irritate everyone around them. They are excessively cheerful, aggressive, or irritable, and they may brag, talk too fast, interrupt conversations, or spend too much money (Gorman, 1996).

In serious cases of depression it is impossible for a person to function at work or at school. Sometimes, depressed individuals cannot even feed or dress themselves. In cases of depression and/or mania that are even more severe, the person may also lose touch with reality and display psychotic symptoms.

How do major mood disorders differ from dysthymic and cyclothymic disorders? As mentioned, the major mood disorders involve more severe emotional changes. Also, major

In major depressive disorders, suicidal impulses can be intense and despair total.

Major mood disorders Disorders marked by lasting extremes of mood or emotion and sometimes accompanied by psychotic symptoms.

Major depressive disorder A mood disorder in which the person has suffered one or more intense episodes of depression.

Bipolar I disorder A mood disorder in which a person has episodes of mania (excited, hyperactive, energetic, grandiose behavior) and also periods of deep depression.

Bipolar II disorder A mood disorder in which a person is mostly depressed (sad, despondent, guilt ridden) but has also had one or more episodes of mild mania (hypomania).

mood disorders more often appear to be **endogenous** (en-DODGE-eh-nus: produced from within) rather than a reaction to external events.

What Causes Mood Disorders?

Depression and other mood disorders have resisted adequate explanation and treatment. Some scientists are focusing on the biology of mood changes. They are interested in brain chemicals and transmitter substances, especially serotonin, noradrenaline, and dopamine levels. Their findings are incomplete, but progress has been made. For example, the chemical *lithium carbonate* can be effective for treating some cases of bipolar depression.

Other researchers seek psychological explanations. Psychoanalytic theory, for instance, holds that depression is caused by repressed anger. This rage is displaced and turned inward as self-blame and self-hate. As discussed in Chapter 11, behavioral theories of depression emphasize learned helplessness (LoLordo, 2001; Seligman, 1989). Cognitive psychologists believe that self-criticism and negative, distorted, or self-defeating thoughts underlie many cases of depression. (This view is discussed in Chapter 13.) Clearly, life stresses trigger many mood disorders (Maier, 2001). This is especially true for people who have personality traits and thinking patterns that make them vulnerable to depression (Dozois & Dobson, 2002).

Gender and Depression

Overall, women are twice as likely as men to experience depression (Kuehner, 2003). Researchers believe that social and environmental conditions are the main reason for this difference (Winstead & Sanchez, 2005). Factors that contribute to women's greater risk of depression include conflicts about birth control and pregnancy, work and parenting, and the strain of providing emotional support for others. Marital strife, sexual and physical abuse, and poverty are also factors. Nationwide, women and children are most likely to live in poverty. As a result, poor women frequently suffer the stresses associated with single parenthood, loss of control over their lives, poor housing, and dangerous neighborhoods (Stoppard & McMullen, 2003). One study found that women in the United States were most likely to be depressed if they had these characteristics: low education, unmarried, Latina, high stress levels, and feelings of hopelessness (Myers et al., 2002)

Is heredity involved in the major mood disorders? Yes, especially in bipolar disorders (McGuffin et al., 2003). As a case in point, if one identical twin is depressed, the other has a 67 percent chance of suffering depression, too. For fraternal twins the probability is 19 percent. This difference may be related to the recent finding that people who have a particular version of a gene are more likely to become depressed when they are stressed (Caspi et al., 2003). As we have noted, psychological causes are important in many cases of depression. But for major mood disorders, biological factors seem to play a larger role. Surprisingly, one additional source of depression is related to the seasons.

Seasonal Affective Disorder

Unless you have experienced a winter of "cabin fever" in the far north, you may be surprised to learn that the rhythms of the seasons underlie some depressions. Researcher Norman Rosenthal has found that some people suffer from **seasonal affective disorder (SAD),** or depression that only occurs during the fall and winter months. Almost anyone can get a little depressed when days are short, dark, and cold. But when a person's symptoms are lasting and disabling, the problem may be SAD. Here are some of the major symptoms of SAD (Rosenthal, 1993):

- **Oversleeping and difficulty staying awake:** Your sleep patterns may be disturbed and waking very early in the morning is common.
- **Fatigue:** You feel too tired to maintain a normal routine.
- **Craving:** You hunger for carbohydrates and sweets, leading to overeating and weight gain.

Endogenous depression Depression that appears to be produced from within (perhaps by chemical imbalances in the brain), rather than as a reaction to life events.

Seasonal affective disorder Depression that occurs only during fall and winter; presumably related to decreased exposure to sunlight.

- **Inability to cope:** You feel irritable and stressed.
- **Social withdrawal:** You become unsocial in the winter but are socially active during other seasons.

Starting in the fall, people with SAD sleep longer but more poorly. During the day they feel tired and drowsy, and they tend to overeat. With each passing day they become more sad, anxious, irritable, and socially withdrawn.

Although their depressions are not severe, many victims of SAD face each winter with a sense of foreboding. SAD is especially prevalent in northern latitudes, where days are very short during the winter (Michalak & Lam, 2002) (▸▸Fig. 12.12). For instance, one study found that 13 percent of college students living in northern New England showed signs of suffering from SAD (Low & Feissner, 1998). The students most likely to be affected were those who had moved from the South to attend college!

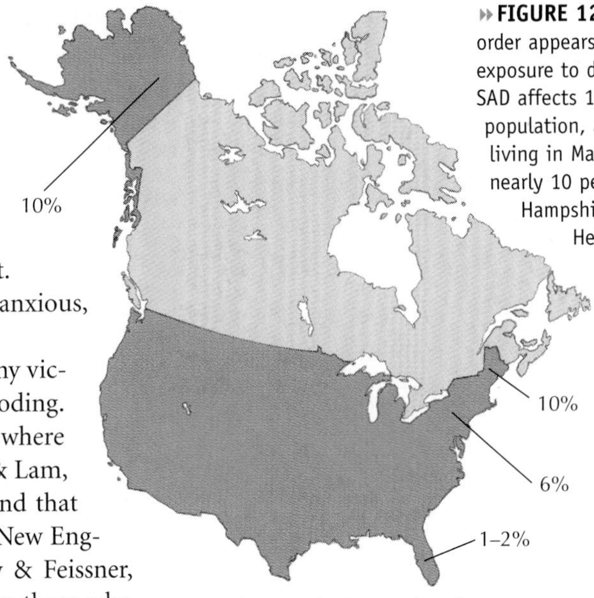

Seasonal depressions are related to the release of more melatonin during the winter. This hormone, which is secreted by the pineal gland in the brain, regulates the body's response to changing light conditions (Wehr et al., 2001). That's why 80 percent of SAD patients can be helped by extra doses of bright light, a remedy called phototherapy (▸▸Fig. 12.13). **Phototherapy** involves exposing SAD patients to one or more hours of very bright fluorescent light each day (Neumeister, 2004). This is best done early in the morning, where it simulates dawn in the summer (Avery et al., 2001). For many SAD sufferers a hearty dose of morning "sunshine" appears to be the next best thing to vacationing in the tropics.

▸▸**FIGURE 12.12** Seasonal affective disorder appears to be related to reduced exposure to daylight during the winter. SAD affects 1 to 2 percent of Florida's population, about 6 percent of the people living in Maryland and New York City, and nearly 10 percent of the residents of New Hampshire and Alaska (Booker & Hellekson, 1992).

10%
10%
6%
1–2%

Rates of seasonal affective disorder, by latitude

▸▸**FIGURE 12.13** An hour or more of bright light a day can dramatically reduce the symptoms of seasonal affective disorder. Treatment is usually necessary from fall through spring. Light therapy typically works best when it is used early in the morning (Lewy et al., 1998).

DISORDERS IN PERSPECTIVE— PSYCHIATRIC LABELING

As we conclude our survey of psychological disorders, a caution is in order. The terms we have reviewed in this chapter aid communication about human problems. But if used carelessly, they can hurt people. Everyone has felt or acted "crazy" during brief periods of stress or high emotion. People with psychological disorders have problems that are more severe or long-lasting than most of us experience. Otherwise, they may not be that different from you or me.

A fascinating classic study carried out by psychologist David Rosenhan illustrates the impact of psychiatric labeling. Rosenhan and several colleagues had themselves committed to mental hospitals with a diagnosis of "schizophrenia" (Rosenhan, 1973). After being admitted, each of these "pseudopatients" dropped all pretense of mental illness. Yet, even though they acted completely normal, none of the researchers was ever recognized by hospital *staff* as a phony patient. Real patients were not so easily fooled. It was not unusual for a patient to say to one of the researchers, "You're not crazy, you're checking up on the hospital!" or, "You're a journalist."

To record his observations, Rosenhan took notes by carefully jotting things on a small piece of paper hidden in his hand. However, he soon learned that stealth was totally unnecessary. Rosenhan simply walked around with a clipboard, recording observations. No one questioned this behavior. Rosenhan's note-taking was just regarded as a symptom of his "illness." This observation clarifies why staff members failed to detect the fake patients.

Phototherapy A treatment for seasonal affective disorder that involves exposure to bright, full-spectrum light.

Because they were in a mental ward, and because they had been *labeled* schizophrenic, anything the pseudopatients did was seen as a symptom of psychopathology.

As Rosenhan's study shows, it is far better to label *problems* than to label people. Think of the difference in impact between saying, "You are experiencing a serious psychological disorder" and saying, "You're a schizophrenic." Which statement would you prefer to have said about yourself?

Social Stigma

An added problem with psychiatric labeling is that it frequently leads to prejudice and discrimination. That is, the mentally ill in our culture are often *stigmatized* (rejected and disgraced). People who have been labeled mentally ill (at any time in their lives) are less likely to be hired. They also tend to be denied housing and they are more likely to be falsely accused of crimes. Thus, people who are grappling with mental illness may be harmed as much by social stigma as they are by their immediate psychological problems (Corrigan & Penn, 1999).

A Look Ahead

Treatments for psychological problems range from counseling and psychotherapy to mental hospitalization and drug therapy. Because they vary greatly, a complete discussion of therapies is found in the next chapter. For now, it's worth noting that many milder mental disorders can be treated successfully. Even major disorders may respond well to drugs and other techniques. It is wrong to fear "former mental patients" or to exclude them from work, friendships, and other social situations. A struggle with major depression or a psychotic episode does not inevitably lead to lifelong dysfunction. Too often, however, it does lead to unnecessary rejection based on groundless fears (Sarason & Sarason, 2005).

Let's conclude with a look at a widely misunderstood problem: By the time you finish reading this page, someone in the United States will have attempted suicide. What can be done about suicide? The upcoming "Psychology in Action" section provides some answers.

 Study Break **Mood Disorders**

Reflect

How are the mentally ill stigmatized in movies and television dramas? Can you think of any positive portrayals (such as the film *A Beautiful Mind*)? How do you think such portrayals affect attitudes about mental disorders?

Learning Check

1. Dysthymic disorder is to depression as cyclothymic disorder is to manic-depression. T or F?
2. Major mood disorders, especially bipolar disorders, often appear to be endogenous. T or F?

3. Learned helplessness is emphasized by _____ theories of depression.

   a. humanistic   b. biological
   c. behavioristic   d. psychoanalytic

4. The drug lithium carbonate has been shown to be an effective treatment for anxiety disorders. T or F?
5. The acronym SAD stands for schizotypal affective disorder. T or F?

Critical Thinking

6. How might relationships contribute to the higher rates of depression experienced by women?

Answers

1. T 2. T 3. c 4. F 5. F 6. Women tend to be more focused on relationships than men are. When listing the stresses in their lives, depressed women consistently report higher rates of relationship problems, such as loss of a friend, spouse, or lover, problems getting along with others, and illnesses suffered by people they care about. Depressed men tend to mention issues such as job loss, legal problems, or work problems (Kendler, Thornton, & Prescott, 2001).

Psychology in Action

Suicide—Lives on the Brink

>SURVEY QUESTIONS< *Why do people commit suicide? Can suicide be prevented?*

"Suicide: A permanent solution to a temporary problem."

We tend to be very concerned about the high rates of murder in North America. Yet for every 3 people who die by homicide, 5 will kill themselves. And there may be as many as 25 attempts for every "successful" suicide (NIMH, 2003). Sooner or later you are likely to be affected by the suicide attempt of someone you know.

What factors affect suicide rates? Suicide rates vary greatly, but some general patterns do emerge.

Sex Men are "better" at suicide than women. Four times as many men as women *complete* suicide, but women make more attempts (NIMH, 2006). Male suicide attempts are more lethal because men typically use a gun or an equally fatal method (Garland & Zigler, 1993). Women most often attempt a drug overdose, so there's a better chance of help arriving before death occurs. Sadly, women are beginning to use more deadly methods and may soon equal men in their likelihood of death by suicide.

Ethnicity Suicide rates vary dramatically from country to country. The rate in the United States is almost 10 times higher than the rate in Azerbaijan and, in turn, the rate in Hungary is over 3 times the U.S. rate (Lester & Yang, 2005). Within the United States, Caucasians generally have higher suicide rates than do non-Caucasians (▸▸Fig 12.14), although rates have increased among African Americans in recent years (Griffin-Fennell & Williams, 2006). Unfortunately, the suicide rate among Native Americans is the highest in the country (suicide rates are equally high among the aboriginal peoples of Australia and New Zealand) (McKenzie, Serfaty, & Crawford, 2003).

Age Suicide rates increase with advancing age. More than half of all suicide victims are over 45 years old (▸▸Fig 12.14). White males 65 years and older are particularly at risk. Of particular concern is the rate of suicide among younger people. Between 1950 and 1990, suicide rates for adolescents and young adults doubled (Durand & Barlow, 2006). Among college students, suicide is the second leading cause of death (Jamison, 2001). School is a factor in some suicides, but only in the sense that suicidal students were not living up to their own

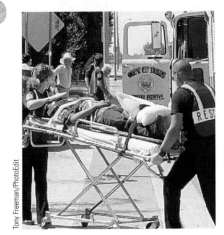
Tony Freeman/PhotoEdit

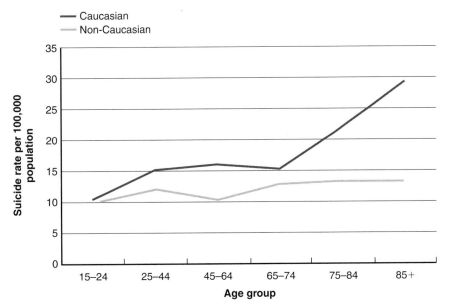

▸▸**FIGURE 12.14** In the United States, suicide rates for Caucasians are higher than those for non-Caucasians. Also, older people have higher suicide rates than younger people (CDC, 2003).

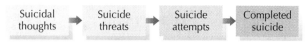

extremely high standards. Many were good students. Other important factors in student suicide are chronic health problems (real or imagined) and interpersonal difficulties (some suicides are rejected lovers, but others are simply withdrawn and friendless people).

Marital Status Marriage (when successful) may be the best natural guard against suicidal impulses. The highest suicide rates are found among the divorced, the next-highest rates occur among the widowed, lower rates are recorded for single persons, and married individuals have the lowest rates of all.

Immediate Causes of Suicide

Why do people try to kill themselves? The best explanation for suicide may simply come from a look at the conditions that precede it. A diagnosable mental disorder (usually depression or substance abuse disorder) is a factor in 90 percent of all suicides (NIMH, 2006). Suicidal people usually have a history of trouble with family, a lover, or a spouse. Often they have drinking or drug abuse problems, sexual adjustment problems, or job difficulties.

The following are all major *risk factors* for suicide (NIMH, 2003; Rudd, Joiner, Jr., & Rajab, 2001): Drug or alcohol abuse; a prior suicide attempt; depression or other mood disorder; feelings of hopelessness or worthlessness; antisocial, impulsive, or aggressive behavior; severe anxiety; panic attacks; family history of suicidal behavior; shame, humiliation, failure, or rejection; and availability of a firearm.

Typically, suicidal people isolate themselves from others, feel worthless, helpless, and misunderstood, and want to die. An extremely negative self-image and severe feelings of *hopelessness* are warnings that the risk of suicide is very high (Beck et al., 1990; Heisel, Flett, & Hewitt, 2003). However, a long history of such conditions is not always necessary to produce a desire for suicide. Anyone may temporarily reach a state of depression severe enough to attempt suicide. Most dangerous for the average person are times of divorce, separation, rejection, failure, and bereavement. Each situation can seem intolerable and motivate an intense desire to die, to escape, or to obtain relief (Boergers, Spirito, & Donaldson, 1998). For young people, feelings of anger and hostility add to the danger. When the impulse to harm others is turned inward, the risk of suicide increases dramatically (Jamison, 2001).

Preventing Suicide

Is it true that people who talk about or threaten suicide are rarely the ones who try it? No, this is a major fallacy. Of every 10 potential suicides, 8 give warning beforehand. A person who threatens suicide should be taken seriously. (See ▸Fig. 12.15.) A suicidal person may say nothing more than "I feel sometimes like I'd be better off dead." Warnings may also come indirectly. If a friend gives you a favorite ring and says, "Here, I won't be needing this anymore," or comments, "I guess I won't get my watch fixed—it doesn't matter anyway," it may be a plea for help.

The warning signs in the list that follows, especially if they are observed in combination, can signal an impending suicide attempt (Leenaars, Lester, & Wenckstern, 2005; Slaby, Garfinkel, & Garfinkel, 1994).

- Withdrawal from contact with others
- Sudden swings in mood
- Recent occurrence of life crisis or emotional shock
- Personality change
- Gift giving of prized possessions
- Depression/hopelessness
- Aggression and/or risk taking
- Single-car accident
- Preoccupation with death
- Drug use

- Death imagery in art
- Direct threats to commit suicide

Is it true that suicide can't be prevented, that the person will find a way to do it anyway? No. Suicide attempts usually come when a person is alone, depressed, and unable to view matters objectively. You *should* intervene if someone seems to be threatening suicide.

It is estimated that about two thirds of all suicide attempts are made by people who do not really want to die. Almost a third more are *ambivalent* or undecided about dying. Only 3 to 5 percent of suicide cases involve people who really want to die. Most people, therefore, are relieved when someone comes to their aid. Remember that suicide is almost always a cry for help and that you *can* help. As suicide expert Edwin Shneidman (1987a) puts it, "Suicidal behavior is often a form of communication, a cry for help born out of pain, with clues and messages of suffering and anguish and pleas for response."

How to Help

What is the best thing to do if someone hints they are thinking about suicide? It helps to know some of the common characteristics of suicidal thoughts and feelings (Shneidman, 1987b; Leenaars, Lester, & Wenckstern, 2005):

1. **Escape.** At times, everyone feels like running away from an upsetting situation. Running away from home, quitting school, abandoning a marriage—these are all departures. Suicide, of course, is the ultimate escape. It helps when suicidal persons see that the natural wish for escape doesn't have to be expressed by ending it all.
2. **Unbearable psychological pain.** Emotional pain is what the suicidal person is seeking to escape. A goal of anyone hoping to prevent suicide should be to reduce the pain in any way possible. Ask the person, "Where does it hurt?" Suicide occurs when pain exceeds a person's resources for coping with pain.
3. **Frustrated psychological needs.** Often, suicide can be prevented if a distressed person's frustrated needs can be identified and eased. Is the person deeply frustrated in his or her search for love, achievement, trust, security, or friendship?
4. **Constriction of options.** The suicidal person feels helpless and decides that death is the *only* solution. The person has narrowed all his or her options solely to death. The rescuer's goal, then, is to help broaden the person's perspective. Even when all the choices are unpleasant, suicidal persons can usually be made to see that their *least unpleasant option* is better than death.

Knowing these patterns will give some guidance in talking to a suicidal person. In addition, your most important task may be to establish *rapport* (a harmonious connection) with the person. You should offer support, acceptance, and legitimate caring.

Remember that a suicidal person feels misunderstood. Try to accept and understand the feelings the person is expressing. Acceptance should also extend to the idea of suicide itself. It is completely acceptable to ask, "Are you thinking of suicide?"

Establishing communication with suicidal persons may be enough to carry them through a difficult time. You may also find it helpful to get day-by-day commitments from them to meet for lunch, share a ride, and the like. Let the person know you *expect* her or him to be there. Such commitments, even though small, can be enough to tip the scales when a person is alone and thinking about suicide.

Don't end your efforts too soon. A dangerous time for suicide is when a person suddenly seems to get better after a severe depression. This often means the person has finally decided to end it all. The improvement in mood is deceptive because it comes from an anticipation that suffering is about to end.

Crisis Intervention

Most cities have mental health crisis intervention teams or centers for suicide prevention. Both have staff members trained to talk with suicidal persons over the phone. Give a person who seems to be suicidal the number of one of these services.

Urge the person to call you or the other number if she or he becomes frightened or impulsive. Or better yet, help the person make an appointment to get psychological treatment (Weishaar, 2006).

The preceding applies mainly to persons who are having mild suicidal thoughts. If a person actually threatens suicide, or if a suicide attempt seems to be imminent, don't worry about overreacting. Immediately seek professional assistance by calling the police, crisis intervention, or a rescue unit. If that is infeasible, ask how the person plans to carry out the suicide. A person who has a *specific, workable plan,* and the means to carry it out, should be asked to accompany you to the emergency ward of a hospital.

Needless to say, you should call immediately if a person is in the act of attempting suicide or if a drug has already been taken. The majority of suicide attempts come at temporary low points in a person's life and may never be repeated. Get involved—you may save a life!

 Study Break   Suicide and Suicide Prevention

Reflect

You're working a suicide hotline and you take a call from a very distressed young man. What risk factors will you look for as he tells you about his anguish?

What are the common characteristics of suicidal thoughts and feelings identified by Edwin Shneidman? If a friend of yours were to express any of these thoughts or feelings, how would you respond?

Learning Check

1. More women than men use guns in their suicide attempts. T or F?
2. While the overall suicide rate has remained about the same, there has been a decrease in adolescent suicides. T or F?

3. Suicide is equally a problem of the rich and the poor. T or F?
4. The highest suicide rates are found among the divorced. T or F?
5. The majority (two thirds) of suicide attempts are made by people who do not want to die. T or F?

Critical Thinking

6. If you follow the history of popular music, see if you can answer this question: What two major risk factors contributed to the 1994 suicide of Kurt Cobain, lead singer for the rock group Nirvana?

Answers 1. F 2. F 3. T 4. T 5. T 6. Drug or alcohol abuse and availability of a firearm.

CHAPTER IN REVIEW

Major Points

- Judgments of normality are relative, but psychological disorders clearly exist and need to be classified, explained, and treated.
- Psychopathology, which involves identifying, classifying, and explaining psychological disorders is worthwhile and necessary.
- Psychologically unhealthy behavior is maladaptive and it involves a loss of adequate control over thoughts, feelings, and actions.
- Maladaptive behavior patterns, unhealthy personality types, and excessive levels of anxiety underlie many mental disorders.
- The most severe forms of psychopathology involve emotional extremes and/or a break with reality.

- Psychological disorders are complex and have multiple causes.
- Suicide is a relatively frequent cause of death that can, in many cases, be prevented.

Summary

How is normality defined, and what are the major psychological disorders?

- Psychopathology refers to maladaptive behavior and to the scientific study of mental disorders.
- Definitions of normality usually take into account the following: subjective discomfort, statistical abnormality, social nonconformity, and the cultural or situational context of behavior.

- Two key elements in judgments of disorder are that a person's behavior must be maladaptive and it must involve a loss of control.
- Major mental disorders include psychotic disorders, dementia, substance related disorders, mood disorders, anxiety disorders, somatoform disorders, dissociative disorders, personality disorders, and sexual or gender identity disorders.
- Insanity is a legal term defining whether a person may be held responsible for his or her actions. Sanity is determined in court on the basis of testimony by expert witnesses.

What is a personality disorder?

- Personality disorders are deeply ingrained maladaptive personality patterns.
- Sociopathy is a common personality disorder. Antisocial persons seem to lack a conscience. They are emotionally unresponsive, manipulative, shallow, and dishonest.

What problems result when a person suffers high levels of anxiety?

- Anxiety disorders, dissociative disorders, and somatoform disorders are characterized by high levels of anxiety, rigid defense mechanisms, and self-defeating behavior patterns.
- The term *nervous breakdown* has no formal meaning. However, "emotional breakdowns" do correspond somewhat to the occurrence of an adjustment disorder.
- Anxiety disorders include generalized anxiety disorder, panic disorder with or without agoraphobia, agoraphobia (without panic), specific phobias, social phobia, obsessive-compulsive disorders, posttraumatic stress disorder, and acute stress disorder.
- Dissociative disorders may take the form of dissociative amnesia, dissociative fugue, or dissociative identity disorder.
- Somatoform disorders center on physical complaints that mimic disease or disability. Four examples of somatoform disorders are hypochondriasis, somatization disorder, somatoform pain disorder, and conversion disorders.

How do psychologists explain anxiety-based disorders?

- The psychodynamic approach emphasizes unconscious conflicts as the cause of disabling anxiety.
- The humanistic approach emphasizes the effects of a faulty self-image.
- The behaviorists emphasize the effects of previous learning, particularly avoidance learning.

- Cognitive theories of anxiety focus on distorted thinking, judgment, and attention.

What are the general characteristics of psychotic disorders?

- Psychosis is a break in contact with reality that is marked by delusions, hallucinations, sensory changes, disturbed emotions, disturbed communication, and personality disintegration.
- An organic psychosis is based on known injuries or diseases of the brain, including damage caused by poisoning and drug abuse.

How do delusional disorders differ from other forms of psychosis?

- Delusional disorders are almost totally based on the presence of delusions of grandeur, persecution, infidelity, romantic attraction, or physical disease.
- The most common delusional disorder is paranoid psychosis. Paranoid persons may be violent if they believe they are threatened.

What forms does schizophrenia take? What causes it?

- Schizophrenia involves a split between thought and emotion, delusions, hallucinations, and communication difficulties.
- Disorganized schizophrenia is marked by extreme personality disintegration and silly, bizarre, or obscene behavior. Social impairment is usually extreme.
- Catatonic schizophrenia is associated with stupor, mutism, and odd postures. Sometimes violent and agitated behavior also occurs.
- In paranoid schizophrenia (the most common type), outlandish delusions of grandeur and persecution are coupled with psychotic symptoms and personality breakdown.
- Current explanations of schizophrenia emphasize a combination of early trauma, environmental stress, inherited susceptibility, and abnormalities in the brain.
- Environmental factors that increase the risk of schizophrenia include viral infection or malnutrition during the mother's pregnancy, birth complications, early psychological trauma, and a disturbed family environment.
- Heredity is a major factor in schizophrenia.
- Recent biochemical studies have focused on the brain transmitter dopamine and its receptor sites.
- The dominant explanation of schizophrenia, and other problems as well, is the stress-vulnerability model.

What are mood disorders? What causes depression?

- Mood disorders primarily involve disturbances of mood or emotion, producing manic or depressive states. Severe mood disorders may include psychotic features.

- In a dysthymic disorder, depression is long lasting, though moderate. In a cyclothymic disorder, people suffer from long-lasting, though moderate, swings between depression and elation.

- Bipolar disorders combine mania and depression. In a bipolar I disorder the person swings between severe mania and severe depression. In a bipolar II disorder the person is mostly depressed, but has had periods of mild mania.

- A major depressive disorder involves extreme sadness and despondency but no signs of mania.

- Seasonal affective disorder (SAD), which occurs during the winter months, is another common form of depression. SAD is typically treated with phototherapy.

- Major mood disorders are partially explained by genetic vulnerability and changes in brain chemistry. Other important factors are loss, anger, learned helplessness, stress, and self-defeating thinking patterns.

Why do people commit suicide? Can suicide be prevented?

- Suicide is statistically related to such factors as age, sex, and marital status.

- In individual cases, the potential for suicide is best identified by a desire to escape, unbearable psychological pain, frustrated psychological needs, and a constriction of options.

- Suicide can often be prevented by the efforts of family, friends, and mental health professionals.

Interactive Learning

Internet addresses frequently change. To find the sites listed here, visit www.thomsonedu/psychology/coon for an updated list of Internet addresses and direct links to relevant sites.

Psychology: A Journey **Companion Website**   Find online quizzes, flash cards, animations, video clips, experiments, interactive assessments, and other helpful study aids for this text at www.thomsonedu.com/psychology/coon.

A Guide to Depressive and Manic Depressive Illness   A complete overview of mood disorders.

Anxiety Disorders   Information and links to sites about anxiety disorders.

Depression after Delivery   A site devoted to providing information about postpartum depression.

DSM-IV Questions and Answers   Answers to common questions about the DSM-IV.

Internet Mental Health   Comprehensive page on mental health, with links to many other sites.

National Alliance for the Mentally Ill   Home page of the group, with links.

National Institute of Mental Health   Links to public information, news and events, and research activities.

Personality Disorders   Multiple links to information on personality disorders and their treatment.

Understanding Schizophrenia   An extensive look at schizophrenia.

ThomsonNOW   Go to www.thomsonedu.com to link to ThomsonNOW, your online study tool. First take the **Pre-Test** for this chapter to get your **Personalized Study Plan**, which will identify topics you need to review and direct you to online resources. Then take the **Post-Test** to determine what concepts you have mastered and what you still need work on.

Psychological Disorders

For additional review, get more practice with *ThomsonNOW*, *WebTutor*, the *Practice Quizzes*, and/or the printed *Study Guide* available with this book.

1. The core feature of abnormal behavior is that it is
   a. statistically unusual
   b. maladaptive
   c. socially nonconforming
   d. a source of subjective discomfort

2. In North America, the most widely used standard for classifying mental disorders is the
   a. PTSD
   b. *Schedule of Personality Dysfunctions*
   c. DSM
   d. *Psychiatrist's Desk Reference*

3. People are said to have "retreated from reality" when they suffer from
   a. psychotic disorders
   b. mood disorders
   c. somatoform disorders
   d. personality disorders

4. A person who has periods of extreme mania suffers from
   a. a somatoform disorder
   b. a mood disorder
   c. an anxiety disorder
   d. a neurosis

5. Koro and dhat are
   a. somatoform disorders
   b. forms of psychosis
   c. folk terminology
   d. organic mental disorders

6. Which of the following is a *legal* concept?
   a. neurosis
   b. psychosis
   c. drapetomania
   d. insanity

7. Which of the following is NOT a type of personality disorder?
   a. schizoid
   b. borderline
   c. neurotic
   d. dependent

8. A person who is impulsive, dishonest, emotionally cold, and manipulative may suffer from
   a. antisocial personality disorder
   b. histrionic personality disorder
   c. dependent personality disorder
   d. obsessive-compulsive personality disorder

9. When prolonged unemployment, a bad marriage, or physical illness pushes a person beyond his or her ability to cope, it is most likely that which of the following problems will occur?
   a. a dissociative disorder
   b. agoraphobia
   c. an adjustment disorder
   d. a conversion disorder

10. Agoraphobia is most often a feature of
    a. adjustment disorder
    b. panic disorder
    c. DSM
    d. obsessive-compulsive disorder

11. According to the _____ view, anxiety disorders are the end result of a faulty self-image.
    a. psychodynamic
    b. humanistic
    c. behavioristic
    d. cognitive

12. Delusions and hallucinations are most characteristic of
    a. neurosis
    b. psychosis
    c. Alzheimer's disease
    d. dysthymic disorder

13. Paranoid psychosis is the most common type of
    a. catatonic schizophrenia
    b. delusional disorder
    c. personality disorder
    d. dementia

14. Which of the following is NOT one of the subtypes of schizophrenia?
    a. erotomanic type
    b. catatonic type
    c. paranoid type
    d. disorganized type

15. Biochemical explanations of schizophrenia have focused on excessive amounts of _____ in the brain.
    a. radioactive sugar
    b. webs and tangles
    c. PCP
    d. dopamine and glutamate

16. The stress-vulnerability model of psychosis explains mental disorders as a product of environmental stresses and
    a. psychological trauma
    b. deviant communication
    c. exposure to the flu virus during pregnancy
    d. heredity

17. Bipolar disorders that are not too severe are called
    a. endogenous disorders
    b. cyclothymic disorders
    c. seasonal affective disorders
    d. dysthymic disorders

18. The fact that lithium carbonate is effective in treating some cases of bipolar depression suggests that the causes of bipolar disorders are at least partly _____.
    a. biological
    b. existential
    c. environmental
    d. neurotic

19. Depression that occurs only in the winter is likely to be classified as
    a. SAD
    b. PTSD
    c. bipolar
    d. endogenous

20. The risk that a person may attempt suicide is greatest if the person has
    a. a concrete, workable plan
    b. had a recent life crisis
    c. withdrawn from contact with others
    d. frustrated psychological needs

ANSWERS 1. b 2. c 3. a 4. b 5. c 6. d 7. c 8. a 9. c 10. b 11. b 12. b 13. b 14. a 15. d 16. d 17. b 18. a 19. a 20. a

Pulse Productions/jupiterimages

CHAPTER

13

Therapies

JOURNEY INTO PSYCHOLOGY: COLD TERROR ON A WARM AFTERNOON

The warm Arizona sun was shining brightly. Outside, an assortment of small birds sang sweetly. Susan's psychology professor could hear them between Susan's frightened sobs.

As psychologists, we meet many students with personal problems. Still, Susan's teacher was surprised to see her at his office door. Her excellent work in class and her healthy, casual appearance left him unprepared for her first words. "I feel like I'm losing my mind," she said. "Can I talk to you?"

In the next hour, Susan described her own personal hell. Her calm appearance hid a world of crippling fear, anxiety, and depression. At work, she was deathly afraid of talking to coworkers and customers. Her social phobia led to frequent absenteeism and embarrassing behavior. At each job she held, it was only a matter of time until she got fired.

At school Susan felt "different" and was sure that other students could tell she was "weird." Several disastrous romances had left her terrified of men. Lately she had been so depressed that she thought of suicide. Often, she became terrified for no apparent reason. Each time, her heart pounded wildly and she felt that she was about to completely lose control.

Susan's request for help was an important turning point. Emotional conflicts had made her existence a nightmare. At a time when she was becoming her own worst enemy, Susan realized she needed help from another person. In Susan's case, that person was a talented psychologist to whom her teacher referred her. With psychotherapy, the psychologist was able to help Susan come to grips with her emotions and regain her balance.

This chapter discusses methods used to alleviate problems like Susan's. First, we will describe therapies that emphasize the value of gaining *insight* into personal problems. Then, we will focus on *behavior therapies* and *cognitive therapies,* which directly change troublesome actions and thoughts. Later, we will conclude with *medical therapies,* which are based on psychiatric drugs and other physical treatments.

▼ **Survey Questions**

PSYCHOTHERAPY—GETTING BETTER BY THE HOUR

>SURVEY QUESTIONS< *How do psychotherapies differ? How did psychotherapy originate?*

Psychotherapy refers to any psychological technique that can bring about positive changes in personality, behavior, or personal adjustment. In most cases, psychotherapy is based on a dialogue between therapists and their clients. Some therapists also use learning principles to directly alter troublesome behaviors.

Therapists have many approaches to choose from: psychoanalysis, desensitization, Gestalt therapy, client-centered therapy, cognitive therapy, and behavior therapy—to name but a few. As we will see, each therapy emphasizes different concepts and methods. For this reason, the best approach for a particular person or problem may vary (Trull, 2005).

Dimensions of Therapy

The terms listed here describe basic aspects of various therapies. Notice that more than one term may apply to a particular therapy. For example, it is possible to have a directive, action-oriented group therapy or a nondirective, individual, insight-oriented therapy.

- **Individual therapy** A therapy involving only one client and one therapist.
- **Group therapy** A therapy session in which several clients participate at the same time.
- **Insight therapy** Any psychotherapy whose goal is to lead clients to a deeper understanding of their thoughts, emotions, and behavior.
- **Action therapy** Any therapy designed to bring about direct changes in troublesome thoughts, habits, feelings, or behavior, without seeking insight into their origins or meanings.
- **Directive therapy** Any approach in which the therapist provides strong guidance.
- **Nondirective therapy** A style of therapy in which clients assume responsibility for solving their own problems; the therapist assists, but does not guide or give advice.
- **Time-limited therapy** Any therapy begun with the expectation that it will last only a limited number of sessions.
- **Supportive therapy** An approach in which the therapist's goal is to offer support, rather than to promote personal change. A person trying to get through an emo-

Psychotherapy Any psychological technique used to facilitate positive changes in a person's personality, behavior, or adjustment.

■ Table 13.1   **Elements of Positive Mental Health**

- Personal autonomy and independence
- A sense of identity
- Feelings of personal worth
- Skilled interpersonal communication
- Sensitivity, nurturance, and trust
- Genuine and honest with self and others
- Self-control and personal responsibility
- Committed and loving personal relationships
- Capacity to forgive others and oneself
- Personal values and a purpose in life
- Self-awareness and motivation for personal growth
- Adaptive coping strategies for managing stresses and crises
- Fulfillment and satisfaction in work
- Good habits of physical health

Source: Adapted from Bergin, 1991; Bloch, 2006.

▸▸**FIGURE 13.1** Primitive "treatment" for mental disorders sometimes took the form of boring a hole in the skull. This example shows signs of healing, which means the patient survived the treatment. Many didn't.

Demonology In medieval Europe, the study of demons and the treatment of persons "possessed" by demons.

tional crisis or one who wants to solve day-to-day problems may benefit from supportive therapy.

- **Positive therapy** Techniques designed to enhance personal strengths, rather than "fix" weaknesses.

Myths

Psychotherapy has been depicted as a complete personal transformation—a sort of "major overhaul" of the psyche. But therapy is *not* equally effective for all problems. Chances of improvement are fairly good for phobias, low self-esteem, some sexual problems, and marital conflicts. More complex problems can be difficult to solve. For many people, the major benefit of therapy is that it provides comfort, support, and a way to make constructive changes (Bloch, 2006; Hellerstein et al., 1998).

In short, it is often unrealistic to expect psychotherapy to undo a person's entire past history. Yet even when problems are severe, therapy may help a person gain a new perspective or learn behaviors to better cope with life. Psychotherapy can be hard work for both clients and therapists. But when it succeeds, few activities are more worthwhile.

It's also a mistake to think that psychotherapy is only used to solve problems or end a crisis. Even if a person is already doing well, therapy can be a way to promote personal growth (Bloch, 2006). Therapists in the positive psychology movement are developing ways to help people make use of their personal strengths. Rather than trying to fix what is "wrong" with a person, they seek to nurture positive traits and actively solve problems (Compton, 2005). ▪ Table 13.1 lists some of the elements of positive mental health that therapists seek to restore or promote.

ORIGINS OF THERAPY—BORED SKULLS AND HYSTERIA ON THE COUCH

Early treatments for mental problems give good reasons to appreciate modern therapies. Archaeological findings dating to the Stone Age suggest that most primitive approaches were marked by fear and superstitious belief in demons, witchcraft, and magic. One of the more dramatic "cures" practiced by primitive "therapists" was a process called *trepanning* (treh-PAN-ing; also sometimes spelled *trephining*). In modern usage, trepanning is any surgical procedure in which a hole is bored in the skull. In the hands of primitive therapists it meant boring, chipping, or bashing holes into a patient's head. Presumably this was done to relieve pressure or release evil spirits (▸▸ Fig. 13.1). Actually, many "patients" didn't survive the "treatment," which suggests that trepanning may have simply been an excuse to kill people who were unusual.

During the Middle Ages, treatments for mental illness in Europe focused on **demonology,** the study of demons and persons plagued by spirits. Medieval "therapists" commonly blamed abnormal behavior on supernatural forces, such as possession by the devil, or on

(left) Supernatural explanations attributed abnormal behavior to the work of the devil or "possession" by demons. A modern analysis of "demonic possession" suggests that some victims were suffering from dissociative disorders (van der Hart, Lierens, & Goodwin, 1996). *(right)* Many other cases of "possession" in medieval Europe and "bewitchment" in colonial New England may be explained by the psychedelic effects of ergot fungus. An ear of rye infested with the fungus (dark areas) is shown here.

curses from witches and wizards. As a cure, they used exorcism to "cast out evil spirits." For the fortunate, exorcism was a religious ritual. More often, physical torture was used to make the body an inhospitable place for the devil to reside. Modern analyses of "demonic possession" suggest that many victims were suffering from epilepsy, schizophrenia (Mirsky & Duncan, 2005), dissociative disorders (van der Hart, Lierens, & Goodwin, 1996), and depression (Thase, 2006).

One reason for the rise of demonology may lie in *ergotism* (AIR-got-ism), a psychotic-like condition caused by ergot poisoning. In the Middle Ages, rye (grain) fields were often infested with ergot fungus. Ergot, we now know, is a natural source of LSD and other mind-altering chemicals. Eating tainted bread could have caused symptoms that were easily mistaken for bewitchment or madness. Pinching sensations, muscle twitches, facial spasms, delirium, and hallucinations are all signs of ergot poisoning (Matossian, 1982). Thus, many people "treated" by demonologists may have been doubly victimized.

(left) Many early asylums were no more than prisons with inmates held in chains. *(right)* One late 19th-century "treatment" was based on swinging the patient in a harness—presumably to calm the patient's nerves.

It wasn't until 1793 that the emotionally disturbed were regarded as "mentally ill" and given compassionate treatment. That was the year a French doctor named Philippe Pinel changed the Bicêtre Asylum in Paris from a squalid "madhouse" into a mental hospital by unchaining the inmates. Although it has been more than 200 years since Pinel began humane treatment, the process of improving care continues today.

When was psychotherapy developed? The first true psychotherapy was created by Sigmund Freud about 110 years ago (Jacobs, 2003). As a physician in Vienna, Freud was intrigued by cases of *hysteria*. People suffering from hysteria have physical symptoms (such as paralysis or numbness) for which no physical causes can be found. (Such problems are now called somatoform disorders.) Slowly, Freud became convinced that hysteria was related to deeply hidden unconscious conflicts. Based on this insight, Freud developed a therapy called psychoanalysis. Because it is the "granddaddy" of more modern therapies, let us examine psychoanalysis in some detail.

PSYCHOANALYSIS—EXPEDITION INTO THE UNCONSCIOUS

>SURVEY QUESTION< *Is Freudian psychoanalysis still used?*

Isn't psychoanalysis the therapy where the patient lies on a couch? Freud's patients usually reclined on a couch during therapy, while Freud sat out of sight taking notes and offering interpretations. This procedure was supposed to encourage a free flow of thoughts and images from the unconscious. However, it is the least important element of psychoanalysis and many modern analysts have abandoned it.

How did Freud treat emotional problems? Freud's theory stressed that "neurosis" and "hysteria" are caused by repressed memories, motives, and conflicts—particularly those stemming from instinctual drives for sex and aggression. Although they are hidden, these forces remain active in the personality and they cause some people to develop rigid ego-defenses and compulsive, self-defeating behavior. Thus, the main goal of **psychoanalysis** is to reduce internal conflicts that lead to emotional suffering (Marcus, 2002).

Freud developed four basic techniques to uncover the unconscious roots of neurosis (Freud, 1949). These are *free association, dream analysis, analysis of resistance,* and *analysis of transference.*

Pioneering psychotherapist Sigmund Freud's famous couch.

Psychoanalysis A Freudian therapy that emphasizes the use of free association, dream interpretation, resistances, and transference to uncover unconscious conflicts.

Free Association

Saying whatever comes to mind is the basis for **free association.** Patients must speak without worrying whether ideas are painful, embarrassing, or illogical. Thoughts are simply allowed to move freely from one idea to the next, without self-censorship. The purpose of free association is to lower defenses so that unconscious thoughts and feelings can emerge (Hoffer & Youngren, 2004).

Dream Analysis

Freud believed that dreams provide a "royal road to the unconscious" because they freely express forbidden desires and unconscious feelings. Such feelings are found in the **latent content** (hidden, symbolic meaning) of dreams. Normally, we only remember a dream's **manifest content** (obvious, visible meaning), which tends to disguise information from the unconscious.

Freud was especially interested in unconscious messages revealed by **dream symbols** (images that have personal or emotional meanings). Let's say a young man reports a dream in which he pulls a pistol from his waistband and aims at a target while his wife watches. The pistol repeatedly fails to discharge, and the man's wife laughs at him. Freud might have seen this as an indication of repressed feelings of sexual impotence, with the gun serving as a disguised image of the penis.

Analysis of Resistance

When free associating or describing dreams, patients may *resist* talking about or thinking about certain topics. Such **resistances** (blockages in the flow of ideas) reveal particularly important unconscious conflicts. As analysts become aware of resistances, they bring them to the patient's awareness so the patient can deal with them realistically. Rather than being roadblocks in therapy, resistances can be challenges and guides (Engle & Arkowitz, 2006).

Analysis of Transference

Transference is the tendency to "transfer" feelings to a therapist that match those the patient had for important persons in his or her past. At times, the patient may act as if the analyst is a rejecting father, an unloving or overprotective mother, or a former lover, for example. As the patient re-experiences repressed emotions, the therapist can help the patient recognize and understand them. Troubled persons often provoke anger, rejection, boredom, criticism, and other negative reactions from others. Effective therapists learn to avoid reacting as others do and playing the patient's habitual resistance and transference "games." This, too, contributes to therapeutic change (Marcus, 2002).

Psychoanalysis Today

What is the status of psychoanalysis today? Traditional psychoanalysis called for three to five therapy sessions a week, often for many years. Today, most patients are only seen once or twice per week, but treatment may still go on for years (Friedman et al., 1998). Because of the huge amounts of time and money this requires, psychoanalysts have become relatively rare. Nevertheless, psychoanalysis made a major contribution to modern therapies by highlighting the importance of unconscious conflicts (Friedman, 2006).

Many therapists have switched to doing **brief psychodynamic therapy,** which uses direct questioning to reveal unconscious conflicts (Binder, 2004). Modern therapists also actively provoke emotional reactions that will lower defenses and provide insights (Davanloo, 1995). Interestingly, brief therapy seems to accelerate recovery. Patients seem to realize that they need to get to the heart of their problems quickly (Messer & Kaplan, 2004).

The development of newer, more streamlined dynamic therapies is in part due to questions about whether traditional psychoanalysis "works." In a classic criticism, Hans Eysenck (1994) suggested that psychoanalysis simply takes so long that patients experience a *spontaneous remission* of symptoms (improvement due to the mere passage of time). How could

Free association In psychoanalysis, the technique of having a client say anything that comes to mind, regardless of how embarrassing or unimportant it may seem.

Latent dream content The hidden or symbolic meaning of a dream, as revealed by dream interpretation and analysis.

Manifest dream content The surface, "visible" content of a dream; dream images as they are remembered by the dreamer.

Dream symbols Images in dreams whose personal or emotional meanings differ from their literal meanings.

Resistance A blockage in the flow of free association; topics the client resists thinking or talking about.

Transference The tendency of patients to transfer feelings to a therapist that correspond to those the patient had for important persons in his or her past.

Brief psychodynamic therapy A modern therapy based on psychoanalytic theory but designed to produce insights more quickly.

we tell if a particular therapy, or the passage of time, is responsible for a person's improvement? Typically, some patients are randomly assigned for treatment, and others are placed on a waiting list. If members of this *waiting-list control group,* who receive no treatment, improve at the same rate as those in therapy, the therapy may be of little value.

How seriously should the possibility of spontaneous remission be taken? It's true that problems ranging from hyperactivity to anxiety improve with the passage of time. However, researchers have confirmed psychoanalysis does, in fact, produce improvement in a majority of patients (Doidge, 1997).

The real value of Eysenck's critique is that it encouraged psychologists to try new ideas and techniques. Researchers began to ask: "When psychoanalysis works, why does it work? What parts of it are essential and which are unnecessary?" Modern therapists have given surprisingly varied answers to these questions. Upcoming sections will acquaint you with some of the therapies currently in use.

 Study Break **Psychotherapy and Psychoanalysis**

Reflect

How has your understanding of psychotherapy changed? How many types of therapy can you name?

Make a list describing what you think it means to be mentally healthy. How well does your list match the items in ■ Table 13.1?

The use of trepanning, demonology, and exorcism all implied that the mentally ill are "cursed." To what extent are the mentally ill rejected and stigmatized today?

Try to free associate (aloud) for 10 minutes. How difficult was it? Did anything interesting surface?

Can you explain, in your own words, the role of dream analysis, resistances, and transference in psychoanalysis?

Learning Check

Match:

_____ 1. Directive therapies
_____ 2. Action therapies
_____ 3. Insight therapies
_____ 4. Nondirective therapies

A. Change behavior
B. Place responsibility on the client
C. The client is guided strongly
D. Seek understanding

5. Pinel is famous for his use of exorcism. T or F?
6. In psychoanalysis, what is an emotional attachment to the therapist by the patient called?

a. free association
b. manifest association
c. resistance
d. transference

Critical Thinking

7. Waiting-list control groups help separate the effects of therapy from improvement related to the mere passage of time. What other type of control group might be needed to learn if therapy is truly beneficial?

Answers

1. C 2. A 3. D 4. B 5. F 6. d 7. Placebo therapy is sometimes used to assess the benefits of real therapy. Placebo therapy superficially resembles the real thing, but it lacks key elements that are thought to be therapeutic.

HUMANISTIC THERAPIES—RESTORING HUMAN POTENTIAL

>SURVEY QUESTION< *What are the major humanistic therapies?*

When most people picture clinical psychologists at work, they probably imagine them doing insight therapy. As stated earlier, insight therapists help clients gain a deeper understanding of their thoughts, emotions, and behavior. Let's sample a variety of insight-oriented approaches, including therapies done at a distance, by telephone or over the Internet.

Better self-knowledge was the goal of traditional psychoanalysis. However, Freud claimed that his patients could expect only to change their "hysterical misery into common unhappiness"! Humanistic therapies are more optimistic. Most assume that it is possible for people to use their potentials fully and live rich, rewarding lives. Psychotherapy is seen as a way to give mental health a chance to emerge.

Client-Centered Therapy

What is client-centered therapy? How is it different from psychoanalysis? Psychoanalysts delve into the unconscious. Psychologist Carl Rogers (1902–1987) found it more beneficial to explore *conscious* thoughts and feelings. The psychoanalyst tends to take a position of authority, stating what dreams, thoughts, or memories "mean." In contrast, Rogers believed that what is right or valuable for the therapist may be wrong for the client. (Rogers preferred the term *client* to *patient* because "patient" implies a person is "sick" and needs to be "cured.") Consequently, the client determines what will be discussed during each session. Thus, **client-centered therapy** (also called **person-centered therapy**) is nondirective and based on insights from conscious thoughts and feelings (Schneider, 2002).

If the client runs things, what does the therapist do? The therapist's job is to create a safe "atmosphere of growth." The therapist provides opportunities for change, but the client must actively seek to solve his or her problems. The therapist cannot "fix" the client (Whitton, 2003).

Health-Promoting Conditions

Rogers believed that effective therapists maintain four basic conditions. First, the therapist offers the client **unconditional positive regard** (unshakable personal acceptance). The therapist refuses to react with shock, dismay, or disapproval to anything the client says or feels. Total acceptance by the therapist is the first step to self-acceptance by the client.

Second, the therapist attempts to achieve genuine **empathy** by trying to see the world through the client's eyes and feeling some part of what the client is feeling.

As a third essential condition, the therapist strives to be **authentic** (genuine and honest). The therapist must not hide behind a professional role. Rogers believed that phony fronts destroy the growth atmosphere sought in client-centered therapy.

Fourth, the therapist does not make interpretations, propose solutions, or offer advice. Instead, the therapist **reflects** (rephrases, summarizes, or repeats) the client's thoughts and feelings. This allows the therapist to act as a psychological "mirror" so clients can see themselves more clearly. Rogers theorized that a person armed with a realistic self-image and greater self-acceptance will gradually discover solutions to life's problems.

Existential Therapy

According to the existentialists, "being in the world" (existence) creates deep anxiety. Each of us must deal with the realities of death. We must face the fact that we create our private world by making choices. We must overcome isolation on a vast and indifferent planet. Most of all, we must confront feelings of meaninglessness.

What do these concerns have to do with psychotherapy? **Existential therapy** focuses on the problems of existence, such as meaning, choice, and responsibility. Like client-centered therapy, it promotes self-knowledge. However, there are important differences. Client-centered therapy seeks to uncover a "true self" hidden behind a screen of defenses. In contrast, existential therapy emphasizes free will, the human ability to make choices. Accordingly, existential therapists believe you can *choose to become* the person you want to be.

Existential therapists try to give clients the *courage* to make rewarding and socially constructive choices. Typically, therapy focuses on *death, freedom, isolation,* and *meaninglessness,* the "ultimate concerns" of existence (Yalom, 1980). These universal human challenges include: an awareness of one's mortality; the responsibility that comes with

Psychotherapist Carl Rogers, who originated client-centered therapy.

Courtesy of Dr. Natalie Rogers

Client-centered (or person-centered) therapy A nondirective therapy based on insights gained from conscious thoughts and feelings; emphasizes accepting one's true self.

Unconditional positive regard An unqualified, unshakable acceptance of another person.

Empathy A capacity for taking another's point of view; the ability to feel what another is feeling.

Authenticity In Carl Rogers's terms, the ability of a therapist to be genuine and honest about his or her own feelings.

Reflection In client-centered therapy, the process of rephrasing or repeating thoughts and feelings expressed by clients so they can become aware of what they are saying.

Existential therapy An insight therapy that focuses on the elemental problems of existence, such as death, meaning, choice, and responsibility; emphasizes making courageous life choices.

freedom to choose; being alone in your own private world; and the need to create meaning in your life.

What does the existential therapist do? The therapist helps clients discover self-imposed limitations in personal identity. To be successful, the client must fully accept the challenge of changing his or her life (Bretherton & Orner, 2004). Interestingly, Buddhists seek a similar state that they call "radical acceptance" (Brach, 2003).

A key aspect of existential therapy is *confrontation,* in which clients are challenged to examine their values and choices and to take responsibility for the quality of their existence (Gerwood, 1998). An important part of confrontation is the unique, intense, here-and-now *encounter* between two human beings. When existential therapy is successful, it brings about a renewed sense of purpose and a reappraisal of what's important in life. Some clients even experience an emotional rebirth, as if they had survived a close brush with death. As Marcel Proust wrote, "The real voyage of discovery consists not in seeing new landscapes but in having new eyes."

Gestalt Therapy

Gestalt therapy is based on the idea that perception, or *awareness,* is disjointed and incomplete in maladjusted persons. The German word *Gestalt* means "whole," or "complete." **Gestalt therapy** helps people rebuild thinking, feeling, and acting into connected wholes. This is achieved by expanding personal awareness; by accepting responsibility for one's thoughts, feelings, and actions; and by filling in gaps in experience (Joyce & Sills, 2001).

What do you mean by gaps in experience? Gestalt therapists believe that we often shy away from expressing or "owning" upsetting feelings. This creates a gap in self-awareness that may become a barrier to personal growth. For example, a person who feels anger after the death of a parent might go for years without fully expressing it. This and similar threatening gaps may impair emotional health.

The Gestalt approach is more directive than client-centered or existential therapy and it emphasizes immediate experience. Working either one-to-one or in a group setting, the Gestalt therapist encourages clients to become more aware of their moment-to-moment thoughts, perceptions, and emotions (Staemmler, 2004). Rather than discussing *why* clients feel guilt, anger, fear, or boredom, they are encouraged to have these feelings in the "here and now" and become fully aware of them. The therapist promotes awareness by drawing attention to a client's posture, voice, eye movements, and hand gestures. Clients may also be asked to exaggerate vague feelings until they become clear. Gestalt therapists believe that expressing such feelings allows people to "take care of unfinished business" and break through emotional impasses.

Gestalt therapy is often associated with the work of Frederick (Fritz) Perls (1969). In all his writings, Perls's basic message comes through clearly: Emotional health comes from knowing what you *want* to do, not dwelling on what you *should* do, *ought* to do, or *should want* to do (Rosenberg & Lynch, 2002). Another way of stating this idea is that emotional health comes from taking full responsibility for one's feelings and actions. For example, it means changing "I can't" to "I won't," or "I must" to "I choose to."

How does Gestalt therapy help people discover their real wants? Above all else, Gestalt therapy emphasizes *present* experience. Clients are urged to stop intellectualizing and talking *about* feelings. Instead, they learn to live now; live here; stop imagining; experience the real; stop unnecessary thinking; taste and see; express rather than explain, justify, or judge; give in to unpleasantness and pain just as to pleasure; and surrender to being as you are. Gestalt therapists believe that, paradoxically, the best way to change is to become who you really are (Joyce & Sills, 2001).

Because of their emphasis on verbal interaction, humanistic therapies may be conducted at a distance, by telephone or e-mail. Let's investigate this possibility.

Gestalt therapy An approach that focuses on immediate experience and awareness to help clients rebuild thinking, feeling, and acting into connected wholes; emphasizes the integration of fragmented experiences.

THERAPY AT A DISTANCE—PSYCH JOCKEYS AND CYBERTHERAPY

How valid are psychological services offered over the phone and on the Internet? For better or worse, psychotherapy and counseling are rapidly becoming high tech. Today, psychological services are available through radio, telephone, videoconferencing, e-mail, and Internet chat rooms (Maheu et al., 2004). What are the advantages and disadvantages of getting help "online"?

Media Psychologists

By now, you have probably heard a phone-in radio psychologist. On a typical program, callers describe problems arising from child abuse, loneliness, love affairs, phobias, sexual adjustment, or depression. The radio psychologist then offers reassurance, advice, or suggestions for getting help. Talk-radio psychology and similar TV programs may seem harmless, but they raise some important questions. For instance, is it reasonable to give advice without knowing anything about a person's background? Could the advice do harm? What good can a psychologist do in 3 minutes or even an hour?

In defense of themselves, media psychologists point out that listeners and viewers may learn solutions to their problems by hearing others talk. Many also stress that their work is educational, not therapeutic. Nevertheless, the question arises, When does advice become therapy? The American Psychological Association urges media psychologists to discuss problems only of a general nature, instead of actually counseling anyone. For example, if a caller complains about insomnia, the radio psychologist should talk about insomnia in general, not probe the caller's personal life.

By giving information, advice, and social support, media psychologists probably do help some people. Even so, a good guide for anyone tempted to call a radio psychologist or accept advice from a TV psychologist might be "let the consumer beware."

Media psychologists have been urged to educate without actually doing therapy on the air. Some overstep this boundary, however. Do you think popular TV psychologist Dr. Phil sometimes goes too far?

Telephone Therapists

The same caution applies to telephone therapists. These "counselors" can be reached through 900-number services for $3 to $4 per minute. To date, there is no evidence that commercial telephone counseling is effective. Successful face-to-face therapy is based on a continuing *relationship* between two people. Telephone therapy is also seriously limited by a lack of visual cues, such as facial expressions and body language (Haas, Benedict, & Kobos, 1996).

It's important to note that legitimate therapists may use the phone to calm, console, or advise clients between therapy sessions. Others are experimenting with actually doing therapy by telephone. For example, after the attack on the World Trade Center towers, many rescue personnel needed counseling. To fill the need, a phone network was created to link emergency workers with psychologists all over the country (Murray, 2001; Shore, 2003). Under the right circumstances, telephone therapy can be as successful as face-to-face therapy (Day & Schneider, 2002). For example, in one study, telephone counseling helped improve success rates for smokers who wanted to quit (Rabius et al., 2004). Other studies have shown that depressed people benefit from telephone therapy (Mohr et al., 2005; Simon et al., 2004). Nevertheless, it's worth saying again that the value of commercial telephone therapists is questionable. Consumers might well ask themselves, How much confidence would I place in a physician who would make a diagnosis over the phone?

Internet Therapy

You can find almost anything on the Internet. Recently, psychological advice, support groups, self-help magazines, and even online therapy have been added to the list. Some services, such as support groups, are free. Online counseling or advice, in contrast, is typically offered for a fee. Some online therapists will "discuss" problems with you through e-mail messages. Others merely answer questions or give advice concerning specific problems.

Online counseling and advice services do have some advantages. For one thing, clients can remain anonymous. Thus, a person who might hesitate to see a psychologist can seek help privately, online. Likewise, the Internet can link people who live in rural areas with psychologists living in large cities. And, compared with traditional office visits, Internet therapy is less expensive.

As with radio talk shows and telephone counselors, many objections can be raised about online psychological services. Clearly, brief e-mail messages are no way to make a diagnosis. And forget about facial expressions or body language—not even tone of voice reaches the online therapist. Typing emotional icons (called "emoticons") like little smiley faces (☺) or frowns (☹) is a poor substitute for real human interaction. Another problem is that e-mail counseling may not be completely confidential and could be intercepted and misused. Of special concern is the fact that "cybershrinks" may or may not be trained professionals (Bloom, 1998). And even if they are, questions exist about whether a psychologist licensed in one state can legally do therapy in another state, via the Internet. Despite such objections, psychologists are actively exploring the possibility of providing therapy over the Internet, at least for certain types of problems (Klein, Richards, & Austin, 2006).

Many of the drawbacks we have discussed can be solved with videoconferencing. A two-way audio-video link allows the client and therapist to see one another on TV screens and to talk via speakerphones. Doing therapy this way still lacks the close personal contact of face-to-face interaction. However, it does remove many of the objections to doing therapy at a distance. It's very likely that "telehealth" services will become a major source of mental health care in coming years (Schopp, Demiris, & Glueckauf, 2006).

Implications

As you can see, psychological services that rely on electronic communication may serve some useful purposes. However, the value of therapy offered by commercial telephone counselors and Internet therapists remains open to question. The very best advice given by media psychologists, telephone counselors, or Internet therapists may be, "You should consider discussing this problem with a psychologist or counselor in your own community."

 Study Break **Insight Therapies**

Reflect

Here's a mnemonic for the elements of client-centered therapy: Picture a therapist saying "I ear u" to a client. The E stands for empathy, A for authenticity, R for reflection, and U for unconditional positive regard.

What would an existential therapist say about the choices you have made so far in your life? Should you be choosing more "courageously"?

You are going to play the role of a therapist for a classroom demonstration. How would you act if you were a client-centered therapist? An existential therapist? A Gestalt therapist?

A neighbor of yours is thinking about getting counseling on the Internet. What would you tell her about the pros and cons of distance therapy?

Learning Check

Match:

_____ 1. Client-centered therapy   **A.** Electronic advice
_____ 2. Gestalt therapy   **B.** Unconditional positive regard
_____ 3. Existential therapy   **C.** Gaps in awareness
_____ 4. Internet therapy   **D.** Choice and becoming

5. The Gestalt therapist tries to *reflect* a client's thoughts and feelings. T or F?
6. Client-centered therapy is directive. T or F?
7. Confrontation and encounter are concepts of existential therapy. T or F?

Critical Thinking

8. How might using the term *patient* affect the relationship between an individual and a therapist?

Answers

1. B 2. C 3. D 4. A 5. F 6. F 7. T 8. The terms *doctor* and *patient* imply a large gap in status and authority between the individual and his or her therapist. Client-centered therapy attempts to narrow this gap by making the person the final authority concerning solutions to his or her problems. Also, the word *patient* implies that a person is "sick" and needs to be "cured." Many regard this as an inappropriate way to think about human problems.

BEHAVIOR THERAPY—HEALING BY LEARNING

>SURVEY QUESTION< *What is behavior therapy?*

Jay repeatedly and vividly imagined himself going into a store to steal something. He then pictured himself being caught and turned over to the police, who handcuffed him and hauled him off to jail. Once there, he imagined calling his wife to tell her he had been arrested for shoplifting. He became very distressed as he faced her anger and his son's disappointment (Kohn & Antonuccio, 2002).

Why would anyone imagine such a thing? Jay's behavior is not as strange as it may seem. His goal was self-control: Jay is a *kleptomaniac* (a compulsive stealer). The method he chose (called *covert sensitization*) is a form of behavior therapy (Corsini, 2001). **Behavior therapy** is the use of learning principles to make constructive changes in behavior. Behavioral approaches include behavior modification, aversion therapy, desensitization, token economies, and other techniques (Forsyth & Savsevitz, 2002).

Behavior therapists believe that deep insight into one's problems is often unnecessary for improvement. Instead, they try to directly alter troublesome thoughts and actions. Jay didn't need to probe into his past or his emotions and conflicts; he simply wanted to break his shoplifting habit.

In general, how does behavior therapy work? Behavior therapists assume that people have *learned* to be the way they are. If they have learned responses that cause problems, then they can change them by *relearning* more appropriate behaviors. Broadly speaking, **behavior modification** refers to any use of classical or operant conditioning to directly alter human behavior (Miltenberger, 2004; Spiegler & Guevremont, 2003). (Some therapists prefer to call this approach *applied behavior analysis*.)

How does classical conditioning work? I'm not sure I remember. Classical conditioning is a form of learning in which simple responses (especially reflexes) are associated with new stimuli. Perhaps a brief review would be helpful. In classical conditioning, a neutral stimulus is followed by an *unconditioned stimulus (US)* that consistently produces an unlearned reaction, called the *unconditioned response (UR)*. Eventually, the previously neutral stimulus begins to produce this response directly. The response is then called a *conditioned response (CR)*, and the stimulus becomes a *conditioned stimulus (CS)*. Thus, for a child the sight of a hypodermic needle (CS) is followed by an injection (US), which causes anxiety or fear (UR). Eventually the sight of a hypodermic (the conditioned stimulus) may produce anxiety or fear (a conditioned response) *before* the child gets an injection. (For a more thorough review of classical conditioning, return to Chapter 6.)

What does classical conditioning have to do with behavior modification? Classical conditioning can be used to associate discomfort with a bad habit, as Jay did. More powerful versions of this approach are called aversion therapy.

Aversion Therapy

Imagine that you are eating an apple. Suddenly you discover that you just bit a large green worm in half. You vomit. Months later you cannot eat an apple again without feeling ill. It's apparent that you have developed a conditioned aversion to apples. (A *conditioned aversion* is a learned dislike or negative emotional response to some stimulus.)

How are conditioned aversions used in therapy? In **aversion therapy,** an individual learns to associate a strong aversion to an undesirable habit such as smoking, drinking, or gambling. Aversion therapy has been used to cure hiccups, sneezing, stuttering, vomiting, nail-biting, bed-wetting, compulsive hair-pulling, alcoholism, and the smoking of tobacco, marijuana, or crack cocaine. Actually, aversive conditioning happens every day. For example, not many physicians who treat lung cancer are smokers, nor do many emergency room doctors drive without using their seat belts (Eifert & Lejuez, 2000).

Behavior therapy Any therapy designed to actively change behavior.

Behavior modification The application of learning principles to change human behavior, especially maladaptive behavior.

Aversion therapy Suppressing an undesirable response by associating it with aversive (painful or uncomfortable) stimuli.

Puffing Up an Aversion

The fact that nicotine is toxic makes it easy to create an aversion that helps people give up smoking. Behavior therapists have found that electric shock, nauseating drugs, and similar aversive stimuli are not required to make smokers uncomfortable. All that is needed is for the smoker to smoke—rapidly, for a long time, at a forced pace. During rapid smoking, clients are told to smoke continuously, taking a puff every 6 to 8 seconds. Rapid smoking continues until the smoker is miserable and can stand it no more. By then, most people are thinking, "I never want to see another cigarette for the rest of my life."

Rapid smoking has long been known as an effective behavior therapy for smoking (Houtsmuller & Stitzer, 1999). Nevertheless, anyone tempted to try rapid smoking should realize that it is very unpleasant. Without the help of a therapist, most people quit too soon for the procedure to succeed. In addition, rapid smoking can be dangerous. It should only be done with professional supervision. (An alternative method that is more practical is described in the "Psychology in Action" section of this chapter.)

Aversive Therapy for Drinking

Another excellent example of aversion therapy was pioneered by Roger Vogler and his associates (1977). Vogler works with alcoholics who were unable to stop drinking. For many clients, aversion therapy is a last chance. While drinking an alcoholic beverage, clients receive a painful (although noninjurious) electric shock to the hand. Most of the time, these shocks occur as the client is beginning to take a drink of alcohol.

These *response-contingent shocks* (shocks that are linked to a response) obviously take the pleasure out of drinking. Shocks also cause the alcohol abuser to develop a conditioned aversion to drinking. Normally, the misery caused by alcohol abuse comes long after the act of drinking—too late to have much effect. But if alcohol can be linked with *immediate* discomfort, then drinking will begin to make the individual very uncomfortable.

Is it really acceptable to treat clients this way? People are often disturbed (shocked?) by such methods. However, clients usually *volunteer* for aversion therapy because it helps them overcome a destructive habit. Indeed, commercial aversion programs for overeating, smoking, and alcohol abuse have attracted many willing customers. And more important, aversion therapy can be justified by its long-term benefits. As behaviorist Donald Baer put it, "A small number of brief, painful experiences is a reasonable exchange for the interminable pain of a lifelong maladjustment."

Desensitization

>SURVEY QUESTION<   *How is behavior therapy used to treat phobias, fears, and anxieties?*

Assume that you are a swimming instructor who wants to help a child named Jamie overcome fear of the high diving board. How might you proceed? Directly forcing Jamie off the high board could be a psychological disaster. Obviously, a better approach would be to begin by teaching her to dive off the edge of the pool. Then she could be taught to dive off the low board, followed by a platform 6 feet above the water and then an 8-foot platform. As a last step, Jamie could try the high board.

Who's Afraid of a Hierarchy?

This rank-ordered series of steps is called a **hierarchy.** The hierarchy allows Jamie to undergo *adaptation.* Gradually, she adapts to the high dive and overcomes her fear. When Jamie has conquered her fear, we can say that *desensitization* (dee-SEN-sih-tih-ZAY-shun) has occurred (Spiegler & Guevremont, 2003).

Desensitization is also based on **reciprocal inhibition** (using one emotional state to block another) (Heriot & Pritchard, 2004). For instance, it is impossible to be anxious and relaxed at the same time. If we can get Jamie onto the high board in a relaxed state, her anxiety and fear will be inhibited. Repeated visits to the high board should cause fear in this situation to disappear. Again we would say that Jamie has been desensitized. Typically,

Hierarchy A rank-ordered series of higher and lower amounts, levels, degrees, or steps.

Reciprocal inhibition The presence of one emotional state can inhibit the occurrence of another, such as joy preventing fear or anxiety inhibiting pleasure.

Feeling a Little Tense? Relax!

The key to desensitization is relaxation. To inhibit fear, you must *learn* to relax. One way to voluntarily relax is by using the **tension-release method.** To achieve deep-muscle relaxation, try the following exercise.

Tense the muscles in your right arm until they tremble. Hold them tight as you slowly count to 10 and then let go. Allow your hand and arm to go limp and to relax completely. Repeat the procedure. Releasing tension two or three times will allow you to feel whether or not your arm muscles have relaxed. Repeat the tension-release procedure with your left arm. Compare it with your right arm. Repeat until the left arm is equally relaxed. Apply the tension-release technique to your

right leg; to your left leg; to your abdomen; to your chest and shoulders. Clench and release your chin, neck, and throat. Wrinkle and release your forehead and scalp. Tighten and release your mouth and face muscles. As a last step, curl your toes and tense your feet. Then release.

Practice the tension-release method until you can achieve complete relaxation quickly (5 to 10 minutes). After you have practiced relaxation once a day for a week or two, you will begin to be able to tell when your body (or a group of muscles) is tense. Also, you will begin to be able to relax on command. This is a valuable skill that you can apply in any situation that makes you feel tense or anxious.

systematic desensitization (a guided reduction in fear, anxiety, or aversion) is attained by gradually approaching a feared stimulus while maintaining relaxation.

What is desensitization used for? Desensitization is primarily used to help people unlearn phobias (intense, unrealistic fears) or strong anxieties. For example, each of these people might be a candidate for desensitization: a teacher with stage fright, a student with test anxiety, a salesperson who fears people, or a newlywed with an aversion to sexual intimacy.

Performing Desensitization

How is desensitization done? First, the client and the therapist *construct a hierarchy.* This is a list of fear-provoking situations, arranged from least disturbing to most frightening. Second, the client is taught *exercises that produce deep relaxation.* (See "Feeling a Little Tense? Relax!") Once the client is relaxed, she or he proceeds to the third step by trying to *perform the least disturbing item* on the list. For a fear of heights (acrophobia), this might be: "(1) Stand on a chair." The first item is repeated until no anxiety is felt. Any change from complete relaxation is a signal that clients must relax again before continuing. Slowly, clients move up the hierarchy: "(2) Climb to the top of a small stepladder"; "(3) Look down a flight of stairs"; and so on, until the last item is performed without fear: "(20) Fly in an airplane."

For many phobias, desensitization works best when people are directly exposed to the stimuli and situations they fear (Bourne, 2005). For something like a simple spider phobia, this exposure can even be done in groups. Also, for some fears (such as fear of riding an elevator) desensitization may be completed in a single session (Sturges & Sturges, 1998).

Vicarious Desensitization

I understand how some fears could be desensitized by gradual approach—as in the case of the child on the high dive. But what if it's not practical to directly act out the steps of a hierarchy? For a fear of heights, the steps of the hierarchy might be acted out. However, if this is impractical the problem can be handled by having clients observe *models* who are performing the feared behavior (Eifert & Lejuez, 2000) (▸▸Fig. 13.2). A model is a person (either live or filmed) who serves as an example for observational learning. If such **vicarious desensitization** (secondhand learning) can't be used, there is yet another option. Fortunately, desensitization works almost as well when a person *vividly imagines* each step in the hierarchy (Yahnke, Sheikh, & Beckman, 2003). If the steps can be visualized without anxiety, fear in the actual

Programs for treating fears of flying combine relaxation, systematic desensitization, group support, and lots of direct exposure to airliners. Many such programs conclude with a brief flight, so that participants can "test their wings."

Christopher A. Record/AP/Wide World Photo

Tension-release method A procedure for systematically achieving deep relaxation of the body.

Systematic desensitization A reduction in fear, anxiety, or aversion brought about by planned exposure to aversive stimuli.

Vicarious desensitization A reduction in fear or anxiety that takes place vicariously ("secondhand") when a client watches models perform the feared behavior.

situation is reduced. Because imagining feared stimuli can be done at a therapist's office, it is the most common way of doing desensitization.

Virtual Reality Exposure

Desensitization is an *exposure therapy.* Like other such therapies, it involves exposing people to feared stimuli until their fears extinguish. In an important new development, psychologists are using virtual reality to treat phobias. Virtual reality is a computer-generated, three-dimensional "world" that viewers enter by wearing a head-mounted video display. **Virtual reality exposure** presents computerized fear stimuli to clients in a realistic, yet carefully controlled fashion (Wiederhold & Wiederhold, 2005). It has already been used to treat acrophobia (fear of heights), fears of flying and driving and public speaking, spider phobias, and claustrophobia (Arbona et al., 2004; Giuseppe, 2005; Hoffman et al., 2003; Lee et al., 2002; Wald and Taylor, 2000). (See ▸▸Fig. 13.3.)

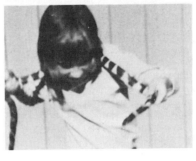

▸▸**FIGURE 13.2** Treatment of a snake phobia by vicarious desensitization. These classic photographs show models interacting with snakes. To overcome their own fears, phobic subjects observed the models (Bandura et al., 1969). (Photos courtesy of Albert Bandura.)

Desensitization has been one of the most successful behavior therapies. A second new technique may provide yet another way to lower fears, anxieties, and psychological pain.

Eye Movement Desensitization

Traumatic events produce painful memories. Disturbing flashbacks often haunts victims of accidents, disasters, molestations, muggings, rapes, or emotional abuse. Recently, Dr. Francine Shapiro developed **eye movement desensitization and reprocessing (EMDR)** to help ease traumatic memories and posttraumatic stress.

In a typical EMDR session, the client is asked to visualize the images that most upset her or him. At the same time, a pencil (or other object) is moved rapidly from side to side in front of the person's eyes. Watching the moving object causes the person's eyes to dart swiftly back and forth. After about 30 seconds, clients describe any memories, feelings, and thoughts that emerged and discuss them with the therapist. These steps are repeated until troubling thoughts and emotions no longer surface (Shapiro, 2001; Shapiro & Forrest, 2004).

A number of studies suggest that EMDR lowers anxieties and takes the pain out of traumatic memories (Ironson et al., 2002; Silver et al., 2005). However, EMDR is highly controversial. Some studies, for example, have found that eye movements add nothing to the

▸▸**FIGURE 13.3** *(left)* Dr. Barbara Rothbaum and Dr. Larry Hodges show how a virtual reality system is used to expose people to feared stimuli. Many clients would rather face feared stimuli in a virtual environment than in a real physical environment. *(right)* A computer image from a virtual elevator. Over an 8-week period, clients who suffered from acrophobia "rode" in the elevator. Each session took them to greater heights. (Image courtesy of Larry Hodges, Thomas Meyer, and Rob Kooper.)

Virtual reality exposure Use of computer-generated images to present fear stimuli. The virtual environment responds to a viewer's head movements and other inputs.

Eye movement desensitization and reprocessing (EMDR) A technique for reducing fear or anxiety; based on holding upsetting thoughts in mind while rapidly moving the eyes from side to side.

treatment. The apparent success of EMDR may simply be based on gradual exposure to upsetting stimuli, as in other forms of desensitization (Cahill, Carrigan, & Frueh, 1999; Davidson & Parker, 2001). On the other hand, some researchers continue to find that EMDR is superior to traditional therapies (Greenwald, 2006; Rogers & Silver, 2002).

Is EMDR a breakthrough? Given the frequency of traumas in modern society, it shouldn't be long before we find out.

Study Break   Behavior Therapy

Reflect

Can you describe three problems for which you think behavior therapy would be an appropriate treatment?

A friend of yours has a dog that goes berserk during thunderstorms. You own a CD of a thunderstorm. How could you use the CD to desensitize the dog? (Hint: The CD player has a volume control.)

Have you ever become naturally desensitized to a stimulus or situation that at first made you anxious (for instance, heights, public speaking, or driving on freeways)? How would you explain your reduced fear?

Learning Check

1. What two types of conditioning are used in behavior modification? _____ and _____
2. Shock, pain, and discomfort play what role in conditioning an aversion?

   a. conditioned stimulus   b. unconditioned response
   c. unconditioned stimulus d. conditioned response

3. If shock is used to control drinking, it must be _____ contingent.

4. What two principles underlie systematic desensitization? _____ and _____
5. When desensitization is carried out through the use of live or filmed models, it is called

   a. cognitive therapy   b. flooding
   c. covert desensitization d. vicarious desensitization

6. The three basic steps in systematic desensitization are: construct a hierarchy, flood the person with anxiety, and imagine relaxation. T or F?
7. In EMDR therapy, computer-generated virtual reality images are used to expose clients to fear-provoking stimuli. T or F?

Critical Thinking

8. Alcoholics who take a drug called Antabuse become ill after drinking alcohol. Why, then, don't they develop an aversion to drinking?
9. A natural form of desensitization often takes place in hospitals. Can you guess what it is?

Answers

1. classical (or respondent), operant   2. c   3. response   4. adaptation, reciprocal inhibition   5. d   6. F   7. F   8. It takes long enough for their discomfort to develop to prevent it from being closely associated with drinking. Fortunately, there are safer, better ways to do aversion therapy (Wilson, 1987).   9. Doctors and nurses learn to relax and remain calm at the sight of blood because of their frequent exposure to it.

OPERANT THERAPIES—ALL THE WORLD IS A SKINNER BOX?

>SURVEY QUESTION< *What role does reinforcement play in behavior therapy?*

Aversion therapy and desensitization are based on classical conditioning. Where does operant conditioning fit in? As you may recall, operant conditioning refers to learning based on the consequences of making a response. The operant principles most often used by behavior therapists to deal with human behavior are:

1. **Positive reinforcement.** Responses that are followed by reward tend to occur more frequently. If children whine and get attention, they will whine more frequently. If you get A's in your psychology class, you may become a psychology major.

2. **Nonreinforcement.** A response that is not followed by reward will occur less frequently.

3. **Extinction.** If a response is not followed by reward after it has been repeated many times, it will go away. After winning three times, you pull the handle on a slot machine 30 times more without a payoff. What do you do? You go away. So does the response of handle pulling (for that particular machine, at any rate).

4. **Punishment.** If a response is followed by discomfort or an undesirable effect, the response will be suppressed (but not necessarily extinguished).

5. **Shaping.** Shaping means rewarding actions that are closer and closer approximations to a desired response. For example, to reward a retarded child for saying "ball," you might begin by rewarding the child for saying anything that starts with a *b* sound.

6. **Stimulus control.** Responses tend to come under the control of the situation in which they occur. If you set your clock 10 minutes fast, it may be easier to leave the house on time in the morning. Your departure is under the stimulus control of the clock, even though you know it is fast.

7. **Time out.** A time-out procedure usually involves removing the individual from a situation in which reinforcement occurs. Time out is a variation of nonreinforcement: It prevents reward from following an undesirable response. For example, children who fight with each other can be sent to separate rooms and allowed out only when they are able to behave more calmly. (For a more thorough review of operant learning, return to Chapter 6.)

As simple as these principles may seem, they have been used very effectively to overcome difficulties in work, home, school, and industrial settings. Let's see how.

Nonreinforcement and Extinction

An extremely overweight mental patient had a persistent and disturbing habit: She stole food from other patients. No one could persuade her to stop stealing or to diet. For the sake of her health, a behavior therapist assigned her a special table in the ward dining room. If she approached any other table, she was immediately removed from the dining room. Because her attempts to steal food went unrewarded, they rapidly disappeared. Additionally, any attempt to steal from others caused the patient to miss her own meal (Ayllon, 1963).

What operant principles did the therapist in this example use? The therapist used *nonreward* to produce *extinction.* The most frequently occurring human behaviors lead to some form of reward. An undesirable response can be eliminated by *identifying* and *removing* the rewards that maintain it. But people don't always do things for food, money, or other obvious rewards. Most of the rewards maintaining human behavior are subtler. *Attention, approval,* and *concern* are common yet powerful reinforcers for humans (▸▸Fig. 13.4).

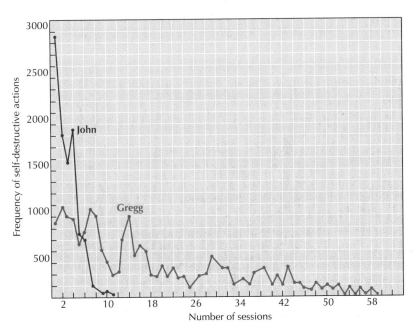

▸▸**FIGURE 13.4** This graph shows extinction of self-destructive behavior in two autistic boys. Before extinction began, the boys received attention and concern from adults for injuring themselves. During extinction, the adults were taught to ignore the boys' self-damaging behavior. As you can see, the number of times that the boys tried to injure themselves declined rapidly. (Adapted from Lovaas & Simons, 1969.)

Nonreward and extinction can eliminate many problem behaviors, especially in schools, hospitals, and institutions. Often, difficulties center around a limited number of particularly disturbing responses. Time out is a good way to remove such responses, usually by refusing to pay attention to a person who is misbehaving. For example, 14-year-old Terrel periodically appeared in the nude in the activity room of a training center for disturbed adolescents. This behavior always generated a great deal of attention from staff and other patients. As an experiment he was placed on time out. The next time he appeared nude, counselors and other staff members greeted him normally and then ignored him. Attention from other patients rapidly subsided. Sheepishly he returned to his room and dressed.

Reinforcement and Token Economies

A distressing problem therapists sometimes face is how to break through to severely disturbed patients who won't talk. Conventional psychotherapy offers little hope of improvement for such patients.

What can be done for them? One widely used approach is based on *tokens* (symbolic rewards, such as plastic chips, that can be exchanged for real rewards). Tokens may be printed slips of paper, check marks, points, or gold stars. Whatever form they take, tokens serve as rewards because they may be exchanged for candy, food, cigarettes, recreation, or privileges, such as private time with a therapist, outings, or watching TV. Tokens are used in mental hospitals, half-way houses, schools for the retarded, programs for delinquents, and ordinary classrooms. They usually produce improvements in behavior (Dickerson, Tenhula, & Green-Paden, 2005; Reitman et al., 2004).

By using tokens, a therapist can *immediately reward* positive responses. For maximum impact, therapists select specific *target behaviors* (actions or other behaviors the therapist seeks to modify). Target behaviors are then reinforced with tokens. For example, a mute mental patient might first be given a token each time he or she says a word. Next, tokens may be given for speaking a complete sentence. Later, the patient could gradually be required to speak more often, then to answer questions, and eventually to carry on a short conversation in order to receive tokens. In this way, deeply withdrawn patients have been returned to the world of normal communication.

Full-scale use of tokens in an institutional setting produces a *token economy*. In a **token economy,** patients are rewarded with tokens for a wide range of socially desirable or productive activities (Spiegler & Guevremont, 2003). They must *pay* tokens for privileges and for engaging in problem behaviors (» Fig. 13.5). For example, tokens are given to patients who get out of bed, dress themselves, take required medication, arrive for meals on time, and so on. Constructive activities, such as gardening, cooking, or cleaning, may also earn tokens. Patients must *exchange* tokens for meals and private rooms, movies, passes, offward activities, and other privileges. They are *charged* tokens for staying in bed, disrobing in public, talking to themselves, fighting, crying, and similar target behaviors (Morisse et al., 1996).

Token economies can radically change a patient's overall adjustment and morale. Patients are given an incentive to change, and they are held responsible for their actions. The use of tokens may seem manipulative, but it actually empowers patients. Many "hopelessly" retarded, mentally ill, and delinquent people have been returned to productive lives by means of token economies (Field et al., 2004).

By the time they are ready to leave, patients may be earning tokens on a weekly basis for maintaining sane, responsible, and productive behavior (Miltenberger, 2004). Typically, the most effective token economies are those that gradually switch from tokens to *social rewards* such as praise, recognition, and approval. Such rewards are what patients will receive when they return to family, friends, and community.

Token economy A therapeutic program in which desirable behaviors are reinforced with tokens that can be exchanged for goods, services, activities, and privileges.

Credit Card

**OXNARD DAY TREATMENT CENTER
CREDIT INCENTIVE SYSTEM**

EARN CREDITS BY		SPEND CREDITS FOR	
MONITOR DAILY	15	COFFEE	5
MENU PLANNING CHAIRMAN	50	LUNCH	10
PARTICIPATE	5	EXCEPT THURSDAY	15
BUY FOOD AT STORE	10	BUS TRIP	5
COOK FOR/PREPARE LUNCH	5	BOWLING	8
WIPE OFF KITCHEN TABLE	3	GROUP THERAPY	5
WASH DISHES	5-10	PRIVATE STAFF TIME	5
DRY AND PUT AWAY DISHES	5	DAY OFF	5-20
MAKE COFFEE AND CLEAN URN	15	WINDOW SHOPPING	5
CLEAN REFRIGERATOR	20	REVIEW WITH DR.	10
ATTEND PLANNING CONFERENCE	1	DOING OWN THING	1
OT PREPARATION	1-5	LATE 1 PER EVERY 10 MIN	
COMPLETE OT PROJECT	5	PRESCRIPTION FROM DR.	10
RETURN OT PROJECT	2		
DUST AND POLISH TABLES	5		
PUT AWAY GROCERIES	3		
CLEAN TABLE	5		
CLEAN 6 ASH TRAYS	2		
CLEAN SINK	5		
CARRY OUT CUPS & BOTTLES	5		
CLEAN CHAIRS	5		
CLEAN KITCHEN CUPBOARDS	5		
ASSIST STAFF	5		
ARRANGE MAGAZINES NEATLY	3		
BEING ON TIME	5		
MONITOR-ANN			

▸▸**FIGURE 13.5** Shown here is a token used in one token economy system. In this instance the token is a card that records the number of credits earned by a patient. Also pictured is a list of credit values for various activities. Tokens may be exchanged for items or for privileges listed on the board. (After photographs by Robert P. Liberman.)

COGNITIVE THERAPY—THINK POSITIVE!

>SURVEY QUESTION< *Can therapy change thoughts and emotions?*

How would a behavior therapist treat a problem like depression? None of the techniques described seem to apply. As we have discussed, behavior therapists usually try to change troublesome actions. However, in recent years cognitive therapists have become interested in what people think, believe, and feel, as well as how they act. In general, **cognitive therapy** helps clients change thinking patterns that lead to troublesome emotions or behaviors (Hall, 2006). For example, compulsive hand-washing can be greatly reduced by changing a client's thoughts and beliefs about dirt and contamination (Jones & Menzies, 1998). Cognitive therapy has been used as a remedy for many problems, but it has been especially successful in treating depression (Chambless & Ollendick, 2001).

Cognitive Therapy for Depression

As you may recall from Chapter 12, cognitive psychologists believe that negative, self-defeating thoughts underlie depression. According to Aaron Beck (1991), depressed persons see themselves, the world, and the future in negative terms. Beck believes this occurs because of major distortions in thinking. The first is **selective perception,** which refers to perceiving only certain stimuli in a larger array. If five good things and three bad things happen during the day, depressed people focus only on the bad. A second thinking error in depression is **overgeneralization,** the tendency to think that an upsetting event applies to other, unrelated situations. An example would be considering yourself a total failure, or

Cognitive therapy A therapy directed at changing the maladaptive thoughts, beliefs, and feelings that underlie emotional and behavioral problems.

Selective perception Perceiving only certain stimuli among a larger array of possibilities.

Overgeneralization Blowing a single event out of proportion by extending it to a large number of unrelated situations.

completely worthless, if you were to lose a part-time job or fail a test. To complete the picture, depressed persons tend to magnify the importance of undesirable events by engaging in **all-or-nothing thinking.** That is, they see events as completely good or bad, right or wrong, and themselves as either successful or failing miserably (J. S. Beck, 2002; Gilbert, 2001).

How do cognitive therapists alter such patterns? Cognitive therapists make a step-by-step effort to correct negative thoughts that lead to depression or similar problems. At first, clients are taught to recognize and keep track of their own thoughts. The client and therapist then look for ideas and beliefs that cause depression, anger, and avoidance. For example, here's how a therapist might challenge all-or-nothing thinking (Burns & Persons, 1982):

> **Client:** I'm feeling even more depressed. No one wants to hire me, and I can't even clean up my apartment. I feel completely incompetent!
>
> **Therapist:** I see. The fact that you are unemployed and have a messy apartment proves that you are completely incompetent?
>
> **Client:** Well . . . I can see that doesn't add up.

Next, clients are asked to gather information to test their beliefs. For instance, a depressed person might list his or her activities for a week. The list is then used to challenge all-or-nothing thoughts, such as "I had a terrible week" or "I'm a complete failure." With more coaching, clients learn to alter their thoughts in ways that improve their moods, actions, and relationships.

Cognitive therapy is as effective as drugs for treating many cases of depression. More important, people who have adopted new thinking patterns are less likely to become depressed again—a benefit that drugs can't impart (Dozois & Dobson, 2004).

In an alternate approach, cognitive therapists look for an *absence* of effective coping skills and thinking patterns, not for the *presence* of self-defeating thoughts (Dobson, Backs-Dermott, & Dozois, 2000). The aim is to teach clients how to cope with anger, depression, shyness, stress, and similar problems. Stress inoculation, which was described in Chapter 11, is a good example of this approach.

Cognitive therapy is a rapidly expanding specialty. Before we leave the topic, let's explore another widely used cognitive therapy.

Rational-Emotive Behavior Therapy

Rational-emotive behavior therapy (REBT) attempts to change irrational beliefs that cause emotional problems. According to Albert Ellis (1995, 2004), the basic idea of rational-emotive behavior therapy is as easy as A-B-C. Ellis assumes that people become unhappy and develop self-defeating habits because they have unrealistic or faulty *beliefs.*

How are beliefs important? Ellis analyzes problems in this way: The letter A stands for an *activating experience,* which the person assumes to be the cause of C, an *emotional consequence.* For instance, a person who is rejected (the activating experience) feels depressed, threatened, or hurt (the consequence). Rational-emotive behavior therapy shows the client that the real problem is what comes between A and C: In between is B, the client's irrational and unrealistic *beliefs.* In this example, an unrealistic belief leading to unnecessary suffering is: "I must be loved and approved by everyone at all times." REBT holds that events do not *cause* us to have feelings. We feel as we do because of our beliefs (Kottler, 2004). (For some examples, see "Ten Irrational Beliefs—Which Do you Hold?")

Ellis (1979, 2004) says that most irrational beliefs come from three core ideas, each of which is unrealistic:

1. I *must* perform well and be approved of by significant others. If I don't, then it is awful, I cannot stand it, and I am a rotten person.

All-or-nothing thinking Classifying objects or events as absolutely right or wrong, good or bad, acceptable or unacceptable, and so forth.

Rational-emotive behavior therapy (REBT) An approach that states that irrational beliefs cause many emotional problems and that such beliefs must be changed or abandoned.

Ten Irrational Beliefs—Which Do You Hold?

Rational-emotive behavior therapists have identified numerous beliefs that commonly lead to emotional upsets and conflicts. See if you recognize any of the following irrational beliefs:

1. I must be loved and approved by almost every significant person in my life or it's awful and I'm worthless.
   Example: "One of my roommates doesn't seem to like me. I must be a total zero."

2. I should be completely competent and achieving in all ways to be a worthwhile person.
   Example: "I don't understand my chemistry class. I guess I really am a stupid person."

3. Certain people I must deal with are thoroughly bad and should be severely blamed and punished for it.
   Example: "The old man next door is such a pain. I'm going to play my stereo even louder the next time he complains."

4. It is awful and upsetting when things are not the way I would very much like them to be.
   Example: "I should have gotten a B in that class. The teacher is unfair."

5. My unhappiness is always caused by external events; I cannot control my emotional reactions.
   Example: "You make me feel awful. I would be happy if it weren't for you."

6. If something unpleasant might happen, I should keep dwelling on it.
   Example: "I'll never forget the time my boss insulted me. I think about it every day at work."

7. It is easier to avoid difficulties and responsibilities than to face them.
   Example: "I don't know why my wife seems angry. Maybe it will just pass by if I ignore it."

8. I should depend on others who are stronger than I am.
   Example: "I couldn't survive if he left me."

9. Because something once strongly affected my life, it will do so indefinitely.
   Example: "My girlfriend dumped me during my junior year in college. I don't know if I can ever trust a woman again."

10. There is always a perfect solution to human problems and it is awful if this solution is not found.
    Example: "I'm so depressed about politics in this country. It all seems hopeless."

(Adapted from J. S. Beck, 2002; Ellis, 2004; Rohsenow & Smith, 1982.)

If any of the listed beliefs sound familiar, you may be creating unnecessary emotional distress for yourself by holding on to unrealistic expectations.

2. You *must* treat me fairly. When you don't, it is horrible, and I cannot bear it.

3. Conditions *must* be the way I want them to be. It is terrible when they are not, and I cannot stand living in such an awful world.

It's easy to see that such beliefs can lead to much grief and needless suffering in a less than perfect world. Rational-emotive behavior therapists are very directive in their attempts to change a client's irrational beliefs and "self-talk." The therapist may directly attack clients' logic, challenge their thinking, confront them with evidence contrary to their beliefs, and even assign "homework." Here, for instance, are some examples of statements that dispute irrational beliefs (after Kottler, 2004):

- "Where is the evidence that you are a loser just because you didn't do well this one time?"
- "Who said the world should be fair? That's your rule."
- "What are you telling yourself to make yourself feel so upset?"
- "Is it really terrible that things aren't working out as you would like? Or is it just inconvenient?"

Many of us would probably do well to give up our irrational beliefs. Improved self-acceptance and a better tolerance of daily annoyances are the benefits of doing so.

The value of cognitive approaches is further illustrated by three techniques (*covert sensitization, thought stopping,* and *covert reinforcement*) described in this chapter's "Psychology in Action" section. A little later you can see what you think of them.

Study Break Operant Therapies and Cognitive Therapies

Reflect

See if you can give a personal example of how the following principles have affected your behavior: positive reinforcement, extinction, punishment, shaping, stimulus control, and time out.

You are setting up a token economy for troubled elementary school children. What target behaviors will you attempt to reinforce? For what behaviors will you charge tokens?

We all occasionally engage in negative thinking. Can you remember a time recently when you engaged in selective perception? Overgeneralization? All-or-nothing thinking?

Which of REBT's irrational beliefs have affected your feelings? Which beliefs would you like to change?

Learning Check

1. Behavior modification programs aimed at extinction of an undesirable behavior typically make use of what operant principles?

   a. punishment and stimulus control b. punishment and shaping

   c. nonreinforcement and time out d. stimulus control and time out

2. Attention can be a powerful _____ for humans.
3. Token economies depend on the time-out procedure. T or F?
4. Tokens basically allow the operant shaping of desired responses or "target behaviors." T or F?
5. According to Beck, selective perception, overgeneralization, and _____ thinking are cognitive habits that underlie depression.
6. REBT teaches people to change the antecedents of irrational behavior. T or F?

Critical Thinking

7. In Aaron Beck's terms, a belief such as "I must perform well or I am a rotten person" involves two thinking errors. These are:

Answers

1. c 2. reinforcer 3. F 4. T 5. all-or-nothing 6. F 7. Overgeneralization and all-or-nothing thinking.

GROUP THERAPY—PEOPLE WHO NEED PEOPLE

>SURVEY QUESTION< *Can psychotherapy be done with groups of people?*

To complete our discussion of psychotherapies, we will begin with a brief look at group therapy. Group therapy has certain advantages, not the least of which is reduced cost. After that, we will try to identify the core features and helping skills that make psychotherapy "work." To conclude, we will explore medical approaches to treating mental disorders.

Group therapy is psychotherapy done with more than one person. Most of the therapies we have discussed can be adapted for use in groups. Psychologists first tried working with groups because there was a shortage of therapists. Surprisingly, group therapy has turned out to be just as effective as individual therapy and it has some special advantages (Burlingame, Fuhriman, & Mosier, 2003).

What are the advantages? In group therapy, a person can *act out* or directly experience problems. Doing so often produces insights that might not occur from merely talking about an issue. In addition, other group members with similar problems can offer support and useful input. Group therapy is especially good for helping people understand their personal relationships (McCluskey, 2002). For reasons such as these, a number of specialized groups have emerged. Because they range from Alcoholics Anonymous to Marriage Encounter, we will sample only a few examples.

Psychodrama

Group therapy Psychotherapy conducted in a group setting to make therapeutic use of group dynamics.

Psychodrama A therapy in which clients act out personal conflicts and feelings in the presence of others who play supporting roles.

One of the first group therapies was developed by Jacob L. Moreno (1953), who called his technique psychodrama. In **psychodrama,** clients act out personal conflicts with others who play supporting roles. Through role-playing, the client re-enacts incidents that cause problems in real life. For example, Don, a disturbed teenager, might act out a typical family fight, with the therapist playing his father and with other clients playing his mother, brothers, and sisters. Moreno believed that insights gained in this way transfer to real-life situations.

Therapists using psychodrama often find that role reversals are helpful. A **role reversal** involves taking the part of another person to learn how he or she feels. For instance, Don might role-play his father or mother, to better understand their feelings. A related method is the **mirror technique,** in which clients observe another person re-enact their behavior. Thus, Don might briefly join the audience and watch as another group member plays his role. This would allow him to see himself as others do. Later, the group may summarize what happened and reflect on its meaning (Turner, 1997).

A group therapy session. Group members offer mutual support while sharing problems and insights.

Family Therapy

Family relationships are the source of great pleasure, and all too often, of great pain. In **family therapy,** husband, wife, and children work as a group to resolve the problems of each family member. Family therapy tends to be brief and focused on specific problems, such as frequent fights or a depressed teenager. For some types of problems, family therapy may be superior to other approaches (Capuzzi, 2003; Pinsof, Wynne, & Hambright, 1996).

Family therapists believe that a problem experienced by one family member is really the whole family's problem. If the entire pattern of behavior in a family doesn't change, improvements in any single family member may not last. Thus, family members work together to improve communication, to change destructive patterns, and to see themselves and each other in new ways. This helps them reshape distorted perceptions and interactions directly, with the very persons with whom they have troubled relationships (Goldenberg & Goldenberg, 2004).

Does the therapist work with the whole family at once? Family therapists treat the family as a unit, but they may not meet with the entire family at each session. If a family crisis is at hand, the therapist may first try to identify the most resourceful family members, who can help solve the immediate problem. The therapist and family members may then work on resolving more basic conflicts and on improving family relationships (Griffin, 2002).

Group Awareness Training

Thirty years ago, the human potential movement led many people to seek personal growth experiences. Often, their interest was expressed by participation in sensitivity training or encounter groups.

What is the difference between sensitivity and encounter groups? Sensitivity groups tend to be less confrontational than encounter groups. Participants in **sensitivity groups** take part in exercises that gently enlarge self-awareness and sensitivity to others. For example, in a "trust walk," participants expand their confidence in others by allowing themselves to be led around while blindfolded.

Encounter groups are based on an honest expression of feelings, and intensely personal communication may take place. Typically, the emphasis is on tearing down defenses and false fronts. Because there is a danger of hostile confrontation, participation is safest when members are carefully screened and a trained leader guides the group. Encounter group "casualties" are rare, but they do occur (Shaffer & Galinsky, 1989).

In business settings, psychologists still use the basic principles of sensitivity and encounter groups—truth, self-awareness, and self-determination—to improve employee relationships. Specially designed encounter groups for married couples are also widely held (Harway, 2004).

There has also been much public interest in various forms of large-group awareness training. **Large-group awareness training** refers to programs that claim to increase self-

Role reversal Taking the role of another person to learn how one's own behavior appears from the other person's perspective.

Mirror technique Observing another person re-enact one's own behavior, like a character in a play; designed to help persons see themselves more clearly.

Family therapy Technique in which all family members participate, both individually and as a group, to change destructive relationships and communication patterns.

Sensitivity group A group experience consisting of exercises designed to increase self-awareness and sensitivity to others.

Encounter group A group experience that emphasizes intensely honest interchanges among participants regarding feelings and reactions to one another.

Large-group awareness training Any of a number of programs (many of them commercialized) that claim to increase self-awareness and facilitate constructive personal change.

awareness and facilitate constructive personal change. Lifespring, Actualizations, the Forum, and similar commercial programs are examples. Like the smaller groups that preceded them, large-group trainings combine psychological exercises, confrontation, new viewpoints, and group dynamics to promote personal change.

Are sensitivity, encounter, and awareness groups really psychotherapies? These experiences tend to be positive, but they produce only moderate benefits (Faith, Wong, & Carpenter, 1995). Moreover, many of the claimed benefits may simply result from a kind of **therapy placebo effect,** in which improvement is based on a client's belief that therapy will help. Positive expectations, a break in daily routine, and an excuse to act differently can have quite an impact. Also, less ambitious goals may be easier to attain. For example, one program succeeded in teaching stress-management techniques in a large group setting (Timmerman, Emmelkamp, & Sanderman, 1998). Because of their versatility, groups undoubtedly will continue to be a major tool for solving problems and improving lives.

PSYCHOTHERAPY—AN OVERVIEW

>SURVEY QUESTION< *What do various therapies have in common?*

How effective is psychotherapy? Judging the outcome of therapy is tricky. Nevertheless, there is ample evidence that therapy is beneficial. Hundreds of studies show a strong pattern of positive effects for psychotherapy and counseling (Barlow, 2004; Lambert & Ogles, 2004). Even more convincing, perhaps, are the findings of a national survey. Nearly 9 out of 10 people who have sought mental health care say their lives improved as a result of the treatment (Kotkin, Daviet, & Gurin, 1996).

In general, then, psychotherapy works (Moras, 2002). Of course, results vary in individual cases. For some people therapy is immensely helpful; for others it is unsuccessful; overall it is effective for more people than not. Speaking more subjectively, a real success, in which a person's life is changed for the better, can be worth the frustration of several cases in which little progress is made.

Although it is common to think of therapy as a long, slow process, this is no longer normally the case (Shapiro et al., 2003). Research shows that about 50 percent of all clients feel better after between 13 and 18 weekly 1-hour therapy sessions. (Unfortunately, today the average client receives only 5 therapy sessions after which only 20 percent of patients feel better; Hansen, Lambert, & Forman, 2002.) (See ▸▸Fig. 13.6.) This means that the majority of clients improve after 6 months of therapy. Such rapid improvement is impressive in view of the fact that people often suffer for several years before seeking help.

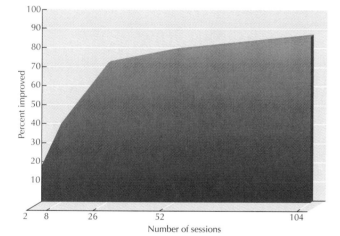

▸▸**FIGURE 13.6** The dose-improvement relationship in psychotherapy. This graph shows the percentage of patients who improved after varying numbers of therapy sessions. Notice that the most rapid improvement took place during the first 6 months of once-a-week sessions. (From Howard et al., 1986b.)

Core Features of Psychotherapy

What do psychotherapies have in common? We have sampled only a few of the many therapies in use today. For a summary of major differences among psychotherapies, see ▪ Table 13.2. To add to your understanding, let us briefly summarize what all techniques have in common.

Psychotherapies of various types share all or most of these goals: restoring hope, courage, and optimism; gaining insight; resolving conflicts; improving one's sense of self; changing unacceptable patterns of behavior; finding purpose; mending interpersonal relations; and learning to approach problems rationally (Frank & Frank, 2004; Seligman, 1998). To accomplish these goals, psychotherapies offer the following:

1. Therapy provides a *caring relationship* between the client and therapist, called a **therapeutic alliance.** Emotional rapport, warmth, friendship, understanding,

Therapy placebo effect Improvement caused not by the actual process of therapy but by a client's expectation that therapy will help.

Therapeutic alliance A caring relationship that unites a therapist and a client in working to solve the client's problems.

■ Table 13.2   Comparison of Psychotherapies

	Insight or Action?	Directive or Nondirective?	Individual or Group?	Therapy's Strength*
Psychoanalysis	Insight	Directive	Individual	Searching honesty
Brief psychodynamic therapy	Insight	Directive	Individual	Productive use of conflict
Client-centered therapy	Insight	Nondirective	Both	Acceptance, empathy
Existential therapy	Insight	Both	Individual	Personal empowerment
Gestalt therapy	Insight	Directive	Both	Focus on immediate awareness
Behavior therapy	Action	Directive	Both	Observable changes in behavior
Cognitive therapy	Action	Directive	Individual	Constructive guidance
Rational-emotive behavior therapy	Action	Directive	Individual	Clarity of thinking and goals
Psychodrama	Insight	Directive	Group	Constructive re-enactments
Family therapy	Both	Directive	Group	Shared responsibility for problems

*This column based in part on Andrews (1989).

acceptance, and empathy are the basis for this relationship. The therapeutic alliance unites the client and therapist as they work together to solve the client's problems. The strength of this alliance has a major impact on whether therapy succeeds (Kozart, 2002; Meier et al., 2006).

2. Therapy offers a *protected setting* in which emotional *catharsis* (release) can take place. Therapy is a sanctuary in which the client is free to express fears, anxieties, and personal secrets without fearing rejection or loss of confidentiality.

3. All therapies to some extent offer an *explanation* or *rationale* for the client's suffering. Additionally, they propose a line of action that will end this suffering.

4. Therapy provides clients with a *new perspective* about themselves and their situations and a chance to practice *new behaviors* (Crencavage & Norcross, 1990). Insights gained during therapy can bring about lasting changes in clients' lives (Grande et al., 2003).

If you recall that our discussion began with trepanning and demonology, it is clear that psychotherapy has come a long way. Still, the search for ways to improve psychotherapy remains an urgent challenge for those who devote their lives to helping others.

The Future of Psychotherapy

What will psychotherapy look like in the future? A group of experts predicted the following (Norcross, Hedges, & Prochaska, 2002):

- There will be an increase in the use of short-term therapy and solution-focused, problem solving approaches.
- More therapy will be provided by master's-level practitioners (counselors, social workers, and psychiatric nurses).
- The use of lower-cost Internet services, telephone counseling, paraprofessionals, and self-help groups will grow.
- The use of psychiatrists and psychoanalysis will decrease.

As you might guess, many of these predicted changes are based on pressures to reduce the cost of mental health services. Another interesting cost-saving measure is the idea that computers may be able to treat some relatively minor problems. In one study, clients worked through 10 computer-guided sessions that helped them identify a problem, form a plan of

■ Table 13.3 Helping Behaviors

To help another person gain insight into a personal problem it is valuable to keep the following comparison in mind.

Behaviors that Help	Behaviors that Hinder
Active listening	Probing painful topics
Acceptance	Judging/moralizing
Reflecting feelings	Criticism
Open-ended questioning	Threats
Supportive statements	Rejection
Respect	Ridicule/sarcasm
Patience	Impatience
Genuineness	Placing blame
Paraphrasing	Opinionated statements

Source: Adapted from Kottler, 2004.

action, and work through carrying out the plan. Most were satisfied with the help they received (Jacobs et al., 2001).

Basic Counseling Skills

A number of general helping skills can be distilled from the various approaches to therapy. These are points to keep in mind if you would like to comfort a person in distress, such as a troubled friend or relative (■ Table 13.3).

Active Listening

People frequently talk "at" each other without really listening. A person with problems needs to be heard. Make a sincere effort to listen to and understand the person. Try to accept the person's message without judging it or leaping to conclusions. Let the person know you are listening, through eye contact, posture, your tone of voice, and your replies (Kottler, 2004).

Clarify the Problem

People who have a clear idea of what is wrong in their lives are more likely to discover solutions. Try to understand the problem from the person's point of view. As you do, check your understanding often. For example, you might ask, "Are you saying that you feel depressed just at school? Or in general?" Remember, a problem well defined is often half solved.

Focus on Feelings

Feelings are neither right nor wrong. By focusing on feelings you can encourage the outpouring of emotion that is the basis for catharsis. Passing judgment on what is said just makes people defensive. For example, a friend confides that he has failed a test. Perhaps you know that he studies very little. If you say, "Just study more and you would do better," he will probably become defensive or hostile. Much more can be accomplished by saying, "You must feel very frustrated" or simply, "How do you feel about it?"

Teams of psychologists and counselors are often assembled to provide support to victims of major accidents and natural disasters. Because their work is stressful and often heart wrenching, relief workers also benefit from on-site counseling. Expressing emotions and talking about feelings are major elements of disaster counseling.

Avoid Giving Advice

Many people mistakenly think that they must solve problems for others. Remember that your goal is to provide understanding and support, not solutions. Of course, it is reasonable to give advice when you are asked for it, but beware of the trap of the "Why don't you . . . ? Yes, but . . ." game. According to psychotherapist Eric Berne (1964), this "game" follows a pattern: Someone says, "I have this problem." You say, "Why don't you do thus and so?" The person replies, "Yes, but . . ." and then tells you why your suggestion won't work. If you make a new suggestion the reply will once again be, "Yes, but . . ." Obviously, the person either knows more about his or her personal situation than you do or he or she has reasons for avoiding your advice. The student described earlier knows he needs to study. His problem is to understand why he doesn't *want* to study.

Accept the Person's Frame of Reference

W. I. Thomas said, "Things perceived as real are real in their effects." Try to resist imposing your views on the problems of others. Because we all live in different psychological worlds, there is no "correct" view of a life situation. A person who feels that his or her viewpoint has been understood feels freer to examine it objectively and to question it. Accepting and understanding the perspective of another person can be especially difficult when cultural differences exist (Draguns, Gielen, & Fish, 2004). (See "Therapy and Culture—A Bad Case of 'Ifufunyane.'")

Therapy and Culture—A Bad Case of "Ifufunyane"

At the age of 23, the patient was clearly suffering from "ifufunyane," a form of bewitchment common in the Xhosa culture of South Africa. However, he was treated at a local hospital by psychiatrists, who said he had schizophrenia and gave him antipsychotic drugs. The drugs helped, but his family shunned his fancy medical treatment and took him to a traditional healer who gave him herbs for his ifufunyane. Unfortunately, he got worse and was readmitted to the hospital. This time, the psychiatrists included the patient's family in his treatment. Together, they agreed to treat him with a combination of antipsychotic drugs *and* traditional herbs. This time, the patient got much better and his ifufunyane was alleviated too (Niehaus et al. 2005).

As this example illustrates, **culturally skilled therapists** are skilled at working with clients from various cultural backgrounds. To be culturally skilled, a counselor must be able to do all of the following (APA, 2003; Draguns, Gielen, & Fish, 2004; Fowers & Davidov, 2006):

- Adapt traditional theories and techniques to meet the needs of clients from non-European ethnic or racial groups
- Be aware of his or her own cultural values and biases
- Establish rapport with a person from a different cultural background
- Be open to cultural differences without resorting to stereotypes
- Treat members of racial or ethnic communities as individuals
- Be aware of a client's ethnic identity and degree of acculturation to the majority society
- Use existing helping resources within a cultural group to support efforts to resolve problems

Cultural awareness has helped broaden our ideas about mental health and optimal development (Draguns, Gielen, & Fish, 2004). It is also worth remembering that cultural barriers apply to communication in all areas of life, not just therapy. Although such differences can be challenging, they are also frequently enriching (Uwe et al., 2006).

Reflect Thoughts and Feelings

One of the best things you can do when offering support to another person is to give feedback by simply restating what is said. This is also a good way to encourage a person to talk. If your friend seems to be at a loss for words, *restate* or *paraphrase* his or her last sentence. Here's an example.

Friend: I'm really down about school. I can't get interested in any of my classes. I flunked my Spanish test, and somebody stole my notebook for psychology.

You: You're really upset about school, aren't you?

Friend: Yeah, and my parents are hassling me about my grades again.

You: You're feeling pressured by your parents?

Friend: Yeah, damn.

You: It must make you angry to be pressured by them.

As simple as this sounds, it is very helpful to someone trying to sort out feelings. Try it. If nothing else, you'll develop a reputation as a fantastic conversationalist!

Silence

Counselors tend to wait longer before responding than do people in everyday conversations. Pauses of 5 seconds or more are not unusual, and interrupting is rare. Listening patiently lets the person feel unhurried and encourages her or him to speak freely.

Questions

Because your goal is to encourage free expression, *open questions* tend to be the most helpful. A *closed question* is one that can be answered yes or no. Open questions call for an open-ended reply. Say, for example, that a friend tells you, "I feel like my boss has it in for me at work." A closed question would be, "Oh yeah? So, are you going to quit?" Open questions, such as, "Do you want to talk about it?" or "How do you feel about it?" are more likely to be helpful.

Culturally skilled therapist A therapist who has the awareness, knowledge, and skills necessary to treat clients from diverse cultural backgrounds.

Maintain Confidentiality

Your efforts to help will be wasted if you fail to respect the privacy of someone who has confided in you. Put yourself in the person's place. Don't gossip.

These guidelines are not an invitation to play "junior therapist." Professional therapists are trained to approach serious problems with skills far exceeding those described here. However, the points made help define the qualities of a therapeutic relationship. They also emphasize that each of us can supply two of the greatest mental health resources available at any cost: friendship and honest communication.

MEDICAL THERAPIES—PSYCHIATRIC CARE

>SURVEY QUESTION< *How do psychiatrists treat psychological disorders?*

Psychotherapy may be applied to anything from a brief crisis to a full-scale psychosis. However, most psychotherapists *do not* treat patients with major depressive disorders, schizophrenia, or other severe conditions. Major mental disorders are more often treated medically (Julien, 2004).

Three main types of **somatic** (bodily) **therapy** are *pharmacotherapy, electroconvulsive therapy,* and *psychosurgery.* Somatic therapy is often done in the context of psychiatric hospitalization. All the somatic approaches have a strong medical slant and they are typically administered by psychiatrists.

Drug Therapies

The atmosphere in psychiatric wards and mental hospitals changed radically in the mid-1950s with the widespread adoption of pharmacotherapy (FAR-meh-koe-THER-eh-pea). **Pharmacotherapy** refers to the use of drugs to treat emotional disturbances. Drugs may relieve the anxiety attacks and other discomforts of milder psychological disorders. More often, however, they are used to combat schizophrenia and major mood disorders.

What sorts of drugs are used in pharmacotherapy? Three major types of drugs are used. **Anxiolytics** (such as Valium) produce relaxation or reduce anxiety. **Antidepressants** are mood-elevating drugs that combat depression. **Antipsychotics** (also called **major tranquilizers**) have tranquilizing effects and, in addition, reduce hallucinations and delusions. (See Table 13.4 for examples of each class of drugs.)

Are drugs a valid approach to treatment? Drugs have shortened hospital stays and they have greatly improved the chances that people will recover from major psychological disorders. Drug therapy has also made it possible for many people to return to the community, where they can be treated on an out-patient basis.

Somatic therapy Any bodily therapy, such as drug therapy, electroconvulsive therapy, or psychosurgery.

Pharmacotherapy The use of drugs to alleviate the symptoms of emotional disturbance.

Anxiolytics Drugs (such as Valium) that produce relaxation or reduce anxiety.

Antidepressants Mood-elevating drugs.

Antipsychotics Drugs that, in addition to having tranquilizing effects, also tend to reduce hallucinations and delusional thinking. (Also called **major tranquilizers.**)

■ Table 13.4 Commonly Prescribed Psychiatric Drugs		
Class	**Examples (Trade Names)**	**Effects**
Minor tranquilizers (antianxiety drugs)	Ativan, Halcion, Librium, Restoril, Valium, Xanax	Reduce anxiety, tension, fear
Antidepressants	Anafranil, Elavil, Nardil, Norpramin, Parnate, Paxil, Prozac, Tofranil, Zoloft	Counteract depression
Antipsychotics (major tranquilizers)	Clozaril, Haldol, Mellaril, Navane, Risperdal, Thorazine	Reduce agitation, delusions, hallucinations, thought disorders

Limitations of Drug Therapy

Few experts would argue for a return to the conditions that existed before pharmacotherapy became available. However, drugs do have drawbacks. For example, 15 percent of patients taking major tranquilizers for long periods develop a neurological disorder that causes rhythmic facial and mouth movements (Chakos et al., 1996). Newer drugs are often hailed as medical "miracles." However, all drugs involve a trade-off between benefits and risks. For example, the drug Clozaril (clozapine) can relieve the symptoms of schizophrenia in some previously "hopeless" cases. But Clozaril is also dangerous: Two out of 100 patients taking the drug suffer from a potentially fatal blood disease (Ginsberg, 2006).

Is the risk worth it? Many experts think it is, because chronic schizophrenia robs people of almost everything that makes life worth living. It's possible, of course, that newer drugs will improve the risk-benefit ratio in the treatment of severe problems like schizophrenia. For example, the drug Risperdal (risperidone) appears to be as effective as Clozaril, without the lethal risk. But, even the best new drugs are not cure-alls. They help some people and relieve some problems, but not all. It is noteworthy that for serious mental disorders a combination of medication and psychotherapy almost always works better than drugs alone. Nevertheless, where schizophrenia and major mood disorders are concerned, drugs will undoubtedly remain the primary mode of treatment (Vasa, Carlino, & Pine, 2006; Walker et al., 2004).

Shock

In **electroconvulsive therapy (ECT)** a 150-volt electrical current is passed through the brain for slightly less than a second. This rather drastic medical treatment for depression triggers a convulsion and causes the patient to lose consciousness for a short time. Muscle relaxants and sedative drugs are given before ECT to soften its impact. Treatments are given in a series of six to eight sessions spread over 3 to 4 weeks.

How does shock help? Actually, it is the seizure activity that is believed to be helpful. Proponents of ECT claim that shock-induced seizures alter the biochemical and hormonal balance in the brain and body, bringing an end to severe depression and suicidal behavior (Fink, 2000) as well as improving long-term quality of life (McCall et al., 2006). Others have charged that ECT works only by confusing patients so they can't remember why they were depressed.

The ECT Debate

Not all professionals support the use of ECT. However, most experts seem to agree on the following: (1) At best, ECT produces only temporary improvement—it gets the patient out of a bad spot, but it must be combined with other treatments; (2) ECT can cause memory losses in some patients; (3) ECT should be used only after other treatments have failed; and (4) to lower the chance of a relapse, ECT should be followed by antidepressant drugs (Sackeim et al., 2001). All told, ECT is considered by many to be a valid treatment for selected cases of depression—

Courtesy of Rodger Casier

The work of artist Rodger Casier illustrates the value of psychiatric care. Despite having a form of schizophrenia, Casier produces artwork that has received public acclaim and has been featured in professional journals.

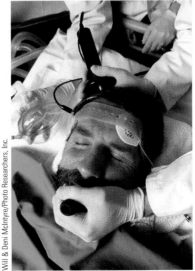

Will & Deni McIntyre/Photo Researchers, Inc.

In electroconvulsive therapy, electrodes are attached to the head, and a brief electrical current is passed through the brain. ECT is used in the treatment of severe depression.

Electroconvulsive therapy (ECT) A treatment for severe depression, consisting of an electric shock passed directly through the brain, which induces a convulsion.

especially when it rapidly ends wildly self-destructive or suicidal behavior (Pagnin et al., 2004). It's interesting to note that most ECT patients feel that the treatment helped them. Most, in fact, would have it done again (Bernstein et al., 1998).

Psychosurgery

The most extreme medical treatment is **psychosurgery** (any surgical alteration of the brain). The best-known psychosurgery is the lobotomy. In the *prefrontal lobotomy* the frontal lobes were surgically disconnected from other brain areas. This procedure was supposed to calm persons who didn't respond to any other type of treatment.

When the lobotomy was first introduced in the 1940s, there were enthusiastic claims for its success. But later studies suggested that some patients were calmed, some showed no change, and some became mental "vegetables." Lobotomies also produced a high rate of undesirable side effects, such as seizures, blunted emotions, major personality changes, and stupor. At about the same time that such problems became apparent, the first antipsychotic drugs became available. Soon after, the lobotomy was abandoned (Mashour, Walker, & Martuza, 2005).

To what extent is psychosurgery used now? Psychosurgery is still considered valid by many neurosurgeons. However, most now use *deep lesioning,* in which small target areas are destroyed in the brain's interior. The appeal of deep lesioning is that it can have specific value as a remedy for some very specific disorders (Mashour, Walker, & Martuza, 2005). For instance, patients suffering from a severe type of obsessive-compulsive disorder may be helped by psychosurgery (Dougherty et al., 2002).

It is worth remembering that psychosurgery cannot be reversed. Whereas a drug can be given or taken away, you can't take back psychosurgery. Critics argue that psychosurgery should be banned altogether; others continue to report success with brain surgery. All things considered, it is perhaps most accurate, even after decades of use, to describe psychosurgery as an experimental technique.

Depending on the quality of the institution, hospitalization may be a refuge or a brutalizing experience. Many state "asylums" or mental hospitals are antiquated and in need of drastic improvement.

Peter Southwick/Stock, Boston

Psychosurgery Any surgical alteration of the brain designed to bring about desirable behavioral or emotional changes.

Mental hospitalization Placing a person in a protected, therapeutic environment staffed by mental health professionals.

Hospitalization

Mental hospitalization for major mental disorders involves placing a person in a protected setting where medical therapy is provided. Hospitalization, by itself, can be a form of treatment. Staying in a hospital takes patients out of situations that may be sustaining their problems. For example, people with drug addictions may find it nearly impossible to resist the temptations for drug abuse in their daily lives. Hospitalization can help them make a clean break from their self-destructive behavior patterns (André et al., 2003).

At their best, hospitals are sanctuaries that provide diagnosis, support, refuge, and therapy. This is generally true of psychiatric units in general hospitals and private psychiatric hospitals. At worst, confinement to an institution can be a brutal experience that leaves people less prepared to face the world than when they arrived. This is more often the case in large state mental hospitals (Gorman, 1996).

In most instances, hospitals are best used as a last resort, after other forms of treatment within the community have been exhausted. Actually, most psychiatric patients do as well with short-term hospitalization as they do with longer periods. For this reason, the average stay in psychiatric hospitals is now just 20 days, rather than 3 to 4 months, as it was 20 years ago.

A new trend in treatment is **partial hospitalization.** In this approach, some patients spend their days in the hospital, but go home at night. Others attend therapy sessions during the evening. A major advantage of partial hospitalization is that patients can go home and practice what they've been learning. Eventually, most return to normal life. Overall, partial hospitalization can be just as effective as full hospitalization (Kiser, Heston, & Paavola, 2006).

Deinstitutionalization

In the last 30 years the population in large mental hospitals has dropped by two thirds. This is largely a result of **deinstitutionalization,** or reduced use of full-time commitment to mental institutions. Long-term "institutionalization" can lead to dependency, isolation, and continued emotional disturbance (Chamberlin & Rogers, 1990). Deinstitutionalization was meant to remedy this problem.

How successful has deinstitutionalization been? In truth, its success has been limited (Talbott, 2004). Many states reduced mental hospital populations primarily as a way to save money. The upsetting result is that many chronic patients have been discharged to hostile communities without adequate care. Many former patients have joined the ranks of the homeless. Sadly, patients who trade hospitalization for unemployment, homelessness, and social isolation all too often end up rehospitalized or in jail (Goldman, 1998).

Large mental hospitals may no longer be warehouses for society's unwanted, but many former patients are no better off in bleak nursing homes, single-room hotels, board-and-care homes, shelters, or jails. One in five of the two million Americans who are in jail or prison are mentally ill—three times the number who are in mental hospitals (Human Rights Watch, 2003). These figures suggest that jails are replacing mental hospitals as our society's "solution" for mental illness. Yet, ironically, high-quality care is available in almost every community. As much as anything, a simple lack of money prevents large numbers of people from getting the help they need (Torrey, 1996).

Half-way houses may be a better way to ease a patient's return to the community (Anthony, Cohen, & Kennard, 1990). **Half-way houses** are short-term group living facilities for people making the transition from an institution (mental hospital, prison, and so forth) to independent living. Typically, they offer supervision and support, without being as restricted and medically oriented as hospitals. They also keep people near their families. Most important, half-way houses can reduce a person's chances of being readmitted to a hospital (Coursey, Ward-Alexander, & Katz, 1990).

Ed Kashi/Corbis

A well-run half-way house can be a humane and cost-effective way to ease former mental patients back into the community (Coursey, Ward-Alexander, & Katz, 1990).

Community Mental Health Programs

Community mental health centers are a bright spot in the area of mental health care. **Community mental health centers** offer a wide range of mental health services and psychiatric care. Such centers try to help people avoid hospitalization and find answers to mental health problems (Burns, 2004). Typically, they do this by providing short-term treatment, counseling, out-patient care, emergency services, and suicide prevention.

If it is like most, the primary aim of the mental health center in your community is to directly aid troubled citizens. Its second goal is likely to be *prevention.* Consultation, education, and **crisis intervention** (skilled management of a psychological emergency) are used to prevent problems before they become serious. Also, some centers attempt to raise the general level of mental health in a community by combating unemployment, delinquency, and drug abuse (Tausig, Michello, & Subedi, 2004).

How have community mental health centers done in meeting their goals? In practice, they have concentrated much more on providing clinical services than they have on preventing problems. This appears to be primarily the result of wavering government support (translation: money). Overall, community mental health centers have succeeded in making psychological services more accessible than ever before. Many of their programs rely on **paraprofessionals** (individuals who work in a near-professional capacity under the supervision of more highly trained staff). Some paraprofessionals are ex-addicts, ex-alcoholics, or ex-patients who have "been there." Many more are persons (paid or volunteer) who have skills in tutoring, crafts, or counseling or who are simply warm, understanding, and skilled at communication. Often, paraprofessionals are more approachable than "doctors." This encourages people to seek mental health services that they might otherwise be reluctant to use (Everly, 2002).

A Look Ahead

In the "Psychology in Action" section that follows we will return briefly to behavioral approaches. There you will find a number of useful techniques that you may be able to apply to your own behavior. You'll also find a discussion of when to seek professional help and how to find it. Here's your authors' professional advice: This is information you won't want to skip.

Study Break   Group Therapies, Psychotherapy Skills, and Medical Therapies

Reflect

Would you rather participate in individual therapy or group therapy? What advantages and disadvantages do you think each has?

Based on your own experience, how valid do you think it is to say that within families "a problem for one is a problem for all"?

What lies at the "heart" of psychotherapy? How would you describe it to a friend?

Which of the basic counseling skills do you already use? Which would improve your ability to help a person in distress?

If a family member of yours became severely depressed, what therapies would be available to him or her? What are the pros and cons of each choice?

Learning Check

1. In psychodrama, people attempt to form meaningful wholes out of disjointed thoughts, feelings, and actions. T or F?
2. Most large-group awareness trainings make use of Gestalt therapy. T or F?
3. Which therapy places great emphasis on role-playing?

   a. psychodrama   b. awareness training
   c. family therapy   d. encounter

4. Emotional _____ (release) in a protected setting is an element of most psychotherapies.
5. To aid a troubled friend, you should focus on facts rather than feelings, and you should critically evaluate what the person is saying to help him or her grasp reality. T or F?
6. ECT is a modern form of pharmacotherapy. T or F?
7. Currently, the frontal lobotomy is the most widely used form of psychosurgery. T or F?

Critical Thinking

8. In your opinion, do psychologists have a duty to protect others who may be harmed by their clients? For example, if a patient has homicidal fantasies about his ex-wife, should she be informed?
9. Residents of Berkeley, California, voted on a referendum to ban the use of ECT within city limits. Do you think that the use of certain psychiatric treatments should be controlled by law?

Answers

1. F 2. F 3. a 4. catharsis 5. F 6. F 7. F 8. According to the law, there is a duty to protect others where a therapist could, with little effort, prevent serious harm. However, this duty can conflict with a client's rights to confidentiality and with client-therapist trust. Therapists often make difficult choices in such situations. 9. The question of who can prescribe drugs, do surgery, and administer ECT is controlled by law. However, psychiatrists strongly object to residents, city councils, or government agencies making medical decisions.

Psychology in Action

Self-Management and Seeking Professional Help

>SURVEY QUESTION< *How are behavioral principles applied to everyday problems?*

"Throw out the snake oil, ladies and gentlemen, and throw away your troubles. Doctor B. Havior Modification is here to put an end to all human suffering."

True? Well, not quite. Behavior therapy is not a cure-all. Its use is often quite complicated and requires a great deal of expertise. Still, behavior therapy offers a straightforward solution to many problems.

Paraprofessional An individual who works in a near-professional capacity under the supervision of a more highly trained person.

As mentioned elsewhere in this book, you should seek professional help when a significant problem exists. For lesser difficulties you may want to try applying behavioral principles yourself (Watson & Tharp, 2007). Let us see how this might be done.

Covert Reward and Punishment—Boosting Your "Willpower"

Therapist: "Have you ever decided to quit smoking cigarettes, watching television too much, eating too much, drinking too much, or driving too fast?"

Client: "Well, one of those applies. I have decided several times to quit smoking."

Therapist: "When have you decided?"

Client: "Usually after I am reminded of how dangerous smoking is—like when I heard that my uncle had died of lung cancer. He smoked constantly."

Therapist: "If you have decided to quit 'several times' I assume you haven't succeeded."

Client: "No, the usual pattern is for me to become upset about smoking and then to cut down for a day or two."

Therapist: "You forget the disturbing image of your uncle's death, or whatever, and start smoking again."

Client: "Yes, I suppose if I had an uncle die every day or so, I might actually quit!"

Sheila Terry/Photo Researchers, Inc.

The use of intensive behavioral principles, such as electric shock, to condition an aversion seems remote from everyday problems. Even naturally aversive actions are difficult to apply to personal behavior. As mentioned earlier, for instance, rapid smoking is difficult for most smokers to carry out on their own. And what about a problem like overeating? It would be difficult indeed to eat enough to create a lasting aversion to overeating. (Although it's sometimes tempting to try.)

In view of such limitations, psychologists have developed an alternative procedure that can be used to curb smoking, overeating, and other habits (Cautela & Kearney, 1986; Watson & Tharp, 2007).

Covert Sensitization In **covert sensitization,** aversive imagery is used to reduce the occurrence of an undesired response. Here's how it's done: Obtain six 3 × 5 cards and on each write a brief description of a scene related to the habit you wish to control. The scene should be so *disturbing* or *disgusting* that thinking about it would temporarily make you very uncomfortable about indulging in the habit. For smoking, the cards might read:

- I am in a doctor's office. The doctor looks at some reports and tells me I have lung cancer. She says a lung will have to be removed and sets a date for the operation.
- I am in bed under an oxygen tent. My chest feels caved in. There is a tube in my throat. I can barely breathe.
- I wake up in the morning and smoke a cigarette. I begin coughing up blood.
- My lover won't kiss me because my breath smells bad.
- Other cards would continue along the same line.

The trick, of course, is to get yourself to imagine or picture vividly each of these disturbing scenes *several times* a day. Imagining the scenes can be accomplished by placing them under *stimulus control.* Simply choose something you do *frequently* each day (such as getting a cup of coffee or getting up from your chair). Next make a rule: Before you can get a cup of coffee or get up from your chair, or whatever you have selected as a cue, you must take out your cards and *vividly picture* yourself engaging in the action you wish to curb (eating or smoking, for example). Then *vividly picture* the scene described on the top card. Imagine the scene for 30 seconds.

Covert sensitization Use of aversive imagery to reduce the occurrence of an undesired response.

After visualizing the top card, move it to the bottom so the cards are rotated. Make up new cards each week. The scenes can be made much more upsetting than the samples given here. The samples are toned down to keep you from being "grossed out."

Covert sensitization can also be used directly in situations that test your self-control. If you are trying to lose weight, for instance, you might be able to turn down a tempting dessert in this way: As you look at the dessert, visualize maggots crawling all over it. If you make this image as vivid and nauseating as possible, losing your appetite is almost a certainty. If you want to apply this technique to other situations, be aware that vomiting scenes are especially effective. Covert sensitization may sound as if you are "playing games with yourself," but it can be a great help if you want to cut down on a bad habit (Cautela & Kearney, 1986). Try it!

Thought Stopping   As discussed earlier, behavior therapists accept that thoughts, like visible responses, can also cause trouble. Think of times when you have repeatedly "put yourself down" mentally or when you have been preoccupied by needless worries, fears, or other negative and upsetting thoughts. If you would like to gain control over such thoughts, thought stopping may help you do it.

In **thought stopping,** aversive stimuli are used to interrupt or prevent upsetting thoughts. The simplest thought-stopping technique makes use of mild punishment to suppress upsetting mental images and internal "talk." Simply place a large, flat rubber band around your wrist. As you go through the day apply this rule: Each time you catch yourself thinking the upsetting image or thought, pull the rubber band away from your wrist and snap it. You need not make this terribly painful. Its value lies in drawing your attention to how often you form negative thoughts and in interrupting the flow of thoughts. Strong punishment is not required.

It seems like this procedure might be abandoned rapidly. Is there an alternative? A second thought-stopping procedure requires only that you interrupt upsetting thoughts each time they occur. Begin by setting aside time each day during which you will deliberately think the unwanted thought. As you begin to form the thought, shout "Stop!" aloud, with conviction. (Obviously, you should choose a private spot for this part of the procedure!)

Repeat the thought-stopping procedure 10 to 20 times for the first 2 or 3 days. Then switch to shouting "Stop!" covertly (to yourself) rather than aloud. Thereafter, thought stopping can be carried out throughout the day, whenever upsetting thoughts occur (Williams & Long, 1991). After several days of practice, you should be able to stop unwanted thoughts whenever they occur.

Covert Reinforcement   Earlier we discussed how punishing images can be used to decrease undesirable responses, such as smoking or overeating. Many people also find it helpful to covertly *reinforce* desired actions. **Covert reinforcement** is the use of positive imagery to reinforce desired behavior. For example, suppose your target behavior is, once again, not eating dessert. If this were the case, you could do the following (Cautela & Kearney, 1986; Watson & Tharp, 2007):

Imagine that you are standing at the dessert table with your friends. As dessert is passed, you politely refuse and feel good about staying on your diet.

These images would then be followed by imagining a pleasant, reinforcing scene:

Imagine that you are your ideal weight. You look really slim in your favorite color and style. Someone you like says to you, "Gee, you've lost weight. I've never seen you look so good."

For many people, of course, actual direct reinforcement (as described in the "Psychology in Action" section of Chapter 6) is the best way to alter behavior. Nevertheless, covert or "visualized" reinforcement can have similar effects. To make use of covert reinforcement, choose one or more target behaviors and rehearse them mentally. Then follow each rehearsal with a vivid, rewarding image.

Thought stopping Use of aversive stimuli to interrupt or prevent upsetting thoughts.

Covert reinforcement Using positive imagery to reinforce desired behavior.

Self-Directed Desensitization—Overcoming Common Fears

You have prepared for 2 weeks to give a speech in a large class. As your turn approaches, your hands begin to tremble. Your heart pounds and you find it difficult to breathe. You say to your body, "Relax!" What happens? Nothing! That's why the first step in desensitization is learning to relax voluntarily, by using the tension-release method described earlier in this chapter. As an alternative, you might want to try imagining a very safe, pleasant, and relaxing scene. Some people find such images as relaxing as the tension-release method (Rosenthal, 1993). Another helpful technique is to do some deep breathing. Typically, a person who is breathing deeply is relaxed. Shallow breathing involves little movement of the diaphragm. If you place your hand on your abdomen, it will move up and down if you are breathing deeply.

Once you have learned to relax, the next step is to identify the fear you would like to control and construct a hierarchy.

Procedure for Constructing a Hierarchy   Make a list of situations (related to the fear) that make you anxious. Try to list at least 10 situations. Some should be very frightening and others only mildly frightening. Write a short description of each situation on a separate 3 × 5 card. Place the cards in order from the least disturbing situation to the most disturbing. Here is a sample hierarchy for a student afraid of public speaking:

1. Being given an assignment to speak in class
2. Thinking about the topic and the date the speech must be given
3. Writing the speech; thinking about delivering the speech
4. Watching other students speak in class the week before the speech date
5. Rehearsing the speech alone; pretending to give it to the class
6. Delivering the speech to my roommate; pretending my roommate is the teacher
7. Reviewing the speech on the day it is to be presented
8. Entering the classroom; waiting and thinking about the speech
9. Being called; standing up; facing the audience
10. Delivering the speech

Using the Hierarchy   When you have mastered the relaxation exercises and have the hierarchy constructed, set aside time each day to work on reducing your fear. Begin by performing the relaxation exercises. When you are completely relaxed, visualize the scene on the first card (the least frightening scene). If you can *vividly* picture and imagine yourself in the first situation twice *without a noticeable increase in muscle tension,* proceed to the next card. Also, as you progress, relax yourself between cards.

Each day, stop when you reach a card that you cannot visualize without becoming tense in three attempts. Each day, begin one or two cards before the one on which you stopped the previous day. Continue to work with the cards until you can visualize the last situation without experiencing tension (techniques are based on Wolpe, 1974).

By using this approach you should be able to reduce the fear or anxiety associated with things such as public speaking, entering darkened rooms, asking questions in large classes, heights, talking to members of the opposite sex, and taking tests (Watson & Tharp, 2007). Even if you are not always able to reduce a fear, you will have learned to place relaxation under voluntary control. This alone is valuable because controlling unnecessary tension can increase energy and efficiency.

Seeking Professional Help—When, Where, and How?

>SURVEY QUESTION<   *How could a person find professional help?*

Chances are good that at some point you, or someone in your family, will benefit from mental health services of one kind or another. In one survey, half of all American households had someone who received mental health treatment during the preceding year (Chamberlin, 2004).

How would I know if I should seek professional help at some point in my life? Although there is no simple answer to this question, the following guidelines may be helpful.

1. If your level of psychological discomfort (unhappiness, anxiety, or depression, for example) is comparable to a level of physical discomfort that would cause you to see a doctor or dentist, you should consider seeing a psychologist or a psychiatrist.
2. Another signal to watch for is significant changes in behavior, such as the quality of your work (or schoolwork), your rate of absenteeism, your use of drugs (including alcohol), or your relationships with others.
3. Perhaps you have urged a friend or relative to seek professional help and were dismayed because he or she refused to do so. If *you* find friends or relatives making a similar suggestion, recognize that they may be seeing things more clearly than you are.
4. If you have persistent or disturbing suicidal thoughts or impulses, you should seek help immediately.

Locating a Therapist

If I wanted to talk to a therapist, how would I find one?   Here are some suggestions that could help you get started.

1. *The yellow pages.* Psychologists are listed in the telephone book under "Psychologist" or in some cases under "Counseling Services." Psychiatrists are generally listed as a subheading under "Physicians." Counselors are usually found under the heading "Marriage and Family Counselors." These listings will usually put you in touch with individuals in private practice.
2. *Community or county mental health centers.* Most counties and many cities offer public mental health services. (These are listed in the phone book.) Public mental health centers usually provide counseling and therapy services directly, and they can refer you to private therapists.
3. *Mental health associations.* Many cities have mental health associations organized by concerned citizens. Groups such as these usually keep listings of qualified therapists and other services and programs in the community.
4. *Colleges and universities.* If you are a student, don't overlook counseling services offered by a student health center or special student counseling facilities.
5. *Newspaper advertisements.* Some psychologists advertise their services in newspapers. Also, low-cost "outreach" clinics occasionally try to make their presence known to the public by advertising. In either case, you should carefully inquire into a therapist's training and qualifications. Without the benefit of a referral from a trusted person, it is wise to be cautious.
6. *Crisis hotlines.* The typical crisis hotline is a telephone service staffed by community volunteers. These people are trained to provide information concerning a wide range of mental health problems. They also have lists of organizations, services, and other resources in the community where you can go for help.

■ Table 13.5 summarizes all of the sources for psychotherapy, counseling, and referrals we have discussed, as well as some additional possibilities.

Options   *How would I know what kind of a therapist to see? How would I pick one?*   The choice between a psychiatrist and a psychologist is somewhat arbitrary. Both are trained to do psychotherapy. A psychiatrist can administer somatic therapy and prescribe drugs; a psychologist can work in conjunction with a physician if such services are needed. Psychologists and psychiatrists can be equally effective as therapists (Seligman, 1995).

Fees for psychiatrists are usually higher, averaging about $160 to $200 an hour. Psychologists average about $100 an hour. Counselors and social workers typically charge about

---

■ Table 13.5   Mental Health Resources

- Family doctors (for referrals to mental health professionals)
- Mental health specialists, such as psychiatrists, psychologists, social workers, or mental health counselors
- Health maintenance organizations (HMOs)
- Community mental health centers
- Hospital psychiatry departments and outpatient clinics
- University- or medical school–affiliated programs
- State hospital outpatient clinics
- Family service/social agencies
- Private clinics and facilities
- Employee assistance programs
- Local medical, psychiatric, or psychological societies

Source: National Institute of Mental Health.

$80 per hour. Group therapy averages only about $40 an hour because the therapist's fee is divided among several people.

Be aware that most health insurance plans will pay for psychological services. If fees are a problem, keep in mind that many therapists charge on a sliding scale, or ability-to-pay basis, and that community mental health centers almost always charge on a sliding scale. In one way or another, help is almost always available for anyone who needs it.

Some communities and college campuses have counseling services staffed by sympathetic paraprofessionals or peer counselors. These services are free or very low cost. As mentioned earlier, paraprofessionals are people who work in a near-professional capacity under professional supervision. **Peer counselors** are nonprofessional persons who have learned basic counseling skills. There is a natural tendency, perhaps, to doubt the abilities of paraprofessionals. However, many studies have shown that paraprofessional counselors are often as effective as professionals (Christensen & Jacobson, 1994).

Also, don't overlook self-help groups, which can add valuable support to professional treatment. Members of a self-help group typically share a particular type of problem, such as eating disorders or coping with an alcoholic parent. **Self-help groups** offer members mutual support and a chance to discuss problems. In many instances helping others also serves as therapy for those who give help (Burlingame & Davies, 2002). For some problems, self-help groups may be the best choice of all (Fobair, 1997; Galanter et al., 2005).

Qualifications   You can usually find out about a therapist's qualifications simply by asking. A reputable therapist will be glad to reveal his or her background. If you have any doubts, credentials may be checked and other helpful information can be obtained from local branches of any of the following organizations. You can also browse the websites listed here:

American Association for Marriage and Family Therapy (www.aamft.org)

American Family Therapy Association (www.afta.org)

American Psychiatric Association (www.psych.org)

American Psychological Association (www.apa.org)

Association of Humanistic Psychology (www.ahpweb.org)

Canadian Psychiatric Association (www.cpa-apc.org)

Canadian Psychological Association (www.cpa.ca)

National Mental Health Association (www.nmha.org)

The question of how to pick a particular therapist remains. The best way is to start with a short consultation with a respected psychiatrist, psychologist, or counselor. This will allow the person you consult to evaluate your difficulty and recommend a type of therapy or a therapist who is likely to be helpful. As an alternative you might ask the person teaching this course for a referral.

Evaluating a Therapist   *How would I know whether or not to quit or ignore a therapist?*   A balanced look at psychotherapies suggests that all *techniques* are about equally successful (Wampold et al., 1997). However, all *therapists* are not equally successful. Far more important than the approach used are the therapist's personal qualities (Norcross, Hedges, & Prochaska, 2002; Okiishi et al., 2003). The most consistently successful therapists are those who are willing to use whatever method seems most helpful for a client. They are also marked by personal characteristics of warmth, integrity, sincerity, and empathy. Former clients consistently rate the person doing the therapy as more important than the type of therapy used (Elliott & Williams, 2003).

It is perhaps most accurate to say that at this stage of development, psychotherapy is an art, not a science. The *relationship* between a client and therapist is the therapist's most basic tool (Hubble, Duncan, & Miller, 1999; Norcross, Hedges, & Prochaska,, 2002). This is why

Peer counselor A nonprofessional person who has learned basic counseling skills.

Self-help group A group of people who share a particular type of problem and provide mutual support to one another.

you must trust and easily relate to a therapist for therapy to be effective. Here are some danger signals to watch for in psychotherapy:

- Sexual advances by therapist
- Therapist makes repeated verbal threats or is physically aggressive
- Therapist is excessively blaming, belittling, hostile, or controlling
- Therapist makes excessive small talk; talks repeatedly about his/her own problems
- Therapist encourages prolonged dependence on him/her
- Therapist demands absolute trust or tells client not to discuss therapy with anyone else

Clients who like their therapist are generally more successful in therapy (Talley, Strupp, & Morey, 1990). An especially important part of the therapeutic alliance is agreement about the goals of therapy (Meier et al., 2006). It is therefore a good idea to think about what you would like to accomplish by entering therapy. Write down your goals and discuss them with your therapist during the first session. Your first meeting with a therapist should also answer all of the following questions (Somberg, Stone, & Claiborn, 1993):

- Will the information I reveal in therapy remain completely confidential?
- What risks do I face if I begin therapy?
- How long do you expect treatment to last?
- What form of treatment do you expect to use?
- Are there alternatives to therapy that might help me as much or more?

It's always tempting to avoid facing up to personal problems. With this in mind, you should give a therapist a fair chance and not give up too easily. But don't hesitate to change therapists or to terminate therapy if you lose confidence in the therapist or if you don't relate well to the therapist as a person.

 Study Break   **Self-Management and Finding Professional Help**

Reflect

How could you use covert sensitization, thought stopping, and covert reinforcement to change your behavior? Try to apply each technique to a specific example.

Just for practice, make a fear hierarchy for a situation you find frightening. Does vividly picturing items in the hierarchy make you tense or anxious? If so, can you intentionally relax using the tension-release method?

Assume that you want to seek help from a psychologist or other mental health professional. How would you proceed? Take some time to actually find out what mental health services are available to you.

Learning Check

1. Covert sensitization and thought stopping combine aversion therapy and cognitive therapy. T or F?
2. Like covert aversion conditioning, covert reinforcement of desired responses is also possible. T or F?
3. Exercises that bring about deep-muscle relaxation are an essential element in covert sensitization. T or F?
4. Items in a desensitization hierarchy should be placed in order from the least disturbing to the most disturbing. T or F?
5. The first step in desensitization is to place the visualization of disturbing images under stimulus control. T or F?
6. Persistent emotional discomfort is a clear sign that professional psychological counseling should be sought. T or F?
7. Community mental health centers rarely offer counseling or therapy themselves; they only do referrals. T or F?
8. In many instances, a therapist's personal qualities have more of an effect on the outcome of therapy than does the type of therapy used. T or F?

Critical Thinking

9. Would it be acceptable for a therapist to urge a client to break all ties with a troublesome family member?

Answers

1. T 2. T 3. F 4. T 5. F 6. T 7. F 8. T 9. Such decisions must be made by clients themselves. Therapists can help clients evaluate important decisions and feelings about significant persons in their lives. However, actively urging a client to sever a relationship borders on unethical behavior.

CHAPTER IN REVIEW

Major Points

- Psychotherapy facilitates positive changes in personality, behavior, or adjustment.
- Before the development of modern therapies, superstition dominated attempts to treat psychological problems.
- Five major categories of psychotherapy are psychodynamic, insight, behavioral, cognitive, and group therapies.
- Psychotherapy is generally effective, although no single form of therapy is superior to others.
- All medical treatments for psychological disorders have pros and cons. Overall, however, their effectiveness is improving.
- Some personal problems can be successfully treated using self-management techniques.
- Everyone should know how to obtain high-quality mental health care in his or her community.

Summary

How do psychotherapies differ? How did psychotherapy originate?

- Psychotherapies may be classified as insight, action, directive, nondirective, or supportive therapies, and combinations of these.
- Therapies may be conducted either individually or in groups, and they may be time limited.
- Primitive approaches to mental illness were often based on belief in supernatural forces.
- Demonology attributed mental disturbance to demonic possession and prescribed exorcism as the cure.
- In some instances, the actual cause of bizarre behavior may have been ergot poisoning.
- More humane treatment began in 1793 with the work of Philippe Pinel in Paris.

Is Freudian psychoanalysis still used?

- Freud's psychoanalysis was the first formal psychotherapy. Psychoanalysis seeks to release repressed thoughts and emotions from the unconscious.
- The psychoanalyst uses free association, dream analysis, and analysis of resistance and transference to reveal health-producing insights.
- Some critics argue that traditional psychoanalysis receives credit for spontaneous remissions of symptoms. However, psychoanalysis is successful for many patients.

- Brief psychodynamic therapy (which relies on psychoanalytic theory but is brief and focused) is as effective as other major therapies.

What are the major humanistic therapies?

- Client-centered (or person-centered) therapy is nondirective and is dedicated to creating an atmosphere of growth.
- Unconditional positive regard, empathy, authenticity, and reflection are combined to give the client a chance to solve his or her own problems.
- Existential therapies focus on the end result of the choices one makes in life. Clients are encouraged through confrontation and encounter to exercise free will and to take responsibility for their choices.
- Gestalt therapy emphasizes immediate awareness of thoughts and feelings. Its goal is to rebuild thinking, feeling, and acting into connected wholes and to help clients break through emotional blockages.
- Media psychologists, telephone counselors, and Internet therapists may, on occasion, do some good. However, each has serious drawbacks, and the effectiveness of telephone counseling and Internet therapy has not been established.
- Therapy by videoconferencing shows more promise as a way to provide mental health services at a distance.

What is behavior therapy?

- Behavior therapists use various behavior modification techniques that apply learning principles to change human behavior.
- In aversion therapy, classical conditioning is used to associate maladaptive behavior (such as smoking or drinking) with pain or other aversive events in order to inhibit undesirable responses.

How is behavior therapy used to treat phobias, fears, and anxieties?

- Classical conditioning also underlies systematic desensitization, a technique used to overcome fears and anxieties. In desensitization, gradual adaptation and reciprocal inhibition break the link between fear and particular situations.
- Typical steps in desensitization are: Construct a fear hierarchy; learn to produce total relaxation; and perform items on the hierarchy (from least to most disturbing).

- Desensitization may be carried out with real settings or it may be done by vividly imagining the fear hierarchy or by watching models perform the feared responses.
- In some cases, virtual reality exposure can be used to present fear stimuli in a controlled manner.
- A new technique called eye movement desensitization and reprocessing (EMDR) shows promise as a treatment for traumatic memories and stress disorders. At present, however, EMDR is highly controversial.

What role does reinforcement play in behavior therapy?

- Behavior modification makes use of operant principles, such as positive reinforcement, nonreinforcement, extinction, punishment, shaping, stimulus control, and time out. These principles are used to extinguish undesirable responses and to promote constructive behavior.
- Nonreward can extinguish troublesome behaviors. Often this is done by simply identifying and eliminating reinforcers, particularly attention and social approval.
- To apply positive reinforcement and operant shaping, tokens are often used to reinforce selected target behaviors.
- Full-scale use of tokens in an institutional setting produces a token economy. Toward the end of a token economy program, patients are shifted to social rewards such as recognition and approval.

Can therapy change thoughts and emotions?

- Cognitive therapy emphasizes changing thought patterns that underlie emotional or behavioral problems. Its goals are to correct distorted thinking and/or teach improved coping skills.
- In a variation of cognitive therapy called rational-emotive behavior therapy (REBT), clients learn to recognize and challenge their own irrational beliefs.

Can psychotherapy be done with groups of people?

- Group therapy may be a simple extension of individual methods or it may be based on techniques developed specifically for groups.
- In psychodrama, individuals enact roles and incidents resembling their real-life problems. In family therapy, the family group is treated as a unit.
- Although they are not literally psychotherapies, sensitivity and encounter groups attempt to encourage positive personality change. In recent years, commercially offered large-group awareness trainings have become popular. However, the therapeutic benefits of such programs are questionable.

What do various therapies have in common?

- To alleviate personal problems, all psychotherapies offer a caring relationship, emotional rapport, a protected setting, catharsis, explanations for the client's problems, a new perspective, and a chance to practice new behaviors.
- Many basic counseling skills underlie a variety of therapies. These include listening actively, helping to clarify the problem, focusing on feelings, avoiding the giving of unwanted advice, accepting the person's perspective, reflecting thoughts and feelings, being patient during silences, using open questions when possible, and maintaining confidentiality.
- The culturally skilled counselor must be able to establish rapport with a person from a different cultural background and adapt traditional theories and techniques to meet the needs of clients from non-European ethnic or racial groups.

How do psychiatrists treat psychological disorders?

- Three medical, or somatic, approaches to treatment are pharmacotherapy, electroconvulsive therapy (ECT), and psychosurgery. All three techniques are controversial to a degree because of questions about effectiveness and side effects.
- Community mental health centers seek to avoid or minimize mental hospitalization. They also seek to prevent mental health problems through education, consultation, and crisis intervention.

How are behavioral principles applied to everyday problems?

- Cognitive techniques can be an aid to managing personal behavior.
- In covert sensitization, aversive images are used to discourage unwanted behavior.
- Thought stopping uses mild punishment to prevent upsetting thoughts.
- Covert reinforcement is a way to encourage desired responses by mental rehearsal.
- Desensitization pairs relaxation with a hierarchy of upsetting images in order to lessen fears.

How could a person find professional help?

- In most communities, a competent and reputable therapist can be located with public sources of information or through a referral.
- Practical considerations such as cost and qualifications enter into choosing a therapist. However, the therapist's personal characteristics are of equal importance.

Interactive Learning

Internet addresses frequently change. To find the sites listed here, visit www.thomsonedu/psychology/coon for an updated list of Internet addresses and direct links to relevant sites.

Psychology: A Journey Companion Website   Find online quizzes, flash cards, animations, video clips, experiments, interactive assessments, and other helpful study aids for this text at www.thomsonedu.com/psychology/coon.

Basics of Cognitive Therapy   An overview of cognitive therapy, with suggested readings.

How to Find Help for Life's Problems   Provides information on psychotherapy and advice on how to choose a psychotherapist.

NetPsychology   Explores the delivery of psychological services on the Internet.

Psychological Self-Help   An online book about self-improvement.

Science & Pseudoscience Review in Mental Health   A review of therapies that are considered to be scientifically dubious.

The Effectiveness of Psychotherapy   A summary of the *Consumer Reports* survey on the effectiveness of psychotherapy.

Types of Therapies   Describes four different approaches to therapy. Also has information about choosing a therapist.

Web Counselor   Typical personal problems are presented along with examples of advice.

ThomsonNOW   Go to www.thomsonedu.com to link to ThomsonNOW, your online study tool. First take the **Pre-Test** for this chapter to get your **Personalized Study Plan,** which will identify topics you need to review and direct you to online resources. Then take the **Post-Test** to determine what concepts you have mastered and what you still need work on.

TEST YOUR KNOWLEDGE

Therapies

For additional review, get more practice with *ThomsonNOW*, *WebTutor*, the *Practice Quizzes*, and/or the printed *Study Guide* available with this book.

1. An approach that is incompatible with insight therapy is
   a. individual therapy
   b. action therapy
   c. nondirective therapy
   d. group therapy

2. Which type of therapy is LEAST likely to bring about personal change?
   a. nondirective therapy
   b. supportive therapy
   c. time-limited therapy
   d. group therapy

3. A scientific explanation of medieval "possessions" by "demons" is related to the effects of
   a. ergot poisoning
   b. trepanning
   c. exorcism
   d. unconscious transference

4. Which of the following is NOT a psychoanalytic concept?
   a. free association
   b. resistance
   c. transference
   d. trepanning

5. When evaluating a therapy, one way to avoid being mislead by a spontaneous remission of symptoms is to use a _____ control group.
   a. nondirective
   b. latent
   c. psychodynamic
   d. waiting-list

6. Carl Rogers did NOT believe in using _____ in therapy.
   a. empathy
   b. authenticity
   c. reflection
   d. confrontation

7. Filling in gaps in immediate self-awareness is one of the principal goals of
   a. REBT
   b. existential therapy
   c. person-centered therapy
   d. Gestalt therapy

8. To date, the most acceptable type of "distance therapy" is
   a. media psychology
   b. commercial telephone counseling
   c. Internet therapy
   d. telehealth

9. Classical conditioning principles are the basis for
   a. aversion therapy
   b. time out
   c. token economies
   d. EMDR

10. Reciprocal inhibition is an important principle in
    a. EMDR
    b. REBT
    c. desensitization
    d. the design of a token economy

11. A psychologist who is interested in overgeneralization and irrational beliefs is obviously a proponent of
    a. exposure therapy
    b. token economies
    c. systematic desensitization
    d. cognitive therapy

12. The B in the A-B-C of REBT stands for
    a. behavior
    b. belief
    c. being
    d. backward

13. The mirror technique is frequently used in
    a. exposure therapy
    b. psychodrama
    c. family therapy
    d. EMDR

14. Research shows that about half of all clients feel better after their first _____ therapy sessions.
    a. 8
    b. 16
    c. 24
    d. 26

15. Emotional rapport, warmth, understanding, acceptance, and empathy are the core of
    a. the therapeutic alliance
    b. large-group awareness training
    c. role reversals
    d. action therapies

16. Culturally skilled therapists do all but one of the following; which does NOT apply?
    a. Be aware of the client's degree of acculturation.
    b. Use helping resources within the client's cultural group.
    c. Adapt standard techniques to match cultural stereotypes.
    d. Be aware of their own cultural values.

17. Major tranquilizers are also known as
    a. anxiolytics
    b. antipsychotics
    c. antidepressants
    d. prefrontal sedatives

18. ECT is classified as a type of
    a. somatic therapy
    b. pharmacotherapy
    c. psychosurgery
    d. deep lesioning

19. Mild punishment is used in which self-management technique?
    a. thought stopping
    b. desensitization
    c. REBT
    d. time out

20. The tension-release method is an important part of
    a. covert reinforcement
    b. thought stopping
    c. desensitization
    d. peer counseling

Social Behavior

JOURNEY INTO PSYCHOLOGY: SIX DEGREES OF SEPARATION

N *"No man is an island, entire of itself."* —John Donne

Here's your assignment: You have been given a message and the name, address, and occupation of the person who should receive it. The "target person" lives somewhere else on earth. You can move the message by e-mail, but you may send it only to a first-name acquaintance. That person, in turn, must forward the message to a first-name acquaintance. The message is to be moved in this fashion until it reaches the target person, whom the previous person must know by name.

Sound impossible? Following up on the pioneering work of social psychologist Stanley Milgram (1967), sociologist Duncan Watts asked more than 60,000 senders to use this method to forward e-mails to 18 target recipients in 13 countries. Like Milgram before him, Watts found that the average number of intermediaries was six (Dodds, Muhamad, & Watts, 2003).

How is that possible? Each of us is part of a rich tapestry of social relationships. You probably know at least dozens of people by name. Each of them knows dozens more people, who each know still more people, and so on. Thus, each social relationship connects with many others. By following all the social links, you could reach millions of people, just six "layers" out. With the recent explosion in popularity of social networking sites like Blogger, Facebook, Friendster, and MySpace, our social world will undoubtedly shrink even more.

Although you may like being alone at times, the fact is, humans are social animals. Imagine if you were deprived of all contact with your family and friends. You would probably find it painfully lonely and disorienting. Social behavior has been the target of an immense amount of study—too much, in fact, for us to cover in detail. Therefore, this chapter is a social psychology "sampler." We hope that you will find the topics interesting and thought provoking.

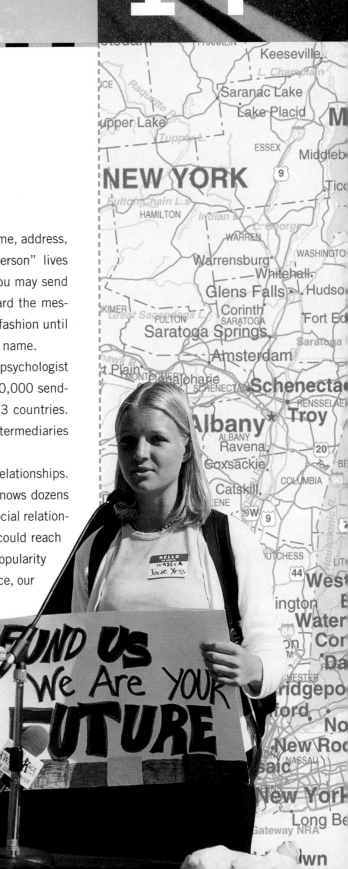

Index Stock Imagery/Jupiterimages

▽ Survey Questions

- Why do people affiliate? What factors influence interpersonal attraction?
- How does group membership affect our behavior?
- What have social psychologists learned about conformity, compliance, obedience, and self-assertion?
- How are attitudes acquired and changed?
- Under what conditions is persuasion most effective?
- Is brainwashing actually possible? How are people converted to cult membership?
- What causes prejudice and intergroup conflict?
- How do psychologists explain human aggression?
- Why are bystanders so often unwilling to help in an emergency?
- What can be done to avoid prejudice and promote social harmony?

AFFILIATION AND ATTRACTION—COME TOGETHER

>SURVEY QUESTIONS< *Why do people affiliate? What factors influence interpersonal attraction?*

Social psychology is the scientific study of how individuals behave, think, and feel in social situations (that is, in the presence, actual or implied, of others) (Baron, Byrne, & Branscombe, 2006). Each of us is immersed in a complex social world of families, teams, crowds, tribes, companies, parties, troops, bands, sects, gangs, crews, clans, communities, and nations. But what brings us together in the first place? The *need to affiliate* (associate with other people) is based on basic human desires for approval, support, friendship, and information. We also seek the company of others to alleviate fear or anxiety. A classic experiment in which college women were threatened with electric shock illustrates this point.

> ### Zilstein's Shock Shop
> A man introduced as Dr. Gregor Zilstein ominously explained to arriving participants, "We would like to give each of you a series of electric shocks . . . these shocks will hurt, they will be painful." In the room was a frightening electrical device that seemed to verify Zilstein's plans. While waiting to be shocked, each woman was given a choice of waiting alone or with other participants. Women frightened in this way more often chose to wait with others; those who expected the shock to be "a mild tickle or tingle" were more willing to wait alone (Schachter, 1959).

Apparently, the frightened women found it comforting to be with others. Should we conclude that "misery loves company"? Actually, that's not entirely correct. In a later experiment, women who expected to be shocked were given the choice of waiting with other future shock recipients, with women waiting to see their college advisers, or alone. Most women chose to wait with other future "victims." In short, misery seems to love miserable company! In general, we prefer to be with people in circumstances similar to our own (Gump & Kulik, 1997).

Is there a reason for that? Yes. Other people provide information that helps us evaluate our own reactions. When a situation is threatening or unfamiliar, or when we are in doubt, *social comparisons* tend to guide our behavior (Kulik, Mahler, & Moore, 2003).

Social Comparison Theory

If you want to know how tall you are, you simply get out a tape measure. But how do you know if you are a good athlete, worker, parent, or friend? How do you know if your views on politics, religion, or hip-hop are unusual or widely shared? When there are no objective

Social psychology The scientific study of how individuals behave, think, and feel in social situations.

standards, the only available yardstick is provided by comparing yourself to others (Miller, 2006).

Social psychologist Leon Festinger (1919–1989) theorized that belonging to groups fills our needs for **social comparison** (comparing your own actions, feelings, opinions, or abilities to those of others). Have you ever "compared notes" with other students after taking an exam? ("How did you do?" "Wasn't that last question hard?") If you have, you were satisfying needs for social comparison (Festinger, 1957).

Typically, we don't make social comparisons randomly or on some absolute scale. Meaningful evaluations are based on comparing yourself with people of similar backgrounds, abilities, and circumstances (Miller, Turnbull, & McFarland, 1988). To illustrate, let's ask a student named Wendy if she is a good tennis player. If Wendy compares herself to a professional, the answer will be no. But this tells us little about her *relative* ability. Within her tennis group, Wendy is regarded as an excellent player. On a fair scale of comparison, Wendy knows she is good and she takes pride in her tennis skills. In the same way, thinking of yourself as successful, talented, responsible, or fairly paid depends entirely on whom you choose for comparison. Thus, a desire for social comparison provides a motive for associating with others and influences which groups we join.

Don't people also affiliate out of attraction for one another? They do, of course. Let's see why.

High school class reunions are notorious for the rampant social comparison they often encourage. Apparently it's hard to resist comparing yourself to former classmates to see how you are doing in life.

Interpersonal Attraction

"Birds of a feather flock together." "Familiarity breeds contempt." "Opposites attract." "Absence makes the heart grow fonder." Are these statements true? Actually, the folklore about friendship is, at best, a mixture of fact and fiction.

What does attract people to each other? **Interpersonal attraction** (affinity to another person) is the basis for most voluntary social relationships (Berscheid & Regan, 2005). As you might expect, we look for friends and lovers who are kind and understanding, who have attractive personalities, and who like us in return (Sprecher, 1998). Deciding whether you would like to know another person can happen very quickly, sometimes within just minutes of meeting (Sunnafrank, Ramirez, & Metts, 2004). In addition, several less obvious factors influence attraction.

Physical Proximity

Our choice of friends (and even lovers) is based more on *physical proximity* (nearness) than we might care to believe. For example, the closer people live to each other, the more likely they are to become friends. Likewise, lovers like to think they have found the "one and only" person in the universe for them. In reality, they have probably found the best match in a 5-mile radius (Buss, 1985)! Marriages are not made in heaven—they are made in schools, businesses, churches, bars, clubs, and neighborhoods.

Proximity promotes attraction by increasing the *frequency of contact* between people. In general, we are attracted to people we see often. (If you have a reluctant sweetheart, be careful not to send too many love letters—she or he might run off with the letter carrier!) In short, there does seem to be a "boy-next-door" or "girl-next-door" effect in romantic attraction, and a "folks-next-door" effect in friendship. Notice, however, that the Internet is making it increasingly easier to maintain frequent contact, which is leading to more and more long-distance friendships and romances (Lawson & Leck, 2006).

Physical Attractiveness

People who are *physically attractive* are regarded as good-looking by others. Beautiful people are generally rated as more appealing than average. This is due, in part, to the *halo effect,* a tendency to generalize a favorable impression to unrelated personal characteristics. Because of it, we assume that beautiful people are also likable, intelligent, warm, witty, mentally

Social comparison Making judgments about ourselves through comparison with others.

Interpersonal attraction Social attraction to another person.

Physical beauty can be socially advantageous because of the widespread belief that "what is beautiful is good." However, physical beauty is generally unrelated to actual personal traits and talents.

healthy, and socially skilled. In reality, physical attractiveness has almost *no* connection to intelligence, talents, or abilities. Perhaps that's why beauty mainly affects our initial interest in getting to know others (Keller & Young, 1996). Later, more meaningful qualities gain in importance (Berscheid, 2000; Miller, Perlman, & Brehm, 2007).

Competence

People who are *competent* have knowledge, ability, or proficiency. All other things being equal, we are more attracted to people who are talented or competent. However, there's an interesting twist to this. In a revealing classic study, college students listened to audiotapes of candidates for a "College Quiz Bowl." Two of the candidates seemed to be highly intelligent. The other two were of average ability. In addition, one "intelligent" candidate and one "average" candidate could be heard to clumsily spill coffee on themselves. Later, students rated the intelligent candidate who blundered as *most* attractive. In contrast, the average person who blundered was rated *least* attractive (Aronson, 1969). Thus, the superior but clumsy person was more attractive than the person who was only superior. Apparently, we like people who are competent but imperfect—which makes them more "human."

Similarity

Take a moment to make a list of your closest friends. What do they have in common (other than the joy of knowing you)? It is likely that their ages are similar to yours and you are of the same sex and ethnicity. There will be exceptions, of course. But similarity on these three dimensions is the general rule for friendships.

Similarity refers to how alike you are to another person in background, age, interests, attitudes, beliefs, and so forth. In everything from casual acquaintance to marriage, similar people are attracted to each other (Figueredo, Sefcek, & Jones, 2006; Miller, Perlman, & Brehm, 2007). And why not? It's reinforcing to see our beliefs and attitudes shared by others. It shows we are "right" and reveals that they are clever people as well (Alicke, Yurak, & Vredenburg, 1996)!

So similarity also influences mate selection? Yes, in choosing a mate we tend to marry someone who is like us in almost every way, a pattern called *homogamy* (huh-MOG-ah-me) (Blackwell & Lichter, 2004). Studies show that married couples are highly similar in age, education, ethnicity, and religion. To a lesser degree, they are also similar in attitudes and opinions, mental abilities, status, height, weight, and eye color. In case you're wondering, homogamy also applies to unmarried couples who are living together (Blackwell & Lichter, 2004). Homogamy is probably a good thing. The risk of divorce is highest among couples with sizable differences in age and education (Tzeng, 1992).

Self-Disclosure

How do people who are not yet friends learn if they are similar? To get acquainted you must be willing to talk about more than just the weather, sports, or nuclear physics. At some point you must begin to share private thoughts and feelings and reveal yourself to others. This process, which is called **self-disclosure,** is essential for developing close relationships. In general, as friends talk, they gradually deepen the level of liking, trust, and self-disclosure (Levesque, Steciuk, & Ledley, 2002).

We more often reveal ourselves to persons we like than to those we find unattractive. Disclosure also requires a degree of trust. Many people play it safe, or "close to the vest," with people they do not know well. Indeed, self-disclosure is governed by unspoken rules about what's acceptable. Moderate self-disclosure leads to *reciprocity* (a return in kind). In contrast, *overdisclosure* exceeds what is appropriate for a relationship or social situation, giving

Self-disclosure The process of revealing private thoughts, feelings, and one's personal history to others.

rise to suspicion and reducing attraction. For example, imagine standing in line at a store and having the stranger in front of you say, "Lately I've been thinking about how I really feel about myself. I think I'm pretty well adjusted, but I occasionally have some questions about my sexual adequacy."

When self-disclosure proceeds at a moderate pace, it builds trust, intimacy, reciprocity, and positive feelings. When it is too rapid or inappropriate, we are likely to "back off" and wonder about the person's motives. It's interesting to note that on the Internet (and especially on social networking websites like MySpace) people often feel freer to express their true feelings, which can lead to genuine, face-to-face friendships (Bargh et al., 2002) but can also lead to some very dramatic overdisclosure (George, 2006).

Excessive self-disclosure is a staple of many television talk shows. Guests frequently reveal intimate details about their personal lives, including private family matters, sex and dating, physical or sexual abuse, major embarrassments, and criminal activities. Viewers probably find such intimate disclosures entertaining, rather than threatening, because they don't have to reciprocate.

LOVING AND LIKING—DATING, RATING, MATING

How does romantic attraction differ from interpersonal attraction? **Romantic love** is based on interpersonal attraction, but it also involves high levels of emotional arousal and/or sexual desire (Berscheid & Regan, 2005; Miller, Perlman, & Brehm, 2007). To get another angle on love, psychologist Zick Rubin (1973) chose to think of it as an attitude we hold toward another person. This allowed him to develop "liking" and "love" scales to measure each "attitude" (see ▸▸Fig. 14.1). Next, he asked dating couples to complete the scales twice, once with their lover in mind and once for a close friend of the same sex.

What were the results? Love for partners and friends differed more than liking did (▪ Table 14.1). (**Liking** is affection without passion or deep commitment.) Basically, dating couples like *and* love their partners, but mostly they just like their friends. Women, however, were a little more "loving" of their friends than men were. Does this reflect real differences in the strength of male friendships and female friendships? Maybe not, because it is more acceptable in our culture for women to express love for one another than it is for men. Nevertheless, another study confirmed that dating couples feel a mixture of love and friendship for their partners. In fact, 44 percent of a group of dating persons named their romantic partner as their closest friend (Hendrick & Hendrick, 1993).

Love and friendship differ in another interesting way. Romantic love, in contrast to simple liking, usually involves deep *mutual absorption*. In other words, lovers (unlike friends) attend almost exclusively to one another. It's not surprising, then, that couples who score high on Rubin's love scale spend more time gazing into each other's eyes than do couples who score low on the scale. And what do lovers see when they gaze into each other's eyes? Generally, romantic partners tend to idealize each other, which helps keep relationships going, despite the fact that nobody's perfect (Murray, Holmes, & Griffin, 1996, 2003).

Love Scale

1. If _____ were feeling bad, my first duty would be to cheer him (her) up.
2. I feel that I can confide in _____ about virtually everything.
3. I find it easy to ignore _____'s faults.

Liking Scale

1. When I am with _____ , we are almost always in the same mood.
2. I think that _____ is unusually well adjusted.
3. I would highly recommend _____ for a responsible job.

▸▸**FIGURE 14.1** Sample love-scale and liking-scale items. Each scale consists of 13 items similar to those shown. Scores on these scales correspond to other indications of love and liking. (Reprinted by permission of Zick Rubin.)

▪ Table 14.1	Average Love and Liking Scores for Date and Same-Sex Close Friend				
Attitude toward Dating Partner			**Attitude toward Close Friend**		
	Love score	*Liking score*		*Love score*	*Liking score*
Women	89.5	88.5	**Women**	65.3	80.5
Men	89.4	84.7	**Men**	55.0	79.1

Source: Rubin, 1970.

Romantic love Love that is associated with high levels of interpersonal attraction, heightened arousal, mutual absorption, and sexual desire.

Liking A relationship based on intimacy, but lacking passion and commitment.

Evolution and Mate Selection

Evolutionary psychology is the study of the evolutionary origins of human behavior patterns. Many psychologists believe that evolution left an imprint on men and women that influences everything from sexual attraction and infidelity to jealousy and divorce. According to David Buss, the key to understanding human mating patterns is to understand how evolved behavior patterns guide our choices (Buss, 2004).

In a study of 37 cultures on 6 continents, Buss found the following patterns: Compared with women, men are more interested in casual sex; they prefer younger, more physically attractive partners; and they get more jealous over real or imagined sexual infidelities than they do over a loss of emotional commitment. Compared with men, women prefer slightly older partners who appear to be industrious, higher in status, or economically successful; women are more upset by a partner who becomes emotionally involved with someone else, rather than one who is sexually unfaithful (Townsend & Wasserman, 1998) (►Fig. 14.2).

Why do such differences exist? Buss and others believe that mating preferences evolved in response to the differing reproductive challenges faced by men and women. As a rule, women must invest more time and energy in reproduction and nurturing the young than men do. Consequently, women evolved an interest in whether their partners will stay with them and whether their mates have the resources to provide for their children (Buss, 2004; Regan et al., 2000).

In contrast, the reproductive success of men depends on their mates' fertility. Men, therefore, tend to look for health, youth, and beauty in a prospective mate, as signs of suitability for reproduction (Regan et al., 2000). This preference, perhaps, is why some older men abandon their first wives in favor of young, beautiful "trophy wives." Evolutionary theory further explains that the male emphasis on their mates' sexual fidelity is based on concerns about the paternity of offspring. From a biological perspective, men do not benefit from investing resources in children they did not sire (Buller, 2005).

Although some evidence supports the evolutionary view of mating, it is important to remember that evolved mating tendencies are subtle at best and easily overruled by other factors. Some mating patterns may simply reflect the fact that men still tend to control the power and resources in most societies (Feingold, 1992).

Whatever the outcome of the debate about evolution and mate selection, it is important to remember this: Potential mates are rated as most attractive if they are kind, secure, intelligent, and supportive (Klohnen & Luo, 2003; Regan et al., 2000). These qualities are love's greatest allies.

Needs for affiliation and interpersonal attraction inevitably bring people together in groups. In the next section we will explore several interesting aspects of group membership. But first, here's a chance to review what you have learned.

According to evolutionary psychologists, women tend to be concerned with whether mates will devote time and resources to a relationship. Men place more emphasis on physical attractiveness and sexual fidelity.

Anthony B. Woods/Stock, Boston

►**FIGURE 14.2** What do people look for when considering potential dating partners? Here are the results of a study in which personal ads were placed in newspapers. As you can see, men were more influenced by looks, and women by success (Goode, 1996).

Evolutionary psychology Study of the evolutionary origins of human behavior patterns.

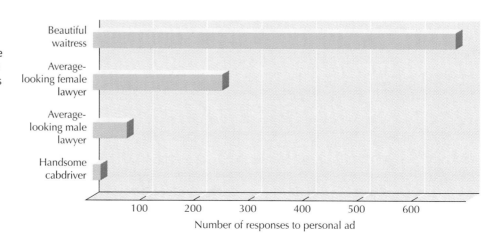

Number of responses to personal ad

Study Break **Affiliation, Friendship, and Love**

Reflect

How has social comparison affected your behavior? Has it influenced who you associate with?

Think of three close friends. Which of the attraction factors described earlier apply to your friendships?

To what extent do Rubin's findings about love and liking match your own experiences?

Learning Check

1. Women threatened with electric shock in an experiment generally chose to wait alone or with other women not taking part in the experiment. T or F?

2. Interpersonal attraction is increased by all but one of the following. (Which does not fit?)

   a. physical proximity   b. competence
   c. similarity   d. overdisclosure

3. High levels of self-disclosure are reciprocated in most social encounters. T or F?

4. Women rate their friends higher on the Love Scale than do men. T or F?

5. The most striking finding about marriage patterns is that most people choose mates whose personalities are quite unlike their own. T or F?

6. Compared with men, women tend to be more upset by sexual infidelity than by a loss of emotional commitment on the part of their mates. T or F?

Critical Thinking

7. How has the Internet altered the effects of proximity on interpersonal attraction?

Answers

1. F 2. d 3. F 4. T 5. F 6. F 7. As mentioned earlier, it is now possible to interact with another person through the Internet. This makes actual physical proximity less crucial in interpersonal attraction, because frequent contact is possible even at great distances. Internet romances are a good example of this possibility.

HUMANS IN A SOCIAL CONTEXT— PEOPLE, PEOPLE, EVERYWHERE

>SURVEY QUESTION< *How does group membership affect our behavior?*

We all belong to many overlapping social groups, and in each, we occupy a *position* in the *structure* of the group. **Social roles** are patterns of behavior expected of persons in various social positions (Breckler, Olson, & Wiggins, 2006). For instance, playing the role of mother, boss, or student involves different sets of behaviors and expectations. Some roles are *ascribed* (they are assigned to a person or are not under personal control): male or female, son, adolescent, inmate. *Achieved roles* are voluntarily attained by special effort: spouse, teacher, scientist, bandleader.

What effect does role-playing have on behavior? Roles streamline daily interactions by allowing us to anticipate what others will do. When a person is acting as a doctor, mother, clerk, or police officer, we expect certain behaviors. However, roles have a negative side too. Many people experience **role conflicts**, in which two or more roles make conflicting demands on them. Consider, for example, a teacher who must flunk a close friend's daughter; a mother who has a full-time job; and a soccer coach whose son is on the team, but isn't a very good athlete. Likewise, the clashing demands of work, family, and school create role conflicts for many students (Hammer, Grigsby, & Woods, 1998; Senécal, Julien, & Guay, 2003).

Bonnie Kamin/PhotoEdit

Roles have a powerful impact on social behavior. What kinds of behavior do you expect from your teachers? What behaviors do they expect from you? What happens if either of you fails to match the other's expectations?

Group Structure, Cohesion, and Norms

Are there other dimensions of group membership? Two important dimensions of any group are its structure and cohesiveness. **Group structure** consists of the network of roles, communication pathways, and power in a group. Organized groups such as an army or an athletic team have a high degree of structure. Informal friendship groups may or may not be very structured.

Social role Expected behavior patterns associated with particular social positions (such as daughter, worker, student).

Role conflict Trying to occupy two or more roles that make conflicting demands on behavior.

Group structure The network of roles, communication pathways, and power in a group.

Group cohesiveness refers to the degree of attraction among group members or the strength of their desire to remain in the group. Members of cohesive groups literally stick together: They tend to stand or sit close together, they pay more attention to one another, and they show more signs of mutual affection. Also, their behavior tends to be closely coordinated (Chansler, Swamidass, & Cammann, 2003). Cohesiveness is the basis for much of the power that groups exert over us. Therapy groups, businesses, sports teams, and the like seek to increase cohesion because it helps people work together better (Craig & Kelly, 1999).

In-groups

Cohesiveness is particularly strong for **in-groups** (groups with which a person mainly identifies). Very likely, your own in-groups are defined by a combination of prominent social dimensions, such as nationality, ethnicity, age, education, religion, income, political values, gender, sexual orientation, and so forth. In-group membership helps define who we are socially. Predictably, we tend to attribute positive characteristics to our in-groups and negative qualities to **out-groups** (groups with which we do not identify). We also tend to exaggerate differences between members of out-groups and our own groups. This sort of "us-and-them" thinking seems to be a basic fact of social life. It also sets the stage for conflict between groups and for racial and ethnic prejudice—topics we will explore later in this chapter.

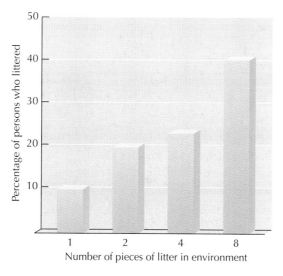

▶▶**FIGURE 14.3** Results of an experiment on norms concerning littering. The prior existence of litter in a public setting implies that littering is acceptable. This encourages others to "trash" the area. (From Cialdini, Reno, & Kallgren, 1990.)

Status

In addition to defining roles, a person's social position within groups determines his or her **status,** or level of social power and importance. Higher status bestows special privileges and respect. For example, in a classic experiment, researchers left dimes in phone booths. When people entered the booths, a researcher approached and said, "Excuse me, I think I left a dime here a few minutes ago. Did you find it?" Seventy-seven percent of the people returned the money when the researcher was well dressed. Only 38 percent returned it to poorly dressed researchers (Bickman, 1974). You don't have to be in a phone booth for this to work. In most situations, we are more likely to comply with a request made by a high-status (well-dressed) person (Guéguen, 2002). Perhaps the better treatment given "higher-status" persons explains some of our society's preoccupation with expensive clothes, cars, and other status symbols.

Norms

We are also greatly affected by group norms. A **norm** is a widely accepted (but often unspoken) standard for appropriate behavior. If you have the slightest doubt about the power of norms, try this test: Walk into a crowded supermarket, get in a checkout line, and begin singing loudly in your fullest voice. Are you the 1 person in 100 who could actually carry out these instructions?

The impact of norms is shown by an interesting study of littering. The question was, Does the amount of trash in an area affect littering? To find out, people were given flyers as they walked into a public parking garage. As you can see in ▶▶Figure 14.3, the more litter there was on the floor, the more likely people were to add to it by dropping their flyer. Apparently, seeing that others had already littered implied a lax norm about whether littering is acceptable. The moral? The cleaner a public area is kept, the less likely people are to "trash" it (Cialdini, Reno, & Kallgren, 1990).

Group cohesiveness The degree of attraction among group members or their commitment to remaining in the group.

In-group A group with which a person identifies.

Out-group A group with which a person does not identify.

Status An individual's position in a social structure, especially with respect to power, privilege, or importance.

Norm A widely accepted standard of conduct for appropriate behavior.

Making Attributions

Every day we must guess how people will act, often from small shreds of evidence. We do this through a process called **attribution.** As we observe others, we make inferences about them. Why did Vonda insult Sutchai? Why did Nick change his college major? Why does Kirti talk so fast when she's around men? In answering such questions we *attribute* people's behavior to various causes. Whether we are right or wrong about the causes of behavior, our conclusions affect how we act. To learn how we fill in the "person behind the mask," let's explore the making of attributions.

Two people enter a restaurant and order different meals. Nell tastes her food, then salts it. Bert salts his food before he tastes it. How would you explain their behavior? In Nell's case, you might assume that the *food* needed salt. If so, you have attributed her actions to an *external cause* (one that lies outside a person). With Bert, you might be more inclined to conclude that he must really *like* salt. If so, the cause of his behavior is internal. *Internal causes,* such as needs, personality traits, and Bert's taste for salt, lie within the person.

In 2005, in the aftermath of Hurricane Katrina, many celebrities, including actor Sean Penn, went to New Orleans to help hurricane victims. As you watched these events, did you attribute the celebrities' actions to selfless concern for the suffering in New Orleans? Or were the celebrities motivated by a selfish desire to hog the limelight? Such attributions greatly affect how we perceive and respond to the social behavior of others.

What effects do such interpretations have? It is difficult to fully understand social behavior without considering the attributions that we make. For instance, let's say that at the last five parties you've been to, you've seen a woman named Macy. Based on this, you assume that Macy likes to socialize. You see Macy at yet another gathering and mention that she seems to like parties. She says, "Actually, I hate these parties, but I get invited to play my tuba at them. My music teacher says I need to practice in front of an audience, so I keep attending these dumb events. Want to hear a Sousa march?"

We seldom know the real reasons for others' actions. That is why we tend to infer causes from *circumstances.* However, in doing so, we often make mistakes like the one with Macy. The most common error is to attribute the actions of others to internal causes (Follett & Hess, 2002; Jones & Nisbett, 1971). This mistake is called the **fundamental attribution error.** We tend to think the actions of others have internal causes even if they are actually caused by external forces or circumstances.

Where our own behavior is concerned, we are more likely to think that external causes explain our actions. In other words, there is an **actor-observer bias** in how we explain behavior. As *observers,* we attribute the behavior of others to their wants, motives, and personality traits (this is the fundamental attribution error). As *actors,* we tend to find external explanations for our own behavior (Gordon & Kaplar, 2002). No doubt you chose your major in school because of what it has to offer. Other students choose *their* majors because of the kind of people they are. Other people who don't leave tips in restaurants are cheapskates. If you don't leave a tip it's because the service was bad. And, of course, other people are always late because they are irresponsible. You are late because you were held up by events beyond your control.

Ye Old Double Standard

Attributions reveal an interesting double standard regarding the abilities of men and women. In a classic study by Kay Deaux and Tim Emswiller (1974), men and women overheard a male or female perform extremely well on a perception task. Each person was then asked to rate whether the test taker's success was due to ability, luck, or some combination of the two. Both men and women attributed male success mainly to skill and women's performances mainly to luck! This was true even though male and female performances were identical.

As early as kindergarten, boys tend to take credit for successes. Girls tend to discount their own performances ("put themselves down") (Burgner & Hewstone, 1993). In general,

Attribution The process of making inferences about the causes of one's own behavior, and that of others.

Fundamental attribution error The tendency to attribute the behavior of others to internal causes (personality, likes, and so forth).

Actor-observer bias The tendency to attribute the behavior of others to internal causes while attributing one's own behavior to external causes (situations and circumstances).

there is a strong tendency to assume, "He's skilled, she's lucky," when judging men and women (Swim & Sanna, 1996). Throughout life, such attributions no doubt haunt many talented and successful women.

SOCIAL INFLUENCE—FOLLOW THE LEADER

>SURVEY QUESTION< *What have social psychologists learned about conformity, compliance, obedience, and self-assertion?*

No topic lies nearer the heart of social psychology than **social influence** (changes in behavior induced by the actions of others). When people interact, they almost always affect one another's behavior (Brehm, & Kassin, & Fein, 2005; Crano, 2000). For example, in a sidewalk experiment, various numbers of people stood on a busy New York City street. On cue they all looked at a sixth-floor window across the street. A camera recorded how many passersby also stopped to stare. The larger the influencing group, the more people were swayed to join in staring at the window (Milgram, Bickman, & Berkowitz, 1969).

Are there different kinds of social influence? Social influence ranges from *mere presence* (changing behavior just because other people are nearby) to intensive indoctrination (brainwashing). Three major forms of social influence are conformity, compliance, and obedience. The gentlest of these three forms of social influence is conformity. We **conform** when we bring our behavior into agreement with the actions, norms, or values of others in the absence of any direct pressure. Compliance is a more directed form of social influence. We **comply** when we change our behavior in response to another person who has little or no authority. Obedience is an even more direct form of social influence. We **obey** when we change our behavior in direct response to the demands of an authority.

Daily behavior is probably most influenced by group pressures for conformity (bringing your behavior into agreement with the actions, norms, or values of others) (Baron, Byrne, & Branscombe, 2006). We all conform to a degree. In fact, some uniformity is a necessity. Imagine being totally unable to anticipate the actions of others. In stores, schools, and homes this would be frustrating and disturbing. On the highways it would be lethal.

Roy Morsch/Corbis

Conformity is a subtle dimension of daily life. Notice the similarities in clothing and hairstyles among these couples.

Social influence Changes in a person's behavior induced by the presence or actions of others.

Conformity Bringing one's behavior into agreement or harmony with norms or with the behavior of others in a group in the absence of any direct pressure.

Compliance Bending to the requests of a person who has little or no authority or other form of social power.

Obedience Conformity to the demands of an authority.

Conformity

When John first started working at the Fleegle Flange Factory, he found it easy to process 300 flanges an hour. Others around him averaged only 200. John's coworkers told him to slow down and take it easy. "I get bored," he said and continued to do 300 flanges an hour. At first John was welcomed, but now conversations broke up when he approached. Other workers laughed at him or ignored him when he spoke. Although he never made a conscious decision to conform, in another week John's output had slowed to 200 flanges an hour. Perhaps the most basic of all group norms is, as John discovered, "Thou shalt conform." Like it or not, life is filled with instances of conformity.

The Asch Experiment

How strong are group pressures for conformity? One of the first experiments on conformity was staged by Solomon Asch (1907–1996). To fully appreciate it, imagine yourself as a subject. Assume that you are seated at a table with six other students. Your task is actually quite simple. On each trial you are shown three lines. Your job is to select the line that matches a "standard" line (➡ Fig. 14.4).

Groupthink—Agreement at Any Cost

As we write this, debate rages about the Iraq war. Why, for example, were no weapons of mass destruction found in Iraq, even though their existence was the major justification for the war in the first place? Was the decision to invade Iraq made by a small group of policymakers with little tolerance for dissenting views? Already, it has been suggested that this war may have been a result of **groupthink**—an urge by decision makers to maintain each other's approval, even at the cost of critical thinking (Singer, 2005).

Groupthink has been blamed for many embarrassments, such as the *Columbia* space shuttle disaster in 2003, and the loss, in 1999, of the $165 million *Mars Climate Orbiter*. An analysis of 19 international crises found that groupthink contributed to most (Schafer & Crichlow, 1996).

The core of groupthink is misguided loyalty. Group members are hesitant to "rock the boat" or question sloppy thinking. This self-censorship leads people to believe they agree more than they actually do (Esser, 1998; Whyte, 2000).

To prevent groupthink, group leaders should take the following steps:

- Define each group member's role as a "critical evaluator."
- Avoid revealing any personal preferences in the beginning.
- State the problem factually, without bias.
- Invite a group member or outside person to play devil's advocate.
- Make it clear that group members will be held accountable for decisions.
- Encourage open inquiry and a search for alternate solutions (Baron, 2005; Chen et al., 1996).

In addition, it is advisable to have a "second-chance" meeting to re-evaluate important decisions. That is, each decision should be reached twice.

In fairness to our decision makers, it is worth noting that the presence of too many alternatives can lead to *deadlock,* which can delay taking necessary action (Kowert, 2002). Regardless, in an age clouded by the threat of war, global warming, and terrorism, even stronger solutions to the problem of groupthink would be welcome. Perhaps we should form a group to think about it?!

As the testing begins, each person announces an answer for the first card. When your turn comes, you agree with the others. "This isn't hard at all," you say to yourself. For several more trials your answers agree with those of the group. Then comes a shock. All six people announce that line 1 matches the standard, and you were about to say line 2 matches. Suddenly you feel alone and upset. You nervously look at the lines again. The room falls silent. Everyone seems to be staring at you. The experimenter awaits your answer. Do you yield to the group?

In this study the other "students" were all actors who gave the wrong answer on about a third of the trials to create group pressure (Asch, 1956). Real students conformed to the group on about one third of the critical trials. Of those tested, 75 percent yielded at least once. People tested alone erred in less than 1 percent of their judgments. Clearly, those who yielded to group pressures were denying what their eyes told them.

Are some people more susceptible to group pressures than others? People with high needs for structure or certainty are more likely to conform. So are people who are anxious, low in self-confidence, or concerned with the approval of others. People who live in cultures that emphasize group cooperation (such as many Asian cultures) are also more likely to conform (Bond & Smith, 1996).

In addition to personal characteristics, certain situations tend to encourage conformity—sometimes with disastrous results. The feature titled "Groupthink—Agreement at Any Cost" offers a prime example.

Group Factors in Conformity

How do groups enforce norms? In most groups, we have been rewarded with acceptance and approval for conformity and threatened with rejection or ridicule for nonconformity. These reactions are called *group sanctions.* Negative sanctions range from laughter, staring, or social disapproval to complete rejection or formal exclusion. If you've ever felt the sudden chill of disapproval by others, you will understand the power of group sanctions.

Wouldn't the effectiveness of group sanctions depend on the importance of the group? Yes. The more important group membership is to a person, the more he or she will be influenced by other group members. The risk of being rejected can be a threat to our sense of

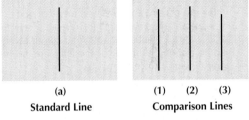

(a)
Standard Line

(1) (2) (3)
Comparison Lines

▸▸**FIGURE 14.4** Stimuli used in Solomon Asch's conformity experiments.

Groupthink A compulsion by members of decision-making groups to maintain agreement, even at the cost of critical thinking.

personal identity (Crano, 2000). That's why the Asch experiments are impressive. Because these were only temporary groups, sanctions were informal and rejection had no lasting importance. Just the same, the power of the group was evident.

What other factors, besides importance of the group, affect the degree of conformity? In the sidewalk experiment described earlier, we noted that large groups had more influence. In Asch's face-to-face groups the size of the majority also made a difference, but a surprisingly small one. In other studies, the number of people who conformed increased dramatically as the majority grew from two to three people. However, a majority of three produced about as much yielding as a majority of eight. The next time you want to talk someone into (or out of) something, take two friends along and see what a difference it makes! (Sometimes it helps if the two are large and mean looking.)

Even more important than the size of the majority is its *unanimity* (total agreement). Having at least one person in your corner can greatly reduce pressures to conform. When Asch gave subjects an ally (who also opposed the majority by giving the correct answer), conformity was lessened. In terms of numbers, a unanimous majority of three is more powerful than a majority of eight with one dissenting. Perhaps this accounts for the rich diversity of human attitudes, beliefs, opinions, and lifestyles. If you can find at least one other person who sees things as you do (no matter how weird), you can be relatively secure in your opposition to other viewpoints. Incidentally, the Internet now makes it much easier to find that other like-minded person.

 Study Break **Groups, Attribution, and Conformity**

Reflect

What are the most prominent roles you play? Which are achieved and which are ascribed? How do they affect your behavior? What conflicts do they create?

Do you commit the fundamental attribution error? Try to think of a specific example that illustrates the concept.

Identify a recent time when you conformed in some way. How did norms, group pressure, sanctions, and unanimity contribute to your tendency to conform?

Learning Check

1. Status refers to a set of expected behaviors associated with a social position. T or F?
2. The fundamental attribution error is to attribute the actions of others to internal causes. T or F?

3. The effect one person's behavior has on another is called _____.
4. Subjects in Solomon Asch's conformity study yielded on about 75 percent of the critical trials. T or F?
5. Nonconformity is punished by negative group _____.
6. Janis used the term _____ to describe a compulsion among decision-making groups to maintain an illusion of unanimity.

Critical Thinking

7. Would it be possible to be completely nonconforming (that is, to not conform to some group norm)?

Answers

1. F 2. T 3. social influence 4. F 5. sanctions 6. groupthink 7. A person who did not follow at least some norms concerning normal social behavior would very likely be perceived as extremely bizarre, disturbed, or psychotic.

COMPLIANCE—A FOOT IN THE DOOR

Pressures to "fit in" and conform are usually indirect. In contrast, the term **compliance** refers to situations in which one person bends to the requests of another person who has little or no authority. These more direct pressures to comply are quite common. For example, a stranger might ask you to borrow your cell phone so he can make a call; a saleswoman might suggest that you buy a more expensive watch than you had planned on; or a coworker might ask you for the money to buy a cappuccino.

What determines whether a person will comply with a request? Many factors could be listed, but three stand out as especially interesting.

Compliance Bending to the requests of a person who has little or no authority or other form of social power.

The Foot-in-the-Door Effect

People who sell door-to-door have long recognized that once they get a foot in the door, a sale is almost a sure thing. To state the **foot-in-the-door effect** more formally, a person who first agrees to a small request is later more likely to comply with a larger demand (Pascual & Guéguen, 2005). For instance, if someone asked you to put a large, ugly sign in your front yard to promote safe driving, you would probably refuse. If, however, you had first agreed to put a small sign in your window, you would later be much more likely to allow the big sign in your yard.

Apparently, the foot-in-the-door effect is based on observing one's own behavior. Seeing yourself agree to a small request helps convince you that you didn't mind doing what was asked. After that, you are more likely to comply with a larger request (Pascual & Guéguen, 2005).

The Door-in-the-Face Effect

Let's say that a neighbor comes to your door and asks you to feed his dogs, water his plants, and mow his yard while he is out of town for a month. This is quite a major request—one that most people would probably turn down. Feeling only slightly guilty, you tell your neighbor that you're sorry but you can't help him. Now, what if the same neighbor returns the next day and asks if you would at least pick up his mail while he is gone. Chances are very good that you would honor this request, even if you might have originally turned it down, too.

Psychologist Robert Cialdini coined the term **door-in-the-face effect** to describe the tendency for a person who has refused a major request to agree to a smaller request. In other words, after a person has turned down a major request ("slammed the door in your face"), he or she may be more willing to comply with a lesser demand. This strategy works because a person who abandons a large request appears to have given up something. In response, many people feel that they must repay her or him by giving in to the smaller request (Cialdini & Goldstein, 2004). In fact, a good way to get another person to comply with a request is to first do a small favor for the person.

The Low-Ball Technique

Anyone who has purchased an automobile will recognize a third way of inducing compliance. Automobile dealers are notorious for convincing customers to buy cars by offering "low-ball" prices that undercut the competition. The dealer first gets the customer to agree to buy at an attractively low price. Then, once the customer is committed, various techniques are used to bump the price up before the sale is concluded.

The **low-ball technique** consists of getting a person committed to act and then making the terms of acting less desirable (Guéguen, Pascual, & Dagot, 2002). Here's another example: A fellow student asks to borrow $25 for a day. This seems reasonable and you agree. However, once you have given your classmate the money, he explains that it would be easier to repay you after payday, in 2 weeks. If you agree, you've succumbed to the low-ball technique. Here's another example: Let's say you ask someone to give you a ride to school in the morning. Only after the person has agreed do you tell her that you have to be there at 6 A.M.

Calvin and Hobbes © 1985 Watterson. Distributed by Universal Press Syndicate. Reprinted with permission. All rights reserved.

Foot-in-the-door effect The tendency for a person who has first complied with a small request to be more likely later to fulfill a larger request.

Door-in-the-face effect The tendency for a person who has refused a major request to subsequently be more likely to comply with a minor request.

Low-ball technique A strategy in which commitment is gained first to reasonable or desirable terms, which are then made less reasonable or desirable.

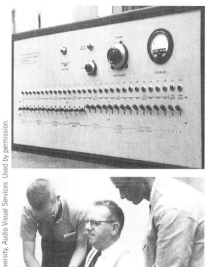

▶▶**FIGURE 14.5** Scenes from Stanley Milgram's classic study of obedience: the "shock generator," strapping a "learner" into his chair, and a "teacher" being told to administer a severe shock to the learner.

OBEDIENCE—WOULD YOU ELECTROCUTE A STRANGER?

When an authority commands obedience, the pressure to conform is greater than when someone with little or no authority requests compliance. A person who has social power in one situation may have very little in another. In those situations where a person has power, she or he is described as an *authority*. Let's investigate obedience, a special type of conformity to the demands of an authority.

The question is this: If ordered to do so, would you shock a man with a heart condition who is screaming and asking to be released? Certainly, few people would obey. Or would they? In Nazi Germany, obedient soldiers (once average citizens) helped slaughter more than 6 million people in concentration camps. Do such inhumane acts reflect deep character flaws? Are they the acts of heartless psychopaths or crazed killers? Or are they simply the result of obedience to authority? What are the limits of obedience? These are questions that puzzled social psychologist Stanley Milgram (1965) when he began a provocative series of studies on obedience.

How did Milgram study obedience? As was true of the Asch experiments, Milgram's research is best appreciated by imagining yourself as a subject. Place yourself in the following situation.

Milgram's Obedience Studies

Imagine answering a newspaper ad to take part in a "learning" experiment at Yale University. When you arrive, a coin is flipped and a second person, a pleasant-looking man in his 50s, is designated the "learner." By chance you have become the "teacher."

Your task is to read a list of word pairs. The learner's task is to memorize them. You are to punish him with an electric shock each time he makes a mistake. The learner is taken to an adjacent room and you watch as he is seated in an "electric chair" apparatus. Electrodes are attached to his wrists. You are then escorted to your position in front of a "shock generator." On this device is a row of 30 switches marked from 15 to 450 volts. Corresponding labels range from "Slight Shock" to "Extreme Intensity Shock" and finally "Danger: Severe Shock." Your instructions are to shock the learner each time he makes a mistake. You must begin with 15 volts and then move one switch (15 volts) higher for each additional mistake (▶▶Fig. 14.5).

The experiment begins, and the learner soon makes his first error. You flip a switch. More mistakes. Rapidly you reach the 75-volt level. The learner moans after each shock. At 100 volts he complains that he has a heart condition. At 150 volts he says he no longer wants to continue and demands to be released. At 300 volts he screams and says he can no longer give answers.

At some point, you begin to protest to the experimenter. "That man has a heart condition," you say; "I'm not going to kill that man." The experimenter says, "Please continue." Another shock and another scream from the learner and you say, "You mean I've got to keep going up the scale? No, sir. I'm not going to give him 450 volts!" The experimenter says, "The experiment requires that you continue." For a time the learner refuses to answer any more questions and screams with each shock (Milgram, 1965). Then he falls chillingly silent for the rest of the experiment.

It's hard to believe many people would do this. What happened? Milgram also doubted that many people would obey his orders. When he polled a group of psychiatrists before the experiment, they predicted that less than 1 percent of those tested would obey. The astounding fact is that 65 percent obeyed completely by going all the way to the 450-volt level. Virtually no one stopped short of 300 volts ("Severe Shock") (▶▶Fig. 14.6).

Was the learner injured? The time has come to reveal that the "learner" was actually an actor who turned a tape recorder on and off in the shock room. No shocks were ever admin-

Quack Like a Duck

Imagine your response to the following events. On the first day of class, your psychology professor begins to establish the basic rules of behavior for the course. Draw a line under the first instruction you think you would refuse to carry out.

1. Seats are assigned and you are told to move to a new location.
2. You are told not to talk during class.
3. Your professor tells you that you must have permission to leave early.
4. You are told to bring your textbook to class at all times.
5. Your professor tells you to use only a pencil for taking notes.
6. You are directed to take off your watch.
7. The professor tells you to keep both hands on your desktop at all times.
8. You are instructed to keep both of your feet flat on the floor.
9. You are told to stand up and clap your hands three times.
10. Your professor says, "Stick two fingers up your nose and quack like a duck."

At what point would you stop obeying such orders? In reality, you might find yourself obeying a legitimate authority long after that person's demands had become unreasonable (Aronson, Wilson, & Akert, 2005). What would happen, though, if a few students resisted orders early in the sequence? Would that help free others to disobey? For an answer, return to the discussion of Milgram's experiment for some final remarks.

---

istered, but the dilemma for the "teacher" was quite real. Subjects protested, sweated, trembled, stuttered, bit their lips, and laughed nervously. Clearly they were disturbed by what they were doing. Nevertheless, most obeyed the experimenter's orders.

Milgram's Follow-Up

Why did so many people obey? Some have suggested that the prestige of Yale University added to subjects' willingness to obey. Could it be that they assumed the professor running the experiment would not really allow anyone to be hurt? To test this possibility, the study was rerun in a shabby office building in nearby Bridgeport, Connecticut. Under these conditions fewer people obeyed (48 percent), but the reduction was minor.

Milgram was disturbed by the willingness of people to knuckle under to authority and senselessly shock someone. In later experiments, he tried to reduce obedience. He found that the distance between the teacher and the learner was important. When subjects were in the *same room* as the learner, only 40 percent obeyed fully. When they were *face-to-face* with the learner and required to force his hand down on a simulated "shock plate," only 30 percent obeyed (▸▸Fig. 14.7). Distance from the authority also had an effect. When the experimenter gave his orders over the phone, only 22 percent obeyed. You may doubt that Milgram's study of obedience applies to you. If so, take a moment to read "Quack Like a Duck."

Implications

Milgram's research raises nagging questions about our willingness to commit antisocial or inhumane acts commanded by a "legitimate authority." The excuse so often given by war criminals—"I was only following orders"—takes on new meaning in this light. Milgram suggested that when directions come from an authority, people rationalize that they are not personally responsible for their actions. In locales as diverse as Vietnam, Rwanda, Bosnia, South Africa, Nicaragua, Sri Lanka, and Laos the tragic result has been "sanctioned massacres" of chilling pro-

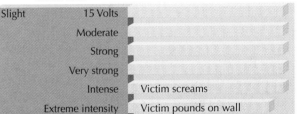

Shock level

Slight	15 Volts	
Moderate		
Strong		
Very strong		
Intense	Victim screams
Extreme intensity	Victim pounds on wall
Danger: severe shock	Victim silent
XXX	450 Volts	Victim silent

10 20 30 40 50 60 70 80 90 100
Percentage of subjects obeying
command at each shock level

▸▸**FIGURE 14.6** Results of Milgram's obedience experiment. Only a minority of subjects refused to provide shocks, even at the most extreme intensities. The first substantial drop in obedience occurred at the 300-volt level (Milgram, 1963).

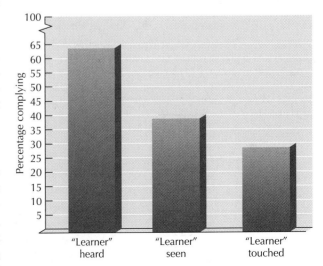

▸▸**FIGURE 14.7** Physical distance from the "learner" had a significant effect on the percentage of subjects obeying orders.

Obedience to authority is often necessary and reasonable; however, it can also be destructive.

portions. Even in everyday life, crimes of obedience are common. In order to keep their jobs, many people obey orders to do things that they know are dishonest, unethical, or harmful (Hamilton & Sanders, 1995).

Let us end on a more positive note. In one of his experiments, Milgram found that group support can greatly reduce destructive obedience. When real subjects saw two other "teachers" (both actors) resist orders and walk out of the experiment, only 10 percent continued to obey. Thus, a personal assertion of courage or moral fortitude by one or two members of a group may free others to disobey misguided or unjust authority. Let's see how assertive people handle difficult social situations.

Assertiveness Training

Have you ever done any of the following?

- Hesitated to question an error on a restaurant bill because you were afraid of making a scene?
- Backed out of asking for a raise or a change in working conditions?
- Said yes when you wanted to say no?
- Been afraid to question a grade that seemed unfair?

If you've ever had trouble with similar situations, *assertiveness training* (instruction in how to be self-assertive) may offer a solution. In assertiveness training, people learn assertive behavior through group exercises, videotapes, and staged conflicts. They also learn to practice honesty, disagreeing, questioning authority, and assertive postures and gestures. As their self-confidence improves, nonassertive clients are taken on "field trips" to shops and restaurants where they practice what they have learned.

Associated Press photographer Jeff Widener snapped this timeless photo of a lone protester literally standing up on his own behalf while he halted a column of tanks during the 1989 pro-democracy rallies in Tiananmen Square in Beijing, China. How many of us would find the courage to assert ourselves against such direct expressions of authority?

The first step in assertiveness training is to convince yourself of three basic rights: You have the right to refuse, to request, and to right a wrong. **Self-assertion** involves standing up for these rights by speaking out in your own behalf.

Is self-assertion just getting things your own way? Not at all. A basic distinction can be made between *self-assertion* and *aggressive* behavior. Self-assertion is a direct, honest expression of feelings and desires. It is not exclusively self-serving. People who are nonassertive are usually patient to a fault. Sometimes their pent-up anger explodes with unexpected fury, which can damage relationships. In contrast to assertive behavior, **aggression** involves hurting another person or achieving one's goals at the expense of another. Aggression does not take into account the feelings or rights of others. It is an attempt to get one's own way no matter what. Assertion techniques emphasize firmness, not attack (■ Table 14.2).

The basic idea in assertiveness training is that each assertive action is practiced until it can be repeated even under stress. For example, let's say it really angers you when a store clerk waits on several people who arrived after you did. To improve your assertiveness in this situation, you would begin by *rehearsing* the dialogue, posture, and gestures you would use to confront the clerk or the other customer. Working in front of a mirror can be very helpful. If possible, you should *role-play* the scene with a friend. Be sure to have your friend take the part of a really aggressive or irresponsible clerk, as well as a cooperative one. Rehearsal and role-playing should also be used when you expect a possible confrontation with someone—for example, if you are going to ask for a raise, challenge a grade, or confront a landlord.

Self-assertion A direct, honest expression of feelings and desires.

Aggression Hurting another person or achieving one's goals at the expense of another person.

■ Table 14.2	**Comparison of Assertive, Aggressive, and Nonassertive Behavior**	
	Actor	**Receiver of Behavior**
Nonassertive behavior	Self-denying, inhibited, hurt, and anxious; lets others make choices; goals not achieved	Feels sympathy, guilt, or contempt for actor; achieves goals at actor's expense
Aggressive behavior	Achieves goals at others' expense; expresses feelings, but hurts others; chooses for others or puts them down	Feels hurt, defensive, humiliated, or taken advantage of; does not meet own needs
Assertive behavior	Self-enhancing; acts in own best interests; expresses feelings; respects rights of others; goals usually achieved; self-respect maintained	Needs respected and feelings expressed; may achieve goal; self-worth maintained

Self-assertion does not supply instant poise, confidence, or self-assurance. However, it is a way of combating anxieties associated with life in an impersonal and sometimes intimidating society. If you are interested in more information, you can consult a book entitled *Your Perfect Right* by Alberti and Emmons (2001).

Study Break   Social Power, Obedience, and Compliance

Reflect

Are you surprised that so many people obeyed orders in Milgram's experiments? Do you think you would have obeyed? How actively do you question authority?

You would like to persuade people to donate to a deserving charity. How, specifically, could you use compliance techniques to get people to donate?

Pick a specific instance when you could have been more assertive. How would you handle the situation if it occurs again? Think of a specific instance when you were angry and acted aggressively. How could you have handled the situation through self-assertion, instead of aggression?

Learning Check

1. The term *compliance* refers to situations in which a person complies with commands made by a person who has authority. T or F?

2. Obedience in Milgram's experiments was related to

   a. distance between learner and teacher
   b. distance between experimenter and teacher
   c. obedience of other teachers
   d. all of these

3. By repeating his obedience experiment in a downtown office building, Milgram demonstrated that the prestige of Yale University was the main reason for subjects' willingness to obey in the original experiment. T or F?

4. The research of Thomas Moriarty and others has highlighted the problem of _____ _____, rather than obedience to authority.

5. In assertiveness training, people learn techniques for getting their way in social situations and angry interchanges. T or F?

6. Nonassertive behavior causes hurt, anxiety, and self-denial in the actor and sympathy, guilt, or contempt in the receiver. T or F?

Critical Thinking

7. Modern warfare allows killing to take place impersonally and at a distance. How does this relate to Milgram's experiments?

Answers

1. F 2. d 3. F 4. passive compliance 5. F 6. T 7. There is a big difference between killing someone in hand-to-hand combat and killing someone by lining up images on a video screen. Milgram's research suggests that it is easier for a person to follow orders to kill another human when the victim is at a distance and removed from personal contact.

ATTITUDES—DOOMSDAY FOR THE SEEKERS

>SURVEY QUESTION< *How are attitudes acquired and changed?*

Hardly a year passes without a doomsday group of one kind or another making the news. In a classic example of such groups, a woman named Mrs. Keech claimed she was receiving messages from alien beings on a planet called Clarion. The aliens told Mrs. Keech that they had detected a fault in the earth's crust that would plunge North America into the ocean, causing an unimaginable disaster. The tragedy would occur on December 21. However, Mrs. Keech and her band of followers, who called themselves the Seekers, had no fear: On December 20 they expected to be met at midnight by a flying saucer and taken to safety in outer space.

The night of December 20 arrived, and the Seekers gathered at Mrs. Keech's house. Many had given up their jobs and possessions to prepare for departure. Expectations were high and commitment was total. But as midnight passed, the world continued to exist. It was a bitter and embarrassing disappointment for the Seekers.

Did the group break up then? Our story now takes an amazing twist—one that intrigued social psychologists. Instead of breaking up, the Seekers became *more* convinced than ever before that they had been right. At about 5 A.M. Mrs. Keech announced she had received a message explaining that the Seekers had saved the world.

Before December 20, the Seekers were uninterested in persuading other people that the world was coming to an end. Now they called newspapers and radio stations to convince others of their accomplishment.

How do we explain this strange turn in behavior? An answer may lie in the concept of *cognitive dissonance,* which also helps explain many aspects of attitude change. We will return to cognitive dissonance in a moment, but first let's answer some basic questions about attitudes.

Belief + Emotion + Action

What is your attitude toward affirmative action, euthanasia, environmental groups, the death penalty, legalized abortion, junk food, psychology? The answers can have far-reaching effects on your behavior. Attitudes are intimately woven into our actions and views of the world. Our tastes, friendships, votes, preferences, and goals are all touched by attitudes.

What specifically is an attitude? An **attitude** is a mixture of belief and emotion that predisposes a person to respond to other people, objects, or groups in a positive or negative way. Attitudes summarize your *evaluation* of objects (Oskamp & Schultz, 2005). As a result, they predict or direct future actions.

"Your attitude is showing," is sometimes said. Actually, attitudes are expressed through beliefs, emotions, and actions. The *belief component* of an attitude is what you believe about a particular object or issue. The *emotional component* consists of your feelings toward the attitudinal object. The *action component* refers to your actions toward various people, objects, or institutions. Consider, for example, your attitude toward gun control. You will have beliefs about whether gun control would affect rates of crime or violence. You will respond emotionally to guns, finding them either attractive and desirable or threatening and destructive. And you will have a tendency to seek out or avoid gun ownership. The action component of your attitude will probably also include support of organizations that urge or oppose gun control. As you can see, attitudes orient us to the social world. In doing so, they prepare us to act in certain ways (Ajzen, 2005). (For another example, see ▶Fig. 14.8.)

Forming Attitudes

How do people acquire attitudes? Attitudes are acquired in several basic ways. Sometimes, attitudes come from *direct contact* (personal experience) with the object of the attitude—such as opposing pollution when a nearby factory ruins your favorite river (Ajzen, 2005). Some attitudes are simply formed through *chance conditioning* (learning that takes place by chance or coincidence) (Olson & Zanna, 1993). Let's say, for instance, that you have had three encounters in your lifetime with psychologists. If all three were negative, you might take an unduly dim view of psychology. In the same way, people often develop strong attitudes toward cities, foods, or parts of the country on the basis of one or two unusually good or bad experiences.

Attitude A learned tendency to respond to people, objects, or institutions in a positive or negative way.

Issue: Affirmative Action

Belief component
Restores justice
Provides equal opportunity

Emotional component
Optimism

Action component
Vote for affirmative action
Donate to groups that support
affirmative action

Belief component
Unfair to majority
Reverse discrimination

Emotional component
Anger

Action component
Vote against affirmative action
Donate to groups that oppose
affirmative action

▸▸**FIGURE 14.8** Elements of positive and negative attitudes toward affirmative action.

Attitudes are also learned through *interaction with others;* that is, through discussion with people holding a particular attitude. For instance, if three of your friends are volunteers at a local recycling center, and you talk with them about their beliefs, you may come to favor recycling, too. More generally, there is little doubt that many of our attitudes are influenced by *group membership.* In most groups, pressures to conform shape our attitudes, just as they do our behavior. *Child rearing* (the effects of parental values, beliefs, and practices) also affects attitudes. For example, if both parents belong to the same political party, chances are 2 out of 3 that their children will belong to that party as adults.

Finally, there can be no doubt that attitudes are influenced by the *mass media* (all media, such as magazines and television, that reach large audiences). Every day we are coaxed, persuaded, and skillfully manipulated by messages in the mass media. Ninety-nine percent of North American homes have a television set, which is on an average of more than 7 hours a day (Steuer & Hustedt, 2002). The information thus channeled into homes has a powerful impact. For instance, frequent viewers mistrust others and overestimate their own chances of being harmed. This suggests that a steady diet of TV violence leads some people to develop a *mean worldview,* in which they regard the world as a dangerous and threatening place (Eschholz, Chiricos, & Gertz, 2003).

Attitudes and Behavior

Why are some attitudes acted on, while others are not? To answer this question, let's consider an example. Assume that a woman named Lorraine knows that automobiles add to air pollution, and she hates smog. Why would Lorraine continue to drive to work every day? Probably it is because the *immediate consequences* of our actions weigh heavily on the choices we make. No matter what Lorraine's attitude may be, it is difficult for her to resist the immediate convenience of driving. Our expectations of how *others will evaluate* our actions are also important. Lorraine may resist taking public transit to work for fear that her coworkers will be critical of her environmental stand. Finally, we must not overlook the effects of long-standing *habits* (Oskamp & Schultz, 2005). Let's say that after years of driving to work Lorraine finally vows to shift to public transit. Two months later it would not be unusual for her behavior to show the effects of habit rather than her good intentions.

In short, there are often large differences between attitudes and behavior—particularly between privately held attitudes and public behavior. However, barriers to action typically fall when a person holds an attitude with *conviction.* If you have *conviction* about an issue it evokes strong feelings, you think about it and discuss it often, and you are knowledgeable about it. Attitudes held with passionate conviction often lead to major changes in personal behavior (Oskamp & Schultz, 2005).

Do you exercise regularly? Like students in the Bennington study, your intentions to exercise are probably influenced by the exercise habits of your reference groups (Terry & Hogg, 1996).

Persuasion. Would you be likely to be swayed by this group's message? Successful persuasion is related to characteristics of the communicator, the message, and the audience.

Reference group Any group that an individual uses as a standard for social comparison.

Persuasion A deliberate attempt to change attitudes or beliefs with information and arguments.

ATTITUDE CHANGE—WHY THE "SEEKERS" WENT PUBLIC

>SURVEY QUESTION< *Under what conditions is persuasion most effective?*

Although attitudes are fairly stable, they do change. Some attitude change can be understood in terms of **reference groups** (any group an individual uses as a standard for social comparison). It is not necessary to have face-to-face contact with other people for them to be a reference group. It depends instead on whom you identify with or whose attitudes and values you care about (Ajzen, 2005).

In the 1930s Theodore Newcomb studied real-life attitude change among students at Bennington College (Alwin, Cohen, & Newcomb, 1991). Most students came from conservative homes, but Bennington was a very liberal school. Newcomb found that most students shifted significantly toward more liberal attitudes during their 4 years at Bennington. Those who didn't change kept their parents and hometown friends as primary reference groups. This is typified by a student who said, "I decided I'd rather stick to my father's ideas." Those who did change identified primarily with the campus community. Notice that all students could count the college and their families as *membership* groups. However, one group or the other tended to become their point of reference.

Persuasion

What about advertising and other direct attempts to change attitudes? Are they effective? **Persuasion** is any deliberate attempt to change attitudes or beliefs through information and arguments (Brock & Green, 2005). Businesses, politicians, and others who seek to persuade us obviously believe that attitudes can be changed. Billions of dollars are spent yearly on television advertising in the United States and Canada alone. Persuasion can range from the daily blitz of media commercials to personal discussion among friends. In most cases, the success or failure of persuasion can be understood if we consider the *communicator,* the *message,* and the *audience.*

At a community meeting, let's say you have a chance to promote an issue important to you (for or against building a nuclear power plant nearby, for instance). Whom should you choose to make the presentation, and how should that person present it? Research suggests that attitude change is encouraged when the following conditions are met.

1. The communicator is likable, expressive, trustworthy, an expert on the topic, and similar to the audience in some respect.
2. The message appeals to emotions, particularly to fear or anxiety.
3. The message also provides a clear course of action that will, if followed, reduce fear or produce personally desirable results.
4. The message states clear-cut conclusions.
5. The message is backed up by facts and statistics.
6. Both sides of the argument are presented in the case of a well-informed audience.
7. Only one side of the argument is presented in the case of a poorly informed audience.
8. The persuader appears to have nothing to gain if the audience accepts the message.
9. The message is repeated as frequently as possible (Aronson, 2004; Oskamp & Schultz, 2005).

You should have little trouble seeing how these principles are applied to sell everything from underarm deodorants to presidents.

Cognitive Dissonance Theory

Cognitions are thoughts. Dissonance means clashing. The influential theory of **cognitive dissonance** states that contradicting or clashing thoughts cause discomfort. That is, we have a need for *consistency* in our thoughts, perceptions, and images of ourselves (Cooper, Mirabile, & Scher, 2005; Festinger, 1957).

What happens if people act in ways that are inconsistent with their attitudes or self-images? Typically, the contradiction makes them uncomfortable. Such discomfort can motivate people to make their thoughts or attitudes agree with their actions (Oskamp & Schultz, 2005). For example, smokers are told on every pack that cigarettes endanger their lives. They light up and smoke anyway. How do they resolve the tension between this information and their actions? They could quit smoking, but it may be easier to convince themselves that smoking is not really so dangerous. To do this, many smokers seek examples of heavy smokers who have lived long lives; they spend their time with other smokers; and they avoid information about the link between smoking and cancer. According to cognitive dissonance theory, we also tend to reject new information that contradicts ideas we already hold. We're all guilty of this "don't bother me with the facts, my mind is made up" strategy at times.

Now recall Mrs. Keech and her doomsday group. Why did their belief in Mrs. Keech's messages *increase* after the world failed to end? Why did the group suddenly become interested in convincing others that they were right? Cognitive dissonance theory explains that after publicly committing themselves to their beliefs, they had a strong need to maintain consistency. In effect, convincing others was a way of adding proof that they were correct (see ■ Table 14.3).

Acting contrary to one's attitudes doesn't always bring about change. How does cognitive dissonance explain that? The amount of justification for acting contrary to your attitudes and beliefs affects how much dissonance you feel. (*Justification* is the degree to which a person's actions are explained by rewards or other circumstances.) In a classic study, college students did an extremely boring task (turning wooden pegs on a board), for a *long* time.

■ Table 14.3   Strategies for Reducing Cognitive Dissonance

LeShawn, who is a college student, has always thought of himself as an environmental activist. Recently, LeShawn "inherited" a car from his parents, who were replacing the family "barge." In the past, LeShawn biked or used public transportation to get around. His parents' old car is an antiquated gas-guzzler, but he has begun to drive it every day. How might LeShawn reduce the cognitive dissonance created by the clash between his environmentalism and his use of an inefficient automobile?

Strategy	Example
Change your attitude	"Cars are not really a major environmental problem."
Add consonant thoughts	"This is an old car, so keeping it on the road makes good use of the resources consumed when it was manufactured."
Change the importance of the dissonant thoughts	"It's more important for me to support the environmental movement politically than it is to worry about how I get to school and work."
Reduce the amount of perceived choice	"My schedule has become too hectic, it's not practical to bike or take the bus anymore."
Change your behavior	"I'm only going to use the car when it's impossible to bike or take the bus."

Source: After Franzoi, 2000.

Cognitive dissonance An uncomfortable clash between self-image, thoughts, beliefs, attitudes, or perceptions and one's behavior.

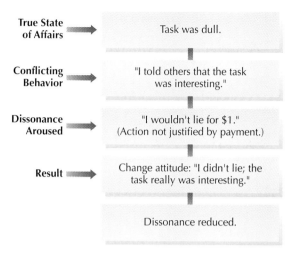

True State of Affairs →	Task was dull.
Conflicting Behavior →	"I told others that the task was interesting."
Dissonance Aroused →	"I wouldn't lie for $1." (Action not justified by payment.)
Result →	Change attitude: "I didn't lie; the task really was interesting."
	Dissonance reduced.

▶**FIGURE 14.9** Summary of the Festinger and Carlsmith (1959) study from the viewpoint of a person experiencing cognitive dissonance.

Afterward, they were asked to help lure others into the experiment by pretending that the task was interesting and enjoyable. Students paid $20 for lying to others did not change their own negative opinion of the task: "That was *really* boring!" Those who were paid only $1 later rated the task as "pleasant" and "interesting." How can we explain these results? Apparently, students paid $20 experienced no dissonance. These students could reassure themselves that anybody would tell a little white lie for $20. Those paid $1 were faced with the conflicting thoughts: "I lied," and "I had no good reason to do it." Rather than admit to themselves that they had lied, these students changed their attitude toward what they had done (Festinger & Carlsmith, 1959) (▶Fig. 14.9).

We are especially likely to experience dissonance after we cause an event to occur that we wish hadn't taken place (Cooper & Fazio, 1984). Let's say that you agree to help a friend move to a new apartment. The big day arrives and you feel like staying in bed. Actually, you wish you had never promised to help. To reduce dissonance, you may convince yourself that the work will actually be "good exercise," "sort of fun," or that your friend really deserves the help. We often make such adjustments in attitudes to minimize cognitive dissonance.

Before we leave the topic of attitudes, let's see what psychologists have learned about brainwashing and other high-pressure attempts to change attitudes.

FORCED ATTITUDE CHANGE— BRAINWASHING AND CULTS

>SURVEY QUESTIONS< *Is brainwashing actually possible? How are people converted to cult membership?*

If you're a history enthusiast, you may associate *brainwashing* with techniques used by the Communist Chinese on prisoners during the Korean War. Through various types of "thought reform," the Chinese were able to coerce some of these prisoners to sign false confessions. More recently, the mass murder/suicide at Jonestown, the Branch Davidian tragedy at Waco, the Heaven's Gate group suicide in San Diego, and Osama bin Laden's al-Qaeda movement have heightened public interest in forced attitude change.

How does it differ from other persuasive techniques? Brainwashing, or forced attitude change, requires a captive audience. If you are offended by a television commercial, you can tune it out. Prisoners in the POW camps are completely at the mercy of their captors. Complete control over the environment allows a degree of psychological manipulation that would be impossible in a normal setting.

Brainwashing

How does captivity facilitate persuasion? Brainwashing typically begins by making the target person feel completely helpless. Physical and psychological abuse, lack of sleep, humiliation, and isolation serve to *unfreeze,* or loosen, former values and beliefs. When exhaustion, pressure, and fear become unbearable, *change* occurs as the person begins to abandon former beliefs. Prisoners who reach the breaking point may sign a false confession or cooperate to gain relief. When they do, they are suddenly rewarded with praise, privileges, food, or rest. From that point on, a mixture of hope and fear, plus pressures to conform, serves to *refreeze* (solidify) new attitudes (Taylor, 2004).

How permanent are changes caused by brainwashing? In most cases, the dramatic shift in attitudes brought about by brainwashing is temporary. Most "converted" prisoners who returned to the United States after the Korean War eventually reverted to their original beliefs. Nevertheless, brainwashing can be powerful, as shown by the success of cults in recruiting new members.

Cults

Exhorted by their leader, some 900 members of the Reverend Jim Jones's People's Temple picked up paper cups and drank purple Kool-Aid laced with the deadly poison cyanide. Psychologically, the mass suicide at Jonestown in 1978 is not so incredible as it might seem. The inhabitants of Jonestown were isolated in the jungles of Guyana, intimidated by guards and lulled with sedatives. They were also cut off from friends and relatives and totally accustomed to obeying rigid rules of conduct, which primed them for Jones's final "loyalty test." Of greater psychological interest is the question of how people reach such a state of commitment and dependency.

Why do people join groups such as the People's Temple? The People's Temple was a classic example of a *cult*. A cult is an authoritarian group in which the leader's personality is more important than the beliefs she or he preaches. Cult members give their allegiance to this person, who is regarded as infallible, and they follow his or her dictates without question. Almost always, cult members are victimized by their leaders in one way or another. For example, in April 1993, David Koresh and members of his Branch Davidian group perished in a fire at their Waco, Texas, compound. Like Jim Jones had done years before in Jonestown, Koresh took nearly total control of his followers' lives. He told them what to eat, dictated sexual mores, and had errant followers paddled. Followers were persuaded to surrender money, property, and even their children and wives. Like Jones, Koresh also took mistresses and had children out of wedlock. And like other cult leaders, Jones and Koresh demanded absolute loyalty and obedience, with tragic results (Reiterman, 1993).

Psychologist and pioneering brainwashing expert Margaret Singer (1921–2003) studied and aided hundreds of former cult members. Her interviews reveal that in recruiting new members, cults use a powerful blend of guilt, manipulation, isolation, deception, fear, and escalating commitment. In this respect, cults employ high-pressure indoctrination techniques not unlike those used in brainwashing (Singer & Addis, 1992; Singer, 2003). In the United States alone, an estimated 2 to 5 million people have succumbed to the lure of cults (Robinson, Frye, & Bradley, 1997).

Greg Smith/Corbis

In the tragic fire at the Branch Davidian compound near Waco, Texas, some members paid with their lives for giving total allegiance to cult leader David Koresh.

Recruitment

Some people studied by Singer were seriously distressed when they joined a cult. Most, however, were simply undergoing a period of mild depression, indecision, or alienation from family and friends (Hunter, 1998). Cult members try to catch potential converts at a time of need—especially when a sense of belonging will be attractive to converts. For instance, many people were approached just after a romance had broken up, or when they were struggling with exams, or were trying to become independent from their families (Sirkin, 1990). At such times, people are easily persuaded that joining the group is all they need to do to be happy again (Hunter, 1998). Adolescents are especially vulnerable to recruitment into cults as they may be seeking a cause to conform to as a replacement for the parental authority they are rebelling against (Richmond, 2004).

Conversion

How is conversion achieved? Often it begins with intense displays of affection and understanding ("love bombing"). Next comes isolation from people who are not cult members, and drills, discipline, and rituals (all-night meditation or continuous chanting, for instance). These rituals wear down physical and emotional resistance, discourage critical thinking, and generate feelings of commitment (Langone, 2002).

Many cults make clever use of the foot-in-the-door technique, described earlier. At first, recruits make small commitments (to stay after a meeting, for example). Then, larger commitments are encouraged (to stay an extra day, to call in sick at work, and so forth). Making a major commitment is usually the final step. The new devotee signs over a bank account or

Bettmann/Corbis

Aftermath of the mass suicide at Jonestown. How do cult-like groups recruit new devotees?

property to the group, moves in with the group, and so forth. Making such major public commitments creates a powerful cognitive dissonance effect. Before long, it becomes virtually impossible for converts to admit they have made a mistake.

Once in the group, members are cut off from family and friends (former reference groups), and the cult can control the flow and interpretation of information to them. Members are isolated from their former value systems and social structures. Conversion is complete when they come to think of themselves more as group members than as individuals. At this point obedience is nearly total (Wexler, 1995).

Implications

Behind the "throne" from which Jim Jones ruled Jonestown was a sign bearing these words: "Those who do not remember the past are condemned to repeat it." Sadly, another cult-related tragedy occurred in 2001. The terrorist attacks on the United States were carried out by followers of cult leader Osama bin Laden. At his direction, they learned hatred and contempt for everyone outside their band of true believers. If there is a lesson to be learned from such destructive cults, it is this: All true spiritual leaders have taught love and compassion. They also encourage followers to question their beliefs and to reach their own conclusions about how to live. In contrast, destructive cults show that it is dangerous to trade personal independence and critical thinking for security (Goldberg, 2001).

 Study Break **Attitudes and Persuasion**

Reflect

Describe an attitude that is important to you. What are its three components?

Which of the various sources of attitudes best explain your own attitudes?

Who belongs to your most important reference group?

Imagine that you would like to persuade voters to support an initiative to preserve a small wilderness area by converting it to a park. Using research on persuasion as a guide, what could you do to be more effective?

How would you explain cognitive dissonance theory to a person who knows nothing about it?

Learning Check

1. Attitudes have three parts: a _____ component, an _____ component, and an _____ component.
2. Which of the following is associated with attitude formation?

   a. group membership   b. mass media
   c. chance conditioning   d. child rearing
   e. all of the preceding f. a and d only

3. In presenting a persuasive message, it is best to give both sides of the argument if the audience is already well informed on the topic. T or F?

4. Much attitude change is related to a desire to avoid clashing or contradictory thoughts, an idea summarized by _____ _____ theory.
5. Brainwashing differs from other persuasive attempts in that brainwashing requires a _____ _____.
6. Which statement about brainwashing is *false*?

   a. The target person is isolated from others.
   b. Attitude changes brought about by brainwashing are usually permanent.
   c. The first step is unfreezing former values and beliefs.
   d. Cooperation with the indoctrinating agent is rewarded.

Critical Thinking

7. Students entering a college gym are asked to sign a banner promoting water conservation. Later, the students shower at the gym. What effect would you expect signing the banner to have on how long students stay in the showers?
8. Cognitive dissonance theory predicts that false confessions obtained during brainwashing are not likely to bring about lasting changes in attitudes. Why?

Answers

1. belief, emotional, action   2. e   3. T   4. cognitive dissonance theory   5. captive audience   6. b   7. Cognitive dissonance theory predicts that students who sign the banner will take shorter showers, to be consistent with their publicly expressed support of water conservation. This is exactly the result observed in a study done by social psychologist Elliot Aronson.   8. Because there is strong justification for such actions, little cognitive dissonance is created when a prisoner makes statements that contradict his or her beliefs.

PREJUDICE—ATTITUDES THAT INJURE

>SURVEY QUESTION< *What causes prejudice and intergroup conflict?*

Love and friendship bind people together. Prejudice, which is marked by suspicion, fear, or hatred, has the opposite effect. **Prejudice** is a negative emotional attitude held toward members of a specific social group. Prejudices may be reflected in the policies of police departments, schools, or government institutions (Dovidio, Glick, & Rudman, 2005). In such cases, prejudice is referred to as *racism, sexism, ageism,* or *heterosexism,* depending on the group affected. Because it is so prevalent and damaging, let's focus on racism.

Both racial prejudice and racism lead to **discrimination,** or unequal treatment of people who should have the same rights as others. Discrimination prevents people from doing things they should be able to do, such as buying a house, getting a job, or attending a high-quality school. For example, in many cities, African Americans have been the target of "racial profiling" in which they are stopped by police without reason. Sometimes, they are merely questioned, but many are cited for minor infractions, such as a cracked taillight or an illegal lane change. For many law-abiding citizens, being detained in this manner is a rude awakening (Plous, 2003). It's also one reason why many African Americans and other persons of color in America distrust police and the legal system (Dovido et al., 2002).

Becoming Prejudiced

How do prejudices develop? One major theory suggests that prejudice is a form of *scapegoating* (blaming a person or a group for the actions of others or for conditions not of their making). Scapegoating, you may recall, is a type of *displaced aggression* in which hostilities triggered by frustration are redirected at "safer" targets (Nelson, 2002). One interesting classic test of this hypothesis was conducted at a summer camp for young men. The men were given a difficult test they were sure to fail. Additionally, completing the test caused them to miss a trip to the movies, which was normally the high point of their weekly entertainment. Attitudes toward Mexicans and Japanese were measured before the test and after the men had failed the test and missed the movie. Subjects in this study, all European Americans, consistently rated members of the two ethnic groups lower after being frustrated (Miller & Bugelski, 1970). This effect was easy to observe after the September 11, 2001, terrorist attacks in the United States, when people who looked "foreign" became targets for displaced anger and hostility.

At times, the development of prejudice (like other attitudes) can be traced to direct experiences with members of the rejected group. A child who is repeatedly bullied by members of a particular ethnic group might develop a lifelong dislike for all members of the group. Yet even subtle influences, such as parents' attitudes, the depiction of people in books and on TV, and exposure to children of other races can have an impact. By the time they are 3 years old, many children show signs of race bias (Katz, 2003). Sadly, once prejudices are established, they prevent us from accepting more positive experiences that could reverse the damage (Wilder, Simon, & Faith, 1996).

Distinguished psychologist Gordon Allport (1958) concluded that there are two important sources of prejudice. *Personal prejudice* occurs when members of another ethnic group are perceived as a threat to one's own interests. For example, members of another group may be viewed as competitors for jobs. *Group prejudice* occurs when a person conforms to group norms. Let's say, for instance, that you have no personal reason for disliking outgroup members. Nevertheless, your friends, acquaintances, or coworkers expect it of you.

The Prejudiced Personality

Other research suggests that prejudice can be a general personality characteristic. Theodore Adorno and his associates (1950) carefully probed what they called the *authoritarian personality* (ah-thor-ih-TARE-ee-un). These researchers started out by studying anti-Semitism.

Prejudice A negative emotional attitude held against members of a particular group of people.

Discrimination Treating members of various social groups differently in circumstances where their rights or treatment should be identical.

In the process, they found that people who are prejudiced against one group tend to be prejudiced against *all* out-groups (Perreault & Bourhis, 1999).

What are the characteristics of the prejudice-prone personality? The **authoritarian personality** is marked by rigidity, inhibition, prejudice, and oversimplification. Authoritarians also tend to be very *ethnocentric*. **Ethnocentrism** refers to placing one's own group "at the center," usually by rejecting all other groups. Put more simply, authoritarians consider their own ethnic group superior to others. In fact, authoritarians think they are superior to everyone who is different, not just other ethnic groups (Altemeyer, 2004; Whitley, 1999).

In addition to rejecting out-groups, authoritarians are overwhelmingly concerned with power, authority, and obedience. To measure these qualities, the *F scale* was created (the *F* stands for "fascism"). This scale is made up of statements such as the ones that follow—to which authoritarians readily agree (Adorno et al., 1950).

Authoritarian Beliefs

- Obedience and respect for authority are the most important virtues children should learn.
- People can be divided into two distinct classes: the weak and the strong.
- If people would talk less and work more, everybody would be better off.
- What this country needs most, more than laws and political programs, is a few courageous, tireless, devoted leaders, in whom the people can put their faith.
- Nobody ever learns anything really important except through suffering.
- Every person should have complete faith in some supernatural power whose decisions are obeyed without question.
- Certain religious sects that refuse to salute the flag should be forced to conform to such patriotic action or else be abolished.

As you can see, authoritarians are rather close-minded (Butler, 2000). As children, authoritarians were usually severely punished. Most learned to fear authority (and to covet it) at an early age. Authoritarians are not happy people.

Even if we discount the obvious bigotry of the authoritarian personality, racial prejudice runs deep in many nations. Let's probe deeper into the roots of such prejudiced behavior.

INTERGROUP CONFLICT—THE ROOTS OF PREJUDICE

An unfortunate by-product of group membership is that it often limits contact with people in other groups. Additionally, groups themselves may come into conflict. Both events tend to foster hatred and prejudice toward the out-group. The bloody clash of opposing forces in Israel, Ireland, Iraq, Africa, and Hometown, U.S.A., are reminders that intergroup conflict is widespread. Daily, we read of jarring strife between political, religious, or ethnic groups.

Shared beliefs concerning *superiority, injustice, vulnerability,* and *distrust* are common triggers for hostility between groups. Pick almost any group in conflict with others and you will find people thinking along these lines: "We are special people who are superior to other groups, but we have been unjustly exploited, wronged, or humiliated [superiority and injustice]. Other groups are a threat to us [vulnerability]. They are dishonest and have repeatedly betrayed us [distrust]. Naturally, we are hostile toward them. They don't deserve our respect or cooperation." (Eidelson & Eidelson, 2003).

In addition to hostile beliefs about other groups, conflicts are almost always amplified by stereotyped images of out-group members (Bar-Tal & Labin, 2001).

What exactly is a stereotype? **Social stereotypes** are oversimplified images of people in various groups. There is a good chance that you have stereotyped images of some of the following: African Americans, European Americans, Hispanics, Jews, women, Christians, old people, men, Asian Americans, blue-collar workers, rednecks, politicians, business exec-

Authoritarian personality A personality pattern characterized by rigidity, inhibition, prejudice, and an excessive concern with power, authority, and obedience.

Ethnocentrism Placing one's own group or race at the center—that is, tending to reject all other groups but one's own.

Social stereotypes Oversimplified images of the traits of individuals who belong to a particular social group.

utives, teenagers, and billionaires. In general, the top three categories on which most stereotypes are based are sex, age, and race (Fiske, 1993a).

Stereotypes tend to simplify people into "us" and "them" categories. Actually, aside from the fact that they always oversimplify, stereotypes often include a mixture of *positive* or *negative* qualities (Fiske et al., 2002) (▸Fig. 14.10). ■ Table 14.4 shows stereotyped images of various national and ethnic groups and their changes over a 34-year period. Notice that many of the qualities listed are desirable. Note too, that although the overall trend was a decrease in negative stereotypes, belief in the existence of some negative traits increased.

▸▸**FIGURE 14.10** Racial stereotypes are common in sports. For example, a study confirmed that many people actually do believe that "White men can't jump." This stereotype implies that African-American basketball players are naturally superior in athletic ability. European-American players, in contrast, are falsely perceived as smarter and harder working than African Americans. Such stereotypes set up expectations that distort the perceptions of fans, coaches, and sportswriters. The resulting misperceptions, in turn, help perpetuate the stereotypes (Stone, Perry, & Darley, 1997).

Even though stereotypes sometimes include positive traits, they are often used to maintain control over other people. When a person is stereotyped, the easiest thing for her or him to do is to abide by others' expectations—even if they are demeaning. That's why no one likes to be stereotyped. Being forced into a small, distorted social "box" is limiting and insulting. Without stereotypes there would be far less hate, prejudice, exclusion, and conflict (Fiske, 1993b).

When a prejudiced person meets a pleasant or likable member of a rejected group, the out-group member tends to be perceived as "an exception to the rule," not as evidence against the stereotype. This prevents prejudiced persons from changing their stereotyped beliefs (Wilder et al., 1996). In addition, some elements of prejudice are unconscious, which makes them difficult to change (Dovido et al., 2002).

Today's racism is often disguised by **symbolic prejudice.** That is, many people realize that crude and obvious racism is socially unacceptable. However, this may not stop them from expressing prejudice in thinly veiled forms when they state their opinions about affirmative action, busing, immigration, crime, and so on. In effect, modern racists find ways to rationalize their prejudice so that it seems to be based on issues other than raw racism. For instance, an African-American candidate and a European-American candidate apply for a job. Both are only moderately qualified for the position. If the person making the hiring decision is European American, who gets the job? As you might guess, the European-

Symbolic prejudice Prejudice that is expressed in disguised fashion.

■ Table 14.4   University Students' Characterization of Ethnic Groups, 1933 and 1967

Trait	Percent Checking Trait 1933	1967	Trait	Percent Checking Trait 1933	1967	Trait	Percent Checking Trait 1933	1967
Americans			**Italians**			**Jews**		
Industrious	48	23	Artistic	53	30	Shrewd	79	30
Intelligent	47	20	Impulsive	44	28	Mercenary	49	15
Materialistic	33	67	Musical	32	9	Grasping	34	17
Progressive	27	17	Imaginative	30	7	Intelligent	29	37
Germans			**Irish**			**Blacks**		
Scientific	78	47	Pugnacious	45	13	Superstitious	84	13
Stolid	44	9	Witty	38	7	Lazy	75	26
Methodical	31	21	Honest	32	17	Ignorant	38	11
Efficient	16	46	Nationalistic	21	41	Religious	24	8

Source: M. Karlins, T. L. Coffman, and G. Walters, "On the fading of social stereotypes. Studies in three generations of college students," *Journal of Personality and Social Psychology* 13 (1969):116. Reprinted with permission of the American Psychological Association.

Ethnic pride is slowly replacing stereotypes and discrimination. For example, the African-American festival of Kwanzaa, a holiday celebrated late in December, emphasizes commitment to family, community, and African culture. However, despite affirmations of ethnic heritage, the problem of prejudice is far from solved.

American candidate is much more likely to be hired. In other words, the European-American candidate will be given "the benefit of the doubt," about his or her abilities, whereas the African-American candidate won't. People making such decisions often believe that they aren't being prejudiced, but they unconsciously discriminate against minorities (Dovidio et al., 2002).

Two experiments, both in unlikely settings and both using children, offer some additional insights into how stereotypes and intergroup tensions develop.

Experiments in Prejudice

What is it like to be discriminated against? In a unique experiment, elementary school teacher Jane Elliot sought to give her pupils direct experience with prejudice. On the first day of the experiment, Elliot announced that brown-eyed children were to sit in the back of the room and that they could not use the drinking fountain. Blue-eyed children were given extra recess time and got to leave first for lunch. At lunch, brown-eyed children were prevented from taking second helpings because they would "just waste it." Brown-eyed and blue-eyed children were kept from mingling, and the blue-eyed children were told they were "cleaner" and "smarter" (Peters, 1971). Eye color might seem like a trivial basis for creating prejudices. However, people primarily use skin color to make decisions about the race of another person (Brown, Dane, & Durham, 1998). Surely, this is just as superficial a way of judging people as eye color is, especially given recent biological evidence that it does not even make genetic sense to talk about "races" (Bonham, Warshauer-Baker, & Collins, 2005). (See "Understand That Race Is a Social Construction" later in this chapter.)

At first, Elliot made an effort to constantly criticize and belittle the brown-eyed children. To her surprise, the blue-eyed children rapidly joined in and were soon outdoing her in the viciousness of their attacks. The blue-eyed children began to feel superior, and the brown-eyed children felt just plain awful. Fights broke out. Test scores of the brown-eyed children fell.

How lasting were the effects of this experiment? The effects were short lived, because two days later the children's roles were reversed. Before long, the same destructive effects occurred again, but this time in reverse. The implications of this experiment are unmistakable. In less than one day it was possible to get children to hate each other because of eye color and *status inequalities* (differences in power, prestige, or privileges). Certainly the effects of a lifetime of real racial or ethnic prejudice are infinitely more powerful and destructive (Clark et al., 1999). (See "Is America Purple?")

Many school districts in the United States have begun requiring students to wear uniforms. Appearance (including gang colors) is one of the major reasons why kids treat each other differently. Uniforms help minimize status inequalities and in-group/out-group distinctions. In Long Beach, California, a switch to uniforms was followed by a 91 percent drop in student assaults, thefts, vandalism, and weapons and drug violations (Ritter, 1998).

Equal-Status Contact

What can be done to combat prejudice? Several lines of thought (including cognitive dissonance theory) suggest that more frequent *equal-status contact* between groups in conflict should reduce prejudice and stereotyping (Olson & Zanna, 1993; Wernet et al., 2003). Equal-status contact refers to interacting on an equal footing, without obvious differences in power or status. In various studies, mixed-race groups have been formed at work, in the laboratory, and at schools. The conclusion from such research is that personal contact with a disliked group tends to induce friendly behavior, respect, and liking. However, these benefits occur only when personal contact is cooperative and on an equal footing (Grack & Richman, 1996).

Is America Purple?

As research shows, it is easy to create prejudice. Pick any simplistic way to divide a group of people into "us" and "them" and popularize it. That's what teacher Jane Elliott did when she divided her class into the brown-eyed kids and the blue-eyed kids. In no time at all, the groups were prejudiced against each other.

But that was just an experiment. It couldn't happen in the real world, right? According to psychologists Conor Seyle and Matthew Newman (2006), we are witnessing just such a real-world example in America today. In order to graphically convey the outcome of the presidential vote in the 2000 election, *USA Today* created a state-by-state map, color coded red and blue to denote states that had voted for the Republican candidate or the Democratic candidate.

Just a few years later, "Red" and "Blue" have become a national shorthand for dividing Americans into opposing camps. The "Reds" are supposed to be Republican, conservative, middle-class, rural, religious, and live in the American heartland. The "Blues" are supposed to be Democrat, liberal, upper class, urban, nonreligious, and live on the coasts. The end result is that the complex American social world is reduced to two oversimplified stereotypes, leading to an increase in between-group prejudice (Mundy, 2004).

This oversimplification ignores the fact that, in many states, the presidential votes are very close. Thus, a state that is "Red" by 51 percent is nevertheless 49 percent "Blue." Besides, many different combinations exist. President Clinton is originally from Arkansas (a "Red" state), but identifies himself as a Southern Baptist and worships in a Methodist church. Is he "Blue"? How do you categorize someone from California (a "Blue" state) who is an economic conservative, attends church occasionally, lives in San Francisco, supports gay marriage, and yet votes Republican?

According to Seyle & Newman (2006), a better approach is to recognize that America is made up of a full spectrum of political,

social, religious, and economic views and that most Americans are "Purple " Thinking this way also highlights the fact that Americans of all political persuasions share more similarities than they do differences when compared to the citizens of other countries. This more tolerant, less polarizing, view of America is reflected in the "Purple America" map (⟩⟩ Fig 14.11) (Gastner, Shalizi, & Newman, 2005). Thinking purple just might result in a more productive national discussion about the important issues facing America today.

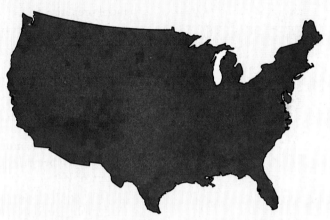

⟩⟩**FIGURE 14.11** Purple America Map. Counties within states voting more than 70 percent Republican appear in red; areas voting more than 70 percent Democratic appear in blue. Shades of purple represent intermediate percentages of voters. (Reprinted by permission of the authors, Michael Gastner, Cosma Shalizi, and Mark Newman, University of Michigan.)

Superordinate Goals

Let us now consider a revealing study done with 11-year-old boys. When the boys arrived at a summer camp, they were split into two groups and housed in separate cabins. At first the groups were kept apart to build up separate group identities and friendships. Soon each group had a flag and a name (the "Rattlers" and the "Eagles") and each had staked out its territory. At this point the two groups were placed in competition with each other. After a number of clashes, disliking between the groups bordered on hatred: The boys baited each other, started fights, and raided each other's cabins (Sherif et al., 1961).

Were they allowed to go home hating each other? As an experiment in reducing intergroup conflict, and to prevent the boys from remaining enemies, various strategies to reduce tensions were tried. Holding meetings between group leaders did nothing. When the groups were invited to eat together, the event turned into a free-for-all. Finally, emergencies that required *cooperation* among members of both groups were staged at the camp. For example, the water supply was damaged so that all the boys had to work together to repair it. Creating this and other *superordinate goals* helped restore peace between the two groups. (A **superordinate goal** exceeds or overrides other lesser goals.)

Cooperation and shared goals seem to help reduce conflict by encouraging people in opposing groups to see themselves as members of a single, larger group (Gaertner et al., 2000). Superordinate goals, in other words, have a "we're all in the same boat" effect on per-

Superordinate goal A goal that exceeds or overrides all others; a goal that renders other goals relatively less important.

ceptions of group membership (Olson & Zanna, 1993). The power of superordinate goals can be seen in the unity that prevailed in the United States (and throughout much of the rest of the world) for months after the September 11 terrorist attacks. Superordinate goals are also an important factor in helping peacekeepers constructively engage with people from other nationalities (Boniecki & Britt, 2003).

Can such goals exist on a global scale? One example might be a desire to avoid nuclear holocaust. Another that comes to mind is the need to preserve the natural environment on a global scale. Still another is the continuing threat posed by terrorism and religious extremism. Politically, such goals may be far from universal. But their superordinate quality is clearly evident.

"Jigsaw" Classrooms

Contrary to the hopes of many, integrating public schools often has little positive effect on racial prejudice. In fact, prejudice may be made worse, and the self-esteem of minority students frequently decreases (Aronson, 2004).

If integrated schools provide equal-status contact, shouldn't prejudice be reduced? Theoretically, yes. But in practice, minority group children often enter schools unprepared to compete on an equal footing. The competitive nature of schools almost guarantees that children will *not* learn to like and understand each other.

With the preceding in mind, social psychologist Elliot Aronson pioneered a way to apply superordinate goals to ordinary classrooms. According to Aronson, such goals are effective because they create **mutual interdependence.** That is, people must depend on one another to meet each person's goals. When individual needs are linked, cooperation is encouraged (Deutsch, 1993).

How has that idea been applied? Aronson has successfully created "jigsaw" classrooms that emphasize cooperation rather than competition. The term *jigsaw* refers to the pieces of a jigsaw puzzle. In a **jigsaw classroom,** each child is given a "piece" of the information needed to complete a project or prepare for a test.

In a typical session, children are divided into groups of five or six and given a topic to study for a later exam. Each child is given his or her "piece" of information and asked to learn it. For example, one child might have information on Thomas Edison's invention of the light bulb; another, facts about his invention of the long-playing phonograph record;

In a "jigsaw" classroom, children help each other prepare for tests. As they teach each other what they know, the children learn to cooperate and to respect the unique strengths of each individual.

Jonathan Nourok/PhotoEdit

and a third, information about Edison's childhood. After the children have learned their parts, they teach them to others in the group. Even the most competitive children quickly realize that they cannot do well without the aid of everyone in the group. Each child makes a unique and essential contribution, so the children learn to listen to and respect each other.

Does the jigsaw method work? Compared to children in traditional classrooms, children in jigsaw groups are less prejudiced, they like their classmates more, they have more positive attitudes toward school, their grades improve, and their self-esteem increases (Aronson, 2004; Walker & Crogan, 1998). Such results are quite encouraging. As art historian Sir Kenneth Clark said, "Racial prejudice . . . debases all human beings—those who are its victims, those who victimize, and in quite subtle ways, those who are merely accessories."

To summarize, prejudice will be reduced when (Pettigrew, 1998):

Mutual interdependence A condition in which people must depend on one another to meet each person's goals.

Jigsaw classroom A method of reducing prejudice; each student receives only part of the information needed to complete a project or prepare for a test.

- Members of different groups have equal status *within the situation* that brings them together.
- Members of all groups seek a common goal.

- Group members must cooperate to reach the goal.
- Group members spend enough time together for cross-group friendships to develop.

Sports teams are an excellent example of a situation in which all of these conditions apply. The close contact and interdependent effort required in team sports often creates lifelong friendships and breaks down the walls of prejudice.

 Study Break **Prejudice and Intergroup Conflict**

Reflect

Mentally scan over the events of the last week. How would they have changed if prejudices of all types ceased to exist?

Think of the most rigid person you know. Does he or she match the profile of the authoritarian personality?

Stereotypes exist for many social categories, even ordinary ones such as "college student" or "unmarried young adult." What stereotypes do you think you face in daily life?

The director of a youth recreation center is concerned about the amount of conflict she is seeing between boys and girls from different racial and ethnic groups. What advice can you give the director?

Learning Check

1. As a basis for prejudice, _____ is frequently related to frustration and displaced _____.

2. The authoritarian personality tends to be prejudiced against all out-groups, a quality referred to as _____.

3. The stereotypes underlying racial and ethnic prejudice tend to evolve from the superordinate goals that often separate groups. T or F?

4. The term *symbolic prejudice* refers to racism or prejudice that is expressed in disguised or hidden form. T or F?

5. Jane Elliot's classroom experiment in prejudice showed that children could be made to dislike one another by frustrating the students. T or F?

6. Research suggests that prejudice and intergroup conflict may be reduced by _____ interaction and _____ goals.

Critical Thinking

7. In court trials, defense lawyers sometimes try to identify and eliminate prospective jurors who have authoritarian personality traits. Can you guess why?

Answers

1. scapegoating, aggression 2. ethnocentrism 3. F 4. T 5. F 6. equal-status, superordinate 7. Because authoritarians tend to believe that punishment is effective, they are more likely to vote for conviction.

AGGRESSION—THE WORLD'S MOST DANGEROUS ANIMAL

>SURVEY QUESTION< *How do psychologists explain human aggression?*

"I know not with what weapons World War III will be fought, but World War IV will be fought with sticks and stones." —Albert Einstein

For a time, the City Zoo of Los Angeles, California, had on display two examples of the world's most dangerous animal—the only animal capable of destroying the Earth and all other animal species. Perhaps you have already guessed which animal it was. In the cage were two college students, representing the species *Homo sapiens!*

The human capacity for aggression is staggering. It has been estimated that 58 million humans were killed by other humans (an average of nearly one person per minute) during the 125-year period ending with World War II. War, homicide, riots, family violence, assassination, rape, assault, forcible robbery, and other violent acts offer sad testimony to the realities of human aggression.

What causes aggression? **Aggression** refers to any action carried out with the intention of harming another

Ritualized human aggression. Violent and aggressive behavior is so commonplace it may be viewed as entertainment. How "natural" is aggressive behavior?

Aggression Any action carried out with the intention of harming another person.

person. Aggression has many potential causes. Brief descriptions of some of the major possibilities follow.

Instincts

Some theorists argue we are naturally aggressive creatures, having inherited a "killer instinct" from our animal ancestors. Ethologists theorize that aggression is a biologically rooted behavior observed in all animals, including humans (Blanchard & Blanchard, 2003). (An *ethologist* is a person who studies the natural behavior patterns of animals.) Noted ethologist Konrad Lorenz (1966, 1974) also believed that humans lack certain innate patterns that inhibit aggression in animals. For example, in a dispute over territory, two wolves may growl, lunge, bare their teeth, and fiercely threaten each other. In most instances, though, neither is killed or even wounded. One wolf, recognizing the dominance of the other, will typically bare its throat in a gesture of submission. The dominant wolf could kill in an instant, but it is inhibited by the other wolf's submissive gesture. In contrast, human confrontations of equal intensity almost always end in injury or death.

The idea that humans are "naturally" aggressive has an intuitive appeal, but many psychologists question it. Many of Lorenz's "explanations" of aggression are little more than loose comparisons between human and animal behavior. Just labeling a behavior as "instinctive" does little to explain it. More important, we are left with the question of why some individuals or human groups (the Arapesh, the Senoi, the Navajo, the Eskimo, and others) show little hostility or aggression. And, thankfully, the vast majority of humans *do not* kill or harm others.

Biology

Despite problems with the instinctive view, aggression may have a biological basis. Physiological studies have shown that some brain areas are capable of triggering or ending aggressive behavior. Also, researchers have found a relationship between aggression and such physical factors as hypoglycemia (low blood sugar), allergy, and specific brain injuries and diseases. For both men and women, higher levels of the hormone testosterone are associated with more aggressive behavior (Banks & Dabbs, 1996; Harris et al., 1996). Perhaps because of their higher testosterone levels, men are 10 times more likely to commit murder than women are (Anderson & Bushman, 2002). However, none of these biological factors can be considered a direct *cause* of aggression (Moore, 2001). Instead, they probably lower the threshold for aggression, making hostile behavior more likely to occur.

The effects of alcohol and other drugs provide another indication of the role of the brain and biology in violence and aggression. A variety of studies show that alcohol is involved in large percentages of murders and violent crimes. Intoxicating drugs also seem to lower inhibitions to act aggressively—often with tragic results (Anderson & Bushman, 2002; Quigley & Leonard, 2000).

To summarize, the fact that we are biologically *capable* of aggression does not mean that aggression is inevitable or "part of human nature." Twenty eminent scientists who studied the question concluded that "Biology does not condemn humanity to war. . . . Violence is neither in our evolutionary legacy nor in our genes. The same species that invented war is capable of inventing peace" (Scott & Ginsburg, 1994; UNESCO, 1990). Humans are fully capable of learning to inhibit aggression. For example, American Quakers and Amish, who live in this country's increasingly violent culture, adopt nonviolence as a way of life (Bandura, 2001).

Frustration

Step on a dog's tail and you may get nipped. Frustrate a human and you may get insulted. The **frustration-aggression hypothesis** states that frustration tends to lead to aggression.

Does frustration always produce aggression? Although the connection is strong, a moment's thought will show that frustration does not *always* lead to aggression. Frustration,

Road rage and some freeway shootings may be a reaction to the frustration of traffic congestion. The fact that automobiles provide anonymity, or a loss of personal identity, may also encourage aggressive actions that would not otherwise occur.

Jon Love/Getty Images

Frustration-aggression hypothesis
States that frustration tends to lead to aggression.

for instance, may lead to stereotyped responding or perhaps to a state of "learned helplessness" (see Chapter 11). Also, aggression can occur in the absence of frustration. This possibility is illustrated by sports spectators who start fights, throw bottles, tear down goal posts, and so forth, after their team has *won*.

Aversive Stimuli

Frustration probably encourages aggression because it is uncomfortable. Various *aversive stimuli,* which produce discomfort or displeasure, can heighten hostility and aggression (Anderson, Anderson, & Deuser, 1996; Morgan, 2005) (▶▶Fig. 14.12). Examples include insults, high temperatures, pain, and even disgusting scenes or odors. Such stimuli probably raise overall arousal levels so that we become more sensitive to *aggression cues* (signals that are associated with aggression) (Carlson, Marcus-Newhall, & Miller, 1990). Aversive stimuli also tend to activate ideas, memories, and expressions associated with anger and aggression (Morgan, 2005).

Some cues for aggression are internal (angry thoughts, for instance). Many are external: Certain words, actions, and gestures made by others are strongly associated with aggressive responses. A raised middle finger, for instance, is an almost universal invitation to aggression in North America. Weapons serve as particularly strong cues for aggressive behavior (Morgan, 2005). The implication of this *weapons effect* seems to be that the symbols and trappings of aggression encourage aggression. A prime example is the fact that murders are almost three times more likely to occur in homes where guns are kept. Nearly 80 percent of the victims in such homes are killed by a family member or acquaintance (Kellermann et al., 1993).

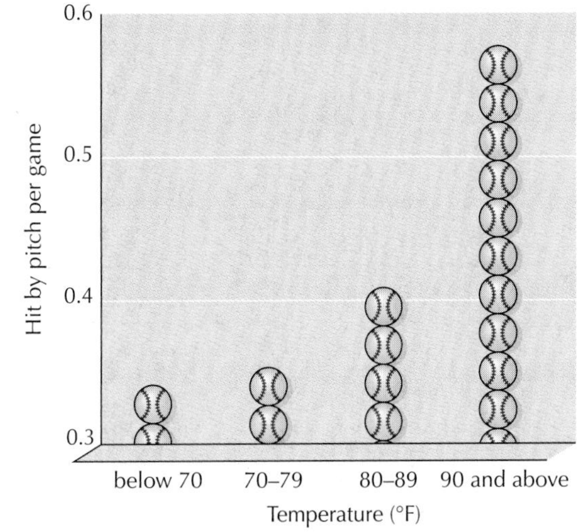

▶▶FIGURE 14.12 Personal discomfort caused by aversive (unpleasant) stimuli can make aggressive behavior more likely. For example, studies of crime rates show that the incidence of highly aggressive behavior, such as murder, rape, and assault, rises as the air temperature goes from warm to hot to sweltering (Anderson, 1989). The results you see here further confirm the heat-aggression link. The graph shows that there is a strong association between the temperatures at major league baseball games and the number of batters hit by a pitch during those games. When the temperature goes over 90 degrees, watch out for that fastball (Reifman, Larrick, & Fein, 1991)!

Social Learning

One of the most widely accepted explanations of aggression is also the simplest. Social learning theory holds that we learn to be aggressive by observing aggression in others (Bandura, 1973). **Social learning theory** combines learning principles with cognitive processes, socialization, and modeling to explain behavior. According to this view, there is no instinctive human programming for fistfighting, pipe bombing, knife wielding, gun loading, 95-mile-an-hour "bean balls," or other violent or aggressive behaviors. Hence, aggression must be learned (▶▶Fig. 14.13). Is it any wonder that people who were the victims of violence during childhood are likely to become violent themselves (Macmillan, 2001)?

Social learning theorists predict that people growing up in nonaggressive cultures will themselves be nonaggressive. Those raised in a culture with aggressive models and heroes will learn aggressive responses (Bandura, 2001). Considered in such terms, it is no wonder that America has become one of the most violent of all countries. A violent crime occurred every 23 seconds in the United States during 2005 (FBI, 2005). Approximately 40 percent of the population owns firearms. Nationally, 70 percent agree that "When a boy is growing up, it is very important for him to have a few fist-fights." Children and adults are treated to an almost nonstop parade of aggressive models, in the media as well as in actual behavior. We are, without a doubt, an aggressive culture.

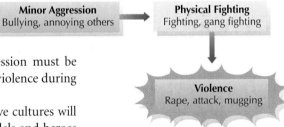

▶▶FIGURE 14.13 Violent behavior among delinquent boys doesn't appear overnight. Usually, their capacity for violence develops slowly, as they move from minor aggression to increasingly brutal acts. Overall aggression increases dramatically in early adolescence as boys gain physical strength and more access to weapons (Loeber & Hay, 1997).

Media Violence

Every day, mainstream media provide an endless stream of bad models, especially concerning violence. TV, movies, computer games, and even music lyrics all contain violence. According to the organization Adults and Children Against Violence Together, young children spend about 35 hours a week in front of TV or computer screens. By the end of elementary school children will have seen about 8,000 murders and 100,000 other violent acts depicted on TV. Eighty percent of popular video games contain violent content. Many popular toys are also linked to violent media (ACT Against Violence, 2005a). And, of course, teenagers and young people are also chronically exposed to violence in the media.

Social learning theory Combines learning principles with cognitive processes, socialization, and modeling to explain behavior.

How much does media violence affect children? As Albert Bandura showed in his studies of imitation (Chapter 6), children may learn new aggressive actions by watching violent or aggressive behavior, or they may learn that violence is "okay." Either way, they are more likely to act aggressively. Heroes on TV are as violent as the villains, and they usually receive praise for their violence. There is now little doubt that widespread exposure to media violence contributes to aggression (Anderson et al., 2003; DeGaetano, 2005). Boys and girls who watch a lot of violence on TV are much more likely to be aggressive as adults (Huesmann et al., 2003). Violent video games are at least as problematic (Bartholow, Bushman, & Sestir, 2006) and even violent song lyrics increase aggressive tendencies (Anderson, Carnagey, & Eubanks, 2003).

In addition to teaching new antisocial actions, media such as TV and video games may disinhibit dangerous impulses that viewers already have. *Disinhibition* (the removal of inhibition) results in acting out behavior that normally would be restrained. For example, many TV programs give the message that violence is acceptable behavior that leads to success and popularity. For some people, this message can lower inhibitions against acting out hostile feelings (Anderson et al., 2003).

Another effect of media violence is that it tends to lower sensitivity to violent acts (Funk, 2005). As anyone who has seen a street fight or a mugging can tell you, TV violence is sanitized and unrealistic. The real thing is gross, ugly, and gut wrenching. Even when media violence is graphic, as it is in many video games, it is experienced in the relaxed and familiar setting of the home. For at least some viewers, this combination diminishes emotional reactions to violent scenes. More than 30 years ago, when Victor Cline and his associates showed a bloody fight film to a group of boys, they found that heavy TV viewers (averaging 42 hours a week) showed much less emotion than those who watched little or no TV (Cline, Croft, & Courrier, 1972). Media, it seems, can cause a *desensitization* (reduced emotional sensitivity) to violence (Huesmann et al., 2003).

Preventing Aggression

What can be done about aggression? Social learning theory implies that "aggression begets aggression." For example, children who are physically abused at home, those who suffer severe physical punishment, and those who merely witness violence in the community are more likely to be involved in fighting, aggressive play, and antisocial behavior at school (Bartholow, Sestir, & Davis, 2005; Macmillan, 2001).

According to social learning theorists, watching a prizefight, sporting event, or violent TV program may increase aggression, rather than drain off aggressive urges. A case in point is provided by psychologist Leonard Eron, who spent 22 years following more than 600 children into adulthood. Eron (1987) observes, "Among the most influential models for children were those observed on television. One of the best predictors of how aggressive a young man would be at age 19 was the violence of the television programs he preferred when he was 8 years old" (▸▸Fig. 14.14). According to Eron, children learn aggressive strategies and actions from TV violence. Because of this, they are more prone to aggress when they face frustrating situations or cues. Others have found that viewers who experience violent media have more aggressive thoughts. As we have noted, violent thoughts often precede violent actions (Anderson, Carnagey, & Eubanks, 2003). Thus, the spiral of aggression might be broken if we did not so often portray it, reward it, and glorify it (Hughes & Hasbrouck, 1996).

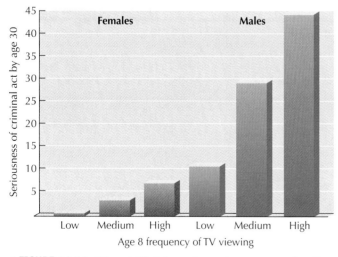

▸▸**FIGURE 14.14** Although TV violence does not cause aggression, it can encourage it. The likelihood of committing criminal acts by age 30 is related to the amount of TV watching a person did when she or he was a child (Eron, 1987). (Graph copyright 1987 by the American Psychological Association, Inc. Reprinted by permission of the author.)

Parents as TV Guides

As the preceding studies show, reducing exposure to violent media is one way to lower aggression. However, other than pulling the plug, what can parents do about media's negative effects on children? Actually, quite a lot. Parents can make a big difference if they do the following (ACT Against Violence, 2005b; Frydman, 1999).

1. Start by creating a safe, warm environment at home and school and by modeling positive ways of getting along in the world. Children typically model parents' behavior including their media viewing habits, and they are guided by parents' reactions to media.
2. Limit total media time so that TV and computer games do not dominate your child's view of the world. If necessary, set schedules for when watching TV or playing video games is allowed. Don't use media as a babysitter.
3. Closely monitor what your child does experience. Change channels or turn off the TV if you object to a program. Be prepared to offer games and activities that stimulate your child's imagination and creativity.
4. Actively seek media your child will enjoy, especially those that model positive behavior and social attitudes.
5. Explore media with your child so that you can counter what is shown. Help your child distinguish between reality and fantasy in media. Reply to distortions and stereotypes as they appear on screen.
6. Discuss the social conflicts and violent solutions shown in media. Ask your child in what ways the situations are unrealistic and why the violence shown would not work in the real world. Encourage the child to propose more mature, realistic, and positive responses to situations.
7. Show by your own disapproval that violent TV and computer game heroes are not the ones to emulate. Remember, children who identify with media characters are more likely to be influenced by media aggression.

By following these guidelines you can help children learn to enjoy television and other media without being overly influenced by programs and advertisers. One study found that elementary school children become less aggressive when they decrease the amount of time they spend watching TV and playing video games (Robinson et al., 2001).

Beyond this, the question remains, How shall we tame the world's most dangerous animal? There is no easy answer, only a challenge of pressing importance (Lench, 2004). For the immediate future, it is clear that we need more people who are willing to engage in helpful, altruistic, **prosocial behavior** (actions that are constructive, altruistic, or helpful to others). In the next section we will examine some of the forces that prevent people from helping others and how to encourage prosocial behavior.

PROSOCIAL BEHAVIOR—HELPING OTHERS

>SURVEY QUESTION< *Why are bystanders so often unwilling to help in an emergency?*

Late one night in 1964, tenants of a Queens, New York, apartment building watched and listened in horror as a young woman named Kitty Genovese was murdered on the sidewalk outside. From the safety of their rooms, no fewer than 38 people heard the agonized screams as her assailant stabbed her, was frightened off, and returned to stab her again.

Kitty Genovese's murder took more than 30 minutes, but none of her neighbors tried to help. None even called the police until after the attack had ended. Perhaps it is understandable that no one wanted to get involved. After all, it could have been a violent lovers' quarrel. Or helping might have meant risking personal injury. But what prevented these people from at least calling the police?

Isn't this an example of the alienation of city life? News reports treated this incident as evidence of a breakdown in social ties caused by the impersonality of the city. Although it is true that urban living can be dehumanizing, this does not fully explain such *bystander apathy* (the unwillingness of bystanders to offer help during emergencies is also referred to as the *bystander effect*). According to landmark work by psychologists John Darley and Bibb

Prosocial behavior Behavior toward others that is helpful, constructive, or altruistic.

Does the person lying on the ground need help? What factors determine whether a person in trouble will receive help in an emergency? Surprisingly, more potential helpers tend to lower the chances that help will be given.

Latané (1968), failure to help is related to the number of people present. Over the years many studies have shown that the *more* potential helpers present, the *less* likely people are to help (Latané, Nida, & Wilson, 1981; Miller, 2006).

Why would people be less willing to help when others are present? In Kitty Genovese's case, the answer is that everyone thought *someone else* would help. The dynamics of this effect are easily illustrated: Suppose that two motorists have stalled at roadside, one on a sparsely traveled country road and the other on a busy freeway. Who gets help first?

On the freeway, where hundreds of cars pass every minute, each driver can assume that someone else will help. Personal responsibility for helping is spread so thin that no one takes action. On the country road, one of the first few people to arrive will probably stop, since the responsibility is clearly theirs. In general, Darley and Latané assume that bystanders are not apathetic or uncaring; they are inhibited by the presence of others.

Bystander Intervention

People must pass through four decision points before giving help. First they must notice that something is happening. Next they must define the event as an emergency. Then they must take responsibility. Finally, they must select a course of action (▸▸Fig. 14.15). Laboratory experiments have shown that each step can be influenced by the presence of other people.

Noticing

What would happen if you fainted and collapsed on the sidewalk? Would someone stop to help? Would people think you were drunk? Would they even notice you? Darley and Latané suggest that if the sidewalk is crowded, few people will even see you. This has nothing to do with people blocking each other's vision. Instead, it is related to widely accepted norms against staring at others in public. People in crowds typically "keep their eyes to themselves."

Is there any way to show that this is a factor in bystander apathy? To test this idea, students were asked to fill out a questionnaire either alone or in a room full of people. While the students worked, a thick cloud of smoke was blown into the room through a vent.

Most students left alone in the room noticed the smoke immediately. Few of the people in groups noticed the smoke until it actually became difficult to see through it. Subjects working in groups politely kept their eyes on their papers and avoided looking at others (or the smoke). In contrast, those who were alone scanned the room from time to time.

▸▸**FIGURE 14.15** This decision tree summarizes the steps a person must take before making a commitment to offer help, according to Darley and Latané's model.

Defining an Emergency

The smoke-filled room also shows the influence others have on defining a situation as an emergency. When subjects in groups finally noticed the smoke, they cast sidelong glances at others in the room. Apparently, they were searching for clues to help interpret what was happening. No one wanted to overreact or act like a fool if there was no emergency. However, as subjects coolly surveyed the reactions of others, they were themselves being watched. In real emergencies, people sometimes "fake each other out" and underestimate the need for action because each person attempts to appear calm. In short, until someone acts, no one acts.

Taking Responsibility

Perhaps the most crucial step in helping is assuming responsibility. In this case, groups limit helping by causing a *diffusion of responsibility* (spreading responsibility among several people).

Is that like the unwillingness of drivers to offer help on a crowded freeway? Exactly. It is the feeling that no one is personally responsible for helping. This problem was demonstrated in an experiment in which students took part in a group discussion over an intercom system. Actually, there was only one real subject in each group; the others were tape-recorded actors. Each subject was placed in a separate room (supposedly to maintain confidentiality), and discussions of college life were begun. During the discussion, one of the "students" simulated an epileptic-like seizure and called out for help. In some cases, subjects thought they were alone with the seizure victim. Others believed they were members of three- or six-person groups.

Subjects who thought they were alone with the "victim" of this staged emergency reported it immediately or tried to help. Some subjects in the three-person groups failed to respond, and those who did were slower. In the six-person groups, over a third of the subjects took no action at all. People in this experiment were obviously faced with a conflict like that in many real emergencies: Should they be helpful and responsible, or should they mind their own business? Many were influenced toward inaction by the presence of others.

People do help in some emergencies. How are these different? It is not always clear what makes the difference. Helping behavior is complex and influenced by many variables. One naturalistic experiment staged in a New York City subway gives a hint of the kinds of things that may be important. When a "victim" (actor) "passed out" in a subway car, he received more help when carrying a cane than when carrying a liquor bottle. More important, however, was the fact that most people were willing to help in either case (Piliavin, Rodin, & Piliavin, 1969).

To better answer the question we need to consider some factors not included in Darley and Latané's account of helping.

Who Will Help Whom?

Many studies suggest that when we see a person in trouble, it tends to cause *heightened arousal* (Dovidio & Penner, 2001). This aroused, keyed-up feeling can motivate us to give aid, but only if the rewards of helping outweigh the costs. Higher costs (such as great effort, personal risk, or possible embarrassment) almost always decrease helping. In addition to general arousal, potential helpers may also feel **empathic arousal.** This means they empathize with the person in need or feel some of the person's pain, fear, or anguish. Helping is much more likely when we are able to take the perspective of others and feel sympathy for their plight (Batson & Powell, 2003).

Empathic arousal is especially likely to motivate helping when the person in need seems to be similar to ourselves (Batson & Powell, 2003). In fact, a feeling of connection to the victim may be one of the most important factors in helping. This, perhaps, is why being in a good mood also increases helping. When we are feeling successful, happy, or fortunate, we may also feel more connected to others (Dovidio & Penner, 2001). In summary, there is a

Empathic arousal Emotional arousal that occurs when you feel some of another person's pain, fear, or anguish.

strong **empathy-helping relationship:** We are most likely to help someone in need when we "feel for" that person and experience emotions such as empathy, sympathy, and compassion (Batson, 2006).

Is there anything that can be done to encourage prosocial behavior? People who see others helping are more likely to offer help themselves. Also, persons who give help in one situation tend to perceive themselves as helpful people. This change in self-image encourages them to help in other situations. One more point is that norms of fairness encourage us to help others who have helped us (Dovidio & Penner, 2001). For all these reasons, helping others not only assists them directly, it encourages others to help too.

"De-victimize" Yourself

If you should find yourself in need of help during an emergency, what can you do to avoid being a victim of bystander apathy? The work we have reviewed here suggests that you should make sure that you are noticed, that people realize there's an emergency, and that they need to take action. Being noticed can be promoted in some situations by shouting "Fire!" Bystanders who might run away from a robbery or an assault may rush to see where the fire is. At the very least, remember not to just scream. Instead, you should call out "Help," or "I need help right now." Whenever possible, define your situation for bystanders. Say, for instance, "I'm being attacked, call the police." Or, "Stop that man, he has my purse." You can also directly assign responsibility to a bystander by pointing to someone and saying, "You, call the police" or "I'm injured, I need you to call an ambulance" (Cummins, 1995).

A Look Ahead

The Psychology in Action section of this chapter returns to the topic of prejudice for some further thoughts about how to promote tolerance. Don't miss this interesting conclusion to our discussion of social psychology.

Empathy-helping relationship
Observation that we are most likely to help someone else when we feel emotions such as empathy and compassion.

Study Break   Aggression and Prosocial Behavior

Reflect

Most people have been angry enough at some time to behave aggressively. Which concepts or theories do you think best explain your own aggressive actions?

An elderly woman is at the side of the road, trying to change a flat tire. She obviously needs help. You are approaching her in your car. What must happen before you are likely to stop and help her?

Learning Check

1. The position of ethologists is that there is no biological basis for aggression. T or F?
2. Higher levels of testosterone are associated with more aggressive behavior. T or F?
3. Frustration and aversive stimuli are more likely to produce aggression when cues for aggressive behavior are present. T or F?

4. Social learning theory holds that exposure to aggressive models helps drain off aggressive energies. T or F?
5. Heavy exposure to television results in lowered emotional sensitivity to violence. T or F?
6. _____ behavior refers to actions that are constructive, altruistic, or helpful to others.
7. Seeing that a person in need is similar to ourselves tends to increase empathic arousal and the likelihood that help will be given. T or F?

Critical Thinking

8. If televised violence contributes to aggressive behavior in our society, do you think it is possible that TV could also promote prosocial behavior?

Answers

1. F 2. T 3. T 4. F 5. T 6. Prosocial 7. T 8. Yes. TV could be used to promote helping, cooperation, charity, and brotherhood in the same way that it has encouraged aggression. Numerous studies show that prosocial behavior on TV increases prosocial behavior by viewers.

Psychology in Action

Multiculturalism—Living with Diversity

>SURVEY QUESTION< *What can be done to avoid prejudice and promote social harmony?*

Today's society is more like a "tossed salad" than a cultural "melting pot." Rather than expecting everyone to be alike, psychologists believe that we must learn to respect and appreciate our differences. **Multiculturalism,** as this is called, gives equal status to different ethnic, racial, and cultural groups. It is a recognition and acceptance of human diversity (Fowers & Richardson, 1996).

Breaking the Prejudice Habit

Most people publicly support policies of equality and fairness. Yet, many still have lingering biases and negative images of African Americans, Latinos, Asian Americans, and other ethnic minorities. How can we make sense of such conflicting attitudes? Patricia Devine, a social psychologist, has shown that a decision to forsake prejudice does not immediately eliminate prejudiced thoughts and feelings. People who are not consciously prejudiced may continue to respond emotionally to members of other ethnic groups (Nosek, Greenwald, & Banaji, 2005). Quite likely this reflects lingering stereotypes and prejudices learned in childhood (Devine et al., 1991; Dion, 2003).

For many people, becoming less prejudiced begins by accepting the value of *openness to the other*, the ability to genuinely appreciate those who differ from us culturally (Fowers & Davidov, 2006). It is important to remember that being open to someone else does not mean that you have to agree with that person or turn your back on your own culture. Openness, in turn, leads to the acceptance of the values of tolerance and equality. People who value tolerance resist intolerant thoughts or feelings, which motivates them to try to alter their own biased reactions (Dovidio & Gaertner, 1999; Zuwerink et al., 1996). But doing so is not easy. Typically, it requires repeated efforts to learn to think, feel, and act differently. Nevertheless, many people have succeeded in overcoming the "prejudice habit" and becoming more open to life experiences in general (Fowers & Davidov, 2006). If you would like to be more open and tolerant, the following points may be helpful to you.

Beware of Stereotyping Stereotypes make the social world more manageable. But placing people in categories almost always causes them to appear more similar than they really are. As a result, we tend to see out-group members as very much alike, even when they are as varied as our friends and family. People who are not prejudiced work hard to actively inhibit stereotyped thoughts and to emphasize fairness and equality. A good way to tear down stereotypes is to get to know individuals from various ethnic and cultural groups (Giliovich, Keltner, & Nisbett, 2005).

Seek Individuating Information When are we most tempted to apply stereotypes? Typically it is when we only have minimal information about a person. Stereotypes help us guess what a person is like and how she or he will act. Unfortunately, these inferences are usually wrong.

One of the best antidotes for stereotypes is **individuating information** (information that helps us see a person as an individual, rather than as a member of a group) (Cameron & Trope, 2004; Click, Zion, & Nelson, 1988). Anything that keeps us from placing a person in a particular social category tends to negate stereotyped thinking. When you meet individuals from various backgrounds, focus on the *person,* not the *label* attached to her or him.

A good example of the effects of individuating information comes from a study in Canada of English-speaking students in a French language program. Students who were "immersed" (spent most of their waking hours with French Canadians) became more posi-

Multiculturalism Giving equal status, recognition, and acceptance to different ethnic and cultural groups.

Individuating information Information that helps define a person as an individual, rather than as a member of a group or social category.

tive toward them. Immersed students were more likely to say they had come to appreciate and like French Canadians; they were more willing to meet and interact with them; and they saw themselves as less different from French Canadians (Lambert, 1987). In fact, with more subtle kinds of symbolic prejudice, such contact may be the best way to reduce intergroup conflict (Dovidio & Gaertner, 1999)

Don't Fall Prey to Just-World Beliefs   Do you believe that the world is basically fair? Even if you don't, you may believe that the world is sufficiently just so that people generally get what they deserve. It may not be obvious, but such beliefs can directly increase prejudiced thinking (Hafer & Bègue, 2005).

As a result of discrimination, social conditions, and circumstances (such as recent immigration), minorities may occupy lower socioeconomic positions. **Just-world beliefs** (belief that people generally get what they deserve) can lead us to assume that minority group members wouldn't be in such positions if they weren't inferior in some way. This bit of faulty thinking amounts to blaming people who are *victims* of prejudice and discrimination for their plight. For example, assuming that a poor person is lazy may overlook the fact that discrimination in hiring has made it very difficult for him or her to find a job.

Be Aware of Self-Fulfilling Prophecies   You may recall from Chapter 1 that people tend to act in accordance with the behavior expected by others. If you hold strong stereotypes about members of various groups, a vicious cycle can occur. When you meet someone who is different from yourself, you may treat her or him in a way that is consistent with your stereotypes. If the other person is influenced by your behavior, she or he may act in ways that seem to match your stereotype. For example, a person who believes that members of another ethnic group are hostile and unfriendly will probably treat people in that group in ways that provoke hostile and unfriendly response. This creates a self-fulfilling prophecy and reinforces belief in the stereotype. (A **self-fulfilling prophecy** is an expectation that prompts people to act in ways that make the expectation come true.)

Remember, Different Does Not Mean Inferior   Some conflicts between groups cannot be avoided. What *can* be avoided is unnecessary **social competition** (rivalry among groups, each of which regards itself as superior to others). The concept of social competition refers to the fact that some individuals seek to enhance their self-esteem by identifying with a group. However, this works only if the group can be seen as superior to others. Because of social competition, groups tend to view themselves as better than their rivals (Baron, Byrne, & Branscombe, 2006). In one survey, every major ethnic group in the United States rated itself as better than any other group (Njeri, 1991).

A person who has high self-esteem does not need to treat others as inferior in order to feel good about himself or herself. Similarly, it is not necessary to degrade other groups in order to feel positive about one's own group identity (Fowers & Davidov, 2006; Messick & Mackie, 1989). In fact, each ethnic group has strengths that members of other groups could benefit from emulating. For instance, African Americans, Asian Americans, and Latinos emphasize family networks that help buffer them from some of the stresses of daily life (Suinn, 1999).

Just-world beliefs Belief that people generally get what they deserve.

Self-fulfilling prophecy An expectation that prompts people to act in ways that make the expectation come true.

Social competition Rivalry among groups, each of which regards itself as superior to others.

Understand That Race Is a Social Construction   From the viewpoint of modern genetics, the concept of race has absolutely no meaning (Bonham, Warshauer-Baker, & Collins, 2005; Sternberg, Grigorenko, & Kidd, 2005). Members of various groups are so varied genetically and human groups have intermixed for so many centuries, that it is impossible to tell, biologically, to what "race" any given individual belongs. Thus, race is an illusion based on superficial physical differences and learned ethnic identities. Certainly people *act as if* different races exist. But this is a matter of social labeling, not biological reality. To assume that any human group is biologically superior or inferior is simply wrong. In fact, the best available evidence suggests that all people are descended from the same ancient ancestors. The origins of our species lie in Africa, about 100,000 years ago. Among early human populations, darker skin is a protective adaptation to sun exposure near the equator (Jablonski & Chaplin, 2000). Biologically, we are all brothers and sisters under the skin (Graves, 2001; Smedley & Smedley, 2005).

Look for Commonalities We live in a society that puts a premium on competition and individual effort. One problem with this is that competing with others fosters desires to demean, defeat, and vanquish them. When we cooperate with others we tend to share their joys and suffer when they are in distress (Aronson, 2004; Lanzetta & Englis, 1989). If we don't find ways to cooperate and live in greater harmony, everyone will suffer. That, if nothing else, is one thing that we all have in common. Everyone knows what it feels like to be different. Greater tolerance comes from remembering those times.

Tolerance and Cultural Awareness

Living comfortably in a multicultural society means being open to other groups. Getting acquainted with a person whose cultural background is different from your own can be a wonderful learning experience. No one culture has all the answers or the best ways of doing things. Multicultural populations enrich a community's food, music, arts, and philosophy. Likewise, openness toward different racial, cultural, and ethnic groups can be personally rewarding (Fowers & Davidov, 2006).

The importance of cultural awareness often lies in subtleties and details. For example, in large American cities, many small stores are owned by Korean immigrants. Some of these Korean-American merchants have been criticized for being cold and hostile to their customers. Refusing to place change directly in customers' hands, for instance, helped trigger an African-American boycott of Korean grocers in New York City. The core of the problem was a lack of cultural awareness on both sides.

In America, if you walk into a store, you expect the clerk to be courteous to you. One way of showing politeness is by smiling. But in the Confucian-steeped Korean culture, a smile is reserved for family members and close friends. If a Korean or Korean American has no reason to smile, he or she just doesn't smile. There's a Korean saying: "If you smile a lot, you're silly." Expressions such as "thank you" and "excuse me" are also used sparingly and strangers rarely touch each other—not even to return change.

Here's another example of how ignorance of cultural practices can lead to needless friction and misunderstanding: An African-American woman who wanted to ease racial tensions took a freshly baked pie to her neighbors across the way, who were Orthodox Jews. At the front door the woman extended her hand, not knowing that Orthodox Jews don't shake women's hands, unless the woman is a close family member. Once she was inside, she picked up a kitchen knife to cut the pie, not knowing the couple kept a kosher household and used different knives for different foods. The woman's well-intentioned attempt at neighborliness ended in an argument! Knowing a little more about each other's cultures could have prevented both of the conflicts just described.

The Journey Continues—Psychology and You

The technological advances of the last 20 years have dramatically changed what is humanly possible. Yet, as a species we still have much in common with people who lived many hundreds of years ago. Although we might like to think otherwise, we cannot count on technology to solve all of our problems. The threat of war, social conflict, crime, prejudice, infectious disease, overpopulation, environmental damage, famine, homicide, economic disaster—these and most other major dilemmas facing us are *behavioral*. Will the human family endure? It's a psychological question.

At the beginning of this book we described psychology as a journey of self-discovery. It is our sincere hope that you have found enough relevance and value here to spark a lifelong interest in psychology. As your personal journey continues, one thing is certain: Many of your greatest challenges and most treasured moments will involve other people. You would be wise to continue adding to your understanding of human behavior. Psychology's future looks exciting. What role will it play in your life?

 Study Break   Multiculturalism

Reflect

Which strategies for breaking the prejudice habit do you already use? How could you apply the remaining strategies to become more tolerant?

Learning Check

1. Multiculturalism refers to the belief that various subcultures and ethnic groups should be blended into a single emergent culture. T or F?

2. Patricia Devine found that many people who hold nonprejudiced beliefs still have prejudiced thoughts and feelings in the presence of minority group individuals. T or F?

3. Individuating information tends to be a good antidote for stereotypes. T or F?

4. Just-world beliefs are the primary cause of social competition. T or F?

Critical Thinking

5. Why is it valuable to learn the terms by which members of various groups prefer to be addressed (for example, Mexican-American, Latino [or Latina], Hispanic, or Chicano [Chicana])?

Answers

1. F   2. T   3. T   4. F   5. Because labels might have negative meanings that are not apparent to persons outside the group. People who are culturally aware allow others to define their own identities, rather than imposing labels on them.

CHAPTER IN REVIEW

Major Points

- Social psychology studies how we behave, think, and feel in social situations.

- We are attracted to other people for reasons that are fairly universal.

- To understand social behavior we must know what roles people play, their status, the norms they follow, and the attributions they make.

- Everyone is affected by pressures to conform, obey, and comply. There are times when it is valuable to resist such pressures.

- Attitudes subtly affect nearly all aspects of social behavior.

- To persuade others, you must be aware of your role as a communicator, the nature of the audience, and messages that will appeal to them.

- Prejudice is reduced by equal-status contact and mutual interdependence.

- Aggression is a fact of life, but humans are not inevitably aggressive.

- We can encourage helping and altruism by removing barriers to prosocial behavior.

- Multicultural harmony can be attained through conscious efforts to be more tolerant of others.

Summary

Why do people affiliate? What factors influence interpersonal attraction?

- Affiliation is tied to needs for approval, support, friendship, and information. Also, affiliation can reduce anxiety.

- Social comparison theory holds that we affiliate to evaluate our actions, feelings, and abilities.

- Interpersonal attraction is increased by proximity, frequent contact, beauty, competence, and similarity.

- Mate selection is characterized by a large degree of similarity on many dimensions.

- Self-disclosure follows a reciprocity norm: Low levels of self-disclosure are met with low levels in return; moderate self-disclosure elicits more personal replies.

- In comparison with liking, romantic love involves higher levels of emotional arousal and it is accompanied by mutual absorption between lovers.

- Evolutionary psychology attributes human mating patterns to the differing reproductive challenges faced by men and women since the dawn of time.

How does group membership affect our behavior?

- Social roles are particular behavior patterns associated with social positions.
- Higher status within groups is associated with special privileges and respect.
- Group structure refers to roles, communication pathways, and power within a group. Group cohesiveness is the degree of attraction among group members.
- Norms are standards of conduct enforced (formally or informally) by groups.
- Attribution theory describes how we perceive the causes of behavior.
- The fundamental attribution error is to think that internal causes explain the actions of other people. In contrast, we tend to attribute our own behavior to external causes.

What have social psychologists learned about conformity, compliance, obedience, and self-assertion?

- Social influence refers to alterations in behavior brought about by the behavior of others. Three forms of social influence, in ascending order of directness, are conformity, compliance, and obedience.
- The famous Asch experiments demonstrated that various group pressure and group sanctions encourage conformity.
- Groupthink refers to compulsive conformity in group decision making.
- Three strategies for gaining compliance are the foot-in-the-door technique, the door-in-the-face approach, and the low-ball technique.
- Many people show a surprising level of passive compliance to unreasonable requests.
- Obedience to authority in Milgram's studies decreased when the "teacher" and "learner" were close to one another, when the authority was absent, and when others refused to obey.
- Self-assertion, as opposed to aggression, involves clearly stating one's wants and needs to others.

How are attitudes acquired and changed?

- Attitudes are learned dispositions made up of a belief component, an emotional component, and an action component.
- Attitudes may be formed by direct contact, interaction with others, child-rearing practices, and group pressures. Peer group influences, reference group membership, the mass media, and chance conditioning also appear to be important in attitude formation.

Under what conditions is persuasion most effective?"

- Effective persuasion occurs when characteristics of the communicator, the message, and the audience are well matched.
- In general, a likable and believable communicator who repeats a credible message that arouses emotion in the audience and states clear-cut conclusions will be persuasive.
- Maintaining and changing attitudes is closely related to cognitive dissonance and our needs to be consistent in our thoughts and actions.

Is brainwashing actually possible? How are people converted to cult membership?

- Brainwashing is a form of forced attitude change. It depends on control of the target person's total environment.
- Three steps in brainwashing are unfreezing, changing, and refreezing attitudes and beliefs.
- Many cults recruit new members with high-pressure indoctrination techniques involving isolation, displays of affection, rituals, intimidation, and escalating commitment.

What causes prejudice and intergroup conflict?

- Prejudice is a negative attitude held toward members of various out-groups. One theory attributes prejudice to scapegoating. A second account says that prejudices may be held for personal reasons (personal prejudice) or simply through adherence to group norms (group prejudice).
- Prejudiced individuals tend to have an authoritarian personality.
- Intergroup conflict gives rise to hostility and the formation of social stereotypes. Status inequalities tend to build prejudice. Equal-status contact tends to reduce it.
- Superordinate goals are a key to reducing intergroup conflict.
- On a smaller scale, jigsaw classrooms (which encourage cooperation through mutual interdependence) have been shown to combat prejudice.

How do psychologists explain human aggression?

- Ethological explanations of aggression attribute it to inherited instincts. Biological explanations emphasize brain mechanisms and physical factors related to thresholds for aggression.
- According to the frustration-aggression hypothesis, frustration and aggression are closely linked.
- Frustration is only one of many aversive stimuli that can arouse a person and make aggression more likely.

Aggression is especially likely to occur when aggression cues are present.

- Social learning theory has focused attention on the role of aggressive models in the development of aggressive behavior.

Why are bystanders so often unwilling to help in an emergency?

- Four decision points that must be passed before a person gives help are: noticing, defining an emergency, taking responsibility, and selecting a course of action.
- Helping is less likely at each point when other potential helpers are present.
- Helping is encouraged by general arousal, empathic arousal, being in a good mood, low effort or risk, and perceived similarity between the victim and the helper.
- For several reasons, giving help tends to encourage others to help too.

What can be done to avoid prejudice and promote social harmony?

- Multiculturalism is an attempt to give equal status to different ethnic, racial, and cultural groups.
- Greater tolerance can be encouraged by neutralizing stereotypes with individuating information; by looking for commonalities with others; and by avoiding the effects of just-world beliefs, self-fulfilling prophecies, and social competition.
- Cultural awareness is a key element in promoting greater social harmony.

Interactive Learning

Internet addresses frequently change. To find the sites listed here, visit www.thomsonedu/psychology/coon for an updated list of Internet addresses and direct links to relevant sites.

Psychology: A Journey Companion Website Find online quizzes, flash cards, animations, video clips, experiments, interactive assessments, and other helpful study aids for this text at www.thomsonedu.com/psychology/coon.

Social Psychology Network A comprehensive site with many links to information about social psychology.

Center for Evolutionary Psychology A primer on evolutionary psychology, a reading list, and links.

Information about Cults and Psychological Manipulation The home page of the International Cultic Studies Association offers a wealth of information about cults.

Implicit Association Test Online tests that purportedly reveal the unconscious roots of prejudice.

Media Violence Discusses research and implications of watching violence on television or other media.

ThomsonNOW Go to www.thomsonedu.com to link to ThomsonNOW, your online study tool. First take the **Pre-Test** for this chapter to get your **Personalized Study Plan,** which will identify topics you need to review and direct you to online resources. Then take the **Post-Test** to determine what concepts you have mastered and what you still need work on.

TEST YOUR KNOWLEDGE | Social Behavior

For additional review, get more practice with *ThomsonNOW*, *WebTutor*, the *Practice Quizzes*, and/or the printed *Study Guide* available with this book.

1. The pattern known as homogamy shows the powerful effect that _____ has on interpersonal attraction.
   a. physical beauty
   b. similarity
   c. competence
   d. physical proximity

2. The fact that men tend to prefer younger, more physically attractive partners is predicted by
   a. evolutionary psychology
   b. the overdisclosure hypothesis
   c. social comparison theory
   d. Rubin's studies of mutual absorption

3. Away from the office, Jan has become friends with Fran, a woman she supervises at work. Jan must do an evaluation of Fran, who hasn't been very efficient lately. It is most likely that Jan will experience
   a. groupthink
   b. role conflict
   c. group sanctions
   d. overdisclosure

4. A common error we all make is to attribute the actions of others to internal causes. This is known as the fundamental
   a. reciprocity norm
   b. role conflict
   c. social comparison
   d. attribution error

5. In Solomon Asch's conformity experiment, subjects yielded to group pressure on about _____ of the critical trials.
   a. 1 percent
   b. 10 percent
   c. one third
   d. two thirds

6. Groupthink is an example of the danger that lies in powerful pressures for group
   a. cohesion
   b. conformity
   c. attribution
   d. reciprocity

7. Which compliance technique involves getting a person committed to act and then making the terms of acting less desirable?
   a. foot in the door
   b. low ball
   c. door in the face
   d. groupthink

8. In Milgram's experiments, the lowest level of obedience occurred when subjects
   a. saw another person refuse to obey
   b. were in the same room with the "learner"
   c. were face to face with the "learner"
   d. received orders over the phone

9. "Achieving one's goals without taking into account the rights of others." This statement describes
   a. self-assertion
   b. overdisclosure
   c. cognitive dissonance
   d. aggression

10. The three parts of an attitude are
    a. internal, external, group
    b. conviction, attribution, absorption
    c. status, norm, cohesion
    d. belief, emotion, action

11. Which of the following is NOT one of the factors that typically determines whether our attitudes are expressed as actions?
    a. empathic arousal
    b. existing habits
    c. immediate consequences
    d. anticipated evaluations by others

12. If you are trying to persuade a well-informed audience, it is usually best to present
    a. one side of the argument
    b. both sides of the argument
    c. the unfreezing, change, refreezing cycle
    d. negative sanctions

13. The amount of cognitive dissonance a person feels is related to how much _____ exists for his or her actions.
    a. reciprocity
    b. justification
    c. chance conditioning
    d. reference

14. Some expressions of prejudice can be thought of as scapegoating or
    a. displaced aggression
    b. empathic arousal
    c. reference group reversal
    d. external attribution

15. One of the reasons that superordinate goals tend to reduce prejudice is that they require cooperation and
    a. social stereotyping
    b. ethnocentrism
    c. unfreezing
    d. equal-status contact

16. Jigsaw classrooms use _____ to create mutual interdependence.
    a. social competition
    b. just world beliefs
    c. self-fulfilling prophecies
    d. superordinate goals

17. The *weapons effect* refers to the impact that _____ have on behavior.
    a. just-world beliefs
    b. aggression cues
    c. self-fulfilling prophecies
    d. televised models

18. The point of view most at odds with the idea that humans are instinctively aggressive is
    a. social learning theory
    b. the frustration-aggression hypothesis
    c. ethology
    d. the aversive stimuli effect

19. People are more likely to help another who is in trouble if
    a. many other helpers are present
    b. a diffusion of responsibility occurs
    c. they experience empathic arousal
    d. desensitization has taken place

20. One of the best antidotes for stereotypes is
    a. accepting just-world beliefs
    b. individuating information
    c. accepting self-fulfilling prophecies
    d. honest social competition

Behavioral Statistics

JOURNEY INTO PSYCHOLOGY: STATISTICS FROM "HEADS" TO "TAILS"

Let's say a friend of yours invites you to try your hand at a "game of chance." He offers to flip a coin and pay you a dollar if the coin comes up heads. If the coin shows tails, you must pay him a dollar. He flips the coin: tails—you pay him a dollar. He flips it again: tails. Again: tails. And again: tails. And again: tails.

At this point you are faced with a choice. Should you continue the game in an attempt to recoup your losses? Or should you assume that the coin is biased and quit before you really get "skinned"? Taking out a pocket calculator (and, of course, the statistics book you carry with you at all times), you compute the odds of obtaining 5 tails in a row from an unbiased coin. The probability is 0.032 (roughly 3 times out of 100).

If the coin really is honest, 5 consecutive tails is a rare event. Wisely, you decide that the coin is probably biased and refuse to play again. (Unless, of course, your "friend" is willing to take "tails" for the next 5 tosses!)

Perhaps a decision could have been made in this hypothetical example without using statistics. But notice how much clearer the situation becomes when it is expressed statistically.

Psychologists try to extract and summarize useful information from the observations they make. To do so, they use two major types of statistics. **Descriptive statistics** summarize or "boil down" numbers so they become more meaningful and easier to communicate to others. In comparison, **inferential statistics** are used for decision making, for generalizing from small samples, and for drawing conclusions. As was the case in the coin-flipping example, psychologists must often base decisions on limited data. Such decisions are much easier to make with the help of inferential statistics. Let's see how statistics are used in psychology.

▼ Survey Questions

- What are descriptive statistics?
- How are statistics used to identify an average score?
- What statistics do psychologists use to measure how much scores differ from one another?
- What are inferential statistics?
- How are correlations used in psychology?

DESCRIPTIVE STATISTICS—PSYCHOLOGY BY THE NUMBERS

Let's say you have completed a study on human behavior. You measured the willingness of hundreds of men and women to take risks with a risk-taking questionnaire. The results seem interesting, but can you really tell what your data reveal, just by looking at a jumble of numbers? To get a clear picture of how people behaved, you will probably turn to descriptive statistics. By summarizing the results of your study, statistics will help you draw valid conclusions about what you observed.

Statistics bring greater clarity and precision to psychological thought and research (Gravetter & Wallnau, 2007). To see how, let's begin by considering three basic types of descriptive statistics: *graphical statistics,* measures of *central tendency,* and measures of *variability.* Let's start with **graphical statistics,** which present numbers pictorially, so they are easier to visualize.

Graphical Statistics

■ Table A.1 shows simulated scores on a test of hypnotic susceptibility given to 100 college students. With such disorganized data, it is hard to form an overall "picture" of the differences in hypnotic susceptibility. But by using a *frequency distribution,* large amounts of information can be neatly organized and summarized. A **frequency distribution** is made by breaking down the entire range of possible scores into classes of equal size. Next, the number of scores falling into each class is recorded. In ■ Table A.2, the raw data from ■ Table A.1 have been condensed into a frequency distribution. Notice how much clearer the pattern of scores for the entire group becomes.

■ Table A.1		Raw Scores of Hypnotic Susceptibility							
55	86	52	17	61	57	84	51	16	64
22	56	25	38	35	24	54	26	37	38
52	42	59	26	21	55	40	59	25	57
91	27	38	53	19	93	25	39	52	56
66	14	18	63	59	68	12	19	62	45
47	98	88	72	50	49	96	89	71	66
50	44	71	57	90	53	41	72	56	93
57	38	55	49	87	59	36	56	48	70
33	69	50	50	60	35	67	51	50	52
11	73	46	16	67	13	71	47	25	77

Descriptive statistics Mathematical tools used to describe and summarize numeric data.

Inferential statistics Mathematical tools used for decision making, for generalizing from small samples, and for drawing conclusions.

Graphical statistics Techniques for presenting numbers pictorially, often by plotting them on a graph.

Frequency distribution A table that divides an entire range of scores into a series of classes and then records the number of scores that fall into each class.

Table A.2 Frequency Distribution of Hypnotic Susceptibility Scores	
Class Interval	Number of Persons in Class
0–19	10
20–39	20
40–59	40
60–79	20
80–99	10

Frequency distributions are often shown *graphically* to make them more "visual." A **histogram,** or graph of a frequency distribution, is made by labeling class intervals on the *abscissa* (horizontal line) and frequencies (the number of scores in each class) on the *ordinate* (vertical line). Next, bars are drawn for each class interval; the height of each bar is determined by the number of scores in each class (»Fig. A.1). An alternate way of graphing scores is the more familiar **frequency polygon** (»Fig. A.2). Here, points are placed at the center of each class interval to indicate the number of scores. Then the dots are connected by straight lines.

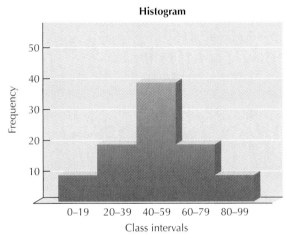

»**FIGURE A.1** Frequency histogram of hypnotic susceptibility scores contained in ▪ Table A.2.

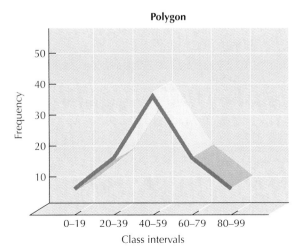

Histogram A graph of a frequency distribution in which the number of scores falling in each class is represented by vertical bars.

Frequency polygon A graph of a frequency distribution in which the number of scores falling in each class is represented by points on a line.

»**FIGURE A.2** Frequency polygon of hypnotic susceptibility scores contained in ▪ Table A.2.

Measures of Central Tendency

Notice in ■Table A.2 that more scores fall in the range 40–59 than elsewhere. How can we show this fact? A measure of **central tendency** is simply a number describing a "typical score" around which other scores fall. A familiar measure of central tendency is the mean, or "average." But as we shall see in a moment, there are other types of "averages" that can be used. To illustrate each we need an example: ■Table A.3 shows the raw data for an imaginary experiment in which two groups of subjects were given a test of memory. Assume that one group was given a drug that might improve memory (let's call the drug Rememberine). The second group received a placebo. Is there a difference in memory scores between the two groups? It's difficult to tell without computing an average.

The Mean

As one type of "average," the **mean** is calculated by adding all the scores for each group and then dividing by the total number of scores. Notice in ■Table A.3 that the means reveal a difference between the two groups.

The mean is sensitive to extremely high or low scores in a distribution. For this reason it is not always the best measure of central tendency. (Imagine how distorted it would be to calculate average yearly incomes from a small sample of people that happened to include a multimillionaire.) In such cases the middle score in a group of scores—called the *median*—is used instead.

The Median

The **median** is found by arranging scores from the highest to the lowest and selecting the score that falls in the middle. In other words, half the values in a group of scores fall below the median and half fall above. Consider, for example, the following weights obtained from a small class of college students: 105, 111, 123, 126, 148, 151, 154, 162, 182. The median for the group is 148, the middle score. Of course, if there is an even number of scores, there will be no "middle score." This problem is handled by averaging the two scores that "share" the middle spot. This procedure yields a single number to serve as the median (see bottom panel of ■Table A.3).

■ **Table A.3   Raw Scores on a Memory Test for Subjects Taking Rememberine or a Placebo**

Subject	Group 1 Rememberine	Group 2 Placebo
1	65	54
2	67	60
3	73	63
4	65	33
5	58	56
6	55	60
7	70	60
8	69	31
9	60	62
10	68	61
Sum	650	540
Mean	65	54
Median	66	60

$$\text{Mean} = \frac{\Sigma X}{N} \text{ or } \frac{\text{Sum of all scores, X}}{\text{number of scores}}$$

$$\text{Mean Group 1} = \frac{65 + 67 + 73 + 65 + 58 + 55 + 70 + 69 + 60 + 68}{10}$$

$$= \frac{650}{10} = 65$$

$$\text{Mean Group 2} = \frac{54 + 60 + 63 + 33 + 56 + 60 + 60 + 31 + 62 + 61}{10}$$

$$= \frac{540}{10} = 54$$

Median = the middle score or the mean of the two middle scores*

Median Group 1 = 55 58 60 65 $\boxed{65\ 67}$ 68 69 70 73

$$= \frac{65 + 67}{2} = 66$$

Median Group 2 = 31 33 54 56 $\boxed{60\ 60}$ 60 61 62 63

$$= \frac{60 + 60}{2} = 60$$

* $\boxed{}$ indicates middle score(s).

The Mode

A final measure of central tendency is the *mode*. The **mode** is simply the most frequently occurring score in a group of scores. If you were to take the time to count the scores in ■Table A.3, you would find that the mode of Group 1 is 65, and the mode of Group 2 is 60. The mode is usually easy to obtain. However, the mode can be an unreliable measure, especially in a small group of scores. The mode's advantage is that it gives the score actually obtained by the greatest number of people.

Measures of Variability

Let's say a researcher discovers two drugs that lower anxiety in agitated patients. However, let's also assume that one drug consistently lowers anxiety by moderate amounts, whereas the second sometimes lowers it by large amounts, sometimes has no effect, or may even

Central tendency The tendency for a majority of scores to fall in the midrange of possible values.

Mean A measure of central tendency calculated by adding a group of scores and then dividing by the total number of scores.

Median A measure of central tendency found by arranging scores from the highest to the lowest and selecting the score that falls in the middle. That is, half the values in a group of scores fall above the median and half fall below.

Mode A measure of central tendency found by identifying the most frequently occurring score in a group of scores.

■ Table A.4 Computation of the Standard Deviation

Group 1 Mean = 65

Score Mean	Deviation (d)	Deviation Squared (d²)
65 − 65 =	0	0
67 − 65 =	2	4
73 − 65 =	8	64
65 − 65 =	0	0
58 − 65 =	−7	49
55 − 65 =	−10	100
70 − 65 =	5	25
69 − 65 =	4	16
60 − 65 =	−5	25
68 − 65 =	3	9
		292

$$SD = \sqrt{\frac{\text{sum of } d^2}{n}} = \sqrt{\frac{292}{10}} = \sqrt{29.2} = 5.4$$

Group 2 Mean = 54

Score Mean	Deviation (d)	Deviation Squared (d²)
54 − 54 =	0	0
60 − 54 =	6	36
63 − 54 =	9	81
33 − 54 =	−21	441
56 − 54 =	2	4
60 − 54 =	6	36
60 − 54 =	6	36
31 − 54 =	−23	529
62 − 54 =	8	64
61 − 54 =	7	49
		1276

$$SD = \sqrt{\frac{\text{sum of } d^2}{n}} = \sqrt{\frac{1276}{10}} = \sqrt{127.6} = 5.4$$

increase anxiety in some patients. Overall, there is no difference in the *average* (mean) amount of anxiety reduction. Even so, an important difference exists between the two drugs. As this example shows, it is not enough to simply know the average score in a distribution. Usually, we would also like to know if scores are grouped closely together or scattered widely.

Measures of **variability** provide a single number that tells how "spread out" scores are. When the scores are widely spread, this number gets larger. When they are close together it gets smaller. If you look again at the example in ■ Table A.3, you will notice that the scores within each group vary widely. How can we show this fact?

The Range

The simplest way would be to use the **range,** which is the difference between the highest and lowest scores. In Group 1 of our experiment, the highest score is 73, and the lowest is 55; thus, the range is 18 (73 − 55 = 18). In Group 2, the highest score is 63, and the lowest is 31; this makes the range 32. Scores in Group 2 are more spread out (are more variable) than those in Group 1.

The Standard Deviation

A better measure of variability is the **standard deviation** (an index of how much a typical score differs from the mean of a group of scores). To obtain the standard deviation, we find the deviation (or difference) of each score from the mean and then square it (multiply it by itself). These squared deviations are then added and averaged (the total is divided by the number of deviations). Taking the square root of this average yields the standard deviation (■ Table A.4). Notice again that the variability for Group 1 (5.4) is smaller than that for Group 2 (where the standard deviation is 11.3).

Standard Scores

A particular advantage of the standard deviation is that it can be used to "standardize" scores in a way that gives them greater meaning. For example, John and Susan both took psychology midterms, but in different classes. John earned a score of 118, and Susan scored 110. Who did better? It is impossible to tell without knowing what the average score was on each test, and whether John and Susan scored at the top, middle, or bottom of their classes. We would like to have one number that gives all this information. A number that does this is the *z-score.*

To convert an original score to a **z-score,** we subtract the mean from the score. The resulting number is then divided by the standard deviation for that group of scores. To illustrate, Susan had a score of 110 in a class with a mean of 100 and a standard deviation of 10. Therefore, her z-score is +1.0 (■ Table A.5). John's score of 118 came from a class having a mean of 100 and a standard deviation of 18; thus his z-score is also +1.0 (see ■ Table A.5). Originally it looked as if John did better on his midterm than Susan did. But we now see that, relatively speaking, their scores were equivalent. Compared to other students, each was an equal distance above average.

Variability The tendency for a group of scores to differ in value. Measures of variability indicate the degree to which a group of scores differ from one another.

Range The difference between the highest and lowest scores in a group of scores.

Standard deviation An index of how much a typical score differs from the mean of a group of scores.

z-score A number that tells how many standard deviations above or below the mean a score is.

■ Table A.5 Computation of a z-score

$$z = \frac{X - \bar{X}}{SD} = \text{or} \frac{\text{score} - \text{mean}}{\text{standard deviation}}$$

$$\text{Susan: } z = \frac{110 - 100}{10} = \frac{+10}{10} = +1.0$$

$$\text{John: } z = \frac{118 - 100}{18} = \frac{+18}{18} = +1.0$$

The Normal Curve

When chance events are recorded, we find that some outcomes have a high probability and occur very often; others have a lower probability and occur infrequently; still others have little probability and occur rarely. As a result, the distribution (or tally) of chance events typically resembles a *normal curve* (⟫Fig. A.3). A **normal curve** is bell-shaped, with a large number of scores in the middle, tapering to very few extremely high and low scores. Most psychological traits or events are determined by the action of a large number of factors. Therefore, like chance events, measures of psychological variables tend to roughly match a normal curve. For example, direct measurement has shown such characteristics as height, memory span, and intelligence to be distributed approximately along a normal curve. In other words, many people have average height, memory ability, and intelligence. However, as we move above or below average, fewer and fewer people are found.

It is very fortunate that so many psychological variables tend to form a normal curve, because much is known about the curve. One valuable property concerns the relationship between the standard deviation and the normal curve. Specifically, the standard deviation measures off set proportions of the curve above and below the mean. For example, in ⟫Figure A.4, notice that roughly 68 percent of all cases (IQ scores, memory scores, heights, or whatever) fall between one standard deviation above and below the mean (±1 SD); 95 percent of all cases fall between ±2 SD; and 99 percent of the cases can be found between ±3 SD from the mean.

▪ Table A.6 gives a more complete account of the relationship between z-scores and the percentage of cases found in a particular area of the normal curve. Notice, for example, that 93.3 percent of all cases fall below a z-score of +1.5. A z-score of 1.5 on a test (no matter what the original, or "raw," score was) would be a good per-

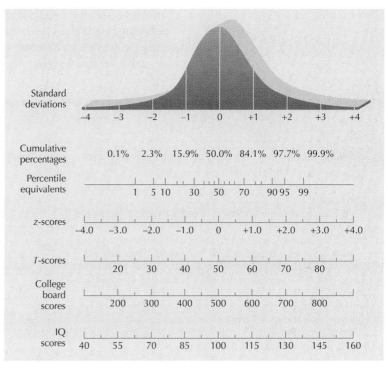

⟫**FIGURE A.3** The normal curve. The normal curve is an idealized mathematical model. However, many measurements in psychology closely approximate a normal curve. The scales you see here show the relationship of standard deviations, z-scores, and other measures to the curve.

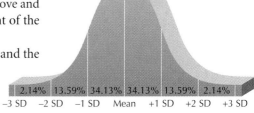

⟫**FIGURE A.4** Relationship between the standard deviation and the normal curve.

z-Score	Percentage of Area to the Left of This Value	Percentage of Area to the Right of This Value
−3.0 SD	00.1	99.9
−2.5 SD	00.6	99.4
−2.0 SD	02.3	97.7
−1.5 SD	06.7	93.3
−1.0 SD	15.9	84.1
−0.5 SD	30.9	69.1
0.0 SD	50.0	50.0
+0.5 SD	69.1	30.9
+1.0 SD	84.1	15.9
+1.5 SD	93.3	06.7
+2.0 SD	97.7	02.3
+2.5 SD	99.4	00.6
+3.0 SD	99.9	00.1

▪ Table A.6 **Computation of a z-score**

Normal curve A bell-shaped distribution, with a large number of scores in the middle, tapering to very few extremely high and low scores.

formance, because roughly 93 percent of all scores fall below this mark. Relationships between the standard deviation (or z-scores) and the normal curve do not change. This makes it possible to compare various tests or groups of scores if they come from distributions that are approximately normal.

Study Break   Descriptive Statistics

Reflect

Let's say you ask 100 people how long they sleep each night and record their answers. How could you show these scores graphically?

To find the average amount of sleep for your subjects, would you prefer to know the most frequent score (the mode), the middle score (the median), or the arithmetic average (the mean)?

How could you determine how much sleep times vary? That is, would you prefer to know the highest and lowest scores (the range), or the average amount of variation (the standard deviation)?

How would you feel about receiving your scores on classroom tests in the form of z-scores?

Do you think the distribution of scores in your study of sleep would form a normal curve? Why or why not?

Learning Check

1. _____ statistics summarize numbers so they become more meaningful or easier to communicate; _____ statistics are used for decision making, generalizing, or drawing conclusions.
2. Histograms and frequency polygons are graphs of frequency distributions. T or F?
3. Three measures of central tendency are the mean, the median, and the _____.
4. If scores are placed in order, from the smallest to the largest, the median is defined as the middle score. T or F?
5. As a measure of variability, the standard deviation is defined as the difference between the highest and lowest scores. T or F?
6. A z-score of −1 tells us that a score fell one standard deviation below the mean in a group of scores. T or F?
7. In a normal curve, 99 percent of all scores can be found between +1 and −1 standard deviations from the mean. T or F?

Answers

1. Descriptive, inferential 2. T 3. mode 4. T 5. F 6. T 7. F

INFERENTIAL STATISTICS—SIGNIFICANT NUMBERS

You would like to know if girls are more verbally aggressive than boys. You observe a group of 5-year-old girls and boys on a playground. After collecting data for a week you find that the girls committed more acts of verbal aggression than the boys. Could this difference just be a meaningless fluctuation in verbal aggression? Or does it show conclusively that girls are more verbally aggressive than boys? Inferential statistics were created to answer just such questions (Sprinthall, 2007).

As stated earlier, *inferential statistics* are techniques that allow us to make inferences. That is, they allow us to generalize from the behavior of small groups of subjects to that of the larger groups they represent. For example, let's say that a researcher studies the effects of a new therapy on a small group of depressed individuals. Is she or he interested only in these particular individuals? Usually not, because except in rare instances, psychologists seek to discover general laws of behavior that apply widely to humans and animals. Undoubtedly the researcher would like to know if the therapy holds any promise for all depressed people.

Samples and Populations

In any scientific study, we would like to observe the entire set, or **population,** of subjects, objects, or events of interest. However, this is usually impossible or impractical. Observing all terrorists, all cancer patients, or all mothers-in-law could be both impractical (because all are large populations) and impossible (because people change political views, may be unaware of having cancer, and change their status as relatives). In such cases, **samples** (smaller cross sections of a population) are selected, and observations of the sample are used to draw conclusions about the entire population.

Population An entire group of animals, people, or objects belonging to a particular category (for example, all college students or all married women).

Sample A smaller subpart of a population.

For any sample to be meaningful, it must be **representative.** That is, the sample group must truly reflect the membership and characteristics of the larger population. In our earlier hypothetical study of a memory drug, it would be essential for the sample of 20 people to be representative of the general population. A very important aspect of representative samples is that their members are chosen at **random.** In other words, each member of the population must have an equal chance of being included in the sample.

Significant Differences

In our imaginary drug experiment, we found that the average memory score was higher for the group given the drug than it was for persons who didn't take the drug (the placebo group). Certainly this result is interesting, but could it have occurred by chance? If two groups were repeatedly tested (with neither receiving any drug), their average memory scores would sometimes differ. How much must two means differ before we can consider the difference "real" (not due to chance)?

Notice that the question is similar to one discussed earlier: How many tails in a row must we obtain when flipping a coin before we can conclude that the coin is biased? In the case of the coin, we noted that obtaining 5 tails in a row is a rare event. Thus, it became reasonable to assume that the coin was biased. Of course, it is possible to get 5 tails in a row when flipping an honest coin. But because this outcome is unlikely, we have good reason to suspect that something other than chance (a loaded coin, for instance) caused the results. Similar reasoning is used in tests of statistical significance.

Tests of **statistical significance** provide an estimate of how often experimental results could have occurred by chance alone. The results of a significance test are stated as a probability. This probability gives the odds that the observed difference was due to chance. In psychology, any experimental result that could have occurred by chance 5 times (or less) out of 100 (in other words, a probability of .05 or less) is considered *significant.* In our memory experiment, the probability is .025 ($p = .025$) that the group means would differ as they do by chance alone. This allows us to conclude with reasonable certainty that the drug actually did improve memory scores.

CORRELATION—RATING RELATIONSHIPS

Psychologists are very interested in detecting relationships between events: Are children from single-parent families more likely to misbehave at school? Is wealth related to happiness? Is there a relationship between childhood exposure to the Internet and IQ at age 20? Is the chance of having a heart attack related to having a hostile personality? All of these are questions about correlation (Silverthorne, 2004).

Many of the statements that psychologists make about behavior do not result from the use of experimental methods. Rather, they come from keen observations and measures of existing phenomena. A psychologist might note, for example, that the higher a couple's socioeconomic and educational status, the smaller the number of children they are likely to have. Or that grades in high school are related to how well a person is likely to do in college. Or even that as rainfall levels increase within a given metropolitan area, crime rates decline. In these instances, we are dealing with the fact that two variables are correlating (varying together in some orderly fashion), or there is a **correlation** between them.

The simplest way of visualizing a correlation is to construct a **scatter diagram.** In a scatter diagram, two measures (grades in high school and grades in college, for instance) are obtained. One measure is indicated by the X axis and the second by the Y axis. The scatter diagram plots the intersection (crossing) of each pair of measurements as a single point. Many such measurement pairs give pictures like those shown in ▸▸Figure A.5.

Representative sample A small, randomly selected part of a larger population that accurately reflects characteristics of the whole population.

Random selection Choosing a sample so that each member of the population has an equal chance of being included in the sample.

Statistical significance The degree to which an event (such as the results of an experiment) is unlikely to have occurred by chance alone.

Correlation The existence of a consistent, systematic relationship between two events, measures, or variables.

Scatter diagram A graph that plots the intersection of paired measures; that is, the points at which paired X and Y measures cross.

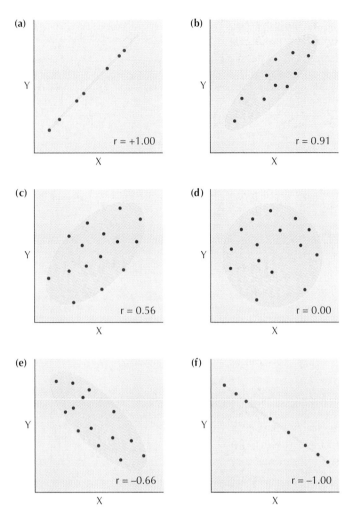

▸▸**FIGURE A.5** Scatter diagrams showing various degrees of relationship for a positive, zero, and negative correlation.

Relationships

▸▸Figure A.5 also shows scatter diagrams of three basic kinds of relationships between variables (or measures). Graphs a, b, and c show *positive relationships* of varying strength. As you can see, in a **positive relationship,** increases in the X measure (or score) are matched by increases on the Y measure (or score). An example would be finding that higher IQ scores (X) are associated with higher college grades (Y). A **zero correlation** suggests that no relationship exists between two measures (see graph d). This might be the result of comparing subjects' hat sizes (X) to their college grades (Y). Graphs e and f both show a **negative relationship** (or correlation). Notice that as values of one measure increase, those of the second become smaller. An example might be the relationship between amount of alcohol consumed and scores on a test of coordination: Higher alcohol levels are correlated with lower coordination scores.

The Correlation Coefficient

The strength of a correlation can also be expressed as a **coefficient of correlation.** This coefficient is simply a number falling somewhere between +1.00 and −1.00. If the number is zero or close to zero, it indicates a weak or nonexistent relationship. If the correlation is +1.00, a **perfect positive relationship** exists; if the correlation is −1.00, a **perfect negative relationship** has been discovered. The most commonly used correlation coefficient is called the Pearson *r*. Calculation of the Pearson *r* is relatively simple, as shown in ▦ Table A.7. (The numbers shown are hypothetical.)

As stated in Chapter 1, correlations in psychology are rarely perfect. Most fall somewhere between zero and plus or minus 1. The closer the correlation coefficient is to +1.00 or −1.00, the stronger the relationship. An interesting example of some typical correlations is provided by a study that compared the IQs of adopted children with the IQs of their biological mothers. At age 4, the children's IQs correlated .28 with their biological mothers' IQs. By age 7 the correlation was .35. And by age 13 it had grown to .38. Over time, the IQs of adopted children become more similar to the IQs of their biological mothers.

Prediction

Correlations often provide highly useful information. For instance, it is valuable to know that there is a correlation between cigarette smoking and lung cancer rates. Another example is the fact that higher consumption of alcohol during pregnancy is correlated with lower birth weight and a higher rate of birth defects. There is a correlation between the number of recent life stresses experienced and the likelihood of emotional disturbance. Many more examples could be cited, but the point is, correlations help us to identify relationships that are worth knowing.

Correlations are particularly valuable for making *predictions.* If we know that two measures are correlated, and we know a person's score on one measure, we can predict his or her score on the other. For example, most colleges have formulas that use multiple correlations to decide which applicants have the best chances for success. Usually the formula includes such predictors as high school GPA, teacher ratings, extracurricular activities, and scores on the *Scholastic Assessment Test* (SAT) or some similar test. Although no single predictor is perfectly correlated with success in college, together the various predictors correlate highly and provide a useful technique for screening applicants.

Positive relationship A mathematical relationship in which increases in one measure are matched by increases in the other (or decreases correspond with decreases).

Zero correlation The absence of a (linear) mathematical relationship between two measures.

Negative relationship A mathematical relationship in which increases in one measure are matched by decreases in the other.

Coefficient of correlation A statistical index ranging from −1.00 to +1.00 that indicates the direction and degree of correlation.

Perfect positive relationship A mathematical relationship in which the correlation between two measures is +1.00.

Perfect negative relationship A mathematical relationship in which the correlation between two measures is −1.00.

■ Table A.7   **IQ and Grade Point Average for Computing Pearson *r***

Student No.	IQ (X)	Grade Point Average (Y)	X Score Squared (X²)	Y Score Squared (Y²)	X Times Y (XY)
1	110	1.0	12,100	1.00	110.0
2	112	1.6	12,544	2.56	179.2
3	118	1.2	13,924	1.44	141.6
4	119	2.1	14,161	4.41	249.9
5	122	2.6	14,884	6.76	317.2
6	125	1.8	15,625	3.24	225.0
7	127	2.6	16,124	6.76	330.2
8	130	2.0	16,900	4.00	260.0
9	132	3.2	17,424	10.24	422.4
10	134	2.6	17,956	6.76	348.4
11	136	3.0	18,496	9.00	408.0
12	138	3.6	19,044	12.96	496.8
Total	1503	27.3	189,187	69.13	3488.7

$$r = \frac{\Sigma XY - \frac{(\Sigma X)(\Sigma Y)}{N}}{\sqrt{\left[\Sigma X^2 - \frac{(\Sigma X)^2}{N}\right]\left[\Sigma Y^2 - \frac{(\Sigma Y)^2}{N}\right]}}$$

$$= \frac{3488.7 - \frac{1503(27.3)}{12}}{\sqrt{\left[189,187 - \frac{(1503)^2}{2}\right]\left[69.13 - \frac{(27.3)^2}{12}\right]}}$$

$$= \frac{69.375}{81.088} = 0.856 = 0.86$$

There is an interesting "trick" you can do with correlations that you may find useful. It works like this: If you *square* the correlation coefficient (multiply *r* by itself), you will get a number telling the **percent of variance** (amount of variation in scores) accounted for by the correlation. For example, the correlation between IQ scores and college grade point average is .5. Multiplying .5 times .5 gives .25, or 25 percent. This means that 25 percent of the variation in college grades is accounted for by knowing IQ scores. In other words, with a correlation of .5, college grades are "squeezed" into an oval like the one shown in graph C, ▸▸ Figure A.5. IQ scores take away some of the possible variation in corresponding grade point averages. If there were no correlation between IQ and grades, grades would be completely free to vary, as shown in ▸▸ Figure A.5, graph D.

Along the same line, a correlation of +1.00 or −1.00 means that 100 percent of the variation in the Y measure is accounted for by knowing the X measure: If you know a person's X score, you can tell exactly what the Y score is. An example that comes close to this state of affairs is the high correlation (.86) between the IQs of identical twins. In any group of identical twins, 74 percent of the variation in the "Y" twins' IQs is accounted for by knowing the IQs of their siblings (the "X's").

Squaring correlations to obtain the *percent variance* accounted for is a useful tool for interpreting the correlations encountered in the media and the psychological literature. For example, sweeping pronouncements about relationships are occasionally made on the basis of correlations in the .25 to .30 range even though the values mean that only 6 to 9 percent of the variance is accounted for by the observed correlation. Such correlations may document relationships worth noting, but they are rarely something to get excited about.

Percent of variance A portion of the total amount of variation in a group of scores.

Correlation and Causation

It is very important to recognize that finding a correlation between two measures does not automatically mean that one causes the other: Correlation does not demonstrate causation. When a correlation exists, the best we can say is that two variables are related. Of course, this does not mean that it is impossible for two correlated variables to have a cause-and-effect relationship. Rather, it means that we cannot *conclude,* solely on the basis of correlation, that a causal link exists. To gain greater confidence that a cause-and-effect relationship exists, an experiment must be performed (see Chapter 1).

Often, two correlated measures are related as a result of the influence of a third variable. For example, we might observe that the more hours students devote to studying, the better their grades. Although it is tempting to conclude that more studying produces (causes) better grades, it is possible (indeed, it is probable) that grades and the amount of study time are both related to the amount of motivation or interest a student has.

The difference between cause-and-effect data and data that reveal a relationship of unknown origin is one that should not be forgotten. Because we rarely run experiments in daily life, the information on which we act is largely correlational. This should make us more humble and more tentative in the confidence with which we make pronouncements about human behavior.

Causation The act of causing some effect.

Study Break Inferential Statistics

Reflect

Informally, you have probably inferred something about a population of people based on the small sample you have observed directly. How could statistics improve the accuracy of your inferences?

If you were trying to test whether a drug causes birth defects, what level of statistical significance would you use? If you were doing a psychology experiment, what level would you be comfortable with?

See if you can identify at least one positive relationship and one negative relationship involving human behavior that you have observed. How strong to you think the correlation would be in each case? What correlation coefficient would you expect to see?

A woman you know drinks more coffee in the winter than she does in the summer. She also has more colds in the winter. She decides to reduce the amount of coffee she drinks to help prevent colds. What can you tell her about correlation and causation?

Learning Check

1. In inferential statistics, observations of a(n) _____ are used to make inferences and draw conclusions about an entire _____.
2. A representative sample can be obtained by selecting members of the sample at _____.
3. If the results of an experiment could have occurred by chance alone less than 25 times out of 100, the result is considered statistically significant. T or F
4. A scatter diagram can be used to plot and visualize a(n) _____ between two groups of scores.
5. In a negative relationship, increases in X scores correspond to decreases in Y scores. T or F?
6. A perfect positive correlation exists when the correlation coefficient is 0.00. T or F?
7. It is important to remember that correlation does not demonstrate _____.

Answers

1. sample, population 2. random 3. F 4. correlation 5. T 6. F 7. causation

---

APPENDIX: BEHAVIORAL STATISTICS IN REVIEW

Major Points

- The results of psychological studies are often expressed as numbers, which must be summarized and interpreted before they have any meaning.
- Summarizing numbers visually, by using various types of graphs, makes it easier to see trends and patterns in the results of psychological investigations.

- It is helpful to know the "average" of a group of scores as well as how much they vary.
- Many psychological measures produce scores that form a normal curve. This is useful because the characteristics of normal curves are well known.
- Some statistical techniques can be used to generalize results from samples to populations, to draw conclu-

sions, and to tell if the results of a study could have occurred by chance.

- When there is a correlation, or consistent relationship, between scores on two measures, knowing a person's score on one measure allows us to predict his or her score on the second measure.

Summary

What are descriptive statistics?

- Descriptive statistics organize and summarize numbers.
- Graphical statistics, such as histograms and frequency polygons, are used to represent numbers pictorially.

How are statistics used to identify an average score?

- Measures of central tendency define the "typical score" in a group of scores.
- The mean is found by adding all the scores in a group and then dividing by the total number of scores.
- The median is found by arranging a group of scores from the highest to the lowest and selecting the middle score.
- The mode is the score that occurs most frequently in a group of scores.

What statistics do psychologists use to measure how much scores differ from one another?

- Measures of variability provide a number that shows how much scores vary.
- The range is the difference between the highest score and the lowest score in a group of scores.
- The standard deviation shows how much, on average, all the scores in a group differ from the mean.
- To change an original score into a standard score (or z-score), you must subtract the mean from the score and then divide the result by the standard deviation.
- Standard scores (z-scores) tell, in standard deviation units, how far above or below the mean a score is. This allows meaningful comparisons between scores from different groups.
- Scores that form a normal curve are easy to interpret because the properties of the normal curve are well known.

What are inferential statistics?

- Inferential statistics are used to make decisions, to generalize from samples, and to draw conclusions.
- Most studies in psychology are based on samples. Findings from representative samples are assumed to also apply to entire populations.
- In psychology experiments, differences in the average performance of groups could occur purely by chance. Tests of statistical significance tell us if the observed differences between groups are common or rare. If a difference is large enough to be improbable, it suggests that the results did not occur by chance alone.

How are correlations used in psychology?

- Pairs of scores that vary together in an orderly fashion are said to be correlated.
- The relationship between two variables or measures can be positive or negative.
- Correlation coefficients tell how strongly two groups of scores are related.
- Correlation alone does not demonstrate cause-and-effect links between variables or measures.

🌐 Interactive Learning

Internet addresses frequently change. To find the sites listed here, visit www.thomsonedu/psychology/coon for an updated list of Internet addresses and direct links to relevant sites.

Psychology: A Journey Companion Website   Find online quizzes, flash cards, animations, video clips, experiments, interactive assessments, and other helpful study aids for this text at www.thomsonedu.com/psychology/coon.

Statistics to Use   If you enter a series of numbers, this site will calculate basic descriptive statistics and more advanced inferential statistics.

ThomsonNOW   Go to www.thomsonedu.com to link to ThomsonNOW, your online study tool. First take the **Pre-Test** for this Appendix to get your **Personalized Study Plan,** which will identify topics you need to review and direct you to online resources. Then take the **Post-Test** to determine what concepts you have mastered and what you still need work on.

Glossary

Ablation Surgical removal of tissue.

Absolute threshold The minimum amount of physical energy necessary to produce a sensation.

Abstract principles Concepts and ideas removed from specific examples and concrete situations.

Accommodation (perceptual) Changes in the shape of the lens of the eye.

Accommodation (Piaget) In Piaget's theory, the modification of existing mental patterns to fit new demands (that is, mental schemes are changed to accommodate new information or experiences).

Acculturative stress Stress caused by the many changes and adaptations required when a person moves to a foreign culture.

Acetylcholine The neurotransmitter released by neurons to activate muscles.

Acquaintance (date) rape Forced intercourse that occurs in the context of a date or other voluntary encounter.

Acquisition The period in conditioning during which a response is reinforced.

Action component How one tends to act toward the object of an attitude.

Action potential The nerve impulse.

Activation-synthesis hypothesis An attempt to explain how dream content is affected by motor commands in the brain that occur during sleep, but are not carried out.

Active listener A person who knows how to maintain attention, avoid distractions, and actively gather information from lectures.

Activity theory Theory stating that the best adjustment to aging occurs when people remain active mentally, socially, and physically.

Actor-observer bias The tendency to attribute the behavior of others to internal causes while attributing one's own behavior to external causes (situations and circumstances).

Acute stress disorder A psychological disturbance lasting up to 1 month following stresses that would produce anxiety in anyone who experienced them.

Adaptation level An internal or mental "average" or "medium" point that is used to judge amounts.

Adaptive behaviors Actions that aid attempts to survive and adapt to changing conditions.

Adjustment disorder An emotional disturbance caused by ongoing stressors within the range of common experience.

Adolescence The culturally defined period between childhood and adulthood.

Adrenal glands Endocrine glands that arouse the body, regulate salt balance, adjust the body to stress, and affect sexual functioning.

Affectional needs Emotional needs for love and affection.

Ageism Discrimination or prejudice based on a person's age.

Aggression Hurting another person or achieving one's goals at the expense of another person.

Aggression cues Stimuli or signals that are associated with aggression and that tend to elicit it.

Aggressive pornography Media depictions of sexual violence or of forced participation in sexual activity.

Agnosia An inability to identify seen objects.

Agoraphobia (without panic) The person fears that something extremely embarrassing will happen to them if they leave the house or enter unfamiliar situations.

Alarm reaction First stage of the general adaptation syndrome (G.A.S.), during which bodily resources are mobilized to cope with a stressor.

Alcohol myopia Shortsighted thinking and perception that occurs during alcohol intoxication.

Algorithm A learned set of rules that always leads to the correct solution of a problem.

All-or-nothing thinking Classifying objects or events as absolutely right or wrong, good or bad, acceptable or unacceptable, and so forth.

Alpha waves Large, slow brain waves associated with relaxation and falling asleep.

Altered state of consciousness (ASC) A condition of awareness distinctly different in quality or pattern from waking consciousness.

Alzheimer's disease An age-related disease characterized by memory loss, mental confusion, and, in its later stages, by a nearly total loss of mental abilities.

Ambivalence Mixed positive and negative feelings or simultaneous attraction and repulsion.

Ambivalent attachment An emotional bond marked by conflicting feelings of affection, anger, and emotional turmoil.

Amphetamine psychosis A loss of contact with reality due to repeated amphetamine use.

Amygdala A part of the limbic system associated with fear responses.

Anal stage The psychosexual stage corresponding roughly to the period of toilet training (ages 1 to 3).

Anal-expulsive personality A disorderly, destructive, cruel, or messy person.

Anal-retentive personality A person who is obstinate, stingy, or compulsive, and who generally has difficulty "letting go."

Androgen Any of a number of male sex hormones, especially testosterone.

Androgyny The presence of both "masculine" and "feminine" traits in a single person (as masculinity and femininity are defined within one's culture).

Andropause A gradual decline in testosterone levels in older men.

Anger control Personal strategies for reducing or curbing anger.

Anhedonia An inability to feel pleasure.

Anima An archetype representing the female principle.

Animal model In research, an animal whose behavior is used to discover principles that may apply to human behavior.

Animus An archetype representing the male principle.

Anorexia nervosa Active self-starvation or a sustained loss of appetite that has psychological origins.

Anosmia Loss or impairment of the sense of smell.

Antecedents Events that precede a response.

Anthropomorphic error The error of attributing human thoughts, feelings, or motives to animals, especially as a way of explaining their behavior.

Antidepressants   Mood-elevating drugs.

Antipsychotics   Drugs that, in addition to having tranquilizing effects, also tend to reduce hallucinations and delusional thinking. (Also called major tranquilizers.)

Antisocial personality   A person who lacks a conscience, is emotionally shallow, impulsive, selfish, and tends to manipulate others.

Anxiety   Apprehension, dread, or uneasiness similar to fear but based on an unclear threat.

Anxiety disorder   Disruptive feelings of fear, apprehension, or anxiety, or distortions in behavior that are anxiety related.

Anxiety reduction hypothesis   Explains the self-defeating nature of avoidance responses as a result of the reinforcing effects of relief from anxiety.

Anxiolytics   Drugs (such as Valium) that produce relaxation or reduce anxiety.

Aphasia   A speech disturbance resulting from brain damage.

Apparent-distance hypothesis   An explanation of the moon illusion stating that the horizon seems more distant than the night sky.

Applied psychology   The use of psychological principles and research methods to solve practical problems.

Approach-approach conflict   Choosing between two positive, or desirable, alternatives.

Approach-avoidance conflict   Being attracted to and repelled by the same goal or activity.

Aptitude   A capacity for learning certain abilities.

Aptitude test   A test that rates a person's potential to learn skills required by various occupations.

Archetype   A universal idea, image, or pattern, found in the collective unconscious.

Architectural psychology   Study of the effects buildings have on behavior and the design of buildings using behavioral principles.

Arousal theory   Assumes that people prefer to maintain ideal, or comfortable, levels of arousal.

Artificial intelligence   Any artificial system (often a computer program) that is capable of human-like problem solving or intelligent responding.

Assertiveness training   Instruction in how to be self-assertive.

Assessment center   A program set up within an organization to conduct in-depth evaluations of job candidates.

Assimilation   In Piaget's theory, the application of existing mental patterns to new situations (that is, the new situation is assimilated to existing mental schemes).

Association cortex   All areas of the cerebral cortex that are not primarily sensory or motor in function.

Astigmatism   Defects in the cornea, lens, or eye that cause some areas of vision to be out of focus.

Attention   Voluntarily focusing on a specific sensory input.

Attentional overload   A stressful condition caused when sensory stimulation, information, and social contacts make excessive demands on attention.

Attention-deficit/hyperactivity disorder (ADHD)   A behavioral problem characterized by short attention span, restless movement, and impaired learning capacity.

Attitude   A learned tendency to respond to people, objects, or institutions in a positive or negative way.

Attitude scale   A collection of attitudinal statements with which respondents indicate agreement or disagreement.

Attribution   The mental process of assigning causes to events. In emotion, the process of attributing arousal to a particular source.

Authenticity   In Carl Rogers's terms, the ability of a therapist to be genuine and honest about his or her own feelings.

Authoritarian parents   Parents who enforce rigid rules and demand strict obedience to authority.

Authoritarian personality   A personality pattern characterized by rigidity, inhibition, prejudice, and an excessive concern with power, authority, and obedience.

Authoritative parents   Parents who supply firm and consistent guidance combined with love and affection.

Autism   A severe disorder involving mutism, sensory spin-outs, sensory blocking, tantrums, unresponsiveness to others, and other difficulties.

Autokinetic effect   The apparent movement of a stationary pinpoint of light displayed in a darkened room.

Autonomic nervous system (ANS)   The system of nerves carrying information to and from the internal organs and glands.

Autonomy versus shame and doubt   A conflict created when growing self-control (autonomy) is pitted against feelings of shame or doubt.

Aversion therapy   Suppressing an undesirable response by associating it with aversive (painful or uncomfortable) stimuli.

Aversive stimulus   A stimulus that is painful or uncomfortable.

Avoidance learning   Learning to make a response in order to postpone or prevent discomfort.

Avoidance-avoidance conflict   Choosing between two negative, undesirable alternatives.

Avoidant attachment   An emotional bond marked by a tendency to resist commitment to others.

Axon   Fiber that carries information away from the cell body of a neuron.

Axon terminals   Branching fibers at the ends of axons.

Babbling   The repetition by infants of meaningless language sounds (including both vowel and consonant sounds).

Bait shyness   An unwillingness or hesitation on the part of animals to eat a particular food.

Barnum effect   The tendency to consider a personal description accurate if it is stated in very general terms.

Base rate   The basic rate at which an event occurs over time; the basic probability of an event.

Basic anxiety   A primary form of anxiety that arises from living in a hostile world.

Basic emotions   The first distinct emotions to emerge in infancy.

Basic needs   The first four levels of needs in Maslow's hierarchy; lower needs tend to be more potent than higher needs.

Basic suggestion effect   The tendency of hypnotized persons to carry out suggested actions as if they were involuntary.

Behavior modification   The application of learning principles to change human behavior, especially maladaptive behavior.

Behavior therapy   Any therapy designed to actively change behavior.

Behavioral assessment   Recording the frequency of various behaviors.

Behavioral contract   A formal agreement stating behaviors to be changed and consequences that apply.

Behavioral dieting   Weight reduction based on changing exercise and eating habits, rather than temporary self-starvation.

Behavioral genetics The study of inherited behavioral traits and tendencies.

Behavioral medicine The study of behavioral factors in medicine, physical illness, and medical treatment.

Behavioral personality theory Any model of personality that emphasizes learning and observable behavior.

Behavioral risk factors Behaviors that increase the chances of disease, injury, or premature death.

Behavioral setting A smaller area within an environment whose use is well defined, such as a bus depot, waiting room, or lounge.

Behaviorism School of psychology that emphasizes the study of overt, observable behavior.

Belief component What a person thinks or believes about the object of an attitude.

Bereavement Period of emotional adjustment that follows the death of a loved one.

Beta waves Small fast brain waves associated with being awake and alert.

Beta-endorphin A natural, painkilling brain chemical similar to morphine.

Biased sample A subpart of a larger population that does not accurately reflect characteristics of the whole population.

Bilingualism An ability to speak two languages.

Binge drinking Consuming five or more drinks in a short time (four drinks for women).

Biodata Detailed biographical information about a job applicant.

Biofeedback Information given to a person about his or her ongoing bodily activities; aids voluntary regulation of bodily states.

Biological aging Physiological changes that accompany growing older.

Biological biasing effect Hypothesized effect that prenatal exposure to sex hormones has on development of the body, nervous system, and later behavior patterns.

Biological predisposition The presumed hereditary readiness of humans to learn certain skills, such as how to use language, or a readiness to behave in particular ways.

Biological rhythm Any repeating cycle of biological activity, such as sleep and waking cycles or changes in body temperature.

Bipolar disorders Emotional disorders involving both depression and mania or hypomania.

Bipolar I disorder A mood disorder in which a person has episodes of mania (excited, hyperactive, energetic, grandiose behavior) and also periods of deep depression.

Bipolar II disorder A mood disorder in which a person is mostly depressed (sad, despondent, guilt ridden) but has also had one or more episodes of mild mania (hypomania).

Bisexual A person romantically and erotically attracted to both men and women.

Blind spot An area of the retina lacking visual receptors.

Bottom-up processing Organizing perceptions by beginning with low-level features.

Brainstem The lowest portions of the brain, including the cerebellum, medulla, pons, and reticular formation.

Brainstorming Method of creative thinking that separates the production and evaluation of ideas.

Brainwashing Engineered or forced attitude change involving a captive audience.

Brief psychodynamic therapy A modern therapy based on psychoanalytic theory but designed to produce insights more quickly.

Brightness constancy The apparent (or relative) brightness of objects remains the same as long as they are illuminated by the same amount of light.

Broca's area A language area related to grammar and pronunciation.

Broken record A self-assertion technique involving repeating a request until it is acknowledged.

Browser Software that facilitates access to text, images, sounds, video, and other information stored in formats used on the Internet.

Bulimia nervosa Excessive eating (gorging) usually followed by self-induced vomiting and/or taking laxatives.

Burnout A job-related condition of mental, physical, and emotional exhaustion.

Bystander apathy Unwillingness of bystanders to offer help during emergencies or to become involved in others' problems.

Caffeinism Excessive consumption of caffeine, leading to dependence and a variety of physical and psychological complaints.

Cannon-Bard theory States that activity in the thalamus causes emotional feelings and bodily arousal to occur simultaneously.

Cardinal trait A personality trait so basic that all of a person's activities relate to it.

Caregiving styles Identifiable patterns of parental caretaking and interaction with children.

Case study An in-depth focus on all aspects of a single person.

Castration Surgical removal of the testicles or ovaries.

Cataplexy A sudden temporary paralysis of the muscles.

Catatonic schizophrenia Schizophrenia marked by stupor, rigidity, unresponsiveness, posturing, mutism, and, sometimes, agitated, purposeless behavior.

Causation The act of causing some effect.

Central nervous system (CNS) The brain and spinal cord.

Central tendency The tendency for a majority of scores to fall in the midrange of possible values.

Central traits The core traits that characterize an individual personality.

Cerebellum A brain structure that controls posture and coordination.

Cerebral cortex The outer layer of the cerebrum.

Character Personal characteristics that have been judged or evaluated; a person's desirable or undesirable qualities.

Chromosomes Thread-like "colored bodies" in the nucleus of each cell that are made up of DNA.

Chronological age A person's age in years.

Circadian rhythms Cyclical changes in bodily functions and arousal levels that vary on a schedule approximating a 24-hour day.

Clairvoyance The purported ability to perceive events at a distance or through physical barriers.

Classical conditioning A form of learning in which reflex responses are associated with new stimuli.

Client-centered (or person-centered) therapy A nondirective therapy based on insights gained from conscious thoughts and feelings; emphasizes accepting one's true self.

Climacteric A point during late middle age when males experience a significant change in health, vigor, or appearance.

Clinical case study   A detailed investigation of a single person, especially one suffering from some injury or disease.

Clinical method   Studying psychological problems and therapies in clinical settings.

Clinical psychologist   A psychologist who specializes in the treatment of psychological and behavioral disturbances or who does research on such disturbances.

Coefficient of correlation   A statistical index ranging from −1.00 to +1.00 that indicates the direction and degree of correlation.

Coercive power   Social power based on the ability to punish others.

Cognition   The process of thinking or mentally processing information (images, concepts, words, rules, and symbols).

Cognitive behaviorism   An approach that combines behavioral principles with cognition (perception, thinking, anticipation) to explain behavior.

Cognitive dissonance   An uncomfortable clash between self-image, thoughts, beliefs, attitudes, or perceptions and one's behavior.

Cognitive interview   Use of various cues and strategies to improve the memory of eyewitnesses.

Cognitive learning   Higher level learning involving thinking, knowing, understanding, and anticipation.

Cognitive map   Internal images or other mental representations of an area (maze, city, campus, and so forth) that underlie an ability to choose alternative paths to the same goal.

Cognitive therapy   A therapy directed at changing the maladaptive thoughts, beliefs, and feelings that underlie emotional and behavioral problems.

Collective unconscious   A mental storehouse for unconscious ideas and images shared by all humans.

Color blindness   A total inability to perceive colors.

Color weakness   An inability to distinguish some colors.

Common traits   Personality traits that are shared by most members of a particular culture.

Community health campaign   A community-wide education program that provides information about how to lessen risk factors and promote health.

Community mental health center   A facility offering a wide range of mental health services, such as prevention, counseling, consultation, and crisis intervention.

Comparison level   A personal standard used to evaluate rewards and costs in a social exchange.

Compensation   Counteracting a real or imagined weakness by emphasizing desirable traits or seeking to excel in the area of weakness or in other areas.

Compliance   Bending to the requests of a person who has little or no authority or other form of social power.

Computer simulations   Computer programs that mimic some aspect of human thinking, decision making, or problem solving.

Concentrative meditation   Mental exercise based on attending to a single object or thought.

Concept   An idea representing a category of related objects or events.

Concept formation   The process of classifying information into meaningful categories.

Conceptual rule   A formal rule for deciding if an object or event is an example of a particular concept.

Concrete operational stage   Period of intellectual development during which children become able to use the concepts of time, space, volume, and number, but in ways that remain simplified and concrete, rather than abstract.

Condensation   Combining several people, objects, or events into a single dream image.

Conditioned emotional response (CER)   An emotional response that has been linked to a previously nonemotional stimulus by classical conditioning.

Conditioned response (CR)   A learned response elicited by a conditioned stimulus.

Conditioned stimulus (CS)   A stimulus that evokes a response because it has been repeatedly paired with an unconditioned stimulus.

Conditioning chamber   An apparatus designed to study operant conditioning in animals; a Skinner box.

Conditions of worth   Internal standards used to judge the value of one's thoughts, actions, feelings, or experiences.

Conduct disorder   A pattern in which children consistently violate rules and behave aggressively and destructively.

Conductive hearing loss   Poor transfer of sounds from the eardrum to the inner ear.

Cones   Visual receptors for colors and daylight visual acuity.

Conflict   A stressful condition that occurs when a person must choose between incompatible or contradictory alternatives.

Conformity   Bringing one's behavior into agreement or harmony with norms or with the behavior of others in a group in the absence of any direct pressure.

Congenital problems   Problems or defects that originate during prenatal development in the womb.

Conjunctive concept   A class of objects that have two or more features in common. (For example, to qualify as an example of the concept an object must be both red *and* triangular.)

Connotative meaning   The subjective, personal, or emotional meaning of a word or concept.

Conscience   The part of the superego that causes guilt when its standards are not met.

Conscious   Region of the mind that includes all mental contents a person is aware of at any given moment.

Consciousness   Mental awareness of sensations, perceptions, memories, and feelings.

Consequences   Effects that follow a response.

Conservation   In Piaget's theory, mastery of the concept that the weight, mass, and volume of matter remains unchanged (is conserved) even when the shape or appearance of objects changes.

Consistency   With respect to child discipline, the maintenance of stable rules of conduct.

Consolidation   Process by which relatively permanent memories are formed in the brain.

Constructive processing   Reorganizing or updating memories on the basis of logic, reasoning, or the addition of new information.

Contact comfort   A pleasant and reassuring feeling human and animal infants get from touching or clinging to something soft and warm, usually their mother.

Context   Information surrounding a stimulus.

Continuous reinforcement   A schedule in which every correct response is followed by a reinforcer.

Control   Altering conditions that influence behavior.

Control group   In a controlled experiment, the group of subjects exposed to all experimental conditions or variables *except* the independent variable.

Control questions   In a polygraph exam, questions that almost always provoke anxiety.

Conventional moral reasoning   Moral thinking based on a desire to please others or to follow accepted rules and values.

Convergent thinking   Thinking directed toward discovery of a single established correct answer; conventional thinking.

Conversion disorder   A bodily symptom that mimics a physical disability but is actually caused by anxiety or emotional distress.

Conviction   Beliefs that are important to a person and that evoke strong emotion.

Cooing   Spontaneous repetition of vowel sounds by infants.

Cooperative play   Play in which two or more children must coordinate their actions; if children don't cooperate the game ends.

Coping statements   Reassuring, self-enhancing statements that are used to stop self-critical thinking.

Correlation   The existence of a consistent, systematic relationship between two events, measures, or variables.

Correlational method   Making measurements to discover relationships between events.

Correlational study   A nonexperimental study designed to measure the degree of relationship (if any) between two or more events, measures, or variables.

Corticalization   An increase in the relative size of the cerebral cortex.

Counseling psychologist   A psychologist who specializes in the treatment of milder emotional and behavioral disturbances.

Counselor   A mental health professional who specializes in helping people with problems not involving serious mental disorder; for example, marriage counselors, career counselors, or school counselors.

Counterirritation   Using mild pain to block more intense or long-lasting pain.

Covert reinforcement   Using positive imagery to reinforce desired behavior.

Covert sensitization   Use of aversive imagery to reduce the occurrence of an undesired response.

Cranial nerves   Major nerves that leave the brain without passing through the spinal cord.

Creative self   The "artist" in each of us that creates a unique identity and style of life.

Cretinism   Stunted growth and mental retardation caused by an insufficient supply of thyroid hormone.

Crisis intervention   Skilled management of a psychological emergency.

Critical incidents   Situations that arise in a job, with which a competent worker must be able to cope.

Critical situations   Situations during childhood that are capable of leaving a lasting imprint on personality.

Critical thinking   An ability to evaluate, compare, analyze, critique, and synthesize information.

Cross-stimulation effect   In group problem solving, the tendency of one person's ideas to trigger ideas from others.

Crowding   A subjective feeling of being overstimulated by a loss of privacy or by the nearness of others (especially when social contact with them is unavoidable).

Crystallized abilities   Abilities that a person has intentionally learned; accumulated knowledge and skills.

CT scan   Computed tomography scan; a computer-enhanced X-ray image of the brain or body.

Cue   An external stimuli that guides responses, especially by signaling the presence or absence of reinforcement.

Cult   A group that professes great devotion to some person and follows that person almost without question; cult members are typically victimized by their leaders in various ways.

Cultural relativity   The idea that behavior must be judged relative to the values of the culture in which it occurs.

Culturally skilled therapist   A therapist who has the awareness, knowledge, and skills necessary to treat clients from diverse cultural backgrounds.

Culture   An ongoing pattern of life, characterizing a society at a given point in history.

Culture-fair test   A test (such as an intelligence test) designed to minimize the importance of skills and knowledge that may be more common in some cultures than in others.

Curve of forgetting   A graph that shows the amount of memorized information remembered after varying lengths of time.

Curvilinear relationship   A relationship that forms a curved line when graphed.

Cyclothymic disorder   Moderate manic and depressive behavior that persists for 2 years or more.

Dark adaptation   Increased retinal sensitivity to light.

Daydream   A vivid waking fantasy.

Death-qualified jury   A jury composed of people who favor the death penalty or at least are indifferent to it.

Decay   When referring to memory, the fading or weakening of memories assumed to occur when memory traces become weaker.

Declarative memory   That part of long-term memory containing specific factual information.

Deductive thought   Thought that applies a general set of rules to specific situations; for example, using the laws of gravity to predict the behavior of a single falling object.

Deep lesioning   Removal of tissue within the brain by use of an electrode.

Deep sleep   Stage 4 sleep; the deepest form of normal sleep.

Defense mechanism   A habitual and often unconscious psychological process used to reduce anxiety.

Deinstitutionalization   Reduced use of full-time commitment to mental institutions to treat mental disorders.

Delayed speech   Speech that begins well after the normal age for language development has passed.

Delta waves   Large, slow brain waves that occur in deeper sleep (stages 3 and 4).

Delusion   A false belief held against all contrary evidence.

Delusional disorder   A psychosis marked by severe delusions of grandeur, jealousy, persecution, or similar preoccupations.

Dementia   Serious mental impairment in old age caused by physical deterioration of the brain.

Demonology   In medieval Europe, the study of demons and the treatment of persons "possessed" by demons.

Dendrites   Neuron fibers that receive incoming messages.

Denial   Protecting oneself from an unpleasant reality by refusing to perceive it.

Denotative meaning   The exact, dictionary definition of a word or concept; its objective meaning.

Density   The number of people in a given space or, inversely, the amount of space available to each person.

Dependent variable   In an experiment, the condition (usually a behavior) that is affected by the independent variable.

Depressant A substance that decreases activity in the body and nervous system.

Depression A state of despondency marked by feelings of powerlessness and hopelessness.

Depressive disorders Emotional disorders primarily involving sadness, despondency, and depression.

Deprivation In development, the loss or withholding of normal stimulation, nutrition, comfort, love, and so forth; a condition of lacking.

Depth cues Perceptual features that impart information about distance and three-dimensional space.

Depth perception The ability to see three-dimensional space and to accurately judge distances.

Description In scientific research, the process of naming and classifying.

Descriptive statistics Mathematical tools used to describe and summarize numeric data.

Desensitization A reduction in emotional sensitivity to a stimulus. Can be used to deliberately reduce fear or anxiety by repeatedly exposing a person to emotional stimuli while the person is deeply relaxed.

Determinism The idea that all behavior has prior causes that would completely explain one's choices and actions if all such causes were known.

Detoxification In the treatment of alcoholism, the withdrawal of the patient from alcohol.

Developmental level An individual's current state of physical, emotional, and intellectual development.

Developmental milestone A significant turning point or marker in personal development.

Developmental psychology The study of progressive changes in behavior and abilities from conception to death.

Developmental task Any skill that must be mastered, or personal change that must take place, for optimal development.

Deviation IQ An IQ obtained statistically from a person's relative standing in his or her age group; that is, how far above or below average the person's score was relative to other scores.

Diagnostic interview An interview used to find out how a person is feeling and what complaints or symptoms he or she has.

Difference threshold A change in stimulus intensity that is detectable to an observer.

Diffusion of responsibility Spreading the responsibility to act among several people; reduces the likelihood that help will be given to a person in need.

Direct instruction Presentation of factual information by lecture, demonstration, and rote practice.

Direct observation Assessing behavior through direct surveillance.

Discovery learning Learning based on insight and understanding.

Discrimination Treating members of various social groups differently in circumstances where their rights or treatment should be identical.

Discriminative stimuli Stimuli that precede rewarded and nonrewarded responses in operant conditioning.

Disease-prone personality A personality type associated with poor health; marked by persistent negative emotions, including anxiety, depression, and hostility.

Disengagement theory of aging Theory stating that it is normal for older people to withdraw from society and from roles they held earlier.

Dishabituation A reversal of habituation.

Disinhibition The removal of inhibition; results in acting out behavior that normally would be restrained.

Disjunctive concept A concept defined by the presence of at least one of several possible features. (For example, to qualify an object must be either blue *or* circular.)

Disorganized schizophrenia Schizophrenia marked by incoherence, grossly disorganized behavior, bizarre thinking, and flat or grossly inappropriate emotions.

Displaced aggression Redirecting aggression to a target other than the actual source of one's frustration.

Displacement Directing emotions or actions toward safe or unimportant dream images.

Dissociative amnesia Loss of memory (partial or complete) for important information related to personal identity.

Dissociative disorder Temporary amnesia, multiple personality, or depersonalization.

Dissociative fugue Sudden travel away from home, plus confusion about one's personal identity.

Dissociative identity disorder The presence of two or more distinct personalities (multiple personality).

Disuse Theory that memory traces weaken when memories are not periodically used or retrieved.

Divergent thought Thinking that produces many ideas or alternatives; a major element in original or creative thought.

Divided attention Allotting mental space or effort to various tasks or parts of a task.

DNA Deoxyribonucleic acid, a molecular structure that contains coded genetic information.

Dogmatism An unwarranted positiveness or certainty in matters of belief or opinion.

Dominant gene A gene whose influence will be expressed each time the gene is present.

Dominant hemisphere A term usually applied to the side of a person's brain that produces language.

Door-in-the-face effect The tendency for a person who has refused a major request to subsequently be more likely to comply with a minor request.

Double approach-avoidance conflict Being simultaneously attracted to and repelled by each of two alternatives.

Double standard Applying different standards for judging the appropriateness of male and female sexual behavior.

Double-blind experiment An arrangement in which both subjects and experimenters are unaware of whether subjects are in the experimental group or the control group.

Down syndrome A genetic disorder caused by the presence of an extra chromosome; results in mental retardation.

Downward comparison Comparing yourself with a person who ranks lower than you on some dimension.

Dream processes Mental filters that hide the true meanings of dreams.

Dream symbols Images in dreams that serve as visible signs of hidden ideas, desires, impulses, emotions, relationships, and so forth.

Drive The psychological expression of internal needs or valued goals. For example, hunger, thirst, or a drive for success.

Drug interaction A combined effect of two drugs that exceeds the addition of one drug's effects to the other.

Drug tolerance A reduction in the body's response to a drug.

Dynamic touch Touch experienced when the body is in motion; a combination of sensations from skin receptors, muscles, and joints.

Dyslexia An inability to read with understanding, often caused by a tendency to misread letters (by seeing their mirror images, for instance).

Dyspareunia Genital pain before, during, or after sexual intercourse.

Dysthymic disorder Moderate depression that persists for 2 years or more.

Early childhood education program Programs that provide stimulating intellectual experiences, typically for disadvantaged preschoolers.

Echo A brief continuation of sensory activity in the auditory system after a sound is heard.

Echolalia A compulsion, sometimes observed in autistic children, to repeat everything that is said.

Educational psychology The field that seeks to understand how people learn and how teachers instruct.

Ego The executive part of personality that directs rational behavior.

Ego ideal The part of the superego representing ideal behavior; a source of pride when its standards are met.

Egocentric thought Thought that is self-centered and fails to consider the viewpoints of others.

Eidetic imagery The ability to retain a "projected" mental image long enough to use it as a source of information.

Ejaculation The release of sperm and seminal fluid by the male at the time of orgasm.

Elaborative rehearsal Rehearsal that links new information with existing memories and knowledge.

Electra conflict A girl's sexual attraction to her father and feelings of rivalry with her mother.

Electrical stimulation of the brain (ESB) Direct electrical stimulation and activation of brain tissue.

Electroconvulsive shock (ECS) An electric current passed directly through the brain, producing a convulsion.

Electroconvulsive therapy (ECT) A treatment for severe depression, consisting of an electric shock passed directly through the brain, which induces a convulsion.

Electrode Any device (such as a wire, needle, or metal plate) used to electrically stimulate nerve tissue or to record its activity.

Electroencephalograph (EEG) A device that detects, amplifies, and records electrical activity in the brain.

Emblems Gestures that have widely understood meanings within a particular culture.

Emotion A state characterized by physiological arousal, changes in facial expression, gestures, posture, and subjective feelings.

Emotional appraisal Evaluating the personal meaning of a stimulus or situation.

Emotional attachment An especially close emotional bond that infants form with their parents, caregivers, or others.

Emotional component One's feelings toward the object of an attitude.

Emotional expression Outward signs that an emotion is occurring.

Emotional feelings The private, subjective experience of having an emotion.

Emotional intelligence Emotional competence, including empathy, self-control, self-awareness, and other skills.

Emotion-focused coping Managing or controlling one's emotional reaction to a stressful or threatening situation.

Empathic arousal Emotional arousal that occurs when you feel some of another person's pain, fear, or anguish.

Empathy A capacity for taking another's point of view; the ability to feel what another is feeling.

Empathy-helping relationship Observation that we are most likely to help someone else when we feel emotions such as empathy and compassion.

Empty nest syndrome Psychological disturbance experienced by some women after their last child leaves home.

Encoding Converting information into a form in which it will be retained in memory.

Encoding failure Failure to store sufficient information to form a useful memory.

Encopresis A lack of bowel control; "soiling."

Encounter group A group experience that emphasizes intensely honest interchanges among participants regarding feelings and reactions to one another.

Endocrine system Glands whose secretions pass directly into the bloodstream or lymph system.

Endogenous depression Depression that appears to be produced from within (perhaps by chemical imbalances in the brain), rather than as a reaction to life events.

Engineering psychology (human factors engineering) A specialty concerned with making machines and work environments compatible with human perceptual and physical capacities.

Engram A "memory trace" in the brain.

Enrichment Deliberately making an environment more novel, complex, and perceptually or intellectually stimulating.

Enuresis An inability to control urination, particularly with regard to bed-wetting.

Environment ("nurture") The sum of all external conditions affecting development, including especially the effects of learning.

Environmental assessment Measurement and analysis of the effects an environment has on the behavior of people within that environment.

Environmental psychology The formal study of how environments affect behavior.

Epinephrine (adrenaline) An adrenal hormone that tends to arouse the body; epinephrine is associated with fear.

Episodic drive A drive that occurs in distinct episodes.

Episodic memory A subpart of declarative memory that records personal experiences that are linked with specific times and places.

Equal-status contact Social interaction that occurs on an equal footing, without obvious differences in power or status.

Erectile disorder An inability to maintain an erection for lovemaking.

Erogenous zones Areas of the body that produce pleasure and/or provoke erotic desire.

Eros Freud's name for the "life instincts."

Escape Reducing discomfort by leaving frustrating situations or by psychologically withdrawing from them.

Escape learning Learning to make a response in order to end an aversive stimulus.

Estrogen Any of a number of female sex hormones.

Estrus Changes in the sexual drives of animals that create a desire for mating; particularly used to refer to females in heat.

Ethnocentrism Placing one's own group or race at the center—that is, tending to reject all other groups but one's own.

Ethologist A person who studies the natural behavior patterns of animals.

Eugenics Selective breeding for desirable characteristics.

Evolutionary psychology Study of the evolutionary origins of human behavior patterns.

Excitement phase The first phase of sexual response, indicated by initial signs of sexual arousal.

Existential therapy An insight therapy that focuses on the elemental problems of existence, such as death, meaning, choice, and responsibility; emphasizes making courageous life choices.

Expectancy Anticipation about the effect a response will have, especially regarding reinforcement.

Expectancy An anticipation concerning future events or relationships.

Experiential intelligence Specialized knowledge and skills acquired through learning and experience.

Experiment A formal trial undertaken to confirm or disconfirm a fact or principle.

Experimental group In a controlled experiment, the group of subjects exposed to the independent variable or experimental condition.

Experimental method Investigating behavior through controlled experimentation.

Experimenter effect Changes in subjects' behavior caused by the unintended influence of an experimenter's actions.

Expert power Social power derived from possession of knowledge or expertise.

Expert systems Computer programs designed to respond as a human expert would; programs based on the knowl-edge and rules that underlie human expertise in specific topics.

Explicit memory A memory that a person is aware of having; a memory that is consciously retrieved.

Expressive behaviors Behaviors that express or communicate emotion or personal feelings.

External cause A cause of behavior that is assumed to lie outside a person.

Extinction The weakening of a conditioned response through removal of reinforcement.

Extracellular thirst Thirst caused by a reduction in the volume of fluids found between body cells.

Extraneous variables Conditions or factors excluded from influencing the outcome of an experiment.

Extrasensory perception (ESP) The purported ability to perceive events in ways that cannot be explained by known capacities of the sensory organs.

Extrinsic motivation Motivation based on obvious external rewards, obligations, or similar factors.

Extrovert A person whose attention is directed outward; a bold, outgoing person.

Eye movement desensitization and reprocessing (EMDR) A technique for reducing fear or anxiety; based on holding upsetting thoughts in mind while rapidly moving the eyes from side to side.

Facial agnosia An inability to perceive familiar faces.

Facial feedback hypothesis States that sensations from facial expressions help define what emotion a person feels.

Fallacy of positive instances The tendency to remember or notice information that fits one's expectations, while forgetting discrepancies.

Familial retardation Mild mental retardation associated with homes that are intellectually, nutritionally, and emotionally impoverished.

Family therapy Technique in which all family members participate, both individually and as a group, to change destructive relationships and communication patterns.

Fantasy Fulfilling unmet desires in imagined achievements or activities.

Feedback Information returned to a person about the effects a response has had; also known as knowledge of results.

Feeling of knowing A feeling that allows people to predict beforehand whether they will be able to remember something.

Female orgasmic disorder A persistent inability to reach orgasm during lovemaking.

Female sexual arousal disorder A lack of physical arousal to sexual stimulation.

Figure-ground organization Part of a stimulus appears to stand out as an object (figure) against a less prominent background (ground).

Five-factor model Proposes that there are five universal dimensions of personality.

Fixation (cognition) In problem solving, a tendency to repeat wrong solutions or faulty responses, especially as a result of becoming blind to alternatives.

Fixation (Freudian) A lasting conflict developed as a result of frustration or overindulgence.

Fixed interval (FI) schedule A reinforcer is given only when a correct response is made after a set amount of time has passed since the last reinforced response. Responses made during the time interval are not reinforced.

Fixed ratio (FR) schedule A set number of correct responses must be made to get a reinforcer. For example, a reinforcer is given for every four correct responses.

Flashbulb memories Memories created at times of high emotion that seem especially vivid.

Flexibility In tests of creativity, flexibility is indicated by the number of different types of solutions produced.

Flextime A work schedule that allows flexible starting and quitting times.

Fluency In tests of creativity, fluency refers to the total number of solutions produced.

Fluid abilities Innate, non-learned abilities based on perceptual, motor, or intellectual speed and flexibility.

fMRI scan Functional magnetic resonance imaging that records brain activity.

Foot-in-the-door effect The tendency for a person who has first complied with a small request to be more likely later to fulfill a larger request.

Forced teaching Accelerated learning at a pace dictated by an adult.

Forcible rape Sexual intercourse carried out against the victim's will, under the threat of violence or bodily injury.

Foreclosed identity The result of shutting down personal growth.

Formal operations stage Period of intellectual development characterized by thinking that includes abstract, theoretical, and hypothetical ideas.

Fovea An area at the center of the retina containing only cones.

Fragile-X syndrome A genetic form of mental retardation caused by a defect in the X chromosome.

Frame of reference An internal perspective relative to which events are perceived and evaluated.

Framing In thought, the terms in which a problem is stated or the way that it is structured.

Fraternal twins Twins conceived from two separate eggs.

Free association In psychoanalysis, the technique of having a client say anything that comes to mind, regardless of how embarrassing or unimportant it may seem.

Free will The idea that human beings are capable of freely making choices or decisions.

Frequency distribution A table that divides an entire range of scores into a series of classes and then records the number of scores that fall into each class.

Frequency polygon A graph of a frequency distribution in which the number of scores falling in each class is represented by points on a line.

Frequency theory Holds that tones up to 4,000 hertz are converted to nerve impulses that match the frequency of each tone.

Frontal lobes A brain area associated with movement, the sense of smell, and higher mental functions.

Frustration A negative emotional state that occurs when one is prevented from reaching a goal.

Frustration-aggression hypothesis States that frustration tends to lead to aggression.

Functional fixedness A rigidity in problem solving caused by an inability to see new uses for familiar objects.

Functional solution A detailed, practical, and workable solution.

Functionalism School of psychology concerned with how behavior and mental abilities help people adapt to their environments.

Fundamental attribution error The tendency to attribute the behavior of others to internal causes (personality, likes, and so forth).

Galvanic skin response (GSR) A change in the electrical resistance (or inversely, the conductance) of the skin, due to sweating.

Gate control theory Proposes that pain messages pass through neural "gates" in the spinal cord.

Gender bias (in research) A tendency for females and female issues to be underrepresented in research, psychological or otherwise.

Gender identity One's personal, private sense of maleness or femaleness.

Gender Psychological and social characteristics associated with being male or female; defined especially by one's gender identity and learned gender roles.

Gender role The pattern of behaviors that are regarded as "male" or "female" by one's culture; sometimes also referred to as a sex role.

Gender role socialization The process of learning gender behaviors considered appropriate for one's sex in a given culture.

Gender role stereotypes Oversimplified and widely held beliefs about the basic characteristics of men and women.

General adaptation syndrome (G.A.S.) A series of bodily reactions to prolonged stress; occurs in three stages: alarm, resistance, and exhaustion.

General intelligence test A test that measures a wide variety of mental abilities.

General solution A solution that correctly states the requirements for success but not in enough detail for further action.

Generalized anxiety disorder The person is in a chronic state of tension and worries about work, relationships, ability, or impending disaster.

Generativity versus stagnation A conflict of middle adulthood in which self-interest is countered by an interest in guiding the next generation.

Genes Specific areas on a strand of DNA that carry hereditary information.

Genetic disorders Problems caused by defects in the genes or by inherited characteristics.

Genetic sex Sex as indicated by the presence of *XX* (female) or *XY* (male) chromosomes.

Genital sex Sex as indicated by the presence of male or female genitals.

Genital stage Period of full psychosexual development, marked by the attainment of mature adult sexuality.

Gerontologist One who scientifically studies aging and its effects.

Gestalt psychology A school of psychology emphasizing the study of thinking, learning, and perception in whole units, not by analysis into parts.

Gestalt therapy An approach that focuses on immediate experience and awareness to help clients rebuild thinking, feeling, and acting into connected wholes; emphasizes the integration of fragmented experiences.

g-factor A general ability factor or core of general intellectual ability that involves reasoning, problem-solving ability, knowledge, memory, and successful adaptation to one's surroundings.

Giftedness Either the possession of a high IQ or special talents or aptitudes.

Goal The target or objective of motivated behavior.

Gonadal sex Sex as indicated by the presence of ovaries (female) or testes (male).

Gonads The primary sex glands; the testes in males and ovaries in females.

Grammar A set of rules for combining language units into meaningful speech or writing.

Graphical statistics Techniques for presenting numbers pictorially, often by plotting them on a graph.

Grief An intense emotional state that follows the death of a lover, friend, or relative.

Group cohesiveness The degree of attraction among group members or their commitment to remaining in the group.

Group intelligence test Any intelligence test that can be administered to a group of people with minimal supervision.

Group prejudice Prejudice held out of conformity to group views.

Group sanctions Rewards and punishments (such as approval or disapproval) administered by groups to enforce conformity among members.

Group structure The network of roles, communication pathways, and power in a group.

Group therapy Psychotherapy conducted in a group setting to make therapeutic use of group dynamics.

Groupthink A compulsion by members of decision-making groups to maintain agreement, even at the cost of critical thinking.

Growth hormone A hormone, secreted by the pituitary gland, that promotes bodily growth.

Growth needs In Maslow's hierarchy, the higher level needs associated with self-actualization.

Growth spurt An often dramatic acceleration in physical growth that coincides with puberty.

Guided imagery Intentional visualization of images that are calming, relaxing, or beneficial in other ways.

Gustation The sense of taste.

Habit A deeply ingrained, learned pattern of behavior.

Habituation A decrease in perceptual response to a repeated stimulus.

Hair cells Receptor cells within the cochlea that transduce vibrations into nerve impulses.

Half-way house A community-based facility for individuals making the transition from an institution (mental hospital, prison, and so forth) to independent living.

Hallucination An imaginary sensation, such as seeing, hearing, or smelling things that don't exist in the real world.

Hallucinogen A substance that alters or distorts sensory impressions.

Halo effect The tendency to generalize a favorable or unfavorable impression to unrelated details of personality.

Handedness A preference for the right or left hand in most activities.

Hardy personality A personality style associated with superior stress resistance.

Hassle (Microstressor) Any distressing, day-to-day annoyance.

Health psychology Study of the ways in which behavioral principles can be used to prevent illness and promote health.

Heredity ("nature") The transmission of physical and psychological characteristics from parents to offspring through genes.

Heterosexism The belief that heterosexuality is better or more natural than homosexuality.

Heterosexual A person romantically and erotically attracted to members of the opposite sex.

Heuristic Any strategy or technique that aids problem solving, especially by limiting the number of possible solutions to be tried.

Hidden observer A detached part of the hypnotized person's awareness that silently observes events.

Hierarchy A rank-ordered series of higher and lower amounts, levels, degrees, or steps.

Hierarchy of human needs Abraham Maslow's ordering of needs, based on their presumed strength or potency.

Higher order conditioning Classical conditioning in which a conditioned stimulus is used to reinforce further learning; that is, a CS is used as if it were a US.

Hippocampus A part of the limbic system associated with emotion and the transfer of information from short-term memory to long-term memory.

Histogram A graph of a frequency distribution in which the number of scores falling in each class is represented by vertical bars.

Homeostasis A steady state of bodily equilibrium.

Homogamy Marriage of two people who are similar to one another.

Homosexual A person romantically and erotically attracted to same-sex persons.

Honesty test A paper-and-pencil test designed to detect attitudes, beliefs, and behavior patterns that predispose a person to dishonest behavior.

Hormonal sex Sex as indicated by a preponderance of estrogens (female) or androgens (male) in the body.

Hormone A glandular secretion that affects bodily functions or behavior.

Human growth sequence The pattern of physical development from conception to death.

Humanism An approach to psychology that focuses on human experience, problems, potentials, and ideals.

Hydrocephaly A buildup of cerebrospinal fluid within brain cavities.

Hyperopia Difficulty focusing nearby objects (farsightedness).

Hypersomnia Excessive day-time sleepiness.

Hypnagogic images Vivid mental images that may occur just as one enters stage 1 sleep.

Hypnosis An altered state of consciousness characterized by narrowed attention and increased suggestibility.

Hypnotic susceptibility One's capacity for becoming hypnotized.

Hypoactive sexual desire A persistent, upsetting loss of sexual desire.

Hypochondriac A person who complains about illnesses that appear to be imaginary.

Hypochondriasis A preoccupation with fears of having a serious disease. Ordinary physical signs are interpreted as proof that the person has a disease, but no physical disorder can be found.

Hypothalamus A small area at the base of the brain that regulates many aspects of motivation and emotion, especially hunger, thirst, and sexual behavior.

Hypothesis The predicted outcome of an experiment or an educated guess about the relationship between variables.

Hypothetical possibilities Suppositions, guesses, or projections.

Icon A mental image or visual representation.

Id The primitive part of personality that remains unconscious, supplies energy, and demands pleasure.

Ideal self An idealized image of oneself (the person one would like to be).

Identical twins Twins who develop from a single egg and have identical genes.

Identification Feeling emotionally connected to a person and seeing oneself as like him or her.

Identification Taking on some of the characteristics of an admired person, usually as a way of compensating for perceived personal weaknesses or faults.

Identity versus role confusion A conflict of adolescence, involving the need to establish a personal identity.

Illogical thought Thought that is intuitive, haphazard, or irrational.

Illusion A misleading or distorted perception.

Illustrators Gestures people use to illustrate what they are saying.

Image Most often, a mental representation that has picture-like qualities; an icon.

Imagery rehearsal Mentally rehearsing and changing a nightmare in an attempt to prevent it from reoccurring.

Imaginary audience The group of people a person imagines is watching (or will watch) his or her actions.

I-message A message that states the effect someone else's behavior has on you.

Imitation An attempt to match one's own behavior to another person's behavior.

Immune system System that mobilizes bodily defenses (such as white blood cells) against invading microbes and other disease agents.

Implicit memory A memory that a person does not know exists; a memory that is retrieved unconsciously.

Imprinting A rapid and relatively permanent type of learning that occurs during a limited period early in life.

Inattentional blindness Failure to perceive a stimulus that is in plain view, but not the focus of attention.

In-basket test A testing procedure that simulates the individual decision-making challenges that executives face.

Incentive value The value of a goal above and beyond its ability to fill a need.

Incongruence State that exists when there is a discrepancy between one's experiences and self-image or between one's self-image and ideal self.

Incongruent person A person who has an inaccurate self-image or whose self-image differs greatly from the ideal self.

Incremental problem solving Thinking marked by a series of small steps that lead to an original solution.

Independent variable In an experiment, the condition being investigated as a possible cause of some change in behavior. The values that this variable takes are chosen by the experimenter.

Individual intelligence test A test of intelligence designed to be given to a single individual by a trained specialist.

Individual traits Personality traits that define a person's unique individual qualities.

Individuating information Information that helps define a person as an individual, rather than as a member of a group or social category.

Inductive thought Thinking in which a general rule or principle is gathered from a series of specific examples; for instance, inferring the laws of gravity by observing many falling objects.

Industrial-organizational psychology A field that focuses on the psychology of work and on behavior within organizations.

Industry versus inferiority A conflict in middle childhood centered around lack of support for industrious behavior, which can result in feelings of inferiority.

Inferential statistics Mathematical tools used for decision making, for generalizing from small samples, and for drawing conclusions.

Information bits Meaningful units of information, such as numbers, letters, words, or phrases.

Information chunks Information bits grouped into larger units.

Informational view Perspective that explains learning in terms of information imparted by events in the environment.

In-group A group with which a person identifies.

Initiative versus guilt A conflict between learning to take initiative and overcoming feelings of guilt about doing so.

Insanity A legal term that refers to a mental inability to manage one's affairs or to be aware of the consequences of one's actions.

Insecure-ambivalent attachment An anxious emotional bond marked by both a desire to be with a parent or caregiver and some resistance to being reunited.

Insecure-avoidant attachment An anxious emotional bond marked by a tendency to avoid reunion with a parent or caregiver.

Insight A sudden mental reorganization of a problem that makes the solution obvious.

Insomnia Difficulty in getting to sleep or staying asleep.

Inspection time The amount of time a person must look at a stimulus to make a correct judgment about it.

Instrumental behaviors Behaviors directed toward the achievement of some goal; behaviors that are instrumental in producing some effect.

Integrity versus despair A conflict in old age between feelings of integrity and the despair of viewing previous life events with regret.

Intellectualization Separating emotion from a threatening or anxiety-provoking situation by talking or thinking about it in impersonal "intellectual" terms.

Intelligence An overall capacity to think rationally, act purposefully, and deal effectively with the environment.

Intelligence quotient (IQ) An index of intelligence defined as a person's mental age divided by his or her chronological age and multiplied by 100.

Interference The tendency for new memories to impair retrieval of older memories, and the reverse.

Internal cause A cause of behavior assumed to lie within a person—for instance, a need, preference, or personality trait.

Internal images Mental images or visual depictions used in memory and thinking.

Internet A digital network that enables computers to communicate with one another through the phone system and other digital links.

Interpersonal attraction Social attraction to another person.

Interpretation Where pain is concerned, the meaning given to a stimulus.

Intersexual person An individual who has genitals suggestive of both sexes.

Interview (personality) A face-to-face meeting held for the purpose of gaining information about an individual's personal history, personality traits, current psychological state, and so forth.

Intimacy versus isolation The challenge of overcoming a sense of isolation by establishing intimacy with others.

Intimate distance The most private space immediately surrounding the body (up to about 18 inches from the skin).

Intracellular thirst Thirst triggered when fluid is drawn out of cells due to an increased concentration of salts and minerals outside the cell.

Intrinsic motivation Motivation that comes from within, rather than from external rewards; motivation based on personal enjoyment of a task or activity.

Introspection To look within; to examine one's own thoughts, feelings, or sensations.

Introvert A person whose attention is focused inward; a shy, reserved, self-centered person.

Intuition Quick, impulsive thought that does not make use of formal logic or clear reasoning.

Intuitive thought Thinking that makes little or no use of reasoning and logic.

Ion channels Tiny openings through the axon membrane.

Iris Circular muscle that controls the amount of light entering the eye.

Isolation Separating contradictory thoughts or feelings into "logic-tight" mental compartments so that they do not come into conflict.

James-Lange theory States that emotional feelings follow bodily arousal and come from awareness of such arousal.

Jigsaw classroom A method of reducing prejudice; each student receives only part of the information needed to complete a project or prepare for a test.

Job analysis A detailed description of the skills, knowledge, and activities required by a particular job.

Job enrichment Making a job more personally rewarding, interesting, or intrinsically motivating; typically involves increasing worker knowledge.

Job satisfaction The degree to which a person is comfortable with or satisfied with his or her work.

Just noticeable difference (JND) Any noticeable difference in a stimulus.

Just-world beliefs Belief that people generally get what they deserve.

Keyword method   As an aid to memory, using a familiar word or image to link two items.

Kinesics   Study of the meaning of body movements, posture, hand gestures, and facial expressions; commonly called body language.

Kinesthetic senses   The senses of body movement and positioning.

Knowledge of results (KR)   Informational feedback.

Language   Words or symbols, and rules for combining them, that are used for thinking and communication.

Large-group awareness training   Any of a number of programs (many of them commercialized) that claim to increase self-awareness and facilitate constructive personal change.

Latency   According to Freud, a period in childhood when psychosexual development is more or less interrupted.

Latent dream content   The hidden or symbolic meaning of a dream, as revealed by dream interpretation and analysis.

Latent learning   Learning that occurs without obvious reinforcement and that remains unexpressed until reinforcement is provided.

Lateralization   Differences between the two sides of the body; especially, differences in the abilities of the brain hemispheres.

Law of effect   Responses that lead to desirable effects are repeated; those that produce undesirable results are not.

Leaderless group discussion   A test of leadership that simulates group decision making and problem solving.

Learned helplessness   A learned inability to overcome obstacles or to avoid punishment; learned passivity and inaction to aversive stimuli.

Learning   Any relatively permanent change in behavior that can be attributed to experience.

Learning disorder   Any problem with thinking, perception, language, attention, or activity levels that tends to impair learning ability.

Learning theorist   A psychologist interested in the ways that learning shapes behavior and explains personality.

Legitimate power   Social power based on a person's position as an agent of an accepted social order.

Lexigram   A geometric shape used as a symbol for a word.

Libido   In Freudian theory, the force, primarily pleasure oriented, that energizes the personality.

Life change units (LCUs)   Numerical values assigned to each life event on the SRRS.

Life expectancy   The average number of years a person of a given sex, race, and nationality can expect to live.

Life skills training   A program that teaches stress reduction, self-protection, decision making, self-control, and social skills.

Life stages   Widely recognized periods of life corresponding to broad phases of development.

Life-span perspective   The study of continuity and change in behavior over a lifetime.

Lifestyle disease   A disease related to health-damaging personal habits.

Light sleep   Stage 1 sleep, marked by small, irregular brain waves and some alpha waves.

Liking   A relationship based on intimacy, but lacking passion and commitment.

Limbic system   A system in the forebrain that is closely linked with emotional response.

Linear relationship   A relationship that forms a straight line when graphed.

Links   Connections built into Internet sites that let you "jump" from one site to the next.

Localization of function   The research strategy of linking specific structures in the brain with specific psychological or behavioral functions.

Lock and key theory   Holds that odors are related to the shapes of chemical molecules.

Logical consequences   Reasonable consequences that are defined by parents.

Logical thought   Drawing conclusions on the basis of formal principles of reasoning.

Logotherapy   A form of existential therapy that emphasizes the need to find and maintain meaning in one's life.

Long sleeper   A person who averages 9 hours of sleep or more per night.

Long-term memory (LTM)   The memory system used for relatively permanent storage of meaningful information.

Low-ball technique   A strategy in which commitment is gained first to reasonable or desirable terms, which are then made less reasonable or desirable.

Lucid dream   A dream in which the dreamer feels awake and capable of normal thought and action.

Maintenance rehearsal   Silently repeating or mentally reviewing information to hold it in short-term memory.

Major depressive disorder   A mood disorder in which the person has suffered one or more intense episodes of depression.

Major mood disorders   Disorders marked by lasting extremes of mood or emotion and sometimes accompanied by psychotic symptoms.

Maladaptive behavior   Behavior that makes it difficult to adapt to the environment and meet the demands of day-to-day life.

Male orgasmic disorder   A persistent inability to reach orgasm during lovemaking.

Management by objectives   A management technique in which employees are given specific goals to meet in their work.

Management techniques   Combining praise, recognition, approval, rules, and reasoning to enforce child discipline.

Mandala   A circular design representing balance, unity, and completion.

Manifest dream content   The surface, "visible" content of a dream; dream images as they are remembered by the dreamer.

Massed practice   A practice schedule in which studying continues for long periods, without interruption.

Mastery training   Reinforcement of responses that lead to mastery of a threat or control over one's environment.

Masturbation   Self-stimulation that causes sexual pleasure or orgasm.

Maternal influences   The aggregate of all psychological effects mothers have on their children.

Maternity blues   A brief and relatively mild state of depression often experienced by mothers 2 or 3 days after giving birth.

Maturation   The physical growth and development of the body and nervous system.

Maximum life span   The biologically defined maximum number of years humans can live under optimal conditions.

Mean   A measure of central tendency calculated by adding a group of scores and then dividing by the total number of scores.

Means–ends analysis   An analysis of how to reduce the difference between the present state of affairs and a desired goal.

Mechanical solution A problem solution achieved by trial and error or by a fixed procedure based on learned rules.

Median A measure of central tendency found by arranging scores from the highest to the lowest and selecting the score that falls in the middle. That is, half the values in a group of scores fall above the median and half fall below.

Medicated birth The common practice in Western medicine of giving painkilling drugs during labor and birth.

Meditation A mental exercise for producing relaxation or heightened awareness.

Medulla The structure that connects the brain with the spinal cord and controls vital life functions.

Melatonin Hormone released by the pineal gland in response to daily cycles of light and dark.

Memory cue Any stimulus associated with a particular memory. Memory cues usually enhance retrieval.

Memory decay The fading or weakening of memories assumed to occur when memory traces become weaker.

Memory task Any task designed to test or assess memory.

Memory The mental system for receiving, encoding, storing, organizing, altering, and retrieving information.

Memory traces Physical changes in nerve cells or brain activity that take place when memories are stored.

Menopause The female "change of life" signaled by the end of regular monthly menstrual periods.

Mental age The average mental ability people display at a given age.

Mental disorder A significant impairment in psychological functioning.

Mental hospitalization Placing a person in a protected, therapeutic environment staffed by mental health professionals.

Mental images Mental pictures or visual depictions used in memory and thinking.

Mental practice Imagining a skilled performance to aid learning.

Mental retardation (developmentally disabled) The presence of a developmental disability, a formal IQ score below 70, or a significant impairment of adaptive behavior.

Mental set A predisposition to perceive or respond in a particular way.

Meta-analysis A statistical technique for combining the results of many studies on the same subject.

Metacognitive skills An ability to manage one's own thinking and problem-solving efforts.

Meta-needs In Maslow's hierarchy, needs associated with impulses for self-actualization.

Microcephaly A disorder in which the head and brain are abnormally small.

Microsleep A brief shift in brain-wave patterns to those of sleep.

Mindfulness meditation Mental exercise based on widening attention to become aware of everything experienced at any given moment.

Minnesota Multiphasic Personality Inventory-2 (MMPI-2) One of the best-known and most widely used objective personality questionnaires.

Mirror technique Observing another person re-enact one's own behavior, like a character in a play; designed to help persons see themselves more clearly.

MMPI-2 profile A graphic representation of an individual's scores on each of the primary scales of the MMPI-2.

Mnemonic Any kind of memory system or aid.

Mock jury A group that realistically simulates a courtroom jury.

Mode A measure of central tendency found by identifying the most frequently occurring score in a group of scores.

Model A person who serves as an example in observational learning.

Mood A low-intensity, long-lasting emotional state.

Mood disorder A major disturbance in mood or emotion, such as depression or mania.

Moon illusion The apparent change in size that occurs as the moon moves from the horizon (large moon) to overhead (small moon).

Moral anxiety Apprehension felt when thoughts, impulses, or actions conflict with the superego's standards.

Moral development The development of values, beliefs, and thinking abilities that act as a guide regarding what is acceptable behavior.

Morphemes The smallest meaningful units in a language, such as syllables or words.

Motherese (or parentese) A pattern of speech used when talking to infants, marked by a higher-pitched voice; short, simple sentences; repetition, slower speech; and exaggerated voice inflections.

Motivation Internal processes that initiate, sustain, and direct activities.

Motor cortex A brain area associated with control of movement.

Motor program A mental plan or model that guides skilled movement.

Motor skill A series of actions molded into a smooth and efficient performance.

MRI scan Magnetic resonance imaging; a three-dimensional image of the brain or body, based on its response to a magnetic field.

Müller-Lyer illusion Two equal-length lines tipped with inward or outward pointing V's appear to be of different lengths.

Multiculturalism Giving equal status, recognition, and acceptance to different ethnic and cultural groups.

Multimedia computerized test A test that uses a computer to present lifelike situations; test takers react to problems posed by the situations.

Multiple approach-avoidance conflict Being simultaneously attracted to and repelled by each of several alternatives.

Multiple aptitude test Test that measures two or more aptitudes.

Multiple intelligences Howard Gardner's theory that there are several specialized types of intellectual ability.

Mutual absorption With regard to romantic love, the nearly exclusive attention lovers give to one another.

Mutual interdependence A condition in which people must depend on one another to meet each person's goals.

Myelin A fatty layer coating some axons.

Myopia Difficulty focusing distant objects (nearsightedness).

Narcolepsy A serious sleep disturbance in which an individual suffers sudden, irresistible sleep attacks.

Natural clinical test A natural event that provides data on a psychological phenomenon.

Natural consequences The effects that naturally tend to follow a particular behavior.

Natural design Human factors engineering that makes use of naturally understood perceptual signals.

Natural selection Darwin's theory that evolution favors those plants and animals best suited to their living conditions.

Naturalistic observation Observing behavior as it unfolds in natural settings.

Near-death experience (NDE) A pattern of subjective experiences that may occur when a person is clinically dead and then resuscitated.

Need An internal deficiency that may energize behavior.

Need for achievement (nAch) The desire to excel or meet some internalized standard of excellence.

Need for power The desire to have social impact and control over others.

Need to affiliate The desire to associate with other people.

Negative after-potential A drop in electrical charge below the resting potential.

Negative correlation A statistical relationship in which increases in one measure are matched by decreases in the other.

Negative instance In concept learning, an object or event that does not belong to the concept class.

Negative reinforcement Occurs when a response is followed by an end to discomfort or by the removal of an unpleasant event.

Negative relationship A mathematical relationship in which increases in one measure are matched by decreases in the other.

Negative self-statements Self-critical thoughts that increase anxiety and lower performance.

Negative transfer Mastery of one task conflicts with learning or performing another.

Neo-Freudian A psychologist who accepts the broad features of Freud's theory but has revised

the theory to fit his or her own concepts.

Nerve A bundle of neuron fibers.

Nerve deafness Deafness caused by damage to the hair cells or auditory nerve.

Network model A model of memory that views it as an organized system of linked information.

Neural intelligence The innate speed and efficiency of a person's brain and nervous system.

Neurilemma A layer of cells that encases many axons.

Neurogenesis The production of new brain cells.

Neurological soft signs Subtle behavioral signs of brain dysfunction, including clumsiness, an awkward gait, poor hand–eye coordination, and other perceptual and motor problems.

Neuron An individual nerve cell.

Neuropeptides Brain chemicals, such as enkephalins and endorphins, that regulate the activity of neurons.

Neurosis An outdated term once used to refer, as a group, to anxiety disorders, somatoform disorders, dissociative disorders, and some forms of depression.

Neurotic anxiety Apprehension felt when the ego struggles to control id impulses.

Neurotransmitter Any chemical released by a neuron that alters activity in other neurons.

Neutral stimulus (NS) A stimulus that does not evoke a response.

Night blindness Blindness under conditions of low illumination.

Night terror A state of panic during NREM sleep.

Nightmare A bad dream that occurs during REM sleep.

Noise pollution Stressful and intrusive noise; usually artificially generated by machinery,

but also including noises made by animals and humans.

Noise-induced hearing loss Damage caused by exposing the hair cells to excessively loud sounds.

Nonhomeostatic drive A drive that is relatively independent of physical deprivation cycles or bodily need states.

non-REM (NREM) sleep Non–rapid eye movement sleep characteristic of stages 2, 3, and 4.

Norepinephrine An adrenal hormone that tends to arouse the body; norepinephrine is associated with anger. (Also known as noradrenaline.)

Norm (social) An accepted (but often unspoken) standard of conduct for appropriate behavior.

Norm (testing) An average score for a designated group of people.

Normal curve A bell-shaped curve characterized by a large number of scores in a middle area, tapering to very few extremely high and low scores.

Obedience Conformity to the demands of an authority.

Object permanence Concept, gained in infancy, that objects continue to exist even when they are hidden from view.

Objective test A test that gives the same score when different people correct it.

Observational learning Learning achieved by watching and imitating the actions of another or noting the consequences of those actions.

Observational record A detailed summary of observed events or a videotape of observed behavior.

Observer bias The tendency of an observer to distort observations or perceptions to match his or her expectations.

Observer effect Changes in behavior brought about by an awareness of being observed.

Obsessive-compulsive disorder An extreme preoccupation with certain thoughts and compulsive performance of certain behaviors.

Occipital lobes Portion of the cerebral cortex where vision registers in the brain.

Oedipus conflict A boy's sexual attraction to his mother, and feelings of rivalry with his father.

Olfaction The sense of smell.

Open teaching Instruction based on active teacher–student discussion.

Open-ended interview An interview in which persons are allowed to freely state their views.

Operant conditioning Learning based on the consequences of responding.

Operant extinction The weakening or disappearance of a nonreinforced operant response.

Operant reinforcer Any event that reliably increases the probability or frequency of responses it follows.

Operant stimulus discrimination The tendency to make an operant response when stimuli previously associated with reward are present and to withhold the response when stimuli associated with nonreward are present.

Operant stimulus generalization The tendency to respond to stimuli similar to those that preceded operant reinforcement.

Operational definition Defining a scientific concept by stating the specific actions or procedures used to measure it. For example, "hunger" might be defined as "the number of hours of food deprivation."

Opponent-process theory (emotional) States that a strong emotional state tends to be followed by an opposite emotional state; also, the strength of both emotional states changes over time.

Opponent-process theory (sensation) Theory of color vision based on three coding systems (red or green, yellow or blue, black or white).

Oral stage The period when infants are preoccupied with the mouth as a source of pleasure and means of expression.

Oral-aggressive personality A person who uses the mouth to express hostility by shouting, cursing, biting, and so forth. Also, one who actively exploits others.

Oral-dependent personality A person who wants to passively receive attention, gifts, love, and so forth.

Organ of Corti Center part of the cochlea, containing hair cells, canals, and membranes.

Organic mental disorder A mental or emotional problem caused by brain diseases or injuries.

Organismic valuing A natural, undistorted, full-body reaction to an experience.

Organizational citizenship Making positive contributions to the success of an organization in ways that go beyond one's job description.

Organizational culture The social climate within an organization.

Orgasm A climax and release of sexual excitement.

Orientation response Bodily changes that prepare an organism to receive information from a particular stimulus.

Originality In tests of creativity, originality refers to how novel or unusual solutions are.

Out-group A group with which a person does not identify.

Overgeneralization Blowing a single event out of proportion by extending it to a large number of unrelated situations.

Overlearning Continuing to study and learn after you first think you've mastered a topic.

Overly permissive parents Parents who give little guidance, allow too much freedom, or do not require the child to take responsibility.

Pain disorder Pain that has no identifiable physical cause and appears to be of psychological origin.

Panic disorder (with agoraphobia) A chronic state of anxiety and brief moments of sudden panic. The person fears that these panic attacks will occur in public places or unfamiliar situations.

Panic disorder (without agoraphobia) The person is in a chronic state of anxiety and also has brief moments of sudden, intense, unexpected panic.

Paranoid psychosis A delusional disorder centered especially on delusions of persecution.

Paranoid schizophrenia Schizophrenia marked by a preoccupation with delusions or by frequent auditory hallucinations related to a single theme, especially grandeur or persecution.

Paraphilias Compulsive or destructive deviations in sexual preferences or behavior.

Paraprofessional An individual who works in a near-professional capacity under the supervision of a more highly trained person.

Parapsychology The study of extranormal psychological events, such as extrasensory perception.

Parasympathetic branch A part of the autonomic nervous system that quiets the body and conserves energy.

Parasympathetic rebound Excess activity in the parasympathetic nervous system following a period of intense emotion.

Parasympathetic system A branch of the autonomic nervous system (ANS) that quiets the body.

Parental styles Identifiable patterns of parental caretaking and interaction with children.

Parentese (motherese) A pattern of speech used when talking to infants, marked by a higher-pitched voice; short, simple sentences; repetition, slower speech; and exaggerated voice inflections.

Parietal lobes Area of the brain where bodily sensations register.

Partial hospitalization An approach in which patients receive treatment at a hospital during the day, but return home at night.

Partial reinforcement A pattern in which only a portion of all responses are reinforced.

Partial reinforcement effect Responses acquired with partial reinforcement are more resistant to extinction.

Participative management An approach to management that allows employees at all levels to participate in decision making.

Passive compliance Passively bending to unreasonable demands or circumstances.

Paternal influences The aggregate of all psychological effects fathers have on their children.

Peak performance A performance during which physical, mental, and emotional states are harmonious and optimal.

Peer counselor A nonprofessional person who has learned basic counseling skills.

Peer group A group of people who share similar social status.

Percent of variance A portion of the total amount of variation in a group of scores.

Perception The mental process of organizing sensations into meaningful patterns.

Perceptual construction A mental model of external events.

Perceptual defense Resistance to perceiving threatening or disturbing stimuli.

Perceptual expectancy (or set) A readiness to perceive in a particular manner, induced by strong expectations.

Perceptual features Basic elements of a stimulus, such as lines, shapes, edges, or colors.

Perceptual habits Well-established patterns of perceptual organization and attention.

Perceptual hypothesis An initial guess regarding how to organize (perceive) a stimulus pattern.

Perceptual learning Changes in perception that can be attributed to prior experience; a result of changes in how the brain processes sensory information.

Perceptual reconstruction A mental model of external events.

Perfect negative relationship A mathematical relationship in which the correlation between two measures is -1.00.

Perfect positive relationship A mathematical relationship in which the correlation between two measures is $+1.00$.

Performance intelligence Intelligence measured by solving puzzles, assembling objects, completing pictures, and other nonverbal tasks.

Peripheral nervous system All parts of the nervous system outside the brain and spinal cord.

Peripheral vision Vision at the edges of the visual field.

Persona The "mask" or public self presented to others.

Personal distance The distance maintained when interacting with close friends (about 18 inches to 4 feet from the body).

Personal interview Formal or informal questioning of job applicants to learn their qualifications and to gain an impression of their personalities.

Personal prejudice Prejudicial attitudes held toward persons who are perceived as a direct threat to one's own interests.

Personal space An area surrounding the body that is regarded as private and subject to personal control.

Personal unconscious A mental storehouse for a single individual's unconscious thoughts.

Personality A person's unique and relatively stable behavior patterns.

Personality disorder A maladaptive personality pattern.

Personality questionnaire A paper-and-pencil test consisting of questions that reveal aspects of personality.

Personality theory A system of concepts, assumptions, ideas, and principles used to understand and explain personality.

Personality trait A stable, enduring quality that a person shows in most situations.

Personality type A style of personality defined by a group of related traits.

Personnel psychology Branch of industrial-organizational psychology concerned with testing, selection, placement, and promotion of employees.

Persuasion A deliberate attempt to change attitudes or beliefs with information and arguments.

PET scan Positron emission tomography; a computer-generated image of brain activity, based on glucose consumption in the brain.

Phallic personality A person who is vain, exhibitionistic, sensitive, and narcissistic.

Phallic stage The psychosexual stage (roughly ages 3 to 6) when a child is preoccupied with the genitals.

Phantom limb The illusory sensation that a limb still exists after it is lost through accident or amputation.

Pharmacotherapy The use of drugs to alleviate the symptoms of emotional disturbance.

Phenylketonuria A genetic disease that allows phenylpyruvic acid to accumulate in the body.

Pheromone An airborne chemical signal.

Phonemes The basic speech sounds of a language.

Phototherapy A treatment for seasonal affective disorder that involves exposure to bright, full-spectrum light.

Physical dependence Physical addiction, as indicated by the presence of drug tolerance and withdrawal symptoms.

Physical environments Natural settings, such as forests and beaches, as well as environments built by humans, such as buildings, ships, and cities.

Physiological changes (in emotion) Alterations in heart rate, blood pressure, perspiration, and other involuntary responses.

Pica Eating or chewing on inedible objects or substances such as chalk, ashes, and the like.

Pictorial depth cues Features found in paintings, drawings, and photographs that impart information about space, depth, and distance.

Pineal gland Gland in the brain that helps regulate body rhythms and sleep cycles.

Pituitary gland The "master gland" whose hormones influence other endocrine glands.

Place theory Theory that higher and lower tones excite specific areas of the cochlea.

Placebo An inactive substance given in the place of a drug in psychological research or by physicians who wish to treat a complaint by suggestion.

Placebo effect Changes in behavior due to expectations that a drug (or other treatment) will have some effect.

Plasticity The capacity of the brain to change in response to experience.

Plateau phase The second phase of sexual response during which physical arousal is further heightened.

Pleasure principle A desire for immediate satisfaction of wishes, desires, or needs.

Polygenic characteristics Personal traits or physical properties that are influenced by many genes working in combination.

Polygraph A device for recording heart rate, blood pressure, respiration, and galvanic skin response; commonly called a "lie detector."

Pons An area on the brainstem that acts as a bridge between the medulla and other structures.

Population An entire group of animals, people, or objects belonging to a particular category (for example, all college students or all married women).

Positive correlation A statistical relationship in which increases in one measure are matched by increases in the other (or decreases correspond with decreases).

Positive instance In concept learning, an object or event that belongs to the concept class.

Positive psychology The study of human strengths, virtues, and effective functioning.

Positive reinforcement Occurs when a response is followed by a reward or other positive event.

Positive relationship A mathematical relationship in which increases in one measure are matched by increases in the other (or decreases correspond with decreases).

Positive self-regard Thinking of oneself as a good, lovable, worthwhile person.

Positive transfer Mastery of one task aids learning or performing another.

Postconventional moral reasoning Moral thinking based on carefully examined and self-chosen moral principles.

Postpartum depression A mild to moderately severe depression that begins within 3 months following childbirth.

Posttraumatic stress disorder (PTSD) A psychological disturbance lasting more than 1 month following stresses that would produce anxiety in anyone who experienced them.

Power assertion The use of physical punishment or coercion to enforce child discipline.

Precognition The purported ability to accurately predict future events.

Preconscious An area of the mind containing information that can be voluntarily brought to awareness.

Preconventional moral reasoning Moral thinking based on the consequences of one's choices or actions (punishment, reward, or an exchange of favors).

Prediction An ability to accurately forecast behavior.

Prejudice A negative emotional attitude held against members of a particular group of people.

Premack principle Any high-frequency response can be used to reinforce a low-frequency response.

Premature ejaculation Ejaculation that consistently occurs before the man and his partner want it to occur.

Preoperational stage Period of intellectual development during which children begin to use language and think symbolically, yet remain intuitive and egocentric in their thought.

Prepared childbirth A collection of techniques designed to manage discomfort and facilitate birth so that the use of painkilling drugs can be avoided or minimized.

Presbyopia Farsightedness caused by aging.

Pressure A stressful condition that occurs when a person must meet urgent external demands or expectations.

Primary appraisal Deciding if a situation is relevant to oneself and if it is a threat.

Primary emotions According to Robert Plutchik's theory, the most basic emotions are fear, surprise, sadness, disgust, anger, anticipation, joy, and acceptance.

Primary motives Innate motives based on biological needs.

Primary reinforcers Nonlearned reinforcers; usually those that satisfy physiological needs.

Primary sexual characteristics Sex as defined by the genitals and internal reproductive organs.

Priming Facilitating the retrieval of an implicit memory by using cues to activate hidden memories.

Private self-consciousness Preoccupation with inner feelings, thoughts, and fantasies.

Proactive interference The tendency for old memories to interfere with the retrieval of newer memories.

Problem finding The active discovery of problems to be solved.

Problem-focused coping Directly managing or remedying a stressful or threatening situation.

Procedural memory Longterm memories of conditioned responses and learned skills.

Programmed instruction Any learning format that presents information in small amounts, gives immediate practice, and provides continuous feedback to learners.

Progressive relaxation A method for producing deep relaxation of all parts of the body.

Projection Attributing one's own feelings, shortcomings, or unacceptable impulses to others.

Projective tests Psychological tests making use of ambiguous or unstructured stimuli.

Prosocial behavior Behavior toward others that is helpful, constructive, or altruistic.

Prototype An ideal model used as a prime example of a particular concept.

Proxemics Systematic study of the human use of space, particularly in social settings.

Pseudopsychology Any false and unscientific system of beliefs and practices that is offered as an explanation of behavior.

Psi phenomena Events that seem to lie outside the realm of accepted scientific laws.

Psyche The mind, mental life, and personality as a whole.

Psychiatric social worker A mental health professional trained to apply social science principles to help patients in clinics and hospitals.

Psychiatrist A medical doctor with additional training in the diagnosis and treatment of mental and emotional disorders.

Psychoactive drug A substance capable of altering attention, memory, judgment, time sense, self-control, mood, or perception.

Psychoanalysis A Freudian therapy that emphasizes the use of free association, dream interpretation, resistances, and transference to uncover unconscious conflicts.

Psychoanalyst A mental health professional (usually a medical doctor) trained to practice psychoanalysis.

Psychoanalytic theory Freudian theory of personality that emphasizes unconscious forces and conflicts.

Psychodrama A therapy in which clients act out personal conflicts and feelings in the presence of others who play supporting roles.

Psychodynamic theory Any theory of behavior that emphasizes internal conflicts, motives, and unconscious forces.

Psychogenic Having psychological origins, rather than physical causes.

Psychokinesis The purported ability to mentally alter or influence objects or events.

Psychological dependence Drug dependence that is based primarily on emotional or psychological needs.

Psychological efficiency Maintenance of good morale, labor relations, employee satisfaction, and similar aspects of work behavior.

Psychological situation A situation as it is perceived and interpreted by an individual, not as it exists objectively.

Psychological trauma A psychological injury or shock, such as that caused by violence, abuse, neglect, separation, and so forth.

Psychologist A person highly trained in the methods, factual knowledge, and theories of psychology.

Psychology of law Study of the psychological and behavioral dimensions of the legal system.

Psychology The scientific study of behavior and mental processes.

Psychoneuroimmunology Study of the links among behavior, stress, disease, and the immune system.

Psychopathology The scientific study of mental, emotional, and behavioral disorders; also, abnormal or maladaptive behavior.

Psychophysics Study of the relationship between physical stimuli and the sensations they evoke in a human observer.

Psychosexual stages The oral, anal, phallic, and genital stages, during which various personality traits are formed.

Psychosis A withdrawal from reality marked by hallucinations and delusions, disturbed thought and emotions, and by personality disorganization.

Psychosocial dilemma A conflict between personal impulses and the social world.

Psychosomatic disorders Illnesses in which psychological factors contribute to bodily damage or to damaging changes in bodily functioning.

Psychosurgery Any surgical alteration of the brain designed to bring about desirable behavioral or emotional changes.

Psychotherapy Any psychological technique used to facilitate positive changes in a person's personality, behavior, or adjustment.

Psychotic disorder A severe mental disorder characterized by a retreat from reality, by hallucinations and delusions, and by social withdrawal.

PsycINFO A searchable, online database that provides brief summaries of the scientific and scholarly literature in psychology.

Puberty The biologically defined period during which a person matures sexually and becomes capable of reproduction.

Public distance Distance at which formal interactions, such as giving a speech, occur (about 12 feet or more from the body).

Public self-consciousness Intense awareness of oneself as a social object.

Punisher Any event that decreases the probability or frequency of responses it follows.

Punishment Any event that follows a response and *decreases* its likelihood of occurring again; the process of suppressing a response.

Pupil The opening at the front of the eye through which light passes.

Quality circle An employee discussion group that makes suggestions for improving quality and solving business problems.

Racism   Racial prejudice that has become institutionalized (that is, it is reflected in government policy, schools, and so forth) and that is enforced by the existing social power structure.

Random assignment   The use of chance (for example, flipping a coin) to assign subjects to experimental and control groups.

Random search strategy   Trying possible solutions to a problem in a more or less random order.

Random selection   Choosing a sample so that each member of the population has an equal chance of being included in the sample.

Range   The difference between the highest and lowest scores in a group of scores.

Rape myths   False beliefs about rape that tend to blame the victim and increase the likelihood that some men will think that rape is justified.

Rapid eye movements (REMs)   Swift eye movements during sleep.

Rating scale   A list of personality traits or aspects of behavior on which a person is rated.

Rational-emotive behavior therapy (REBT)   An approach that states that irrational beliefs cause many emotional problems and that such beliefs must be changed or abandoned.

Rationalization   Justifying your behavior by giving reasonable and "rational," but false, reasons for it.

Reaction formation   Preventing dangerous impulses from being expressed in behavior by exaggerating opposite behavior.

Readiness   A condition that exists when maturation has advanced enough to allow the rapid acquisition of a particular skill.

Reality principle   Delaying action (or pleasure) until it is appropriate.

Reality testing   Obtaining additional information to check on the accuracy of perceptions.

Recall   To supply or reproduce memorized information with a minimum of external cues.

Receptor sites   Areas on the surface of neurons and other cells that are sensitive to neurotransmitters or hormones.

Recessive gene   A gene whose influence will be expressed only when it is paired with a second recessive gene.

Reciprocal inhibition   The presence of one emotional state can inhibit the occurrence of another, such as joy preventing fear or anxiety inhibiting pleasure.

Recoding   Reorganizing or modifying information to assist storage in memory.

Recognition memory   An ability to correctly identify previously learned information.

Redintegrative memories   Memories that are reconstructed or expanded by starting with one memory and then following chains of association to other, related memories.

Reference group   Any group that an individual uses as a standard for social comparison.

Referent power   Social power gained when one is used as a point of reference by others.

Referred pain   Pain that is felt in one part of the body but comes from another.

Reflection   In client-centered therapy, the process of rephrasing or repeating thoughts and feelings expressed by clients so they can become aware of what they are saying.

Reflective intelligence   An ability to become aware of one's own thinking habits.

Reflex   An innate, automatic response to a stimulus; for example, an eye blink.

Reflex arc   The simplest behavior, in which a stimulus provokes an automatic response.

Refractory period   A short time period after orgasm during which males are unable to again reach orgasm.

Refusal skills training   Program that teaches youths how to resist pressures to begin smoking. (Can also be applied to other drugs and health risks.)

Regression   Retreating to an earlier level of development or to earlier, less demanding habits or situations.

Reinforcement   Any event that increases the probability that a particular response will occur.

Reinforcement value   The subjective value a person attaches to a particular activity or reinforcer.

Relational concept   A concept defined by the relationship between features of an object or between an object and its surroundings (for example, "greater than," "lopsided").

Relaxation response   The pattern of internal bodily changes that occurs at times of relaxation.

Relearning   Learning again something that was previously learned. Used to measure memory of prior learning.

Reliability   The ability of a test to yield nearly the same score each time it is given to the same person.

REM rebound   The occurrence of extra rapid eye movement sleep following REM sleep deprivation.

REM sleep   Sleep marked by rapid eye movements and a return to stage 1 EEG patterns.

Reminding system   Pain based on small nerve fibers; reminds the brain that the body has been injured.

Replicate   To reproduce or repeat.

Representative sample   A small, randomly selected part of a larger population that accurately reflects characteristics of the whole population.

Representativeness heuristic   A tendency to select wrong answers because they seem to match pre-existing mental categories.

Repression   Unconsciously preventing painful or dangerous thoughts from entering awareness.

Research method   A systematic approach to answering scientific questions.

Resistance   A blockage in the flow of free association; topics the client resists thinking or talking about.

Resolution   The fourth phase of sexual response, involving a return to lower levels of sexual tension and arousal.

Respondent reinforcement   Reinforcement that occurs when an unconditioned stimulus closely follows a conditioned stimulus.

Response   Any muscular action, glandular activity, or other identifiable aspect of behavior.

Response chaining   The assembly of separate responses into a series of actions that lead to reinforcement.

Response cost   Removal of a positive reinforcer after a response is made.

REST   Restricted Environmental Stimulation Therapy.

Resting potential   The electrical charge of a neuron at rest.

Reticular activating system (RAS)   A part of the reticular formation that activates the cerebral cortex.

Reticular formation (RF)   A network within the medulla and brainstem; associated with attention, alertness, and some reflexes.

Retina   The light-sensitive layer of cells at the back of the eye.

Retrieval   Recovering information from storage in memory.

Retroactive interference   The tendency for new memories to interfere with the retrieval of old memories.

Reversibility of thought Recognition that relationships involving equality or identity can be reversed (for example, if A = B, then B = A).

Reward Anything that produces pleasure or satisfaction; a positive reinforcer.

Reward power Social power based on the capacity to reward a person for acting as desired.

Rhodopsin The light-sensitive pigment in the rods.

Rods Visual receptors for dim light that produce only black and white sensations.

Role conflict Trying to occupy two or more roles that make conflicting demands on behavior.

Role reversal Taking the role of another person to learn how one's own behavior appears from the other person's perspective.

Romantic love Love that is associated with high levels of interpersonal attraction, heightened arousal, mutual absorption, and sexual desire.

Rorschach Technique A projective test comprised of ten standardized inkblots.

Rote learning Learning that takes place mechanically, through repetition and memorization, or by learning rules.

Run of luck A statistically unusual outcome (as in getting 5 heads in a row when flipping a coin) that could still occur by chance alone.

Sample A smaller subpart of a population.

Scaffolding The process of adjusting instruction so that it is responsive to a beginner's behavior and supports the beginner's efforts to understand a problem or gain a mental skill.

Scapegoating Blaming a person or a group of people for conditions not of their making.

Scatter diagram A graph that plots the intersection of paired measures; that is, the points at which paired X and Y measures cross.

Schachter's cognitive theory States that emotions occur when physical arousal is labeled or interpreted on the basis of experience and situational cues.

Schedule of reinforcement A rule or plan for determining which responses will be reinforced.

Schizophrenia A psychosis characterized by delusions, hallucinations, apathy, and a "split" between thought and emotion.

Scientific jury selection Using social science principles to choose members of a jury.

Scientific management (Theory X) An approach to managing employees that emphasizes work efficiency.

Scientific method Testing the truth of a proposition by careful measurement and controlled observation.

Scientific observation A systematic empirical investigation that is structured to answer questions about the world.

Seasonal affective disorder (SAD) Depression that occurs only during fall and winter; presumably related to decreased exposure to sunlight.

Secondary appraisal Deciding how to cope with a threat or challenge.

Secondary elaboration Making a dream more logical and complete while remembering it.

Secondary motives Motives based on learned needs, drives, and goals.

Secondary reinforcer A learned reinforcer; often one that gains reinforcing properties by association with a primary reinforcer.

Secondary sexual characteristics Sexual features other than the genitals and reproductive organs—breasts, body shape, facial hair, and so forth.

Secondary traits Traits that are inconsistent or relatively superficial.

Secure attachment A stable and positive emotional bond.

Selective attention Giving priority to a particular incoming sensory message.

Selective perception Perceiving only certain stimuli among a larger array of possibilities.

Self A continuously evolving conception of one's personal identity.

Self archetype An unconscious image representing, unity, wholeness, completion, and balance.

Self-actualization The process of fully developing one's personal potentials.

Self-actualizer One who is living creatively and making full use of his or her potentials.

Self-assertion A direct, honest expression of feelings and desires.

Self-concept A person's perception of his or her own personality traits.

Self-disclosure The process of revealing private thoughts, feelings, and one's personal history to others.

Self-efficacy Belief in your capacity to produce a desired result.

Self-esteem Regarding oneself as a worthwhile person; a positive evaluation of oneself.

Self-fulfilling prophecy An expectation that prompts people to act in ways that make the expectation come true.

Self-handicapping Arranging to perform under conditions that usually impair performance, so as to have an excuse for a poor showing.

Self-help group A group of people who share a particular type of problem and provide mutual support to one another.

Self-image Total subjective perception of one's body and personality (another term for self-concept).

Self-managed team A work group that has a high degree of freedom with respect to how it achieves its goals.

Self-recording Self-management based on keeping records of response frequencies.

Self-regulated learning Active, self-guided learning.

Self-reinforcement Praising or rewarding oneself for having made a particular response (such as completing a school assignment).

Self-testing Evaluating learning by posing questions to yourself.

Semantic memory A subpart of declarative memory that records impersonal knowledge about the world.

Semantics The study of meanings in words and language.

Sensate focus Form of therapy that directs a couple's attention to natural sensations of sexual pleasure.

Sensation A sensory impression; also, the process of detecting physical energies with the sensory organs.

Sensitive period During development, a period of increased sensitivity to environmental influences. Also, a time during which certain events must take place for normal development to occur.

Sensitivity group A group experience consisting of exercises designed to increase self-awareness and sensitivity to others.

Sensorimotor stage Stage of intellectual development during which sensory input and motor responses become coordinated.

Sensorineural hearing loss Loss of hearing caused by damage to the inner ear hair cells or auditory nerve.

Sensory adaptation A decrease in sensory response to an unchanging stimulus.

Sensory analysis   Separation of sensory information into important elements.

Sensory coding   Codes used by the sense organs to transmit information to the brain.

Sensory conflict theory   Explains motion sickness as the result of a mismatch between information from vision, the vestibular system, and kinesthesis.

Sensory deprivation (SD)   Any major reduction in the amount or variety of sensory stimulation.

Sensory gating   Alteration of sensory messages in the spinal cord.

Sensory memory   The first stage of memory, which holds an exact record of incoming information for a few seconds or less.

Sensory neuron   A nerve cell that carries information from the senses toward the CNS.

Separation anxiety disorder   Severe and prolonged distress displayed by children when they are separated from their parents or caregivers.

Separation anxiety   Distress displayed by infants when they are separated from their parents or principal caregivers.

Serial position effect   The tendency to make the most errors in remembering the middle items of an ordered list.

Set point (for fat)   The proportion of body fat that tends to be maintained by changes in hunger and eating.

Sex drive   The strength of one's motivation to engage in sexual behavior.

Sex   One's biological classification as female or male.

Sexism   Institutionalized prejudice against members of either sex, based solely on their gender.

Sex-linked trait   Traits other than sex that are influenced by genes carried on an *X* chromosome (or, rarely, on a *Y* chromosome).

Sexual and gender identity disorders   Any of a wide range of difficulties with sexual identity, deviant sexual behavior, or sexual adjustment.

Sexual aversion   Persistent feelings of fear, anxiety, or disgust about engaging in sex.

Sexual orientation   One's degree of emotional and erotic attraction to members of the same sex, opposite sex, or both sexes.

Sexual script   An unspoken mental plan that defines a "plot," dialogue, and actions expected to take place in a sexual encounter.

Sexually transmitted disease (STD)   A disease that is typically passed from one person to the next by intimate physical contact; a venereal disease.

Shape constancy   The perceived shape of an object is unaffected by changes in its retinal image.

Shaping   Gradually molding responses to a final desired pattern.

Short-term memory (STM)   The memory system used to hold small amounts of information for relatively brief time periods.

Shyness   A tendency to avoid others plus uneasiness and strain when socializing.

Signal   In early language development, any behavior, such as touching, vocalizing, gazing, or smiling, that allows nonverbal interaction and turn-taking between parent and child.

Simultaneous color contrast   Changes in perceived hue that occur when a colored stimulus is displayed on backgrounds of various colors.

Single-blind experiment   An arrangement in which subjects remain unaware of whether they are in the experimental group or the control group.

Situational demands   Unstated expectations that define desirable or appropriate behavior in various settings and social situations.

Situational determinants   External conditions that strongly influence behavior.

Situational judgment test   Presenting realistic work situations to applicants in order to observe their skills and reactions.

Situational test   Simulating real-life conditions so that a person's reactions may be directly observed.

Size constancy   The perceived size of an object remains constant, despite changes in its retinal image.

Size–distance invariance   The strict relationship between the distance an object lies from the eyes and the size of its image.

Skin receptors   Sensory organs for touch, pressure, pain, cold, and warmth.

Skin senses   The senses of touch, pressure, pain, heat, and cold.

Sleep apnea   Repeated interruption of breathing during sleep.

Sleep deprivation   Being prevented from getting desired or needed amounts of sleep.

Sleep hormone   A sleep-promoting substance found in the brain and spinal cord.

Sleep patterns   The order and timing of daily sleep and waking periods.

Sleep spindles   Distinctive bursts of brain-wave activity that indicate a person is asleep.

Sleep stages   Levels of sleep identified by brain-wave patterns and behavioral changes.

Sleep-deprivation psychosis   A major disruption of mental and emotional functioning brought about by sleep loss.

Sleeptalking   Speaking that occurs during NREM sleep.

Social anxiety   A feeling of apprehension in the presence of others.

Social comparison   Making judgments about ourselves through comparison with others.

Social competition   Rivalry among groups, each of which regards itself as superior to others.

Social development   The development of self-awareness, attachment to parents or caregivers, and relationships with other children and adults.

Social distance   Distance at which impersonal interaction takes place (about 4 to 12 feet from the body).

Social distance scale   A rating of the degree to which a person would be willing to have contact with a member of another group.

Social environment   An environment defined by a group of people and their activities or interrelationships (such as a parade, revival meeting, or sports event).

Social exchange   Any exchange between two people of attention, information, affection, favors, or the like.

Social exchange theory   Theory stating that rewards must exceed costs for relationships to endure.

Social influence   Changes in a person's behavior induced by the presence or actions of others.

Social learning theory (of behavior)   Combines learning principles with cognitive processes, socialization, and modeling to explain behavior.

Social learning theory (of personality)   An explanation of personality that combines learning principles, cognition, and the effects of social relationships.

Social markers   Visible or tangible signs that indicate a person's social status or role.

Social motives Learned motives acquired as part of growing up in a particular society or culture.

Social nonconformity Failure to conform to societal norms or the usual minimum standards for social conduct.

Social norms Unspoken rules that define acceptable and expected behavior for members of a group.

Social phobia An intense, irrational fear of being observed, evaluated, embarrassed, or humiliated by others in social situations.

Social power The capacity to control, alter, or influence the behavior of another person.

Social psychology The scientific study of how individuals behave, think, and feel in social situations.

Social Readjustment Rating Scale (SRRS) A scale that rates the impact of various life events on the likelihood of illness.

Social referencing Observing others in social situations to obtain information or guidance.

Social reinforcer Reinforcement based on receiving attention, approval, or affection from another person.

Social role Expected behavior patterns associated with particular social positions (such as daughter, worker, student).

Social smile Smiling elicited by social stimuli, such as seeing a parent's face.

Social stereotypes Oversimplified images of the traits of individuals who belong to a particular social group.

Social support Close, positive relationships with other people.

Solitary play Playing alone.

Soma The main body of a neuron or other cell.

Somatic pain Pain from the skin, muscles, joints, and tendons.

Somatic system The system of nerves linking the spinal cord with the body and sense organs.

Somatic therapy Any bodily therapy, such as drug therapy, electroconvulsive therapy, or psychosurgery.

Somatization disorder Afflicted persons have numerous physical complaints. Typically, they have consulted many doctors, but no organic cause for their distress can be identified.

Somatoform disorder Physical symptoms that mimic disease or injury for which there is no identifiable physical cause.

Somatosensory area A receiving area for bodily sensations.

Somesthetic senses Sensations produced by the skin, muscles, joints, viscera, and organs of balance.

Somnambulism Sleepwalking; occurs during NREM sleep.

Source traits Basic underlying traits, or dimensions, of personality; each source trait is reflected in a number of surface traits.

Spaced practice Practice spread over many relatively short study sessions. (Massed practice, in comparison, continues for long periods without interruption.)

Special aptitude test Test to predict a person's likelihood of succeeding in a particular area of work or skill.

Specific goal A goal with a clearly defined and measurable outcome.

Specific phobia An intense, irrational fear of specific objects, activities, or situations.

Speed of processing The speed with which a person can mentally process information.

Spinal nerves Major nerves that carry sensory and motor messages in and out of the spinal cord.

"Split-brain" operation Cutting the corpus callosum.

Spontaneous recovery The reappearance of a learned response after its apparent extinction.

Sports psychology Study of the psychological and behavioral dimensions of sports performance.

SQ4R method An active study-reading technique based on these steps: survey, question, read, recite, reflect, and review.

Squeeze technique Method for inhibiting ejaculation by compressing the tip of the penis.

Stage ESP The simulation of ESP for the purpose of entertainment.

Stage hypnosis Use of hypnosis to entertain; often, merely a simulation of hypnosis for that purpose.

Stage of exhaustion Third stage of the general adaptation syndrome (G.A.S.), at which time the body's resources are exhausted and serious health consequences occur.

Stage of resistance Second stage of the general adaptation syndrome (G.A.S.), during which bodily adjustments to stress stabilize, but at a high physical cost.

Standard deviation An index of how much a typical score differs from the mean of a group of scores.

State-dependent learning Memory influenced by one's bodily state at the time of learning and at the time of retrieval. Improved memory occurs when the bodily states match.

Statistical abnormality Abnormality defined on the basis of an extreme score on some dimension, such as IQ or anxiety.

Statistical significance The degree to which an event (such as the results of an experiment) is unlikely to have occurred by chance alone.

Status An individual's position in a social structure, especially with respect to power, privilege, or importance.

Status inequalities Differences in the power, prestige, or privileges of two or more persons or groups.

Stereoscopic vision Perception of space and depth caused chiefly by the fact that the eyes receive different images.

Sterilization Medical procedures such as vasectomy or tubal ligation that make a man or a woman infertile.

Stimulant A substance that increases activity in the body and nervous system.

Stimulation deafness Damage caused by exposing the hair cells to excessively loud sounds.

Stimulus Any physical energy that has some effect on an organism and that evokes a response.

Stimulus control Stimuli present when an operant response is acquired tend to control when and where the response is made.

Stimulus discrimination The learned ability to respond differently to similar stimuli.

Stimulus drives Drives based on needs for exploration, manipulation, curiosity, and stimulation.

Stimulus generalization The tendency to respond to stimuli similar to, but not identical to, a conditioned stimulus.

Stimulus motives Innate needs for stimulation and information.

Storage Holding information in memory for later use.

Stress The mental and physical condition that occurs when a person must adjust or adapt to the environment.

Stress disorder A significant emotional disturbance caused by stresses outside the range of normal human experience.

Stress inoculation Use of positive coping statements to control fear and anxiety.

Stress management The application of behavioral strategies to reduce stress and improve coping skills.

Stress reaction The physical response to stress, consisting mainly of bodily changes related to autonomic nervous system arousal.

Stressor A specific condition or event in the environment that challenges or threatens a person.

Stress-vulnerability model Attributes psychosis to a combination of environmental stress and inherited susceptibility.

Striving for superiority According to Adler, this basic drive propels us toward perfection.

Stroboscopic movement Illusion of movement in which an object is shown in rapidly changing series of positions.

Structuralism The school of thought concerned with analyzing sensations and personal experience into basic elements.

Stuttering Chronic hesitation or stumbling in speech.

Style of life The pattern of personality and behavior that defines the pathway each person takes through life.

Subcortex All brain structures below the cerebral cortex.

Subjective well-being General life satisfaction combined with frequent positive emotions and relatively few negative emotions.

Subjects Animals or people whose behavior is under scientific investigation.

Sublimation Working off unmet desires, or unacceptable impulses, in activities that are constructive.

Subliminal perception Perception of a stimulus below the threshold for conscious recognition.

Substance related disorder Abuse of or dependence on a mood- or behavior-altering drug.

Sudden infant death syndrome (SIDS) The sudden, unexplained death of an apparently healthy infant.

Superego A judge or censor for thoughts and actions.

Superordinate goal A goal that exceeds or overrides all others; a goal that renders other goals relatively less important.

Superstitious behavior A behavior repeated because it seems to produce reinforcement, even though it is actually unnecessary.

Suppression A conscious effort to put something out of mind or to keep it from awareness.

Surface traits The visible or observable traits of one's personality.

Surrogate mother A substitute mother (often an inanimate dummy in animal research).

Survey method Using questionnaires and surveys to poll large groups of people.

Syllogism A format for analyzing logical arguments.

Symbolic prejudice Prejudice that is expressed in disguised fashion.

Symbolization The nonliteral expression of dream content.

Sympathetic branch A part of the autonomic nervous system (ANS) that activates the body at times of stress.

Synapse The microscopic space between two neurons, over which messages pass.

Synesthesia Experiencing one sense in terms normally associated with another sense; for example, "seeing" colors when a sound is heard.

Syntax Rules for ordering words when forming sentences.

Systematic desensitization A reduction in fear, anxiety, or aversion brought about by planned exposure to aversive stimuli.

Task analysis Breaking complex skills into their subparts.

Taste aversion An active dislike for a particular food.

Taste bud The receptor organ for taste.

Teaching strategy A plan for effective teaching.

Telepathy The purported ability to directly know another person's thoughts.

Temperament The hereditary physical core of personality, including sensitivity, activity levels, prevailing mood, irritability, and adaptability.

Temporal lobes Areas that include the sites where hearing registers in the brain.

Tension-release method A procedure for systematically achieving deep relaxation of the body.

Teratogen Radiation, a drug, or other substance capable of altering fetal development in nonheritable ways that cause birth defects.

Term schedule A written plan that lists the dates of all major assignments for each of your classes for an entire semester or quarter.

Terminal decline An abrupt decline in measured intelligence about 5 years before death.

Territorial behavior Any behavior that tends to define a space as one's own or that protects it from intruders.

Territorial markers Objects and other signals whose placement indicates to others the "ownership" or control of a particular area.

Test anxiety High levels of arousal and worry that seriously impair test performance.

Test standardization Establishing standards for administering a test and interpreting scores.

Testosterone A male sex hormone, secreted mainly by the testes and responsible for the development of many male sexual characteristics.

Thalamus A brain structure that relays sensory information to the cerebral cortex.

Thanatologist A specialist who studies emotional and behavioral reactions to death and dying.

Thanatos The death instinct postulated by Freud.

Thematic Apperception Test (TAT) A projective test consisting of 20 different scenes and life situations about which respondents make up stories.

Theory A system of ideas designed to interrelate concepts and facts in a way that summarizes existing data and predicts future observations.

Theory of mind A child's current understanding of the mind, including the desires, beliefs, intentions, and feelings of others.

Theory Y A management style that emphasizes human relations at work and that views people as industrious, responsible, and interested in challenging work.

Therapeutic alliance A caring relationship that unites a therapist and a client in working to solve the client's problems.

Therapy placebo effect Improvement caused not by the actual process of therapy but by a client's expectation that therapy will help.

Thought stopping Use of aversive stimuli to interrupt or prevent upsetting thoughts.

Threshold The point at which a nerve impulse is triggered.

Thyroid gland Endocrine gland that helps regulate the rate of metabolism.

Tip-of-the-tongue (TOT) state The feeling that a memory is available but not quite retrievable.

Token economy A therapeutic program in which desirable behaviors are reinforced with tokens that can be exchanged for goods, services, activities, and privileges.

Token reinforcer A tangible secondary reinforcer such as money, gold stars, poker chips, and the like.

Top-down processing Applying higher-level knowledge to rapidly organize sensory information into a meaningful perception.

Trait profile A graph of the scores obtained on several personality traits.

Trait theorist A psychologist interested in classifying, analyzing, and interrelating traits to understand personality.

Trait-situation interaction The influence that external settings or circumstances have on the expression of personality traits.

Tranquilizer A drug that lowers anxiety and reduces tension.

Transference The tendency of patients to transfer feelings to a therapist that correspond to those the patient had for important persons in his or her past.

Transformation (Piaget) The mental ability to change the shape or form of a substance (such as clay or water) and to perceive that its volume remains the same.

Transformation rules Rules by which a simple declarative sentence may be changed to other voices or forms (past tense, passive voice, and so forth).

Transition period Time span during which a person leaves an existing life pattern behind and moves into a new pattern.

Traumatic stresses Extreme events that cause psychological injury or intense emotional pain.

Trichromatic theory Theory of color vision based on three cone types: red, green, and blue.

Trust versus mistrust A conflict early in life about learning to trust others and the world.

Twin study A comparison of the characteristics of twins who were raised together or separated at birth; used to identify the relative impact of heredity and environment.

Two-way bilingual education A program in which English-speaking children and children with limited English proficiency are taught half the day in English and half in a second language.

Type A personality A personality type with an elevated risk of heart disease; characterized by time urgency, anger, and hostility.

Type B personality All personality types other than Type A; a low cardiac-risk personality.

Unconditional positive regard An unqualified, unshakable acceptance of another person.

Unconditioned response (UR) An innate reflex response elicited by an unconditioned stimulus.

Unconditioned stimulus (US) A stimulus innately capable of eliciting a response.

Unconscious The region of the mind that is beyond awareness, especially impulses and desires not directly known to a person.

Uncritical acceptance The tendency to believe generally positive or flattering descriptions of oneself.

Understanding (problem solving) A deeper comprehension of the nature of a problem.

Understanding (psychology) Understanding is achieved when the causes of a behavior can be stated.

Undifferentiated schizophrenia Schizophrenia lacking the specific features of catatonic, disorganized, or paranoid types.

Upward comparison Comparing yourself with a person who ranks higher than you on some dimension.

Vaginismus Muscle spasms of the vagina.

Validity The ability of a test to measure what it purports to measure.

Validity scales Scales that tell whether test scores should be invalidated for lying, inconsistency, or "faking good."

Variability The tendency for a group of scores to differ in value. Measures of variability indicate the degree to which a group of scores differ from one another.

Variable Any condition that changes or can be made to change; a measure, event, or state that may vary.

Variable interval (VI) schedule A reinforcer is given for the first correct response made after a varied amount of time has passed since the last reinforced response. Responses made during the time interval are not reinforced.

Variable ratio (VR) schedule A varied number of correct responses must be made to get a reinforcer. For example, a reinforcer is given after three to seven correct responses; the actual number changes randomly.

Verbal intelligence Intelligence measured by answering questions involving vocabulary, general information, arithmetic, and other language- or symbol-oriented tasks.

Vestibular senses The senses of balance, position in space, and acceleration.

Vicarious classical conditioning Classical conditioning brought about by observing another person react to a particular stimulus.

Vicarious desensitization A reduction in fear or anxiety that takes place vicariously ("second hand") when a client watches models perform the feared behavior.

Virtual reality exposure Use of computer-generated images to present fear stimuli. The virtual environment responds to a viewer's head movements and other inputs.

Visceral pain Pain originating in the internal organs.

Visible spectrum That part of the electromagnetic spectrum to which the eyes are sensitive.

Visual acuity The sharpness of visual perception.

Vocational interest test A paper-and-pencil test that assesses a person's interests and matches them to interests found among successful workers in various occupations.

Waking consciousness A state of normal, alert awareness.

Warning system Pain based on large nerve fibers; warns that bodily damage may be occurring.

Weapons effect The observation that weapons serve as strong cues for aggressive behavior.

Weber's law The just noticeable difference is a constant proportion of the original stimulus intensity.

Weekly time schedule A written plan that allocates time for study, work, and leisure activities during a one-week period.

Wellness A positive state of good health; more than the absence of disease.

Wernicke's area An area related to language comprehension.

Wish fulfillment Freudian belief that many dreams express unconscious desires.

Withdrawal of love Withholding affection to enforce child discipline.

Withdrawal symptoms Physical illness and discomfort following the withdrawal of a drug.

Work efficiency Maximum output (productivity) at lowest cost.

Working memory Another name for short-term memory,

especially as it is used for thinking and problem solving.

World Wide Web   A system of information "sites" accessible through the Internet.

X **chromosome**   The female chromosome contributed by the mother; produces a female when paired with another *X* chromosome, and a male when paired with a *Y* chromosome.

Y **chromosome**   The male chromosome contributed by the father; produces a male when paired with an *X* chromosome. Fathers may give either an *X* or a *Y* chromosome to their offspring.

Yerkes-Dodson law   A summary of the relationships among arousal, task complexity, and performance.

You-message   Threatening, accusing, bossing, lecturing, or criticizing another person.

Zener cards   A deck of 25 cards bearing various symbols and used in early parapsychological research.

Zero correlation   The absence of a (linear) mathematical relationship between two measures.

Zone of proximal development   Refers to the range of tasks a child cannot yet master alone, but that she or he can accomplish with the guidance of a more capable partner.

z-score   A number that tells how many standard deviations above or below the mean a score is.

References

AAMR. (2004). *Montreal declaration on intellectual disabilities.* Washington: American Association on Mental Retardation. Retrieved August 21, 2006, from http://www.aamr.org/pdf/DeclarationMTL.pdf.

Abel, T., & Lattal, K. M. (2001). Molecular mechanisms of memory acquisition, consolidation and retrieval. *Current Opinion in Neurobiology, 11*(2), 180–187.

Abrams, D. B., Brown, R., Niaura, R. S., Emmons, K., et al. (2003). *The tobacco dependence treatment handbook: A guide to best practices.* New York: Guilford.

Accordino, D. B., Accordino, M. P., & Slaney, R. B. (2000). An investigation of perfectionism, mental health, achievement, and achievement motivation in adolescents. *Psychology in the Schools, 37*(6), 535–545.

ACT Against Violence (2005a). *Facts related to media violence.* Washington: Adults and Children Against Violence Together. Retrieved October 18, 2006, from http://www.actagainstviolence.com/materials/handouts/FamilyMV1.pdf.

ACT Against Violence (2005b). *Early violence prevention.* Washington: Adults and Children Against Violence Together. Retrieved October 18, 2006, from http://www.actagainstviolence.com/violprevent/index.html.

Adams, J. (1988). *Conceptual blockbusting.* New York: Norton.

Adamson, K. (2004). *Kate's journey: Triumph over adversity.* Redondo Beach, CA: Nosmada Press.

Addis, K. M., & Kahana, M. J. (2004). Decomposing serial learning: What is missing from the learning curve? *Psychonomic Bulletin & Review, 11*(1), 118–174.

Adler, S. A., & Orprecio, J. (2006). The eyes have it: Visual pop-out in infants and adults. *Developmental Science, 9,* 189–206.

Adorno, T. W., Frenkel-Brunswik, E., Levinson, D. J., & Sanford, R. N. (1950). *The authoritarian personality.* New York: Harper.

Ahima, R. S., & Osei, S. Y. (2004). Leptin signaling. *Physiology & Behavior, 81,* 223–241.

Ajzen, I. (2005). *Attitudes, personality and behaviour* (2nd ed.). New York: McGraw-Hill.

Akerstedt, T., Hume, K., Minors, D., & Waterhouse, J. (1993). Regulation of sleep and naps on an irregular schedule. *Sleep, 16*(8), 736–743.

Alarcon, R. D. (1995). Culture and psychiatric diagnosis: Impact on DSM-IV and ICD-10. *Psychiatric Clinics of North America, 18*(3), 449–465.

Alberti, R., & Emmons, M. (2001). *Your perfect right* (8th ed.). San Luis Obispo, CA: Impact.

Alberto, P. A., & Troutman, A. C. (2006). *Applied behavior analysis for teachers* (7th ed.). Englewood Cliffs, NJ: Prentice Hall

Alcock, J. E. (2003). Give the null hypothesis a chance: Reasons to remain doubtful about the existence of psi. *Journal of Consciousness Studies, 10*(6–7), 29–50.

Alcock, J. E., Burns, J., & Freeman, A. (2003). *Psi wars: Getting to grips with the paranormal.* Exeter, UK: Imprint Academic Press.

Alicke, M. D., Yurak, T. J., & Vredenburg, D. S. (1996). Using personal attitudes to judge others. *Journal of Research in Personality, 30*(1), 103–119.

Allen, K., Blascovich, J., & Mendes, W. B. (2002). Cardiovascular reactivity in the presence of pets, friends, and spouses: The truth about cats and dogs. *Psychosomatic Medicine, 64*(5), 727–739.

Allgower, A., Wardle, J., & Steptoe, A. (2001). Depressive symptoms, social support, and personal health behaviors in young men and women. *Health Psychology, 20*(3), 223–227.

Allport, G. W. (1958). *The nature of prejudice.* Garden City, NY: Anchor Books, Doubleday.

Allport, G. W. (1961). *Pattern and growth in personality.* New York: Holt.

Altemeyer, B. (2004). Highly dominating, highly authoritarian personalities. *Journal of Social Psychology, 144*(4), 421–447.

Altman, L. K. (2002). AIDS threatens to claim 65M more lives by '20. *Arizona Daily Star,* July 3, A7.

Altschuler, G. C. (2001). Battling the cheats. *The New York Times: Education,* Jan. 7, 15.

Alvarado, N. (1994). Empirical validity of the Thematic Apperception Test. *Journal of Personality Assessment, 63*(1), 59–79.

Alvino, J., & the Editors of *Gifted Children Monthly.* (1996). *Parents' guide to raising a gifted child.* New York: Ballantine.

Alwin, D. F., Cohen, R. L., & Newcomb, T. M. (1991). *Political attitudes over the life span. The Bennington women after fifty years.* Madison, WI: University of Wisconsin Press.

Amabile, T., Hadley, C. N., & Kramer, S. J. (2002). Creativity under the gun. *Harvard Business Review, 80*(8), 52–61.

Amato, P. R., & Fowler, F. (2002). Parenting practices, child adjustment, and family diversity. *Journal of Marriage & Family, 64*(3), 703–716.

Ambady, N., & Rosenthal, R. (1993). Half a minute: Predicting teacher evaluations from thin slices of nonverbal behavior and physical attractiveness. *Journal of Personality & Social Psychology, 64,* 431–441.

American Lung Association (2006). Secondhand smoke fact sheet. Retrieved July 19, 2006, from http://www.lungusa.org/site/pp.asp?c=dvLUK9O0E&b=35422.

Ancis, J. R., Chen, Y., & Schultz, D. (2004). Diagnostic challenges and the so-called culture-bound syndromes. In J. R. Ancis (Ed.), *Culturally responsive interventions: Innovative approaches to working with diverse populations.* New York: Brunner-Routledge.

Anderson, C. A. (2004). An update on the effects of violent video games. *Journal of Adolescence, 27,* 113–122.

Anderson, C. A., & Bushman, B. J. (2002). Human aggression. *Annual Review of Psychology, 53,* 27–51.

Anderson, C. A., Anderson, K. B., & Deuser, W. E. (1996). Examining an affective aggression framework. *Personality & Social Psychology Bulletin, 22*(4), 366–376.

Anderson, C. A., Berkowitz, L, Donnerstein, E., Huesmann, L R., et al. (2003). The influence of media violence on youth. *Psychological Science in the Public Interest, 4*(3), 81–110.

Anderson, C. A., Carnagey, N. L., & Eubanks, J. (2003). Exposure to violent media: The effects of songs with violent lyrics on aggressive thoughts and feelings. *Journal of Personality & Social Psychology, 84*(5), 960–971.

Anderson, J. R. (2005). *Cognitive psychology and its implications* (6th ed.). New York: Worth.

Anderson, M. C. (2001). Active forgetting: Evidence for functional inhibition as a source of memory failure. *Journal of Aggression, Maltreatment & Trauma, 4*(2), 185–210.

Anderson, M. C., & Bell, T. (2001). Forgetting our facts: The role of inhibitory processes in the loss of propositional knowledge. *Journal of Experimental Psychology: General, 130*(3), 544–570.

Anderson, M. C., & Green, C. (2001, March 15). Suppressing unwanted memories by executive control. *Nature, 410,* 366–369.

Anderson, M. C., Ochsner, K. N., Kuhl, B., Cooper, J., et al. (2004). Neural systems underlying the suppression of unwanted memories. *Science, 303,* 232–235.

Anderson, N. H. (1989). Functional memory and on-line attribution. In J. N. Bassili (Ed.), *On-line cognition in person perception.* Mahwah, NJ: Erlbaum.

Andrasik, F. (2003). Behavioral treatment approaches to chronic headache. *Neurological Sciences, 24*(Suppl2), S80–S85.

André, C., Jaber-Filho, J. A., Carvalho, M., Jullien, C., et al. (2003). Predictors of recovery following involuntary hospitalization of violent substance abuse patients. *The American Journal on Addictions, 12*(1), 84–89.

Andresen, J. (2000). Meditation meets behavioural medicine: The story of experimental research on meditation. *Journal of Consciousness Studies, 7*(11–12), 17–73.

Annett, M., & Manning, M. (1990). Arithmetic and laterality. *Neuropsychologia, 28*(1), 61–69.

Annett, M. (2002). *Handedness and brain asymmetry: The right shift theory.* Hove, UK: Psychology Press.

Anthony, W. A., Cohen, M., & Kennard, W. (1990). Understanding the current facts and principles of mental health systems planning. *American Psychologist, 45*(11), 1249–1252.

Antle, M. C., & Mistlberger, R. E. (2005). Circadian rhythms. In I. Q. Whishaw & B. Kolb (Eds.), *The behavior of the laboratory rat: A handbook with tests.* London: Oxford.

Antony, M. M. (2004). *10 simple solutions to shyness: How to overcome shyness, social anxiety & fear of public speaking.* Oakland, CA: New Harbinger.

APA. (2000). 2000 APA directory survey. Retrieved June 7, 2006, from http://research.apa.org/2000membershipt4.pdf.

APA. (2003). Guidelines on multicultural education, training, research, practice, and organizational change for psychologists. *American Psychologist, 58*(5), 377–402.

APA. (2005). 2005 APA directory survey. Retrieved June 7, 2006, from http://research.apa.org/profile2005t3.pdf.

Arbona, C. B., Osma, J., Garcia-Palacios, A., Quero, S., et al. (2004). Treatment of flying phobia using virtual reality: Data from a 1-year follow-up using a multiple baseline design. *Clinical Psychology & Psychotherapy, 11*(5), 311–323.

Ariely, D., & Wertenbroch, K. (2002). Procrastination, deadlines, and performance: Self-control by precommitment. *Psychological Science, 13*(3), 219–224.

Armeli, S., Gunthert, K. C., & Cohen, L. H. (2001). Stressor appraisals, coping, and post-event outcomes: The dimensionality and antecedents of stress-related growth. *Journal of Social & Clinical Psychology, 20*(3), 366–395.

Arnett, J. J., & Tanner, J. L. (Eds.). (2006). *Emerging adults in America: Coming of age in the 21st century.* Washington: American Psychological Association.

Arnett, J. J. (2000). Emerging adulthood. *American Psychologist, 55*(5), 469–480.

Arnett, J. J. (2004). *Emerging adulthood: The winding road from late teens through the twenties.* New York: Oxford University Press.

Arnett, J. J., & Galambos, N. L. (Eds.). (2003). *New directions for child and adolescent development: Exploring cultural conceptions of the transition to adulthood.* San Francisco: Jossey-Bass.

Aronoff, J., Barclay, A. M., & Stevenson, L. A. (1988). The recognition of threatening facial stimuli. *Journal of Personality & Social Psychology, 54*(4), 647–655.

Aronow, E., Altman Weiss, K., & Reznikoff, M. (2001). *A practical guide to the Thematic Apperception Test: The TAT in clinical practice.* New York: Brunner-Routledge.

Aronson, E. (1969). Some antecedents of interpersonal attraction. In W. J. Arnold & D. Levine (Eds.), *Nebraska Symposium on Motivation*. Lincoln: University of Nebraska Press.

Aronson, E. (2004). *The social animal* (9th ed.). New York: Worth.

Aronson, E., Wilson, T. D., & Akert, R. M. (2005). *Social psychology* (5th ed.). Englewood Cliffs, NJ: Prentice Hall.

Arthur, W., & Doverspike, D. (2001). Predicting motor vehicle crash involvement from a personality measure and a driving knowledge test. *Journal of Prevention & Intervention in the Community, 22*(1), 35–42.

Artz, S. (2005). To die for: Violent adolescent girls' search for male attention. In D. J. Pepler, K. C. Madsen, C. D. Webster, & K. S. Levene (Eds.), *The development and treatment of girlhood aggression*. Mahwah, NJ: Erlbaum.

Ary, D. V., Duncan, T. E., Biglan, A., Metzler, C. W., et al. (1999). Development of adolescent problem behavior. *Journal of Abnormal Child Psychology, 27*(2), 141–150.

Asch, S. E. (1956). Studies of independence and conformity: A minority of one against a unanimous majority. *Psychological Monographs, 70*(Whole No. 416).

Ash, D. W., & Holding, D. H. (1990). Backward versus forward chaining in the acquisition of a keyboard skill. *Human Factors, 32*(2), 139–146.

Ashby, F. G., & Maddox, W. T. (2005). Human category learning. *Annual Review of Psychology, 56*, 149–78.

Aslin, R. N., & Smith, L. B. (1988). Perceptual development. *Annual Review of Psychology, 39*, 435–473.

Asmundson, G. J. G., & Taylor, S. (2005). *It's not all in your head*. London: Psychology Press.

Assanand, S., Pinel, J. P. J., & Lehman, D. R. (1998). Personal theories of hunger and eating. *Journal of Applied Social Psychology, 28*(11), 998–1015.

Ausubel, D. P. (1978). In defense of advance organizers: A reply to the critics. *Review of Educational Research, 48*, 251–257.

Avery, D. H., Eder, D. N., Bolte, M. A., Hellekson, C. J., et al. (2001). Dawn simulation and bright light in the treatment of SAD. *Biological Psychiatry, 50*(3), 205–216.

Ayers, L., Beaton, S., & Hunt, H. (1999). The significance of transpersonal experiences, emotional conflict, and cognitive abilities in creativity. *Empirical Studies of the Arts, 17*(1), 73–82.

Ayllon, T. (1963). Intensive treatment of psychotic behavior by stimulus satiation and food reinforcement. *Behavior Research and Therapy, 1*, 53–61.

Ayllon, T., & Azrin, N. H. (1965). The measurement and reinforcement of behavior of psychotics. *Journal of the Experimental Analysis of Behavior, 8*, 357–383.

Baard, P. P., Deci, E. L., & Ryan, R. M. (2004). Intrinsic need satisfaction: A motivational basis of performance and well-being in two work settings. *Journal of Applied Social Psychology, 34*(10), 2045–2068.

Bachman, J. G., & Johnson, L. D. (1979). The freshmen. *Psychology Today, 13*, 78–87.

Baddeley, A. D. (2003). Working memory: Looking back and looking forward. *Nature Reviews Neuroscience, 4*(10), 829–839.

Baehr, E. K., Revelle, W., & Eastman, C. I. (2000). Individual differences in the phase and amplitude of the human circadian temperature rhythm with an emphasis on morningness-eveningness. *Journal of Sleep Research, 9*, 117–127.

Baer, J. M. (1993). *Creativity and divergent thinking*. Hillsdale, NJ: Erlbaum.

Bailey, C. H., & Kandel, E. R. (2004). Synaptic growth and the persistence of long-term memory: A molecular perspective. In M. S. Gazzaniga (Ed.), *The cognitive neurosciences* (3rd ed.). Cambridge, MA: MIT Press.

Bailey, L. M., & McKeever, W. F. (2004). A large-scale study of handedness and pregnancy/birth risk events: Implications for genetic theories of handedness. *Laterality: Asymmetries of Body, Brain & Cognition, 9*(2), 175–188.

Baillargeon, R. (1991). Reasoning about the height and location of a hidden object in 4.5- and 6.5-month-old infants. *Cognition, 38*(1), 13–42.

Baillargeon, R. (2004). Infants' reasoning about hidden objects: Evidence for event-general and event-specific expectations. *Developmental Science. 7*(4), 391–424.

Baillargeon, R., De Vos, J., & Graber, M. (1989). Location memory in 8-month-old infants in a non-search AB task. *Cognitive Development, 4*, 345–367.

Bain, S. K., & Allin, J. D. (2005). Stanford-Binet Intelligence Scales, Fifth Edition. *Journal of Psychoeducational Assessment, 23*(1), 87–95.

Balch, W. R., & Lewis, B. S. (1996). Music-dependent memory. *Journal of Experimental Psychology: Learning, Memory, & Cognition, 22*(6), 1354–1363.

Balk, D. E., Lampe, S., Sharpe, B., Schwinn, S., et al. (1998). TAT results in a longitudinal study of bereaved college students. *Death Studies, 22*(1), 3–21.

Bandura, A. (1971). *Social learning theory*. New York: General Learning Press.

Bandura, A. (1973). *Aggression: A social learning analysis*. Englewood Cliffs, NJ: Prentice-Hall.

Bandura, A. (2001). Social cognitive theory: An agentic perspective. *Annual Review of Psychology, 52*, 1–26.

Bandura, A., & Walters, R. (1959). *Adolescent aggression*. New York: Ronald.

Bandura, A., Blanchard, E. B., & Ritter, B. (1969). Relative efficacy of desensitization and modeling approaches for inducing behavioral, affective, and attitudinal changes. *Journal of Personality & Social Psychology, 13*(3), 173–199.

Bandura, A., Ross, D., & Ross, S. A. (1963). Vicarious reinforcement and imitative learning. *Journal of Abnormal and Social Psychology, 67*, 601–607.

Banich, M. T. (2004). *Cognitive neuroscience and neuropsychology* (2nd ed.). Boston: Houghton Mifflin.

Banks, A., & Gartrell, N. K. (1995). Hormones and sexual orientation: A questionable link. *Journal of Homosexuality, 28*(3–4), 247–268.

Banks, T., & Dabbs, Jr., J. M. (1996). Salivary testosterone and cortisol in delinquent and violent urban subculture. *Journal of Social Psychology, 136*(1), 49–56.

Barabasz, A. (2000). EEG markers of alert hypnosis. *Sleep & Hypnosis, 2*(4), 164–169.

Barber, T. X. (2000). A deeper understanding of hypnosis: Its secrets, its nature, its essence. *American Journal of Clinical Hypnosis, 42*(3–4), 208–272.

Bard, C., Fleury, M., & Goulet, C. (1994). Relationship between perceptual strategies and response adequacy in sport situations. *International Journal of Sport Psychology, 25*(3), 266–281.

Bargh, J. A., McKenna, K. Y. A., & Fitzsimons, G. M. (2002). Can you see the real me? Activation and expression of the "true self" on the Internet. *Journal of Social Issues, 58*(1), 33–48.

Barkataki, I., Kumari, V., Das, M., Taylor, P. et al. (2006). Volumetric structural brain abnormalities in men with schizophrenia or antisocial personality disorder. *Behavioural Brain Research, 169*(2), 239–247.

Barlow, D. H. (2000). Unraveling the mysteries of anxiety and its disorders from the perspective of emotion theory. *American Psychologist, 55*, 1247–1263.

Barlow, D. H. (2002). *Anxiety and its disorders* (2nd ed.). New York: Guilford.

Barlow, D. H. (2004). Psychological treatments. *American Psychologist, 59*(9), 869–878.

Barnier, A. J., McConkey, K. M., & Wright, J. (2004). Posthypnotic amnesia for autobiographical episodes: Influencing memory accessibility and quality. *International Journal of Clinical and Experimental Hypnosis, 52*(3), 260–279.

Baron, I. S. (2005). Test review: Wechsler intelligence scale for children (4th ed.). (WISC-IV). *Child Neuropsychology, 11*(5), 471–475.

Baron, R. A., Byrne, D. E., & Branscombe, N. R. (2006). *Social psychology* (11th ed.). Boston: Allyn & Bacon.

Baron, R. S. (2005). So right it's wrong: Groupthink and the ubiquitous nature of polarized group decision making In M. P. Zanna (Ed.), *Advances in experimental social psychology* (Vol. 37). San Diego, CA: Elsevier.

Barrett, D. (1993). The "committee of sleep": A study of dream incubation for problem solving. *Dreaming, 3*(2), 115–122.

Barrick, M. R., Moun, M. K., & Judge, T. A. (2001). Personality and performance at the beginning of the new millennium. *International Journal of Selection & Assessment, 9*(1–2), 9–30.

Barron, F. (1958). The psychology of imagination. *Scientific American, 199*(3), 150–170.

Barrowcliff, A. L., & Haddock, G. (2006). The relationship between command hallucinations and factors of compliance: A critical review of the literature. *Journal of Forensic Psychiatry & Psychology, 17*(2), 266–298.

Bar-Tal, D., & Labin, D. (2001). The effect of a major event on stereotyping: Terrorist attacks in Israel and Israeli adolescents' perceptions of Palestinians, Jordanians and Arabs. *European Journal of Social Psychology, 31*(3), 265–280.

Bartholow, B. D., & Anderson, C. A. (2002). Effects of violent video games on aggressive behavior. *Journal of Experimental Social Psychology, 38*(3), 283–290.

Bartholow, B. D., Bushman, B. J., & Sestir, M. A. (2006). Chronic violent video game exposure and desensitization to violence: Behavioral and event-related brain potential data. *Journal of Experimental Social Psychology, 42*(4), 532–539.

Bartholow, B. D., Sestir, M. A., & Davis, E. B. (2005). Correlates and consequences of exposure to video game violence: Hostile personality, empathy, and aggressive behavior. *Personality & Social Psychology Bulletin, 31*(11), 1573–1586.

Bartlett, J. C., & Searcy, J. (1993). Inversion and configuration of faces. *Cognitive Psychology, 25*(3), 281–316.

Bartz, W. R. (2002). Teaching skepticism via the CRITIC acronym. *Skeptical Inquirer*, Sept-Oct, 42–44.

Basson, R., Brotto, L. A., Laan, E., Redmond, G., et al. (2005). Assessment and management of women's sexual dysfunctions: Problematic desire and arousal. *Journal of Sexual Medicine, 2*(3), 291–300.

Bath, H. (1996). Everyday discipline or control with care. *Journal of Child & Youth Care, 10*(2), 23–32.

Batson, C. D. (2006). "Not all self-interest after all": Economics of empathy-induced altruism. In D. De Cremer, M. Zeelenberg, & J. K. Murnighan (Eds.), *Social psychology and economics*. Mahwah, NJ: Erlbaum.

Batson, C. D., & Powell, A. A. (2003). Altruism and prosocial behavior. In T. Millon, & M. J. Lerner (Eds.), *Handbook of psychology: Personality and social psychology* (Vol. 5). New York: Wiley.

Batterham, R. L., Cohen, M. A., Ellis, S. M., Le Roux, C. E., et al. (2003). Inhibition of food intake in obese subjects by peptide YY3–36. *New England Journal of Medicine, 349*, 941–948.

Baum, A., & Posluszny, D. M. (1999). Health psychology. *Annual Review of Psychology, 50*, 137–163.

Baumeister, R. F., Campbell, J. D., Krueger, J. I., & Vohs, K. D. (2003). Does high self-esteem cause better performance, interpersonal success, happiness, or healthier lifestyles? *Psychological Science in the Public Interest, 4*(1), 1–44.

Baumrind, D. (1991). The influence of parenting style on adolescent competence and substance use. *Journal of Early Adolescence, 11*(1), 56–95.

Baumrind, D. (2005). Patterns of parental authority and adolescent autonomy. In J. Smetana (Ed.), *New directions for child development: Changes in parental authority during adolescence*. San Francisco: Jossey-Bass.

Baumrind, D., Larzelere, R. E., & Cowan, P. A. (2002). Ordinary physical punishment: Is it harmful? *Psychological Bulletin, 128*(4), 580–589.

Bearman, P. S., Moody, J., & Stovel, K. (2004). Chains of affection: The structure of adolescent romantic and sexual networks. *American Journal of Sociology, 110*(1), 44–91.

Beck, A. T. (1991). Cognitive therapy. *American Psychologist, 46*(4), 368–375.

Beck, A. T. (2004). Cognitive patterns in dreams and daydreams. In R. I. Rosner, & W. J. Lyddon (Eds.), *Cognitive therapy and dreams.* New York: Springer Publishing.

Beck, A. T., & Greenberg, R. L. (1974). *Coping with depression.* Institute For Rational Living.

Beck, A. T., Brown, C., Berchick, R. J., Stewart, B. L., et al. (1990). Relationship between hopelessness and ultimate suicide. *American Journal of Psychiatry, 147*(2), 190–195.

Beck, B. L., Koons, S. R., & Milgrim, D. L. (2000). Correlates and consequences of behavioral procrastination. *Journal of Social Behavior & Personality, 15*(5), 3–13.

Beck, J. S. (2002). Beck therapy approach. In M. Hersen & W. H. Sledge (Eds.), *Encyclopedia of psychotherapy.* San Diego: Academic Press.

Beck, R. C. (2004). *Motivation: Theories and principles* (5th ed.). Englewood Cliffs, NJ: Prentice Hall.

Beebe, B., Gerstman, L., Carson, B., Dolins, M., Zigman, A., Rosenweig, H., Faughey K., & Korman, M. (1982). Rhythmic communication in the mother-infant dyad. In M. Davis (Ed.), *Interaction rhythms, periodicity in communicative behavior.* New York: Human Sciences Press.

Behrend, D. A., Beike, D. R., & Lampinen, J. M. (2004). *The self and memory.* Hove, UK: Psychology Press.

Beirne-Smith, M., Patton, J., & Shannon, K. (2006). *Mental retardation: An introduction to intellectual disability* (7th ed.). Englewood Cliffs, NJ: Prentice Hall.

Belenky, G., Wesensten, N. J., Thorne, D. R., Thomas, M. L., et al. (2003). Patterns of performance degradation and restoration during sleep restriction and subsequent recovery: A sleep dose-response study. *Journal of Sleep Research, 12*(1), 1–12.

Beljan, J. R., Rosenblatt, L. S., Hetherington, N. W., Layman, J., et al. (1972). Human performance in the aviation environment. *NASA Contract no 2-6657, Pt. Ia,* 253–259.

Bellezza, F. S., Six, L. S., & Phillips, D. S. (1992). A mnemonic for remembering long strings of digits. *Bulletin of the Psychonomic Society, 30*(4), 271–274.

Belsky, J. (1996). Parent, infant, and social-contextual antecedents of father-son attachment security. *Developmental Psychology, 32*(5), 905–913.

Bem, S. L. (1974). The measurement of psychological androgyny. *Journal of Consulting & Clinical Psychology, 42*(2), 155–162.

Bem, S. L. (1981). Gender schema theory. A cognitive account of sex typing. *Psychological Review, 88,* 354–364.

Benbow, C. P. (1986). Physiological correlates of extreme intellectual precocity. *Neuropsychologia, 24*(5), 719–725.

Benjafield, J. G. (2004). *A history of psychology* (2nd ed.). Boston: Allyn & Bacon.

Benloucif, S., Bennett, E. L., & Rosenzweig, M. R. (1995). Norepinephrine and neural plasticity: The effects of xylamine on experience-induced changes in brain weight, memory, and behavior. *Neurobiology of Learning & Memory, 63*(1), 33–42.

Bensafi, M., Zelano, C., Johnson, B., Mainland, J., Khan, R., & Sobel, N. (2004). Olfaction: From sniff to percept. In M. S. Gazzaniga (Ed.), *The cognitive neurosciences* (3rd ed.). Cambridge, MA: MIT Press.

Ben-Shakhar, G., & Dolev, K. (1996). Psychophysiological detection through the guilty knowledge technique: Effect of mental countermeasures. *Journal of Applied Psychology, 81*(3), 273–281.

Bensley, L., & Van Eenwyk, J. (2001). Video games and real-life aggression. *Journal of Adolescent Health, 29*(4), 244–257.

Benson, H. (1977). Systematic hypertension and the relaxation response. *The New England Journal of Medicine, 296,* 1152–1156.

Benson, J., Greaves, W., O'Donnell, M., & Taglialatela, J. (2002). Evidence for symbolic language processing in a Bonobo (Pan paniscus). *Journal of Consciousness Studies, 9*(12), 33–56.

Bergin, A. E. (1991). Values and religious issues in psychotherapy and mental health. *American Psychologist, 46,* (4), 394–403.

Berne, E. (1964). *Games people play.* New York: Grove.

Bernstein, H. J., Beale, M. D., Burns, C., & Kellner, C. H. (1998). Patient attitudes about ECT after treatment. *Psychiatric Annals, 28*(9), 524–527.

Bernthal, M. J. (2003) The effects of professional wrestling viewership on children. *The Sport Journal, 6*(3). Retrieved August 1, 2006, from http://www.thesportjournal.org/2003Journal/Vol6-No3/wrestling.htm.

Berntsen, D., & Thomsen, D. K. (2005). Personal memories for remote historical events: Accuracy and clarity of flashbulb memories related to World War II. *Journal of Experimental Psychology: General, 134*(2), 242–257.

Berry, J. W. (1990). The psychology of acculturation. In R. A. Dienstbier, & J. J. Berman (Eds.), *Nebraska Symposium on Motivation 1989: Cross-cultural perspectives, 37.* Lincoln: University of Nebraska Press.

Berry, J. W., Phinney, J. S, Sam, D. L., & Vedder, P. (2005). *Immigrant youth in cultural transition.* Mahwah, NJ: Erlbaum.

Berscheid, E., & Regan, P. (2005). *The psychology of interpersonal relationships.* Englewood Cliffs, NJ: Prentice Hall.

Berscheid, E. (2000). Attraction. In A. Kazdin (Ed.), *Encyclopedia of psychology.* Washington: American Psychological Association.

Bersoff, D. M. (1999). Why good people sometimes do bad things: Motivated reasoning and unethical behavior. *Personality & Social Psychology Bulletin, 25*(1), 28–39.

Bertsch, G. J. (1976). Punishment of consummatory and instrumental behavior: A review. *Psychological Record, 26,* 13–31.

Betancur, C., Velez, A., Cabanieu, G., le Moal, M., et al. (1990). Association between left-handedness and allergy: A reappraisal. *Neuropsychologia, 28*(2), 223–227.

Beyerstein, B. L., & Beyerstein, D. F. (1992). *The write stuff: Evaluations of graphology.* Buffalo, NY: Prometheus.

Bickman, L. (1974). Clothes make the person. *Psychology Today,* April, 48–51.

Binder, J. L. (2004). *Key competencies in brief dynamic psychotherapy: Clinical practice beyond the manual.* New York: Guilford.

Binks, P.G., Waters, W. F., & Hurry, M. (1999). Short-term total sleep deprivations does not selectively impair higher cortical functioning. *Sleep, 22*(3), 328–334.

Birch, J., & McKeever, L. M. (1993). Survey of the accuracy of new pseudoisochromatic plates. *Ophthalmic & Physiological Optics, 13*(1), 35–40.

Birnbaum, M. H. (2004). Human research and data collection via the Internet. *Annual Review of Psychology, 55,* 803–832.

Blackmore, S. (1989). What do we really think? A survey of parapsychologists and sceptics. *Journal of the Society for Psychical Research, 55*(814), 251–262.

Blackmore, S. (2001). Giving up the ghosts. *Skeptical Inquirer, March-April,* 25.

Blackmore, S. (2004). *Consciousness: An introduction.* New York: Oxford University Press.

Blackwell, D. L., & Lichter, D. T. (2004). Homogamy among dating, cohabiting, and married couples. *Sociological Quarterly, 45*(4), 719–737.

Blair, K. S., Richell, R. A., Mitchell, D. G. V., Leonard, A., et al. (2006). They know the words, but not the music: Affective and semantic priming in individuals with psychopathy. *Biological Psychology, 73*(2), 114–123.

Blakemore, C., & Cooper, G., (1970). Development of the brain depends on the visual environment. *Nature, 228,* 477–478.

Blanchard, D. C., & Blanchard, R. J. (2003). What can animal aggression research tell us about human aggression? *Hormones & Behavior, 44*(3), 171–177.

Blanchard, E. B., Kuhn, E., Rowell, D. L., Hickling, E. J., et al. (2004). Studies of the vicarious traumatization of college students by the September llth attacks: Effects of proximity, exposure and connectedness. *Behaviour Research & Therapy, 42*(2), 191–205.

Bloch, S. (2006). *Introduction to the psychotherapies* (4th ed.). New York: Oxford University Press.

Blood, A. J., & Zatorre, R. J. (2001). Intensely pleasurable responses to music correlate with activity in brain regions implicated in reward and emotion. *Proceedings National Academy of Sciences, 98*(20) 11818–11823.

Bloom, B. (1985). *Developing talent in young people.* New York: Ballantine.

Bloom, J. W. (1998). The ethical practice of WebCounseling. *British Journal of Guidance & Counselling, 26*(1), 53–59.

Blunt, A., & Pychyl, T. A. (2005). Project systems of procrastinators: A personal project-analytic and action control perspective. *Personality & Individual Differences, 38*(8), 1771–1780.

Boergers, J., Spirito, A., & Donaldson, D. (1998). Reasons for adolescent suicide attempts. *Journal of the American Academy of Child & Adolescent Psychiatry, 37*(12), 1287–1293.

Bohannon, J. N., & Stanowicz, L. B. (1988). The issue of negative evidence: Adult responses to children's language errors. *Developmental Psychology, 24*(5), 684–689.

Boivin, D. B., Czeisler, C. A., & Waterhouse, J. W. (1997). Complex interaction of the sleep-wake cycle and circadian phase modulates mood in healthy subjects. *Archives of General Psychiatry, 54*(2), 145–152.

Boldero, J. M., Moretti, M. M., Bell, R. C., & Francis, J. J. (2005). Self-discrepancies and negative affect: A primer on when to look for specificity, and how to find it. *Australian Journal of Psychology, 57*(3), 139–147.

Bonanno, G. A., Papa, A., Lalande, K., Westphal, M., et al. (2004). The importance of being flexible. *Psychological Science, 15*(7), 482–487.

Bond, R., & Smith, P. B. (1996). Culture and conformity: A meta-analysis of studies using Asch's (1952, 1956) line judgment task. *Psychological Bulletin, 119,* 111–137.

Bongard, S., al'Absi, M., & Lovallo, W. R. (1998). Interactive effects of trait hostility and anger expression on cardiovascular reactivity in young men. *International Journal of Psychophysiology, 28*(2), 181–191.

Bonham, V., Warshauer-Baker, E., & Collins, F. S. (2005). Race and ethnicity in the genome era: The complexity of the constructs. *American Psychologist, 60*(1), 9–15.

Boniecki, K. A., & Britt, T. W. (2003). Prejudice and the peacekeeper. In T. W. Britt & A. B Adler (Eds.), *The psychology of the peacekeeper: Lessons from the field. Psychological dimensions to war and peace.* Westport, CT: Praeger.

Booker, J. M., & Hellekson, C. J. (1992). Prevalence of seasonal affective disorder in Alaska. *American Journal of Psychiatry, 149*(9), 1176–1182.

Bootzin, R. R., & Epstein, D. R. (2000). Stimulus control. In K. L. Lich & C. M. Morin (Eds.), *Treatment of late life insomnia.* Thousand Oaks, CA: Sage.

Borlongan, C. V., Sanberg, P. R., & Freeman, T. B. (1999). Neural transplantation for neurodegenerative disorders. *Lancet, 353*(Suppl. 1), S29–30.

Bornstein, M. H., & Tamis-LeMonda, C. S. (2001). Mother-infant interaction. In A. Fogel & G. Bremner (Eds.), *Blackwell handbook of infant development.* London: Blackwell.

Bornstein, R. F. (1996). Sex differences in dependent personality disorder prevalence rates. *Clinical Psychology: Science & Practice, 3*(1), 1–12.

Borod, J. C., Bloom, R. L., Brickman, A. M., Nakhutina, L., et al. (2002). Emotional processing deficits in individuals with unilateral brain damage. *Applied Neuropsychology, 9*(1), 23–36.

Bouchard, Jr., T. J. (1983). Twins—Nature's twice-told tale. *Yearbook of science and the future,* 66–81. Chicago: Encyclopedia Britannica.

Bouchard, Jr., T. J. (2004). Genetic influence on human psychological traits: A survey. *Current Directions in Psychological Science, 13*(4), 148–151.

Bouchard, Jr., T. J., Lykken, D. T., McGue, M., Segal, N. L., et al. (1990). Sources of human psychological differences: The Minnesota study of twins reared apart. *Science, 250,* 223–228.

Bourne, E. J. (2005). *The anxiety & phobia workbook* (4th ed.). Oakland, CA: New Harbinger.

Bovbjerg, D. H., Redd, W. H., Jacobsen, P. B., Manne, S. L., et al. (1992). An experimental analysis of classically conditioned nausea during cancer chemotherapy. *Psychosomatic Medicine, 54*(6), 623–637.

Bower, G. H. (1981). Mood and memory. *American Psychologist, 36,* 129–148.

Bower, G. H., & Springston, F. (1970). Pauses as recoding points in letter series. *Journal of Experimental Psychology, 83,* 421–430.

Boyle, S. H., Williams, R. B., Mark, D., Brummett, B. H., et al. (2004). Hostility as a predictor of survival in patients with coronary artery disease. *Psychosomatic Medicine, 66*(5), 629–632.

Brach, T. (2003). *Radical acceptance.* New York: Bantam Books

Bradley, R. H., & Corwyn, R. F. (2002). Socioeconomic status and child development. *Annual Review of Psychology, 53,* 377–399.

Bradshaw, S. D. (2006). Shyness and difficult relationships: Formation is just the beginning. In D. C. Kirkpatrick, D. S. Duck, & M. K. Foley (Eds.), *Relating difficulty: The processes of constructing and managing difficult interaction.* Mahwah, NJ: Erlbaum.

Brainerd, C. J. (2003). Jean Piaget, learning research, and American education. In B. J. Zimmerman & D. H. Schunk (Eds.), *Educational psychology: A century of contributions.* Mahwah, NJ: Erlbaum.

Brannon, L. (1996). Gender. Boston: Allyn & Bacon.

Brannon, L., & Feist, J. (2007). *Health psychology: An introduction to behavior and health* (6th ed.). Belmont, CA: Wadsworth.

Bransford, J. D., & McCarrell, N. S. (1977). A sketch of cognitive approach to comprehension: Some thoughts about understanding what it means to comprehend. In P. N. Johnson-Laird & P. C. Wason (Eds.), *Thinking: Readings in cognitive science.* Cambridge, MA: Cambridge University Press.

Braun, A. R., Balkin, T. J., & Herscovitch, P. (1998). Dissociated pattern of activity in visual cortices and their projections during human rapid eye movement sleep. *Science, 279*(5347), 91–95.

Braun, K. A., Ellis, R., & Loftus, E. F. (2002). Make my memory: How advertising can change memories of the past. *Psychology and Marketing, 19,* 1–23.

Braun, S. (2001). Seeking insight by prescription. *Cerebrum, 3*(2), 10–21.

Breckler, S. J., Olson, J., & Wiggins, E. (2006). *Social psychology alive.* Belmont, CA: Wadsworth.

Brehm, S. S., & Kassin, S. M., & Fein, S. (2005). *Social psychology* (6th ed.). Boston: Houghton Mifflin.

Breslau, N., Johnson, E. O., Hiripi, E., & Kessler, R. (2001). Nicotine dependence in the United States. *Archives of General Psychiatry, 58*(9), 810–816.

Bressi, C., Albonetti, S., & Razzoli, E. (1998). "Communication deviance" and schizophrenia. *New Trends in Experimental & Clinical Psychiatry, 14*(1), 33–39.

Bretherton, R., & Orner, R. J. (2004). Positive psychology and psychotherapy: An existential approach. In P. A. Linley & S. Joseph (Eds.), *Positive psychology in practice.* New York: Wiley.

Brewer, K. R., & Wann, D. L. (1998). Observational learning effectiveness as a function of model characteristics. *Social Behavior & Personality, 26*(1), 1–10.

Brewer, N., & Wells, G. L. (2006). The confidence-accuracy relationship in eyewitness identification: Effects of lineup instructions, foil similarity, and target-absent base rates. *Journal of Experimental Psychology: Applied, 12*(1), 11–30.

Bridges, K. M. B. (1932). Emotional development in early infancy. *Child Development, 3,* 324–334.

Bridges, L. J. (2003). Trust, attachment, and relatedness. In M. H. Bornstein, L. Davidson, C. L. M. Keyes, & K. Moore (Eds.), *Well-being: Positive development across the life course.* Mahwah, NJ: Erlbaum.

Brock, T. C., & Green, M. C. (Eds.). (2005). *Persuasion: Psychological insights and perspectives* (2nd ed.). Thousand Oaks, CA: Sage.

Brothen, T., & Wambach, C. (2001). Effective student use of computerized quizzes. *Teaching of Psychology, 28*(4), 292–294.

Brown, A. M. (1990). Development of visual sensitivity to light and color vision in human infants: A critical review. *Vision Research, 30*(8), 1159–1188.

Brown, A. S. (2004). *The déjà vu experience.* New York: Psychology Press.

Brown, A. S., Cohen, P., Harkavy-Friedman, J., Babulas, V., et al. (2001). Prenatal rubella, premorbid abnormalities, and adult schizophrenia. *Biological Psychiatry, 49*(6), 473–486.

Brown, L. M. (2005). *Girlfighting: Betrayal and rejection among girls.* New York: New York University Press.

Brown, P. (1990). The name game. *Journal of Mind and Behavior, 11,* 385–406.

Brown, R. L., Leonard, T., Saunders, L. A., & Papasouiotis, O. (1997). A two-item screening test for alcohol and other drug problems. *Journal of Family Practice, 44*(2), 151–160.

Brown, R., & McNeill, D. (1966). The "tip of the tongue" phenomenon. *Journal of Verbal Learning & Verbal Behavior, 5*(4), 325–337.

Brown, S. A., Tapert, S. F., Granholm, E., & Delis, D. C. (2000). Neurocognitive functioning of adolescents: Effects of protracted alcohol use. *Alcoholism: Clinical & Experimental Research, 24*(2), 164–171.

Brown, S. G., Roy, E., Rohr, L., & Bryden, P. (2006). Using hand performance measures to predict handedness. *Laterality: Asymmetries of Body, Brain & Cognition, 11*(1), 1–14.

Brown, T. A., & Barlow, D. H. (2007). *Casebook in abnormal psychology* (3rd ed.). Belmont, CA: Thomson/Wadsworth.

Brown, T. D., Dane, F. C., & Durham, M. D. (1998). Perception of race and ethnicity. *Journal of Social Behavior & Personality, 13*(2), 295–306.

Browne, N., & Keeley, S. (2007). *Asking the right questions: A guide to critical thinking* (8th ed.). Englewood Cliffs, NJ: Prentice Hall.

Brownell, K. D. (2003). *Food fight.* New York: McGraw-Hill.

Bruch, M. A. (2001). Shyness and social interaction. In R. Crozier, & L. Alden (Eds.), *International handbook of social anxiety.* Sussex, England: Wiley.

Bruer, J. T. (2001). A critical and sensitive period primer. In D. B. Bailey, Jr., J. T. Bruer, F. J. Symons, & J. W. Lichtman, (Eds.), *Critical thinking about critical periods.* Baltimore, MD: Paul H. Brookes Publishing.

Bruner, J. (1973). *Going beyond the information given.* New York: Norton.

Bruner, J. (1983). *Child's Talk.* New York: Norton.

Bryan, J. H., & Walbek, N. H. (1970). Preaching and practicing generosity: Children's actions and reactions. *Child Development, 41,* 329–353.

Bryden, P. J., & Bruyn, J., Fletcher, P. (2005). Handedness and health: An examination of the association between different handedness classifications and health disorders. *Laterality: Asymmetries of Body, Brain & Cognition, 10*(5), 429–440.

Buchwald, A. (1965). Psyching out. *The Washington Post,* June 20.

Buddie, A. M. (2004). Alternatives to twelve-step programs. *Journal of Forensic Psychology Practice, 4*(3), 61–70.

Budney, A. J., & Hughes, J. R. (2006). The cannabis withdrawal syndrome. *Current Opinion in Psychiatry, 19*(3), 233–238.

Buehner, M. J., & May, J. (2003). Rethinking temporal contiguity and the judgement of causality: Effects of prior knowledge, experience, and reinforcement procedure. *Quarterly Journal of Experimental Psychology A: Human Experimental Psychology, 56A*(5), 865–890.

Buller, D. J. (2005). *Adapting minds: Evolutionary psychology and the persistent quest for human nature.* Cambridge, MA: MIT Press.

Bunde, J., & Suls, J. (2006). A quantitative analysis of the relationship between the cook-medley hostility scale and traditional coronary artery disease risk factors. *Health Psychology, 25*(4), 493–500.

Burchinal, M. R., Roberts, J. E., Riggins, R., Zeisel, S. A., et al. (2000). Relating quality of center-based child care to early cognitive and language development longitudinally. *Child Development, 71*(2), 339–357.

Burger, J. M., & Lynn, A. L. (2005). Superstitious behavior among American and Japanese professional baseball players. *Basic & Applied Social Psychology, 27*(1), 71–76.

Burgess, C. A., & Kirsch, I. (1999). Expectancy information as a moderator of the effects of hypnosis on memory. *Contemporary Hypnosis, 16*(1), 22–31.

Burgess, M. C. R., & Weaver, G. E. (2003). Interest and attention in facial recognition. *Perceptual & Motor Skills, 96*(2), 467–480.

Burgner, D., & Hewstone, M. (1993). Young children's causal attributions for success and failure. *British Journal of Developmental Psychology, 11*(2), 125–129.

Burlingame, G. M., Fuhriman, A., & Mosier, J. (2003). The differential effectiveness of group psychotherapy: A meta-analytic perspective. *Group Dynamics: Theory, Research, and Practice, 7*(1), 3–12.

Burlingame, G., & Davies, R. (2002). Self-help groups. In M. Hersen & W. H. Sledge (Eds.), *Encyclopedia of psychotherapy.* San Diego: Academic Press.

Burnett, R. C., Medin, D. L., Ross, N. O., & Blok, S. V. (2005). Ideal is typical. *Canadian Journal of Experimental Psychology. Special Issue on 2003 Festschrift for Lee R. Brooks, 59*(1), 3–10.

Burns, D. D., & Persons, J. (1982). Hope and hopelessness: A cognitive approach. In L. E. Abt & I. R. Stuart (Eds.), *The newer therapies: A sourcebook.* New York: Van Nostrand Reinhold.

Burns, T. (2004). *Community mental health teams: A guide to current practices.* New York: Oxford.

Burton, C. M., & King, L. A. (2004). The health benefits of writing about intensely positive experiences. *Journal of Research in Personality, 38*(2), 150–163.

Burtt, H. E. (1941). An experimental study of early childhood memory: Final report. *Journal of General Psychology, 58,* 435–439.

Bushman, B. J., & Anderson, C. A. (2001). Media violence and the American public. *American Psychologist, 56*(6/7), 477–489.

Bushnell, L. W., Sai, F., & Mullin, L. T. (1989). Neonatal recognition of the mother's face. *British Journal of Developmental Psychology, 7*(1), 3–15.

Bushnell, M. C., Villemure, C., & Duncan, G. H. (2004). Psychophysical and neurophysiological studies of pain modulation by attention. In D. D. Price & M. C. Bushnell (Eds.), *Psychological methods of pain control: Basic science and clinical perspectives.* Seattle, WA: IASP Press.

Buss, D. M. (1985). Human mate selection. *American Scientist, 73,* 47–51.

Buss, D. M. (2000). The evolution of happiness. *American Psychologist, 55,* 15–23.

Buss, D. M. (2004). *Evolutionary psychology: The new science of the mind* (2nd ed.). Boston: Allyn & Bacon.

Butcher, J. N. (2005). *A beginner's guide to the MMPI-2* (2nd ed.). Washington: American Psychological Association.

Butcher, J. N., Mineka, S., & Hooley, J. (2004). *Abnormal psychology and modern life* (12th ed.). Boston: Allyn & Bacon.

Butcher, J. N. (Ed.). (2006). *MMPI-2: A practitioner's guide*. Washington: American Psychological Association.

Butkovic, A., & Bratko, D. (2003). Generation and sex differences in sensation seeking: Results of the family study. *Perceptual and Motor Skills, 97*(3, Pt 1), 965–970.

Butler, J. C. (2000). Personality and emotional correlates of right-wing authoritarianism. *Social Behavior & Personality, 28*(1), 1–14.

Butler, M. G. (2001). *Overcoming social anxiety and shyness: A self-help guide using cognitive behavioral techniques*. New York: New York University Press.

Butler, R. (1954). Curiosity in monkeys. *Scientific American, 190*(18), 70–75.

Byrne, S. M., & McLean, N. J. (2002). The cognitive-behavioral model of bulimia nervosa: A direct evaluation. *International Journal of Eating Disorders, 31*, 17–31.

Cahill, S. P., Carrigan, M. H., & Frueh, B. C. (1999). Does EMDR work? and if so, why? *Journal of Anxiety Disorders, 13*(1–2), 5–33.

Cahn, B. R., & Polich, J. (2006). Meditation states and traits: EEG, ERP, and neuroimaging studies. *Psychological Bulletin, 132*(2), 180–211.

Callahan, C. M. (2006). Giftedness. In G. G. Bear & K. M. Minke, (Eds.), *Children's needs III: Development, prevention, and intervention*. Washington: National Association of School Psychologists.

Camara, W. J., & Schneider, D. L. (1994). Integrity tests. *American Psychologist, 49*(2), 112–119.

Cameron, J. A., & Trope, Y. (2004). Stereotype-biased search and processing of information about group members. *Social Cognition, 22*(6), 650–672.

Cameron, J., & Pierce, W. D. (2002). *Rewards and intrinsic motivation: Resolving the controversy*. Westport, CO: Bergin & Garvey.

Cameron, L. D., & Nicholls, G. (1998). Expression of stressful experiences through writing. *Health Psychology, 17*(1), 84–92.

Campbell, L., Campbell, B., & Dickinson, D. (2003). *Teaching and learning through multiple intelligences* (3rd ed.). Boston: Allyn & Bacon.

Campos, A., Amor, A., & González, M. A. (2004). The importance of the keyword-generation method in keyword mnemonics. *Experimental Psychology, 51*(2), 125–131.

Canli, T., Desmond, J. E., Zhao, Z., Glover, G., et al. (1998). Hemispheric asymmetry for emotional stimuli detected with fMRI. *Neuroreport, 9*(14) 3233–3239.

Cannon, W. B. (1932). *The wisdom of the body*. New York: Norton.

Cannon, W. B. (1934). Hunger and thirst. In C. Murchinson (Ed.), *Handbook of general experimental psychology*. Worcester, MA: Clark University Press.

Cannon, W. B., & Washburn, A. L. (1912). An explanation of hunger. *American Journal of Physiology, 29*, 444–454.

Caplan, P. J. (1995). *They say you're crazy*. Reading, MA: Addison-Wesley.

Capuzzi, D. (2003). *Approaches to group counseling*. Englewood Cliffs, NJ: Prentice Hall.

Cardenas, D. D., & Jensen, M. P. (2006). Treatments for chronic pain in persons with spinal cord injury: A survey study. *Journal of Spinal Cord Medicine, 29*(2):109–117.

Cardoso, S. H. (2000). Our ancient laughing brain. *Cerebrum, 2*(4), 15–30.

Carlson, M., Marcus-Hewhall, A., & Miller, N. (1990). Effects of situational aggression cues: A quantitative review. *Journal of Personality & Social Psychology, 58*(4), 622–633.

Carlson, N. R. (2005). *Physiology of behavior* (8th ed.). Boston: Allyn & Bacon.

Carnagey, N. L., & Anderson, C. A. (2004). Violent video game exposure and aggression: A literature review. *Minerva Psichiatrica, 45*(1), 1–18.

Carney, P. R., Geyer, J. D., & Berry, R. B. (Eds.). (2005). *Clinical sleep disorders*. Philadelphia, PA: Lippincott Williams & Wilkins.

Carney, R. N., & Levin, J. R. (2001). Remembering the names of unfamiliar animals: Keywords as keys to their kingdom. *Applied Cognitive Psychology, 15*(2), 133–143.

Carney, R. N., & Levin, J. R. (2003). Promoting higher-order learning benefits by building lower-order mnemonic connections. *Applied Cognitive Psychology, 17*(5), 563–575.

Carroll, D. W. (2004). *Psychology of language* (4th ed.). Belmont, CA: Wadsworth.

Carroll, J. M., & Russell, J. A. (1996). Do facial expressions signal specific emotions? Judging emotion from the face in context. *Journal of Personality & Social Psychology, 70*(2), 205–218.

Carskadon, M. A., Acebo, C., & Jenni, O. C. (2004). Regulation of adolescent sleep: Implications for behavior. *Annals of the New York Academy of Science, 1021*, 276–291.

Carter, R. (1998). *Mapping the mind*. Berkeley, CA: University of California Press.

Cartwright, D. (2002a). *Psychoanalysis, violence and rage-type murder: Murdering minds*. New York: Brunner-Routledge.

Cartwright, D. (2002b). The narcissistic exoskeleton: The defensive organization of the rage-type murderer. *Bulletin of the Menninger Clinic, 66*(1), 1–18.

Cartwright, R., & Lamberg, L. (1992). *Crisis dreaming*. New York: HarperCollins.

Casey, P. (2001). Multiple personality disorder. *Primary Care Psychiatry, 7*(1), 7–11.

Caspi, A. Sugden, K., Moffitt, T. E., Taylor, A., et al. (2003). Influence of life stress on depression: Moderation by a polymorphism in the 5-HTT gene. *Science, 301*(5631), 386–389.

Caspi, A., Roberts, B. W., & Shiner, R. L. (2005). Personality development: Stability and change. *Annual Review of Psychology, 56*, 453–484.

Cassady, J. C. (2004). The influence of cognitive test anxiety across the learning-testing cycle. *Learning & Instruction, 14*(6), 569–592.

Castro, J. R., & Rice, K. G. (2003). Perfectionism and ethnicity: Implications for depressive symptoms and self-reported academic achievement. *Cultural Diversity and Ethnic Minority Psychology, 9*(1), 64–78.

Castro, J., Gila, A., Gual, P., Lahortiga, F., et al. (2004). Perfectionism dimensions in children and adolescents with anorexia nervosa. *Journal of Adolescent Health, 35*(5), 392–398.

Catalano, R., Novaco, R., & McConnell, W. (1997). A model of the net effect of job loss on violence. *Journal of Personality & Social Psychology, 72*(6), 1440–1447.

Cattell, R. B. (1965). *The scientific analysis of personality*. Baltimore: Penguin.

Cattell, R. B. (1973). Personality pinned down. *Psychology Today*, July, 40–46.

Cautela, J. R., & Kearney, A. J. (1986). *The covert conditioning handbook*. New York: Springer.

Cavaco, S., Anderson, S. W., Allen, J. S., Castro-Caldas, A., et al. (2004). The scope of preserved procedural memory in amnesia. *Brain: A Journal of Neurology, 127*(8), 1853–1867.

CDC. (2003). *Deaths, percent of total deaths, and death rates for 15 leading causes of death in 5-year age groups, by race and sex: United States, 2000*. Centers for Disease Control and National Center for Health Statistics, National Vital Statistics System. Downloaded September 20, 2006, from http://www.cdc.gov/nchs/datawh/statab/unpubd/mortabs/lcwk1_10.htm.

CDC. (2005). Annual smoking-attributable mortality, years of potential life lost, and productivity losses: United States, 1997–2001. *Centers for Disease Control and Prevention Morbidity and Mortality Weekly Report, 54*(25), 625–628.

Cecil, H., Evans, R. J., & Stanley, M. A. (1996). Perceived believability among adolescents of health warning labels on cigarette packs. *Journal of Applied Social Psychology, 26*(6), 502–519.

Chakos, M. H., Alvir, J. M. J., Woerner, M., & Koreen, A. (1996). Incidence and correlates of tardive dyskinesia in first episode of schizophrenia. *Archives of General Psychiatry, 53*(4), 313–319.

Chamberlin, J. (2004). Survey says: More Americans are seeking mental health treatment. *Monitor on Psychology*, July/Aug., 17.

Chamberlin, J., & Rogers, J. A. (1990). Planning a community-based mental health system. *American Psychologist, 45*(11), 1241–1244.

Chambers, R. A., Taylor, J. R., & Potenza, M. N. (2003). Developmental neurocircuitry of motivation in adolescence: A critical period of addiction vulnerability. *American Journal of Psychiatry, 160*(6), 1041–1052.

Chambless, D. L., & Ollendick, T. H. (2001). Empirically supported psychological interventions. *Annual Review of Psychology, 52*, 685–716.

Chamorro-Premuzic, T., & Furnham, A. (2003). Personality predicts academic performance. *Journal of Research in Personality, 37*(4), 319–338.

Chan, R. W., Raboy, B., & Patterson, C. J. (1998). Psychosocial adjustment among children conceived via donor insemination by lesbian and heterosexual mothers. *Child Development, 69*(2), 443–457.

Chance, P. (2006). *Learning and behavior* (5th ed.). Belmont, CA: Wadsworth.

Chansler, P. A., Swamidass, P. M., & Cammann, C. (2003). Self-managing work teams: An empirical study of group cohesiveness in "natural work groups" at a Harley-Davidson Motor Company plant. *Small Group Research, 34*(1), 101–120.

Chao, R., & Tseng, V. (2002). Parenting of Asians. In M. H. Bornstein (Ed.), *Handbook of parenting* (Vol. 4): *Social conditions and applied parenting* (2nd ed.). Mahwah, NJ: Erlbaum.

Chapman, R. A. (Ed.). (2006). *The clinical use of hypnosis in cognitive behavior therapy: A practitioner's casebook*. New York: Springer Publishing.

Chassin, L., Presson, C. C., Sherman, S. J., & Kim, K. (2003). Historical changes in cigarette smoking and smoking-related beliefs after 2 decades in a midwestern community. *Health Psychology, 22*(4), 347–353.

Chaves, J. F. (2000). Hypnosis. In A. Kazdin (Ed.), *Encyclopedia of psychology*. Washington: American Psychological Association.

Cheek, J., & Buss, A. H. (1979). *Scales of shyness, sociability and self-esteem and correlations among them*. Unpublished research, University of Texas. (Cited by Buss, 1980.)

Chen, K., & Kandel, D. B. (1995). The natural history of drug use from adolescence to the mid-thirties in a general population sample. *American Journal of Public Health, 85*(1), 41–47.

Chen, Z., Lawson, R. B., Gordon, L. R., & McIntosh, B. (1996). Groupthink: Deciding with the leader and the devil. *Psychological Record, 46*(4), 581–590.

Cheng, H., Cao, Y., & Olson, L. (1996). Spinal cord repair in adult paraplegic rats: Partial restoration of hind limb function. *Science, 273*(5274), 510.

Chess, S., & Thomas, A. (1986). *Know your child*. New York: Basic.

Chesson, A. L., Anderson, W. M., Littner, M., Davila, D., et al. (1999). Practice parameters for the nonpharmacologic treatment of chronic insomnia. *Sleep, 22*, 1128–33.

Cheyne, J. A. (2005). Sleep paralysis episode frequency and number, types, and structure of associated hallucinations. *Journal of Sleep Research, 14*(3), 319–324.

Cheyne, J. A., Rueffer, S. D., & Newby-Clark, I. R. (1999). Hypnagogic and hypnopompic hallucinations during sleep paralysis: Neurological and cultural construction of the night-mare. *Consciousness & Cognition, 8*, 319–337.

Chomsky, N. (1975). *Reflections on language*. New York: Pantheon.

Chomsky, N. (1986). *Knowledge of language*. New York: Praeger.

Christensen, A., & Jacobson, N. S. (1994). Who (or what) can do psychotherapy. *Psychological Science, 5*(1), 8–14.

Christensen, D. (1999). Mind over matter. *Science News, 156*, 142–143.

Christian, K. M., & Thompson, R. F. (2005). Long-term storage of an associative memory trace in the cerebellum. *Behavioral Neuroscience, 119*(2), 526–537.

Christophersen, E. R., & Mortweet, S. L. (2003). *Parenting that works: Building skills that last a lifetime*. Washington: American Psychological Association.

Cialdini, R. B., & Goldstein, N. J. (2004). Social influence: Compliance and conformity. *Annual Review of Psychology, 55,* 591–621.

Cialdini, R. B., Eisenberg, N., & Green, B. L., Rhoads, K., et al. (1998). Undermining the undermining effect of reward on sustained interest. *Journal of Applied Social Psychology, 28*(3), 249–263.

Cialdini, R. B., Reno, R. R., & Kallgren, C. A. (1990). A focus theory of normative conduct: Recycling the concept of norms to reduce littering in public places. *Journal of Personality & Social Psychology, 58*(6), 1015–1026.

Ciarrochi, J., Dean, F. P., & Anderson, S. (2002). Emotional intelligence moderates the relationship between stress and mental health. *Personality & Individual Differences, 32*(2), 197–209.

Cinciripini, P. M., Wetter, D. W., & McClure, J. B. (1997). Scheduled reduced smoking. *Addictive Behaviors, 22*(6), 759–767.

Clark, D., Boutros, N., & Mendez, M. (2005). *The brain and behavior* (2nd ed.). Cambridge, MA: Cambridge University Press.

Clark, R., Anderson, N. B., Clark, V. R., & Williams, D. R. (1999). Racism as a stressor for African Americans. *American Psychologist, 54*(10), 805–816.

Click, P., Zion, C., & Nelson, C. (1988). What mediates sex discrimination in hiring decisions? *Journal of Personality & Social Psychology, 55*(2), 178–186.

Cline, V. B., Croft, R. G., & Courrier, S. (1972). Desensitization of children to television violence. *Journal of Personality & Social Psychology, 27,* 360–365.

Cnattingius, S., Signorello, L. B., Ammerén, G., Clausson, B., et al. (2000). Caffeine intake and the risk of first-trimester spontaneous abortion. *New England Journal of Medicine, 343*(25), 1839–845.

Cohen, P., Cohen, J., Kasen, S., Velez, C. N., et al. (1993). An epidemiological study of disorders in late adolescence: I. Age- and gender-specific prevalence. *Journal of Child Psychology & Psychiatry, 6,* 851–867.

Cole, J. (1995). *Pride and a daily marathon.* Cambridge, MA: MIT Press.

Coles, C. D., & Black, M. M. (2006). Introduction to the special issue. *Journal of Pediatric Psychology. Special Issue: Prenatal Substance Exposure: Impact on Children's Health, Development, School Performance, and Risk Behavior, 31*(1), 1–4.

Colin, A. K., Moore, K., & West, A. N. (1996). Creativity, oversensitivity, and rate of habituation. *EDRA: Environmental Design Research Association, 20*(4), 423–427.

Collins, A. M., & Quillian, M. R. (1969). Retrieval time from semantic memory. *Journal of Verbal Learning and Verbal Behavior, 8,* 240–247.

Collins, N. L., Cooper, M. L., Albino, A., & Allard, L. (2002). Psychosocial vulnerability from adolescence to adulthood: A prospective study of attachment style differences in relationship functioning and partner choice. *Journal of Personality, 70*(6), 965–1008.

Collins, W. A., & Gunnar, M. R. (1990). Social and personality development. *Annual Review of Psychology, 41,* 387–416.

Collop, N. A. (2005). Obstructive sleep apnea: treatment overview and controversies. In P. R. Carney, J. D. Geyer, & R. B. Berry (Eds.), *Clinical sleep disorders.* Philadelphia, PA: Lippincott Williams & Wilkins.

Comer, R. J. (2005). *Fundamentals of abnormal psychology* (4th ed.). New York: Worth.

Compton, W. C. (2005). *An introduction to positive psychology.* Belmont, CA: Wadsworth.

Conway, A. R. A., Cowan , N., & Bunting, M. F. (2001). The cocktail party phenomenon revisited. *Psychonomic Bulletin & Review, 8*(2), 331–335.

Conway, M. A., Cohen, G., & Stanhope, N. (1992). Very long-term memory for knowledge acquired at school and university. *Applied Cognitive Psychology, 6*(6), 467–482.

Cooper, J., & Fazio, R. H. (1984). A new look at dissonance theory. *Advances in Experimental Social Psychology, 17,* 226–229.

Cooper, J., Mirabile, R., & Scher, S. J. (2005). Actions and attitudes: The theory of cognitive dissonance. In T. C. Brock & M. C. Green (Eds.), *Persuasion: Psychological insights and perspectives* (2nd ed.). Thousand Oaks, CA: Sage.

Cooper, M. J. (2005). Cognitive theory in anorexia nervosa and bulimia nervosa: Progress, development and future directions. *Clinical Psychology Review, 25*(4), 511–531.

Cooper, R. P., Abraham, J., Berman, S., & Staska, M. (1997). The development of infants' preference for motherese. *Infant Behavior and Development, 20*(4), 477–488.

Corballis, M. C. (2002). *From hand to mouth: The origins of language.* Princeton, NJ: Princeton University Press.

Coren, S. (1992). *The left-hander syndrome.* New York: Free Press.

Coren, S. (1996). *Sleep thieves.* New York: Free Press.

Coren, S., Ward, L. M., & Enns, J. T. (2004). *Sensation and perception* (6th ed.). New York: Wiley.

Corkin, S. (2002). What's new with the amnesic patient H.M.? *Nature Reviews Neuroscience, 3,* 153–160.

Cormier, J. F., & Thelen, M. H. (1998). Professional skepticism of multiple personality disorder. *Professional Psychology: Research and Practice, 29*(2), 163–167.

Correa-Chávez, M., Rogoff, B., & Arauz, R. M. (2005). Cultural patterns in attending to two events at once. *Child Development, 76*(3), 664–678.

Corrigan, P. W., & Penn, D. L. (1999). Lessons from social psychology on discrediting psychiatric stigma. *American Psychologist, 54*(9), 765–776.

Corrigan, P. W., & Watson, A. C. (2005). Findings from the National Comorbidity Survey on the frequency of violent behavior in individuals with psychiatric disorders. *Psychiatry Research, 136*(2-3), 153–162.

Corrigan, P. W., Watson, A. C., Gracia, G., Slopen, N., et al. (2005). Newspaper stories as measures of structural stigma. *Psychiatric Services, 56*(5), 551–556.

Corsini, R. J. (2001). *Handbook of innovative therapy* (2nd ed.). York: Wiley.

Costa, Jr., P. T., & McCrae, R. R. (2006). Trait and factor theories. In J. C. Thomas, D. L. Segal, & M. Hersen (Eds.), *Comprehensive handbook of personality & psychopathology* (Vol. 1): *Personality and everyday functioning.* New York: Wiley.

Côté, J. E., & Levine, C. (2002). *Identity formation, agency, and culture.* Hillsdale, NJ: Erlbaum.

Coursey, R. D., Ward-Alexander, L., & Katz, B. (1990). Cost-effectiveness of providing insurance benefits for posthospital psychiatric halfway house stays. *American Psychologist, 45*(10), 1118–1126.

Court, J. H., & Court, P. C. (2001). Repression: R. I. P. *Australian Journal of Clinical & Experimental Hypnosis, 29*(1), 8–16.

Cowan, N. (2001). The magical number 4 in short-term memory. *Behavioral & Brain Sciences, 24*(1), 87–185.

Cowan, N. (2005). *Working memory capacity.* Hove, UK: Psychology Press.

Cowden, C. R. (2005). Worry and its relationship to shyness. *North American Journal of Psychology, 7*(1), 59–69.

Cowles, J. T. (1937). Food tokens as incentives for learning by chimpanzees. *Comparative Psychology,* Monograph, *14*(5, Whole No. 71).

Craig, L. (2006). Does father care mean fathers share?: A comparison of how mothers and fathers in intact families spend time with children. *Gender & Society, 20*(2), 259–281.

Craig, T. Y., & Kelly, J. R. (1999). Group cohesiveness and creative performance. *Group Dynamics, 3*(4), 243–256.

Craik, F. I. M. (1970). The fate of primary items in free recall. *Journal of Verbal Learning and Verbal Behavior, 9,* 143–148.

Craik, F. I. M., & Bialystok, E. (2005). Intelligence and executive control: Evidence from aging and bilingualism. *Cortex, 41*(2), 222–224.

Crano, W. D. (2000). Milestones in the psychological analysis of social influence. *Group Dynamics: Theory, Research, and Practice, 4*(1), 68–80.

Cravatt, B. F., Prospero-Garcia O., Siuzdak G., Gilula, N. B., et al. (1995). Chemical characterization of a family of brain lipids that induce sleep. *Science, 268*(5216), 1506–1509.

Crawley, S. B., & Sherrod, K. B. (1984). Parent-infant play during the first year of life. *Infant Behavior & Development, 7,* 65–75.

Crencavage, L. M., & Norcross, J. C. (1990). Where are the commonalities among the therapeutic common factors? *Professional Psychology: Research & Practice, 21*(5), 372–378.

Crisp, A., Gowers, S., Joughin, N., McClelland, L. et al. (2006). Anorexia nervosa in males: similarities and differences to anorexia nervosa in females. *European Eating Disorders Review. Special Issue: Anorexia Nervosa, 14*(3), 163–167.

Cronk, N. J., Slutske, W. S., Madden, P. A. F., Bucholz, K. K., et al. (2005). Risk for separation anxiety disorder among girls: Paternal absence, socioeconomic disadvantage, and genetic vulnerability. *Journal of Abnormal Psychology, 113*(2), 237–247.

Crooks, R., & Bauer, K. (2005). *Our sexuality* (9th ed.). Belmont, CA: Wadsworth.

Crosby, R. A., & Yarber, W. L. (2001). Perceived versus actual knowledge about correct condom use among U.S. adolescents: results from a national study. *Journal of Adolescent Health, 28*(5), 415–420.

Crown, C. L., Feldstein, S., Jasnow, M. D., Beebe, B., & Jaffe, J. (2002). The cross-modal coordination of interpersonal timing. *Journal of Psycholinguistic Research, 31*(1), 1–23.

Crowther, J. H., Sanftner, J., Bonifazi, D. Z., & Shepherd, K. L. (2001). The role of daily hassles in binge eating. *International Journal of Eating Disorders, 29,* 449–454.

Csikszentmihalyi, M. (1997). *Creativity.* New York: HarperCollins.

Cull, W. L., Shaughnessy, J. J., & Zechmeister, E. B. (1996). Expanding understanding of the expanding-pattern-of-retrieval mnemonic. *Journal of Experimental Psychology: Applied, 2*(4) 365–378.

Cummings, M. R. (2006) *Human heredity: Principles and issues* (7th ed.). Belmont CA: Wadsworth.

Cummins, D. D. (1995). *The other side of psychology.* New York: St. Martins.

Czeisler, C. A., Duffy, J. F., Shanahan, T. L., Brown, E. N., et al. (1999). Stability, precision, and near-24-hour period of the human circadian pacemaker. *Science, 284,* 2177–2181.

Czeisler, C. A., Richardson, G. S., Zimmerman, J. C., Moore-Ede, M. C., et al. (1981). Entrainment of human circadian rhythms by light-dark cycles: A reassessment. *Photochemistry, Photobiology, 34,* 239–247.

Daniels, H. (2005). Vygotsky and educational psychology: Some preliminary remarks. *Educational & Child Psychology, 22*(1), 6–17.

Darley, J. M., & Latane, B. (1968). Bystander intervention in emergencies: Diffusion of responsibility. *Journal of Personality & Social Psychology, 8,* 377–383.

Darley, J. M. (2000). Bystander phenomenon. In A. E. Kazdin (Ed.), *Encyclopedia of psychology* (Vol. 1). Washington: American Psychological Association.

Darley, J. M., & Latané, B. (1968). Bystander intervention in emergencies: Diffusion of responsibility. *Journal of Personality & Social Psychology, 8,* 377–383.

Darling, C. A., Davidson, J. K., & Passarello, L. C. (1992). The mystique of first intercourse among college youth: The role of partners, contraceptive practices, and psychological reactions. *Journal of Youth & Adolescence, 21*(1), 97–117.

Darou, W. S. (1992). Native Canadians and intelligence testing. *Canadian Journal of Counselling, 26*(2), 96–99.

Daruna, J. H. (2004). *Introduction to psychoneuroimmunology.* Amsterdam: Elsevier.

Darwin, C. (1872). *The expression of emotion in man and animals.* Chicago: University of Chicago Press.

Das, J. P. (2000). Mental retardation. In A. Kazdin (Ed.), *Encyclopedia of psychology.* Washington: American Psychological Association.

Dauvilliers, Y., Cervena, K, Carlander, B., Espa, F., et al. (2004). Dissociation in circadian rhythms in a pseudohypersomnia form of fatal familial insomnia. *Neurology, 63*(12), 2416–2418.

Davanloo, H. (1995). Intensive short-term dynamic psychotherapy. *International Journal of Short-Term Psychotherapy, 10*(3–4), 121–155.

Davidson, P. R., & Parker, K. C. H. (2001). Eye movement desensitization and reprocessing (EMDR): A meta-analysis. *Journal of Consulting & Clinical Psychology, 69*(2), 305–316.

Davidson, R. J., Kabat-Zinn, J., Schumacher, J., Rosenkranz, M., et al. (2003). Alternations in brain and immune function produced by mindfulness meditation. *Psychosomatic Medicine, 65*(4), 564–570.

Davidson, T. L. (2000). Latent learning. In A. E. Kazdin (Ed.), *Encyclopedia of psychology* (Vol. 4). Washington: American Psychological Association.

Davis, D., & Follette, W. C. (2002). Rethinking the probative value of evidence. *Law & Human Behavior, 26*(2), 133–158.

Davis, M. R., McMahon, M., & Greenwood, K. M. (2005). The efficacy of mnemonic components of the cognitive interview: Towards a shortened variant for time-critical investigations. *Applied Cognitive Psychology, 19*(1), 75–93.

Davison, G. C., & Neale, J. M. (2006). *Abnormal psychology* (10th ed.). San Francisco: Jossey-Bass.

Dawson, G., & Toth, K. (2006). Autism spectrum disorders. In D. Cicchetti & D. J. Cohen (Eds.), *Developmental psychopathology (Vol 3): Risk, disorder, and adaptation* (2nd ed.). Hoboken, NJ: Wiley.

De Jong, P. J., & Muris, P. (2002). Spider phobia. *Journal of Anxiety Disorders, 16*(1), 51–65.

de las Fuentes, C., & Vasquez, M. J. T. (1999). Immigrant adolescent girls of color. In N. G. Johnson, M. C. Roberts, & J. Worell (Eds.), *Beyond appearance*. Washington: American Psychological Association.

de Leon, C. F. M. (2005). Social engagement and successful aging. *European Journal of Ageing, 2*(1), 64–66.

de Rios, M. D., & Grob, C. S. (2005). Editors' introduction: Ayahuasca use in cross-cultural perspective. *Journal of Psychoactive Drugs, 37*(2), 119–121.

Deaux, K., & Emswiller, T. (1974). Explanation of successful performance on sex-linked tasks: What is skill for the male is luck for the female. *Journal of Personality & Social Psychology, 29*, 80–85.

Deckers, L. (2005). *Motivation: Biological, psychological, and environmental* (2nd ed.). Boston: Allyn & Bacon.

Deckro, G. R., Ballinger, K. M., Hoyt, M., Wilcher, M., et al. (2002). The evaluation of a mind/body intervention to reduce psychological distress and perceived stress in college students. *Journal of American College Health, 50*(6), 281–287.

Deeb, S. S. (2004). Molecular genetics of color-vision deficiencies. *Visual Neuroscience, 21*(3), 191–196.

DeGaetano, G. (2005). The impact of media violence on developing minds and hearts.

In S. Olfman (Ed.), *Childhood lost: How American culture is failing our kids*. Westport, CT: Praeger Publishers.

Deinzer, R., Kleineidam, C., Stiller-Winkler, R., Idel, H., et al. (2000). Prolonged reduction of salivary immunoglobulin A (sIgA) after a major academic exam. *International Journal of Psychophysiology, 37*, 219–232.

Delgado, B. M., & Ford, L. (1998). Parental perceptions of child development among low-income Mexican American families. *Journal of Child & Family Studies, 7*(4), 469–481.

Delpero, W. T., O'Neill, H., Casson, E., & Hovis, J. (2005). Aviation-relevent epidemiology of color vision deficiency. *Aviation, Space, and Environmental Medicine, 76*(2), 127–133.

Demos, J. N. (2005). *Getting started with neurofeedback*. New York: Norton.

Denmark, F. L., Rabinowitz, V. C., & Sechzer, J. A. (2005). *Engendering psychology: Women and gender revisited* (2nd ed.). Boston: Allyn & Bacon.

Denollet, J., & Van Heck, G. L. (2001). Psychological risk factors in heart disease. *Journal of Psychosomatic Research, 51*(3), 465–468.

Derlega, V. J., Winstead, B. A., & Jones, W. H. (2005). *Personality: Contemporary theory and research* (3rd ed.). Belmont, CA: Wadsworth.

Deutsch, M. (1993). Educating for a peaceful world. *American Psychologist, 48*(5), 510–517.

Devine, P. G., Monteith, M. J., Zuerink, J. R., & Elliot, A. J. (1991). Prejudice with and without compunction. *Journal of Personality & Social Psychology, 60*(6), 817–830.

Devlin, B., Daniels, M., & Roeder, K. (1997). The heritability of IQ. *Nature, 388*(6641), 468–471.

Devoto, A., Lucidi, F., Violani, C., & Bertini, M. (1999). Effects of different sleep reductions on daytime sleepiness. *Sleep, 22*(3), 336–343.

Di Marzo, V., Goparaju, S. K., Wang, L., Liu, J., et al. (2001). Leptin-regulated endocannabinoids are involved in maintaining food intake. *Nature, 410*(6830), 822–825.

Diano, S., Farr, S. A., Benoit, S. C., McNay, E. C., et al. (2006). Ghrelin controls hippocampal spine synapse density and memory performance. *Nature Neuroscience, 9*, 381–388.

Dickens, W. T., & Flynn, J. R. (2001). Heritability estimates versus large environmental effects: The IQ paradox resolved. *Psychological Review, 108*, 346–369

Dickerson, F. B., Tenhula, W. N., & Green-Paden, L. D. (2005). The token economy for schizophrenia: Review of the literature and recommendations for future research. *Schizophrenia Research, 75*(2-3), 405–416.

Dickinson, D. K., & Tabors, P. O. (Eds.). (2001). *Beginning literacy with language*. Baltimore: Paul H. Brookes.

Dieter, J. N. I., & Emory, E. K. (1997). Supplemental stimulation of premature infants. *Journal of Pediatric Psychology, 22*(3), 281–295.

Dinan, T. G. (2001). Stress, depression and cardiovascular disease. *Stress & Health: Journal of the International Society for the Investigation of Stress, 17*(2), 65–66.

Dingus, T. A., Klauer, S. G., Neale, V. L., Petersen, A., et al. (2006). The 100-Car Naturalistic Driving Study, Phase II – Results of the 100-car field experiment. *National Highway Traffic Safety Administration Report No. DOT HS 810 593*. Retrieved June 15, 2006, from http://www-nrd.nhtsa.dot.gov/departments/nrd-13/driver-distraction/PDF/100CarMain.pdf.

Dinkmeyer, D. Sr., McKay, G. D., & Dinkmeyer, D. Jr. (1997). *The parent's handbook*. Circle Pines, MN: American Guidance Service.

Dion, K. L. (2003). Prejudice, racism, and discrimination. In T. Millon & M. J. Lerner (Eds.), *Personality and social psychology. The comprehensive handbook of psychology* (Vol. 5). New York: Wiley.

Dirkzwager, A. J. E., Bramsen, I., & Van Der Ploeg, H. M. (2001). The longitudinal course of posttraumatic stress disorder symptoms among aging military veterans. *Journal of Nervous & Mental Disease, 189*(12), 846–853.

Dobelle, W. H. (2000). Artificial vision for the blind by connecting a television camera to the visual cortex. *American Society of Artificial Internal Organs, 46*, 3–9.

Dobson, K. S., Backs-Dermott, G. J., & Dozois, D. J. A. (2000). Cognitive and cognitive-behavioral therapies. In C. R. Snyder & R. E. Ingram (Eds.), *Handbook of psychological change: Psychotherapy processes and practices for the 21st century*. New York: Wiley.

Dodds, P. S., Muhamad, R., & Watts, D. J. (2003). An experimental study of search in global social networks. *Science, 301*(5634), 827–829.

Doidge, N. (1997). Empirical evidence for the efficacy of psychoanalytic psychotherapies and psychoanalysis. *Psychoanalytic Inquiry, Suppl.*, 102–150.

Dollard, J., & Miller, N. E. (1950). *Personality and psychotherapy: An analysis in terms of learning, thinking and culture*. New York: McGraw-Hill.

Domhoff, W. (2003). *The scientific study of dreams: Neural networks, cognitive development, and content analysis*. Washington: American Psychological Association.

Domingo, R. A., & Goldstein-Alpern, N. (1999). "What dis?" and other toddler-initiated, expressive language-learning strategies. *Infant-Toddler Intervention, 9*(1), 39–60.

Domjan, M. (2006). *The principles of learning and behavior* (5th ed.). Belmont, CA: Wadsworth.

Dooling, D. J., & Lachman, R. (1971). Effects of comprehension on retention of prose. *Journal of Experimental Psychology, 88*, 216–222.

Doran, S. M., Van Dongen, H. P., & Dinges, D. F. (2001). Sustained attention performance during sleep deprivation. *Archives of Italian Biology, 139*, 253–267.

Dorman, M. F., & Wilson, B. S. (2004). The design and function of cochlear implants. *American Scientist, 92*(Sept-Oct), 436–445.

Dosher, B. A., & Ma, J. (1998). Output loss or rehearsal loop? *Journal of Experimental Psychology: Learning, Memory, & Cognition, 24*(2), 316–335.

Dougall, A. L., & Baum, A. (2003). Stress, coping, and immune function. In M. Gallagher & R. J. Nelson (Eds.), *Handbook of psychology: Biological psychology* (Vol. 3). New York: John Wiley.

Dougherty, D. D., Baer, L., Cosgrove, G. R., Cassem, E. H., et al. (2002). Prospective long-term follow-up of 44 patients who received cingulotomy for treatment-refractory obsessive-compulsive disorder. *American Journal of Psychiatry, 159*(2), 269–275.

Dovidio, J. E., & Penner, L. A. (2001). Helping and altruism. In M. Hewstone & M. Brewer (Eds.), *Handbook of social psychology*. London: Blackwell.

Dovidio, J. F., & Gaertner, S. L. (1999). Reducing prejudice: Combating intergroup biases. *Current Directions in Psychological Science, 8*(4), 101–105.

Dovidio, J. F., Glick, P., & Rudman, L. A. (Eds.). (2005). *On the nature of prejudice: Fifty years after Allport*. Malden, MA: Blackwell.

Dovido, J. F., Gaertner, S. L., Kawakami, K., & Hodson, G. (2002). Why can't we just get along? *Cultural Diversity and Ethnic Minority Psychology, 8*(2), 88–102.

Dowling, K. W. (2005). The effect of lunar phases on domestic violence incident rates. *Forensic Examiner, 14*(4), 13–18.

Dozois, D. J. A., & Dobson, K. S. (Eds.). (2004). *The prevention of anxiety and depression: Theory, research, and practice*. Washington: American Psychological Association.

Dozois, D. J. A., & Dobson, K. S. (2002). Depression. In M. M. Antony & D. H. Barlow (Eds.), *Handbook of assessment and treatment planning for psychological disorders*. New York: Guilford.

Draguns, J. G., Gielen, U. P., & Fish, J. M. (2004). Approaches to culture, healing, and psychotherapy. In U. P. Gielen, J. M. Fish, & J. G. Draguns (Eds.), *Handbook of culture, therapy, and healing*. Mahwah, NJ: Lawrence Erlbaum.

Drigotas, S. M., Rusbult, C. E., Wieselquist, J., & Whitton, S. W. (1999). Close partner as sculptor of the ideal self: Behavioral affirmation and the Michelangelo phenomenon. *Journal of Personality & Social Psychology, 77*(2), 293–323.

Drolet, G., Dumont, E. C., Gosselin, I., Kinkead, R., et al. (2001). Role of endogenous opioid system in the regulation of the stress response. *Progress in Neuro-Psychopharmacology & Biological Psychiatry, 25*(4), 729–741.

Druckman, D., & Bjork, R. A. (1994). *Learning, remembering, believing: Enhancing human performance*. Washington: National Academy Press.

DSM-IV-TR: Diagnostic and statistical manual of mental disorders (5th ed.). (2000). Washington: American Psychiatric Association.

Duclos, S. E., & Laird, J. D. (2001). The deliberate control of emotional experience through control of expressions. *Cognition and Emotion, 15,* 27–56.

Duffy, J. F., & Wright, Jr., K. P. (2005). Entrainment of the human circadian system by light. *Journal of Biological Rhythms, 20*(4), 326–338.

Dulewicz, V., & Higgs, M. (2000). Emotional intelligence. *Journal of Managerial Psychology, 15*(4), 341–372.

Duncan, J., Seitz, R. J., Kolodny, J., Bor, D., et al. (2000). A neural basis for general intelligence. *Science, 289,* 457–460.

Duncker, K. (1945). On problem solving. *Psychological Monographs, 58*(270).

Durand, V. M., & Barlow, D. H. (2006). *Essentials of abnormal psychology* (4th ed.). Belmont, CA: Thomson/Wadsworth.

Durham, M. D., & Dane, F. C. (1999). Juror knowledge of eyewitness behavior. *Journal of Social Behavior & Personality, 14*(2), 299–308.

Durrant, J. E., & Janson, S. (2005). Legal reform, corporal punishment and child abuse: The case of Sweden. *International Review of Victimology, 12,* 139–158.

Dutton, D., & Aron, A. (1974). Some evidence for heightened sexual attraction under conditions of high anxiety. *Journal of Personality & Social Psychology, 30,* 510–517.

Dywan, J., & Bowers, K. S. (1983). The use of hypnosis to enhance recall. *Science, 222,* 184–185.

Dzokoto, V. A., & Adams, G. (2005). Understanding genital-shrinking epidemics in West Africa: Koro, juju, or mass psychogenic illness? *Culture, Medicine and Psychiatry, 29*(1), 53–78.

Ebbinghaus, H. (1885). *Memory: A contribution to experimental psychology.* Translated by H. A. Ruger, & C. E. Bussenius, 1913. New York: New York Teacher's College, Columbia University.

Eckerman, D. A. (1999). Scheduling reinforcement about once a day. *Behavioural Processes, 45*(1-3), 101–114.

Eichenbaum, H., & Fortin, N. J. (2005). Bridging the gap between brain and behavior: Cognitive and neural mechanisms of episodic memory. *Journal of the Experimental Analysis of Behavior, 84*(3), 619–629.

Eidelson, R. J., & Eidelson, J. I. (2003). Dangerous ideas. *American Psychologist, 58*(3), 182–192.

Eifert, G. H., & Lejuez, C. W. (2000). Aversion therapy. In A. E. Kazdin (Ed.), *Encyclopedia of psychology.* Washington: American Psychological Association.

Eimas, P. D., Quinn, P. C., & Cowan, P. (1994). Development of exclusivity in perceptually based categories of young infants. *Journal of Experimental Child Psychology, 58*(3), 418–431.

Eisenberg, N., Valiente, C., Fabes, R. A., Smith, C. L., et al. (2003). The relations of effortful control and ego control to children's resiliency and social functioning. *Developmental Psychology, 39*(4), 761–776.

Eisler, J. A., Justice, Jr., J. B., & Neill, D. B. (2004). Individual differences in reward sensitivity: Implications for psychostimu-

lant abuse vulnerability. *North American Journal of Psychology, 6*(3), 527–544.

Ekman, P. (1993). Facial expression and emotion. *American Psychologist, 48*(4), 384–392.

Ekman, P., & Rosenberg, E. (1997). *What the face reveals.* New York: Oxford University Press.

Ekman, P., Levenson, R. W., & Friesen, W. V. (1983). Autonomic nervous system activity distinguishes among emotions. *Science, 223,* 1208–1210.

Eliot, L. (1999). *What's going on in there?* New York: Bantam

Elli, K. A., & Nathan, P. J. (2001). The pharmacology of human working memory. *International Journal of Neuropsychopharmacology, 4*(3), 299–313.

Ellickson, P. L., Martino, S. C., & Collins, R. L. (2004). Marijuana use from adolescence to young adulthood. *Health Psychology, 23*(3), 299–307.

Elliott, M., & Williams, D. (2003). The client experience of counselling and psychotherapy. *Counselling Psychology Review, 18*(1), 34–38.

Ellis, A. (1979). The practice of rational-emotive therapy. In A. Ellis & J. Whiteley (Eds.), *Theoretical and empirical foundations of rational-emotive therapy.* Monterey, CA: Brooks/Cole.

Ellis, A. (1995). Changing rational-emotive therapy (RET) to rational emotive behavior therapy (REBT). *Journal of Rational-Emotive & Cognitive Behavior Therapy, 13*(2), 85–89.

Ellis, A. (2004). Why rational emotive behavior therapy is the most comprehensive and effective form of behavior therapy. *Journal of Rational-Emotive & Cognitive Behavior Therapy, 22*(2), 85–92.

Emmorey, K., Grabowski, T., McCullough, S., Damasio, H., et al. (2003). Neural systems underlying lexical retrieval for sign language. *Neuropsychologia, 41*(1), 85–95.

Emurian, H. H. (2005). Web-based programmed instruction: Evidence of rule-governed learning. *Computers in Human Behavior, 21*(6), 893–915.

Engle, D. E., & Arkowitz, H. (2006). *Ambivalence in psychotherapy: Facilitating readiness to change.* New York: Guilford.

Enns, J. T., & Coren, S. (1995). The box alignment illusion. *Perception & Psychophysics, 57*(8), 1163–1174.

Enns, M. W., Cox, B. J., & Clara, I. P. (2005). Perfectionism and neuroticism: A longitudinal study of specific vulnerability and diathesis-stress models. *Cognitive Therapy and Research, 29*(4), 463–478.

Erickson, C. D., & Al-Timimi, N. R. (2001). Providing mental health services to Arab Americans. *Cultural Diversity and Ethnic Minority Psychology, 7*(4), 308–327.

Ericsson, K. A. (2000). How experts attain and maintain superior performance. *Journal of Aging & Physical Activity, 8*(4), 366–372.

Ericsson, K. A., & Charness, N. (1994). Expert performance. *American Psychologist, 49*(8), 725–747.

Ericsson, K. A., & Chase, W. G. (1982). Exceptional memory. *American Scientist, 70,* 607–615.

Ericsson, K. A., Delaney, P. F., Weaver, G., & Mahadevan, R. (2004). Uncovering the structure of a memorist's superior "basic" memory capacity. *Cognitive Psychology, 49*(3), 191–237.

Erikson, E. H. (1963). *Childhood and society.* New York: Norton.

Erlacher, D., & Schredl, M. (2004). Dreams reflecting waking sport activities: A comparison of sport and psychology students. *International Journal of Sport Psychology, 35*(4), 301–308.

Eron, L. D. (1987). The development of aggressive behavior from the perspective of a developing behaviorism. *American Psychologist, 42,* 435–442.

Eschholz, S., Chiricos, T., & Gertz, M. (2003). Television and fear of crime: Program types, audience traits, and the mediating effect of perceived neighborhood racial composition. *Social Problems, 50*(3), 395–415.

Espie, C. A. (2002). Insomnia. *Annual Review of Psychology, 53,* 215–243.

Esser, J. K. (1998). Alive and well after 25 years: A review of groupthink research. *Organizational Behavior & Human Decision Processes, 73*(2-3), 116–141.

Esterling, B. A., L'Abate, L., Murray, E. J., & Pennebaker, J. W. (1999). Empirical foundations for writing in prevention and psychotherapy: Mental and physical health outcomes. *Clinical Psychology Review, 19*(1), 79–96.

Ethical principles of psychologists and code of conduct. (2002). The American Psychological Association. *American Psychologist, 57*(12), 1060–1073.

Ethier, K. A., Kershaw, T., Niccolai, L., Lewis, J. B., et al. (2003). Adolescent women underestimate their susceptibility to sexually transmitted infections. *Sexually Transmitted Infections, 79,* 408–411.

Everly, G. S. (2002). Thoughts on peer (paraprofessional) support in the provision of mental health services. *International Journal of Emergency Mental Health, 4*(2), 89–92.

Ewen, R. B. (2003). *An introduction to theories of personality* (6th ed.). Hillsdale, NJ: Lawrence Erlbaum.

Ewing, G. (2001). Altruistic, egoistic, and normative effects on curbside recycling. *Environment & Behavior, 33*(6), 733–764.

Eyer, D. E. (1994). Mother-infant bonding: A scientific fiction. *Human Nature, 5*(1), 69–94.

Eysenck, H. J. (1994). The outcome problem in psychotherapy: What have we learned? *Behaviour Research & Therapy, 32*(5), 477–495.

Eysenck, H. J. (Ed.). (1981). *A model for personality.* New York: Springer-Verlag.

Fabrega, Jr., H. (2004). Culture and the origins of psychopathology. In U. P. Gielen, J. M. Fish, & Draguns, J. G. (Eds.), *Handbook of culture, therapy, and healing.* Mahwah, NJ: Erlbaum.

Fahim, C., Stip, E., Mancini-Marïe, A., Mensour, B., et al. (2005). Brain activity during emotionally negative pictures in schizophrenia with and without flat affect: An fMRI study. *Psychiatry Research: Neuroimaging, 140*(1), 1–15.

Fahle, M., & Poggio, T. (Eds.). (2002). *Perceptual learning.* Cambridge, MA: MIT Press.

Fain, G. L. (2003). *Sensory transduction.* Sunderland, MA: Sinauer.

Faith, M. S., Wong, F. Y., & Carpenter, K. M. (1995). Group sensitivity training: Update, meta-analysis, and recommendations. *Journal of Counseling Psychology, 42*(3), 390–399.

Falkowski, C. (2000). *Dangerous Drugs.* Center City, MN: Hazelden Information Education.

Farah, M. (2004). *Visual agnosia* (2nd ed.). Cambridge, MA: MIT Press.

Farrimond, T. (1990). Effect of alcohol on visual constancy values and possible relation to driving performance. *Perceptual & Motor Skills, 70*(1), 291–295.

Farroni, T., Massaccesi, S., Pividori, D., & Johnson, M. H. (2004). Gaze following in newborns. *Infancy, 5*(1), 39–60.

FBI. (2005). *Crime in the United States, 2005.* Washington: Federal Bureau of Investigation. Retrieved October 17, 2006, from http://www.fbi.gov/ucr/05cius/.

Feingold, A. (1992). Gender differences in mate selection preferences. *Psychological Bulletin, 111,* 304–341.

Feist, J., & Feist, G. J. (2006). *Theories of personality* (6th ed.). New York: McGraw-Hill.

Feldhusen, J. F., & Goh, B. E. (1995). Assessing and accessing creativity: An integrative review of theory, research, and development. *Creativity Research Journal, 8*(3), 231–247.

Feldman, D. H. (2004). Piaget's stages: The unfinished symphony of cognitive development. *New Ideas in Psychology, 22*(3), 175–231.

Fellous, J.-M., & LeDoux, J. E. (2005). Toward basic principles for emotional processing: What the fearful brain tells the robot. In J.-M. Fellous & M. A. Arbib, (Eds.), *Who needs emotions?: The brain meets the robot.* New York: Oxford University Press.

Fenn, K. M., Nusbaum, H. C., & Margoliash, D. (2003). Consolidation during sleep of perceptual learning of spoken language. *Nature, 425*(6958), 614–616.

Fernald, A. (1989). Intonation and communicative intent in mothers' speech to infants: Is the melody the message? *Child Development, 60*(6), 1497–1510.

Fernald, A., Perfors, A., & Marchman, V. A. (2006). Picking up speed in understanding: Speech processing efficiency and vocabulary growth across the 2nd year. *Developmental Psychology, 42*(1), 98–116.

Féron, F., Perry, C., Cochrane, J., Licina, P., et al. (2005). Autologous olfactory ensheathing cell transplantation in human spinal cord injury. *Brain: A Journal of Neurology, 128*(12), 2951–2960.

Ferrari, J. R., & Scher, S. J. (2000). Toward an understanding of academic and nonacademic tasks procrastinated by students: The use of daily logs. *Psychology in the Schools, 37*(4), 359–366.

Festinger, L. (1957). *A theory of cognitive dissonance.* Evanston, IL: Row Peterson.

Festinger, L., & Carlsmith, J. M. (1959). Cognitive consequences of forced compliance. *Journal of Abnormal and Social Psychology, 58,* 203–210.

Field, C. E., Nash, H. M., Handwerk, M. L., & Friman, P. C. (2004). A modification of the token economy for nonresponsive youth in family-style residential care. *Behavior Modification, 28*(3), 438–457.

Fields, R. M., & Margolin, J. (2001). *Coping with trauma.* Washington: American Psychological Association.

Figueredo, A. J., Sefcek, J. A., & Jones, D. N. (2006). The ideal romantic partner personality. *Personality & Individual Differences, 41*(3), 431–441.

Fink, M. (2000). Electroshock revisited. *American Scientist, 88*(March-April), 162–167.

Fink, M., & Taylor, M. A. (2003). *Catatonia: A clinician's guide to diagnosis and treatment.* London: Cambridge University Press.

First, M. B., & Pincus, H. A. (2002). The DSM-IV text revision: Rationale and potential impact on clinical practice. *Psychiatric Services, 53,* 288–292.

Fischer, A. H., Manstead, A. S. R., Rodriquez Mosquera, P. M., et al. (2004). Gender and culture differences in emotion. *Emotion, 4*(1), 87–94.

Fisher, R. P., & Geiselman, R. E. (1987). Enhancing eyewitness memory with the cognitive interview. In M. M. Gruneberg, P. E. Morris, & R. N. Sykes (Eds.), *Practical aspects of memory: Current research and issues.* Chinchester, U.K.: Wiley.

Fisher, S., & Greenberg, R. P. (1996). *Freud scientifically reappraised.* Hoboken, NJ: Wiley.

Fiske, S. T. (1993a). Social cognition and social perception. *Annual Review of Psychology, 44,* 155–194.

Fiske, S. T., (1993b). Controlling other people. *American Psychologist, 48*(6), 621–628.

Fiske, S. T., Cuddy, A. J. C., Glick, P., & Xu, J. (2002). A model of (often mixed) stereotype content. *Journal of Personality & Social Psychology, 82*(6), 878–902.

Flanagan, M. B., May, J. G., & Dobie, T. G. (2004). The role of vection, eye movements and postural instability in the etiology of motion sickness. *Journal of Vestibular Research: Equilibrium & Orientation, 14*(4), 335–346.

Flavell, J. H. (1992). Cognitive development: Past, present, and future. *Developmental Psychology, 28*(6), 998–1005.

Fleming, J. (1974). Field report: The state of the apes. *Psychology Today,* Jan., 46.

Fobair, P. (1997). Cancer support groups and group therapies. *Journal of Psychosocial Oncology, 15*(3–4), 123–147.

Fochtmann, L. J. (1995). Intractable sneezing as a conversion symptom. *Psychosomatics, 36*(2), 103–112.

Folkman, S., & Moskowitz, J. T. (2004). Coping. *Annual Review of Psychology, 55,* 745–774.

Follett, K., & Hess, T. M. (2002). Aging, cognitive complexity, and the fundamental attribution error. *Journals of Gerontology: Series B: Psychological Sciences and Social Sciences, 57B*(4), 312–323.

Fontaine, K. R., Redden, D. T., Wang, C., Westfall, A. O., et al. (2003). Years of life lost due to obesity. *Journal of the American Medical Association, 289,* 187–193.

Fontenelle, D. H. (1989). *How to live with your children.* Tucson, AZ: Fisher Books.

Foo, P., Warren, W. H., Duchon, A., & Tarr, M. J. (2005). Do humans integrate routes into a cognitive map? Map- versus landmark-based navigation of novel shortcuts. *Journal of Experimental Psychology: Learning, Memory, & Cognition, 31*(2), 195–215.

Ford, D. Y., & Moore, J. L. (2006). Being gifted and adolescent: Issues and needs of students of color. In F. A. Dixon & S. M. Moon (Eds.), *The handbook of secondary gifted education.* Waco, TX: Prufrock Press.

Forney, W. S., Forney, J. C., & Crutsinger, C. (2005). Developmental stages of age and moral reasoning as predictors of juvenile delinquents' behavioral intention to steal clothing. *Family & Consumer Sciences Research Journal, 34*(2), 110–126.

Forsyth, J. P., & Savsevitz, J. (2002). Behavior therapy: Historical perspective and overview. In M. Hersen & W. H. Sledge (Eds.), *Encyclopedia of psychotherapy.* San Diego: Academic Press.

Fosse, R., Stickgold, R., & Hobson, J. A. (2001). The mind in REM sleep: Reports of emotional experience. *Sleep: Journal of Sleep & Sleep Disorders Research, 24*(8), 947–955.

Foster, C. A., Witcher, B. S., Campbell, W. K., & Green, J. D. (1998). Arousal and attraction. *Journal of Personality & Social Psychology, 74*(1), 86–101.

Foster, G., & Ysseldyke, J. (1976). Expectancy and halo effects as a result of artificially induced teacher bias. *Contemporary Educational Psychology, 1,* 37–45.

Fowers, B. J., & Davidov, B. J. (2006). The virtue of multiculturalism: Personal transformation, character, and openness to the other. *American Psychologist, 61*(6), 581–594.

Fowers, B. J., & Richardson, F. C. (1996). Why is multiculturalism good? *American Psychologist, 51*(6), 609–621.

Foxhall, K. (2000). Suddenly, a big impact on criminal justice. *APA Monitor,* Jan. 36–37.

Frank, J. D., & Frank, J. (2004). Therapeutic components shared by all psychotherapies. In A. Freeman, M. J. Mahoney, P. DeVito, & D. Martin (Eds.), *Cognition and psychotherapy* (2nd ed.). New York: Springer.

Franken, R. E. (2007). *Human motivation.* Belmont, CA: Wadsworth.

Franzoi, S. L. (2000). *Social psychology.* New York: McGraw-Hill.

Fraser, C. (2002). Fact and fiction: A clarification of phantom limb phenomena. *British Journal of Occupational Therapy, 65*(6), 256–260.

Fredrickson, B. L. (2001). The role of positive emotions in positive psychology. *American Psychologist, 56*(3), 218–226.

Fredrickson, B. L. (2003). The value of positive emotions. *American Scientist, 91,* 330–335.

Fredrickson, B. L., & Branigan, C. (2005). Positive emotions broaden the scope of attention and thought-action repertoires. *Cognition & Emotion, 19*(3), 313–332.

Freeman, D., & Garety, P. A. (2004). *Paranoia: the psychology of persecutory delusions.* New York: Routledge.

Freiwald, W. A., & Kanwisher, N. G. (2004). Visual selective attention: Insights from brain imaging and neurophysiology. In M. S. Gazzaniga (Ed.), *The cognitive neurosciences* (3rd ed.). Cambridge, MA: MIT Press.

French, C. C., Fowler, M., McCarthy, K., & Peers, D. (1991). A test of the Barnum effect. *Skeptical Inquirer, 15*(4), 66–72.

French, S. E., Kim, T. E., & Pillado, O. (2006). Ethnic identity, social group membership, and youth violence. In N. G. Guerra & E. P. Smith (Eds.), *Preventing youth violence in a multicultural society.* Washington: American Psychological Association.

Freud, S. (1900). *The interpretation of dreams.* London: Hogarth.

Freud, S. (1949). *An outline of psychoanalysis.* New York: Norton.

Fried, P. A., O'Connell, C. M., & Walkinson, B. (1992). 60- and 72-month follow-up of children prenatally exposed to marijuana, cigarettes, and alcohol. *Journal of Developmental & Behavioral Pediatrics, 13*(6), 383–391.

Fried, P.A., & Smith, A. M. (2001) A literature review of the consequences of prenatal marihuana exposure. *Neurotoxicology and Teratology, 23*(1), 1–11.

Friedman, H. S. (2002). *Health psychology* (2nd ed.). Englewood Cliffs, NJ: Prentice-Hall.

Friedman, L. (2006). What is psychoanalysis? *Psychoanalytic Quarterly, 75*(3), 689–713.

Friedman, L. J. (2004). Erik Erikson on generativity: A biographer's perspective. In E. de St. Aubin, D. P. McAdams, & T.-C. Kim (Eds.), *The generative society: Caring for future generations.* Washington: American Psychological Association.

Friedman, M., & Rosenman, R. H. (1983). *Type A behavior and your heart.* New York: Knopf.

Friedman, R. C. Bucci, W., Christian, C., Drucker, P., et al. (1998). Private psychotherapy patients of psychiatrist psychoanalysts. *American Journal of Psychiatry, 155,* 1772–1774.

Frydman, M. (1999). Television, aggressiveness and violence. *International Journal of Adolescent Medicine & Health, 11*(3–4), 335–344.

Fukuda, K., & Ishihara, K. (2001). Age-related changes of sleeping pattern during adolescence. *Psychiatry & Clinical Neurosciences, 55*(3), 231–232.

Funder, D. C. (2004). *The personality puzzle* (3rd ed.). New York: Norton.

Funk, J. B. (2005). Children's exposure to violent video games and desensitization to violence. *Child and Adolescent Psychiatric Clinics of North America, 14*(3), 387–404.

Furnham, A., Chamorro-Premuzic, T., & Callahan, I. (2003). Does graphology predict personality and intelligence? *Individual Differences Research, 1*(2), 78–94.

Gable, S. L., Reis, H. T., Impett, E., & Asher, E. R. (2004). What do you do when things go right? The intrapersonal and interpersonal benefits of sharing positive events. *Journal of Personality & Social Psychology, 87,* 228–245.

Gadzella, B. M. (1995). Differences in processing information among psychology course grade groups. *Psychological Reports, 77,* 1312–1314.

Gaertner, S. L., Dovidio, J. F., Banker, B. S., Houlette, M., et al. (2000). Reducing intergroup conflict: From superordinate goals to decategorization, recategorization, and mutual differentiation. *Group Dynamics, 4*(1), 98–114.

Galambos, N. L., Barker, E. T., & Tilton-Weaver, L. C. (2003). Who gets caught at maturity gap? A study of pseudomature, immature and mature adolescents. *International Journal of Behavioral Development, 27*(3), 253–263.

Galanter, M., Hayden, F., Castañeda, R., & Franco, H. (2005). Group therapy, self-help groups, and network therapy. In R. J. Frances, S. I. Miller, & A. H. Mack (Eds.), *Clinical textbook of addictive disorders* (3rd ed.). New York: Guilford.

Galati, D., Scherer, K. R., & Ricci-Bitti, P. E. (1997). Voluntary facial expression of emotion: Comparing congenitally blind with normally sighted encoders. *Journal of Personality & Social Psychology, 73*(6), 1363–1379.

Galea, S., & Resnick, H. (2005). Posttraumatic stress disorder in the general population after mass terrorist incidents: Considerations about the nature of exposure. *CNS Spectrums, 10*(2), 107–115.

Galea, S., Ahern, J., Resnick, H., Kilpatrick, D., et al. (2002). Psychological sequelae of the September 11 terrorist attacks in New York City. *New England Journal of Medicine, 346*(13), 982–987.

Ganis, G., Thompson, W. L., & Kosslyn, S. M. (2004). Brain areas underlying visual mental imagery and visual perception: An fMRI study. *Cognitive Brain Research, 20*(2), 226–241.

Ganster, D. C., Fox, M. L., & Dwyer, D. J. (2001). Explaining employees' health care costs: A prospective examination of stressful job demands, personal control, and physiological reactivity. *Journal of Applied Psychology, 86,* 954–964.

Garbarino, S., Beelke, M., Costa, G., Violani, C., et al. (2002). Brain function and effects of shift work: implications for clinical neuropharmacology. *Neuropsychobiology, 45,* 50–56.

Garbarino, S., Mascialino, B., Penco, M. A., Squarcia, S., et al. (2004). Professional shift-work drivers who adopt prophylactic naps can reduce the risk of car accidents during night work. *Sleep: Journal of Sleep & Sleep Disorders Research, 27*(7), 1295–1302.

Gardner, H. (2002). The pursuit of excellence through education. In M. Ferrari (Ed.), *Learning from extraordinary minds.* Mahwah, NJ: Erlbaum.

Gardner, H. (2003). *Multiple intelligences after twenty years.* Invited Address, American Educational Research Association, April, 2003. Retrieved July 7, 2005, from http://www.pz.harvard.edu/PIs/HG_MI_after_20_years.pdf.

Gardner, H. (2004). *Frames of mind* (Tenth-anniversary edition). New York: Basic.

Gardner, R. A., & Gardner, B. T. (1989). *Teaching sign language to chimpanzees.* Albany, NY: State University of New York Press.

Garland, A. F., & Zigler, E. (1993). Adolescent suicide prevention. *American Psychologist, 48*(2), 169–182.

Garnets, L. D. (2002) Sexual orientation in perspective. *Cultural Diversity & Ethnic Minority Psychology, 8,* 115–129.

Garnets, L. D., & Kimmel, D. (1991). Lesbian and gay male dimensions in the psychological study of human diversity. *Psychological perspectives on human diversity in America.* Washington: American Psychological Association.

Gastner, M. T., Shalizi, C. R., & Newman, M. E. J. (2005). Maps and cartograms of the 2004 US presidential election results. *Advances in Complex Systems, 8*(1), 117–123.

Gates, A. I. (1958). Recitation as a factor in memorizing. In J. Deese (Ed.), *The psychology of learning.* New York: McGraw-Hill.

Gathchel, R. J., & Oordt, M. S. (2003). Insomnia. In R. J. Gatchel & M. S. Oordt (Eds.), *Clinical health psychology and primary care: Practical advice and clinical guidance for successful collaboration.* Washington: American Psychological Association.

Gayle, H. (2000). An overview of the global HIV/AIDS epidemic, with a focus on the United States. *AIDS, 14*(Suppl. 2), S8–S17.

Gazzaniga, M. S. (1970). *The bisected brain.* New York: Plenum.

Gazzaniga, M. S. (2005). Forty-five years of split-brain research and still going strong. *Nature Reviews Neuroscience, 6*(8), 653–659.

Geary, N. (2004). Endocrine controls of eating: CCK, leptin, and ghrelin. *Physiology & Behavior, 81*(5), 719–733.

Gedo, J. E. (2002). The enduring scientific contributions of Sigmund Freud. *Perspectives in Biology & Medicine, 45,* 200–211.

Gegenfurtner, K. R., & Kiper, D. C. (2003). Color vision. *Annual Review of Neuroscience, 26,* 181–206.

Geiselman, R. E., Fisher, R. P., MacKinnon, D. P., & Holland, H. L. (1986). Eyewitness memory enhancement with the cognitive interview. *American Journal of Psychology, 99,* 385–401.

Geliebter, A., & Aversa, A. (2003). Emotional eating in overweight, normal weight, and underweight individuals. *Eating Behaviors, 3*(4), 341–347.

Genesee, F., Paradis., J., & Crago, M. (2004). *Dual language development and disorders: A handbook on bilingualism and second language learning.* London: Paul Brookes.

George, A. (2006). Living online: The end of privacy? *New Scientist, 2659* (Sept 18), 50–51.

Georgiades, A., Serwood, A., Gullette, E. C., Babyak, M. A., et al. (2000). Effects of exercise and weight loss on mental stress–induced cardiovascular responses in individuals with high blood pressure. *Hypertension, 36,* 171–176.

Germain, A., Krakow, B., Faucher, B., Zadra, A., et al. (2004). Increased mastery elements associated with imagery rehearsal treatment for nightmares in sexual assault survivors with PTSD. *Dreaming, 14*(4), 195–206.

German, T. P., & Barrett, H. C. (2005). Functional fixedness in a technologically sparse culture. *Psychological Science, 16*(1), 1–5.

German, T. P., & Defeyter, M. A. (2000). Immunity to functional fixedness in young children. *Psychonomic Bulletin & Review, 7*(4), 707–712.

Gersh, R. D. (1982). Learning when not to shoot. *Santa Barbara News Press,* June 20.

Gershoff, E. T. (2002). Corporal punishment by parents and associated child behaviors and experiences: A meta-analytic and theoretical review. *Psychological Bulletin, 128*(4), 539–579.

Gerwood, J. B. (1998). The legacy of Viktor Frankl. *Psychological Reports, 82*(2), 673–674.

Geschwind, N. (1979). Specializations of the human brain. *Scientific American, 241,* 180–199.

Gewirtz, J. C., & Davis, M. (1998). Application of Pavlovian higher-order conditioning to the analysis of the neural substrates of fear conditioning. *Neuropharmacology, 37*(4–5), 453–459.

Gibson, E. J., & Walk, R. D. (1960). The "visual cliff." *Scientific American, 202*(4), 67–71.

Gibson, K. R. (2002). Evolution of human intelligence: The roles of brain size and mental construction. *Brain, Behavior & Evolution, 59*(1–2), 10–20.

Gilbert, P. (2001). *Overcoming depression.* New York: Oxford.

Giliovich, T., Keltner, D., & Nisbett, R. (2005). *Social psychology.* New York: Norton.

Gill, S. T. (1991). Carrying the war into the never-never land of psi. *Skeptical Inquirer, 15*(1), 269–273.

Gillberg, M., & Akerstedt, T. (1998). Sleep loss performance: No "safe" duration of a monotonous task. *Physiology & Behavior, 64*(5), 599–604.

Ginet, M., & Py, J. (2001). A technique for enhancing memory in eyewitness testimonies for use by police officers and judicial officials: The cognitive interview. *Travail Humain, 64*(2), 173–191.

Ginott, H. G. (1965). *Between parent and child: New solutions to old problems.* New York: Macmillan.

Ginsberg, D. L. (2006). Fatal agranulocytosis four years after clozapine discontinuation. *Primary Psychiatry, 13*(2), 32–33.

Giuseppe, R. (2005). Virtual reality in psychotherapy: Review. *CyberPsychology & Behavior. Special Use of Virtual Environments in Training and Rehabilitation: International Perspectives, 8*(3), 220–230.

Gladwell, M. (2005). *Blink: The power of thinking without thinking.* New York: Little, Brown.

Gleason, J. B. (2005). *The development of language* (6th ed.). Boston: Allyn & Bacon.

Glisky, M. L., Williams, J. M., & Kihlstrom, J. F. (1996). Internal and external mental imagery perspectives and performance on two tasks. *Journal of Sport Behavior, 19*(1), 3–18.

Gobet, F., & Simon, H. A. (1996). Recall of random and distorted chess positions: Implications for the theory of expertise. *Memory & Cognition, 24*(4), 493–503.

Goel, V., & Grafman, J. (1995). Are the frontal lobes implicated in "planning" functions? Interpreting data from the Tower of Hanoi. *Neuropsychologia, 33*(5), 623–642.

Goel, V., & Dolan, R. J. (2004). Differential involvement of left prefrontal cortex in inductive and deductive reasoning. *Cognition, 93*(3), 109–121.

Gogate, L. J., Bahrick, L. E., & Watson, J. D. (2000). A study of multimodal motherese: The role of temporal synchrony between verbal labels and gestures, *Child Development, 71*(4), 878–894.

Goldberg, C. (2001). Of prophets, true believers, and terrorists. *The Dana Forum on Brain Science, 3*(3), 21–24.

Golden, J. (2005). *Message in a bottle: The making of fetal alcohol syndrome.* Cambridge, MA: Harvard University Press.

Goldenberg, H., & Goldenberg, I. (2004). *Family therapy: An overview* (6th ed.). Pacific Grove, CA: Brooks/Cole.

Goldman, H. H. (1998). Deinstitutionalization and community care. *Harvard Review of Psychiatry, 6*(4), 219–222.

Goldstein, E. B. (2005). *Cognitive psychology: Connecting mind, research and everyday experience.* Belmont, CA: Wadsworth.

Goldstein, E. B. (2007). *Sensation and perception* (7th ed.). Belmont, CA: Wadsworth.

Goleman, D. (1995). *Emotional intelligence.* New York: Bantam.

Goodall, J. (1990). *Through a window: My thirty years with the chimpanzees of the Gombe.* Boston: Houghton Mifflin.

Goode, E. (1996). Gender and courtship entitlement: Responses to personal ads. *Sex Roles, 34*(3–4), 141–169.

Goodwin, R. D., Fergusson, D. M., & Horwood, L. J. (2005). Childhood abuse and familial violence and the risk of panic attacks and panic disorder in young adulthood. *Psychological Medicine, 35*(6), 881–890.

Gopnik, A., Meltzoff, A. N., & Kuhl, P. K. (2000). *The scientist in the crib: What early learning tells us about the mind.* New York: HarperCollins.

Gordon, A. K., & Kaplar, M. E. (2002). A new technique for demonstrating the actor-observer bias. *Teaching of Psychology, 29*(4), 301–303.

Gordon, T. (2000). Parent effectiveness training: The proven program for raising responsible children. New York: Three Rivers Press.

Gorman, J. M. (1996). *The essential guide to mental health.* New York: St. Martin's Griffin.

Gosling, S. D., Vazire, S., Srivastave, S., & John, O. P. (2004). Should we trust Web-based studies? *American Psychologist, 59*(2), 93–104.

Gottlieb, G. (1998). Normally occurring environmental and behavioral influences on gene activity: From central dogma to probabilistic epigenesis. *Psychological Review, 105*(4), 792–802.

Gottselig, J. M., Bassetti, C. L., & Achermann, P. (2002). Power and coherence of sleep spindle frequency activity following hemispheric stroke. *Brain, 125,* 373–383.

Gould, E., & Gross, C. G. (2002). Neurogenesis in adult mammals: Some progress and problems. *Journal of Neuroscience, 22*(3), 619–623.

Gould, E., Reeves, A. J., & Gross, C. G. (1999). Neurogenesis in the neocortex of adult primates. *Science, 286*(5439), 548.

Grabe, M. (2006). *Integrating technology for meaningful learning.* Boston: Houghton Mifflin.

Grack, C., & Richman, C. L. (1996). Reducing general and specific heterosexism through cooperative contact. *Journal of Psychology & Human Sexuality, 8*(4), 59–68.

Grande, T., Rudolf, G., Oberbracht, C., & Pauli-Magnus, C. (2003). Progressive changes in patients' lives after psychotherapy. *Psychotherapy Research, 13*(1), 43–58.

Grandner, M. A., & Kripke, D. F. (2004). Self-reported sleep complaints with long and short sleep: A nationally representative sample. *Psychosomatic Medicine, 66,* 239–241.

Granrud, C. E. (2004). Visual metacognition and the development of size constancy. In D. T. Levin (Ed.), *Thinking and seeing: Visual metacognition in adults and children.*

Grant, B. F., & Dawson, D. A. (1997). Age at onset of alcohol use and its association with DSM-IV alcohol abuse and dependence. *Journal of Substance Abuse, 9,* 103.

Grant, B. F., Hasin, D. S., Stinson, F. S., Dawson, D. A., et al. (2006). The epidemiology of DSM-IV panic disorder and agoraphobia in the United States: Results from the National Epidemiologic Survey on Alcohol and Related Conditions. *Journal of Clinical Psychiatry, 67*(3), 363–374.

Grant, I., Gonzalez, R., Carey, C., & Natarajan, L. (2001). Long-term neurocognitive consequences of marijuana. In *National Institute on Drug Abuse Workshop on Clinical Consequences of Marijuana,* August 13, 2001, Rockville, MD.

Graves, J. L. (2001). *The emperor's new clothes.* Piscataway, NJ: Rutgers University Press.

Gravetter, F. J., & Wallnau, L. B. (2007). *Statistics for the behavioral sciences* (7th ed.). Belmont, CA: Wadsworth.

Greenberg, D. L. (2004). President Bush's false 'flashbulb' memory of 9/11/01. *Applied Cognitive Psychology, 18*(3), 363–370.

Greene, D., & Lepper, M. R. (1974). How to turn play into work. *Psychology Today,* Sept., 49.

Greenfield, P. M. (1997). You can't take it with you: Why abilities assessments don't cross cultures. *American Psychologist, 52,* 1115–1124.

Greenglass, E. R., Burke, R. J., & Moore, K. A. (2003). Reactions to increased workload: Effects on professional efficacy of nurses. *Applied Psychology: An International Review, 52*(4), 580–597.

Greenwald, R. (2006). Eye movement desensitization and reprocessing with traumatized youth. In N. B. Webb (Ed.), *Working with traumatized youth in child welfare: Social work practice with children and families.* New York: Guilford.

Gregory, R. L. (1990). *Eye and brain: The psychology of seeing.* Princeton, NJ: Princeton University Press.

Gregory, R. L. (2003). Seeing after blindness. *Nature Neuroscience, 6*(9), 909–910.

Griffin, D. R. (1992). *Animal minds.* Chicago: University of Chicago Press.

Griffin, W. A. (2002). Family therapy. In M. Hersen & W. H. Sledge (Eds.), *Encyclopedia of psychotherapy.* San Diego: Academic Press.

Griffin-Fennell, F., & Williams, M. (2006). Examining the complexities of suicidal behavior in the African American community. *Journal of Black Psychology, 32*(3), 303–319.

Grigorenko, E. L., & Sternberg, R. J. (2003). The nature-nurture issue. In A. Slater & G. Bremner (Eds.), *An introduction to developmental psychology.* Malden, MA: Blackwell.

Grigorenko, E. L. (2005). The inherent complexities of gene-environment interactions. *Journals of Gerontology: Series B: Psychological Sciences & Social Sciences. Special Research on Environmental Effects in Genetic Studies of Aging, 60B*(1,SpecIssue), 53–64.

Grobstein, P., & Chow, K. L. (1975). Perceptive field development and individual experience. *Science, 190,* 352–358.

Gross, J. J. (2001). Emotion regulation in adulthood: Timing is everything. *Current Directions in Psychological Science, 10*(6), 214–219.

Grubin, D., & Madsen, L. (2005). Lie detection and the polygraph: A historical review. *Journal of Forensic Psychiatry & Psychology, 16*(2), 357–369.

Grunbaum, J. A., Kann, L., Kinchen, S., & Ross, J., et al. (2004). Youth Risk Behavior Surveillance: United States, 2003. *Centers for Disease Control and Prevention Morbidity and Mortality Weekly Report Surveillance Summary, 53*(SS02), 1–96.

Gruner, C. R., & Tighe, M. R. (1995). Semantic differential measurements of connotations of verbal terms and their doublespeak facsimiles in sentence contexts. *Psychological Reports, 77*(3, Pt. 1), 778.

Grzegorek, J. L., Slaney, R. B., Franze, S., & Rice, K. G. (2004). Self-criticism, dependency, self-esteem, and grade point average satisfaction among clusters of perfectionists and nonperfectionists. *Journal of Counseling Psychology, 51*(2), 192–200.

Guastello, D. D., & Guastello, S. J. (2003). Androgyny, gender role behavior, and emotional intelligence among college students and their parents. *Sex Roles, 49*(11–12), 663–673.

Guéguen, N. (2002). Status, apparel and touch: Their joint effects on compliance to a request. *North American Journal of Psychology, 4*(2), 279–286.

Guéguen, N., Pascual, A., & Dagot, L. (2002). Low-ball and compliance to a request: An application in a field setting. *Psychological Reports, 91*(1), 81–84.

Gullette, D. L., & Lyons, M. A. (2005). Sexual sensation seeking, compulsivity, and HIV risk behaviors in college students. *Journal of Community Health Nursing, 22*(1), 47–60.

Gump, B. B., & Kulik, J. A. (1997). Stress, affiliation, and emotional contagion. *Journal of Personality & Social Psychology, 72*(2), 305–319.

Gur, R. E., Cowell, P., Turetsky, B. I., Gallacher, F., et al. (1998). A follow-up magnetic resonance imaging study of schizophrenia. *Archives of General Psychiatry, 55*(2), 145–152.

Gustavsson, J. P., Weinryb, R. M., Göransson, S., Pedersen, N. L., et al. (1997). Stability and predictive ability of personality traits across 9 years. *Personality & Individual Differences, 22*(6), 783–791.

Haas, L. J., Benedict, J. G., & Kobos, J. C. (1996). Psychotherapy by telephone: Risks and benefits for psychologists and consumers. *Professional Psychology: Research & Practice, 27*(2), 154–160.

Haber, R. N., & Haber, L. (2000). Eidetic imagery. In A. E. Kazdin, (Ed.), *Encyclopedia of psychology* (Vol. 3). Washington: American Psychological Association.

Haber, R. N. (1969). Eidetic images; with biographical sketches. *Scientific American, 220*(12), 36–44.

Haber, R. N. (1970). How we remember what we see. *Scientific American, 222,* 104–112.

Haddad, S. (2003). Islam and attitudes toward U.S. policy in the Middle East: Evidence from survey research in Lebanon. *Studies in Conflict & Terrorism, 26*(2), 135–154.

Hadwin, A. F., Kirby, J. R., & Woodhouse, R. A. (1999). Individual differences in notetaking, summarization and learning from lectures. *Alberta Journal of Educational Research, 45*(1), 1–17.

Haenschel, C., Vernon, D. J., Dwivedi, P., Gruzelier, J. H., et al. (2005). Event-related brain potential correlates of human auditory sensory memory-trace formation. *Journal of Neuroscience, 25*(45), 10494–10501.

Hafer, C. L., & Bègue, L. (2005). Experimental research on just-world theory: problems, developments, and future challenges. *Psychological Bulletin, 131*(1), 128–167.

Haier, R. J., Jung, R. E., Yeo, R. A., Head, K, et al. (2004). Structural brain variation and general intelligence. *NeuroImage, 23,* 425–433.

Haier, R. J., Siegel, B. V., Nuechterlein, K. H., Hazlett, E., et al. (1988). Cortical glucose metabolic rate correlates of abstract reasoning and attention studied with positron emission tomography. *Intelligence, 12,* 199–217.

Haier, R. J., White, N. S., & Alkire, M. T. (2003). Individual differences in general intelligence correlate with brain function during nonreasoning tasks. *Intelligence, 31*(5), 429–441.

Halbert, J., Crotty, M., & Cameron, I. D. (2002). Evidence for the optimal management of acute and chronic phantom pain. *Clinical Journal of Pain, 18*(2), 84–92.

Hall, C. (1966a). *The meaning of dreams.* New York: McGraw-Hill.

Hall, C. (1974a). What people dream about. In R. L. Woods & H. B. Greenhouse (Eds.), *The new world of dreams: An anthology.* New York: Macmillan.

Hall, J. (2006). *What is clinical psychology?* (4th ed.). New York: Oxford University Press.

Hallahan, D. P., & Kauffman, J. M. (2006). *Exceptional learners* (10th ed.). Boston: Allyn & Bacon.

Halpern, D. F. (2003). *Thought and knowledge: An introduction to critical thinking* (4th ed.). Mahwah, NJ: Erlbaum.

Hamilton, V. L., & Sanders, J. (1995). Crimes of obedience and conformity in the workplace. *Journal of Social Issues, 51*(3), 67–88.

Hammer, L. B., Grigsby, T. D., & Woods, S. (1998). The conflicting demands of work, family, and school among students at an urban university. *Journal of Psychology, 132*(2), 220–226.

Hancock, P. A., & Ganey, H. C. N. (2003). From the inverted-U to the extended-U: The evolution of a law of psychology. *Journal of Human Performance in Extreme Environments, 7*(1), 5–14.

Hanley, S. J., & Abell, S. C. (2002). Maslow and relatedness: Creating an interpersonal model of self-actualization. *Journal of Humanistic Psychology, 42*(4), 37–56.

Hansell, J. H., & Damour, L. (2004). *Abnormal psychology.* San Francisco: Jossey-Bass.

Hansen, C. J., Stevens, L. C., & Coast, J. R. (2001). Exercise duration and mood state. *Health Psychology, 20*(4), 267–275.

Hansen, N. B., Lambert, M. J., & Forman, E. M. (2002). The psychotherapy dose-response effect and its implications for treatment delivery services. *Clinical Psychology: Science & Practice, 9*(3), 329–334.

Harding, D. J., Fox, C., & Mehta, J. D. (2002). Studying rare events through qualitative case studies. *Sociological Methods & Research, 31*(2), 174–217.

Harding, R. W., Morgan, F. H., Indermaur, D., Ferrante, A. M., et al. (1998). Road rage and the epidemiology of violence. *Studies on Crime & Crime Prevention, 7*(2), 221–238.

Hare, R. D. (2006). Psychopathy: A Clinical and forensic overview. *Psychiatric Clinics of North America, 29*(3), 709–724.

Harker, L., & Keltner, D. (2001). Expressions of positive emotion in women's college yearbook pictures and their relationship to personality and life outcomes across adulthood. *Journal of Personality & Social Psychology, 80*(1), 112–124.

Harlow, H. F., & Harlow, M. K. (1962). Social deprivation in monkeys. *Scientific American, 207,* 136–146.

Harlow, J. M. (1868). Recovery from the passage of an iron bar through the head. *Publications of the Massachusetts Medical Society, 2,* 327–347.

Harrigan, J. A. (2006). Proxemics, kinesics, and gaze. In J. A. Harrigan, R. Rosenthal, & K. R. Scherer (Eds.), *The new handbook of methods in nonverbal behavior research.* New York: Oxford University Press.

Harris, J. A., Rushton, J. P., Hampson, E., & Jackson, D. N. (1996). Salivary testosterone and self-report aggressive and prosocial personality characteristics in men and women. *Aggressive Behavior, 22*(5), 321–331.

Harris, J. R., & Liebert, R. M. (1991). *The child.* Englewood Cliffs, NJ: Prentice Hall.

Harrison, P. J., & Weinberger, D. R. (2005). Schizophrenia genes, gene expression, and neuropathology: On the matter of their convergence. *Molecular Psychiatry, 10*(1), 40–68.

Hart, B., & Risley, T. R. (1999). *The social world of children learning to talk.* Baltimore, MD: Paul H. Brookes

Hart, D., & Carlo, G. (2005). Moral development in adolescence. *Journal of Research on Adolescence. Special Issue: Moral Development, 15*(3), 223–233.

Hartgens, F., & Kuipers, H. (2004). Effects of androgenic-anabolic steroids in athletes. *Sports Medicine, 34*(8), 513–54.

Hartlep, K. L., & Forsyth, G. A. (2000). The effect of self-reference on learning and retention. *Teaching of Psychology, 27*(4), 269–271.

Hartmann, P., Reuter, M., & Nyborg, H. (2006). The relationship between date of birth and individual differences in personality and general intelligence: A large-scale study. *Personality & Individual Differences, 40*(7), 1349–1362.

Harway, M. (Ed.), (2004). *Handbook of couples therapy.* San Francisco, CA: Jossey-Bass.

Hashibe, M., Straif, K., Tashkin, D. P., Morgenstern, H., et al. (2005). Epidemiologic review of marijuana use and cancer risk. *Alcohol, 35*(3), 265–275.

Hauck, F. R., Moore, C. M., Herman, S. M., Donovan, M., et al. (2002). The contribution of prone sleeping position to the racial disparity in sudden infant death syndrome. *Pediatrics, 110,* 772–780.

Hauri, P., & Linde, S. (1990). *No more sleepless nights.* New York: Wiley.

Hayes, C. (1951). *The ape in our house.* New York: Harper & Row.

Hayne, H., & Rovee-Collier, C. (1995). The organization of reactivated memory in infancy. *Child Development, 66*(3), 893–906.

Heath, R. G. (1963). Electrical self-stimulation of the brain in man. *American Journal of Psychiatry, 120,* 571–577.

Heiman, J. R. (2002). Sexual dysfunction: Overview of prevalence, etiological factors, and treatments. *Journal of Sex Research. Special Promoting Sexual Health & Responsible Sexual Behavior, 39*(1), 73–78.

Heimann, M., & Meltzoff, A. N. (1996). Deferred imitation in 9- and 14-month-old infants. *British Journal of Developmental Psychology, 14,* 55–64.

Heinrichs, R. W. (2001). *In search of madness.* New York: Oxford.

Heinze, H. J., Hinrichs, H., Scholz, M., Burchert, W., & Mangun, G. R. (1998). Neural mechanisms of global and local processing. *Journal of Cognitive Neuroscience, 10*(4), 485–498.

Heisel, M. J., Flett, G. L., & Hewitt, P. L. (2003). Social hopelessness and college student suicide ideation. *Archives of Suicide Research, 7*(3), 221–235.

Hellerstein, D. J., Rosenthal, R. N., Pinsker, H., Samstag, L. W., et al. (1998). A randomized prospective study comparing supportive and dynamic therapies. *Journal of Psychotherapy Practice & Research, 7*(4), 261–271.

Hellige, J. B. (1993). *Hemispheric asymmetry.* Cambridge, MA: Harvard University Press.

Helms, J. E. (1992). Why is there no study of cultural equivalence in standardized ability testing? *American Psychologist, 47*(9), 1083–1101.

Helson, R., & Srivastava, S. (2002). Creative and wise people. *Personality & Social Psychology Bulletin, 28*(10), 1430–1440.

Henderson, N. D. (1982). Human behavior genetics. *Annual Review of Psychology, 33,* 403–440.

Hendrick, S. S., & Hendrick, C. (1993). Lovers as friends. *Journal of Social & Personal Relationships, 10*(3), 459–466.

Henman, L. D. (2001). Humor as a coping mechanism. *Humor: International Journal of Humor Research, 14*(1), 83–94.

Hepper, P. G., Wells, D. L., & Lynch, C. (2005). Prenatal thumb sucking is related to postnatal handedness. *Neuropsychologia, 43*(3), 313–315.

Hepper, P.G., McCartney, G. R., & Shannon, E. A. (1998). Lateralised behaviour in first trimester human foetuses. *Neuropsychologia, 36*(6), 531–534.

Hergenhahn, B. R., & Olson, M. H. (2005). *Introduction to the theories of learning* (7th ed.). Englewood Cliffs, NJ: Prentice Hall.

Hergenhahn, B. R., & Olson, M. (2007). *An introduction to theories of personality* (7th ed.). Englewood Cliffs, NJ: Prentice Hall.

Hergenhahn, B. R. (2005). *An introduction to the history of psychology* (5th ed.). Belmont, CA: Wadsworth.

Heriot, S. A., & Pritchard, M. (2004). 'Reciprocal Inhibition as the Main Basis of Psychotherapeutic Effects' by Joseph Wolpe (1954). *Clinical Child Psychology & Psychiatry, 9*(2), 297–307.

Hermann, B., Seidenberg, M., Sears, L., Hansen, R., et al. (2004). Cerebellar atrophy in temporal lobe epilepsy affects procedural memory. *Neurology, 63*(11), 2129–2131.

Herrmann, D. J., Yoder, C. Y., Gruneberg, M., & Payne, D. G. (2006). *Applied cognitive psychology: A textbook.* Mahwah, NJ: Erlbaum.

Herrnstein, R. J., & Murray, C. (1994). *The Bell Curve: Intelligence and class structure in American life.* New York: Macmillan.

Herxheimer, A., & Waterhouse, J. (2003). The prevention and treatment of jet lag. *British Medical Journal, 326*(7384), 296–297.

Herz, R. S. (2001). Ah sweet skunk! *Cerebrum, 3*(4), 31–47.

Hettich, P. I. (2005). *Connect college to career: Student guide to work and life transition.* Belmont, CA: Wadsworth.

Higbee, K. L., Clawson, C., DeLano, L., & Campbell, S. (1990). Using the link mnemonic to remember errands. *Psychological Record, 40*(3), 429–436.

Higham, P. A., & Gerrard, C. (2005). Not all errors are created equal: Metacognition

and changing answers on multiple-choice tests. *Canadian Journal of Experimental Psychology. Special Issue on 2003 Festschrift for Lee R. Brooks, 59*(1), 28–34.

Hilgard, E. R . (1994) Neodissociation theory. In S. J. Lynn & J. W. Rhue (Eds.), *Dissociation: Clinical, theoretical and research perspectives.* New York: Guilford.

Hilgard, E. R. (1968). *The experience of hypnosis.* New York: Harcourt Brace Jovanovich.

Hilgard, E. R. (1977). *Divided consciousness.* New York: Wiley.

Hilsenroth, M. J. (2000). Rorschach test. In A. Kazdin (Ed.), *Encyclopedia of psychology.* Washington: American Psychological Association.

Hinkel, E. (Ed.). (2005). *Handbook of research in second language teaching and learning.* Mahwah, NJ: Erlbaum.

Hinterberger, T., Kübler, A., Kaiser, J., Neumann, N., et al. (2003). A brain-computer interface (BCI) for the locked-in: Comparison of different EEG classifications for the thought translation device. *Clinical Neurophysiology, 114*(3), 416–425.

Hittner, J. B., & Daniels, J. R. (2002). Gender-role orientation, creative accomplishments and cognitive styles. *Journal of Creative Behavior, 36*(1), 62–75.

"HIV/AIDS." (2004). *UNAIDS 2004 Report on the global AIDS epidemic.* New York: United Nations.

Hobson, J. A. (2000). Dreams: Physiology. In A. Kazdin (Ed.), *Encyclopedia of psychology.* Washington: American Psychological Association.

Hobson, J. A. (2001). *The dream drugstore.* Cambridge, MA: MIT Press.

Hobson, J. A. (2005). Sleep is of the brain, by the brain and for the brain. *Nature, 437*(7063), 1254–1256.

Hobson, J. A., Pace-Schott, E. F., & Stickgold, R. (2000). Dream science 2000. *Behavioral & Brain Sciences, 23*(6), 1019–1035; 1083–1121.

Hobson, J. A., Pace-Schott, E. F., Stickgold, R., & Kahn, D. (1998). *Current Opinion in Neurobiology, 8*(2), 239–244.

Hodgson, R., & Miller, P. (1982). *Selfwatching.* New York: Facts on File.

Hofer, B. K., & Yu, S. L. (2003). Teaching self-regulated learning through a "Learning to Learn" course. *Teaching of Psychology, 30*(1), 30–33.

Hoff, E. (2006). How social contexts support and shape language development. *Developmental Review, 26*(1), 55–88.

Hoffer, A., & Youngren, V. R. (2004). Is free association still at the core of psychoanalysis? *International Journal of Psychoanalysis, 85*(6), 1489–1492.

Hoffman, H. G., Garcia-Palacios, A., Carlin, A., Furness, T. A., et al. (2003). Interfaces that heal: Coupling real and virtual objects to treat spider phobia. *International Journal of Human-Computer Interaction, 16*(2), 283–300.

Hogan, E. H., Hornick, B. A., & Bouchoux, A. (2002). Focus on communications: Communicating the message: Clarifying the controversies about caffeine. *Nutrition Today, 37,* 28–35.

Hogben, D., & Lawson, M. J. (1992). Superiority of the keyword method for backward

recall in vocabulary acquisition. *Psychological Reports, 71*(3, Pt. 1), 880–882.

Hoge, C. W., Castro, C. A., Messer, S. C., McGurk, D., et al. (2004). Combat duty in Iraq and Afghanistan, mental health problems, and barriers to care. *New England Journal of Medicine, 351*(1), 13–22.

Hohwy, J., & Rosenberg, R. (2005). Unusual experiences, reality testing and delusions of alien control. *Mind & Language, 20*(2), 141–162.

Holden, C. (1980). Twins reunited. *Science 80,* Nov., 55–59.

Holmes, J., & Adams, J. W. (2006). Working memory and children's mathematical skills: Implications for mathematical development and mathematics curricula. *Educational Psychology, 26*(3), 339–366.

Holmes, P. S., & Collins, D. J. (2001). The PETTLEP approach to motor imagery: A functional equivalence model for sport psychologists. *Journal of Applied Sport Psychology, 13*(1), 60–83.

Holmes, T. H., & Rahe, R. H. (1967). The social readjustment rating scale. *Journal of Psychosomatic Research, 11*(2), 213–218.

Holtzen, D. W. (2000). Handedness and professional tennis. *International Journal of Neuroscience, 105*(1–4), 101–111.

Horgan, J. (2005). The forgotten era of brain chips. *Scientific American, 293*(4), 66–73.

Horn, J., Nelson, C. E., & Brannick, M. T. (2004). Integrity, conscientiousness, and honesty. *Psychological Reports, 95*(1), 27–38.

Horn, R. R., Williams, A. M., Scott, M. A., & Hodges, N. J. (2005). Visual search and coordination changes in response to video and point-light demonstrations without KR. *Journal of Motor Behavior, 37*(4), 265–274.

Horne, R. S. C., Andrew, S., Mitchell, K., Sly, D. J., et al. (2001). Apnoea of prematurity and arousal from sleep. *Early Human Development, 61*(2), 119–133.

Hortman, G. (2003). What do facial expressions convey? *Emotion, 3*(2), 150–166.

Horvath, L. S., Milich, R., Lynam, D., Leukefeld, C., et al. (2004) Sensation seeking and substance use: A cross-lagged panel design. *Individual Differences Research, 2*(3), 175–183.

Hosch, H. M., & Cooper, D. S. (1982). Victimization as a determinant of eyewitness accuracy. *Journal of Applied Psychology, 67,* 649–652.

Houtsmuller, E. J., & Stitzer, M. L. (1999). Manipulation of cigarette craving through rapid smoking: Efficacy and effects on smoking behavior. *Psychopharmacology, 142*(2), 149–157.

Howard, I. P., & Rogers, B. J. (2001a). *Seeing in depth* (Vol. 1): *Basic mechanisms.* Toronto: Porteous.

Howard, I. P., & Rogers, B. J. (2001b). *Seeing in depth* (Vol. 2): *Depth perception.* Toronto: Porteous.

Howard, K. I., Kopta, S. M., Krause, M. S., & Orlinsky, D. E. (1986). The dose-effect relationship in psychotherapy. *American Psychologist, 41,* 159–164.

Howes, C. (1997). Children's experiences in center-based child care as a function of teacher background and adult:child ratio. *Merrill-Palmer Quarterly, 43*(3), 404–425.

Hsia, Y., & Graham, C. H. (1997). Color blindness. In A. Byrne & D. R. Hilbert (Eds.), *Readings on color* (Vol. 2): *The science of color.* Cambridge, MA: MIT Press.

Hubble, M.A., Duncan, B. L., & Miller, S. D. (Eds.). (1999). *The heart and soul of change: What works in therapy.* Washington: American Psychological Association.

Hubel D. H., & Wiesel, W. N. (2005). *Brain & visual perception: The story of a 25-year collaboration.* New York: Oxford University Press.

Huebner, R. (1998). Hemispheric differences in global/local processing revealed by same-different judgements. *Visual Cognition, 5*(4), 457–478.

Huesmann, L R., Moise-Titus, J., Podolski, C.-L., & Eron, L. D. (2003). Longitudinal relations between children's exposure to TV violence and their aggressive and violent behavior in young adulthood: 1977–1992. *Developmental Psychology. Special Issue: Violent children, 39*(2), 201–221.

Huesmann, L. R., Moise-Titus, J., Podolski, C., & Eron, L. D. (2003). Longitudinal relations between children's exposure to TV violence and their aggressive and violent behavior in young adulthood: 1977–1992. *Developmental Psychology, 39*(2), 201–221.

Hughes, J. N., & Hasbrouck, J. E. (1996). Television violence: Implications for violence prevention. *School Psychology Review, 25*(2), 134–151.

Hughes, J. R., Oliveto, A. H., Liguori, A., Carpenter, J., et al. (1998). Endorsement of DSM-IV dependence criteria among caffeine users. *Drug & Alcohol Dependence, 52*(2), 99–107.

Human Rights Watch. (2003). *Ill-equipped: U.S. prisons and offenders with mental illness.* New York: Holt.

Humphries, S. A., Johnson, M. H., & Long, N. R. (1996). An investigation of the gate control theory of pain using the experimental pain stimulus of potassium iontophoresis. *Perception & Psychophysics, 58*(5), 693–703.

Hunt, E. B. (1995). *Will we be smart enough? A cognitive analysis of the coming workforce.* New York: Russell Sage Foundation.

Hunt, R. R., & Ellis, H. C. (2004). *Fundamentals of cognitive psychology* (7th ed.). New York: McGraw-Hill.

Hunter, E. (1998). Adolescent attraction to cults. *Adolescence, 33*(131), 709–714.

Hunter, J. P., Katz, J., & Davis, K. D. (2003). The effect of tactile and visual sensory inputs on phantom limb awareness. *Brain, 126*(3), 579–589.

Hutchinson, S. R. (2004). Survey research. In K. deMarrais & S. D. Lapan (Eds.), *Foundations for research: Methods of inquiry in education and the social sciences. Inquiry and pedagogy across diverse contexts.* Mahwah, NJ: Erlbaum.

Hyde, J. S. (2004). *Half the human experience: The psychology of women* (6th ed.). Boston: Houghton Mifflin.

Hyde, J. S., & DeLamater, J. D. (2006). *Understanding human sexuality* (9th ed.). New York: McGraw-Hill.

Hyman, R. (1996a). Evaluation of the military's twenty-year program on psychic spying. *Skeptical Inquirer, 20*(2), 21–23.

Hyman, R. (1996b). The evidence for psychic functioning: Claims vs. reality. *Skeptical Inquirer, 20*(2), 24–26.

Hysenbegasi, A., Hass, S. L., & Rowland, C. R. (2005). The impact of depression on the academic productivity of university students. *Journal of Mental Health Policy & Economics, 8*(3), 145–151.

Iosif, A., & Ballon, B. (2005). Bad moon rising: The persistent belief in lunar connections to madness. *Canadian Medical Association Journal, 173*(12), 1498–1500.

Ironson, G., Freud, B., Strauss, J. L., & Williams, J. (2002). Comparison for two treatments for traumatic stress: A community-based study of EMDR and prolonged exposure. *Journal of Clinical Psychology, 58*(1) 113–128.

Isaak, M. I., & Just, A. (1995). Constraints on thinking in insight and invention. In R. J. Sternberg & J. E. Davidson (Eds.), *The nature of insight.* Cambridge, MA: MIT Press.

Izard, C. E. (1977). *Human emotions.* New York: Plenum.

Izard, C. E. (1990). Facial expressions and the regulation of emotions. *Journal of Personality & Social Psychology, 58*(3), 487–498.

Izard, C. E., Fantauzzo, C. A., Castle, J. M., Haynes, O. M., Rayias, M. F., & Putnam, P. H. (1995). The ontogeny and significance of infants' facial expressions in the first 9 months of life. *Developmental Psychology, 31*(6), 997–1013.

Jablonski, N.G., & Chaplin, G. (2000). The evolution of human skin coloration. *Journal of Human Evolution, 39*(1), 57–106.

Jackson, T., Fritch, A., Nagasaka, T., & Gunderson, J. (2002). Towards explaining the association between shyness and loneliness. *Social Behavior & Personality, 30*(3), 263–270.

Jackson, T., Towson, S., & Narduzzi, K. (1997). Predictors of shyness. *Social Behavior & Personality, 25*(2), 149–154.

Jacob, A., Prasad, S., Boggild, M., & Chandratre, S. (2004). Charles Bonnet syndrome: Elderly people and visual hallucinations. *British Medical Journal, 328*(7455), 1552–1554.

Jacobs, M. (2003). *Sigmund Freud.* Thousand Oaks, CA: Sage.

Jacobs, M. K., Christensen, A., Snibbe, J. R., Dolezal-Wood, S., et al. (2001). A comparison of computer-based versus traditional individual psychotherapy. *Professional Psychology: Research & Practice, 32*(1), 92–96.

Jacobs, S. R., & Dodd, D. K. (2003). Student burnout as a function of personality, social support, and workload. *Journal of College Student Development, 44*(3), 2003, 291–303.

Jaffe, J., Beatrice, B., Feldstein, S., Crown, C. L., & Jasnow, M. D. (2001). Rhythms of dialogue in infancy. *Monographs of the Society for Research in Child Development, 66*(2), vi–131.

Jamison, K. R. (2001). Suicide in the young: An essay. *Cerebrum, 3*(3), 39–42.

Janssen, S. A., & Arntz, A. (2001). Real-life stress and opioid-mediated analgesia in novice parachute jumpers. *Journal of Psychophysiology, 15*(2), 106–113.

Janus, S. S., & Janus, C. L. (1993). *The Janus report.* New York: Wiley.

Jarvin, L., & Sternberg, R. J. (2003). Alfred Binet's contributions to educational psychology. In B. J. Zimmerman & D. H. Schunk (Eds.), *Educational psychology: A century of contributions.* Mahwah, NJ: Erlbaum.

Jay, T. B. (2003). *Psychology of language.* Upper Saddle River, NJ: Prentice Hall.

Jeffery, R. W., & Wing R. R. (2001). The effects of an enhanced exercise program on long-term weight loss. *Obesity Research, 9*(Suppl. 3), O193.

Jenkins, J. G., & Dallenbach, K. M. (1924). Oblivescence during sleep and waking. *American Journal of Psychology, 35,* 605–612.

Jerabek, I., & Standing, L. (1992). Imagined test situations produce contextual memory enhancement. *Perceptual & Motor Skills, 75*(2), 400.

Johnson, K. E., & Mervis, C. B. (1997). Effects of varying levels of expertise on the basic level of categorization. *Journal of Experimental Psychology: General, 126*(3), 248–277.

Johnson, K. J., & Fredrickson, B. L. (2005). "We all look the same to me": Positive emotions eliminate the own-race bias in face recognition. *Psychological Science, 16*(11), 875–881.

Johnson, S. (2005). *Everything bad is good for you: How today's popular culture is actually making us smarter.* New York: Riverhead.

Johnson, S. M., & White, G. (1971). Self-observation as an agent of behavioral change. *Behavior Therapy, 2,* 488–497.

Johnson, T. J. (2002). College students' self-reported reasons for why drinking games end. *Addictive Behaviors, 27*(1), 145–153.

Jones, B. T. (2003). Alcohol consumption on the campus. *Psychologist, 16*(10), 523–525.

Jones, E. E., & Nisbett, R. E. (1971). The actor and observer: Divergent perceptions of the causes of behavior. In E. E. Jones, D. E. Kanouse, H. H. Kelley, R. E. Nisbett, et al. (Eds.), *Attribution: Perceiving the causes of behavior.* Morristown, NJ: General Learning Press.

Jones, G. V., & Martin, M. (2001). Confirming the X-linked handedness gene as recessive, not additive. *Psychological Review, 108*(4), 811–813.

Jones, L., & Petruzzi, D. C. (1995). Test anxiety: A review of theory and current treatment. *Journal of College Student Psychotherapy, 10*(1), 3–15.

Jones, M. K., & Menzies, R. G. (1998). Danger ideation reduction therapy (DIRT) for obsessive-compulsive washers. *Behaviour Research & Therapy, 36*(10), 959–970.

Jones, S. S., & Hong, H.-W. (2001). Onset of voluntary communication: Smiling looks to mother. *Infancy, 2*(3), 353–370.

Jouvet, M. (1999). *The paradox of sleep.* Boston, MA: MIT Press.

Joyce, P., & Sills, C. (2001). *Skills in Gestalt counseling & psychotherapy.* Newbury Park: Sage.

Juliano, L. M., & Griffiths, R. R. (2004). A critical review of caffeine withdrawal: Empirical validation of symptoms and signs, incidence, severity, and associated features. *Psychopharmacology, 176*(1), 1–29.

Julien, R. M. (2005). *A primer of drug action: A comprehensive guide to the actions, uses, and side effects* (10th ed.). New York: Worth.

Jurma, W. E., & Powell, M. L. (1994). Perceived gender roles of managers and effective conflict management. *Psychological Reports, 74*(1), 104–106.

Jussim, L., & Harber, K. D. (2005). Teacher expectations and self-fulfilling prophecies: Knowns and unknowns, resolved and unresolved controversies. *Personality & Social Psychology Review, 9*(2), 131–155.

Kagan, J. (1971). *Change and continuity in infancy.* New York: Wiley.

Kagan, J. (2004). New insights into temperament. *Cerebrum, 6*(1), 51–66.

Kagan, J. (2005). Personality and temperament: Historical perspectives. In M. Rosenbluth, S. H. Kennedy, & R. M. Bagby (Eds.), *Depression and personality: Conceptual and clinical challenges.* Washington: American Psychiatric Publishing.

Kahneman, D. (2003). A perspective on judgment and choice. *American Psychologist, 58*(9), 697–720.

Kahneman, D., & Tversky, A. (1972). Subjective probability: A judgment of representativeness. *Cognitive Psychology, 3,* 430–454.

Kahneman, D., & Tversky, A. (1973). On the psychology of prediction. *Psychological Review, 80,* 237–251.

Kahneman, D., Slovic, P., & Tversky, A. (1982). *Judgment under uncertainty: Heuristics and biases.* Cambridge, MA: Cambridge University Press.

Kaitz, M., Zvi, H., Levy, M., Berger, A., et al. (1995). The uniqueness of mother-own-infant interactions. *Infant Behavior & Development, 18*(2), 247–252.

Kalal, D. M. (1999). Critical thinking in clinical practice: Pseudoscience, fad psychology, and the behavioral therapist. *The Behavior Therapist, 22*(4), 81–84.

Kalat, J. W., & Shiota, M. N. (2007). *Emotion.* Belmont, CA: Wadsworth.

Kalat, J. W. (2007). *Biological psychology* (8th ed.). Belmont, CA: Wadsworth.

Kallio, S., & Revonsuo, A. (2003). Hypnotic phenomena and altered states of consciousness: A multilevel framework of description and explanation. *Contemporary Hypnosis, 20*(3), 111–164.

Kamimori, G. H., Johnson, D., Thorne, D., & Belenky, G. (2005). Multiple caffeine doses maintain vigilance during early morning operations. *Aviation, Space, & Environmental Medicine, 76*(11), 1046–1050.

Kamin, L. J. (1981). *The intelligence controversy.* New York: Wiley.

Kandel, E. R., Schwartz, J. H., & Jessell, T. M. (2003). *Principles of neuroscience* (5th ed.). New York: McGraw-Hill.

Kaplan, P. S. (1998). *The human odyssey.* Pacific Grove, CA: Brooks/Cole.

Kapleau, P. (1966). *The three pillars of Zen.* New York: Harper & Row.

Kapur, S., & Lecrubier, Y. (Eds.) (2003). *Dopamine in the pathophysiology and treatment of schizophrenia: New findings.* Washington: Taylor & Francis.

Karon, B. P., & Widener, A. J. (1997). Repressed memories and World War II: Lest we forget! *Professional Psychology: Research & Practice, 28*(4), 338–340.

Kasser, T., & Ryan, R. M. (1993). A dark side of the American dream: Correlates of financial success as a central life aspiration. *Journal of Personality & Social Psychology, 65*(2), 410–422.

Kasser, T., & Ryan, R. M. (1996). Further examining the American dream: Differential correlates of intrinsic and extrinsic goals. *Personality & Social Psychology Bulletin, 22*(3), 280–287.

Kassin, S. M. (2005). On the psychology of confessions: Does innocence put innocents at risk? *American Psychologist, 60*(3), 215–228.

Kassin, S. M., Tubb, V. A., Hosch, H. M., & Memon, A. (2001). On the "general acceptance" of eyewitness testimony research. *American Psychologist, 56*(5), 405–416.

Kataria, S. (2004). A clinical guide to pediatric sleep: Diagnosis and management of sleep problems. *Journal of Developmental & Behavioral Pediatrics, 25*(2), 132–133.

Katz, P. A. (2003). Racists or tolerant multiculturalists? *American Psychologist, 58*(11), 897–909.

Kaufman, A. S. (2000). Intelligence tests and school psychology: Predicting the future by studying the past. *Psychology in the Schools, 37*(1), 7–16.

Kaufman, L., & Kaufman, J. H. (2000). Explaining the moon illusion. *Proceedings of the National Academy of Sciences, 97*(1), 500–505.

Kawai, K., Sugimoto, K., Nakashima, K., Miura, H., et al. (2000). Leptin as a modulator of sweet taste sensitivities in mice. *Proceedings: National Academy of Sciences, 97*(20), 11044–11049.

Kearney, C. A., Sims, K. E., Pursell, C. R., & Tillotson, C. A. (2003). Separation anxiety disorder in young children: A longitudinal and family analysis. *Journal of Clinical Child & Adolescent Psychology, 32*(4), 593–598.

Kebbell, M. R., & Wagstaff, G. F. (1998). Hypnotic interviewing: The best way to interview eyewitnesses? *Behavioral Sciences & the Law, 16*(1), 115–129.

Keefe, F. J., Abernethy, A. P., & Campbell, L. C. (2005). Psychological approaches to understanding and treating disease-related pain. *Annual Review of Psychology, 56,* 601–630.

Keel, P. K., & Klump, K. L. (2003). Are eating disorders culture-bound syndromes? Implications for conceptualizing their etiology. *Psychological Bulletin, 129*(5), 747–769.

Keller, M. C., & Young, R. K. (1996). Mate assortment in dating and married couples. *Personality & Individual Differences, 21*(2), 217–221.

Kellermann, A. L., Rivara, F. P., Rushforth, N. B., Banton, J. G., et al. (1993). Gun ownership as a risk factor for homicide in the home. *New England Journal of Medicine, 329*(15), 1084–1091.

Kelley, H. H. (1950). The warm-cold variable in first impressions of persons. *Journal of Personality, 18,* 431–439.

Kelly, I. W. (1999). "Debunking the debunkers": A response to an astrologer's debunking of skeptics. *Skeptical Inquirer,* Nov-Dec, 37–43.

Kelly, M. P., Strassberg, D. S., & Turner, C. M. (2006). Behavioral assessment of couples' communication in female orgasmic disorder. *Journal of Sex & Marital Therapy, 32*(2), 81–95.

Kendler, K. S., Thornton, L. M., & Prescott, C. A. (2001). Gender differences in the rates of exposure to stressful life events and sensitivity to their depressogenic effects. *American Journal of Psychiatry, 158*(4), 587–593.

Kennaway, D. J., & Wright, H. (2002). Melatonin and circadian rhythms. *Current Topics in Medicinal Chemistry, 2,* 199–209.

Kennedy, P. R., & Bakay, R. A. (1998). Restoration of neural output from a paralyzed patient by a direct brain connection. *Neuroreport, 9*(8), 1707–1711.

Kenneth, M., Carpenter, K. M., & Hasin, D. S. (1998). Reasons for drinking alcohol. *Psychology of Addictive Behaviors, 12*(3), 168–184.

Kernis, M. H., & Goldman, B. M. (2005). Authenticity, social motivation, and psychological adjustment. In J. P. Forgas, K. D. Williams, & S. M. Laham (Eds.), *Social motivation: Conscious and unconscious processes.* New York: Cambridge University Press.

Kety, S. S. (1979). Disorders of the human brain. *Scientific American, 241,* 202–214.

Keysers, C., Xiao, D.–K., Földiák, P., & Perrett, D. I. (2005). Out of sight but not out of mind: The neurophysiology of iconic memory in the superior temporal sulcus. *Cognitive Neuropsychology, 22*(3-4), 316–332.

Kiecolt-Glaser, J. K., McGuire, L. Robles, T. F., & Glaser, R. (2002). Emotions, morbidity, and immunity. *Annual Review of Psychology, 53,* 83–107.

Killen, J. D., & Fortmann, S. P. (1997). Craving is associated with smoking relapse: Findings from three prospective studies. *Experimental & Clinical Psychopharmacology, 5*(2), 137–142.

Kim, S. (2000). Bogglers. *Discover,* Dec., 98.

Kim-Cohen, J., Moffitt, T. E., Caspi, A., & Taylor, A. (2004). Genetic and environmental processes in young children's resilience and vulnerability to socioeconomic deprivation. *Child Development, 75*(3), 651–668.

King, N. J., Muris, P., & Ollendick, T. H. (2005). Childhood fears and phobias: Assessment and treatment. *Child & Adolescent Mental Health, 10*(2), 50–56.

Kinnunen, L. H., Moltz, H., Metz, J., & Cooper, M. (2004). Differential brain activation in exclusively homosexual and heterosexual men produced by the selective serotonin reuptake inhibitor, fluoxetine. *Brain Research, 1024*(1–2), 251–254.

Kirsch, I., (2005). The flexible observer and neodissociation theory. *Contemporary Hypnosis, 22*(3), 121–122.

Kirsch, I., & Lynn, S. J. (1995). The altered state of hypnosis. *American Psychologist, 50*(10), 846–858.

Kirsch, I., & Sapirstein, G. (1998). Listening to Prozac but hearing placebo: A meta-analysis of antidepressant medication. *Prevention & Treatment, 1*(June 26), Article 0002a.

Kirsh, S. J. (2005). *Children, adolescents, and media violence: a critical look at the research.* Newbury Park: Sage.

Kiser, L. J., Heston, J. D., & Paavola, M. (2006). Day treatment centers/Partial hospitalization settings. In T. A. Petti & C. Salguero (Eds.), *Community child & adolescent psychiatry: A manual of clinical practice and consultation.* Washington: American Psychiatric Publishing.

Kisilevsky, B. S., Hains, S. M. J., Jacquet, A. Y., Granier-Deferre, C., et al. (2004). Maturation of fetal responses to music. *Developmental Science, 7*(5), 550–559.

Kitayama, S., Markus, H. R., & Kurokawa, M. (2000). Culture, emotion, and well-being: Good feelings in Japan and the United States. *Cognition & emotion, 14,* 93–124.

Kjellgren, A., Sundequist, U., Norlander, T., & Archer, T. (2001). Effects of flotation-REST on muscle tension pain. *Pain Research & Management, 6*(4), 181–189.

Klaus, M. H., Kennell, J. H., & Klaus, P. H. (1995). *Bonding.* Reading, MA: Addison-Wesley.

Klein, B., Richards, J. C., & Austin, D. W. (2006). Efficacy of internet therapy for panic disorder. *Journal of Behavior Therapy & Experimental Psychiatry, 37*(3), 213–238.

Klein, D. W., & Kihlstrom, J. F. (1986). Elaboration, organization, and the self-reference effect in memory. *Journal of Experimental Psychology: General, 115,* 26–38.

Klein, K., & Boals, A. (2001a). The relationship of life event stress and working memory capacity. *Applied Cognitive Psychology, 15*(5), 565–579.

Klein, K., & Boals, A. (2001b). Expressive writing can increase working memory capacity. *Journal of Experimental Psychology: General, 130*(3), 520–533.

Kleinke, C. L., Peterson, T. R., & Rutledge, T. R. (1998). Effects of self-generated facial expressions on mood. *Journal of Personality and Social Psychology, 74*(1), 272–279.

Klohnen, E. C., & Luo, S. (2003). Interpersonal attraction and personality: What is attractive—self similarity, ideal similarity, complementarity or attachment security? *Journal of Personality & Social Psychology, 85*(4), 709–722.

Knaus, W. J., & Ellis, A. (2002). *The procrastination workbook: Your personalized program for breaking free from the patterns that hold you back.* Oakland, CA: New Harbinger Press.

Knight, J. (2005). The truth about lying. *Nature, 428,* 692–694.

Knoops, K. T. B., de Groot, L. C., Kromhout, D., Perrin, A., et al. (2004). Mediterranean diet, lifestyle factors, and 10-year mortality in elderly European men and women. *Journal of the American Medical Association, 292*(12), 1433–1439.

Koch, C. (2004). *The quest for consciousness: A neurobiological approach.* Englewood, CO: Roberts and Co.

Koch, W. H., & Pratarelli, M. E. (2004). Effects of intro/extraversion and sex on social internet use. *North American Journal of Psychology, 6*(3), 371–382.

Koepke, J. E., & Bigelow, A. E. (1997). Observations of newborn suckling behavior. *Infant Behavior & Development, 20*(1), 93–98.

Kohlberg, L. (1969). The cognitive-developmental approach to socialization. In A. Goslin (Ed.), *Handbook of socialization theory and research.* Chicago: Rand McNally.

Kohlberg, L. (1981). *Essays on moral development* (Vol. 1): *The philosophy of moral development.* San Francisco: Harper.

Kohn, C. S., & Antonuccio, D. O. (2002). Treatment of kleptomania using cognitive and behavioral strategies. *Clinical Case Studies, 1*(1), 25–38.

Köke, A., Schouten J. S., Lamerichs-Geelen. M. J. H., Lipsch J. S. M., et al. (2004). Pain reducing effect of three types of transcutaneous electrical nerve stimulation in patients with chronic pain: A randomized crossover trial. *Pain, 108*(1–2), 36–42.

Kolb, B. (1990). Recovery from occipital stroke: A self-report and an inquiry into visual processes. *Canadian Journal of Psychology, 44*(2), 130–147.

Kolb, B., Gibb, R., & Gorny, G. (2003). Experience-dependent changes in dendritic arbor and spine density in neocortex vary with age and sex. *Neurobiology of Learning & Memory, 79*(1), 1–10.

Kolb, B., & Whishaw, I. Q. (1998). Brain plasticity and behavior. *Annual Review of Psychology, 49,* 43–64.

Kolb, B., & Whishaw, I.Q. (2005). *Introduction to brain and behavior* (2nd ed.). New York: Freeman-Worth.

Korol, C., Craig, K. D., & Firestone, P. (2003). Dissociative and somatoform disorders. In P. Firestone & W. L. Marshall (Eds.), *Abnormal psychology: Perspectives* (2nd ed.). Toronto: Prentice Hall.

Kosslyn, S. M. (1983). *Ghosts in the mind's machine.* New York: Norton.

Kosslyn, S. M. (1985). Stalking the mental image. *Psychology Today,* May, 23–28.

Kosslyn, S. M. (2005). Mental images and the brain. *Cognitive Neuropsychology, 22*(3–4), 333–347.

Kosslyn, S. M., Ball, T. M., & Reiser, B. J. (1978). Visual images preserve metric spatial information: Evidence from studies of image scanning. *Journal of Experimental Psychology: Human Perception and Performance, 4,* 47–60.

Kosslyn, S. M., Seger, C., Pani, J. R., & Hillger, L. A. (1990). When is imagery used in everyday life? A diary study. *Journal of Mental Imagery, 14*(3–4), 131–152.

Kosslyn, S. M., Thompson, W. L., Costantini-Ferrando, M. F., Alpert, N. M., et al. (2000). Hypnotic visual illusion alters color processing in the brain. *American Journal of Psychiatry, 157*(8), 1279–1284.

Kosson, D. S., Suchy, Y., Mayer, A. R., & Libby, J. (2002). Facial affect recognition in criminal psychopaths. *Emotion, 2*(4), 398–411.

Kotkin, M., Daviet, C., & Gurin, J. (1996). The Consumer Reports mental health survey. *American Psychologist, 51*(10), 1080–1082.

Kottler, J. A. (2004). *Introduction to therapeutic counseling.* Belmont, CA: Wadsworth.

Kowert, P. A. (2002). *Groupthink or deadlock: When do leaders learn from their advisors?* SUNY series on the presidency. Albany, NY: State University of New York Press.

Kozart, M. F. (2002). Understanding efficacy in psychotherapy. *American Journal of Orthopsychiatry, 72*(2), 217–231.

Krakow, B., & Zadra, A. (2006). Clinical management of chronic nightmares: Imagery rehearsal therapy. *Behavioral Sleep Medicine, 4*(1), 45–70.

Krakow, B., & Krakow, J. K. (2002). *Turning nightmares into dreams.* Albuquerque, NM: New Sleepy-Times.

Krall, E. A., Garvey, A. J., & Garcia, R. I. (2002). Smoking relapse after 2 years of abstinence: Findings from the VA Normative Aging Study. *Nicotine & Tobacco Research, 4*(1), 95–100.

Krantz, D. S., & McCeney, M. K. (2002). Effects of psychological and social factors on organic disease. *Annual Review of Psychology, 53,* 341–369.

Kratofil, P. H., Baberg, H. T., & Dimsdale, J. E. (1996). Self-mutilation and severe self-injurious behavior associated with amphetamine psychosis. *General Hospital Psychiatry, 18*(2), 117–120.

Ksir, C. J., Hart, C. L., & Ray, O. S. (2006). *Drugs, society, and human behavior* (11th ed.). New York: McGraw-Hill.

Kubovy, M., & Gepshtein, S. (2003). Grouping in space and in space-time: An exercise in phenomenological psychophysics. In R. Kimchi, M. Behrmann & C. R. Olson (Eds.), *Perceptual organization in vision: Behavioral and neural perspectives.* Mahwah, NJ: Erlbaum.

Kuehner, C. (2003). Gender differences in unipolar depression: an update of epidemiological findings and possible explanations. *Acta Psychiatrica Scandinavica, 108*(3), 163–174.

Kuhl, P. K. (2004). Early language acquisition: Cracking the speech code. *Nature Reviews Neuroscience, 5*(11), 831–841.

Kuhn, C. M., & Wilson, W. A. (2001). Our dangerous love affair with Ecstasy. *Cerebrum, 3*(2), 22–33.

Kulik, J., Mahler, H. I. M., & Moore, P. J. (2003). Social comparison affiliation under threat: Effects on recovery from major surgery. In P. Salovey & A. J. Rothman (Eds.), *Social psychology of health: Key readings in social psychology.* New York: Psychology Press.

Kumaran, D., & Maguire, E. A. (2005). The human hippocampus: Cognitive maps or relational memory? *Journal of Neuroscience, 25*(31), 7254–7259.

Kunkel, M. A. (1993). A teaching demonstration involving perceived lunar size. *Teaching of Psychology, 20*(3), 178–180.

Kusseling, F. S., Shapiro, M. F., Greenberg, J. M., & Wenger, N. S. (1996). Understanding why heterosexual adults do not practice safer sex: A comparison of two samples. *AIDS Education & Prevention, 8*(3), 247–257.

LaBar, K. S., & LeDoux, J. E. (2002). Emotional learning circuits in animals and man. In R. J. Davidson, K. R. Scherer, & H. H. Goldsmith (Eds.), *Handbook of affective sciences.* New York: Oxford University Press.

LaBerge, L., Petit, D., Simard, C., Vitaro, F., et al. (2001). Development of sleep patterns in early adolescence. *Journal of Sleep Research, 10*(1), 59–67.

LaBerge, S. (2000). Lucid dreaming: Evidence and methodology. In F. E. Pace-Schott, M. Solms, M. Blagrove, & S. Harnad (Eds.), *Sleep and dreaming: Scientific advances and reconsiderations.* Cambridge, UK: Cambridge University Press.

LaBerge, S. P. (1985). *Lucid dreaming.* Los Angeles: Tarcher.

Labov, W. (1973). The boundaries of words and their meanings. In C. J. N. Bailey & R. W. Shuy (Eds.), *New ways of analyzing variation in English.* Washington: Georgetown University Press.

Lacayo, A. (1995). Neurologic and psychiatric complications of cocaine abuse. *Neuropsychiatry, Neuropsychology, & Behavioral Neurology, 8*(1), 53–60.

Lackner, J. R., & DiZio, P. (2005). Vestibular, proprioceptive, and haptic contributions to spatial orientation. *Annual Review of Psychology, 56,* 115–147.

Lamb, M. R., & Yund, E. W. (1996). Spatial frequency and attention. *Perception & Psychophysics, 58*(3), 363–373.

Lambert, M. J. (1999). Are differential treatment effects inflated by researcher therapy allegiance? *Clinical Psychology: Science & Practice, 6*(1), 127–130.

Lambert, M. J., & Ogles, B. M. (2004). The efficacy and effectiveness of psychotherapy. In M. J. Lambert (Ed.), *Bergin and Garfield's handbook of psychotherapy and behaviour change* (5th ed.). New York: Wiley.

Lambert, W. E. (1987). The effects of bilingual and bicultural experiences on children's attitudes and social perspectives. In P. Homel, M. Palij, & D. Aaronson (Eds.), *Childhood bilingualism.* Hillsdale, NJ: Erlbaum.

Lance, C. E., LaPointe, J. A., & Stewart, A. M. (1994). A test of the context dependency of three causal models of halo rater error. *Journal of Applied Psychology, 79*(3), 332–340.

Landau, J. D., & Bavaria A. J. (2003). Does deliberate source monitoring reduce students' misconceptions about psychology? *Teaching of Psychology, 30,* 311–314.

Langer, E. J. (2000). Mindful learning. *Current Directions in Psychological Science, 9,* 220–223.

Langleben, D. D., Loughead, J. W., Bilker, W. B., Ruparel, K., et al. (2005). Telling truth from lie in individual subjects with fast event-related fMRI. *Human Brain Mapping, 26*(4), 262–272.

Langleben, D. D., Schroeder, L, Maldjian, J. A., Gur, R. C., et al. (2002). Brain activity during simulated deception: An event-related functional magnetic resonance study. *NeuroImage, 15,* 727–732.

Langone, M. D. (2002). Cults, conversion, science, and harm. *Cultic Studies Review, 1*(2), 178–186.

Lanzetta, J. T., & Englis, B. G. (1989). Expectations of cooperation and competition and their effects on observers' vicarious emotional responses. *Journal of Personality & Social Psychology, 56*(4), 543–554.

Larner, A. J., Moss, J., Rossi, M. L., & Anderson, M. (1994). Congenital insensitivity to pain. *Journal of Neurology, Neurosurgery & Psychiatry, 57*(8), 973–974.

Larsen, R. J., & Buss, D. M. (2005). *Personality psychology* (2nd ed.). New York: McGraw-Hill.

Larsen, R. J., & Kasimatis, M. (1990). Individual differences in entrainment of mood to the weekly calendar. *Journal of Personality & Social Psychology, 58*(1), 164–171.

Larsen, R.J., & Prizmic, Z. (2004) Affect regulation. In R. Baumeister & K. D. Voohs (Eds.), *Handbook of self-regulation: Research, theory, and applications.* London: Guilford.

Larsson, B., Carlsson, J., Fichtel, Å., & Melin, L. (2005). Relaxation treatment of adolescent headache sufferers: Results from a school-based replication series. *Headache: The Journal of Head & Face Pain, 45*(6), 692–704.

Larsson, J.-O., Larsson, H., & Lichtenstein, P. (2004). Genetic and environmental contributions to stability and change of ADHD symptoms between 8 and 13 years of age: A longitudinal twin study. *Journal of the American Academy of Child & Adolescent Psychiatry, 43*(10), 1267–1275.

Latané, B., Nida, S. A., & Wilson, D. W. (1981). The effects of group size on helping behavior. In J. P. Rushton & R. M. Sorrentino (Eds.), *Altruism and helping behavior: Social, personality and developmental perspectives.* Hillsdale, NJ: Erlbaum.

Lattal, K. A., Reilly, M. P., & Kohn, J. P. (1998). Response persistence under ratio and interval reinforcement schedules. *Journal of the Experimental Analysis of Behavior, 70*(2), 165–183.

Laub, J. H., & Sampson, R. J. (2003). *Shared beginnings, divergent lives: Delinquent boys to age 70.* Cambridge, MA: Harvard University Press.

Laurent, G., Stopfer, M., Friedrich, R. W., Rabinovich, M. I., et al. (2001). Odor encoding as an active, dynamical process. *Annual Review of Neuroscience, 24,* 263–297.

Lavie, P. (2001). Sleep-wake as a biological rhythm. *Annual Review of Psychology, 52,* 277–303.

Lawson, H. M., & Leck, K. (2006). Dynamics of Internet dating. *Social Science Computer Review, 24*(2), 189–208.

Lay, C., & Verkuyten, M. (1999). Ethnic identity and its relation to personal self-esteem. *Journal of Social Psychology, 139*(3), 288–299.

Lazar, S. W. (2005). Mindfulness research. In C. K. Germer, R. D. Siegel, & P. R. Fulton (Eds.), *Mindfulness and psychotherapy.* New York: Guilford.

Lazar, S. W., Bush, G., Gollub, R. L., Fricchione, G. L., et al. (2000). Functional brain mapping of the relaxation response and meditation. *Neuroreport, 11*(7), 1581–1585.

Lazarus, R. S. (1991a). Progress on a cognitive-motivational-relational theory of emotion. *American Psychologist, 46*(8), 819–834.

Lazarus, R. S. (1991b). Cognition and motivation in emotion. *American Psychologist, 46*(4), 352–367.

Lazev, A. B., Herzog, T. A., & Brandon, T. H. (1999). Classical conditioning of environmental cues to cigarette smoking. *Experimental and Clinical Psychopharmacology, 7*(1), 56–63.

Leal, M. C., Shin, Y. J., Laborde, M.-L., Calmels, M.-N., et al. (2003). Music perception in adult cochlear implant recipients. *Acta Oto-Laryngologica, 123*(7), 826–835.

Leary, M. R. (2004). *Introduction to behavioral research methods* (4th ed.). Boston: Allyn and Bacon.

Leavens, D. A., & Hopkins, W. D. (1998). Intentional communication by chimpanzees. *Developmental Psychology, 34*(5), 813–822.

LeBlanc, G., & Bearison, D. J. (2004). Teaching and learning as a bi-directional activity: Investigating dyadic interactions between child teachers and child learners. *Cognitive Development, 19*(4), 499–515.

LeDoux, J. (1996). *The emotional brain: The mysterious underpinnings of emotional life.* New York: Simon & Schuster.

LeDoux, J. (1999). The power of emotions. In R. Conlan (Ed.), *States of mind.* New York: Wiley.

LeDoux, J. E., & Gorman, J. M. (2001). A call to action: Overcoming anxiety through active coping. *American Journal of Psychiatry. 158*(12), 1953–1955.

Lee, J. M., Ku, J. H., Jang, D. P., Kim, D., et al. (2002). Virtual reality system for treatment of the fear of public speaking using image-based rendering and moving pictures. *CyberPsychology & Behavior, 5*(3), 191–195.

Lee, M., Zimbardo, P. G., & Bertholf, M. (1977). Shy murderers. *Psychology Today,* Nov., 68–70.

Leenaars, A. A., Lester, D., & Wenckstern, S. (2005). Coping with: The art and the research. In R. I. Yufit & D. Lester (Eds.), *Assessment, treatment, and prevention of suicidal behavior.* New York: Wiley.

Leeper, R. W. (1935). A study of a neglected portion of the field of learning: The development of sensory organization. *Pedagogical Seminary & Journal of Genetic Psychology, 46,* 41–75.

Lefcourt, H. M. (2003). Humor as a moderator of life stress in adults. In C. E. Schaefer (Ed.), *Play therapy with adults.* New York: Wiley.

Lehman, D. R., Chiu, C., & Schaller, M. (2004). Psychology and culture. *Annual Review of Psychology, 55,* 689–714.

Leichtman, M. (2004). Projective tests: The nature of the task. In M. J. Hilsenroth & D. L. Segal (Eds.), *Comprehensive handbook of psychological assessment* (Vol. 2): *Personality assessment.* New York: Wiley.

Leiter, M. P., & Maslach, C. (2005). *Banishing burnout: Six strategies for improving your relationship with work.* San Francisco, CA: Jossey-Bass.

Lejuez, C. W., Eifert, G. H., Zvolensky, M. J., & Richards, J. B. (2000). Preference between onset predictable and unpredictable administrations of 20% carbon-dioxide-enriched air. *Journal of Experimental Psychology: Applied, 6*(4), 349–358.

Lench, H. C. (2004). Anger management: Diagnostic differences and treatment implications. *Journal of Social & Clinical Psychology, 23*(4), 512–531.

Lenton, A. P., & Bryan, A. (2005). An affair to remember: The role of sexual scripts in perceptions of sexual intent. *Personal Relationships, 12*(4), 483–498.

Lenzenweger, M. F., & Gottesman, I. I. (1994). Schizophrenia. In V. S. Ramachandran (Ed.), *Encyclopedia of human behavior.* San Diego, CA: Academic.

Leor, J., Poole, W. K., & Kloner, R. A. (1996). Sudden cardiac death triggered by earthquake. *The New England Journal of Medicine, 334*(7), 413.

Lepore, F. E. (2002). When seeing is not believing. *Cerebrum, 4*(2), 23–38.

Lessow-Hurley, J. (2005). *Foundations of dual language instruction* (4th ed.). Boston: Allyn & Bacon.

Lester, D., & Yang, B. (2005). Regional and time-series studies of suicide in nations of the world. *Archives of Suicide Research, 9*(2), 123–133.

Lettvin, J. Y. (1961). Two remarks on the visual system of the frog. In W. Rosenblith (Ed.), *Sensory communication.* Cambridge, MA: MIT Press.

Levant, R. F. (2001). Men and masculinity. In J. Worell (Ed.), *Encyclopedia of women and gender.* San Diego: Academic Press.

Levant, R. F. (2003). Treating male alexithymia. In L. B. Silverstein & T. J. Goodrich (Eds.), *Feminist family therapy: Empowerment in social context.* Washington: American Psychological Association.

LeVay, S. (1993). *The sexual brain.* Cambridge, MA: MIT Press.

Levenston, G. K., Patrick, C. J., Bradley, M. M., & Lange, P. J. (2000). The psychopathic observer. *Journal of Abnormal Psychology, 109,* 373–385.

Levesque, M. J., Steciuk, M., & Ledley, C. (2002). Self-disclosure patterns among well-acquainted individuals. *Social Behavior & Personality, 30*(6), 579–592.

Levi, A. M. (1998). Are defendants guilty if they were chosen in a lineup? *Law & Human Behavior, 22*(4), 389–407.

Levin, R., & Fireman, G. (2002). Nightmare prevalence, nightmare distress, and self-reported psychological disturbance. *Sleep: Journal of Sleep & Sleep Disorders Research, 25*(2), 205–212.

Levinson, A. (1999). Memory champ an absent-minded lady. *Tucson Daily Star,* Feb.

Levitsky, D. A., Nussbaum, M., Halbmaier, C.A., & Mrdjenovic, G. (2003). *The Freshman 15: a model for the study of techniques to curb the 'epidemic' of obesity.* Society for the Study of Ingestive Behavior: Annual Meeting, July 15–19, University of Groningen, Haren, The Netherlands.

Levy, J., & Reid, M. (1976). Cerebral organization. *Science,* 337–339.

Lewis, M., & Brooks-Gunn, J. (1979). *Social cognition and the acquisition of self.* New York: Plenum.

Lewis, M. (1995). Self-conscious emotions. *American Scientist, 83*(Jan–Feb), 68–78.

Lewy, A. J., Bauer V. K., Cutler, N. L., Sack, R. L., et al. (1998). Morning vs evening light treatment of patients with winter depression. *Archives of General Psychiatry, 55*(10), 890–896.

Leyendecker, B., Harwood, R. L., Comparini, L., & Yalçinkaya, A. (2005). Socioeconomic status, ethnicity, and parenting. In T. Luster & L. Okagaki (Eds.), *Parenting: An ecological perspective* (2nd ed.). Mahwah, NJ: Erlbaum.

Lichtman, A. H., & Martin, B. R. (2006). Understanding the pharmacology and physiology of cannabis dependence In R. Roffman & R. S. Stephens (Eds.), *Cannabis dependence. Its nature, consequences and treatment.* New York: Cambridge University Press.

Liddell, S. K. (2003). *Grammar, gesture and meaning in American Sign Language.* Cambridge, MA: Cambridge University Press.

Lieberman, D. A. (2004). *Learning and memory: An integrative approach.* Belmont, CA: Wadsworth.

Lilienfeld, S. O. (1999). Projective measures of personality and psychopathology. *Skeptical Inquirer,* (Sept./Oct.), 32–39.

Lilienfeld, S. O., Fowler, K. A., Lohr, J. M., & Lynn, S. (2005). Pseudoscience, non-science & nonsense in clinical psychology: Dangers and remedies. In R. H. Wright & N. A. Cummings (Eds.), *Destructive trends in mental health: The well-intentioned path to harm.* New York: Routledge.

Lindemann, B. (2000). A taste for umami. *Nature Neuroscience, 3,* 99–100.

Lindemann, B. (2001). Receptors and transduction in taste. *Nature, 413,* 219–25.

Linden, W. (2005). *Stress management: From basic science to better practice.* Thousand Oaks, CA: Sage.

Lindsay, E. W., Mize, J., & Pettit, G. S. (1997). Differential pay patterns of mothers and fathers of sons and daughters. *Sex Roles, 37*(9–10), 643–661.

Linton, M. (1979). I remember it well. *Psychology Today,* July, 81–86.

Liu, Y., Gao, J., Liu, H., & Fox, P. T. (2000). The temporal response of the brain after eating revealed by functional MRI. *Nature, 405,* 1058–1062.

Liu X, Matochik, J. A., Cadet, J. L., & London, E. D. (1998). Smaller volume of prefrontal lobe in polysubstance abusers. *Neuropsychopharmacology, 18*(4), 243–252.

Loeber, R., & Hay, D. (1997). Key issues in the development of aggression and violence from childhood to early adulthood. *Annual Review of Psychology, 48,* 371–410.

Loehlin, J. C., McCrae, R. R., Costa, P. T., & John, O. (1998). Heritabilities of common and measure-specific components of the Big Five personality factors. *Journal of Research in Personality, 32*(4), 431–453.

Loftus, E. F., & Bernstein, D. M. (2005). Rich false memories: The royal road to success. In A.F. Healy (Ed.), *Experimental cognitive*

psychology and its applications. Washington: American Psychological Association.

Loftus, E. F. (1980). *Memory.* Reading MA: Addison-Wesley.

Loftus, E. F. (2003). Make-believe memories. *American Psychologist, 58*(11), 867–873.

Loftus, E. F. (2003). Memory in Canadian courts of law. *Canadian Psychology, 44*(3), 207–212.

Loftus, E. F., & Ketcham, K. (1994). *The myth of repressed memory: False memories and allegations of abuse.* New York: St. Martin's Press.

Loftus, E., & Palmer, J. C. (1974). Reconstruction of automobile destruction: An example of interaction between language and memory. *Journal of Verbal Learning and Verbal Behavior, 13,* 585–589.

LoLordo, V. M. (2001). Learned helplessness and depression. In M. E. Carroll & J. B. Overmier (Eds.), *Animal research and human health: Advancing human welfare through behavioral science.* Washington: American Psychological Association.

López, S. R., & Guarnaccia, P. J. (2000). Cultural psychopathology: Uncovering the social world of mental illness. *Annual Review of Psychology, 51,* 571–598.

Lorenz, K. (1966). *On aggression.* Translated by M. Kerr-Wilson. New York: Harcourt Brace Jovanovich.

Lorenz, K. (1974). *The eight deadly sins of civilized man.* Translated by M. Kerr-Wilson. New York: Harcourt Brace Jovanovich.

Lovaas, O., & Simmons, J. (1969). Manipulation of self-destruction in three retarded children. *Journal of Applied Behavior Analysis, 2,* 143–157.

Low, K. G., & Feissner, J. M. (1998). Seasonal affective disorder in college students: Prevalence and latitude. *Journal of American College Health, 47*(3), 135–137.

Lucas, F., & Sclafani, A. (1990). Hyperphagia in rats produced by a mixture of fat and sugar. *Physiology & Behavior, 47*(1), 51–55.

Luce, G. G. (1965). *Current research on sleep and dreams.* Health Service Publication, No. 1389. U.S. Department of Health, Education and Welfare.

Luchins, D. J., Cooper, A. E., Hanrahan, P., & Rasinski, K. (2004). Psychiatrists' attitudes toward involuntary hospitalization. *Psychiatric Services, 55*(9), 1058–1060.

Luckasson, R., Borthwick-Duffy, S., Buntinx, W. H. E., Coulter, D. L., et al. (2002). *Mental retardation: Definition, classification, and systems of supports* (10th ed.). Washington: American Association on Mental Retardation.

Lumley, M. A. (2004). Alexithymia, emotional disclosure, and health: A program of research. *Journal of Personality. Special Emotions, Personality, and Health, 72*(6), 1271–1300.

Lundh, L., Berg, B., Johansson, H., Nilsson, L., et al. (2002). Social anxiety is associated with a negatively distorted perception of one's own voice. *Cognitive Behaviour Therapy, 31*(1), 25–30.

Luria, A. R. (1968). *The mind of a mnemonist.* New York: Basic Books.

Luster, T., & Dubow, E. (1992). Home environment and maternal intelligence as

predictors of verbal intelligence. *Merrill-Palmer Quarterly, 38*(2), 151–175.

Lustig, C., May, C. P., & Hasher, L. (2001). Working memory span and the role of proactive interference. *Journal of Experimental Psychology: General, 130*(2), 199–207.

Lykken, D. T. (1998). *A tremor in the blood: Uses and abuses of the lie detector.* New York: Plenum.

Lykken, D. T. (2001). Lie detection. In W. E. Craighead & C. B. Nemeroff (Eds.), *The Corsini Encyclopedia of psychology and behavioral science* (3rd ed.). New York: Wiley.

Lynch, K. B., Geller, S. R., & Schmidt, M. G. (2004). Multi-year evaluation of the effectiveness of a resilience-based prevention program for young children. *Journal of Primary Prevention, 24*(3), 335–353.

Lynch, T. R., Robins, C. J., Morse, J. Q., & MorKrause, E. D. (2001). A mediational model relating affect intensity, emotion inhibition, and psychological distress. *Behavior Therapy, 32*(3), 519–536.

Lynn, S. J., & Kirsch, I. (2006). Introduction: Definitions and early history. In S. J. Lynn & I. Kirsch (Eds.), *Essentials of clinical hypnosis: An evidence-based approach.* Washington: American Psychological Association.

Lyons, A. C., & Chamberlain, K. (2006). *Health psychology.* Cambridge, MA: Cambridge University Press.

Lyubomirsky, S., & Tucker, K. L. (1998). Implications of individual differences in subjective happiness for perceiving, interpreting, and thinking about life events. *Motivation & Emotion, 22*(2), 155–186.

Maas, J. (1999). *Power sleep.* New York: HarperCollins.

Mack, A. (2002). Is the visual world a grand illusion? *Journal of Consciousness Studies, 9*(5–6), 102–110.

Mackintosh, N. J. (2003). Pavlov and associationism. *Spanish Journal of Psychology, 6*(2), 177–184.

Macklin, C. B., & McDaniel, M. A. (2005). The bizarreness effect: Dissociation between item and source memory. *Memory, 13*(7), 682–689.

MacLeod, C. M. (2005). The Stroop task in cognitive research. In A. Wenzel & D. C. Rubin (Eds.), *Cognitive methods and their application to clinical research.* Washington: American Psychological Association.

Macmillan, R. (2001). Violence and the life course. *Annual Review of Sociology, 27,* 1–22.

Maddi, S. R. (2006). Hardiness: The courage to grow from stresses. *Journal of Positive Psychology, 1*(3), 160–168.

Maddock, J., & Glanz, K. (2005). The relationship of proximal normative beliefs and global subjective norms to college students' alcohol consumption. *Addictive Behaviors, 30*(2), 315–323.

Maddock, J. E., Laforge, R. G., Rossi, J. S., & O'Hare, T. (2001). The College Alcohol Problems Scale. *Addictive Behaviors, 26,* 385–398.

Maguire, E. A., Frackowiak, R. S. J., & Frith, C. D. (1997). Recalling routes around

London: Activation of the hippocampus in taxi drivers. *The Journal of Neuroscience, 17*(8), 7103–7110.

Maguire, E. A., Valentine, E. R., Wilding, J. M., & Kapur, N. (2003). Routes to remembering: The brains behind superior memory. *Nature Neuroscience, 6*(1), 90–95.

Mah, K., & Binik, Y. M. (2001). The nature of human orgasm: A critical review of major trends. *Clinical Psychology Review, 21*(6), 823–856.

Maheu, M. M., Pulier, M. L., Wilhelm, F. H., McMenamin, J. P., et al. (2004). *The mental health professional and the new technologies: A handbook for practice today.* Mahwah, NJ: Lawrence Erlbaum.

Maier, N. R. F. (1949). *Frustration.* New York: McGraw-Hill.

Maier, S. F. (2001). Exposure to the stressor environment prevents the temporal dissipation of behavioral depression/learned helplessness. *Biological Psychiatry, 49*(9), 763–773.

Mailis-Gagnon, A., & Israelson, D. (2005). *Beyond pain: Making the mind-body connection.* Ann Arbor, MI: University of Michigan Press.

Malaspina, D., Reichenberg, A., Weiser, M., Fennig, S., et al. (2005). Paternal age and intelligence: Implications for age-related genomic changes in male germ cells. *Psychiatric Genetics, 15*(2), 117–125.

Manalo, E. (2002). Uses of mnemonics in educational settings: A brief review of selected research. *Psychologia: An International Journal of Psychology in the Orient, 45*(2), 69–79.

Mandler, J. M., & McDonough, L. (1998). On developing a knowledge base in infancy. *Developmental Psychology, 34*(6), 1274–1288.

Mangels, J. A., Picton, T. W., & Craik, F. I. M. (2001). Attention and successful episodic encoding: An event-related potential study. *Brain Research, 11,* 77–95.

Manne, S. (2003). Coping and social support. In A. Nezu, C. Nezu, & P. Geller (Eds.), *Handbook of health psychology* (Vol. 9). New York: Wiley.

Manschreck, T. C. (1996). Delusional disorder: The recognition and management of paranoia. *Journal of Clinical Psychiatry, 57*(3, Suppl), 32–38.

Mansouri, A., & Adityanjee. (1995). Delusion of pregnancy in males: A case report and literature review. *Psychopathology, 28*(6), 307–311.

Mantyla, T. (1986). Optimizing cue effectiveness: Recall of 600 incidentally learned words. *Journal of Experimental Psychology: Learning, Memory, & Cognition, 12*(1), 66–71.

Marcus, E. (2002). Psychoanalytic psychotherapy and psychoanalysis: An overview. In M. Hersen & W. H. Sledge (Eds.), *Encyclopedia of psychotherapy.* San Diego: Academic Press.

Marks, D. F. (2000). *The psychology of the psychic.* Buffalo, NY: Prometheus.

Markus, H. R., & Nurius, P. (1986). Possible selves. *American Psychologist, 41,* 954–969.

Markus, H. R., Uchida, Y., Omoregie, H., Townsend, S. S. M., et al. (2006). Going for the gold: Models of agency in Japanese and American contexts. *Psychological Science, 17*(2), 103–112.

Marsiglia, F. F., Kulis, S., Hecht, M. L., & Sills, S. (2004). Ethnicity and ethnic identity as predictors of drug norms and drug use among preadolescents in the US southwest. *Substance Use & Misuse, 39*(7), 1061–1094.

Martens, R., & Trachet, T. (1998). *Making sense of astrology.* Amherst, MA: Prometheus.

Martin, A. J., & Marsh, H. W. (2003). Fear of failure: Friend or foe? *Australian Psychologist, 38*(1), 31–38.

Martin, C. L., & Fabes, R. A. (2001). The stability and consequences of young children's same-sex peer interactions. *Developmental Psychology, 37*(3), 431–446.

Martin, G., & Pear, J. (2003). *Behavior modification* (7th ed.). Upper Saddle River, NJ: Prentice Hall.

Martin, S. (1995). Field's status unaltered by the influx of women. *APA Monitor,* Jan., 9.

Martin, W. L. B., & Freitas, M. B. (2002). Mean mortality among Brazilian left- and right-handers: Modification or selective elimination. *Laterality, 7*(1), 31–44.

Martinez-Gonzalez, M. A., Gual, P., Lahortiga, F., Alonso, Y., et al. (2003). Parental factors, mass media influences, and the onset of eating disorders in a prospective population-based cohort. *Pediatrics, 111,* 315–320.

Mashour, G. A., Walker, E. E., & Martuza, R. L. (2005). Psychosurgery: Past, present, and future. *Brain Research Reviews, 48*(3), 409–419.

Masi, G., Mucci, M., & Millepiedi, S. (2001). Separation anxiety disorder in children and adolescents. *CNS Drugs, 15*(2), 93–104.

Maslach, C., Schaufeli, W. B., & Leiter, M. P. (2001). Job burnout. *Annual Review of Psychology, 52,* 397–422.

Maslow, A. (1954). *Motivation and personality.* New York: Harper & Row.

Maslow, A. (1971). *The farther reaches of human nature.* New York: Viking.

Maslow, A. H. (1967). Self-actualization and beyond. In J. F. T. Bugental (Ed.), *Challenges of humanistic psychology.* New York: McGraw-Hill.

Maslow, A. H. (1969). *The psychology of science.* Chicago: Henry Regnery.

Maslow, A. H. (1970). *Motivation and personality.* New York: Harper & Row.

Masse, L. C., & Tremblay, R. E. (1997). Behavior of boys in kindergarten and the onset of substance use during adolescence. *Archives of General Psychiatry, 54*(1), 62–68.

Masten, A. S. (2001). Ordinary magic: Resilience processes in development. *American Psychologist, 56*(3), 227–238.

Masters, J. L., & Holley, L. M. (2006). A glimpse of life at 67: The modified future-self worksheet. *Educational Gerontology, 32*(4), 261–269.

Masters, W. H., & Johnson, V. E. (1966). *Human sexual response.* Boston: Little, Brown.

Masters, W. H., & Johnson, V. E. (1970). *The pleasure bond: A new look at sexuality and commitment.* Boston: Little, Brown.

Matheny, K. B., Brack, G. L., McCarthy, C. J., & Penick, J. M. (1996). The effectiveness of cognitively-based approaches in treating stress-related symptoms. *Psychotherapy, 33*(2), 305–320.

Matossian, M. K. (1982). Ergot and the Salem witchcraft affair. *American Scientist, 70,* 355–357.

Matson, J. L., Sevin, J. A., Fridley, D., & Love, S. R. (1990). Increasing spontaneous language in three autistic children. *Journal of Applied Behavior Analysis, 23*(2), 223–227.

Matthews, G., Deary, I. J., & Whiteman, M. C. (2003). *Personality traits* (2nd ed.). New York: Cambridge University Press.

Matthews, P. H., & Matthews, M. S. (2004). Heritage language instruction and giftedness in language minority students: Pathways toward success. *Journal of Secondary Gifted Education, 15*(2), 50–55.

Mayer, J. D., & Hanson, E. (1995). Mood-congruent judgment over time. *Personality & Social Psychology Bulletin, 21*(3), 237–244.

Mayer, J. D. (2005). A tale of two visions: Can a new view of personality help integrate psychology? *American Psychologist, 60*(4), 294–307.

Mayer, J. D., Salovey, P., Caruso, D. R., & Sitarenios, G. (2001). Emotional intelligence as standard intelligence. *Emotion, 1*(3), 232–242.

Mayer, R. E. (2004). Should there be a three-strikes rule against pure discovery learning? *American Psychologist, 59*(1), 14–19.

Mazur, J. E. (2006). *Learning and behavior* (6th ed.). Englewood Cliffs, NJ: Prentice Hall.

McBride, W. J., Murphy, J. M., & Ikemoto, S. (1999). Localization of brain reinforcement mechanisms. *Behavioural Brain Research, 101*(2), 129–152.

McCall, W. V., Prudic, J., Olfson, M., & Sackeim, H. (2006). Health-related quality of life following ECT in a large community sample. *Journal of Affective Disorders, 90*(2–3), 269–274.

McCarley, R. W. (1998). Dreams: Disguise of forbidden wishes or transparent reflections of a distinct brain state? In R. M. Bilder & F. F. LeFever (Eds.), *Neuroscience of the mind on the centennial of Freud's Project for a Scientific Psychology.* New York: New York Academy of Sciences.

McCarthy, B. W. (1995). Bridges to sexual desire. *Journal of Sex Education & Therapy, 21*(2), 132–141.

McClelland, D. C. (1961). *The achieving society.* New York: Van Nostrand.

McClelland, D. C. (1965). Achievement and entrepreneurship. *Journal of Personality & Social Psychology, 1,* 389–393.

McClelland, D. C. (1975). *Power: the inner experience.* New York: Irvington.

McClelland, D. C. (1994). The knowledge-testing-educational complex strikes back. *American Psychologist, 49*(1), 66–69.

McClelland, D. C., & Cheriff, A. D. (1997). The immunoenhancing effects of humor on secretory IgA and resistance to respiratory infections. *Psychology & Health, 12*(3), 329–344.

McClelland, D. C., & Pilon, D. A. (1983). Sources of adult motives in patterns of parent behavior in early childhood. *Journal of Personality & Social Psychology, 44,* 564–574.

McClelland, J. L., & Rogers, T. T. (2003). The parallel distributed processing approach to semantic cognition. *Nature Reviews Neuroscience, 4*(4), 310–322.

McCluskey, U. (2002). The dynamics of attachment and systems-centered group psychotherapy. *Group Dynamics, 6*(2), 131–142.

McCrae, R. R., & Costa, P. T. (1990). *Personality in adulthood.* New York: Guilford.

McCrae, R. R., & Costa, P. T. (2001). A five-factor theory of personality. In L. A. Pervin & O. P. John (Eds.), *Handbook of personality.* New York: Guilford.

McCrae, R. R., & Terracciano, A. (2005). Universal features of personality traits from the observer's perspective: Data from 50 cultures. *Journal of Personality & Social Psychology, 88*(3), 547–561.

McDonald, J. K., Yanchar, S. C., & Osguthorpe, R. (2005). Learning from programmed instruction: Examining implications for modern instructional technology. *Educational Technology Research & Development, 53*(2), 84–98.

McGuffin, P., Rijsdijk, F., Andrew, M., Sham, P., et al. (2003). The heritability of bipolar affective disorder and the genetic relationship to unipolar depression. *Archives of General Psychiatry, 60*(5), 497–502.

McIntosh, W. D., Harlow, T. F., & Martin, L. L. (1995). Linkers and nonlinkers: Goal beliefs as a moderator of the effects of everyday hassles on rumination, depression, and physical complaints. *Journal of Applied Social Psychology, 25*(14), 1231–1244.

McKay, A. (2005). Sexuality and substance use: The impact of tobacco, alcohol, and selected recreational drugs on sexual function. *Canadian Journal of Human Sexuality, 14*(1–2), 47–56.

McKeever, W. F. (2000). A new family handedness sample with findings consistent with X-linked transmission. *British Journal of Psychology, 91*(1), 21–39.

McKeever, W. F., Cerone, L. J., Suter, P. J., & Wu, S. M. (2000). Family size, miscarriage-proneness, and handedness. *Laterality, 5*(2), 111–120.

McKenna, M. W., & Ossoff, E. P. (1998). Age differences in children's comprehension of a popular television program. *Child Study Journal, 28*(1), 52–68.

McKenzie, K., Serfaty, M., & Crawford, M. (2003). Suicide in ethnic minority groups. *British Journal of Psychiatry, 183*(2), 100–101.

McKim, W. A. (2003). *Drugs and behavior* (5th ed.). Upper Saddle River, NJ: Prentice Hall.

McLewin, L. A., & Muller, R. T. (2006). Childhood trauma, imaginary companions, and the development of pathological dissociation. *Aggression & Violent Behavior, 11*(5), 531–545.

McLoyd, V. C., & Smith, J. (2002). Physical discipline and behavior problems in African American, European American, and Hispanic children: Emotional support as a moderator. *Journal of Marriage & Family, 64*(1), 40–53.

McMahon, S., & Koltzenburg, M. (2005). *Wall & Melzacks textbook of pain* (5th ed.). London: Churchill Livingstone.

McNally, R. J., & Clancy, S. A. (2005). Sleep paralysis, sexual abuse, and space alien abduction. *Transcultural Psychiatry, 42*(1), 113–122.

McNally, R. J., Clancy, S. A., & Barrett, H. M. (2004). Forgetting trauma? In D. Reisberg & P. Hertel (Eds.), *Memory & emotion.* New York: Oxford University Press.

McNamara, D. S., & Scott, J. L. (2001). Working memory capacity and strategy use. *Memory & Cognition, 29*(1), 10–17.

Medhus, E. (2001). *When the bough breaks: The making of a terrorist.* www.drmedhus.com.

Mehrabian, A. (2000). Beyond IQ. *Genetic Social, & General Psychology Monographs, 126,* 133–239.

Mehren, E. (1994). Study finds most child care lacking. *The Los Angeles Times,* April 8, E-5.

Meier, P. S., Donmall, M. C., McElduff, P., Barrowclough, C., et al. (2006). The role of the early therapeutic alliance in predicting drug treatment dropout. *Drug & Alcohol Dependence, 83*(1), 57–64.

Meltzoff, A. N. (2005). Imitation and other minds: The "Like Me" Hypothesis. In S. Hurley & N. Chater (Eds.), *Perspectives on imitation: From neuroscience to social science* (Vol. 2): *Imitation, human development, and culture.* Cambridge, MA: MIT Press.

Meltzoff, A. N., & Prinz, W. (2002). *The imitative mind: Development, evolution, and brain bases.* Cambridge, MA: Cambridge University Press.

Melzack, R., & Katz, J. (2004). The gate control theory: Reaching for the brain. In T. Hadjistavropoulos & Craig, K. D. (Eds.), *Pain: Psychological perspectives.* Mahwah, NJ: Erlbaum.

Melzack, R., & Wall, P. D. (1996). *The Challenge of Pain.* Harmondworth, UK: Penguin.

Melzack, R. (1999). From the gate to the neuromatrix. *Pain. Special issue: A tribute to Patrick D. Wall* (Suppl. 6), pS121–S126.

Mendolia, M. (2002). An index of self-regulation of emotion and the study of repression in social contexts that threaten or do not threaten self-concept. *Emotion, 2*(3), 215–232.

Meneses, G. D., & Beerlipalacio, A. (2005). Recycling behavior: A multidimensional approach. *Environment & Behavior, 37*(6), 837–860.

Mercer, J. (2006). *Understanding attachment: Parenting, child care, and emotional development.* Westport, CT: Praeger.

Merritt, J. M., Stickgold, R., Pace-Schott, E., Williams, J., et al. (1994). Emotion profiles in the dreams of men and women. *Consciousness & Cognition, 3*(1), 46–60.

Mesquita, B., & Markus, H. R. (2004). Culture and emotion: Models of agency as sources of cultural variation in emotion. In A. S. R. Manstead, S. R. Antony, N. Frijda, & A. Fischer (Eds.), *Feelings and emotions: The Amsterdam symposium.* New York: Cambridge University Press.

Messer, S. B., & Kaplan, A. H. (2004). Outcomes and factors related to efficacy of brief psychodynamic therapy. In D. P. Charman (Ed.), *Core processes in brief psychodynamic psychotherapy: Advancing effective practice.* Mahwah, NJ: Lawrence Erlbaum.

Messick, D. M., & Mackie, D. M. (1989). Intergroup relations. *Annual Review of Psychology, 40,* 45–81.

Meyer, G. J., Finn, S. E., Eyde, L. D., Kay, G. G., et al. (2001). Psychological testing and psychological assessment. *American Psychologist, 56*(2) 128–165.

Michael, D., & Chen, S. (2006). *Serious games: Games that educate, train, and inform.* Boston, MA: Thomson Course Technology.

Michalak, E. E., & Lam, R. W. (2002). Seasonal affective disorder: The latitude hypothesis revisited. *Canadian Journal of Psychiatry, 47*(8), 787–788.

Michalko, M. (1998). *Cracking creativity.* Berkeley, CA: Ten Speed Press.

Middaugh, S. J., & Pawlick, K. (2002). Biofeedback and behavioral treatment of persistent pain in the older adult: A review and a study. *Applied Psychophysiology & Biofeedback, 27*(3), 185–202.

Mielke, H. W. (1999). Lead in the inner cities. *American Scientist, 87*(Jan. –Feb.), 62–73.

Milgram, S. (1963). Behavioral study of obedience. *Journal of Abnormal & Social Psychology, 67,* 371–378.

Milgram, S. (1965). Some conditions of obedience and disobedience to authority. *Human Relations, 18,* 56–76.

Milgram, S. (1967). The small-world problem. *Psychology Today,* May, 61–67.

Milgram, S., Bickman, L., & Berkowitz, L. (1969). Note on the drawing power of crowds of different size. *Journal of Personality & Social Psychology, 13,* 79–82.

Miller, D. T. (2006). *An invitation to social psychology.* Belmont, CA: Wadsworth.

Miller, D. T., Turnbull, W., & McFarland, C. (1988). Particularistic and universalistic evaluation in the social comparison process. *Journal of Personality & Social Psychology, 55*(6), 908–917.

Miller, E. K., & Cohen, J. D. (2001). An integrative theory of prefrontal cortex function. *Annual Review of Neuroscience, 24,* 167–202.

Miller, G. A. (1956). The magical number seven, plus or minus two: Some limits on our capacity for information processing. *Psychological Review, 48,* 337–442.

Miller, G. A. (1999). On knowing a word. *Annual Review of Psychology, 50,* 1–19.

Miller, G. E., Cohen, S., & Ritchey, A. K. (2002). Chronic psychological stress and the regulation of pro-inflammatory cytokines. *Health Psychology, 21*(6), 531–541.

Miller, M. A., & Rahe, R. H. (1997). Life changes scaling for the 1990s. *Journal of Psychosomatic Research, 43*(3), 279–292.

Miller, N. E. (1944). Experimental studies of conflict. In J. McV. Hunt (Ed.), *Personality and the behavior disorders* (Vol. 1). New York: Ronald Press.

Miller, N. E., & Bugelski. R. (1970). The influence of frustration imposed by the in-group on attitudes expressed toward out-groups. In R. I. Evans & R. M. Rozelle (Eds.), *Social psychology in life.* Boston: Allyn & Bacon.

Miller, N., Pedersen, W. C., Earleywine, M., & Pollock, V. E. (2003). A theoretical model of triggered displaced aggression. *Personality & Social Psychology Review, 7*(1), 75–97.

Miller, R., Perlman, D., & Brehm, S. S. (2007). *Intimate relationships* (4th ed.). New York: McGraw-Hill.

Miller, W. R., & Munoz, R. F. (2005). *Controlling your drinking: Tools to make moderation work for you.* New York: Guilford.

Millman, R. B., & Ross, E. J. (2003). Steroid and nutritional supplement use in professional athletes. *American Journal on Addictions, 12*(Suppl2), S48–S54.

Milne, R., & Bull, R. (2002). Back to basics: A componential analysis of the original cognitive interview mnemonics with three age groups. *Applied Cognitive Psychology, 16*(7), 743–753.

Milner, B. (1965). Memory disturbance after bilateral hippocampal lesions. In P. Milner & S. Glickman (Eds.), *Cognitive processes and the brain.* Princeton, NJ: Van Nostrand.

Miltenberger, R. G. (2004). *Behavior modification* (3rd ed.). Belmont, CA: Wadsworth.

Miltner, W. H. R., Krieschel, S., Hecht, H., Trippe, R., et al. (2004). Eye movements and behavioral responses to threatening and nonthreatening stimuli during visual search in phobic and nonphobic subjects. *Emotion, 4*(4), 323–339.

Milton, J., & Wiseman, R. (1997). *Guidelines for extrasensory perception research.* Hertfordshire, UK: University of Hertfordshire Press.

Milton, J., & Wiseman, R. (1999). A meta-analysis of mass-media tests of extrasensory perception. *British Journal of Psychology, 90*(2), 235–240.

Minda, J. P., & Smith, J. D. (2001). Prototypes in category learning: The effects of category size, category structure, and stimulus complexity. *Journal of Experimental Psychology: Learning, Memory, and Cognition, 27,* 775–799.

Mineka, S., & Hamida, S. B. (1998). Observational and nonconscious learning. In W. T. O'Donohue (Ed.), *Learning and behavior therapy.* Boston: Allyn & Bacon.

Minton, H. L. (2000). Psychology and gender at the turn of the century. *American Psychologist, 55*(6), 613–615.

Miotto, K., Darakjian, J., Basch, J., Murray, S., et al. (2001). Gamma-hydroxybutyric acid: Patterns of use, effects and withdrawal. *American Journal on Addictions, 10*(3), 232–241.

Mirsky, A. F., & Duncan, C. C. (2005). Pathophysiology of mental illness: A view from the fourth ventricle. *International Journal of Psychophysiology, 58*(2–3), 162–178.

Mirsky, A. F., Bieliauskas, L. A., French, L. M., Van Kammen, D. P., et al. (2000). A 39-year followup on the Genain quadruplets. *Schizophrenia Bulletin, 26*(3), 699–708.

Mischel, W. (2004). Toward an integrative science of the person. *Annual Review of Psychology, 55,* 1–22.

Mischel, W., & Shoda, Y. (1998). Reconciling processing dynamics and personality dispositions. *Annual Review of Psychology, 49,* 229–258.

Mischel, W., Shoda, Y., & Smith, R. E. (2004). *Introduction to personality: Toward an integration* (7th ed.). Hoboken, NJ: Wiley.

Mistlberger, R. E. (2005). Circadian regulation of sleep in mammals: Role of the suprachiasmatic nucleus. *Brain Research Reviews, 49*(3), 429–454.

Mitchell, D. (1987). Firewalking cults: Nothing but hot air. *Laser,* Feb., 7–8.

Mitru, G., Millrood, D.L., & Mateika, J. H. (2002). The impact of sleep on learning and behavior in adolescents. *Teachers College Record, 104*(4), 704–726.

Miyake, A. (2001). Individual differences in working memory. *Journal of Experimental Psychology: General, 130*(2), 163–168.

Mogg, K., Bradley, B. P., Hyare, H., & Lee, S. (1998). Selective attention to food-related stimuli in hunger. *Behaviour Research & Therapy, 36*(2), 227–237.

Moghaddam, B. (2002). Stress activation of glutamate neurotransmission in the prefrontal cortex. *Biological Psychiatry, 51*(10), 775–787.

Mohr, D. C., Hart, S. L., Julian, L., Catledge, C., et al. (2005). Telephone-administered psychotherapy for depression. *Archives of General Psychiatry, 62*(9), 1007–1014.

Mokdad, A. H., Marks, J. S., Stroup, D. F., & Gerberding, J. L. (2004). Actual causes of death in the United States, 2000. *Journal of the American Medical Association, 291*(March 10), 1238–1245.

Monahan, J., Steadman, H. J., Silver, E., Appelbaum, P. S., et al. (2001). *Rethinking risk assessment: The MacArthur Study of Mental Disorder and Violence.* New York, Oxford University Press.

Montgomery, P., & Dennis, J. (2004). A systematic review of non-pharmacological therapies for sleep problems in later life. *Sleep Medicine Reviews, 8*(1), 47–62.

Moore, T. O. (2001). Testosterone and male behavior: Empirical research with hamsters does not support the use of castration to deter human sexual aggression. *North American Journal of Psychology, 3*(3), 503–520.

Moore-Ede, M. C., Sulzman, F. M., & Fuller, C. A. (1982). *The clocks that time us.* Cambridge, MA: Harvard University Press.

Moras, K. (2002). Research on psychotherapy. In M. Hersen & W. H. Sledge (Eds.), *Encyclopedia of psychotherapy.* San Diego: Academic Press.

Morelli, G. A., Rogoff, B., Oppenheim, D., & Goldsmith, D. (1992). Cultural variation in infants' sleeping arrangements. *Developmental Psychology, 28*(4), 604–613.

Moreno, J. L. (1953). *Who shall survive?* New York: Beacon.

Morgan, J. P. (Ed.). (2005). *Psychology of aggression.* Hauppauge, NY: Nova Science Publishers.

Morgenstern, J., Labouvie, E., McCrady, B. S., Kahler, C. W., et al. (1997). Affiliation with Alcoholics Anonymous after treatment: A study of its therapeutic effects and mechanisms of action. *Journal of Consulting & Clinical Psychology, 65*(5), 768–777.

Morisse, D., Batra, L., Hess, L., & Silverman, R. (1996). A demonstration of a token economy for the real world. *Applied & Preventive Psychology, 5*(1), 41–46.

Moritz, A. P., & Zamchech, N. (1946). Sudden and unexpected deaths of young soldiers. *American Medical Association Archives of Pathology, 42,* 459–494.

Morrison, R. G., & Wallace, B. (2001). Imagery vividness, creativity and the visual arts. *Journal of Mental Imagery, 25*(3–4), 135–152.

Mosher, W. D., Chandra, C., & Jones, J. (2005). *Sexual behavior and selected health measures: Men and women 15–44 years of age, United States, 2002.* Atlanta: Centers for Disease Control. Retrieved August 25, 2006, from http://www.cdc.gov/nchs/data/ad/ad362.pdf.

Most, S. B., Scholl, B. J., Clifford, E. R., & Simons, D. J. (2005). What you see is what you set: Sustained inattentional blindness and the capture of awareness. *Psychological Review, 112*(1), 217–242.

Mundy, A. (2004). Divided we stand. *American Demographics, 26*(5), 26–31.

Munsey, C. (2006). RxP legislation made historic progress in Hawaii. *APA Monitor,* June, 42.

Murray, B. (2001). A daunting unbelievable experience. *Monitor on Psychology,* Nov., 18.

Murray, J. B. (2002). Phencyclidine (PCP): A dangerous drug, but useful in schizophrenia research. *Journal of Psychology, 136*(3), 319–327.

Murray, S. H., Touyz, S. W., & Beumont, P. J. V. (1996). Awareness and perceived influence of body ideals in the media: A comparison of eating disorder patients and the general community. Eating Disorders: *The Journal of Treatment & Prevention, 4*(1), 33–46.

Murray, S. L., Holmes, J. G., & Griffin, D. W. (1996). The self-fulfilling nature of positive illusions in romantic relationships. *Journal of Personality & Social Psychology, 71*(6), 1155–1180.

Murray, S., Holmes, J. G., & Griffin, D. W. (2003). Reflections on the self-fulfilling effects of positive illusions. *Psychological Inquiry, 14*(3–4), 2003, 289–295.

Mussen, P. H., Conger, J. J., Kagan, J., & Geiwitz, J. (1979). *Psychological development: A life span approach.* New York: Harper & Row.

Mustanski, B. S., Chivers, M. L., & Bailey, J. M. (2002). A critical review of recent biological research on human sexual orientation. *Annual Review of Sex Research, 13,* 89–140.

Myers, H. F., Lesser, I., Rodriguez, N., Mira, C. B., et al. (2002). Ethnic differences in clinical presentation of depression in adult women. *Cultural Diversity & Ethnic Minority Psychology, 8*(2), 138–156.

Nagel, T. (1974). What is it like to be a bat? *The Philosophical Review, 83*, 435–450.

Nairne, J. S. (2002). Remembering over the short-term. *Annual Review of Psychology, 53*, 53–81.

Naitoh, P., Kelly, T. L., & Englund, C. E. (1989). *Health effects of sleep deprivation.* U.S. Naval Health Research Center Report, No. 89–46.

Nakamichi, M. (2004). Tool-use and tool-making by captive, group-living orangutans (Pongo pygmaeus abelii) at an artificial termite mound. *Behavioural Processes, 65*(1), 87–93.

Nakamura, J., & Csikszentmihalyi, M. (2002). The concept of flow. In C. R. Snyder & S. J. Lopez (Eds.), *Handbook of positive psychology.* New York: Oxford.

Nakamura, J., & Csikszentmihalyi, M. (2003). The motivational sources of creativity as viewed from the paradigm of positive psychology. In L. G. Aspinwall & U. M. Staudinger (Eds.), *A psychology of human strengths: Fundamental questions and future directions for a positive psychology.* Washington: American Psychological Association.

National Academy of Sciences. (2002). *The polygraph and lie detection.* Washington, DC: National Academy of Sciences.

National Institute of Child Health and Human Development. (1999). The NICHD Study of Early Child Care, Bethesda, MD: National Institute of Child Health and Human Development.

Nau, S. D., & Lichstein, K. L. (2005). Insomnia: Causes and treatments. In P. R. Carney, J. D. Geyer, & R. B. Berry (Eds.), *Clinical sleep disorders.* Philadelphia, PA: Lippincott Williams & Wilkins.

NCCDPHP (National Center for Chronic Disease Prevention and Health Promotion). (2004). *Health effects of cigarette smoking.* Retrieved July 19, 2006, from http://www.cdc.gov/Tobacco/factsheets/HealthEffectsofCigaretteSmoking_Factsheet.htm

Neath, I., & Surprenant, A. (2003). *Human memory* (2nd ed.). Belmont, CA: Wadsworth.

Needles, D. J., & Abramson, L. Y. (1990). Positive life events, attributional style, and hopefulness: Testing a model of recovery from depression. *Journal of Abnormal Psychology, 99*(2), 156–165.

Nehlig, A. (Ed.). (2004). *Coffee, tea, chocolate, and the brain.* Boca Raton, FL: CRC Press.

Neisser, U., Boodoo, G., Bouchard, T. J., Boykin, A. W., et al. (1996). Intelligence: Knowns & unknowns. *American Psychologist, 51*, 77–101.

Nelson, C. A. (1999). How important are the first 3 years of life? *Applied Developmental Science, 3*(4), 235–238.

Nelson, G., & and Prilleltensky, I. (Eds.). (2005). *Community psychology: In pursuit of liberation and well-being.* New York: Palgrave MacMillan.

Nelson, T. D. (2002). *Psychology of prejudice.* Boston: Allyn & Bacon.

Nelson, T. D. (2005). Ageism: Prejudice against our feared future self. *Journal of Social Issues, 61*(2), 207–221.

Neter, E., & Ben-Shakhar, G. (1989). The predictive validity of graphological inferences: A meta-analytic approach. *Personality and Individual Differences, 10*(7), 737–745.

Neufeld, R. W. J., Carter, J. R., Nicholson, I. R., & Vollick, D. N. (2003). Schizophrenia. In P. Firestone & W. L. Marshall (Eds.), *Abnormal psychology: Perspectives* (2nd ed.). Toronto: Prentice Hall.

Neuman, G. A., & Baydoun, R. (1998). An empirical examination of overt and covert integrity tests. *Journal of Business & Psychology, 13*(1), 65–79.

Neumeister, A. (2004). Neurotransmitter depletion and seasonal affective disorder: Relevance for the biologic effects of light therapy. *Primary Psychiatry. Special Neurotransmitter Depletion, 11*(6), 44–48.

Nevid, J. S., & Greene, B. (2005). *Abnormal psychology in a changing world, media and research update* (5th ed.). Upper Saddle River, NJ: Prentice Hall.

Newman, A. W., & Thompson, J. W. (2001). The rise and fall of forensic hypnosis in criminal investigation. *Journal of the American Academy of Psychiatry & the Law, 29*(1), 75–84.

Ng, S. H. (2002). Will families support their elders? Answers from across cultures. In T. Nelson (Ed.), *Ageism: Stereotyping and prejudice against older persons.* Cambridge, MA: MIT Press.

Niaura, R., Todaro, J. F., Stroud, L., Spiro, A., et al. (2002). Hostility, the metabolic syndrome, and incident coronary heart disease. *Health Psychology, 21*(6), 588–593.

Nickell, J. (2001). John Edward: Hustling the bereaved. *Skeptical Inquirer,* Nov. –Dec., 19–22.

Nickerson, R. S., & Adams, M. J. (1979). Long-term memory for a common object. *Cognitive Psychology, 11,* 287–307.

NIDA. (2006). *Tobacco addiction.* National Institute on Drug Abuse, NIH Publication Number 06-4342. Retrieved July 24, 2006, from http://www.nida.nih.gov/PDF/RRTobacco.pdf.

Niedzwienska, A. (2004). Metamemory knowledge and the accuracy of flashbulb memories. *Memory, 12*(5), 603–613.

Niehaus, D. J. H., Stein, D. J., Koen, L., Lochner, C., et al. (2005). A case of "Ifufunyane": A Xhosa culture-bound syndrome. *Journal of Psychiatric Practice, 11*(6), 411–413.

Nielsen, D. M., & Metha, A. (1994). Parental behavior and adolescent self-esteem in clinical and nonclinical samples. *Adolescence, 29*(115), 525–542.

Nielsen, M., & Dissanayake, C. (2004). Pretend play, mirror self-recognition and imitation: A longitudinal investigation through the second year. *Infant Behavior & Development, 27*(3), 342–365.

NIMH. (2001). *Facts about anxiety disorders.* Bethesda, MD: National Institute of Mental Health. Retrieved September 20, 2006, from http://www.nimh.nih.gov/publicat/NIMHadfacts.pdf.

NIMH. (2003). *In harm's way: Suicide in America.* Bethesda, MD: National Institute of Mental Health. Retrieved September 21, 2006, from http://www.nimh.nih.gov/publicat/harmsway.cfm.

NIMH. (2006). *The numbers count: Mental disorders in America.* Bethesda, MD: National Institute of Mental Health. Retrieved September 14, 2006, from http://www.nimh.nih.gov/publicat/numbers.cfm.

Nisbett, R. E. (2005). Heredity, environment, and race differences in IQ: A commentary on Rushton and Jensen (2005). *Psychology, Public Policy, and Law, 11*(2), 302–310.

Njeri, I. (1991). Beyond the melting pot. *Los Angeles Times,* Jan. 13, E-1, E-8.

Noble, P. (1997). Violence in psychiatric inpatients. *International Review of Psychiatry, 9*(2–3), 207–216.

Noice, H., & Noice, T. (1999). Long-term retention of theatrical roles. *Memory, 7*(3), 357–382.

Noland, J. S., Singer, L. T., Short, E. J., Minnes, S., et al. (2005). Prenatal drug exposure and selective attention in preschoolers. *Neurotoxicology & Teratology, 27*(3), 429–438.

Nolen-Hoeksema, S. (2004). *Abnormal psychology* (3rd ed.). New York: McGraw-Hill.

Norcross, J. C. (Ed.) (2002). *Psychotherapy relationships that work.* New York: Oxford.

Norcross, J. C., Hedges, M., & Prochaska, J. O. (2002). The face of 2010: A Delphi poll on the future of psychotherapy. *Professional Psychology: Research & Practice, 33*(3), 316–322.

Nori, G. (1998). Glucagon and the control of meal size. In: Smith, G. P. (Ed.), *Satiation: From gut to brain.* New York: Oxford University Press.

Norlander, T., Bergman, H., & Archer, T. (1998). Effects of flotation rest on creative problem solving and originality. *Journal of Environmental Psychology, 18*(4), 399–408.

Norlander, T., Bergman, H., & Archer, T. (1999). Primary process in competitive archery performance: Effects of flotation REST. *Journal of Applied Sport Psychology, 11*(2), 194–209.

Norris, R. M., & Weinman, J. A. (1996). Psychological change following a long sail training voyage. *Personality & Individual Differences, 21*(2), 189–194.

North, C. S. (1987). *Welcome silence.* New York: Simon & Schuster.

Northcutt, R. G. (2004). Taste buds: Development and evolution. *Brain, Behavior & Evolution, 64*(3), 198–206.

Norton, P. (2003). *Teaching with technology: Designing opportunities to learn.* Belmont, CA: Wadsworth.

Nosek, B. A., Greenwald, A. G., & Banaji, M. R. (2005). Understanding and using the implicit association test: II. Method variables and construct validity. *Personality & Social Psychology Bulletin, 31*(2), 166–180.

Nurnberger, J. I., & Zimmerman, J. (1970). Applied analysis of human behaviors: An alternative to conventional motivational inferences and unconscious determination in therapeutic programming. *Behavior Therapy, 1,* 59–69.

Oakley, D. A., Whitman, L. G., & Halligan, P. W. (2002). Hypnotic imagery as a treatment for phantom limb pain. *Clinical Rehabilitation, 16*(4), 368–377.

Oatley, K., & Jenkins, J. M. (1992). Human emotions: Function and dysfunction. *Annual Review of Psychology, 45,* 55–85.

Obhi, S. S., & Haggard, P. (2004). Free will and free won't. *American Scientist, 92*(July–Aug), 358–365.

Ochoa, J. G., & Pulido, M. (2005). Parasomnias. In P. R. Carney, J. D. Geyer, & R. B. Berry (Eds.), *Clinical sleep disorders.* Philadelphia, PA: Lippincott Williams & Wilkins.

O'Conner, T. G., Marvin, R. S., Rutter, M., Olrick, J. T., & et al. (2003). Child-parent attachment following early institutional deprivation. *Development & Psychopathology, 15*(1), 19–38.

O'Connor, M. G., Sieggreen, M. A., Bachna, K., Kaplan, B., et al. (2000). Long-term retention of transient news events. *Journal of the International Neuropsychological Society, 6*(1), 44–51.

O'Craven, K. M., & Kanwisher, N. (2000). Mental imagery of faces and places activates corresponding stimulus-specific brain regions. *Journal of Cognitive Neuroscience, 12*(6), 1013–1023.

Ogloff, J. R. P. (2006). Psychopathy/antisocial personality disorder conundrum. *Australian & New Zealand Journal of Psychiatry, 40*(6), 519–528.

Ohayon, M. M., Guilleminault, C., & Priest, R. G. (1999). Night terrors, sleepwalking, and confusional arousals in the general population. *Journal of Clinical Psychiatry, 60*(4), 268–276.

O'Keeffe, C., & Wiseman, R. (2005). Testing alleged mediumship: Methods and results. *British Journal of Psychology, 96*(2), 165–179.

Okiishi, J., Lambert, M. J., Nielsen, S. L., & Ogles, B. M. (2003). Waiting for supershrink: An empirical analysis of therapist effects. *Clinical Psychology & Psychotherapy, 10*(6), 361–373.

Olds, M. E., & Fobes, J. L. (1981). The central basis of motivation: Intracranial self-stimulation studies. *Annual Review of Psychology, 32,* 523–574.

Olio, K. A. (2004). The truth about "false memory syndrome." In P. J. Caplan & L. Cosgrove (Eds.), *Bias in psychiatric diagnosis. A project of the association for women in psychology.* Northvale, NJ: Jason Aronson.

Olson, J. M., & Zanna, M. P. (1993). Attitudes and attitude change. *Annual Review of Psychology, 44,* 117–154.

Olszewski, P. K., Li, D., Grace, M. K., Billington, C. J., et al. (2003). Neural basis of orexigenic effects of ghrelin acting within lateral hypothalamus. *Peptides, 24*(4), 597–602.

O'Neill, B. (2003). *Don't believe everything you read online.* BBC News: http://news.bbc.co.uk, March 8.

O'Neill, P. (2005) The ethics of problem definition. *Canadian Psychology, 46,* 13–20.

Ones, D. S., & Viswesvaran, C. (2001). Integrity tests and other criterion-focused occupational personality scales (COPS) used in personnel selection. *International Journal of Selection & Assessment, 9*(1–2), 31–39.

Ones, D. S.,Viswesvaran, C., & Schmidt, F. L. (2003). Personality and absenteeism: A meta-analysis of integrity tests. *European Journal of Personality. Special Issue: Personality and Industrial, Work and Organizational Applications, 17*(Suppl1), S19–S38.

Onwuegbuzie, A. J. (2000). Academic procrastinators and perfectionistic tendencies among graduate students. *Journal of Social Behavior & Personality, 15*(5), 103–109.

Ooki, S. (2005). Genetic and environmental influences on the handedness and footedness in Japanese twin children. *Twin Research and Human Genetics, 8*(6), 649–656.

Ord, T. J., Martins E. P., Thakur S., Mane K. K., et al. (2005). Trends in animal behaviour research (1968–2002): Ethoinformatics and the mining of library databases. *Animal Behaviour, 69*(6), 1399–1413.

Orleans, C. T. (2000). Promoting the maintenance of health behavior change. *Health Psychology, 19*(Suppl. 1), 76–83.

Orleans, C. T., Gruman, J., & Hollendonner, J. K. (1999). Rating our progress in population health promotion: Report card on six behaviors. *American Journal of Health Promotion 14*(2), 75–82.

Ornstein, R., & Ehrlich, P. (1989). *New world new mind.* New York: Simon & Schuster.

O'Roark, A. M. (2001). Personality assessment, projective methods and a triptych perspective. *Journal of Projective Psychology & Mental Health, 8*(2), 116–126.

Osgood, C. E. (1952). The nature and measurement of meaning. *Psychological Bulletin, 49,* 197–237.

Oskamp, S., & Schultz, P. W. (2005). *Attitudes and opinions* (3rd ed.). Mahwah, NJ: Erlbaum.

Oster, H. (2005). The repertoire of infant facial expressions: a ontogenetic perspective. In J. Nadel & D. Muir (Eds.), *Emotional development: Recent research advances.* New York: Oxford University Press.

Overmier, J. B., & LoLordo, V. M. (1998). Learned helplessness. In W. T. O'Donohue, (Ed.), *Learning and behavior therapy.* Boston, MA: Allyn & Bacon.

Oyserman, D., Bybee, D., Terry, K., & Hart-Johnson, T. (2004). Possible selves as roadmaps. *Journal of Research in Personality, 38*(2), 130–149.

Pagano, R. R., & Warrenburg, S. (1983). Meditation. In R J. Davidson, G. E. Schwartz, & D. Shapiro (Eds.), *Consciousness and self-regulation* (153–210). New York: Plenum.

Page, K. (1999, May 16). The graduate. *Washington Post Magazine, 152,* 18–20.

Pagnin, D., de Queiroz, V., Pini, S., & Cassano, G. B. (2004). Efficacy of ECT in Depression: A meta-analytic review. *Journal of ECT, 20*(1), 13–20.

Palm, K., & Gibson, P. (1998). Recovered memories of childhood sexual abuse: Clinicians' practices and beliefs. *Professional Psychology: Research & Practice, 29*(3), 257–261.

Palmer, S. E. (1992). Common region: A new principle of perceptual grouping. *Cognitive Psychology, 24*(3), 436–447.

Panksepp, J., & Pasqualini, M. S. (2005). The search for the fundamental brain/mind sources of affective experience. In J. Nadel & D. Muir (Eds.), *Emotional development: Recent research advances.* New York: Oxford University Press.

Papa, F. J., Aldrich, D., & Schumacker, R. E. (1999). The effects of immediate online feedback upon diagnostic performance. *Academic Medicine, 74*(Suppl. 10), S16–S18.

Paradis, C. M., Solomon, L. Z., Florer, F., & Thompson, T. (2004). Flashbulb memories of personal events of 9/11 and the day after for a sample of New York City residents. *Psychological Reports, 95*(1), 304–310.

Park, D. C., Smith, A. D., & Cavanaugh, J. C. (1990). Metamemories of memory researchers. *Memory & Cognition, 18*(3), 321–327.

Parke, R. D. (2004). Development in the family. *Annual Review of Psychology, 55,* 365–399.

Parker, A., Ngu, H., & Cassaday, H. J. (2001). Odour and Proustian memory. *Applied Cognitive Psychology, 15*(2), 159–171.

Parker, J. D. A. (2001). The relevance of emotional intelligence for clinical psychology. In R. Schulze & R. D. Roberts (Eds.), *Emotional intelligence: An international handbook.* Ashland, OH: Hogrefe & Huber.

Pascual, A., & Guéguen, N. (2005). Foot-in-the-door and Door-in-the-face: A comparative meta-analytic study. *Psychological Reports, 96*(1), 122–128.

Patterson, C. J. (2002). Lesbian and gay parenthood. In M. Bornstein (Ed.), *Handbook of Parenting* (Vol. 3). Mahwah, NJ: Erlbaum.

Paulhus, D. L. (1998). Interpersonal and intrapsychic adaptiveness of trait self-enhancement. *Journal of Personality and Social Psychology, 74*(5), 1197–1208.

Paulsson, T., & Parker, A. (2006). The effects of a two-week reflection-intention training program on lucid dream recall. *Dreaming, 16*(1), 22–35.

Pavlidis, I., Eberhardt, N. L., & Levine, J. A. (2002). Seeing through the face of deception. *Nature, 415*(6867), 35.

Pavlov, I. P. (1927). *Conditioned reflexes.* New York: Dover.

Penfield, W. (1957). Brain's record of past a continuous movie film. *Science News Letter,* April 27, 265.

Penfield, W. (1958). *The excitable cortex in conscious man.* Springfield, IL: Charles C Thomas.

Pennebaker, J. W. (2004). *Writing to heal: A guided journal for recovering from trauma and emotional upheaval.* Oakland, CA: New Harbinger Press.

Peplau, L. A. (2003). Human sexuality: How do men and women differ? *Current Directions in Psychological Science, 12*(2), 37–40.

Perin, C. T. (1943). A quantitative investigation of the delay of reinforcement gradient. *Journal of Experimental Psychology, 32,* 37–51.

Perls, F. (1969). *Gestalt therapy verbatim.* Lafayette, CA: Real People Press.

Perreault, S., & Bourhis, R. Y. (1999). Ethnocentrism, social identification, and discrimination. *Personality & Social Psychology Bulletin, 25*(1), 92–103.

Perry, R. P. (2003). Perceived (academic) control and causal thinking in achievement settings. *Canadian Psychology, 44*(4), 312–331.

Perry, R. P., Hladkyj, S., Pekrun, R. H., & Pelletier, S. T. (2001). Academic control and action control in the achievement of college students: A longitudinal field study. *Journal of Educational Psychology, 93*(4), 776–789.

Perugini, E. M., Kirsch, I., Allen, S. T., Coldwell, E, et al. (1998). Surreptitious observation of responses to hypnotically suggested hallucinations. *International Journal of Clinical & Experimental Hypnosis, 46*(2), 191–203.

Pervin, L. A., Cervone, D., & John, O. P. (2005). *Personality: Theory and research* (9th ed.). Hoboken, NJ: Wiley.

Pesant, N., & Zadra, A. (2006). Dream content and psychological well-being: A longitudinal study of the continuity hypothesis. *Journal of Clinical Psychology, 62*(1), 111–121.

Pescatello, L. S. (2001). Exercising for health. *Western Journal of Medicine, 174*(2), 114–118.

Peters, W. A. (1971). *A class divided.* Garden City, NY: Doubleday.

Peterson, C., & Vaidya, R. S. (2001). Explanatory style, expectations, and depressive symptoms. *Personality & Individual Differences, 31*(7), 1217–1223.

Peterson, L. R., & Peterson, M. J. (1959). Short-term retention of individual verbal items. *Journal of Experimental Psychology, 58,* 193–198.

Peterson, S. E. (1992). The cognitive functions of underlining as a study technique. *Reading Research & Instruction, 31*(2), 49–56.

Petri, H. L., & Govern, J. M. (2004). *Motivation: Theory, research, and applications* (5th Ed.). Belmont, CA: Wadsworth.

Pett, M. A., & Johnson, M. J. M. (2005). Development and psychometric evaluation of the Revised University Student Hassles Scale. *Educational & Psychological Measurement, 65*(6), 984–1010.

Pettigrew, T. F. (1998). Intergroup contact theory. *Annual Review of Psychology, 49,* 65–85.

Pettit, G. S., Brown, E. G., Mize, J., & Lindsey, E. (1998). Mothers' and fathers' socializing behaviors in three contexts. *Merrill-Palmer Quarterly, 44*(2), 173–193.

Peverly, S. T., Brobst, K. E., Graham, M., & Shaw, R. (2003). College adults are not good at self-regulation. *Journal of Educational Psychology, 95*(2), 335–346.

Phillips, D. P., Liu, G. C., Kwok, K., Jarvinen, J., et al. (2001). The Hound of the Baskervilles effect: Natural experiment on the influence of psychological stress on timing of death. *British Medical Journal, 323*(7327), 1443–1446

Piaget, J. (1951, original French, 1945). *The psychology of intelligence.* New York: Norton.

Piaget, J. (1952). *The origins of intelligence in children.* New York: International University Press.

Pickel, K. L., French, T. A., & Betts, J. M. (2003). A cross-modal weapon focus effect: The influence of a weapon's presence on memory for auditory information. *Memory, 11*(3), 277–292.

Piek, J. P. (2006). *Infant motor development.* Champaign, Il: Human Kinetics Publishers.

Pierce, W. D., & Cheney, C. D (2004). *Behavior analysis and learning* (3rd ed.). Mahwah, NJ: Erlbaum.

Pierrehumbert, B., Ramstein, T., Karmaniola, A., Miljkovitch, R., et al. (2002). Quality of child care in the preschool years. *International Journal of Behavioral Development, 26*(5), 385–396.

Pierrel, R., & Sherman, J. G. (1963). Train your pet the Barnabus way. *Brown Alumni Monthly,* Feb., 8–14.

Piliavin, I. M., Rodin, J., & Piliavin, J. A. (1969). Good samaritanism: An underground phenomenon? *Journal of Personality & Social Psychology, 13,* 289–299.

Pillow, D. R., Zautra, A. J., & Sandler, I. (1996). Major life events and minor stressors: Identifying mediational links in the stress process. *Journal of Personality & Social Psychology, 70*(2), 381–394.

Pinel, J. P.J., Assanand, S., & Lehman, D. R. (2000). Hunger, eating, and ill health. *American Psychologist, 55*(10), 1105–1116.

Pinker, S., & Jackendoff, R. (2005). The faculty of language: What's special about it? *Cognition, 95*(2), 201–236.

Pinsof, W. M., Wynne, L. C., & Hambright, A. B. (1996). The outcomes of couple and family therapy. *Psychotherapy, 33*(2), 321–331.

Pizam, A., Jeong, G.-H., Reichel, A., Van Boemmel, H., et al. (2004). The relationship between risk-taking, sensation-seeking, and the tourist behavior of young adults: A cross-cultural study. *Journal of Travel Research, 42,* 251–260.

Pliner, P., & Mann, N. (2004). Influence of social norms and palatability on amount consumed and food choice. *Appetite, 42*(2), 227–237.

Plous, S. (2003). *Understanding prejudice and discrimination.* New York: McGraw-Hill.

Plutchik, R. (2001). The nature of emotions. *American Scientist, 89,* 344–350.

Plutchik, R. (2003). *Emotions and life: Perspectives from psychology, biology, and evolution.* Washington: American Psychological Association.

Pogatchnik, S. (1990). Kids' TV gets more violent, study finds. *The Los Angeles Times,* Jan. 26, F, 1, 27.

Poland, J., & Caplan, P. J. (2004). The deep structure of bias in psychiatric diagnosis. In P. J. Caplan & L. Cosgrove (Eds.), *Bias in psychiatric diagnosis. A project of the association for women in psychology.* Lanham, MD: Jason Aronson.

Polemikos, N., & Papaeliou, C. (2000). Sidedness preference as an index of organization of laterality. *Perceptual & Motor Skills, 91*(3, Pt. 2), 1083–1090.

Polivy, J., & Herman, C. P. (2002). Causes of eating disorders. *Annual Review of Psychology, 53,* 187–213.

Pollner, M. (1998). The effects of interviewer gender in mental health interviews. *Journal of Nervous & Mental Disease, 186*(6), 369–373.

Pollock, V. E., Briere, J., Schneider, L., Knop, J., et al. (1990). Childhood antecedents of antisocial behavior. *American Journal of Psychiatry, 147*(10), 1290–1293.

Pope, H. G., Gruber, A. J., & Yurgelun-Todd, D. (1995). The residual neuropsychological effects of cannabis. *Drug & Alcohol Dependence, 38*(1), 25–34.

Porac, C., Friesen, I. C., Barnes, M. P., & Gruppuso, V. (1998). Illness and accidental injury in young and older adult left- and right-handers: Implications for genetic theories of hand preference. *Developmental Neuropsychology, 14*(1), 157–172.

Porter, K., Babiker, A. G., Darbyshire, J. H., & Pezzotti, P. (2003). Determinants of survival following HIV-1 seroconversion after the introduction of HAART. *The Lancet,* Oct. 18, 362, 1267–1274.

Posada, G., Jacobs, A., Richmond, M. K., Carbonell, O. A., et al. (2002). Maternal caregiving and infant security in two cultures. *Developmental Psychology, 38*(1), 67–78.

Poulton, R. G., & Andrews, G. (1996). Change in danger cognitions in agoraphobia and social phobia during treatment. *Behaviour Research & Therapy, 34*(5–6), 413–421.

Powell, A. L., & Thelen, M. H. (1996). Emotions and cognitions associated with bingeing and weight control behavior in bulimia. *Journal of Psychosomatic Research, 40*(3), 317–328.

Powell, D. H. (2004). Behavioral treatment of debilitating test anxiety among medical students. *Journal of Clinical Psychology, 60*(8), 853–865.

Powell, R. A., Symbaluk, D. G., & Macdonald, S. E. (2005). *Introduction to learning and behavior* (2nd ed.). Belmont, CA: Wadsworth.

Preckel, F., Holling, H., & Wiese, M. (2006). Relationship of intelligence and creativity in gifted and non-gifted students: An investigation of threshold theory. *Personality & Individual Differences, 40*(1), 159–170.

Premack, A. J., & Premack, D. (1972). Teaching language to an ape. *Scientific American, 227*(4), 92–99.

Premack, D., & Premack, A. J. (1983). *The mind of an ape.* New York: Norton.

Priluck, R., & Till, B. D. (2004). The role of contingency awareness, involvement, and need for cognition in attitude formation. *Journal of the Academy of Marketing Science, 32*(3), 329–344.

Provencher, M. D., Dugas, M. J., & Ladouceur, R. (2004). Efficacy of problem-solving training and cognitive exposure in the treatment of generalized anxiety disorder: A case replication series. *Cognitive & Behavioral Practice, 11*(4), 404–414.

Puca, R. M., & Schmalt, H. (1999). Task enjoyment: A mediator between achievement motives and performance. *Motivation & Emotion, 23*(1), 15–29.

Pychyl, T. A., Lee, J. M., Thibodeau, R., & Blunt, A. (2000). Five days of emotion: An experience sampling study of undergraduate student procrastination. *Journal of Social Behavior & Personality, 15*(5), 239–254.

Quednow, B. B., Jessen, F., Kühn, K.-W., Maier, W., et al. (2006). Memory deficits in abstinent MDMA (ecstasy) users: Neuropsychological evidence of frontal dysfunction. *Journal of Psychopharmacology, 20*(3), 373–384.

Quigley, B. M., & Leonard, K. E. (2000). Alcohol, drugs, and violence. In V. B. Van Hasselt & M. Hersen (Eds.), *Aggression and violence: An introductory text.* Boston: Allyn & Bacon.

Rabius, V., McAlister, A. L., Geiger, A., Huang, P., et al. (2004). Telephone counseling increases cessation rates among young adult smokers. *Health Psychology, 23*(5), 539–541.

Rachman, S. (2004). *Anxiety* (2nd. ed.), New York: Routledge.

Rainville, P. (2004). Pain & emotions. In D. D. Price & M. C. Bushnell (Eds.), *Psychological methods of pain control: Basic science and clinical perspectives.* Seattle, WA: IASP Press.

Ramachandran, V. S. (1995). 2-D or not 2-D—that is the question. In R. Gregory, J. Harris, P. Heard, & D. Rose (Eds.), *The artful eye.* Oxford: Oxford University Press.

Ramanaiah, N. V., Detwiler, F. R. J., & Byravan, A. (1995). Sex-role orientation and satisfaction with life. *Psychological Reports, 77*(3, Dec., Pt. 2), 1260–1262.

Ramsay, M. C., Reynolds, C. R., & Kamphaus, R. W. (2002). *Essentials of behavioral assessment.* New York: Wiley.

Randi, J. (1983). Science and the chimera. In G. O. Abell & B. Singer (Eds.), *Science and the paranormal.* New York: Scribner's.

Randi, J. (1997). *An encyclopedia of claims, frauds, and hoaxes of the occult and supernatural.* New York: St. Martin's Press.

Rathus, R., Nevid, J., & Fichner-Rathus, L. (2005). *Human sexuality in a world of diversity* (6th ed.). Boston: Allyn & Bacon.

Rau, H., Bührer, M., & Weitkunat, R. (2003). Biofeedback of R-wave-to-pulse interval normalizes blood pressure. *Applied Psychophysiology and Biofeedback, 28*(1), 37–46.

Rau, P. R. (2005). *Drowsy driver detection and warning system for commercial vehicle drivers: Field operational test design, data analyses, and progress.* National Highway Traffic Safety Administration Paper Number 05-0192. Retrieved July 24, 2006, from http://www-nrd.nhtsa.dot.gov/pdf/nrd-01/esv/esv19/05-0192-W.pdf.

Rau, W., & Durand, A. (2000). The academic ethic and college grades: Does hard work help students to "make the grade"? *Sociology of Education, 73*(1), 19–38.

Reed, J. D., & Bruce, D. (1982). Longitudinal tracking of difficult memory retrievals. *Cognitive Psychology, 14,* 280–300.

Reeve, J. (2004). *Understanding motivation and emotion* (4th Ed.). New York: Wiley.

Regan, P. C., Levin, L., Sprecher, S., Christopher, F. S., et al. (2000). Partner preferences: What characteristics do men and women desire in their short-term sexual and long-term romantic partners? *Journal of Psychology & Human Sexuality, 12*(3), 1–21.

Reid, M. R., Mackinnon, L. T., & Drummond, P. D. (2001). The effects of stress management on symptoms of upper respiratory tract infection, secretory immunoglobulin A, and mood in young adults. *Journal of Psychosomatic Research, 51*(6), 721–728.

Reid, P. T. (2002). Multicultural psychology. *Cultural Diversity & Ethnic Minority Psychology, 8*(2), 103–114.

Reiff, S., Katkin, E. S., & Friedman, R. (1999). Classical conditioning of the human blood pressure response. *International Journal of Psychophysiology, 34*(2), 135–145.

Reifman, A. S., Larrick, R. P., & Fein, S. (1991). Temper and temperature on the diamond: The heat-aggression relationship in major league baseball. *Personality & Social Psychology Bulletin, 17*(5), 580–585.

Reiss, M., Tymnik, G., Koegler, P., Koegler, W., et al. (1999). Laterality of hand, foot, eye, and ear in twins. *Laterality, 4*(3), 287–297.

Reiss, S., & Havercamp, S. M. (2005). Motivation in developmental context: A new method for studying self-actualization. *Journal of Humanistic Psychology, 45*(1), 41–53.

Reiterman, T. (1993). Parallel roads led to Jonestown, Waco. *The Los Angeles Times,* April 23, A-24.

Reitman, D., Murphy, M. A., Hupp, S. D. A., & O'Callaghan, P. M. (2004). Behavior change and perceptions of change: Evaluating the effectiveness of a token economy. *Child & Family Behavior Therapy, 26*(2), 17–36.

Renner, M. J., & Mackin, R. S. (1998). A life stress instrument for classroom use. *Teaching of Psychology, 25*(1), 46–48.

Rentfrow, P. J., & Gosling, S. D. (2003). The do re mi's of everyday life: The structure and personality correlates of music preferences. *Journal of Personality & Social Psychology, 84*(6), 1236–1256.

Rescorla, R. A. (1987). A Pavlovian analysis of goal-directed behavior. *American Psychologist, 42,* 119–126.

Rescorla, R. A. (2004). Spontaneous recovery. *Learning & Memory, 11*(5), 501–509.

Restak, R. M. (2001). *The secret life of the brain.* New York: The Dana Press.

Reznick, J. S., & Goldfield, B. A. (1992). Rapid change in lexical development in comprehension and production. *Developmental Psychology, 28*(3), 406–413.

Rhine, J. B. (1953). *New world of the mind.* New York: Sloane.

Rice, M. E. (1997). Violent offender research and implications for the criminal justice system. *American Psychologist, 52*(4), 414–423.

Richards, J. M., & Gross, J. J. (2000). Emotion regulation and memory: The cognitive costs of keeping one's cool. *Journal of Personality & Social Psychology, 79*(3), 410–424.

Richardson, D. R., & Green, L. R. (1999). Social sanction and threat explanations on gender effects in direct and indirect aggression. *Aggressive Behavior, 25,* 425–434.

Richmond, L. J. (2004). When spirituality goes awry: Students in cults. *Professional School Counseling, 7*(5), 367–375.

Ridenour, T. A., Maldonado-Molina M., Compton, W. M., Spitznagel, E. L., et al. (2005). Factors associated with the transition from abuse to dependence among substance abusers: Implications for a measure of addictive liability. *Drug & Alcohol Dependence, 80*(1), 1–14.

Riefer, D. M., Keveri, M. K., & Kramer, D. L. (1995). Name that tune: Eliciting the tip-of-the-tongue experience using auditory stimuli. *Psychological Reports, 77*(3) (Pt. 2), 1379–1390.

Rieke, M. L., & Guastello, S. J. (1995). Unresolved issues in honesty and integrity testing. *American Psychologist,* June, 458–459.

Riley, W., Jerome, A., Behar, A., & Zack, S. (2002). Feasibility of computerized scheduled gradual reduction for adolescent smoking cessation. *Substance Use & Misuse, 37*(2), 255–263.

Riquelme, H. (2002). Can people creative in imagery interpret ambiguous figures faster than people less creative in imagery? *Journal of Creative Behavior, 36*(2), 105–116.

Ritter, J. (1998). Uniforms changing the culture of the nation's classrooms. *USA Today,* Oct. 15, 1A, 2A.

Roberti, J. W. (2004). A review of behavioral and biological correlates of sensation seeking. *Journal of Research in Personality, 38*(3), 256–279.

Roberts, D. F., Foehr, U. G., & Rideout, V. (2005). *Generation M: Media in the lives of 8-18 year-olds.* Kaiser Family Foundation March 2005. Retrieved July 30, 2006, from http://www.kff.org/entmedia/7251.cfm.

Roberts, R. E., Phinney, J. S., Masse, L. C., Chen, Y. R., et al. (1999). The structure of ethnic identity of young adolescents from diverse ethnocultural groups. *Journal of Early Adolescence, 19*(3), 301–322.

Robertson, I. S. (2001). *Problem solving.* Hove, UK: Psychology Press.

Robins, R. W., Gosling, S. D., & Craik, K. H. (1998). Psychological science at the crossroads. *American Scientist, 86*(July–Aug), 310–313.

Robinson, A., & Clinkenbeard, P. R. (1998). Giftedness. *Annual Review of Psychology, 49,* 117–139.

Robinson, B., Frye, E. M., & Bradley, L. J. (1997). Cult affiliation and disaffiliation. *Counseling & Values, 41*(2), 166–173.

Robinson, T. N., Wilde, M. L., Navracruz, L. C., Haydel, K. F., et al. (2001). Effects of reducing children's television and video game use on aggressive behavior. *Archives of Pediatrics & Adolescent Medicine, 155*(1), 17–23.

Robinson-Riegler, B., & McDaniel, M. (1994). Further constraints on the bizarreness effect: Elaboration at encoding. *Memory & Cognition, 22*(6), 702–712.

Robson, P. (1984). Prewalking locomotor movements and their use in predicting standing and walking. *Child Care, Health & Development, 10,* 317–330.

Rock, A. (2004). *The mind at night: The new science of how and why we dream.* New York: Basic Books.

Rodd, Z. A., Bell, R. L., McQueen, V. K., Davids, M. R., et al. (2005). Chronic ethanol drinking by alcohol-preferring rats increases the sensitivity of the posterior ventral tegmental area to the reinforcing effects of ethanol. *Alcoholism: Clinical & Experimental Research, 29*(3), 358–366.

Roeckelein, J. E. (2004). *Imagery in psychology: A reference guide.* Westport, CT: Praeger.

Roediger, H. L., & McDermott, K. B. (1995). Creating false memories: Remembering words not presented on lists. *Journal of Experimental Psychology: Learning, Memory, & Cognition, 21*(4), 803–814.

Roediger, III, H. L., & Amir, N. (2005). Implicit memory tasks: Retention without conscious recollection. In A. Wenzel & D. C. Rubin (Eds.), *Cognitive methods and their application to clinical research.* Washington: American Psychological Association.

Rogers, C. R. (1959). A theory of therapy, personality, and interpersonal relationships, as developed in the client-centered framework. In S. Koch (Ed.), *Psychology: A study of a science* (Vol. 3). New York: McGraw-Hill.

Rogers, C. R. (1961). *On becoming a person.* Boston: Houghton Mifflin.

Rogers, S., & Silver, S. M. (2002). Is EMDR an exposure therapy? A review of trauma protocols. *Journal of Clinical Psychology, 58*(1), 43–59.

Rohsenow, D. J., & Smith R. E. (1982). Irrational beliefs as predictors of negative affective states. *Motivation and Emotion, 6,* 299–301.

Roid, G. H. (2003). *Stanford-Binet Intelligence Scales, Fifth Edition, Examiner's Manual.* Itasca, IL: Riverside.

Roos, P. E., & Cohen, L. H. (1987). Sex roles and social support as moderators of life stress adjustment. *Journal of Personality & Social Psychology, 52,* 576–585.

Rosch, E. (1977). Classification of real-world objects: Origins and representations in cognition. In P. N. Johnson-Laird & P. C. Wason (Eds.), *Thinking: Reading in cognitive science.* Cambridge, MA: Cambridge University Press.

Rosen, G., Hugdahl, K., Ersland, L., Lundervold, A., et al. (2001). Different brain areas activated during imagery of painful and non-painful 'finger movements' in a subject with an amputated arm. *Neurocase, 7*(3), 255–260.

Rosen, L. A., Booth, S. R., Bender, M. E., McGrath, M. L., et al. (1988). Effects of sugar (sucrose) on children's behavior. *Journal of Consulting & Clinical Psychology, 56*(4), 583–589.

Rosenberg, L. B. (1994). *The effect of interocular distance upon depth perception when using stereoscopic displays to perform work within virtual and telepresent environments.* USAF AMRL Technical Report (Wright-Patterson),Jul.,AL/CF-TR-1994-0052.

Rosenberg, S. S., & Lynch, J. E. (2002). Fritz Perls revisited: A micro-assessment of a live clinical session. *Gestalt Review, 6*(3), 184–202.

Rosenhan, D. L. (1973). On being sane in insane places. *Science, 179,* 250–258.

Rosenkranz, M.A., Jackson, D. C., Dalton, K. M., Dolski, I., et al. (2003). Affective style and in vivo immune response: Neurobehavioral mechanisms. *Proceedings of the National Academy of Sciences, 100,* 11148–11152.

Rosenthal, R. (1965). Clever Hans: A case study of scientific method. Introduction to a reissue of *Clever Hans: (The horse of Mr. Von Osten),* by O. Pfungst. New York: Holt.

Rosenthal, R. (1973). The Pygmalion effect lives. *Psychology Today,* Sept., 56–63.

Rosenthal R. (1994). Science and ethics in conducting, analyzing, and reporting psychological research. *Psychological Science, 5,* 127–134.

Rosenthal, T. L. (1993). To soothe the savage breast. *Behavior Research & Therapy, 31*(5), 439–462.

Rosenthal, T. L., & Rosenthal, R. (1980). *The vicious cycle of stress reaction.* Copyright, Renate & Ted Rosenthal, Stress Management Clinic, Department of Psychiatry, University of Tennessee College of Medicine, Memphis, Tennessee.

Rosenzweig, M. R., Breedlove, S. M., & Watson, N. V. (2004). Biological psychology: *An introduction to behavioral and cognitive neuroscience* (4th ed.). Sunderland, MA: Sinauer Associates.

Rosnow, R. L. (2006). *Writing papers in psychology: A student guide to research papers, essays, proposals, posters, and handouts* (7th ed.). Belmont, CA: Wadsworth.

Ross, H. E., & Plug, C. (2002). *The mystery of the moon illusion.* Oxford: Oxford University Press.

Ross, M., Heine, S. J., Wilson, A. E., & Sugimori, S. (2005). Cross-cultural discrepancies in self-appraisals. *Personality and Social Psychology Bulletin, 31*(9), 1175–1188.

Rowe, B. (2007). *College awareness guide: What students need to know to succeed in college.* Upper Saddle River, NJ: Prentice Hall.

Rubenstein, C. (2002). What turns you on? *My Generation,* July–Aug., 55–58.

Rubin, D. C. (1985). The subtle deceiver: Recalling our past. *Psychology Today,* Sept., 38–-46.

Rubin, Z. (1970). Measurement of romantic love. *Journal of Personality & Social Psychology, 16,* 265–273.

Rubin, Z. (1973). *Liking and loving: An invitation to social psychology.* New York: Holt.

Rudd, M. D., Joiner, Jr., T. E., & Rajab, M. H. (2001). *Treating suicidal behavior.* New York: Guilford.

Ruder, M., & Bless, H. (2003). Mood and the reliance on the ease of retrieval heuristic. *Journal of Personality & Social Psychology, 85*(1), 20–32.

Rueckl, J. G., & Galantucci, B. (2005). The locus and time course of long-term morphological priming. *Language & Cognitive Processes, 20*(1), 115–138.

Rummens, J., Beiser, M., & Noh, S. (Eds.). (2003). *Immigration, ethnicity and health.* Toronto: University of Toronto Press.

Runco, M. A. (2003). Idea evaluation, divergent thinking, and creativity. In M. A. Runco (Ed.). *Critical creative processes. Perspectives on creativity research.* Cresskill, NJ: Hampton Press.

Runco, M. A. (2004). Creativity. *Annual Review of Psychology, 55,* 657–687.

Rushton, J. P., & Jensen, A. R. (2005). Thirty years of research on race differences in cognitive ability. *Psychology, Public Policy, & Law, 11,* 235–294.

Russell, S., & Norvig, P. (2003). *Artificial intelligence: A modern approach* (2nd. ed.). Englewood Cliffs, NJ: Prentice Hall.

Russo, M. B., Brooks, F. R., Fontenot, J., Dopler, D. M., et al. (1998). Conversion disorder presenting as multiple sclerosis. *Military Medicine, 163*(10), 709–710.

Rutledge, T., & Linden, W. (1998). To eat or not to eat: Affective and physiological mechanisms in the stress-eating relationship. *Journal of Behavioral Medicine, 21*(3), 221–240.

Ryan, M. P. (2001). Conceptual models of lecture learning. *Reading Psychology, 22*(4), 289–312.

Ryan, R. M., & Deci, E. L. (2000). Self-determination theory and the facilitation of intrinsic motivation, social development, and well-being. *American Psychologist, 55,* 68–78.

Ryff, C. D., & Keyes, C. L. (1995). The structure of psychological well-being revisited. *Journal of Personality & Social Psychology, 69*(4), 719–727.

Ryff, C. D., & Singer, B. (2000). Interpersonal flourishing. *Personality and Social Psychology Review, 4,* 30–44.

Ryff, C. D. (1995). Psychological well-being in adult life. *Current Directions in Psychological Science, 4*(4), 99–104.

Ryff, C. D., Singer, B. H., & Palmersheim, K. A. (2004). Social inequalities in health and well-being: The role of relational and religious protective factors. In O. G. Brim, C. D. Ryff, & R. C. Kessler (Eds.), *How healthy are we?: A national study of well-being at midlife.* Chicago, IL: University of Chicago Press.

Saadeh, W., Rizzo, C. P., & Roberts, D. G. (2002). Spanking. *Clinical Pediatrics, 41*(2), 87–88.

Sackeim, H. A., Haskett, R. F., Mulsant, B. H., Thase, M. E., et al. (2001). Continuation pharmacotherapy in the prevention of relapse following electroconvulsive therapy. *Journal of the American Medical Association, 285,* 1299–1307.

Sahelian, R. (1998). *5-HTP.* Wakefield, RI: Moyer Bell.

Salmon, P. (2001). Effects of physical exercise on anxiety, depression, and sensitivity to stress: A unifying theory. *Clinical Psychology Review, 21*(1), 33–61.

Salovey, P., & Mayer, J. (1997). *Emotional development and emotional intelligence.* New York: Basic Books.

Salthouse, T. A. (2004). What and when of cognitive aging. *Current Directions in Psychological Science, 13*(4), 140–144.

SAMHAS (Substance Abuse and Mental Health Services Administration). (2005). Rockville, MD: *Overview of Findings from the 2004 National Survey on Drug Use and Health.* Rockville, MD: Office of Applied Studies, NSDUH Series H-27, DHHS Publication No. SMA 05-4061. Retrieved July 18, 2006, from http://www.oas. samhsa.gov/nsduh/2k4nsduh/ 2k4overview/2k4overview.pdf.

Sankofa, B. M., Hurley, E. A., Allen, B. A., & Boykin, A. W. (2005). Cultural expression and black students' attitudes toward high achievers. *Journal of Psychology: Interdisciplinary & Applied, 139*(3), 247–259.

Sansone, R. A., Sansone, L. A., & Righter, E. L. (1998). Panic disorder. *Journal of Women's Health, 7*(8), 983–989.

Santrock, J. W., & Halonen, J. S. (2007). *Connections to college success.* Belmont, CA: Wadsworth.

Santrock, J. W. (2007). *Child development* (11th ed.). New York: McGraw-Hill.

Sarason, I. G., & Sarason, B. R. (2005). *Abnormal psychology* (11th ed.). Mahwah, NJ: Prentice Hall.

Sateia, M. J., & Nowell, P. D. (2004). Insomnia. *Lancet, 364*(9449), 1959–1973.

Saunders, T., Driskell, J. E., Johnston, J. H., & Salas, E. (1996). The effect of stress inoculation training on anxiety and performance. *Journal of Occupational Health Psychology, 1*(2), 170–186.

Savage-Rumbaugh, E. S., Murphy, J., Sevcik, R. A., Brakke, K. E., et al. (1993). Language comprehension in ape and child. *Monographs of the Society for Research in Child Development, Serial No. 233* (Vol. 58, Nos. 3–4).

Savage-Rumbaugh, S., & Lewin, R. (1996). *Kanzi.* New York: Wiley.

Savage-Rumbaugh, S., Sevcik, R. A., Brakke, K. E., Rumbaugh, D. M., et al. (1990). Symbols: Their communicative use, comprehension, and combination by bonobos (Pan paniscus). *Advances in Infancy Research, 6,* 221–278.

Savage-Rumbaugh, S., Shanker, S., & Taylor, T. (1998). *Apes, language, and mind.* New York: Oxford.

Saxton, M., Houston-Price, C., & Dawson, N. (2005). The prompt hypothesis: Clarification requests as corrective input for grammatical errors. *Applied Psycholinguistics, 26*(3), 393–414.

Schachter, S. (1959). *Psychology of affiliation.* Stanford, CA: Stanford University Press.

Schachter, S., & Wheeler, L. (1962). Epinephrine, chlorpromazine and amusement. *Journal of Abnormal and Social Psychology, 65,* 121–128.

Schacter, D. L. (1996). *Searching for memory: The brain, the mind, and the past.* New York: Basic Books.

Schacter, D. L. (2000). Memory: Memory systems. In A. Kazdin (Ed.), *Encyclopedia of psychology.* Washington: American Psychological Association.

Schacter, D. L. (2001). *The seven sins of memory.* Boston: Houghton Mifflin.

Schacter, D. L., Norman, K. A., & Koutstaal, W. (1998). The cognitive neuroscience of constructive memory. *Annual Review of Psychology, 49,* 289–318.

Schafer, M., & Crichlow, S. (1996). Antecedents of groupthink: A quantitative study. *Journal of Conflict Resolution, 40*(3), 415–435.

Schaie, K. W. (1994). The course of adult intellectual development. *American Psychologist, 49*(4), 304–313.

Schaie, K. W. (2005). *Developmental influences on adult intelligence: The Seattle longitudinal study.* London, England: Oxford University Press.

Scheck, B., Neufeld, P., & Dwyer, J. (2000). *Actual innocence.* New York: Doubleday.

Schick, T., & Vaughn, L. (2001). *How to think about weird things: Critical thinking for a new age.* New York: McGraw-Hill.

Schilling, M. A. (2005). A "Small-World" network model of cognitive insight. *Creativity Research Journal, 17*(2-3), 131–154.

Schiraldi, G. R., & Brown, S. L. (2001). Primary prevention for mental health: Results of an exploratory cognitive-behavioral college course. *Journal of Primary Prevention, 22*(1), 55–67.

Schleicher, S. S., & Gilbert, L. A. (2005). Heterosexual dating discourses among college students: Is there still a double standard? *Journal of College Student Psychotherapy, 19*(3), 7–23.

Schlosberg, H. (1954). Three dimensions of emotion. *Psychological Review, 61,* 81–88.

Schmitt, D. P., & Allik, J. (2005). Simultaneous administration of the Rosenberg Self-Esteem Scale in 53 nations: Exploring the universal and culture-specific features of global self-esteem. *Journal of Personality & Social Psychology, 89*(4), 623–642.

Schmitt, E. (2001). U.S. now more diverse, ethnically and racially. *The New York Times,* April 1, A-18.

Schmolck, H., Buffalo, E. A., & Squire, L. R. (2000). Memory distortions develop over time: Recollections of the O. J. Simpson trial verdict after 15 and 32 months. *Psychological Science, 11*(1), 39–45.

Schneider, K. J. (2002). Humanistic psychotherapy. In M. Hersen & W. H. Sledge (Eds.), *Encyclopedia of psychotherapy.* San Diego: Academic Press.

Schneider, K. J., Bugental, J. F. T., & Pierson, J. F. (2001). Introduction. *The Handbook of Humanistic Psychology,* Thousand Oaks, CA: Sage.

Schneiderman, N., Antoni, M. H., Saab, P. G., & Ironson, G. (2001). Health psychology: Psychological and biobehavioral aspects of chronic disease management. *Annual Review of Psychology, 52,* 555–580.

Schooler, C. (1998) Environmental complexity and the Flynn effect. In U. Neisser (Ed.), *The rising curve: Long-term gains in IQ and related measures.* Washington: American Psychological Association.

Schopp, L. H., Demiris, G., & Glueckauf, R. L. (2006). Rural backwaters or frontrunners? Rural telehealth in the vanguard of psychology practice. *Professional Psychology: Research & Practice, 37*(2), 165–173.

Schouten, S. A. (1994). An overview of quantitatively evaluated studies with mediums and psychics. *Journal of the American Society for Psychical Research, 88*(3), 221–254.

Schreiber, E. H., & Schreiber, D. E. (1999). Use of hypnosis with witnesses of vehicular homicide. *Contemporary Hypnosis, 16*(1), 40–44.

Schreiber, F. R. (1973). *Sybil.* Chicago: Regency.

Schroeder, J. E. (1995). Self-concept, social anxiety, and interpersonal perception skills. *Personality & Individual Differences, 19*(6), 955–958.

Schuel, H., Chang, M. C., Burkman, L. J., Picone, R. P., et al. (1999) Cannabinoid receptors in sperm. In G. Nahas, K. M. Sutin, D. Harvey, & S. Agurell (Eds.), *Marihuana and medicine.* Totowa, NJ: Humana Press.

Schuetze, P., & Eiden, R. D. (2006). The association between maternal cocaine use during pregnancy and physiological regulation in 4- to 8-week-old infants: An examination of possible mediators and moderators. *Journal of Pediatric Psychology. Special Issue: Prenatal Substance Exposure: Impact on Children's Health, Development, School Performance, and Risk Behavior, 31*(1), 15–26.

Schultheiss, O. C., Wirth, M. M., & Stanton, S. J. (2004). Effects of affiliation and power motivation arousal on salivary progesterone and testosterone. *Hormones & Behavior, 46*(5), 592–599.

Schultz, D. P., & Schultz, S. E. (2005). *Theories of personality* (8th ed.). Belmont, CA: Wadsworth.

Schultz, H. T. (2004). Good and bad movie therapy with good and bad outcomes. *The Amplifier: Official Newsletter of APA Division 46, Media Psychology, Fall/Winter 2004.* Retrieved October 25, 2005, from http://www.apa.org/divisions/div46/Amp%20Winter%2005/for%20Website/ampwinter05.html#therapy.

Schum T. R., Kolb, T. M., McAuliffe T. L., Simms, M., et al. (2002). Sequential acquisition of toilet-training skills: A descriptive study of gender and age differences in normal children. *Pediatrics, 3,* e48. Retrieved July 4, 2006, from http://pediatrics.aappublications.org/cgi/content/abstract/109/3/e48.

Schum, T. R., McAuliffe, T. L., Simms, M. D., Walter, J. A., et al. (2001). Factors associated with toilet training in the 1990s. *Ambulatory Pediatrics, 1*(2), 79–86.

Schuster, M. A., Stein, B. D., Jaycox, L. H., Collins, R. L., et al. (2001). A national survey of stress reactions after the September 11, 2001, terrorist attacks. *New England Journal of Medicine, 345*(20), 1507–1512.

Schwartz, B. L. (2002). *Tip-of-the-tongue states: Phenomenology, mechanism, and lexical retrieval.* Hillsdale, NJ: Erlbaum.

Schwartz, M. S., & Andrasik, F. (Eds.). (2003). *Biofeedback: A practitioner's guide* (3rd ed.). New York: Guilford.

Sclafani, A., & Springer, D. (1976). Dietary obesity in adult rats: Similarities to hypothalamic and human obesity syndromes. *Psychology and Behavior, 17,* 461–471.

Scoboria, A., Mazzoni, G., Kirsch, I., & Milling, L. S. (2002). Immediate and persisting effects of misleading questions and hypnosis on memory reports. *Journal of Experimental Psychology: Applied, 8*(1), 26–32.

Scott, J. P., & Ginsburg, B. E. (1994). The Seville statement on violence revisited. *American Psychologist, 49*(10), 849–850.

Scott, L., & O'Hara, M. W. (1993). Self-discrepancies in clinically anxious and depressed university students. *Journal of Abnormal Psychology, 102*(2), 282–287.

Scurfield, R. M. (2002). Commentary about the terrorist acts of September 11, 2001: Posttraumatic reactions and related social and policy issues. *Trauma Violence & Abuse, 3*(1), 3–14.

Seal, D. W., & Palmer-Seal, D. A. (1996). Barriers to condom use and safer sex talk among college dating couples. *Journal of Community & Applied Social Psychology, 6*(1), 15–33.

Searcy, W. A., & Nowicki, S. (2005). *The evolution of animal communication: Reliability and deception in signaling systems.* Princeton, NJ: Princeton University Press.

Seckel, A. (2000). *The art of optical illusions.* London: Carlton Books.

Segerdahl, P., Fields, W., & Savage-Rumbaugh, S. (2005). *Kanzi's primal language: The cultural initiation of primates into language.* New York: Palgrave MacMillan,

Segerstrom, S., & Miller, G. E. (2004). Psychological stress and the human immune system: A meta-analytic study of 30 years of inquiry. *Psychological Bulletin, 130*(4), 601–630.

Seidman, B. F. (2001). Medicine wars. *Skeptical Inquirer,* Jan.–Feb., 28–35.

Seitz, A., & Watanabe, T. (2005). A unified model for perceptual learning. *Trends in Cognitive Sciences, 9*(7), 329–334.

Sekuler, R., & Blake, R. (2006). *Perception* (5th ed.). New York: McGraw-Hill.

Seligman, M. E. P., & Csikszentmihalyi, M. (2000). Positive psychology: An introduction. *American Psychologist, 55,* 5–14.

Seligman, M. E. P. (1972). For helplessness: Can we immunize the weak? In *Readings in psychology today* (2nd ed.). Del Mar, CA: CRM.

Seligman, M. E. P. (1989). Research in clinical psychology: Why is there so much depression today? In I. S. Cohen (Ed.), *The G. Stanley Hall lecture series* (Vol. 9). Washington: American Psychological Association.

Seligman, M. E. P. (1994). *What you can change and what you can't.* New York: Knopf.

Seligman, M. E. P. (1995). The effectiveness of psychotherapy. *American Psychologist, 50*(12), 965–974.

Seligman, M. E. P. (1998). Why therapy works. *APA Monitor, 29*(12), 2.

Seligman, M. E. P. (2002). *Authentic happiness: Using the new positive psychology to realize your potential for lasting fulfillment.* New York: Free Press/Simon and Schuster.

Selye, H. (1976). *The stress of life.* New York: Knopf.

Senécal, C., Julien, E., & Guay, F. (2003). Role conflict and academic procrastination: A self-determination perspective. *European Journal of Social Psychology, 33*(1), 135–145.

Seybolt, D. C., & Wagner, M. K. (1997). Self-reinforcement, gender-role, and sex of participant in prediction of life satisfaction. *Psychological Reports, 81*(2) 519–522.

Seyle, D. C., & Newman, M. L. (2006). A house divided? The psychology of red and blue America. *American Psychologist, 61*(6), 571–580.

Shaffer, D. R. (2002). *Developmental psychology.* Belmont, CA: Wadsworth

Shaffer, J. B., & Galinsky, M. D. (1989). *Models of group therapy.* Englewood Cliffs, NJ: Prentice Hall.

Shafir, E. (1993). Choosing versus rejecting: Why some options are both better and worse than others. *Memory and Cognition, 21,* 546–556.

Shafton, A. (1995). *Dream reader.* Albany, NY: SUNY Press.

Shalev, A. Y. (2001). What is posttraumatic stress disorder? *Journal of Clinical Psychiatry, 62*(Suppl. 17), 4–10.

Shapiro, D. A., Barkham, M., Stiles, W. B., Hardy, G. E., et al. (2003). Time is of the essence: A selective review of the fall and rise of brief therapy research. *Psychology & Psychotherapy: Theory, Research & Practice, 76*(3), 211–235.

Shapiro, F. (2001). *Eye movement desensitization and reprocessing: Basic principles, protocols and procedures* (2nd ed.). New York: Guilford.

Shapiro, F., & Forrest, M. S. (2004). *EMDR: The breakthrough therapy for overcoming anxiety, stress, and trauma.* New York: Basic Books.

Shapiro, S. L., & Walsh, R. (2006). The meeting of meditative disciplines and Western psychology: A mutually enriching dialogue. *American Psychologist, 61*(3), 227–239.

Shaywitz, B. A., Shaywitz, S. E., Pugh, K. R., Constable, R. T., et al. (1995). Sex differences in functional organization of the brain for language. *Nature, 373*(6515), 607–609.

Sheldon, K. M., Ryan, R. M., Rawsthorne, L. J., & Ilardi, B. (1997). Trait self and true self: Cross-role variation in the Big-Five personality traits and its relations with psychological authenticity and subjective well-being. *Journal of Personality & Social Psychology, 73*(6), 1380–1393.

Shepard, R. N. (1975). Form, formation, and transformation of internal representations. In R. L. Solso (Ed.), *Information processing and cognition: The Loyola Symposium.* Hillsdale, NJ: Erlbaum.

Sherif, M., Harvey, O. J., White, B. J., Hood, W. R., & Sherif, C. W. (1961). *Intergroup cooperation and competition: The Robbers Cave experiment.* Norman, OK: University of Oklahoma Press.

Shneerson, J. M. (2005). *Sleep medicine: A guide to sleep and its disorders* (2nd ed.). London: Blackwell.

Shneidman, E. S. (1987a). At the point of no return. *Psychology Today,* March, 54–58.

Shneidman, E. S. (1987b). Psychological approaches to suicide. In G. R. VandenBos & B. K. Bryant (Eds.), *Cataclysms, crises, and catastrophes: Psychology in action.* Washington: American Psychological Association.

Shore, H. (2003). Personal communication.

Shurkin, J. N. (1992). *Terman's kids.* Boston, MA: Little, Brown.

Siau, Keng L. (1996). Group creativity and technology. *Journal of Creative Behavior, 29*(3), 201–216.

Siegel, R. K. (2005). *Intoxication: The universal drive for mind-altering substances.* Rochester, VT: Park Street Press.

Siegler, R. S. (2004). *Children's thinking* (4th ed.). Mahwah, NJ: Erlbaum.

Siegler, R. S., DeLoache, J. S., & Eisenberg, N. (2006). *How children develop* (2nd ed.). New York: Worth.

Siever, L. J., & Koenigsberg, H. W. (2000). The frustrating no-man's-land of borderline personality disorder. *Cerebrum, 2*(4), 85–99.

Silver, S. M., Rogers, S., Knipe, J., & Colelli, G. (2005). EMDR therapy following the 9/11 terrorist attacks: A community-based intervention project in New York City. *International Journal of Stress Management, 12*(1), 29–42.

Silverthorne, C. (2004). *Common sense statistics* (4th ed.). New York: McGraw-Hill.

Simeon, D., Guralnik, O., Knutelska, M., & Schmeidler, J. (2002). Personality factors associated with dissociation: Temperament, defenses, and cognitive schemata. *American Journal of Psychiatry, 159,* 489–491.

Simister, J., & Cooper, C. (2005), Thermal stress in the U.S.A.: Effects on violence and on employee behaviour. *Stress & Health, 21,* 3–15.

Simner, M. L., & Goffin, R. D. (2003). A position statement by the international graphonomics society on the use of graphology in personnel selection testing. *International Journal of Testing, 3*(4), 353–364.

Simon, G. E, Ludman, E. J., Tutty, S., Operskalski, B., et al. (2004). Telephone psychotherapy and telephone care management for primary care patients starting antidepressant treatment. *Journal of the American Medical Association, 292,* 935–942.

Simons, D. J., & Chabris, C. F. (1999). Gorillas in our midst: Sustained inattentional blindness for dynamic events. *Perception, 28,* 1059–1074.

Simons, D. J., & Levin, D. T. (1998). Failure to detect changes to people during a real-world interaction. *Psychonomic Bulletin & Review, 5*(4), 644–649.

Simons, J. S., Dodson, C. S., Bell, D., & Schacter, D. L. (2004). Specific- and partial-source memory: Effects of aging. *Psychology & Aging, 19*(4), 689–694.

Simonton, D. K., & Baumeister, R. F. (2005). Positive psychology at the summit. *Review of General Psychology. Special Positive Psychology, 9*(2), 99–102.

Simpson, D. D., Joe, G. W., Fletcher, B. W., Hubbard, R. L, et al. (1999). A national evaluation of treatment outcomes for cocaine dependence. *Archives of General Psychiatry, 57*(6), 507–514.

Singer, J. D. (2005). Explaining foreign policy: U.S. decision-making and the Persian Gulf War. *Political Psychology, 26*(5), 831–834.

Singer, M. T. (2003). *Cults in our midst: The continuing fight against their hidden menace* (rev. ed.). San Francisco: Jossey-Bass.

Singer, M. T., & Addis, M. E. (1992). Cults, coercion, and contumely. *Cultic Studies Journal, 9*(2), 163–189.

Singleton, J. L., & Newport, E. L. (2004). When learners surpass their models: The acquisition of American Sign Language from inconsistent input. *Cognitive Psychology, 49*(4), 370–407.

Sinha, R., Garcia, M., Paliwal, P., Kreek, M. J., et al. (2006). Stress-induced cocaine craving and hypothalamic-pituitary-adrenal responses are predictive of cocaine relapse outcomes. *Archives of General Psychiatry, 63*(3), 324–331.

Sipos, A., Rasmussen, F., Harrison, G., Tynelius, P., et al. (2004). Paternal age and schizophrenia: A population based cohort study. *British Medical Journal, 329*(7474), 1070.

Sirkin, M. I. (1990). Cult involvement: A systems approach to assessment and treatment. *Psychotherapy, 27*(1), 116–123.

Skeels, H. M. (1966). Adult status of children with contrasting early life experiences. *Monograph of the Society for Research in Child Development, 31*(3), 105.

Skinner, B. F. (1938). *The behavior of organisms: An experimental analysis.* New York: Appleton-Century-Crofts.

Skipton, L. H. (1997). The many faces of character. *Consulting Psychology Journal: Practice & Research. 49*(4), 235–245

Slaby, A. E., Garfinkel, B. D., & Garfinkel, L. F. (1994). *No one say my pain.* New York: Norton.

Slater, A., Mattock, A., & Brown, E. (1990). Size constancy at birth: Newborn infants' responses to retinal and real size. *Journal of Experimental Child Psychology, 49*(2), 314–322.

Slater, A., Mattock, A., Brown, E., & Bremner, J. G. (1991). Form perception at birth: Cohen and Younger (1984) revisited. *Journal of Experimental Child Psychology, 51*(3), 395–406.

Slot, L. A. B., & Colpaert, F. C. (1999). Recall rendered dependent on an opiate state. *Behavioral Neuroscience, 113*(2), 337–344.

Slotkin, T. A. (1998). Fetal nicotine or cocaine exposure: which one is worse? *The Journal of Pharmacology & Experimental Therapeutics, 285*(3), 931–945

Smedley, A., & Smedley, B. D. (2005). Race as biology is fiction, racism as a social problem is real. *American Psychologist, 60*(1), 16–26.

Smith, A. P. (2005). Caffeine at work. *Human Psychopharmacology: Clinical & Experimental, 20*(6), 441–445.

Smith, A. P., Clark, R., & Gallagher, J. (1999). Breakfast cereal and caffeinated coffee: Effects on working memory, attention, mood and cardiovascular function. *Physiology & Behavior, 67*(1), 9–17.

Smith, C., Carey, S., & Wiser, M. (1985). On differentiation: A case study of the development of the concepts of size, weight, and density. *Cognition, 21*(3), 177–237.

Smith, J. L., & Cahusac, P. M. B. (2001). Right-sided asymmetry in sensitivity to tickle. *Laterality, 6*(3), 233–238.

Smith, K. E., Landry, S. H., & Swank, P. R. (2000). Does the content of mothers' verbal stimulation explain differences in children's development of verbal and nonverbal cognitive skills? *Journal of School Psychology, 38*(1), 27–49.

Smith, L. (2002). Piaget's model. In U. Goswami (Ed.), *Blackwell handbook of childhood cognitive development.* Malden, MA: Blackwell.

Smith, T. W., Glazer, K., Ruiz, J. M., & Gallo, L. C. (2004). Hostility, anger, aggressiveness, and coronary heart disease: An interpersonal perspective on personality, emotion, and health. *Journal of Personality. Special Emotions, Personality, and Health, 72*(6), 1217–1270.

Smith, T. W., Ruiz, J. M., & Uchino, B. N. (2004). Mental activation of supportive ties, hostility, and cardiovascular reactivity to laboratory stress in young men and women. *Health Psychology, 23*(5), 476–485.

Smyth, M. M., & Waller, A. (1998). Movement imagery in rock climbing. *Applied Cognitive Psychology, 12*(2), 145–157.

Sobel, E., Shine, D., DiPietro, D., & Rabinowitz, M. (1996). Condom use among HIV/infected patients in South Bronx, New York. *AIDS, 10*(2), 235–236.

Sobolewski, J. M., & Amato, P. R. (2005). Economic hardship in the family of origin and children's psychological well-being in adulthood. *Journal of Marriage and Family, 67*(1), 141–156.

Solomon, J. L., Marshall, P., & Gardner, H. (2005). Crossing boundaries to generative wisdom: An analysis of professional work. In R. J. Sternberg & J. Jordan (Eds.), *A handbook of wisdom: Psychological perspectives.* New York: Cambridge University Press.

Solowij, N., Stephens, R. S., Roffman, R. A., Babor, T., et al. (2002). Cognitive functioning of long-term heavy cannabis users seeking treatment. *Journal of the American Medical Association, 287,* 1123–1131.

Solso, R. L., MacLin, M. K., & MacLin, O. H. (2005). *Cognitive psychology* (7th ed.). Allyn & Bacon.

Somberg, D. R., Stone, G., & Claiborn, C. D. (1993). Informed consent: Therapist's beliefs and practices. *Professional Psychology: Research & Practice, 24*(2), 153–159.

Sommers-Flanagan, J., & Sommers-Flanagan, R. (2002). *Clinical interviewing* (3rd ed.). New York: Wiley.

Soussignan, R. (2002). Duchenne smile, emotional experience, and autonomic reactivity: A test of the facial feedback hypothesis. *Emotion, 2*(1), 52–74.

Spector, P. E. (2005). Industrial and organizational psychology: *Research and practice* (4th ed.). New York: Wiley.

Spence, S., & David, A. (Eds.). (2004). *Voices in the brain: The cognitive neuropsychiatry of auditory verbal hallucinations.* London: Psychology Press.

Sperry, R. W. (1968). Hemisphere deconnection and unity in conscious awareness. *American Psychologist, 23,* 723–733.

Spiegler, M. D., & Guevremont, D. C. (2003). *Contemporary behavior therapy* (4th ed.). Belmont, CA: Wadsworth.

Spinella, M. (2005). Compulsive behavior in tobacco users. *Addictive Behaviors, 30*(1), 183–186.

Spiro Wagner, P., & Spiro, C. S. (2005). *Divided minds: Twin sisters and their journey through schizophrenia.* New York, St. Martin's Press, 2005

Sporer, S. L. (2001). Recognizing faces of other ethnic groups. *Psychology, Public Policy, and Law, 7*(1), 36–97

Sprecher, S. (1998). Insiders' perspectives on reasons for attraction to a close other. *Social Psychology Quarterly, 61*(4), 287–300.

Springer, S. P., & Deutsch, G. (1998). *Left brain, right brain.* New York: Freeman.

Sprinthall, R. C. (2007). *Basic statistical analysis* (8th ed.). Boston: Allyn & Bacon.

Squire, L. R. (2004). Memory systems of the brain: A brief history and current perspective. *Neurobiology of Learning & Memory, 82,* 171–177.

Squire, L. R., & Zola-Morgan, S. (1988). Memory: Brain systems and behavior. *Trends in Neurosciences, 11*(4), 170–175.

Srivastava, S., John, O. P., Gosling, S. D., & Potter, J. (2003). Development of personality in early and middle adulthood: Set like plaster or persistent change? *Journal of Personality & Social Psychology, 84*(5), 1041–1053.

Sroufe, L. A., Egeland, B., Carlson, E., & Collins, W. A. (2005). Placing early attachment experiences in developmental context: The Minnesota Longitudinal Study. In K. E. Grossmann, K. Grossmann, & E. Waters (Eds.), *Attachment from infancy to adulthood: The major longitudinal studies.* New York: Guilford.

Staemmler, F.-M. (2004). Dialogue and interpretation in Gestalt therapy: Making sense together. *International Gestalt Journal, 27*(2), 33–57.

Stanovich, K. E. (2004). *How to think straight about psychology* (7th ed.). Boston: Allyn & Bacon.

Steblay, N. M. (1992). A meta-analytic review of the weapon focus effect. *Law and Human Behavior, 16,* 413–424.

Stein, M. D., & Friedmann, P. D. (2005). Disturbed sleep and its relationship to alcohol use. *Substance Abuse, 26*(1), 1–13.

Stein, M. T., & Ferber, R. (2001). Recent onset of sleepwalking in early adolescence. *Journal of Development, Behavior, and Pediatrics, 22,* S33–S35.

Stemler, S. E., & Sternberg, R. J. (2006). Using situational judgment tests to measure practical intelligence. In J. A. Weekley & R. E. Ployhart (Eds.), *Situational judgment tests: Theory, measurement, and application.* Mahwah, NJ: Erlbaum.

Stephan, W., Berscheid, E., & Walster, E. (1971). Sexual arousal and heterosexual perception. *Journal of Personality & Social Psychology, 20*(1), 93–101.

Stephens, K., Kiger, L., Karnes, F. A., & Whorton, J. E. (1999). Use of nonverbal measures of intelligence in identification of culturally diverse gifted students in rural areas. *Perceptual & Motor Skills, 88*(3, Pt. 1), 793–796.

Stern, D. (1982). Some interactive functions of rhythm changes between mother and infant. In M. Davis (Ed.), *Interaction rhythms, periodicity in communicative behavior.* New York: Human Sciences Press.

Stern, S. L., Dhanda, R., & Hazuda, H. P. (2001). Hopelessness predicts mortality in older Mexican and European Americans. *Psychosomatic Medicine, 63*(3), 344–351.

Sternberg, R. J., & Grigorenko, E. L. (2006). Cultural intelligence and successful intelligence. *Group & Organization Management, 31*(1), 27–39.

Sternberg, R. J. (2000). The holy grail of general intelligence. *Science, 289,* 399–401.

Sternberg, R. J. (2001). Is there a heredity-environment paradox? In R. J. Sternberg & E. L. Grigorenko (Eds.), *Environmental effects on cognitive abilities.* Mahwah, NJ: Erlbaum.

Sternberg, R. J. (2004). Culture and intelligence. *American Psychologist, 59*(5), 325–338.

Sternberg, R. J., & Davidson, J. D. (1982). The mind of the puzzler. *Psychology Today,* June.

Sternberg, R. J., & Grigorenko, E. L. (2005). Cultural explorations of the nature of intelligence. In A. F. Healy (Ed.), *Experimental cognitive psychology and its applications.* Washington: American Psychological Association.

Sternberg, R. J., & Lubart, T. I. (1995). *Defying the crowd.* New York: The Free Press.

Sternberg, R. J., Grigorenko, E. L., & Kidd, K. K. (2005). Intelligence, race, and genetics. *American Psychologist, 60*(1), 46–59.

Steuer, F. B., & Hustedt, J. T. (2002). *TV or No TV? A primer on the psychology of television.* Lanham, MD: University Press of America.

Stewart, A. J., & Ostrove, J. M. (1998). Women's personality in middle age. *American Psychologist, 53*(11), 1185–1194.

Stewart-Williams, S. (2004). The placebo puzzle: Putting together the pieces. *Health Psychology, 23*(2), 198–206.

Stickgold, R., & Walker, M. (2004). To sleep, perchance to gain creative insight? *Trends in Cognitive Sciences, 8*(5), 191–192.

Stipek, D. (2001). *Motivation to learn* (4th ed.). Boston: Allyn & Bacon.

Stöber, J. (2004). Dimensions of test anxiety: Relations to ways of coping with pre-exam anxiety and uncertainty. *Anxiety, Stress & Coping: An International Journal, 17*(3), 213–226.

Stokes, D. M. (2001). The shrinking file-drawer. *Skeptical Inquirer,* (May–June), 22–25.

Stokoe, W. C. (2001). *Language in hand: Why sign came before speech.* Washington: Gallaudet University Press.

Stolerman, I. P., & Jarvis, M. J. (1995) The scientific case that nicotine is addictive. *Psychopharmacology, 117*(1), 2–10.

Stone, J., Perry, Z. W., & Darley, J. M. (1997). "White men can't jump." *Basic and Applied Social Psychology, 19*(3), 291–306.

Stoppard, J. M., & McMullen, L. M. (Eds.). (2003). *Situating sadness: Women and depression in social context.* New York: New York University Press.

Strack. F., Martin, L. L., & Stepper, S. (1988). Inhibiting and facilitating conditions of facial expressions: A non-obtrusive test of the facial feedback hypothesis. *Journal of Personality & Social Psychology, 54,* 768–777.

Straneva, P. A., Maixner, W., Light, K. C., Pedersen, C. A., et al. (2002). Menstrual cycle, beta-endorphins, and pain sensitivity in premenstrual dysphoric disorder. *Health Psychology, 21*(4), 358–367.

Straub, R. (2002). *Health psychology.* New York: Worth.

Strayer, D. L., Drews, F. A., & Johnston, W. A. (2003). Cell phone-induced failures of visual attention during simulated driving. *Journal of Experimental Psychology: Applied, 9*(1), 23–32.

Strickler, E. M., & Verbalis, J. G. (1988). Hormones and behavior: The biology of thirst and sodium appetite. *American Scientist,* May-June, 261–267.

Strongman, K. T. (2003). *The psychology of emotion: From everyday life to theory* (5th Ed.). New York: Wiley.

Strote, J., Lee, J. E., & Wechsler, H. (2002). Increasing MDMA use among college students: Results of a national survey. *Journal of Adolescent Health, 30*(1), 64–72.

Sturges, J. W., & Sturges, L. V. (1998). In vivo systematic desensitization in a single-session treatment of an 11-year old girl's elevator phobia. *Child & Family Behavior Therapy, 20*(4), 55–62.

Stuss, D. T., & Alexander, M. P. (2000). The anatomical basis of affective behavior, emotion and self-awareness: A specific role of the right frontal lobe. In G. Hatano, N. Okada, & H. Tanabe (Eds.), *Affective minds. The 13th Toyota conference.* Amsterdam: Elsevier.

Stuss, D. T., & Levine, B. (2002). Adult clinical neuropsychology. *Annual Review of Psychology, 53,* 401–433.

Suedfeld, P., & Borrie, R. A. (1999). Health and therapeutic applications of chamber and flotation restricted environmental stimulation therapy (REST). *Psychology & Health., 14*(3), 545–566.

Sugimoto, K., & Ninomiya, Y. (2005). Introductory remarks on umami research: Candidate receptors and signal transduction mechanisms on umami. *Chemical Senses, 30*(Suppl. 1), p i21–i22, 2005.

Suinn, R. M. (1975). *Fundamentals of behavior pathology* (2nd ed.). New York: Wiley.

Suinn, R. M. (1999). Scaling the summit: Valuing ethnicity. *APA Monitor,* March, 2.

Suinn, R. M. (2001). The terrible twos—Anger and anxiety. *American Psychologist, 56*(1), 27–36.

Sullivan, M. J., Johnson, P. I., Kjelberg, B. J., Williams, J., et al. (1998). Community leadership opportunities for psychologists. *Professional Psychology: Research and Practice, 29*(4), 328–331.

Sumathipala, A., Siribaddana, S. H., & Bhugra, D. (2004). Culture-bound syndromes: The story of dhat syndrome. *British Journal of Psychiatry, 184*(3), 200–209.

Sumerlin, J. R., & Bundrick, C. M. (1996). Brief Index of Self-Actualization: A measure of Maslow's model. *Journal of Social Behavior & Personality, 11*(2), 253–271.

Sumi, K., & Kanda, K. (2002). Relationship between neurotic perfectionism, depression, anxiety, and psychosomatic symptoms. *Personality & Individual Differences, 32*(5), 817–826.

Sunnafrank, M., Ramirez, A., & Metts, S. (2004). At first sight: Persistent relational effects of get-acquainted conversations. *Journal of Social & Personal Relationships, 21*(3), 361–379.

Suzuki, L., & Aronson, J. (2005). The cultural malleability of intelligence and its impact on the racial/ethnic hierarchy. *Psychology, Public Policy, & Law, 11,* 320–327.

Swaak, J., de Jong, T., & van Joolingen, W. R. (2004). The effects of discovery learning and expository instruction on the acquisition of definitional and intuitive knowledge. *Journal of Computer Assisted Learning, 20*(4), 225–234.

Swim, J. K., & Sanna, L. J. (1996). He's skilled, she's lucky: A meta-analysis of observers' attributions for women's and men's successes and failures. *Personality & Social Psychology Bulletin, 22*(5), 507–519.

Synhorst, L. L., Buckley, J. A., Reid, R., Epstein, M. H., et al. (2005). Cross informant agreement of the Behavioral and Emotional Rating Scale-2nd Edition (BERS-2) parent and youth rating scales. *Child & Family Behavior Therapy, 27*(3), 1–11.

Szabo, A. (2003). The acute effects of humor and exercise on mood and anxiety. *Journal of Leisure Research, 35*(2), 152–162.

Talbott, J. A. (2004). Deinstitutionalization: Avoiding the disasters of the past. *Psychiatric Services. Special Issue: A Tribute to John A. Talbott, M.D., 55*(10), 1112–1115.

Talley, P. F., Strupp, H. H., & Morey, L. C. (1990). Matchmaking in psychotherapy: Patient-therapist dimensions and their impact on outcome. *Journal of Consulting & Clinical Psychology, 58*(2), 182–188.

Tamis-LeMonda, C. S., Bornstein, M. H., & Baumwell, L. (2001). Maternal responsiveness and children's achievement of language milestones. *Child Development, 72,* 748–767.

Tanner, J. M. (1973). Growing up. *Scientific American, 229,* 34–43.

Taraban, R., Rynearson, K., & Kerr, M. (2000). College students' academic performance and self-reports of comprehension strategy use. *Reading Psychology, 21*(4) 283–308

Tardif, T. Z., & Sternberg, R. J. (1988). What do we know about creativity? In R. J. Sternberg (Ed.), *The nature of creativity.* Cambridge, MA: Cambridge University Press.

Taris, T. W., Bakker, A. B., Schaufeli, W. B., Stoffelsen, J., et al. (2005). Job control and burnout across occupations. *Psychological Reports, 97*(3), 955–961.

Tausig, M., Michello, J., & Subedi, S. (2004). *A sociology of mental illness* (2nd ed.). Englewood Cliffs, NJ: Prentice Hall.

Taylor, K. (2004). *Brainwashing: The science of thought control.* New York: Oxford University Press.

Taylor, S. E. (2002). Classical conditioning. In M. Hersen, & W. H. Sledge (Eds.), *Encyclopedia of psychotherapy.* San Diego: Academic Press.

Taylor, S. E. (2006). *Health psychology* (6th ed.). New York: McGraw-Hill.

Taylor, S. E., Kemeny, M. E., Reed, G. M., Bower, J. E., et al. (2000). Psychological resources, positive illusions, and health. *American Psychologist, 55*(1), 99–109.

Taylor, S. E., Lerner, J. S., Sherman, D. K., Sage, R. M., et al. (2003). Are self-enhancing cognitions associated with healthy or unhealthy biological profiles? *Journal of Personality & Social Psychology, 85*(4), 605–615.

Taylor-Seehafer, M., & Rew, L. (2000). Risky sexual behavior among adolescent women. *Journal of Social Pediatric Nursing, 5*(1), 15–25.

"Teen sex: Not for love." (1989). *Psychology Today,* May, 10.

Terman, L. M., & Merrill, M. A. (1937, revised, 1960). *Stanford-Binet Intelligence Scale.* Boston: Houghton Mifflin.

Terman, L. M., & Oden, M. (1959). *The gifted group in mid-life* (Vol. 5): *Genetic studies of genius.* Stanford, CA: Stanford University Press.

Terry, D. J., & Hogg, M. A. (1996). Group norms and the attitude-behavior relationship. *Personality & Social Psychology Bulletin, 22*(8), 776–793.

Thase, M. E. (2006). Major depressive disorder. In F. Andrasik (Ed.), *Comprehensive handbook of personality and psychopathology* (Vol. 2): *Adult psychopathology.* New York: Wiley.

Thelen, E. (2000). Infancy: Perception and motor development. In A. Kazdin (Ed.), *Encyclopedia of psychology.* Washington: American Psychological Association.

Thiessen, E. D., Hill, E. A., & Saffran, J. R. (2005). Infant-directed speech facilitates word segmentation. *Infancy, 7*(1), 53–71.

Thomas, E. M. (2004). *Aggressive behaviour outcomes for young children: Change in parenting environment predicts change in behaviour.* Ottawa, ON: Statistics Canada. Retrieved March 22, 2005, from http://www.statcan.ca/cgi-bin/downpub/listpub.cgi?catno=89-599-MIE2004001.

Thompson, R. A., & Nelson, C. A. (2001). Developmental science and the media. *American Psychologist, 56*(1), 5–15.

Thompson, R. F. (2005). In search of memory traces. *Annual Review of Psychology, 56,* 1–23.

Tidwell, M. O., Reis, H. T., & Shaver, P. R. (1996). Attachment, attractiveness, and social interaction. *Journal of Personality & Social Psychology, 71*(4), 729–745.

Tierny, J. (1987). Stitches: Good news; Better health linked to sin, sloth. *Hippocrates,* Sept./Oct., 30–35.

Till, B. D., & Priluck, R. L. (2000). Stimulus generalization in classical conditioning: An initial investigation and extension. *Psychology & Marketing, 17*(1), 55–72.

Timmerman, C. K., & Kruepke, K. A. (2006). Computer-assisted instruction, media richness, and college student performance. *Communication Education, 55*(1), 73–104.

Timmerman, I. G. H., Emmelkamp, P. M. G., & Sanderman, R. (1998). The effects of a stress-management training program in individuals at risk in the community at large. *Behaviour Research & Therapy, 36*(9), 863–875.

Tipples, J., Atkinson, A. P., & Young, A. W. (2002). The eyebrow frown: A salient social signal. *Emotion, 2*(3), 288–296.

Tobler, N. S., Roona, M. R., Ocshorn, P., Marshall, D. G., et al. (2000). School-based adolescent drug prevention programs: 1998 meta-analysis. *Journal of Primary Prevention, 20,* 275–337.

Tolman, E. C., & Honzik, C. H. (1930). Degrees of hunger, reward and non-reward, and maze performance in rats. *University of California Publications in Psychology, 4,* 21–256.

Tolman, E. C., Ritchie, B. F., & Kalish, D. (1946). Studies in spatial learning: II. Place learning versus response learning. *Journal of Experimental Psychology, 36,* 221–229.

Tomasello, M. (2003). *Constructing a language: A usage-based theory of language acquisition.* Cambridge, MA: Harvard University Press.

Toneatto, T., Sobell, L. C., Sobell, M. B., & Rubel, E. (1999). Natural recovery from cocaine dependence. *Psychology of Addictive Behaviors, 13*(4), 259–268.

Torrey, E. F. (1996). *Out of the shadows.* New York: John Wiley & Sons.

Tourangeau, R. (2004). Survey research and societal change. *Annual Review of Psychology, 55,* 775–801.

Townsend, J. M., & Wasserman, T. (1998). Sexual attractiveness. *Evolution & Human Behavior, 19*(3), 171–191.

Toyota, H., & Kikuchi, Y. (2005). Encoding richness of self-generated elaboration and spacing effects on incidental memory. *Perceptual & Motor Skills, 101*(2), 621–627.

Trainor, L. J., & Desjardins, R. N. (2002). Pitch characteristics of infant-directed speech affect infants' ability to discriminate vowels. *Psychonomic Bulletin & Review, 9*(2), 335–340.

Travis, F., Arenander, A., & DuBois, D. (2004). Psychological and physiological characteristics of a proposed object-referral/self-referral continuum of self-awareness. *Consciousness & Cognition, 13,* 401–420.

Treffert, D. A., & Christensen, C. D. (2005). Inside the mind of a savant. *Scientific American, 293*(6), 108–113.

Trehub, S. E., Unyk, A. M., & Trainor, L. J. (1993a). Adults identify infant-directed music across cultures. *Infant Behavior & Development, 16*(2), 193–211.

Trehub, S. E., Unyk, A. M., & Trainor, L. J. (1993b). Maternal singing in cross-cultural perspective. *Infant Behavior & Development, 16*(3), 285–295.

Troll, L. E., & Skaff, M. M. (1997). Perceived continuity of self in very old age. *Psychology & Aging, 12*(1), 162–169.

Truax, S. R. (1983). Active search, mediation, and the manipulation of cue dimensions: Emotion attribution in the false feedback paradigm. *Motivation and Emotion, 7,* 41–60.

Trull, T. (2005). *Clinical psychology* (7th ed.). Belmont, CA: Wadsworth.

Tsai, G., & Coyle, J. T. (2002). Glutamatergic mechanisms in schizophrenia. *Annual Review of Pharmacology & Toxicology, 42,* 165–179.

Tse, L. (1999). Finding a place to be: Ethnic identity exploration of Asian Americans. *Adolescence, 34*(133), 121–138.

Tugade, M. M., Fredrickson, B. L., & Barrett, L. F. (2004). Psychological resilience and positive emotional granularity: Examining the benefits of positive emotions on coping and health. *Journal of Personality. Special Emotions, Personality, & Health, 72*(6), 1161–1190.

Tulving, E. (2002). Episodic memory. *Annual Review of Psychology, 53,* 1–25.

Turiel, E. (2006).Thought, emotions, and social interactional processes in moral development. In M. Killen & J. G. Smetana, (Eds.), *Handbook of moral development.* Mahwah, NJ: Erlbaum.

Turkheimer, E., Haley, A., Waldron, M., D'Onofrio, B. M., et al. (2003). Socioeconomic status modifies heritability of IQ in young children. *Psychological Science, 14,* 623–628.

Turner, S. J. M. (1997). The use of the reflective team in a psychodrama therapy group. *International Journal of Action Methods, 50*(1) 17–26.

Tversky, A., & Kahneman, D. (1981). The framing of decisions and the psychology of choice. *Science, 211,* 453–458.

Tversky, A., & Kahneman, D. (1982). Judgments of and by representativeness. In D. Kahneman, P. Slovic, & A. Tversky (Eds.), *Judgment under uncertainty: Heuristics and biases.* Cambridge, MA: Cambridge University Press.

Twenge, J. M., & Campbell, W. K. (2001). Age and birth cohort differences in self-esteem. *Personality & Social Psychology Review, 5*(4), 321–344.

Tye-Murray, N., Spencer, L., & Woodworth, G. G. (1995). Acquisition of speech by children who have prolonged cochlear implant experience. *Journal of Speech & Hearing Research, 38*(2), 327–337.

Tzeng, M. (1992). The effects of socioeconomic heterogamy and changes on marital dissolution for first marriages. *Journal of Marriage and Family, 54,* 609–619.

Underwood, B. J. (1957). Interference and forgetting. *Psychological Review, 64,* 49–60.

UNESCO. (1990). The Seville statement on violence. *American Psychologist, 45*(10), 1167–1168.

Unsworth, G., & Ward, T. (2001). Video games and aggressive behaviour. *Australian Psychologist, 36*(3), 184–192.

Urbina, S. (2004). *Essentials of psychological testing.* New York: Wiley.

U.S. Department of Energy Human Office of Science. (2005). *About the Human Genome Project.* Washington: U.S. Department of Energy. Retrieved September 3, 2005, from http://www.ornl.gov/sci/techresources/Human_Genome/project/about.shtml.

USDHHS (U.S. Department of Health and Human Services). (2004). *The health consequences of smoking: A report of the Sur-geon General, Executive summary.* Retrieved July 19, 2006, from http://www.cdc.gov/tobacco/sgr/sgr_2004/pdf/executivesummary.pdf.

Gielen, U. P., Fish, J. M., & Draguns, J. G. (Eds.). (2006). *Handbook of culture, therapy, and healing.* Mahwah, NJ: Lawrence Erlbaum.

Vaillant, G. E. (2002). *Aging well.* Boston: Little, Brown.

Vaillant, G. E. (2005). Alcoholics Anonymous: Cult or cure? *Australian and New Zealand Journal of Psychiatry, 39*(6), 431–436.

Vaillant, G. E., & Mukamal, K. (2001). Successful aging. *American Journal of Psychiatry, 158*(6), 839–847.

Valins, S. (1966). Cognitive effects of false heart-rate feedback. *Journal of Personality & Social Psychology, 4,* 400–408.

Valins, S. (1967). Emotionality and information concerning internal reactions. *Journal of Personality & Social Psychology, 6,* 458–463.

Van der Hart, O., Lierens, R., & Goodwin, J. (1996). Jeanne Fery: A sixteenth-century case of dissociative identity disorder. *Journal of Psychohistory, 24*(1), 18–35.

van Dierendonck, D., & Te Nijenhuis, J. (2005). Flotation restricted environmental stimulation therapy (REST) as a stress-management tool: A meta-analysis. *Psychology & Health, 20*(3), 405–412.

van Elst, L. T., Valerius, G., Büchert, M., Thiel, T., et al. (2005). Increased prefrontal and hippocampal glutamate concentration in schizophrenia: Evidence from a magnetic resonance spectroscopy study. *Biological Psychiatry, 58*(9), 724–730.

Van Goozen, S. H. M., Cohen-Kettenis, P. T., Gooren, L. J. G., & Frijda, N. H. (1995). Gender differences in behaviour: Activating effects of cross-sex hormones. *Psychoneuroendocrinology, 20*(4), 343–363.

Van Lawick-Goodall, J. (1971). *In the shadow of man.* New York: Houghton Mifflin.

Van Rooij, J. J. F. (1994). Introversion-extraversion: Astrology versus psychology. *Personality & Individual Differences, 16*(6), 985–988.

Vandell, D. L. (2004). Early child care: The known and the unknown. *Merrill-Palmer Quarterly. Special Issue: The maturing of the human developmental sciences: Appraising past, present, and prospective agendas, 50*(3), 387–414.

VandenBos, G. R., & Bryant, B. K. (Eds.). (1987). *Cataclysms, crises, and catastrophes: Psychology in action.* Washington: American Psychological Association.

Vasa, R. A., Carlino, A. R., & Pine, D. S. (2006). Pharmacotherapy of depressed children and adolescents: Current issues and potential directions. *Biological Psychiatry, 59*(11), 1021–1028.

Velakoulis, D., & Pantelis, C. (1996). What have we learned from functional imaging studies in schizophrenia? *Australian & New Zealand Journal of Psychiatry, 30*(2), 195–209.

Venezia, M., Messinger, D. S., Thorp, D., & Mundy, P. (2004). The development of anticipatory smiling. *Infancy, 6*(3), 397–406.

Videon, T. M. (2005). Parent-child relations and children's psychological well-being: Do dads matter? *Journal of Family Issues, 26*(1), 55–78.

Viegener, B. J., Perri, M. G., Nezu, A. M., Renjilian, D. A., et al. (1990). Effects of an intermittent, low-fat, low-calorie diet in the behavioral treatment of obesity. *Behavior Therapy, 21*(4), 499–509.

Viveros, M. P., Llorente, R., Moreno, E., & Marco, E. M. (2005). Behavioural and neuroendocrine effects of cannabinoids in critical developmental periods. *Behavioural Pharmacology, 16*(5–6), 353–362.

Vogler, R. E., & Bartz, W. R. (1992). *Teenagers and alcohol.* Philadelphia: Charles Press.

Vogler, R. E., Weissbach, T. A., Compton, J. V., & Martin, G. T. (1977). Integrated behavior change techniques for problem drinkers in the community. *Journal of Consulting and Clinical Psychology, 45,* 267–279.

Volkow, N. D., Gillespie, H., Mullani, N., & Tancredi, L. (1996). Brain glucose metabolism in chronic marijuana users at baseline and during marijuana intoxication. *Psychiatry Research: Neuroimaging, 67*(1), 29–38.

Volpicelli, J. R., Ulm, R. R., Altenor, A., & Seligman, M. E. P. (1983). Learned mastery in the rat. *Learning and Motivation, 14,* 204–222.

Vygotsky, L. S. (1962). *Thought and language.* Cambridge, MA: MIT Press.

Vygotsky, L. S. (1978). *Mind in society.* Cambridge, MA: Harvard University Press.

Wager, T. D., Rilling, J. K., Smith, E. E., Sokolik, A., et al. (2004). Placebo-induced changes in fMRI in the anticipation and experience of pain. *Science, 303*(Feb. 20), 1162–1166.

Wagstaff, G., Brunas-Wagstaff, J., Cole, J., & Wheatcroft, J. (2004). New directions in forensic hypnosis: Facilitating memory with a focused meditation technique. *Contemporary Hypnosis, 21*(1), 14–27.

Waid, W. M., & Orne, M. T. (1982). The physiological detection of deception. *American Scientist, 70*(July/Aug.), 402–409.

Wainright, J. L., Russell, S. T., & Patterson, C. J. (2004). Psychosocial adjustment, school outcomes, and romantic relationships of adolescents with same-sex parents. *Child Development, 75*(6), 1886–1898.

Wakefield, J. C. (1992). The concept of mental disorder. *American Psychologist, 47*(3), 373–388.

Wald, J., & Taylor, S. (2000). Efficacy of virtual reality exposure therapy to treat driving phobia. *Journal of Behavior Therapy & Experimental Psychiatry, 31*(3–4), 249–257.

Walker, E., Kestler, L. Bollini, A., & Hochman, K. M. (2004). Schizophrenia: Etiology and course. *Annual Review of Psychology, 55,* 401–430.

Walker, I., & Crogan, M. (1998). Academic performance, prejudice, and the Jigsaw classroom. *Journal of Community & Applied Social Psychology, 8*(6), 381–393

Walker, M. P., & Stickgold, R. (2006). Sleep, memory, and plasticity. *Annual Review of Psychology, 57,* 139–166.

Wallach, M. A., & Kogan, N. (1965). *Modes of thinking in young children.* New York: Holt.

Walster, E. (1971). Passionate love. In B. I. Murstein (Ed.), *Theories of attraction and love.* New York: Springer.

Walton, C. E., Bower, M. L., & Bower, T. G. (1992). Recognition of familiar faces by newborns. *Infant Behavior & Development, 15*(2), 265–269.

Wampold, B. E., Minami T., Tierney, S. C., Baskin, T. W., et al. (2005). The placebo is powerful: Estimating placebo effects in medicine and psychotherapy from randomized clinical trials. *Journal of Clinical Psychology, 61*(7), 835–854.

Wampold, B. E., Mondin, G. W., Moody, M., Stich, E., et al. (1997). A meta-analysis of outcome studies comparing bona fide psychotherapies. *Psychological Bulletin, 122*(3), 203–215.

Wandersman, A., & Florin, P. (2003). Community interventions and effective prevention. *American Psychologist, 58*(6/7), 441–448.

Wang, Q., & Conway, M. A. (2004). The stories we keep: Autobiographical memory in American and Chinese middle-aged adults. *Journal of Personality, 72*(5), 911–938.

Wang, S. S., & Brownell, K. D. (2005). Public policy and obesity: The need to marry science with advocacy. *Psychiatric Clinics of North America, 28*(1), 235–252.

Ward, C., & Rana-Deuba, A. (1999). Acculturation and adaptation revisited. *Journal of Cross-Cultural Psychology, 30*(4), 422–442.

Ward, J. (2006). *The student's guide to cognitive neuroscience.* Hove, UK: Psychology Press.

Warren, D. J., & Normann, R. A. (2005). Functional reorganization of primary visual cortex induced by electrical stimulation in the cat. *Vision Research, 45,* 551–565.

Waterfield, R. (2002). *Hidden depths: The story of hypnosis.* London: Macmillan.

Watson, D. L., & Tharp, R. G. (2007). *Self-directed behavior* (9th ed.). Belmont, CA: Wadsworth.

Watson, J. B. (1913). Psychology as the behaviorist views it. *Psychological Review, 20,* 158–177.

Watson, J. B. (1994). Psychology as the behaviorist views it. Special Issue: The centennial issue of the Psychological Review. *Psychological Review, 101*(2), 248–253.

Way, I., vanDeusen, K. M., Martin, G., Applegate, B., et al. (2004). Vicarious trauma: A comparison of clinicians who treat survivors of sexual abuse and sexual offenders. *Journal of Interpersonal Violence, 19*(1), 49–71.

Wechsler, H., & Wuethrich, B. (2002). *Dying to drink.* Emmaus, PA: Rodale Books.

Wechsler, H., Lee, J. E., Kuo, M., Seibring, M., et al. (2002). Trends in college binge drinking during a period of increased prevention efforts. *Journal of American College Health, 50*(5), 203–217.

Wedding, D., & Corsini, R. J. (2005). *Case studies in psychotherapy* (4th ed.). Belmont, CA: Wadsworth.

Weekley, J. A., & Jones, C. (1997). Video-based situational testing. *Personnel Psychology, 50*(1), 25–49.

Weems, C. F. (1998). The evaluation of heart rate biofeedback using a multi-element design. *Journal of Behavior Therapy & Experimental Psychiatry, 29*(2), 157–162.

Wehr, T. A., Duncan, W. C., Sher, L., Aeschbach, D., et al. (2001). A circadian signal of change of season in patients with seasonal affective disorder. *Archives of General Psychiatry, 58*(12), 1108–1114.

Weinberg, R. A. (1989). Intelligence and IQ. *American Psychologist, 44*(2), 98–104.

Weintraub, M. I. (1983). *Hysterical conversion reactions.* New York: SP Medical & Scientific Books.

Weishaar, M. E. (2006). A cognitive-behavioral approach to suicide risk reduction in crisis intervention. In A. R. Roberts & K. R. Yeager, (Eds.), *Foundations of evidence-based social work practice.* New York: Oxford University Press.

Weisskirch, R. S. (2005). Ethnicity and perceptions of being a "typical American" in relationship to ethnic identity development. *International Journal of Intercultural Relations, 29*(3), 355–366.

Weissman, A. M., Jogerst, G. J., & Dawson, J. D. (2003). Community characteristics associated with child abuse in Iowa. *Child Abuse & Neglect, 27*(10), 1145–1159.

Weiten, W. (1998). Pressure, major life events, and psychological symptoms. *Journal of Social Behavior & Personality, 13*(1), 51–68.

Weitzman, E. R. (2004). Poor mental health, depression, and associations with alcohol consumption, harm, and abuse in a national sample of young adults in college. *Journal of Nervous & Mental Disease, 192*(4), 269–277.

Wells, G. L. (2001). Police lineups: Data, theory, and policy. *Psychology, Public Policy, & Law, 7*(4), 791–801.

Wells, G. L., & Olsen, E. A. (2003). Eyewitness testimony. *Annual Review of Psychology, 54,* 277–295.

Wernet, S. P., Follman, C., Magueja, C., & Moore-Chambers, R. (2003). Building bridges and improving racial harmony: An evaluation of the Bridges Across Racial Polarization Program. In J. J. Stretch, E. M. Burkemper, W. J. Hutchison, & J. Wilson (Eds.), *Practicing social justice.* New York: Haworth Press.

Wertheimer, M. (1959). *Productive thinking.* New York: Harper & Row.

Wesensten, N. J., Belenky, G., Kautz, M. A., Thorne, D. R., et al. (2002). Maintaining alertness and performance during sleep deprivation: Modafinil versus caffeine. *Psychopharmacology, 159*(3), 238–247.

Wessel, I., & Wright, D. B. (Eds.). (2004). *Emotional memory failures.* Hove, UK: Psychology Press.

West, R., & Sohal, T. (2006). "Catastrophic" pathways to smoking cessation: Findings from national survey. *British Medical Journal, 332*(7539), 458–460.

West, T. G. (1997). *In the mind's eye.* Buffalo, NY: Prometheus.

Wexler, M. N. (1995). Expanding the group-think explanation to the study of contemporary cults. *Cultic Studies Journal, 12*(1), 49–71.

White, G. L., & Taytroe, L. (2003). Personal problem-solving using dream incubation: Dreaming, relaxation, or waking cognition? *Dreaming, 13*(4), 193–209.

Whitley, B. E. (1999). Right-wing authoritarianism, social dominance orientation, and prejudice. *Journal of Personality & Social Psychology, 77*(l), 126–134.

Whitton, E. (2003). *Humanistic approach to psychotherapy.* New York: Wiley.

Whyte, G. (2000). Groupthink. In A. E. Kazdin (Ed.), *Encyclopedia of psychology* (Vol. 4). Washington: American Psychological Association.

Widiger, T. A. (2005). Classification and diagnosis: Historical development and contemporary issues. In J. E. Maddux & B. A. Winstead (Eds.), *Psychopathology: Foundations for a contemporary understanding.* Mahwah, NJ: Erlbaum.

Widner, Jr., R. L., Otani, H., & Winkelman, S. E. (2005). Tip-of-the-tongue experiences are not merely strong feeling-of-knowing experiences. *Journal of General Psychology, 132*(4), 392–407.

Wiederhold, B. K., & Wiederhold, M. D. (2005). Acrophobia. In B. K. Wiederhold & M. D. Wiederhold, *Virtual reality therapy for anxiety disorders: Advances in evaluation and treatment.* Washington: American Psychological Association.

Wiederhold, B. K., & Wiederhold, M. D. (2005). Posttraumatic stress disorder. In B. K. Wiederhold & M. D. Wiederhold (Eds.), *Virtual reality therapy for anxiety disorders: Advances in evaluation and treatment.* Washington: American Psychological Association.

Wiederman, M. W. (2001). Gender differences in sexuality: Perceptions, myths, and realities. *Family Journal-Counseling & Therapy for Couples & Families, 9*(4), 468–471.

Wigfield, A., & Eccles, J. (Eds.). (2002). *Development of achievement motivation.* San Diego: Academic Press.

Wilder, D. A., Simon, A. F., & Faith, M. (1996). Enhancing the impact of counter-stereotypic information. *Journal of Personality & Social Psychology, 71*(2), 276–287.

Wilding, J., & Valentine, E. (1994a). Memory champions. *British Journal of Psychology, 85*(2), 231–244.

Wilding, J., & Valentine, E. (1994b). Mnemonic wizardry with the telephone directory: But stories are another story. *British Journal of Psychology, 85*(4), 501–509.

Wilkinson, D., & Abraham, C. (2004). Constructing an integrated model of the antecedents of adolescent smoking. *British Journal of Health Psychology, 9*(3), 315–333.

Wilkinson, M. (2006). The dreaming mind-brain: A Jungian perspective. *Journal of Analytical Psychology, 51*(1), 43–59.

Williams, D. G., & Morris, G. (1996). Crying, weeping or tearfulness in British and Israeli adults. *British Journal of Psychology, 87*(3), 479–505.

Williams, G., Cai, X. J., Elliott, J. C., & Harrold, J. A. (2004). Anabolic neuropeptides. *Physiology & Behavior. Special Issue: Reviews on Ingestive Science, 81*(2), 211–222.

Williams, R. (1989). *The trusting heart: Great news about Type A behavior.* New York: Random House.

Williams, R. B., Barefoot, J. C., & Schneiderman, N. (2003). Psychosocial risk factors for cardiovascular disease: More than one culprit at work. *JAMA: Journal of the American Medical Association, 290*(16), 2190–2192.

Williams, R. L., & Eggert, A. (2002). Notetaking predictors of test performance. *Teaching of Psychology, 29*(3), 234–236.

Williams, R. L., & Long, J. D. (1991). *Toward a self-managed life style.* Boston: Houghton Mifflin.

Williamson, D. A., Ravussin, E., Wong, M.-L., Wagner, A., et al. (2005). Microanalysis of eating behavior of three leptin deficient adults treated with leptin therapy. *Appetite, 45,* 75–80.

Willoughby, T., Wood, E., Desmarais, S., Sims, S., et al. (1997). Mechanisms that facilitate the effectiveness of elaboration strategies. *Journal of Educational Psychology, 89*(4), 682–685.

Wilson, G. L. (2002). *Groups in context: Leadership and participation in small groups* (6th ed.). New York: McGraw-Hill.

Wilson, G. T. (1987). Chemical aversion conditioning as a treatment for alcoholism: A re-analysis. *Behaviour Research and Therapy, 25*(6), 503–516.

Winger, G., Woods, J. H., Galuska, C. M., & Wade-Galuska, T. (2005). Behavioral perspectives on the neuroscience of drug addiction. *Journal of the Experimental Analysis of Behavior, 84*(3), 667–681.

Wingood, G.M., DiClemente, R.J., Bernhardt, J.M., Harrington, K., et al. (2003). A prospective study of exposure to rap music videos and African American female adolescents' health. *American Journal of Public Health, 93,* 437–439.

Winner, E. (2003). Creativity and talent. In M. H. Bornstein, L. Davidson, C. L. M. Keyes, & K. Moore (Eds.), *Well-being: Positive development across the life course.* Mahwah, NJ: Erlbaum.

Winstead, B. A., & Sanchez, J. (2005). Gender and psychopathology. In J. E. Maddux & B. A. Winstead (Eds.), *Psychopathology: Foundations for a contemporary understanding.* Mahwah, NJ: Erlbaum.

Wise, R. A., & Safer, M. A. (2004). What US judges know and believe about eyewitness testimony. *Applied Cognitive Psychology, 18*(4), 427–443.

Witherington, D. C., Campos, J. J., Anderson, D. I., Lejeune, L., & Seah, E. (2005). Avoidance of heights on the visual cliff in newly walking infants. *Infancy, 7*(3), 285–298.

Withers, N. W., Pulvirenti, L., Koob, G. F., & Gillin, J. C. (1995). Cocaine abuse and dependence. *Journal of Clinical Psychopharmacology, 15*(1), 63–78.

Witt, C. M. Jena, S., Selim, D., Brinkhaus, B., et al. (2006). Pragmatic randomized trial evaluating the clinical and economic effectiveness of acupuncture for chronic low back pain. *American Journal of Epidemiology Advance Access* (E-Publication). Retrieved July 13, 2006, from http://aje.oxfordjournals.org/cgi/reprint/kwj224v1.

Wixted, J. T. (2005). A theory about why we forget what we once knew. *Current Directions in Psychological Science, 14*(1), 6–9.

Wolfe, J. M., Kluender, K. R., Levi, D. M., Bartoshuk, L. M., et al. (2005). *Sensation & perception.* Sunderland, MA: Sinauer Associates.

Wolpe, J. (1974). *The practice of behavior therapy* (2nd ed.). New York: Pergamon.

Wolpin, M., Marston, A., Randolph, C., & Clothier, A. (1992). Individual difference correlates of reported lucid dreaming frequency and control. *Journal of Mental Imagery, 16*(3–4), 231–236.

Wood, E., & Willoughby, T. (1995). Cognitive strategies for test-taking. In E. Wood, V. Woloshyn, & T. Willoughby (Eds.), *Cognitive strategy instruction for middle and high schools.* Cambridge, MA: Brookline Books.

Wood, J. M., Nezworski, M. T., Lilienfeld, S. O., & Garb, H. N. (2003). The Rorschach Inkblot test, fortune tellers, and cold reading. *Skeptical Inquirer, 27*(4), 29–33.

Wood, W., & Eagly, A. H. (2002). A cross-cultural analysis of the behavior of women and men. *Psychological Bulletin, 128,* 699–727.

Woodhill, B. M., & Samuels, C. A. (2004). Desirable and undesirable androgyny: A prescription for the twenty-first century. *Journal of Gender Studies, 13*(1), 15–28.

Woods, S. C., Schwartz, M. W, Baskin, D. G., & Seeley, R J. (2000). Food intake and the regulation of body weight. *Annual Review of Psychology, 51,* 255–277.

Worthen, J. B., & Marshall, P. H. (1996). Intralist and extralist sources of distinctiveness and the bizarreness effect. *American Journal of Psychology, 109*(2), 239–263.

Wraga, M., Shephard, J. M., Church, J. A., Inati, S., et al. (2005). Imagined rotations of self versus objects: An fMRI study. *Neuropsychologia, 43*(9), 1351–1361.

Wu, C. W.H., & Kaas, J. H. (2002). The effects of long-standing limb loss on anatomical reorganization of the somatosensory afferents in the brainstem and spinal cord. *Somatosensory & Motor Research, 19*(2), 153–163.

Wulf, G., Mc Connel, N., Gärtner, M., & Schwarz, A. (2002). Enhancing the learning of sport skills through external-focus feedback. *Journal of Motor Behavior, 34*(2), 171–182.

Wyatt, J. W., Posey, A., Welker, W., & Seamonds, C. (1984). Natural levels of similarities between identical twins and between unrelated people. *The Skeptical Inquirer, 9,* 62–66.

Wynne, C. D. L. (2004). The perils of anthropomorphism. *Nature, 428*(6983), 606.

X Day, S., & Schneider, P. L. (2002). Psychotherapy using distance technology. *Journal of Counseling Psychology, 49*(4), 499–503.

Yahnke, B. H., Sheikh, A. A., & Beckman, H. T. (2003). Imagery and the treatment of phobic disorders. In A. A. Sheikh (Ed.), *Healing images: The role of imagination in health.* Amityville, NY: Baywood Publishing.

Yalom, I. D. (1980). *Existential psychotherapy.* New York: Basic.

Yarmey, A. D. (2003). Eyewitness identification: Guidelines and recommendations for identification procedures in the United States and in Canada. *Canadian Psychology, 44*(3), 181–189.

Yeh, C. J. (2003). Age, acculturation, cultural adjustment, and mental health symptoms of Chinese, Korean, and Japanese immigrant youths. *Cultural Diversity & Ethnic Minority Psychology, 9*(1), 34–48.

Yehuda, R. (2002). Post-traumatic stress disorder. *New England Journal of Medicine, 346*(2), 108–114.

Yokota, F., & Thompson, K. M. (2000). Violence in G-rated animated films. *Journal of the American Medical Association, 283*(20), 2716.

Yonas, A., Elieff, C. A., & Arterberry, M. E. (2002). Emergence of sensitivity to pictorial depth cues: Charting development in individual infants. *Infant Behavior & Development. Special Issue: Variability in Infancy, 25*(4), 495–514.

Yoshida, M. (1993). Three-dimensional electrophysiological atlas created by computer mapping of clinical responses elicited on stimulation of human subcortical structures. *Stereotactic & Functional Neurosurgery, 60*(1–3), 127–134.

Yost, W. A. (2007) *Fundamentals of hearing: An introduction* (5th ed.). San Diego: Elsevier.

Zarcadoolas, C., Pleasant, A., & Greer, D. S. (2006). *Advancing health literacy: A framework for understanding and action.* San Francisco: Jossey-Bass.

Zellner, D. A., Harner, D. E., & Adler, R. L. (1989). Effects of eating abnormalities and gender on perceptions of desirable body shape. *Journal of Abnormal Psychology, 98*(1), 93–96.

Zemishlany, Z., Aizenberg, D., & Weizman, A. (2001). Subjective effects of MDMA ("Ecstasy") on human sexual function. *European Psychiatry, 16*(2), 127–130.

Zimbardo, P. G., Pilkonis, P. A., & Norwood, R. M. (1978). The social disease called shyness. *In Annual editions, personality and adjustment 78/79.* Guilford, CT: Dushkin.

Zohar, D. (1998). An additive model of test anxiety: Role of exam-specific expectations. *Journal of Educational Psychology, 90,* 330–340.

Zola, S. M., & Squire, L. R. (2001). Relationship between magnitude of damage to the hippocampus and impaired recognition in monkeys. *Hippocampus, 11,* 92–98.

Zuckerman, M. (1990). The psychophysiology of sensation seeking. *Journal of Personality, 58*(1), 313–345.

Zuckerman, M. (1996). Item revisions in the Sensation Seeking Scale Form V (SSS-V). *EDRA: Environmental Design Research Association, 20*(4), 515.

Zuckerman, M. (2000). Sensation seeking. In A. Kazdin (Ed.), *Encyclopedia of psychology.* Washington: American Psychological Association.

Zuckerman, M. (2002). Genetics of sensation seeking. In J. Benjamin, R. P. Ebstein, & R. H. Belmaker (Eds.), *Molecular genetics and the human personality.* Washington: American Psychiatric Publishing.

Zuwerink, J. R., Devine, P. G., Monteith, M. J., & Cook, D. A. (1996). Prejudice toward Blacks: With and without compunction? *Basic & Applied Social Psychology, 18*(2), 131–150.

Name Index

Subject Index

TO THE OWNER OF THIS BOOK:

I hope that you have found *Psychology: A Journey*, 3rd edition, useful. So that this book can be improved in a future edition, would you take the time to complete this sheet and return it? Thank you.

School and address: _____

_____

Department: _____

Instructor's name: _____

1. What I like most about this book is: _____

_____

_____

2. What I like least about this book is: _____

_____

_____

3. My general reaction to this book is: _____

_____

_____

4. The name of the course in which I used this book is: _____

_____

5. Were all of the chapters of the book assigned for you to read? _____

   If not, which ones weren't? _____

6. In the space below, or on a separate sheet of paper, please write specific suggestions for improving this book and anything else you'd care to share about your experience in using this book.

_____

_____

_____

_____

_____

_____

BUSINESS REPLY MAIL
FIRST-CLASS MAIL   PERMIT NO. 34   BELMONT CA

POSTAGE WILL BE PAID BY ADDRESSEE

Attn: Michele Sordi, Publisher

Wadsworth/Thomson Learning
10 Davis Dr
Belmont CA 94002-9801

OPTIONAL:

Your name: _____Date: _____

May we quote you, either in promotion for *Psychology: A Journey,* 3rd edition, or in future
publishing ventures?

      Yes _____ No _____

Sincerely yours,

Dennis Coon and John Mitterer